Ref.
Histo

Historic
Documents
of 2003

Historic
Documents
of 2003

Includes Cumulative Index, 1999–2003

CQ PRESS

A Division of Congressional Quarterly Inc.
Washington, D.C.

Historic Documents of 2003
Editors: Martha Gottron, John Felton, and Bruce Maxwell
Production and Associate Editor: Kerry V. Kern
Indexer: Victoria Agee

CQ Press
1255 22nd Street, N.W., Suite 400
Washington, D.C. 20037
(202) 729-1900; toll-free 1-866-4CQ-PRESS (1-866-427-7737)
www.cqpress.com

Printed and bound in the United States of America
08 07 06 05 04   5 4 3 2 1

∞The paper used in this publication exceeds the requirements of the American National Standard for Information Sciences—Permanence of Paper for Printed Library Materials, ANSI Z39.48-1992.

The Library of Congress cataloged the first issue of this title as follows:

Historic documents. 1972—
Washington. Congressional Quarterly Inc.

1. United States—Politics and government—1945 —Yearbooks.
2. World politics—1945 —Yearbooks. I. Congressional Quarterly Inc.
E839.5H57   917.3'03'9205   72-97888
ISBN 1-56802-857-1
ISSN 0892-080X

Contents

June

the official announcement that Hispanics were now the largest
minority group in the United States.

Two decisions handed down June 23, 2003: first, the main majority and dissenting opinions in the case of *Grutter v. Bollinger,* in
which the Supreme Court ruled 5–4 that achieving a diverse student body was a compelling state interest that justified the use of
race as one of several considerations in admitting students so
long as applications were evaluated individually and race was not
used in a "mechanical way"; second, the majority opinion in the
case of *Gratz v. Bollinger,* in which the Court struck down, 6–3,
the University of Michigan's undergraduate admissions policy
because its point system automatically awarded a set number
of points to minority students, making it an impermissible quota
system.

The majority, concurring, and dissenting opinions in the case of
United States v. American Library Association Inc., in which the
Supreme Court on June 23, 2003, upheld, 6–3, the Children's
Internet Protection Act (PL 106–554), which required public
libraries receiving certain federal subsidies to install antipornog-
raphy filters on computers used by the public for access to the
Internet.

First, the majority opinion in the case of *Lawrence v. Texas,* in
which the Supreme Court, on June 26, 2003, by a 6–3 vote,
struck down as unconstitutional state laws that criminalized sex
between mutually consenting gay adults; second, the majority
opinion in the case of *Goodridge v. Department of Public Health,*
in which the Supreme Judicial Court of Massachusetts ruled 4–3
on November 18, 2003, that the state's ban on gay marriage was
a violation of the state's constitution.

"Democratic Security and Defense," a policy issued June 29,
2003, by President Alvaro Uribe of Colombia.

July

"The Employment Situation: June 2003," a report issued July 3,
2003, by the Bureau of Labor Statistics in the Department of
Labor.

October

November

Preface

Iraq and the Middle East, sub-Saharan Africa, and tax cuts, security issues, jobs, and deficits in America are only some of the topics of national and international interest chosen for *Historic Documents of 2003*. This edition marks the thirty-second volume of a CQ Press project that began with *Historic Documents of 1972*. This series allows students, librarians, journalists, scholars, and others to research and understand the most important issues of the year through primary source documents. These primary sources have often been excerpted to highlight the most important parts of lengthy documents written for a specialized audience. In our judgment, the official statements, news conferences, speeches, special studies, and court decisions presented here will be of lasting interest.

This edition also includes some new features, such as a new design to make both the introductions and the documents more readable, and formal source citations for the documents. For more details, please see "How to Use This Book" (page xx).

Historic Documents of 2003 begins with "Overview of 2003," which puts key events and issues from around the world in political, historical, or social context. The balance of the book is organized chronologically, with each "article" comprising an introduction and one or more related documents on a specific event, issue, or topic. The introduction preceding each document provides context, background, and an account of continuing developments during the year, when relevant.

As events, issues, and consequences become more complex and far-reaching, these introductions and documents yield important information and deepen understanding about the world in which we live. The editors of this series believe these introductions will become increasingly useful as memories of current events fade.

How to Use This Book

The eighty articles in this edition each begin with a comprehensive introduction, followed by one or more historic documents. The articles are arranged in chronological order. If you know the approximate date of the report, speech, statement, court decision, or other document you are looking for, glance through the titles for that month in the table of contents or in the monthly tables of contents that appear throughout the volume at the start of each month's introductions and documents.

If the table of contents does not lead you directly to the document you want, turn to the index at the end of the book. There you may find references not only to the particular document you seek but also to other entries on the same or a related subject. The index in this volume is a five-year cumulative index of *Historic Documents* covering the years 1999–2003. There is a separate volume, *Historic Documents Index, 1972–2002,* that may also be useful.

Each article begins with the heading "Introduction" and the discussion that directly follows in sans serif type provides the historical and intellectual context for the selected document(s). A thin rule designates the start of the official document, followed by the formal title (in quotation marks) or informal title (without quotation marks). The documents are reproduced in roman type with unjustified line breaks. The spelling, capitalization, and punctuation of the original or official copy have been retained. Where the full text is not given, omissions of material are indicated by ellipses. Insertions within the documents by the editors to clarify information are enclosed within brackets.

Full citations to the print or online source, including the Internet URL addresses noting where the documents have been obtained, appear at the end of each document. If documents were not available on the Internet, this also has been noted.

Overview of 2003

Iraq was at the forefront of the world's agenda all through 2003, dominating public debate and roiling international diplomacy as had no single matter since the height of the Vietnam War more than three decades earlier. The year began with an intensely bitter dispute over a plan by President George W. Bush to invade Iraq and oust its president, Saddam Hussein. At year's end, having achieved that goal, Bush was presiding over the biggest, most complex, and most problem-fraught nation-building exercise the United States had tackled since the post–World War II period.

The war in Iraq was supposed to be a fairly simple affair, at least according to the prewar rhetoric of Bush administration officials. Long-repressed Iraqis, glad to be released from Saddam's clutches, would greet invading U.S. troops as liberators and then coalesce around Washington's vision of a unified, democratic Iraq, lighting a beacon of hope for the entire Middle East. The United States, with aid from Britain and a small number of allies, needed just three weeks in late March and early April 2003 to topple Saddam and another three weeks to dismantle the rest of his regime.

Both the prewar and postwar periods, however, were anything but simple. Before a single shot was fired in Iraq, European leaders fought among themselves over whether to support Bush's call for war. The United Nations, which had been remarkably unified on its approach to Iraq in late 2002, again became the scene of diplomatic squabbling that had paralyzed it many times in the past.

Postwar Iraq resembled none of the scenarios that Pentagon officials had envisioned during the lengthy planning of the war and its aftermath. While most Iraqis appeared delighted to be rid of Saddam and his brutal regime, most also appeared eager to see the backs of their new American overlords.

U.S. administrators repeatedly shifted their plans in response to grim realities, most importantly the military's inability to guarantee security in a nation where ethnic and religious factions suddenly had freedom to assert themselves.

Almost from the day—May 1, 2003—that Bush declared an end to major combat in Iraq, the people of Iraq found themselves victimized by terrorism. Car bombings, suicide bombings, mortar attacks, sniper shootings—these were among the weapons that kept Iraq on edge all through the last eight months of the year. Many of the victims were international soldiers and aid workers whose stated missions were to help Iraqis rebuild their wounded society. Among them were employees of the United Nations and the International Committee of the Red Cross, whose neutrality offered them no protection. The majority of the victims of postwar bombings and other violence were Iraqis, many of them Iraqis who cooperated with the occupying powers. Those responsible for the attacks did not make themselves known but were assumed to be diehard loyalists of Saddam's regime and religious extremists who seized an opportunity to strike at the West. Saddam himself disappeared from view for eight months but was found on December 13, bearded and grubby, hiding in a hole in the ground near his hometown.

American soldiers had an easier time finding Saddam than his alleged weapons of mass destruction. In the months before the war, Bush had said Iraq's programs to develop biological, chemical, and nuclear weapons posed a "grave and gathering danger" to Americans and, therefore, justified a war to oust Saddam from power. Bush's aides also insisted before the war that they knew exactly where the Iraqi regime was building and storing those weapons, discounting UN weapons inspectors who had been unable to find the weapons during a three-month search. Starting in April teams of U.S. soldiers and weapons experts combed through the locations where Iraq's weapons were supposed to be hidden, but none were found. Undaunted, the administration asserted that Iraq had been developing "weapons of mass destruction-related programs," if not the weapons themselves, and that the removal of Saddam made Americans safer in any event.

At least three other countries—North Korea, Iran, and Libya—apparently had been trying to develop similar weapons, but the Bush administration used diplomatic, rather than military, means to deal with them. North Korea's program was by far the most dangerous. Western experts were convinced the communist regime of Kim Jong Il already had built at least one or two nuclear bombs, and in 2002 North Korean officials announced plans to develop more. In this case, the U.S. administration had an important ally, China, which hosted two series of multinational talks in 2003 attempting to persuade North Korea to halt its weapons programs. The talks failed to produce that result by year's end, but they did offer a reasonable prospect for a negotiated solution.

Another member of the "axis of evil" that Bush had identified in his 2002 State of the Union address (along with Iraq and North Korea) was Iran, where a moderate, elected government was struggling to gain authority from the Islamist clerics who had been in charge since 1979. U.S. officials had long suspected Iran was trying to build nuclear weapons, but Tehran insisted it was developing only nuclear power. An intervention by European diplomats in October secured Iran's agreement to open its nuclear facilities to UN inspection. The first inspections appeared to verify U.S. suspicions, leading to more inspections—and the prospect for another diplomatic standoff—at the end of the year.

Libya made a surprise appearance in 2003 on the list of countries whose weapons programs came under international scrutiny. Libya and its erratic leader, Muammar Qaddafi, had topped the list of "rogue" regimes routinely denounced by the United States in the 1970s and 1980s, but it had long since been supplanted by others, notably Iraq. In March Qaddafi initiated a diplomatic overture to Britain that ultimately led to his agreement to renounce his programs to develop chemical and nuclear weapons. Inspections uncovered a sizable stockpile of chemical weapons and a nuclear weapons program that was more advanced than U.S. officials suspected—but still years away from producing a bomb.

The attention paid to Iraq and these other nations tended to obscure the struggle for stability in Afghanistan, which had been the opening chapter in Bush's war against terrorism. An interim government headed by moderate leader Hamid Karzai had some modest success in extending its authority beyond the capital, Kabul, and curbing the influence of powerful warlords who ruled much of the countryside. At year's end leaders of Afghanistan's many factions were negotiating a new constitution intended to set the stage for the country's first-ever elections in mid-2004. As in Iraq, the political process was in constant danger of being overwhelmed by violence, in this case from supporters of the ousted Taliban regime and the al Qaeda terrorist network. Al Qaeda's leader, Osama bin Laden, remained at large, presumably in the rugged mountains of Pakistan along the border with Afghanistan.

Bin Laden and fellow extremists had gained substantial sympathy in Islamic countries with an agenda of complaints about the United States and other "infidel" Western countries. One of bin Laden's main complaints—the presence of U.S. military bases in Saudi Arabia, the birthplace of Islam—was removed from that agenda in 2003. Apparently by mutual agreement, the Bush administration and Saudi leaders decided in April to close those bases and withdraw the 5,000 or so U.S. personnel who had been stationed there. The U.S. military did not move far, however—just down the Persian Gulf to Qatar and to other countries in the Gulf region and East Africa.

The other principal item on bin Laden's stated agenda was the Israeli-Palestinian conflict, which remained a festering sore. For the first time since the current violence began in September 2000, there was a brief flurry of hope for a diplomatic settlement in mid-2003. The hope had two sources: Palestinian leader Yasir Arafat's agreement to appoint a prime minister, Mahmoud Abbas, to negotiate peace with the Israelis, and Bush's embrace of an internationally supported "roadmap" to peace. Bush met jointly in June with Abbas and Israeli prime minister Ariel Sharon, and he promised to "ride herd" on them as they took the difficult journey along the roadmap.

A suicide bombing in August, coupled with hesitations on both sides, threw the peace talks off track, and Bush quietly withdrew. Moderate Israelis and Palestinians drew up counterproposals that demonstrated the technical possibility of achieving peace, but these efforts had no formal backing from decision makers. Sharon in December threatened to impose a unilateral solution based on what he called "disengagement" from the Palestinians.

Ending Wars in Africa

Aside from the Middle East, the region that had been most troubled by conflict in the early years of the twenty-first century was sub-Saharan Africa. More than a dozen countries had been plagued by wars over political power, natural resources, ethnic differences, or a combination of those factors. Many of these conflicts appeared to be headed to peaceful conclusions as of 2003, leaving a legacy of hundreds of thousands of deaths, unbelievable misery, and ravaged natural resources. The biggest war of all—for control of the Democratic Republic of the Congo—wound down to a low level as leaders from various factions began competing for political power in possible elections in 2005.

One of the year's most remarkable developments was the relatively prompt international response to two crises in Africa that had threatened to become immense humanitarian tragedies, as had so many other conflicts on the continent. In May UN officials warned of a possible genocide in eastern Congo, where the last embers of a huge international war were still glowing. After just a few weeks' hesitation by the great powers at the United Nations, France and other countries responded with an emergency peacekeeping force that prevented a small-scale massacre from developing into a much bigger one. Similarly, a conflict in Liberia was contained by the presence of a small contingent of U.S. Marines—bolstered by three warships that Bush posted off the coast. Liberia's warlord-president, Charles Taylor, fled the country and went into exile, opening the possibility that the long-troubled West African country might finally enjoy a respite of peace.

Neither of these interventions was costly in terms of lives or money, but together they may have saved many lives and soothed the consciences of

Western policy makers still troubled by the failure to act against the genocide in Rwanda in 1994. Rwanda itself held its first-ever contested presidential election in August. Although far from a model of democracy, the election victory for incumbent president Paul Kagame, the man who had doused the fires of genocide, appeared to reflect the will of Rwanda's still-conflicted people.

Deficits, Controversies, and Threats

After two years of disappointing growth following a mild recession in 2001, the U.S. economy showed signs of getting back on track in 2003. Interest rates and inflation remained low, business investment picked up toward the end of the year, and investors began to return to the stock market. Two disturbing trends raised questions about the durability of the recovery, however. Job creation remained stagnant throughout the year, with the country in the longest hiring slump since the end of the Great Depression in the 1930s. The federal budget, which had been in surplus in 2000, had sunk to a $374 billion deficit in 2003—the highest dollar level in history. The hangover from the recession and spending to finance the war on terrorism and the invasion of Iraq contributed to the deficit, as did the massive tax cuts pressed by President Bush and passed by the Republican-led Congress in 2001 and 2003.

Jobs and the deficit were clearly going to be issues on the presidential campaign trail in 2004. A field of contenders for the Democratic nomination was already challenging the president on both issues, arguing that he had not done enough to put Americans back to work and that Bush was irresponsible for pursuing tax cuts when the deficit was spiraling out of control. Bush defended the tax cuts as the best way to promote economic growth and job creation, claimed that the deficit was "manageable" and justified in the face of economic slowdown and security threats, and vowed that he would not be satisfied until every American who wanted a job had one.

Politics was also at the core of a major overhaul of the Medicare program. The legislation, which Bush triumphantly signed into law at an elaborate ceremony in Washington, provided a prescription drug benefit for retirees starting in 2006, at an estimated cost of $435 billion over ten years. Passage of the reform was a crucial boost for Bush's impending run for reelection—allowing him to claim credit for expanding a popular social program originally put in place and long-championed by Democrats. Although enough Democrats supported the bill to enable its passage, others, including its leading opponent, Massachusetts senator Edward M. Kennedy, said the law did more for the insurance and pharmaceutical companies than for seniors. They pledged to try to repeal some of the more controversial elements of the bill, including provisions that effectively barred importation of cheaper prescription drugs from Canada and that prohibited the U.S. government from directly negotiating with the drug companies for price discounts.

Another matter poised to become a campaign issue was same-sex marriage. In December the Massachusetts supreme court ruled that the state's ban on gay marriage violated the state constitution. Gay couples would be able to marry in that state starting on May 17, 2004, pending action by the state legislature. The decision renewed calls for passage of an amendment to the U.S. Constitution banning same-sex marriages and put both Bush and his Democratic rivals in a political hot seat—any position they took was likely to offend some segment of the voting public. Bush, who had repeatedly said he was opposed to gay marriage, avoided taking a stand on a constitutional amendment until mid-December and then gave it only qualified support.

The Massachusetts ruling came five months after the U.S. Supreme Court reversed an earlier decision and struck down a state law that criminalized sexual relations between two people of the same gender. The Court majority said the constitutional guarantee of liberty extended to the right of mutually consenting adults to engage in private sexual activity without fear of government intervention. In another important and controversial civil rights case, the Supreme Court endorsed the limited use of affirmative action in college and university admissions policies aimed at creating a diverse student body. The decision was widely hailed by corporations, professional associations, and prominent members of the armed forces, all of whom said that well-educated and well-trained students of all races and ethnicities were crucial to the continued vitality of the country.

The sweeping breadth of the majority opinions in the sodomy and affirmative action cases was matched by the majority opinion in a ruling, issued at the end of the year, that upheld the key elements of the 2002 campaign finance reform. That measure was aimed at curbing the influence of big money in federal elections. The majority unequivocally endorsed Congress's authority "to anticipate and respond to concerns about circumvention of [campaign finance] regulations," squarely rejecting the challengers' claims that the new law violated the right of free speech.

Key elements of President Bush's controversial handling of terrorist suspects were being challenged in court throughout 2003. The administration scored an important victory in June when a federal appeals court upheld the Justice Department's right to keep secret the identities of 726 immigrants—most of them Muslims—it had detained while it looked for information linking them to terrorists. The Bush administration said the confidentiality was required to help foil future terrorist attacks.

On another issue, appeals courts took opposite views on the question of whether foreign nationals captured by American troops in Afghanistan during the war there in 2001 and held at a military prison at Guantanamo Naval Base in Cuba should have access to U.S. courts to challenge their detention. One court said that under the Constitution the courts had no jurisdiction over foreign nationals held on foreign territory; the other said the courts were obliged, even in national emergencies, to ensure that the executive branch did not ride "roughshod" over the rights of citizens and aliens. The Supreme Court agreed in November to review the issue. At year's end the Court was still considering whether to hear a similar issue raised by Yasir Esam Hamdi, a U.S. citizen who was captured in Afghanistan in 2001 and labeled an "enemy combatant." Hamdi was held incommunicado by the U.S. Navy until December 3, 2003, when the Bush administration reversed course and said that he would be allowed to consult a lawyer.

As controversial as the handling of terrorist suspects was the Justice Department's use of its domestic police powers to hunt down and detain those suspects. Civil liberties advocates said the new powers given to the Federal Bureau of Investigation and other law enforcement agencies were too broad, cloaked in too much secrecy, and not subject to enough checks and balances. A month-long national speaking tour by Attorney General John D. Ashcroft to defend the USA Patriot Act against allegations that it was infringing on civil liberties appeared to do little to quell anxieties about the law. Congress gave scant attention to President Bush's proposals for strengthening the law—made public on the eve of the second anniversary of the September 11, 2001, terrorist attacks on New York and Washington—and new support appeared to be gathering for repealing some parts of the law that its opponents found most objectionable.

Two health scares erupted in 2003. A previously unknown, highly infectious respiratory disease, known as SARS (for Severe Acute Respiratory Syndrome) broke out in China in 2002 and spread to some thirty countries before being contained in mid-2003. The disease infected more than 8,000 people, mostly in Asia, left nearly 800 people dead, rocked the global economy for several months, and sent waves of panic throughout the world. In late December the U.S. secretary of agriculture announced that a dairy cow in Washington state had tested positive for mad cow disease (bovine spongiform encephalopathy, or BSE). Consumption of certain parts of infected cattle could cause a rare but incurable wasting brain disease in humans. The government assured consumers that the food supply was safe and quickly introduced new rules to keep infected cows from contaminating the food chain. Nonetheless, consumers were frightened, and more than thirty countries banned imports of American beef.

Corporate Corruption

A wave of corporate scandals that began with the bankruptcy of the Enron Corporation in late 2001 continued all through 2003. The year's major new development was the revelation that some of the nation's largest mutual funds had allowed special favors for select investors, often at the expense of the vast majority of their clients. More than 70 million Americans had invested in retirement accounts and other forms of savings with mutual funds—largely because they were relatively easy to use and had appeared to be bastions of integrity. An investigation by New York State Attorney General Eliot Spitzer sparked numerous inquiries that raised serious questions about the practices at dozens of mutual funds. Some investors responded by pulling their money out of the funds targeted by the investigations, but most Americans had few attractive alternative options for investing their savings.

Other cases of misdeeds in the nation's executive suites and boardrooms came to light during the year, as well as additional information about some of the major scandals that had arisen in 2002. Among the most notable companies joining the scandal parade were Freddie Mac, the nation's second largest financier of home mortgages; HealthSouth, owner of a chain of rehabilitation nursing centers; and Parmalat, one of Europe's major food producers.

Investigative reports detailed how some leading corporate officials had mismanaged their companies and how their boards of directors let them get away with it. Perhaps the most graphic description of corporate misbehavior came in a blow-by-blow report on the events leading to the bankruptcy of telecommunications giant WorldCom; that report said the company's board had routinely rubber-stamped decisions by executives and approved billion-dollar deals without examining any of the details. By 2003 the company was taking aggressive steps to reinvent itself.

John Felton and Martha Gottron

January

Lula on His Inauguration as President of Brazil

January 1, 2003

INTRODUCTION

Luiz Inacio Lula da Silva—known universally as Lula—was sworn into office as president of Brazil on January 1, 2003. A former autoworker who grew up in extreme poverty and rose to prominence as a radical leftist labor leader during the 1970s and 1980s, Lula confounded supporters and skeptics alike with his conservative fiscal policies and his cautious approach to addressing the country's social ills during his first year in office.

Lula da Silva had scored a landslide electoral victory in October 2002 on the basis of widespread discontent with the results of the free-trade and free-market economic policies of his two-term predecessor, Fernando Henrique Cardoso. Lula promised a brighter future, especially for the nearly 50 million Brazilians (almost 28 percent of the total population of 180 million) who lived in poverty. With his many campaign promises, Lula created high expectations among the poor, but he asked for their patience as he struggled first with the need to right the country's listing economy. At least initially, he had remarkable success both in managing expectations for change and in winning broad domestic and international support for reviving the economy. *(Background, Historic Documents of 2002, p. 774)*

Lula's Inaugural Address

Lula's inauguration was a momentous occasion in Brazilian history, marking the first transfer of power from one elected president to another in four decades and, more symbolically, the first time that a leftist union leader, born to the nation's underclass of impoverished workers, had been elected to the presidency. Nearly all of his thirty-five predecessors, whether those who had assumed power through coups or the few who had won legitimate elections, had come from the military or the nation's elite upper classes. The hopes that Lula inspired were evident on inauguration day, as an estimated 200,000 people gathered in a park outside the national Congress building in Brasilia. When the newly sworn-in president began to speak, thousands in the crowd chanted "Lula, Lula," until he managed to calm them.

Obviously aware that the world was watching to see if he really had set aside his radical past, Lula sprinkled his inaugural speech with assurances that he did not plan a dramatic upheaval. "Change" was the first word of the speech, but Lula quickly added that it would be "change with courage and caution . . . a gradual and continual process, not a simple act of will; nor simply an act of willful rapture." He also urged his countrymen to exercise "patience and perseverance" each day.

Despite Brazil's rich agricultural resources, millions of Brazilians regularly suffered from hunger—estimates ranged from 15 million to 50 million (the latter figure being the number of Brazilians who lived on incomes of less than one dollar a day). In his inaugural speech, Lula repeated his campaign pledge for a Zero Hunger (*Fome Zero* in Portuguese) program. He offered no details but simply quoted his pledge immediately after his election: "If, when I conclude my term of office, all Brazilians have breakfast, lunch, and supper, I will have fulfilled my mission in life." Lula also repeated his promise of a "peaceful, organized, and well-planned" land reform, consisting primarily of settling families on millions of hectares of "idle land" and providing them with credit and technical assistance.

The new president pledged to tackle double-digit inflation, which had been sapping the Brazilian economy for years. Again, he offered no specifics in terms of policy prescriptions except to say that Brazil needed to increase its exports and stimulate its domestic economy.

One of the few reminders of Lula's radical past was his call for a "genuine social pact for change," which he said would feature social security reform, tax reform, political reform, and labor law reform. These reforms would be guided by a National Counsel for Economic and Social Development, a committee of business leaders, workers, and others that Lula appointed later in January.

Many Brazilian citizens seemed well aware that Lula faced enormous obstacles in keeping his many promises. "I hope he's going to change things, but it's a huge challenge for him," Fabiane Cristina, a babysitter living in Brasilia told the Associated Press. A public opinion survey for the *Folha De São Paulo* newspaper showed 80 percent of Brazilians expecting Lula's government to be "excellent" or "good," and the same newspaper said in an editorial: "Very rarely has a president taken up office with such a high level of expectations at one extreme, and fears at the other."

Balancing Promises and Reality

Some of the government's earliest challenges came with Lula's pledged "Zero Hunger" campaign. Government agencies were slow to implement some of the programs Lula announced with great fanfare, including distribution of electronic cards providing cash for more than a million of the poorest Brazilians to buy food. Several highly publicized missteps also embarrassed the government, among them a case, revealed by a newspaper, in which a check for nearly $30,000 donated by a famous model to the anti-hunger campaign went uncashed for more than a month. Some of Lula's own supporters demonstrated a degree of impatience, including a leftist group of peasants, called the Landless Movement, which resumed a campaign of invading and "squatting" on untilled land owned by wealthy farmers or businesses.

Keeping another campaign promise, Lula in April introduced a substantial increase in the national minimum wage. The increase, to $71 a month, applied mostly to government employees. In an April 7 speech marking his first hundred days in office, Lula said he would have liked an even higher minimum wage, but the $71 figure "is the most that prudence and care advise at the moment."

To make room in the tight budget for his promised social programs, Lula squeezed spending in nearly all other government accounts. One of his first official acts was to postpone the purchase of a dozen jets for the air force, saving at least $700 million. He also took several symbolic steps to economize, including traveling by commercial jet to Europe for a conference at which he pleaded with world business leaders for investments in Brazil.

Lula used his enormous personal popularity to win support for his programs in the bicameral national Congress, where his Workers Party had only a minority of seats and needed support from other parties to get legislation passed. The first major political battle of Lula's tenure came on the issue of autonomy for the Brazilian central bank. Lula in 2002 had endorsed a plan by then-president Cardoso giving the bank guaranteed independence as arbiter of monetary policy—a position generally associated with conservative, probusiness factions. In early April Lula won support in Congress from across the political spectrum for a constitutional amendment assuring increased autonomy for the central bank. The bank promptly raised its key interest rates to more than 26 percent in hopes of curbing double-digit inflation, prompting widespread complaints that economic recovery was being choked. One of the loudest complaints on that score came from Lula's vice president, former businessman José Alencar.

Even tougher challenges faced Lula in reforming pensions and the country's tax codes, two areas that had contributed to Brazil's mammoth public debt. Retired senior government employees in many cases were entitled to pensions that greatly exceeded their final salaries; this retirement system accounted for approximately 40 percent of the government's total payroll. The government in May proposed raising retirement ages and reducing pension payouts, leading to a public employee strike in July and a protest demonstration at Congress in August. After the legislature approved the bulk of Lula's pension and tax reforms, the Workers Party in December voted to expel four leftist legislators who had voted against the changes. One of the four, Batista de Araujo, called the government "reactionary" and "right-wing"—adjectives that no one would have considered using to describe Lula before his election.

Fixing the Economy

As a candidate in 2002, Lula had faced deep skepticism, both domestically and internationally, about his intentions concerning Brazil's enormous debt. The government and related agencies owed approximately $260 billion to creditors, and many skeptics were convinced that, once elected, Lula would attempt to repudiate some or all of that debt to pay for the social programs he was promising voters. Candidate Lula insisted that was not his intent, but fresh in the minds of skeptics was the recent experience in neighboring Argentina, which repudiated billions of dollars of commercial debt in late 2001 when that country fell into a deep economic crisis. *(Economic recovery in Argentina, p. 824; crisis in Argentina, Historic Documents of 2002, p. 89)*

The skepticism continued even after Lula, in August 2002, endorsed promises that Cardoso made the International Monetary Fund (IMF) to secure a $30 billion loan—the largest the IMF had ever made to any country. Chief among those promises was that Brazil would maintain a "primary budget surplus"—a surplus in government spending before interest payments—of at least 3.75 percent of gross domestic product. Maintaining such a surplus would sharply curtail government spending, especially on social programs.

Once in office Lula confounded the skeptics—and many of his most radical supporters—by keeping Cardoso's pledges to the IMF. In fact, the new government proved even better at pinching *reals* than its conservative predecessor. On February 7, 2003, finance minister Antonio Palocci announced that the targeted primary budget surplus would be raised to 4.25 percent as a further hedge against the deficit. This new target, coupled with a willingness to back autonomy for the central bank, reassured domestic and international investors but annoyed many of the president's core constituents, who saw the moves as favoring business interests at the expense of the working classes.

The economic results, at least through the rest of 2003, were positive. Inflation dropped from a high of 15 percent at the end of 2002 to below

10 percent in mid-2003 and was expected to fall further to about 6 percent during 2004. In response, the central bank in June began progressively cutting its prime lending; on December 18 the bank set a new rate of 16.5 percent—high by international standards but Brazil's lowest level in more than two years. For the first time since worldwide financial crises in 1997–1998, Brazil again appeared to be an attractive place for foreign investors. The factor known as "country risk"—the premium investors demanded before buying Brazilian rather than U.S. bonds—fell during the year from 24 percentage points to less than 6 points.

Although these indicators showed new strength for the Brazilian economy, the improvements did not necessarily translate into better lives for all Brazilians. Unemployment stubbornly remained at about 13 percent overall and exceeded 20 percent in São Paolo, the largest city. Real, after-inflation wages remained stagnant, as did consumer demand for products and services. Most polls showed that Brazilians remained hopeful, but Lula's personal approval rating slowly dropped during the year; by December only about two-thirds of those polled approved of his performance in office, down from record-high levels when he took office.

Lula's cautious stewardship of the budget and economy won a significant reward in November, when the IMF agreed to a $14 billion loan. That figure included $6 billion of new lending and the release of $8 billion that the IMF had withheld from the original $30 billion loan pending Brazil's fiscal performance during the year. In a further sign of international confidence in Lula's government, the IMF also allowed Brazil to delay, until 2005–2006, about $5.5 billion in repayments on principal from the $30 billion loan. Economists and business leaders praised the new IMF lending as demonstrating continued confidence in Lula's government.

Brazilian-U.S. Relations

In previous decades relations between Brazil and the United States often had been strained, generally because Brazilian leaders resented what they viewed as Washington's interference in Latin American economic and political matters. Lula's election at first seemed to portend yet another period of distrust between the giants of South and North America. As a candidate, Lula had harshly criticized U.S. negotiating positions during international trade talks, and one top U.S. official suggested Brazil's only export customer would be Antarctica if it failed to fall into line. Lula also enjoyed warm relations with the two leftist Latin American leaders most disliked by Washington: Cuban dictator Fidel Castro, and Venezuela's embattled president Hugo Chavez. *(Venezuela, p. 279)*

Lula's relations with Washington got off to a rocky start early in his tenure when he opposed the Bush administration's war in Iraq. But on June 21

Lula became the first foreign critic of that war to visit President George W. Bush at the White House. The two men—both known for stressing personal ties over the intricate details of government policy—appeared to develop a good working relationship.

As expected, trade proved to be the most contentious issue between Brazil and the United States. In his inaugural address, Lula indicated that he would take a tough line defending Brazil's interest in two multilateral trade negotiations: the talks among thirty-four Western Hemisphere countries (except Cuba) aimed at creating a hemispheric tariff-free trading community known as the Free Trade Area of the Americas (FTAA), and the international negotiations toward a new trade agreement among nearly one hundred fifty members of the World Trade Organization (WTO). Directly challenging the negotiating positions of the United States and the European Union, Lula said he would "seek to eliminate the outrageous agricultural subsidies practiced in the developed countries" that undermined Brazilian food exports and the "unjustifiable barriers to our exports of industrial goods." Lula made no mention of Brazil's own barriers against international trade, primarily its restrictions on foreign competition with Brazilian banks, public utilities, and other service industries.

The opposing agendas on trade matters came to a head in mid-September, when Brazil led twenty other developing countries in blocking U.S. and European positions in the current round of WTO talks at Cancun, Mexico. The collapse of those negotiations was a major setback to plans for the latest in a series of worldwide agreements since the 1960s to reduce trade barriers.

The scenario was similar—with slightly different results—during negotiations in Miami during mid-November on the FTAA. Once again, Brazil demanded that the United States open its markets to greater imports of food and other products from developing countries in Latin America, and U.S. officials insisted such issues should be handled instead in the faltering WTO negotiations. The result was an implied concession by all involved that the original goal of a broad free trade agreement for the Western Hemisphere was no longer possible. Instead, negotiators said they would work toward a scaled-back version leading to only a few tariff reductions and other trade incentives. Washington also turned its attention to smaller-scale trade agreements, including one signed on December 17 with four of the five Central American countries (Costa Rica had dropped out of the talks).

Following are excerpts from the speech by Luiz Inacio Lula da Silva, on January 1, 2003, upon his inauguration as the thirty-sixth president of Brazil.

Inauguration Speech of Brazilian President Luiz Inacio Lula da Silva

Change. This is the key word. It was the great message from Brazilian Society in the October elections.

Hope finally triumphed over fear as society decided it was time to tread a new path.

In face of the exhaustion of a model that, rather than generating growth, has produced stagnation, unemployment and hunger; in face of the failure of a culture of individualism, selfishness, indifference to one's neighbor, family and of community disintegration; in face of threats to national sovereignty; the overwhelming precariousness of public safety; disrespect for the elderly and disillusionment of youth. In face of the Country's economic, social and moral stalemate, Brazilian society opted for change; and has itself taken the steps to promote such change.

It was for this that the Brazilian people elected me President of the Republic: to change. This was the meaning underlying each vote in my favor, and in that of my brave running mate José Alencar.

And I am here on this day, so longingly sought after by preceding generations in the struggle, to reaffirm my deepest and most essential commitments; to reiterate, to each citizen, man and woman, of my Country, the meaning of each word uttered during the course of the campaign. To imprint change of an intensely practical nature.

To announce that the time has come to transform Brazil into the Nation of which we have always dreamed. A dignified, sovereign Nation, aware of its own importance in the international scenario and, at the same time, capable of sheltering, welcoming and treating all its children with justice.

Yes, we will change. Change with courage and caution. With humility and boldness; change in the awareness that change is a gradual and continuous process, not a simple act of will; nor simply an act of willful rapture. Change through dialogue and negotiation; without upheavals or precipitation; in order for the results to be consistent and long lasting.

Brazil is a vast country, a continent of huge human, ecological and social complexities, with a population of almost 175 million. We cannot leave it adrift, at the whim of the winds, lacking a true national development plan, and truly strategic planning.

If we want to transform Brazil, so that we may dwell in a nation where everyone can walk tall, we will have to exercise two virtues on a day-to-day basis: patience and perseverance.

We must keep our many and legitimate social aspirations under control, so that they can be fulfilled at the right pace and at the right time. We must tread this path with our eyes open, and walk with well-considered, precise and steady steps. For the simple reason that no one can harvest fruits without first planting the tree.

But we shall embark upon change immediately, since, as the popular saying goes, a long journey begins with the first steps.

This is an extraordinary Country. From Amazonia to Rio Grande do Sul, among populations that live on the beaches, in the hinterland and along river banks, wherever I have been, I have met mature, seasoned and optimistic people. People who never cease to be youthful and young at heart. People who have experience of suffering, but who also know joy; who trust in themselves and in their own resourcefulness.

I believe in a glorious future for Brazil, because our joy is greater than our sorrow. Our strength is mightier than our poverty. Our hope out-strips our fear.

The Brazilian people, in more recent and in more remote historical times, have provided indubitable proof of their magnanimity and gen-erosity. They have given proof of their capacity to mobilize the nation's spirit in large-scale civic endeavors. It is my desire, prior to anything else, to summon my people for just such a large-scale civic endeavor: a national endeavor against hunger.

In a country that has so much fertile land and so many people willing to work, there ought to be no cause to speak of hunger. Nonetheless, millions of Brazilians, in the countryside and in the cities, in underprivi-leged rural areas and on the outskirts of the cities, at this very moment, have nothing to eat.

They survive miraculously below the poverty line, when they do not die in misery, begging for a crust of bread.

This story is an old one. Brazil experienced the wealth of the sugar mills and cane plantations in the early colonial era—but never overcame hunger. It proclaimed its independence and abolished slavery—but never overcame hunger. It saw the wealth of the gold fields of Minas Gerais and of coffee plantations in the Paraíba valley—but never overcame hunger. It industrialized and established remarkably diversified industrial capacity—but it never overcame hunger.

This cannot continue. So long as one of our Brazilian brothers or sisters is hungry, we can only be overwhelmed by shame.

It is for this reason that I have placed, among the priorities of my Government, a food security program to be known as Zero Hunger ('Fome Zero'). As I said in my first speech after the election, if, when I conclude my term of office, all Brazilians can have breakfast, lunch and supper, I will have fulfilled my mission in life.

It is for this that I issue this summons: let us put an end to hunger in our Country! We shall transform the ending of hunger into a great national cause, similar to such causes of the past as the founding of Petrobrás [the national oil company], and the memorable struggle to restore our Country's democracy.

This is a cause that can and should be embraced by all, regardless of social class, political party or ideological distinctions. In face of the cries of those oppressed by the bane of hunger, the ethical imperative of joining forces, skills and instruments to defend that which is most sacred must prevail: the dignity of human beings.

To this end it is essential that peaceful, organized and well-planned land reform be carried out. We shall ensure access to the land for those who wish to work; not merely as a matter of social justice, but so that the fields of Brazil can produce more and yield more food for all our tables; that they may yield wheat, soybeans, fruits, and our daily rice and beans.

That country people may have their dignity restored to them, in the knowledge that, upon rising with the sun, with each stroke of their hoes or of their tractors, they are contributing to the well being of all Brazilians, both in the countryside and in the cities.

We shall also foster family agriculture, cooperatives, and other forms of communal economy. These are perfectly compatible with our strong support for livestock raising, corporate farms, industrial farming and agribusiness. Indeed, they are complementary from both the economic and social standpoints. We can only be proud of these goods that we produce and ship to market.

Land reform shall be carried on idle land, on the millions of hectares that are today available to settle families and plant seeds that shall sprout luxuriantly, fostered by lines of credit, scientific research and technical assistance.

We shall do this without in any way affecting farms that are productive. This shall be so because productive land is its own justification and such land shall be stimulated to produce ever more, as in the example provided by the huge mountain of grain that we harvest each year.

Today, so many regions of the Country have been duly settled. Fields stretch beyond where the eye can see. There are places where we have achieved levels of productivity that exceed those of Australia and the United States. We must cherish this immense, splendid productive heritage.

On the other hand, it is absolutely essential that the country's growth be restored, in order to generate jobs and distribute income. I wish here to reaffirm my commitment to production, and to Brazilian men and women who want to work and live in dignity from the fruit of their labor.

I have said before and I now repeat: job creation shall be my obsession.

In this regard, we shall work to overcome our current vulnerabilities and to create favorable macroeconomic conditions for the resumption of sustained growth, for which stability and responsible management of public finances are essential elements.

In order to advance in this direction we must combat inflation implacably, export more, add value to our products and act with energy and creativity at the international forums of globalized trade. Likewise, it is necessary that we strongly stimulate our domestic market, and strengthen micro and small companies. It is also necessary to invest in technological training and in the infrastructure required to transport our production.

In order to place Brazil back on the path of growth and to generate the jobs that are so sorely needed, what is lacking is a genuine social pact for change; an alliance that brings us all together with a single aim, the productive capital that generates the essential wealth of the Nation; in order that Brazil may overcome its current stagnation; in order that the Country might resume navigation of the open seas of social and economic development.

The social pact will be equally decisive for achieving the reforms that Brazilian society clamors for, and that I have committed myself to, bringing about: social security reform, tax reform, political reform, and reform of the labor laws, aside from land reform. This set of reforms will provide the driving force for a new cycle of national development.

An essential instrument for this pact in favor of change shall be the National Counsel for Economic and Social Development, which I propose to install this January, to bring together businessmen, workers, and leaders of the various segments of civil society.

We are at a particularly propitious moment for this; a rare moment in the life of a people. A moment in which the President of the Republic has the Nation's will on his side.

Business, the political parties, the armed forces and workers are united. Men, women, the elderly and youth, are united as brothers with the same purpose of contributing so that the Country can fulfill its historic destiny of prosperity and justice.

Aside from the support of the vast majority of organizations and social movements, we can also count upon enthusiastic participation of millions of Brazilian men and women who wish to join this crusade for the resumption of growth, against hunger, unemployment and social inequality. It is a powerful energy of solidarity that our campaign has awakened and that we cannot afford to allow to go to waste; an extraordinary ethical-political energy, in which we shall become fully immersed as our government seeks channels for expression.

In view of all this, I believe in the social pact. It is with this same spirit that I have selected my ministers from among the best leaders of each of Brazil's economic and social segments. And we shall work as a team, without favoring personalities, for the good of Brazil. And we shall adopt a new style of government, with absolute transparency and permanent stimulus for popular participation.

Combating corruption and defending ethics in dealings with public affairs shall be central and permanent goals of my Government. We must face up to and vanquish this veritable culture of impunity that prevails in certain segments of public life.

We shall not allow corruption, tax evasion and waste to continue depriving the population of resources that are its due and which are sorely needed to assist in the grim struggle for survival.

Being honest means more than merely not stealing and not allowing others to steal. It also entails efficiency, transparency and eliminating all waste of public resources, with the aim of achieving concrete social outcomes.

I am convinced that, in this manner, we have a unique chance to overcome the principal obstacles to our Country's sustained development. Believe me: I do not intend to waste this opportunity, achieved through the efforts of many millions of Brazilian men and women.

Under my leadership, the Executive branch will maintain a constructive relationship with other branches of the Republic, paying exemplary respect to their independence and the exercise of their high constitutional functions.

I, who have had the honor of being a member of this House, hope to be able to count upon the contribution of the National Congress, through meticulous debate, in ensuring the feasibility of the structural reforms that our Country requires of us all.

In my government, Brazil will be at the center of attention. What Brazil needs to do, in all areas, is to plunge within itself in order to create forces to enable it to expand its horizons

Taking such a plunge does not imply closing doors and windows to the world. Brazil can and must have a development plan that consists, at the same time, of a national and universal approach. This means simply that we must acquire greater confidence in ourselves, in our capacity to establish short, medium and long-term objectives, and work to fulfill them. The principal characteristic of the model that we wish to work towards is an expansion of domestic savings and of our own investment capacity. Likewise, Brazil must enhance the status of its human capital by investing in knowledge and technology.

Above all, we must produce. Because the wealth that matters is the wealth that is generated by our own hands; the wealth produced by our machines, by our intelligence and by our sweat.

Brazil is huge. Despite all the cruelty and discrimination, especially against indigenous and black communities, and despite the inequality and pain that must never be forgotten, the Brazilian people have created an admirable work of resistance and national construction.

They have, over centuries, created a Nation that is pluralistic and diversified, contradictory even; but where people from the most extreme points of its territory understand each other. From the enchanted beings ('encantados') of Amazonia to the African deities ('orixás') of Bahia; from the 'frevo' rhythm of Pernambuco to the 'samba' schools of Rio de Janeiro; from the drum beat of Maranhão to the baroque style of Minas Gerais; from the modern architecture of Brasilia to the 'sertaneja' music of the interior—the multiplicity of its cultures extends like an arc and is reflected in the cultures of São Paulo, of Paraná, of Santa Catarina, of Rio Grande do Sul and of the Central-West.

This is a nation where everyone speaks the same language; shares the same fundamental values; feels that they are Brazilian. A Nation where miscegenation and syncretism imposed their own original contribution to the world. Where Jews and Arabs speak to each other without fear, where all immigrants receive a welcome, because we know that in a short space of time, through our own capacity for assimilation and mutual affection, each immigrant is soon transformed into yet another Brazilian.

This nation, raised under tropical skies, needs to state what it stands for. Domestically, doing justice to the struggle in which its children are committed. And internationally, affirming its sovereign and creative presence as a nation of this world.

Our foreign policy shall also reflect the desire for change manifested at the ballot box. Under my Government, Brazil's diplomatic efforts will be guided by a humanistic perspective directed, above all else, at providing instruments for the Nation's development. Through our foreign trade, through the obtaining of advanced technologies and through the quest for productive investment, Brazil's foreign relations will aim at improving the living conditions of Brazilian men and women, at increasing income levels and generating dignified jobs. Trade negotiations are today of vital importance. With respect to the FTAA [Free Trade Area of the Americas], through understandings with Mercosur [a South American free trade area], the European Union and the World Trade Organization, Brazil will combat protectionism, struggle to eliminate trade barriers and attempt to obtain fairer and more appropriate conditions for fostering the Nation's development. We shall seek to eliminate the outrageous agricultural subsidies practiced in the developed countries, that harm our farmers by denying them their comparative advantages. With the same ardor, we shall take pains to remove unjustifiable barriers to our exports of industrial goods. In all of these forums, it is essential that we maintain spaces and flexibility for our own development policies in the areas of social and regional development, the environment, agriculture, industry and technology. We shall never overlook the fact that human beings are the final objective of the results of such negotiations. It would be of little use for us to participate in such diversified efforts on so many fronts if they do not result in direct benefits for our people. We shall be watching these negotiations closely, since nowadays they extend far beyond mere tariff reductions and encompass a broad spectrum of normative issues. We shall ensure that they do not create unwarranted restrictions to the sovereign right of the Brazilian people to decide upon the model of development they desire.

The greatest priority of our foreign policy during my Government will be the building of a politically stable, prosperous and united South America, founded upon ideals of democracy and social justice. To this end, decisive action is required to revitalize Mercosur that has been so weakened by the crises afflicting each of its member states, and by narrow and sometimes self-serving standpoints in relation to integration. Mercosur, and likewise South American integration as a whole, is primarily a political project. Nonetheless, this project rests upon economic and commercial foundations that need urgently to be repaired and strengthened. We shall also deal with the social, cultural and scientific-technological aspects of the integration process. We shall stimulate joint ventures and organize rich intellectual and artistic exchanges among the countries of South America. We shall provide support for the necessary institutional arrangements designed to enable a veritable Mercosur and South American identity to flourish. Currently, several of our neighbors are facing difficult circumstances. We shall contribute, when called upon and within the scope of our possibilities, to finding peaceful solutions to crises, based upon dialogue, in line with democratic principles and respecting the constitutional provisions of each country. Likewise, we shall maintain concrete cooperation efforts and substantive dialogue with all countries of Latin America.

We shall seek to maintain with the United States of America a mature partnership, based upon reciprocal interests and mutual respect. We shall seek to strengthen understandings and cooperation with the European Union and its Member States, as well as with other important industrialized countries such as Japan. We shall deepen our relations with such large developing countries as China, India, Russia and South Africa, among others. We reaffirm the deep ties that unite us to the African continent and our willingness actively to contribute so that its vast potentialities can be developed. We aim not only to explore the potential benefits of greater economic exchanges, and of a greater Brazilian presence in the international market, but also to stimulate incipient elements of multi-polarity in the contemporary international scenario.

The democratization of international relations, without hegemonies of any kind whatsoever, is as important for the future of Mankind as the consolidation and development of democracy within each State. We shall exalt the value of multilateral organizations, and especially of the United Nations, which has the prime mandate for preserving international peace and security. Resolutions of the Security Council must be duly enforced. International crises, such as the situation in the Middle East, should be resolved by peaceful means and negotiation. We support a reform of the Security Council, to make it more representative of contemporary realities, with developed and developing countries from the various regions of the world among its permanent members.

We face challenges at the present time, such as terrorism and organized crime, that can only be resolved through international cooperation based upon the principles of multilateralism and of International Law. We shall lend support to efforts targeted at making the UN and its agencies flexible and effective instruments for promoting social and economic development, including combating poverty, inequalities and all forms of discrimination, defending of human rights and preservation of the environment.

Indeed: we have a message for the world. We must display our national project, democratically, through an open dialogue, before other nations of the planet. Because we are new; we are the innovation that a civilization has fearlessly drafted; drafted on the body, soul and heart of a people, often without acquiescence of the elites, of institutions, or even of the State.

It is true that the deterioration of social ties in Brazil over the past two decades, as a consequence of economic policies that did not favor growth and brought on an ominous cloud that has jeopardized customary standards of tolerance in Brazilian society. Heinous crimes, massacres and lynchings have become commonplace, especially in the large cities, constituting an experience similar to war of all against all.

For this reason, I begin my term of office firmly resolved to place the federal government, in partnership with the States, at the service of a much more vigorous and efficient public security policy. A policy that, combined with actions in areas including health and education, targeted at preventing violence, deterring crime and reestablishing security for citizens, men and women. If we are able once more to walk in peace through our streets and squares, we will have made an extraordinary step forward in our national project of building, in this corner of the Americas, a bastion of tolerance, democratic pluralism, respectful coexistence, in which differences are respected.

Brazil has much to offer itself and to the world. It is for this reason that we must demand so much of ourselves. We must demand even more than we had thought; because we have not as yet finished making our mark on history; and because we have not yet fulfilled the great planetary mission that awaits us.

This is because, in this new historical, social, cultural and economic endeavor, Brazil will have to count, above all, upon itself. It will have to think with its own head, walk on its own legs, and listen to the dictates of its own heart. And all of us will have to learn, with renewed intensity, to love this our country, to love our flag, to love our struggle, and to love our people.

Each one of us Brazilians knows that what we have achieved to date is no small feat; we know also, however, that we can do much more.

When I look back upon my own life as a migrant from the Northeast, as a boy who sold peanuts and oranges on the docks at Santos, who became a lath operator and union leader and who one day founded the Worker's Party (PT), and who believed in what he was doing, and who is now taking office as the Nation's supreme ruler, I perceive, with full clarity and conviction, that we can achieve much more. And that, to do so, all we need is to believe in ourselves; in our own strength and in our own creative capacity, and in our willingness to act.

We are all aware that, today, we are embarking upon a new chapter of the history of Brazil. Not as a submissive Nation, relinquishing its sovereignty; nor as an unjust nation, passively watching the suffering of its poorer citizens; but rather, as a bold and noble Nation, bravely asserting its position in the world; like any other nation, without distinctions of class, race, sex or belief.

This is a country that can, and will, make a veritable qualitative quantum leap. It is the Country of the new millennium. Its agricultural prowess, its urban and industrial structure, its fantastic biodiversity, its cultural wealth, its love of nature, its creativity, its intellectual and scientific capabilities, its human warmth, its love of novelty and innovation, and, above all, the innate qualities and powers of its people.

What we are experiencing today, at this moment, my colleagues, brothers and sisters, from all over Brazil, can be summarized in a few brief words. Today is the day when Brazil has reencountered itself.

I give thanks to God for having brought me so far: I am now the number one public servant of my Country.

I ask God for wisdom to govern, for discernment to judge, for serenity to administer, for courage to decide, and for a heart the size of Brazil so as to make me feel united to each citizen, man and woman, in this country, day-to-day, over the next four years.

Long live the Brazilian People!

Source: Brazil. Embassy of Brazil in London. Speech Given by President Luiz Inacio Lula Da Silva on the Occasion of His Accession to the Presidency in Brasilia, Brazil. January 1, 2003. www.brazil.org.uk/page.php?cid=1499 (accessed May 29, 2003).

State of the Union Address and Democratic Response

January 28, 2003

INTRODUCTION

President George W. Bush used his third State of the Union address on January 28, 2003, to strengthen his case for an impending war with Iraq. Addressing Congress and the American people—but also sending an unmistakable message to the world at large and Iraqi leader Saddam Hussein in particular—the president said he considered Iraq to be a legitimate target in the war against terrorism. "A brutal dictator, with a history of reckless aggression . . . with ties to terrorism . . . will not be permitted to dominate a vital region and threaten the United States," Bush said. Less than two months later, on March 20, Bush launched the overwhelming power of the U.S. military on a war that succeeded in ousting Saddam from power in just three weeks. Rebuilding Iraq after the war and establishing a democracy, as Bush promised, proved to be a much more difficult task that was still, haltingly, under way at year's end.

Although the looming war overshadowed all other considerations at the time, Bush also sought in his State of the Union address to bolster support for a domestic agenda clearly aimed at giving him, and his fellow Republicans who controlled Congress, a sturdy platform for the 2004 elections. The president proposed tax cuts to stimulate the shaky economy and a Medicare "reform" plan to give senior citizens the prescription drug benefit he had promised in his 2000 campaign.

Most opinion polls conducted just before the annual speech gave the president generally high approval ratings but showed growing public unease with his handling of the economy and foreign affairs. According to the polls, most Americans did not yet feel that the economy was on the road to recovery or that Bush's expensive tax cut passed by Congress in 2001 had provided much of a stimulus for jobs and investment. An increasing portion of the public also expressed doubt about the wisdom of the impending war with Iraq. Depending on the timing and questions used in the polls, a half or more of Americans said Bush had not yet made a compelling case for the expenditure of blood and money to oust the Iraqi leader. *(Iraq war, pp. 40, 135, 933; U.S. economy, pp. 68, 441)*

Warning to Iraq

The 2003 State of the Union speech marked Bush's fourth major attempt in a year to explain why he believed Saddam's Iraq presented a security threat to the United States. The first was the previous State of the Union address, delivered January 29, 2002, in which Bush listed Iraq, along with Iran and North Korea, as part of an "axis of evil" that, he said, had ties to terrorist groups and had developed, or were developing, biological, chemical, and nuclear weapons (the so-called weapons of mass destruction). Bush again pressed his case with a forceful speech to the United Nations General Assembly on September 12, 2002, calling on the UN's Security Council to enforce its numerous resolutions requiring Iraq to give up its weapons of mass destruction. One month later, on October 7, 2002, Bush gave a nationally televised address in which he said that Iraq "on any given day" could attack the United States or its allies with biological or chemical weapons or could give such weapons to terrorist groups. These three speeches, coupled with intensive political maneuvering and diplomatic efforts by Bush's aides, led Congress in October 2002 to adopt a resolution (PL 107–243) authorizing the use of U.S. armed force against Iraq, and the UN Security Council in November 2002 to adopt Resolution 1441 demanding that Iraq give up its weapons of mass destruction. *(2002 State of the Union address, Historic Documents of 2002, p. 33; Bush speech to the United Nations, Historic Documents of 2002, p. 612; U.S. and UN resolutions on Iraq, Historic Documents of 2002, p. 713)*

In his 2003 State of the Union address, Bush was not yet ready to declare war on Iraq because diplomatic efforts were still under way to determine the UN's next step. But by January 29 there was little doubt that a war was in the offing within a few weeks or months; the only question was whether the UN Security Council would specifically authorize it.

Bush offered no new arguments in his address, but he did seek to draw a clear link between Iraq's leader and international terrorism. The president summarized UN reports and U.S. intelligence information on Iraq's presumed arsenals of biological and chemical weapons and its presumed attempts to acquire nuclear weapons. Bush also said the United States had evidence that Saddam "aids and protects terrorists, including members of al Qaeda," the group that Bush said carried out the September 11, 2001, terrorist attacks in New York City and Washington, D.C. *(Attacks, Historic Documents of 2001, p. 614)*

Acknowledging that diplomacy was still ongoing at the UN, Bush said: "We will consult [with other countries], but let there be no misunderstanding:

If Saddam Hussein does not fully disarm, for the safety of our people, and for the peace of the world, we will lead a coalition to disarm him."

Uranium from Niger

For the second consecutive year, a small number of words in a Bush State of the Union address generated intense international controversy. In 2002 Bush's claim that Iran, Iraq, and North Korea constituted an "axis of evil" reverberated around the world as political leaders, diplomats, and policy experts debated the wisdom of lumping the three countries into the same category. That claim came into dispute almost from the moment the words left Bush's mouth. In contrast, sixteen words in Bush's 2003 address came into serious question only months later.

As part of his laundry list of Saddam's alleged support for terrorists and his attempts to develop weapons of mass destruction, Bush said: "The British government has learned that Saddam Hussein recently sought significant quantities of uranium from Africa." The president offered no other details. *(Iraqi weapons issue, p. 874)*

Very little of the initial reporting and commentary on Bush's speech mentioned this allegation, which referred to reports that Iraq had attempted, as recently as 2000, to buy a uranium substance known as "yellow cake" from Niger. Mohamed El Baradei, director general of the International Atomic Energy Agency, told the UN Security Council on March 8 that documents allegedly verifying the Iraq-Niger connection were "not authentic." Several news reports in subsequent months revealed that the Central Intelligence Agency had concluded in 2002 that the Iraq-Niger allegation was not true. Even so, the matter did not develop into a major controversy until July 6, when the *New York Times* published a column in which Joseph C. Wilson IV, a former U.S. ambassador, said he had investigated the Iraq-Niger report in 2002 at the CIA's request and had found no evidence to support it. The next day, White House officials acknowledged that the information cited by Bush was incorrect and should not have been used in the State of the Union address.

Two separate but related controversies then developed. One centered on why the White House used the incorrect information and why the CIA did not attempt to have the statement deleted from Bush's speech. A second flare-up emerged after a veteran Washington columnist, Robert Novak, alleged that the CIA sent Wilson to investigate the Niger information on the recommendation of his wife, who was a covert CIA agent.

CIA director George J. Tenet attempted on July 11 to calm the first controversy by accepting responsibility for his agency's approval of Bush's statement in the State of the Union speech. "The president had every reason to believe that the text presented to him was sound," Tenet said in a statement. "These sixteen words [about Iraq and Africa] should never have been included in the text written for the president." Most Republicans on Capitol Hill accepted Tenet's statement as the final word on the matter, but many Democrats did not and pressed the issue in House and Senate Intelligence committee hearings in mid-July. Tenet himself reportedly muddied the waters during the hearings by saying that a CIA weapons expert had recommended that the Niger reference be removed from Bush's speech, but the White House insisted on retaining it. The Senate on July 16 rejected a proposal by Democrats to establish a special commission to investigate the administration's handling of intelligence information about Iraq. Stephen J. Hadley, Bush's deputy national security adviser, on July 22 said he was responsible for allowing the Niger reference in the speech. Hadley's assertion failed to quell the dispute, and finally, on July 30, Bush himself accepted ultimate responsibility. "I take personal responsibility for everything I say, absolutely," he said during a rare news conference at the White House. The president offered no explanation for why he had used the erroneous information.

The related flap over Wilson's wife developed in August, when Wilson alleged that unnamed "senior" White House officials had leaked her name to columnist Novak in an effort to intimidate anyone who might have information discrediting its case against Iraq. News reports noted that federal law made it a crime to disclose the identity of covert intelligence operatives. After several weeks of speculation about which White House officials might have been involved, news reports on September 28 revealed that Tenet had asked the Justice Department to investigate the matter. In a statement, the White House pledged to cooperate in the probe, the results of which had not been made public by year's end. Attorney General John Ashcroft on December 30 recused himself from any role in the case; this action came after months of pressure by Democrats for an independent investigation.

AIDS Initiative

One of the most dramatic moments in Bush's speech was his focus on AIDS, the incurable disease that had killed about 25 million people worldwide in the previous decades and was spreading at an alarming rate, most recently in the world's two most populous countries, China and India. Bush had devoted little attention to the AIDS pandemic earlier in his presidency, and the issue only recently had received sympathetic attention from conservative Republicans in Congress. One of those who had been vocal about the need for increased U.S. funding to battle AIDS was the new Senate majority leader, Bill Frist, the Tennessee Republican who also was a medical doctor and had regularly traveled to Africa to treat AIDS patients as a volunteer.

In solemn tones, Bush recited some of the grim statistics about the AIDS crisis, particularly in Africa. But Bush also noted that the cost of drugs used to counter the symptoms of AIDS had fallen sharply—a development, he said, that "places a tremendous possibility within our grasp." The president said he would ask Congress to appropriate $15 billion over the next five years for anti-AIDS programs in Africa and the Caribbean; of that, $10 billion was to be what Bush called "new money," over and above his previous requests. Bush won wide praise for this initiative, although many anti-AIDS activists faulted him for plans to spend the money through U.S. agencies (which Congress had barred from funding programs that distributed condoms) rather than the United Nations international campaign against AIDS. Congress quickly passed legislation (PL 108–25) authorizing the $15 billion Bush requested (at a rate of $3 billion a year). But Bush himself later pared back his initiative, seeking only $2 billion in actual spending for fiscal year 2004. After much wrangling during the year, Congress eventually agreed to spend something closer to the president's original request: $2.4 billion. That money was included in two different portions of a massive catch-all appropriations bill (HR 2800) still pending at year's end. *(AIDS reports, p. 780)*

Domestic Issues

Even while continuing to focus attention on Iraq and other foreign issues, Bush used his State of the Union speech to outline an ambitious agenda on domestic matters. He could be confident that a Republican-controlled Congress would enact major pieces of his agenda, enabling him to go into the 2004 presidential elections with a list of accomplishments that any Democratic challenger could not hope to match.

Much of the initial attention focused on a surprise proposal: Bush's call for $1.2 billion in funding for a crash research program to develop hydrogen fuel cells as a future method of powering automobiles. But the key domestic element of Bush's speech was his call for yet another tax cut, the second major one of his presidency. Bush said the economy needed another boost—beyond that provided by low interest rates and the $1.35 trillion, ten-year tax cut enacted by Congress in 2001. The centerpiece of his new plan was the elimination of taxes on most stock dividends paid to individuals; this proposal was expected to account for more than one-half of the total ten-year $726 billion cost of Bush's tax cut. Bush insisted that cutting taxes would be so effective in stimulating the economy that, ultimately, tax revenues would grow with the creation of new jobs. He used this controversial argument to dispute assertions by critics that his tax cuts and defense spending increases would drive up the deficit for years to come.

If Bush expected his tax plan to energize a sluggish stock market, he miscalculated. Driven more by fear of the impending war with Iraq than by the prospect of lower taxes on their earnings, investors responded initially by selling more stocks than they bought. The stock markets began climbing steadily only in May, after major combat in Iraq had ended.

By far the most controversial element of Bush's tax plan was the elimination of most taxes on stock dividends. Democrats derided the proposal as "no millionaire left behind," a satirical reference to Bush's 2001 changes in federal education funding that he called "no child left behind." Even many Republicans on Capitol Hill were nervous about a proposal that so clearly benefited only a narrow slice of the taxpaying public. Ultimately, Republican congressional leaders crafted a compromise plan that reduced taxes on capital gains and dividends and accelerated some of the individual income tax cuts enacted in 2001. That package carried an estimated price tax of $350 billion over ten years, about half of what Bush had proposed. Congress cleared the tax cut on May 23, and Bush signed it into law (PL 108–27) five days later. *(Economy, p. 68)*

Another presidential priority was what Bush called a "reform" of the Medicare system, combined with a new prescription drug benefit for senior citizens. Under the president's proposal, senior citizens could opt to continue their existing Medicare coverage for most health care costs except for prescription drugs, but they would have to sign up for a private health care provider to receive coverage for prescriptions. The president said his budget would provide "an additional $400 billion over the next decade to reform and strengthen Medicare" by subsidizing what he called a health care "choice" for seniors.

As could be expected with such a politically touchy subject, Bush's Medicare plan provoked a lengthy and hard-fought battle in Congress that ended in late November with passage of a Republican-drafted compromise. The final bill, signed into law (PL 108–173) by Bush on December 8, created a complex scheme to provide senior citizens with limited prescription drug coverage beginning in 2006. The bill also provided tens of billions of dollars worth of subsidies to health insurers (to encourage them to set up alternatives to Medicare) and to employers (to encourage them to continue offering health coverage to their retirees). Most Republicans in Congress supported the final version and boasted that it gave them, and Bush, a strong platform to claim support from senior citizens. Most Democrats opposed the measure as offering too little benefit for seniors and too much in subsidies for pharmaceutical and health insurance companies. *(Health insurance, p. 846)*

Democratic Response

The official Democratic response to Bush's speech was delivered by Washington governor Gary Locke, who sought to focus attention on the nation's faltering economy. "Some say it's a recovery, but there's no recovery in our states and cities. There's no recovery in our rural communities," he said. Noting rising unemployment, which had topped 6 percent, Locke added: "After gaining 22 million jobs in eight years [during the administration of Democrat Bill Clinton], we've now lost 2 million jobs in the past two years since President Bush took office—100,000 lost last month alone." Locke also criticized Bush's tax-cutting proposal as "upside down economics" that would not stimulate the economy and instead would "weaken our economic future" by bloating the federal budget deficit. Locke offered few specific alternatives to Bush's proposals.

Democrats on Capitol Hill joined Locke in challenging many of the president's domestic proposals, notably the tax cut and the reliance on the private insurance companies as an alternative to the Medicare program. Some Democrats also said Bush had not yet made what Sen. Edward M. Kennedy of Massachusetts called a "convincing case for war" in Iraq.

Following are the texts of the State of the Union address delivered January 29, 2003, by President George W. Bush to a joint session of Congress and the Democratic response by Governor Gary Locke of Washington.

President Bush's 2003 State of the Union Address

Mr. Speaker, Vice President Cheney, Members of Congress, distinguished guests, fellow citizens:

Every year, by law and by custom, we meet here to consider the state of the union. This year, we gather in this chamber deeply aware of decisive days that lie ahead.

You and I serve our country in a time of great consequence. During this session of Congress, we have the duty to reform domestic programs vital to our country . . . and we have the opportunity to save millions of lives abroad from a terrible disease. We will work for a prosperity that is broadly shared . . . and we will answer every danger and every enemy that threatens the American people.

In all these days of promise and days of reckoning, we can be confident. In a whirlwind of change, and hope, and peril, our faith is sure, our resolve is firm, and our union is strong.

This country has many challenges. We will not deny, we will not ignore, we will not pass along our problems to other Congresses, other Presidents, and other generations. We will confront them with focus, and clarity, and courage.

During the last two years, we have seen what can be accomplished when we work together. To lift the standards of our public schools, we achieved historic education reform—which must now be carried out in every school, and every classroom, so that every child in America can read, and learn, and succeed in life. To protect our country, we reorganized our government and created the Department of Homeland Security— which is mobilizing against the threats of a new era. To bring our economy out of recession, we delivered the largest tax relief in a generation. To insist on integrity in American business, we passed tough reforms, and we are holding corporate criminals to account.

Some might call this a good record. I call it a good start. Tonight I ask the House and Senate to join me in the next bold steps to serve our fellow citizens.

Our first goal is clear: We must have an economy that grows fast enough to employ every man and woman who seeks a job.

After recession, terrorist attacks, corporate scandals, and stock market declines, our economy is recovering—yet it is not growing fast enough, or strongly enough. With unemployment rising, our Nation needs more small businesses to open, more companies to invest and expand, more employers to put up the sign that says, "Help Wanted."

Jobs are created when the economy grows; the economy grows when Americans have more money to spend and invest; and the best, fairest way to make sure Americans have that money is not to tax it away in the first place.

I am proposing that all the income tax reductions set for 2004 and 2006 be made permanent and effective this year. And under my plan, as soon as I have signed the bill, this extra money will start showing up in workers' paychecks. Instead of gradually reducing the marriage penalty, we should do it now. Instead of slowly raising the child credit to a thousand dollars, we should send the checks to American families now.

This tax relief is for everyone who pays income taxes—and it will help our economy immediately. Ninety-two million Americans will keep—this year—an average of almost $1,100 more of their own money. A family of four with an income of $40,000 would see their federal income taxes fall from $1,178 to $45 per year. And our plan will improve the bottom line for more than 23 million small businesses.

You, the Congress, have already passed all these reductions, and promised them for future years. If this tax relief is good for Americans three, or five, or seven years from now, it is even better for Americans today.

We also strengthen the economy by treating investors equally in our tax laws. It is fair to tax a company's profits. It is not fair to again tax the shareholder on the same profits. To boost investor confidence, and to help the nearly 10 million seniors who receive dividend income, I ask you to end the unfair double taxation of dividends.

Lower taxes and greater investment will help this economy expand. More jobs mean more taxpayers—and higher revenues to our government. The best way to address the deficit and move toward a balanced budget is to encourage economic growth—and to show some spending discipline in Washington, D.C. We must work together to fund only our most important priorities. I will send you a budget that increases discretionary spending by four percent next year—about as much as the average family's income is expected to grow. And that is a good benchmark for us: Federal spending should not rise any faster than the paychecks of American families.

A growing economy, and a focus on essential priorities, will also be crucial to the future of Social Security. As we continue to work together to keep Social Security sound and reliable, we must offer younger workers a chance to invest in retirement accounts that they will control and they will own.

Our second goal is high-quality, affordable health care for all Americans.

The American system of medicine is a model of skill and innovation— with a pace of discovery that is adding good years to our lives. Yet for many people, medical care costs too much—and many have no coverage at all. These problems will not be solved with a nationalized health care system that dictates coverage and rations care. Instead, we must work toward a system in which all Americans have a good insurance policy . . . choose their own doctors . . . and seniors and low-income Americans receive the help they need. Instead of bureaucrats, and trial lawyers, and HMOs, we must put doctors, and nurses, and patients back in charge of American medicine.

Health care reform must begin with Medicare, because Medicare is the binding commitment of a caring society. We must renew that commitment by giving seniors access to the preventive medicine and new drugs that are transforming health care in America.

Seniors happy with the current Medicare system should be able to keep their coverage just the way it is. And just like you, the members of Congress, members of your staffs, and other federal employees, all seniors should have the choice of a health care plan that provides prescription drugs. My budget will commit an additional $400 billion over the next decade to reform and strengthen Medicare. Leaders of both political parties have talked for years about strengthening Medicare—I urge the members of this new Congress to act this year.

To improve our health care system, we must address one of the prime causes of higher costs—the constant threat that physicians and hospitals will be unfairly sued. Because of excessive litigation, everybody pays more for health care—and many parts of America are losing fine doctors. No one has ever been healed by a frivolous lawsuit—and I urge the Congress to pass medical liability reform.

Our third goal is to promote energy independence for our country, while dramatically improving the environment.

I have sent you a comprehensive energy plan to promote energy efficiency and conservation, to develop cleaner technology, and to produce more energy at home. I have sent you Clear Skies legislation that mandates a 70 percent cut in air pollution from power plants over the next 15 years. I have sent you a Healthy Forests Initiative, to help prevent the catastrophic fires that devastate communities, kill wildlife, and burn away millions of acres of treasured forest.

I urge you to pass these measures, for the good of both our environment and our economy. Even more, I ask you to take a crucial step, and protect our environment in ways that generations before us could not have imagined. In this century, the greatest environmental progress will come about, not through endless lawsuits or command and control regulations, but through technology and innovation. Tonight I am proposing $1.2 billion in research funding so that America can lead the world in developing clean, hydrogen-powered automobiles.

A simple chemical reaction between hydrogen and oxygen generates energy, which can be used to power a car—producing only water, not exhaust fumes. With a new national commitment, our scientists and engineers will overcome obstacles to taking these cars from laboratory to showroom—so that the first car driven by a child born today could be powered by hydrogen, and pollution-free. Join me in this important innovation—to make our air significantly cleaner, and our country much less dependent on foreign sources of energy.

Our fourth goal is to apply the compassion of America to the deepest problems of America. For so many in our country—the homeless, the fatherless, the addicted—the need is great. Yet there is power—wonder-working power—in the goodness, and idealism, and faith of the American people.

Americans are doing the work of compassion every day—visiting prisoners, providing shelter to battered women, bringing companionship to lonely seniors. These good works deserve our praise . . . they deserve our personal support . . . and, when appropriate, they deserve the assistance of our government. I urge you to pass both my faith-based initiative and the Citizen Service Act—to encourage acts of compassion that can transform America, one heart and one soul at a time.

Last year, I called on my fellow citizens to participate in USA Freedom Corps, which is enlisting tens of thousands of new volunteers across America. Tonight I ask Congress and the American people to focus the spirit of service and the resources of government on the needs of some of our most vulnerable citizens—boys and girls trying to grow up without guidance and attention . . . and children who have to go through a prison gate to be hugged by their mom or dad. I propose a $450 million initiative to bring mentors to more than a million disadvantaged junior high students and children of prisoners. Government will support the training and recruiting of mentors, yet it is the men and women of America who will fill the need. One mentor, one person, can change a life forever—and I urge you to be that one person.

Another cause of hopelessness is addiction to drugs. Addiction crowds out friendship, ambition, moral conviction, and reduces all the richness of life to a single destructive desire. As a government, we are fighting illegal drugs by cutting off supplies, and reducing demand through anti-drug education programs. Yet for those already addicted, the fight against drugs is a fight for their own lives.

Too many Americans in search of treatment cannot get it. So tonight I propose a new $600 million program to help an additional 300,000 Americans receive treatment over the next three years.

Our Nation is blessed with recovery programs that do amazing work. One of them is found at the Healing Place Church in Baton Rouge, Louisiana. A man in the program said, "God does miracles in people's lives, and you never think it could be you." Tonight, let us bring to all Americans who struggle with drug addiction this message of hope: The miracle of recovery is possible, and it could be you.

By caring for children who need mentors, and for addicted men and women who need treatment, we are building a more welcoming society—a culture that values every life. And in this work we must not overlook the weakest among us. I ask you to protect infants at the very hour of birth, and end the practice of partial-birth abortion. And because no human life should be started or ended as the object of an experiment, I ask you to set a high standard for humanity and pass a law against all human cloning.

The qualities of courage and compassion that we strive for in America also determine our conduct abroad. The American flag stands for more than our power and our interests. Our Founders dedicated this country to the cause of human dignity—the rights of every person and the possibilities of every life. This conviction leads us into the world to help the afflicted, and defend the peace, and confound the designs of evil men. In Afghanistan, we helped to liberate an oppressed people . . . and we will continue helping them secure their country, rebuild their society, and educate all their children—boys and girls. In the Middle East, we will continue to seek peace between a secure Israel and a democratic Palestine. Across the earth, America is feeding the hungry; more than 60 percent of international food aid comes as a gift from the people of the United States.

As our Nation moves troops and builds alliances to make our world safer, we must also remember our calling, as a blessed country, to make this world better. Today, on the continent of Africa, nearly 30 million people have the AIDS virus—including three million children under the age of 15. There are whole countries in Africa where more than one-third of the adult population carries the infection. More than four million require immediate drug treatment. Yet across that continent, only 50,000 AIDS victims—only 50,000—are receiving the medicine they need.

Because the AIDS diagnosis is considered a death sentence, many do not seek treatment. Almost all who do are turned away. A doctor in rural South Africa describes his frustration. He says, "We have no medicines . . . many hospitals tell [people], 'You've got AIDS. We can't help you. Go home and die.'"

In an age of miraculous medicines, no person should have to hear those words. AIDS can be prevented. Anti-retroviral drugs can extend life for many years. And the cost of those drugs has dropped from $12,000 a year to under $300 a year—which places a tremendous possibility within our grasp.

Ladies and gentlemen, seldom has history offered a greater opportunity to do so much for so many. We have confronted, and will continue to confront, HIV/AIDS in our own country. And to meet a severe and urgent crisis abroad, tonight I propose the Emergency Plan for AIDS Relief—a work of mercy beyond all current international efforts to help the people of Africa. This comprehensive plan will prevent seven million new AIDS infections . . . treat at least two million people with life-extending drugs . . . and provide humane care for millions of people suffering from AIDS, and for children orphaned by AIDS. I ask the Congress to commit $15 billion over the next five years, including nearly $10 billion in new money, to turn the tide against AIDS in the most afflicted nations of Africa and the Caribbean.

This Nation can lead the world in sparing innocent people from a plague of nature. And this Nation is leading the world in confronting and defeating the man-made evil of international terrorism.

There are days when the American people do not hear news about the war on terror. There is never a day when I do not learn of another threat, or receive reports of operations in progress, or give an order in this global war against a scattered network of killers. The war goes on, and we are winning.

To date we have arrested, or otherwise dealt with, many key commanders of al-Qaeda. They include a man who directed logistics and

funding for the September 11th attacks . . . the chief of al-Qaeda operations in the Person Gulf who planned the bombings of our embassies in
East Africa and the USS *Cole* . . . an al-Qaeda operation chief from
Southeast Asia . . . a former director of al-Qaeda's training camps in
Afghanistan . . . a key al-Qaeda operative in Europe . . . and a major al-
Qaeda leader in Yemen. All told, more than 3,000 suspected terrorists
have been arrested in many countries. And many others have met a different fate. They are no longer a problem for the United States and our
friends and allies.

We are working closely with other nations to prevent further attacks.
America and coalition countries have uncovered and stopped terrorist
conspiracies targeting the American embassy in Yemen . . . the American
embassy in Singapore . . . a Saudi military base . . . and ships in the
straits of Hormuz, and the straits of Gibraltar. We have broken al-Qaeda
cells in Hamburg, and Milan, and Madrid, and London, and Paris—as
well as Buffalo, New York.

We have the terrorists on the run, and we are keeping them on the run.
One by one, the terrorists are learning the meaning of American justice.

As we fight this war, we will remember where it began—here, in our
own country. This government is taking unprecedented measures to protect our people and defend our homeland. We have intensified security
at the borders and ports of entry . . . posted more than 50,000 newly
trained federal screeners in airports . . . begun inoculating troops and
first responders against smallpox . . . and are deploying the Nation's first
early warning network of sensors to detect biological attack. And this
year, for the first time, we are beginning to field a defense to protect this
Nation against ballistic missiles.

I thank the Congress for supporting these measures. I ask you tonight
to add to our future security with a major research and production effort
to guard our people against bio-terrorism, called Project Bioshield. The
budget I send you will propose almost $6 billion to quickly make avail-
able effective vaccines and treatments against agents like anthrax,
butolinum toxin, Ebola, and plaque. We must assume that our enemies
would use these diseases as weapons, and we must act before the dangers
are upon us.

Since September 11th, our intelligence and law enforcement agencies
have worked more closely than ever to track and disrupt the terrorists.
The FBI is improving its ability to analyze intelligence, and transforming
itself to meet new threats. And tonight, I am instructing the leaders of
the FBI, Central Intelligence, Homeland Security, and the Department
of Defense to develop a Terrorist Threat Integration Center, to merge
and analyze all threat information in a single location. Our government
must have the very best information possible, and we will use it to make
sure the right people are in the right places to protect our citizens.

Our war against terror is a contest of will, in which perseverance is power. In the ruins of two towers, at the western wall of the Pentagon, on a field in Pennsylvania, this Nation made a pledge, and we renew that pledge tonight: Whatever the duration of this struggle, and whatever the difficulties, we will not permit the triumph of violence in the affairs of men—free people will set the course of history.

Today, the gravest danger in the war on terror . . . the gravest danger facing America and the world . . . is outlaw regimes that seek and possess nuclear, chemical, and biological weapons. These regimes could use such weapons for blackmail, terror, and mass murder. They could also give or sell those weapons to their terrorist allies, who would use them without the least hesitation.

This threat is new; America's duty is familiar. Throughout the 20th century, small groups of men seized control of great nations . . . built armies and arsenals . . . and set out to dominate the weak and intimidate the world. In each case, their ambitions of cruelty and murder had no limit. In each case, the ambitions of Hitlerism, militarism, and communism were defeated by the will of free peoples, by the strength of great alliances, and by the might of the United States of America. Now, in this century, the ideology of power and domination has appeared again, and seeks to gain the ultimate weapons of terror. Once again this Nation and our friends are all that stand between a world at peace, and a world of chaos and constant alarm. Once again, we are called to defend the safety of our people, and the hopes of all mankind. And we accept this responsibility.

America is making a broad and determined effort to confront these dangers. We have called on the United Nations to fulfill its charter, and stand by its demand that Iraq disarm. We are strongly supporting the International Atomic Energy Agency in its mission to track and control nuclear materials around the world. We are working with other governments to secure nuclear materials in the former Soviet Union, and to strengthen global treaties banning the production and shipment of missile technologies and weapons of mass destruction.

In all of these efforts, however, America's purpose is more than to follow a process—it is to achieve a result: the end of terrible threats to the civilized world. All free nations have a stake in preventing sudden and catastrophic attack. We are asking them to join us, and many are doing so. Yet the course of this Nation does not depend on the decisions of others. Whatever action is required, whenever action is necessary, I will defend the freedom and security of the American people.

Different threats require different strategies. In Iran, we continue to see a government that represses its people, pursues weapons of mass destruction, and supports terror. We also see Iranian citizens risking intimidation and death as they speak out for liberty, human rights, and democracy. Iranians, like all people, have a right to choose their own government, and determine their own destiny—and the United States supports their aspirations to live in freedom.

On the Korean peninsula, an oppressive regime rules a people living in fear and starvation. Throughout the 1990s, the United States relied on a negotiated framework to keep North Korea from gaining nuclear weapons. We now know that the regime was deceiving the world, and developing those weapons all along. And today the North Korean regime is using its nuclear program to incite fear and seek concessions. America and the world will not be blackmailed. America is working with the countries of the region—South Korea, Japan, China, and Russia—to find a peaceful solution, and to show the North Korean government that nuclear weapons will bring only isolation, economic stagnation, and continued hardship. The North Korean regime will find respect in the world, and revival for it people, only when it turns away from its nuclear ambitions.

Our Nation and the world must learn the lessons of the Korean peninsula, and not allow an even greater threat to rise up in Iraq. A brutal dictator, with a history of reckless aggression . . . with ties to terrorism . . . with great potential wealth . . . will not be permitted to dominate a vital region and threaten the United States.

Twelve years ago, Saddam Hussein faced the prospect of being the last casualty in a war he had started and lost. To spare himself, he agreed to disarm of all weapons of mass destruction. For the next 12 years, he systematically violated that agreement. He pursued chemical, biological, and nuclear weapons even while inspectors were in his country. Nothing to date has restrained him from his pursuit of these weapons—not economic sanctions, not isolation from the civilized world, not even cruise missile strikes on his military facilities. Almost three months ago, the United Nations Security Council gave Saddam Hussein his final chance to disarm. He has shown instead his utter contempt for the United Nations, and for the opinion of the world.

The 108 U.N. weapons inspectors were not sent to conduct a scavenger hunt for hidden materials across a country the size of California. The job of the inspectors is to verify that Iraq's regime is disarming. It is up to Iraq to show exactly where it is hiding its banned weapons . . . lay those weapons out for the world to see . . . and destroy them as directed. Nothing like this has happened.

The United Nations concluded in 1999 that Saddam Hussein had biological weapons materials sufficient to produce over 25,000 liters of anthrax—enough doses to kill several million people. He has not accounted for that material. He has given no evidence that he has destroyed it.

The United Nations concluded that Saddam Hussein had materials sufficient to produce more than 38,000 liters of botulinum toxin—

enough to subject millions of people to death by respiratory failure. He has not accounted for that material. He has given no evidence that he has destroyed it.

Our intelligence officials estimate that Saddam Hussein had the materials to produce as much as 500 tons of sarin, mustard, and VX nerve agent. In such quantities, these chemical agents also could kill untold thousands. He has not accounted for these materials. He has given no evidence that he has destroyed them.

U.S. intelligence indicates that Saddam Hussein had upwards of 30,000 munitions capable of delivering chemical agents. Inspectors recently turned up 16 of them, despite Iraq's recent declaration denying their existence. Saddam Hussein has not accounted for the remaining 29,984 of these prohibited munitions. He has given no evidence that he has destroyed them.

From three Iraqi defectors we know that Iraq, in the late 1990s, had several mobile biological weapons labs. These are designed to produce germ warfare agents, and can be moved from place to place to evade inspectors. Saddam Hussein has not disclosed these facilities. He has given no evidence that he has destroyed them.

The International Atomic Energy Agency confirmed in the 1990s that Saddam Hussein had an advanced nuclear weapons development program, had a design for a nuclear weapon, and was working on five different methods of enriching uranium for a bomb. The British government has learned that Saddam Hussein recently sought significant quantities of uranium from Africa. Out intelligence sources tell us that he has attempted to purchase high strength aluminum tubes suitable for nuclear weapons production. Saddam Hussein has not credibly explained these activities. He clearly has much to hide.

The dictator of Iraq is not disarming. To the contrary, he is deceiving. From intelligence sources, we know, for instance, that thousands of Iraqi security personnel are at work hiding documents and materials from the U.N. inspectors—sanitizing inspection sites, and monitoring the inspectors themselves. Iraqi officials accompany the inspectors in order to intimidate witnesses. Iraq is blocking U-2 surveillance flights requested by the United Nations. Iraqi intelligence officers are posing as the scientists inspectors are supposed to interview. Real scientists have been coached by Iraqi officials on what to say. And intelligence sources indicate that Saddam Hussein has ordered that scientists who cooperate with U.N. inspectors in disarming Iraq will be killed, along with their families.

Year after year, Saddam Hussein has gone to elaborate lengths, spent enormous sums, taken great risks, to build and keep weapons of mass destruction—but why? The only possible explanation, the only possible use he could have for those weapons, is to dominate, intimidate, or attack. With nuclear arms or a full arsenal of chemical and biological weapons, Saddam Hussein could resume his ambitions of conquest in the Middle East, and create deadly havoc in the region. And this Congress and the American people must recognize another threat. Evidence from intelligence sources, secret communications, and statements by people now in custody, reveal that Saddam Hussein aids and protects terrorists, including members of al-Qaeda. Secretly, and without fingerprints, he could provide one of his hidden weapons to terrorists, or help them develop their own.

Before September 11, 2001, many in the world believed that Saddam Hussein could be contained. But chemical agents and lethal viruses and shadowy terrorist networks are not easily contained. Imagine those 19 hijackers with other weapons, and other plans—this time armed by Saddam Hussein. It would take just one vial, one canister, one crate slipped into this country to bring a day of horror like none we have ever known. We will do everything in our power to make sure that day never comes.

Some have said we must not act until the threat is imminent. Since when have terrorists and tyrants announced their intentions, politely putting us on notice before they strike? If this threat is permitted to fully and suddenly emerge, all actions, all words, and all recriminations would come too late. Trusting in the sanity and restraint of Saddam Hussein is not a strategy, and it is not an option.

This dictator, who is assembling the world's most dangerous weapons, has already used them on whole villages—leaving thousands of his own citizens dead, blind, or disfigured. Iraqi refugees tell us how forced confessions are obtained—by torturing children while their parents are made to watch. International human rights groups have catalogued other methods used in the torture chambers of Iraq: electric shock, burning with hot irons, dripping acid on the skin, mutilation with electric drills, cutting out tongues, and rape.

If this is not evil, then evil has no meaning. And tonight I have a message for the brave and oppressed people of Iraq: Your enemy is not surrounding your country—your enemy is ruling your country. And the day he and his regime are removed from power will be the day of your liberation.

The world has waited twelve years for Iraq to disarm. America will not accept a serious and mounting threat to our country, our friends, and our allies. The United States will ask the U.N. Security Council to convene on February 5th to consider the facts of Iraq's ongoing defiance of the world. Secretary of State Powell will present information and intelligence about Iraq's illegal weapons programs; its attempts to hide those weapons from inspectors; and its links to terrorist groups. We will consult, but let there be no misunderstanding: If Saddam Hussein does not fully disarm, for the safety of our people, and for the peace of the world, we will lead a coalition to disarm him.

Tonight I also have a message for the men and women who will keep the peace, members of the American Armed Forces: Many of you are assembling in and near the Middle East, and some crucial hours may lie ahead. In those hours, the success of our cause will depend on you. Your training has prepared you. Your honor will guide you. You believe in America, and America believes in you.

Sending Americans into battle is the most profound decision a president can make. The technologies of war have changed. The risks and suffering of war have not. For the brave Americans who bear the risk, no victory is free from sorrow. This Nation fights reluctantly, because we know the cost, and we dread the days of mourning that always come.

We seek peace. We strive for peace. And sometimes peace must be defended. A future lived at the mercy of terrible threats is no peace at all. If war is forced upon us, we will fight in a just cause and by just means—sparing, in every way we can, the innocent. And if war is forced upon us, we will fight with the full force and might of the United States military—and we will prevail. And as we and our coalition partners are doing in Afghanistan, we will bring to the Iraqi people food, and medicines, and supplies . . . and freedom.

Many challenges, abroad and at home, have arrived in a single season. In two years, America has gone from a sense of invulnerability to an awareness of peril . . . from bitter division in small matters to calm unity in great causes. And we go forward with confidence, because this call of history has come to the right country.

Americans are a resolute people, who have risen to every test of our time. Adversity has revealed the character of our country, to the world, and to ourselves.

America is a strong Nation, and honorable in the use of our strength. We exercise power without conquest, and sacrifice for the liberty of strangers.

Americans are a free people, who know that freedom is the right of every person and the future of every nation. The liberty we prize is not America's gift to the world, it is God's gift to humanity.

We Americans have faith in ourselves—but not in ourselves alone. We do not claim to know all the ways of Providence, yet we can trust in them, placing our confidence in the loving God behind all of life, and all of history.

May He guide us now, and may God continue to bless the United States of America.

Source: U.S. Congress. House. *State of the Union Message: Message from the President of the United States Transmitting a Report on the State of the Union.* 108th Cong., 1st sess., 2003. H. Doc. 108–1. January 28, 2003. http://purl.access.gpo.gov/GPO/LPS26932 (accessed May 31, 2003).

Democratic Response to the State of the Union Address

I'm Gary Locke, the governor of Washington State. It's an honor to give the response to President Bush on behalf of my family, my state, my fellow Democratic Governors, and the Democratic Party. Tonight, I'd like to offer our view of how to strengthen America.

My grandfather came to this country from China nearly a century ago, and worked as a servant. Now, I serve as governor just one mile from where my grandfather worked. It took our family a hundred years to travel that mile—it was a voyage we could only make in America. The values that sustained us—education, hard work, responsibility and family—guide me every day. I want every person to have the chance this country gave our family.

But like many of you, I am concerned about the challenges now before us.

Tonight, President Bush spoke about the threats we face from terrorists and dictators abroad.

Many of the young Americans who fought in Afghanistan—and who tonight are still defending our freedom—were trained in Washington State. We are so grateful to them, to all the members of our armed services and their families—and we pray for their safe return. But the war against terror is not over. Al Qaeda still targets Americans. Osama Bin Laden is still at large. As we rise to the many challenges around the globe, let us never lose sight of who attacked our people here at home.

We also support the President in working with our allies and the United Nations to eliminate the threat posed by Saddam Hussein and Kim Jong Il of North Korea. Make no mistake: Saddam Hussein is a ruthless tyrant, and he must give up his weapons of mass destruction. We support the President in the course he has followed so far—working with Congress, working with the United Nations, insisting on strong and unfettered inspections. We need allies today in 2003, just as much as we needed them in Desert Storm and just as we needed them on D-Day in 1944, when American soldiers—including my father—fought to vanquish the Nazi threat. We must convince the world that Saddam Hussein is not America's problem alone—he's the world's problem. And we urge President Bush to stay this course for we are far stronger when we stand with other nations than when we stand alone.

I have no doubt that together, we can meet these global challenges.

But to be strong abroad we need to be strong at home. And today, in too many ways, our country is headed in the wrong direction. We are missing the opportunity to strengthen America for the future. Democrats have a positive, specific plan to turn our nation around.

Today, the economy is limping along. Some say it's a recovery, but for far too many Americans there's no recovery in our states and cities. There's no recovery in our rural communities. There's no recovery for working Americans and for those searching for jobs to feed and clothe their families.

After gaining 22 million jobs in eight years, we've now lost two million jobs in the last two years since President Bush took office—100,000 jobs lost last month alone.

Two years ago, the federal budget was in surplus. Now, this administration's policies will produce massive deficits of over a trillion dollars over the next decade.

These policies have powerful and painful consequences. States and cities now face our worst budget crises since World War II. We're being forced to cut vital services from police to fire to health care—and many are being forced to raise taxes. We need a White House that understands the challenges our communities and people are facing across America.

We Democrats have a plan to restore prosperity—so the United States once again becomes the great job engine it was in the 1990s. It's rooted in three principles. It must give our economy an immediate jump-start; it must benefit middle-class families rather than just a few; and it must be fiscally responsible, so we have the savings to strengthen Social Security and protect our homeland.

Our plan provides over a hundred billion dollars in tax relief and investments, right now:

- Tax relief for middle class and working families—immediately.
- Incentives for businesses to invest and create jobs—this year.
- Substantial help for cities and states like yours and mine—now.
- Extended unemployment benefits—without delay for nearly a million American workers who have already exhausted their benefits.
- And all without passing on the bill to our children and grandchildren through exploding budget deficits for years to come.

Now, as you heard tonight, President Bush has a very different plan. We think it's upside down economics: it does too little to stimulate the economy now and does too much to weaken our economic future. It will create huge, permanent deficits that will raise interest rates, stifle growth, hinder homeownership and cut off the avenues of opportunity that have let so many work themselves up from poverty.

We believe every American should get a tax cut. That's the way to create broad based growth. But we shouldn't spend hundreds of billions of dollars on a plan that helps neither the economy nor the families that need it most—while making it harder to save Social Security and invest in health care and education. Think about it: Under the President's proposal to eliminate taxes on stock dividends, the top one percent—that's people who earn over $300,000 a year—would get more tax relief than the bottom 95 percent of taxpayers combined. That's wrong. It's irresponsible and it won't create jobs. Let's choose the right course—the successful and fair course—for our economy.

We have another urgent priority: homeland security. In this unprecedented fight against terror, the frontlines are in our own neighborhoods and communities.

And this one hits home. In 1999, an Al Qaeda operative tried to enter my state with a trunk full of explosives. Thankfully, he was caught in time. Now, a year and a half after September 11th, America is still far too vulnerable. Last year Congress authorized $2.5 billion in vital new resources to protect our citizens—for equipment for firefighters and police, to protect ports, to guard against bioterrorism, to secure nuclear power plants, and more. It's hard to believe, but President Bush actually refused to release the money. Republicans now say we can't afford it. Democrats say: If we're serious about protecting our homeland, we can and we must.

Now, to strengthen America at home, there's much more to do.

You and I know that education is the great equalizer, the hope of democracy, and the key to the information economy of the future. In my state we have raised test scores, cut class sizes, trained teachers, launched innovative reading programs, offered college scholarships even as the federal government cut its aid to deserving students. Democrats worked with President Bush to pass a law that demands more of our students and invests more in our schools. But his budget fails to give communities the help they need to meet these new, high standards. We say we want to leave no child behind, but our schools need more than kind words about education from Washington, D.C.—we need a real partnership to renew our schools.

Tonight, we also heard the president talk about health care. Too many seniors can't afford the remarkable new drugs that can save lives—some are skimping on food to pay for needed medicine. On this issue, the contrast is clear. Democrats insist on a Medicare prescription drug benefit for all seniors. President Bush says he supports a prescription drug benefit—but let's read the fine print: his plan only helps seniors who leave traditional Medicare. Our parents shouldn't be forced to give up their doctor or join an HMO to get the medicine they need. That wouldn't save Medicare—it would privatize it. And it would put too many seniors at too much risk—just when they need the security of Medicare.

And, finally, let's talk about the environment and energy. Environmental protection has been a tremendous bipartisan success story over three decades. Our air and water are cleaner. In communities in my state and yours, conservation is a way of life. But the administration is determined to roll back much of this progress. Our nation should lead global efforts to promote environmental responsibility—not shun them. And instead of opening up Alaska's wilderness to oil drilling, we should be committed to a national policy to reduce our dependence on oil by promoting American technology and sustainability.

Yes, the Republican Party now controls the executive branch and both houses of Congress. But we Democrats will hold the administration and congressional leaders accountable. We will work to create jobs and strengthen homeland security. We will fight to protect a woman's right to choose and we will fight for affirmative action, equal opportunity and diversity in our schools and our workplaces. Above all, we will demand that this government advance our common purpose and not pander to narrow special interests.

That's the vision of the Democratic Party—in statehouses, in Congress, and in the homes of millions of Americans. We believe it's the best course for our nation. It is the vision we will work for—and stand for—in the coming years.

This is not an easy time. But I often think about my grandfather, arriving by steamship a hundred years ago. He had no family here; he spoke no English. I can only imagine how he must have felt as he looked out at his new country. There are millions of families like mine—people whose ancestors dreamed the American Dream and worked hard to make it come true. They transformed adversity into opportunity. Yes, these are challenging times—but the American family . . . the American Dream . . . has prevailed before. That's the character of our people and the hallmark of our country. The lesson of our legacy is, if we work together, and make the right choices, we will become a stronger, more united and more prosperous nation.

Good night and God Bless America.

Source: State of Washington. Office of the Governor. *Governor Gary Locke's Remarks: Democratic Response to the State of the Union.* January 28, 2003. www.governor.wa.gov/speeches/speech-view.asp?SpeechSeq=385 (accessed May 31, 2003).

European Leaders on the Prospect of a War in Iraq

January 30 and February 10, 2003

INTRODUCTION

Early in 2003 the looming prospect of a war in Iraq caused the gravest crisis in U.S.-European relations since World War II. European leaders split sharply on the wisdom and necessity of going to war in Iraq. Some, led by British prime minister Tony Blair, agreed with U.S. president George W. Bush that Iraqi leader Saddam Hussein posed a serious threat to world peace and had to be ousted from power. Others, notably the leaders of France, Germany, and Russia, argued that a war of Western nations against Iraq could destabilize the Middle East and possibly lead to an upsurge in Islamist terrorism.

In many ways, the transatlantic arguments about going to war in Iraq exposed a more fundamental dispute about the U.S. role in the world. Since assuming the presidency in 2001, Bush had adopted what many observers, especially in Europe, considered to be a unilateralist approach to foreign policy by rejecting United Nations treaties on climate change and a new International Criminal Court, pursuing a controversial missile defense program, violating free trade precepts for domestic political benefit, and generally throwing around its weight as the world's sole economic and military superpower. The Bush administration naturally rejected this characterization of its actions but nevertheless made clear that the United States could and would act according to what it saw as its own interests, whether other countries liked the results or not.

The hard feelings generated by the prewar feuding continued long after major combat in Iraq ended in late April. National leaders who had opposed the war were reluctant to heed U.S. pleas for money and peacekeeping troops to reconstruct Iraq afterward. In December the Pentagon revived the dispute by announcing that U.S. commercial contracts for rebuilding Iraq would be awarded only to companies from countries that had supported the war. Ironically, the Pentagon announcement came on the same day that President Bush began calling foreign leaders—including some who had opposed the war—to request that they forgive Iraq's prewar debts, which totaled billions of dollars. Former secretary of state James A. Baker III, acting as Bush's personal envoy, met with European leaders later in December and was able to smoothe over that dispute by opening the possibility that some European companies might be able to bid on contract work in Iraq. The split within Europe over Iraq also contributed to the collapse in December of final negotiations on a new constitution for the European Union (EU) when it expanded from fifteen to twenty-five members in 2004. *(Post-war Iraq, p. 933; EU expansion, p. 492)*

The Split Within Europe

Bush launched his first verbal assault on Iraq in November 2001, about two months after the September 11 terrorist attacks that killed nearly 3,000 people in New York City and Washington, D.C. At the time, most U.S. allies reacted cautiously and expressed hope that Bush would not take any military action against Iraq without approval from the United Nations Security Council. Bush escalated his rhetoric during the first half of 2002, making it clear that he had decided on the necessity of "regime change" in Iraq. Even so, he agreed to work through the UN, and careful diplomacy by Secretary of State Colin Powell in November 2002 won the Security Council's unanimous endorsement of Resolution 1441 demanding that Saddam give up his prohibited weapons of mass destruction or face "serious consequences." The resolution required Iraq to allow unfettered access to its military facilities by two teams of UN weapons inspectors. The inspections began in late November 2002 but had made only limited progress by early 2003. *(Iraq background, Historic Documents of 2001, p. 849; Historic Documents of 2002, p. 612)*

It soon became evident that the unanimity of the UN action belied deep-seated differences among world leaders about what to do with Iraq. The Bush administration clearly viewed the UN resolution as a necessary formality before taking the next steps: giving Saddam a final ultimatum, which he almost certainly would reject, then going to war to oust him from power. Britain's Blair appeared to endorse this view as well, although he was careful to emphasize the need for additional diplomacy before going to war. But many other world leaders argued against what they called a rush into war. French president Jacques Chirac and others insisted that the UN goal was eliminating Iraq's illicit weapons, not ousting Saddam from power. Therefore, they argued, the UN weapons inspectors needed to be given more time to continue searching for the biological and chemical weapons that Iraq, in the mid-1990s, had admitted building and the nuclear weapons program that U.S. officials insisted Iraq also was hiding.

This fundamental dispute came to a head in January when Chirac and German chancellor Gerhard Schroeder stepped up their criticism of Bush's war plans. Schroeder said flatly on January 22 that Germany, which had just taken up a two-year post on the Security Council, would vote against any resolution authorizing war against Iraq. During this same period leaders of several formerly communist countries in Eastern Europe indicated their support for the U.S. position. Defense Secretary Donald H. Rumsfeld on January 21 said these differing views reflected a split between "old Europe" (meaning long-established powers such as France and Germany) and "new Europe" (meaning the Eastern European countries that were eager to join NATO and the European Union). Rumsfeld's comment inflamed an already tense situation.

The split within Europe broke wide open on January 30, when Blair and seven other European leaders published a letter in the *Wall Street Journal* and major European newspapers expressing solidarity with Bush's hard-line stand against Iraq. The letter, which had been initiated by a *Journal* editor, repeatedly stressed the need for "unity" between Europe and the United States and endorsed Bush's view that Saddam posed a "threat" to the rest of the world. "Our goal is to safeguard world peace and security by ensuring that this [Iraqi] regime gives up its weapons of mass destruction," the eight leaders wrote. "Our governments have a common responsibility to face this threat. Failure to do so would be nothing less than negligent to our citizens and to the wider world." In addition to Blair, those signing the letter were the prime ministers of Denmark, Hungary, Italy, Poland, Portugal, and Spain, and the president of the Czech Republic. Several of the leaders courted political trouble by signing such a letter because public opinion in their countries ran strongly against a war and against close cooperation with Bush.

The letter sparked widespread debate within Europe, with much of the attention focused on the participation of the leaders of the Czech Republic, Hungary, and Poland—the first three Eastern European countries to be admitted into NATO (in 1999) and three of ten pending candidates for membership in the European Union. In a January 31 editorial, Britain's liberal *Guardian* newspaper warned of "trouble to come as they, and the seven other new EU members, begin to challenge the predominance of the West Europeans." Many other commentators said that, in reality, Iraq was not the fundamental cause of divisions among European countries. "The problem is relations with the United States," Italian foreign policy expert Sergio Romano told the *New York Times*. "That is the real issue." According to this view, Britain, Italy, and the newly independent countries of Eastern Europe used the Iraq issue to align themselves with Washington, the sole remaining superpower, while France and Germany sought to demonstrate their independence.

Chirac and Schroeder formally staked out their defiant stance on February 10. They did so in an especially provocative manner, by aligning themselves with Russian president Vladimir Putin, whose own relations with Bush had cycled between periods of sweetness and stress. After a meeting in Paris between Chirac and Putin, the two leaders issued a statement cosigned by Schroeder demanding that Iraq comply with UN Security Council resolutions but also warning that "the use of force could only be a last resort." The three leaders said they were "determined to allow every opportunity for the peaceful disarmament of Iraq." And in a not-so-subtle reminder of international politics, they insisted their view "coincides with that of a large number of countries, within the Security Council in particular."

In historical terms, Schroeder's participation in the February 10 statement was by far the most significant. French leaders ever since Charles de Gaulle (in the 1950s and 1960s) had made a habit of opposing U.S. foreign policy positions—although rarely in such blunt terms as did Chirac in this case. Ever since the collapse of the Soviet Union in 1991, Russian leaders had been careful to distance themselves from some aspects of U.S. policy. But Schroeder broke with posture of all his predecessors since the end of World War II that any serious disagreements with Washington should be aired quietly, in private—not flaunted in public. Schroeder had adopted his stance during his successful reelection campaign in 2002, in essence riding a powerful wave of antiwar sentiment in Germany.

On the same day the three leaders issued their statement, European war opponents moved beyond rhetoric with a diplomatic step that severely complicated U.S. war planning. At a NATO meeting in Brussels, representatives of Belgium, France, and Germany blocked a U.S. proposal for the alliance to defend Turkey (a NATO member bordering Iraq) in the event of war in Iraq. This highly unusual step was a severe shock to an alliance long accustomed to smoothing over disagreements to maintain the appearance of unity. Nicholas Burns, the U.S. ambassador to NATO, said the alliance was facing "a serious test of its credibility to an ally, Turkey." NATO's rebuff later contributed to the refusal of Turkey's parliament to allow the United States to open a northern front against Iraq by traveling through Turkish territory.

No one expected these moves to be the final shots in the intra-European war of words, and indeed they were not. On February 16 the leaders of ten more European countries signed a letter supporting Washington's position on Iraq. Among them were the remaining seven candidates for membership in the European Union. That letter brought to eighteen the number of European leaders siding with the United States, including those of all ten countries eagerly awaiting EU membership early in 2004.

The intervention of these smaller countries appeared to be more than Chirac could bear. Following an EU meeting in Brussels on February 17, Chirac sarcastically said the leaders from Central and Eastern Europe who had signed the pro-U.S. letters were "badly brought up" and had missed "an opportunity to keep quiet." Adopting a threatening tone, Chirac warned that candidates for EU membership were hurting themselves. In particular, he said Bulgaria and Romania, which were hoping to join the EU in 2007, "could hardly find a better way" to jeopardize their EU candidacies.

These remarks, coupled with similarly undiplomatic comments by the French defense and foreign ministers, brought a shocked response from across the continent. "We thought we were preparing for war with Saddam Hussein and not Jacques Chirac," Czech deputy foreign minister Alexandr Vondra said. Blair rushed to the defense of his colleagues in "new" Europe, stating that "they have as much right to speak up as Great Britain or France or any other member of the European Union today."

Tensions among European leaders continued straight through the rest of the year and culminated in the collapse, on December 13, of a summit meeting that was supposed to ratify a new constitution for the European Union. Many of the same divisions that had surfaced in the Iraq debate were still evident, as France and Germany successfully resisted efforts by smaller and poorer countries, notably Poland and Spain, to gain a greater say in EU decision making.

Returning to the UN

The immediate impact of the transatlantic dispute over Iraq was to expose the underlying divisions within the UN Security Council on how to enforce Saddam's full compliance with Resolution 1441. The Bush administration insisted the resolution was self-enforcing because its references to Iraq's "material breach" of all previous UN resolutions and its warning of "significant consequences" for Iraq's continued failure to comply provided adequate legal justification for any future military action by the United States and its allies. The French were leaders in insisting that Resolution 1441 did not provide the legal basis for war, and so a second resolution authorizing military action would be necessary. In effect, the United States viewed Resolution 1441 as a way to establish, once again, that Iraq would not comply with UN disarmament demands; by contrast, the leaders of France and some other countries considered the resolution a means of using new weapons inspections to avoid war.

The Bush administration had long made clear that it did not intend to seek a second resolution authorizing war, and it held to that position well into February. That position became untenable only when Britain's Blair found himself on the losing side of public opinion at home. Protest marches and opinion surveys demonstrated that a majority of Britons either opposed a war against Iraq or would approve of British participation only if the war was specifically sanctioned by a UN resolution. In a meeting at Camp David on January 30, Blair prevailed upon Bush to seek a UN resolution authorizing war, setting in motion several weeks of fevered diplomacy.

Even as it returned to the UN, the administration found itself in a bind: It had to engage in diplomacy to convince other countries on the Security Council that it was serious about seeking a second resolution, but at the same time had to deploy tens of thousands of troops to the Middle East to maintain a realistic timetable for war and to present Iraq with a credible threat of force. Ultimately, the highly publicized military preparations undermined the U.S. diplomacy, while the diplomacy gave the military additional time to put troops and equipment in place for the war.

The key step in the administration's diplomacy was a ninety-minute presentation to the Security Council on February 5 in which Powell offered snippets of intelligence information bolstering the case that Saddam possessed weapons of mass destruction and was hiding them from the UN inspectors. While much of the world watched on television, Powell played recordings of conversations (intercepted by U.S. intelligence agencies) in which Iraqi military officials seemed to be discussing how to trick the UN inspectors; showed satellite photos of facilities that Powell said were intended to produce biological and chemical weapons—including some sites being cleaned up just before the arrival of UN inspectors; and revealed portions of U.S. intelligence reports on Iraqi actions that appeared to demonstrate plans for acquiring nuclear weapons. Powell was accompanied by CIA director George J. Tenet, whose presence was intended to be an endorsement of the presentation by the U.S. intelligence community. Powell called the information he presented "an accumulation of facts and disturbing patterns of behavior." Added together, he said, the information showed "Saddam Hussein's contempt for the will of this council, his contempt for the truth, and most damning of all, his utter contempt for human life."

Powell's presentation was by far the most detailed case the United States had ever made that Iraq was building and hiding weapons of mass destruction. Even so, it appeared to persuade only those who already accepted that case and had little impact on those who were skeptical about the U.S. charges or who simply wanted to give the UN inspectors more time to do their work in Iraq. Opinion polls showed that most Americans, as well as a sizable majority in Britain, accepted the validity of Powell's charges, while strong majorities in most European countries remained unconvinced that Saddam Hussein presented an imminent threat outside his own country.

Role of the UN Inspectors

At least in theory, the whole point of UN involvement in the Iraq issue was to force Saddam Hussein to reveal, and then allow the destruction of, the weapons of mass destruction he was presumed to have developed. As soon as they set foot in Iraq in late November 2002, the inspectors pressed Saddam's regime to follow through on its promised cooperation. *(Details on weapons inspections, p. 874)*

The Security Council received regular reports from the heads of the two weapons inspection missions: Swedish diplomat Hans Blix, who was in charge of finding biological and chemical weapons and long-range missions in Iraq, and Mohamed El Baradei, head of the International Atomic Energy Agency, which looked for signs of a nuclear weapons program in Iraq. On each occasion the two men said Iraq's cooperation was limited. Blix, a cautious diplomat, used uncharacteristically blunt language only once, on January 27 when he gave the council a detailed list of questions about weapons Iraq was supposed to have destroyed and said Iraq "appears not to have come to a genuine acceptance, even today, of the disarmament which was demanded of it." The United States eagerly embraced that statement as proving the point that Saddam never could be trusted. Washington's use of that report for its own purposes apparently distressed Blix, who took his assignment of looking for Iraq's weapons seriously and wanted the necessary time and resources to carry out his job. Thereafter, Blix used much more cautious wording in his reports to the council, a caution that angered the Bush administration.

The inspectors ultimately were reduced to the role of bit actors in a much larger drama than the search for weapons hidden in Iraq's cities and deserts. Opponents of a war used the ongoing inspections to argue that the UN's goal of disarming Iraq could be accomplished without a bloody and expensive war. The United States and its allies drew the exact opposite conclusion, that Iraq was continuing to play a cat-and-mouse game with the inspectors and never would disarm as long as Saddam remained in power.

Iraq and al Qaeda

One important element of the Bush administration's prewar strategy was to demonstrate a link between the Iraqi regime and international terrorism, specifically the al Qaeda terrorist group said to have been responsible for the September 11, 2001, attacks against the United States. But Bush and his key aides never succeeded in proving the Iraq-terrorism link.

Ever since his first major statement denouncing Saddam in November 2001, Bush had suggested the Iraqi leader had collaborated with terrorists, or at least could offer weapons to them that ultimately could be used against the U.S. interests. In his October 2002 speech in Cincinnati, for example, Bush said Iraq had acquired unmanned planes that could be used to attack the United States or its allies with biological or chemical weapons. The president himself said there was no evidence that Iraq played a role in the September 11 attacks, but some of his aides, including Vice President Dick Cheney, often hinted at a link. The one piece of evidence they cited was a disputed report that the alleged leader of the September 11 attacks, Mohammed Atta of Egypt, had met with a senior Iraqi intelligence official in Prague in April 2001; the Iraqi official, who was captured by U.S. forces after the invasion, reportedly said he had not met with Atta. Many intelligence officials and experts on terrorism said the Bush administration had no solid evidence to support its claims, but many Americans seemed convinced. Numerous opinion polls showed that half or more of Americans believed Saddam somehow had played a role in the September 11 attacks.

The administration's fullest explanation of its case linking Iraq with al Qaeda terrorism came in Powell's February 5 presentation to the Security Council. Powell said the key connection was a terrorist network headed by Abu Musab al-Zarqawi, a Palestinian born in Jordan who Powell called "an associate and collaborator" of al Qaeda leader Osama bin Laden. Powell said Zarqawi's network had established a camp in northeastern Iraq that was used to train terrorists to make and use poisons, including a deadly toxic agent known as ricin. Powell said Zarqawi had received medical treatment in Baghdad for two months in mid-2002, during which "nearly two dozen terrorists converged on Baghdad and established a base of operations there." Powell also said the U.S. government had evidence that Zarqawi's group had financed or supported terrorists who assassinated an American diplomat, Laurence Foley, in Amman, Jordan, in October 2002.

News reports raised numerous questions about both the details and substance of Powell's allegations. The *Washington Post* on February 6 quoted U.S. officials as acknowledging that Zarqawi and his group were not controlled by either the Iraqi government or al Qaeda, as Powell had suggested. The group, in fact, operated in a small Kurdish area of northeastern Iraq that was totally outside the control of the Baghdad government. Intelligence experts quoted by the *Post* and other news organizations said the U.S. government had legitimate suspicions about the actions and motives of Zarqawi's group but no solid information proving that it was a connecting link between Saddam's secular government and the militant Islamist al Qaeda group. News organizations also reported in late January and early February that the inability of U.S intelligence agencies to produce proof of Iraq's support of al Qaeda terrorism had angered top White House and Pentagon officials, who insisted such proof existed.

Failure of UN Negotiations

In one sense, the international diplomacy of February and March 2003 centered on the search for a majority of votes on the Security Council. The greater issue, however, was whether the United Nations would be part of the ultimate step in dealing with Iraq or would be shunted off to the sidelines. The Bush administration had made clear that the United States would take whatever action it felt necessary in Iraq regardless of whether it had formal support from the UN. For other nations on the fence, that stance meant a painful choice between siding with the world's sole remaining superpower or daring to be seen in opposition.

To gain passage of a second resolution authorizing war, the United States and its allies (principally Britain and Spain) needed the votes of nine of the fifteen countries represented on the Security Council and, just as important, either positive votes or at least abstentions from the three other nations with veto power—France, China, and Russia. As diplomacy got under way, six Security Council nations were considered to be undecided: Angola, Cameroon, Chile, Guinea, Mexico, and Pakistan.

By late January it had become clear that the principal diplomatic antagonists were the United States and France. Bush, Powell, and their aides worked the telephones, calling world leaders asking for support of a resolution authorizing war. French president Chirac and his foreign minister, Dominique de Villepin, did the same in opposition. An indefatigable traveler, Villepin even went to the capitals of the three African nations serving on the council to appeal for support of the French position. Because it seemed clear that France would use its veto to block a resolution, the Bush administration set its sites on securing what it viewed as a symbolic victory: the votes of nine Security Council members in favor of a war resolution.

As with any search for votes in a legislative context, both sides dangled incentives. The French offered aid to the African countries, two of which (Cameroon and Guinea) Paris had controlled during the colonial era. The Bush administration also offered aid and other incentives to the undecided nations. None of these efforts at horse-trading had much success and in some cases backfired. Bush administration officials tried to win Chile's vote, for example, by promising to push harder for action on a U.S.-Chile bilateral trade agreement that had been stalled in the Senate. Chilean leaders reportedly responded by insisting that Washington should push for the treaty anyway because it benefited both countries. By late February Washington had little hope of getting the nine votes it wanted.

Any doubt about the eventual outcome of the diplomacy was erased on March 5 when France, Germany, and Russia issued an even more forceful version of their statement a month earlier opposing war. This statement said the three countries "will not let the proposed resolution pass that would authorize the use of force." Two days later, the United States, Britain, and Spain introduced a revised proposal setting a March 17 deadline for Iraq to destroy its prohibited weapons. This resolution had no serious chance of passage and clearly was intended as yet another warning to Saddam. When the March 17 deadline came, the allies withdrew the resolution, and Bush issued his last ultimatum, demanding that Saddam leave Iraq within forty-eight hours. Saddam stayed put, and the invasion of Iraq began on March 20.

The failure of diplomacy led to recriminations on both sides of the Atlantic, with pro- and antiwar factions accusing each other of having acted in bad faith. Bush administration officials insisted that Chirac had used his support for inspections as a pretext for avoiding a war because he wanted to protect French commercial interests in Iraq. French officials, by contrast, said the Bush administration never had any true interest in diplomacy or weapons inspections but used both merely to build support for a protracted war. In the United States, most news reports indicated that the Bush administration had expended far less effort on diplomacy than it had on preparing for a war. Critics were particularly harsh in contrasting the 1990–1991 diplomacy of Bush's father, George H. W. Bush—who spent countless hours building international support for the Gulf war that ended Iraq's invasion of Kuwait—with the tentative efforts of George W. Bush, who made few telephone calls to fellow leaders and who met personally only with leaders whose support he already had.

Following are the texts of two statements by European leaders on the prospect of war in Iraq: first, a letter published January 30, 2003, by the Wall Street Journal *and several major European newspapers supporting the U.S. position of confronting the government of Iraq with the prospect of war if it failed to give up its presumed arsenal of weapons of mass destruction, signed by Jose Maria Aznar, Jose-Manuel Durão Barroso, Silvio Berlusconi, Tony Blair, Peter Medgyessy, Leszek Miller, Andres Fogh Rasmussen (the prime ministers, respectively, of Spain, Portugal, Italy, the United Kingdom, Hungary, Poland, and Denmark), and Vaclav Havel, the president of the Czech Republic; second, a declaration issued February 10, 2003, in Paris by French president Jacques Chirac, Russian president Vladimir Putin, and German chancellor Gerhard Schroeder, arguing that war against Iraq should be a "last resort."*

European Leaders on Supporting the Prospect of War in Iraq

The real bond between the U.S. and Europe is the values we share: democracy, individual freedom, human rights and the rule of law. These values crossed the Atlantic with those who sailed from Europe to help create the United States of America. Today they are under greater threat than ever.

The attacks of Sept. 11 showed just how far terrorists—the enemies of our common values—are prepared to go to destroy them. Those outrages were an attack on all of us. In standing firm in defense of these principles, the governments and people of the U.S. and Europe have amply demonstrated the strength of their convictions. Today more than ever, the trans-Atlantic bond is a guarantee of our freedom.

We in Europe have a relationship with the U.S. which has stood the test of time. Thanks in large part to American bravery, generosity and farsightedness, Europe was set free from the two forms of tyranny that devastated our continent in the 20th century: Nazism and communism. Thanks, too, to the continued cooperation between Europe and the U.S. we have managed to guarantee peace and freedom on our continent. The trans-Atlantic relationship must not become a casualty of the current Iraqi regime's persistent attempts to threaten world security.

In today's world, more than ever before, it is vital that we preserve that unity and cohesion. We know that success in the day-to-day battle against terrorism and the proliferation of weapons of mass destruction demands unwavering determination and firm international cohesion on the part of all countries for whom freedom is precious.

The Iraqi regime and its weapons of mass destruction represent a clear threat to world security. This danger has been explicitly recognized by the U.N. All of us are bound by Security Council Resolution 1441, which was adopted unanimously. We Europeans have since reiterated our backing for Resolution 1441, our wish to pursue the U.N. route, and our support for the Security Council at the Prague NATO Summit and the Copenhagen European Council.

In doing so, we sent a clear, firm and unequivocal message that we would rid the world of the danger posed by Saddam Hussein's weapons of mass destruction. We must remain united in insisting that his regime be disarmed. The solidarity, cohesion and determination of the international community are our best hope of achieving this peacefully. Our strength lies in unity.

The combination of weapons of mass destruction and terrorism is a threat of incalculable consequences. It is one at which all of us should feel concerned. Resolution 1441 is Saddam Hussein's last chance to disarm using peaceful means. The opportunity to avoid greater confrontation rests with him. Sadly this week the U.N. weapons inspectors have confirmed that his long-established pattern of deception, denial and non-compliance with U.N. Security Council resolutions is continuing.

Europe has no quarrel with the Iraqi people. Indeed, they are the first victims of Iraq's current brutal regime. Our goal is to safeguard world peace and security by ensuring that this regime gives up its weapons of mass destruction. Our governments have a common responsibility to face this threat. Failure to do so would be nothing less than negligent to our own citizens and to the wider world.

The U.N. Charter charges the Security Council with the task of pre-serving international peace and security. To do so, the Security Council must maintain its credibility by ensuring full compliance with its resolutions. We cannot allow a dictator to systematically violate those resolutions. If they are not complied with, the Security Council will lose its credibility and world peace will suffer as a result. We are confident that the Security Council will face up to its responsibilities.

> **Source:** Jose Maria Aznar, Jose-Manuel Durão Barroso, Silvio Berlusconi, Tony Blair, Vaclav Havel, Peter Medgyessy, Leszek Miller, and Anders Fogh Rasmussen. *United We Stand* (statement issued to newspapers). January 30, 2003. http://64.0.91.34 (accessed October 14, 2003).

French, Russian, and German Leaders on Opposition to War in Iraq

Russia, Germany and France, in close coordination, reaffirm that the disarmament of Iraq, in accordance with the relevant UN resolutions since Resolution 687, is the common aim of the international community, and that it must be pursued to its conclusion within the shortest possible period.

There is a debate over the means to achieve this. This debate must continue in the spirit of friendship and respect that characterises our relations with the United States. It should be inspired by the principles of the United Nations Charter, as stated recently by Mr. Kofi Annan.

Resolution 1441, adopted unanimously by the Security Council, provides a framework whose possibilities have not yet been thoroughly explored.

The inspections conducted by UNMOVIC and the IAEA have already yielded results. Russia, Germany and France favour the continuation of inspections and the substantial strengthening of their human and technical capabilities by all possible means and in consultation with the inspectors, within the framework of Resolution 1441.

There is still an alternative to war. The use of force could only be a last resort. Russia, Germany and France are determined to allow every opportunity for the peaceful disarmament of Iraq.

It is up to Iraq to cooperate actively with UNMOVIC and the IAEA in their work so that they can complete the inspections. The Iraqi regime must face up to its responsibilities in full.

Russia, Germany and France note that the position they express coincides with that of a large number of countries, within the Security Council in particular.

Source: France. Embassy of France in the United States. *Situation in Iraq.* February 10, 2003. www.info-france-usa.org/news/statmnts/2003/chirac021003.asp (accessed October 16, 2003).

February

New Constitution Adopted for Serbia and Montenegro

February 4, 2003

INTRODUCTION

The Federal Republic of Yugoslavia finally ceased to exist in 2003, a decade after its partial collapse led to Europe's deadliest conflicts since World War II. Serbia and Montenegro, the last two constituent republics of Yugoslavia, created a new federation simply called Serbia and Montenegro, which came into being with the adoption of a new constitution in late January and early February.

In reality, there was little of substance to this new country. It consisted of two unequal parts: Serbia, with a population of about 10 million, and Montenegro, with only about 650,000 people. The union was mostly a marriage of convenience that few expected to survive a three-year trial period, during which each republic would work through its own economic and political problems. There were plenty of problems, especially in Serbia, which had been the center of gravity in the former Yugoslavia. Serbia's reformist prime minister, Zoran Djindic, was assassinated in March, reportedly by a criminal gang; repeated attempts to elect someone to the largely ceremonial office of president failed because of voter apathy; the economy continued to suffer as a result of wars during the 1990s and long-term mismanagement; and parliamentary elections in December saw the resurgence of hard-line nationalist politicians who had spawned those wars. At year's end pro-Western democratic factions were under intense international pressure to set aside their feuding so they could form a new government.

The End of Yugoslavia

Yugoslavia had been a creation of post–World War I idealism coupled with practicality. It was an experiment in multiethnic nation building in one of the most unstable corners of Europe. The Western powers who redrew the map of Europe after the war created the Kingdom of Serbs, Croats, and

Slovenes, by attaching five lands to the central core of Serbia: Bosnia-Herzegovina (then divided between Muslims and ethnic Croats), Croatia (the homeland of Croats), Macedonia (divided between ethnic Albanians and Bulgarians), Montenegro (a Serbian country), and Slovenia (home of the Slovenes). Croatia and Slovenia had been part of the Austro-Hungarian empire, which fell apart during the war, and all or parts of the other lands had long been dominated by the Ottoman empire, which collapsed at the end of World War I. The kingdom changed its name to Yugoslavia—the Land of Southern Slavs—in 1929.

After World War II, communist ruler Josip Broz Tito came to power in Belgrade. Tito steered a course independent of Moscow and kept a firm hand on Yugoslavia for thirty-five years, until his death in 1980. Communism in Eastern Europe began its rapid collapse in 1989, and two years later Yugoslavia began a long and bloody implosion. Croatia and Slovenia voted to secede from Yugoslavia in 1991, and Bosnia and Macedonia followed suit in 1992. Serbia allowed Macedonia and Slovenia to slip away, but the secessions of Bosnia and Croatia (both of which had large Serbian minorities) set off ethnic wars that raged until 1995 and killed hundreds of thousands of people. The end of the wars left only Serbia and Montenegro within the Yugoslav federation, but in 1997 Montenegro's leader, Milo Djukanovic, began campaigning for independence. Yet another war came in 1999, when the NATO alliance bombed Serbia to force it to release its grip on Kosovo, a province where the Albanian majority wanted independence. *(Bosnia, p. 460; Kosovo, p. 1138)*

Serbia was devastated by the wars, all of which had been promoted by the Serbian nationalist leader, Slobodan Milosevic. When Milosevic ran for reelection as Yugoslav president in 2000, and declared himself the victor despite clear evidence he had lost, thousands of Serbs rose in rebellion and forced him from office. Milosevic was succeeded in October 2000 by the actual winner of that election, Vojislav Kostunica, who espoused a milder brand of Serbian nationalism. *(Milosevic ouster, Historic Documents of 2000, p. 833)*

In Montenegro, the status of the Yugoslav federation was a divisive issue. Djukanovic pushed for independence but, in 2000, failed to win a majority for that stance. The prospect of a final breakup of Yugoslavia concerned other European leaders, who feared such a step would encourage the further division of countries into ministates based on ethnic or religious differences. In particular, European Union (EU) officials sought to head off a move toward formal independence of Kosovo from Serbia, as this might spark yet another war. Other concerns were that the Serbian-dominated areas of Bosnia might seek independence or—even more provocatively—union with Serbia, or that the minority of Albanian Muslims in Macedonia might seek independence or even union with Albania. *(Albanian rebellion in Macedonia, Historic Documents of 2001, p. 554)*

Seeking to slow Montenegro's drive for independence, the EU in March 2002 negotiated a compromise under which Yugoslavia would be replaced by a "union" of Serbia and Montenegro, each of which would be sovereign states linked by a parliament, a president, a court, and a "council of ministers" responsible primarily for defense and foreign affairs. Belgrade was to remain the capital, although the union's court was to be located in Posgorica, Montenegro's capital. A key point of the compromise was that after three years either state could hold a referendum on seeking independence. Neither state could block the other's independence.

The dissolution of Yugoslavia and the creation of the new entity were accomplished in a three-step process. The Serbian parliament approved the arrangement on January 27. The Montenegrin parliament followed suit two days later. Finally, on February 4 both chambers of the Yugoslav parliament voted in favor by a wide margin; nearly all the "no" votes came from Serbian nationalists, who saw the step as yet another blow to Belgrade's prestige. "I think it was a good country and I don't know why so many remain keen to destroy it," Aleksandar Simic, a member of the Socialist Party formerly headed by Milosevic, said of the death of Yugoslavia. Most public opinion polls showed widespread indifference in both Serbia and Montenegro to the final end of Yugoslavia and the creation of its replacement. One of the most common reactions was that the new nation's name was too long to shout out at a soccer match.

The new Serbia-Montenegro parliament began work on March 3; its 126 deputies were elected by the legislatures of each country. The parliament named as president Svetozar Marovic, a Montenegrin politician who had opposed independence for his country. Ironically, support for the new federation appeared to grow during the year in Montenegro—where support for independence previously had been strongest—and to diminish in Serbia— where many people previously had been anxious to hold on to a semblance of past glory as the center of a larger nation.

Djindjic Assassinated

The ouster of Milosevic in 2000 ended a dictatorship but also forced Serbia to establish a democratic form of government, a task that most other Eastern European countries (including Montenegro) had confronted a decade earlier following the collapse of communism. In broad terms, the Serbian polity was divided into two general camps: those who wanted to emulate Western-style democratic and free-market economic systems and those who sought a return to the nationalist and state-driven economic policies of the Milosevic era.

Pro-Western reformers won the initial round, gaining control of the Serbian parliament in elections shortly after the fall of Milosevic. But that victory contained the seeds of further dissension. The reformers who took over the Serbian government were led by Zoran Djindjic, the charismatic head of the Democratic Party. Djindjic had been a vocal opponent of Milosevic for a decade and fervently wanted to cast Serbia's fate with the West, hopefully as a member of the EU. Djindjic's chief rival was Kostunica, who had been the consensus candidate among opposition groups for the 2000 Yugoslav presidential elections that Milosevic tried to steal. Kostunica, who shared Milosevic's nationalism but opposed his brutal tactics, appeared less interested than Djindjic in transforming Serbian society along Western lines.

The key event in the early years of the post-Milosevic era was a decision by Djindjic and his government to hand Milosevic over to the United Nations tribunal, seated at The Hague, Netherlands, that was hearing war crimes cases stemming from the Balkan wars of the 1990s. The tribunal had indicted Milosevic on charges of genocide and other war crimes. The United States and European countries had promised Serbia more than $1 billion in economic aid—but only if Milosevic was sent to The Hague to face the charges against him. The Djindjic government complied with this demand in June 2001, a step that brought the promised aid and international praise but also was harshly condemned by Serbian nationalists, including Kostunica. Djindjic's willingness to offer up Milosevic in exchange for foreign aid was characteristic of his deal-making style of government. Supporters said he maneuvered deftly to keep the reform process on track; critics said he compromised important goals simply to hold onto power. *(Milosevic trial, Historic Documents of 2001, p. 826)*

In 2002 Kostunica sought to exchange his presidency of Yugoslavia—by now little more than a figurehead position—for that of the presidency of Serbia, in which post he would be better able to challenge Djindjic. Serbia held two presidential elections in 2002. Each time Kostunica won a solid majority, but the results were invalidated because voter turnout fell below the required 50 percent threshold. Kostunica angrily denounced Djindjic for discouraging voters from going to the polls.

The feuding between Djindjic and Kostunica paralyzed the government and prevented it from implementing important economic and political reforms. Political infighting also diverted attention from some of Serbia's continuing problems, including the operations of criminal gangs. Milosevic used paramilitary units operated by some of these gangs to bolster his power, attack his enemies, and carry out the bloody purges of Croats and Muslims in Bosnia. The Djindjic government failed to crack down on the gangs, as it had promised, and by early 2003 most observers said criminal enterprises thriving on drugs, thefts, and prostitution were stronger than ever.

Ultimately, Djindjic paid with his life for his inability to thwart the gangs. Shortly after noon on March 12, 2003, as Djindjic was about to enter government headquarters in downtown Belgrade, snipers fired three shots; two bullets hit him in the abdomen and chest, and the third struck his nearby car. Djindjic was rushed to a hospital, where he died.

The government immediately declared a state of emergency and set up roadblocks around the capital. Pro-government politicians and Western leaders condemned the assassination as an attack on the process of political and economic reform in Serbia.

Within hours, officials attributed the assassination to criminal gangs, citing in particular a drug-running enterprise run by Milorad Lukovic (also known as Legija, or "legion" after his former service in the French foreign legion). During the Milosevic years Lukovic had headed an especially notorious paramilitary unit. Lukovic had sided with Djindjic in the uprising against Milosevic in 2000, but in February 2003 the gang leader published an open letter in which he accused the prime minister of being "dangerously unpatriotic" and warned that his days were numbered. Lukovic's statement had finally provoked the government into action; officials had planned to issue arrest warrants for Lukovic and key members of his gang, known as the Zemun Clan, on March 12, the day of the assassination.

An estimated 500,000 people turned out for Djindjic's funeral in Belgrade on March 15. The show of respect was remarkable, in part, because Djindjic had fallen steeply in popularity because his reforms had not brought the economic prosperity that Serbians so desperately craved after a decade of war and upheaval. In the weeks after the assassination government security forces arrested several thousand suspected members of criminal gangs, including several leaders of Lukovic's Zemun Clan. Lukovic himself remained at large.

International human rights groups, and many domestic critics of the government, said the crackdown had developed into a political vendetta; as evidence, they cited the arrests of two associates of Kostunica. In late April police said forty-five people had been charged in connection with the assassination, including the elusive Lukovic and a prominent nationalist politician—Voijislav Seselj—who in February had surrendered to the UN tribunal to face war crimes charges. Thirty-six alleged members of the Lukovic gang went on trial on December 22, all on charges related to the Djindjic assassination. Among them was Zvezdan Jovanovi, one of the alleged snipers. Reuters news service reported on December 25 that Jovanovi had said Djindjic was killed to prevent him from handing war crimes suspects over to the Hague tribunal.

Djindjic's Democratic Party selected Zoran Zivkovic, a former interior minister, as the new prime minister. Zivkovic lacked Djindjic's charisma and penchant for deal making, but he demonstrated a greater zeal than his predecessor for reform within the government. Under his leadership the government enacted several economic and political reform measures that had been stalled while Djindjic was alive. Zivkovic also targeted the military, which remained dominated by generals who rose through the ranks in the Milosevic years. By late summer the government had fired sixteen top-ranking generals, including the head of the intelligence service and the corps that had carried out the attacks against Albanian Muslims in Kosovo province in 1998–1999. Zivkovic said the changes would allow for a "young and reformed army leadership."

The Old Order Surges Back

Public sympathy for Djindjic's reformist allies wore thin in the months after the assassination, and by the fall the haggard coalition was torn apart by new charges of corruption and incompetence. Acknowledging on November 13 that his government lacked enough parliamentary support to enact new legislation, Zivkovic called new legislative elections for December 28, one year ahead of schedule. Three days later, on November 16, a third attempt to elect a new president of Serbia failed, again because of low turnout. This time Kostunica did not run, and his party urged voters to stay away from the polls. But in a sign of deep trouble for the government, the top vote-getter was Tomislav Nikolic, who represented the hard-line nationalist Serbian Radical Party; that party's real leader was Voijislav Seselj, who was in jail at the Hague, waiting trial on war crimes charges.

The failed presidential election turned out to be an indicator of public dissatisfaction with the government, and possibly even the yearning of many Serbians for the old days of supposed Serbian glory under Milosevic. In a strong turnout on December 28, the clear victor was Seselj's Serbian Radical Party, which won nearly 28 percent of the vote—enough for 81 seats in the 250-seat parliament. The old Milosevic party, the Socialist Party of Serbia, collected just over 7 percent of the vote, enough for 22 seats. Party officials said one of those seats would be offered to Milosevic, still on trial at the Hague.

Three pro-government reformist parties, including Djindjic's Democratic Party, captured about one-third of the vote, enough for 94 seats—well short of the majority needed to form a new government. That left Kostunica's Democratic Party of Serbia as the power broker; it won 18 percent of the vote, or enough for 53 seats. Before the election, Kostunica had harshly criticized the other three reform parties and had ruled out serving in a coalition with them. At year's end, European leaders were pressing Kostunica to negotiate a deal with those parties to form a government—most likely with him at the head as prime minister. Most analysts expected a prolonged period of deal making before a new government could take office. Even then, any coalition was certain to be so fragmented that more elections, and more political upheaval, were in Serbia's future.

Following are excerpts from an unofficial translation of the Constitutional Charter of the State Union of Serbia and Montenegro, established February 4, 2003, following the dissolution of the former Republic of Yugoslavia.

"Constitutional Charter of the State Union of Serbia and Montenegro"

Proceeding from the equality of the two member states, the state of Montenegro and the state of Serbia which includes the Autonomous Province of Vojvodina and the Autonomous Province of Kosovo and Metohija, the latter currently under international administration in accordance with UN SC resolution 1244, and on the basis of the Proceeding Points for the Restructuring of Relations between Serbia and Montenegro of 14 March 2002.

The National Assembly of the Republic of Serbia, the Assembly of the Republic of Montenegro and the Federal Assembly have adopted the following:

I

The name

Article 1
The name of the State union shall be Serbia and Montenegro.

Principle of equality

Article 2
Serbia and Montenegro shall be based on the equality of the two member states, the state of Serbia and the state of Montenegro.

Goals

Article 3
The goals of Serbia and Montenegro shall be:

- respect for the human rights of all persons within its competence,
- preservation and promotion of human dignity, equality and the rule of law,

- integration in European structures, the European Union in particular,
- harmonization of its legislation and practices with European and international standards
- introduction of market economy based on free enterprise, competition and social justice, and
- establishment and ensurance of an unhindered operation of the common market on its territory through coordination and harmonization of the economic systems of the member states in line with the principle and standards of the European Union.

Symbols

Article 4
Serbia and Montenegro shall have a flag, an anthem and a coat-of-arms as specified by the laws of Serbia and Montenegro.

The territory

Article 5
The territory of Serbia and Montenegro shall consist of the territories of the member states of Serbia and Montenegro.

The border of Serbia and Montenegro shall be inviolable.

The boundary between the member states shall be unchangeable, except by mutual consent.

Seat of institutions

Article 6
The administrative centre of Serbia and Montenegro shall be in Belgrade.

The seat of the Parliament of Serbia and Montenegro and the Council of Ministers shall be in Belgrade and the seat of the Court of Serbia and Montenegro in Podgorica.

Citizenship

Article 7
A citizen of a member state shall be also a citizen of Serbia and Montenegro.

A citizen of a member state shall have the same rights and duties in the other member state as its own citizens, except for the right to vote.

II

The Charter of Human and Minority Rights and Civil Liberties

Article 8
A Charter of Human and Minority Rights and Civil Liberties, forming an integral part of the Constitutional Charter, shall be adopted under the procedure and in the manner set forth for the adoption of the Constitutional Charter.

Exercise of human and minority rights and civil liberties

Article 9
The member states shall regulate, ensure and protect human and minority rights and civil liberties on their territories.

The achieved level of human and minority rights, individual and collective, and of civil liberties may not be reduced.

Serbia and Montenegro shall monitor the implementation of human and minority rights and civil liberties and shall ensure their protection if such protection is not ensured in the member states.

Direct implementation of international treaties

Article 10
Provisions of international treaties on human and minority rights and civil liberties applicable on the territory of Serbia and Montenegro shall apply directly.

III

Principles of market economy

Article 11
Economic relations in Serbia and Montenegro shall be based on market economy that rest on free enterprise, competition, liberal trade policies and the protection of property.

Serbia and Montenegro shall coordinate and harmonize the economic systems of the member states.

Common Market

Article 12
Serbia and Montenegro shall have a common market.

The member states shall be responsible for an unhindered operation of the common market.

Freedom of movement

Article 13
The movement of people, goods, services and capital shall be free in Serbia and Montenegro.

The prevention of the free flow of people, goods, services and capital between the state of Serbia and the state of Montenegro shall be prohibited.

IV

International Personality

Article 14
Serbia and Montenegro shall be a single subject of international law and a member of international, global and regional organizations, the membership of which is contingent on international personality.

The member states may become members of the international, global and regional organizations, the membership of which is not contingent on international personality.

Establishment and maintenance of international relations

Article 15
Serbia and Montenegro shall establish international relations with other states and with international organizations and shall conclude international treaties and agreements.

The member states [may] maintain international relations, conclude international agreements and establish missions in other states, unless this is contrary to the competences of Serbia and Montenegro and the interests of the other member state.

Supremacy of international law

Article 16
Ratified international agreements and the generally accepted rules of international law shall have precedence over the law of Serbia and Montenegro and over the law of the member states.

V

Establishment of the competences of the State union of Serbia and Montenegro

Article 17
Serbia and Montenegro shall have those competences entrusted to it by the present Constitutional Charter.

The member states may jointly entrust to Serbia and Montenegro the carrying out of additional affairs from their competences.

Financing of the competences of the State union of Serbia and Montenegro

Article 18
The member states shall provide finances for the carrying out of the entrusted competences and additional affairs of Serbia and Montenegro.

VI

1. The Parliament of Serbia and Montenegro

Competences

Article 19
The Parliament of Serbia and Montenegro shall decide on the Constitutional Charter as a supreme legal act of Serbia and Montenegro in the manner set forth by the Constitutional Charter and pass law and other acts on:

- institutions established in accordance with the Constitutional Charter and their operation;

- implementation of international law and conventions that have established the obligation of cooperation between Serbia and Montenegro and international courts;
- declaration and lifting of a state of war, with prior consent of the Assemblies of the member states;
- military and defence matters;
- membership of Serbia and Montenegro, as an international legal subject, in international organizations, and the rights and obligations stemming from that membership, with prior consent of relevant bodies of the member states;
- identification of borders of Serbia and Montenegro, with prior consent of the Assembly of a member state on whose territory the border extends;
- issues related to the standardization, intellectual property, measurements, precious metals and statistics;
- policies of immigration and asylum, visa system and integrated border management in accordance with the standards of the European Union;
- ratification of international treaties and agreement of Serbia and Montenegro;
- annual revenue and expenditure necessary for funding the activities transferred to Serbia and Montenegro at the proposal of relevant bodies of the member states and the Council of Ministers;
- prevention and removal of obstacles to a free flow of goods, services, persons and capital within Serbia and Montenegro;
- election of the President and the Council of Ministers of Serbia and Montenegro;
- the flag, anthem and the coat-of-arms of Serbia and Montenegro.

The Parliament of Serbia and Montenegro shall also carry out the affairs from the competences of Serbia and Montenegro as set forth in the Constitutional Charter.

The Parliament of Serbia and Montenegro shall adopt its rules of procedure.

Composition and election

Article 20

The Parliament of Serbia and Montenegro shall be unicameral consisting of 126 members, of whom 91 shall come from Serbia and 35 from Montenegro.

Members of Parliament of Serbia and Montenegro shall be elected from each member state in accordance with European and democratic standards under the laws of the member states. In the first two years after the promulgation of the Constitutional Charter, Members of Parliament shall be directly elected, in proportion to the representation in the National Assembly of Serbia and the Assembly of Montenegro.

In the first elections, Members of Parliament shall be elected from among the Deputies in the National Assembly of Serbia, in the National Assembly of Montenegro and the Federal Assembly. If a member state holds parliamentary elections in that same period, the composition of its delegation to the Parliament of Serbia and Montenegro shall be proportionally adjusted to the election results.

After this initial period, Members of Parliament of Serbia and Montenegro shall be elected in direct elections.

Members of Parliament shall be elected for a term of office of four years. . . .

Withdrawal from the State union of Serbia and Montenegro

Article 60

Upon the expiry of a three-year period the member state shall have the right to initiate the procedure for a change of the state status, i.e. for withdrawal from the State union of Serbia and Montenegro.

A decision to withdraw from the State union of Serbia and Montenegro shall be made after a referendum has been held. The Law on Referendum shall be passed by a member state, taking into account recognized democratic standards.

If Montenegro withdraws from the State union of Serbia and Montenegro, the international documents related to the Federal Republic of Yugoslavia, particularly United Nations Security Council Resolution 1244, shall pertain and apply fully to Serbia as its successor.

The member state that exercises the right of withdrawal shall not inherit the right to international legal personality and all outstanding issues shall be regulated separately between the successor state and the state that has become independent.

If both member states declare in a referendum that they are in favour of changing the state status, i.e. in favour of independence, all outstanding issues shall be resolved in the succession procedure, as was the case with the former Socialist Federal Republic of Yugoslavia. . . .

Source: Serbia and Montenegro. Ministry of Foreign Affairs. The Constitutional Charter of the State Union of Serbia and Montenegro, unofficial translation. February 4, 2003. www.mfa.gov.yu/Facts/charter_e.html (accessed June 1, 2003).

President's Economic Report, Economic Advisers' Report

February 7, 2003

INTRODUCTION

The U.S. economy, mired for two years in a desultory recovery from the mild recession of 2001, showed signs of getting back on track toward the end of 2003. The economy grew at an annual rate of 3.1 percent for the year, including a scorching pace of 8.2 percent in the third quarter. Inflation and interest rates remained low, while productivity grew at its fastest pace in twenty years. Consumer spending continued as the main driver of the recovery, while business investment in equipment began to pick up toward the end of the year. The value of the dollar declined against other currencies, stimulating growth in American exports. Investors started coming back to a rising stock market, whose sudden slump in 1999 and 2000 had contributed to the downturn and wobbly recovery.

Two disturbing trends raised questions about the durability of the recovery, however. Job creation remained stagnant throughout 2003, showing little sign of growing fast enough to bring down the unemployment rate, which stayed in the 6 percent range, and the federal budget deficit climbed to its highest dollar level ever—$374 billion at the end of the 2003 fiscal year, and it was projected to reach nearly $500 billion in fiscal 2004. The return of large budget deficits required Congress to enact a record increase of nearly $1 trillion in the legal limit on the national debt.

The U.S. economy, the world's largest, was not the only one to begin performing better as the year ended. European economies also began to climb out of recession or near-recession. Moves by the governments of Austria, France, Germany, and Italy to curb their bloated labor costs contributed to forecasts of positive if still sluggish growth in 2004. Asian countries, whose economies took a beating during the spring and early summer due to the spread of a respiratory disease known as Severe Acute Respiratory Syndrome

(SARS), regained their footing in the second half of the year. Despite having been hit hardest by SARS and its economic fallout, China reported that its economy grew at a rate of 9.1 percent in 2003. Japan, the world's second largest economy, began slowly to pull out of a prolonged depression. Even Latin America and Africa showed some hopeful signs of bringing their long-troubled economies under control. *(SARS outbreak, p. 121; Overview of global economy, p. 751)*

Several forces were in play, however, that analysts said could affect the pace of the global recovery. Among these were the high budget and current account deficits in the United States, as well as a dollar that was declining in value against other currencies. Economists feared that both situations could eventually raise interest rates. A rising tide of protectionism in the wake of the failure of the world's trade ministers in September to reach accommodation on agricultural subsidies and other trade rules could also slow recovery by raising prices. *(Trade talks, p. 740)*

U.S. president George W. Bush remained steadfast in his contention that the massive tax cuts he pushed through Congress in 2001 and 2003 would foster spending and investment, thus stimulating economic growth and job creation. Bush and his aides also argued that the budget deficit was appropriate given the country's need to oust Iraqi leader Saddam Hussein and fight an international war against terrorism. In the final months of the year, Bush touted the spurt in economic growth as evidence that he was correct. But Democratic presidential candidates charged that the dismal record of job creation was evidence that Bush's economic policies were a failure. The president was even beginning to hear criticism from conservative Republicans that the budget deficits had grown too large. *(Jobs, p. 441; deficits, p. 678)*

An Uncertain First Half

Uncertainty was the word that best described the economy as 2003 began. After growing at a rate of 4 percent in the third quarter of 2002, the economy slowed to a 1.4 percent annual growth rate in the fourth quarter, as Bush and his administration prepared the country for an invasion of Iraq aimed at ridding that country of its alleged weapons of mass destruction as well as its leader, Saddam Hussein. Continuing fears of another terrorist attack like the one of September 11, 2001, and unease over threats by North Korea that it was developing nuclear weapons contributed to the wariness. So did the outbreak in the spring of the deadly and previously unknown strain of influenza known as SARS. Although SARS was confined largely to East Asia and was contained by the end of June, fears that it would quickly spread throughout the world compounded general unease about the future. *(Preparing for war, p. 40)*

In his State of the Union message at the end of January, President Bush called for another round of tax cuts to stimulate the economy. He asked for $726 billion in cuts and tax credits, in addition to the $1.3 trillion ten-year tax cut he had pushed through Congress in 2001. In both his State of the Union address and his annual economic report to Congress, Bush argued that the additional tax stimulus would create jobs and thus ultimately raise tax revenues. At a news conference releasing the economic report February 7, Glenn Hubbard, chairman of the president's Council of Economic Advisers, predicted that the economy would grow enough over the next five years for the Treasury to recoup 40 percent of the costs of the tax cut. *(State of the Union Address, p. 18; economic report, p. 68; 2001 tax cuts, Historic Documents of 2001, p. 400)*

The centerpiece of the Bush proposal was the elimination of most taxes on stock dividends paid to individuals, a proposal that Democrats derided as "no millionaire left behind," a play on the Bush education initiative known as "no child left behind." Concerns about the fairness of the proposal along with its sheer size also made many congressional Republicans nervous, and Bush was ultimately forced to accept a tax cut that totaled $330 billion over ten years along with $20 billion in aid to the states. The key provisions of the bill, which was signed into law on May 28 (PL 108–27), reduced the tax rate on dividends and capital gains to 15 percent through 2008, accelerated some of the individual income tax cuts enacted in 2001, and increased the per-child tax credit from $600 to $1,000 in 2003 and 2004.

Growth remained slow in the first quarter of 2003, staying at the same 1.4 percent annual rate recorded in the last quarter of 2002. (The figure for first-quarter growth was later revised to 2 percent, when the government did a routine five-year adjustment of its statistics to keep them comparable over the long run.) Expectations for the second quarter were not high. The United States invaded Iraq on March 20, quickly and successfully overthrowing the government, but then was mired in what looked to be a long and costly period of trying to stabilize that country. At home, the jobless picture appeared to worsen, as the unemployment rate grew from 5.7 percent in January to 6.4 percent, its high point for the year. At the end of June, the Federal Reserve lowered interest rates another quarter of a percentage point, to 1 percent, saying that the economy had yet to show "sustainable growth." It was the thirteenth reduction the Federal Reserve had made in the key federal funds rate since the beginning of 2001, and the new level was the lowest since 1958. The Federal Reserve also began to talk of the "remote" possibility of deflation, a period of sustained low or falling prices that could result in lower output and wages, which could further depress prices.

As it turned out, growth in the second quarter was much better than expected. Boosted by a 46 percent increase in defense spending largely attributable to the Iraq war, the economy grew at a (revised) rate of 3.3 percent.

Consumer spending, which drove the economy and which some analysts feared might be weakening, rose 3.8 percent, boosted by an increase in home construction of 6.6 percent. Nonresidential spending, the broadest measure of investment, rose 8 percent. That was welcome news, since business investment, considered a main key to a sustained recovery, had been flat since the recession of 2001.

Cautious Optimism in the Second Half

Economists expected growth to pick up even more in the third quarter, but they were stunned when preliminary figures showed that the economy had charged ahead by 7.2 percent. (The revised figures, announced in November, put third-quarter growth at 8.2 percent.) Much of the credit was given to a provision of the tax-cut measure that called for a $400 increase in the child tax credit for 2003, which was to be refunded immediately. The Treasury Department sent out more than 12 million checks totaling $14 billion to parents in August just in time to cover back-to-school expenses. "The tax relief we passed is working," President Bush told a cheering crowd of workers at an aluminum processing plant in Ohio on October 30 when the preliminary quarterly figures were announced. It was the fastest rate of quarterly growth since 1984. Fueled by the rebate checks and housing refinancings, consumer spending grew at a 6.4 percent annual rate. Manufacturers began to build their inventories for the first time in six months. For the first time in eight months, the economy added jobs in September, although nowhere near enough to have much of an impact on the jobless rate.

No one expected the economy to continue to grow at such a fast past, but many analysts predicted that fourth-quarter growth would be in the 5 percent range. (Preliminary figures issued at the end of January 2004 put it at 4 percent, which was somewhat disappointing in its fall-off from the third quarter but nonetheless a sound rate of growth.)

One reason for renewed confidence that the economy was finally on track for recovery was the performance of the stock market. After falling in the three previous years, the market began a rally in March that brought the Dow Jones industrial average above 10,000 points on December 11 for the first time in eighteen months. Overall the Dow Jones index gained 25 percent in 2004, while the Nasdaq index, composed of information and other high-tech stocks, rose 50 percent. Standard and Poor's (S&P) 500 stock index rose 26 percent. Many stocks, particularly of the large companies represented in the S&P 500 and the smaller companies represented in the Russell 2000 index, finished the year higher than they were when those two indexes peaked in 2000, and many investors had recouped most if not of all their losses of the past few years.

Nonetheless, various indicators during the fourth quarter indicated that the economy was still not in full recovery. After reaching its highest level in fourteen months in November, consumer confidence as measured by the Conference Board, a private research group, dropped off again in December. Sales of existing homes fell 4.6 percent in November. Many analysts had expected a smaller decrease and expressed concern that housing sales and construction, which had helped sustain growth throughout the economic slowdown, might finally have reached their limits of expansion. In what might have been the most disappointing news, the Labor Department reported in early January 2004 that, while the unemployment rate for December fell to 5.7 percent, the economy had created a net of only 1,000 new jobs—well below the 50,000 to 100,000 that many analysts had predicted and far below the 200,000 a month needed to bring the jobless rate down. The Labor Department said that most of the decline in the jobless rate was attributable to discouraged unemployed workers who dropped out of the labor market.

Effects of Slow Growth

Toward the end of 2003 state governments began to emerge from three years of budget deficits as state tax revenues picked up in the face of higher overall economic growth. (Unlike the federal government, many states were prohibited by their constitutions from running deficits and thus had to take politically painful actions, such as spending cuts and tax increases, to keep their budgets in balance.) According to the National Conference of State Legislatures, only ten states were facing budget shortfalls as they entered the new fiscal year, compared with thirty-one a year earlier. Officials for many states said they were not out of the woods yet and still needed to cope with long-term spending demands to cover increased health care and education costs. One of the states in the deepest budget trouble was California, where voters in October showed their displeasure with the state's troubled finances by recalling Democratic governor Gray Davis and replacing him with actor and political neophyte Arnold Schwarzenegger. *(California recall, p. 1005)*

In any economic downturn the people who were usually hurt most were the poor and near poor. It was thus not surprising that more people fell into poverty in 2002. According to a Census Bureau report released September 26, the poverty rate for 2002 was 12.1 percent, up from 11.7 percent in 2001. That translated into 34.6 million people living below the poverty line in 2002, nearly 1.7 million more than in 2001. Of those, 14.1 million lived in severe poverty, defined as incomes below half of the poverty line, up from 13.4 million in 2001. (The poverty threshold was $18,392 for a family of four and $9,183 for a single individual.) This was the second year in a row that poverty had increased after declining for four consecutive years.

The Census Bureau also reported that median household money income fell 1.1 percent, or $500, from $42,900 in 2001 to $42,409 in 2002. Since its peak in 1999, median income had fallen $1,506.The number of people without health insurance also rose in 2002, to 43.6 million—an increase of 2.4 million over 2001, and the largest annual increase in a decade. *(Health insurance coverage, p. 846)*

A survey of twenty-five large cities, released by the U.S. Conference of Mayors in December, reported that requests for emergency food assistance had gone up 17 percent in the last year, while requests for emergency shelter had increased by 13 percent. The report said that unemployment, low-paying jobs, high housing costs, substance abuse, and high energy and utility costs all contributed to the hunger problem.

Following are the text of President George W. Bush's annual report to Congress, The Economic Report of the President, *and excerpts from* The Annual Report of the Council of Economic Advisers, *both released February 7, 2003.*

"The Economic Report of the President"

To the Congress of the United States:

The economy is recovering from the effects of the slowdown that began in the middle of 2000 and led to the subsequent recession. The American economy has been hit hard by the events of the past three years, most tragically by the effects of the terrorist attacks of September 11, 2001. Our economy and investor confidence were hurt when we learned that some corporate leaders were not playing by the rules. The combined impact of these events, along with the three-year decline in stock values that impacted business investment, slowed growth in 2002. Despite these challenges, the economy's underlying fundamentals remain solid—including low inflation, low interest rates, and strong productivity gains. Yet the pace of the expansion has not been satisfactory; there are still too many Americans looking for jobs. We will not be satisfied until every part of our economy is vigorous and every person who wants a job can find one.

We are taking action to restore the robust growth that creates jobs. In January, I proposed a growth and jobs plan to add needed momentum to our economic recovery. We will accelerate the tax relief already approved by Congress and give it to Americans now, when it is most needed. Lowering tax rates and moving more Americans into the lowest tax bracket will help our economy grow and create jobs. Faster marriage tax relief and a faster increase in the child tax credit will especially help middle-class families, and should take effect now. We will take steps to encourage small business investment, helping them to expand and create jobs. We will end the unfair double taxation of corporate income received by individuals. By putting more money back in the hands of shareholders, strengthening investor confidence in the market, and encouraging more investment, we will have more growth and job creation. These steps will allow Americans to keep more of their own money to spend, save, or invest. They will boost the economy, ensure that the recovery continues, and provide long-term economic benefits through higher productivity and higher incomes.

As our economy recovers, we also have an obligation to help Americans who have lost their jobs. That is why we extended unemployment payments for workers who lost their jobs and improved incentives for investment to create new jobs. I also proposed a bold new program of reemployment accounts to help workers searching for jobs.

Our commitment to a strong economy does not stop with these important steps. We will continue to strengthen investor confidence in the integrity of our markets. We will develop better ways to train workers for new jobs. We will make the Nation's regulations and tax code less onerous and more reflective of the demands of a dynamic economy, and expand opportunities for open trade and stronger growth in all nations, especially for emerging and developing economies.

Our Nation's economic progress comes from the innovation and hard work of Americans in a free market that creates opportunities no other system can offer. Government does not create wealth, but instead creates the economic environment in which risk takers and entrepreneurs create jobs. With the right policies focused on growth and jobs, strong economic fundamentals—and hard work—I am confident we will extend economic opportunity and prosperity to every corner of America.

George W. Bush
The White House
February 2003

Source: U.S. Executive Office of the President. Economic Report of the President Transmitted to the Congress. February 7, 2003. http://purl.access. gpo.gov/GPO/LPS5348 (accessed September 27, 2003).

"The Annual Report of the Council of Economic Advisers"

Chapter 1

Macroeconomic Performance in 2002

The U.S. economy solidified its forward progress in 2002, with the third quarter of the year marking the fourth consecutive quarter of economic growth. This progress followed a contraction in 2001 that was deeper and longer than initial data suggested, but still mild by historical standards. Real gross domestic product (GDP) declined by 0.6 percent during the first three quarters of 2001, about one-fourth the average percentage decline over the previous seven recessions. Growth resumed in the fourth quarter of 2001—despite the terrorist attacks in September—and real GDP rose at an annual rate of 3.4 percent in the first three quarters of 2002. . . . Although economic activity probably weakened in the fourth quarter, the ongoing improvement in productivity growth, together with lean inventories, foreshadowed a return to more normal levels of production and job growth in the quarters ahead.

The economic recovery of 2002 resulted from a constellation of factors, including the resiliency of the economy after the terrorist attacks and the lagged effects of stimulative monetary and fiscal policy in 2001. Although the Federal Reserve lowered the Federal funds rate only once in 2002—by half a percentage point on November 6—the 475-basis-point reduction over the course of 2001 continued to stimulate the economy throughout the year. (A basis point is 0.01 percentage point.) Monetary stimulus was complemented by fiscal stimulus, in the form of the tax rate reductions included in the Economic Growth and Taxpayer Relief Reconciliation Act of 2001 (EGTRRA) and the investment incentives in the Job Creation and Worker Assistance Act (JCWAA) of 2002. In the long run, EGTRRA's reductions in marginal tax rates will raise potential output by increasing labor supply and encouraging the entrepreneurial activities that are the building blocks of economic growth. In the short run, however, the tax cuts buoyed disposable income and helped keep consumption high. Robust consumption, in turn, was a crucial locus of strength in the overall economy, contributing an average of 2.1 percentage points to real GDP growth during the first three quarters of the year. Additionally, the tax incentives in JCWAA, which the President signed in March, provided needed support to investment at a time when stability in this component of final demand was especially important.

In 2002 discussions of both economic activity and economic policy paid particular attention to the valuation of the economy's stock of productive assets. One of the more favorable developments for many Americans in 2002 was the continued appreciation of their most important investment: their home. Housing prices rose 6.2 percent from the third quarter of 2001 to the third quarter of 2002, following an 8.7 percent increase in the same period a year earlier. As discussed below, housing values were buoyed not only by low mortgage interest rates, which reached levels not seen in more than a generation, but also by rising demand, continuing strength in purchases of second homes, and ongoing improvements in mortgage finance. Strength in housing values contributed to robust increases in residential investment, providing another important impetus to final demand in 2002.

In the aggregate, however, the appreciation in housing wealth was overshadowed by continued losses in the stock market. Like those for all of the world's major equity exchanges, U.S. stock indexes lost ground in 2002, continuing a general slide that began in the spring of 2000. From the market's high point in the first quarter of 2000 to the fourth quarter of 2002, stockholders lost nearly $7 trillion in equity wealth. These losses continued to weigh heavily on economic growth and job creation in 2002, by reducing the wealth of consumers and raising the cost of equity capital for investing firms. The precise reasons for the bear market of 2000-02 are subject to debate, but the market's 3-year slide was probably influenced by two general factors: a decline in expected profit growth and an increase in the premium that investors required to hold risky assets. These factors continued to play important roles in the first three quarters of 2002 as the stock market continued its decline. Specifically, corporate accounting scandals called into question the reported profits of some firms, while risk premiums (as measured by the difference, or spread, between the yields of corporate bonds and those of U.S. Treasuries) rose to near-record levels. Although some observers attributed most of the market's decline to the corporate scandals, it is worth noting that equity prices fell around the world, even in countries with different accounting systems and governance institutions.

The stock market's decline has caused some to question the productivity improvements of the late 1990s. Yet even though investors may have over-estimated the value of particular technology-intensive investments, it would be a mistake to infer that technological improvements hold little promise for future economic growth. Detailed analyses of the sources of productivity growth indicate that the post-1995 productivity improvement owes much to the U.S. economy's ability to profit from technological innovation. If technology continues to progress at its recent pace, rising productivity will continue to bring about improvements in living standards that compare quite favorably with the more modest gains of only one or two decades ago.

In the short run, however, economic growth is determined by demand factors as well as by the economy's technology and potential to supply goods and services. The next section discusses the individual components of GDP from the demand side. There and elsewhere in the chapter, the discussion pays particular attention to the links between asset markets (which set the prices for stocks, bonds, and houses) and the components of real aggregate demand (consumption, investment, government purchases, and net exports).

GDP and Its Components in 2002

Consumption

Consumption continued to be the prime locomotive for the recovery in 2002, rising at an annual rate of 3.0 percent over the first three quarters of the year. (GDP data for the fourth quarter were not yet available as this *Report* went to press.) Expenditure on consumer durables was especially strong, in large part because of strong motor vehicle sales. Zero-percent financing offers and other aggressive sales promotions sent automobile sales soaring to more than 18 million units at an annual rate in July and August. (Automobile sales were also especially strong in December.) Largely as a result, expenditure on consumer durables accounted for more than 1.7 percentage points of GDP growth in the third quarter. Consumption of nondurable goods was especially strong in the first quarter, rising 7.9 percent at an annual rate, but tailed off afterward. Finally, consumption of services remained robust, accounting for about 1 percentage point of GDP growth in each of the first three quarters of the year. . . .

The Housing Market and Consumption. Along with healthy growth of disposable income, another positive determinant of consumption growth in 2002 was the strength of the housing market. (The sources of this strength . . . include record low mortgage rates and continued growth in housing demand, fueled in part by high immigration and the demand for second homes.) Housing wealth is more widely distributed among American families than stock market wealth, and housing equity continued to rise in 2002. A common way for this equity to support consumption is through borrowing against home equity: the outstanding value of revolving home equity loans at commercial banks rose from $155.5 billion in December 2001 to $212.3 billion in December 2002. Another way that homeowners can tap the equity in their homes, for higher consumption or for spending on home improvements, is by refinancing their outstanding mortgages when interest rates have fallen. Of course, simply refinancing a mortgage at a lower interest rate can reduce monthly mortgage payments and free up extra cash. Many refinancers, however, choose to remove equity from their homes by taking out a new mortgage with a larger principal than the amount outstanding on the original mortgage. These "cash-out" refinancings boomed in 2002 as a result of the continued appreciation in housing prices and declining long-term interest rates. According to the Federal Home Loan Mortgage Corporation (Freddie Mac), holders of conventional, conforming mortgages liquefied about $59 billion in equity in the first three quarters of 2002. . . .

Nonresidential Investment

Nonresidential investment was one of the weakest components of demand in 2002. In the first three quarters of the year, business fixed investment declined at an annual rate of 3.1 percent, in large part because of a precipitous 17.8 percent fall in investment in structures. The other, larger component of business fixed investment, equipment and software, fell at an annual rate of 2.7 percent in the first quarter of the year, but then rebounded to rise at an annual rate of 5.0 percent in the second and third quarters. In light of the weak investment performance, many observers wondered whether the economy suffered from a capital overhang, built up by excessive investment in the years immediately before the 2001 recession. As discussed in last year's *Report*, this possibility is hard to verify, because it requires an estimate of the "correct" amount of capital relative to the economy's output, a figure that is hard to know with certainty. Yet as the 2002 *Report* also noted, some empirical evidence had emerged in 2001 indicating that a modest overhang had developed the previous year for some capital goods, notably servers, routers, switches, optical cabling, and large trucks. However, evidence that a widespread overhang continues to hinder overall investment outside of a few particular industries is harder to find. In any case, the growth rate of capital services has fallen sharply over the past 2 years, from an average of more than 5.9 percent a year from 1998 to 2000 to 3.6 percent in 2001 and about 3.4 percent in 2002. This low rate of growth means that any general capital overhang that had developed by 2000 is likely to have been significantly reduced by the end of 2002.

Another important business investment development in 2002 was the change in business inventories. In 2001 firms drew down $61.4 billion in real inventories (in 1996 dollars), but real inventory investment turned positive in the second and third quarters of 2002. Although the level of inventory investment remained modest, the change in that investment after the drawdown of 2001 added several percentage points to GDP growth, especially in the first quarter. As the year drew to a close, inventory-to-sales ratios remained close to their lowest levels in years, suggesting further room for inventory expansion in 2003.

Although the short-term outlook for investment in both inventories and equipment and software is positive, the outlook for investment in structures is more uncertain. One potential positive influence on structures investment going forward is the Congress' passage of a terrorism risk insurance bill in late 2002, which will facilitate the construction of projects that are difficult to insure privately against terrorist attacks. Yet vacancy rates for both office and industrial space remained high in 2002, suggesting that the rebound in structures investment may not begin for some time. . . .

Residential Investment

In contrast to the softness in nonresidential investment, residential investment grew briskly in 2002, sparked by the lowest mortgage interest rates in more than a generation. After hitting a recent peak of 8.64 percent in May 2000, interest rates for conventional, fixed-rate 30-year loans fell to 5.93 percent by the end of December 2002, their lowest level since 1965. Low mortgage rates contributed to the 6.8 percent increase in single family housing starts over their already high level of 2001, while boosting sales of new homes to record levels near the end of the year. The strength of housing construction during the past 3 years stands in contrast to past business cycles, when housing starts were not nearly as robust. . . .

Strong housing construction is also a natural consequence of rising housing prices, although that rise moderated to an annual rate of 3.4 percent in the third quarter of 2002 from an annual rate of about 9 percent in the first half of the year. The continued appreciation of housing during the last several years has led some observers to contend that the housing market is caught in a bubble, in which buyers pay high prices for assets simply because they hope to sell those assets to other investors at even higher prices, a scheme that collapses quickly when no further purchasers can be found. Proponents of the housing bubble theory noted that houses were particularly expensive relative to rents, which indicated that high shelter costs alone did not explain the entire rise in housing prices. Housing prices also rose much more quickly than the median household income in 2001, which left the price-to-income ratio at its highest level in more than two decades.

Because it is difficult to know the precise motivations of the millions of persons who buy homes (or any other assets), it is impossible to know for sure whether any sharp increase in home prices is a bubble. Yet the high transactions costs involved in selling houses make a bubble in the housing market unlikely. Moreover, new sources of housing demand have emerged in the past two decades to support the fundamental value of owner-occupied houses. One is the growth in purchases of second homes by baby-boomers, many of whom are now in their prime earning years. Perhaps more important is the recent surge in immigration into the United States. In the 10 years preceding the 2000 Census, the number of foreign-born residents in the United States rose by 11.3 million, or 57 percent, compared with an increase of only 5.7 million in the previous 10-year period. As a result, the share of foreign-born individuals in the total U.S. resident population reached 11.1 percent in the 2000 Census. This is well above their 4.7 percent share in 1970 and comparable to the 13 to 15 percent shares recorded during the golden age of immigration from 1860 to 1920.

By itself, a surge in immigration would be expected to raise shelter costs in general, but not necessarily the price of homes relative to rents. Yet there is evidence that the timing of the immigration wave, along with recent developments in mortgage finance, has raised demand for owner-occupied homes separately from the demand for rental housing. Some recent research has pointed out that immigrants who arrived in the 1980s have only recently been able to make the transition to home ownership, because it takes time to save for a down payment. Also, developments in mortgage finance over the 1990s have made home purchases more affordable by narrowing the spread between mortgage interest rates and benchmark U.S. Treasury yields. The liberalization of mortgage finance would be expected to exert a strong, independent effect on home demand, by enlarging the pool of potential buyers of any nationality. This liberalization could well have combined with improvements in the financial positions of previous immigrants to result in a strong source of housing demand in the past several years. According to the 2001 American Housing Survey, sponsored by the Department of Housing and Urban Development, foreign-born residents have accounted for a sizable share of first-time home purchases since 1997, when the increase in house prices began in earnest. The survey shows that there were more than 5.7 million foreign-born homeowners in the United States in 2001, and more than 20 percent of them had purchased their first house since 1997. Although many of these new homeowners were members of minority groups, the rate of homeownership among minorities still lags behind that of whites. To redress this imbalance, in June 2002 the Administration announced an initiative to add 5.5 million minority homeowners by the end of the decade.

Net Exports

Although the output of the U.S. economy remained below potential in 2002, its growth rate still outpaced those of many other industrialized countries. Slow growth among many of the United States' major trading partners, in turn, contributed to slow growth in U.S. exports compared with that of imports. Exports rose at an annual rate of 7.4 percent during the first three quarters of the year, while imports grew 11.1 percent. This discrepancy between the rates of growth in exports and imports led to an increase in the U.S. trade deficit, so that net exports exerted a drag on GDP growth in the first half of the year. (Net exports were essentially unchanged in the third quarter.)

Because changes in the trade deficit are often quantitatively important for year-to-year changes in GDP growth, U.S. trade performance is an important concern. Imports and exports both provide benefits to consumers and firms. Imports provide U.S. firms with a wider variety of low-cost inputs, and consumers with wider variety and lower prices for goods. Moreover, competition from international producers induces domestic firms to raise their productivity, which raises incomes in the long run. Trade therefore boosts consumer satisfaction at home and ensures that American producers remain competitive, by increasing the size of the market in which they operate. In light of the benefits of trade to both Americans and foreigners, the Administration has made the expansion of trade a central policy objective. . . .

Government Purchases

The war on terrorism continued to exert upward pressure on Federal Government purchases in 2002. In late March the President requested that the Congress provide an additional appropriation of $27.1 billion, primarily to fund this effort. More than half of this amount was allocated to activities of the Department of Defense and various intelligence agencies. Most of the rest was needed for homeland security (mainly for the new Transportation Security Administration) and for the emergency response and recovery efforts in New York City. Although most of this spending was required for one-time outlays only, it nevertheless contributed to the 6.4 percent annual rate of increase in real Federal Government purchases in the first three quarters of 2002. State and local government purchases rose at a more moderate 1.7 percent annual rate during the same period.

The Labor Market, Productivity, and Real Wages

Although the labor market improved in 2002 after weakness in the wake of the September 2001 attacks, most major labor market indicators showed little progress over the course of the year. The unemployment rate hovered between 5.5 and 6.0 percent throughout the year, after rising 1.8 percentage points in 2001. Nonfarm payroll employment in 2002 was similarly weak, with 181,000 jobs lost during the year, compared with 1.4 million jobs lost the previous year. As in past business cycles, the decline in manufacturing employment has been especially pronounced. Factory employment fell by 592,000 in 2002, following a decline of 1.3 million in 2001 and about 100,000 in 2000. Another feature of previous business cycles that has recurred in the past 2 years is the increase in the number of workers who report a long unemployment spell. Like the overall unemployment rate, the number of workers unemployed for 26 weeks or more rose in 2001 and remained high in 2002. . . .

In other ways, however, the recent behavior of the labor market has been different from that in past business cycles. One difference is the high fraction of job losers who reported a permanent rather than temporary separation in 2001. In the government's monthly Current Population Survey, each respondent who reports a job loss is asked whether he or she expects to return to work with the same employer. (Those who expect to return are typically on an explicitly temporary layoff, although this need not be the case.) Research from the Bureau of Labor Statistics found that, in the initial quarters of the four recessions before 1990, slightly more than half of job losers were permanently separated from their previous employers, with the rest on temporary layoff. In the three quarters after the business cycle peak of 1990, however, the share of permanent job losers rose to almost three quarters, and the comparable proportion for the March 2001 peak is nearly 90 percent.

The rising proportion of job losers facing a permanent separation in recessions may reflect structural changes in the labor market during the past two decades, including the rise in temporary help employment. A firm facing a transitory increase in demand may use a temporary worker (formally employed by a temporary help firm) rather than add staff to its regular work force. When demand falls, the firm would then permanently sever the relationship with this worker; in the past the firm might have placed one of its own workers on temporary layoff. This explanation is consistent with the sharp rise in temporary help employment over the past 20 years as well as the sharp drop in 2001. Yet it is important to keep in mind that the fraction of workers losing their jobs in 2001 remained well below that in recent recessions, because of the mildness of the 2001 contraction. Although year-to-year fluctuations in the labor market are of immediate concern, sustained improvements in the living standards of American workers depend on more structural, long-term factors. . . . [T]hese factors include the flexibility and dynamism of the American labor market, which matches millions of workers with new jobs each month and provides incentives for investments that make workers more productive. Indeed, pro-growth labor market policies in the United States have helped the economy achieve a sizable increase in labor productivity growth since 1995. When this increase began, many economists were skeptical that it was permanent, because productivity growth in a given quarter or year can be strongly influenced by the business cycle.

Indeed, macroeconomic research has long established the procyclicality of productivity as a stylized fact, with output per worker rising faster in expansions than in recessions. This productivity pattern can be explained by the reluctance of firms to hire early in a recovery, before they are sure that a robust recovery has taken hold. This reluctance means that existing employees must work harder to fill the higher number of orders when demand first begins to rise. The resulting increase in worker effort causes output to rise faster than hours worked, so that the data indicate an increase in productivity even without any improvement in the underlying technology of production. Economists therefore prefer to observe improved productivity performance over an extended period before pronouncing that a change in productivity growth has taken place.

As productivity growth has stayed high since 1995, the productivity improvement has increasingly come to be seen as lasting. Data from 2001 and 2002 only strengthen this conclusion. During the seven quarters ending in the third quarter of 2002—a period that includes a recession and a recovery—labor productivity grew at an annual rate of 3.2 percent, somewhat higher than the annual rate of 2.5 percent from 1995 to 2000 and much higher than the 1.4 percent trend from 1973 to 1995. (A formal analysis of recent productivity data is presented later in the chapter.) An improvement of only about 2 percentage points in productivity growth may not sound impressive, but over time even a small increase in productivity growth brings about a large improvement in living standards. For example, growth in productivity of 1.4 percent a year implies that productivity doubles every 50 years, but growth of 2.5 percent implies a doubling every 28 years.

Strong productivity growth also helps to keep inflation down, by allowing real wages to grow without an increase in unit labor costs, which would drive up firms' costs of production and therefore push output prices upward. Indeed, another bright spot in 2002 was the behavior of inflation and real wages. The consumer price index (CPI) rose 2.4 percent in 2002 (December to December), close to its 1.6 percent rate of increase in 2001. The core CPI, which does not include the volatile food and energy components, rose 1.9 percent.

Inflation is difficult to measure, because of the dynamic nature of consumers' choices . . . and it is not directly linked to long-run living standards. Nonetheless, low inflation is fundamental to a healthy economy. High and variable inflation not only can cloud the relative price signals needed to allocate resources efficiently, but also can introduce other distortions through the income tax. Additionally, bringing inflation down from high levels typically requires sustained (and costly) increases in unemployment. The low inflation observed in 2002 gave policymakers the flexibility to support the fledgling recovery without being overly concerned that they would increase price pressures in doing so.

Taken together, rapid productivity growth and low inflation meant that real wages continued to grow in 2002. As measured by the employment cost index, real compensation for private industry workers grew 2.1 percent over the four quarters ending in the third quarter of 2002. This compares with real compensation growth of only 1.3 percent during the same period a year earlier. Although increases in benefits (such as employer payments for health insurance) accounted for much of the acceleration in total compensation growth, annualized real growth in wages and salaries also accelerated, from 0.9 percent to 1.7 percent across the same two periods.

In short, the sluggish performance of the labor market in 2002 was an unwelcome development for many workers and their families, as well as a matter of concern for policymakers. But rapid productivity growth, low inflation, and healthy real wage gains set the stage for future improvements in both unemployment and job growth in the years ahead.

Macroeconomic Policy and the Budget Outlook

The U.S. economy has suffered a number of serious setbacks in the past 3 years, including the terrorist attacks of September 2001, the significant loss of stock market wealth since 2000, and the recent corporate accounting scandals. Yet the contraction of 2001 was one of the mildest on record, with recovery proceeding steadily, if modestly, in 2002. One reason for the economy's stability in the face of these adverse developments was the stance of macroeconomic policy, both monetary (set by the Federal Reserve) and fiscal (set by the President and the Congress). . . .

Monetary Policy
In 2001, faced with signs of a slowing of economic activity, the Federal Reserve reduced its policy interest rate, the Federal funds rate, 11 times during the year, from 6.50 percent to 1.75 percent. The Federal Reserve then held the funds rate steady through most of 2002, until a further half-percentage-point cut on November 6 brought it down to 1.25 percent. Although the Federal funds rate thus remained constant for most of 2002, earlier rate reductions continued to stimulate the economy throughout the year. Understanding the reasons for this lag requires an understanding of the channels through which monetary policy affects the economy. A lowering of interest rates stimulates demand through four main channels: encouraging consumption (particularly of durables), stimulating business investment (by lowering the cost of capital), promoting residential investment (as seen from the booming housing sector), and lowering the foreign exchange value of the dollar (which tends to raise exports and lower imports). All of these effects take time to be felt.

Consumers must plan how best to take advantage of lower borrowing costs, firms must plan new investments, and importers and exporters must determine how any change in the dollar's exchange value will affect their prices and costs.

Measuring the size of these effects as well as the time needed for them to be fully expressed is an active area of macroeconomic research. . . .

Results from both model-based and data-based methods suggest that monetary policy changes take effect only after a lag of several months, but that these effects are long-lasting, so that the rate reductions in 2001 are likely to have stimulated the economy throughout 2002. To gain a sense of the magnitudes involved, one well-known model of the economy predicts that, holding other factors constant, a 1-percentage-point decrease in the Federal funds rate raises real GDP by 0.6 percent above its baseline level after 1 year. This effect of monetary stimulus on real GDP rises to 1.7 percent after 2 years. Data-based methods broadly concur with this assessment: one study shows that the typical decrease in the funds rate raises output steadily in subsequent quarters, reaching a maximum effect on output after about 18 months. Both methods therefore imply that interest rate cuts in 2001 continued to exert considerable economic stimulus in 2002.

Fiscal Policy

An important goal of fiscal policy is to promote growth by limiting the share of output commanded by the government. In 2001 the Congress and the Administration made major progress along these lines with passage of the Economic Growth and Tax Relief Reconciliation Act, which featured a broad-based cut in marginal tax rates. The long-term benefits of such a policy are clear, as high marginal tax rates discourage the entrepreneurship and risk taking on which the strength of the U.S. economic system depends. Yet although the goal of EGTRRA was to improve long-term living standards and limit the size of the government, the legislation conferred important short-term benefits as well, thanks to the way in which the tax rate reductions were set in place and the timing of the act's passage. A new lower tax rate of 10 percent was introduced at the bottom range of the previous 15 percent bracket, and taxpayers in 2001 were given an advance rebate on their likely savings due to this reduction.

Rebate checks ($300 for most single taxpayers, $600 for most married couples filing jointly) arrived in mailboxes in the summer of 2001. The timing of the resulting $36 billion infusion of spendable income into the economy could not have been more favorable. Although the depth of the 2001 recession would not be known until revised GDP figures were announced the next year, GDP had already declined by 0.6 percent at an annual rate in the first quarter of 2001 and by 1.6 percent in the second quarter. As estimated from the traditional relationship between overall GDP and current income, the tax plan added about 1.2 percentage points of growth at an annual rate in the third quarter. As a result, without the checks, third-quarter GDP would have declined at an annual rate of 1.5 percent rather than the 0.3 percent rate actually observed. In the fourth quarter, tax relief continued to add 1.2 percentage points to the annual rate of real GDP growth, so that instead of rising at an annual rate of 2.7 percent, GDP would have risen by only 1.5 percent in the absence of the rebates.

The rebate checks mailed in 2001 represented only a small fraction of the tax relief from the EGTRRA package. In addition to lowering marginal tax rates, EGTRRA increases the incentives for saving, for making bequests to heirs, and for investment. As a result, tax relief from EGTRRA probably helped the private sector create 800,000 jobs by the end of 2002 relative to the baseline level without tax relief, while raising GDP growth by about 0.5 percentage point over the course of that year.

In March 2002 the President signed the Job Creation and Worker Assistance Act, which implemented a tax policy especially appropriate for the fledgling recovery. The act promoted investment by allowing firms to immediately write off (that is, expense) 30 percent of the value of qualified investments in the year of purchase for investments made through September 11, 2004. . . . [G]overnment policies can significantly improve growth by removing tax distortions that penalize investment or other productive activities. For example, introducing expensing lowers the cost of capital, thereby making more investment opportunities profitable on an after-tax basis. The act stimulates investment by allowing partial expensing through most of 2004. In addition to reducing the tax-adjusted cost of investment, the act extended unemployment benefits to workers who have exhausted their regular benefits. This enhanced the role of unemployment insurance as one of the economy's most important automatic stabilizers.

The Federal Budget

After 4 years of surpluses, the unified Federal budget recorded a deficit of $158 billion in fiscal 2002, or about 1.5 percent of GDP. The return of the deficit was primarily due to four factors: the lingering effects of the recession of 2001, the stock market plunge, increased Federal expenditure necessitated by the war on terrorism, and the costs of homeland security. Recessions tend to increase budget deficits because they lead to higher outlays (for unemployment insurance, for example) at the same time that they reduce tax receipts (because taxable income falls). The decline in receipts during the most recent downturn in the business cycle has been especially pronounced. Total receipts in fiscal 2002 were $1,853 billion, having fallen $138 billion, or about 7 percent, from their level in fiscal 2001. This represented a much larger percentage decrease in receipts than in previous, far more severe recessions. One of the most important reasons for the dramatic decline in receipts given the mildness of the 2001 contraction was the coincident decline in the stock market. The stock market's decline reduced capital gains receipts in addition to reducing taxes on wage and salary income for workers whose jobs are closely tied to equity markets. More detailed information on the precise sources of the decline in receipts will not be available until the Treasury completes its regular annual examination of individual tax returns. Even with the decline in receipts, however, the budget deficit was relatively small as a fraction of GDP compared with those seen in previous periods of war and recession.

The President's Jobs and Growth Initiative

On January 7, 2003, the President proposed a plan to enhance the long-term growth of the economy while supporting the emerging recovery. At the start of 2003 the consensus of private forecasters predicted accelerating growth in real GDP over the course of the year, which would raise investment, reduce unemployment, and increase job growth. This consensus view is reflected in the Administration's outlook, discussed below. Yet the recovery in investment could be delayed by weaker-than-expected profit growth, higher required rates of return arising from geopolitical and other risks, or a prolonged period during which companies focus on repairing their balance sheets. More general risks to recovery in 2003 include an increased sense of caution, which could lead households to pull back on their spending plans, and the potential for further terrorist attacks. To insure against these near-term risks while boosting long-term growth, the President has proposed a focused set of initiatives. Specifically, the President's plan would:

- Accelerate to January 1, 2003, many features of the 2001 tax cut that are currently scheduled to be phased in over several years. These include the reductions in marginal income tax rates, additional marriage penalty relief, a larger child credit, and a wider 10 percent income tax bracket
- Eliminate the double taxation of corporate income by excluding dividends from individual taxable income
- Increase expensing limits for small business investment, raising to $75,000 the amount that small businesses may deduct from their taxable income in the year the investment takes place
- Provide $3.6 billion to the States to fund Personal Reemployment Accounts for unemployed workers. These accounts would allow eligible workers to spend up to $3,000 to defray the costs of finding or training for a new job. Workers could keep any unspent balance in their account if they find work within 13 weeks of going on unemployment.

Accelerating the marginal tax rate reductions would insure against a softening of consumption by putting more money in consumers' pockets through long-term tax cuts, which have been shown to be more effective than temporary cuts in boosting near-term spending. Ending the double tax on corporate income would increase the ability of corporations to raise equity capital, providing near-term support to investment while improving the long-term efficiency of capital markets. . . . The provisions also support investment by small firms. Higher expensing limits would make it easier for small firms to expand by reducing the tax-adjusted cost of capital; lower marginal tax rates would increase growth incentives for small business owners whose business income is taxed at individual rates. Finally, Personal Reemployment Accounts . . . would provide unemployed workers with a new set of incentives as they look for work. Accounts of this type, which reward unemployed workers for finding jobs quickly, have been shown in experiments in several States to increase the speed with which unemployed workers find new jobs. Moreover, by allowing workers a choice between using the funds to support their job search and using them for job training expenses, the accounts are well suited for the dynamic U.S. labor market.

The Effect of Tax Relief on Interest Rates

One of the most widely discussed issues in fiscal policy concerns the effect of tax relief on interest rates. It is widely agreed that, in the immediate aftermath of a permanent tax cut, consumption increases because consumers have more disposable income. This increase in consumption raises GDP in the near term, especially if the economy is operating below its potential, with large amounts of unused labor and capital. In the long run, lower tax rates have somewhat complicated, offsetting effects on GDP. On the negative side, if the reduction in tax rates is not accompanied by spending reductions, it will increase the budget deficit and may reduce national saving. Lower national saving, in turn, will shrink the pool of loanable funds available in capital markets, which increases interest rates and reduces investment. Ultimately, lower investment leads to a smaller stock of productive capital, resulting in lower wages, lower productivity, and lower output. Offsetting this, however, is the positive effect of tax relief that operates through improved incentives to work and take risks, for example by creating a new firm or by making a new investment. Incentives to undertake these activities improve after a cut in marginal tax rates, because the tax reduction allows more of the rewards to be captured by workers, entrepreneurs, and investors and not by the government. When tax relief extends to capital income (such as dividends), as proposed in the President's most recent jobs and growth initiative, an additional positive effect arises through stronger incentives to save. These positive effects on GDP operating through improved incentives also have an impact on future budget deficits and investment, because deficits will be less onerous if the economy grows in response to the improved investment climate.

Assessing the ultimate effect of tax relief on GDP and future government debt thus requires gauging both the negative effects that arise through higher interest rates and the positive effects that come from improved incentives. Unfortunately, measuring the effect through incentive channels is difficult, because there have been few episodes of large, broad-based tax relief during the last several decades. Moreover, even these historical episodes occurred amid a host of other economic developments, making it difficult to isolate the direct effect of lower taxes on working and saving.

Obtaining a rough estimate of the interest rate effect is less difficult, because widely accepted economic theory allows precise predictions of how much an increase in the stock of debt should affect interest rates. The first step in making this calculation is to note that an additional dollar of government debt does not reduce the capital stock by a full dollar. About 40 cents of the additional debt will be offset by larger capital inflows from abroad, so that the U.S. capital stock would fall by only about 60 cents. The next step is to translate this 60-cent-per-dollar decrease in the capital stock into an ultimate change in long-term interest rates. This is done by noting that the interest rate on a bond should be closely related to the marginal product that physical capital earns in the marketplace. This is so because the two should converge to the point where investors are indifferent between holding financial securities or holding physical capital in their portfolios. Reducing the physical capital stock will increase the marginal return to capital in the marketplace by making capital scarce relative to other factors of production; the key question is by how much this marginal return rises. Some calculations . . . imply that interest rates rise by about 3 basis points for every $200 billion in additional government debt.

Given this relationship between government debt and interest rates, concerns that higher interest rates would choke off the stimulative effects of recent tax reductions seem unwarranted. For example, this relationship implies that the $1.3 trillion in tax relief included in EGTRRA would raise interest rates by only about 19 basis points—a modest cost to be set against the long-term incentive-based benefits expected from lower marginal tax rates.

The modest effect of government debt on interest rates does not mean that tax cuts pay for themselves with higher output. Although the economy grows in response to tax reductions (because of higher consumption in the short run and improved incentives in the long run), it is unlikely to grow so much that lost tax revenue is completely recovered by the higher level of economic activity. The small effect of debt on interest rates does show, however, that attempts to stimulate the economy by raising taxes in order to lower interest rates are likely to be unsuccessful, especially if the taxes raised are those that discourage private saving and investment. The resulting reduction in interest rates will probably be too small to outweigh the negative effects of tax increases that work through distorted incentives. Further, the modest effect of increased debt on interest rates suggests that policymakers should not be afraid to use fiscal policy when doing so improves the long-run health of the economy. As long as the change in fiscal policy does not bring about large, systemic imbalances in the economy—such as a high debt-to-GDP ratio, or rapidly rising interest costs as a share of Federal outlays—policymakers should not be paralyzed by the fear that any benefits from tax reductions are likely to be undone by the increase in interest rates they bring about.

Developments in the Rest of the World

Growth in many of the United States' major trading partners was even more disappointing in 2002 than was growth at home. Although growth in Canada, America's largest trading partner, was a surprisingly robust 4.0 percent during the four quarters ending in the third quarter of 2002, growth elsewhere lagged far behind. The economy of the United Kingdom grew only 2.1 percent over the same period; growth rates in Germany (0.4 percent), Italy (0.5 percent), France (1.0 percent), Japan (1.3 percent), and Mexico (1.8 percent) were even lower. Low demand for U.S. exports combined with the emerging recovery in the United States (which increased U.S. demand for imports) sent the U.S. trade deficit to a record high in 2002.

Discussion of the U.S. position in international markets is often framed in terms of the current account, a broader measure of international transactions. In addition to the trade balance in goods and services, the current account includes net investment income, net compensation of resident alien workers, and net unilateral transfers. Because the trade component is by far the largest in the current account balance, the widening in the trade deficit in 2002 contributed strongly to the widening in the current account deficit. The latter reached a record 4.9 percent of GDP in the second quarter of 2002 before falling slightly, to 4.8 percent, in the third quarter.

One advantage of framing international finance discussions in terms of the current account is that, as a matter of national accounting, the current account balance equals the difference between net national saving and net national investment. For example, if U.S. saving were smaller than U.S. investment in a given period, the difference—the excess of investment over saving—must have been financed by foreigners. In the process of financing U.S. investment, foreign investors obtain U.S. assets, either in portfolio form (that is, as stocks, bonds, or other financial securities) or though direct controlling ownership of physical capital. These assets then generate investment income in the form of dividends, interest payments, and profits that can be repatriated to the investors abroad. Balance of payments data therefore resemble a "sources and uses of funds" statement for the Nation as a whole, providing useful information on the amounts of internal and external investment financing. High levels of investment in the late 1990s meant that the U.S. capital stock grew quickly in the late 1990s, but the accumulation of past current account deficits requires an increasing portion of the income earned by this capital to flow abroad. Over the past year, the U.S. current account deficit has widened because net investment has been essentially flat while net saving has fallen. . . .

The relationship between the current account deficit and net investment by foreigners in U.S. assets also makes clear how changes in international demand for U.S. assets can affect the trade balance, and vice versa. Consider an increase in foreigners' demand for U.S. assets. Their resulting accumulation of U.S. assets can affect international trade flows through an appreciation of the dollar, because foreigners must obtain dollars in order to purchase U.S. assets. Appreciation of the dollar tends to make imports cheaper for U.S. residents, and U.S. exports more expensive to consumers abroad; both these effects move the trade balance (and the current account) toward deficit. . . .

. . . Recent increases in the current account deficit have led to some concerns that continued current account deficits (and the increase in the United States' international debt that would result) might not be sustainable. Clearly, debt cannot increase without limit. Because debt has to be serviced by the repatriation of capital income abroad, the ratio of a country's debt to its income has to stabilize at some point.

Yet the United States today is far from the point at which servicing its international debt becomes an onerous burden. In fact, until last year, more investment income was generated by U.S. investment in foreign countries than by foreign investments inside the United States, even though the net international investment position of the United States moved into deficit almost two decades ago. . . . Given the United States' negative international investment position, the fact that, until 2002, more investment income flowed into the United States than flowed out of it implies that the rates of return on U.S. investment abroad were higher than the returns enjoyed by foreign investors in the United States. (Further analysis of international investment data indicates that these differences in rates of return are especially pronounced for direct investment, and less so for portfolio investment.) Although debt service became a net transfer from the United States to the rest of the world in

2002, this debt service is unlikely to amount to a significant portion of U.S. output in the foreseeable future.

Near-term developments in the U.S. current account depend on a number of factors. One of the most important is the rate of economic growth in the rest of the world. Faster growth abroad raises the demand for U.S. exports, which reduces the trade and current account deficits. A second factor affecting the U.S. current account is the propensity of U.S. residents to save. [S]aving rates fell sharply in the 1990s, as noted . . . this may have stemmed from the strong appreciation in the stock market, which allowed wealth to grow quickly without any increase in active saving out of disposable income. The retrenchment in asset prices that began in early 2000 may encourage some consumers to increase their active saving to pre-1995 levels. For any given level of domestic investment, an increase in the saving rate lessens the need to borrow from abroad and thereby reduces the current account deficit. In any event, it is far preferable to reduce the current account deficit by saving more than by reducing investment, because lower investment results in slower growth in the capital stock, a lower growth rate of labor productivity, and slower growth in living standards.

A third factor affecting the evolution of the current account is the future demand by foreign investors for U.S. assets. To the extent that foreign investors reduce their demand for U.S. assets and substitute holdings in other countries for those assets, the real exchange value of the dollar will fall, holding other factors constant. Conversely, the real value of the dollar will rise with an increase in the demand for U.S. assets. Such an increase in demand might result from continued productivity growth in the United States or from an increase in the perceived safety of U.S. assets relative to the rest of the world.

Moderate changes in foreign demand for dollar-denominated assets need not have large disruptive effects on the U.S. economy. Gradual shifts in the terms of trade would engender offsetting increases or decreases in the growth of consumption and imports, leaving real GDP little affected. In fact, if productivity growth remains relatively high in the United States while inflation remains low, a moderate shift in global demand away from U.S. assets and the subsequent decline in the real value of the dollar may not even require a change in the nominal exchange rate, because the real value of the dollar falls with a constant nominal exchange rate when inflation at home is lower than inflation abroad.

Moreover, history has shown that even a substantial decline in the value of the dollar need not result in sharply lower prices for U.S. stocks, bonds, or other assets. From the fourth quarter of 1985 to the fourth quarter of 1990, the real, trade-weighted exchange value of the dollar fell by nearly 24 percent while the current account deficit shrank from more than 3 percent of GDP to less than 1 percent. At the same time, however, stock prices rose by about 47 percent while long-term interest rates (which move inversely to bond prices) fell by more than 1 percentage point.

In the end, the key determinant of the sustainability of the U.S. international debt position is continued confidence in the economic policies of the United States. As long as the United States pursues its current market-oriented, pro-growth policies, there is no reason to believe that the current account deficit represents a problem for continued economic growth.

The Economic Outlook

The economy continues to display supply-side characteristics favorable to long-term growth. Productivity growth remains strong, and inflation remains low and stable. Real GDP is expected to grow faster than its 3.1 percent potential rate during the next 4 years, and then to grow at a 3.1 percent annual rate during the balance of the budget window. . . .

Near-Term Outlook

The Administration expects that aggregate economic activity will have weathered a quarter of weakness at the end of 2002, following which it will gather strength during 2003, with real GDP growing 3.4 percent during the four quarters of the year. The unemployment rate, which was 5.9 percent in the fourth quarter of 2002, is projected to edge down about 0.3 percentage point by the fourth quarter of 2003.

As discussed earlier, real GDP growth in 2002 was accounted for by solid growth in consumption, a modest pickup in exports, and an increase in inventory investment. Although investment in equipment and software was slow, it stabilized during the first quarter of 2002 and began to grow in the second and third quarters, foreshadowing one way in which the composition of growth is projected to differ next year: the growth rate of equipment and software investment is projected to pick up in 2003. (Another difference is that the contribution of inventory investment is projected to wane.) Several factors are expected to lead to a rebound in equipment and software investment. Any capital overhang that might have arisen during the late-1990s investment boom has been reduced, because the level of investment fell in 2001; expectations of future GDP growth have stabilized after falling during 2001; and the replacement cycle is approaching for the short-lived capital goods put in place during the investment boom of 1999 and 2000. At the same time, the financial foundations for investment remain positive: real short-term interest rates are low, and prices of computers are falling more rapidly than they did in 2000. (Computer investment accounted for a third of all nonresidential investment growth from 1995 to 2000.) Less bright is the outlook for nonresidential structures, which still appears weak even after 2 years of decline. Even so, structures investment is projected to stabilize around the second half of 2003, as the maturing recovery generates higher occupancy rates for office buildings and greater demand for commercial properties. The recent passage of legislation for terrorism risk insurance may unblock some planned investments in structures that were held up because of lack of insurance.

Real exports, which turned up in 2002, are projected to improve further during 2003, reflecting the widely held expectation of stronger growth among the United States' trading partners and the lagged effects of the past year's decline in the dollar. Although real imports and exports are expected to grow at similar rates during the four quarters of 2003, the United States imports more than it exports, and therefore the dollar value of imports is expected to increase more than the dollar value of exports. As a result, net exports are likely to become more negative during the course of 2003.

Less change is expected for the largest component of aggregate demand, consumption, which is expected to remain robust in 2003. The negative influence of the stock market decline on household wealth, and thus on consumption, is expected to wane as this decline recedes into history. Consumption growth will also be supported by fiscal stimulus and the lagged effects of recent interest rate cuts. Finally, low interest rates will continue to support the purchase of consumer durables, just as they did for much of 2002. . . .

Long-Term Outlook

The Administration forecasts real annual GDP growth to average 3.4 percent during the first 4 years of the projection. As this is somewhat above the expected rate of increase in productive capacity, the unemployment rate is projected to decline as a consequence. In 2007 and 2008, real GDP growth is projected to continue at its long-run potential rate of 3.1 percent. The growth rate of the economy over the long run is determined by the growth rates of its supply-side components, which include population, labor force participation, productivity, and the workweek. . . .

The Administration expects nonfarm labor productivity to grow at a 2.1 percent annual average pace over the forecast period, virtually the same as that recorded from the business cycle peak in 1990 through the third quarter of 2002. This projection is notably more conservative than the nearly 2I percent average rate actually recorded since 1995. The cautious projection of productivity growth guards against several downside risks:

- Nonresidential fixed investment has fallen about 12 percent since its peak in mid-2000. The slower pace of investment means that the near-term growth of capital services is likely to be reduced from its average pace from 1995 to 2002, leading to a lesser contribution to productivity growth from the use of these capital services.

- [A]bout half of the post-1995 structural productivity acceleration is attributable to growth in total factor productivity (TFP) outside of the computer sector. This growth is due to technological progress, better business organization, and other factors that are hard to identify. Although there is no reason to expect this process to slow, the Administration forecast adopts a cautious view of the pace of TFP growth, setting it near its longer term average rather than at the higher post-1995 pace.

In addition to productivity, growth of the labor force . . . is projected to contribute 1.0 percentage point a year to growth of potential output on average through 2008. Labor force growth results from growth in the working-age population and changes in the labor force participation rate. The Bureau of the Census projects that the working-age population will grow at an average annual rate of 1.1 percent through 2008.

The labor force participation rate is expected to be roughly flat through 2008, although it may begin to decline around that year, which is the year that the oldest baby-boomers (those born in 1946) reach the early-retirement age of 62.

In sum, potential real GDP is projected to grow at about a 3.1 percent annual pace, slightly above the average pace since 1973. Actual real GDP growth during the 6-year forecast period is projected to be slightly higher, at 3.2 percent, because the civilian employment rate . . . makes a small (0.1 percentage point) and transitory contribution to growth through 2006. This contribution then ends as the unemployment rate stabilizes at 5.1 percent. . . .

Conclusion

The Administration believes that the economy is likely to grow somewhat faster than in the projection presented here, as the long-run benefits from the full reductions in marginal tax rates and the dividend exclusion are felt. These should lead to increases in labor force participation and increased entrepreneurial activity. The Administration, however, chooses to adopt conservative economic assumptions that are close to the consensus of professional forecasters. As such, the assumptions provide a prudent, cautious basis for the budget projections. Yet the Administration's policies are designed to enhance U.S. economic growth, not just maintain it. . . .

Source: Council of Economic Advisers. The Annual Report of the Council of Economic Advisers. February 7, 2003. http://purl.access.gpo.gov/GPO/LPS5348 (accessed September 27, 2003).

March

UN Secretary General on the First Session of the International Criminal Court

March 11, 2003

INTRODUCTION

An international court to try cases of genocide and war crimes began work in 2003, more than fifty years after such a court was first proposed. Eighteen judges from around the world held their first meeting at The Hague, the Netherlands, on March 11 and heard United Nations Secretary General Kofi Annan declare them to be "the embodiment of our collective conscience." The judges set about writing regulations and getting their procedures in order and were expected to hear their first case, dealing with the war in the Democratic Republic of Congo, in 2004. *(Congo war, p. 288)*

One country—the United States—dissented vocally and vigorously from the general world view that the International Criminal Court would be a good thing. The administration of President George W. Bush heatedly objected to the court and put enormous pressure on other countries to exempt U.S. citizens from its jurisdiction. By the end of 2003 more than seventy countries had signed agreements promising not to surrender U.S. citizens to the court's jurisdiction. *(Background, Historic Documents of 2002, p. 605)*

Even as the new court was getting under way, two other UN-established courts continued to work their way through dozens of cases stemming from murderous conflicts in the 1990s. The International Criminal Tribunal for the Former Yugoslavia, also based at The Hague, heard genocide and war crimes cases involving wars in Bosnia, Croatia, and Kosovo. Its most notable case dealt with former Yugoslav president Slobodan Milosevic, whose trial began in 2001 and was expected to drag on well into 2004. The International Criminal Tribunal for Rwanda, based at Arusha, Tanzania, continued hearing dozens of cases from the massive 1994 genocide in Rwanda. That tribunal had been heavily criticized internationally for its slow pace of work, and in late July Annan took the Rwandan cases away from Carla Del Ponte, who had been in charge of prosecutions for both the

Yugoslavia and Rwanda tribunals. *(Rwanda prosecutions, Historic Documents of 1999, p. 860; Yugoslavia prosecutions, Historic Documents of 2001, p. 826)*

The new International Criminal Court had no direct relationship to the long-established International Court of Justice, which also operated at The Hague. The latter court dealt with civil disputes involving international law, such as boundary disagreements and violations of treaties.

Establishing the Court

First proposed following World War II, the International Criminal Court was established under a treaty that was debated for decades and finally negotiated during a UN-sponsored conference in Rome in mid-1998. The minimum number of sixty countries ratified the treaty early in 2002, putting the document into legal effect on July 1, 2002. By February 2003 a total of eighty-five nations had ratified the treaty. Meeting at UN headquarters in New York, representatives of those nations elected eighteen judges, including seven women, from nations as diverse as Costa Rica, Ghana, Latvia, and Samoa. Irish jurist Maureen Harding Clark, who served as a part-time judge on the Yugoslavia war crimes tribunal, was the top vote-getter among the judges.

The eighteen judges were sworn in during March 11 ceremonies at The Hague, witnessed by Annan and Queen Beatrix of the Netherlands. Conspicuous by its absence was the U.S. government, which refused to send a representative. China, India, Israel, Russia, and Turkey were among the other prominent countries that had refused either to sign or ratify the Rome treaty and accept the court's jurisdiction. The judges elected Philippe Kirsch, a Canadian specialist in international law, as their first presiding judge.

Annan, who had campaigned tirelessly for the court after watching the United Nations fail to deal adequately with the wars in Rwanda and the former Yugoslavia, told the new judges of two reasons why their court was needed to establish "personal responsibility" for crimes against humanity. "First, persons who are tempted or pressured to commit unspeakable crimes must be deterred, by the knowledge that one day they will be individually called to account. That deterrence was missing in the past. It is needed today as much as ever, and it will be needed in the future," Annan said. "And second, only by clearly identifying the individuals responsible for these crimes can we save whole communities from being held collectively guilty. It is that notion of collective guilt which is the true enemy of peace, since it encourages communities to nurture hatred against each other from one generation to the next."

In April the ninety nations that by that time had ratified the Rome Treaty nominated Luis Moreno Ocampo as the court's first prosecutor. An Argentine human rights lawyer, Ocampo had gained international fame in the

1980s for prosecuting military officials responsible for his country's "dirty war," in which thousands of people died or disappeared. Ocampo took the oath of office as the court's prosecutor on June 16. He said a month later that the first case brought before the court probably would involve the giant war in the Democratic Republic of the Congo. Ocampo noted that he could present cases only for war crimes violations committed after July 1, 2002, when the court legally came into being.

U.S. Objections

The administration of President Bill Clinton signed the Rome Treaty at the end of 2000, just before he left office, but the Senate never took action to ratify it. Demonstrating its displeasure with the accord, the Bush administration in May 2002 took the unusual step of informing the United Nations that the United States would not honor the Clinton administration's signature, a step that effectively withdrew the prior endorsement. Bush's aides argued that U.S. soldiers serving with international peacekeeping operations, American businessmen, or even journalists or religious figures traveling overseas might be singled out for politically motivated prosecution by a court displeased with U.S. policies. The Bush administration dismissed several compromises that Rome treaty negotiators had made in hopes of swaying the United States to support the court. Among other things, the court's prosecutor could issue indictments only in cases where national courts were unable or unwilling to handle genocide or war crimes cases. To be prosecuted, an individual had to be considered responsible for "systematic or widespread" war crimes, not a single abuse such as the killing of one person. Moreover, indictments had to be approved by a panel of judges, not simply issued by the prosecutor.

Under intense pressure from the Bush administration, the UN Security Council in July 2002 agreed to exempt U.S. members of international peacekeeping forces from potential prosecution by the court for one year. That exemption was extended for another year in July 2003.

The Bush administration took a further step, demanding that other countries sign agreements promising never to extradite U.S. citizens or officials to the International Criminal Court. As a stick, Congress in 2002 passed and Bush signed the American Servicemembers Protection Act explicitly threatening to withhold U.S. aid to those countries that did not sign such agreements. By early 2003 some three dozen countries, most of them poor nations in Africa, Asia, and Latin America, had signed nonextradition agreements.

The Bush administration's position came into direct conflict with the European Union (EU) in June. The EU, some of whose members had opposed Washington's war in Iraq, urged its fifteen members, and ten nations up for membership, not to sign the agreements exempting U.S. citizens from juris-diction of the international court. That brought a formal complaint from the State Department, which warned that the EU's opposition to U.S. policy on the matter could be "very damaging." The dispute continued through the rest of the year, with a senior U.S. official—Undersecretary of State John R. Bolton—arguing on November 2 that it was the EU that was forcing an "unfair choice upon our friends and allies." Bolton made no reference to the fact that the United States was itself pressuring countries to sign exemp-tion agreements by threatening to withhold foreign aid.

Following through on its threat, the Bush administration announced on July 1 that it was withholding more than $48 million in military aid to thirty-five countries that had refused to sign the agreements. None of the affected aid programs were sizable in scope; the biggest single program jeopard-ized was $5 million for Colombia, which already had received more than $100 million during the 2003 fiscal year for antidrug programs. Facing the threatened aid cutoff, Colombia on September 18 signed the agreement demanded by Washington.

With the start of the 2004 fiscal year on October 1, the administration announced it was withholding another $89 million in aid to thirty-two coun-tries that still had not signed nonextradition agreements.

Following is the text of "International Criminal Court Judges Embody 'Our Collective Conscience,'" an address by United Nations Secretary General Kofi Annan, delivered March 11, 2003, at a ceremony at The Hague, the Netherlands, marking the swearing-in of the eighteen judges of the new International Criminal Court.

"International Criminal Court Judges Embody 'Our Collective Conscience' "

It has taken mankind many years to reach this moment.

By the solemn undertaking they have given here in open court, these 11 men and seven women, representing all regions of the world and many different cultures and legal traditions, have made themselves the embodiment of our collective conscience.

For centuries, and especially in the last century, that conscience has been shocked by unspeakable crimes: crimes whose victims were counted not in tens, but in tens of thousands—even in millions.

By 1945, those crimes had cost humanity so dear that it was deemed necessary to set up special tribunals, in Nuremberg and Tokyo, to judge the main perpetrators. Those tribunals established a principle of vital importance: that those who take part in gross violations of international humanitarian law cannot shelter behind the authority of the State in whose name they did so. They must take personal responsibility for their acts, and face the consequences.

Ever since then, the international community has sought to establish a permanent international criminal court to try and punish those who commit genocide, war crimes and crimes against humanity. These include mass murder, enslavement, rape, torture, and other abhorrent crimes—not only against people of other nations, but also against their own.

A big step forward was taken in the past decade, with the establishment of the International Criminal Tribunals for the Former Yugoslavia and for Rwanda. These have already shown that it is feasible to bring to impartial justice, before a judiciary representing the world's great legal systems, persons both high and low who are accused of crimes against humanity.

Yet it has taken fifty years to agree on the form this court should take, and the extent of its powers. There were many considerations that had to be carefully evaluated—in particular, the implications such a court might have for the delicate process of dismantling tyrannies and replacing them with more democratic regimes, committed to uphold human rights.

There are times when we are told that justice must be set aside in the interests of peace. It is true that justice can only be dispensed when the peaceful order of society is secure. But we have come to understand that the reverse is also true: without justice, there can be no lasting peace.

Certainly there is a place in every court for mercy and compassion. But mercy can be shown only when guilt and responsibility have been clearly established and acknowledged.

And individual responsibility is of crucial importance, for two reasons.

First, persons who are tempted or pressured to commit unspeakable crimes must be deterred, by the knowledge that one day they will be individually called to account. That deterrence was missing in the past. It is needed today as much as ever, and it will be needed in the future.

And second, only by clearly identifying the individuals responsible for these crimes can we save whole communities from being held collectively guilty. It is that notion of collective guilt which is the true enemy of peace, since it encourages communities to nurture hatred against each other from one generation to the next.

As for compassion, those most entitled to it are, of course, the victims of crime.

For those who have been slaughtered, all we can do is seek to accord them in death the dignity and respect they were so cruelly denied in life.

To the survivors, who are also the witnesses, and to the bereaved, we owe a justice that also brings healing. And that means that you, the judges, will have to show great patience and compassion, as well as an unfailing resolve to arrive at the truth. There must be justice, not only in the end result, but also in the process.

Above all, however, this court is for those who might be victims in the future. If the court lives up to our expectations, they will not be victims, because would-be violators will be deterred.

That is why it is so important that you, the judges, and all the officials of the Court, demonstrate in all your actions and decisions an unimpeachable integrity and impartiality.

In all your functions—judicial, administrative and representational—you must act without fear or favour, guided and inspired by the provisions of the Rome Statute. The wisdom of your judgements must be such as to command universal respect for international justice and the force of law. The honesty and efficiency of the Court's administration must be beyond reproach.

All your work must shine with moral and legal clarity, bringing life to the provisions of the Rome Statute and helping the States parties to discharge their share of responsibility. That assistance will be an important part of your task.

Of crucial importance is one responsibility that States parties must discharge in the very near future: the choice of a prosecutor. The importance of that function can hardly be exaggerated. As we know from the experience of the International Tribunals for the Former Yugoslavia and Rwanda, the decisions and public statements of the prosecutor will do more than anything else to establish the reputation of the Court, especially in the first phases of its work.

It is, therefore, vital that a person of the highest calibre be found to undertake that grave responsibility. This surely is a time to set aside national interests, and focus exclusively on the qualifications of the individual candidates. Once that choice is made, States will also have a responsibility to cooperate with the Court—in effecting arrests of those indicted, in providing evidence, and in enforcing sentences once imposed. That cooperation is essential, if the Court is to succeed.

The commitment shown thus far augurs well for the future. The United Nations looks forward to working with the International Criminal Court in this cause, which is the cause of all humanity.

Source: United Nations. *International Criminal Court Judges Embody 'Our Collective Conscience' Says Secretary-General to Inaugural Meeting in The Hague.* Press release SG/SM/8628, L/3027. March 11, 2003. www.un.org/ News/Press/docs/2003/sgsm8628.doc.htm (accessed July 13, 2003).

U.S. Court of Appeals Rulings on Detentions of Terrorism Suspects

March 11 and December 18, 2003

INTRODUCTION

The Bush administration faced increasing scrutiny of its blanket policy of secret, indefinite imprisonment of foreigners—and even some U.S. citizens—in connection with its declared war against terrorism. U.S. courts, which had given the administration broad leeway during the first year or so following the September 11, 2001, terrorist attacks against the United States, began taking a closer look during 2003 at various legal issues surrounding the long-running detentions of suspects. In particular, judges started questioning the administration's contention that the court system had no business involving itself in those issues.

After the September 11 attacks, and then the U.S.-led war to oust the Islamist government of Afghanistan later in 2001, the United States military and law enforcement agencies detained at least 2,000 people who were suspected of having some connection with international terrorist groups. *(Background, Historic Documents of 2001, p. 642; Historic Documents of 2002, p. 830)*

The detentions fell into several categories:

- In the United States, more than 700 foreigners were arrested and detained on immigration charges and then questioned about their possible connections to terrorists, notably the al Qaeda network said to be responsible for the September 11 attacks. The government detained another 400 or so people in the United States as part of its post-September 11 roundup; most were held on various criminal charges, and some were held as "material witnesses" because the government suspected they might have information about terrorists. *(Foreign detainees in the United States, p. 310)*

- Three U.S. citizens were detained and held as "enemy combatants"—people who allegedly had supported the al Qaeda network or the extremist Taliban regime in Afghanistan, which had opened its territory to al Qaeda in the 1990s. One of these citizens, John Walker Lindh, allegedly had fought for the Taliban in Afghanistan, where he was captured in late 2001. In July 2002 he pleaded guilty to three charges of aiding the Taliban and was sentenced to twenty years in prison. The cases of two others were more complex and were still pending as of the end of 2003: Yaser Esam Hamdi, who also was captured in Afghanistan in 2001 and had been held incommunicado by the U.S. Navy ever since; and Jose Padilla, who was arrested in Chicago in May 2002 on suspicion that he had plotted with al Qaeda to build a "dirty bomb" mixing radioactive material and conventional explosives. Padilla also was held incommunicado by the U.S. Navy. It was not known whether any charges had been filed against either Hamdi or Padilla as of the end of 2003.
- More than 600 people were captured in Afghanistan, during and after the war there, and then transferred to a new U.S. military prison at Guantanamo Naval Base on the southeastern tip of Cuba. By 2003 that prison reportedly had a capacity of about 660 people. Nearly 100 people who had been held there eventually were sent back to Afghanistan or other countries and released, but several hundred remained in detention all through 2002 and 2003. As of the end of 2003 none of the detainees at Guantanamo had been charged with a crime. Several of the detainees, however, were expected to be among the first people tried by new military tribunals the Bush administration established to deal with terrorism-related cases outside the jurisdiction of the U.S. court system.
- The U.S. military held several hundred suspected terrorists at new prisons it had built at the Bagram air base just north of Kabul, Afghanistan, and at a U.S. naval base on the British-owned island of Diego Garcia, in the Indian Ocean. The exact number of people held at these prisons was not made public, although news reports said the Bagram prison had a capacity of at least 100 prisoners. These detainees reportedly included the two most senior al Qaeda officials who had been captured by the United States: Khalid Shaikh Mohammed, alleged by the United States to have been the al Qaeda operations chief who planned the September 11 attacks; and Abu Zubaydah, allegedly another top al Qaeda commander. These two men, plus other detainees at those facilities, reportedly were subjected to intense interrogations that stopped just short of torture, which the U.S. military said it did not use. The *New York Times* reported on March 9 that Mohammed and other detainees at Bagram and Diego Garcia occasionally were deprived of sleep, food, and medicine and

were subjected to psychological stresses, such as being forced to stand or kneel in uncomfortable positions for long periods. *(Al Qaeda, p. 1050)*

- According to news reports, an unknown number of terrorism suspects were held at other secret locations controlled by the United States military and intelligence services, including a Central Intelligence Agency facility in Thailand. Others were turned over to the security services of "friendly" Arab countries—including Egypt, Jordan, and Saudi Arabia—that often were accused by human rights organizations of using torture in their investigations.

Guantanamo Bay Detainees

Internationally, by far the best-known U.S. detainees were the 600 or so people held at the military prison in Guantanamo. These were the only U.S. detainees whose status was monitored by any outsiders; the International Committee of the Red Cross made regular visits to the prison but provided few public statements about what it had found. The Pentagon also allowed groups of journalists to visit the prison periodically, but the reporters were not allowed to interview any of the prisoners. In early 2002 television footage of hooded and handcuffed detainees living in open-air, chain-link fence cells caused an international outcry. The Pentagon later built a more permanent facility and prohibited the filming of living conditions there. The Bush administration insisted that the detainees were given proper food and medical care, were allowed to observe religious rituals (nearly all the detainees were Muslim), and were generally given the same treatment accorded prisoners of war under the Geneva Convention. The administration said it did not consider the detainees to be formal prisoners of war, however.

The U.S. government made public no specific information about the individuals being held at Guantanamo, such as their names, nationalities, or reasons for being held. The names of some of the detainees became known when they were flown back to Afghanistan or Pakistan and released. Defense Secretary Donald H. Rumsfeld in September gave a succinct summary of the administration position on the detainees: "Our interest is in not trying them and letting them out," he said. "Our interest is in—during this global war on terror—keeping them off the streets, and so that's what's taking place."

Despite such statements, the Bush administration came under increasing pressure during the year to initiate legal proceedings for those detainees against whom the U.S. had evidence of supporting terrorism and to release the others. Some of the pressure came from lawsuits filed on behalf of the detainees, some from humanitarian organizations, and some from lawyers and judges in Australia and Britain, two close U.S. allies that had some of their citizens held at Guantanamo.

The most important legal cases were three lawsuits filed in 2002 on behalf of sixteen Guantanamo detainees. One lawsuit dealt with twelve Kuwaitees; the others dealt with two Britons and two Australians. All three suits sought a writ of habeas corpus for the detainees—essentially a statement by the courts that they had jurisdiction over the detainees. All the men had been captured in Afghanistan or Pakistan in late 2001 or early 2002, and all denied having fought for, or been associated with, either al Qaeda or the Taliban government of Afghanistan. Several men reportedly insisted they had been volunteers for various humanitarian organizations and had been captured and turned over to the United States by warlords or local groups in Afghanistan or Pakistan in exchange for bounties offered by the Pentagon.

The cases reached the federal district court in Washington, D.C., in August 2002, where they were consolidated into one case. Judge Colleen Kollar-Kotelly rejected the habeas corpus pleas, saying that U.S. courts had no jurisdiction over the Guantanamo Bay prison because it was located within foreign territory—the island of Cuba. A lease signed in 1903 gave the United States total control over the base but recognized Cuba's continued sovereignty over the land. As a result, the base was Cuban, not a U.S. territory, Judge Kollar-Kotelly ruled. She based her opinion on a post-World War II case decided by the Supreme Court in 1950—*Johnson v. Eisentrager*—that said foreign nationals arrested overseas by U.S. authorities did not have access to U.S. courts.

Judge Kollar-Kotelly's ruling was upheld on March 11 by a three-judge panel of the U.S. Court of Appeals for the District of Columbia. Writing for the panel, circuit court judge A. Raymond Randolph said U.S. courts could not claim jurisdiction in the sovereign territory of another country—even if the United States had total effective control over that territory. "No court in this country has jurisdiction to grant habeas relief to the Guantanamo detainees, even if they have not been adjudicated enemies of the United States," Randolph wrote. "If the Constitution does not entitle the detainees to due process, and it does not, they cannot invoke the jurisdiction of our courts to test the constitutionality or the legality of restraints on their liberty."

Attorney General John D. Ashcroft said the ruling validated the administration's position that it was under no obligation to provide legal rights for the Guantanamo detainees. "In times of war, the president must be able to protect our nation from enemies who seek to harm innocent Americans," he said.

Attorneys representing the detainees said they would appeal the ruling. Kristine Huskey and Thomas Wilner, the attorneys for the Kuwaitees, said the appellate court's ruling had held "for the first time in any context that the United States may jail foreigners abroad with no rights whatsoever, including the right to go before an impartial forum to establish their inno-cence." A similar argument came from Sergio Vieira de Mello, the United Nations High Commissioner for Human Rights, who said the United States had put the detainees into a "judicial black hole" at Guantanamo. "There is a new concept . . . of a territory where no law applies," he said of the court's ruling. Vieira de Mello was killed in August by the suicide bombing of a UN compound in Baghdad, where he was serving as the head of the UN's post-war mission to Iraq. *(Postwar Iraq, p. 933)*

International pressure reportedly led Secretary of State Colin Powell to write Defense Secretary Rumsfeld a letter in April asking for quicker action to resolve the cases of Guantanamo detainees—especially those who were citizens of Australia, Britain, Pakistan, Spain, and Russia. State Department officials told reporters that Powell expressed concern that the lengthy deten-tions had angered allies and other friendly nations.

Explicit criticism of the indefinite detentions came in October from the International Committee of the Red Cross (ICRC), the only independent agency with any regular access to the detainees. After meeting with some of the detainees, ICRC official Christophe Girod told the *New York Times* on October 9 that "the open-endedness of the situation and its impact on the mental health of the population [at Guantanamo] has become a major problem." At that point nearly two dozen detainees had attempted suicide, some more than once, but none of the attempts had been successful. After months of silence about the detention, Girod and other Red Cross officials said they decided to speak out because the U.S. government had not responded to requests to resolve the cases of the detainees. "One cannot keep these detainees in this pattern, this situation, indefinitely," Girod told the *Times.*

As of the end of 2003, the Pentagon had transferred about ninety pris-oners out of Guantanamo. Four of the men were sent to Saudi Arabia, where they would be subject to that country's court system, and the rest were released in their home countries. Despite these releases, the overall population at Guantanamo reportedly held fairly steady at about 650 because new detainees were brought in, from other facilities, to replace those who were released.

Supreme Court Steps In

In the months after the District of Columbia appellate court decision, most legal observers suggested that the Supreme Court would allow it to stand by refusing to consider an appeal. The Court had a majority of five gener-ally conservative judges who were expected to show deference to the administration's prerogatives on national security issues. Indeed, Chief Jus-tice William H. Rehnquist had written in a 1998 book that courts correctly had "muted" civil liberties concerns during times of war. In arguing to the Court that it should not take the case, Solicitor General Theodore B. Olson stated bluntly that the court system had no business interfering in the detention of those held at Guantanamo. Their status, Olson said in a brief, was a matter "constitutionally committed to the executive branch" and not to the courts.

On November 10 the Supreme Court appeared to reject Olson's argument, saying that it would accept the appeal of the circuit court ruling eight months earlier. As usual, the Court did not explain its decision to take the case. Some of the commentary on the decision, however, noted that at least some of the justices appeared to reject another of Olson's assertions: that it was up to the executive branch, not to the courts, to decide whether the Guantanamo base was U.S. territory in any practical sense. Olson's brief had stated that the detainees were held "outside the sovereign territory" of the United States. In its notice, the Court eliminated that phrase. The Court was scheduled to hear arguments in the case in March 2004, by which time the administration was planning to begin putting at least some of the detainees before military tribunals, which were also outside the jurisdiction of the court system.

In mid-December an Australian lawyer became the first civilian lawyer to meet with a detainee at Guantanamo. Under pressure from the Australian government, the Bush administration on November 25 agreed to allow the two Australian detainees to have independent legal representation. Two weeks later, lawyer Stephen Kenney spent nearly five days with his client, David Hicks, an Australian citizen who had been captured in Afghanistan and held at Guantanamo because he allegedly had fought for the Taliban regime. Although he had not yet been charged with any crime, Hicks was expected to be one of the first detainees put before a military tribunal. After his visit with Hicks, Kenney told reporters that his client had been placed in a "legal and moral black hole."

Similarly tough language had come on November 26 from one of Britain's senior judges, Lord Steyn, who said in a speech that the U.S. government had deprived the detainees of "any rights whatsoever. As a lawyer brought up to admire the ideals of American democracy and justice, I would have to say that I regard this as a monstrous failure of justice."

The year's final legal action on the Guantanamo situation came December 18 from a three-judge panel of the Court of Appeals for the Ninth Circuit, in San Francisco. Adopting the opposite position of the appellate court in Washington, that panel ruled that the Guantanamo detainees did come under the jurisdiction of the U.S. court system. The executive branch needed to have flexibility to protect the country, Judge Stephen Reinhardt wrote in the 2–1 majority. "However, even in times of national emergency—indeed, particularly in such times—it is the obligation of the judicial branch to ensure the preservation of our constitutional values and to prevent the executive branch from running roughshod over the rights of citizens and aliens alike."

The San Francisco panel ruled in a case brought by a California man, Belaid Gherebi, who said his brother from Libya, Falen Gherebi, was being held at Guantanamo. Because the Supreme Court already had agreed to consider the earlier case, the decision of the San Francisco panel had no immediate legal effect, other than to bolster the arguments of those who contended that Guantanamo detainees should be given at least some legal rights under U.S. law.

U.S. Citizens as Enemy Combatants

In theory, at least, U.S. citizens automatically had more legal rights in the United States under the Constitution than did foreigners—especially foreigners held outside U.S. territory. But two U.S. citizens who were caught in the post-September 11 antiterrorism sweep ended up in legal limbos not much different from those of the detainees at Guantanamo Bay. As of 2003 U.S. citizens Hamdi and Padilla had both been detained in U.S. Navy brigs: Hamdi since shortly after his capture in Afghanistan in late 2001 and Padilla since shortly after his arrest at Chicago's O'Hare International Airport in May 2002. The government designated each man as an "enemy combatant" because of his alleged participation in terrorism plots and had denied them any legal representation.

Other parties filed habeas corpus suits on behalf of the men, and those cases traveled similar paths. Hamdi was a U.S. citizen because he was born in Louisiana; both of his parents were citizens of Saudi Arabia. His father filed suit in federal district court in Virginia in June 2002 and won a ruling in August 2002 from Judge Robert G. Doumar that the government needed to provide information justifying Hamdi's continued detention. That ruling was overturned January 8, 2003, by a unanimous three-judge appellate panel, which said the courts could not intervene in the case because Hamdi had been captured overseas; the panel also argued that courts should be "deferential" to the executive branch in times of conflict. The full Fourth Circuit Court of Appeals upheld that ruling on July 9, on an 8–4 vote. Hamdi's lawyer appealed the decision.

On December 3, as the Supreme Court was considering whether to take up the appeal, the Bush administration abruptly reversed course and announced that Hamdi would be allowed to consult a lawyer. The Pentagon released a statement announcing that this decision was "a matter of discretion" and did not establish a precedent for similar cases. Legal experts said the abrupt change of position appeared to be an attempt by the administration to strengthen its argument, before the Supreme Court, that Hamdi was not being held unfairly. News reports also quoted Pentagon officials as saying that the interrogations of Hamdi had been completed, so allowing him to see a lawyer no longer posed any security concerns.

The Supreme Court agreed on January 10, 2004, to hear Hamdi's case. As in the case of the Guantanamo detainees, the Supreme Court decision to consider the appeal amounted to the rejection of an assertion by the Bush administration that the courts had no jurisdiction in these terrorism-related prosecutions.

Padilla had been arrested at the Chicago airport in May 2002 after he returned from a trip to Pakistan. At first he was held as a material witness and transferred to a detention center in New York City. After a judge appointed a lawyer for Padilla—but before another judge was to hear a challenge to his detention—President Bush designated Padilla as an enemy combatant. Padilla was then transferred to a naval brig in South Carolina, where he was held incommunicado. Government officials reportedly had said that two sources had sworn that Padilla conspired with al Qaeda members to produce a dirty bomb.

In December 2002 Michael Mukasey, chief judge of the Federal District Court in Manhattan, said Bush had the authority to detain Padilla if there was evidence of his involvement in terrorism. But Mukasey ruled that Padilla had the legal right to be represented by a lawyer and to contest his status as an enemy combatant.

A year later, on December 18, 2003, a three-judge panel of the Second Circuit Court of Appeals in New York ruled by a 2–1 vote that Bush lacked the legal power to detain Padilla as an enemy combatant because Congress had never authorized such a status. "Presidential authority does not exist in a vacuum, and this case involves not whether those responsibilities should be aggressively pursued, but whether the president is obligated, in the circumstances presented here, to share them with Congress," the judges ruled. The panel ordered the Pentagon to release Padilla within thirty days but said the government also had the option of transferring him to the civilian court system—where he could face criminal charges or be held as a material witness. Padilla's status was unresolved as of the end of 2003.

The Bush administration had designated at least one other man as an "enemy combatant," but he was not a U.S. citizen and little was known about his case. The man was Ali Saleh Kahlah al-Marri, a citizen of Qatar who had graduated from Bradley University in Illinois. Declaring that he had been a "sleeper agent" for al Qaeda, Bush formally designated him as an enemy combatant in June 2003.

A broad criticism of the Bush administration's use of the enemy combatant procedure came early in the year from the American Bar Association (ABA). By a vote of 368–76 on February 10 at its midwinter meeting, the bar association's policy board, the House of Delegates, declared that U.S. citizens should not be held incommunicado and should be given access to lawyers and a court review of their status.

Plans for Military Tribunals

After nearly two years of discussion, the Bush administration in late 2003 appeared to be putting the finishing touches on its plans to try at least some terrorism suspects before closed military courts known as tribunals. The administration's first plans for the tribunals, announced in late 2001, were heavily criticized by legal experts as poorly drawn and contradictory. Subsequent revisions during 2002 and 2003 appeared to address some of the criticism, apparently in the hope of giving the tribunals a measure of international credibility. Even so, the plans continued to draw significant criticism. On August 12, for example, the ABA's House of Delegates criticized the military's plan to allow security agents to eavesdrop on conversations between terrorism suspects and their military lawyers and to restrict the access of lawyers to the evidence used against their clients.

The administration planned to open the first tribunals in 2004, using them to hear the cases of six of the detainees at the Guantanamo Bay prison— reportedly including at least three of the four Australians and Britons held there. The administration had said it would seek the death penalty in significant cases heard by the tribunals. But at the request of the British and Australian governments, the administration agreed during 2003 that their citizens would not be subjected to the death penalty if found guilty. Some legal experts said that concession would undermine the argument for imposing the death penalty against defendants from other countries.

The Pentagon on November 25 said it was conducting a final review of the rules for the tribunals. "Clarifications" of previous rules and additional legal "assurances" would be added "where appropriate," the Pentagon's statement said. Defense Secretary Rumsfeld on December 31 said retired major general John Altenburg, a former U.S. Army lawyer, would approve all charges presented to the tribunals and would appoint the members of the panels.

Following are excerpts from two documents: first, the decision of the U.S. Court of Appeals for the District of Columbia, issued March 11, 2003, in the case of Khaled A. F. Al Odah, et al. v. United States of America, *in which the court ruled that U.S. courts did not have jurisdiction over the status of foreigners held as terrorism suspects at a military detention center at Guantanamo Bay Naval Base in Cuba; second, the decision of the U.S. Court of Appeals for the Ninth Circuit, in San Francisco, issued December 18, 2003, in the case of* Falen Gherebi v. George Walker Bush; Donald H. Rumsfeld, *in which the court ruled that U.S. courts did have jurisdiction over the status of foreigners detained at the Guantanamo base.*

Khaled A. F. Al Odah, et al. v. United States of America

... In response to the attacks of September 11, 2001, and in the exercise of its constitutional powers, Congress authorized the President "to use all necessary and appropriate force against those nations, organizations, or persons he determines planned, authorized, committed, or aided" the attacks and recognized the President's "authority under the Constitution to take action to deter and prevent acts of international terrorism against the United States." The President declared a national emergency, and, as Commander in Chief, dispatched armed forces to Afghanistan to seek out and subdue the al Qaeda terrorist network and the Taliban regime that had supported and protected it. During the course of the Afghanistan campaign, the United States and its allies captured the aliens whose next friends bring these actions.

In one of the cases (*Al Odah v. United States*, No. 02–5251), fathers and brothers of twelve Kuwaiti nationals detained at Camp X-Ray in Guantanamo Bay brought an action in the form of a complaint against the United States, President George W. Bush, Secretary of Defense Donald H. Rumsfeld, Chairman of the Joint Chiefs of Staff Gen. Richard B. Myers, Brig. Gen. Rick Baccus, whom they allege is the Commander of Joint Task Force 160, and Col. Terry Carrico, the Commandant of Camp X-Ray/Camp Delta. None of the plaintiffs' attorneys have communicated with the Kuwaiti detainees. The complaint alleges that the detainees were in Afghanistan and Pakistan as volunteers providing humanitarian aid; that local villagers seeking bounties seized them and handed them over to United States forces; and that they were transferred to Guantanamo Bay sometime between January and March 2002. ... They seek a declaratory judgment and an injunction ordering that they be informed of any charges against them and requiring that they be permitted to consult with counsel and meet with their families.

Rasul v. Bush (No. 02–5288) is styled a petition for a writ of habeas corpus on behalf of three detainees, although it seeks other relief as well. The next friends bringing the petition are the father of an Australian detainee, the father of a British detainee, and the mother of another British detainee. ... The petition claims that the Australian detainee was living in Afghanistan when the Northern Alliance captured him in early December 2001; that one of the British detainees traveled to Pakistan for an arranged marriage after September 11, 2001; and that the other British detainee went to Pakistan after that date to visit relatives and continue his computer education. . . . They seek a writ of habeas corpus, relief from unlawful custody, access to coiunsel, an end to interrogations, and other relief.

Habib v. Bush (No. 02–5284) is also in the form of a petition for writ of habeas corpus and is brought by the wife of an Australian citizen, acting as his next friend. Naming President Bush, Secretary Rumsfeld, Brig. Gen. Baccus, and Lt. Col. William Cline as defendants, the petition alleges that Habib traveled to Pakistan to look for employment and a school for his children; that after Pakistani authorities arrested him in October 2001, they transferred him to Egyptian authorities, who handed him over to the United States military; and that the military moved him from Egypt to Afghanistan and ultimately to Guantanamo Bay in May 2002. . . . Habib seeks a writ of habeas corpus, legally sufficient process to establish the legality of his detention, access to counsel, an end to all interrogations of him, and other relief.

The district court held that it lacked jurisdiction. Believing no court would have jurisdiction, it dismissed the complaint and the two habeas corpus petitions with prejudice. In the court's view all of the detainees' claims went to the lawfulness of their custody and thus were cognizable only in habeas corpus. Relying upon *Johnson v. Eisentrager* (1950), the court ruled that it did not have jurisdiction to issue writs of habeas corpus for aliens detained outside the sovereign territory of the United States. . . .

II.

. . . In each of the three cases, the detainees deny that they are enemy combatants or *enemy* aliens. Typical of the denials is this paragraph from the petition in *Rasul*:

> The detained petitioners are not, and have never been, members of Al Qaida or any other terrorist group. Prior to their detention, they did not commit any violent act against any American person, nor espouse any violent act against any American person or property. On information and belief, they had no involvement, direct or indirect, in either the terrorist attacks on the United States September 11, 2001, or any act of international terrorism attributed by the United States to al Qaida or any terrorist group.

(As the district court pointed out, an affidavit from the father of the Australian detainee in *Rasul* admitted that his son had joined the Taliban forces.) Although the government asked the district court to take judicial notice that the detainees are "enemy combatants," the court declined and assumed the truth of their denials.

This brings us to the first issue: whether the Supreme Court's decision in *Johnson v. Eisentrager*, which the district court found dispositive, is distinguishable on the ground that the prisoners there were "enemy aliens.". . . .

Despite the government's argument to the contrary, it follows that none of the Guantanamo detainees are within the category of "enemy aliens," at least as *Eisentrager* used the term. They are nationals of Kuwait, Australia, or the United Kingdom. Our war in response to the attacks of September 11, 2001, obviously is not against these countries. It is against a network of terrorists operating in secret throughout the world and often hiding among civilian populations. An "alien friend" may become an "alien enemy" by taking up arms against the United States, but the cases before us were decided on the pleadings, each of which denied that the detainees had engaged in hostilities against America.

Nonetheless the Guantanamo detainees have much in common with the German prisoners in *Eisentrager*. They too are aliens, they too were captured during military operations, they were in a foreign country when captured, they are now abroad, they are in the custody of the American military, and they have never had any presence in the United States. For the reasons that follow we believe that under *Eisentrager* these factors preclude the detainees from seeking habeas relief in the courts of the United States. . . .

[The court reviewed previous decisions in which courts had held that foreigners were not accorded the same constitutional rights as U.S. citizens.]

The consequence is that no court in this country has jurisdiction to grant habeas relief . . . to the Guantanamo detainees, even if they have not been adjudicated enemies of the United States. We cannot see why, or how, the writ may be made available to aliens abroad when basic constitutional protections are not. This much is at the heart of *Eisentrager*. If the Constitution does not entitle the detainees to due process, and it does not, they cannot invoke the jurisdiction of our courts to test the constitutionality or the legality of restraints on their liberty. *Eisentrager* itself directly tied jurisdiction to the extension of constitutional provisions: "in extending constitutional protections beyond the citizenry, the Court has been at pains to point out that it was the alien's presence within its territorial jurisdiction that gave the Judiciary power to act." Thus, the "privilege of litigation has been extended to aliens, *whether friendly or enemy*, only because permitting their presence in the country implied protection." (emphasis added). In arguing that *Eisentrager* turned on the status of the prisoners as enemies, the detainees do not deny that if they are in fact in that category, if they engaged in international terrorism or were affiliated with al Qaeda, the courts would not be open to them. Their position is that the district court should have made these factual determinations at the threshold, before dismissing for lack of jurisdiction. But the Court in *Eisentrager* did not decide to avoid all the problems exercising jurisdiction would have caused, only to confront the same problems in determining whether jurisdiction exists in the first place. . . .

We have thus far assumed that the detainees are not "within any territory over which the United States is sovereign," *Eisentrager*. The detainees dispute the assumption. They say the military controls Guantanamo Bay, that it is in essence a territory of the United States, that the government exercises sovereignty over it, and that in any event *Eisentrager* does not turn on technical definitions of sovereignty or territory.

The United States has occupied the Guantanamo Bay Naval Base under a lease with Cuba since 1903, as modified in 1934. In the 1903 Lease, "the United States recognizes the continuance of the ultimate sovereignty of the Republic of Cuba" over the naval base. ("So long as the United States of America shall not abandon the said naval station at Guantanamo or the two Governments shall not agree to a modification of its present limits, the station shall continue to have the territorial area that it now has. . . ."). . . .

The text of the leases, quoted above, shows that Cuba—not the United States—has sovereignty over Guantanamo Bay. . . .

[The court reviewed arguments over whether the United States had control of Guantanamo Bay, even though it lacked sovereignty.]

. . . But under *Eisentrager*, control is surely not the test. Our military forces may have control over the naval base at Guantanamo, but our military forces also had control over the Landsberg prison in Germany [the prison where the Germans who were the subject of the *Eisentrager* case were held.]

We also disagree with the detainees that the *Eisentrager* opinion interchanged "territorial jurisdiction" with "sovereignty," without attaching any particular significance to either term. When the Court referred to "territorial jurisdiction," it meant the territorial jurisdiction of the United States courts, as for example in these passages quoted earlier: "in extending constitutional protections beyond the citizenry, the Court has been at pains to point out that it was the alien's presence within its territorial jurisdiction that gave the Judiciary power to act" and "the scenes of their offense, their capture, their trial and their punishment were all beyond the territorial jurisdiction of United States courts". Sovereignty, on the other hand, meant then—and means now—supreme dominion exercised by a nation. The United States has sovereignty over the geographic area of the States and, as the *Eisentrager* Court recognized, over insular possessions. Guantanamo Bay fits within neither category. . . .

Source: U.S. United States Court of Appeals for the District of Columbia Circuit. *Khaled A.F. Al Odah, et al. v. United States of America.* No. 02–5251. March 11, 2003. www.ll.georgetown.edu/federal/judicial/dc/opinions/02opinions/02-5251a.pdf (accessed April 12, 2003).

Falen Gherebi v. George Walker Bush; Donald H. Rumsfeld

This case presents the question whether the Executive Branch may hold uncharged citizens of foreign nations in indefinite detention in territory under the "complete jurisdiction and control" of the United States while effectively denying them the right to challenge their detention in any tribunal anywhere, including the courts of the U.S. The issues we are required to confront are new, important, and difficult.

In the wake of the devastating terrorist attacks on September 11, 2001, Congress authorized the President to

> "use all necessary and appropriate force against those nations, organizations, or persons he determines planned, authorized, committed, or aided the terrorist attacks that occurred on September 11, 2001, or harbored such organizations or persons, in order to prevent any future acts of international terrorism against the United States by such nations, organizations or persons."

Pursuant to that authorization, the President sent U.S. forces to Afghanistan to wage a military operation that has been commonly termed—but never formally declared—a "war" against the Taliban government and the terrorist network known as Al Queda.

Starting in early January 2002, the Armed Forces began transferring to Guantanamo, a United States naval base located on territory physically situated on the island of Cuba, scores of individuals who were captured by the American military during its operations in Afghanistan. The captured individuals were labeled "enemy combatants." Now, for almost two years, the United States has subjected over six hundred of these captives to indefinite detention, yet has failed to afford them any means to challenge their confinement, to object to the failure to recognize them as prisoners of war, to consult with legal counsel, or even to advance claims of mistaken capture or identity. Despite U.S. officials' recent stated intention to move to begin a sorting of the detainees, electing which to release and which to try before military tribunals on criminal charges, and the administration's designation several months ago of six detainees (including two Britons and one Australian) deemed eligible for military trials, no military tribunal has actually been convened. Nor has a single Guantanamo detainee been given the opportunity to consult an attorney, had formal charges filed against him, or been permitted to contest the basis of his detention in any way. Moreover, top U.S. officials, including

Secretary of Defense Rumsfeld, have made it clear that the detainees may be held in their present circumstances until this country's campaign against terrorism ends. The administration has, understandably, given no indication whether that event will take place in a matter of months, years, or decades, if ever. . . .

. . . Belaid Gherebi filed an amended next-friend habeas petition in this Court, on behalf of his brother Faren, in which the standing issue is not present. In his February 2003 Amended Petition, Gherebi alleged violations of the U.S. Constitution and the Third Geneva Convention arising out of his involuntary detention at Guantanamo, a naval base "under the exclusive and complete jurisdiction of the respondents," and he further claimed that, "Respondents have characterized Gherebi as an 'unlawful combatant,' and have denied him status as a prisoner of war, have denied him rights under the United States Constitution, . . . have denied him access to the United States Courts," and have denied him access to legal counsel. The government did not respond. Thereafter, Gherebi urged this Court to resolve the "threshhold question" of federal subject matter jurisdiction in a motion to grant his petition summarily. At that point, the government moved to dismiss Gherebi's petition without prejudice to its being re-filed in the district court, or alternatively, to transfer it to the district court so that the district judge could decide the question of jurisdiction. A motions panel of this Court granted the government's request, transferring Gherebi's petition to the United States District Court for the Central District of California. After additional motions were filed with the district court urging summary disposition of the jurisdictional question, that court issued a reasoned order on May 13, 2003 dismissing Gherebi's petition for lack of jurisdiction. The court held that *Johnson v. Eisentrager* controlled and foreclosed jurisdiction over Gherebi's petition in any federal court because Guantanamo "is not within sovereign U.S. territory." In so holding, the court described its conclusion as "reluctant," and expressed hope that "a higher court w[ould] find a principled way" to provide the remedy of habeas corpus.

On appeal before this Court, Gherebi argues that (1) the district court erred in holding that *Johnson v. Eisentrager* precludes the district courts of this nation from exercising jurisdiction over his petition; and (2) the District Court for the Central District of California has jurisdiction to hear the writ because the custodians of the prisoners are within the jurisdiction of the court. We agree with Gherebi on both points. In so holding, we underscore that the issue before us is not whether Gherebi's detention will withstand constitutional inquiry, but rather whether the courts of the United States are entirely closed to detainees held at Guantanamo indefinitely—detainees who would appear to have no effective right to seek relief in the courts of any other nation or before any international judicial body.

We recognize that the process due "enemy combatant" habeas petitioners may vary with the circumstances and are fully aware of the unprecedented challenges that affect the United States' national security interests today, and we share the desire of all Americans to ensure that the Executive enjoys the necessary power and flexibility to prevent future terrorist attacks. However, even in times of national emergency—indeed, particularly in such times—it is the obligation of the Judicial Branch to ensure the preservation of our constitutional values and to prevent the Executive Branch from running roughshod over the rights of citizens and aliens alike. Here, we simply cannot accept the government's position that the Executive Branch possesses the unchecked authority to imprison indefinitely any persons, foreign citizens included, on territory under the sole jurisdiction and control of the United States, without permitting such prisoners recourse of any kind to any judicial forum, or even access to counsel, regardless of the length or manner of their confinement. We hold that no lawful policy or precedent supports such a counter-intuitive and undemocratic procedure, and that, contrary to the government's contention, *Johnson* [*v. Eisentrager*] neither requires nor authorizes it. In our view, the government's position is inconsistent with fundamental tenets of American jurisprudence and raises most serious concerns under international law.

Accordingly, we reverse the ruling of the district court that jurisdiction over Gherebi's habeas petition does not lie. Because we also conclude that personal jurisdiction may be asserted against respondent Rumsfeld in the Central District of California, we remand the matter to the district court for further proceedings consistent with this opinion. We do not resolve here, and leave to the district court to decide, the distinct and important question whether a transfer to a different district court may be appropriate. . . .

Source: U.S. United States Court of Appeals for the Ninth Circuit. *Falen Gherebi v. George Walker Bush; Donald H. Rumsfeld.* No. 03–55785. December 18, 2003. www.ca9.uscourts.gov/ca9/newopinions.nsf/ 429E2096892C3D8388256E00005FEB65/$file/0355785final.pdf?openelement (accessed April 12, 2003).

World Health Organization on the Worldwide SARS Outbreak

March 15 and 16, 2003

INTRODUCTION

A previously unknown, highly infectious respiratory disease broke out in China in late 2002 and spread to some thirty countries before being contained in mid-2003. Severe Acute Respiratory Syndrome (SARS), as the atypical pneumonia came to be known, infected more than 8,000 people, mostly in Asia, left nearly 800 people dead, rocked the global economy for several months, caused political unrest in China, and sent waves of fear throughout the world.

The disease first came to the attention of the World Health Organization (WHO) in February 2003. The UN agency issued a global health alert on March 15 and kicked off a remarkable collaboration among medical scientists and health experts around the world to determine the cause of the disease, find ways to treat it, and stop its spread.

Experts quickly focused on a previously unknown strain of a corona virus, a virus that in milder forms was responsible for about one-third of all common colds. The SARS virus was much more deadly, however, with about one in every ten victims dying; the mortality rate was about one in five for people over age sixty. Because corona viruses were known to cause severe and often fatal illness in cats, dogs, cattle, poultry, and other animals, researchers began to focus on a possible link between the human SARS virus and a similar virus found in the civet, a weasel-like animal related to the mongoose that was considered a delicacy in China's Guangdong province. Other exotic animals used as food in that area were also under investigation.

Researchers also quickly found that there was no specific treatment for SARS. Medical personnel began to treat it as they would other atypical pneumonias, which included using ventilating machines to help severely effected patients breathe. When it became apparent that health care workers were among those most vulnerable to contracting the disease, hospitals began isolating patients and in some cases their health care workers, and health officials began quarantining family members and others who had come into contact with patients. It was the extensive use of isolation, monitoring, and quarantine that eventually brought the outbreak under control. Laboratories around the world were working on a vaccine for the disease, but experts predicted that it would be at least two or three years before one was found, if it could be found at all.

WHO lifted its health alert for SARS on July 5, twenty days after the last case of SARS was reported, in Taiwan. Health officials warned that because SARS was caused by a virus, it might break out again later in the year during the regular flu season. Individual cases of SARS were reported in Singapore and Taiwan in the second half of the year, but they were contained and no widespread outbreak of the disease occurred. At the end of the year, attention was focused on a suspected case of SARS in the Guangdong province. Health officials there and in neighboring Hong Kong immediately stepped up precautions to prevent any possible spread of the disease to the general population.

The first suspected cases of SARS in the United States were confirmed on March 19. Only days before, the federal Centers for Disease Control and Prevention (CDC) in Atlanta had activated emergency procedures for coordinating information on SARS with other countries and for investigating suspect cases in the United States. In October the CDC reported that 164 people were infected with SARS and that none of them had died. The CDC had used similar emergency procedures only twice before, for mosquito-borne West Nile virus in 2002 and for the anthrax scare in 2001. *(Anthrax scare, Historic Documents of 2001, p. 672)*

The Outbreak of SARS

SARS was thought to have emerged first in Guangdong province in southern China in November 2002, but Chinese officials did not publicly report the disease until February 11, 2003, when they informed WHO that there were 300 cases of an "acute respiratory syndrome" in the province, including five deaths. A month later Vietnam and Hong Kong were both experiencing outbreaks of the disease. It was thought that SARS began to spread outside of China when a physician who had been treating patients in Guangdong province became infected and traveled to Hong Kong. Days later other guests of the hotel in which he stayed began to show symptoms of the infection, but by that time many of them had traveled to other countries where they unknowingly infected fellow travelers, family members, and the doctors and nurses from whom they sought care.

On March 15 WHO issued an alert, declaring the new disease to be a "worldwide health threat" and urging air travelers and crew members who developed SARS-like symptoms to seek medical care immediately and to inform health care workers about their recent travel. The rare alert came as the United States and its allies were poised to attack Iraq in a bid to oust its leader, Saddam Hussein, and rid that country of its presumed weapons of mass destruction. Speculation that the mysterious disease might be some form of bioterrorism exacerbated the public's fears about SARS, even though most public health officials downplayed that likelihood. *(Iraq war, p. 135)*

In an updated report on March 16, WHO described in more detail the outbreaks that had appeared in Canada, China, Hong Kong, Indonesia, the Philippines, Singapore, Thailand, and Vietnam. Over the next few weeks SARS cases appeared in about twenty other countries around the globe, including Taiwan, which had a severe outbreak. Other countries in Europe, Africa, and elsewhere in Asia were able to quickly contain the disease before it developed into a full-blown outbreak. For the first time in its history, WHO also issued advisories urging travelers to postpone unnecessary trips to areas experiencing severe outbreaks. The first travel warning, affecting Guangdong province and neighboring Hong Kong, was issued April 2. Later WHO extended the warnings to several other cities and countries in Asia as well as the city of Toronto, Canada.

Containing the Disease

In the early days of the disease, health care workers did not realize how contagious the disease was or exactly how it was transmitted. As a result many of the first victims of SARS were the health workers who cared for infected patients. Doctors quickly suspected that SARS was passed from person to person primarily through droplets produced when an infected person coughed or sneezed. They thus began to isolate patients and the hospital workers who cared for them and to urge anyone who had come into contact with a patient to stay home for ten days, the usual length of time it took for symptoms to develop after exposure. As a precaution millions of people, particularly in the badly affected countries in Asia, began to wear surgical masks whenever out in public.

Beyond the vulnerability of family members and health care personnel, air travel was recognized as the biggest source of possible contamination. In addition to specific travel warnings from WHO, individual countries took a variety of steps to stop the spread of SARS. Some countries stopped giving visas to people from highly affected countries. Other countries, including the United States, screened passengers arriving from affected countries and isolated those that showed SARS symptoms. Some countries used infrared machines that could identify airline passengers with elevated temperatures, one of the first indications of a possible SARS infection. Health officials in some countries also tracked down every person that came in close contact with SARS patients, including fellow travelers, urging or requiring them to stay home and monitoring them for symptoms of the disease. Companies that did business in affected countries or areas also took steps to contain the spread of the disease. Business trips and conventions were postponed or cancelled, and workers with SARS-like symptoms were encouraged to stay out of the office for at least ten days.

These isolation, quarantine, and monitoring tactics were largely successful once put into place and aggressively followed. Vietnam, which had the first recognized case of SARS, moved quickly to keep infected and exposed people in a Hanoi hospital separate from healthy populations, thus preventing a SARS outbreak there from worsening. Severe outbreaks of SARS in Hong Kong and Singapore began to ease in late April.

The worst outbreak outside Asia occurred in Toronto; it was believed that SARS was brought there by a traveler from Asia. City and country officials sharply protested WHO's travel advisory for Toronto, issued on April 23, insisting that the disease was contained. WHO lifted the advisory on April 29, citing an ebb in the epidemic and noting that Canada agreed to step up screening at the Toronto airport, using infrared temperature-taking machines that could detect anyone with a fever for further screening. Some observers criticized WHO's quick reversal, saying that it looked like the health organization was caving in to the heavy pressure from the Canadian government. Canadian officials were pleased; even before the advisory had been issued, Canada was estimated to be losing as much as $30 million a day as a result of SARS. A new cluster of cases in Toronto in late May left Canadian officials admitting that they had let down their guard too quickly, but authorities quickly contained the new outbreak through strict quarantine measures.

China's Cover-Up

The country with by far the greatest number of SARS cases was China, which reported some 5,000 cases and nearly 350 deaths before the disease was contained. Chinese officials were widely faulted for covering up the existence of the disease for nearly three months, during which time it spread both in and outside of China. China's normally secretive government typically suppressed bad news of any sort, both from its own people and the world. Observers speculated that the government may not have wanted news of the disease to emerge in the midst of a transition of power, which had begun in the fall and was not completed until March 15, when new Communist Party leader Hu Jintao formally replaced Jiang Zemin as president. *(Reforms in China, p. 1173)*

Even with the WHO global health alert, Chinese officials responded slowly to the potential for SARS to spread through the world's largest population.

For example, the country's largest trade fair opened April 15 in Guangzhou, the capital of Guangdong province, even though thousands of foreign businesses had decided not to attend.

Damage to China's reputation for failing to come to grips with SARS was frequently compared to the aftermath of the 1989 Tiananmen Square debacle when the Chinese Army used tanks to crush a student-led pro-democracy movement. One leading Chinese scientist told the *Washington Post* that when he "went to France, my colleagues looked at me and said, 'We might be able to understand Tiananmen Square. That was your internal affair. But here your failure has cost lives around the world.' I could only agree."

Along with international pressure and a sudden downturn in its economy, the Chinese government was beginning to receive pressure from its own citizens, who were using cell phones and computers to spread more accurate information about the course of the disease in China than the government was revealing. Those pressures, together with a worrisome rise in the number of cases appearing in Beijing, apparently caused the government to reassess its position. On April 18 Chinese leaders publicly declared a nationwide war on SARS and ordered officials to stop covering up the extent of the disease. The health minister, who earlier in April had said the disease was under control, was fired, as was the mayor of Beijing, who had said the city was safe. WHO medical investigators said the city probably had about 200 cases, although the official report was 37 cases. Health care workers said they were told to underreport cases so that WHO would not issue a travel advisory for Beijing (but WHO issued a travel warning on April 23). On April 20 Chinese officials raised the number of confirmed cases of SARS in the city to 346, adding that there were another 402 suspected cases. Those numbers continued to climb over the next several days.

To arrest the spread of the disease in Beijing, a city of 14 million, officials closed all public schools for two weeks beginning April 24. They also imposed a quarantine on thousands of Beijing residents who might have been exposed to SARS patients. This included confining more than 2,000 health workers and patients inside the Beijing University People's Hospital complex. "It's a strong step, but maybe they should have been this serious earlier," one health worker told the *New York Times*.

City authorities eventually closed down all entertainment venues, including theaters and karaoke bars, and prohibited swimming, boating, and fishing in Beijing's reservoirs. As many as 2 million people might have fled the city to avoid contamination. Civil unrest was reported in some rural areas. Villagers in one town overturned an ambulance that they thought was transferring a SARS patient to a local hospital.

On May 8 WHO extended travel advisories to two more provinces in China as well as to Taipei, the capital of Taiwan, where a severe outbreak had begun in late April. On May 16 Taiwan's health minister resigned, accepting responsibility for the island's failure to contain the disease. By May 18 experts agreed that the SARS outbreaks were under control everywhere but in China and Taiwan. WHO gradually began to lift its country alerts and travel warnings. The Beijing travel warning was the last to be lifted, on June 24. WHO removed countries from its watch list when no new cases had appeared for twenty days. On July 5 Taiwan, the last country on the watch list, was removed, and WHO announced that the disease had been contained. "We do not mark the end of SARS today, but we observe a milestone: the global SARS outbreak has been contained," declared Gro Harlem Brundtland, the general director of WHO. The organization reported that 8,349 people had contracted the disease and that 812 had died. Late in the year, WHO reported that further evaluation showed that the number of SARS infections was actually 8,099, and there were 774 deaths.

The Economic Toll

SARS exacted not only a steep human toll, but a severe economic one as well. Canceled travel plans quickly affected the travel and tourism industry, while general anxiety over being exposed to the disease began to hurt restaurants, retail stores, and the entertainment industry. The hardest hit were those in the affected countries in Asia, particularly China, Hong Kong, Singapore, and Taiwan. In early April passenger volume at Hong Kong international airport, normally the busiest in Asia, dropped to 50 percent of normal, and 25 percent of the flights into and out of Hong Kong were canceled. The number of visitors to Singapore fell 60 percent. Already financially unstable, Air Canada filed for bankruptcy after WHO warned people not to travel to Toronto.

The economic slowdown also affected countries that were not experiencing the disease. The Australian airline Qantas, for example, laid off 1,000 employees in early April because of the loss of business attributable to SARS. Shipments of manufactured goods from affected parts of Asia were held up or cancelled. Even places like New York's Chinatown felt the impact as people decided to avoid contact with anything Asian.

The SARS outbreak pushed Hong Kong into its third recession in six years, and Singapore teetered on the edge of recession. J.P. Morgan Chase & Company cut its forecast for economic growth in Malaysia twice in one month because of the impact of the disease. It also reported that growth in China, which had the fastest growing economy in the world, dropped from an annual rate of 10 percent in the first quarter to −2 percent in the second.

The economic downturn was particularly hard for the Asian countries that were just beginning to grow again after being swamped by a major financial crisis in 1997–1998. Fortunately for the countries involved, the SARS downturn was relatively short-lived. Hong Kong's gross domestic product grew at an annual rate 6.4 percent in the third quarter of 2003. Singapore ended the year with positive growth of 0.8 percent, and China grew at a rate of 8.5 percent. *(International economic picture, p. 751; 1997–1998 financial crisis, Historic Documents of 1998, p. 722)*

Aftermath

In the aftermath of the SARS emergency, scientists continued to hunt for the origin of the SARS virus and a vaccine to prevent it. They also searched for a better understanding of how to diagnose and treat the disease, while health officials assessed their readiness for dealing with future outbreaks of SARS or SARS-like diseases. In September WHO announced that it was testing a new surveillance program in China aimed at alerting hospitals to potential SARS cases. WHO also urged China to enact stricter regulations for its trade in exotic animals used for food, as this had been implicated as a possible source of the SARS virus.

Over initial U.S. objections, WHO won greater authority to intervene in countries that refused to admit they might be having a health crisis. WHO would no longer have to wait for a country to report a health threat before sending in an investigative team to verify whether the country was implementing adequate containment measures. The administration of George W. Bush, which had frequently balked at giving United Nations agencies additional powers, sought to postpone a discussion of the new authority but gave in when it realized that WHO had nearly universal support for the expansion.

In the United States the CDC outlined a strategy, widely lauded by the public health community, to help individual physicians cope with any future outbreak of SARS. "It's a good plan," said Georges Benjamin, the director of the American Public Health Association. "Every practicing physician needs to have a plan that answers such questions as what room are you going to use to examine someone? How will you decontaminate that room." But in December a study conducted by researchers at the University of Louisiana for the CDC concluded that the country was ill prepared to deal with a major outbreak of SARS. "The current shortage of epidemiologists, public health nurses and other personnel in the U.S. will reach a crisis stage in the event of an epidemic," the report said. "If these positions are not restored, an otherwise containable epidemic may spread rapidly."

Following are the texts of two press releases issued March 15 and 16, 2003, by the World Health Organization: first, "World Health Organization Issues Emergency Travel Advisory: Severe Acute Respiratory Syndrome (SARS) Spreads Worldwide," an announcement that Severe Acute Respiratory Syndrome had spread worldwide; second, "Severe Acute Respiratory Syndrome (SARS)—Multi-Country Outbreak—Update," a summary of outbreaks in individual countries.

"World Health Organization Issues Emergency Travel Advisory: SARS"

During the past week, WHO has received reports of more than 150 new suspected cases of Severe Acute Respiratory Syndrome (SARS), an atypical pneumonia for which cause has not yet been determined. Reports to date have been received from Canada, China, Hong Kong Special Administrative Region of China, Indonesia, Philippines, Singapore, Thailand, and Viet Nam. Early today, an ill passenger and companions who travelled from New York, United States, and who landed in Frankfurt, Germany were removed from their flight and taken to hospital isolation.

Due to the spread of SARS to several countries in a short period of time, the World Health Organization today has issued emergency guidance for travellers and airlines.

"This syndrome, SARS, is now a worldwide health threat," said Dr. Gro Harlem Brundtland, Director General of the World Health Organization. "The world needs to work together to find its cause, cure the sick, and stop its spread."

There is presently no recommendation for people to restrict travel to any destination. However in response to enquiries from governments, airlines, physicians and travellers, WHO is now offering guidance for travellers, airline crew and airlines. The exact nature of the infection is still under investigation and this guidance is based on the early information available to WHO.

Travellers Including Airline Crew: All travellers should be aware of main symptoms and signs of SARS which include:

- high fever (>38°C)

AND

- one or more respiratory symptoms including cough, shortness of breath, difficulty breathing

AND one or more of the following:

- close contact with a person who has been diagnosed with SARS [Close contact means having cared for, having lived with, or having had direct contact with respiratory secretions and body fluids of a person with SARS.]
- recent history of travel to areas reporting cases of SARS.

In the unlikely event of a traveller experiencing this combination of symptoms they should seek medical attention and ensure that information about their recent travel is passed on to the health care staff. Any traveller who develops these symptoms is advised not to undertake further travel until they have recovered.

Airlines: Should a passenger or crew member who meets the criteria above travel on a flight, the aircraft should alert the destination airport. On arrival the sick passenger should be referred to airport health authorities for assessment and management. The aircraft passengers and crew should be informed of the person's status as a suspect case of SARS. The passengers and crew should provide all contact details for the subsequent 14 days to the airport health authorities. There are currently no indications to restrict the onward travel of healthy passengers, but all passengers and crew should be advised to seek medical attention if they develop the symptoms highlighted above. There is currently no indication to provide passengers and crew with any medication or investigation unless they become ill.

In the absence of specific information regarding the nature of the organism causing this illness, specific measures to be applied to the aircraft cannot be recommended. As a general precaution the aircraft may be disinfected in the manner described in the WHO Guide to Hygiene and Sanitation in Aviation.

As more information has become available, WHO-recommended SARS case definitions have been revised as follows:

Suspect Case

A person presenting after 1 February 2003 with history of :

- high fever (>38°C)

AND

- one or more respiratory symptoms including cough, shortness of breath, difficulty breathing

AND one or more of the following:

- close contact with a person who has been diagnosed with SARS
- recent history of travel to areas reporting cases of SARS

Probable Case

A suspect case with chest x-ray findings of pneumonia or Respiratory Distress Syndrome

OR

A person with an unexplained respiratory illness resulting in death, with an autopsy examination demonstrating the pathology of Respiratory Distress Syndrome without an identifiable cause.

Comments

In addition to fever and respiratory symptoms, SARS may be associated with other symptoms including: headache, muscular stiffness, loss of appetite, malaise, confusion, rash, and diarrhea.

Until more is known about the cause of these outbreaks, WHO recommends that patients with SARS be isolated with barrier nursing techniques and treated as clinically indicated. At the same time, WHO recommends that any suspect cases be reported to national health authorities.

WHO is in close communication with all national authorities and has also offered epidemiological, laboratory and clinical support. WHO is working with national authorities to ensure appropriate investigation, reporting and containment of these outbreaks. . . .

> **Source:** World Health Organization. "World Health Organization Issues Emergency Travel Advisory: Severe Acute Respiratory Syndrome (SARS) Spreads Worldwide." Geneva, Switzerland. March 15, 2003. www.who. int/csr/don/2003_03_15/en/ (accessed June 1, 2003).

"Severe Acute Respiratory Syndrome—Multi-Country Outbreak—Update"

As of 15 March 2003, reports of over 150 cases of Severe Acute Respiratory Syndrome (SARS), an atypical pneumonia of unknown aetiology, have been received by the World Health Organization (WHO) since 26 February 2003. WHO is coordinating the international investigation of this outbreak and is working closely with health authorities in the affected countries to provide epidemiological, clinical and logistical support as required.

SARS was first recognised on the 26 February 2003 in Hanoi, Viet Nam. The causative agent has yet to be identified. The main symptoms and signs include high fever (>38 degrees C), cough, shortness of breath or breathing. A proportion of patients with SARS develop severe pneumonia; some of whom have needed ventilator support. As of 15 March, four deaths have been reported.

As of 15 March the majority of cases have occurred in people who have had very close contact with other cases and over 90% of cases have occurred in health care workers.

The mode of transmission and the causative agent have yet to be determined. Aerosol and/or droplet spread is possible as is transmission from body fluids. Respiratory isolation, strict respiratory and mucosal barrier nursing are recommended for cases. Cases should be treated as clinically indicated. . . .

An epidemic of atypical pneumonia had previously been reported by the Chinese government starting in November 2002 in Guangdong Province. This epidemic is reported to be under control.

Hanoi, Viet Nam

On the 26 February 2003, a man (index case) was admitted to hospital in Hanoi with a high fever, dry cough, myalgia and mild sore throat. Over the next four days he developed increasing breathing difficulties, severe thrombocytopenia, and signs of Adult Respiratory Distress Syndrome and required ventilator support. Despite intensive therapy he died on the 13 March after being transferred to Hong Kong Special Administrative Region of China.

On 5 March, seven health care workers who had cared for the index case also became ill (high fever, myalgia, headache and less often sore throat). The onset of illness ranged from 4 to 7 days after admission of the index case.

As of 15 March, 43 cases have been reported in Viet Nam. At least five of these patients are currently requiring ventilator support. Two deaths have occurred. With the exception of one case (the son of a health care worker) all cases to date have had direct contact with the hospital where the index case had first received treatment.

Hong Kong Special Administrative Region of China

On 12 March 2003, 20 health care workers developed influenza-like symptoms (high fever, headache and lower respiratory symptoms). Since then the number of reported cases has increased daily.

As of 15 March, over 100 reported cases have been hospitalised, at least two of whom are receiving ventilatory support. One death (index case from Viet Nam) has been reported.

Singapore

On 13 March 2003, the Ministry of Health in Singapore reported three cases of SARS in people who had recently returned to Singapore after travelling to Hong Kong Special Administrative Region of China.

As of 15 March 2003, 13 additional cases have been reported. All 13 of these cases have had very close contact with one or more of the initial three cases.

All 16 cases are reported to be in a stable condition and are being cared for in isolation.

Thailand

As of 15 March 2003, one imported case has been reported in Thailand. The case (a health care worker) travelled to Thailand on the 11 March from Hanoi, Viet Nam. The case is known to have had close contact with the Hanoi index case and to have been unwell on arrival in Thailand. The case was immediately isolated on arrival in Thailand and reported to be in a stable condition and is being cared for in isolation. There is no evidence of transmission of SARS in Thailand.

Canada

As of 15 March 2003, seven cases have been reported in Canada; two of whom have died. The cases have occurred in two separate extended family clusters. In both clusters at least one member of the family had travelled to Hong Kong Special Administrative Region of China within a week of developing symptoms.

Philippines and Indonesia

Unconfirmed reports of a single case in the Philippines to date. However one close contact of the Hanoi index case is under observation in an isolation facility. This person is reported to be well.

Unconfirmed reports of a single case in Indonesia were received on the 15 March. However further reports have confirmed that this person does not fulfill the case definition. As of 16 March, there are therefore no reported cases in Indonesia.

New York, USA—Frankfurt, Germany

On 15 March 2003, a health care worker from Singapore who was visiting New York boarded a flight from New York to Frankfurt. The health care worker was known to be unwell and to have had recent close contact with a reported case of SARS in Singapore. German health authorities were notified and the health care worker was transferred to an isolation unit in Frankfurt as soon as the flight landed. There is no evidence of transmission in Germany.

Laboratory Investigation

Various specimens have been collected from cases and post-mortum examinations. A wide range of laboratory tests have been conducted to date but no agent has been definitively identified. Laboratory investigations are continuing.

International Response

WHO is assisting affected countries in responding to the various outbreaks. Extensive epidemiological and clinical investigation are ongoing in all affected countries.

WHO/Global Outbreak Alert and Response Network team of epidemiologists, case management, infection control experts and laboratory experts is assisting the Vietnamese health authorities. The following organisations are contributing personnel and materials to the Hanoi team:

* Centers for Disease Control and Prevention, Atlanta, United States
* Centre of International Health, Australia
* Epicentre
* Institut National de Veille Sanitaire, France
* Institut Pasteur, France and Viet Nam
* Médecins Sans Frontières
* National Health Service, Department of Health, United Kingdom
* Robert Koch Institute, Germany
* Central Field Epidemiology Group Smittskyddsinstitutet (SMI), Sweden

Bilateral assistance has also been mobilised from France and Japan. WHO is providing epidemiological support to health authorities in Hong Kong.

Travel Advice

There is presently no recommendations to restrict travel to any destination. However, guidance has been issued by WHO and is available.

Further Information

Throughout this outbreak, WHO plans to update its web site on a daily basis.

> **Source:** World Health Organization. "Severe Acute Respiratory Syndrome (SARS)—Multi-Country Outbreak—Update." Geneva, Switzerland. March 16, 2003. www.who.int/csr/don/2003_03_16/en/ (accessed June 1, 2003).

President Bush on the
Prospect of War with Iraq

March 17 and 19, 2003

INTRODUCTION

After months of signaling his intentions, President George W. Bush in late March launched a war that quickly toppled the regime of Iraqi leader Saddam Hussein. Bush on March 17 demanded that Saddam leave Iraq within forty-eight hours. Two days later, when Saddam refused to comply, Bush ordered air strikes against Baghdad, quickly followed by a full-scale land invasion by more than 150,000 U.S. and British troops. U.S. troops gained control of most of Baghdad on April 9, symbolically ending Saddam's twenty-four years as Iraq's dictatorial leader. Saddam himself was not captured until December; he was found hiding in a hole at a farmhouse in central Iraq. In the meantime, the U.S. military battled with the remnants of Saddam's regime. The U.S.-led occupying authority had mixed success in providing the basics of daily life for war-weary Iraqi citizens, and Iraq's political and religious leaders bickered over the country's future. *(Prewar diplomacy, p. 40; postwar Iraq, pp. 933, 1189)*

In many ways the Iraq war of 2003 brought to completion the Persian Gulf War of 1991. The United States and dozens of allies had waged the earlier war to expel invading Iraqi forces from neighboring Kuwait. But the U.S. president at that time—Bush's father, George H.W. Bush—had heeded the advice of his generals and allies not to take the war to Baghdad. The junior Bush heeded the advice of many of his aides, who argued that Saddam still posed a threat, not only to his neighbors but also to the United States and its allies. *(Persian Gulf War, Historic Documents of 1991, p. 101)*

A Final Warning

By mid-March few people doubted that an invasion of Iraq was about to begin. Tens of thousands of U.S. and British troops were massed in Kuwait waiting for instructions to cross the border, and five U.S. aircraft carrier battle groups were positioned within striking range of Iraq. One of the doubters, if later reports from some of his aides were accurate, was Saddam Hussein. Scurrying several times each day among his palaces and underground bunkers in the Baghdad area, listening only to a handful of trusted aides, Saddam may have believed that Bush was bluffing, that a last-minute deal might somehow avert a war, that his armies would repel the invaders, or possibly even that he could survive the U.S. onslaught and then return to power once his enemies in Washington lost interest in Iraq.

Saddam apparently did not believe Bush's words on March 17, broadcast live around the world at 8 P.M. eastern standard time. Bush announced that Saddam and his two sons "must leave Iraq within forty-eight hours. Their refusal to do so will result in military conflict, commenced at a time of our choosing." Addressing other Iraqis, Bush said: "The tyrant will soon be gone. The day of your liberation is near."

Fifty hours and fifteen minutes later, again speaking from the White House, Bush announced that U.S. and allied forces "are in the early stages of military operations to disarm Iraq, to free its people, and to defend the world from grave danger." The president had authorized an initial round of air strikes in hopes of killing Saddam and had given his generals the go-ahead for the long-planned land invasion of Iraq.

"Now that conflict has come, the only way to limit its duration is to apply decisive force," Bush told the world. "And I assure you, this will not be a campaign of half measures, and we will accept no outcome but victory."

Shifting, and Disputed, Rationales for War

To a greater degree than any other recent conflict involving U.S. forces, the war in Iraq was justified on grounds that shifted periodically and were challenged by some allies as well as by some of the evidence accumulated by intelligence agencies. According to opinion polls, Bush succeeded in convincing most Americans that the war was justified and necessary. His most important international ally—British prime minister Tony Blair—faced substantial public opposition and found himself on the defensive about the war all through the rest of the year. Opinion polls in most other countries showed intense opposition to Bush's war plans.

From the standpoint of international law, Bush's principal argument was that Iraq had flaunted more than a dozen United Nations Security Council resolutions requiring it to dispose of biological and chemical weapons, as well as medium-range missiles, that it was presumed to have developed before the 1991 Persian Gulf War. Iraq in 1995 admitted having produced large quantities of these weapons but insisted all had been destroyed during or right after the 1991 war—a claim that few international observers believed. The United States also insisted that Iraq had resumed its attempt to develop nuclear weapons in violation of UN resolutions.

UN weapons inspectors, who returned to Iraq in November 2002 after an absence of four years, found limited evidence of work on biological and chemical weapons and discovered that Iraq had produced missiles with a slightly greater range than allowed by UN resolutions. The inspectors found no evidence that Iraq had made substantial progress in building nuclear weapons, however.

Bush's critics said the inspectors should be allowed to continue their work, but by February senior U.S. officials were arguing that military force was the only way to get Iraq to give up its banned weapons. The UN inspections were halted just before the outbreak of the war in March. Following the war, U.S. intelligence and military agencies took over the task of looking for Iraq's banned weapons, but by year's end there had been no significant findings. The futility of the weapons search led Bush and his aides to play down the issue in the months after the war. *(Weapons inspections, p. 874)*

Bush's second, somewhat related, line of argument in favor of war was that Iraq had aligned itself with terrorist groups and might give or sell its weapons of mass destruction to terrorists, who could use them against the United States or its allies. In all his speeches about Iraq, Bush placed his confrontation with Saddam Hussein within the context of the war against terrorism that began after the September 11, 2001, attacks against the United States. "The danger is clear: using chemical, biological, or, one day, nuclear weapons obtained with the help of Iraq, the terrorists could fulfill their stated ambitions and kill thousands or hundreds of thousands of innocent people in our country or any other," Bush said in his March 17 "ultimatum" speech. The evidence for this argument was tenuous and subject to a great deal of dispute, both within the U.S. government and internationally. Most experts on terrorism noted that Saddam, a secularist, had little in common with Islamist terrorists and in recent years had not shown any inclination to give weapons or other support to them (an exception was his support for the Abu Nidal Palestinian terrorist faction in the 1970s and 1980s). CIA director George J. Tenet, for example, told Congress in 2002 that Saddam was likely to give biological and chemical weapons to terrorist groups only if he was under threat of an imminent attack.

Bush on occasion cited a third argument for what U.S. officials euphemistically called "regime change" in Iraq: Ending Saddam's tyranny would result in the formation of a democratic government in Iraq. The president offered no evidence for this expectation, and in fact took the argument much further. A democratic government in Iraq, he said in January, "would serve as a dramatic and inspiring example of freedom for other nations in the region." Some of Bush's aides said the democratic example set by a "new" Iraq would prove to skeptics that Arabs were capable of creating and living with democracy, would unleash powerful forces of reform in the Middle East, and would lead ultimately to the toppling of other long-entrenched dictatorships and the creation of democratic, forward-looking societies that would live in peace with one another (including Israel). Breath-taking in its scope, this idealistic vision of a transformed Middle East was greeted with skepticism by most experts on the region, but it did generate support for the war from some liberals in the United States and internationally who normally opposed Bush's policies.

Assembling a "Coalition" for War

For months Bush had said he preferred, and expected, to have allies for any war in Iraq but would go it alone if necessary. Despite this unilateral-ist rhetoric, some cooperation from other countries was essential. A massive land invasion of Iraq had to start from somewhere nearby, and Kuwait and Turkey were the obvious locations. Long-range U.S. bombers would have to fly over the airspace of a dozen or more countries, each of which would have to give its permission for the overflights. A U.S.-only war would have stretched the country's all-volunteer military to the breaking point, forc-ing the Pentagon to pour into Iraq the bulk of its active forces and an unac-ceptably high portion of its reserve and national guard units.

Bush began his quest for international support with one significant ally, British prime minister Tony Blair, who had used similar arguments for con-fronting and, if necessary, ousting Saddam Hussein from power. Blair com-mitted 44,000 British Marines to the war, constituting about one-fourth of the total ground forces that would invade Iraq. Australian prime minister John Howard echoed the Bush-Blair sentiments about Iraq and sent 3,000 troops to the region. In January and February Bush won diplomatic sup-port for war from seventeen other European countries, only one of which (Poland) had an army large enough to contribute more than a few hundred troops to combat or support missions.

The cooperation of Kuwait was never in doubt. The victims of Iraq's inva-sion in 1990, Kuwaitis were still anxious for the removal of Saddam, who they suspected had never truly given up his claim on their country as Iraq's "nineteenth province." Large contingents of U.S. and British armed forces arrived in Kuwait during late 2002 to begin training and logistical prepara-tions for the invasion of Iraq.

Saudi Arabia, the major staging ground for the 1991 Persian Gulf War, played a much smaller role in 2003. By mutual agreement, the United States was in the process of winding down its military operations in the kingdom, and Saudi leaders were anxious to avoid appearing as cooper-ating too closely with the invasion of an Arab neighbor. *(Saudi Arabia devel-opments, p. 227)*

The last major ally whose participation was needed was Turkey—Iraq's neighbor to the north. Pentagon planners had long expected that Ankara would allow more than 60,000 troops, including the U.S. Army's Fourth Infantry Division, to cross Turkish territory as they headed to open a northern front against Iraq. The Pentagon sent two dozen cargo ships with all the division's tanks and heavy equipment to Turkey, where they arrived in late February. But on March 1 a motion to allow the U.S. deployment failed in Turkey's parliament by a margin of three votes. The rebuff was a major embarrassment for Ankara's new Islamist government, which had been promised $6 billion in U.S. aid in exchange for Turkey's cooperation in the war. The parliament did agree at the last minute, on March 20, to allow U.S. planes to use Turkish airspace for combat missions in Iraq, and on April 2 Turkey approved the use of its territory for shipments of food, fuel, medicine, and other nonmilitary supplies to U.S. forces in Iraq. Also, Turkey ultimately heeded U.S. pleas that it keep its own troops out of northern Iraq. Turkey had long insisted that it would not allow Kurds to establish an independent state in northern Iraq—thus formalizing a de facto Iraqi Kurdistan that had existed for several years—for fear that this would inflame the nationalist aspirations of Kurds living in Turkey. Early in April, under U.S. pressure, Turkey backed off threats to invade northern Iraq to prevent the consolidation of Kurdish control of that region.

Early Days of the War

Although it had been clear for weeks that a war was inevitable, the United States managed to introduce elements of surprise into the actual start of fighting. After Bush on March 17 issued his ultimatum demanding that Saddam and his two sons leave Iraq within forty-eight hours, it was widely assumed that the first strike against Iraq would take place at least three days later—so Bush could argue that he had given Saddam plenty of time to comply. But Bush gave the go-ahead for the first air strikes on Baghdad on the evening of May 19 (the predawn hours of March 20 in Iraq), just after the forty-eight hour deadline expired. Bush acted in response to an intelligence tip that Saddam was meeting with his sons and other top aides in a house in southern Baghdad. U.S. cruise missiles destroyed the house, causing a display of explosions shown on television around the world but failing to kill the Iraqi leader, who apparently had moved elsewhere.

U.S. and British ground forces began their assault on Iraq in the morning of March 20 (Iraq time), with the first convoys of tanks, armored personnel carriers, and other vehicles crossing the heavily fortified border between Kuwait and Iraq. Overhead, a handful of Iraqi missiles flew toward coalition positions in Kuwait (with one landing near the headquarters of the First Marine Expeditionary Force), while scores of coalition planes and missiles attacked key Iraqi military installations.

In the weeks leading up to the 2003 war, many military experts had predicted that the United States and Britain would precede the ground assault with a massive display of aerial bombardment, often referred to as "shock and awe" after the name of a book predicting the future of warfare. The experts said the use of use of so-called smart (electronically targeted) bombs and missiles would be more effective in quickly disabling Iraqi forces than the thirty-nine-day aerial bombardment that preceded the ground assault of the 1991 Persian Gulf War had been. Missiles and bombs hit Baghdad and other targets from March 19 onward—often producing huge explosions that television networks showed endlessly—but the opening days of the 2003 war failed to produce the spectacular aerial fireworks that military analysts had predicted.

U.S. military officials said the experts simply had overdramatized the expectations for the results of an initial air assault on Saddam's centers of power. The goal of the initial air strikes, according to the Pentagon, was to damage specific targets at the center of the Iraqi regime in hopes that some of Saddam's key aides might try to overthrow him, or at least that some generals might surrender to save themselves. Officials also said Bush agreed to speed up the land-based portion of the invasion because of reports that several oil wells in southern Iraq had been set ablaze. U.S. Marines arrived at the huge Rumaila oilfield in time to prevent wide-scale sabotage; only nine of the more than one thousand wells had been torched. Meanwhile, U.S. Special Operations forces—some of whom had been operating secretly in Iraq for weeks—moved to take over remote airfields and other military targets that were poorly defended by Iraqi troops.

The land assault from Kuwait was launched in three major directions. Forces headed straight for Baghdad, with the U.S. Army's Third Infantry Division spearheading the charge along the Euphrates River to the southwest of the capital and the U.S. First Marine Division generally following the Tigris River to the southeast. Separately, British marines headed toward Basra, Iraq's second-largest city, just north of the Kuwait border, and the port city of Umm Qasr at the head of the Persian Gulf.

All the land forces moved quickly at first, encountering only modest resistance. After just one day U.S. troops had covered one-third of the distance to Baghdad, and Umm Qasr had been captured (although not fully pacified) by March 23. British marines laid siege to Basra but did not gain substantial control there until the first week of April.

Intense desert sandstorms slowed the infantry advance on March 24 and plagued military operations for several days afterwards. The Iraqi government also scored a temporary public relations coup on March 24 by showing televised footage of two U.S. pilots who had been captured after their Apache helicopter—one of the army's most sophisticated weapons—was downed near the city of Karbala southwest of Baghdad.

During the run-up to the war, Vice President Dick Cheney had been the most vocal among senior U.S. officials who confidently predicted that many Iraqi civilians, and even soldiers, would greet the coalition forces as "liberators." Officials were especially certain of a warm reception from the majority of Iraqis, concentrated in the southern half of the country, who adhered to the Shi'ite branch of Islam. Because Saddam's government, consisting mostly of Sunni Muslims, had brutally suppressed them, the Shi'ites were thought to be anxious for the dictator's overthrow.

Advancing coalition forces encountered many friendly Iraqis but nothing like the throngs of cheering people Cheney and others in Washington had expected. A more common reaction among Iraqis appeared to be an insistent demand that the United States quickly provide the food, electricity, and most importantly jobs that had been so scarce during the previous two decades of war and international sanctions.

The coalition met another reaction that war-planners apparently had not expected: gangs of well-armed, fiercely determined resistance fighters who suddenly appeared from among the civilian population, ambushed U.S. and British forces in the dead of night, then melted back into the populace. Reportedly organized by Saddam's son Uday, these fighters were known as the "Saddam *fedayeen,*" or volunteers for Saddam.

The severity of these militia attacks apparently stunned coalition commanders, who had been prepared for set-piece battles with large Iraqi military units but not for guerrilla warfare. Lieutenant General William Wallace, commander of U.S. ground forces in Iraq, on March 30 set off an uproar in the news media by telling reporters that coalition forces were facing a different, more determined, enemy than the war plans had suggested. This comment, coupled with criticism of the Pentagon's tactics from some of the retired generals hired as war analysts by television networks, produced several days of public doubt about the course of the war. During this same period U.S. and British forces found themselves facing unexpected resistance in Iraq's southern cities. In the end, however, the fierce guerrilla resistance caused only a minor delay in the inevitable course of the war, proving to be more of a distraction than a serious obstacle for the U.S. military. Iraq's regular military, including the once-powerful Republican Guard, put up scattered resistance throughout the war, but it had never been fully reconstructed after the 1991 Persian Gulf War and was heavily pounded by coalition bombs and missiles. Iraqi warplanes never took to the skies to challenge the invaders; indeed, Baghdad had ordered some of its planes buried in hopes of shielding them from American bombers.

Yet another surprise, at least to some, was something that did not happen during the war: The Iraqi military did not attack coalition forces with the biological and chemical weapons that Bush insisted Saddam had been hiding from UN weapons inspectors. During much of the war coalition troops donned hot and heavy protective gear in anticipation of attacks by poison gas or biological toxins that never came.

One of the war's most memorable dramas began March 23, when twelve U.S. army soldiers went missing after their supply convoy was ambushed near the southern city of Nasiriyah. Iraqi television later aired footage of five of the soldiers, who had been captured, along with what appeared to be the bodies of five others. One week later, acting on a tip from an Iraqi civilian, U.S. special operations forces raided a hospital in Nasiriyah and rescued one of the missing soldiers, Private Jessica Lynch, a nineteen-year-old army supply clerk. Pentagon photographs of the pretty, blonde soldier strapped onto a flag-draped cot being loaded into a helicopter captured the country's attention and gave Americans a heroic figure to celebrate. Sensationalized news reports said Lynch had suffered numerous wounds while trying to fight off her captors. After recovering from her ordeal, Lynch said she had little memory of the events leading to her capture but, in any event, denied the reports that she had fought against the Iraqi military unit.

Driving onto Baghdad

With U.S. and British forces still struggling to overcome surprisingly strong resistance in the south, the Bush administration decided on March 29 to stick to the original plan of concentrating on capturing Baghdad. This meant sending army and marine units north even as fighting was continuing along the supply lines to their rear, a potentially dangerous move usually shunned by the military. Officials reportedly concluded that the possible payoff—the rapid capture of Baghdad and the overthrow of Saddam's regime—was worth the risk.

The gamble paid off. A classic pincer movement, with army forces approaching from one direction and marines from another, forced Saddam to divide his already-weakened forces. After a remarkably fast three-day sprint, the Third Infantry Division reached the Baghdad airport west of the city on April 3, achieving a military objective that, in modern times, usually meant the capital city itself would fall after the defenders realized they had no hope of survival. Then came another surprising move. Rather than adopting the classic procedure of surrounding the city and mounting a siege, the army's generals decided to plunge right in. Beginning on April 6, small units of tanks and other armored vehicles pushed into the city and encountered surprisingly little resistance. The U.S. Army found few of the obstacles—such as antitank trenches, landmines, and destroyed bridges—that defenders usually employ to slow the advance of attackers.

In terms of symbolism, the climax of the war came on April 9 when U.S. forces gained effective control of much of Baghdad. The city's fall came swiftly when marines entered from the eastern suburbs and joined army brigades that controlled the western and southern portions of the city. U.S. forces quickly occupied key government installations and symbols of Saddam's power, including some of his many palaces. The capture of the city finally ignited the jubilation among Iraqis—especially in the poorer parts of the capital—that U.S. officials had predicted. Thousands of cheering people greeted the American troops.

The event that most symbolized Saddam's fall from power was the toppling of a thirty-foot-tall, cast iron statue in central Baghdad depicting the dictator in a triumphal pose, his right arm raised in a salute. After three Iraqis wrapped a noose around the statue's neck, U.S. Marines attached the rope to a tank and pulled "Saddam" to the ground. Jubilant men and boys spat on the statue and attacked it with garbage and shoes (an Arab insult), wreaking on this stand-in for Saddam the vengeance so many Iraqis had long sought against the dictator.

Saddam himself disappeared and was presumed to have fled to his home area of Tikrit, north of the capital, generally considered the base of his support among Iraq's Sunni minority. The marines moved quickly into Tikrit and gained effective control of that city. Army soldiers found the bedraggled former dictator eight months later, on December 12, hiding in a hole at a farmhouse a few miles south of Tikrit. *(Capture of Saddam, p. 1189)*

The dark side of the capture of Baghdad was the collapse of government authority, which enabled criminal gangs and desperate Iraqis to engage in unrestrained looting for several days. All government offices, and many private buildings left unprotected by the U.S. military, were looted down to the bare walls. Gangs also broke into the national library and museum, looting thousands of books and many priceless antiquities. Initial reports suggested that the museum had been stripped of nearly all its valuable holdings, but subsequent inventories revealed that many items had been saved, and hundreds of others were found or returned.

Bush Declares an End to Major Combat

The Pentagon announced on April 14 that the bulk of the fighting in Iraq was finished. "The major combat operations are over, because the major Iraqi units on the ground cease to show coherence," Major General Stanley McChrystal, vice director of the Pentagon's joint staff told reporters in Washington. Navy ships, including two of the five aircraft carrier battle groups that had taken part in the war, and many of the air force planes that had dropped thousands of bombs and missiles on Iraq, headed to their home bases by mid-April. But even as these units left the region, others were just beginning their deployment in Iraq. The U.S. Army's Fourth Infantry Division, which was to have spearheaded a northern front until its deployment was blocked by Turkey, arrived in Kuwait after the fall of Baghdad and began heading into Iraq a few days later. The First Armored Division began its move into Iraq early in May. The arrival of these army units enabled the Pentagon to withdraw the marines and some of the army units that had been in the region for months and had borne the brunt of the fighting.

The White House, which carefully choreographed all of Bush's appearances, used every theatrical technique at its disposal in arranging for a dramatic announcement by the president that the main fighting in Iraq was over. On May 1 Bush flew in a navy jet to the aircraft carrier *Abraham Lincoln,* which was then steaming toward San Diego Harbor, and stepped out of the cockpit wearing a pilot's flight suit. In a twenty-minute speech to the sailors aboard the carrier, broadcast live by television, Bush stopped just short of declaring victory but said "major combat operations in Iraq have ended." Even so, the president again placed the Iraq war in the context of the "war on terror" he had declared after the September 11 attacks. "The liberation of Iraq is a crucial advance in the campaign against terror," he said. "We have removed an ally of al Qaeda, and cut off a course of terrorist funding. And this much is certain: No terrorist network will gain weapons of mass destruction from the Iraqi regime, because that regime is no more." The president did not mention international criticism of the Iraq war, including from such key allies as France and Germany, nor did he discuss the heated debate within the United Nations that preceded the conflict. Bush cited just three allies who, he said, "shared in the hardships of war": Australia, Britain, and Poland.

Obviously intended by the White House as a jumping-off point for Bush's 2004 reelection campaign, Bush's appearance on the aircraft carrier later became something of an embarrassment for the administration. As the chaos of postwar Iraq deepened in late October, news reports disputed the White House version of who had arranged for the posting on the carrier of a huge "Mission Accomplished" banner, which served as a backdrop for Bush's speech. White House officials had insisted at the time that sailors had put the banner on the ship, but it was later revealed that the banner actually was a product of the administration's public relations apparatus.

In another development clearly not intended by the White House, the president's May 1 speech served as an important dividing line for the counting of U.S. war casualties. As of May 1, 115 U.S. service personnel had died in combat. From May 1 through the rest of 2003 an additional 212 U.S. personnel were killed in hostilities (such as bombings or firefights with guerrillas). By year's end, a total of 2,751 U.S. personnel had been injured in Iraq. Britain forces suffered 52 deaths, and other countries reported a total of 35 deaths among troops in Iraq during 2003.

Civilian Casualties

In his March 19 speech announcing the war, Bush pledged that coalition forces "will make every effort to spare innocent civilians from harm." The careful wording of that statement recognized that some civilians inevitably would be harmed in a conflict as large as the invasion of Iraq. Several thousand civilians did die, and many more were wounded, in the first month of large-scale combat and in the months of instability that followed. As of year's end, no official estimates of civilian casualties had been made by the U.S. government or other agencies in Iraq. Shortly after the war, the Associated Press (AP) canvassed sixty Iraqi hospitals and estimated that at least 3,400 Iraqi civilians died. Acknowledging that its survey was "fragmentary," the AP said the actual total "is sure to be significantly higher." Another survey, by the *Los Angeles Times,* of twenty-seven hospitals in Baghdad and surrounding areas found at least 1,700 deaths and more than 8,000 war-related injuries among civilians.

Counting civilian casualties was difficult enough, but assigning responsibility for them was virtually impossible. During the conflict each side accused the other of endangering civilians. The Iraqi government insisted that U.S. bombs and missiles were deliberately aimed at residential neighborhoods in Baghdad. In turn, U.S. and British military officials said Iraq had used civilians as "human shields" against attack and had placed military installations in neighborhoods, knowing they would be targeted.

In a report issued December 12, Human Rights Watch said its investigations in Iraq, between late April and early June, had found that both sides had caused civilian casualties. Iraqi forces, the group said, had "committed a number of violations of international humanitarian law," for example by locating ammunition dumps in mosques and hospitals and by having some military units wear civilian clothing. Coalition forces "took precautions to spare civilians," Human Rights Watch said, but still caused many civilian deaths and injuries. In particular, the group faulted U.S. and British forces for using thousands of "cluster bombs" (each containing dozens or hundreds of tiny bomblets). Coalition ground forces "repeatedly used these weapons in attacks on Iraqi positions in residential areas," resulting in an unknown number of civilian casualties, the group said.

Following are the texts of two documents: first, a speech by President George W. Bush, delivered from the White House on March 17, 2003, setting an ultimatum for Iraqi leader Saddam Hussein and his sons to leave the country within forty-eight hours; second, a speech by President Bush, delivered from the White House on March 19, 2003, announcing that U.S. and British forces had begun attacking Iraq.

President Bush's Address to the Nation on Iraq, March 17, 2003

My fellow citizens, events in Iraq have now reached the final days of decision. For more than a decade, the United States and other nations have pursued patient and honorable efforts to disarm the Iraqi regime without war. That regime pledged to reveal and destroy all its weapons of mass destruction as a condition for ending the Persian Gulf war in 1991.

Since then, the world has engaged in 12 years of diplomacy. We have passed more than a dozen resolutions in the United Nations Security Council. We have sent hundreds of weapons inspectors to oversee the disarmament of Iraq. Our good faith has not been returned.

The Iraqi regime has used diplomacy as a ploy to gain time and advantage. It has uniformly defied Security Council resolutions demanding full disarmament. Over the years, U.N. weapon inspectors have been threatened by Iraqi officials, electronically bugged, and systematically deceived. Peaceful efforts to disarm the Iraqi regime have failed again and again because we are not dealing with peaceful men.

Intelligence gathered by this and other governments leaves no doubt that the Iraq regime continues to possess and conceal some of the most lethal weapons ever devised. This regime has already used weapons of mass destruction against Iraq's neighbors and against Iraq's people.

The regime has a history of reckless aggression in the Middle East. It has a deep hatred of America and our friends. And it has aided, trained, and harbored terrorists, including operatives of Al Qaida.

The danger is clear: Using chemical, biological or, one day, nuclear weapons obtained with the help of Iraq, the terrorists could fulfill their stated ambitions and kill thousands or hundreds of thousands of innocent people in our country or any other.

The United States and other nations did nothing to deserve or invite this threat. But we will do everything to defeat it. Instead of drifting along toward tragedy, we will set a course toward safety. Before the day of horror can come, before it is too late to act, this danger will be removed.

The United States of America has the sovereign authority to use force in assuring its own national security. That duty falls to me as Commander in Chief, by the oath I have sworn, by the oath I will keep.

Recognizing the threat to our country, the United States Congress voted overwhelmingly last year to support the use of force against Iraq. America tried to work with the United Nations to address this threat because we wanted to resolve the issue peacefully. We believe in the mission of the United Nations. One reason the U.N. was founded after the Second World War was to confront aggressive dictators actively and early, before they can attack the innocent and destroy the peace.

In the case of Iraq, the Security Council did act in the early 1990s. Under Resolutions 678 and 687, both still in effect, the United States and our allies are authorized to use force in ridding Iraq of weapons of mass destruction. This is not a question of authority. It is a question of will.

Last September, I went to the U.N. General Assembly and urged the nations of the world to unite and bring an end to this danger. On November 8th, the Security Council unanimously passed Resolution 1441, finding Iraq in material breach of its obligations and vowing serious consequences if Iraq did not fully and immediately disarm.

Today, no nation can possibly claim that Iraq has disarmed, and it will not disarm so long as Saddam Hussein holds power. For the last 4 1/2 months, the United States and our allies have worked within the Security Council to enforce that Council's longstanding demands. Yet, some permanent members of the Security Council have publicly announced they will veto any resolution that compels the disarmament of Iraq. These governments share our assessment of the danger but not our resolve to meet it.

Many nations, however, do have the resolve and fortitude to act against this threat to peace, and a broad coalition is now gathering to enforce the just demands of the world. The United Nations Security Council has not lived up to its responsibilities, so we will rise to ours.

In recent days, some governments in the Middle East have been doing their part. They have delivered public and private messages urging the dictator to leave Iraq, so that disarmament can proceed peacefully. He has thus far refused.

All the decades of deceit and cruelty have now reached an end. Saddam Hussein and his sons must leave Iraq within 48 hours. Their refusal to do so will result in military conflict, commenced at a time of our choosing. For their own safety, all foreign nationals, including journalists and inspectors, should leave Iraq immediately.

Many Iraqis can hear me tonight in a translated radio broadcast, and I have a message for them: If we must begin a military campaign, it will be directed against the lawless men who rule your country and not against you. As our coalition takes away their power, we will deliver the food and medicine you need. We will tear down the apparatus of terror, and we will help you to build a new Iraq that is prosperous and free. In a free Iraq, there will be no more wars of aggression against your neighbors, no more poison factories, no more executions of dissidents, no more torture chambers and rape rooms. The tyrant will soon be gone. The day of your liberation is near.

It is too late for Saddam Hussein to remain in power. It is not too late for the Iraqi military to act with honor and protect your country by permitting the peaceful entry of coalition forces to eliminate weapons of mass destruction. Our forces will give Iraqi military units clear instructions on actions they can take to avoid being attacked and destroyed. I urge every member of the Iraqi military and intelligence services: If war comes, do not fight for a dying regime that is not worth your own life.

And all Iraqi military and civilian personnel should listen carefully to this warning: In any conflict, your fate will depend on your actions. Do not destroy oil wells, a source of wealth that belongs to the Iraqi people. Do not obey any command to use weapons of mass destruction against anyone, including the Iraqi people. War crimes will be prosecuted. War criminals will be punished. And it will be no defense to say, "I was just following orders."

Should Saddam Hussein choose confrontation, the American people can know that every measure has been taken to avoid war and every measure will be taken to win it. Americans understand the costs of conflict because we have paid them in the past. War has no certainty, except the certainty of sacrifice. Yet, the only way to reduce the harm and duration of war is to apply the full force and might of our military, and we are prepared to do so.

If Saddam Hussein attempts to cling to power, he will remain a deadly foe until the end. In desperation, he and terrorist groups might try to conduct terrorist operations against the American people and our friends. These attacks are not inevitable. They are, however, possible. And this very fact underscores the reason we cannot live under the threat of blackmail. The terrorist threat to America and the world will be diminished the moment that Saddam Hussein is disarmed.

Our Government is on heightened watch against these dangers. Just as we are preparing to ensure victory in Iraq, we are taking further actions to protect our homeland. In recent days, American authorities have expelled from the country certain individuals with ties to Iraqi intelligence services. Among other measures, I have directed additional security of our airports and increased Coast Guard patrols of major seaports. The Department of Homeland Security is working closely with the Nation's Governors to increase armed security at critical facilities across America.

Should enemies strike our country, they would be attempting to shift our attention with panic and weaken our morale with fear. In this, they would fail. No act of theirs can alter the course or shake the resolve of this country. We are a peaceful people. Yet we're not a fragile people, and we will not be intimidated by thugs and killers. If our enemies dare to strike us, they and all who have aided them will face fearful consequences.

We are now acting because the risks of inaction would be far greater. In 1 year, or 5 years, the power of Iraq to inflict harm on all free nations would be multiplied many times over. With these capabilities, Saddam Hussein and his terrorist allies could choose the moment of deadly conflict when they are strongest. We choose to meet that threat now, where it arises, before it can appear suddenly in our skies and cities.

The cause of peace requires all free nations to recognize new and undeniable realities. In the 20th century, some chose to appease murderous dictators, whose threats were allowed to grow into genocide and global war. In this century, when evil men plot chemical, biological, and nuclear terror, a policy of appeasement could bring destruction of a kind never before seen on this Earth.

Terrorists and terror states do not reveal these threats with fair notice, in formal declarations, and responding to such enemies only after they have struck first is not self-defense; it is suicide. The security of the world requires disarming Saddam Hussein now.

As we enforce the just demands of the world, we will also honor the deepest commitments of our country. Unlike Saddam Hussein, we believe the Iraqi people are deserving and capable of human liberty. And when the dictator has departed, they can set an example to all the Middle East of a vital and peaceful and self-governing nation.

The United States, with other countries, will work to advance liberty and peace in that region. Our goal will not be achieved overnight, but it can come over time. The power and appeal of human liberty is felt in every life and every land. And the greatest power of freedom is to overcome hatred and violence and turn the creative gifts of men and women to the pursuits of peace.

That is the future we choose. Free nations have a duty to defend our people by uniting against the violent. And tonight, as we have done before, America and our allies accept that responsibility.

Good night, and may God continue to bless America.

Source: Bush, George W. "Address to the Nation on Iraq." *Weekly Compilation of Presidential Documents* 39, no. 12 (March 24, 2003): 338–341. Washington, D.C., National Archives and Records Administration. http://frwebgate.access.gpo.gov/cgi-bin/getdoc.cgi?dbname=2003_presidential_documents&docid=pd24mr03_txt-9 (accessed July 18, 2003).

President Bush's Address to the Nation on Iraq, March 19, 2003

My fellow citizens, at this hour, American and coalition forces are in the early stages of military operations to disarm Iraq, to free its people, and to defend the world from grave danger.

On my orders, coalition forces have begun striking selected targets of military importance to undermine Saddam Hussein's ability to wage war. These are opening stages of what will be a broad and concerted campaign. More than 35 countries are giving crucial support, from the use of naval and air bases, to help with intelligence and logistics, to the deployment of combat units. Every nation in this coalition has chosen to bear the duty and share the honor of serving in our common defense.

To all the men and women of the United States Armed Forces now in the Middle East, the peace of a troubled world and the hopes of an oppressed people now depend on you. That trust is well placed. The enemies you confront will come to know your skill and bravery. The people you liberate will witness the honorable and decent spirit of the American military.

In this conflict, America faces an enemy who has no regard for conventions of war or rules of morality. Saddam Hussein has placed Iraqi troops and equipment in civilian areas, attempting to use innocent men, women, and children as shields for his own military, a final atrocity against his people.

I want Americans and all the world to know that coalition forces will make every effort to spare innocent civilians from harm. A campaign on the harsh terrain of a nation as large as California could be longer and more difficult than some predict. And helping Iraqis achieve a united, stable, and free country will require our sustained commitment.

We come to Iraq with respect for its citizens, for their great civilization, and for the religious faiths they practice. We have no ambition in Iraq, except to remove a threat and restore control of that country to its own people.

I know that the families of our military are praying that all those who serve will return safely and soon. Millions of Americans are praying with you for the safety of your loved ones and for the protection of the inno-cent. For your sacrifice, you have the gratitude and respect of the American people. And you can know that our forces will be coming home as soon as their work is done.

Our Nation enters this conflict reluctantly. Yet our purpose is sure. The people of the United States and our friends and allies will not live at the mercy of an outlaw regime that threatens the peace with weapons of mass murder. We will meet that threat now, with our Army, Air Force, Navy, Coast Guard and Marines, so that we do not have to meet it later with armies of firefighters and police and doctors on the streets of our cities.

Now that conflict has come, the only way to limit its duration is to apply decisive force. And I assure you, this will not be a campaign of half measures, and we will accept no outcome but victory.

My fellow citizens, the dangers to our country and the world will be overcome. We will pass through this time of peril and carry on the work of peace. We will defend our freedom. We will bring freedom to others, and we will prevail.

May God bless our country and all who defend her.

Source: Bush, George W. "Address to the Nation on Iraq." *Weekly Compilation of Presidential Documents* 39, no. 12 (March 24, 2003: 342–343. Washington, D.C., National Archives and Records Administration. http://frwebgate.access.gpo.gov/cgi-bin/getdoc.cgi?dbname=2003_presidential_ documents&docid=pd24mr03_txt-15 (accessed July 18, 2003).

April

GAO on Integrating Terrorist Watch Lists

April 15, 2003

INTRODUCTION

Despite calls from President George W. Bush for the creation of a "consolidated terrorism watch list" in his July 16, 2002, homeland security strategy report, little progress occurred until a report released April 30, 2003, by the General Accounting Office (GAO) called attention to the fact that the watch lists had not been integrated and that major technological barriers had to be overcome before the process could be completed.

Stung by continuing criticisms that key federal agencies were unable and sometimes unwilling to share information about suspected international terrorists, President Bush on September 16, 2003, ordered the Department of Homeland Security (DHS) to create a single terrorist "watch list" accessible by federal, state, and local law enforcement agencies. The new Terrorist Screening Center, under the aegis of the Federal Bureau of Investigation (FBI), was in place by mid-November, two weeks ahead of the December 1 deadline set in Bush's directive. But the actual integration of twelve separate watch lists, maintained by nine different federal agencies, was sometime off in the future. "We will have it all integrated in the months ahead," DHS secretary Tom Ridge said December 29.

Legislators had been demanding an integrated system since the terrorist attacks on New York and Washington on September 11, 2001. They argued that failure to integrate information on watch lists had allowed suspected terrorists to enter and leave the country undetected. One egregious example involved two of the September 11 terrorists. The Central Intelligence Agency (CIA) had identified the two as al Qaeda members but did not put them on a watch list until after the State Department had issued them visas to enter the country. A month later the pair helped hijack the plane that was crashed into the Pentagon. *(Congressional investigation, p. 544; terrorist attacks, Historic Documents of 2001, pp. 614, 624)*

Merging the watch lists was proving to be a difficult job. The twelve lists were designed to serve different purposes and collected different kinds of information. They did not use compatible computer hardware or software, and policies and procedures for sharing the information among agencies also differed widely; in several cases it did not exist at all. Another major stumbling block turned out to be turf battles between various agencies that were loath to give up control of their watch lists. Moreover, the Department of Homeland Security was simultaneously working on other complicated programs for tracking foreign visitors as they entered and left the country, and it was unclear how data from these new programs would be integrated with existing watch lists and other tracking programs. *(Border security, p. 218)*

Even as the government tried to increase the ability of its counterterrorism organizations to share watch list information, the Justice Department stopped the FBI from obtaining information that could help it track suspected terrorists who bought guns in the United States. Although the FBI matched prospective gun buyers to terrorist watch lists, Justice Department policy prohibited the agency from obtaining any details about the purchasers on the terrorist list if firearms background checks showed that the purchasers were otherwise legally entitled to buy guns. One critic of the policy called it "mind-boggling."

A Dozen Different Watch Lists

In the aftermath of the terrorist attacks on the World Trade Center and the Pentagon, numerous investigations pointed to the failure of the various intelligence agencies to share information and coordinate their findings about potential terrorists and terrorist plots. The CIA and FBI came in for a large share of blame for failing to "connect the dots" indicating that a major terrorist action was being plotted. Numerous initiatives were undertaken to improve the nation's counterintelligence capabilities and prevent future terrorist attacks. The most far-reaching was the creation in 2002 of the Department of Homeland Security, which folded into a single new department twenty-two federal agencies with some jurisdiction over the nation's borders, transportation services, and infrastructure components, such as telephones and computer systems, along with emergency management and some security agencies. *(New department, Historic Documents of 2002, p. 530)*

Over some objections, it was decided not to include the intelligence-gathering functions of the CIA and FBI in the new department, but agreement was widespread that the two agencies should better coordinate their intelligence gathering and analysis. In his 2003 State of the Union address, President George W. Bush announced plans to create a Terrorist Threat Integration Center (TTIC) to review all intelligence on terrorism collected both overseas and at home and to compile a comprehensive assessment of terrorist threats to the United States. The center was set up in the spring of 2003 under the supervision of the director of central intelligence. At the same time, the FBI and CIA intelligence analysis operations were moved into the same physical office building to facilitate the integration.

Bush called for the creation of a "consolidated terrorism watch list" in his July 2002 homeland security strategy. In October 2003 George Tenet, the director of central intelligence, indicated that the CIA was working with the State Department to make its "Tip-off" watch list into a master list that would "serve as a point of contact and coordination" for all the government's watch lists. The State Department list included the names of some 110,000 known or suspected terrorists and was used to check visa applicants. But little more happened until the report by the GAO called attention to the fact that nine agencies had developed twelve different watch lists, all intended to serve different purposes. In addition to the State Department's Tip-off list, the watch lists included the Transportation Security Administration's "no-fly" list of terror suspects prohibited from boarding airplanes, and the FBI's National Crime Information Center list of convicted felons, fugitives, and other people wanted by the police. In addition to the nine agencies that maintained the lists, about fifty other federal agencies, many state and local law enforcement agencies, and some private entities had access to one or more of these lists.

The GAO report said that about half the lists were not available to state and local law enforcement officials. None of the lists were compatible with each other. The lists did not include the same pieces of information, and incompatible computer systems made comparing or merging the information all but impossible. Furthermore, the report said, no two agencies had the same policy and procedures for determining what information to share with whom under what circumstances. The GAO said consolidating and standardizing the lists would offer faster access, reduce duplication, and increase consistency, thus reducing costs and improving the reliability of the data.

The release of the report unleashed a new round of criticism, with legislators complaining not only that the list consolidation had not happened but also that there was no schedule for getting the job done. Several legislators also suggested that some of the key agencies involved were dragging their feet because they were reluctant to share information with other agencies. Others said the problem was made worse by what Rep. Henry A. Waxman, D-Calif., called the administration's "ping-pong approach," with the White House shifting responsibility for dealing with integration first to the FBI and then to the Department of Homeland Security. "This is not a recipe for success," Waxman said.

In response, Bush on September 16 issued a directive establishing a Terrorist Screening Center that would be in operation twenty-four hours a day, seven days a week, to provide information on suspected terrorists to police, airport security personnel, immigration personnel, and others. The center, to be housed within the TTIC, was placed under the direction of the

FBI, which was to work with the CIA, the Justice Department, the Department of Homeland Security, the State Department, and others to set up a process for screening and sharing information on suspected terrorists. Sen. Charles E. Grassley, R-Iowa, who had requested the GAO report, called the announcement "a welcome change from the bureaucratic inaction we've seen with the watch lists. Now it's up to the FBI to demonstrate the technological savvy needed to maintain a list that can be accessed by all the appropriate agencies."

As they had in the past, civil liberties advocates pointed to numerous cases of mistaken identity in the wake of the September 11 attacks and cautioned that any integrated watch list had to include proper safeguards to ensure accurate information. "Our greatest concern is that innocent people might be wrongly labeled as terrorists, with little or no recourse to clear their names," Anthony Romero, the executive director of the American Civil Liberties Union, said in a statement. "The government must tell us how it plans to keep this watch list from turning into a blacklist that will inevitably ruin innocent lives."

Secretary Ridge said the center was expected to be up and running by December 1. On December 29 he said that center had been operational since the middle of November, with officials at the center checking numerous databases to determine if specific individuals appeared on any terrorism watch list. The center had already helped state and local law enforcement officials identify suspicious individuals, Ridge said, but he acknowledged that the watch lists themselves had not yet been consolidated into a single master list. Ridge promised that the center would "have it all integrated in the months ahead."

Terrorists and Gun Purchases

In its efforts to share intelligence about suspected terrorists, the FBI continued to be frustrated by Attorney General John Ashcroft's insistence on a narrow interpretation of the Brady law, the federal gun control law that required a background check before a person could buy a gun from a federally licensed dealer. Soon after the terrorist attacks in September 2001 the Justice Department stopped the FBI from comparing a list of 1,200 detainees rounded up by the government against a list of approved gun purchasers, arguing that the law prohibited the gun purchase records from being used for law enforcement purposes. The action was controversial at the time in part because the FBI reportedly had found two matches before the comparisons were stopped. It was also controversial because Ashcroft was a member of the National Rifle Association, which opposed the background checks and had made overturning the Brady law one of its top priorities. *(FBI gun checks, Historic Documents of 2001, p. 722)*

The controversy flared up again in May 2003 when a Congressional Research Service report said international terrorists could easily exploit the nation's gun laws and their lax enforcement to obtain assault guns and explosives because would-be gun purchasers were not checked against terrorist watch lists. The report cited an al Qaeda training manual, found by U.S. forces in Afghanistan, which noted how easy it was to obtain firearms legally in the United States and urged its readers to "obtain an assault rifle legally . . . learn how to use it properly and go and practice in the areas allowed for such training." In at least two cases after the September 11 terrorist attacks, the FBI had arrested people with terrorist connections who had purchased guns. One was a Michigan felon who bought firearms for the militant group Hezbollah at a gun show. The other was a Seattle man said to have been trying to set up a firearms training camp for al Qaeda in Oregon.

In November the *Washington Post* reported that in late spring the FBI began to check the names of gun purchasers against its terrorist watch list, the Violent Gang and Terrorist Organization File, which contained more than 10,000 names, mostly of suspected terrorists and their associates. According to the *Post's* sources, more than a dozen suspects on the watch list had tried to buy guns. However, because of the Justice Department's narrow interpretation of the Brady law, the FBI was prevented from obtaining details of the gun purchase if the background check showed that the person was otherwise entitled to buy a gun. Under the Brady law, guns could not be sold to felons, illegal immigrants, convicted domestic abusers, people for whom arrest warrants had been issued, and those found by a court to be mentally ill. If the gun purchaser did not fall into any of these categories, the FBI could not even obtain the location of the gun store involved in the transaction or the address of the purchaser—two pieces of information that law enforcement officials said would be extremely useful in tracking down suspects. The FBI could obtain information about those whose background checks barred them from buying guns.

A Justice Department official told the *Post* that "being a suspected member of a terrorist organization doesn't disqualify a person from owning a gun any more than being under investigation for a non-terrorism felony would." Sen. Frank J. Lautenberg, D-N.J., told the *Post* that the Justice Department policy was "mind-boggling." Under that policy, he said, "we could have a nationwide lookout for a known terrorist within our borders, but if he obtained a weapon, the Justice Department's policy is to refuse to reveal his location to law enforcement officials."

Within days of the *Post* story, the Justice Department revised its order. The FBI could still not get details about gun buyers cleared by the background checks, but it would be given three days to run additional checks on prospective gun buyers who appeared on its terrorist watch list. The FBI could use the extra time to uncover information that would stop the purchase and thus enable the FBI to obtain information on the buyer. The Justice

Department indicated that only one prospective gun purchaser on the terrorist list had been blocked from buying guns. However, an unnamed FBI official told the *Post* that twelve other suspects on the watch list had been allowed to buy guns because they did not fall into any of the prohibited categories. Lautenberg said the new directive was not good enough. "The Justice Department treats it like a game, in which the FBI gets only three days to prove a negative before a terrorist gets to anonymously obtain firearms," he told the *Post*. "Why in the world does the FBI need to fight the Justice Department to find the location of a terrorist suspect who is obtaining weapons?"

Following are excerpts from "Information Technology: Terrorist Watch Lists Should Be Consolidated to Promote Better Integration and Sharing," a report prepared by the General Accounting Office at the request of Sens. Charles E. Grassley, R-Iowa, and Carl Levin, D-Mich.; the report was dated April 15, 2003, but not publicly released until April 30, 2003.

"Information Technology: Terrorist Watch Lists Should Be Consolidated"

Results in Brief

Generally, the federal government's approach to developing and using terrorist and criminal watch lists in performing its border security mission is diffuse and nonstandard, largely because these lists were developed and have evolved in response to individual agencies' unique mission needs and the agencies' respective legal, cultural, and technological environments. More specifically, nine federal agencies—which spanned the Departments of Defense, Justice, State, Transportation, and the Treasury—have developed and maintain 12 watch lists. [The nine agencies are the State Department's Bureau of Intelligence and Research and Bureau of Consular Affairs; the Justice Department's Federal Bureau of Investigation, Immigration and Naturalization Service, U.S. Marshals Service, and U.S. National Central Bureau of Interpol; the Department of Defense's Air Force Office of Special Investigations; the Transportation

Department's Transportation Security Administration; and the Treasury Department's U.S. Customs Service. The Immigration and Naturalization Service, the Transportation Security Administration, and the Customs Bureau were incorporated into the new Department of Homeland Security on March 1, 2003.] These lists contain a wide variety of data; most contain biographical data, such as name and date of birth, and a few contain biometric data, such as fingerprints. Beyond the nine agencies that have developed and maintain these watch lists, about 50 other federal agencies and many state and local government entities have access to one or more of these lists.

Nonstandardization also extends to the policies and procedures governing whether and how agencies share watch lists. Specifically, two of the nine federal agencies do not have such policies and procedures, and the remaining seven have differing ones. For example, one of the agencies' policies included guidance on sharing with other federal agencies as well as state and local governments, but another addressed sharing only with federal agencies. As a general rule, the federal agencies that have watch lists share the lists among themselves. However, half of these agencies share their respective lists with state and local agencies, and one-fourth share them with private entities. The extent to which such sharing is accomplished electronically is constrained by fundamental differences in watch list system architectures (that is, the hardware, software, network, and data characteristics of the systems).

The number and variability of federal watch lists, combined with the commonality of purpose of these lists, point to opportunities to consolidate and standardize them. Appropriately exploiting these opportunities offers certain advantages—such as faster access, reduced duplication, and increased consistency—which can reduce costs and improve data reliability. Some of the agencies that have developed and maintain watch lists acknowledged these opportunities, as does the President's homeland security strategy. To this end, Office of Homeland Security officials stated in public forums during the course of our review that watch list consolidation activities were under way as part of efforts to develop a set of integrated blueprints—commonly called an enterprise architecture—for the new Department of Homeland Security (DHS). According to DHS's Chief Information Officer, responsibility for the consolidation effort has been transferred to DHS.

To strengthen our nation's homeland security capability, we are recommending that the Secretary of DHS take a series of steps aimed at ensuring that watch lists are appropriately and effectively standardized, consolidated, and shared. In commenting on a draft of this report, DHS—as well as other departments that develop and maintain watch lists and that commented on the draft—generally agreed with our findings and recommendations. . . .

Background

The President's national strategy for homeland security and the Homeland Security Act of 2002 provide for securing our national borders against terrorists. Terrorist and criminal watch lists are important tools for accomplishing this end.

Simply stated, watch lists can be viewed as automated databases that are supported by certain analytical capabilities. To understand the current state of watch lists, and the possibilities for improving them, it is useful to view them within the context of such information technology management disciplines as database management and enterprise architecture management.

Overview of the President's Homeland Security Strategy and the Homeland Security Act

Since the September 11th terrorist attacks, homeland security—including securing our nation's borders—has become a critical issue. To mobilize and organize our nation to secure the homeland from attack, the administration issued, in July 2002, a federal strategy for homeland security. Subsequently, the Congress passed and the President signed the Homeland Security Act, which established DHS in January 2003. Among other things, the strategy provides for performance of six mission areas, each aligned with a strategic objective, and identifies major initiatives associated with these mission areas. One of the mission areas is border and transportation security.

For the border and transportation security mission area, the strategy and the act specify several objectives, including ensuring the integrity of our borders and preventing the entry of unwanted persons into our country. To accomplish this, the strategy provides for, among other things, reform of immigration services, large-scale modernization of border crossings, and consolidation of federal watch lists. It also acknowledges that accomplishing these goals will require overhauling the border security process. This will be no small task, given that the United States shares a 5,525 mile border with Canada and a 1,989 mile border with Mexico and has 95,000 miles of shoreline. Moreover, each year, more than 500 million people legally enter our country, 330 million of them noncitizens. More than 85 percent enter via land borders, often as daily commuters.

Overview of the Border Security Process

Our nation's current border security process for controlling the entry and exit of individuals consists of four primary functions: (1) issuing visas, (2) controlling entries, (3) managing stays, and (4) controlling exits. The federal agencies involved in these functions include the Department of State's Bureau of Consular Affairs and its Bureau of Intelligence and Research, as well as the Justice Department's Immigration and Naturalization Service (INS), the Treasury Department's U.S. Customs Service (Customs), and the Transportation Department's Transportation Security Administration (TSA).

The process begins at the State Department's overseas consular posts, where consular officers are to adjudicate visa applications for foreign nationals who wish to enter the United States. In doing so, consular officials review visa applications, and sometimes interview applicants, prior to issuing a visa. One objective of this adjudication process is to bar from entry any foreign national who is known or suspected to have engaged in terrorist activity, is likely to engage in such activity, or is a member or supporter of a known terrorist organization.

Foreign nationals (and any other persons attempting to enter the United States, such as U.S. citizens) are to be screened for admission into the United States by INS or Customs inspectors. Generally, this consists of questioning the person and reviewing entry documents. Since October 2002, males aged 16 or over from certain countries (for example, Iran, Iraq, Syria, and the Sudan) are also required to provide their name and U.S. address and to be photographed and fingerprinted. In addition, airline officials use information provided by TSA to screen individuals attempting to travel by air. As discussed in the next section, requirements for checking a person against a watch list differ somewhat, depending upon whether the person arrives at a land-, air-, or seaport.

After foreign nationals are successfully screened and admitted, they are not actively monitored unless they are suspected of illegal activity and come under the scrutiny of a law enforcement agency, such as the Department of Justice's Federal Bureau of Investigation (FBI). Also, when foreign nationals depart the country, they are not screened unless they are males aged 16 years or over from certain countries referenced above, or are leaving by air. According to TSA, all passengers on departing flights are screened prior to boarding the plane.

The Role of Watch Lists in the Border Security Process

Watch lists are important tools that are used by federal agencies to help secure our nation's borders. These lists share a common purpose—to provide decisionmakers with information about individuals who are known or suspected terrorists and criminals, so that these individuals can either be prevented from entering the country, apprehended while in the country, or apprehended as they attempt to exit the country. . . . [W]atch lists collectively support nine federal agencies in performing the four primary functions in the border security process. Specifically:

- When a person applies for a visa to enter the United States, State Department consular officials are to check that person against one or more watch lists before granting a visa.
- When a person attempts to enter the United States by air or sea, INS or Customs officials are required to check that person against watch lists before the person is allowed to enter the country. In addition, when a person attempts to enter the United States by air, INS or Custom officials check him or her against watch lists provided by TSA prior to allowing him or her to board the plane. Persons arriving at land borders may be checked, but there is no requirement to do so. The exception, as previously discussed, is for males aged 16 or over from certain countries, who are required to be checked.
- Once a watch list identifies a person as a known or suspected terrorist, INS, Customs, or airline officials are to contact the appropriate law enforcement or intelligence organization (for example, the FBI), and a decision will be made regarding the person's entry and the agency's monitoring of the person while he or she is in the country.
- When a person exits the country by plane, airline officials are to check that person against watch lists.

In performing these roles, the agencies use information from multiple watch lists. For example, U.S. National Central Bureau for Interpol officials told us that they provide information to the agencies involved in entry control, exit control, and stay management.

President's Strategy Recognizes Problems with Watch Lists and Proposes Improvements

In addition to highlighting the importance of watch lists for border security, the President's national strategy cites problems with these lists, including limited sharing. According to the July 2002 strategy, in the aftermath of the September 11th attacks it became clear that vital watch list information stored in numerous and disparate federal databases [w]as not available to the right people at the right time. In particular, federal agencies that maintained information about terrorists and other criminals had not consistently shared it. The strategy attributed these sharing limitations to legal, cultural, and technical barriers that resulted in the watch lists being developed in different ways, for different purposes, and in isolation from one another.

To address these limitations, the strategy calls for integrating and reducing variations in watch lists and overcoming barriers to sharing the lists. It also calls for developing an enterprise architecture for border security and transportation. . . .More specifically, the strategy provides for developing a consolidated watch list that would bring together the information on known or suspected terrorists contained in federal agencies' respective lists. . . .

Watch Lists Contain Different Types of Data

The 12 watch lists do not all contain the same types of data, although some types are included in all of the lists. At the same time, some types of data are included in only a few of the lists. More specifically, all of the lists include the name and date of birth; 11 include other biographical information (for example, passport number and any known aliases); 9 include criminal history (for example, warrants and arrests); 8 include biometric data (for example, fingerprints); 3 include immigration data (for example, visa type, travel dates, departure country, destination country, country visited, arrival dates, departure dates, and purpose of travel); and 2 include financial data (for example, large currency transactions).

Watch List Sharing Is Governed by Varying Policies and Procedures

Effective sharing of information from watch lists and of other types of data among multiple agencies can be facilitated by agencies' development and use of well-coordinated and aligned policies and procedures that define the rules governing this sharing. One effective way to implement such policies and procedures is to prepare and execute written watch list exchange agreements or memorandums of understanding. These agreements would specify answers to such questions as what data are to be shared with whom, and how and when they are to be shared.

Not all of the nine agencies have policies and procedures governing the sharing of watch lists. In particular, two of the agencies reported that they did not have any policies and procedures on watch list sharing. In addition, of the seven that reported having such policies and procedures, one did not require any written agreements. Further, the policies and procedures of the seven have varied. For example, one agency's policies included guidance on sharing with other federal agencies as well as with state and local governments, but another's addressed sharing only with other federal agencies. In addition, each agency had different policies and procedures on memorandums of understanding, ranging from one agency's not specifying any requirements to others' specifying in detail that such agreements should include how, when, and where data would be shared with other parties.

The variation in policies and procedures governing the sharing of information from watch lists can be attributed to the fact that each agency has developed its own policies and procedures in response to its own specific needs. In addition, the agencies reported that they received no direction from the Office of Homeland Security identifying the needs of the government as a whole in this area. As a result, federal agencies do not have a consistent and uniform approach to sharing watch list information.

Federal Agency Watch List Data Sharing and Supporting System Architectures Vary

The President's homeland security strategy and recent legislation call for increased sharing of watch lists, not only among federal agencies, but also among federal, state, and local government entities and between government and private-sector organizations. Currently, sharing of watch list data is occurring, but the extent to which it occurs varies, depending on the entities involved. Further, these sharing activities are not supported by systems with common architectures. This is because agencies have developed their respective watch lists, and have managed their use, in isolation from each other, and in recognition of each agency's unique legal, cultural, and technological environments. The result is inconsistent and limited sharing.

Watch List Sharing Varies

According to the President's homeland security strategy, watch list data sharing has to occur horizontally among federal agencies as well as vertically among federal, state, and local governments in order for the country to effectively combat terrorism. In addition, recent federal homeland security legislation, including the Homeland Security Act, 16 USA PATRIOT ACT of 2001, and the Enhanced Border Security and Visa Entry Reform Act of 2002 require, among other things, increased sharing of homeland security information both among federal agencies and across all levels of government.

The degree to which watch list data are being shared is not consistent with the President's strategy and recent legislative direction on increased data sharing. Specifically, while federal agencies report that they are generally sharing watch list data with each other, they also report that sharing with organizations outside of the federal government is limited. That is, five of the nine agencies reported that they shared data from their lists with state and local agencies, and three reported that they shared data with private industry.

As noted above, federal agencies are sharing either all or some of their watch list data with each other. However, this sharing is the result of each agency's having developed and implemented its own interfaces with other federal agencies' watch lists. The consequence is the kind of overly complex, unnecessarily inefficient, and potentially ineffective network that is associated with unstructured and nonstandard database environments. In particular, this environment consists of nine agencies—with 12 watch lists—that collectively maintain at least 17 interfaces; one agency's watch list alone has at least 4 interfaces.

A key reason for the varying extent of watch list sharing is the cultural differences among the government agencies and private-sector organizations involved in securing U.S. borders. According to the President's strategy, cultural differences often prevent agencies from exchanging or integrating information. We also recently reported that differences in agencies' cultures has been and remains one of the principal impediments to integrating and sharing information from watch lists and other information.

Historically, legal requirements have also been impediments to sharing, but recent legislation has begun addressing this barrier. Specifically, the President's strategy and our past work have reported on legal requirements, such as security, privacy, and other civil liberty protections, that restrict effective information sharing. To address this problem, Congress has recently passed legislation that has significantly changed the legal framework for information sharing, which, when fully implemented, should diminish the effect of existing legal barriers. In particular, Congress has enacted legislation providing for agencies to have increased access to other agencies' information and directing more data sharing among agencies. For example, section 701 of the USA PATRIOT ACT broadened the goals of regional law enforcement's information sharing to cover terrorist activities. The Enhanced Border Security and Visa Entry Reform Act expanded law enforcement and intelligence information sharing about aliens seeking to enter or stay in the United States. Most recently, the Homeland Security Act provides the newly created DHS with wide access to information held by federal agencies relating to "threats of terrorism" against the United States. Section 891 expresses the "sense of Congress" that "Federal, state, and local entities should share homeland security information to the maximum extent practicable." Further, section 892 of the Act requires the President to prescribe and implement procedures for the sharing of "homeland security information" among federal agencies and with state and local agencies, and section 895 requires the sharing of grand jury information.

Watch List Sharing Is Not Supported by a Common Architecture

The President's homeland security strategy stresses the importance of information sharing and identifies, among other things, the lack of a common systems architecture—and the resultant incompatible watch list systems and data—as an impediment to systems interoperating effectively and efficiently. To address this impediment, the strategy proposes developing a "system of systems" that would allow greater information sharing across federal agencies as well as among federal agencies, state and local governments, private industry, and citizens.

In order for systems to work more effectively and efficiently, each system's key components have to meet certain criteria. In particular, their operating systems and applications have to conform to certain standards that are in the public domain, their databases have to be built according to explicitly defined and documented data schemas and data models, and their networks have to be connected. More specifically, critical system components would have to adhere to common standards, such as open systems standards, to ensure that different systems interoperate. One source for open system standards is the International Organization for Standardization. Also, these systems' data would have to have common— or at least mutually understood—data definitions so that data could, at a minimum, be received and processed, and potentially aggregated and analyzed. Such data definitions are usually captured in a data dictionary. Further, these systems would have to be connected to each other via a telecommunications network or networks. When system components and data do not meet such standards, additional measures have to be employed, such as acquiring or building and maintaining unique system interfaces (hardware and software) or using manual workarounds. These measures introduce additional costs and reduce efficiency and effectiveness.

The 12 automated watch list systems do not meet all of these criteria. For example, they use three different types of operating systems, each of which stores data and files differently. Overcoming these differences requires the use of software utilities to bridge the differences between systems. Without such utilities, for example, a Windows-based system cannot read data from a diskette formatted by a UNIX-based system.

Also, nine of the systems do not have software applications that comply with open system standards. In these cases, agencies may have had to invest time and resources in designing, developing, and maintaining unique interfaces so that the systems can exchange data.

Further, five of the systems' databases do not have a data dictionary, and of the remaining seven systems that do have data dictionaries, at least one is not sharing its dictionary with other agencies. Without both the existence and sharing of these data dictionaries, meaningful under-standing of data received from another agency could require an added investment of time and resources to interpret and understand what the received data mean. Moreover, aggregation and analysis of the data received with the data from other watch lists may require still further investment of time and resources to restructure and reformat the data in a common way.

Last, seven of the systems are not connected to a network outside of their agencies or departments. Our experience has shown that without network connectivity, watch list data sharing among agencies can occur only through manual intervention. According to several of these agencies, the manual workarounds are labor-intensive and time-consuming, and they limit the timeliness of the data provided. For example, data from the TIPOFF system are shared directly with the National Automated Immigration Lookout System through a regular update on diskette. Those data are then transferred from the National Automated Immigra-tion Lookout System to the Interagency Border Inspection System.

The President's strategy attributes these differences to the agencies' building their own systems to meet agency-specific mission needs, goals, and policies, without knowledge of the information needs and policies of the government as a whole. This approach has resulted in an overly complex, unnecessarily inefficient, and potentially ineffective federal watch list sharing environment.

Opportunities Exist for Consolidating Watch Lists and Improving Information Sharing

As addressed in the preceding sections of this report, federal watch lists share a common purpose and support the border security mission. Never-theless, the federal government has developed, maintains, and—along with state and local governments and private entities—uses 12 separate watch lists, some of which contain the same types of data. However, this prolifer-ation of systems, combined with the varying policies and procedures that govern the sharing of each, as well as the architectural differences among the automated lists, create strong arguments for list consolidation. The advantages of doing so include faster access, reduced duplication, and increased consistency, which can reduce costs and improve data reliability.

Most of the agencies that have developed and maintain watch lists did not identify consolidation opportunities. Of the nine federal agencies that operate and maintain watch lists, seven reported that the current state and configuration of federal watch lists meet their mission needs, and that they are satisfied with the level of watch list sharing. However, two agencies supported efforts to consolidate these lists. The State Department's Bureau of Consular Affairs and the Justice Department's U.S. Marshals Service agreed that some degree of watch list consolidation would be beneficial and would improve information sharing. Both cited as advantages of consolidation the saving of staff time and financial resources by limiting the number of labor-intensive and time-consuming data transfers, and one also cited the reduction in duplication of data that could be realized by decreasing the number of agencies that maintain lists.

The President's strategy also recognizes that watch list consolidation opportunities exist and need to be exploited. More specifically, the strategy states that the events of September 11th raised concerns regarding the effectiveness of having multiple watch lists and the lack of integration and sharing among them. To address these problems, the strategy calls for integrating the numerous and disparate systems that support watch lists as a way to reduce the variations in watch lists and remove barriers to sharing them.

To implement the strategy, Office of Homeland Security officials have stated in public settings that they were developing an enterprise architecture for border and transportation security, which is one of the six key mission areas of the newly created DHS. They also reported the following initial projects under this architecture effort: (1) developing a consolidated watch list that brings together information on known or suspected terrorists in the federal agencies' watch lists, and (2) establishing common metadata or data definitions for electronic watch lists and other information that is relevant to homeland security. However, the Office of Homeland Security did not respond to our inquiries about this effort, and thus we could not determine the substance, status, and schedule of any watch list consolidation activities. Since then, the DHS Chief Information Officer told us that DHS has assumed responsibility for these efforts.

Conclusions

Our nation's success in achieving its homeland security mission depends in large part on its ability to get the right information to the right people at the right time. Terrorist and criminal watch lists make up one category of such information. To date, the federal watch list environment has been characterized by a proliferation of systems, among which information sharing is occurring in some cases but not in others. This is inconsistent with the most recent congressional and presidential direction. Our experience has shown that even when sharing is occurring, costly and overly complex measures have had to be taken to facilitate it. Cultural and technological barriers stand in the way of a more integrated, normalized set of watch lists, and agencies' legal authorities and individuals' civil liberties are also relevant considerations. To improve on the current situation, central leadership—spanning not only the many federal agencies engaged in maintaining and using watch lists, but also the state and local government and the private-sector list users—is crucial to introducing an appropriate level of watch list standardization and consolidation while still enforcing relevant laws and allowing agencies to (1) operate appropriately within their unique mission environments and (2) fulfill their unique mission needs. Currently, the degree to which such leadership is occurring, and the substance and status of consolidation and standardization efforts under way, are unclear. In our view, it is imperative that Congress be kept fully informed of the nature and progress of such efforts.

Recommendations for Executive Action

To promote better integration and sharing of watch lists, we recommend that DHS's Secretary, in collaboration with the heads of the departments and agencies that have and use watch lists, lead an effort to consolidate and standardize the federal government's watch list structures and policies. To determine and implement the appropriate level of watch list consolidation and standardization, we further recommend that this collaborative effort include

1. updating the watch list information provided in this report, as needed, and using this information to develop an architectural understanding of our nation's current or "as is" watch list environment;
2. defining the requirements of our nation's target or "to be" watch list architectural environment, including requirements that address any agency-unique needs that can be justified, such as national security issues and civil liberty protections;
3. basing the target architecture on achievement of the mission goals and objectives contained in the President's homeland security strategy and on congressional direction, as well as on opportunities to leverage state and local government and private-sector information sources;

4. developing a near-term strategy for implementing the target architecture that provides for the integration of existing watch lists, as
   well as a longer-term strategy that provides for migrating to a more
   consolidated and standardized set of watch lists;
5. ensuring that these strategies provide for defining and adopting
   more standard policies and procedures for watch list sharing and
   addressing any legal issues affecting, and cultural barriers to, greater
   watch list sharing; and
6. developing and implementing the strategies within the context of
   the ongoing enterprise architecture efforts of each of the collaborating departments and agencies.

In addition, we recommend that the Secretary report to Congress by
September 30, 2003, and every 6 months thereafter, on the status and
progress of these efforts, as well as on any legislative action needed to
accomplish them. . . .

Source: U.S. General Accounting Office. "Information Technology: Terrorist Watch Lists Should Be Consolidated to Promote Better Integration
and Sharing." GAO–03–332. April 15, 2003 (publicly released April 30,
2003). www.gao.gov/new.items/d03322.pdf (accessed July 10, 2003).

National Academy of Public Administration and EPA on Clean Air Regulations

April 21 and August 27, 2003

INTRODUCTION

The Bush administration and environmental advocates continued to do battle during 2003 on a broad range of environmental policies. By far the most controversial was an administration plan to relax a key provision of the Clean Air Act that was intended to force industrial polluters to install improved air pollution control equipment when they expanded or modernized their plants. After nearly three years of debate, the administration adopted a final version of its plan in August 2003—but a federal court in December blocked it from taking effect, at least temporarily.

Ever since taking office in January 2001, President George W. Bush and his aides had adopted or proposed numerous policies changing federal regulations governing air and water pollution, logging in the national forests, oil and gas development on public lands, and other environmental matters. Administration officials said the policies of the Clinton administration had been too stringent in many cases and had cost the nation thousands of jobs. Bush said his goal was to "balance" environmental protections and national economic growth. Environmental advocacy groups, and their supporters on Capitol Hill, said Bush was catering to the interests of big business by weakening laws and regulations intended to protect the health of the American populace and preserve the country's natural resources for future generations. *(Background, Historic Documents of 2001, p. 212; Historic Documents of 2002, p. 894)*

Whitman Resigns at EPA

Christine Todd Whitman, the administration's leading moderate on environmental issues, announced on May 21 that she was resigning as administrator of the Environmental Protection Agency (EPA), effective June 27. A former governor of New Jersey, Whitman said she was resigning of her own accord, so she could return to New Jersey to spend more time with her family. She said she was proud of the EPA's work under her tenure. "Our work has been guided by the strong belief that environmental protection and economic prosperity can and must go hand-in-hand, that the true measure of the value of any environmental policy is in the environmental results it produces," she stated in her resignation letter to Bush.

It was no secret, however, that Whitman had spent much of her time trying to protect the EPA's regulatory role against demands by the White House for new policies that put more emphasis on the free market and less on government regulations. She had been in office less than three months when she was told by the White House to roll back a rule proposed by former president Bill Clinton (1993–2001) reducing the amount of lead permitted in the nation's drinking water. That decision prompted a national outcry that ultimately forced the administration to reverse course and accept Clinton's proposal. The incident also exposed Whitman's weak position within an administration dominated by former officials from major industries. White House officials also overruled Whitman on global warming, for example, by forcing the EPA to rewrite its reports on the subject in such a way as to cast doubt on the extent to which human actions were causing the climate to change.

Bush chose another Republican governor, Michael O. Leavitt of Utah, as Whitman's successor. In announcing the appointment August 11, Bush said Leavitt would promote the roles of state and local governments in protecting the environment because "he rejects the old ways of command and control from above." The thrust of many of the administration's environmental policies had been to transfer decision making to states and localities. Leavitt's nomination won broad support in the Senate, with senators on both sides of the environmental policy divide seeing him as an acceptable successor to Whitman. Sen. Hillary Rodham Clinton, D-N.Y., held up Leavitt's nomination for several weeks to protest what she said had been the EPA's politically driven decision to declare the air in New York City safe to breathe immediately after the destruction of the World Trade Center towers in the September 11, 2001, terrorist attacks. Clinton relented on October 27, after the administration agreed to additional air-quality tests in New York. The Senate confirmed Leavitt the next day, by a vote of 88–8, and he took office November 6.

Background on New Source Review

By far the most controversial of the Bush administration's environmental policies was its plan for air pollution regulations governing thousands of power plants, oil refineries, and other industrial plants. A key provision Congress added in 1977 to the Clean Air Act, called "new source review," required industrial polluters to upgrade their pollution control equipment whenever they expanded or made major repairs or modifications to their plants. "Routine maintenance" did not trigger a requirement for upgraded pollution controls. In writing this provision, Congress intended that new sources of pollution should be less damaging to the environment than old ones had been. Many polluters, however, used the "routine maintenance" exemption to avoid adding expensive new pollution control equipment; in some cases, they claimed that even major expansions of their plants merely were routine maintenance. Among the plants most directly affected by the regulation were power plants in the Midwest and Ohio River Valley that were fueled by high-sulfur coal. Much of the air pollution from these and other industrial plants blew "downwind" to the northeastern and mid-Atlantic states.

The Clinton administration, along with several states, took some major industrial polluters to court, claiming they had abused the routine mainte-nance loophole. Upon taking office in 2001, the Bush administration announced its intention to revise the new source regulation. Officials said the existing regulation, as enforced by the Clinton administration, had dis-couraged companies from modernizing their plants and thus had the unin-tended consequence of keeping heavily polluting equipment in service years past when it should have been replaced. Environmental groups and officials in several northeastern states agreed that the law had discouraged some companies from strengthening their pollution controls—but they argued that the new source review provision should be toughened, not weakened, as they said the administration wanted to do.

Reportedly because of the controversy, the administration delayed pub-lic announcement of its precise plans until after the midterm elections in November 2002, which produced solid gains for Republicans in Congress. The EPA on December 31, 2002, announced its "final" proposal for new source review regulations. That proposal gave industrial polluters substan-tially more flexibility than in the past to modernize and even expand their plants without adding new pollution control equipment.

On January 1, 2003, the day after the administration's announcement, the attorneys general of nine northeastern states—Connecticut, Maine, Maryland, Massachusetts, New Hampshire, New Jersey, New York, Rhode Island, and Vermont—filed suit in federal court in Washington to block the proposed rule. Senate opponents of the new rule also tried to delay it from taking effect, but they were rebuffed on a 50–46 vote on January 22.

National Academy Study of Administration Plans

The administration's plan was subjected to numerous studies by advocates on all sides of the question, but perhaps the most extensive examination was made public on April 21 by the National Academy of Public Administration, an independent advisory organization. A panel of experts appointed by the academy studied the history of the new source review provision, at the request of Congress, and issued its findings in "A Breath of Fresh Air: Reviving the New Source Review Program." The panel's report concluded that new source review was not working as Congress intended and needed to be "fundamentally reformed and strongly enforced against past violations by existing facilities." The panel's assessment of the law's past performance was in accord with Bush administration policy, but its conclusions about how to fix the law were not.

New source review had worked, as Congress intended, to require "modern, cleaner" equipment at new industrial plants, the panel said. But many existing industrial plants had avoided installing new pollution-control equipment even while they increased their production—and pollution. That produced an "unfair burden" on industries that did modernize their pollution controls, the panel said. A more important consequence, it added, was "thousands of premature human deaths, and many thousand cases of acute illnesses and chronic diseases caused by air pollution."

The panel made seven recommendations for short-term and long-term steps to fix the new source review provision, some that would require congressional action and others that could be done by the administration through better enforcement and new regulations. The panel recommended that all existing plants that had not upgraded their pollution equipment since 1977 (when Congress enacted the new source review provision) should be required to do so within ten years, that the EPA and Justice Department should "vigorously" enforce the existing new source review requirements, and that the goal of all regulations should be to reduce the actual levels of air pollution.

Using careful language, the panel challenged key elements of the Bush administration's proposed changes to new source review, arguing that they would create more and bigger "loopholes" for industrial facilities to continue polluting with old equipment. In particular, the panel rejected the administration's proposal that industries be allowed to choose the "baseline" period against which their future pollution emissions would be measured. Giving industries this option "will only broaden the loopholes and aggravate the administrative problems identified by the panel that have allowed many older high-emitting facilities to avoid the NSR [new source review] requirements for installing modern equipment," the panel said. Another major weakness of the administration plan was that it allowed industries to monitor and report their own levels of pollution—a form of "self policing" that had failed in the past, the panel said.

EPA Puts New Proposal into Effect

Throughout the first half of 2003 the EPA held public hearings and solicited public comments on its proposed changes to the new source review rules.

The EPA also took a step that surprised many observers: It pursued several legal cases that state governments and the Clinton administration had brought against major corporations for violating the "old" new source review requirements. On April 9 the administration announced agreements under which Archer Daniels Midland Co. (ADM) and Alcoa Inc. would upgrade air pollution control equipment at plants in the South and Midwest. ADM was the nation's largest producer of ethanol. The government claimed the company had failed to report accurately on pollution generated by some of its plants and had expanded production at others without installing new pollution control equipment. The company agreed to spend $351 million to comply with the law, including $213 million for new equipment at fifty-two plants in sixteen states. Alcoa agreed to cut air pollution emissions from a coal-fired power plant that provided energy for its aluminum smelting plant in Rockdale, Texas, near Austin.

Yet another settlement—the largest ever reached under the Clean Air Act—came on April 18. In that case, the Dominion Virginia Power Company agreed to upgrade pollution control equipment at eight coal-fueled power plants in Virginia and West Virginia. The estimated cost of the upgrades was $1.2 billion, plus the company agreed to pay $5.3 million in federal fines and $14 million for environmental programs in several states. The state of New York had sued the company in 1999, charging that it violated the new source review provision by expanding production without improving pollution controls. Connecticut, New Jersey, and the EPA joined the suit, and in 2000 they reached a tentative settlement with the company. In 2001 the Bush administration's announced plans to change the new source review provision put that settlement on hold. The three states pursued the case, however, and the Bush administration ultimately joined in—a step that put pressure on the company to settle on virtually the same terms as had been agreed nearly three years earlier. New York attorney general Eliot L. Spitzer said the successful settlement "proves that you need vigorous state enforcement at a time when the feds are not vigorously enforcing the law." Tough enforcement of the existing new source review provision also was upheld in August, when a federal court found Ohio Edison had violated the law by expanding a power plant without installing new pollution control equipment.

The Bush administration on August 27 again announced a "final" version of its proposed revisions to the new source review provision. The announcement was made by acting EPA administrator Marianne Horinko, thus putting in place one of the administration's most controversial environmental policies before incoming administrator Leavitt took office. Top environmental officials in Leavitt's administration in Utah had opposed the Bush proposal.

This new, final version was substantially the same as the one announced the previous December 31. The EPA clarified one significant point that had been left vague in the earlier proposal: the scope of a plant expansion that would trigger the requirement for upgrading pollution controls. The earlier proposal had used the cost of expanding a plant as the standard but had left the details unclear. The new proposal set a precise standard: an industrial firm would be required to upgrade its pollution controls only if the cost of its proposed modernization exceeded 20 percent of the cost of replacing the plant's overall production equipment; for example, if a power plant replaced a boiler that cost more than 20 percent of the total price of replacing all the equipment needed for that unit to produce electricity, its pollution controls would have to be modernized.

In her announcement, Horinko said the new rule "will result in safer, more efficient operation of these [industrial] facilities and, in the case of power plants, more reliable operations that are environmentally sound and provide more affordable energy." Spokesmen for industrial firms affected by the rule said they were pleased. Thomas R. Kuhn, president of the Edison Electric Institute (the electric utility trade association), said the rule would "lift a major cloud of uncertainty, boosting our efforts to provide affordable, reliable electric service and cleaner air."

Environmental groups and legal officers for the northeastern states most affected by industrial air pollution called the new rule a "giveaway" to industry and pledged to step up their lawsuits to block it. The Natural Resources Defense Council estimated that the administration's rule would exempt 17,000 existing power plants, oil refineries, paper mills, and other factories from having to install new pollution control equipment.

The opponents received ammunition for their cause from a study issued August 22 by the General Accounting Office (GAO), the investigative arm of Congress. That study said the EPA had relied solely on "anecdotal" information from the affected industries—rather than independent scientific studies—to conclude that the new rule would have only minimal impacts on human health and the economy. Environmental groups said the GAO study bolstered their claims that the Bush administration was more interested in protecting industry than in enforcing environmental regulations.

President Bush, who had generally stayed out of the new source review controversy, defended his administration's approach during a September 15 visit to a large power plant in Monroe, Michigan. "Regulations intended to enhance air quality made it really difficult for companies to do that which is necessary, to not only produce more energy, but to do it in a cleaner way," Bush said. "It makes sense to change those regulations."

In a follow-up study for Congress issued October 21, the GAO confirmed the criticism of environmental groups that the administration's new rule would give industries broad leeway to determine on their own whether their plant expansions would require upgrading pollution controls. In effect, the GAO said, companies could "self-police" their pollution controls, which "makes it difficult for EPA, state and local agencies, and the public to verify company compliance" with the new source review regulations.

The GAO report also said the new rule would make it difficult for the administration and states to pursue existing lawsuits against companies that allegedly had evaded the old regulations for upgrading their pollution controls. On November 6, the *New York Times* reported that the administration had decided to drop its investigations into some fifty power plants for past violations. That news brought another round of complaints from the northeastern states, which said they would file their own lawsuits to enforce the law against those plants.

The year's final development on the issue took place December 24, when a three-judge panel of the U.S. Circuit Court of Appeals for the District of Columbia temporarily blocked the EPA's August 27 rule from taking effect. The court granted a request for an injunction against the rule that had been sought by attorneys general from twelve states and representatives of several cities.

Broader Air Quality Issues

The controversy over the new source review regulation took place even as the Bush administration, industry groups, and environmental advocates were sparring over other air pollution issues. For much of the year, the forum for the debate was a set of administration proposals that would revise key sections of the Clean Air Act. Bush proposed the changes in 2002, wrapping them together in legislation he called a "Clear Skies Initiative." A central feature of Bush's plan called for an expansion of current rules allowing industrial firms to trade "credits" for their emissions of nitrogen oxide and sulfur dioxide, which were among the major pollutants produced by burning fossil fuels. Bush also proposed allowing industries to trade credits for their emissions of mercury, another toxic chemical. Under the trading system, plants that could not meet standards for reducing their pollution could buy, or trade, emission allowances from other plants that exceeded the standards. This system, called "cap and trade," was used during the 1980s and 1990s to reduce emissions by power plants of sulfur dioxide, which caused a form of pollution known as acid rain.

Bush's Clear Skies plan languished in Congress because of opposition from environmental groups, Democrats, and a handful of moderate Republicans. While endorsing the general cap-and-trade concept, critics said Bush's proposal would weaken overall controls on pollution. Opponents also insisted that any new regulations should require reduced emissions by electric utilities and other industries of carbon dioxide—a "greenhouse gas" that most scientists said was a major cause of global climate change. Bush during his 2000 election campaign had proposed regulating carbon dioxide emissions, but after taking office reversed course; aides said his campaign position on the issue had been a "mistake." *(Climate change, p. 861)*

With its Clear Skies initiative blocked on Capitol Hill, the administration moved during the year to put the same provisions into effect through regulations. In back-to-back announcements, the EPA on December 15 proposed rules limiting emissions of mercury by coal-fired power plants and on December 17 proposed rules limiting emissions of sulfur dioxide and nitrogen oxide. The first rule would give the electric power industry fifteen years, until 2018, to reduce the overall national emissions of mercury by about 70 percent—from forty-eight tons down to fifteen tons. The second rule set a 2015 deadline for industry to reduce overall emissions of sulfur dioxide by 70 percent and of nitrogen oxides by 65 percent. The EPA on December 19 proposed yet another rule regulating emissions of mercury by the chemical industry.

EPA officials said the new regulations would substantially reduce air pollution, over the long haul, beyond what Congress had required in the 1970 Clean Air Act. Announcing the mercury regulation, EPA administrator Leavitt said it would require "the largest single industry investment in any clean air program in U.S. history."

Representatives of environmental groups countered that the new rules would allow more pollution, over a longer period of years, than any rules that had been considered by the Clinton administration and even some earlier plans the Bush administration had considered. "As expected, the Bush administration's plan to clean up air pollution is too little, too late," John Walke, of the Natural Resources Defense Council, said. "It's no wonder power companies and industry lobbyists are cheering this plan."

Other Environment Issues

The Bush administration and environmental advocates sparred on numerous other issues during 2003, including:

- **Clean water.** A series of reports, some of them by the EPA's inspector general, raised questions about the government's enforcement of the Clean Water Act. On May 20 the EPA inspector general reported that an agency computer system was so outmoded that it was failing to keep track of the sources of water pollution. On June 6 the *Washington Post* reported that another EPA internal study, covering 1999 through 2001, had found that about 25 percent of the nation's largest industrial plants and water treatment facilities were in "significant noncompliance" with regulations under the Clean Water Act. The EPA took enforcement action against only about 15 percent of the violators, but fewer than half of them were required to pay fines, the newspaper said. Another internal investigation by the EPA appeared to show that the agency was overstating the percentage of the American public with access to safe drinking water. The EPA's "Draft Report on the Environment," released June 23, said that 94 percent of the population was served by community water systems "that met all health-based standards." EPA documents obtained by the *Washington Post,* however, estimated that only 79–84 percent of the population had safe drinking water—a difference of between 28 million and 42 million people.

On March 7 the EPA temporarily exempted the oil and gas industry from a new requirement that construction sites between one and five acres in size have adequate systems to control the runoff of storm water containing chemicals and metals from disturbed soils. Construction sites larger than five acres had been subject to this requirement since 1990, and the Clinton administration in 1999 proposed a rule subjecting smaller sites to the requirement as well. The Bush administration retained the Clinton rule but gave a two-year exemption to oil and gas wells and pipelines.

- **National forests.** The Bush administration made significant headway during 2003 on several aspects of plans to open the national forests to expanded logging, mining, oil and gas development, and other forms of commercial activity. Bush in 2002 had proposed a multipart plan, which he called the "Healthy Forests Initiative," that would allow logging companies to "thin" forests that had become overgrown and, thus, were subject to wildfires. Opponents blocked the plan in Congress, but the U.S. Forest Service and the Bureau of Land Management implemented most of it with revised regulations. On a separate but related matter, the administration on June 9 said it was reinstating a regulation developed by the Clinton administration barring the construction of roads in 58.5 million acres of national forests. Former president Clinton had developed this "roadless" plan to curtail logging and other forms of development in the forests, but the Bush administration had initially tried to repeal it. Even while reinstating the rule, however, Bush administration said state governors could seek exemptions from the ban on roads. Environmental groups said governors of several western states would use this exemption to expedite logging. The first big exemption came December 23, when the Agriculture Department announced that 300,000 acres of the Tongass National Forest in Alaska would be opened for the construction of roads, and thus for logging. With 16.8 million acres, the Tongass forest was the nation's largest, and it had become a national symbol of the political and legal struggles between environmental groups and industry.

- **Enforcing environmental laws.** News reports, and an internal investigation by the EPA's inspector general, appeared to bolster claims by some environmental groups that the federal government had cut back its enforcement of environmental laws. The *New York Times* on April 28 quoted EPA criminal investigators as saying they had been taken off cases of alleged pollution-control violations and assigned instead to investigating terrorism incidents, including alleged "eco-terrorism" by extreme environmental groups. Some EPA investigators also had been assigned as security guards for then-administrator Whitman as she traveled around the country, the *Times* said. The report by the EPA's inspector general, released October 10, confirmed that the agency had "shifted priorities, budget, and personnel" from purely environmental matters to "homeland security" concerns, such as providing security at the annual Superbowl game and Fourth of July celebrations. Moreover, the report said, the EPA for years had failed to provide the funding and personnel needed to enforce existing regulations.

- **Oil and gas development.** The Bush administration took steps to open millions of acres of public lands—most of it in western states—to oil and gas exploration. In August the Bureau of Land Management instructed its field offices in Colorado, Montana, New Mexico, Utah, and Wyoming to allow oil and gas development on public lands they controlled. Director Kathleen Clarke said the bureau's goal was to "ensure the timely development of these critical energy resources in an environmentally sound manner." Environmental groups said the administration was giving priority to energy development and failing to conserve public lands for future generations. The administration failed to win congressional approval for its much more controversial plan to allow oil drilling in the Alaska National Wildlife Refuge. That plan required congressional approval because the refuge was a "wilderness" area protected from development by law. The House had approved Bush's plan to drill for oil in the wilderness, but the Senate had blocked it repeatedly. The "final" version of an energy-promotion bill (HR 6) considered by Congress in 2003 did not include the administration's Alaska provision. *(Energy issues, p. 1014)*

- **Pesticides.** The administration on February 1 said it would help U.S. businesses win exemptions from an international treaty that banned the use of methyl bromide, a pesticide. Use of the substance had been banned by the 1985 Montreal Protocol on Substances That Deplete the Ozone Layer. That treaty sought to curb the use of chemicals and gases that depleted the ozone layer, a part of the Earth's upper atmosphere that absorbed most of the sun's ultraviolet-B radiation. Pesticide producers and farm groups said they needed to continue using methyl bromide because there were no effective substitutes for it.

- **Wetlands.** The Bush administration in December backed away from a plan that would have made it easier for homebuilders and other developers to drain millions of acres of wetlands. The plan, which had been under consideration by the EPA for more than a year, would have removed federal protection from "isolated wetlands"—small swamps and other marshy areas that were not connected to larger systems of wetlands. The plan also would have removed federal protection of "intermittent streams," most of which were creeks in western states that contained water only in the spring. The National Association of Home Builders had called for changes in wetlands protections, saying its members were confronted with too many regulations. The Bush administration at first agreed, but EPA administrator Leavitt on December 16 said existing regulations would be maintained. Legal experts said the changes that had been considered by the administration would have been challenged in court, leading to a lengthy legal battle the administration had no guarantee of winning.

Following are two documents: first, the executive summary from "A Breath of Fresh Air: Reviving the New Source Review Program," a report issued April 21, 2003, by a panel of experts appointed by the National Academy of Public Administration; second, the text of "EPA Announces Next Step to Improve the New Source Review Program," a statement issued August 27, 2003, by the Environmental Protection Agency announcing final changes to the new source review program of the Clean Air Act.

"A Breath of Fresh Air: Reviving the New Source Review Program"

Executive Summary

The New Source Review program (NSR) is a critical tool enacted by Congress 25 years ago to protect public health and improve the nation's air quality. But, as applied to existing facilities, NSR is not working as Congress intended. Thus NSR should be fundamentally reformed and strongly enforced against past violations by existing facilities.

The complicated NSR program has been effective in controlling air pollution from newly built industrial facilities and utilities, but it has performed poorly in reducing pollution from the nation's oldest and dirtiest factories and power plants. The result is unfair to facilities that have invested in upgrading their equipment to reduce pollution while others have avoided controlling their pollution. NSR's unpredictable and lengthy permitting process is also detrimental to facilities that must change operations quickly to compete effectively. Finally, NSR is not having the positive effect on the health of individuals, or on the quality of the nation's air, that Congress intended.

In this report commissioned by Congress, a Panel of the National Academy of Public Administration (the Academy) recommends that the oldest and dirtiest facilities be given a firm deadline to install cleaner equipment or close down. The Panel further recommends that Congress continue requiring NSR permits for new plants, but also replace NSR as it applies to existing facilities with a simpler, more effective, performance-based program.

In 1977, when Congress added NSR to the Clean Air Act, it gave the Environmental Protection Agency (EPA) and the states an essential tool for reducing air pollution from factories and power plants, thus protecting public health. The Panel finds that Congress intended the NSR program would lead to a reduction in emissions through the development and application of cleaner technologies as sources wore out and were replaced or modernized over time. By making NSR applicable to existing sources only when they modified and increased emissions, Congress did not envision that these existing sources would run in perpetuity, but that they would be replaced or would install lower-emitting technologies, leading to a reduction in overall emissions. Thus, Congress believed that NSR's requirements for controlling pollution from such facilities would help to achieve the nation's air quality standards, while encouraging industries to develop and install new, cleaner technologies for preventing or controlling air pollution.

NSR is fundamentally two programs, both requiring permits for releasing air pollution. The first requires that new major sources be built with modern, cleaner equipment to minimize air pollution. The second requires that similar upgrades be installed when existing plants are modified in ways that may significantly increase their emissions.

The Panel's research indicates that the NSR permitting process works as Congress intended for new industrial facilities. Pre-construction permits for newly built sources have promoted development and installation of cleaner technologies in various industry sectors throughout the country, and those cleaner facilities have helped to protect air quality. The Panel believes the success of the program for new sources is primarily due to two factors: fairly straightforward decisions about whether a proposed new source is covered by NSR; and an early EPA lawsuit to enforce NSR's requirement for pre-construction permits at brand new sources.

But NSR has not been as effective in reducing air pollution when changes at existing sources are likely to increase emissions. Instead—

contrary to Congressional intent—many large, highly polluting facilities have continued to operate and have expanded their production (and pollution) over the past 25 years without upgrading to cleaner technologies. This avoidance of NSR requirements has delayed the reduction in emissions that Congress expected to result eventually from the NSR program. The result: thousands of premature human deaths, and many thousand additional cases of acute illnesses and chronic diseases caused by air pollution.

The Academy Panel finds that, as applied to existing sources, NSR has *not* protected the environment and public health to the extent that Congress intended, and that EPA's implementation of NSR for existing facilities has:

- Allowed the persistence of old, polluting equipment and production technology;
- Created incentives for more polluting facilities to continue operating, breaking the link between capital investments and upgrading equipment to prevent or control pollution;
- Failed to accommodate adequately industries with short-product cycles and large-scale batch production, affecting them in ways that may reduce their competitiveness;
- Produced a mixed record of promoting cleaner technologies;
- Placed heavy administrative burdens on regulators by requiring complicated applicability determinations, by allowing facilities to self-police their compliance with NSR, and by making enforcement difficult; and
- Created uneven and unfair burdens on newer facilities and those with upgraded equipment, on states that are downwind of older facilities with excess emissions, and on communities of color or low-income that are often located near older, more polluting facilities.

A combination of factors has prevented NSR from being effective in reducing emissions from existing facilities. They are:

- The structure of the NSR regulatory program—because it applies only to new or modified facilities, relies on industry self-determinations of applicability, and offers broad regulatory loopholes;
- Lack of EPA's early enforcement against existing facilities that did not obtain NSR permits for modifications—which would have clarified requirements for complying with NSR and would have deterred further violations;
- Pervasive data gaps and no requirement to report emissions—which have handicapped EPA, as well as state and local air agencies, in monitoring the compliance of regulated facilities and analyzing whether NSR is reducing pollution; and

• Insufficient focus on performance-based approaches to achieve desired environmental results.

For those reasons, the Academy Panel believes that the NSR program, as applied to existing sources, must be fundamentally reformed. Protection of the public health and welfare from air pollution is a critical goal of the Clean Air Act; and a strengthened and reformed NSR program can serve, as Congress intended, as an important tool to further that goal. Decisions on reforming NSR and continuing vigorous enforcement against past violations by existing facilities will directly affect the health of individuals—particularly children, the elderly, and asthmatics. Therefore, efforts to reform the NSR program should ensure that NSR provides enhanced protection of health and the environment and should carefully avoid creating even broader loopholes or more exemptions from NSR's requirements.

Summary of Academy Panel's Recommendations

In brief, the Panel's core recommendations for reforming NSR include:

1: End Grandfathering.
Congress should end grandfathering of major sources with high emission levels as soon as possible. Within the next ten years, all major sources that have not obtained an NSR permit since 1977 should upgrade their equipment and lower their emissions to levels that are equivalent to the reductions achieved by the current BACT [Best Available Control Technology] or LAER [Lowest Achievable Emission Rate] performance standards.1

2: Retain NSR for Newly Built Sources.
Congress should continue to require that all newly built major sources of any criteria air pollutant must obtain NSR pre-construction permits, operate at levels that meet the BACT or LAER performance standards and fulfill all other requirements of the current NSR program, such as obtaining offsets in nonattainment areas.

3: Continue to Enforce NSR Vigorously.
EPA and the Department of Justice should continue their investigations and enforcement actions to correct past violations of NSR, especially for changes at existing facilities. These actions will produce significant environmental benefits, deter future violations, and encourage other modified facilities to comply with NSR until Congress has adopted the Panel's other recommended reforms.

4: Reform NSR for Existing Sources Using a Performance-Based System.
Congress should amend the Clean Air Act to reform NSR for existing
sources, replacing it with a compulsory, three-tier performance-based
system that will require facilities to reduce air pollution. Emission limits
for each tier will be based on the lower emissions produced by the clean-
est technologies available. With the development of newer technologies
that can reduce emissions further, NSR's applicable performance standards will then be likely to decline over time.

The three performance tiers are:

Tier 1: Cap-and-Trade: A national or regional multi-pollutant cap-and-
trade system for all fossil fuel-fired power plants, industrial boilers, and
similar facilities that can monitor their emissions continuously, or can
model their emissions reliably.
Tier 2: Cap-and-Net: Emission limits based on the BACT or LAER
performance standards and covering an entire facility with multiple
emission sources that cannot reliably monitor or model and report its emissions on a continuous basis, and thus cannot participate in the cap-and-
trade system of Tier 1.
Tier 3: Unit Cap: Unit-specific emission limits for individual sources
where neither the cap-and-trade nor cap-and-net approaches of Tiers 1 and
2 can feasibly be adopted.

Under any of the three tiers, so long as an existing facility is performing in compliance with all applicable emission limits and has demonstrated that its emissions are reduced and will stay at levels equivalent to
the BACT or LAER performance standards, it may make modifications
without applying for an NSR pre-construction permit.

**5: Improve EPA and State Information Systems and Public
Accountability.**
Congress should require facilities to conduct frequent emission monitoring and to report regularly the results to a centralized database that is
maintained by EPA and the states and made accessible to the public.
Congress should also appropriate adequate funds for EPA to operate a
comprehensive, easily used clearinghouse of technologies that can meet
the BACT or LAER performance standards.

6. Establish Clear Requirements for Compliance.
All NSR reforms should specify clearly how facilities can verify and demonstrate that they are meeting applicable emission limits and
performance standards so that compliance—and enforcement when necessary—will be more predictable, more efficient, and less complicated for
EPA, state and local governments, affected facilities, and the public.

7. Prepare for the Future.

The Panel recommends that Congress' NSR reforms should anticipate future environmental challenges and more effectively integrate the NSR program with other elements of the Clean Air Act, such as Title V operating permits and state implementation plans. Most importantly, the Panel recommends that Congress adopt these reforms in a manner that provides future regulatory certainty for the regulated community, while ensuring that public health and the environment will be protected.

In conclusion, Panel believes that its recommendations preserve the primary goal of Congress for the NSR program: protecting public health by the eventual installation of modern, cleaner technologies, thereby reducing air pollution and improving overall air quality. The Panel's recommendations also provide a workable solution to the problems that have made it so difficult for existing facilities to make changes and still comply with NSR.

Furthermore, the Panel's suggested reforms are designed to stimulate markets for developing and installing improved technologies for preventing or controlling air pollution. They also will eliminate the inequities in the current implementation of the NSR program by closing loopholes, remedying the noncompliance now evident among existing sources, and addressing NSR's ineffectiveness for certain industrial sectors.

Source: National Academy of Public Administration. "A Breath of Fresh Air: Reviving the New Source Review Program." Report by a Panel of the National Academy of Public Administration for the U.S. Congress and the Environmental Protection Agency. Funded by the U.S. Environmental Protection Agency under contract number 68–D–01–047. April 21, 2003. www.napawash.org/Pubs/Fresh Air Full Report.pdf (accessed April 1, 2004).

"EPA Announces Next Step to Improve the New Source Review Program"

EPA is establishing an equipment replacement provision as part of the routine maintenance, repair and replacement exclusion of the New Source Review (NSR) permitting program. Today's rule makes the program more effective and responsive to today's environmental, economic and energy challenges.

"The changes we are making in this rule will provide industrial facilities and power plants with the regulatory certainty they need," said Acting Administrator Marianne Horinko. "This rule will result in safer, more efficient operation of these facilities and, in the case of power plants, more reliable operations that are environmentally sound and provide more affordable energy."

"While today's rule is an important step in improving the New Source Review program, I also remind everyone that existing authorities under the Clean Air Act, including the Acid Rain Amendments of 1990, already control emissions from these facilities and will do so in the future," added Horinko.

Under the Clean Air Act Amendments of 1990, an Acid Rain control program was established that capped emissions of SO2 from power plants. The program went into effect in 1995, and SO2 emissions from these sources have already been reduced more than 40 percent from 1980 levels in a program widely acknowledged as both efficient and effective.

"Enforcement plays an important role in any pollution abatement effort," Horinko said, "but the most effective and efficient way to control emissions is through comprehensive approaches like those successful in controlling acid rain pollutants. These same approaches are embodied in the President's Clear Skies legislation now before Congress."

In today's action EPA is finalizing changes to the definition of "equipment replacement" under NSR. These changes were proposed in December 2002. EPA opened a 120 day comment period and held five public hearings across the country to ensure ample opportunity for public comment on the proposed changes. EPA received over 150,000 written comments and heard from over 450 individuals who participated in the public hearings. After reviewing the comments, EPA decided to move forward to finalize part of the proposed rule. Today's final rule applies only to the equipment replacement part of the proposal.

Congress established the New Source Review program as part of the 1977 Clean Air Act to help control emissions from major new stationary sources of pollution. The NSR program does not generally apply to existing sources, but it does apply if they make a modification that results in a significant emissions increase.

The action taken today promotes the central purposes of the Clean Air Act, "to protect and enhance the quality of the Nation's air resources so as to promote the public health and welfare and the productive capacity of its populations." (Clean Air Act section 101). Under this rule, an equipment replacement activity will be excluded from NSR if:

- it involves replacement of any existing component(s) of a process unit with an identical or functionally equivalent component(s);
- the fixed capital cost of the replaced component, plus the costs of

any repair and maintenance activities that are part of the replacement activity (such as labor, contract services, major equipment rental, etc.), does not exceed 20 percent of the replacement value of the entire process unit;

- the replacement(s) does not change the basic design parameters of the process unit; and
- the replacement(s) does not cause the unit to exceed any emissions limits.

The rule allows sources to use the following approaches to determine the replacement value of a new process unit:

- replacement cost;
- invested cost, adjusted for inflation;
- the insurance value of the equipment, where the insurance value covers complete replacement of the process unit; or
- another accounting procedure, based on Generally Accepted Accounting Principles.

In addition, the final rule also:

- defines a "process unit;"
- specifically delineates the boundary of a process unit for certain specified industries;
- defines a "functionally equivalent" replacement; and
- defines how an owner or operator establishes basic design parameters for electric utility steam generating units and for other types of process units.

Source: U.S. Environmental Protection Agency. Office of Public Affairs. "EPA Announces Next Step to Improve the New Source Review Program." August 27, 2003. www.epa.gov/newsroom/headline2_082703.htm (accessed April 1, 2004).

International "Roadmap" for Peace in the Middle East

April 30, 2003

INTRODUCTION

After standing on the sidelines of the Israeli-Palestinian conflict for most of his first two years in office, President George W. Bush in 2003 waded in and pledged to stay committed. But the president quickly learned the painful lesson that had troubled most of his recent predecessors: Negotiating peace between Israel and its Arab antagonists required sustained diplomacy and a willingness to pressure both sides to make compromises. Bush quietly withdrew from the diplomatic scene when his pressure on the Palestinians failed to bear fruit after a few weeks of effort.

Taking advantage of the vacuum left by the U.S. withdrawal and by continued infighting among the Palestinians, Israeli prime minister Ariel Sharon in December issued a threat to impose his own solution to the conflict. Sharon called his plan "disengagement" and said it would involve withdrawing from a small part of the territories Israel had captured in the 1967 war, closing some of the Jewish settlements in those territories, and completing a wall, then under construction, that would separate Israel and the remaining settlements from most of the Palestinians in the West Bank. *(Sharon plan, p. 1200)*

As these diplomatic and political maneuverings were under way, violence between Israelis and Palestinians continued, though at a somewhat less intense level than during the previous two-plus years. The year saw the familiar cycle of suicide bombings and other attacks by Palestinians against Israelis (an uprising the Palestinians called the Intifada), and an Israeli military response that included assassinations of Palestinian extremists and tight restrictions on the daily lives of Palestinians. The deaths and injuries from the violence represented just the most visible—at least to the outside world—damage caused by the continuing Israeli-Palestinian conflict. The economies of both communities remained stuck in deep recession. By and large Palestinians suffered more than Israelis because military restrictions kept thousands out of work, and some international aid programs that had underpinned the Palestinian economy ran out of money. *(Details on the year's violence and economic problems, p. 751; background, Historic Documents of 2002, p. 927)*

"New" Israeli and Palestinian Governments

The opening events of 2003 offered little hope that any moves toward peace would be successful. On January 5 two suicide bombers set off their weapons in downtown Tel Aviv, killing 23 people (other than themselves) and injuring more than 100. It was the deadliest attack inside Israel in nearly a year; in response, Israeli helicopters fired missiles at suspected Palestinian terrorist bases in Gaza City.

The violence came in the middle of an Israeli election campaign, necessitated by the collapse the previous October of the "national unity" coalition that had governed Israel since early 2001. Although Sharon's hard-line policies toward the Palestinians clearly had not succeeded in stopping suicide bombings and other forms of violence, the latest attacks strengthened the political stance of those who supported such policies—or even tougher ones. On election day, January 28, Israeli voters chose no clear winner but did select a loser: the center-left Labor Party, which had dominated the political scene for the first thirty years of the country's existence. Led by Amram Mitzna, a former general who advocated renewed peace talks, the party won only 19 seats in the Knesset, by far its fewest ever. Sharon's rightist Likud coalition won 37 seats, one of its poorest showings in recent decades and far from the majority needed in the 120-seat parliament. Perhaps the most successful party was a relatively new one that opposed the subsidies and other benefits that Israel long had given to Orthodox Jews. The Shinui Party, whose name meant "change," won 15 seats, drawing much of its strength from disillusioned former Labor Party supporters. Religious and other special-interest parties won the remaining seats.

Sharon appealed to Labor to join him in another unity government, saying the country needed unity and stability "before the crisis deepens further." Labor declined the invitation and after a month of deal making Sharon had formed a new 68-seat majority based on an unlikely marriage of convenience of Likud, Shinui, and several right-wing parties.

Political maneuvering was under way on the other side of the divide, as well, where Palestinian leader Yasir Arafat faced pressure both internationally and from within his own community. Siding with Sharon's long-standing demand, President Bush in 2002 had called on Palestinians to elect new leaders "not compromised by terror"—in other words, to replace Arafat.

More radical Palestinians, notably the Islamist organizations Hamas and Islamic Jihad, had undercut Arafat's popularity among his people by taking a more aggressive stance toward Israel, especially through the sponsorship of suicide bombings and other violence. Many Palestinians, of all political persuasions, were frustrated by the corruption and inefficiency of Arafat's Palestinian Authority.

Yielding to these pressures, Arafat agreed on February 14 to appoint a prime minister to run the Palestinian Authority's day-to-day administration and to represent the Palestinians in any direct negotiations with Israel. On March 7 he nominated one of his longtime aides, Mahmoud Abbas (better known as Abu Mazen) for the post. Widely considered a moderate who opposed terrorism, Abbas had often clashed with Arafat in the past and was unafraid to challenge him. Moreover, Abbas reportedly was one of only two Palestinian leaders whom Israel considered to be acceptable negotiating partners; the other was the speaker of the Palestinian parliament, Ahmed Qureia. The Palestinian legislature approved the Abbas appointment on March 10 and handed an early political victory to him by limiting Arafat's powers to interfere in his administration. One crucial point was left unclear, however: Who would control the dozen or so official Palestinian police and paramilitary security services? Abbas insisted he should be in charge of these services, but Arafat resisted, apparently fearing the loss of a key aspect of his authority. Arafat and some of his key aides also sought to undermine Abbas's credibility among the Palestinian people, saying that he had been appointed under pressure from the United States and Israel.

Publishing the Roadmap

Abbas formally accepted the appointment as Palestinian prime minister on March 19, just a few hours before the United States and a handful of allies launched a massive war in Iraq. That war quickly succeeded in ousting dictator Saddam Hussein, but it also changed the overall political dynamics of the Middle East. Israel no longer had to consider Saddam's regime as a potential military threat. The region's Arab leaders now had to take into account the U.S. occupation of Iraq and Washington's stated determination to promote democracy and economic reform in the region. *(Iraq war, p. 135; Arab world issues, p. 955)*

The successful Iraq war also changed the Bush administration's calculations about the Israeli-Palestinian dispute. During 2002 the administration had joined diplomats from the United Nations, the European Union, and Russia in drafting a Middle East peace plan called the "roadmap"; the four sides called themselves the "quartet." That plan envisioned creation of a Palestinian state within the Gaza strip and portions of the West Bank by 2005, and it called on both Israel and the Palestinians to take conciliatory steps to make long-term peace possible. At Sharon's request, however, Bush had agreed in December 2002 to withhold official publication of the roadmap plan until after the Israeli elections. Sharon staunchly opposed the roadmap as offering too many concessions to the Palestinians.

The ouster of Saddam on April 9, followed on April 29 by the formal installation of Abbas as Palestinian prime minister, finally gave the Bush administration the justification it had sought for pressing ahead with the roadmap. An additional source of encouragement was British prime minister Tony Blair, who had been Bush's most important international ally in the Iraq war but had made it clear he also wanted more attention paid to settling the Israeli-Palestinian conflict.

On April 30 diplomats representing the United States and its partners in the quartet formally handed copies of the roadmap proposal to Sharon and Abbas. At the White House, Bush called Abbas "a man I can work with, and I look forward to working with him and will work with him for the sake of peace." The White House issued a statement calling on "both sides" to carry out the responsibilities assigned them by the peace plan.

Those responsibilities included politically difficult steps for both Israeli and Palestinian leaders. The roadmap called on Israel to dismantle an estimated seventy Jewish settlement "outposts" that had been built in the West Bank since March 2001 without formal Israeli government authorization; freeze "all settlement activity," in other words to stop the expansion of existing Jewish settlements in the territories and to prevent the development of new ones; stop all military attacks on Palestinian civilians; stop demolition of Palestinian homes, olive groves, and other property as collective punishment for terrorist attacks; and withdraw the army in stages from the parts of the West Bank and Gaza strip it had occupied during the Intifada. The roadmap instructed the Palestinians to declare an "unequivocal end to violence and terrorism" and "undertake visible efforts" to block individuals and groups from carrying out violent attacks against Israelis; dismantle "terrorist capabilities and infrastructure," including the confiscation of illegal weapons; reform and consolidate the Palestinian security services; and prepare for eventual Palestinian statehood, including holding elections, drafting a constitution, and creating democratic institutions.

The steps in the roadmap were divided into three phases, with several difficult tasks expected to be undertaken in the first phase. Among those were the Palestinian cease-fire and actions to halt terrorism, as well as Israel's dismantlement of the unauthorized settlements and gradual withdrawal of troops from the West Bank. The roadmap called for these initial steps to be completed by June 2003—a deadline established when diplomats negotiated the roadmap in mid-2002. By the time the roadmap was published, the deadline had become an impossible one, given the continued mistrust between the two sides. Critics said this unrealistic deadline demonstrated the fundamental unworkability of the roadmap, but the Bush administration said the deadlines still served as important goals for both sides.

In keeping with most previous attempts at a comprehensive Israeli-Palestinian peace, the roadmap left the most controversial issues for the end of the process, scheduled vaguely as "2004–2005." These issues included the future of the more than 3 million Palestinians and their descendants who had lived as refugees ever since the 1948 Arab-Israeli war, and the status of Jerusalem, which was claimed by each side as its capital.

Palestinian extremists delivered their reaction to the roadmap even before it was made public. Two suicide bombings in Tel Aviv on April 28 and 29 killed six people and wounded several dozen others. Israel responded with raids in Gaza and the West Bank that, over a three-day period, killed nearly twenty Palestinians.

Officially, Israeli and Palestinian leaders said they welcomed the roadmap peace plan, but they quickly reverted to form, each demanding that the other side carry out its responsibilities first. Sharon and Abbas held an inconclusive meeting on May 17; it was the first time Sharon had met with a top-level Palestinian leader since he became prime minister more than two years earlier.

Sharon also met with U.S. diplomats to demand major changes in the roadmap. The thrust of his demands was to relieve Israel of any responsibility to ease its restrictions on Palestinians, or halt its settlement activity, until after the Palestinians had taken decisive action to halt terrorism. The Bush administration on May 22 assured Sharon that his concerns would be taken into consideration, and three days later the Israeli cabinet approved the roadmap by a narrow margin; one opponent called the plan a "sugar-coated cyanide pill." The cabinet made its approval contingent on fourteen changes that, if adopted, would have made the peace plan unacceptable for Palestinians. The key change demanded by the cabinet was that the Palestinians officially surrender any right for refugees to return to their former homes inside Israel. Palestinian leaders considered this so-called right of return to be one of their trump cards in any negotiations with Israel.

A Brief Period of U.S. Diplomacy

Israel's hedged approval of the roadmap set in motion a flurry of diplomacy that—at least for a few weeks—offered the first hope in nearly three years for a peaceful resolution of the Israeli-Palestinian conflict. In anticipation of an expected visit to the region by President Bush, Sharon and Abbas met again on May 29 and agreed to a limited Israeli troop pullback from parts of the occupied territories. Israel in subsequent days also announced the easing of some travel restrictions on Palestinians, released about one hundred Palestinian prisoners from jail, and announced plans to remove some of the unauthorized settlements. The Bush administration named John Wolf, a veteran diplomat, as the new U.S. special envoy for Middle East peace; his predecessor, retired general Anthony Zinni, had achieved little of substance during several trips to the region in 2001 and 2002.

Bush began his visit to the region by meeting with Arab leaders, including Abbas, at the Egyptian resort city Sharm el-Sheik on June 3. The Arabs agreed to support the peace process and denounced the "culture of extremism and violence" in the Middle East. Bush met the following day with Abbas and Sharon at Aqaba, a Jordanian port city. Photographs of the three men, deep in conversation under palm trees on a hot day, seemed to herald a fresh start for the long-stalled peace negotiations. In public, Abbas and Sharon both made the statements Bush had come to hear: Abbas that he renounced terrorism and was calling for an end to the Palestinian uprising, Sharon that he was ordering dismantlement of unauthorized settlements. Bush praised the pledges by both leaders and said the United States, in turn, was "committed" to the cause of peace. Bush later told reporters he had warned Abbas and Sharon that he would "ride herd" on them to keep their promises.

In subsequent weeks both sides took some of the steps they had promised, despite continued suicide bombings and Israeli attacks on Palestinian extremists. Aided by Egyptian diplomats, Abbas negotiated with the main Palestinian extremist groups—Hamas, Islamic Jihad, and the al Aqsa Martyrs Brigade. After direct intervention by Secretary of State Colin Powell and Bush's national security adviser, Condoleezza Rice, Hamas and Islamic Jihad on June 29 agreed to a three-month cease-fire of all attacks against Israel; Arafat's Fatah faction said it would honor a cease-fire for six months. Israel, which did not pledge a reciprocal cease-fire, nevertheless dismantled several unauthorized settlements, most of them uninhabited, and withdrew the army from the northern part of the Gaza strip.

The next six weeks presented one of the calmest periods since the Palestinian uprising began in September 2000. Despite a handful of violent incidents, Abbas and Sharon met twice (on July 1 and July 20), and each pledged to keep the peace process going if only the other side would stick to its promises. Hoping for an Israeli concession that would increase his credibility among Palestinians, Abbas pressed for Sharon to release hundreds of Palestinians from jail. Sharon complied by releasing fifty-four prisoners, including a Palestinian Authority security official, on July 3, but then refused to release others. Abbas came under attack from within the Palestinian leadership—reportedly including Arafat—and he threatened to resign on July 8. A week later Abbas and Arafat worked out a power-sharing deal that kept Abbas on the job but failed to resolve differences over how to approach the negotiations with Israel.

With the peace process in danger of stalling, Bush summoned the two leaders to the White House for separate meetings. Abbas was the first to arrive, on July 25. Bush offered Abbas new words of encouragement and a small reward: The president said an Israeli plan to drive a security fence, or wall, deep into the West Bank was "a problem." It was the most direct criticism Bush had ever made of the wall, which Sharon's government said was needed to keep suicide bombers out of Israel and Palestinians said would divide many West Bank communities. Bush met with Sharon on July 29 and softened his tone about the wall, saying it would be "irrelevant" if Palestinians would halt terrorism against Israel.

The peace talks reached another crisis point on August 5 when Abbas cancelled a scheduled meeting with Sharon, complaining about Israel's plans for releasing Palestinian prisoners. The government had said it would release about 350 jailed Palestinians (in addition to about 250 who had been released in several groups during previous weeks); Abbas wanted a pledge that most of the 6,000 Palestinians in Israeli jails would be freed. Israel went ahead with its plans on August 6, releasing 339 Palestinians, none of them considered "security prisoners" who had committed serious acts of violence against Israel.

For all practical purposes, the halting drive toward peace came to an end on August 19 when a Palestinian suicide bomber exploded his device on a bus in Jerusalem, killing twenty people and wounding several dozen others. Abbas ordered Palestinian security services to arrest those who had planned the attack, but his belated attempt to crack down on the militants was overtaken by events. Israel responded to the bombing by freezing all talks with the Palestinians, halting its military withdrawals from the West Bank, moving troops into Jenin and Nablus, and killing yet another Hamas official, Abu Shanab, who had been one of the group's chief advocates of the cease-fire. Hamas declared the cease-fire dead, and the familiar cycle of attacks and counterattacks resumed.

An angry and frustrated Abbas on September 6 submitted his resignation as prime minister. It was his third threat to resign since he had first accepted the job, and this time Arafat accepted it.

Why the Roadmap Failed

The departure of Abbas put the peace process on hold—at best—and led all sides to assess why the hopes that had emerged on a sunny day in Aqaba in June had collapsed just three months later. Israelis and Palestinians again blamed the other side for failing to follow through on promises. Some officials on both sides also blamed the Bush administration for not putting enough pressure on the opposite side.

Writing in a November report for the Jaffe Center for Security Studies in Jerusalem, Israeli political analyst Mark Heller argued that the basic flaw of the latest peace process was that it did nothing to change the way each side viewed the other. "Neither [side] was genuinely committed to closing the chapter of the three-year intifada and reengaging in serious peace negotiations, if only because neither believed that the other was similarly committed," Heller said. Both sides "appeared to be acting out of fatigue and a desire to pause and regroup," as well as in response to international and domestic pressure.

Heller and many other Middle East policy experts also said the Bush administration had an unrealistic view of Abbas's ability to act independently of Arafat and to crack down on Hamas and Islamic Jihad, which had more public support than he did. Until Abbas did so, Sharon refused to take steps—such as freezing settlements or ending restrictions on Palestinian travel—that might have strengthened Abbas's leadership; Sharon argued that any Israeli concessions would reward terrorism. This mutual intransigence developed into the latest in a long serious of vicious cycles in the Israeli-Palestinian conflict.

Some critics also faulted the roadmap for its step-by-step approach. The concept of incremental moves was borrowed from earlier peace plans, notably the Israel-Palestinian portion of the 1978 Camp David peace agreement between Israel and Egypt, and the 1993 Oslo accord under which Israel and the Palestinians agreed to make peace. The level of violence and mistrust was now so great, some observers said, that the conflict could be ended only with a giant step to a permanent agreement resolving all the major issues. Others, including key Bush administration officials, called such a move impractical, noting that former president Clinton's failure to achieve a comprehensive agreement in 2000 had led to the current cycle of violence. *(Camp David agreement, Historic Documents of 1978, p. 605; Oslo accords, Historic Documents of 1993, p. 747; Clinton negotiations, Historic Documents of 2000, p. 494)*

Finally, the Bush administration's actions, or lack of them, also played a role in the failure of the roadmap, according to most observers. After pledging at Aqaba to "ride herd" on both sides, Bush essentially backed away from personal involvement in the peace process aside from his separate meetings at the White House with Abbas and Sharon. Secretary of State Powell made just two trips to the region during the early stages of the year's peace process—in contrast to the ambitious shuttle diplomacy that several of his predecessors had used to win agreements. Bush sent diplomats to monitor Israeli and Palestinian compliance with the roadmap, but their findings were never made public. "You cannot monitor things in this situation . . . with such a low profile," former Israeli peace negotiator Yossi Beilin told the *Washington Post.*

Following is the text of "A Performance-Based Roadmap to a Permanent Two-State Solution to the Israeli-Palestinian Conflict," released April 30, 2003, by the "quartet" that had developed it: the United States, the United Nations, the European Union, and Russia.

"Roadmap to a Permanent Two-State Solution to the Israeli-Palestinian Conflict"

The following is a performance-based and goal-driven roadmap, with clear phases, timelines, target dates, and benchmarks aiming at progress through reciprocal steps by the two parties in the political, security, economic, humanitarian, and institution-building fields, under the auspices of the Quartet [the United States, European Union, United Nations, and Russia]. The destination is a final and comprehensive settlement of the Israel-Palestinian conflict by 2005, as presented in President Bush's speech of 24 June, and welcomed by the EU, Russia and the UN in the 16 July and 17 September Quartet Ministerial statements.

A two-state solution to the Israeli-Palestinian conflict will only be achieved through an end to violence and terrorism, when the Palestinian people have a leadership acting decisively against terror and willing and able to build a practicing democracy based on tolerance and liberty, and through Israel's readiness to do what is necessary for a democratic Palestinian state to be established, and a clear, unambiguous acceptance by both parties of the goal of a negotiated settlement as described below. The Quartet will assist and facilitate implementation of the plan, starting in Phase I, including direct discussions between the parties as required. The plan establishes a realistic timeline for implementation. However, as a performance-based plan, progress will require and depend upon the good faith efforts of the parties, and their compliance with each of the obligations outlined below. Should the parties perform their obligations rapidly, progress within and through the phases may come sooner than indicated in the plan. Non-compliance with obligations will impede progress.

A settlement, negotiated between the parties, will result in the emergence of an independent, democratic, and viable Palestinian state living side by side in peace and security with Israel and its other neighbors. The settlement will resolve the Israel-Palestinian conflict, and end the occupation that began in 1967, based on the foundations of the Madrid Conference, the principle of land for peace, UNSCRs [United Nations Security Council Resolutions] 242, 338 and 1397, agreements previously reached by the parties, and the initiative of Saudi Crown Prince Abdullah—endorsed by the Beirut Arab League Summit—calling for acceptance of Israel as a neighbor living in peace and security, in the context of a comprehensive settlement. This initiative is a vital element of international efforts to promote a comprehensive peace on all tracks, including the Syrian-Israeli and Lebanese-Israeli tracks.

The Quartet will meet regularly at senior levels to evaluate the parties' performance on implementation of the plan. In each phase, the parties are expected to perform their obligations in parallel, unless otherwise indicated.

Phase I: Ending Terror And Violence, Normalizing Palestinian Life, and Building Palestinian Institutions—Present to May 2003

In Phase I, the Palestinians immediately undertake an unconditional cessation of violence according to the steps outlined below; such action should be accompanied by supportive measures undertaken by Israel. Palestinians and Israelis resume security cooperation based on the Tenet work plan to end violence, terrorism, and incitement through restructured and effective Palestinian security services. Palestinians undertake comprehensive political reform in preparation for statehood, including drafting a Palestinian constitution, and free, fair and open elections upon the basis of those measures. Israel takes all necessary steps to help normalize Palestinian life. Israel withdraws from Palestinian areas occupied from September 28, 2000 and the two sides restore the status quo that existed at that time, as security performance and cooperation progress. Israel also freezes all settlement activity, consistent with the Mitchell report.

At the outset of Phase I:

- Palestinian leadership issues unequivocal statement reiterating Israel's right to exist in peace and security and calling for an immediate and unconditional ceasefire to end armed activity and all acts of violence against Israelis anywhere. All official Palestinian institutions end incitement against Israel.
- Israeli leadership issues unequivocal statement affirming its commitment to the two-state vision of an independent, viable, sovereign Palestinian state living in peace and security alongside Israel, as expressed by President Bush, and calling for an immediate end to violence against Palestinians everywhere. All official Israeli institutions end incitement against Palestinians.

Security

- Palestinians declare an unequivocal end to violence and terrorism and undertake visible efforts on the ground to arrest, disrupt, and restrain individuals and groups conducting and planning violent attacks on Israelis anywhere.

- Rebuilt and refocused Palestinian Authority security apparatus begins sustained, targeted, and effective operations aimed at confronting all those engaged in terror and dismantlement of terrorist capabilities and infrastructure. This includes commencing confiscation of illegal weapons and consolidation of security authority, free of association with terror and corruption.

- GOI [Government of Israel] takes no actions undermining trust, including deportations, attacks on civilians; confiscation and/or demolition of Palestinian homes and property, as a punitive measure or to facilitate Israeli construction; destruction of Palestinian institutions and infrastructure; and other measures specified in the Tenet work plan.

- Relying on existing mechanisms and on-the-ground resources, Quartet representatives begin informal monitoring and consult with the parties on establishment of a formal monitoring mechanism and its implementation.

- Implementation, as previously agreed, of U.S. rebuilding, training and resumed security cooperation plan in collaboration with outside oversight board (U.S.–Egypt–Jordan). Quartet support for efforts to achieve a lasting, comprehensive cease-fire.
  — All Palestinian security organizations are consolidated into three services reporting to an empowered Interior Minister.
  — Restructured/retrained Palestinian security forces and IDF [Israeli Defense Forces] counterparts progressively resume security cooperation and other undertakings in implementation of the Tenet work plan, including regular senior-level meetings, with the participation of U.S. security officials.

- Arab states cut off public and private funding and all other forms of support for groups supporting and engaging in violence and terror.

- All donors providing budgetary support for the Palestinians channel these funds through the Palestinian Ministry of Finance's Single Treasury Account.

- As comprehensive security performance moves forward, IDF withdraws progressively from areas occupied since September 28, 2000 and the two sides restore the status quo that existed prior to September 28, 2000. Palestinian security forces redeploy to areas vacated by IDF.

Palestinian Institution-Building

- Immediate action on credible process to produce draft constitution for Palestinian statehood. As rapidly as possible, constitutional committee circulates draft Palestinian constitution, based on strong parliamentary democracy and cabinet with empowered prime minister, for public comment/debate. Constitutional committee proposes draft document for submission after elections for approval by appropriate Palestinian institutions.

- Appointment of interim prime minister or cabinet with empowered executive authority/decision-making body.
- GOI fully facilitates travel of Palestinian officials for PLC [Palestinian Legislative Council] and Cabinet sessions, internationally supervised security retraining, electoral and other reform activity, and other supportive measures related to the reform efforts.
- Continued appointment of Palestinian ministers empowered to undertake fundamental reform. Completion of further steps to achieve genuine separation of powers, including any necessary Palestinian legal reforms for this purpose.
- Establishment of independent Palestinian election commission. PLC reviews and revises election law.
- Palestinian performance on judicial, administrative, and economic benchmarks, as established by the International Task Force on Palestinian Reform.
- As early as possible, and based upon the above measures and in the context of open debate and transparent candidate selection/electoral campaign based on a free, multi-party process, Palestinians hold free, open, and fair elections.
- GOI facilitates Task Force election assistance, registration of voters, movement of candidates and voting officials. Support for NGOs [non-governmental organizations] involved in the election process.
- GOI reopens Palestinian Chamber of Commerce and other closed Palestinian institutions in East Jerusalem based on a commitment that these institutions operate strictly in accordance with prior agreements between the parties.

Humanitarian Response

- Israel takes measures to improve the humanitarian situation. Israel and Palestinians implement in full all recommendations of the Bertini report to improve humanitarian conditions, lifting curfews and easing restrictions on movement of persons and goods, and allowing full, safe, and unfettered access of international and humanitarian personnel.
- AHLC [Ad-Hoc Liaison Committee] reviews the humanitarian situation and prospects for economic development in the West Bank and Gaza and launches a major donor assistance effort, including to the reform effort.

- GOI and PA [Palestinian Authority] continue revenue clearance process and transfer of funds, including arrears, in accordance with agreed, transparent monitoring mechanism.

Civil Society

- Continued donor support, including increased funding through PVOs/NGOs, for people to people programs, private sector development and civil society initiatives.

Settlements

- GOI immediately dismantles settlement outposts erected since March 2001.
- Consistent with the Mitchell Report, GOI freezes all settlement activity (including natural growth of settlements).

Phase II: Transition—June 2003-December 2003

In the second phase, efforts are focused on the option of creating an independent Palestinian state with provisional borders and attributes of sovereignty, based on the new constitution, as a way station to a permanent status settlement. As has been noted, this goal can be achieved when the Palestinian people have a leadership acting decisively against terror, willing and able to build a practicing democracy based on tolerance and liberty. With such a leadership, reformed civil institutions and security structures, the Palestinians will have the active support of the Quartet and the broader international community in establishing an independent, viable, state.

Progress into Phase II will be based upon the consensus judgment of the Quartet of whether conditions are appropriate to proceed, taking into account performance of both parties. Furthering and sustaining efforts to normalize Palestinian lives and build Palestinian institutions, Phase II starts after Palestinian elections and ends with possible creation of an independent Palestinian state with provisional borders in 2003. Its primary goals are continued comprehensive security performance and effective security cooperation, continued normalization of Palestinian life and institution-building, further building on and sustaining of the goals outlined in Phase I, ratification of a democratic Palestinian constitution, formal establishment of office of prime minister, consolidation of political reform, and the creation of a Palestinian state with provisional borders.

- International Conference: Convened by the Quartet, in consultation with the parties, immediately after the successful conclusion of Palestinian elections, to support Palestinian economic recovery and launch a process, leading to establishment of an independent Palestinian state with provisional borders.
  — Such a meeting would be inclusive, based on the goal of a comprehensive Middle East peace (including between Israel and Syria, and Israel and Lebanon), and based on the principles described in the preamble to this document.
  — Arab states restore pre-intifada links to Israel (trade offices, etc.).
  — Revival of multilateral engagement on issues including regional water resources, environment, economic development, refugees, and arms control issues.
- New constitution for democratic, independent Palestinian state is finalized and approved by appropriate Palestinian institutions. Further elections, if required, should follow approval of the new constitution.
- Empowered reform cabinet with office of prime minister formally established, consistent with draft constitution.
- Continued comprehensive security performance, including effective security cooperation on the basis laid out in Phase I.
- Creation of an independent Palestinian state with provisional borders through a process of Israeli-Palestinian engagement, launched by the international conference. As part of this process, implementation of prior agreements, to enhance maximum territorial contiguity, including further action on settlements in conjunction with establishment of a Palestinian state with provisional borders.
- Enhanced international role in monitoring transition, with the active, sustained, and operational support of the Quartet.
- Quartet members promote international recognition of Palestinian state, including possible UN membership.

Phase III: Permanent Status Agreement and End of the Israeli-Palestinian Conflict—2004–2005

Progress into Phase III, based on consensus judgment of Quartet, and taking into account actions of both parties and Quartet monitoring. Phase III objectives are consolidation of reform and stabilization of Palestinian institutions, sustained, effective Palestinian security performance, and Israeli-Palestinian negotiations aimed at a permanent status agreement in 2005.

- Second International Conference: Convened by Quartet, in consultation with the parties, at beginning of 2004 to endorse agreement reached on an independent Palestinian state with provisional borders and formally to launch a process with the active, sustained, and operational support of the Quartet, leading to a final, permanent status resolution in 2005, including on borders, Jerusalem, refugees, settlements; and, to support progress toward a comprehensive Middle East settlement between Israel and Lebanon and Israel and Syria, to be achieved as soon as possible.

- Continued comprehensive, effective progress on the reform agenda laid out by the Task Force in preparation for final status agreement.
- Continued sustained and effective security performance, and sustained, effective security cooperation on the basis laid out in Phase I.
- International efforts to facilitate reform and stabilize Palestinian institutions and the Palestinian economy, in preparation for final status agreement.
- Parties reach final and comprehensive permanent status agreement that ends the Israel-Palestinian conflict in 2005, through a settlement negotiated between the parties based on UNSCR 242, 338, and 1397, that ends the occupation that began in 1967, and includes an agreed, just, fair, and realistic solution to the refugee issue, and a negotiated resolution on the status of Jerusalem that takes into account the political and religious concerns of both sides, and protects the religious interests of Jews, Christians, and Muslims worldwide, and fulfills the vision of two states, Israel and sovereign, independent, democratic and viable Palestine, living side-by-side in peace and security.
- Arab state acceptance of full normal relations with Israel and security for all the states of the region in the context of a comprehensive Arab-Israeli peace.

Source: U.S. Department of State. Office of the Spokesman. "A Performance-Based Roadmap to a Permanent Two-State Solution to the Israeli-Palestinian Conflict." April 30, 2003. www.state.gov/r/pa/prs/ps/2003/20062.htm (accessed May 1, 2003).

May

2003 HISTORIC DOCUMENTS

Indian and Pakistani Prime Ministers on the Dispute over Kashmir

May 2 and 6, 2003

INTRODUCTION

One year after they traded threats of yet another war, India and Pakistan took limited but important steps in 2003 toward resolving their half-century-long dispute over Kashmir. The two governments restored full diplomatic relations, and Pakistan's military leader, President Pervez Musharraf, offered a significant concession from his country's long-standing demands about the future of Kashmir. Musharraf and his Indian counterpart, Prime Minister Atal Bihari Vajpayee, were expected to meet at a regional summit session early in 2004—their first face-to-face encounter in nearly two years.

Kashmir had been in dispute between the two countries ever since 1947 when Britain, the colonial power, divided the Indian subcontinent between India, with its mostly Hindu population, and Pakistan, with its mostly Muslim population. Although most of its people were Muslim, Kashmir ended up within India's borders. The two countries fought wars over Kashmir in 1947–1948 and 1965, after which Pakistan gained control over about one-third of the province. Islamist guerrillas, trained and armed by Pakistan, began systematic attacks against the Indian government of Kashmir in 1989; India responded with brutally repressive tactics. The conflict resulted in tens of thousands of deaths over the next decade. India and Pakistan both tested nuclear weapons in 1998, and the two countries fought another inconclusive skirmish over Kashmir the following year. Yet another confrontation came after Pakistani guerrillas in December 2001 attacked the Indian parliament building in New Delhi, killing nine people. The two countries massed more than 1 million troops along their borders and threatened war against each other in the spring of 2002. U.S. diplomats helped avert a war by convincing Musharraf to suppress the guerrillas.

The repeated conflicts, and threats of new ones, were both the cause and effect of political stresses in both India and Pakistan. Vajpayee headed a Hindu nationalist coalition whose members considered Indian control of Kashmir as nonnegotiable; any concession to Pakistan was seen as violating India's fundamental interests. Vajpayee tried to moderate some of the extremist elements of his coalition but could not ignore their influence.

Musharraf was in a much more difficult position, in fact the same state of affairs in which he found himself after the September 2001 terrorist attacks against the United States. He was still under pressure from Washington to root out members of the al Qaeda terrorist network, and of the former Taliban regime in Afghanistan, who had taken refuge in the mountains of Pakistan's northwest province. India—and to a lesser extent the United States—continued to demand that Musharraf dismantle the Islamic extremist groups that the Pakistani military had used for more than a decade to fight Indian control of Kashmir. But every step that Musharraf took to comply with these foreign pressures undermined his status at home, where there still was strong public support for the extremist groups that had done Pakistan's bidding in Afghanistan and Kashmir. Islamic political parties did well in regional and national parliamentary elections in 2002, demonstrating clearly that Musharraf's military government still lacked legitimacy in the minds of many Pakistanis. *(Background, Historic Documents of 2002, pp. 165, 325)*

More Threats

The threat of war in April-May 2002 was headed off when Musharraf promised the United States that Islamist guerrillas would not be allowed to attack India from Pakistani territory. Musharraf had already arrested more than 2,000 alleged extremists and banned four of the dozen-some organizations said to have been responsible for terrorist activities in Kashmir. Among the banned groups were Jaish-e-Muhammed and Lashkar-e-Taiaba, both of which India accused of carrying out the December 2001 attack on the Indian parliament. But later in 2002 the government released most of those it had arrested, including top leaders of the banned groups. The groups themselves continued operating under new names.

The *Washington Post,* in February 2003, quoted Hafiz Sayeed—the founder of Lashkar-e-Taiaba—as claiming that the group's "jihad" campaign had continued even while he was imprisoned. "India should believe me that it is beyond General Musharraf to blow a whistle and stop the jihad in Kashmir," Sayeed told the *Post.*

In a related step, Musharraf reorganized Pakistan's powerful Inter-Services Intelligence (ISI) agency, which had been responsible for funneling aid and weapons to the extremist groups in Kashmir. He fired the agency's chief, but he then gave the general a job heading a private company reportedly owned by the military.

The controversy over just what Pakistan had done to crack down on the guerrillas erupted again on February 8, when India—citing continued cross-border attacks on Kashmir—expelled Pakistan's acting ambassador and four of his aides. India accused the ambassador, acting high commissioner Jalil Abbas Jilani, of passing money to the guerrillas, a charge he denied. Pakistan responded by ousting the Indian ambassador to Islamabad. Four days later India tested a new cruise missile, capable of hitting any point in Pakistan with a nonnuclear warhead; Pakistan responded early in March by formally unveiling a new medium-range missile capable of carrying a nuclear warhead into northern India. These tit-for-tat events were followed in mid-March by an episode of heavy shelling across the Kashmir border and then a series of guerrilla attacks within Kashmir that killed several dozen people. In the deadliest attack, on March 24, guerrillas shot dead twenty-four Hindu civilians in a small village.

A Thaw in Relations

Despite the continuing violence, and accompanying hot rhetoric from both sides, Vajpayee on April 18 moved to lower the temperature by offering to hold talks with Pakistan. "Guns will not solve the matter, but brotherhood will," he said during a visit to Kashmir, adding that he was extending a "hand of friendship" to Pakistan. Ten days later Pakistani prime minister Mir Zafarullah Khan Jamali called Vajpayee, thanked him for his comments, and invited him to Islamabad. It was the first substantive high-level contact between the two countries since a failed summit between Vajpayee and Musharraf in July 2001.

Two subsequent car bombings and other attacks signaled that guerrillas hoped to derail any move toward peace. Hard-line factions of Vajpayee's coalition also tried to intervene, announcing—apparently without authorization from the prime minister himself—that the invitation to Islamabad had been rejected.

Even so, the political leaders moved ahead. Speaking in parliament on May 2, Vajpayee said he was offering to send India's ambassador back to Pakistan and allow the restoration of air transportation between the two countries. "We are committed to the improvement of relations with Pakistan, and are willing to grasp every opportunity for doing so," he said.

Responding to Vajpayee's proffer, Prime Minister Jamali said on May 6 that Pakistan agreed to the restoration of full diplomatic relations and transportation links with India. Jamali said that during his earlier telephone conversation with Vajpayee "I sensed a positive desire on his part to break the impasse in our relationship. . . ."

India and Pakistan announced on July 10 that their respective leaders would meet in January 2004 at the annual Summit of the South Asian Association for Regional Cooperation, scheduled to take place in Islamabad. That group's 2003 summit had to be called off because India refused to attend. At the 2002 summit, in Katmandu, Musharraf approached Vajpayee unexpectedly, and the two men shook hands and exchanged a few words but reportedly had no substantive discussions.

Yet another sign that the latest moves toward peace might be in earnest was a two-day conference of legislators, journalists, and academics held at the Marriott Hotel in Islamabad. The delegation of thirty-three Indian legislators reportedly was the largest ever to visit Pakistan. The conference got under way on August 9, the same day that India's new ambassador presented his credentials to Musharraf. Vajpayee sent a conciliatory statement to the conference: "Violence and bloodshed cannot provide any solutions," he said. "We can live together only if we let each other live." Musharraf held a private meeting with the Indian legislators after the conference ended on August 12.

As so often in the past, the atmosphere suddenly turned chilly again two weeks later, on August 25, when two bombs hidden in taxis killed 52 people and wounded nearly 150 in Bombay (now known as Mumbai). It was the worst attack in a west coast Indian city since 1993, when a series of bombs exploded at the stock exchange and other buildings, killing more than 260 people. No group claimed responsibility for the latest bombing, but Indian authorities blamed an outlawed Indian Muslim group that reportedly had links to the Pakistan-based Lashkar-e-Taiaba.

Three days after the bombing, Indian security forces stormed a hotel in Srinigar, the summer capital of Kashmir, where Islamist extremists were holding hostages; four people died in the attack. Vajpayee was visiting Kashmir at the time, and he used the incident to voice his frustration: "Talks have not even begun. People are dying in terrorist violence. How can you have meaningful talks now?" A Pakistani foreign ministry spokesman responded by saying "the onus" was on India to ease tensions: "It can do so by ending repression and human rights violations in Indian-held Kashmir."

Violence in Kashmir escalated in September and October, killing more than 350 people. Repeating an often-used script from the past, India blamed the killings on attacks by insurgents from Pakistan, while separatist groups in Kashmir insisted the Indian government's repression had inspired a thirst for vengeance among the local population. Adding to the tumult and uncertainty was a split in one of the leading Muslim groupings in the region. The All Parties Hurriyat Conference—a coalition of twenty-four political and religious groups in Kashmir—split in early September between those favoring a merger with Pakistan and those favoring full independence for the region. The split appeared to strengthen those factions that demanded independence.

The first positive step in nearly three months came on November 25, when the Indian and Pakistani armies agreed to a cease-fire in what had become routine shootings across the frontier, known as the Line of Control, that divided Kashmir. Ostensibly launched to celebrate the end of the Muslim holy month of Ramadan, it was the first formal cease-fire since the outbreak of guerrilla fighting in Kashmir in 1989. Ever since then, troops had regularly fired automatic rifles, and occasionally artillery, across the border simply to assert each side's claim to territory held by the other.

Musharraf's Concession

Vajpayee had initiated the year's first round of conciliation back in April when he offered talks with Pakistan. Musharraf unexpectedly opened a second round in December with what many observers considered the most important Pakistani concession in years. In an interview with the Reuters news service on December 17, Musharraf said he had put "aside" Pakistan's long-standing demand that the future of Kashmir should be decided by a referendum among the territory's people. The United Nations Security Council had called for such a referendum in 1948 and 1950, at the conclusion of the first India-Pakistan war over Kashmir. Ever since, Pakistan had demanded such a referendum, obviously hoping that the Muslim-majority in Kashmir would vote for incorporation into Pakistan—or at least independence from India. India had adamantly opposed such a vote.

"We are for United Nations Security Council resolutions," Musharraf told Reuters. "However, now we have left that aside. If we want to resolve this issue, both sides need to talk to each other with flexibility, coming beyond stated positions, meeting halfway somewhere." Musharraf said he was shifting position because the recent thaw in relations had generated an "expectation" of peace among the people in both countries. "If the leadership doesn't rise to the occasion, it is a pity, and I think we'll disappoint our public again," he said.

Some observers, in both India and Pakistan, noted that Musharraf in the past had signaled a possible willingness to compromise on the referendum issue, but he had never been so explicit. His new statement brought immediate praise from India, where foreign minister Yashwant Sinha said "he welcomed any change in or modification" of Pakistan's referendum demand. The U.S. State Department also called Musharraf's statement "constructive."

Hard-line Islamist factions in Pakistan did not see the president's new flexibility as a positive development, however. The religious coalition Mutahida Majlis-e-Amal, which in 2002 had won regional elections giving it control of the Northwest Frontier province, issued a statement calling Musharraf's position a "betrayal of Kashmiris."

Assassination Attempts

Musharraf's latest move toward peace with India came in the context of new attacks on his presidency. On December 14, and again on December 25, Musharraf narrowly survived assassination attempts. In the first attack, a remote-controlled bomb exploded at a bridge in the city of Rawalpindi less that one minute after the president's motorcade had passed. An electronic jamming system in Musharraf's limousine apparently delayed the triggering of the bomb. The second attack came in the same vicinity as the first: Drivers in two bomb-laden pickup trucks rammed into the rear of the president's motorcade. The resulting explosions killed fifteen people and cracked the windshield of Musharraf's car, but the president and his driver escaped unhurt. The December 14 attack was similar to a failed bombing of Musharraf's motorcade during a visit to the city of Karachi in April 2002.

Musharraf's decision in 2001 to side with the United States in its war against terrorism had made him an enemy of Islamist extremist groups, notably the al Qaeda terrorist network. Government officials and independent observers said Islamist extremists, possibly even one or more of the groups that the Pakistani military had supported in Afghanistan and Kashmir, almost certainly carried out the attacks. Three alleged members of one of those groups, Haruk ul-Islam, had been sentenced to prison for involvement in the April 2002 bombing attempt. In September tape recordings attributed to senior al Qaeda leader Ayman Zawahiri said Pakistan's military had an "Islamic duty" to oust Musharraf from power.

Musharraf insisted he was not intimidated by the attacks against him. In a television interview broadcast the night of the December 25 attempt, he said the incident "has further strengthened my resolve."

In addition to failing to kill Musharraf, the attacks did not derail a political compromise the president had struck earlier in December with the Islamist political opposition. Under that deal, Musharraf was to be given extraordinary political powers in exchange for his pledge to step down as military leader at the end of 2004. Ever since he ousted the country's elected government in a 1999 coup, Musharraf had retained his command of the military as well as his leadership of the civilian government. Musharraf assumed the title of president in 2000, and in 2002 he won a disputed referendum that authorized him to remain in office for five years. Parliamentary elections later in 2002 led to the installation of a civilian government headed by Prime Minister Jamali, but Musharraf retained real power.

On December 29 the lower house of parliament, the national assembly, approved the compromise arrangement in the form of amendments to the constitution. The bill won overwhelming approval, although the vote was boycotted by representatives of parties headed by the two former elected prime ministers (Nawaz Sharif and Benazir Bhutto, both living in exile).

Three days later, in a sequence of votes orchestrated by the government, both houses of parliament and the legislatures of the four provinces voted overwhelmingly to give Musharraf a vote of "confidence." These votes were boycotted by most opposition lawmakers.

Following are the texts of two documents: first, an address May 2, 2003, in the Indian parliament by Prime Minister Atal Bihari Vajpayee, in which he called for restoration of diplomatic relations and civil aviation links between India and Pakistan; second, a statement issued May 6, 2003, by Pakistani prime minister Mir Zafarullah Khan Jamali, responding positively to Vajpayee's speech.

"Prime Minister Vajpayee's Statement in Parliament on Pakistan"

I received a telephone call on the evening of 28th April, from Prime Minister [PM] Jamali of Pakistan. PM Jamali conveyed his appreciation and thanks for the comments I had made in Srinagar and my remarks about India-Pakistan relations contained in my statement in the two Houses of Parliament. He also condemned terrorism.

As Honourable members are aware, we are committed to the improvement of relations with Pakistan, and are willing to grasp every opportunity for doing so. However, we have repeatedly expressed the need to create a conducive atmosphere for a sustained dialogue, which necessarily requires an end to cross border terrorism and the dismantling of its infrastructure.

We discussed ways of carrying forward our bilateral relations. In this regard, I emphasized the importance of economic cooperation, cultural exchanges, people-to-people contacts and civil aviation links. These would create an environment in which difficult issues in our bilateral relations could be addressed. PM Jamali suggested resumption of sporting links between the two countries. We agreed that, as a beginning, these measures could be considered.

In this context, it has been decided to appoint a High Commissioner [ambassador] to Pakistan and to restore the civil aviation links on a reciprocal basis.

I also emphasized the importance of substantive progress on the decisions for regional trade and economic cooperation taken at the SAARC [South Asian Association for Regional Cooperation] Kathmandu Summit. Agreements arrived at Kathmandu [site of the SSAARC summit in 2002] must be implemented.

Source: India. Embassy of India in Washington, D.C. "Prime Minister Vajpayee's Statement in Parliament on Pakistan." New Delhi, India. May 2, 2003. www.indianembassy.org/pm/pm_may_02_03.htm (accessed June 6, 2003).

Pakistani Prime Minister Mir Zafarullah Khan Jamali's Statement

During my phone call to Prime Minister Vajpayee on 28 April 2003, I sensed a positive desire on his part to break the impasse in our relationship and to take steps which would lead to improved relations between Pakistan and India. The entire international community is watching with hope and expectation the movement towards a future of peace, security and prosperity in South Asia.

I have sent a formal invitation to Prime Minister Vajpayee to visit Pakistan. He is welcome to visit Pakistan whenever he wishes to do so.

The current global situation is marked by several challenges facing the international community. It is our duty to deal with these challenges collectively and constructively. The fight against terrorism is a case in point. Pakistan condemns terrorism in all its forms and manifestations and would continue to cooperate with the international community to eliminate this scourge. Of equal importance is the promotion of regional peace and security in regions of the world suffering from tensions and unresolved conflicts.

Encouraged by the recent positive developments and in order to set the stage for a meaningful dialogue with India, I have decided on the following measures:

   i. Since the majority of travellers between India and Pakistan use train and bus services, these will be resumed immediately on acceptance by India.
  ii. Resumption of airlink between India and Pakistan to facilitate travel of the people between the two countries.
 iii. Immediate release of all Indian fishermen, 22 Sikh youth and the 14 crew members of the Indian cargo boat "Raj Laxhmi."
  iv. Resumption of sports ties beginning with cricket and hockey.
   v. In addition to exchange of the two High Commissioners, we also propose restoration of the full strength of the missions of the two countries in their respective capitals.

In order to give impetus to SAARC to make it a more effective regional body, I have decided:

a. To place additional seventy eight items on the positive list [this is a list of items allowed to trade between India and Pakistan]. It is my hope that this will clear the way for a more meaningful SAARC role for the promotion of regional trade.
b. We will soon approach the Secretary General, SAARC to ascertain the convenience of the Member States for convening the 12th SAARC Summit in Islamabad well before the end of the current year.
c. Pakistan is also willing to host SAF [South Asia Federation] games as soon as possible.

Nuclear realities in our region impose certain obligations and responsibilities on our two countries. It is, therefore, important for both India and Pakistan to engage in serious discussions for nuclear and strategic stability in our region. In this context, Pakistan supports the Confidence Building Measures outlined in the MOU [Memorandum of Understanding] signed in Lahore in February 1999 and we hope that a reconvened dialogue will enable us to conclude substantive and result oriented measures for arms restraint and promotion of security in our region.

We believe that all outstanding issues between Pakistan and India must be addressed sincerely and constructively and in a composite manner through a sustained dialogue with a sense of priority.

It is my hope that India will seize the moment, put aside the acrimony of the past and purposefully move forward with Pakistan to peacefully resolve all issues, including the core issue of Jammu and Kashmir. Such a commitment is in the interest of harmony and stability in the region and for the prosperity of its billion-plus people. We should begin talks from where they were left off at Agra [at a summit meeting between Indian prime minister Vajpayee and Pakistani president Pervez Mushsarraf in 2001] and work out an agenda for a tiered dialogue including Summit level interaction.

It is a matter of great satisfaction for me that in the endeavour we have undertaken, I enjoy the fullest support of the people and all major political parties whom I have consulted. With this national consensus we are ready to engage in a serious and substantive dialogue with India.

I want to assure my Kashmiri brothers and sisters as well as the people of Pakistan that at all stages, their interests will be of supreme importance.

Source: Pakistan. Ministry of Foreign Affairs. "Prime Minister's Statement." Islamabad, Pakistan. May 6, 2003. www.forisb.org/pm03-05-06.htm (accessed June 6, 2003).

GAO on Tracking Foreign Visitors and Improving Border Security

May 13, 2003

INTRODUCTION

The administration of President George W. Bush unveiled ambitious new plans in 2003 for tracking the millions of foreign visitors entering and leaving the United States every year. Perhaps the most ambitious was a program that would require digital fingerprints, photographs, and other biometric information to be embedded in visas and passports starting in October 2004. The first phase of that program, in which all foreign visitors arriving in the United States by air would have their fingerprints and photographs digitally recorded upon their entry, was scheduled to begin on January 5, 2004.

The stated purpose of the program, which was mandated by Congress, was to prevent terrorists or other criminals from slipping into the country and to help ensure that foreign visitors did not overstay their visas. But the plans for the program, known as US-VISIT (for United States Visitors and Immigrant Status Indicator Technology), raised many questions, including whether the federal government had the staffing and technical capacity both to gather the information and to make effective use of it. Critics raised privacy concerns and questioned whether the government was willing to commit the billions of dollars they said was necessary to make the program effective. A report issued by the General Accounting Office (GAO) in September called the program "a very risky endeavor."

The administration took several other steps during the year to improve security at the nation's land, air, and sea borders. Among them were an increased capacity to detect radioactive materials, a computerized system to monitor the whereabouts of foreign students in the United States, and a requirement that visa applicants have face-to-face interviews at U.S. consular officers as a condition for receiving a visa. All these activities were in addition to aviation security programs aimed at screening passengers, luggage, and cargo for weapons, explosives, or other dangerous items. *(Aviation security, p. 720)*

The changes resulted from reassessments of U.S. visa policies in the wake of the terrorist attacks on September 11, 2001, in which nineteen foreign nationals hijacked commercial airliners and crashed them into the World Trade Center towers in New York and the Pentagon outside Washington, killing nearly 3,000 people. All nineteen had come into the country under visas they had obtained legally. Evidence after the attacks showed that closer monitoring of their entry and their whereabouts while in the United States might have led to their detection and detention or deportation before the attacks. The Central Intelligence Agency, for example, had identified two of the men as terrorist suspects, but that information did not reach the State Department until after that agency had already granted them visas. One of the terrorists came in under a student visa but never showed up at the school. In an especially embarrassing moment, six months after the attacks the Immigration and Naturalization Service (INS) sent student visas for two of the hijackers to a Florida flight school.

Keeping track of the Americans and foreigners crossing the border was a massive job. According to data kept by the INS (which was folded into the Department of Homeland Security [DHS] in March 2003), the agency conducted 453 million border inspections in 2002 to determine whether the travelers were legally entitled to enter the country. About 363 million of those inspections occurred at 166 land border crossings with Mexico and Canada. Roughly two-thirds of these involved foreign nationals; the other one-third were Americans. The great majority of the land crossings involved residents of the border area who crossed frequently. About 43 million foreign nationals and 30 million Americans arrived at airports; the remainder entered through seaports.

Evidence of Insecure Borders

In numerous reports reviewing various aspects of the system for keeping track of visitors to the United States, the GAO found that too few personnel, too little training, and ill-defined or vague procedures left security gaps in the government's system for detecting unwelcome aliens and keeping them out of the country. The daunting task of ensuring that everyone entering the country was who they said they were was illustrated early in the year when the GAO reported that its investigators were able to get into the country using fake identifications. In testimony before the Senate Finance Committee on January 30 and the House Judiciary Subcommittee on Immigration and Border Security on May 13, Robert J. Cramer, the head of GAO's office of special investigations, detailed how its agents used off-the-shelf computer graphic software to create phony driver's licenses and birth certificates. They then used those false documents to enter the United States from Jamaica, Barbados, Mexico, and Canada. INS and customs agents "never questioned the authenticity of the counterfeit documents, and our agents encountered no difficulty entering the country using them," Cramer reported.

On two occasions, Cramer said, immigration officials did not ask for any identification at all. At one crossing, a park that straddled the border between British Columbia and Washington state, a GAO agent was able to walk across the border in both directions without being stopped or questioned by immigration and customs officials of either country. American citizens were not required to show passports upon returning to the United States from other countries in the Western Hemisphere. They were required, however, to show proof of citizenship such as a birth certificate or baptismal record or to attest verbally that they were citizens. American citizens also had to show photo identification, such as a driver's license.

"Bouncers at college bars could spot the kind of fake IDs that were used by investigators," Sen. Charles E. Grassley, R-Iowa, chairman of the Finance Committee, said at the January 30 hearing. "The officials in charge of border security need to be at least that good at their jobs."

Biometric Identifiers

In part to overcome such counterfeiting problems, the federal government in October announced that the US-VISIT program would begin on January 5, 2004. Electronic fingerprints (one of each index finger) and digital photographs would be taken of all visa-holders entering the United States through 115 airports and 14 seaports. Land border biometric processing was scheduled to begin in 2005. Initially the biometric information would be used to verify the identity of the visa-holder. Upon departure, visitors would have to repeat the fingerprinting process and scan their travel documents into a computer database. When fully operational, US-VISIT was intended to integrate the biometric information collected at entry and exit points with data from about twenty other programs, including watch lists, to help the government quickly identify suspected terrorists and other unwanted aliens, to prevent visa and passport fraud, and to keep travelers from overstaying their visas.

The next step under the plan was to be the embedding of machine-readable biometric identifiers in every U.S. visa issued after October 26, 2004, as well as in all passports issued by the twenty-seven countries participating in the visa-waiver program. Those countries included most of Europe, Brunei, Japan, Singapore, Australia, and New Zealand. Visitors from those countries that did not have a machine-readable passport would be required to obtain a visa to enter the country. The biometric identifiers and the entry-exit program had been mandated by Congress in various pieces of legislation enacted both before and after the terrorist attacks of September 11, 2001. The Immigration and Naturalization Service, under the direction of the Justice Department, began a new entry-and-exit tracking program in 2002 that began to take digital fingerprints from foreign nationals of five countries the United States said sponsored terrorism as well as from other suspect aliens. That program, known as the National Security Entry-Exit Registration System (NSEERS), became the US-VISIT program when INS was folded into the Department of Homeland Security. *(NSEERS program, Historic Documents of 2002, p. 842)*

The DHS ran a trial of the initial biometric identification program in November at Atlanta's Hartsfield Jackson International Airport and declared it a success. More than 20,000 arriving passengers were voluntarily finger-printed and photographed. "Several" incidents of visa fraud were uncovered, and "several" people were matched to names in the FBI's crime database. But many observers voiced serious concerns about the program, question-ing the reliability of the biometrics as well as the data they were being matched against, whether it contained enough privacy protections, whether it would cause unacceptably long delays at checkpoints, and whether the government was capable of putting together and running such a highly inte-grated system involving hundreds of millions of individual pieces of data. The government had already missed its deadline for integrating several different watch lists into a master list that border inspectors could consult to see if a foreign national were a terrorist suspect, a visa violator, or the subject of an outstanding arrest warrant. *(Watch lists, p. 155)*

In a report released in September, the GAO described the US-VISIT pro-gram as "a risky endeavor" for several reasons. The mission left little room for error, the GAO said; "the missed entry of just one person" bent on harming the United States could have serious consequences. Yet the program was large and complex in scope, involving modification and expansion of facilities at most land border checkpoints and in many airports. It involved the integration of sev-eral existing programs that were not currently compatible with each other and were already known to have problems. The government did not have enough people, tools, or processes in place to manage the program, nor had it set up an accountable management structure to ensure that the program would be carried out as designed. The government had not set specific performance standards to determine whether the system was working as expected, and the costs of implementing the system were "enormous." The GAO said that DHS estimates put the cost at $7.2 billion through fiscal 2014, but this did not include the cost to the State Department of implementing the visa biometric program, which was estimated to cost another $15 billion through fiscal 2014.

Closing Loopholes

The federal government took several other steps in 2003 to tighten its border security. Beginning in March travelers arriving in the United States by land, sea, or air began to be screened for radiological materials. About 7,000 portable radiation detectors were distributed to agents at border checkpoints. The detec-tors, which each cost about $2,500, were the size of a pager and usually were clipped on to an inspector's belt. DHS officials said they expected that all 18,000 border inspectors would be equipped with the detectors by the middle of 2004. "We think this is an important way of improving our capability of detecting radiological materials including dirty bombs and the material that could be used to make dirty bombs," said Robert C. Bonner, commissioner of the DHS Bureau of Customs and Border Protection. A dirty bomb was one that used conventional explosives to spread radioactive material. In May 2002 Jose Padilla, a U.S. citizen, was arrested at Chicago's O'Hare Airport on suspicion of working with al Qaeda to build a dirty bomb. As of end of 2003 no formal charges had been brought against Padilla, who was being held incommunicado by the U.S. Navy. *(Detentions of terrorism suspects, p. 310)*

The State Department issued a number of new regulations dealing with visas. As of August 1 visa applicants were required to have face-to-face interviews with consular officers before a visa could be issued. Visa applicants, and the American universities and businesses that recruited foreign students and workers, said the new rules were adding weeks and sometimes months to the applications process. The travel and tourism industry also complained about the long delays, saying that travelers were beginning to take their business elsewhere. State Department officials said they hoped to minimize the delays but argued that the new rules were necessary to protect the country. "In the post–9/11 environment, we do not believe that the issues at stake allow us the luxury of erring on the side of expeditious processing," one official told a congressional committee.

To speed up the process for tracking the whereabouts of foreign students, the INS revamped the Student and Exchange Visitor Program to require colleges to enter data about the academic status and addresses of foreign students directly into a national computer database. Previously the colleges had been required to maintain similar files on campus. However, shortly after the program began in mid-February, some colleges began to complain that it took hours to log on to the computer and that sometimes the computer accepted data on a student only to delete it hours or days later.

In August DHS and the State Department announced the immediate suspension of two programs that allowed foreigners to be in the United States without a visa long enough to change planes. One program, called Transit Without Visa, allowed foreign passengers in transit to another country to leave the international airport and make a connection on a domestic flight, if need be. There were about 381,000 such travelers in 2002, mostly from Latin America and Asia. A second program, called International to International, allowed passengers to be in the United States without a visa if they were connecting with a flight to another country and did not leave the airport's international transit lounge. There were about 233,000 such passengers in 2002. The two departments said they had received specific intelligence that certain terrorist organizations, including al Qaeda, were planning to use these programs to hijack planes arriving in or departing the United States.

The GAO pointed to another loophole that it urged the government to close. The agency examined 240 visas, issued between September 11, 2001, and the end of 2002, that were granted and then revoked because it was learned that the people might have links to terrorism. It found that the State Department did not always immediately inform INS and the FBI of the revocations and that the INS and FBI were not routinely investigating or locating those persons who remained in the United States even though their visa had been withdrawn. As a result, the GAO said as many as thirty foreign nationals suspected of terrorism ties could still be in the country.

Following is the text of "Counterfeit Documents Used to Enter the United States from Certain Western Hemisphere Countries Not Detected," testimony presented May 13, 2003, by Robert J. Cramer, managing director of the General Accounting Office's Office of Special Investigations, before the House Judiciary Subcommittee on Immigration, Border Security, and Claims.

"Counterfeit Documents Used to Enter the United States Not Detected"

Mr. Chairman and Members of the Committee:

I am here today to discuss the results of security tests we performed in which agents of the Office of Special Investigations (OSI), acting in an undercover capacity, entered the United States from various countries in the Western Hemisphere using counterfeit documentation and fictitious identities. This work was initially undertaken at the request of the Senate Finance Committee and was continued at your request. The purpose of our tests was to determine whether U.S. government officials conducting inspections at ports of entry would detect the counterfeit identification documents. . . .

In summary, we created counterfeit identification documents in order to establish fictitious identities for our agents by using off-the-shelf computer graphic software that is available to any purchaser. The agents entered the United States from Jamaica, Barbados, Mexico, and Canada using fictitious names, counterfeit driver's licenses and birth certificates. Bureau of Customs & Border Protection (BCBP) staff never questioned the authenticity of the counterfeit documents, and our agents encountered no difficulty entering the country using them. On two occasions, BCBP staff did not ask for any identification when our agents entered the United States from Mexico and Canada. We have briefed BCBP officials on the results and methods of our work.

Background

Immigration regulations require that all persons who arrive at a U.S. port of entry be inspected by a government official. A U.S. citizen traveling from countries in the Western Hemisphere, such as those we visited for purposes of these tests, is not required to show a passport when entering the United States but is required to prove citizenship. BCBP accepts as proof of citizenship documents, such as a United States' state or federally issued birth certificate or a baptismal record, and photo identification such as a driver's license. However, since the law does not require that U.S. citizens who enter the United States from Western Hemisphere countries present documents to prove citizenship they are permitted to establish U.S. citizenship by oral statements alone.

Border Crossings

U.S. Border Crossing from Jamaica

Two of our agents traveling on one-way tickets from Jamaica arrived at an airport in the United States. After landing at the U.S. airport, the two agents proceeded to the immigration checkpoint and presented to BCBP immigration inspectors counterfeit driver's licenses in fictitious names along with fictitious birth certificates purportedly issued by two different states. One BCBP inspector asked one of the agents for his date of birth, and inquired about where and when the agent had obtained the birth certificate. The agent stated that he had obtained the birth certificate about 4 or 5 years earlier. A different BCBP inspector did not question the second agent. The BCBP inspectors did not recognize any of the documents presented as counterfeit and allowed the agents to enter the United States.

U.S. Border Crossing from Barbados

Barbados immigration officials provide visitors entering Barbados with a two-part immigration form to complete. They collect one part and return the second part to the visitor stamped with the date of entry into Barbados. Visitors are instructed to return the second part to immigration officials upon departing Barbados. In May 2003, two of our agents departed Barbados and provided Barbados immigration officials with unstamped immigration forms in fictitious names. Barbados officials accepted the forms without questioning why they were not stamped.

Two agents traveled on one-way tickets from Barbados and arrived at an airport in the United States. The two agents separately proceeded to the immigration checkpoint and were checked by the same BCBP immigration inspector. One agent was asked for his passport, and he responded that did not have one. The agent provided a fictitious birth certificate and a Customs declaration form. The BCBP inspector reviewed the documents and asked for picture identification. In response to this request, the agent provided a counterfeit driver's license. The BCBP inspector then asked the agent several questions, reviewed the documents again, asked additional questions, and instructed the agent to proceed through Customs. The agent provided the BCBP customs officer with the Customs form and subsequently left the airport without any further scrutiny.

The second agent had a similar experience. The BCBP immigration inspector asked for a passport. The agent explained that he did not have one and provided a counterfeit birth certificate. The BCBP inspector then asked for picture identification and the agent offered to produce a driver's license. The BCBP inspector did not ask to see the driver's license but asked several questions and then instructed the agent to proceed to Customs. The agent turned in his Customs form to a Customs official and then left the airport without any further scrutiny.

The BCBP immigration inspector did not question any of the counterfeit documents.

U.S. Border Crossings from Mexico

On two occasions our agents crossed the border from Mexico into the United States. On one occasion, at a land border crossing, a BCBP immigration inspector asked our agent if he was a U.S. citizen and whether he had brought anything across the border from Mexico. After the agent responded that he was a U.S. citizen and that he was not bringing anything into the United States from Mexico, the inspector allowed him to proceed without requiring any proof of identity.

On a subsequent occasion at the same border crossing, two of our agents were asked for identification by separate BCBP inspectors. Both agents presented counterfeit driver's licenses and were allowed to cross into the United States.

U.S. Border Crossings from Canada

On three occasions our agents crossed the border from Canada into the United States. The first border crossing occurred when two agents entered the United States through a sea port of entry from Canada. On that occasion, the agents were not asked to show identification. On a subsequent occasion, two agents, driving a rented car with Canadian plates, using fictitious names and counterfeit documents, crossed the border into the United States at a Canadian border crossing. A BCBP immigration inspector asked for identification and was provided the counterfeit documents. After the inspector reviewed the documents, the agents were allowed to cross the border.

During the Canadian land border crossing, the agents discovered a further potential security problem. A park straddles the U.S. and Canada at this border crossing. One of our agents was able to walk across this park into the United States from Canada without being stopped or questioned by any U.S. government official. Later, that agent walked back to Canada through this park without being inspected by Canadian authorities.

Conclusion

We recognize that weaknesses in inspection processes for entrants into the United States raise complex issues, and we are currently performing an evaluation of those processes, which will be reported to Congress in the coming months. Although BCBP inspects millions of people who enter the United States and detects thousands of individuals who attempt to enter illegally each year, the results of our work indicate that BCBP inspectors are not readily capable of detecting counterfeit identification documents. Further, people who enter the United States are not always asked to present identification. While current law does not require that U.S. Citizens who enter the U.S. from Western Hemisphere countries provide documentary proof of U.S. citizenship, this does provide an opportunity for individuals to enter the United States illegally.

Mr. Chairman, this completes my prepared statement. We will be pleased to respond to any questions you or other members of the committee may have at this time.

Source: U.S. Congress. General Accounting Office. "Counterfeit Documents Used to Enter the United States From Certain Western Hemisphere Countries Not Detected." Statement of Robert J. Cramer before the Subcommittee on Immigration, Border Security, and Claims, House Committee on the Judiciary. GAO–03–713T. May 13, 2003. www.gao.gov/new.items/d03713t.pdf (accessed June 12, 2003).

Saudi Arabian Crown Prince Abdullah on Bombings in Riyadh

May 13, 2003

INTRODUCTION

Saudi Arabia, one of the world's most conservative societies, experienced unprecedented turmoil during 2003 as its leaders and people grappled with the consequences of terrorism, economic and political stagnation, religious extremism, and the war in Iraq. Deadly bombings in May and November—apparently aimed at forcing American and other foreigners to leave the kingdom—finally convinced Saudi leaders that they could no longer ignore homegrown Islamic terrorism. The government launched a cautious program of political reform, and a few voices of dissent were raised against the fundamentalist brand of Islam that had a tight grip on nearly all aspects of Saudi daily life. The United States, which for six decades had decreed the security of Saudi oil to be a vital American interest, dramatically scaled back its military presence in that country and shifted its attention to neighboring Iraq.

The U.S.-led war in Iraq was a contributing factor to many of the year's developments in Saudi Arabia. In January, as the war drew near, Saudi leaders desperately tried to head it off by urging Iraqi leader Saddam Hussein to go into exile. Saddam stayed put until the United States and a handful of allies toppled him during a lightening-fast war in March and April. Then, the new reality of an American occupation of an Arab country in the heart of the Middle East provoked reactions from Saudi extremists, including those responsible for two waves of suicide bombings in Riyadh. Others in Saudi Arabia may have taken a different message from the events in Iraq, a message that authoritarian regimes in the Middle East were not necessarily permanent. *(Iraq war, pp. 40, 135, 874, 933)*

Another underlying factor for many of the events in Saudi Arabia was the economy. The country's enormous oil wealth for decades financed lavish lifestyles for the royal family and extensive social programs for ordinary Saudi citizens. But the dependence on a single, extractive industry led to boom-and-bust cycles as oil prices fluctuated. A sharp drop in oil prices during most of the 1990s sent the economy plunging; by 2003 the per capita income had fallen to about $10,500—relatively high by Middle Eastern standards but little more than half what it had been two decades earlier. Unemployment soared to about 25 percent and was concentrated among young people, who made up more than half the Saudi population of 22 million people. Joblessness even touched middle-class, college-educated Saudis who had grown accustomed to guaranteed government jobs. The result was a combustible mix of young, unemployed workers looking for someone to blame, and a fundamentalist religious establishment eager to place the blame on the West (especially the United States) and the Saudi royal family.

Riyadh Bombings

Saudi Arabia had experienced turmoil and terrorism in the past, notably the assassination of King Faisal by a nephew in 1975; a takeover of the Grand Mosque in Mecca by Muslim fundamentalists in 1979; a bloody riot by Iranian pilgrims in Mecca in 1987; a 1995 car bombing of a U.S.-run military training facility in Riyadh that killed seven people, including five Americans; and the 1996 bombing, by Iranian-backed militants, of an apartment complex in Dhahran that killed nineteen U.S. servicemen. Then, on September 11, 2001, fifteen Saudi citizens were among the nineteen young Arab men who hijacked four airliners in the United States and killed nearly 3,000 people. President George W. Bush said the hijackings were sponsored by the al Qaeda terrorist group, headed by Osama bin Laden, a self-exiled member of a wealthy Saudi Arabian family. *(Dhahran bombing, Historic Documents of 1996, p. 672; U.S. hijackings, Historic Documents of 2001, p. 614)*

None of these events had prompted Saudi Arabia to come to grips with the societal forces that made the country a prime candidate for instability. Under enormous pressure from the Bush administration, the Saudi government in late 2002 and early 2003 froze the bank accounts of some organizations linked to terrorist cells and rounded up several hundred suspected terrorists. But the government continued to deny publicly that al Qaeda had any links to or presence in Saudi Arabia or that terrorists were using the country's fundamentalist form of Islam, known as Wahhabism, to justify their actions. Perhaps most startling to American ears, many Saudis, including senior government officials, insisted that none of the September 11 hijackers were Saudi nationals.

That attitude of denial changed quickly in 2003 after terrorists made their presence unmistakably known. On May 1 the U.S. State Department warned Americans to avoid Saudi Arabia because intelligence information pointed to a likely attack against "American interests" there. A week later, police in Riyadh fought a gun battle with suspected terrorists, then seized more than eight hundred pounds of explosives and a large cache of weapons from their hideout. The government said it was pursuing nineteen terrorists, all but two of them Saudis, who were members of a recently formed al Qaeda cell. Several of these terrorists were said to have trained in Afghanistan, where al Qaeda had been based until the United States invaded that country in late 2001. In an unusual step acknowledging al Qaeda's presence, the government published photographs of the suspects and offered a reward for information about them. *(Afghanistan, p. 1089)*

On May 12, during a visit to the Saudi capital by Secretary of State Colin Powell, gunmen attacked three residential compounds in the city and set off car bombs, killing thirty-five people, including sixteen Saudi citizens, eight Americans, two Britons, and nine suicide attackers. Nearly two hundred people were injured. A smaller bombing the following day damaged a U.S.-Saudi business in Riyadh. The attacks were the first against nonmilitary targets in Saudi Arabia. The heavily guarded residential compounds targeted in the attacks housed hundreds of Americans and other foreign nationals. Many well-to-do Saudi citizens also lived in these compounds, which offered them safety and a relaxed atmosphere free of interference from the religious police who enforced Islamic laws against consumption of alcohol and other Western vices.

Crown Prince Abdullah bin Abdul Aziz addressed the nation the day after the bombings and offered the Saudi government's most direct acknowledgment ever of the religious roots of some Middle Eastern terrorism. Abdullah had been the de facto head of the Saudi government since 1996, a year after his elder brother, King Fahd, suffered a debilitating stroke. "There can be no acceptance or justification for terrorism," Abdullah said. "Nor is there a place for any ideology which promotes it, or beliefs which condone it. We specifically warn anyone who tries to justify these crimes in the name of the religion. And we say that anyone who tries to do so will be considered a full partner of the terrorists and will share their fate."

U.S. ambassador Robert W. Jordan said that, prior to the bombings, his embassy had sent Saudi officials two letters requesting stepped-up security for several specific locations where Americans lived in the capital, but nothing had been done. In response, a Saudi spokesman said the U.S. request had not been specific enough to allow for action before the bombings. After the bombings, the government reportedly cooperated with a team of nearly seventy agents from the FBI, CIA, and other U.S. agencies investigating al Qaeda's links to the attacks. In subsequent months Saudi police arrested more than six hundred men suspected of involvement in the May attacks or terrorism generally. The most important of those arrested appeared to be Ali Abd al-Rahman al-Faqasi al-Ghamdi, described by Saudi officials as one of al Qaeda's senior representatives in the kingdom.

Perhaps most shocking to many Saudis was the discovery in June of an al Qaeda cell in Mecca, the city held sacred by all Muslims because it was Mohammed's birthplace. In November a gun battle took place in Mecca between suspected al Qaeda members and the police. In both incidents, police discovered bombs and other weapons.

The May bombings brought home to top Saudi leaders—as previous U.S. warnings apparently had not—the danger of terrorism from within the country. In subsequent days U.S. and Saudi officials were quoted as saying both countries now understood their joint interest in combating al Qaeda and other terrorist groups. Adel Jubeir, foreign policy adviser to Crown Prince Abdullah, flew to Washington and told reporters the bombings were a "massive jolt" that awoke Saudis to the fact that they were in "the same boat" as Americans in dealing with terrorism. Another Saudi official acknowledged to the *Washington Post* that the bombings represented "an attack on the royal family" as well as the United States. "That is the harsh reality."

On June 8 Saudi interior minister Prince Nayef bin Abdul Aziz—who before the bombings had suggested that al Qaeda did not exist in his country—for the first time said the terrorist organization was behind the bombings. Then on June 12 the government said more than one thousand fundamentalist clerics had been fired or suspended for preachings that advocated intolerance and fostered terrorism. The country's highest religious body, the Council of Senior Clerics, on August 17 issued a statement denouncing terrorists and those who help them as "criminals" who violated Islamic law.

Any illusion that the government's crackdown had eliminated the threat of terrorism in Saudi Arabia was shattered on November 9, when an enormous car bomb exploded at another residential compound in Riyadh. The blast killed eighteen people and wounded more than one hundred others. The bombing occurred during a visit to the capital by Deputy Secretary of State Richard L. Armitage, echoing the bombing in May during a visit by Secretary of State Powell. Armitage said the bombing demonstrated that al Qaeda was attempting to destabilize the Saudi government. Unlike the May bombing, however, this attack was aimed primarily at Arabs from other countries, rather than Westerners and wealthy Saudis. That fact appeared to anger many Saudis, as did the timing of the attack—during the holy month of Ramadan. "The terrorists who carried out these bombings have proved that they have no faith," Saleh al-Tuwaiji, vice president of the Riyadh Red Crescent Society (the equivalent of the Red Cross) told the government's English-language newspaper, *Arab News.*

By December it appeared that Saudi terrorists were focusing their attacks on the government, specifically the agencies responsible for Riyadh's new crackdown against terrorism. On December 4 terrorists tried to assassinate the kingdom's senior antiterrorism official, Major General

Abdul Aziz al-Huweirini. The general was "moderately wounded," according to a subsequent report by the *New York Times,* and his brother was more seriously wounded. Also in early December the police defused a car bomb planted outside the headquarters of a Saudi intelligence agency, and a senior official of the government's internal security agency narrowly escaped a bombing on December 29.

Rising U.S. Anger

Despite the new-found convergence of U.S. and Saudi interests in combating terrorism, the middle part of 2003 saw relations between the two countries plummet to the lowest point in three decades. The level of mistrust and anger between the two countries had not been as great since the Arab oil embargo against the United States and some of its allies following the 1973 Arab-Israeli war. *(Oil embargo, Historic Documents of 1974, p. 221)*

Members of Congress, in both political parties, fanned the flames of resentment against what they called Saudi indifference to the threat of terrorism. "I think what 9-11 showed in large picture, and yesterday's bombing showed again, is the fact that once again the Saudi elite are never going to get along with the terrorists and that they are just going to have to have the courage to break with them," Sen. Charles E. Schumer, D-N.Y., said after the May bombings, in comments echoed across Capitol Hill.

The central concern in Washington was Saudi Arabia's long history of tolerating, and even promoting, religious charitable organizations that allegedly funneled money to al Qaeda and other terrorist groups. U.S. intelligence agencies said the Saudi government and private individuals had donated millions of dollars to charities that were supposed to support schools, hospitals, and other causes but in fact were little more than fronts for terrorists. Some U.S. officials and analysts described Saudi funding of these charities as the equivalent of bribes or "protection money" to spare the country from terrorism.

After the May 12 bombings the Saudi government began moving against some of these charities, but in a cautious manner that did little to stem U.S. criticism. Perhaps the most significant step was a crackdown against a large, government-funded charity known as the Al-Haramain Islamic Foundation, which funded several thousand schools and mosques that promoted the Wahhabi brand of Islam around the world. In June the Saudi government said it had ordered al-Haramain to close all ten of its worldwide offices, arrested several of its fundraisers, and forced the resignations of many of its board members. The government also curtailed cash donations to religious charities generally, for example by removing charity boxes from shopping malls and other public places.

The question of possible Saudi government support for terrorist groups severely strained U.S.-Saudi relations during the summer, after the Bush administration suppressed portions of a congressional report on the September 11 hijackings. A special joint panel of the House and Senate Intelligence committees released the report on July 24, but the administration forced the panel to black out twenty-eight pages that reportedly discussed links between Saudi charities and the al Qaeda network. *(Intelligence committee report, p. 544)*

Congressional leaders and the Saudi government both pressed for release of the withheld information. Members of Congress said they wanted the American public to see hard evidence of Saudi support for terrorism, and the Saudis said they could refute the information once it had been made public. Saudi foreign minister Prince Saud al-Faisal flew to Washington and on July 29 asked Bush personally to release the information, but the president refused, saying such a step would "compromise" the ongoing investigation into the September 11 attacks. Prince Saud told reporters he understood Bush's concerns but wanted to demonstrate that his country's was being wrongly accused of supporting terrorism. "Everyone is having a field day casting aspersions about Saudi Arabia," he said.

News reports early in August said much of the secret portion of the report dealt with the actions of two Saudi citizens who might have had some connection with the Saudi government, possibly even as intelligence agents, who appeared to have had contact with some of the September 11 hijackers. The role of one of the men, Omar al-Bayoumi, had been previously reported publicly. According to various reports, he had befriended two of the hijackers when they first arrived in the United States in January 2000, had helped them find housing in the San Diego area, and had introduced them to members of the Arab community there. The role of the other man named in the report, Osama Basnan, was less clear, except that U.S. investigators considered him an "associate" of al-Bayoumi, and the congressional report labeled him as "an extremist and bin Laden associate." Saudi government spokesmen said neither man was a government employee, much less an intelligence agent.

Basnan's name sparked another line of inquiry and public controversy because he and his wife had received checks, reportedly totaling more than $100,000, from Prince Bandar bin Sultan, the Saudi ambassador to the United States, and his wife, Princess Haifa al-Faisal. Bandar and other Saudi officials said the payments were for medical bills incurred by Basnan's wife.

U.S. Military Leaves the Kingdom

The May bombings of Western targets in Riyadh came despite an action by the Bush administration to remove one of the prime stated causes of anti-American terrorism in the Middle East: the vast U.S. military presence in Saudi Arabia. The United States in 1991 had used Saudi Arabia as the launching pad for the Persian Gulf War, which ended Iraq's occupation of neighboring Kuwait. Washington then created a large military presence in the kingdom, including one of the world's most sophisticated air bases, the Prince Sultan base near Riyadh. As of early 2003 about 5,000 U.S. servicemen, and hundreds of civilian support personnel for the U.S. government and private military contractors, were based in Saudi Arabia.

Al Qaeda leader bin Laden repeatedly denounced the presence of U.S. forces in Saudi Arabia, saying the "infidels" were violating the sacred ground where Islam took root. Moreover, the large U.S. military presence stoked resentment among Saudis of U.S. policies elsewhere in the Middle East, particularly what was perceived as Washington's uncritical support for Israel.

In early February news reports suggested that the Saudi government had decided to ask the United States to withdraw its forces as soon as the Iraq war was over. It was unclear at that time whether the Bush administration had agreed with the decision, or even had suggested it. As part of its preparations for the war in Iraq, the Pentagon already had moved key air force operations to a base in Qatar, and other units were being redeployed to Kuwait and other countries in the Persian Gulf region. In any event, Defense Secretary Donald H. Rumsfeld on April 29 met with his Saudi counterpart, Prince Sultan bin Abdul Aziz, and agreed that all but about 400–500 U.S. combat forces would be withdrawn by the summer. "It is now a safer region because of the change of regime in Iraq," Rumsfeld said, referring to the overthrow of Iraqi leader Saddam Hussein three weeks earlier.

Prospects for Political Reform

Political and social reform came slowly in Saudi Arabia, but the movement toward reform appeared to be undeniable during 2003. In Saudi Arabia all real political power was held by senior members of the Saudi royal family. Political meetings were banned, most of the news media was controlled by the government, and public discussion of controversial issues was severely limited. The closest thing to public participation in Saudi life was the process called *majlis,* in which senior princes met regularly with members of the public and accepted written appeals for money for favorable government decisions. The national government also had an unelected advisory council, known as the *Shura,* but it had no political power. *(Lack of freedoms in Arab countries, p. 955)*

The movement toward reform started in January when Crown Prince Abdullah published what he called a plan for "internal reform and enhanced political participation" in the Arab world. Abdullah offered few specifics, but the mere mention of reform from the leader of the Arab world's richest and most conservative monarchy sparked comment and interest throughout the region. Abdullah gave interviews to foreign and domestic reporters calling for reforms, and even King Fahd, in a rare statement, advocated reform that "happens gradually and easily, avoiding damaging speed."

Despite their vague nature, such statements seemed to spark a remarkable—for Saudi Arabia—flurry of public debate. Several small protest rallies were held during the year, only one of which, on October 15, resulted in scuffles between demonstrators and the police. Saudi newspapers showed an increasing willingness to report information not officially sanctioned by the government. After the May 12 Riyadh bombings several local newspapers carried reports about terrorism that, in the past, would not have been allowed. Even so, there was a limit to how far the government would allow journalists to go. In late May the government forced the firing of Jamal Khashoggi, the outspoken editor of the *al-Watan* newspaper, owned by members of the royal family. His offense had been to allow the publication of several articles linking terrorism to Islamic fundamentalism. Khashoggi later reappeared as a "media advisor" to the Saudi ambassador in London.

The government's most concrete step toward political reform came on October 13 when the cabinet announced plans for elections for municipal councils in fourteen cities. Even that step was limited, however, because only half the seats on the councils were to be filled through elections (the other members would be appointed), and no date was set for the voting. Even so, observers said that just mentioning elections represented a major change for the government.

Six weeks later the *New York Times* published a dramatic plea for reform by Mansour al-Nogaidan, a columnist for the *Al Riyadh* newspaper who said that, as a young man, he had been a "Wahhabi extremist" and had set fire to video stores selling Western movies and burned down a charity for widows and orphans. Al-Nogaidan's column, which was widely distributed in Saudi Arabia, denounced the country's religious extremism and resistance to modernity. "Only when we see ourselves the way the rest of the world sees us—a nation that spawns terrorists—and think about why that is and what it means will we be able to take the first step toward correcting that image and eradicating its roots," he wrote.

Following is the text of an address to the nation delivered May 13, 2003, by Saudi Arabian crown prince Abdullah bin Abdul Aziz one day after a series of bombings in Riyadh killed thirty-five people.

Address to the Nation by Crown Prince Abdullah bin Abdul Aziz

In the name of God, most compassionate, most merciful

My fellow citizens:

May God's peace and blessing be upon you.

The tragic, bloody and painful events that took place in the heart of our dear capital, Riyadh, last night, in which innocent citizens and residents were killed or injured, prove once again that terrorists are criminals and murderers with total disregard for any Islamic and human values or decency. They are no different from vicious animals whose only concern is to shed blood and bring terror to those innocents under God's protection.

These tragic events should serve as a warning to the unwary, and should restore sanity to the deluded. The perpetrators are but a small group of deviants whose objective is to do harm to our society by doing damage to its security.

On the other hand, the whole Saudi nation, old and young, men and women, stand shoulder-to-shoulder in condemning this heinous act and expressing their rejection of those who perpetrated it. We will be steadfast in defending our homeland, the cradle of Islam, and the heart of the Arab world.

If these murderers believe that their criminal and bloody act will shake our nation or its unity, they are mistaken. And if they believe they can disrupt the security and tranquility of our nation, they are dreaming. This is because the Saudi people, who have embraced the Holy Book as their guide and the Shari'a as their way of life, and who have rallied behind their leaders, who in turn embraced them, will not permit a deviant few to shed the blood of the innocent which God Almighty, in His infinite wisdom and justice, has sanctified. The entire Saudi nation, and not just its valiant security forces, will not hesitate to confront the murderous criminals.

There can be no acceptance or justification for terrorism. Nor is there a place for any ideology which promotes it, or beliefs which condone it. We specifically warn anyone who tries to justify these crimes in the name of religion. And we say that anyone who tries to do so will be considered a full partner to the terrorists and will share their fate. As revealed in the Holy Qur'an: "If a man kills a believer intentionally, his recompense is Hell, to abide therein (forever): and the wrath and the curse of God are upon him, and a dreadful penalty is prepared for him."

Further, as revealed in the Holy Qur'an, the taking of an innocent life is a crime against all of humanity. In the words of the Prophet (God's peace and mercy be upon him): "He who kills a resident living in peace among you, will never breathe the air of heaven."

These messages, which do not require any interpretation, provide clear evidence that the fate of those murderers is damnation on earth and the fury of Hell in the thereafter.

I vow to my fellow citizens and to the friends who reside among us, that the State will be vigilant about their security and well-being. Our nation is capable, by the Grace of God Almighty and the unity of its citizens, to confront and destroy the threat posed by a deviant few and those who endorse or support them. With the help of God Almighty, we shall prevail.

Source: Saudi Arabia. Royal Embassy of Saudi Arabia in Washington, D.C. Information Office. "Address to the Nation by Crown Prince Abdullah Bin Abdulaziz." May 13, 2003. http://saudiembassy.net/press_release/ releases/03-PR-0513-Abdullah-terrorism.htm (accessed June 6, 2003).

UN Security Council on
Peace Agreement for
Ivory Coast

May 13, 2003

INTRODUCTION

Diplomatic and military intervention by France helped end a civil war that threatened to tear apart Ivory Coast—which for decades had been one of the most prosperous and stable countries in Africa. French diplomats brokered a peace agreement in January among the warring factions, and a French military force of about 4,000 troops helped enforce a cease-fire. But even the intervention by France, the country's colonial power, could not make the peace process go smoothly. Most of the year was taken up with backtracking by one side or another, and it was not until late December that competing armies began pulling back from the frontlines and politicians seemed ready to work together under an interim government. *(Background, Historic Documents of 2002, p. 251)*

Background to the War

Ivory Coast was the latest of three small countries in West Africa to descend into civil war and chaos. Liberia and Sierra Leone had endured bloody wars in the region all through the 1990s; both of those wars were driven primarily by the desire of competing factions to control the trade in diamonds and other natural resources. Greed also played a role in Ivory Coast, which was the world's biggest producer of cacao seeds, used to make cocoa. But ethnicity and political power were the main driving forces behind conflict in Ivory Coast, which was divided among five major tribal groups and, just as important, between the mostly Muslim (and poor) north and the mostly Christian (and more prosperous) south. *(Liberia war, p. 767; Sierra Leone background, Historic Documents of 2002, p. 247)*

The country's civil war had its roots in a December 1999 military coup, led by General Robert Guei, against the elected civilian president, who had ordered the arrest of opposition politicians. Guei, in turn, was driven from office by popular discontent in 2000 when he attempted to rig elections. Politician Laurent Gbagbo, from the south, eventually won elections that most observers said were deeply flawed—largely because the most prominent northern politician, Alassane Ouattara, was prevented from running by a recently enacted provision that allowed only candidates whose parents had both been born in Ivory Coast. While aimed directly at Ouattara, this provision was one of several new anti-immigrant laws promoted by the powerful southern minority, which claimed it wanted to protect the "Ivorian" nature of the country. An estimated 25 percent of the country's 16 million residents were immigrants (most of them Muslim) from Burkina Faso, Mali, and other nearby countries who had sought jobs in the cacao fields of Ivory Coast. Resentment of the immigrants was fueled, in large part, by an economic decline resulting from long-term depression in cocoa prices.

The resulting political instability suddenly broke into civil war on September 19, 2002, when soldiers from the north staged a mutiny and tried to oust Gbagbo from power. The attempted coup was crushed, but the mutinous soldiers fled to the north, where they established a guerrilla army called the Patriotic Movement of Ivory Coast, which quickly gained control of nearly all the northern half of the country. In November 2002 the government and rebels signed a cease-fire, to be monitored by a peacekeeping force of 2,500 French soldiers and several hundred troops from other West African countries. Hundreds of thousands of people fled their homes during this initial round of fighting; among them, according to the United Nations, were an estimated 500,000 immigrants (350,000 from Burkina Faso, 100,000 from Guinea, and 50,000 from Mali) who fled a renewed anti-immigrant campaign mounted by the government.

Later in 2002 more fighting broke out in western Ivory Coast, where two new guerrilla groups emerged: the Movement for Justice and Peace, and the Ivorian Patriotic Movement of the Great West. Bolstered by fighters from Liberia, each of these groups gained control of areas bordering Guinea and Liberia. The new groups reportedly had some links to, but were not controlled by, the northern rebels. By early January 2003 these new guerrilla groups had advanced toward Abidjan, the country's commercial capital.

Peace Agreement Signed

With the war threatening to spiral out of control, the French government in January summoned representatives of the government, the three rebel movements, and Ivory Coast's civilian political parties to a peace conference in Linas-Marcoussis, a suburb of Paris. The bargaining lasted for more than a week, with the central sticking point being a rebel demand that Gbagbo resign. French diplomats negotiated a compromise under which all parties would participate in an interim "government of national reconciliation" headed jointly by Gbagbo and a prime minister acceptable to all the opposition forces. This government would serve until elections could be held in 2005. Gbagbo reportedly resisted the agreement, but he came under intense pressure to accept it from French officials and the leaders of other African countries. The agreement was announced on January 24, and the following day Gbagbo met in Paris with French president Jacques Chirac and said he had accepted the accord. Gbagbo named Seydou Diarra as the prime minister. A Muslim from the northern part of the country, Diarra had served as prime minister under General Guei but was widely respected by most of the country's factions.

The signing of the peace accord sparked huge protests in Abidjan, where mobs attacked the French embassy to denounce what the army and many of Gbagbo's supporters called a French-imposed "victory" for the guerrillas. The demonstrators were especially angered by reports that one of the rebel leaders was to be given the key defense and interior ministries. Suddenly caught in the middle, Gbagbo insisted he had no choice but to sign the agreement. "When you do not win the war you discuss and compromise," he said. "I did not win the war." Gbagbo's remarks failed to calm the situation, however, and for several days French soldiers in Abidjan found themselves confronting angry crowds and even, at one point, units of the Ivorian army. The mobs targeted French residents and businesses, demanding that they leave the country and never return. More than 15,000 French citizens lived in Ivory Coast, and all but a few thousand fled during the rioting. Gbagbo again wavered, implying that the had not really approved the peace agreement, which he referred to as mere "propositions." Subsequent news reports suggested that Gbagbo initiated, or at least approved, the protests in hopes that he could set the peace agreement aside.

With the rioting threatening to unravel the entire peace agreement, the UN Security Council on February 5 endorsed both the agreement and the presence of French and West African peacekeeping troops in Ivory Coast. The council authorized the troops to take all necessary actions to protect themselves, as well as "civilians threatened with imminent violence." Once again under strong international pressure, Gbagbo moved back to the position he had taken in Paris of endorsing the peace agreement. In a televised address on February 7 he called for calm and asked his supporters to "try this medicine" of the peace accord.

Diarra began work as prime minister on February 10, but the country and the peace process were on hold for several weeks as Gbagbo, opposition forces, and foreign diplomats negotiated frantically to salvage the peace accord. Under yet another agreement, reached March 8, the rebels relinquished their claim to the defense and interior ministry posts. Even so, nine guerrilla leaders appointed to other positions failed to show up for work until mid-April. One of the last to arrive was Guillaume Soro, spokesman for the northern guerrilla army, the Ivory Coast Patriotic Movement, who assumed the position of government communications minister. What was advertised as a "final" cease-fire took effect May 4; it involved the government, all guerrilla groups, and neighboring Liberia, which had supported some of the rebels.

On May 13 the UN Security Council again put its stamp of approval on the broader peace agreement. The council unanimously adopted a resolution establishing a small UN mission of up to seventy-six military observers, plus civilian diplomats, to monitor both the cease-fire and the country's political agreements. The task of keeping the competing armies separated continued to be assigned to the French troops (now with about 4,000 troops on the ground) and the West African force (with about 1,300 troops).

Yet another crisis came in September, when rebel leaders withdrew from the government, charging that Gbagbo had refused to delegate any power to them. Tensions rose again, especially in November when the northern rebels (now calling themselves the New Forces) began talking about formally seceding from the rest of the country. At this point the West African countries whose troops had been stationed in Ivory Coast appealed to the United Nations to replace their soldiers with a new UN mission. The Security Council agreed to consider that request early in 2004, and diplomats said it was likely that Secretary General Kofi Annan would recommend a UN peacekeeping force of about 6,000 troops. If approved by the council, such a force almost certainly would be based on contributions from the same West African countries.

A breakthrough came December 4, when Gbagbo met with the top military commander of the northern rebels, Soumaila Bakayoko, and reached agreement on yet another plan to carry out the underlying peace accord that had been dangling since January. Within days the army and rebel forces began withdrawing from their frontline positions and dismantling roadblocks. On December 13 French peacekeepers began collecting weapons handed in by both government troops and rebel fighters. The year's final move back toward reconciliation came on December 22, when the rebel leaders said they would rejoin the government. The first cabinet meeting of the newly reconstituted government was planned for early January 2004.

Humanitarian Situation

The long-delayed resumption of the peace process offered the prospect that international aid agencies finally would be able to begin helping the tens of thousands of people who had been forced from their homes during the waves of fighting. The UN's Office for the Coordination of Humanitarian Affairs estimated at year's end that about 1 million of Ivory Coast's 16 million residents had been displaced. Most of these people were living with relatives or had fled to neighboring countries; few had taken refugee in formal camps established by aid agencies. As a result, the UN office said Ivory Coast's displaced people "remain a largely invisible problem."

Reports by journalists and aid agencies said rebel soldiers and warlords were terrorizing civilians, especially in the north. The interim government had not yet established authority over the region, and guerilla leaders had never been able to exercise discipline over the thousands of fighters who had flocked to their cause.

Following is the text of United Nations Security Council Resolution 1479, adopted May 13, 2003, approving the creation of a small UN mission to monitor the implementation of a peace agreement in Ivory Coast.

"United Nations Security Council Resolution 1479"

The Security Council,

Reaffirming its resolution 1464 (2003) of 4 February 2003, the statement by its President of 20 December 2002, as well as its resolutions 1460 (2003) of 30 January 2003 and 1467 (2003) of 18 March 2003,

Reaffirming also its strong commitment to the sovereignty, independence, territorial integrity and unity of Côte d'Ivoire and reaffirming also its opposition to any attempts to seize power by unconstitutional means,

Recalling the importance of the principles of good-neighbourliness, noninterference and regional cooperation,

Further recalling its full support for the efforts of the Economic Community of West African States (ECOWAS) and France to promote a peaceful settlement of the conflict, and reiterating its appreciation for the efforts of the African Union to reach a settlement,

Reaffirming its endorsement of the agreement signed by the Ivorian political forces at Linas-Marcoussis on 24 January 2003 (S/2003/99) ("Linas-Marcoussis Agreement"), approved by the Conference of Heads of State on Côte d'Ivoire held in Paris on 25 and 26 January,

Noting with satisfaction the conclusions reached at the meeting in Accra, 6-8 March 2003, under the chairmanship of the President of Ghana, the current presidency of ECOWAS,

Noting with satisfaction the appointment of the Government of National Reconciliation and the cabinet meeting on 3 April 2003, attended by all the constituent political groups, in the presence of the Presidents of Ghana, Nigeria and Togo,

Welcoming the report of the Secretary-General on 26 March 2003 and the recommendations therein,

Noting the existence of challenges to the stability of Côte d'Ivoire and determining that the situation in Côte d'Ivoire constitutes a threat to international peace and security in the region,

1. *Reaffirms* its strong support for the Secretary-General's Special Representative and approves his full authority for the coordination and conduct of all the activities of the United Nations system in Côte d'Ivoire;

2. *Decides* to establish, for an initial period of six months, a United Nations Mission in Côte d'Ivoire (MINUCI), with a mandate to facilitate the implementation by the Ivorian parties of the Linas-Marcoussis Agreement, and including a military component on the basis of option (b) identified in the Secretary-General's report, complementing the operations of the French and ECOWAS forces;

3. *Approves* the establishment of a small staff to support the Special Representative of the Secretary-General on political, legal, civil affairs, civilian police, elections, media and public relations, humanitarian and human rights issues, and the establishment of a military liaison group whose tasks shall include:
   • Providing advice to the Special Representative on military matters;
   • Monitoring the military situation, including the security of Liberian refugees and reporting to the Special Representative thereon;
   • Establishing liaison with the French and ECOWAS forces for the purpose of advising the Special Representative on military and related developments;
   • Establishing also liaison with the Forces armées nationales de Côte d'Ivoire (FANCI) and the forces nouvelles, in order to build confidence and trust between the armed groups, in cooperation with the French and ECOWAS forces, in particular concerning helicopters and combat aircraft;
   • Providing input to forward planning on disengagement, disarmament and demobilization and identifying future tasks, in order to advise the Government of Côte d'Ivoire and support the French and ECOWAS forces;
   • Reporting to the Special Representative of the Secretary-General on the above issues;

4. *Stresses* that the military liaison group should be initially composed of 26 military officers and that up to 50 additional officers may be progressively deployed when the Secretary-General determines that there is a need and that security conditions permit;

5. *Requests* that in addition to the recommendations made in the Secretary-General's report regarding the organization of MINUCI, in particular its reference to the human rights components of the mission, special attention be given to the gender component within the staff of MINUCI and to the situation of women and girls, consistent with resolution 1325 (2000);

6. *Renews* its appeal to all Ivorian political forces to implement fully and without delay the Linas-Marcoussis Agreement and *invites* the government of national reconciliation to this end to develop a timetable for implementing the Linas-Marcoussis Agreement and to communicate this timetable to the Monitoring Committee;

7. *Recalls* the importance of sparing no effort, in keeping with the spirit of the Linas-Marcoussis Agreement, to enable the Government of National Reconciliation fully to exercise its mandate during this transitional period;

8. *Emphasizes again* the need to bring to justice those responsible for the serious violations of human rights and international humanitarian law that have taken place in Côte d'Ivoire since 19 September 2002, and *reiterates* its demand that all Ivorian parties take all the necessary measures to prevent further violations of human rights and international humanitarian law, particularly against civilian populations whatever their origins;

9. *Stresses* the importance of an early start to the process of disarmament, demobilization and reintegration;

10. *Requests* all Ivorian parties to cooperate with MINUCI in the execution of its mandate, to ensure the freedom of movement of its personnel throughout the country and the unimpeded and safe movement of the personnel of humanitarian agencies, and to support efforts to find safe and durable solutions for refugees and displaced persons;

11. *Requests* the ECOWAS forces and the French forces, in the execution of their mandate in accordance with resolution 1464 (2003), to continue to work in close consultation with the Special Representative and the Monitoring Committee, and to continue to report to the Council periodically on all aspects of the implementation of their respective mandates;

12. *Welcomes* the complete ceasefire reached on 3 May between FANCI and the forces nouvelles for the entire territory of Côte d'Ivoire, in particular the West, and *welcomes* the intention of ECOWAS forces and the French forces to lend their full support in the implementation of this ceasefire;

13. *Renews* its appeal to all the States in the region to support the peace process by refraining from any action that might undermine the security and territorial integrity of Côte d'Ivoire, particularly the movement of armed groups and mercenaries across their borders and the illicit trafficking and proliferation in the region of arms, especially small arms and light weapons;

14. *Urges* all Ivorian parties to refrain from any recruitment or use of mercenaries or foreign military units and *expresses* its intention to consider possible actions to address this issue;

15. *Demands* that, in accordance with its resolution 1460 (2003), all parties to the conflict who are recruiting or using children in violation of the international obligations applicable to them, immediately halt such recruitment or use of children;

16. *Emphasizes again* the urgent need to provide logistic and financial support to the ECOWAS force including through an appropriate trust fund established by ECOWAS to this effect, and *calls on* the member States to provide substantial international aid to meet the emergency humanitarian needs and permit the reconstruction of the country, and in this context stresses that the return of internally displaced persons, particularly to the north of the country, would be important for the process of reconstruction;

17. *Stresses* the importance of the regional dimension of the conflict and its consequences for neighbouring States and invites the donor community to help the neighbouring States to face the humanitarian and economic consequences of the crisis;

18. *Requests* the Secretary-General to report to the Council every three months on the implementation of this resolution and to provide monthly updates;

19. *Decides* to remain actively seized of the matter.

Source: United Nations. Security Council. *Resolution 1479.* S/RES/1479 (2003). May 13, 2003. www.un.org/Docs/sc/unsc_resolutions03.html (accessed January 19, 2004).

Russian President Putin on the State of the Nation

May 16, 2003

INTRODUCTION

President Vladimir Putin tightened his grip on Russian politics and society during the year, but most analysts said he appeared unable or unwilling to press ahead with the reforms he said were necessary to making Russia a thriving free-market democracy. Political parties beholden to the Kremlin won a strong majority in parliamentary elections in December, and Putin himself seemed nearly certain to win a second term in presidential elections scheduled for March 2004.

Russia's controversial war against pro-independence, Islamic guerrillas in Chechnya entered a new phase in 2003. Putin's government staged two elections that were supposed to give the rebellious province a measure of self-rule and a democratic government. Critics said Moscow rigged the elections to ratify its continued control of Chechnya. The Chechen guerrillas appeared to shift their fight for independence into an all-out terrorist campaign. More than a dozen bombings and other terrorist attacks in Moscow, southern Russia, and Chechnya killed nearly four hundred people during the year. Although sponsorship of the attacks rarely was certain, the government blamed nearly all of them on Chechen rebels, and observers said the Kremlin probably was right in most cases.

Putin: Pessimism and Reforms

A former secret service agent during the Soviet Union era, Putin was suddenly elevated to the presidency at the beginning of 2000 by his mentor, Boris Yeltsin. Yeltsin had presided over the rapid and messy transformation of Russia from communism to democracy and free markets following the collapse of the Soviet Union. Putin won election as president in his own right in 2000 on a platform of promising to continue and stabilize the reforms Yeltsin had initiated. But Putin also demonstrated a penchant for authoritarianism by systematically dismantling independent television stations and hounding the so-called oligarchs"—brash entrepreneurs who had acquired enormous wealth and influence by acquiring huge state-owned businesses in the chaotic early 1990s. *(Background, Historic Documents of 2000, p. 171)*

Early in his tenure Putin pushed through several important reforms, notably a new flat-rate income tax system, a revamped court system based on enforcement of laws rather than political whim, and a legalization of the sale of private property. The economy, which had gone into a deep freeze during the early 1990s and almost collapsed in a 1998 financial crisis, surged ahead starting in 2000 as world oil prices rose and Russia became a major oil exporter.

By 2003, however, the pace of reform had slowed dramatically, and many domestic and international commentators began talking about the "stagnation" or even "death" of the process by which Russia was supposed to be transformed into a Western-style modern society. After visiting Moscow in February, experts from the International Monetary Fund said the reform process had stalled as Russia confronted some of its most difficult issues, such as selling off the state-controlled natural gas monopoly and revamping its banking system.

Putin seemed to have a pessimistic view of the situation, based on his annual address summarizing the state of the nation, delivered to the parliament on May 16. Putin said he rejected the view, which he said was held by some, that "all our problems have now been solved." Instead, he said: "We face serious threats. Our economic foundation has become more solid, but it is still not stable enough and [is] still very weak. Our political system remains insufficiently developed and our state apparatus is not very effective. Most sectors of our economy are not competitive. Meanwhile, our population continues to fall and the fight against poverty is progressing far too slowly. The international situation remains complicated and competition in the world economy is as intense as ever." Elaborating on this last phrase, he added that "highly developed economies" used their power to "push Russia out of promising world markets when they have the chance."

Faced with all these challenges, Putin said Russia had no choice but to press ahead with the reforms that would make it "a country with a flourishing civil society and stable democracy" and a "competitive market economy." Putin offered several specific goals, including doubling the gross domestic product over ten years, ensuring that all the country's goods and services were "competitive" on the international marketplace, and strengthening the currency (the ruble) so it could be traded as a hard currency on world markets. He offered no clear proposals—in the form of legislation, regulations, or other specific steps—to reach any of these goals, however.

Putin Tightens His Grip

In subsequent months Putin and his government appeared to take few concrete steps to address the problems he had identified in his May 16 speech.
Reform legislation in the parliament essentially was on hold, apparently awaiting legislative elections in December and the planned presidential election in
2004. The government also seemed preoccupied with fighting its enemies.

Along with Chechen guerrillas, Putin's Kremlin appeared to identify two
possible sources of internal dissent as enemies: independent journalists and
the handful of oligarchs who had not been jailed or forced into exile because
of alleged corruption. The government had systematically gone after journalists and news media organizations that were critical of the Kremlin. The
most important case was the government's takeover of the independent NTV
station in Moscow in 2001, leaving the country with no nongovernmental
source of television news. Journalists from that station later formed another
one, TVS, but the Kremlin shut it down on June 23, alleging that the debt-
ridden station could not pay its bills. The legislature passed, and Putin
signed, a law barring the news media from engaging in "advocacy" during
election campaigns, a broad category that included most forms of reporting
and analysis on politics. This apparent move by the Kremlin to avoid journalistic criticism proved too much even for the country's generally compliant
constitutional court, which invalidated much of it on October 30.

The Kremlin's campaign against Russia's rich oligarchs entered a new
phase on October 25 when prosecutors arrested Mikhail Khodorkovsky, the
chairman and majority owner of Yukos Oil, the country's largest company. With
an estimated worth of about $8 billion, Khodorkovsky generally was consid-
ered the richest man in Russia; like the other oligarchs, he had developed a
business empire by purchasing state-owned enterprises at fire-sale prices during the early 1990s. He was seized at gunpoint while on a plane in Siberia
and sent back to Moscow, where he was jailed on charges of tax evasion and
fraud charges. The government also froze trading on nearly half of the shares
in Yukos Oil and refused Khodorkovsky's request that he be freed on bail.

The arrest of Khodorkovsky provoked a storm of protest both domestically
and internationally. The Russian stock market plunged steeply, and Putin's
own chief of staff, Alexander Voloshin, resigned in protest. Prime Minister
Mikhail Kasyanov, another Putin appointee, publicly questioned the suspension of Yukos shares. European Union (EU) diplomats suggested the incident
raised serious questions about Russia's commitment to the rule of law.

The jailed Khodorkovsky later resigned his official positions at Yukos and
hinted that he might run against Putin in the 2004 elections. Most analysts
suggested the country's richest man would have trouble generating public
sympathy and support, but Khodorkovsky did have enormous wealth to use
in a campaign, if the government allowed it. Putin at first attempted to distance himself from the controversy, calling it an "isolated" case. But after

meeting with EU officials in Rome on November 6, Putin said the arrest was "guided by the desire to instill law and order in the country and have everybody abide by the law and fight corruption." Khodorkovsky remained in jail at year's end, and the government was preparing for the trial of his business partner, Vasily Shakhnovsky, on tax evasion charges.

The jailing of Khodorkovsky may have unnerved Westerners and many members of Russia's entrepreneurial class, but it did nothing to damage the electoral prospects for parties aligned with Putin. In anticipation of December 7 parliamentary elections—the first in four years—the Kremlin created a new political party, United Russia, which had no platform other than supporting Putin's policies. Putin himself was barred by law from campaigning on behalf of any party, but he skirted the prohibition by repeatedly calling on voters to endorse a "strong, united Russia."

Putin's party won 37 percent of the vote, the highest achieved by any single party since the collapse of the Soviet Union. Two other parties that generally supported the Kremlin received an additional 21 percent, giving the government a strong majority in the 450-seat lower house of parliament, the Duma.

The clear losers in the vote were the once-powerful Communist Party, which received only 12.7 percent of the vote (about half of its previous showing in 1999), and two pro-Western parties that had been the staunchest advocates of democratic, free-market reforms. Because they fell below a minimum threshold, those two parties failed to win a bloc of seats in parliament for the first time since the first free legislative elections in 1993. Only seven members of those parties managed to win seats in their individual districts.

Putin heralded the election as "another step in strengthening democracy," but most international observers were far less complimentary. A report based on the findings of five hundred international observers said the vote "calls into question Russia's willingness to move toward European standards for democratic elections." In particular, the report by the Council of Europe and the Organization for Security and Cooperation in Europe cited "the extensive use of the state apparatus and media favoritism to benefit the largest pro-presidential party." At year's end the Kremlin was attempting to recruit candidates to run against Putin in the March 2004 presidential election; Putin's strategists reportedly feared that voter turnout would fall below the required 50 percent threshold if there was no credible opposition.

Chechnya: Elections and Terrorism

The Russian military in 2000 declared victory in its short and bloody war to suppress guerrillas fighting for the independence of Chechnya, in the

Caucasus region of southern Russia. But the war—the second of its kind, following a longer and even bloodier campaign in the mid-1990s—continued to bedevil both Russia and Chechnya throughout 2003. *(Background, Historic Documents of 2002, p. 763)*

Putin's government claimed to have developed a permanent solution to its Chechnya problem: a new constitution promising the region a measure of autonomy (but not independence) from Russia and an elected local government. The constitution was submitted to a referendum in Chechnya on March 23, and nearly 97 percent of voters endorsed it, the government said. International human rights groups and election observers questioned the validity of the vote, noting that it took place under intense army security and that thousands of Russian troops were allowed to vote.

With the new constitution in place, the government organized a presidential election, which was held October 6. Akhmad Kadyrov, who had been appointed acting president by the Kremlin in 2000, easily won the election, with about 80 percent of the vote, after the names of two major challengers were quietly removed from the ballot. Most international observers called the election a sham; even the U.S. State Department, which had muted its criticism of Putin and his government, said the election "did not meet international standards for free and fair elections." The new constitution called for elections for a new parliament, but no date had been set as of year's end.

The two elections in Chechnya did nothing to halt the guerrilla campaign against Russian control of the region and may, in fact, have contributed to an upsurge of suicide bombings and other acts of terrorism inside both Chechnya and Russia proper. A wave of bombings in 1999 killed three hundred people and provoked Yeltsin and his then-prime minister Putin, into sending the Russian army into Chechnya. Most of the fighting over the next three years took place in Chechnya, but in October 2002 Chechen guerrillas seized a theater in Moscow and took about 750 people hostage. Russian commandoes pumped a knockout gas into the theater before they stormed the building; all 41 guerrillas died in the assault, as did 129 of the hostages who choked on the gas.

Already nervous about their government's ability to deal with terrorism, Russians were frightened by what seemed an unending series of attacks during 2003. Nearly all the attacks involved suicide bombs, and most of the bombers were young women; the handful who could be identified were Chechens. Russians called them "black widows"; Chechen guerrillas called them *shakhidy,* or martyrs.

Some of the attacks took place in Chechnya, where the targets usually were Russian troops or government facilities. The first major bombing of the year took place May 12 near a government building in northern Chechnya; more than fifty people were killed. A suicide bombing a month later killed fourteen people near a Russian military base just outside Russia.

The attacks that most unnerved Russians were those against civilian targets in Russia proper, starting July 5 when two young women set off bombs outside a rock music concert in Moscow, killing fourteen people in addition to themselves. On August 1 at least fifty people died when a truck bomb exploded outside a military hospital in southern Russia. A commuter train line in southern Russia was attacked twice: on September 3, when two bombs exploded killing six people, and again on December 5, when a suicide bomb killed forty-five people and wounded more than one hundred fifty others. That bombing took place just two days before Russia's parliamentary elections, and Putin called it "an attempt to destabilize the country" before the vote. Another attack in Moscow came on December 9 when a female suicide bomber set off an explosion outside a hotel in the center of the city, killing five people (in addition to herself) and wounding thirteen. Authorities said the bomber may have intended to attack the parliament building across the street from the hotel.

Bush and Putin

Putin's relationship with the United States—and in particular with President George W. Bush—appeared to become more complicated than in the past. The two men developed a good working relationship at their first meetings in 2001 despite numerous disagreements on such issues as Bush's plan for an antimissile defense system. After the September 11, 2001, terrorist attacks against the United States, Putin aligned Russia with Washington more closely than ever before by arranging for the U.S. military to use bases in Central Asian countries that once had been part of the Soviet Union. *(Background, Historic Documents of 2001, pp. 614, 624)*

Early in 2003 Putin aligned himself with France and Germany in opposition to Bush's planned war against Iraq. Even that provocative stance failed to upset the Bush-Putin relationship, however. The two leaders appeared to be on cordial terms during two meetings, one held in St. Petersburg in May to celebrate the city's 300th anniversary, and a second in September at the Camp David retreat outside Washington. However, in his private conversations with Putin later in the year, Bush complained about signs of growing authoritarianism in Russia, the *Washington Post* reported in December. *(Putin and Iraq, p. 40)*

Following are excerpts from "Annual Presidential Address to the Federal Assembly of the Russian Federation," the state of the nation address by President Vladimir Putin, delivered May 16, 2003, to the Russian parliament.

"Annual Presidential Address to the Federal Assembly of the Russian Federation"

Today, in accordance with the Constitution, I have come to report to you on the state of the nation. I would like to begin with a brief summing up of the situation. Last year's results are in many ways a continuation of the work begun three years ago. Over these last three years not only have we worked hard to clear the mountain of problems that life itself forces us to tackle practically on a daily basis, we have also achieved some positive results.

Now we must take the next step and focus all our decisions and all our action on ensuring that in a not too far off future, Russia will take its recognised place among the ranks of the truly strong, economically advanced and influential nations. This is an entirely new challenge we must take up, and it represents an entirely new stage in our country's development. We could not take up this challenge earlier because we faced a great number of more urgent problems that we had to tackle first. But now we have this new opportunity in our hands and we must use it.

Russia must become and will become a country with a flourishing civil society and stable democracy, a country that fully guarantees human rights and civil and political freedoms. Russia must become and will become a country with a competitive market economy, a country that gives reliable protection to property rights and provides the economic freedoms that allow its people to work honestly and make money without fear and limitations.

Russia will be a strong country, a country with modern, well-equipped and mobile Armed Forces able to defend our nation and its allies and protect the national interests of our state and its citizens.

Through all of this, we will create the conditions for people to enjoy a decent life and enable Russia to take its place as an equal in the community of most developed nations. Not only will people feel proud of such a country, they will strive to multiply its wealth. They will remember and respect our great history.

This is our strategic objective.

But if we are to achieve this objective, we must consolidate, we must mobilise our intellectual forces and unite the efforts of the state authorities, civil society and all the people of this land.

We must set out a program of clear and comprehensible objectives that we will use to achieve the consolidation we need if we are to resolve the major national problems we face.

Why do I think this of such vital importance?

Our entire historical experience shows that a country like Russia can live and develop within its existing borders only if it is a strong nation. All of the periods during which Russia has been weakened, whether politically or economically, have always and inexorably brought to the fore the threat of the country's collapse.

Yes, certain of our achievements over these last years make it possible to speak of stabilisation. Some people even have the impression that all our problems have now been solved, that Russia now has a perfectly bright and predictable future ahead of it, and that everything now is just a question of whether the economy should grow by four or by six percent a year, and of how much we should spend.

I would like to say that this is not the case. We face serious threats. Our economic foundation has become more solid, but it is still not stable enough and still very weak. Our political system remains insufficiently developed and our state apparatus is not very effective. Most sectors of our economy are not competitive. Meanwhile, our population continues to fall and the fight against poverty is progressing far too slowly. The international situation remains complicated and competition in the world economy is as intense as ever.

All around us are countries with highly developed economies. We need to look in the face the fact that these countries push Russia out of promising world markets when they have the chance. And their obvious economic advantages serve as fuel for their growing geopolitical ambitions.

The proliferation of nuclear weapons continues in our world today. Terrorism threatens the world and endangers the security of our citizens. Certain countries sometimes use their strong and well-armed national armies to increase their zones of strategic influence rather than fighting these evils we all face.

Can Russia have any real hope of standing up to these threats if our society is splintered into little groups and if we all busy ourselves only with the narrow interests of our particular group? And if instead of becoming a thing of the past parasitic moods are only growing? And what is helping feed these moods but a bureaucracy that instead of trying to look after and build up our national wealth often happily lets it get frittered away.

It is my conviction that without consolidation at the least around basic national values and objectives, we will not be able to withstand these threats.

I would like to recall that throughout our history Russia and its people have accomplished and continue to accomplish a truly historical feat, a great work performed in the name of our country's integrity and in the name of bringing it peace and a stable life. Maintaining a state spread over such a vast territory and preserving a unique community of peoples while keeping up a strong presence on the international stage is not just an immense labour, it is also a task that has cost our people untold victims and sacrifice.

Such has been Russia's historic fate over these thousand and more years. Such has been the way Russia has continuously emerged as a strong nation. It is our duty never to forget this, and we should remember it now, too, as we examine the threats we face today and the main challenges to which we must rise.

The results we have achieved through our common efforts over these last three years show that we can rise to these challenges. Yes, we have already managed to deal with a good many of our problems, including some that only recently seemed impossible to resolve.

We have finally re-established the unity of our country, in law and in fact. We have reinforced state authority and brought federal power closer to the regions. Having re-established a common legal space, we were able to turn our attention to the division of powers between the federal and regional authorities. There is still a lot do here, but at least we are now hard at work on this issue. We have begun work on building up effective local authorities that have the financial resources to do their jobs. I choose my words carefully here, as we have only just begun addressing this task.

The adoption of the third part of the Russian Civil Code marked an important stage in our work on codifying our laws. The new Labour Code has also been passed. Modernised legislation and ongoing dialogue with trade unions and employers are now beginning to shape a civilised labour market.

We have made great strides towards creating a genuinely independent court system. We have adopted the new Criminal Procedural, Civil Procedural and Arbitration Procedural Codes, thereby assuring additional guarantees for human rights.

We have improved the electoral system. We now have the conditions we need for the development of a real civil society, and also for the establishment of genuinely strong political parties.

We have made considerable headway in tax reform and have begun military reform. We have managed to make progress on the complex issue of reforming land relations, a matter that had been at a standstill. I would just like to remind you that for a whole decade this question was a serious economic obstacle on the road to democracy and the market.

We have taken the first steps towards reforming the pension system, the infrastructure monopolies and the housing and utilities sector.

Together we have overcome an absolutely unacceptable situation in which certain parts of the country had for all intents and purposes placed themselves beyond the scope of federal jurisdiction. The supremacy of the Russian Constitution and federal laws, as well as the obligation to pay taxes to the national treasury have now become the norm for all the regions of the Russian Federation.

I would like here to add a few important remarks on a subject that is sensitive for all of us. Last year's address spoke of the need to reintegrate the Chechen Republic into the country's political and legal space, of the need for free elections and the establishment of effectively functioning regional authorities in the republic. Frankly speaking, few people believed in these words at that time. Now a year has gone by and reality has proven to us that together we can achieve a great deal. Once again I would like to thank everyone who supported this policy we have pursued and who took an active part in it. And I of course wish to thank all those who helped organise the referendum on the constitution in Chechnya itself.

I wish to express particular thanks to the people of Chechnya today. I thank them for their courage, for the fact that they did not let themselves be intimidated in the past and will not let themselves be intimidated today, and for that wisdom that is so inherent in people who are simple and yet always so sensitive to the truth. People in Chechnya felt in their hearts their responsibility and where their human interest lies. And finally, the referendum showed that the Chechen people rightfully considers itself an inalienable part of the united multi-ethnic community of peoples that make up Russia.

It is true that we have had to pay a high price to restore Russia's territorial integrity, and we bow our heads in memory of our fallen soldiers and of the Chechen civilians who lost their lives, in memory of all those who at the price of their lives did not allow this country to be torn apart and did their duty right to the end.

The constitutional referendum marked the end of these troubled times in Chechnya, these years during which bandits grabbed power in the republic and the people found themselves literally thrown back into a medieval world in which they lost even their most basic human rights. These were times when public executions became regular events on the streets of Chechen towns and villages, when thousands of people became living goods in the hands of slave traders, and when neither schools nor institutes nor hospitals functioned.

All of this is over now.

But we still a great deal of work to do before life in Chechnya returns completely to normal. Now, on a democratic basis and in accordance with the constitution approved by the referendum, the Chechen people must elect a president and parliament for their republic and establish local government. We must draw up and sign an agreement on the division of powers between the federal and the Chechen authorities, and of course we must get the Chechen economy working again.

We also have to transfer the organisation of law enforcement in Chechnya to the republic's own police force. Also, as part of the ongoing process of political regulation, we are working together with you, esteemed colleagues, on preparing the ground for an amnesty that will pave the way back to peaceful life for those who for various reasons did not lay down their arms earlier, but who now wish to do so.

We will face difficult conditions as we carry out this work. It is clear that what remains of the bandits will attempt to intimidate the people of Chechnya through threats, murders and terrorist acts and will try to disrupt and prevent the political regulation process that is gathering steam and moving ahead. We see today that the terrorist acts committed by these bandits are more and more often targeting the civilian population, ordinary people.

But we will see our work through to the end and the people of Chechnya will live a normal life worthy of a human being.

Respected Assembly,

Three years ago we identified the biggest threats to Russia as being demographic decline, economic weakness and a state that did not function effectively.

Have we made headway with solving these problems? Yes and no. We have had some successes, but there have also been some serious failures. Let us take an honest look at this today.

One of the most serious threats we identified was the decrease in the Russian population due above all to a falling birth rate and rising mortality rate. . . .

Another of the serious issues that was named three years ago was the increasing globalisation of the economy and of public international life in general in the modern world. No country today, no matter how big and how wealthy, can develop successfully in isolation from the rest of the world. On the contrary, the biggest success comes to those countries that consciously use their energy and intelligence to integrate themselves into the world economy.

We have taken some big steps forward on the road to international integration over the last three years.

Above all, Russia was invited in June last year to become a full member of the G-8 group of the world's most highly developed nations. Together with our partners in this group we work on safeguarding our own national interests and on finding solutions to the common problems that affect all of us in the modern world. One important example of this cooperation is the global partnership on non-proliferation of weapons of mass destruction. Programs to dismantle, treat and process these weapons will help us improve the environmental situation in a number of Russian regions.

I would like to note that our credit rating today is the highest it has been so far in new Russian history. A number of Russian companies have now joined the ranks of major European and world corporations. Some of these companies have, for the first time in the last 90 years, begun serious expansion into world markets, becoming visible players on the international economic stage and real rivals for foreign firms.

We have also made a lot of progress towards joining the World Trade Organisation.

Finally, Russia's economic weakness was named as a real strategic challenge for the country three years ago.

How far have we come since then in addressing that challenge?

There have been positive changes over this period. Economic growth has continued. Gross domestic product rose by 20 percent over these three years. Investment in fixed capital increased by more than 30 percent. Our exports increased by more than a quarter in physical volume, and exports of cars, equipment, and means of transport rose by more than 70 percent in physical volume terms. Overall, this is a decent result.

For the first time in the last fifty years, Russia went from importing grain to exporting it. Since 1999, exports of Russian foodstuffs have tripled. . . .

But at the same time, despite these positive changes, we are forced to admit that the economic results we have achieved are still very, very modest.

First, we still have a quarter of our citizens with incomes below the survival minimum. A quarter of the country's population!

Second, our economic growth is still very unstable. In 2000, industrial output rose throughout the whole year, but in 2002, it showed an increase only for a total of six months and as a result, unemployment began to rise.

Third, the economic growth rate is slowing down. In 2000, we enjoyed growth of 10 percent, but by last year the growth rate had slowed down to only slightly more than 4 percent. A lower growth rate inevitably also slows down the rate of social development and prevents us from resolving many of the other problems we face. . . .

The last three years have shown us what we really can achieve if we work together towards a common goal.

These three years have shown us that Russia does not have to be fated to suffer crises and decay, and that the Russian people is full of talent, initiative and enterprising spirit, that our people know how to work, that they deserve a better life, and that they can achieve this better life if only we do not get in their way. At the very least we must not get in the way, and it would better still if we help.

I think that our ultimate goal should be to return Russia to its place among the prosperous, developed, strong and respected nations.

But this will only be possible when Russia gains economic power and when it no longer depends on the favours of the international financial organisations or on the unpredictable ups and downs of the foreign trade situation.

We can achieve this kind of Russia only through sustainable and rapid growth, growth drawing on all factors, internal and external, traditional and modern, Russian and foreign.

And finally, sustainable and rapid growth is only possible if we produce competitive goods. Everything we have must be competitive—goods and services, technology and ideas, business and the state itself, private companies and state agencies, entrepreneurs and civil servants, students and teachers, science and culture.

But some people make an opposition between economic growth and reforms. They say it is dangerous to keep pushing economic growth, and that it is more important to carry out structural reforms. I would like to express my point of view on this question, which is that this opposition between growth and reform is debatable, to say the least. We do not need reforms purely for the sake of reform. We do not need a permanent revolution.

It is clear that private initiative, both from Russian business and from foreign companies working in Russia, is the driving force of economic growth. It is also clear that Russian business must itself become modern, enterprising, flexible and mobile. It must become the worthy successor to the great traditions of Russian entrepreneurship, and some added patriotism would not go amiss.

Again I repeat, our country's success depends to a great extent on the successes of our businesspeople.

Finally, there can be no opposition between a policy of pursuing economic growth and a social welfare policy. I would like to emphasise that we need economic growth above all in order to improve the living standards of our people. The solution to a whole range of vital problems depends directly on economic growth. This includes a quality diet, well-built and comfortable housing and reliable electricity and hot water supply. It also includes a good education and modern healthcare, protection from accidents and natural disasters, and finally, a longer life expectancy.

We have said that intense competition is an inherent part of the modern world. And so our ability to compete and our readiness to fight for resources and influence directly determines the situation within the country and Russia's authority in international affairs. . . .

Russia's development prospects and the solution to many of our problems will to a large degree be determined by the results of the main political event of the year - the elections to the State Duma. I cannot ignore this very important event in the life of the country. It is an important step in the formation of our democracy.

In recent years, relations between the executive and legislative branches have significantly improved. Instead of conflict, we have constructive cooperation based on substantial exchange of opinion and balanced criticism. We have interaction.

I see the most important sign of the cultural recovery of our society as being the solidarity shown by politicians on issues such as the war on international terrorism, preserving the territorial integrity of the country and supporting our foreign policy efforts. I can say without exaggeration that I am truly grateful to these political figures of our country. And they are political figures of the most varied political orientation.

I would also like to thank the representatives of all deputy organisations for their active collective work.

At the same time, certain features of our national political life also cause concern. Above all, procedures for financing political parties are still "a deep dark secret" for voters. The market for election campaign and other political technologies is to a significant degree currently one of the sectors of the shadow economy. I hope that very soon our collective work will ensure a greater transparency of party life, and give people more objective information. And as a result, more chances to make the right choice.

The lack of transparency of financial operations on the political stage are often accompanied by an incoherence of ideological position, and sometimes, quite frankly, a certain political insincerity. I will explain what I mean: sometimes deputies who are supposed to be liberals and supporters of progressive economic theories in practice vote for bills that are ruinous for the state budget. And they know what they are doing. And deputies who are not afraid of publicly calling entrepreneurs nothing but "robbers" and "blood-letters" shamelessly lobby the interests of large companies.

Parliamentary parties are a part of the state political machine, and at the same time they are a part of civil society. I would say that they are the most influential part, and so the most responsible. We are all interested in furthering interaction of party structures with the regions and with citizens and public organisations.

It is clear that active contact with the people cannot and must not be limited to pre-election debates and election campaigns. Only a daily link between the state and society, which can and must be provided by the large parties, can protect the government from making serious political errors.

We often talk of the greatness of Russia. But a great Russia is not just a great state. It is above all a modern, developed society, which does not just arise by itself.

A truly developed civil society only emerges when the functions of the state machine are radically reduced, and distrust between various social groups is overcome.

But most importantly, this will only become possible if we can achieve the kind of national unity we need to examine and address the strategic tasks our country faces. This national unity is impossible to achieve without the active participation of political parties.

I consider the upcoming elections to the State Duma as another step in the development of our multi-party system, the development of a greater openness of intentions, greater effectiveness of actions, and greater responsibility before the people of Russia.

A strong and responsible government based on the consolidation of society is vital to preserve the country. Without strong power, it will also be impossible to move forward into the future.

I would like to stress once again that we are facing serious problems and threats. And we need to be clever and strong to survive in the bitter competitive struggle in the world.

But we must not merely survive. We must possess significant economic, intellectual, moral and military advantages. Only in this way will we maintain our position among the greatest powers on the planet.

And I consider that our most important tasks, which I have already mentioned today and which I repeat, are the following:

- to double the gross domestic product;
- to overcome poverty;
- to modernise the Armed Forces.

I think that our society is capable of achieving these results in the period up to 2010. I consider the basis for achieving these goals to be a consolidation of public forces, the solid foundation of the Constitution of the Russian Federation and guaranteed rights and freedoms of our citizens.

I call on everyone who considers the above tasks to be a priority for the country to mobilise their intellectual forces, develop common approaches and agree on a program of action.

I have already said that I support the general policy to strengthen the role of parties in public life. And taking into account the results of the upcoming elections to the State Duma, I think it will be possible to form a professional, effective government, supported by a parliamentary majority.

To conclude my address, I would like to say that unification of our efforts is possible, if the main political forces take civil responsibility for collective work.

I am certain that Russia will rise to a height that is worthy of its potential.

The consolidation of all our intellectual, authoritative and moral resources will allow Russia to achieve the greatest goals.

Great goals worthy of a great people.

Let us wish one another success.

Thank you very much for your attention.

Source: Russian Federation. Office of the President. "Annual Presidential Address to the Federal Assembly of the Russian Federation." May 16, 2003. http://194.226.82.50/eng/text/speeches/2003/05/160000_44692.shtml (accessed July 2, 2003).

WHO Framework Convention on Tobacco Control

May 21, 2003

INTRODUCTION

The World Health Organization (WHO) reached a long-sought goal on May 21, 2003, when its 192 member nations unanimously adopted an international treaty aimed at reducing the number of smokers and deaths caused by smoking-related diseases, such as lung cancer, chronic lung disease, and tuberculosis. An estimated 1.1 billion people smoked worldwide, and 4.9 million died each year from tobacco use. According to WHO projections, without a major effort to reduce smoking, the number of deaths was expected to double to 10 million a year by 2030, with the additional deaths coming largely from developing countries.

The Framework Convention on Tobacco Control attacked tobacco use on several fronts. It called for a ban on tobacco advertising, warning labels that covered at least 30 percent of the packaging on all smoking products, and a listing of all ingredients on the package. The treaty also urged governments to pass laws banning smoking indoors, put high taxes on tobacco products, and get tough on tobacco smuggling.

The next challenge, which most observers said would be much harder than drafting the treaty, was to get at least forty countries to ratify it so that it could go into effect. By the end of the year, eighty-six countries had signed the treaty, the first step in the ratification process, but only five countries—Fiji, Malta, Norway, Seychelles, and Sri Lanka—had ratified the document. Two of the biggest manufacturers and users of cigarettes, China and the United States, were among the holdouts. China, with an estimated 350 million smokers and about 750,000 deaths each year attributable to smoking, signed the treaty on November 10. Days later it announced that it would put larger health warnings on cigarette packages but did not indicate whether it would eventually ratify the treaty. The United

States, which had initially opposed the treaty, had not signed it as of the end of 2003.

On the home front, however, the Justice Department stepped up the war against tobacco manufacturers in March, asking that the country's five largest cigarette makers be required to forfeit $289 billion in "ill-gotten gains." The demand came in new papers the Justice Department filed as part of a federal lawsuit against the tobacco companies initiated by the Clinton administration in 1999. That the Bush administration was pursuing the case so aggressively came as a surprise to many observers, who noted that Attorney General John Ashcroft had indicated he was not in favor of the suit going forward.

In other action, a controversial plan to give federal relief to financially stressed tobacco farmers in exchange for giving the Food and Drug Administration (FDA) authority to regulate tobacco products was revived in Congress, but talks broke down in October over the scope of the authority to be given to the FDA.

Tobacco Treaty

The Framework Convention on Tobacco Control was viewed by some as the most important international public health effort ever undertaken. The treaty was a top priority for WHO general director Gro Harlem Brundtland, who said on May 21 that it could "save billions of lives and protect people's health for generations to come." The major provisions of the treaty called on national governments to:

- Ban all tobacco advertising, promotion, and sponsorship. Those countries whose constitutions prohibited such outright bans were asked to put restrictions on tobacco advertising and promotion.
- Require that health warnings take up at least 30 percent of the packaging and that all ingredients in the product be listed. The labeling could not make "false," "misleading," or "deceptive" statements or create the impression that product was less harmful than other tobacco products. Terms such as "low-tar, light, ultra-light, or mild" were considered false or misleading.
- Enact laws protecting people from exposure to secondhand smoke in public places and workplaces.
- Take steps to reduce smuggling, including requiring manufacturers to label each cigarette packet to indicate its final sales destination.
- Prohibit the sale of cigarettes to underage youth.

Although the treaty did not directly call on nations to increase their taxes on cigarettes and other tobacco products, it encouraged them to do so as a means for discouraging their purchase and use. It did ask countries to prohibit tax- and duty-free sales.

The unanimous adoption of the treaty by the World Health Assembly belied the difficult negotiations that at times nearly derailed the treaty. Throughout the talks, which began in 2000, the United States pressed for a provision that would allow individual countries to opt out of specific provisions of the treaty. The Bush administration said such a provision was necessary to ensure that the United States would not have to adopt constitutionally questionable policies. The administration also argued that ratification by the Senate might be impossible to win if the treaty could not be amended. U.S. officials pressed the issue even after negotiators rejected the opt-out provision in the final text of the treaty, adopted March 3. Anti-smoking advocates said administration opposition was related to helping out the U.S. cigarette makers, who were big contributors to the president's election campaign. "This looks like an American effort to blow up the treaty, or to neutralize it for the benefit of Philip Morris and other cigarette makers," Matthew Myers of the Campaign for Tobacco-Free Kids said in April. *(Negotiations begin, Historic Documents of 2000, p. 538)*

On May 18 Tommy G. Thompson, the secretary of health and human services and the head of the U.S. delegation to the World Health Assembly, announced that the United States would support the treaty. "I'm going to support it—much to the surprise of many around the world," Thompson said. "I'm not going to make any changes. We have no reservations. The delegation here, headed by me, is in support of the tobacco treaty." Thompson added that he did not know whether President George W. Bush would sign the treaty, and the administration had not done so by year's end.

Thompson did not explain the reversal in policy, but many observers suggested that the United States wanted to ensure that it could participate in the international meetings that would determine how to implement the treaty. Only countries that had voted for the treaty were permitted to join those talks. The United States was particularly interested in the talks on cigarette smuggling, a worldwide problem that had been linked with funding for terrorist activities.

Another major point of contention during the negotiations was whether to finance tobacco control programs in poor countries. Thirty-two African countries called for funding for developing countries that grew tobacco to help them switch to other crops. They also asked that tobacco companies be made liable for their products and that they compensate poor nations for the health care burden tobacco use imposed on them. The United States, Germany, and Japan were among those opposing that proposal. The final text of the treaty did not mandate such funding but strongly encouraged richer countries to provide financial assistance for developing countries that were trying to reduce their reliance on tobacco crops.

Although only five countries ratified the treaty by the end of the year, many independently took steps to reduce smoking. Among them, France adopted new regulations requiring larger labels and starker warnings, such as "Smoking kills." The United Kingdom outlawed cigarette ads in magazines, newspapers, and billboards. Ireland was set to impose a ban on smoking in all public places, including restaurants and pubs, as of January 1, 2004. Many jurisdictions in the United States had imposed similar bans on smoking.

Justice Department Lawsuit

The Justice Department's demand that the tobacco companies forfeit $289 billion was the first time since the civil suit was filed in 1999 that the government had put a dollar amount on how much it believed the tobacco companies should pay for manipulating the nicotine levels in cigarettes, lying about the potential dangers to health from smoking, and pitching their products to teenagers. The department backed up that demand with 1,400 pages of documents filed with the U.S. District Court for the District of Columbia, in preparation for the trial that was scheduled to begin in September 2004.

Many of the potentially damning documents came from the files of the companies involved in the suit: Philip Morris USA, R. J. Reynolds, Lorillard, Brown and Williamson, and Liggett Group. In summary, the department's filing said, "defendant's scheme to defraud permeated and influenced all facets of defendants' conduct—research, product development, advertising, marketing, legal, public relations, and communications—in a manner that has resulted in extraordinary profits for the past half-century, but has had devastating consequences for the public's health."

The tobacco companies rejected these claims in its own filings. An attorney for Brown and Williamson told the *New York Times* that many of the Justice Department's proposed findings of fact bore little relationship to the law. "They've put everything and the kitchen sink into these documents in the hopes that something sticks," he said. Antismoking groups applauded the department, however. "With these filings, the Justice Department has documented that the tobacco industry continues to violate the law by marketing to our children and by deceiving the American public," said William V. Corr, executive vice president of the Campaign for Tobacco-Free Kids. Corr and others also expressed some surprise that the department was taking what appeared to be a very aggressive stance against the companies, noting that as a U.S. senator, attorney general John Ashcroft had opposed the lawsuit. After moving to the Justice Department as part of the Bush administration, Ashcroft had moved to cut funding for the legal team working on the suit and also talked about trying to reach a settlement because he thought the government had a weak case. "For this Justice Department to pursue this case so aggressively is very significant," Corr said.

FDA Regulatory Authority

In 1995 the Food and Drug Administration kicked off a major controversy when it asserted that it had the authority to regulate nicotine as an addictive and dangerous drug and, with the backing of the Clinton administration, issued a proposed set of regulations restricting the sale and marketing of tobacco products. After the regulations became final in 1996, the tobacco companies immediately filed suit, and in 2000 the Supreme Court overturned the regulations, saying that the FDA had overstepped its authority and would have to obtain explicit authority from Congress if it wanted to regulate tobacco products. *(FDA regulations, Historic Documents of 1995, p. 670; Supreme Court decision, Historic Documents of 2000, p. 556)*

Public health advocates and antismoking forces pushed legislation to give FDA the required authority. Congress took no action, however, until 2003 when an unusual convergence of interests emerged among tobacco farmers and their congressional supporters and supporters of tobacco regulation. In short, the idea was for legislators from tobacco states to vote for FDA regulatory authority in exchange for support from antismoking legislators on a plan for the federal government to buy out the tobacco quota program, which determined who could grow tobacco and how much they could sell. Tobacco farmers said the seventy-year-old quota program kept prices inflated and was restricting their ability to compete with foreign growers. Many beleaguered farmers said they would use the buyout money to retire from tobacco farming altogether.

An agreement was worked out in the Senate in July to pursue the joint legislation, but the negotiations fell apart in late September and early October, primarily over language granting regulatory authority to the FDA. Democrats on the Senate Health Committee said that the legislative proposal offered by the Republicans and backed by Philip Morris, the largest cigarette maker in the nation, was not strong enough. Antismoking advocates were also concerned that language allowing only Congress to ban cigarettes was so vaguely worded that tobacco companies could challenge even the smallest change in tobacco products as outside the FDA's regulatory authority. "The vague language was a loophole that could prevent FDA from taking any steps to reduce the harm caused by tobacco," said Myers of the Campaign for Tobacco-Free Kids.

Mark Berlind, a lawyer for Altria, Philip Morris's parent company, said that the language was necessary to protect the interests of the tobacco companies and that the antismoking lobby was in reality seeking to give the FDA authority to ban tobacco products. Philip Morris, which controlled about half of all tobacco products sold in the United States, was the only tobacco company to support regulatory authority for the FDA. The other companies opposed it, saying that advertising restrictions would make it harder for them to compete with Philip Morris.

In this annual report on cigarettes, the Federal Trade Commission (FTC) said that tobacco manufacturers spent $11.2 billion on advertising and promotion in the United States in 2001, the latest year for which such figures were available. That was a 17 percent increase over 2000 and came despite the settlement with forty-six states in 1998 that banned cigarette advertising on billboards and public transportation, and limited sponsorships and giveaways of cigarette samples and merchandise branded with logos. Despite the increase in spending on advertising, cigarette sales during the year dropped 3.8 percent. *(Tobacco settlement, Historic Documents of 1998, p. 842)*

The FTC reported that the companies spent most of their advertising money ($4.8 billion) on "retail value added," that is, the costs associated with offers such as "buy one pack, get one free." They also spent $4.5 billion on promotional allowances, such as payments to retailers for prime display space and volume discounts to wholesalers. The total advertising figure did not count lobbying or campaign contributions. Nor did it count the $79.4 million it spent on adverting aimed at reducing youth smoking.

Following are excerpts from the Annex to the World Health Organization's Framework Convention on Tobacco Control, adopted May 21, 2003, by the Fifty-Sixth World Health Assembly in Geneva, Switzerland.

"Framework Convention on Tobacco Control"

Preamble

The Parties to this Convention,

Determined to give priority to their right to protect public health,

Recognizing that the spread of the tobacco epidemic is a global problem with serious consequences for public health that calls for the widest possible international cooperation and the participation of all countries in an effective, appropriate and comprehensive international response,

Reflecting the concern of the international community about the devastating worldwide health, social, economic and environmental consequences of tobacco consumption and exposure to tobacco smoke,

Seriously concerned about the increase in the worldwide consumption and production of cigarettes and other tobacco products, particularly in developing countries, as well as about the burden this places on families, on the poor, and on national health systems,

Recognizing that scientific evidence has unequivocally established that tobacco consumption and exposure to tobacco smoke cause death, disease and disability, and that there is a time lag between the exposure to smoking and the other uses of tobacco products and the onset of tobacco-related diseases,

Recognizing also that cigarettes and some other products containing tobacco are highly engineered so as to create and maintain dependence, and that many of the compounds they contain and the smoke they produce are pharmacologically active, toxic, mutagenic and carcinogenic, and that tobacco dependence is separately classified as a disorder in major international classifications of diseases,

Acknowledging that there is clear scientific evidence that prenatal exposure to tobacco smoke causes adverse health and developmental conditions for children,

Deeply concerned about the escalation in smoking and other forms of tobacco consumption by children and adolescents worldwide, particularly smoking at increasingly early ages,

Alarmed by the increase in smoking and other forms of tobacco consumption by women and young girls worldwide and keeping in mind the need for full participation of women at all levels of policy-making and implementation and the need for gender-specific tobacco control strategies,

Deeply concerned about the high levels of smoking and other forms of tobacco consumption by indigenous peoples,

Seriously concerned about the impact of all forms of advertising, promotion and sponsorship aimed at encouraging the use of tobacco products,

Recognizing that cooperative action is necessary to eliminate all forms of illicit trade in cigarettes and other tobacco products, including smuggling, illicit manufacturing and counterfeiting,

Acknowledging that tobacco control at all levels and particularly in developing countries and in countries with economies in transition requires sufficient financial and technical resources commensurate with the current and projected need for tobacco control activities,

Recognizing the need to develop appropriate mechanisms to address the long-term social and economic implications of successful tobacco demand reduction strategies,

Mindful of the social and economic difficulties that tobacco control programmes may engender in the medium and long term in some developing countries and countries with economies in transition, and recognizing their need for technical and financial assistance in the context of nationally developed strategies for sustainable development,

Conscious of the valuable work being conducted by many States on tobacco control and commending the leadership of the World Health Organization as well as the efforts of other organizations and bodies of the United Nations system and other international and regional intergovernmental organizations in developing measures on tobacco control,

Emphasizing the special contribution of nongovernmental organizations and other members of civil society not affiliated with the tobacco industry, including health professional bodies, women's, youth, environmental and consumer groups, and academic and health care institutions, to tobacco control efforts nationally and internationally and the vital importance of their participation in national and international tobacco control efforts,

Recognizing the need to be alert to any efforts by the tobacco industry to undermine or subvert tobacco control efforts and the need to be informed of activities of the tobacco industry that have a negative impact on tobacco control efforts,

Recalling Article 12 of the International Covenant on Economic, Social and Cultural Rights, adopted by the United Nations General Assembly on 16 December 1966, which states that it is the right of everyone to the enjoyment of the highest attainable standard of physical and mental health,

Recalling also the preamble to the Constitution of the World Health Organization, which states that the enjoyment of the highest attainable standard of health is one of the fundamental rights of every human being without distinction of race, religion, political belief, economic or social condition,

Determined to promote measures of tobacco control based on current and relevant scientific, technical and economic considerations,

Recalling that the Convention on the Elimination of All Forms of Discrimination against Women, adopted by the United Nations General Assembly on 18 December 1979, provides that States Parties to that Convention shall take appropriate measures to eliminate discrimination against women in the field of health care,

Recalling further that the Convention on the Rights of the Child, adopted by the United Nations General Assembly on 20 November 1989, provides that States Parties to that Convention recognize the right of the child to the enjoyment of the highest attainable standard of health,

Have agreed, as follows:

[Part I, articles 1 and 2, omitted.]

Part II: Objective, Guiding Principles and General Obligations

Article 3

Objective

The objective of this Convention and its protocols is to protect present and future generations from the devastating health, social, environmental and economic consequences of tobacco consumption and exposure to tobacco smoke by providing a framework for tobacco control measures to be implemented by the Parties at the national, regional and international levels in order to reduce continually and substantially the prevalence of tobacco use and exposure to tobacco smoke.

Article 4

Guiding principles

To achieve the objective of this Convention and its protocols and to implement its provisions, the Parties shall be guided, inter alia, by the principles set out below:

1. Every person should be informed of the health consequences, addictive nature and mortal threat posed by tobacco consumption and exposure to tobacco smoke and effective legislative, executive, administrative or other measures should be contemplated at the appropriate governmental level to protect all persons from exposure to tobacco smoke.

2. Strong political commitment is necessary to develop and support, at the national, regional and international levels, comprehensive multisectoral measures and coordinated responses, taking into consideration:

   (a) the need to take measures to protect all persons from exposure to tobacco smoke;

   (b) the need to take measures to prevent the initiation, to promote and support cessation, and to decrease the consumption of tobacco products in any form;

   (c) the need to take measures to promote the participation of indigenous individuals and communities in the development, implementation and evaluation of tobacco control programmes that are socially and culturally appropriate to their needs and perspectives; and

   (d) the need to take measures to address gender-specific risks when developing tobacco control strategies.

3. International cooperation, particularly transfer of technology, knowledge and financial assistance and provision of related expertise, to establish and implement effective tobacco control programmes, taking into consideration local culture, as well as social, economic, political and legal factors, is an important part of the Convention.

4. Comprehensive multisectoral measures and responses to reduce consumption of all tobacco products at the national, regional and international levels are essential so as to prevent, in accordance with public health principles, the incidence of diseases, premature disability and mortality due to tobacco consumption and exposure to tobacco smoke.

5. Issues relating to liability, as determined by each Party within its jurisdiction, are an important part of comprehensive tobacco control.

6. The importance of technical and financial assistance to aid the economic transition of tobacco growers and workers whose livelihoods are seriously affected as a consequence of tobacco control programmes in developing country Parties, as well as Parties with economics in transition, should be recognized and addressed in the context of nationally developed strategies for sustainable development.

7. The participation of civil society is essential in achieving the objective of the Convention and its protocols.

Article 5

General obligations

1. Each Party shall develop, implement, periodically update and review comprehensive multisectoral national tobacco control strategies, plans and programmes in accordance with this Convention and the protocols to which it is a Party.

2. Towards this end, each Party shall, in accordance with its capabilities:
   (a) establish or reinforce and finance a national coordinating mechanism or focal points for tobacco control; and
   (b) adopt and implement effective legislative, executive, administrative and/or other measures and cooperate, as appropriate, with other Parties in developing appropriate policies for preventing and reducing tobacco consumption, nicotine addiction and exposure to tobacco smoke.

3. In setting and implementing their public health policies with respect to tobacco control, Parties shall act to protect these policies from commercial and other vested interests of the tobacco industry in accordance with national law.

4. The Parties shall cooperate in the formulation of proposed measures, procedures and guidelines for the implementation of the Convention and the protocols to which they are Parties.

5. The Parties shall cooperate, as appropriate, with competent international and regional intergovernmental organizations and other bodies to achieve the objectives of the Convention and the protocols to which they are Parties.

6. The Parties shall, within means and resources at their disposal, cooperate to raise financial resources for effective implementation of the Convention through bilateral and multilateral funding mechanisms.

Part III: Measures Relating to the Reduction of Demand for Tobacco

Article 6

Price and tax measures to reduce the demand for tobacco

1. The Parties recognize that price and tax measures are an effective and important means of reducing tobacco consumption by various segments of the population, in particular young persons.

2. Without prejudice to the sovereign right of the Parties to determine and establish their taxation policies, each Party should take account of its national health objectives concerning tobacco control and adopt or maintain, as appropriate, measures which may include:
   (a) implementing tax policies and, where appropriate, price policies, on tobacco products so as to contribute to the health objectives aimed at reducing tobacco consumption; and
   (b) prohibiting or restricting, as appropriate, sales to and/or importations by international travellers of tax-and duty-free tobacco products.

3. The Parties shall provide rates of taxation for tobacco products and trends in tobacco consumption in their periodic reports to the Conference of the Parties, in accordance with Article 21.

Article 7

Non-price measures to reduce the demand for tobacco

The Parties recognize that comprehensive non-price measures are an effective and important means of reducing tobacco consumption. Each Party shall adopt and implement effective legislative, executive, administrative or other measures necessary to implement its obligations pursuant to Articles 8 to 13 and shall cooperate, as appropriate, with each other directly or through competent international bodies with a view to their implementation. The Conference of the Parties shall propose appropriate guidelines for the implementation of the provisions of these Articles.

Article 8

Protection from exposure to tobacco smoke
1. Parties recognize that scientific evidence has unequivocally established that exposure to tobacco smoke causes death, disease and disability.
2. Each Party shall adopt and implement in areas of existing national jurisdiction as determined by national law and actively promote at other jurisdictional levels the adoption and implementation of effective legislative, executive, administrative and/or other measures, providing for protection from exposure to tobacco smoke in indoor workplaces, public transport, indoor public places and, as appropriate, other public places.

Article 9

Regulation of the contents of tobacco products
The Conference of the Parties, in consultation with competent international bodies, shall propose guidelines for testing and measuring the contents and emissions of tobacco products, and for the regulation of these contents and emissions. Each Party shall, where approved by competent national authorities, adopt and implement effective legislative, executive and administrative or other measures for such testing and measuring, and for such regulation.

Article 10

Regulation of tobacco product disclosures
Each Party shall, in accordance with its national law, adopt and implement effective legislative, executive, administrative or other measures requiring manufacturers and importers of tobacco products to disclose to governmental authorities information about the contents and emissions of tobacco products. Each Party shall further adopt and implement effective measures for public disclosure of information about the toxic constituents of the tobacco products and the emissions that they may produce.

Article 11

Packaging and labelling of tobacco products

1. Each Party shall, within a period of three years after entry into force of this Convention for that Party, adopt and implement, in accordance with its national law, effective measures to ensure that:

   (a) tobacco product packaging and labelling do not promote a tobacco product by any means that are false, misleading, deceptive or likely to create an erroneous impression about its characteristics, health effects, hazards or emissions, including any term, descriptor, trademark, figurative or any other sign that directly or indirectly creates the false impression that a particular tobacco product is less harmful than other tobacco products. These may include terms such as "low tar", "light", "ultra-light", or "mild"; and

   (b) each unit packet and package of tobacco products and any outside packaging and labelling of such products also carry health warnings describing the harmful effects of tobacco use, and may include other appropriate messages. These warnings and messages:

      (i) shall be approved by the competent national authority,

      (ii) shall be rotating,

      (iii) shall be large, clear, visible and legible,

      (iv) should be 50% or more of the principal display areas but shall be no less than 30% of the principal display areas,

      (v) may be in the form of or include pictures or pictograms.

2. Each unit packet and package of tobacco products and any outside packaging and labelling of such products shall, in addition to the warnings specified in paragraph 1(b) of this Article, contain information on relevant constituents and emissions of tobacco products as defined by national authorities.

3. Each Party shall require that the warnings and other textual information specified in paragraphs 1(b) and paragraph 2 of this Article will appear on each unit packet and package of tobacco products and any outside packaging and labelling of such products in its principal language or languages.

4. For the purposes of this Article, the term "outside packaging and labelling" in relation to tobacco products applies to any packaging and labelling used in the retail sale of the product.

Article 12

Education, communication, training and public awareness

Each Party shall promote and strengthen public awareness of tobacco control issues, using all available communication tools, as appropriate.

Towards this end, each Party shall adopt and implement effective legislative, executive, administrative or other measures to promote:

(a) broad access to effective and comprehensive educational and public awareness programmes on the health risks including the addictive characteristics of tobacco consumption and exposure to tobacco smoke;

(b) public awareness about the health risks of tobacco consumption and exposure to tobacco smoke, and about the benefits of the cessation of tobacco use and tobacco-free lifestyles as specified in Article 14.2;

(c) public access, in accordance with national law, to a wide range of information on the tobacco industry as relevant to the objective of this Convention;

(d) effective and appropriate training or sensitization and awareness programmes on tobacco control addressed to persons such as health workers, community workers, social workers, media professionals, educators, decision-makers, administrators and other concerned persons;

(e) awareness and participation of public and private agencies and non-governmental organizations not affiliated with the tobacco industry in developing and implementing intersectoral programmes and strategies for tobacco control; and

(f) public awareness of and access to information regarding the adverse health, economic, and environmental consequences of tobacco production and consumption.

Article 13

Tobacco advertising, promotion and sponsorship

1. Parties recognize that a comprehensive ban on advertising, promotion and sponsorship would reduce the consumption of tobacco products.

2. Each Party shall, in accordance with its constitution or constitutional principles, undertake a comprehensive ban of all tobacco advertising, promotion and sponsorship. This shall include, subject to the legal environment and technical means available to that Party, a comprehensive ban on cross-border advertising, promotion and sponsorship originating from its territory. In this respect, within the period of five years after entry into force of this Convention for that Party, each Party shall undertake appropriate legislative, executive, administrative and/or other measures and report accordingly in conformity with Article 21.

3. A Party that is not in a position to undertake a comprehensive ban due to its constitution or constitutional principles shall apply restrictions on all tobacco advertising, promotion and sponsorship. This shall include, subject to the legal environment and technical means available to that Party, restrictions or a comprehensive ban

on advertising, promotion and sponsorship originating from its territory with cross-border effects. In this respect, each Party shall undertake appropriate legislative, executive, administrative and/or other measures and report accordingly in conformity with Article 21.

4. As a minimum, and in accordance with its constitution or constitutional principles, each Party shall:

   (a) prohibit all forms of tobacco advertising, promotion and sponsorship that promote a tobacco product by any means that are false, misleading or deceptive or likely to create an erroneous impression about its characteristics, health effects, hazards or emissions;

   (b) require that health or other appropriate warnings or messages accompany all tobacco advertising and, as appropriate, promotion and sponsorship;

   (c) restrict the use of direct or indirect incentives that encourage the purchase of tobacco products by the public;

   (d) require, if it does not have a comprehensive ban, the disclosure to relevant governmental authorities of expenditures by the tobacco industry on advertising, promotion and sponsorship not yet prohibited. Those authorities may decide to make those figures available, subject to national law, to the public and to the Conference of the Parties, pursuant to Article 21;

   (e) undertake a comprehensive ban or, in the case of a Party that is not in a position to undertake a comprehensive ban due to its constitution or constitutional principles, restrict tobacco advertising, promotion and sponsorship on radio, television, print media and, as appropriate, other media, such as the internet, within a period of five years; and

   (f) prohibit, or in the case of a Party that is not in a position to prohibit due to its constitution or constitutional principles restrict, tobacco sponsorship of international events, activities and/or participants therein.

5. Parties are encouraged to implement measures beyond the obligations set out in paragraph 4.

6. Parties shall cooperate in the development of technologies and other means necessary to facilitate the elimination of cross-border advertising.

7. Parties which have a ban on certain forms of tobacco advertising, promotion and sponsorship have the sovereign right to ban those forms of cross-border tobacco advertising, promotion and sponsorship entering their territory and to impose equal penalties as those applicable to domestic advertising, promotion and sponsorship originating from their territory in accordance with their national law. This paragraph does not endorse or approve of any particular penalty.

8. Parties shall consider the elaboration of a protocol setting out appropriate measures that require international collaboration for a comprehensive ban on cross-border advertising, promotion and sponsorship.

Article 14

Demand reduction measures concerning tobacco dependence and cessation

1. Each Party shall develop and disseminate appropriate, comprehensive and integrated guidelines based on scientific evidence and best practices, taking into account national circumstances and priorities, and shall take effective measures to promote cessation of tobacco use and adequate treatment for tobacco dependence.
2. Towards this end, each Party shall endeavour to:
   (a) design and implement effective programmes aimed at promoting the cessation of tobacco use, in such locations as educational institutions, health care facilities, workplaces and sporting environments;
   (b) include diagnosis and treatment of tobacco dependence and counselling services on cessation of tobacco use in national health and education programmes, plans and strategies, with the participation of health workers, community workers and social workers as appropriate;
   (c) establish in health care facilities and rehabilitation centres programmes for diagnosing, counselling, preventing and treating tobacco dependence; and
   (d) collaborate with other Parties to facilitate accessibility and affordability for treatment of tobacco dependence including pharmaceutical products pursuant to Article 22. Such products and their constituents may include medicines, products used to administer medicines and diagnostics when appropriate.

Part IV: Measures Relating to the Reduction of the Supply of Tobacco

Article 15

Illicit trade in tobacco products

1. The Parties recognize that the elimination of all forms of illicit trade in tobacco products, including smuggling, illicit manufacturing and counterfeiting, and the development and implementation

of related national law, in addition to subregional, regional and global agreements, are essential components of tobacco control.

2. Each Party shall adopt and implement effective legislative, executive, administrative or other measures to ensure that all unit packets and packages of tobacco products and any outside packaging of such products are marked to assist Parties in determining the origin of tobacco products, and in accordance with national law and relevant bilateral or multilateral agreements, assist Parties in determining the point of diversion and monitor, document and control the movement of tobacco products and their legal status. In addition, each Party shall:

   (a) require that unit packets and packages of tobacco products for retail and wholesale use that are sold on its domestic market carry the statement: *"Sales only allowed in (insert name of the country, subnational, regional or federal unit)"* or carry any other effective marking indicating the final destination or which would assist authorities in determining whether the product is legally for sale on the domestic market; and

   (b) consider, as appropriate, developing a practical tracking and tracing regime that would further secure the distribution system and assist in the investigation of illicit trade.

3. Each Party shall require that the packaging information or marking specified in paragraph 2 of this Article shall be presented in legible form and/or appear in its principal language or languages.

4. With a view to eliminating illicit trade in tobacco products, each Party shall:

   (a) monitor and collect data on cross-border trade in tobacco products, including illicit trade, and exchange information among customs, tax and other authorities, as appropriate, and in accordance with national law and relevant applicable bilateral or multilateral agreements;

   (b) enact or strengthen legislation, with appropriate penalties and remedies, against illicit trade in tobacco products, including counterfeit and contraband cigarettes;

   (c) take appropriate steps to ensure that all confiscated manufacturing equipment, counterfeit and contraband cigarettes and other tobacco products are destroyed, using environmentally-friendly methods where feasible, or disposed of in accordance with national law;

   (d) adopt and implement measures to monitor, document and control the storage and distribution of tobacco products held or moving under suspension of taxes or duties within its jurisdiction; and

   (e) adopt measures as appropriate to enable the confiscation of proceeds derived from the illicit trade in tobacco products.

5. Information collected pursuant to subparagraphs 4(a) and 4(d) of this Article shall, as appropriate, be provided in aggregate form by the Parties in their periodic reports to the Conference of the Parties, in accordance with Article 21.

6. The Parties shall, as appropriate and in accordance with national law, promote cooperation between national agencies, as well as relevant regional and international intergovernmental organizations as it relates to investigations, prosecutions and proceedings, with a view to eliminating illicit trade in tobacco products. Special emphasis shall be placed on cooperation at regional and subregional levels to combat illicit trade of tobacco products.

7. Each Party shall endeavour to adopt and implement further measures including licensing, where appropriate, to control or regulate the production and distribution of tobacco products in order to prevent illicit trade.

Article 16

Sales to and by minors

1. Each Party shall adopt and implement effective legislative, executive, administrative or other measures at the appropriate government level to prohibit the sales of tobacco products to persons under the age set by domestic law, national law or eighteen. These measures may include:

   (a) requiring that all sellers of tobacco products place a clear and prominent indicator inside their point of sale about the prohibition of tobacco sales to minors and, in case of doubt, request that each tobacco purchaser provide appropriate evidence of having reached full legal age;

   (b) banning the sale of tobacco products in any manner by which they are directly accessible, such as store shelves

   (c) prohibiting the manufacture and sale of sweets, snacks, toys or any other objects in the form of tobacco products which appeal to minors; and

   (d) ensuring that tobacco vending machines under its jurisdiction are not accessible to minors and do not promote the sale of tobacco products to minors.

2. Each Party shall prohibit or promote the prohibition of the distribution of free tobacco products to the public and especially minors.

3. Each Party shall endeavour to prohibit the sale of cigarettes individually or in small packets which increase the affordability of such products to minors.

4. The Parties recognize that in order to increase their effectiveness, measures to prevent tobacco product sales to minors should, where appropriate, be implemented in conjunction with other provisions contained in this Convention.

5. When signing, ratifying, accepting, approving or acceding to the Convention or at any time thereafter, a Party may, by means of a binding written declaration, indicate its commitment to prohibit the introduction of tobacco vending machines within its jurisdiction or, as appropriate, to a total ban on tobacco vending machines. The declaration made pursuant to this Article shall be circulated by the Depositary to all Parties to the Convention.

6. Each Party shall adopt and implement effective legislative, executive, administrative or other measures, including penalties against sellers and distributors, in order to ensure compliance with the obligations contained in paragraphs 1-5 of this Article.

7. Each Party should, as appropriate, adopt and implement effective legislative, executive, administrative or other measures to prohibit the sales of tobacco products by persons under the age set by domestic law, national law or eighteen.

Article 17

Provision of support for economically viable alternative activities
Parties shall, in cooperation with each other and with competent international and regional intergovernmental organizations, promote, as appropriate, economically viable alternatives for tobacco workers, growers and, as the case may be, individual sellers.

[Parts V through XI omitted.]

Source: United Nations. World Health Organization. Fifty-Sixth World Health Assembly. *Framework Convention on Tobacco Control.* WHA56.1. May 21, 2003. www.who.int/entity/tobacco/fctc/text/en/fctc_en.pdf (accessed July 13, 2003).

National Referendum in Venezuela on the Presidency of Hugo Chavez

May 29, 2003

INTRODUCTION

A fiercely determined Hugo Chavez managed to hold on to power as president of Venezuela in 2003—beating back a general strike that crippled the country's economy and generally outfoxing the divided opposition. Chavez survived two petition drives demanding a referendum on his presidency, and at year's end was facing a third. By then it was clear that Chavez—a former army paratrooper who relished a fight—was determined to stay in office through the end of his term in 2007, no matter what the cost to Venezuela economically or politically.

Chavez had come to power in 1998 on the basis of populist rhetoric that appealed to the millions of impoverished Venezuelans—many of them of Indian ancestry—who had not benefited from the wealth generated by the country's oil industry. Chavez promised schools, health clinics, and other social services for the poor. Although he delivered more promises than results, he remained popular in the enormous slums of Caracas and other cities throughout the nation and won reelection in 2000 under a new constitution that increased his power.

The opposition, which had united under the name Coordinadora Demcrática (Democratic Coordinator), consisted of business leaders and some labor unions. Opponents accused Chavez of destroying the economy and attempting to create a leftist dictatorship through a series of legal changes that emasculated the legislature. A group of opposition business and military leaders staged a coup in April 2002 that put Chavez out of power for just two days. After that episode, Chavez deftly maneuvered all through 2002 and 2003 as the opposition, and even international statesmen (including former U.S. president Jimmy Carter), failed in repeated attempts to negotiate a settlement that would end the country's turmoil. *(Background, Historic Documents of 2002, p. 201)*

General Strike Collapses

The opposition had begun the general strike on December 2, 2002, and for more than a month had won broad backing for an economic protest against Chavez. The vast majority of major businesses (but not small ones) closed their doors or opened for only a few hours each day. Most important, all but about 5,000 of the 40,000 employees of the state-owned oil company, Petroleos de Venezuela S.A. (known to Venezuelans as PDVSA, or "pedevesa") walked off the job, severely crippling oil production. At the height of the strike, in early December 2002, daily production was down to about 150,000 barrels a day, compared to normal production of about 3 million barrels a day. Chavez sent the army to take the place of oil company workers, and by late January production was back up to about one-third of prestrike levels.

The goal of the strike was to force Chavez to agree to call a referendum on February 2 on whether he should step down as president. The opposition had gathered 3 million signatures on a petition demanding such a referendum—far more than was required under the constitution. But the Supreme Court on January 22 blocked the vote on a minor technicality, effectively deflating both the drive for a referendum and the general strike that was intended to back it up. On February 2, the day of the long-sought referendum, opposition leaders were reduced to gathering signatures for yet another attempt at a vote. By that time most striking workers had gone back to their jobs, and the general strike clearly had failed in all respects except to damage the economy. Government officials said the strike had cost the country's economy $6 billion—about 5 percent of the prestrike annual gross domestic product.

The failure of the strike also led to discord among opposition leaders, who had been united only by their determination to get rid of Chavez. By early February the forty-some groups that made up the Coordinadora Demcrática were floating competing proposals for the next step. Some still wanted a referendum recalling Chavez, while others called for a constitutional amendment reducing Chavez's term from six years to four years—ending later in 2003. In the meantime, opposition leaders participated in sporadic negotiations with government representatives; the talks were mediated by Cesar Gaviria, the secretary general of the Organization of American States (OAS), who had spent much of the previous year in Caracas trying to develop a compromise solution to the country's political stalemate. Carter also met with Chavez and opposition leaders during the strike in January but failed to produce an agreement. Aides from his think tank in Atlanta (the Carter Center) participated in subsequent talks.

Chavez struck out at the opposition in February, after the failure of the strike, accusing the two most prominent general strike leaders of treason: Carlos Fernandez, head of the country's largest business federation, and

Carlos Ortega, head of the Venezuelan Workers Confederation. A judge then ordered the two men arrested; Fernandez was taken into custody on February 20 and placed under house arrest. Ortega went into hiding and on March 14 turned up in Costa Rica, where he was granted political asylum.

Except for the strike's cutoff of oil exports to the United States and other countries, most of the impact of Venezuela's turmoil had been felt domestically. That changed on February 24, when Chavez accused the governments of Colombia, Spain, and the United States of interfering in Venezuelan affairs. All had voiced concern about the crackdown on opposition leaders, and the U.S. government had appeared to support the failed coup attempt against Chavez in 2001. The Colombian government also had accused Chavez of supporting leftist guerrillas in Colombia, a charge Chavez denied. The next day, bombs exploded at the Spanish embassy and the Colombian consulate in Caracas, slightly injuring four people and damaging several buildings. The U.S. embassy briefly closed its doors on February 26; officials said there had been a "credible threat" to the building and embassy employees. Chavez denied that his government was involved in the bombings, but leaflets found near the diplomatic posts echoed the president's hot language against foreign intervention. *(Conflict in Colombia, p. 425)*

Political Agreement Signed, then Ignored

The long-running political negotiations mediated by the OAS and the Carter Center finally produced an agreement on May 23; it was signed in Caracas on May 29 by opposition leaders and Vice President Jose Vincent Rangel, and witnessed by Gaviria and Francisco Diez, representing the Carter Center. The key point in the agreement was a call for a referendum on whether Chavez should remain in office, to be held after August 19, 2003. That date was the midpoint of Chavez's six-year term; the constitution allowed such a referendum after that point. Although the agreement provided for what the opposition long claimed it wanted—a vote on Chavez's rule—it was not much of a victory. During the political turmoil of 2002 Chavez had offered to hold such a referendum after the August 19 date, but opponents had held out for the earlier vote on February 2. When the general strike failed to force Chavez to resign or accept the earlier date, the August vote became the most realistic option for the opposition. Gaviria called the accord "a good agreement for all Venezuelans."

In a statement praising the willingness of Chavez and his opponents to reach an ageement, Carter warned that implementation would be "the most important and difficult phase in this process of lessening the crisis in Venezuela." Having participated in some of the negotiations over the preceding six months, Carter understood the depth of feeling on both sides—

and his warning of difficult days ahead was prescient. As demonstrations continued, opposition leaders gathered signatures for a petition and confidently predicted that Chavez's days in office were drawing to a close. On August 20 the opposition delivered more than 100 boxes said to contain petitions signed by more than 3 million registered voters, well over the 2.4 million minimum required by the constitution. Chavez remained defiant, calling the signatures "illegal" and bragging that if the opponents managed to get their referendum, "we'll beat them."

Once again, Chavez's confidence was not misplaced. On September 12, the National Electoral Council—controlled by Chavez supporters—ruled the petitions invalid on several technical grounds, most importantly because they were gathered before August 19. The constitution itself was vague about the ground rules for a referendum, stating only that a vote was possible after the midterm of a presidency. On September 26 the electoral council established rules that clearly were intended to undermine the opposition's prospects. Under the rules, the opposition was required to gather the 2.4 million signatures within a four-day period (Chavez had been demanding a one-day limit for signature-gathering, comparing the process to an election). The council would then determine the validity of the signatures within thirty days; if the minimum was met, the council would then establish a referendum date within ninety-seven days—pushing a referendum, at its earliest, into 2004.

The opposition began its signature drive on November 24, with the process monitored by more than fifty international observers from the OAS and the Carter Center. Except for isolated cases of intimidation, the process went smoothly, and on November 28 the OAS and Carter Center issued a statement saying the signature drive "was completely peaceful and without major obstacles that would have impeded the free exercise of constitutional rights." Chavez rejected that statement, claiming that the signature drive was a "mega-fraud" intended to upset the constitution. Chavez also directly challenged Gaviria's personal endorsement of the process: "I think you overstepped the mark, Dr. Gaviria."

Several violent incidents in the following weeks heightened tension in anticipation of the signature-verification process. Unidentified gunmen attacked opposition demonstrators and several media outlets.

Once again, on December 19, the opposition delivered signed petitions to the elections council. Leaders said 250 boxes, delivered under an armed escort, contained 3.4 million signatures, 1 million more than the required minimum. The council's director said work on verifying the signatures would begin on January 5, 2004. On December 23 opposition leaders gave the council another set of more than 1 million signatures on petitions demanding referendum votes on 26 legislators who supported Chavez. The president's supporters, in turn, were gathering signatures on petitions seeking to recall 37 opposition legislators.

*Following is the text of the "Agreement Between the Repre-
sentatives of the Government of the Bolivarian Republic of
Venezuela and the Political and Social Groups Supporting It,
and the Coordinadora Democrática and the Political and Civil
Society Organizations Supporting It," signed May 29, 2003, in
Caracas, calling for a national referendum on the presidency
of Hugo Chavez after August 19, 2003.*

"Agreement Between the Republic of Venezuela and the Coordinadora Democrática"

1. We, the undersigned members of the Forum for Negotiation and
Agreement, representing the national government and the political and
social groups supporting it, as well as the political and civil society
organizations comprising the Coordinadora Democrática, hereby sign
this Agreement in a spirit of tolerance, in order to contribute to
strengthening the climate of peace in the country. It is in this spirit that
we reaffirm the principles and mechanisms that brought us to this table,
as set forth in the Executive Summary agreed by the parties from the
time it was established, as well as our conviction with regard to finding a
constitutional, peaceful, democratic, and electoral solution.

2. We express our full adherence to and respect for the Constitution
of the Bolivarian Republic of Venezuela The rule of law is based on
respect for this Constitution and for the legal system that underpins it.
The Constitution envisions a system of values and norms to govern fundamental principles of social and political coexistence, and establishes
mechanisms for reconciling differences. Any change in response to recent
experiences with the political process should be based on these norms
and should preferably be made through consensus.

3. We are aware that at this historic moment, we must agree upon
fundamentals for ensuring a participatory, pluralist, robust and genuinely
representative democracy, where we shall continue to have room for all,
and where social justice, tolerance, equal opportunity, the rule of law
and democratic coexistence are the essential values. We are aware that

these values must be held above any political or partisan strife and that they must guide policy, especially in areas where there is a preponderant social interest.

4. We wish to state our conviction that Venezuela and the Venezuelan people will continue along the path of democracy, with a sense of fraternity, respect for the beliefs of each and every Venezuelan, and the desire for reconciliation.

5. We are aware that our society must consolidate pluralism, as embodied in the Constitution, where policy exercised by all actors in national life is consistent with the values of the Constitution. Venezuela needs the cooperation of all to continue along the path of peace and democracy, so that each and everyone may express his or her ideas, adopt his or her respective position, and choose from among the various political options that exist.

6. We express our adherence to the principles enshrined in the Inter-American Democratic Charter, which proclaims the right of peoples to live in democracy and the obligation of governments and all citizens to promote and defend it. In light of the provisions of Article 6 of the Constitution of the Bolivarian Republic of Venezuela concerning participatory democracy, all sectors share the values set forth therein—such as those that advocate that power may only be exercised according to the rule of law; the holding of free, fair, and transparent elections; the separation and independence of branches of government; representative democracy reinforced and enriched by ongoing, ethical, and responsible citizen participation within a legal framework; strict respect for human rights, the rights of workers, and freedom of expression, information, and the press; and the elimination of all forms of discrimination and intolerance. Both parties, also recognize the close links between democracy and the war on poverty, between democracy and development, and between democracy and the effective exercise of human rights.

7. We invoke the principles of the Charter of the Organization of American States (OAS); the American Convention on Human Rights; international law as the standard of conduct among states in their reciprocal relations; respect for sovereignty and the principle of nonintervention; the principle of self-determination; the juridical equality of all states; and the peaceful settlement of disputes.

8. We ratify the validity of and our full adherence and commitment to the "Declaration against Violence and for Peace and Democracy", signed on February 18, 2003, which should be considered an integral part of this Agreement.

9. We fully agree that monopoly on the use of force by the State through the National Armed Forces and the metropolitan, state, and municipal police is a basic and inalienable prerogative in combating violence and guaranteeing the essence of a democratic state. The role of the police shall be determined by civilian authorities exercising the powers

conferred on them by the Constitution and the law. This requires full compliance with the legal provisions and judicial decisions governing Citizen Safety Coordination. In any event, the possession of weapons by the police or any other security force having national, state, or municipal jurisdiction must be regulated in strict accordance with the law. None of these forces should be used as an instrument for arbitrary or excessive repression or to engage in actions that connote political intolerance.

10. We agree to undertake a vigorous campaign to effectively disarm the civilian population, on the basis of the law passed by the National Assembly, making sovereign use of all mechanisms and resources provided for therein, and with the technical support of the international institutions. We, the parties, shall abide by the conclusions of the Forum for Dialogue conducted by the National Assembly in its quest for a consensus plan for disarmament of the civilian population.

11. We urge the parliamentary groups of opinion represented in the National Assembly to finalize the law on the formation of the Truth Commission, to enable it to help shed light on the events of April 2002 and cooperate with the judicial bodies in identifying and punishing those responsible.

12. In pursuance of the objective established in the Executive Summary of seeking agreement as a means of contributing to resolution of the crisis in the country through the electoral process, we, the parties, agree that this resolution of the crisis should be achieved through application of Article 72 of the Constitution of the Bolivarian Republic of Venezuela, which provides for the possible holding of revocatory referenda on the mandates of all those holding positions and serving as magistrates as a result of popular election, where they have served one-half of the term for which they were elected (governors, mayors, regional legislators and representatives in the National Assembly), or will have served one-half of their term in the course of this year, as is the case of the President of the Republic, in accordance with the judgment of the Supreme Court of Justice of February 13, 2003. Such referenda, including those already called for and those that may be called for in future, will be possible if they are formally requested by the requisite number of voters and approved by the new National Electoral Council, once it has been established that the constitutional and legal requirements have been met.

13. We agree that it is essential to have as soon as possible a trustworthy, transparent and impartial electoral arbiter, to be designated in the manner prescribed in the Constitution. In that connection, the work under way in the National Assembly is considered to be of the utmost importance. We, the two parties, state our willingness to assist in facilitating understanding in all matters relating to the formation and workings of the Electoral Arbiter, without interfering with the standard procedure being conducted by the National Legislature.

14. We are committed to freedom of expression, as enshrined in our constitutional and legal provisions; to the American Convention on Human Rights and the Inter-American Democratic Charter. We, the two parties, intend to work with the public and private media to promote their espousal of the aims set forth in this document and in the Declaration against Violence and for Peace and Democracy. In particular, we intend to work with the public and private media with a view to quelling violence and with respect to their role in making citizens aware, in an equitable and impartial manner, of their political options, which would contribute significantly to creating the most conducive climate to the successful conduct of electoral processes and referenda provided for in Article 72 of the Constitution.

15. We assume that the Constitution and laws of the Republic provide for the appropriate and necessary requirements and mechanisms in order for the competent Public Authority to proceed with the timely financing of revocatory referenda and any other mechanism for popular consultation, which must be conducted once the admissibility has been confirmed by the competent public body. With regard to the Republic Plan, this Plan will be activated in response to a request from the electoral authorities, under the same terms and conditions that have applied in previous electoral processes.

16. The OAS, the Carter Center, and the United Nations have expressed their willingness to provide such technical assistance as the competent authorities of the Bolivarian Republic of Venezuela might request of them for holding any type of electoral consultation; any such request shall be in accordance with the principle of law contained in the Constitution of the Republic. This technical assistance could range from preparatory or pre-election activities to actual electoral observation. With regard to direct support that may be given to the CNE, emphasis should be placed on the willingness of these three organizations to collaborate with both human and material resources which they have offered.

17. Once the pertinent legal and constitutional requirements have been met, the CNE shall determine the date for the revocatory referenda already requested, as well as any that may be requested later, in an expeditious and timely manner, in accordance with the Law on Suffrage and Political Participation, and we, the parties, agree neither to propose nor to promote amendments to that law.

18. We, the parties, recognize the support and facilitation provided to this Forum by the representatives of the OAS, particularly its Secretary General, by the Carter Center, and by the UNDP, which, upon the signature of this agreement, constructively concludes its task. We recognize the importance of the follow-up work these institutions may conduct in the future for the execution of this agreement and we intend to continue to avail ourselves of international assistance.

19. Lastly, we, the parties, agree to establish the joint follow-up body provided for in Article 7 of the Declaration against Violence and for Peace and Democracy, each appointing two representatives to open channels of communication and take measures for the effective fulfillment of the provisions of that Declaration and of this agreement, maintaining contact with the international facilitation when the parties consider it necessary.

Source: Organization of American States. *Agreement Between the Representatives of the Government of the Bolivarian Republic of Venezuela and the Political and Social Groups Supporting It, and the Coordinadora Democrática and the Political and Civil Society Organizations Supporting It.* Caracas, Venezuela. May 29, 2003. www.oas.org/OASpage/eng/Venezuela/Agreement052303en.htm (accessed January 16, 2003).

UN Security Council on Threats to Peace in Congo

May 30, 2003

INTRODUCTION

A huge and complex series of conflicts in the Democratic Republic of Congo reached another turning point in 2003, possibly toward lasting peace, with the signing of political agreements and the installation of an interim government representing some of the main parties to the war. The new government was supposed to pave the way toward democratic elections in mid-2005—an event that, if it happened, might finally lead this central African nation to the peace and prosperity that had eluded it for many years.

Congo's conflicts—often referred to as "Africa's First World War"—had been under way in one form or another since 1998 and had involved a half-dozen nations and dozens of guerrilla groups. Much of the fighting had sputtered out by 2001, and peace agreements in 2002 set the stage for the political transition that began in July 2003 when President Joseph Kabila was joined in the government by four vice presidents, among them the leaders of the two main rebel groups. In May 2003 fighting among guerrilla factions in eastern portions of the country had threatened to spiral into massive bloodletting. Quick intervention by a United Nations-authorized military contingent calmed the situation, and by year's end the relatively low level of conflict in the region did not appear likely to upset the immediate prospects for national peace.

The war was by far the largest and bloodiest in the world at the close of the twentieth century and the beginning of the twenty-first. Because nearly all the fighting took place in dense forests in remote regions—out of view of journalists, international officials, and aid workers—it was impossible for the world to know with any certainty the full extent of the carnage. One relief agency, the International Rescue Committee, conducted statistical surveys in an attempt to estimate the number of deaths and their causes. The committee in 2001 estimated the death toll at about 2.5 million—more than had died in any other conflict since World War II. An updated study released in April 2003 put the estimate at 3.3 million. The

committee said the vast majority of Congo's deaths—at least 85 percent—
were not from actual fighting but from malnutrition and disease. Murders
and other human rights violations committed during the final stages of the
war were likely to be the first cases brought before the newly established
International Criminal Court, which had jurisdiction over cases of genocide
and war crimes. *(Criminal court, p. 99)*

The death toll was just the beginning of Congo's humanitarian disaster
resulting from the war. According to UN estimates, nearly half of the country's 50 million people were uprooted from their homes at least once, and
more than 3 million remained homeless in late 2003. Half or more of the
several hundred thousand combatants were children whose lives were permanently scarred by the killings they carried out and witnessed. The economy ceased to exist on an organized basis except for wide-scale looting of
natural resources, and nearly all semblance of educational and health systems collapsed. In short, a land with vast quantities of some of the Earth's
richest natural resources—among them cobalt, copper, diamonds, and timber—had been reduced to one of the world's half-dozen poorest countries.
*(Background, Historic Documents of 2000, p. 978; Historic Documents of
2001, p. 159; Historic Documents of 2002, p. 546)*

Transitional Government Established

Meeting in Pretoria, South Africa, government representatives and key rebel
leaders reached agreement on March 7 on specific provisions to implement
an overall political accord signed in December 2002. Among other things,
the rebel forces were to be incorporated into the national army, and a transitional government would be established with representatives from Kabila's
government and the main rebel groups. Kabila would have four vice presidents: one of his own choosing, one each from the two main rebel groups,
and one representing opposition political parties. Presidential and parliamentary elections were to be held in two years, by mid-2005. These details
were then incorporated into a final political agreement signed in Sun City,
South Africa, on April 2. Secretary General Kofi Annan hailed that accord
and pledged that the United Nations would "do its utmost" to help. But, he
added, international support "will be of little value" unless the country's leaders kept the promises they had just made. "The agreement you have signed
is your agreement. It is your responsibility to implement it, and to resolve
the problems you will encounter in doing so, making use of the institutions
that you have decided to put in place," he said.

The first formal step under the agreement was Kabila's inauguration on
April 7 as president of the interim government. He had been president of
the Congo since shortly after his father, Laurent Kabila, was assassinated
in 2001; neither father nor son was elected. The swearing-in of the four vice

presidents was delayed by several weeks of squabbling, especially over plans for a unified military incorporating the Congolese army and the main guerrilla groups. That issue was resolved in late June, and the four vice presidents finally took their posts on July 17. They included rebel leaders Jean-Pierre Bemba, head of the Movement for the Liberation of Congo (a guerrilla group that had been backed by Uganda); Azarias Ruberwa Manywa, of the Congolese Rally for Democracy-Goma (one of several splinter factions of a rebel force backed by Rwanda); Abdoulaye Yerodia Ndombasi, an ally of Kabila; and longtime civilian opposition leader Arthur Z'Ahidi Ngoma. "There is no doubt, it's irreversible," Ruberwa said of the peace process. "We are here as partners and not as belligerents." Despite such positive-sounding words, the nation's new political leaders devoted much of their time in subsequent weeks to arguing over such matters as their salaries and the relative size of their offices. Several cabinet members refused to swear loyalty to Kabila and agreed to assume their jobs only after the oath of office was rewritten.

A two-chamber interim parliament took office on August 22 and was assigned such monumental tasks as establishing the mechanics of a democratic political system in a country long ruled by dictators and guerrillas. Its 620 members included representatives from previously banned political parties, ethnic groups, and many of the former rebel alliances. The parliament in December 2003 approved a law providing for an independent commission to supervise elections in 2005, but as of year's end it had not moved to appoint members to that body.

Continued Fighting in Ituri

Peace agreements and the withdrawal of most foreign forces had sharply reduced fighting in most of Congo by late 2002, but conflict continued in much of heavily forested eastern Congo, particularly in North and South Kivu provinces and the Ituri region of Orientale province adjacent to Uganda. The departure of thousands of Rwandan and Ugandan troops left a vacuum that was quickly filled by numerous guerrilla groups, most based on tribal affiliations. Many of these groups had been aligned either with Rwanda or Uganda at the height of the war; some repeatedly switched their loyalties and alliances to secure momentary advantage, such as territorial gain or access to minerals.

At the start of 2003 UN officials and international aid agencies estimated that more than 150,000 people in Ituri had been made homeless by persistent conflict among various guerrilla factions, including those representing the two main local tribal groups, the Hema and the Lendu. Aid workers and other observers reported terrifying incidents in which guerrillas had torched villages, burned people alive, and raped women and children in front of their families. A special UN investigation mission on January 15 said it had confirmed some of the most horrific charges of rape, torture, and even cannibalism by some guerrilla groups. The mission's report led the Security Council to demand, on January 15, that the militias stop their "massacres and systematic violations of human rights." The council's statement specifically cited reports that some of the violations had been committed by one of the main guerrilla groups in northeastern Congo, the Congolese Liberation Movement, headed by Jean-Pierre Bemba. For much of the war it had been aligned with troops from Uganda.

Some of the year's worst fighting occurred around the town of Bunia, the capital of the gold-mining Ituri region, where an estimated 25,000 well-armed guerrillas representing the Hema and Lendu tribal groups fought with each other to gain the upper hand before and after Uganda withdrew its troops on May 7. Rebels were seen slaughtering civilians of all ages, and fighters early in May twice broke into UN compounds. Tens of thousands of people fled their homes to escape the fighting in the Ituri region; more than 10,000 of them took shelter at Bunia's decrepit airport. Two volunteers for the International Committee of the Red Cross were found dead on Bunia's streets on May 11. A Hema guerrilla group called the Union of Congolese Patriots won the first round, driving the last Lendu fighters from the city on May 12. The Lendu militia took over much of the surrounding countryside and preyed on civilians there.

Months earlier, Uganda had warned that its departure might lead to further conflict. Several international human rights groups had echoed that warning, noting that an estimated 50,000 people already had been killed in the region during the war. In anticipation of Uganda's withdrawal, the UN planned to station a 1,500-member peacekeeping battalion, led by Bangladesh, in the Bunia region—but those troops were not expected to arrive until August, at the earliest. As a stopgap, about 700 lightly armed Uruguayan troops, who were part of the UN's Congo peacekeeping mission, arrived in the Bunia area in April, but they had no mandate to protect civilians and were forced to watch helplessly as the slaughter went on around them.

By May 12 the UN Security Council was meeting in urgent sessions to put together a rapid military response to head off what some officials warned might become an enormous humanitarian catastrophe in the region. Diplomats talked openly about their fears that the tribal conflict in Ituri might escalate into a smaller-scale replay of the 1994 genocide in neighboring Rwanda. In that tragedy, extremist Hutus determined to exterminate the country's minority Tutsi population overwhelmed an undermanned UN peacekeeping force. As many as 800,000 people died in the Rwandan genocide, an event that also served as a precursor to the conflict in Congo because the Hutu militias eventually were driven out of Rwanda and fled to Congo (then known as Zaire). *(Rwanda, p. 1069)*

On May 16 leaders of five of the warring Ituri factions signed a cease-fire agreement negotiated by UN diplomats during a meeting in Tanzania. That brought a lull in the fighting, but given the long history of broken cease-fires in Congo no one was willing to trust the combatants. Dozens of wounded continued to descend on Bunia from surrounding areas, and by late May UN officials had counted the bodies of more than 430 people killed since Uganda's departure. Some of the bodies likely had been cannibalized, the officials said. The UN's worst fears about the safety of its own people seemed to be confirmed on May 20 when the bodies of two unarmed UN military observers were found north of Bunia; the bodies had been brutalized.

Emergency Force Approved

After more than two weeks of diplomatic negotiations in New York, the UN Security Council on May 30 adopted Resolution 1484 authorizing a French-led military force to intervene in Bunia to guarantee an end to the fighting there until September 1, when the new UN peacekeeping force was supposed to be in place. The Security Council authorized the temporary mission under Chapter VII of the UN charter, which meant its troops could use whatever force was necessary to stabilize the security situation and, if necessary, protect the civilian population. French leadership of the force was controversial because many people in central Africa, particularly in Rwanda, held France partly responsible for the 1994 genocide; France had been a strong ally of the Hutu-led Rwandan government at the time and had opposed tough UN intervention to stop the slaughter. Even so, most critics set aside their concerns in hopes that France would now act to avert yet another mass slaughter in the region.

The first small contingent of troops arrived in Bunia on June 6 and was greeted by cheering civilians. They also were greeted, a day later, by an outbreak of fighting that forced them to take refuge in the UN compound. On June 10 the French commander said his emergency force would try to protect civilians in the city but would not venture into the countryside nor try to disarm the thousands of rebel fighters. "Separating the factions is not part of my mission," Brig. Gen. Jean Paul Thonier said. A delegation of diplomats from the UN Security Council arrived in Bunia on June 12 and met with guerrilla leaders, civilians, and aid workers. The desperate humanitarian situation deeply shocked the diplomats, who vowed to take whatever steps were needed to prevent the fighting from again raging out of control. The diplomats also warned "outside parties"—meaning Rwanda and Uganda—to halt their supply of weapons to Congo's guerrillas and to stop exploiting the country's diamonds and other resources.

The French-led emergency force quickly stabilized the situation in Bunia, most importantly by ordering the Hema guerrillas to leave. But fighting continued in surrounding areas. More than 100 people died in a series of attacks in late July by Lendu guerrillas on Hema villages north of the city.

Bangladeshi units from the new longer-term UN peacekeeping force began arriving in Bunia in mid-August and took over control of the city from the emergency force on September 1. In addition to the troops from Bangladesh, and the Uruguayan forces that had remained in the city, the new force included soldiers from Indonesia, India, Nepal, and Pakistan. The UN peacekeepers engaged in sporadic clashes with guerrilla groups in October and November.

Annan reported to the Security Council on November 17 that the relatively rapid deployment of the French-led emergency force "helped to stave off an impending humanitarian crisis." Also important from the UN's institutional point of view, he noted that the quick action "demonstrated the benefits of the international community working effectively and creatively in matters of peace and security." Annan did not say so directly, but that statement clearly was intended to contrast the UN's success in this case with at least two of its most embarrassing failures: the inability to halt the Rwandan genocide and the Security Council's disagreements early in 2003 over Iraq. *(Iraq, p. 40)*

Securing the Rest of Congo

Fears about a possible genocide got the world's attention for a few weeks, but the much bigger and more difficult task of securing peace in the rest of Congo proceeded in much the same way as had the earlier stages of the war: off the radar screen of world leaders and the public. On May 27 Annan sent the Security Council a report arguing that Congo was at "an intersection of peace and war" and needed a sustained commitment of help from the international community. Specifically, Annan called for boosting the authorized strength of the UN's peacekeeping mission (called the UN Organization Mission in the Democratic Republic of Congo, or MONUC, in the French initials) to 10,800 troops from the previous level of 8,700, which had been authorized just six months earlier. Annan proposed adding a contingent of nearly 800 peacekeepers in Kinshasa, the capital, and nearly tripling, from 1,400 to 3,800, the number of troops sent to Ituri after the emergency French-led force left in September.

Annan's proposal won broad support on the Security Council, but the United States initially voiced its reluctance, arguing that no peacekeeping force of any realistic size could guarantee peace in Congo unless the country's political and guerrilla leaders had the willpower to end the fighting.

Washington's attitude changed in July when President George W. Bush visited Africa and heard appeals from local leaders for an expanded UN presence in Congo. The council on July 28 unanimously approved Annan's request for a larger force, as well as his plea that it be given a toughened mandate to use "all necessary means" to enforce the peace in eastern Congo. The council also imposed a one-year embargo on all weapons sales to guerrilla groups in the eastern provinces—a move aimed primarily at Rwanda and Uganda. Representatives of those countries (along with Burundi, which also intervened in earlier stages of the war) formally pledged on September 25 to halt arms shipments and all other forms of interference in Congo.

Among the many uncertainties in Congo at year's end was the prospect for success of a promised campaign to return the thousands of fighters to civilian life—a process that diplomats referred to as "disarmament, demobilization, repatriation, resettlement, and reintegration." UN peacekeepers and international aid agencies attempted to supervise that process and offered incentives for fighters to give up their weapons. But many of the warriors had never held any other kind of job, and it would take years to restore the country's economy so they could exchange rifles and machetes for useful employment.

Plunder of Congo's Resources

Ever since the outbreak of the Congo war in 1998, it had been clear that the principal motivating factor for the foreign armies—and for many of the domestic guerrilla groups aligned with them—was the exploitation of Congo's natural wealth. Laurent Kabila reportedly turned timber resources and diamond mines in southern Congo over to Zimbabwe's army in exchange for its support of his government. In the northeast, the interventions of Rwanda and Uganda masked the plundering by those countries of gold and coltan, a mineral used in the manufacture of mobile telephones.

A UN-appointed "panel of experts" investigated the "illegal exploitation" of Congo's natural resources and issued several reports, including one in October 2002 that alleged involvement by numerous international companies and government officials in Congo, Rwanda, Zimbabwe, and other countries. In its final report to the UN, dated October 23, the panel said some of the companies and individuals it had named a year earlier had since withdrawn from Congo or agreed to stop exploiting the country's resources. Other cases needed to be investigated further, the panel said.

During 2003, the experts added, there had been a "temporary reduction in the volume of illegally exploited resources" as foreign armies left Congo and were replaced by armed militias and the Congolese military. But until the country developed a strong, democratically elected government that controlled its territory, the panel warned, "illegal exploitation will continue and serve as the motivation and the fuel for continued conflicts in the region, to the detriment of the Congolese people, who have suffered too much for too long."

The panel offered two suggestions to Congo's government. One was breaking up the large government-owned companies that traditionally had controlled the country's mineral resources and funneled profits into the hands of high-placed individuals, notably long-serving dictator Mobutu Sese Seko, who was ousted in 1997. The panel said the government also should consider establishing a "natural resources fund" that would use proceeds from the sale of gold, diamonds, and other resources to finance job-creation programs and social services, the panel said. Such a fund should be managed by an "autonomous" agency free of political control, the panel said.

Following is the text of Resolution 1484, adopted May 30, 2003, by the United Nations Security Council, authorizing an Interim Emergency Multinational Force to stabilize the security in the city of Bunia, in the Ituri province of northeastern Congo.

"United Nations Security Council Resolution 1484"

The Security Council,

Recalling its previous resolutions and statements by its President on the Democratic Republic of the Congo, in particular the statement of 16 May 2003,

Determined to promote the peace process at the national level, and in particular to facilitate the early establishment of an inclusive transitional government in the Democratic Republic of the Congo,

Expressing its utmost concern at the fighting and atrocities in Ituri, as well as the gravity of the humanitarian situation in the town of Bunia,

Reaffirming its full support for the political process initiated by the Ituri Pacification Commission, calling for its swift resumption and for the establishment of an effective inclusive security mechanism in this framework, to complement and support the existing Ituri Interim administration,

Recognizing the urgent need for a secure base to allow the full functioning of the institutions of the Ituri Interim Administration, and recognizing that the Engagement to Relaunch the Ituri pacification process, signed in Dar es Salaam on 16 May 2003, reaffirms the Ituri parties' commitment to the Ituri Interim Administration, and commits them to join a process of cantonment and demilitarization,

Commending the United Nations Organization Mission in the Democratic Republic of the Congo (MONUC) for its efforts in order to stabilize the situation in Bunia and to support the political process in Ituri, in particular the effective performance of its Uruguayan contingent deployed there, recognizing the need to support the work of MONUC in the field, and deploring attacks on MONUC and consequent loss of life,

Taking note of the request of the Secretary-General to the Council in his letter dated 15 May 2003 and *taking note also* of the support for this request expressed in the letter to the Secretary-General from the President of the Democratic Republic of the Congo and also by the Ituri parties on 16 May 2003 in Dar es Salaam, as well as the support expressed in the letters to the Secretary-General from the President of Rwanda and from the Minister of State for Foreign Affairs of Uganda, as requested by the Secretary-General, for the deployment of a multinational force in Bunia,

Determining that the situation in the Ituri region and in Bunia in particular constitutes a threat to the peace process in the Democratic Republic of the Congo and to the peace and security in the Great Lakes region,

Acting under Chapter VII of the Charter of the United Nations,

1. *Authorizes* the deployment until 1 September 2003 of an Interim Emergency Multinational Force in Bunia in close coordination with MONUC, in particular its contingent currently deployed in the town, to contribute to the stabilization of the security conditions and the improvement of the humanitarian situation in Bunia, to ensure the protection of the airport, the internally displaced persons in the camps in Bunia and, if the situation requires it, to contribute to the safety of the civilian population, United Nations personnel and the humanitarian presence in the town;

2. *Stresses* that this Interim Emergency Multinational Force is to be deployed on a strictly temporary basis to allow the Secretary-General to reinforce MONUC's presence in Bunia and in this regard, authorizes the Secretary-General to deploy, within the overall authorized MONUC ceiling, of a reinforced United Nations presence to Bunia, and requests him to do so by mid-August 2003;

3. *Calls on* Member States to contribute personnel, equipment and other necessary financial and logistic resources to the multinational

force and invites contributing Member States to inform the leadership of the force and the Secretary-General;

4. *Authorizes* the Member States participating in the Interim Emergency Multinational Force in Bunia to take all necessary measures to fulfil its mandate;

5. *Demands* that all the parties to the conflict in Ituri and in particular in Bunia cease hostilities immediately and reiterates that international humanitarian law must be respected, and that there will be no impunity for violators;

6. *Strongly condemns* the deliberate killing of unarmed MONUC personnel and staff of humanitarian organizations in Ituri and demands that the perpetrators be brought to justice;

7. *Demands* that all Congolese parties and all States in the Great Lakes region respect human rights, cooperate with the Interim Emergency Multinational Force and with MONUC in the stabilization of the situation in Bunia and provide assistance as appropriate, that they provide full freedom of movement to the Force, and that they refrain from any military activity or from any activity that could further destabilize the situation in Ituri, and in this regard, *demands also* the cessation of all support, in particular weapons and any other military materiel, to the armed groups and militias, and further demands that all Congolese parties and all States in the region actively prevent the supply of such support;

8. *Calls on* all Member States and in particular those in the Great Lakes region to provide all necessary support to facilitate the swift deployment in Bunia of the Interim Emergency Multinational Force;

9. *Requests* the leadership of the Interim Emergency Multinational Force in Bunia to report regularly to the Council through the Secretary-General, on the implementation of its mandate;

10. *Decides* to remain actively seized of the matter.

Source: United Nations. Security Council. *Resolution 1484.* May 30, 2003. http://daccess-ods.un.org/access.nsf/Get?OpenAgent&DS=S/RES/1484%20(2003)&Lang=E&Area=UNDOC (accessed June 1, 2003).

June

2003 HISTORIC DOCUMENTS

European Space Agency on Space Probe Launch

June 2, 2003

INTRODUCTION

Three unmanned missions to explore the surface of Mars were undertaken in 2003 by the United States and the European Space Agency (ESA) in hopes of determining whether the Red Planet ever had water or any signs of life. One U.S. mission landed successfully at the beginning of January 2004, and another was scheduled to reach the planet later that month. The apparent success of the first mission reenergized the U.S. space program, which was still reeling from the fiery breakup of the *Columbia* space shuttle in February, which killed all seven astronauts on board. *(*Columbia *disaster, p. 631)*

However, the ESA's *Mars Express* probe sent back no signals after its targeted landing date of December 24. Repeated attempts to establish contact with the probe were not successful as of early January 2004. The apparent failure was a bitter disappointment for the European Union, which never before had sponsored such an ambitious space project. Japan also conceded the failure of its long-troubled Mars mission, which was launched in 1998 but veered off course.

The year was a successful one in space for China, which became the third nation to send an astronaut into orbit of Earth. Yang Liwei, a lieutenant colonel, circled the Earth for twenty-one hours and returned safely on October 16. Only the United States and the Soviet Union (followed by its successor, Russia) had managed to put astronauts into orbit since the dawn of the space age in the 1950s and 1960s. China's achievement spurred Asian rivals India and Japan to speed up their plans for similar missions.

The Race for Mars

For decades Mars had been the most tantalizing objective for space missions, mostly because scientists considered it the only planet in the solar system, other than Earth, that might once have had water and thus the possibility to sustain some form of life. But getting to, or even near, Mars had proven difficult. Of the thirty missions sent to Mars by the United States, the former Soviet Union, and Russia between 1962 and 2001, all but twelve failed for one reason or another. The most recent of the unqualified successes were two orbiting laboratories sent by the United States: *Mars Odyssey,* which in October 2001 began a planned three-year project of mapping the planet's chemical elements and minerals, and *Global Surveyor,* which had been carefully mapping the planet since September 1997.

Putting cameras and other scientific equipment into orbit around Mars was difficult enough, but landing an unmanned vehicle on the Martian surface so it could photograph the scenery first hand, and even analyze soil samples, proved to be among the most technically challenging tasks that space programs ever faced. The first such U.S. missions to succeed were the *Viking 1* and *Viking 2,* both of which dropped landers onto the Martian surface in 1976. The landers took thousands of photographs and analyzed the soil and weather conditions: *Viking 1* for more than six years and *Viking 2* for more than three years. The Soviet Union successfully landed only one vehicle on Mars, in 1971, but it stopped transmitting after only two minutes.

From both scientific and public relations points of view, one of the U.S. space program's most successful missions ever was the Mars *Pathfinder* mission, which in 1997 sent the *Sojourner* rover to the Martian surface, where it roamed for about one hundred yards. Together, over an eleven-week period, *Pathfinder's* landing vehicle and rover sent back to Earth thousands of images and technical studies that gave scientists and the public their best views yet of what Mars really was like. However, a follow-up mission, the Mars *Polar Lander,* joined the long list of space failures in 1999 when it lost contact with Earth. That failure, combined with the loss the same year of the Mars *Climate Orbiter*—because of a simple engineering mistake—dispirited the U.S. space program and prompted a major reassessment of attempts by the National Aeronautics and Space Administration (NASA) to speed up its projects while trimming costs. *(Pathfinder mission, Historic Documents of 1997, p. 509; Mars mission failures, Historic Documents of 1999, p. 711)*

Given that checkered history, NASA and the ESA expressed both high hopes and caution when they sent new missions to Mars. The missions were launched on June 2 and 3, timed to take advantage of the relative nearness of Earth and Mars as they orbited around the sun.

The British-led European mission was the first to be launched, on June 2, aboard a Russian rocket fired from the Soviet Union's old Baikonur field in Kazakhstan. The *Mars Express* was so named because it was developed relatively quickly at a total cost of about $345 million—less than half of comparable U.S. missions. The *Express* carried a surface-rover dubbed *Beagle 2,* in honor of the ship that took scientist Charles Darwin on his landmark nineteenth-century expedition. The project was funded by the British National Space Centre and private sponsors, including Britain's Open University, whose professor Colin Pillinger was the mission's driving force. Weighing 143 pounds, the *Beagle 2* was tiny in comparison to U.S. and Russian Martian landing vehicles, but it was crammed with newly developed scientific gear that private sponsors said could have commercial applications on Earth.

Most aspects of the mission's trip to Mars seemed to go well, and hopes were high on December 19 when the *Beagle 2* successfully separated from the *Express* and headed toward the surface. The *Express* itself succeeded in establishing an orbit of Mars, the beginning of its own mission of using a high-powered radar to search for water or ice as deep as three miles beneath the Martian surface. But then came Christmas eve, December 24, when the *Beagle 2* was supposed to land on the surface near Mars' equator, its descent slowed by a parachute and its actual landing cushioned by three air bags. The space agency listened for the *Beagle 2's* expected first signals back to the orbiting *Express,* but none came. Repeated attempts over the next two weeks by *Express* and by the *Mars Odyssey* to pick up a signal from the *Beagle 2* failed, and by early January the mission's managers were forced to acknowledge the likelihood either that the lander either had been seriously damaged in its descent or its communications equipment had failed. David Southwood, the European Space Agency's science director, admitted he was "very sad" about the apparent failure. "*Beagle 2* was the cherry on the cake and one of the bitter-sweet aspects of this is that *Mars Express,* the mother ship, is performing beautifully," he told reporters.

The apparent loss of *Beagle 2* was all the more troubling for its sponsors because at least one of the simultaneous U.S. missions seemed to be off to a fully successful start. NASA on June 3 had launched two separate missions carrying identical 400-pound vehicles that were to explore the surface of Mars. The combined cost of the two missions was about $800 million. Named by schoolchildren in a nationwide contest, one was called the *Spirit* and was scheduled to land on Mars early in January 2004; the other, called *Opportunity,* was to arrive later that month. Slowed by a parachute and totally encased in air bags, *Spirit* landed safely on January 3, 2004, and quickly began transmitting its first images back to Earth. It was the first successful landing on Mars since *Sojourner's* arrival in 1997. "This is a big night for NASA," the agency's administrator, Sean O'Keefe said, celebrating *Spirit's* arrival and reflecting on the loss of the *Columbia* space shuttle almost exactly eleven months earlier.

There were to be no celebrations of space exploration by Japan, which in 1998 had launched its first attempted probe of Mars, the *Nozomi* ("hope" in Japanese) *Planet B.* The orbiter was intended to determine whether the planet had a magnet field and if its upper atmosphere was affected by "solar wind"—the stream of particles emitted by the sun. But the ill-named probe went off course during its journey, and several maneuvers to put it back on course used up most of its fuel. Moreover, some of the probe's communications and electrical equipment apparently was damaged by solar flares. On December 9, one month short of the probe's planned arrival at Mars, Japan's space agency, JAXA, gave up trying to get it back on course and abandoned the mission.

Other Observations of Mars

Scientists were swamped with new data about Mars during 2003, even before the anticipated arrival of the latest spacecraft at year's end. Important new observations came from the two U.S. platforms orbiting the planet—*Mars Odyssey* and *Global Surveyor*—and from the Hubble telescope.

Chief among the conclusions drawn from the year's cache of data was that Mars almost certainly never was a warm and wet place, as generations of science fiction writers had imagined it to be. After reviewing findings by the *Global Surveyor,* scientists on August 22 said they had found no evidence of limestone formations on Mars. The presence of limestone would have indicated the almost-certainty that Mars once had oceans that, after evaporating for some reason, left behind limestone or other carbonates, which are formed by water and carbon dioxide. Philip R. Christensen, a scientist at Arizona State University who led a team examining data from *Global Surveyor's* thermal emission spectrometer, said the absence of limestone "really points to a cold, frozen, icy Mars that has probably always been that way." Christensen and other scientists said water may well have been present on Mars, and might still be there, but it probably took the form of ice rather than vast oceans or rivers.

Mars Odyssey provided some of the evidence that snow and ice might have been among the forces that created some of the features of the Martian surface, including gullies and layers of loose rock and sediment. Christensen said these findings proved that Mars had a "dynamic geologic history."

The best large-scale photographs ever of Mars were generated in August by the Hubble telescope, which took advantage of the relative closeness of the planet to Earth (at that point the distance was about 35 million miles, the closest since the year 57,617 BC). Among the photographs published by NASA was an especially clear one showing the ice cap at the south pole of Mars and a giant crater called the Hellas basin.

China Heads into Space

The surge of China's economy during the 1990s offered evidence that the nation of more than 1 billion people was about to take its place among the world's great powers. Since the mid-twentieth century space programs had been visible evidence of great-power status. China began launching orbital satellites in the 1970s, but several embarrassing rocket failures during the 1990s appeared to stall the country's space program, including its bid for a sizable share of the business of sending commercial communications satellites into orbit.

Early in the 1990s China began a secret program, reportedly code-named Project 921, to put an astronaut in space. China based its program on rockets and other equipment it purchased from cash-strapped Russia, and in 1996 China announced plans for a manned space program. Gradually, the secretive government in Beijing also offered hints that it had even more ambitious space plans, including lunar explorations, a space observatory similar to the U.S. Hubble telescope, and even a possible space station.

Early in October Chinese news media reported that the country's first manned mission to space would be launched by the middle of the month, in time for an important meeting of the country's political leaders in Beijing. The launch came on October 15 when the *Shenzhou 5* spacecraft (the name meant "Divine Vessel" in Chinese) was sent into orbit from a secret site in the Gobi desert. Colonel Yang, reportedly selected at the last minute from a pool of three finalists for the mission, orbited the Earth fourteen times over a twenty-hour period and returned safely to another secret location in Inner Mongolia. China's new president, Hu Jintao, praised Yang as a "hero" and said his mission heralded the country's status as a great power in the fields of science and technology.

Galileo Ends Successful Tour of Jupiter

One of the oldest and most successful U.S. space missions came to an end in 2003 after sending back volumes of information about the giant planet Jupiter and its moons. Launched in 1989, the spacecraft *Galileo* was troubled by repeated equipment malfunctions but still managed to send back more than 14,000 images after its arrival in the Jovian neighborhood in 1995. *Galileo*'s most famous photographs were of active volcanoes on Jupiter's moon Io, the moon of an asteroid, and comet Shoemaker-Levy 9 crashing into Jupiter's atmosphere.

Battered by radiation and running out of fuel, *Galileo* was nearing the end of its active life in 2003, and NASA considered allowing it to remain in orbit around Jupiter. Ultimately, the space agency decided not to risk the chance that *Galileo* might crash into the moon Europa and contaminate it with microbes that it might be carrying on board. On September 21 engineers sent the spacecraft plunging into the atmosphere of Jupiter at a speed of more than 100,000 miles an hour—a fiery suicide that was almost certain to destroy any living contaminates. Some of the scientists and engineers gathered at the Jet Propulsion Laboratory in Pasadena, California—headquarters of the *Galileo* mission—wept as *Galileo* ended its long mission.

New Findings on Age of the Universe

Photographs and data sent back to Earth by the Hubble telescope and other spacecraft gave scientists more information than ever before about the early years of the universe—which was estimated to be more than 13 billion years old. In February 2003 NASA released an image that scientists said gave the best picture yet of the universe in its infancy, shortly after it was created by the so-called Big Bang. The image was a composite of thermal studies made over the course of a year by the Wilkinson Microwave Antisotropy Probe, a satellite orbiting about 1 million miles above the Earth. It showed a faint glow that, scientists said, appeared to be a remnant of the Big Bang. "We have a map of the earliest light of the universe that is complete, and it is stunning to look at," physicist Lyman Page of Princeton University said of the image.

Data sent by the Hubble telescope offered other perspectives on the infancy of the universe. In June scientists unveiled X-ray observations from Hubble that appeared to show the formation of stars when the universe was "only" 1 billion years old. In July astronomers said Hubble had found the oldest known planet. Formed about 12.7 billon years ago, the planet was estimated to be about twice as large as Jupiter; it orbited burned-out stars in a cluster known as M4, which is 7,200 light-years from Earth. Before this observation, scientists believed that the very first planets could not have been formed until much later, perhaps in the range of 4.6 billion years ago, when the solar system was created.

Following are excerpts from "Mars Express En Route for the Red Planet," a June 2, 2003, announcement by the European Space Agency of the launch of the Mars Express space probe, which was intended to land an unmanned rover on Mars.

"*Mars Express* En Route for the Red Planet"

The European Mars Express space probe has been placed successfully in a trajectory that will take it beyond the terrestrial environment and on the way to Mars—getting there in late December.

This first European Space Agency [ESA] probe to head for another planet will enter an orbit around Mars, from where it will perform detailed studies of the planet's surface, its subsurface structures and its atmosphere. It will also deploy Beagle 2, a small autonomous station which will land on the planet, studying its surface and looking for possible signs of life, past or present.

The probe, weighing in at 1.120 kg, was built on ESA's behalf by a European team led by Astrium. It set out on its journey to Mars aboard a Soyuz-Fregat launcher, under Starsem operational management. The launcher lifted off from Baïkonur in Kazakhstan on 2 June at 23.45 local time. An interim orbit around the Earth was reached following a first firing of the Fregat upper stage. One hour thirty-two minutes after lift off, the probe was injected into its interplanetary orbit.

"Europe is on its way to Mars to stake its claim in the most detailed and complete exploration ever done of the Red Planet. We can be very proud of this and of the speed with which have achieved this goal", said David Southwood, ESA's Director of Science witnessing the launch from Baikonur. Contact with Mars Express has been established by ESOC, ESA's satellite control centre, located in Darmstadt, Germany.

The probe is pointing correctly towards the Sun and has deployed its solar panels. All on-board systems are operating faultlessly. Two days from now, the probe will perform a corrective maneuvre that will place it in a Mars-bound trajectory, while the Fregat stage, trailing behind, will vanish into space—there will be no risk of it crashing into and contaminating the Red Planet.

Mars Express will then travel away from Earth at a speed exceeding 30 km/s (3 km/s in relation to the Earth), on a six-month and 400 million kilometre journey through the solar system. Once all payload operations have been checked out, the probe will be largely deactivated. During this period, the spacecraft will contact Earth only once a day. Mid-journey correction of its trajectory is scheduled for September.

Following reactivation of its systems at the end of November, Mars Express will get ready to release Beagle 2. The 60 kg capsule containing the tiny lander does not incorporate its own propulsion and steering system and will be released into a collision trajectory with Mars, on 20 December. It will enter the Martian atmosphere on Christmas day, after five days' ballistic flight.

As it descends, the lander will be protected in the first instance by a heat-shield; two parachutes will then open to provide further deceleration. With its weight down to 30 kg at most, it will land in an equatorial region known as Isidis Planitia. Three airbags will soften the final impact. This crucial phase in the mission will last just ten minutes, from entry into the atmosphere to landing.

Meanwhile, the Mars Express probe proper will have performed a series of maneuvres through to a capture orbit. At this point its main motor will fire, providing the deceleration needed to acquire a highly elliptical transition orbit. Attaining the final operational orbit will call for four more firings. This 7.5 hour quasi-polar orbit will take the probe to within 250 km of the planet.

Having landed on Mars, Beagle 2—named after HMS Beagle, on which Charles Darwin voyaged round the world, developing his evolutionary theory—will deploy its solar panels and the payload adjustable workbench, a set of instruments (two cameras, a microscope and two spectrometers) mounted on the end of a robot arm.

It will proceed to explore its new environment, gathering geological and mineralogical data that should, for the first time, allow rock samples to be dated with absolute accuracy. Using a grinder and corer, and the "mole", a wire-guided mini-robot able to borrow its way under rocks and dig the ground to a depth of 2 m, samples will be collected and then examined in the GAP automated mini-laboratory, equipped with 12 furnaces and a mass spectrometer. The spectrometer will have the job of detecting possible signs of life and dating rock samples.

The Mars Express orbiter will carry out a detailed investigation of the planet, pointing its instruments at Mars for between half-an-hour and an hour per orbit and then, for the remainder of the time, at Earth to relay the information collected in this way and the data transmitted by Beagle 2.

The orbiter's seven on-board instruments are expected to provide considerable information about the structure and evolution of Mars. A very high resolution stereo camera, the HRSC, will perform comprehensive mapping of the planet at 10 m resolution and will even be capable of photographing some areas to a precision of barely 2 m. The OMEGA spectrometer will draw up the first mineralogical map of the planet to 100 m precision.

This mineralogical study will be taken further by the PFS spectrometer—which will also chart the composition of the Martian atmosphere, a prerequisite for investigation of atmospheric dynamics. The MARSIS radar instrument, with its 40 m antenna, will sound the surface to a depth of 2 km, exploring its structure and above all searching for pockets of water.

Another instrument, ASPERA, will be tasked with investigating interaction between the upper atmosphere and the interplanetary medium. The focus here will be on determining how and at what rate the solar wind, in the absence of a magnetic field capable of deflecting it, scattered the bulk of the Martian atmosphere into space. Atmospheric investigation will also be performed by the SPICAM spectrometer and the MaRS experiment, with special emphasis on stellar occultation and radio signal propagation phenomena.

The orbiter mission should last at least one Martian year (687 days), while Beagle 2 is expected to operate on the planet's surface for 180 days. This first European mission to Mars incorporates some of the objectives of the Euro-Russian Mars 96 mission, which came to grief when the Proton launcher failed. And indeed a Russian partner is cooperating on each of the orbiter's instruments. Mars Express forms part of an international Mars exploration programme, featuring also the U.S. probes Mars Surveyor and Mars Odyssey, the two Mars Exploration Rovers and the Japanese probe Nozomi. Mars Express may perhaps, within this partnership, relay data from the NASA rovers while Mars Odyssey may, if required, relay data from Beagle 2.

The mission's scientific goals are of outstanding importance. Mars Express will, it is hoped, supply answers to the many questions raised by earlier missions—questions concerning the planet's evolution, the history of its internal activity, the presence of water below its surface, the possibility that Mars may at one time have been covered by oceans and thus have offered an environment conducive to the emergence of some form of life, and even the possibility that life may still be present, somewhere in putative subterranean aquifers. In addition the lander doing direct analysis of the soil and the environment comprises a truly unique mission.

Mars Express, drawing heavily on elements of the Rosetta spacecraft awaiting to be launched to a comet next year, paves the way for other ESA-led planetary missions, with Venus Express planned for 2005 and the BepiColombo mission to Mercury at the end of the decade. It is a precursor too for continuing Mars mission activity under Aurora, the programme of exploration of our solar system.

Source: European Space Agency. "*Mars Express* En Route for the Red Planet." ESA PR 36–2003. June 2, 2003. www.esa.int/SPECIALS/ Mars_Express/SEMIKNS1VED_2.html (accessed July 27, 2003).

Justice Department on Treatment of Post– September 11 Detainees

June 2, 2003

INTRODUCTION

The Bush administration's round-up of hundreds of Middle Eastern men in the United States following the September 11, 2001, terrorist attacks came under harsh criticism during 2003. The independent inspector general of the Justice Department reported that many of the 762 people detained in late 2001 and early 2002 had been denied basic legal rights as the government used all its powers to keep them in prison while it looked for information linking them to terrorists. Some of the detainees also had been subject to "unduly harsh" treatment, including physical and verbal abuse, the investigation showed. Only one of the detainees was charged in connection with the September 11 attacks, but more than 500 hundred of them were deported because they had violated U.S. immigration laws.

The inspector general's report was one of the few detailed public examinations of a range of secret actions by the Bush administration in response to the September 11 attacks. In addition to detaining immigrants, the administration arrested and kept in secret detention two U.S. citizens who it called "enemy combatants," and it built a prison at Guantanamo Naval Base in Cuba to house several hundred men who had been captured in Afghanistan, where they allegedly had fought for the former Taliban regime or the al Qaeda terrorist network. The U.S. government also held an estimated 100 suspected terrorists at an air base in Afghanistan. The government released information about only a handful of the terrorist suspects in Afghanistan, including one of the top al Qaeda leaders, but no information about the status or identity of the others had ever been made public. *(Enemy combatants and Guantanamo detainees, p. 135)*

Background

In the weeks after the September 11 attacks, the government detained 738 foreigners—nearly all of them Muslim men from Middle Eastern and South Asian countries—on charges of immigration law violations, such as over-staying visas. Another 24 people were already being held by the Immigration and Naturalization Service (INS) on immigration charges and were then held for further investigations on terrorism grounds. This total of 762 people were held on what the government called the "INS Custody List." The government said 505 of them eventually were deported. One, Zacarias Moussaoui, was charged publicly with a terrorism-related crime; his case was pending at a federal court in Virginia. As of June 2003 the remaining 256 detainees had been charged with nonterrorism crimes or were awaiting deportation proceedings. *(Background, Historic Documents of 2002, p. 833)*

With very few exceptions, the government held all the detainees in secret, refusing to make public any information about the individuals involved, such as their names, nationalities, or reasons for being held. News organizations and civil liberties groups filed suit to force disclosure of detainees names, but a three-judge appeals court rejected that request on June 17.

In addition to the 762 foreigners held on immigration violations, the government detained nearly 400 others in connection with its investigations into the September 11 attacks. About 300 of these people reportedly were detained on criminal charges not related to immigration violations. The government released no information about those individuals or why they were held, according to the Center for National Security Studies, a Washington organization that filed lawsuits to force release of the information. News reports said another 50 or so were held as "material witnesses"—people who authorities suspected might have some information about the September 11 hijackers or other terrorist cases.

Inspector General's Findings

The Bush administration began rounding up immigrants and American citizens with Arabic-sounding names immediately after the September 11 attacks. All nineteen of the alleged September 11 hijackers were Arabs; fifteen of them were natives of Saudi Arabia, and most were in the United States illegally. Civil liberties groups and advocates for the rights of immigrants sought information about the hundreds of people who had been detained, but the Justice Department refused on national security grounds. During 2002, as some of the detainees were released or deported, some information about them became available and raised questions about the treatment of those who were being held in New York area jails. Justice

Department inspector general Glenn A. Fine responded to those reports by opening an investigation into the detentions; his report was made public on June 2. Fine's report dealt only with the 762 people who had been detained for alleged violations of immigration laws; he did not investigate the handling of other cases stemming from the September 11 hijackings, including those of U.S. citizens.

The essence of Fine's report was that federal officials had used every tool at their disposal to keep the detainees in jail until the FBI could determine whether they had any connection to the September 11 hijackings or any other terrorist plots. Under normal circumstances, immigrants found to have overstayed their visas or entered the country illegally were not held for lengthy periods of time. In this case, however, violations of immigration law became the tool that authorities used to keep the detainees in custody. This was accomplished in several ways, according to Fine's report:

- The FBI office in New York City made "little attempt" to distinguish between immigrants who might have some connection to the September 11 attacks and those who were "encountered coincidentally" during investigations of the attacks, the report said. Hundreds of immigrants were swept into the FBI's net and held for weeks or even months "regardless of the strength of the evidence or the origin" of the information that led to their arrest.
- The Justice Department issued a "no bond" policy for all of the detainees, prohibiting them from posting a bond so they could be released pending the investigations. INS lawyers questioned the legality of this policy, but Justice Department officials overruled the concerns.
- The INS delayed telling the detainees why they were being held, in most cases well past the seventy-two-hour period that was standard practice in immigration cases. Some immigrants were not informed of the charges against them until after they had been detained a month or more. This delay, Fine said, "affected the detainees in several ways, from their ability to understand why they were being held, to their ability to obtain legal counsel, to their ability to request a bond hearing."
- The department established an unusual procedure, called "hold until cleared," under which each detainee was jailed until the FBI cleared him as a terrorism suspect; in other words, each detainee was presumed to pose a risk to the United States until the FBI was able to prove otherwise. This "hold until cleared" policy was never put in writing, Fine said, but it was "clearly understood and applied" throughout the Justice Department. Fine's report said Justice Department officials originally assumed that FBI agents would be able to process the detainee cases quickly, within a matter of a few days at most. But lengthy delays resulted because the FBI did not give "sufficient prior-

ity" to resolving these cases. The bureau, he said, failed to assign enough agents to these cases or pulled agents off the detainee cases for other work. Detainees were held on average for eighty days while the FBI investigated their cases. Some continued to be held for weeks or months, even after the FBI had cleared them, usually because of administrative mix-ups.

Fine also reported incidents in which detainees had been abused or treated harshly, particularly at the Metropolitan Detention Center in Brooklyn, New York—a facility run by the federal Bureau of Prisons. Eighty-four detainees were held at that facility, and Fine said many of them were subjected to "unduly harsh" conditions. Detainees were kept in the cells for twenty-three hours a day, their cells were illuminated all night long, and they were allowed just one telephone call each week to a lawyer and one call a month to family members—and often these calls were denied them. Prison officials appeared to make it as difficult as possible for the detainees to obtain legal counsel, the report said. For example, detainees often were given wrong names or telephone numbers for lawyers, and then were told they had used up their one weekly phone call when they got a wrong number or a busy signal. Family members, friends, lawyers, or even law enforcement personnel who inquired about individual detainees often were told they were not being held at the Brooklyn prison—even when they were.

Fine also reported a "pattern of physical and verbal abuse" of some detainees by some officials at the Brooklyn prison, especially in the early months after the September 11 attacks. The verbal abuse included threatening comments by prison guards to the effect that the detainees did not deserve decent treatment. Some detainees were subjected to physical abuse, such as being pushed into walls, the report said. Fine said he based this assessment on statements by detainees, but he noted that all prison personnel denied having witnessed or participated in abuse of detainees.

In his June 2 report, Fine said he had been told that the Bureau of Prisons had destroyed hundreds of hours of videotape showing the handling or movement of detainees at the Brooklyn prison. On December 18, however, Fine issued a second report saying that many of the tapes had been found and that they confirmed the allegations of physical abuse. "We did not find that the detainees were brutally beaten, but we found evidence that some officers slammed detainees against the wall, twisted their arms and hands in painful ways, stepped on their leg restraint chains, and punished them by keeping them restrained for long periods of time," Fine wrote in his report. "We determined that the way these [prison] officers handled some detainees was in many respects unprofessional, inappropriate, and in violation of [Bureau of Prisons] policy." Fine said as many as twenty guards at the prison had abused prisoners; he recommended that twelve of those who were still employed at the prison be disciplined or given counseling.

Fine made twenty-one recommendations for changes in federal policies and procedures to eliminate the problems he had found. Among the major recommendations were that the FBI develop "clearer and more objective criteria" for the mass arrests of illegal aliens in terrorism cases, that the FBI assign enough agents to investigate the cases of detained terrorism suspects, and that government agencies communicate more clearly with each other about the rules in such cases. Fine's recommendations would apply to future investigations and would be of no help to the 762 post–September 11 detainees, nearly all of whom already had been deported or dealt with in some fashion by the criminal justice system.

In his report, and in subsequent testimony on Capitol Hill, Fine acknowledged that federal officials faced "monumental challenges" in the wake of the September 11 attacks. Department officials, he said, "worked tirelessly and with enormous dedication over an extended period to meet these challenges." He also noted that few of the 762 detainees were entirely innocent of wrongdoing; nearly all had "violated immigration laws" in one way or another.

Reaction to the Findings

Civil liberties groups and advocates for the rights of immigrants praised Fine's report, saying it had verified many of the concerns they had expressed about the government's secret detentions. David G. Cole, a Georgetown University law professor who had filed lawsuits on behalf of the detainees, said the report showed "what happens when the government throws off the ordinary rules that ensure that we don't lock up people until we have some sound reason to believe they're engaging in some illegal activity."

One of the detainees told the *New York Times* that "it feels good to have someone saying that we shouldn't have had to go through all that we did." The newspaper said Shanaz Mohammed was held at the Brooklyn prison for eight months before he was deported to Trinidad on an immigration violation. "I think America overreacted a great deal by singling out all Arabnamed men like myself. We were all looked at as terrorists, we were all abused," he told the *Times.*

In its initial responses, the Justice Department defended its actions toward the detainees as justified in the circumstances following the September 11 attacks. "Our policy is to use all legal tools available to protect innocent Americans from terrorist attacks," department spokeswoman Barbara Comstock said in a statement. "We make no apologies for finding every legal way possible to protect the American people from further terrorist attacks." In a letter accompanying Fine's report, Deputy Attorney General Larry D. Thompson said criticism of Justice Department officials was "unfair" because of the pressure to respond to the September 11 attacks.

In subsequent weeks and months, however, Justice Department officials said they were taking seriously the changes Fine had recommended to correct the problems he had uncovered. Addressing a conference of the American Civil Liberties Union on June 14, FBI Director Robert Mueller said Fine had done "a very good job of pointing out areas where we can do better." The bureau, and the Justice Department, were in the process of making changes that would provide clearer criteria for identifying which illegal immigrants should be held as terrorism suspects, improve the conditions under which detainees were held in prison, and give immigration authorities, rather than the FBI, more control over the detention process, Mueller said.

Fine followed up his report by documenting the responses to his findings by the Justice Department and the new Homeland Security Department, which had taken over the immigration law enforcement functions of the former Immigration and Naturalization Service. In a follow-up issued September 8, Fine said the two departments were taking his recommendations "seriously" but that "significant work remains" before they could be fully implemented. Only two of the twenty-one recommendations in the report had been fully adopted, Fine said; both involved new standards for the detention of immigration-law violators at federal prisons.

The Justice Department on November 20 sent Fine a report with updated information about its actions to implement his recommendations. After reviewing that report, Fine said the department "has taken significant and responsible steps" to put his recommendations into effect. As of year's end, Fine had not yet made public his review of an updated report submitted by the Homeland Security Department.

Secrecy of the Detentions

The Bush administration shrouded many of its actions in response to the September 11 attacks in secrecy, citing the need for confidentiality as it sought to block future terrorist attacks. Among the administration's most closely guarded secrets were the identities of the 762 immigrant detainees. The Justice Department refused repeated requests by families of detainees, news organizations, civil liberties groups, and others to identify who was being held, or even to enumerate their nationalities or the category of charges against them.

On June 17 the Bush administration scored a major victory when the federal appeals court in Washington ruled, on a 2–1 vote, that the Justice Department had no legal obligation to release the names of the detainees. Judge David B. Sentelle, writing for himself and Judge Karen LeCraft Henderson, cited numerous past rulings in which courts had deferred to the executive branch in national security cases. "The need for deference in this case is just as strong as in earlier cases," Sentelle said. "America faces an enemy just as real as its former cold war foes, with capabilities beyond the capacity of the judiciary to explore." Judges, he wrote, "are in an extremely poor position to second-guess the executive's judgment in this area of national security."

Judge David S. Tatel sharply dissented, saying his colleagues had given "uncritical deference to the government's vague, poorly explained arguments for withholding broad categories of information about the detainees."

The ruling overturned a decision issued in August 2002 by District Court Judge Gladys Kessler, who had said the government's insistence on keeping the detainees' names secret was based on "pure speculation" about adverse consequences. The case had been filed in December 2001 by the Center for National Security Studies, the American Civil Liberties Union, Human Rights Watch, and other groups. The plaintiffs appealed the decision to the Supreme Court, which upheld the appeals court ruling early in 2004.

Also before the Supreme Court was a similar case, involving an Algerian man in Miami, whose journey through the legal system had been shrouded in total secrecy, except for one administrative mistake. The government had sought, and won from federal courts, a ban on the publication of any information concerning the man's case—including the very existence of the man's habeas corpus petition. Some information about the case leaked out when the Eleventh Circuit Court of Appeals in Atlanta inadvertently posted part of a legal filing on its Web site. The posting identified the man as Mohamed Kamel Bellahouel, a restaurant waiter who, according to the FBI, had served two of the September 11 hijackers and possibly gone to a movie with a third hijacker. The Supreme Court on November 4 agreed to hear the case, but had not taken action by year's end.

Registration of Selected Immigrants

The Bush administration on December 1 announced that it was ending one of the most sweeping and controversial of its post–September 11 policies: a registration requirement for all men and boys over the age of sixteen in the United States from twenty-five Arab and Muslim countries, most in the Middle East or South Asia. Between late 2002 and April 2003, 83,519 people had followed orders to show up at government offices where they were asked questions about their residences, jobs, bank accounts, and other personal details. The government said 13,743 of those who showed up to register were detained at least briefly; deportation proceedings were initiated against some of them. *(Background, Historic Documents of 2002, p. 842)*

The administration began the registration requirement in hopes of catching individuals who might have information about the al Qaeda terrorist network, which was responsible for the September 11 attacks. In the days before the final April 25 deadline, government offices in many metropolitan areas were swamped with thousands of men waiting to register, many of whom expressed fear that they would be arrested and deported.

Administration officials initially called the registration program a success, saying it gave the government information that was needed to counter terrorism. A spokesman for the Homeland Security Department acknowledged in November, however, that the registration program had not caught a single person with known ties to terrorist organizations. Civil liberties groups and organizations representing Arab- and Asian-Americans denounced the program, saying it unfairly targeted men solely because of their religion or ethnic background. Several foreign governments also protested the program, which they said created the impression that their citizens somehow had something to do with terrorism.

Following are excerpts from "The September 11 Detainees: A Review of the Treatment of Aliens Held on Immigration Charges in Connection with the Investigation of the September 11 Attacks," a report issued June 2, 2003, by the Office of the Inspector General at the U.S. Department of Justice.

"The September 11 Detainees"

Chapter One

Introduction

I. Background

On September 11, 2001, terrorists hijacked four airplanes and flew two of them into the World Trade Center Towers in New York City and one into the Pentagon in Arlington, Virginia. The fourth plane crashed into a field in southwestern Pennsylvania before it could strike a target in Washington, D.C. The attacks killed more than 3,100 people, including all 246 people aboard the 4 airplanes.

The Federal Bureau of Investigation (FBI) immediately initiated a massive investigation, called "PENTTBOM," into this coordinated terrorist attack. The FBI investigation focused on identifying the terrorists who hijacked the airplanes and anyone who aided their efforts. In addition, the FBI worked with other federal, state, and local law enforcement agencies to prevent follow-up attacks in this country and against U.S. interests abroad.

Shortly after the attacks, the Attorney General directed the FBI and other federal law enforcement personnel to use "every available law enforcement tool" to arrest persons who "participate in, or lend support to, terrorist activities." One of the principal responses by law enforcement authorities after the September 11 attacks was to use the federal immigration laws to detain aliens suspected of having possible ties to terrorism. Within 2 months of the attacks, law enforcement authorities had detained, at least for questioning, more than 1,200 citizens and aliens nationwide. Many of these individuals were questioned and subsequently released without being charged with a criminal or immigration offense. Many others, however, were arrested and detained for violating federal immigration law.

Our review determined that the Immigration and Naturalization Service (INS) detained 762 aliens as a result of the PENTTBOM investigation. Of these 762 aliens, 24 were in INS custody on immigration violations prior to the September 11 attacks. The remaining 738 aliens were arrested between September 11, 2001, and August 6, 2002, as a direct result of the FBI's PENTTBOM investigation. All 762 detainees were placed on what became known as an "INS Custody List" because of the FBI's assessment that they may have had a connection to the September 11 attacks or terrorism in general, or because the FBI was unable, at least initially, to determine whether they were connected to terrorism.

The Government held these aliens in a variety of federal, local, and private detention facilities across the United States while the FBI investigated them for ties to the September 11 attacks or terrorism in general. These facilities included several Federal Bureau of Prisons (BOP) institutions such as the Metropolitan Detention Center in Brooklyn, New York; the Federal Detention Center in Oakdale, Louisiana; and the U.S. Penitentiary in Leavenworth, Kansas; INS facilities such as the Krome Service Processing Center in Miami, Florida; and state and local facilities under contract with the INS to house federal immigration detainees, such as the Passaic County Jail in Paterson, New Jersey, and the Hudson County Correctional Center in Kearny, New Jersey.

Soon after these detentions began, the media began to report allegations of mistreatment of the detainees. For example, detainees and their attorneys alleged that the detainees were not informed of the charges against them for extended periods of time; were not permitted contact with attorneys, their families, and embassy officials; remained in detention even though they had no involvement in terrorism; or were physically abused, verbally abused, and mistreated in other ways while detained.

Several individual detainees and non-profit organizations filed lawsuits against the Department of Justice (Department) protesting the lack of public information about the detainees and the length and conditions of the detainees' confinement. For example, the Center for National Security Studies brought suit against the Department under the Freedom of Information Act seeking information about the detainees, including their names and where they were being held. Five detainees filed a class action lawsuit alleging they were physically abused, verbally abused, and held without a legitimate immigration or law enforcement purpose long after they received final removal or voluntary departure orders. In addition, advocacy organizations such as Amnesty International and the Lawyers Committee for Human Rights issued reports asserting mistreatment of the detainees or mishandling of their cases.

Pursuant to our responsibilities under the USA PATRIOT Act (Patriot Act) and the Inspector General Act, the Department of Justice Office of the Inspector General (OIG) initiated this review to examine the treatment of detainees arrested in connection with the Department's September 11 terrorism investigation. Specifically, the OIG's review focused on:

- Issues affecting the length of the detainees' confinement, including the process undertaken by the FBI and others to clear individual detainees of a connection to the September 11 attacks or terrorism in general;
- Bond determinations for detainees;
- The removal process and the timing of removal; and
- Conditions of confinement experienced by detainees, including their access to legal counsel.

We focused our review on INS detainees housed at two facilities—the BOP's Metropolitan Detention Center (MDC) in Brooklyn and the Passaic County Jail (Passaic) in Paterson, New Jersey. We chose these two facilities because they held the majority of September 11 detainees and were the focus of many complaints about detainee mistreatment.

Our review did not seek to examine all aspects of the Department's terrorism investigation, including the specific investigative techniques involved in the September 11 investigation or the decisions made by federal, state, and local law enforcement on why to detain specific individuals. Additional issues beyond the scope of this review include the reasons and justifications for the Department's decision to limit public release of information concerning arrests related to the ongoing terrorism investigation, its decision to close immigration proceedings to the public, and its use of voluntary interviews for certain categories of aliens. Several lawsuits related to these issues are ongoing. In addition, our review did not examine the Department's use of material witness warrants to detain certain individuals in connection with its terrorism investigation, another issue currently being litigated in the courts.

Rather, our review focused on the treatment of aliens who were held on federal immigration charges in connection with the September 11 investigation. We examined the reasons why many of the detainees experienced prolonged confinement. In addition, we examined the detainees' conditions of confinement, including their access to counsel, access to medical care, and allegations of physical or verbal abuse by correctional officers.

In this report, we discuss the actions of senior managers at the Department, the FBI, the INS, and the BOP, who established the broad policies and led the investigation in response to the September 11 attacks; the actions of the INS, which processed and detained many of the aliens arrested in the aftermath of September 11; and the actions of the BOP, which housed many of the detainees.

In conducting our review, we were mindful of the circumstances confronting the Department and the country as a result of the September 11 attacks, including the massive disruptions they caused. The Department was faced with monumental challenges, and Department employees worked tirelessly and with enormous dedication over an extended period to meet these challenges. It is also important to note that nearly all of the 762 aliens we examined violated immigration laws, either by overstaying their visas, by entering the country illegally, or some other immigration violation.

[Sections II and III omitted.]

Chapter Nine

OIG Recommendations

We recognize the tremendous challenges the FBI, INS, BOP, and other Department components faced as they responded to the September 11 attacks and mobilized to prevent additional attacks during a chaotic period. We also recognize the dedication exhibited by many Department employees in response to the attacks. Without diminishing their contributions in any way, we believe the Department can learn from the experience in the aftermath of the September 11 attacks, and we therefore offer a series of recommendations to address the issues we examined in our review.

I. Uniform Arrest and Detainee Classification Policies
The FBI New York Field Office and its Joint Terrorism Task Force (JTTF) aggressively pursued thousands of PENTTBOM leads in the weeks and months after the terrorist attacks. Many leads that resulted in

an alien's arrest on immigration charges were quite general in nature, such as a landlord reporting suspicious activity by an Arab tenant. However, we found the FBI and INS in New York City did little to distinguish the aliens arrested as the subjects of PENTTBOM leads or where there was evidence of ties to terrorism from those encountered coincidentally to such leads with no indication of any ties to terrorism.

The FBI's New York Field Office took an aggressive stance when it came to deciding whether any aliens arrested on immigration charges were "of interest" to its terrorism investigation. Witnesses both inside and outside the FBI told us that the New York FBI interpreted and applied the term "of interest" to the September 11 investigation quite broadly. Consequently, all aliens in violation of their immigration status that the JTTF encountered in the course of pursuing PENTTBOM leads—whether or not the subjects of the leads—were arrested, classified as September 11 detainees, and subjected to the full FBI clearance investigation, regardless of the factual circumstances of the aliens' arrest or the absence of evidence connecting them to the September 11 attacks or terrorism. This contrasted with procedures used elsewhere in the country, where aliens were assessed individually before being considered "of interest" to the terrorism investigation and therefore subject to the full FBI clearance investigations.

Moreover, the FBI's initial "interest" classification had an enormous impact on the detainees because it determined whether they would be housed in a high-security BOP facility like the MDC or in a less restrictive setting like Passaic. In addition, the decision to label an alien a "September 11 detainee" versus a "regular immigration detainee" significantly affected whether bond would be available and the timing of the detainee's removal or release.

1. We believe the Department and the FBI should develop clearer and more objective criteria to guide its classification decisions in future cases involving mass arrests of illegal aliens in connection with terrorism investigations. For example, the FBI could develop generic screening protocols (possibly in a checklist format) to help agents make more consistent and uniform assessments of an illegal alien's potential connections to terrorism. These protocols might require some level of evidence linking the alien to the crime or issues in question, and might include an FBI database search or a search of other intelligence and law enforcement databases.

   In addition, the FBI should consider adopting a tiered approach to detainee background investigations that acknowledges the differing levels of inquiry that may be appropriate to clear different detainees of connections to terrorism. For example, a more streamlined inquiry might be appropriate when the FBI has no information that a detainee has ties to terrorism, while a more comprehensive background investigation would be appropriate in other cases.

2. The FBI should provide immigration authorities (now part of the Department of Homeland Security (DHS)) and the BOP with a written assessment of an alien's likely association with terrorism shortly after an arrest (preferably within 24 hours). This, in turn, would assist the immigration authorities in assigning the detainee to an appropriate detention facility and the BOP in determining the appropriate security level within a particular facility. In addition, the FBI should promptly communicate any changes in its assessment of the detainee's connection to terrorism so that the DHS and BOP can make appropriate adjustments to the detainee's conditions of confinement.

3. The FBI did not characterize many of the September 11 detainees' potential connections to terrorism and consequently they were treated as "of undetermined interest" to the terrorism investigation. In these cases the INS, in an understandable abundance of caution, treated the alien as a September 11 detainee subject to the "hold until cleared/no bond" policies applicable to all September 11 detainees. This lack of a characterization by the FBI also resulted in prolonged confinement for many detainees, sometimes under extremely harsh conditions. Unless the FBI labels an alien "of interest" to its terrorism investigation within a limited period of time, we believe the alien should be treated as a "regular" immigration detainee and processed according to routine procedures. In any case, the DHS should establish a consistent mechanism to notify the FBI of its plans to release or deport such a detainee.

II. Inter-Agency Cooperation on Detainee Issues

The INS relied on the FBI to provide evidence about the detainees that it could use in bond and removal proceedings. When this information was not forthcoming in a timely manner, the INS had to request multiple continuances in bond hearings and other immigration proceedings in an effort to maintain the detainees in custody. In many of these cases, the INS's arguments against granting bond to the Immigration Court were based on little more than the fact the detainees were arrested in connection with PENTTBOM leads.

4. Unless the federal immigration authorities, now part of the DHS, work closely with the Department and the FBI to develop a more effective process for sharing information and concerns, the problems inherent in having aliens detained under the authority of one agency while relying on an investigation conducted by another agency can result in delays, continuing conflicts, and concerns about

accountability. At a minimum, we recommend that immigration officials in the DHS enter into an Memorandum of Understanding (MOU) with the Department and the FBI to formalize policies, responsibilities, and procedures for managing a national emergency that involves alien detainees. An MOU should specify a clear chain of command for any inter-agency working group. Further, the MOU should specify information sharing and reporting requirements for all members of such an inter-agency working group.

III. FBI Clearance Process

While we appreciate the enormous demands placed on the FBI in the aftermath of the terrorist attacks, we found the FBI did not adequately staff or assign sufficient priority to its process for clearing September 11 detainees of a connection to terrorism. Agents responsible for clearance investigations often were assigned to other duties, which substantially delayed the completion of detainee clearance investigations. Even after the clearance decisions were centralized at FBI Headquarters, FBI officials failed to provide sufficient resources to complete the detainee clearance process in a timely manner. The FBI took, on average, 80 days to clear a September 11 detainee.

5. We believe it critical for the FBI to devote sufficient resources in its field offices and at Headquarters to conduct timely clearance investigations on immigration detainees, especially if the Department institutes a "hold until cleared" policy. The FBI should assign sufficient resources to conduct the clearance investigations in a reasonably expeditious manner, sufficient resources to provide timely information to other agencies (in this case, additional FBI agents to support the SIOC Working Group), and sufficient resources to review in a timely manner the results of inquiries of other agencies (in this case, completed CIA checks). In addition, FBI Headquarters officials who coordinated the detainee clearance process and FBI field office supervisors whose agents were conducting the investigations should impose deadlines on agents to complete background investigations or, in the alternative, reassign the cases to other agents.

6. We understand the resource constraints confronting the Department in the days and weeks immediately following the September 11 attacks. We also recognize that decisions needed to be made quickly and often without time to consider all the ramifications of these actions. However, within a few weeks of the terrorist attacks it became apparent to many Department officials that some of the early policies developed to support the PENTTBOM investigation were causing problems and should be revisited. Examples of areas of concern included the FBI's criteria for expressing interest in a

detainee and the "hold until cleared" policy. We believe the Department should have, at some point earlier in the PENTTBOM investigation, taken a closer look at the policies it adopted and critically examined the ramifications of those policies in order to make appropriate adjustments. We recommend that the Department develop a process that forces it to reassess early decisions made during a crisis situation and consider any improvements to those policies.

IV. Notices to Appear

Under federal regulation, the INS was required to decide whether to file immigration charges against an alien within 48 hours of his arrest. However, the regulation contained no requirement with respect to when the INS must notify the alien or Immigration Court about the charges. No statute or regulation explicitly stated when the INS was required to serve the Notice to Appear (NTA) on the alien or the Immigration Court. We found the INS did not consistently serve September 11 detainees with NTAs within its stated goal of 72 hours after arrest. Part of the delay can be traced to the INS's practice in the first several months after the terrorist attacks to having all NTAs reviewed for legal sufficiency at INS Headquarters. Another factor was the miscommunication that resulted when detainees arrested in New York City were transferred to the INS Newark District without having been served NTAs. INS Newark District officials assumed the detainees had been served in New York, while INS New York District officials incorrectly assumed that INS Headquarters had forwarded the NTAs to the INS Newark District for service. These delays affected the detainees' ability to obtain legal counsel and postponed the detainees' opportunity to seek a bond re-determination hearing.

7. We recommend that the immigration authorities in the DHS issue instructions that clarify, for future events requiring centralized approvals at a Headquarters' level, which District or office is responsible for serving NTAs on transferred detainees: either the District in which the detainee was arrested or the District where the detainee is transferred.
8. We recommend that the DHS document when the charging determination is made, in order to determine compliance with the "48-hour rule." We also recommend that the DHS convert the 72-hour NTA service objective to a formal requirement. Further, we recommend that the DHS specify the "extraordinary circumstances" and the "reasonable period of time" when circumstances prevent the charging determination within 48 hours. We also recommend that the DHS provide, on a case-by-case basis, written justification for imposing the "extraordinary circumstances" exception and place a copy of this justification in the detainee's A-File.

V. Raising Issues of Concern to Senior Department Officials

Department officials established the "hold until cleared" policy believing that the FBI's clearance process for September 11 detainees would take just a few days. However, in many cases the clearance process stretched on for months and created dilemmas for INS attorneys who handled bond and removal proceedings. The slow pace of the FBI's background investigations, coupled with the lack of individualized evidence connecting specific detainees to terrorism, left INS attorneys with little evidence to argue for continued confinement of the detainees.

The evidence indicated that attorneys in the INS's Office of General Counsel made efforts to raise with some Department officials the issue of whether the INS could refuse to accept bond set by an Immigration Judge when the Government failed to appeal or block a detainee's departure from the country when he had received a final removal order. Yet, when these efforts were unsuccessful, INS officials did not raise the issue at higher levels in the Department or submit their legal concerns in writing until months later.

9. We recommend that Offices of General Counsel throughout the Department establish formal processes for identifying legal issues of concern—like the perceived conflict between the Department's "hold until cleared" policy and immigration laws and regulations—and formally raise significant concerns, in writing, to agency senior management and eventually Department senior management for resolution. Such processes will be even more important now that immigration responsibilities have transferred from the Department to the DHS.

VI. BOP Housing of Detainees

At least 84 September 11 detainees arrested on immigration charges in connection with the September 11 investigation were confined at the MDC. The BOP housed these detainees in its ADMAX SHU under extremely restrictive conditions. While the BOP played no role in deciding which detainees were "of interest" or "of high interest" to the FBI, once detainees were transferred to one of its facilities the BOP assumed responsibility for the detainees' conditions of confinement.

The BOP combined a series of existing policies and procedures that applied to inmates in other contexts to create highly restrictive conditions of confinement for September 11 detainees held at the MDC and other BOP facilities. For example, the BOP initially designated September 11 detainees as witness security (WITSEC) inmates, a categorization that restricted public knowledge of and access to the detainees. This designation frustrated efforts by detainees' attorneys, family members, consular officials, and even law enforcement officers to determine the detainees' location, given how tightly information about WITSEC inmates is held. In addition, the BOP's initial communications blackout and its policy of permitting detainees one legal call per week (coupled with arbitrary policies on whether reaching an answering machine counted as the legal call), severely limited the detainees' ability to contact and consult with legal counsel.

10. We recommend that the BOP establish a unique Special Management Category other than WITSEC for aliens arrested on immigration charges who are suspected of having ties to terrorism. Such a classification should identify procedures that permit detainees' reasonable access to telephones more in keeping with the detainees' status as immigration detainees who may not have retained legal representation by the time they are confined rather than as pre-trial inmates who most likely have counsel. In addition, BOP officials should train their staff on any new Special Management Category to avoid repeating situations such as when MDC staff mistakenly informed people inquiring about a specific September 11 detainee that the detainee was not held at the facility.

11. Given the highly restrictive conditions under which the MDC housed September 11 detainees, and the slow pace of the FBI's clearance process, we believe the BOP should consider requiring written assessments from immigration authorities and the FBI prior to placing aliens arrested solely on immigration charges into highly restrictive conditions, such as disciplinary segregation in its ADMAX SHU. Absent such a particularized assessment from the FBI and immigration authorities, the BOP should consider applying its traditional inmate classification procedures to determine the level of secure confinement required by each detainee.

12. We found delays of days and sometimes weeks between when the FBI notified the BOP that a September 11 detainee had been cleared of ties to terrorism and when the BOP notified the MDC that the detainee could be transferred from its ADMAX SHU to the facility's general population, where conditions were decidedly less severe. We recommend that BOP Headquarters develop procedures to improve the timeliness by which it informs local BOP facilities when the detention conditions of immigration detainees can be normalized.

13. We found evidence indicating a pattern of physical and verbal abuse by some MDC corrections staff against some September 11 detainees. While the OIG is continuing its administrative investigation into these matters, we believe MDC and BOP management should take aggressive and proactive steps to educate its staff on proper methods of handling detainees (and inmates) confined in highly restrictive conditions of confinement, such as the ADMAX SHU. The BOP must be vigilant to ensure that individuals in its custody are not subjected to harassment or more force than necessary to accomplish appropriate correctional objectives.

14. BOP and MDC officials anticipated that some September 11 detainees might allege they were subject to abuse during their confinement. Consequently, they took steps to help prevent or refute such allegations by installing cameras in each ADMAX SHU cell and requiring staff to videotape all detainees' movements outside their cells. Unfortunately, the MDC destroyed the tapes after 30 days. We recommend that the BOP issue new procedures requiring that video-tapes of detainees with alleged ties to terrorism housed in ADMAX SHU units be retained for at least 60 days.

15. We recommend that the BOP ensure that all immigration detainees housed in a BOP facility receive full and timely written notice of the facility's policies, including procedures for filing complaints. We found that the MDC failed to consistently provide September 11 de-tainees with details about its Administrative Remedy Program, the formal process for filing complaints of abuse.

16. Some MDC correctional staff asked detainees "are you okay" as a way to inquire whether they wanted their once-a-week legal telephone call. Detainees told the OIG that they misunderstood this question and, consequently, unknowingly waived their opportunity to place a legal call. We recommend that the BOP develop a national policy re-quiring detainees housed in SHUs to affirm their request for or refusal of a legal telephone call, and that such affirmance or refusal be recorded in the facility's Legal Call Log.

17. We recommend that the MDC examine its ADMAX SHU policies and practices in light of the September 11 detainees' experiences to ensure their appropriateness and necessity. For example, we found that while the MDC offered September 11 detainees exercise time in the facility's open-air recreation cell, they failed to provide suitable clothing during the winter months that would enable the detainees to take advantage of this opportunity. In addition, we found that the MDC kept both lights on in the detainees' cells 24 hours a day for several months after they had the ability to turn off at least one of the cell lights.

VII. Oversight of Detainees Housed in Contract Facilities

18. INS Newark District staff conducted insufficient and irregular visits to September 11 detainees held at Passaic. We also found that Passaic officials did not always inform Newark staff when detainees were placed in the SDU and that Newark officials did not always maintain required records for SDU detainees. Consequently, Newark staff was unable to consistently monitor detainee housing conditions, health issues, or resolve complaints. We recommend that the DHS amend its detention standards to mandate that District Detention and Removal personnel visit immigration detainees at contract facilities like Passaic frequently, with special emphasis on those detainees placed in SDUs,

in order to monitor matters such as housing conditions, health concerns, and complaints of abuse. District visits should include an interview of and a review of the records for detainees housed in SDUs. We further recommend that the DHS issue procedures to mandate that contract detention facilities transmit documentation to the appropriate DHS field office that describes the reasons why immigration detainees have been sent to SDUs.

19. We recommend that DHS field offices conduct weekly visits with detainees arrested in connection with a national emergency like the September 11 attacks to ensure that they are housed according to FBI threat assessments and BOP classifications (or other appropriate facility classification systems). In addition, the DHS should ensure that the detainees have adequate access to counsel, legal telephone calls, and visitation privileges consistent with their classification.

VIII. *Other Issues*

20. How long the INS legally could hold September 11 detainees after they have received final orders of removal or voluntary departure orders in order to conduct FBI clearance checks was the subject of differing opinions within the INS and the Department. A February 2003 opinion by the Department's Office of Legal Counsel concluded, however, that the INS could hold a detainee beyond the normal removal time for this purpose. That issue is also a subject in an ongoing lawsuit.

    Regardless of the outcome of the court case, we concluded that the Department failed to turn its attention in a timely manner to the question of its authority to detain such individuals. Where policies are implemented that could result in the prolonged confinement of illegal aliens, we recommend that the Department carefully examine, at an early stage, the limits on its legal authority to detain these individuals.

21. The INS failed to consistently conduct Post-Order Custody Reviews of September 11 detainees held more than 90 days after receiving final orders of removal. These custody reviews are required by immigration regulations to assess if detainees' continued detention is warranted. We understand that under Department policy in effect at the time, the INS was not permitted to remove September 11 detainees until it received FBI clearances. We believe the INS nevertheless should have conducted the custody reviews, both because they are required by regulation and because such reviews may have alerted Department officials even more directly that a number of aliens were being held beyond the 90-day removal period. We recommend that the DHS ensure that its field offices consistently conduct Post-Order Custody Reviews for all detainees who remain in its custody after the 90-day removal period.

Chapter Ten

Conclusions

In the aftermath of the September 11 terrorist attacks, the Department of Justice used the federal immigration laws to detain aliens who were suspected of having ties to the attacks or terrorism in general. More than 750 aliens who had violated immigration laws were arrested and detained in connection with the FBI's investigation into the attacks, called PENTTBOM. Our review examined the treatment of these detainees, including their processing, bond decisions, the timing of their removal or release, their access to counsel, and their conditions of confinement. To examine these issues, we focused on the detainees held at the BOP's Metropolitan Detention Center in Brooklyn, New York, and at the Passaic County Jail in Paterson, New Jersey, because the majority of September 11 detainees were held in these two facilities, and because many complaints arose regarding their treatment.

In conducting our review, we were mindful of the circumstances confronting the Department and the country as a result of the September 11 attacks, including the massive disruptions they caused. The Department was faced with monumental challenges, and Department employees worked tirelessly and with enormous dedication over an extended period to meet these challenges.

It is also important to note that nearly all of the 762 aliens we examined violated immigration laws, either by overstaying their visas, by entering the country illegally, or some other immigration violation. In other times, many of these aliens might not have been arrested or detained for these violations. However, the September 11 attacks changed the way the Department, particularly the FBI and the INS, responded when encountering aliens who were in violation of their immigration status. It was beyond the scope of this review to examine the specific law enforcement decisions regarding who to arrest or detain. Rather, we focused primarily on the treatment of the aliens who were detained.

While recognizing the difficult circumstances confronting the Department in responding to the terrorist attacks, we found significant problems in the way the September 11 detainees were treated. The INS did not serve notices of the immigration charges on these detainees within the specified timeframes. This delay affected the detainees in several ways, from their ability to understand why they were being held, to their ability to obtain legal counsel, to their ability to request a bond hearing.

In addition, the Department instituted a policy that these detainees would be held until cleared by the FBI. Although not communicated in writing, this "hold until cleared" policy was clearly understood and applied throughout the Department. The policy was based on the belief—which turned out to be erroneous—that the FBI's clearance process would proceed quickly. Instead of taking a few days as anticipated, the clearance process took an average of 80 days, primarily because it was understaffed and not given sufficient priority by the FBI.

We also found that the FBI and the INS in New York City made little attempt to distinguish between aliens who were subjects of the PENTTBOM investigation and those encountered coincidentally to a PENTTBOM lead. Even in the chaotic aftermath of the September 11 attacks, we believe the FBI should have taken more care to distinguish between aliens who it actually suspected of having a connection to terrorism from those aliens who, while possibly guilty of violating federal immigration law, had no connection to terrorism but simply were encountered in connection with a PENTTBOM lead. Alternatively, by early November 2001, when it became clear that the FBI could not complete its clearance investigations in a matter of days or even weeks, the Department should have reviewed those cases and kept on the list of September 11 detainees only those for whom it had some basis to suspect a connection to terrorism.

The FBI's initial classification decisions and the untimely clearance process had enormous ramifications for the September 11 detainees. The Department instituted a "no bond" policy for all September 11 detainees. The evidence indicates that the INS raised concerns about this blanket "no bond" approach, particularly when it became clear that the FBI's clearance process was slow and the INS had little information in many individual cases on which to base its continued opposition to bond. The INS also raised concerns about the legality of holding aliens to conduct clearance investigations after they had received final orders of removal or voluntary departure orders. We found that the Department did not address these legal issues in a timely way.

The FBI's classification of the detainees and the slow clearance process also had important ramifications on their conditions of confinement. Many aliens characterized by the FBI as "of high interest" to the September 11 investigation were detained at the MDC under highly restrictive conditions. While the FBI's classification decisions needed to be made quickly and were based on less than complete information, we believe the FBI should have exercised more care in the process, since it resulted in the MDC detainees being kept in the highest security conditions for a lengthy period. At the least, the FBI should have conducted more timely clearance checks, given the conditions under which the MDC detainees were held.

Our review also raised various concerns about the treatment of these detainees at the MDC. For example, we found that MDC staff frequently—and mistakenly—told people who inquired about a specific September 11 detainee that the detainee was not held at the facility when, in fact, the opposite was true. In addition, the MDC's restrictive and inconsistent policies on telephone access for detainees prevented them from obtaining legal counsel in a timely manner.

With regard to allegations of abuse, the evidence indicates a pattern of physical and verbal abuse by some correctional officers at the MDC against some September 11 detainees, particularly during the first months after the attacks. Although most correctional officers denied any such physical or verbal abuse, our interviews and investigation of specific complaints developed evidence that abuse had occurred.

We also concluded that, particularly at the MDC, certain conditions of confinement were unduly harsh, such as illuminating the detainees' cells for 24 hours a day. Further, we found that MDC staff failed to inform MDC detainees in a timely manner about the process for filing complaints about their treatment.

The September 11 detainees held at Passaic had much different, and significantly less harsh, experiences than the MDC detainees. The Passaic detainees were housed in the facility's general population and treated like other INS detainees held at the facility. Although we received some allegations of physical and verbal abuse, we did not find evidence of a pattern of abuse at Passaic as we did at the MDC. However, we found that the INS did not conduct sufficient and regular visits to Passaic to ensure the conditions of confinement were appropriate.

In sum, while the chaotic situation and the uncertainties surrounding the detainees' connections to terrorism explain some of these problems, they do not explain them all. We believe the Department should carefully consider and address the issues described in this report, and we therefore offered a series of recommendations regarding the systemic problems we identified in our review. They include recommendations to ensure a timely clearance process; timely service of immigration charges; careful consideration of where to house detainees with possible connections to terrorism, and under what kind of restrictions; better training of staff on the treatment of these detainees; and better oversight of the conditions of confinement. We believe these recommendations, if fully implemented, will help improve the Department's handling of detainees in other situations, both larger scale and smaller scale, that may arise in the future.

Source: U.S. Department of Justice. Office of the Inspector General. *The September 11 Detainees: A Review of the Treatment of Aliens Held on Immigration Charges in Connection with the Investigation of the September 11 Attacks.* June 2, 2003. www.usdoj.gov/oig/special/03-06/index.htm (accessed June 2, 2003).

Investigative Report on WorldCom Fraud

June 9, 2003

INTRODUCTION

A wave of corporate scandal that began in late 2001 with the bankruptcy of Enron Corporation continued into 2003 as regulators and prosecutors uncovered new cases of wrongdoing at several large, publicly traded companies. The two biggest companies caught up in the scandal—Enron and WorldCom—were still in bankruptcy during the year. Enron planned to break itself into two smaller companies, and WorldCom planned to change its name (to MCI) and emerge from bankruptcy in 2004.

Investigations continued into improper dealings at more than a dozen other companies that had fallen on hard times in the previous year, including Adelphia, K-Mart, and Tyco. Three other large companies made an appearance on the big-time corporate scandal sheet: HealthSouth, which owned rehabilitation hospitals; Freddie Mac, the country's second largest financier of home mortgages; and Parmalat, one of Europe's biggest food companies.

During the latter part of 2003 the corporate scandals were overshadowed, at least temporarily, by other cases of wrongdoing at the highest levels of American capitalism. Many of the country's largest mutual funds—the companies that managed stockholdings for more than 90 million Americans—were found to have engaged in financial schemes that benefited a few people at the expense of ordinary investors. The New York Stock Exchange was forced into a major shakeup when it became known that the board had agreed to pay its chairman, Richard Grasso, $140 million in deferred compensation. *(Stock market scandals, p. 693)*

Several dozen former corporate officials caught up in the current wave of scandal had pleaded guilty to civil and criminal charges—in most cases to avoid prison or win reduced sentencing. As of the end of 2003, however, only one of those had been a chief executive: Martin L. Grass, the former head of the troubled drugstore chain, Rite Aid Corporation. He was awaiting sentencing at year's end. The company's former chief counsel, Franklin

C. Brown, achieved a different distinction on October 17, becoming the first senior executive convicted by a jury. He was found guilty of conspiracy, obstruction of justice, witness tampering, and lying to the Securities and Exchange Commission (SEC).

One entire company—the Arthur Andersen accounting firm—was convicted of obstructing justice in June 2002 because of its role in the shredding of documents at Enron. That conviction forced Arthur Anderson to fold; parts of the former accounting giant were picked up by other firms. *(Corporate scandal background, Historic Documents of 2001, p. 857; Historic Documents of 2002, pp. 391, 1032)*

WorldCom's House of Phony Numbers

WorldCom, a telecommunications firm that grew to become a giant during the 1990s by aggressive mergers, filed for bankruptcy in July 2002, surpassing Enron as the largest U.S. company (in terms of stated financial size) ever to enter that ignoble state. Subsequent revelations showed that the company's founder, Bernard J. Ebbers, had built an empire on accounting schemes that exaggerated revenues and disguised debt, making WorldCom appear to be profitable even when it was losing money. *(WorldCom background, Historic Documents of 2002, p. 393)*

As it moved through the bankruptcy process, WorldCom enjoyed one significant advantage over Enron: It had real assets and business that could form the basis for a revived company. Enron, by contrast, had based its business growth largely on speculation and hype, neither of which had any value in bankruptcy proceedings.

WorldCom also appeared to have the advantage of a solid management team that took over after Ebbers, other top officials, and the board of directors were forced out. The new chairman and chief executive offer was Michael D. Cappellas, who had headed Compaq Computer Corp. before its merger with Hewlett-Packard. Cappellas brought on a new board of outsiders, sold off unprofitable subsidiaries, laid off about 30,000 of the company's 85,000 employees, and focused on the company's core business, the long-distance carrier MCI. Cappellas also moved the company headquarters from Clinton, Mississippi (near Ebber's hometown), to Ashburn, Virginia, a suburb of Washington, D.C., where MCI had been based.

The company's first major step toward regaining public confidence was its agreement on May 19 to pay investors $500 million to settle civil fraud charges the SEC had filed in June 2002 and then broadened five months later. Although it was the largest fine the SEC had ever imposed on a company, the $500 million was only a fraction of the losses investors had incurred because of the WorldCom debacle; one estimate by the *Washington Post* put the losses in stocks and bonds at about $175 billion. A federal judge in Washington approved the settlement in July, after the amount was boosted to $750 million in response to wide criticism that the company was getting off too easily.

Another major step came October 31, when U.S. Bankruptcy Judge Arthur J. Gonzalez, in New York, approved WorldCom's reorganization plan, a step that officials said would enable the company to emerge from bankruptcy early in 2004—an extraordinarily quick turnaround, given the size and complexity of the case. The plan would erase about $35 billion in company debt, generally by paying back creditors an average of thirty-six cents on the dollar. Cappellas said the company also would change its name to MCI once the bankruptcy proceedings were completed.

A key aspect of WorldCom's reorganization was a radical restructuring of corporate governance. On August 19 the company's new board—which had been hand-picked by Cappellas—approved a set of seventy-eight recommendations formulated by Richard C. Breeden, a former chairman of the SEC who had been appointed by the bankruptcy court to monitor WorldCom's management. Key changes included the naming of an outsider as chairman of the board (thus separating the jobs of chairman and chief executive officer, commonly held by the same person); barring management officers, except for the chief executive, from serving on the board; limiting the terms of directors to ten years and requiring at least one director to leave the board each year; giving investors a greater say in the selection of directors; making it easier for investors to offer resolutions at the company's annual meetings; and requiring the company to change its outside auditor every ten years. Several of these changes were to be put into the company's articles of incorporation— making it difficult for a future board to backtrack on the reforms.

Breeden's reforms were aimed at curing ills that became evident from an investigation, headed by former U.S. attorney general Richard Thornburgh, into WorldCom's failures. Thornburgh had been retained by the New York bankruptcy court to identify those who were responsible for WorldCom's collapse. He issued reports in November 2002 and on June 9, 2003. The latter report, known as the "Thornburgh Report," portrayed WorldCom's old board of directors as a prime example of a board that took management claims for granted and failed to ask probing questions.

Thornburgh said the board had placed "virtually no checks or restraints" on Ebbers. His chief financial officer, Scott D. Sullivan, routinely "rubberstamped" management plans for acquisitions and debt (including some costing billions of dollars) without examining details and failed to demand any kind of realistic long-range planning. "While the degree of responsibility varies greatly, WorldCom could not have failed as a result of the actions of a limited number of individuals," Thornburgh reported. "Rather, there was a broad breakdown of the system of internal controls, corporate governance and individual responsibility, all of which worked together to create a culture in which few persons took responsibility until it was too late." While acknowledging that it would have taken courage for employees or board members to speak out about abuses, Thornburgh expressed disappointment that "those with the responsibility to protect shareholders did not act sooner."

A second, related investigation—authorized by three members of World-Com's new board—detailed the accounting schemes and other financial maneuvers the company had engaged in to hide its troubles from investors, the public, and even its outside auditors. The report of that investigation also was made public June 9; the investigation was conducted by William McLucas, a former director of the SEC enforcement division.

The report focused heavily on Ebbers, arguing that he was unable to manage the company he had built during the 1990s by buying other companies, notably MCI. Pressed by Wall Street to continue producing double-digit revenue growth even in a downturn of the telecommunications industry, Ebbers "did not provide the leadership or managerial attention that would enable WorldCom to meet those expectations legitimately," the report said. Ebbers gave Wall Street, his board, and his employees a "substantially false picture" of the company's status, even while he was getting information that was at odds with that picture and that showed WorldCom was meeting its revenue projections "through financial gimmickry," McLucas said. The actual fraud was carried out by Sullivan and controller Donald Myers, McLucas said. There was "clear evidence" that Ebbers knew of "certain practices" used to inflate revenues, but there was no "direct evidence" that Ebbers knew about or participated in other fraudulent schemes. McLucas was less harsh in describing the failings of WorldCom's board than was Thornburgh, but he did say the board was "so passive and reliant" on Ebbers and Sullivan for information that it had not learned about the ongoing fraud at the company.

With WorldCom appearing to be on the road to recovery, the major question left hanging at the end of 2003 was the price to be paid by the company's former executives. Ebbers faced trouble on two fronts: Shareholders in the original MCI had filed a class-action suit charging that he and Sullivan had perpetrated a fraud with WorldCom's 1999 takeover of MCI, and Oklahoma attorney general Drew Edmonson on August 27 filed criminal charges against WorldCom and six former executives, including Ebbers, saying they had violated state securities laws by falsifying information given to investors. Federal investigators had not brought any civil or criminal charges against Ebbers as of year's end. News reports said Ebbers was having trouble repaying an estimated $400 million that he had borrowed from the company.

Sullivan was indicted in August 2002 on federal fraud charges, to which he pleaded not guilty. His trial was scheduled to begin early in 2004. Two other former senior executives, former controller Myers and former accounting director Buford Yates Jr., pleaded guilty to fraud charges in 2002 and agreed to testify against Sullivan.

Sorting out the Enron Mess

Enron, which in late 2001 had led the parade of large companies caught engaging in financial shenanigans, remained in bankruptcy throughout 2003. The company had claimed to be the seventh largest in the United States, but by 2003 it had been reduced to a shell of its former self, having lost most of its employees and much of its business. After nearly eighteen months under bankruptcy protection, Enron on July 11 filed its plan to emerge from bankruptcy, possibly during 2004. The plan called for Enron to be split into two: CrossCountry Energy Corp. would retain Enron's interests in three natural gas pipelines in North America, and Prisma Energy International Inc. would take over Enron's stakes in nineteen overseas pipelines and energy facilities.

The filing said Enron owed some 20,000 creditors an estimated $67 billion; the latter figure was about one-third of the total claims that had been made by creditors. Under the company's plan, the creditors would receive a maximum of about eighteen cents on each dollar that Enron said they were owed.

A bankruptcy examiner, lawyer Neal Batson, filed two reports during 2003 detailing many of the phony financial transactions that got Enron into trouble. The New York bankruptcy court released Batson's first report on March 5. It described six types of schemes Enron had used to inflate its reported revenues and disguise its debts and losses. In most cases the schemes violated the spirit of generally accepted accounting principles, Batson said. But, he suggested, Enron and its accountant at the time, Arthur Andersen, maneuvered between the lines of propriety in such a way that many of the schemes might technically have been legal—even if they gave a false picture of the company's finances.

Batson reported on November 24 that Enron's former chairman, Kenneth L. Lay, and former chief executive, Jeffrey K. Skilling, were in a "circle of responsibility" for the company's demise, although it was unclear whether the men were legally liable. Top company executives had not exercised their fiduciary responsibilities, Batson said. In particular, they had "failed to respond appropriately to the existence of 'red flags' indicating that certain senior officers" had constructed financial schemes to make the company appear profitable. Batson suggested that Enron file suit to force Lay and Skilling to make good on loans they had received from the company and then repaid with stock that later became almost worthless. Lay had borrowed $94 million and Skilling had borrowed $2 million, Batson's report said. Both Lay and Skilling had denied knowing about Enron's financial fraud, and neither had been charged with a crime as of the end of 2003.

Andrew S. Fastow, the company's former chief financial officer who allegedly had created the off-the-book partnerships and other maneuvers to inflate the company's value, had been charged with nearly one hundred counts of fraud, money laundering, and other crimes. He pleaded innocent and was awaiting trial, possibly in 2004. David W. Delainey, who headed two Enron divisions, pleaded guilty to insider trading charges on October 30. He was the highest-ranking former Enron official to admit to any crimes. Delainey agreed to pay nearly $8 million in civil and criminal penalties and to cooperate with federal investigators as they continued to probe the fraud at Enron. He also faced a possible prison sentence of up to ten years.

Enron's troubles continued to have repercussions at other companies that had participated in its fraudulent behavior. On July 28, J.P. Morgan Chase and Citigroup, two of the nation's largest financial institutions, settled charges brought against them by the Securities and Exchange Commission and Manhattan district attorney Robert M. Morganthau. The banks had loaned Enron hundreds of millions of dollars under terms that disguised the debt, or in some cases even made the loans appear as revenue; it was one of many ways the company hid its true financial picture from investors and regulators. In one case, for example, Enron borrowed $500 million from Citigroup and paid the money back a few days later—simply so it could book the $500 million as operating cash flow.

Documents made public as part of the July 28 settlement made it clear that top officials at the banks were aware that Enron was misreporting the lending. However, they apparently were not aware that the company was misrepresenting other aspects of its business, as well. As a result, they ended up being Enron's biggest creditors when it went bankrupt. Summing up the charges against the two banks, SEC enforcement director Stephen Cutler said: "If you know that you are helping a company mislead its investors, then you are in violation of securities laws." The banks were not penalized in the settlement, but they were required to sign statements promising not to engage in similar transactions in the future.

Merrill Lynch & Company, another major financial services company, on September 17 settled a case stemming from its participation in Enron deals during 1999. The deals had enabled Enron to report inflated profits. In settling the case, Merrill Lynch pledged never again to engage in deals that might mislead investors. The company also established a committee to review complex financial transactions with third parties (such as entities related to Merrill's direct customer)—and to have that committee's work monitored by an independent auditor approved by the Justice Department. Three former senior Merrill Lynch executives were indicted on charges in connection with a fraudulent 1999 deal with Enron. That case was pending as of the end of 2003.

Reforms at the SEC

The steady stream of allegations about corporate misconduct that emerged in 2002 led inevitably to questions about what federal regulators had been doing—or not doing—to safeguard the interests of investors and the general public. Most of these questions were directed at the Securities and Exchange Commission, which was charged with ensuring that publicly traded companies told shareholders the truth about their finances. The SEC appeared to have been quick to go after companies once wrongdoing became obvious, but many critics said the agency had been unable or unwilling to ferret out corporate misdeeds.

The SEC itself became the subject of ridicule in late 2002 when it bungled its way through the naming of a new, congressionally mandated board to oversee the accounting profession. In September the commission named William L. Webster, former director of the CIA and FBI, to head the new board. Six weeks later, commission chairman Harvey L. Pitt resigned under pressure because he had failed to tell fellow commissioners that Webster had chaired the audit committee of a company that had been under fire for accounting irregularities. Webster resigned his post, as well. *(Background, Historic Documents of 2002, p. 1032)*

President George W. Bush in January 2003 named William H. Donaldson to succeed Pitt. He had been the head of a midsize investment firm (Donaldson, Lufkin, and Jenrette) and was a former chairman of the New York Stock Exchange and AETNA insurance. After three months on the job, Donaldson told the *Washington Post* that the extent of corporate wrongdoing was greater than he had understood. "I am surprised at how prevalent it is in the economy," he said. "I'm surprised at the day-in and day-out, steady level of malfeasance that comes in under the radar."

The SEC in May chose William J. McDonough as the new chairman of the accounting board. He had been president and chief executive officer of the Federal Reserve Bank of New York. McDonough took office on June 11, and the board began revising the rules governing the work of accountants and auditors at publicly traded companies. The board also started regular inspections of the four largest remaining accounting firms and announced plans for annual inspections of all accounting firms that had one hundred or more clients.

One of McDonough's first tasks was bolstering the credibility of the new accounting board, which had created its own public relations debacle. In February news organizations reported that board members had voted to pay themselves $450,000 annually and the chairman $560,000. In establishing the board in 2002, as part of the Sarbanes-Oxley Act (PL 107–204), Congress had authorized its members and staff to be paid at "market" rates—but the pay rates far exceeding those paid members of Congress and cabinet officers raised eyebrows around Washington.

The SEC also adopted nearly two dozen rules changes and new requirements during the year intended to deal with some of the problems that had emerged in the recent wave of scandal. Many of the changes were mandated by the Sarbanes-Oxley Act. For example, on May 27 the commission adopted rules requiring companies to file annual reports certifying their internal controls over financial reporting, and on August 6 the commission required increased disclosure by public companies of their procedures for selecting members of board of directors.

The commission faced at least one unprecedented situation during the year: It was unable to spend all the money Congress had given it. Reacting to complaints that the agency never had enough accountants and lawyers to review corporate financial filings, Congress gave the SEC a major budget increase for fiscal year 2003. Donaldson said in July the agency would be unable to spend $103 million allocated for new hires. "You don't want to rush and hire willy-nilly at the cost of having the quality of work decline," he told the *New York Times.*

Other Corporate Scandals

More than a dozen other large companies were caught up in various scandals during 2003, among them:

- **Freddie Mac.** The quasi-government home mortgage financing company known as Freddie Mac acknowledged in late 2003 that it had misreported about $5 billion in earnings over the previous three years. The company agreed on December 10 to pay a $125 million fine to its regulatory agency, the Office of Federal Housing Enterprise Oversight. That body issued a report saying that Freddie Mac's board "deferred to management almost completely" and failed to question items that should have gotten its attention. Under pressure, the company fired two successive chief executive officers (one in June and another in August) before settling on a new chief in December.
- **Adelphia Communications Corp.** Adelphia, the country's sixth-largest cable television firm, filed for bankruptcy in June 2002. A month later its founder, John J. Rigas, and his sons Michael J. and Timothy J., were arrested on charges of stealing several hundred million dollars from the company. The government's charges alleged that the three men had used the company as their "personal piggy bank," had hidden debts, and ultimately had cost investors more than $60 billion. John Rigas was expected to go on trial early in 2004.
- **HealthSouth.** The nation's largest chain of rehabilitation hospitals—long considered a model of the for-prohibit health care business—found itself in need of rehabilitation after March, when a giant pattern of fraud was uncovered. By the end of the year, federal prosecutors had counted nearly $3 billion worth of what they alleged were fraudulent accounting tricks dating to 1996. On November 3 Richard M. Scrushy, the company's founder and former chief executive, was indicted on eighty-five counts, including securities fraud and money

laundering. Scrushy pleaded innocent. Sixteen other HealthSouth officers were indicted on various fraud-related charges earlier in the year; fourteen of them pleaded guilty.

In essence, the charges were similar to those levied against Enron, WorldCom, and other much larger companies—that HealthSouth inflated revenues and assets in an attempt to bolster its stock price. The company's troubles became public knowledge on March 19, when the SEC sued the company and Scrushy, based on a guilty plea entered by a former chief financial officer who acknowledged falsely certifying financial records. Scrushy allegedly had used questionable bonuses and other payments from the company to buy numerous homes, boats, automobiles, and fine art paintings.

- **K-Mart.** Once the country's leading discount retailer, K-Mart emerged as a smaller, thoroughly reorganized company on May 6, just fifteen months after filing for bankruptcy protection. The new company had 1,500 stores, 600 fewer than before it entered bankruptcy, putting it even further behind the new industry leaders, Wal-Mart and Target. The company in January accused twenty-five former executives of obtaining improper loans and said some executives had used company planes for personal travel, improperly cut off payments to suppliers, and, in one case, ordered $850 million in merchandise for stores without proper authorization.

- **Tyco International.** Competition was fierce for the honor—or dishonor—of being the leading symbol of corporate corruption during the 2001–2003 wave of scandal. One of the strongest candidates was Dennis Kozlowski, who had built Tyco from a small industrial company to a giant international conglomerate. Like some of the other companies that had fallen on hard times, much of Tyco's reported profits were based on misleading accounting schemes.

Kozlowski, Tyco's chairman and chief executive, attracted wide public attention, not because of the accounting irregularities, but because of his alleged habit of using Tyco to pay for his extravagant lifestyle. Among other things, Tyco reportedly paid for the $1 million birthday party Kozlowski threw for his wife on the island of Sardinia; videos of the event showed scantily clad dancers and a life-size ice sculpture replica of Michelangelo's David. Along with former chief financial officer Mark H. Swartz, Kozlowski was indicted in June 2002 on several charges of violating New York state laws, including securities fraud, the theft of more than $600 million from an employee program, running a criminal enterprise, and evading about $1 million on sales taxes on art purchases. Kozlowski and Swartz went on trial in late September; the trial was still under way at year's end.

Tyco's new chairman, Edward Breen, faced the monumental task of restoring the company's tarnished image. The job was not made any easier by continuing revelations of past misdeeds, including accounting problems costing at least $265 million at its ADT fire alarm division and an indictment in February of former general counsel Mark Belnick on charges of stealing $12 million by accepting an unapproved bonus. The company announced in March that it would close 300 plants by 2006 in hopes of cutting its costs by about $1 billion.

- **Parmalat.** Several European firms had been caught engaging in fraudulent schemes similar to those concocted by some U.S. companies, but all were of relatively small scale until Parmalat joined the parade in September. The giant Italian food-processing company—best known internationally for its reconstituted milk products—acknowledged that it owed banks and bondholders about $7 billion. That figure later was revised to about $10 billion and was still rising at year's end. The company filed for bankruptcy on December 24, saying it had overstated its 2002 revenue by nearly $5 billion. As with some of the U.S. firms, much of Parmalat's trouble was traced to its longtime chief executive, Calisto Tanzi, who reportedly admitted on December 29 that he had used more than $600 million in company money to finance another firm owned by his family. The U.S. Securities and Exchange Commission filed fraud charges on December 29, saying Parmalat had illegally sold $1.5 billion in bonds and other securities in the United States from 1998 to 2002.

Following are excerpts from the Second Interim Report of the Bankruptcy Court Examiner, referred to as the "Thornburgh Report," in the case of WorldCom, Inc., made public June 9, 2003. The report analyzed alleged improper financial dealings by the company and its executives, including former chairman and chief executive officer Bernard Ebbers.

The "Thornburgh Report"

Summary of Observations

The WorldCom story is not limited to the massive accounting fraud that has been publicly reported. Aside from these issues, the Examiner's continued investigation into other matters has uncovered additional deceit, deficiencies and a disregard for the most basic principles of corporate governance.

The Examiner has identified significant problems with respect to virtually every area reviewed, including acquisitions, strategic planning, debt management, credit facilities, loans to Mr. [Bernard J.] Ebbers [former WorldCom chairman and chief executive officer], Mr. Ebbers' $70 million forward sale, employee compensation, and internal controls. The observations of the Examiner regarding these matters, which are detailed in later sections of this Report, may be summarized as follows:

- WorldCom was dominated by Messrs. Ebbers and Sullivan [Scott D. Sullivan, former chief financial officer], with virtually no checks or restraints placed on their actions by the Board of Directors or other Management. Significantly, although many present or former officers and Directors of WorldCom told us they had misgivings regarding decisions or actions by Mr. Ebbers or Mr. Sullivan during the relevant period, there is no evidence that these officers and Directors made any attempts to curb, stop or challenge the conduct by Mr. Ebbers or Mr. Sullivan that they deemed questionable or inappropriate. Instead, it appears that the Company's officers and Directors went along with Mr. Ebbers and Mr. Sullivan, even under circumstances that suggested corporate actions were at best imprudent, and at worst inappropriate and fraudulent.
- The Company's approach to acquisitions and significant outsourcing transactions was ad hoc and opportunistic. Our examination has revealed little meaningful or coherent strategic planning at World-Com. Further, in many instances, the Company's decision-making was marked by a striking absence of proper corporate governance protocols.
- WorldCom Management provided the Company's Directors with extremely limited information regarding many acquisition transactions. Several multibillion dollar acquisitions were approved by the Board of Directors following discussions that lasted for 30 minutes or less and without the Directors receiving a single piece of paper regarding the terms or implications of the transactions.
- The process surrounding the Company's decision to acquire Intermedia Communications, Inc. ("Intermedia") in September 2000 is particularly troubling. In what one former Director described an "ego deal" for Mr. Ebbers, WorldCom responded to a perceived threat that a competitor could acquire Intermedia (or Digex, Inc. ("Digex"), a Web hosting company controlled by Intermedia) by agreeing to pay $6 billion for the company, based upon approximately 60-90 minutes of due diligence and a 35-minute telephonic Board meeting for which some Directors received no more than two hours notice. The facts raise substantial doubt concerning Management's basis for recommending the transaction and the adequacy of the information provided to the Board. As a former Director stated, "God himself could not have made the decision in one day." The

Directors were not provided with any written materials or analyses concerning this potential transaction. Although numerous people involved with the Board's consideration of the Intermedia transaction now state that they were disturbed by the deal at the time, no Director or anyone else voiced any objection to the cursory consideration by the Board.

- The concerns related to the Intermedia acquisition become even more acute when viewed in the light of subsequent developments. Shortly after the acquisition agreement was announced on September 5, 2000, minority shareholders of Digex filed a lawsuit challenging the transaction. This litigation, and the declining value of other Intermedia assets, gave WorldCom an opportunity to abandon the proposed acquisition. Rather than do so, WorldCom Management, at the apparent direction of Mr. Ebbers, and without consulting the Board of Directors, entered into an agreement to settle the Digex shareholder litigation and signed an amended merger agreement with Intermedia in February 2001. Although a February 15, 2001 WorldCom press release stated that the Board had approved the settlement, the Company's outside Directors were not even polled at the time with respect to whether they wanted to continue with the transaction. In March 2001, the Board passively adopted and endorsed the prior acts of Management, without objection. All told, the acquisition of Intermedia was a dismal failure, producing massive losses for WorldCom. The Examiner believes that a vigilant Board of Directors would have rejected Management's actions.

- Another troubling transaction is WorldCom's $2 billion acquisition of SkyTel Communications, Inc. ("SkyTel") in 1999. That transaction, which was of questionable strategic benefit to WorldCom, was approved by the Board after a presentation by Management lasting about 15 minutes and, again, without a single piece of paper being provided to the Board. The Board members interviewed by the Examiner did not appear troubled by this lack of consideration because the acquisition was for "only" $2 billion. The Examiner believes that a transaction of that magnitude deserved far greater consideration and deliberation.

- The Examiner also has substantial questions concerning the process by which WorldCom adopted its Tracker stock structure in November 2000. [This structure divided WorldCom into two groups for stock exchange listing purposes: the WorldCom Group, containing the high growth portions of the Company (data, Internet, Web hosting and international); and the MCI Group, containing the slower-growth, but higher cash flow, businesses (consumer, small business, wholesale long-distance, paging, voice and dial-up Internet access)]. Our investigation identified little evidence of a thoughtful strategic plan for the Tracker stocks. Instead, it appears that, as stated by one former WorldCom Director, the Tracker stocks were merely the "flavor of the month."

- The Examiner also has concerns regarding the allocation of assets, debt and expenses between the WorldCom Group and the MCI Group under the Tracker stock structure. The Examiner is investigating whether these allocations were intended to burden disproportionately the MCI Group businesses and what the effect of such allocations may be on inter-company claims and creditors.

- The Examiner is also concerned about the Company's tendency to utilize its debt offerings and credit facilities to further a practice pursuant to which it paid off existing investors or lenders with newly-borrowed funds, while growing its debt to a level that became ultimately unserviceable. WorldCom's ability to borrow monies was facilitated by its massive accounting fraud, as it allowed the Company to falsely present itself as creditworthy and "investment grade," when in fact its debt was below "investment grade."

- There is no evidence of meaningful debt planning by WorldCom. Indeed, there is no evidence that Company Management or the Board reasonably monitored the Company's debt level or its ability to satisfy its outstanding obligations. A prime example of inadequate planning was the Company's use of the proceeds from a massive $11.9 billion debt offering in May 2001, which WorldCom projected would satisfy its cash needs for the ensuing 18 months. In fact, WorldCom spent the proceeds in about eight months.

- Messrs. Ebbers and Sullivan had virtually unfettered discretion to commit the Company to billions of dollars in debt obligations with virtually no meaningful Board oversight. WorldCom issued more than $25 billion in debt securities in the four years preceding its bankruptcy. With respect to such offerings, Messrs. Ebbers and Sullivan comprised the entirety of the Company's Pricing Committee. The Board passively "rubber-stamped" proposals from Messrs. Ebbers or Sullivan regarding additional borrowings, most often via unanimous consent resolutions that were adopted after little or no discussion.

- The Company's drawdown on a $2.65 billion line of credit in May 2002 raises significant issues. Despite public statements by Mr. Sullivan early in May 2002 that "certainly there is liquidity in the Company . . . we're in a very solid situation," the evidence establishes that WorldCom had a desperate need for cash at the time. The Company had to meet several large payment obligations and its debt had been downgraded. Moreover, Mr. Sullivan said that "the "money [from the credit facility] won't be used for anything. The money will be sitting on the balance sheet in cash; it will be invested for a few weeks" and repaid when WorldCom completed a $5 billion secured financing in June 2002. However, it appears that at the time Mr. Sullivan made those statements, WorldCom already had decided to use a portion of the proceeds from the line of credit to make payments with respect to the Company's accounts receivable credit program. As the Company's Treasurer told us in an interview, WorldCom merely "robbed Peter to pay Paul."

- The facts and circumstances surrounding the Company's loans of more than $400 million to Mr. Ebbers raise additional and very serious corporate governance concerns. The Compensation and Stock Option Committee of the Board of Directors (the "Compensation Committee") agreed to provide enormous loans and a guaranty for Mr. Ebbers without initially informing the full Board or taking appropriate steps to protect the Company. As the loans and guaranty increased, the Compensation Committee failed to perform appropriate due diligence that would have demonstrated that the collateral was insufficient to support the credit extended to Mr. Ebbers, in light of his substantial other loans and obligations. The Board was similarly at fault for not raising any questions about the loans and merely rubber stamping the actions of the Compensation Committee.

- A forward sale of three million WorldCom shares by Mr. Ebbers in September 2000, in which he received proceeds of over $70 million, also raises questions. Mr. Ebbers had a strong and widely known opposition to any WorldCom employee selling stock of the Company. In early September 2000, Mr. Ebbers received the first of his loans from WorldCom, for $50 million, because the Compensation Committee did not want him to make good on his threat to sell any of his WorldCom stock to meet margin obligations. At this same time, the Compensation Committee also awarded Mr. Ebbers a $10 million cash retention bonus. These amounts were apparently not enough, as Mr. Ebbers asked the Compensation Committee for an additional loan in late September 2000. When the Compensation Committee refused his request, Mr. Ebbers entered into a forward sale of three million shares of WorldCom stock and received a payment of over $70 million. Coincidentally or not, the price of WorldCom stock dropped $2.25 a share on October 4, 2000, the day after the public announcement of the forward sale. Instead of taking reasonable measures to protect WorldCom and its shareholders from Mr. Ebbers' deteriorating personal finances, the Compensation Committee later that month magnified the problem by providing a $75 million guaranty and an additional $25 million loan to Mr. Ebbers. Ultimately, the loans to Mr. Ebbers reached over $400 million.

- The timing and circumstances of the forward sale are also problematic in other respects. Specifically, WorldCom received legal advice from outside counsel for WorldCom that the proposed sale might be inappropriate, particularly since it was to occur shortly before a negative earnings announcement. Despite this, the Company permitted the sale by Mr. Ebbers without adequately investigating the likelihood that the sale violated insider trading laws and despite the fact that the sale violated a Company policy that prohibited such transactions near the time of an earnings announcement.

- The Ebbers loans, guaranty and forward sale of stock are troubling for an additional reason. These fundings revealed the extent of Mr. Ebbers' business activities that were not related to WorldCom. The Board should have questioned these extensive non-WorldCom business activities as inconsistent with the need for Mr. Ebbers to devote his time and attention to managing the business of a large and complex company such as WorldCom. The need for Mr. Ebbers to devote his full attention to WorldCom matters became even more urgent when the downturn in the telecommunications industry began in 2000. The Board, however, did nothing to attempt to persuade Mr. Ebbers to divest himself of these non-WorldCom businesses or otherwise limit his non-WorldCom business activities. To the contrary, the Compensation Committee and the Board provided massive funding that facilitated Mr. Ebbers' personal business activities.

- The Examiner is continuing to review the process by which salaries, bonuses, stock options and other compensation were determined at WorldCom. Our investigation has revealed that there was a significant disparity between the way compensation matters were supposed to be handled in theory, and how they were actually handled. Despite public pronouncements to the contrary, Mr. Ebbers dominated compensation decisions. He was, for example, given almost complete discretion to authorize and allocate a $240 million retention bonus program in 2000 that involved large, up-front cash payments to over 500 executives. Mr. Ebbers awarded Mr. Sullivan and himself $10 million cash bonuses under this program, notwithstanding the fact that they had received retention bonuses of $7.5 million and $1.85 million, respectively, one year earlier, and notwithstanding that other company executives received a combination of cash and stock as retention bonuses.

- Mr. Sullivan paid part of his $10 million cash bonus to some of his subordinates, many of whom had received large retention bonuses directly from the Company. Mr. Sullivan gave $10,000 personal checks to at least seven employees, and additional $10,000 personal checks to the spouses of several of these employees. Although the

Examiner has not identified any information linking these payments to illegal conduct, four of the individuals who received these payments have pled guilty to criminal fraud charges relating to the Company's accounting practices.

- The fact that WorldCom's accounting irregularities went undetected for so long attests to substantial problems with the Company's internal controls. The Audit Committee of the Board of Directors and the Internal Audit Department appear to have acted in good faith and, to their considerable credit, they took significant and responsible steps once accounting irregularities were discovered in the spring of 2002. However, it seems clear that the Audit Committee over the years barely scratched the surface of any potential accounting or financial reporting issues. Moreover, the Internal Audit Department adopted an operational audit function, rather than acting as WorldCom's "internal control police." Finally, it appears that the Audit Committee, the Internal Audit Department and Arthur Andersen allowed their missions to be limited and shaped in ways that served to conceal and perpetuate the Company's accounting fraud.

- The Examiner is troubled by several of his preliminary observations regarding the "risk based" audits Arthur Andersen performed during the relevant period. Although Arthur Andersen considered World-Com to be a "maximum risk" client, it appears that it designed the WorldCom audits to accommodate primarily the needs and desires of the Company's senior Management to the detriment of its own performance. The conduct of Arthur Andersen raises significant questions regarding its audit plan and communication with Management and the Audit Committee.

- WorldCom prepared MonRev [monthly revenue] reports, which identified the revenue of the Company on a monthly and quarterly basis. The Examiner is aware that "Special MonRev" reports were prepared for, and provided to, Arthur Andersen in the third and fourth quarters of 2001. These "Special" MonRev reports contained manipulated data that masked the amounts of certain "corporate adjustments, affecting revenues" and were different than the actual MonRev reports relied on by the Company.

- Accordingly, the Examiner has identified numerous occasions—on acquisitions, debt offerings, loans to Mr. Ebbers and other matters—on which the WorldCom Board was not adequately informed about significant corporate matters before giving its approval. The Examiner is troubled that no WorldCom attorneys (including in-house and outside counsel) appear to have believed that it was their responsibility to advise the Board of their fiduciary obligations to become adequately informed, even in instances where it seems likely that the Board lacked sufficient information. The

Examiner recognizes that the WorldCom culture was not generally supportive of a strong legal function, but this should not have prevented counsel from fulfilling their obligations to their corporate client.

- All told, the Examiner believes that WorldCom's conferral of practically unlimited discretion upon Messrs. Ebbers and Sullivan, combined with passive acceptance of Management's proposals by the Board of Directors, and a culture that diminished the importance of internal checks, forward-looking planning and meaningful debate or analysis formed the basis for the Company's descent into bankruptcy. As set forth above and in the remainder of this Second Interim Report, there are many persons and entities that share responsibility for WorldCom's downfall and the losses suffered by the Company's shareholders and creditors. While the degree of responsibility varies greatly, WorldCom could not have failed as a result of the actions of a limited number of individuals. Rather, there was a broad breakdown of the system of internal controls, corporate governance and individual responsibility, all of which worked together to create a culture in which few persons took responsibility until it was too late.

The Examiner understands that stepping forward to raise questions, whether it be on questionable accounting, lack of data provided to the Board of Directors, or other issues, would have involved acts of courage—possibly risking jobs in some instances. The Examiner further understands that WorldCom's most senior Management, especially Mr. Ebbers and Mr. Sullivan, enjoyed enormous power and substantial respect at various times, making the decision to take a stand that much more difficult. Nevertheless, the Examiner is disappointed that those with the responsibility to protect shareholders did not act sooner.

This Second Interim Report identifies a plethora of troubling and problematic matters. However, it should not be read as telling the entire or final story. Unfortunately, the Examiner believes that the extent of the breakdowns at WorldCom will eventually be determined to extend even beyond the Examiner's findings and observations. . . .

Source: U.S. United States Bankruptcy Court, Southern District of New York. In re: WORLDCOM, INC, Debtors. *Second Interim Report of Dick Thornburgh, Bankruptcy Court Examiner.* Chapter 11, Case No. 02–15533. June 9, 2003. www.elawforworldcom.com/Worldcomdefault.asp (accessed February 5, 2004).

Census Bureau on Increases in the Hispanic Population

June 18, 2003

INTRODUCTION

The U.S. Census Bureau on June 18 officially declared the Hispanic population to be the largest minority group in the United States. There were 38.8 million Hispanics in the United States in July 2002—13 percent of the total population. The African American population, which had been the largest minority for decades, numbered 38.3 million. The Census Bureau counted all people in the United States, including illegal immigrants, most of whom were Hispanic. According to one estimate, about 35–45 percent of all foreign-born Hispanic adults in the United States—about 5 million people—had entered the country illegally.

The Census Bureau had been anticipating that Hispanics would overtake blacks as the largest minority group since the 2000 Census showed that the Hispanic population had grown by 60 percent in the 1990s, from 22 million in 1990 to 35 million in 2000. Between April 1, 2000, and July 1, 2002, Hispanics added 3.5 million to their numbers, a little more than half through immigration and the rest through what the bureau called "natural increase," the difference between births and deaths. The growth rate was nearly 9 percent—four times the growth rate for the U.S. population overall.

"This is an important event in this country—an event that we know is the result of the growth of a vibrant and diverse population that is vital to America's future," said Charles Louis Kincannon, director of the Census Bureau, announcing the finding to the convention of the League of United Latin American Citizens in Orlando, Florida. Similar sentiments were expressed by Roberto Suro, director of the Pew Hispanic Center. "If you consider that the black-white divide has been the basic social construct in American history for 300 years, this marks a change. This is the official reminder that we are moving into new territory."

That territory was not easy to define, largely because the Hispanic population was a diverse mix culturally, geographically, and racially. While most Hispanics were of Mexican origin, there were significant populations from

Cuba, the Caribbean, and Central and South America. Although often considered a community of immigrants who flowed back and forth across the Mexican border between jobs on one side and their families on the other, the fact was that 60 percent Hispanics were born in the United States and thus were automatically U.S. citizens. Although Hispanics were still geographically concentrated in the Southwest and Florida, they were moving in increasing numbers to areas where they had previously not lived. North Carolina, Arkansas, and Georgia had the highest percentage growth rates in Hispanic populations in the 1990s, and Hispanic populations more than doubled in seven midwestern states.

Hispanics were an increasingly influential component of American society. Hispanic authors, musicians, and movie stars had all gained wide mainstream acceptance. Mexican restaurants and fast-food chains were spread across the country. Spanish phrases and slang were commonplace. Makers of consumer goods were pitching their products specifically to Hispanic audiences. Hispanics were being elected and appointed to local, state, and national positions in ever-increasing numbers. Non-Hispanic members of Congress with large Latino constituencies were taking Spanish classes. But Hispanics as a group also confronted some significant problems, including relatively high levels of unemployment and poverty and low levels of education. Hispanics who came into the country illegally also faced the difficulty of living in fear of discovery and deportation, possibly being forced to leave behind an American family.

It remained to be seen whether Hispanics could translate their numbers into political power. Although the majority of Hispanics identified themselves as Democratic, they did not tend to vote as a block. In the 2000 presidential election, for example, about 35 percent voted for Republican George W. Bush. In the October 2003 recall election in California, exit polls showed that while 54 percent of Hispanics voted against recalling Democratic governor Gray Davis, only 52 percent voted for Democratic lieutenant governor Cruz Bustamante, a third-generation Mexican-American, to replace him. Even though he had pledged to overturn a state law that would have allowed illegal immigrants to obtain state driver's licenses, 30 percent of Hispanics voted for the winner, movie star Arnold Schwarzenegger, himself an immigrant. "A significant segment of the Latino community felt that it was time for a change, just like the rest of California," explained Marcelo Gaete of the National Association of Latino elected and Appointed Officials Educational Fund. *(California recall election, p. 1005)*

Diversity among Hispanics

In tandem with Kincannon's announcement, the Census Bureau released "The Hispanic Population in the United States, 2002," a report based on data from the Annual Demographic Supplement to the March 2002 Current Population survey. The report said that almost 67 percent of Hispanics were of Mexican origin, slightly more than 14 percent were originally from Central and South America, nearly 9 percent were from Puerto Rico, and nearly 4 percent from Cuba. Mexican Hispanics tended to live in the West and South, Puerto Ricans in the Northeast, and Cubans in the South. Nearly 46 percent of all Hispanics lived in central cities and about the same proportion lived outside a central city but within a metropolitan area. Only about 9 percent lived outside a metropolitan area.

More than 34 percent of Hispanics in the United States were under eighteen, making the group younger than either whites or blacks. Less than 60 percent of Hispanics twenty-five and older had graduated from high school; 11 percent had college degrees. But 27 percent had not completed ninth grade. Mexicans were less likely than other Hispanics to have graduated from high school. Hispanics were more likely than non-Hispanic whites to be unemployed and to live in poverty. In March 2002, when the data for the report were collected, 8.1 percent of Hispanics were jobless compared with 5.1 percent for non-Hispanic whites.

A Closer Look

Surveys and studies released in 2003 attempted to paint a more detailed picture of the Hispanic community. One report, released by the Lewis Mumford Center for Comparative Urban and Regional Research at the State University of New York in Albany, looked at differences among Hispanics based on their race. Although Hispanics were considered a single ethnic group by the Census Bureau, they were a diverse group racially. The 2000 Census was the first to ask people to classify themselves by both ethnicity and race. About 50 percent of all Hispanics classified themselves as white, about 3 percent classified themselves as black, and the remaining 47 percent considered themselves "some other race." About 97 percent of those who called themselves "some other race" said they were Latino, a classification that usually implied some indigenous Indian ancestry. The Census Bureau, however, used the terms *Latino* and *Hispanic* interchangeably.

The study by the Lewis Mumford Center found distinct differences among the three racial categorizations that suggested black and "other race" Hispanics faced more barriers than did white Hispanics. For example, white Hispanics had higher incomes and lower jobless rates than either black Hispanics or those who said they were some other race, while black Hispanics were better educated. Median household income for white Hispanics was $39,900, the report said, about $5,000 more than the median income for black Hispanics and $2,500 more than for Hispanics of some other race. The jobless rate was 8 percent for white Hispanics, 10 percent for those of "other race," and 12 percent for black Hispanics. But black Hispanics were better educated, averaging twelve years of school, compared with eleven for white Hispanics and ten for Hispanics in the "other race" category. "The point of the report," said its lead researcher, "is that if we take seriously the way people talk about their race, and the reality of their lives, we find that there are real distinctions between white and black Latinos and Hispanics who say they are some other race."

A spokeswoman for the National Council of LaRaza, a Latino civil rights and research organization, said the study confirmed "what we've been saying all along: that Latinos who come to the U.S. are affected by how Americans view race." Suro of the Pew Hispanic Center was not so quick to agree, saying that researchers needed to consider nationality as well as race. His group had earlier released a study showing that a majority of Hispanics identified more closely with their country of origin than with their racial identity.

A *New York Times*/CBS poll conducted in mid-July 2003 found that nearly 70 percent of foreign-born Hispanics said they identified more with the United States than with their country of origin. More than 65 percent said they could not recall a specific instance where they felt discriminated against because of their ethnicity. More than 65 percent also said they came to the United States in search of work and economic opportunity, compared with 9 percent who said freedoms were their primary incentive and 6 percent who said they were looking for a different culture or lifestyle. About 80 percent said they took jobs that American workers did not want.

Politically, the poll found that Hispanics were about twice as likely to call themselves Democrats as Republicans and to believe that the Democratic Party was more likely to be responsive to their needs. But Hispanics also tended to be more conservative than many Democrats on social issues, such as homosexuality and abortion. They also favored tax cuts and school vouchers, two issues widely endorsed by Republicans.

The poll also found that Hispanics were more optimistic about the future than non-Hispanics. Asked if they thought life for the next generation would be better or worse than life today, 64 percent of Hispanics born in the United States and 83 percent of foreign-born Hispanics said it would be better. Only 39 percent of non-Hispanics thought life would be better for their children.

A study by the Pew Hispanic Center, released in October, looked at the changing demographics within the Hispanic community and found that by 2020 the children of immigrants would emerge as the largest sector within the ethnic group. That shift, the study said, a result of the high fertility rate among Hispanic immigrants, would have a "very sizeable impact" on schools and the labor force. According to the study, second-generation Hispanics (those born in the United States but having at least one foreign parent) would increase in size from 28 percent of the Hispanic population in 2000 to 47 percent in 2020. As a result, the number of Hispanics in American schools was expected to double, from 4.4 million in 2000 to 9.0 million in 2020. At the same time, Hispanics were expected to account for more than half of the increase in the labor force during the twenty-year period. An additional 12.6 million Hispanic workers were expected to enter the labor force by 2020, compared with just 11.6 million non-Hispanic workers. Second-generation Hispanics were projected to make up nearly half of the increase in the Hispanic workforce and almost a quarter of the increase in the total workforce.

The report observed that second-generation Hispanics were likely to be substantially bilingual, unlike their first-generation parents who were predominantly Spanish-speakers. The second generation was also likely to be better educated, and these differences in language and education were likely to make second-generation Latinos higher wage earners than their parents. But the report also cautioned that more than 60 percent of the second generation was still younger than eighteen and thus much remained to be determined about their future. In particular, the report observed that "their ultimate educational profile, and hence their economic status, will be determined largely by the course of an education system that is facing demands for change at almost every level." The study did make one prediction with certainty: Given the numbers of second-generation Hispanics, "their future will be a matter of national interest."

Following are excerpts from "The Hispanic Population in the United States: March 2002," a report released June 18, 2003, by the Census Bureau in conjunction with the official announcement that Hispanics were now the largest minority group in the United States.

"The Hispanic Population in the United States: March 2002"

This report describes the Hispanic population in the United States in 2002, providing a profile of demographic and socioeconomic characteristics, such as geographic distribution, age, educational attainment, earnings, and poverty status. These characteristics are compared with those of the non-Hispanic White population, and because Hispanics are a heterogeneous group, variability within the Hispanic population is also discussed. The findings are based on data collected by the Census Bureau in the Annual Demographic Supplement to the March 2002 Current Population Survey (CPS).

People of Hispanic origin were able to report their origin as Mexican, Puerto Rican, Cuban, Central and South American, or some other Latino origin on the CPS questionnaire. Hispanics may be of any race.

Population Size and Composition

More than one in eight people in the United States are of Hispanic origin.
In 2002, there were 37.4 million Latinos in the civilian noninstitutional population of the United States, representing 13.3 percent of the total. Among the Hispanic population, two-thirds (66.9 percent) were of Mexican origin, 14.3 percent were Central and South American, 8.6 percent were Puerto Rican, 3.7 percent were Cuban, and the remaining 6.5 percent were of other Hispanic origins.

Hispanics are more geographically concentrated than non-Hispanic Whites.
Hispanics were more likely than non-Hispanic Whites to reside in the West and the South and less likely to live in the Northeast and the Midwest. In 2002, the regional distribution of the Hispanic population ranged from 44.2 percent in the West to 7.7 percent in the Midwest, while the distribution of non-Hispanic Whites ranged from 33.3 percent in the South to 19.2 percent in the West.

Latinos of Mexican origin were more likely to live in the West (54.6 percent) and the South (34.3 percent); Puerto Ricans were most likely to live in the Northeast (58.0 percent); and Cubans were highly concentrated in the South (75.1 percent). Most Central and South Americans were found in three of the four regions: the Northeast (31.5 percent) the South (34.0 percent), and the West (29.9 percent).

Hispanics are more likely than non-Hispanic Whites to live inside central cities of metropolitan areas.
Nearly half of all Hispanics lived in central cities within a metropolitan area (45.6 percent) compared with slightly more than one-fifth of non-Hispanic Whites (21.1 percent). In 2002, 45.7 percent of Hispanics lived outside central cities but within a metropolitan area, compared with 56.8 percent of non-Hispanic Whites. The percentage of Hispanics living in nonmetropolitan areas (8.7 percent) was much smaller than the percentage of non-Hispanic Whites (22.1 percent). Among Latino groups, Puerto Ricans were more likely than other groups to live in a

central city within a metropolitan area (57.4 percent), while Cubans were more likely than other groups to live outside the central city but within a metropolitan area (76.9 percent).

Hispanics are more likely than non-Hispanic Whites to be under age 18.
In 2002, 34.4 percent of Hispanics were under 18, compared with 22.8 percent of non-Hispanic Whites. Relatively few Latinos were 65 and older (5.1 percent), in contrast with non-Hispanic Whites (14.4 percent). In addition, a smaller proportion of Hispanics than non-Hispanic Whites were 18 to 64 (60.5 percent compared with 62.9 percent, respectively); and conversely, a larger proportion of the Hispanic population than the non-Hispanic White population were 25 to 44: 33.2 percent compared with 28.4 percent, respectively. Among Hispanics, 14.3 percent were 45 to 64, while 25.7 percent of non-Hispanic Whites were these ages.

Among Latinos, the Mexican-origin population had the highest proportion under age 18 (37.1 percent), and the Cuban origin population had the lowest (19.6 percent). The proportion 65 and older ranged from approximately 4.0 percent for Mexicans to 22.6 percent for Cubans.

Two in five Hispanics are foreign born.
In 2002, 40.2 percent (or 15 million) of the Hispanic population in the United States was foreign born. Among the foreign-born Hispanic population in 2002, 52.1 percent entered the United States between 1990 and 2002, another 25.6 percent came in the 1980s, and the remainder (22.3 percent) entered before 1980.

Although 73.3 percent of those who entered before 1970 had obtained citizenship by 2002, only 29.9 percent of those who entered between 1980 and 1989, and 7.3 percent of those who entered between 1990 and 2002 had become citizens by 2002.

Family Household Size and Marital Status

Hispanics live in family households that tend to be larger than those of non-Hispanic Whites.
In 2002, 26.5 percent of family households in which a Hispanic person was the householder consisted of five or more people. In contrast, only 10.8 percent of non-Hispanic White family households were this large. Among Hispanic family households, Mexican family households were most likely to have five or more people (30.8 percent).

Family households with only two people represented 25.9 percent of Hispanic family households but 48.7 percent of non-Hispanic White family households. Among Hispanics, Cuban family households were most likely to have only two people (43.1 percent).

Among the population aged 15 years and older, Hispanics were more likely never to have been married than non-Hispanic Whites (36.3 percent compared with 24.5 percent, respectively), while non-Hispanic Whites were more likely to have been divorced than Hispanics (10.0 percent compared with 6.6 percent, respectively).

Educational Attainment

More than two in five Hispanics aged 25 and older have not graduated from high school.

The Hispanic population aged 25 and older was less likely to have graduated from high school than non-Hispanic Whites (57.0 percent and 88.7 percent, respectively). In addition, more than one-quarter of Hispanics had less than a ninth-grade education (27.0 percent), compared with only 4.0 percent of non-Hispanic Whites. The proportion with a bachelor's degree or more was much lower for Hispanics (11.1 percent) than for non-Hispanic Whites (29.4 percent).

Educational attainment varies among Hispanics.

Among Latinos 25 years and older, other Hispanics, Cubans, Puerto Ricans, and Central and South Americans were more likely to have at least graduated from high school (74.0 percent, 66.8 percent, 70.8 percent, and 64.7 percent, respectively) than were Mexicans (50.6 percent). Similarly, the proportion that had attained at least a bachelor's degree ranged from 18.6 percent for Cubans, 17.3 percent for Central and South Americans, and 19.7 percent for other Hispanics to 7.6 percent for Mexicans.

Economic Characteristics

Hispanics are much more likely than non-Hispanic Whites to be unemployed.

In March 2002, 8.1 percent of Hispanics in the civilian labor force aged 16 and older were unemployed, compared with only 5.1 percent of non-Hispanic Whites. Among Latino groups, 8.4 percent of Mexicans, 9.6 percent of Puerto Ricans, 6.8 percent of Central and South Americans, 6.1 percent of Cubans, and 8.6 percent of other Hispanics were unemployed.

Hispanics and non-Hispanic Whites have different occupational distributions.

In 2002, Hispanics were more likely than non-Hispanic Whites to work in service occupations (22.1 percent and 11.6 percent, respectively). In addition, Hispanics were twice as likely to be employed as operators and laborers than non-Hispanic Whites (20.8 percent and 10.9 percent, respectively). Conversely, only 14.2 percent of Hispanics were in managerial or professional occupations, compared with 35.1 percent of non-Hispanic Whites. Among Latino groups, Central and South Americans were more likely than other groups to work in service occupations (27.3 percent), while Mexicans were less likely than other groups to work in managerial or professional occupations (11.9 percent).

Hispanic workers earn less than non-Hispanic White workers.
Among full-time, year-round workers in 2002, 26.3 percent of Hispanics and 53.8 percent of non-Hispanic Whites earned $35,000 or more. Among Latino full-time, year-round workers, Mexicans had the lowest proportion earning $35,000 or more.

In addition, the proportion of workers making $50,000 or more was 12.4 percent for Hispanics, compared with 31.8 percent for non-Hispanic Whites. Mexicans had the lowest proportion of workers earning $50,000 or more (10.6 percent).

Hispanics are more likely than non-Hispanic Whites to live in poverty.
In 2002, 21.4 percent of Hispanics were living in poverty, compared with 7.8 percent of non-Hispanic Whites. Hispanics represented 13.3 percent of the total population but constituted 24.3 percent of the population living in poverty. In addition, Hispanic children younger than 18 years of age were much more likely than non-Hispanic White children to be living in poverty (28.0 percent compared with 9.5 percent, respectively). Hispanic children represented 17.7 percent of all children in the United States but constituted 30.4 percent of all children in poverty.

Source: Ramirez, Roberto R., and G. Patricia de la Cruz. "The Hispanic Population in the United States: March 2002." *Current Population Reports,* P20–545. U.S. Census Bureau, Washington D.C. June 18, 2003. www.census.gov/prod/2003pubs/p20-545.pdf (accessed June 20, 2003).

Supreme Court on Affirmative Action

June 23, 2003

INTRODUCTION

In what some observers said were the most important civil rights rulings in a generation, the Supreme Court on June 23, 2003, endorsed the use of affirmative action, under limited conditions, in university and college admissions. In a pair of split decisions, the Supreme Court said universities could use race as a "plus factor" in admissions policies aimed at creating a diverse student body so long as each application was evaluated individually and race was not used in a "mechanical way."

By a 5–4 vote, the Court approved the University of Michigan's use of race to ensure that its law school enrolled a "critical mass" of African Americans, Hispanics, and Native Americans because each applicant was reviewed individually, and the law school did not set explicit quotas for the number of minorities to be admitted. At the same time, the Court, by a 6–3 vote, struck down as an impermissible quota system the university's undergraduate admissions program because it automatically awarded a set number of points to minority applicants.

The rulings represented the first time the Court had addressed the issue of affirmative action in higher education since the landmark case of *University of California Regents v. Bakke* in 1978, which outlawed fixed quotas but seemed to permit the consideration of race as a factor in admissions. Some commentators observed that between the *Bakke* decision in 1978 and the Court's decisions in 2003, the debate about affirmative action had shifted from arguing about how best to overcome decades of racial discrimination to how best to ensure a racially and ethnically diverse student body. Justice Sandra Day O'Connor unequivocally endorsed diversity as a compelling government interest in her majority opinion upholding the consideration of race as a factor in admissions to Michigan's law school. "In order to cultivate a set of leaders with legitimacy in the eyes of the citizenry, it is necessary that the path to leadership be visibly open to talented and qualified individuals of every race and ethnicity," O'Connor wrote.

O'Connor's statement was lauded by dozens of corporations, including some of the largest in the country, which had filed legal briefs supporting the university. These businesses stressed the need for racial and ethnic diversity in the nation's colleges and universities if companies were to compete successfully in the global marketplace. Prominent members of the armed forces cited a similar need to ensure a successful military, while professional organizations argued that diversity among doctors, lawyers, and other professionals was needed to ensure that minority populations were well served.

The four dissenters in the law school case and some constitutional scholars complained that the rulings just made the whole issue more opaque, allowing schools to obfuscate what were still clearly racial preferences. Other commentators noted that the two decisions and the many concurring and dissenting opinions written by the justices in the two cases reflected society's unease with the issue. "There is a deep yearning in the public and especially among elites that this issue sort of go away, so we don't have to face the terrible trade-offs between the desire for proportional representation in our elite institutions on the one hand and the vastly unequal levels of preparation and credentialing among different racial groups," Yale University law professor Peter Schuck told the *New York Times.*

The Center for Individual Rights, which brought the legal challenge to Michigan's policies, said it planned to monitor changes in university admissions policies and perhaps challenge any school that said it was considering applications individually but still using a "mechanistic system" of the sort the Court barred. Ward Connerly, a wealthy Sacramento businessman, said, "It may be time for us to pay a visit to the state of Michigan and let the voters decide if they want to use race as a factor in admissions. The Court said they may use race, they didn't say they *have* to use race." Connerly announced on July 8 that he was proceeding with an effort to put an initiative barring affirmative action programs on Michigan's 2004 ballot. Connerly had sponsored the successful California referendum in 1996 in which voters ended state affirmative action programs. Washington state voters adopted a similar restriction in 1998, and Florida banned race as a factor in college admissions in 2000.

The Administration's Balancing Act

That affirmative action remained a politically potent issue was reflected in the Bush administration's careful balancing act regarding the Michigan cases. The federal government was not a party to the case and was under no obligation to file a brief. But Bush came under intense pressure from both those supporting and opposing the Michigan admissions policies to take a stand on such an important issue. His decision was made all the more sensitive because the briefs in the case were due in mid-January, just a month after the White House had engineered the ouster of Republican Senate leader Trent Lott of Mississippi, who had made public comments that appeared to endorse racial segregation. *(Lott resignation, Historic Documents of 2002, p. 969)*

Speaking from the White House on January 15, 2003, Bush announced that although he supported "diversity of all kinds," his administration would support the challenge to the Michigan admissions policies because they amounted to racial quotas that were "divisive, unfair, and impossible to square with the Constitution." Predictably, those comments won praise from Bush's core conservative Republican supporters and condemnation from civil rights groups, some of whom observed that Bush himself benefited from a form of affirmative action as a "legacy" admission at Yale University, from which his father and grandfather graduated. But Bush's comments supporting diversity and opposing quotas also seemed designed to appeal to voters in the middle of the spectrum, who, according to most opinion polls, tended to oppose racial quotas and preferences when they were labeled as such but to approve of diversity as a societal goal.

At the same time, the brief the administration filed was far less sweeping than the president's remarks might have led listeners to understand. Instead of directly calling on the Supreme Court to overturn *Bakke* altogether or discussing whether diversity was such a "compelling government interest" that it justified considering race as a factor in admissions, the brief simply argued that the admissions policies were unconstitutional because the university could have achieved the same goal of diversity using race-neutral policies. The hard edge of Bush's comments also may have been softened when the two most prominent blacks in his administration, Secretary of State Colin Powell and National Security Advisor Condoleezza Rice, publicly announced their disagreement with Bush's position.

In the wake of the Court's decision, Bush released a carefully worded statement in which he applauded "the Supreme Court for recognizing the value of diversity on our nation's campuses" and noted that the "decisions seek a careful balance between the goal of campus diversity and the fundamental principle of equal treatment under the law."

Remedying Past Discrimination and Ensuring Diversity

Before its rulings in the Michigan cases, the Court had last ruled on affirmative action in university admissions in 1978 when it struck down the admissions policy at the University of California medical school at Berkeley because it explicitly reserved sixteen out of one hundred slots for minorities. Six separate opinions were written, none of which were endorsed by a majority of the Court. Four justices would have upheld the admissions policy on the grounds that race could be considered to remedy past racial discrimination. Four other justices would have overturned the admissions policy as a violation of the Civil Rights Act of 1964, without addressing the constitutionality of the admissions policy. The ninth justice, Lewis F. Powell Jr., cast the decisive vote striking down the admissions policy as a violation of both the Civil Rights Act and the Equal Protection Clause of the Constitution. In his opinion, Powell held that a diverse student body was a compelling state interest that justified use of race as "one element in a range of factors a university properly may consider" in deciding whom to admit. Although no other justice signed Powell's opinion, it gradually became the foundation of admissions policies used by public and private colleges and universities across the nation.

In the ensuring years, the Supreme Court began narrowing the reach of affirmative action programs in other venues such as the workplace. Those decisions raised uncertainty that the Powell decision in *Bakke* would stand if the Supreme Court were to revisit the issue. That uncertainty was increased in 1996 when the Court let stand an appeals court ruling striking down an affirmative action plan the University of Texas's law school used to ensure racial diversity among its students. In the case of *Hopwood v. Texas*, the appeals court said that achieving a racially diverse student body was not a compelling state interest under the Fourteenth Amendment of the Constitution. The appeals court acknowledged Powell's opinion but said that the Court's later rulings had raised doubts about its validity.

In response to the *Hopwood* decision, Texas developed an admissions policy that guaranteed a slot in the state university system to any high school student, regardless of race, who graduated in the 10 percent of the class. Bush was governor of Texas at the time. Florida and California followed similar policies. In addition, in California and Texas applicants' socioeconomic status was taken into consideration, with students from poor neighborhoods or low-income families or with parents who did not attend college given extra weight. Studies had generally found that these policies achieved a significant degree of diversity in undergraduate schools but were much less effective at the graduate level.

Given the seeming contradiction between Powell's opinion in the *Bakke* case and the *Hopwood* decision, it appeared to be only a matter of time before another challenge was lodged against the use of race in college admissions. When that challenge came, however, American society had undergone a noticeable change in its attitudes about race, one that reflected its experience with an increasingly diverse American population as well as with globalization. The nation's major corporations and military establishments, which generally had been slow to embrace racial integration, increasingly recognized the value of racial and ethnic diversity in their ranks and were actively recruiting qualified blacks, Hispanics, Asians, women, and other minorities. A diverse workforce helped companies avoid discrimination suits, but it also gave companies entrée to and credibility in markets previously closed to them not only in the United States but around the world.

Unlike in 1978, when few companies took an active role in the *Bakke* case, more than 300 companies, professional associations, labor unions, and military officers signed on to friend-of-the-Court briefs attesting to the need for a diverse and well-educated workforce. Among the companies were Microsoft, Bank One, General Motors, Coca Cola, General Mills, 3M, ChevronTexaco, Pfizer, and Johnson and Johnson. Military leaders filing briefs in support of the university included two former defense secretaries, William Perry and William Cohen; three former chairmen of the Joint Chiefs of Staff, Admiral William Crowe, General John M. Shalikashvili, and General Hugh Shelton; and retired general Norman Schwarzkopf.

Consideration of Race a Permissible Factor

The test of Justice Powell's premise that diversity justified the use of racial preferences under narrowly tailored circumstances came in a pair of cases involving two different admissions policies at the University of Michigan, one used in the law school and the other in the undergraduate program. The law school admissions policy at issue in the case of *Grutter v. Bollinger* required that each application be assessed not only on academic ability but on the applicant's talents, experiences, and potential based on a number of factors including how an applicant might contribute to diversity on campus. The policy did not define diversity, but it did confirm a commitment to enrolling a "critical mass" of African Americans, Hispanics, and Native Americans.

Writing for the majority, Justice O'Connor reaffirmed Powell's view that attaining diversity in a university setting was a compelling state interest. "Effective participation by members of all racial and ethnic groups in the civil life of our nation is essential of the dream of one nation, indivisible, is to be realized," she wrote. She also rejected arguments that the law school admission policy was at base a quota system. The law school undertook a "highly individualized, holistic review of each applicant's file," O'Connor wrote, in which race counted as a "plus" factor but was not treated in a "mechanical way." O'Connor's opinion was endorsed by Justices John Paul Stevens, David H. Souter, Ruth Bader Ginsburg, and Stephen G. Breyer.

Writing the main dissent for himself and Justices Anthony M. Kennedy, Antonin Scalia, and Clarence Thomas, Chief Justice William H. Rehnquist argued that the law school's goal of achieving a critical mass of underrepresented minority students was tantamount to a constitutionally impermissible quota. The policy, he said, was "a carefully managed program designed to ensure proportionate representation of applicants from selected minority groups."

The case of *Gratz v. Bollinger* challenged the admissions policies at the university's undergraduate school. That policy awarded 20 points, out of 150, for applicants who were members of underrepresented minority groups—African Americans, Hispanics, and American Indians. Specific numbers of points were also awarded for other factors, such as alumni connections and athletics. A student who scored 100 points was guaranteed entry to the university's main undergraduate school. The inclusion of points for race meant that nearly all qualified minority applicants were admitted, while many qualified white applicants were turned away. Writing the majority opinion, Chief Justice Rehnquist said this policy did not provide the "individualized consideration" that the *Bakke* decision required. O'Connor, who wrote a concurring opinion, underlined that point, saying that unlike the law school admission policy, the undergraduate policy was a "nonindividualized, mechanical one." Scalia, Kennedy, and Thomas joined Rehnquist's opinion. Breyer agreed with the majority's judgment but not with its reasoning. Souter, Stevens, and Ginsburg all dissented, but did not agree on the reasoning underlying their dissents.

A Road Map to Follow

Most large public universities expressed relief that the Court had upheld the limited use of race in college admissions. Although many universities already followed practices that they said would pass constitutional scrutiny under the Court's rulings, they nonetheless were pleased to have the constitutionality of those practices confirmed. University of Michigan president Mary Sue Coleman called the rulings a "tremendous victory" and said the Court "provided two important signals. The first is a green light to pursue diversity in the college classroom. The second is a road map to get us there." On August 28 the school announced that it was instituting an undergraduate admissions policy similar to the one used by the law school. Academic achievement, including high school grades and curriculum and test scores, would be given the highest priority, but race would still be a factor. Coleman estimated that abandoning the point system to evaluate the 25,000 applications the college received to fill 5,000 freshman slots would cost an additional $1.5–2 million.

The University of Texas announced that it was considering reinstating its race-conscious admissions policies in both graduate and undergraduate admissions in time for the start of the 2004–2005 school year. Officials said the university would retain its race-neutral policy of admitting the top students from each of the state's high schools. The Court's rulings also appeared to resolve a dilemma for Louisiana State University, which was subject both to the *Hopwood* decision barring affirmative action and to a separate federal district court order requiring desegregation.

Several conservative organizations said the rulings showed the importance of ensuring that the next appointment to the Supreme Court was opposed to affirmative action. "It's outrageous that the majority in favor of these racial preferences was formed by Republican appointees," said Clint Bullock, vice president of the Institute for Justice, which joined in the challenge to Michigan's policies. "Conservatives will want to make sure that anyone appointed to the court in this administration is a strong and sure opponent of racial preferences."

Following are excerpts from the main majority and dissenting opinions in the case of Grutter v. Bollinger, *in which the Supreme Court ruled 5–4 that achieving a diverse student body was a compelling state interest that justified the use of race as one of several considerations in admitting students so long as applications were evaluated individually and race was not used in a "mechanical way"; and from the majority opinion in the case of* Gratz v. Bollinger, *in which the Court struck down, 6–3, the University of Michigan's undergraduate admissions policy because its point system automatically awarded a set number of points to minority students, making it an impermissible quota system. The decisions were handed down June 23, 2003.*

Grutter v. Bollinger

No. 02–241

Barbara Grutter, Petitioner	On writ of certiorari to the
v.	United States Court of Appeals
Lee Bollinger et al.	for the Sixth Circuit

[June 23, 2003]

JUSTICE O'CONNOR delivered the opinion of the Court.

This case requires us to decide whether the use of race as a factor in student admissions by the University of Michigan Law School (Law School) is unlawful.

I

A

The Law School ranks among the Nation's top law schools. It receives more than 3,500 applications each year for a class of around 350 students.

Seeking to "admit a group of students who individually and collectively are among the most capable," the Law School looks for individuals with "substantial promise for success in law school" and "a strong likelihood of succeeding in the practice of law and contributing in diverse ways to the well-being of others.". . . More broadly, the Law School seeks "a mix of students with varying backgrounds and experiences who will respect and learn from each other.". . . In 1992, the dean of the Law School charged a faculty committee with crafting a written admissions policy to implement these goals. In particular, the Law School sought to ensure that its efforts to achieve student body diversity complied with this Court's most recent ruling on the use of race in university admissions (*Regents of University of California v. Bakke* (1978)]. . . . Upon the unanimous adoption of the committee's report by the Law School faculty, it became the Law School's official admissions policy.

The hallmark of that policy is its focus on academic ability coupled with a flexible assessment of applicants' talents, experiences, and potential "to contribute to the learning of those around them.". . . The policy requires admissions officials to evaluate each applicant based on all the information available in the file, including a personal statement, letters of recommendation, and an essay describing the ways in which the applicant will contribute to the life and diversity of the Law School. . . . In reviewing an applicant's file, admissions officials must consider the applicant's undergraduate grade point average (GPA) and Law School Admissions Test (LSAT) score because they are important (if imperfect) predictors of academic success in law school. . . . The policy stresses that "no applicant should be admitted unless we expect that applicant to do well enough to graduate with no serious academic problems.". . .

The policy makes clear, however, that even the highest possible score does not guarantee admission to the Law School. . . . Nor does a low score automatically disqualify an applicant. . . . Rather, the policy requires admissions officials to look beyond grades and test scores to other criteria that are important to the Law School's educational objectives. . . . So-called " 'soft' variables" such as "the enthusiasm of recommenders, the quality of the undergraduate institution, the quality of the applicant's essay, and the areas and difficulty of undergraduate course selection" are all brought to bear in assessing an "applicant's likely contributions to the intellectual and social life of the institution.". . .

The policy aspires to "achieve that diversity which has the potential to enrich everyone's education and thus make a law school class stronger than the sum of its parts.". . . The policy does not restrict the types of diversity contributions eligible for "substantial weight" in the admissions process, but instead recognizes "many possible bases for diversity admissions.". . . The policy does, however, reaffirm the Law School's longstanding

commitment to "one particular type of diversity," that is, "racial and ethnic diversity with special reference to the inclusion of students from
groups which have been historically discriminated against, like African-
Americans, Hispanics and Native Americans, who without this commitment might not be represented in our student body in meaningful numbers.". . . By enrolling a " 'critical mass' of [underrepresented] minority
students," the Law School seeks to "ensur[e] their ability to make unique
contributions to the character of the Law School.". . .

The policy does not define diversity "solely in terms of racial and ethnic status.". . . Nor is the policy "insensitive to the competition among
all students for admission to the [L]aw [S]chool.". . . Rather, the policy
seeks to guide admissions officers in "producing classes both diverse and
academically outstanding, classes made up of students who promise to
continue the tradition of outstanding contribution by Michigan Graduates to the legal profession.". . .

B

Petitioner Barbara Grutter is a white Michigan resident who applied to
the Law School in 1996 with a 3.8 grade point average and 161 LSAT
score. The Law School initially placed petitioner on a waiting list, but
subsequently rejected her application. In December 1997, petitioner filed
suit. . . . Petitioner alleged that respondents discriminated against her on
the basis of race in violation of the Fourteenth Amendment; Title VI of
the Civil Rights Act of 1964, 78 Stat. 252, 42 U.S.C. § 2000d; and
Rev. Stat. § 1977, as amended, 42 U.S.C. § 1981.

Petitioner further alleged that her application was rejected because the
Law School uses race as a "predominant" factor, giving applicants who
belong to certain minority groups "a significantly greater chance of admission than students with similar credentials from disfavored racial groups.". . .
Petitioner also alleged that respondents "had no compelling interest to justify their use of race in the admissions process.". . . Petitioner requested
compensatory and punitive damages, an order requiring the Law School to
offer her admission, and an injunction prohibiting the Law School from
continuing to discriminate on the basis of race. . . .

During the 15-day bench trial [before the District Court], the parties
introduced extensive evidence concerning the Law School's use of race in
the admissions process. Dennis Shields, Director of Admissions when
petitioner applied to the Law School, testified that he did not direct his
staff to admit a particular percentage or number of minority students,
but rather to consider an applicant's race along with all other factors. . . .
Shields testified that at the height of the admissions season, he would
frequently consult the so-called "daily reports" that kept track of the

racial and ethnic composition of the class (along with other information such as residency status and gender). . . . This was done, Shields testified, to ensure that a critical mass of underrepresented minority students would be reached so as to realize the educational benefits of a diverse student body. . . . Shields stressed, however, that he did not seek to admit any particular number or percentage of underrepresented minority students. . . .

Erica Munzel, who succeeded Shields as Director of Admissions, testified that " 'critical mass' " means " 'meaningful numbers' " or " 'meaningful representation,' " which she understood to mean a number that encourages underrepresented minority students to participate in the classroom and not feel isolated. . . . Munzel stated there is no number, percentage, or range of numbers or percentages that constitute critical mass. . . . Munzel also asserted that she must consider the race of applicants because a critical mass of underrepresented minority students could not be enrolled if admissions decisions were based primarily on undergraduate GPAs and LSAT scores. . . .

The current Dean of the Law School, Jeffrey Lehman, also testified. . . . When asked about the extent to which race is considered in admissions, Lehman testified that it varies from one applicant to another. . . . In some cases, according to Lehman's testimony, an applicant's race may play no role, while in others it may be a " 'determinative' " factor. . . .

The District Court heard extensive testimony from Professor Richard Lempert, who chaired the faculty committee that drafted the 1992 policy. Lempert emphasized that the Law School seeks students with diverse interests and backgrounds to enhance classroom discussion and the educational experience both inside and outside the classroom. . . . When asked about the policy's " 'commitment to racial and ethnic diversity with special reference to the inclusion of students from groups which have been historically discriminated against,' " Lempert explained that this language did not purport to remedy past discrimination, but rather to include students who may bring to the Law School a perspective different from that of members of groups which have not been the victims of such discrimination. . . . Lempert acknowledged that other groups, such as Asians and Jews, have experienced discrimination, but explained they were not mentioned in the policy because individuals who are members of those groups were already being admitted to the Law School in significant numbers. . . .

Kent Syverud was the final witness to testify about the Law School's use of race in admissions decisions. Syverud was a professor at the Law School when the 1992 admissions policy was adopted and is now Dean of Vanderbilt Law School. In addition to his testimony at trial, Syverud submitted several expert reports on the educational benefits of diversity. Syverud's testimony indicated that when a critical mass of underrepresented minority students is present, racial stereotypes lose their force because nonminority students learn there is no " 'minority viewpoint' " but rather a variety of viewpoints among minority students. . . .

Dr. Stephen Raudenbush, the Law School's expert, focused on the predicted effect of eliminating race as a factor in the Law School's admission process. In Dr. Raudenbush's view, a race-blind admissions system would have a " 'very dramatic,' " negative effect on underrepresented minority admissions. . . . He testified that in 2000, 35 percent of underrepresented minority applicants were admitted. . . . Dr. Raudenbush predicted that if race were not considered, only 10 percent of those applicants would have been admitted. . . . Under this scenario, underrepresented minority students would have comprised 4 percent of the entering class in 2000 instead of the actual figure of 14.5 percent. . . .

In the end, the District Court concluded that the Law School's use of race as a factor in admissions decisions was unlawful. . . . Sitting en banc, the Court of Appeals reversed the District Court's judgment. . . . The Court of Appeals first held that Justice Powell's opinion in *Bakke* was binding precedent establishing diversity as a compelling state interest. . . . The Court of Appeals also held that the Law School's use of race was narrowly tailored because race was merely a "potential 'plus' factor" and because the law School's program was "virtually identical" to the Harvard admissions program described approvingly by Justice Powell and appended to his *Bakke* opinion. . . .

We granted certiorari . . . to resolve the disagreement among the Courts of Appeals on a question of national importance: Whether diversity is a compelling interest that can justify the narrowly tailored use of race in selecting applicants for admission to public universities. . . .

II

A

We last addressed the use of race in public higher education over 25 years ago. In the landmark *Bakke* case, we reviewed a racial set-aside program that reserved 16 out of 100 seats in a medical school class for members of certain minority groups. . . . The decision produced six separate opinions, none of which commanded a majority of the Court. Four Justices would have upheld the program against all attack on the ground that the government can use race to "remedy disadvantages cast on minorities by past racial prejudice.". . . . Four other Justices avoided the constitutional question altogether and struck down the program on statutory grounds. . . . Justice Powell provided a fifth vote not only for invalidating the set-aside program, but also for reversing the state court's injunction against any use of race whatsoever. The only holding for the Court in *Bakke* was that a "State has a substantial interest that legitimately may be served by a properly devised admissions program involving the competitive consideration of race and ethnic origin.". . . Thus, we reversed that part of the lower court's judgment that enjoined the university "from any consideration of the race of any applicant.". . .

Since this Court's splintered decision in *Bakke,* Justice Powell's opinion announcing the judgment of the Court has served as the touchstone for constitutional analysis of race-conscious admissions policies. Public and private universities across the Nation have modeled their own admissions programs on Justice Powell's views on permissible race-conscious policies. . . . We therefore discuss Justice Powell's opinion in some detail.

Justice Powell began by stating that "[t]he guarantee of equal protection cannot mean one thing when applied to one individual and something else when applied to a person of another color. If both are not accorded the same protection, then it is not equal.". . . In Justice Powell's view, when governmental decisions "touch upon an individual's race or ethnic background, he is entitled to a judicial determination that the burden he is asked to bear on that basis is precisely tailored to serve a compelling governmental interest.". . . Under this exacting standard, only one of the interests asserted by the university survived Justice Powell's scrutiny.

First, Justice Powell rejected an interest in " 'reducing the historic deficit of traditionally disfavored minorities in medical schools and in the medical profession' " as an unlawful interest in racial balancing. . . . Second, Justice Powell rejected an interest in remedying societal discrimination because such measures would risk placing unnecessary burdens on innocent third parties "who bear no responsibility for whatever harm the beneficiaries of the special admissions program are thought to have suffered.". . . Third, Justice Powell rejected an interest in "increasing the number of physicians who will practice in communities currently underserved," concluding that even if such an interest could be compelling in some circumstances the program under review was not "geared to promote that goal.". . .

Justice Powell approved the university's use of race to further only one interest: "the attainment of a diverse student body.". . . With the important proviso that "constitutional limitations protecting individual rights may not be disregarded," Justice Powell grounded his analysis in the academic freedom that "long has been viewed as a special concern of the First Amendment.". . . Justice Powell emphasized that nothing less than the " 'nation's future depends upon leaders trained through wide exposure' to the ideas and mores of students as diverse as this Nation of many peoples.". . .

Justice Powell was, however, careful to emphasize that in his view race "is only one element in a range of factors a university properly may consider in attaining the goal of a heterogeneous student body.". . . For Justice Powell, "[i]t is not an interest in simple ethnic diversity, in which a specified percentage of the student body is in effect guaranteed to be members of selected ethnic groups," that can justify the use of race. Rather, "[t]he diversity that furthers a compelling state interest encompasses a far broader array of qualifications and characteristics of which racial or ethnic origin is but a single though important element.". . .

. . . [F]or the reasons set out below, today we endorse Justice Powell's view that student body diversity is a compelling state interest that can justify the use of race in university admissions.

B

The Equal Protection Clause provides that no State shall "deny to any person within its jurisdiction the equal protection of the laws.". . . Because the Fourteenth Amendment "protect[s] *persons,* not *groups,*" all "governmental action based on race—a group classification long recognized as in most circumstances irrelevant and therefore prohibited— should be subjected to detailed judicial inquiry to ensure that the *personal* right to equal protection of the laws has not been infringed." We are a "free people whose institutions are founded upon the doctrine of equality.". . .

We have held that all racial classifications imposed by government "must be analyzed by a reviewing court under strict scrutiny.". . . This means that such classifications are constitutional only if they are narrowly tailored to further compelling governmental interests. "Absent searching judicial inquiry into the justification for such race-based measures," we have no way to determine what "classifications are 'benign' or 'remedial' and what classifications are in fact motivated by illegitimate notions of racial inferiority or simple racial politics.". . . We apply strict scrutiny to all racial classifications to " 'smoke out' illegitimate uses of race by assuring that [government] is pursuing a goal important enough to warrant use of a highly suspect tool.". . .

Context matters when reviewing race-based governmental action under the Equal Protection Clause. . . . In *Adarand Constructors, Inc. v. Pena* [1995], we made clear that strict scrutiny must take " 'relevant differences' into account.". . . Indeed as we explained, that is its "fundamental purpose. . . . Not every decision influenced by race is equally objectionable and strict scrutiny is designed to provide a framework for carefully examining the importance and the sincerity of the reasons advanced by the governmental decisionmaker for the use of race in that particular context.

III

A

With these principles in mind, we turn to the question whether the Law School's use of race is justified by a compelling state interest. Before this Court, as they have throughout this litigation, respondents assert only one justification for their use of race in the admissions process: obtaining "the educational benefits that flow from a diverse student body.".... In other words, the Law School asks us to recognize, in the context of higher education, a compelling state interest in student body diversity....

... Today, we hold that the Law School has a compelling interest in attaining a diverse student body.

The Law School's educational judgment that such diversity is essential to its educational mission is one to which we defer. The Law School's assessment that diversity will, in fact, yield educational benefits is substantiated by respondents and their *amici*....

We have long recognized that, given the important purpose of public education and the expansive freedoms of speech and thought associated with the university environment, universities occupy a special niche in our constitutional tradition.... In announcing the principle of student body diversity as a compelling state interest, Justice Powell invoked our cases recognizing a constitutional dimension, grounded in the First Amendment, of educational autonomy: "The freedom of a university to make its own judgments as to education includes the selection of its student body.".... From this premise, Justice Powell reasoned that by claiming "the right to select those students who will contribute the most to the 'robust exchange of ideas,'" a university "seek[s] to achieve a goal that is of paramount importance in the fulfillment of its mission.".... Our conclusion that the Law School has a compelling interest in a diverse student body is informed by our view that attaining a diverse student body is at the heart of the Law School's proper institutional mission, and that "good faith" on the part of a university is "presumed" absent "a showing to the contrary.".....

As part of its goal of "assembling a class that is both exceptionally academically qualified and broadly diverse," the Law School seeks to "enroll a 'critical mass' of minority students.".... The Law School's interest is not simply "to assure within its student body some specified percentage of a particular group merely because of its race or ethnic origin.".... That would amount to outright racial balancing, which is patently unconstitutional.... Rather, the Law School's concept of critical mass is defined by reference to the educational benefits that diversity is designed to produce.

These benefits are substantial. As the District Court emphasized, the Law School's admissions policy promotes "cross-racial understanding," helps to break down racial stereotypes, and "enables [students] to better understand persons of different races.". . . These benefits are "important and laudable," because "classroom discussion is livelier, more spirited, and simply more enlightening and interesting" when the students have "the greatest possible variety of backgrounds.". . .

The Law School's claim of a compelling interest is further bolstered by its *amici,* who point to the educational benefits that flow from student body diversity. In addition to the expert studies and reports entered into evidence at trial, numerous studies show that student body diversity promotes learning outcomes, and "better prepares students for an increasingly diverse workforce and society, and better prepares them as professionals.". . .

These benefits are not theoretical but real, as major American businesses have made clear that the skills needed in today's increasingly global marketplace can only be developed through exposure to widely diverse people, cultures, ideas, and viewpoints. . . . What is more, high-ranking retired officers and civilian leaders of the United States military assert that, "[b]ased on [their] decades of experience," a "highly qualified, racially diverse officer corps . . . is essential to the military's ability to fulfill its principle mission to provide national security.". . . The primary sources for the Nation's officer corps are the service academies and the Reserve Officers Training Corps (ROTC), the latter comprising students already admitted to participating colleges and universities. . . . At present, "the military cannot achieve an officer corps that is *both* highly qualified and racially diverse unless the service academies and the ROTC used limited race-conscious recruiting and admissions policies.". . . To fulfill its mission, the military "must be selective in admissions for training and education for the officer corps, *and* it must train and educate a highly qualified, racially diverse officer corps in a racially diverse setting.". . .

We have repeatedly acknowledged the overriding importance of preparing students for work and citizenship, describing education as pivotal to "sustaining our political and cultural heritage" with a fundamental role in maintaining the fabric of society. . . . This Court has long recognized that "education . . . is the very foundation of good citizenship.". . . For this reason, the diffusion of knowledge and opportunity through public institutions of higher education must be accessible to all individuals regardless of race or ethnicity. . . .

Effective participation by members of all racial and ethnic groups in the civic life of our Nation is essential if the dream of one Nation, indivisible, is to be realized.

Moreover, universities, and in particular, law schools, represent the training ground for a large number of our Nation's leaders. . . . Individuals with law degrees occupy roughly half the state governorships, more than half the seats in the United States Senate, and more than a third of the seats in the United States House of Representatives. . . .

In order to cultivate a set of leaders with legitimacy in the eyes of the citizenry, it is necessary that the path to leadership be visibly open to talented and qualified individuals of every race and ethnicity. All members of our heterogeneous society must have confidence in the openness and integrity of the educational institutions that provide this training. As we have recognized, law schools "cannot be effective in isolation from the individuals and institutions with which the law interacts.". . . Access to legal education (and thus the legal profession) must be inclusive of talented and qualified individuals of every race and ethnicity, so that all members of our heterogeneous society may participate in the educational institutions that provide the training and education necessary to succeed in America. . . .

B

Even in the limited circumstance when drawing racial distinctions is permissible to further a compelling state interest, government is still "constrained in how it may pursue that end: [T]he means chosen to accomplish the [government's] asserted purpose must be specifically and narrowly framed to accomplish that purpose.". . . The purpose of the narrow tailoring requirement is to ensure that "the means chosen 'fit' . . . th[e] compelling goal so closely that there is little or no possibility that the motive for the classification was illegitimate racial prejudice or stereotype.". . .

To be narrowly tailored, a race-conscious admissions program cannot use a quota system—it cannot "insulat[e] each category of applicants with certain desired qualifications from competition with all other applicants.". . . Instead, a university may consider race or ethnicity only as a "'plus' in a particular applicant's file," without "insulat[ing] the individual from comparison with all other candidates for the available seats.". . . In other words, an admissions program must be "flexible enough to consider all pertinent elements of diversity in light of the particular qualifications of each applicant, and to place them on the same footing for consideration, although not necessarily according them the same weight.". . .

We find that the Law School's admissions program bears the hallmarks of a narrowly tailored plan. As Justice Powell made clear in *Bakke,* truly individualized consideration demands that race be used in a flexible, nonmechanical way. It follows from this mandate that universities cannot establish quotas for members of certain racial groups or put members of those groups on separate admissions tracks. . . . Nor can universities insulate applicants who belong to certain racial or ethnic groups from the competition for admission. . . . Universities can, however, consider race or ethnicity more flexibly as a "plus" factor in the context of individualized consideration of each and every applicant. . . .

We are satisfied that the Law School's admissions program, like the Harvard plan described by Justice Powell, does not operate as a quota. Properly understood, a "quota" is a program in which a certain fixed number or proportion of opportunities are "reserved exclusively for certain minority groups.". . .

The Law School's goal of attaining a critical mass of underrepresented minority students does not transform its program into a quota. As the Harvard plan described by Justice Powell recognized, there is of course "some relationship between numbers and achieving the benefits to be derived from a diverse student body, and between numbers and providing a reasonable environment for those students admitted.". . . "[S]ome attention to numbers," without more, does not transform a flexible admissions system into a rigid quota. . . .

THE CHIEF JUSTICE believes that the Law School's policy conceals an attempt to achieve racial balancing, and cites admissions data to contend that the Law School discriminates among different groups within the critical mass. . . . But, as THE CHIEF JUSTICE concedes, the number of underrepresented minority students who ultimately enroll in the Law School differs substantially from their representation in the applicant pool and varies considerably for each group from year to year. . . .

That a race-conscious admissions program does not operate as a quota does not, by itself, satisfy the requirement of individualized consideration. When using race as a "plus" factor in university admissions, a university's admissions program must remain flexible enough to ensure that each applicant is evaluated as an individual and not in a way that makes an applicant's race or ethnicity the defining feature of his or her application. The importance of this individualized consideration in the context of a race-conscious admissions program is paramount. . . .

Here, the Law School engages in a highly individualized, holistic review of each applicant's file, giving serious consideration to all the ways an applicant might contribute to a diverse educational environment. The Law School affords this individualized consideration to applicants of all races. . . .

We also find that . . . the Law School's race-conscious admissions program adequately ensures that all factors that may contribute to student body diversity are meaningfully considered alongside race in admissions decisions. With respect to the use of race itself, all underrepresented minority students admitted by the Law School have been deemed qualified. By virtue of our Nation's struggle with racial inequality, such students are both likely to have experiences of particular importance to the Law School's mission, and less likely to be admitted in meaningful numbers on criteria that ignore those experiences. . . .

The Law School does not, however, limit in any way the broad range of qualities and experiences that may be considered valuable contributions to student body diversity. To the contrary, the 1992 policy makes clear "[t]here are many possible bases for diversity admissions," and provides examples of admittees who have lived or traveled widely abroad, are fluent in several languages, have overcome personal adversity and family hardship, have exceptional records of extensive community service, and have had successful careers in other fields. . . .

What is more, the Law School actually gives substantial weight to diversity factors besides race. The Law School frequently accepts nonminority applicants with grades and test scores lower than underrepresented minority applicants (and other nonminority applicants) who are rejected. . . . This shows that the Law School seriously weighs many other diversity factors besides race that can make a real and dispositive difference for nonminority applicants as well. By this flexible approach, the Law School sufficiently takes into account, in practice as well as in theory, a wide variety of characteristics besides race and ethnicity that contribute to a diverse student body. . . .

Petitioner and the United States argue that the Law School's plan is not narrowly tailored because race-neutral means exist to obtain the educational benefits of student body diversity that the Law School seeks. We disagree. Narrow tailoring does no require exhaustion of every conceivable race-neural alternative. Nor does is require a university to choose between maintaining a reputation for excellence or fulfilling a commitment to provide educational opportunities of all racial groups. . . .

We acknowledge that "there are serious problems of justice connected with the idea of preference itself.". . . Narrow tailoring, therefore, requires that a race-conscious admissions program not unduly harm members of any racial group. Even remedial race-based governmental action generally "remains subject to continuing oversight to assure that it will work the least harm possible to other innocent persons competing for the benefit.". . . To be narrowly tailored, a race-conscious admissions program must not "unduly burden individuals who are not members of the favored racial and ethnic groups.". . .

We are satisfied that the Law School's admissions program does not. Because the Law School considers "all pertinent elements of diversity," it can (and does) select nonminority applicants who have greater potential to enhance student body diversity over underrepresented minority applicants. . . . We agree that, in the context of its individualized inquiry into the possible diversity contributions of all applicants, the Law School's race-conscious admissions program does not unduly harm nonminority applicants.

We are mindful, however, that "[a] core purpose of the Fourteenth Amendment was to do away with all governmentally imposed discrimination based on race.". . . Accordingly, race-conscious admissions policies must be limited in time. This requirement reflects that racial classifications, however compelling their goals, are potentially so dangerous that they may be employed no more broadly than the interest demands. Enshrining a permanent justification for racial preferences would offend this fundamental equal protection principle. We see no reason to exempt race-conscious admissions programs from the requirement that all governmental use of race must have a logical end point. The Law School, too, concedes that all "race-conscious programs must have reasonable durational limits.". . .

In the context of higher education, the durational requirement can be met by sunset provisions in race-conscious admissions policies and periodic reviews to determine whether racial preferences are still necessary to achieve student body diversity. . . .

The requirement that all race-conscious admissions programs have a termination point "assure[s] all citizens that the deviation from the norm of equal treatment of all racial and ethnic groups is a temporary matter, a measure taken in the service of the goal of equality itself.". . .

We take the Law School at its word that it would "like nothing better than to find a race-neutral admissions formula" and will terminate its race-conscious admissions program as soon as practicable. . . . It has been 25 years since Justice Powell first approved the use of race to further an interest in student body diversity in the context of public higher education. Since that time, the number of minority applicants with high grades and test scores has indeed increased. . . . We expect that 25 years from now, the use of racial preferences will no longer be necessary to further the interest approved today.

IV

In summary, the Equal Protection Clause does not prohibit the Law School's narrowly tailored use of race in admissions decisions to further a compelling interest in obtaining the educational benefits that flow from a diverse student body. Consequently, petitioner's statutory claims based on Title VI and 42 U.S.C. § 1981 also fail. . . . The judgment of the Court of Appeals for the Sixth Circuit, accordingly, is affirmed.

It is so ordered.

CHIEF JUSTICE REHNQUIST, with whom JUSTICE SCALIA, JUSTICE KENNEDY, and JUSTICE THOMAS join, dissenting.

I agree with the Court that, "in the limited circumstance when drawing racial distinctions is permissible," the government must ensure that its means are narrowly tailored to achieve a compelling state interest. . . . I do not believe, however, that the University of Michigan Law School's (Law School) means are narrowly tailored to the interest it asserts. The Law School claims it must take the steps it does to achieve a "critical mass" of underrepresented minority students. . . . But its actual program bears no relation to this asserted goal. Stripped of its "critical mass" veil, the Law School's program is revealed as a naked effort to achieve racial balancing.

As we have explained many times, "[a]ny preference based on racial or ethnic criteria must necessarily receive a most searching examination.". . . Our cases establish that, in order to withstand this demanding inquiry, respondents must demonstrate that their methods of using race " 'fit' " a compelling state interest "with greater precision than any alternative means.". . .

Before the Court's decision today, we consistently applied the same strict scrutiny analysis regardless of the government's purported reason for using race and regardless of the setting in which race was being used. We rejected calls to use more lenient review in the face of claims that race was being used in "good faith" because " '[m]ore than good motives should be required when government seeks to allocate its resources by way of an explicit racial classification system.' ". . . We likewise rejected calls to apply more lenient review based on the particular setting in which race is being used. Indeed, even in the specific context of higher education, we emphasized that "constitutional limitations protecting individual rights may not be disregarded.". . .

Although the Court recites the language of our strict scrutiny analysis, its application of that review is unprecedented in its deference.

Respondents' asserted justification for the Law School's use of race in the admissions process is "obtaining 'the educational benefits that flow from a diverse student body.' ". . . They contend that a "critical mass" of underrepresented minorities is necessary to further that interest. . . . Respondents and school administrators explain generally that "critical mass" means a sufficient number of underrepresented minority students to achieve several objectives: To ensure that these minority students do not feel isolated or like spokespersons for their race; to provide adequate opportunities for the type of interaction upon which the educational benefits of diversity depend; and to challenge all students to think critically and reexamine stereotypes. . . . These objectives indicate that "critical mass" relates to the size of the student body. . . . Respondents further claim that the Law School is achieving "critical mass.". . .

In practice, the Law School's program bears little or no relation to its asserted goal of achieving "critical mass." Respondents explain that the Law School seeks to accumulate a "critical mass" of *each* underrepresented minority group. . . . But the record demonstrates that the Law School's admissions practices with respect to these groups differ dramatically and cannot be defended under any consistent use of the term "critical mass."

From 1995 through 2000, the Law School admitted between 1,130 and 1,310 students. Of those, between 13 and 19 were Native American, between 91 and 108 were African-Americans, and between 47 and 56 were Hispanic. If the Law School is admitting between 91 and 108 African-Americans in order to achieve "critical mass," thereby preventing African-American students from feeling "isolated or like spokespersons for their race," one would think that a number of the same order of magnitude would be necessary to accomplish the same purpose for Hispanics and Native Americans. Similarly, even if all of the Native American applicants admitted in a given year matriculate, which the record demonstrates is not at all the case, how can this possibly constitute a "critical mass" of Native Americans in a class of over 350 students? In order for this pattern of admission to be consistent with the Law School's explanation of "critical mass," one would have to believe that the objectives of "critical mass" offered by respondents are achieved with only half the number of Hispanics and one-sixth the number of Native Americans as compared to African-Americans. But respondents offer no race-specific reasons for such disparities. Instead, they simply emphasize the importance of achieving "critical mass," without any explanation of why that concept is applied differently among the three underrepresented minority groups.

These different numbers, moreover, come only as a result of substantially different treatment among the three underrepresented minority groups, as is apparent in an example offered by the Law School and highlighted by the Court: The school asserts that it "frequently accepts nonminority applicants with grades and test scores lower than under-represented minority applicants (and other nonminority applicants) who are rejected.". . . Specifically, the Law School states that "[s]ixty-nine minority applicants were rejected between 1995 and 2000 with at least a 3.5 [Grade Point Average (GPA)] and a [score of] 159 or higher on the [Law School Admissions Test (LSAT)]" while a number of Caucasian and Asian-American applicants with similar or lower scores were admitted. . . .

Review of the record reveals only 67 such individuals. Of these 67 individuals, 56 were Hispanic, while only 6 were African-American, and only 5 were Native American. This discrepancy reflects a consistent practice. For example, in 2000, 12 Hispanics who scored between a 159–160 on the LSAT and earned a GPA of 3.00 or higher applied for admission and only 2 were admitted. . . . Meanwhile, 12 African-Americans in the same range of qualifications applied for admission and all 12 were admitted. . . . Likewise, that same year, 16 Hispanics who scored between a 151–153 on the LSAT and earned a 3.00 or higher applied for admission and only 1 of those applicants was admitted. . . . Twenty-three similarly qualified African-Americans applied for admission and 14 were admitted. . . .

These statistics have a significant bearing on petitioner's case. Respondents have *never* offered any race-specific arguments explaining why significantly more individuals from one underrepresented minority group are needed in order to achieve "critical mass" or further student body diversity. They certainly have not explained why Hispanics, who they have said are among "the groups most isolated by racial barriers in our country," should have their admission capped out in this manner. . . . True, petitioner is neither Hispanic nor Native American. But the Law School's disparate admissions practices with respect to these minority groups demonstrate that its alleged goal of "critical mass" is simply a sham. Petitioner may use these statistics to expose this sham, which is the basis for the Law School's admission of less qualified underrepresented minorities in preference to her. Surely strict scrutiny cannot permit these sort of disparities without at least some explanation.

Only when the "critical mass" label is discarded does a likely explanation for these numbers emerge. The Court states that the Law School's goal of attaining a "critical mass" of underrepresented minority students is not an interest in merely "assur[ing] within its student body some specified percentage of a particular group merely because of its race or ethnic origin.". . . The Court recognizes that such an interest "would amount to outright racial balancing, which is patently unconstitutional.". . . The Court concludes, however, that the Law School's use of race in admissions, consistent with Justice Powell's opinion in *Bakke,* only pays "[s]ome attention to numbers.". . .

But the correlation between the percentage of the Law School's pool of applicants who are members of the three minority groups and the percentage of the admitted applicants who are members of these same groups is far too precise to be dismissed as merely the result of the school paying "some attention to [the] numbers.". . . [F]rom 1995 through 2000 the percentage of admitted applicants who were members of these minority groups closely tracked the percentage of individuals in the school's applicant pool who were from the same groups.

For example, in 1995, when 9.7% of the applicant pool was African-American, 9.4% of the admitted class was African-American. By 2000, only 7.5% of the applicant pool was African-American, and 7.3% of the admitted class was African-American. This correlation is striking. Respondents themselves emphasize that the number of underrepresented minority students admitted to the Law School would be significantly smaller if the race of each applicant were not considered. . . . But, as the examples above illustrate, the measure of the decrease would differ dramatically among the groups. The tight correlation between the percentage of applicants and admittees of a given race, therefore, must result from careful race based planning by the Law School. It suggests a formula for admission based on the aspirational assumption that all applicants are equally qualified academically, and therefore that the proportion of each group admitted should be the same as the proportion of that group in the applicant pool. . . .

Not only do respondents fail to explain this phenomenon, they attempt to obscure it. . . . But the divergence between the percentages of underrepresented minorities in the applicant pool and in the *enrolled* classes is not the only relevant comparison. In fact, it may not be the most relevant comparison. The Law School cannot precisely control which of its admitted applicants decide to attend the university. But it can and, as the numbers demonstrate, clearly does employ racial preferences in extending offers of admission. Indeed, the ostensibly flexible nature of the Law School's admissions program that the Court finds appealing . . . appears to be, in practice, a carefully managed program designed to ensure proportionate representation of applicants from selected minority groups.

I do not believe that the Constitution gives the Law School such free rein in the use of race. The Law School has offered no explanation for its actual admissions practices and, unexplained, we are bound to conclude that the Law School has managed its admissions program, not to achieve a "critical mass," but to extend offers of admission to members of selected minority groups in proportion to their statistical representation in the applicant pool. But this is precisely the type of racial balancing that the Court itself calls "patently unconstitutional.". . .

Finally, I believe that the Law School's program fails strict scrutiny because it is devoid of any reasonably precise time limit on the Law School's use of race in admissions. We have emphasized that we will consider "the planned duration of the remedy" in determining whether a race-conscious program is constitutional. . . . Our previous cases have required some limit on the duration of programs such as this because discrimination on the basis of race is invidious.

The Court suggests a possible 25-year limitation on the Law School's current program. . . . Respondents, on the other hand, remain more ambiguous, explaining that "the Law School of course recognizes that race-conscious programs must have reasonable durational limits, and the Sixth Circuit properly found such a limit in the Law School's resolve to cease considering race when genuine race-neutral alternatives become available.". . . These discussions of a time limit are the vaguest of assurances. In truth, they permit the Law School's use of racial preferences on a seemingly permanent basis. Thus, an important component of strict scrutiny—that a program be limited in time—is casually subverted.

The Court, in an unprecedented display of deference under our strict scrutiny analysis, upholds the Law School's program despite its obvious flaws. We have said that when it comes to the use of race, the connection between the ends and the means used to attain them must be precise. But here the flaw is deeper than that; it is not merely a question of "fit" between ends and means. Here the means actually used are forbidden by the Equal Protection Clause of the Constitution.

Source: U.S. Supreme Court of the United States. *Grutter v. Bollinger et al.* No. 02–241, 539. U.S. ____ (2003). June 23, 2003. http://supct.law. cornell.edu/supct/html/02-241.ZS.html (accessed July 26, 2003).

Gratz v. Bollinger

No. 02–516

| Jennifer Gratz and Patrick Hamacher, Petitioners *v.* Lee Bollinger et al. | On Writ of Certiorari to the United States Court of Appeals for the Sixth Circuit |

[June 23, 2003]

CHIEF JUSTICE REHNQUIST delivered the opinion of the Court.

We granted certiorari in this case to decide whether "the University of Michigan's use of racial preferences in undergraduate admissions violate[s] the Equal Protection Clause of the Fourteenth Amendment, Title VI of the Civil Rights Act of 1964 (42 U.S.C. § 2000d), or 42 U.S.C. § 1981.". . . Because we find that the manner in which the University considers the race of applicants in its undergraduate admissions guidelines violates these constitutional and statutory provisions, we reverse that portion of the District Court's decision upholding the guidelines.

I

[A omitted.]

B

The University has changed its admissions guidelines a number of times during the period relevant to this litigation, and we summarize the most significant of these changes briefly. The University's Office of Undergraduate

Admissions (OUA) oversees the LSA admissions process. In order to promote consistency in the review of the large number of applications received, the OUA uses written guidelines for each academic year. Admissions counselors make admissions decisions in accordance with these guidelines.

OUA considers a number of factors in making admissions decisions, including high school grades, standardized test scores, high school quality, curriculum strength, geography, alumni relationships, and leadership. OUA also considers race. During all periods relevant to this litigation, the University has considered African-Americans, Hispanics, and Native Americans to be "underrepresented minorities," and it is undisputed that the University admits "virtually every qualified . . . applicant" from these groups. . . .

Beginning with the 1998 academic year, the OUA [adopted] a "selection index," on which an applicant could score a maximum of 150 points. This index was divided linearly into ranges generally calling for admissions dispositions as follows: 100–150 (admit); 95–99 (admit or postpone); 90–94 (postpone or admit); 75–89 (delay or postpone); 74 and below (delay or reject).

Each application received points based on high school grade point average, standardized test scores, academic quality of an applicant's high school, strength or weakness of high school curriculum, in-state residency, alumni relationship, personal essay, and personal achievement or leadership. Of particular significance here, under a "miscellaneous" category, an applicant was entitled to 20 points based upon his or her membership in an underrepresented racial or ethnic minority group. . . .

In all application years from 1995 to 1998, the guidelines provided that qualified applicants from underrepresented minority groups be admitted as soon as possible in light of the University's belief that such applicants were more likely to enroll if promptly notified of their admission. Also from 1995 through 1998, the University carefully managed its rolling admissions system to permit consideration of certain applications submitted later in the academic year through the use of "protected seats." Specific groups—including athletes, foreign students, ROTC candidates, and underrepresented minorities—were "protected categories" eligible for these seats. A committee called the Enrollment Working Group (EWG) projected how many applicants from each of these protected categories the University was likely to receive after a given date and then paced admissions decisions to permit full consideration of expected applications from these groups. If this space was not filled by qualified candidates from the designated groups toward the end of the admissions season, it was then used to admit qualified candidates remaining in the applicant pool, including those on the waiting list.

During 1999 and 2000, the OUA used the selection index, under which every applicant from an underrepresented racial or ethnic minority group was awarded 20 points. Starting in 1999, however, the University established an Admissions Review Committee (ARC), to provide an additional level of consideration for some applications. Under the new system, counselors may, in their discretion, "flag" an application for the ARC to review after determining that the applicant (1) is academically prepared to succeed at the University, (2) has achieved a minimum selection index score, and (3) possesses a quality or characteristic important to the University's composition of its freshman class, such as high class rank, unique life experiences, challenges, circumstances, interests or talents, socioeconomic disadvantage, and underrepresented race, ethnicity, or geography. After reviewing "flagged" applications, the ARC determines whether to admit, defer, or deny each applicant. . . .

[C omitted.]

II

[A omitted.]

B

Petitioners argue, first and foremost, that the University's use of race in undergraduate admissions violates the Fourteenth Amendment. Specifically, they contend that this Court has only sanctioned the use of racial classifications to remedy identified discrimination, a justification on which respondents have never relied. . . . Petitioners further argue that "diversity as a basis for employing racial preferences is simply too open-ended, ill-defined, and indefinite to constitute a compelling interest capable of supporting narrowly-tailored means.". . . But for the reasons set forth today in *Grutter v. Bollinger* . . . the Court has rejected these arguments of petitioners.

Petitioners alternatively argue that even if the University's interest in diversity can constitute a compelling state interest, the District Court erroneously concluded that the University's use of race in its current freshman admissions policy is narrowly tailored to achieve such an interest. Petitioners argue that the guidelines the University began using in 1999 do not "remotely resemble the kind of consideration of race and ethnicity that Justice Powell endorsed in *Bakke*.". . . Respondents reply that the University's current admissions program *is* narrowly tailored and avoids the problems of the Medical School of the University of California at Davis program (U. C. Davis) rejected by Justice Powell. They claim that their program "hews closely" to both the admissions program described by Justice Powell as well as the Harvard College admissions program that he endorsed. . . . Specifically, respondents contend that the LSA's policy provides the individualized consideration that "Justice Powell considered a hallmark of a constitutionally appropriate admissions program.". . . For the reasons set out below, we do not agree.

It is by now well established that "all racial classifications reviewable under the Equal Protection Clause must be strictly scrutinized.". . .

To withstand our strict scrutiny analysis, respondents must demonstrate that the University's use of race in its current admission program employs "narrowly tailored measures that further compelling governmental interests.". . . We find that the University's policy, which automatically distributes 20 points, or one-fifth of the points needed to guarantee admission, to every single "underrepresented minority" applicant solely because of race, is not narrowly tailored to achieve the interest in educational diversity that respondents claim justifies their program.

In *Bakke,* Justice Powell reiterated that "[p]referring members of any one group for no reason other than race or ethnic origin is discrimination for its own sake.". . . He then explained, however, that in his view it would be permissible for a university to employ an admissions program in which "race or ethnic background may be deemed a 'plus' in a particular applicant's file.". . . He explained that such a program might allow for "[t]he file of a particular black applicant [to] be examined for his potential contribution to diversity without the factor of race being decisive when compared, for example, with that of an applicant identified as an Italian-American if the latter is thought to exhibit qualities more likely to promote beneficial educational pluralism.". . . Such a system, in Justice Powell's view, would be "flexible enough to consider all pertinent elements of diversity in light of the particular qualifications of each applicant.". . .

Justice Powell's opinion in *Bakke* emphasized the importance of considering each particular applicant as an individual, assessing all of the qualities that individual possesses, and in turn, evaluating that individual's ability to contribute to the unique setting of higher education. The admissions program Justice Powell described, however, did not contemplate that any single characteristic automatically ensured a specific and identifiable contribution to a university's diversity. . . . Instead, under the approach Justice Powell described, each characteristic of a particular applicant was to be considered in assessing the applicant's entire application.

The current LSA policy does not provide such individualized consideration. The LSA's policy automatically distributes 20 points to every single applicant from an "underrepresented minority" group, as defined by the University. The only consideration that accompanies this distribution of points is a factual review of an application to determine whether an individual is a member of one of these minority groups. Moreover, unlike Justice Powell's example, where the race of a "particular black applicant" could be considered without being decisive, . . . the LSA's automatic distribution of 20 points has the effect of making "the factor of race . . . decisive" for virtually every minimally qualified underrepresented minority applicant. . . .

Also instructive in our consideration of the LSA's system is the example provided in the description of the Harvard College Admissions Program, which Justice Powell both discussed in, and attached to, his opinion in *Bakke*. The example was included to "illustrate the kind of significance attached to race" under the Harvard College program. . . . It provided as follows:

> "The Admissions Committee, with only a few places left to fill, might find itself forced to choose between A, the child of a successful black physician in an academic community with promise of superior academic performance, and B, a black who grew up in an inner-city ghetto of semi-literate parents whose academic achievement was lower but who had demonstrated energy and leadership as well as an apparently abiding interest in black power. If a good number of black students much like A but few like B had already been admitted, the Committee might prefer B; and vice versa. If C, a white student with extraordinary artistic talent, were also seeking one of the remaining places, his unique quality might give him an edge over both A and B. Thus, the critical criteria are often individual qualities or experience *not dependent upon race but sometimes associated with it*.". . . (emphasis added).

This example further demonstrates the problematic nature of the LSA's admissions system. Even if student C's "extraordinary artistic talent" rivaled that of Monet or Picasso, the applicant would receive, at most, five points under the LSA's system. . . . At the same time, every single underrepresented minority applicant, including students A and B, would automatically receive 20 points for submitting an application. Clearly, the LSA's system does not offer applicants the individualized selection process described in Harvard's example. Instead of considering how the differing backgrounds, experiences, and characteristics of students A, B, and C might benefit the University, admissions counselors reviewing LSA applications would simply award both A and B 20 points because their applications indicate that they are African-American, and student C would receive up to 5 points for his "extraordinary talent.". . .

Respondents contend that "[t]he volume of applications and the presentation of applicant information make it impractical for [LSA] to use the . . . admissions system" upheld by the Court today in *Grutter.* . . . But the fact that the implementation of a program capable of providing individualized consideration might present administrative challenges does not render constitutional an otherwise problematic system. . . . Nothing in Justice Powell's opinion in *Bakke* signaled that a university may employ whatever means it desires to achieve the stated goal of diversity without regard to the limits imposed by our strict scrutiny analysis.

We conclude, therefore, that because the University's use of race in its current freshman admissions policy is not narrowly tailored to achieve respondents' asserted compelling interest in diversity, the admissions policy violates the Equal Protection Clause of the Fourteenth Amendment. We further find that the admissions policy also violates Title VI and 42 U.S.C. § 1981. Accordingly, we reverse that portion of the District Court's decision granting respondents summary judgment with respect to liability and remand the case for proceedings consistent with this opinion.

It is so ordered.

Source: U.S. Supreme Court of the United States. *Gratz et al. v. Bollinger et al.* No. 02–516, 539. U.S. ____ (2003). June 23, 2003. http://supct.law.cornell.edu/supct/html/02-516.ZD2.html (accessed July 26, 2003).

Supreme Court on Internet Filters at Public Libraries

June 23, 2003

INTRODUCTION

The Supreme Court on June 23, 2003, endorsed, for the first time, a form of government regulation of the Internet. In a 6–3 ruling in *United States v. American Library Association Inc.,* the Court upheld as constitutional a 2000 law that sought to force public libraries to install software filters that block pornography from computers used by patrons to access the Internet. Opponents—led by the American Library Association (ALA)—had condemned the law as an infringement on free speech, but the Court majority ruled that the government had a legitimate interest in protecting children from the vast amount of obscene and pornographic material available on the Internet.

The Court had blocked two previous congressional attempts to shield children from the darker side of the Internet. In 1997 the Court struck down the Communications Decency Act, which was part of the massive Telecommunications Act of 1996 (PL 104–104). That law had attempted to prohibit owners of Internet sites from knowingly putting "patently offensive material" within the reach of minors. *(Historic Documents of 1997, p. 444)*

Then in 2002 the Court blocked enforcement of a 1998 law, the Child Online Protection Act (PL 105–277), that made it a crime to disseminate material over the Internet that was "harmful to minors." The Supreme Court sent a case involving that law back to the Third Circuit Court of Appeals for further review. That circuit court declared the law unconstitutional in March 2003, but on October 14 the Supreme Court agreed to consider a Bush administration appeal of that ruling.

In a related area, the Supreme Court also had overturned a law that had banned distribution over the Internet of computer-generated "virtual" pornography that appeared to involve children. The Court struck down that law (the Child Pornography Prevention Act—PL 104–208) in April 2002.

Filtering Pornography

The case involving antipornography filters on library computers was controversial because it brought to the fore such issues as free speech, congressional spending powers, and the public interest in protecting minors from pornography. An additional question—one the courts were still attempting to come to terms with—involved the constitutionality and practicality of government regulation of a new, global form of mass communications, the Internet.

Congress had waded into these issues in 2000 when it passed the Children's Internet Protection Act (known as CIPA, PL 106–554), requiring schools and public libraries to install software that would block pornography on computers that might be used by children to gain access to the Internet. Libraries that failed to install this software (known as a filter) by July 2002 risked losing two kinds of federal funds: a subsidized rate (known as the "e-rate") for their access to the Internet and grants for information technology programs under the Library Services and Technology Act.

Opponents of the law, headed by the ALA and the American Civil Liberties Union, filed suit to block application of the law to public libraries (but not schools). Under a special provision of the law, the suit went straight to a three-judge panel of the Third U.S. Circuit Court based in Philadelphia. That panel ruled unanimously in May 2002 that the law represented an unconstitutional infringement on free speech guarantees. The panel based its decision largely on the fact that filtering software programs were unreliable and tended to block many Internet sites that did not contain pornography (a result called "overblocking"); among the blocked sites were those with information on sexually transmitted diseases. The Court also noted that filtering programs failed to block some sites that should have been blocked (called "underblocking").

The government's appeal of that decision took the issue to the Supreme Court, which heard oral arguments March 4 and issued a decision June 23. Because of the complexities and uncertainties raised by the disputed law, the Court found itself fractured along several lines. Four justices (Chief Justice William Rehnquist and Justices Sandra Day O'Connor, Antonin Scalia, and Clarence Thomas) held that the law was constitutional on its face because it represented a legitimate use by Congress of its spending power. Two justices—Anthony M. Kennedy and Stephen G. Breyer—agreed that the law should be allowed to stand, but each raised concerns and suggested the law could be challenged if libraries made it difficult to gain access to some Internet sites. The remaining three justices—Ruth Bader Ginsburg, David H. Souter, and John Paul Stevens—argued that the law was an unconstitutional restriction on free speech. All nine justices appeared to agree on just one legal point in the case, that Congress did have the right to block children (defined as those under the age of seventeen) from viewing pornographic material in schools and public libraries, either on the Internet or in traditional publications.

Writing the plurality opinion, Rehnquist argued that the law did not cross any of the barriers the Court had traditionally used to define an unconstitutional infringement of free speech. Computer terminals in public libraries did not constitute a "public forum"—such as a street corner or a public meeting—where free speech had broad protections, Rehnquist wrote. "Internet terminals are not acquired by a library in order to create a public forum for Web publishers to express themselves," the opinion said. "Rather, a library provides such access for the same reasons it offers other library resources: to facilitate research, learning, and recreational pursuits by furnishing materials of requisite and appropriate quality. The fact that a library reviews and affirmatively chooses to acquire every book in its collection, but does not review every Web site that it makes available, is not a constitutionally relevant distinction."

Moreover, the plurality decision said, Congress had "wide latitude to attach conditions to the receipt of federal assistance," such as the grants and subsidies received by libraries. The Internet filtering requirement was an acceptable condition, the justices ruled, because it did not induce libraries to violate the Constitution.

This legal reasoning by the plurality of four justices might not have carried the day had it not been for a practical consideration cited by Kennedy and Breyer. For both of them, the crux of the matter appeared to be that Congress had stipulated that libraries could temporarily disable the filtering software at the request of adult users who wanted to gain access to blocked sites for "bona fide research or other lawful purposes."

Kennedy offered this summary of his view: "If, on the request of an adult user, a librarian will unblock filtered material or disable the Internet software filter without significant delay, there is little to this case." Breyer, as well, argued that requiring an adult patron to ask for the filtering software to be turned off was no more "onerous" than traditional practices such a segregating sensitive material in closed stacks.

In a vaguely worded sentence of his opinion, however, Kennedy suggested that the issue might not be entirely settled. The law might be challenged on an "as-applied" basis if some libraries could not unblock specific Web sites or if it could be shown that "an adult user's election to view constitutionally protected material is burdened in some other substantial way." Several commentators suggested that Kennedy's remark amounted to an invitation to library patrons to monitor application of the law to ensure that their rights were not infringed.

Stevens submitted a strongly worded dissent in which he said Congress had wielded a "statutory blunderbuss" that violated the First Amendment protections of free speech. Rather than using the threat of a federal funds cutoff to mandate filters on all library computers, he said, Congress should have allowed libraries to employ "less restrictive alternatives," such as installing filters on computers reserved for use by minors.

In his dissent joined by Ginsburg, Souter argued that a library would be guilty of censorship if—on its own—it prevented an adult from viewing certain Web sites while using a library computer. The government would then be engaging in censorship by requiring libraries to install filters that effectively prevented adults from viewing those sites, he argued.

Reaction and FCC Regulations

Supporters of the filtering law claimed victory and said the Court's decision upheld the principle that children should not be exposed to pornography. Bruce Taylor, president and chief counsel of the conservative National Law Center for Children and Families, said the decision meant that "the courts are not going to let the pornographers and the pedophiles take over the libraries."

The American Library Association expressed disappointment with the Court's decision. But the association also said Kennedy's and Breyer's opinions indicated that libraries could disable Internet filters when asked to do so by adult patrons. The association advised libraries that the Court decision meant the law "is constitutional only if the mandated filters can be readily disabled upon the request of adult library users. Users do not have to explain why they are making the request."

That guidance was affirmed by the Federal Communications Commission (FCC), which had been told by Congress to determine whether libraries were complying with the filtering law. In a July 24 regulation, the commission said libraries should develop procedures for unblocking access to Web sites when asked to do so by adults. The FCC also said libraries had to comply with the law's filtering requirements by July 1, 2004.

Officials at numerous libraries said they objected to the law on free speech grounds, even though the Supreme Court had ruled the law did not violate the Constitution. Many librarians also objected to the cost of buying, installing, and maintaining the filters. Chicago library commissioner Mary Dempsey said her system received about $500,000 each year in federal subsidies but expected to pay about $150,000 to buy the filtering software and $25,000 to $50,000 each year to maintain it. Citing both free speech objections and the cost of filtering software, a small number of libraries said they would give up federal funds rather than comply with the law.

Viruses and Worms

Pornography on the Internet was annoying and offensive to many people, but by 2003 other Internet problems were costing businesses and individuals millions of dollars. The most damaging of these problems were viruses and worms—technological flaws deliberately spread via e-mail by mischief-causing individuals. Experts defined a virus as a piece of software code that caused damage to a computer after the user activated it (usually inadvertently), most often by opening an e-mail attachment. A worm was a program that spread automatically, either through e-mail or through a Web site. Several major virus and worm attacks caused massive disruptions of Internet traffic during 2003.

The first attack began on January 25, when Internet monitors reported that a computer worm had infected nearly 40,000 computers, severely slowing Internet service in many parts of the world. Banking and emergency response systems were among those affected, raising questions about the safety of important services that relied on the Internet. Called Slammer and Sapphire, the worm infected computers using a popular database program, SQL Server 2000, sold by the Microsoft Corporation.

A worm named Blaster began spreading across the world in the spring and quickly infected hundreds of thousands of computers, according to the CERT Coordination Center, a federally funded computer incidence response unit at Carnegie Mellon University. By mid-September Blaster had caused an estimated $525 million in damages to computer systems and lost business productivity. Another worm, called SoBig, spread rapidly through e-mail in mid-August and clogged the e-mail in-boxes of millions of homes and businesses, costing estimated damages of at least $500 million within the first two weeks.

Testifying on September 10 to a subcommittee of the House Committee on Government Reform, Richard D. Pethia, director of the CERT Coordination Center, said: "With more government and private sector organizations increasing their dependence on the Internet, our ability to carry on business reliably is at risk" because of the malicious use of viruses and worms.

A common element to all the computer viruses and worms was that they exploited flaws in widely used software programs—most important the personal computer operating systems, Internet browsers, and other products of the Microsoft Corporation, which had a monopoly in the industry. Microsoft had made available corrections (called patches) for many of these flaws, but millions of consumers failed to install the corrections or simply were unaware of the problem. Pethia and other experts said software manufacturers often perpetuated problems by repeating the same flaws in new versions of their products.

Reacting to growing public concern about the safety of Microsoft products, company chief executive Steven A. Ballmer on October 10 announced a series of steps, beginning with a monthly schedule of security updates for the most popular software programs. Ballmer said Microsoft also would begin shipping its widely used "Windows" operating systems with security protections already activated; previously, these protections were disabled until the user turned them on. Computer industry executives generally welcomed these steps by Microsoft, but some executives said the company should have acted years earlier to improve the quality of its products so they would be less vulnerable to malicious attack.

Spam

Unsolicited junk e-mail messages, known as "spam," were clogging business and individual in-boxes by the billions. By mid-2003, according to some estimates, spam messages accounted for at least half of all e-mail messages received in the United States. One study, released in January by Ferris Research, estimated that spam was costing U.S. businesses about $8.9 billion in lost employee productivity and wasted computer space. A survey conducted in October by the Pew Internet and American Life Project found that one-quarter of computer users said they had cut back on their use of e-mail because of spam.

While nearly everyone—except the spammers—agreed that spam e-mail was costly and annoying, there was little agreement about what could be done to stop it. Dozens of state legislatures passed laws attempting to prohibit or ban spam messages, but these measures had little impact because most spam moved across state lines and spam e-mailers had little regard for legal niceties. California in September enacted the toughest antispam legislation, providing for fines of up to $1 million for those convicted of sending unsolicited messages within the state. The Federal Trade Commission (FTC) attempted to enforce truth-in-advertising laws against spammers that engaged in deceptive marketing, but the agency had trouble locating the responsible parties, who often hid behind multiple identities, some of them stolen from legitimate businesses.

Responding to growing public outrage against spam, Congress in December passed legislation (PL 108–187) that gave e-mail users limited protections against unsolicited messages. Dubbed the "Can Spam Act" by its sponsors, the law gave computer users the right to opt out of future solicitations by junk e-mailers and gave state and federal officials authority to prosecute and fine spammers who ignored the rules. The law also authorized the FTC to create a "do not spam" registry, similar to a "do not call" telemarketing law (PL 108–82) that had proved highly popular.

Sponsors called the law a "first step" that would limit the growth of unsolicited e-mail. Critics said the law was too timid, in part because it did not outlaw spam or give consumers the right to take legal action against spammers. A few prominent spam e-mailers said they would change their practices to comply with the federal law, suggesting that its provisions would do little to stop billions of unwanted messages from reaching the in boxes of e-mail users.

The European Union (EU) also adopted antispam regulations, which went into effect on October 31. Those rules required companies to get a recipient's consent before sending bulk e-mail. Enforcement of the rules was left up to individual EU member nations.

Following are excerpts from the majority opinion, concurring opinions, and dissenting opinions in the case of United States v. American Library Association Inc., *in which the Supreme Court on June 23, 2003, upheld, 6–3, the Children's Internet Protection Act (PL 106–554), which required public libraries receiving certain federal subsidies to install antipornography filters on computers used by the public for access to the Internet.*

●——●

United States v. American Library Association Inc.

No. 02-361

United States, et al., appellants
v.
American Library Association, Inc., et al.

On Appeal from the United States District Court for the Eastern District of Pennsylvania

[June 23, 2003]

CHIEF JUSTICE REHNQUIST, delivered the opinion of the court.

To address the problems associated with the availability of Internet pornography in public libraries, Congress enacted the Children's Internet Protection Act (CIPA), 114 Stat. 2763A–335. Under CIPA, a public library may not receive federal assistance to provide Internet access unless it installs software to block images that constitute obscenity or child pornography, and to prevent minors from obtaining access to material that is harmful to them. The District Court held these provisions facially invalid on the ground that they induce public libraries to violate patrons' First Amendment rights. We now reverse. . . .

By connecting to the Internet, public libraries provide patrons with a vast amount of valuable information. But there is also an enormous amount of pornography on the Internet, much of which is easily obtained. The accessibility of this material has created serious problems for libraries, which have found that patrons of all ages, including minors, regularly search for online pornography. Id., at 406. Some patrons also expose others to pornographic images by leaving them displayed on Internet terminals or printed at library printers.

Upon discovering these problems, Congress became concerned that the E-rate [subsidized Internet access rates for public libraries and schools] and LSTA [Library Services and Technology Act] programs were facilitating access to illegal and harmful pornography. Congress learned that adults "us[e] library computers to access pornography that is then exposed to staff, passersby, and children," and that "minors acces[s] child and adult pornography in libraries."

But Congress also learned that filtering software that blocks access to pornographic Web sites could provide a reasonably effective way to prevent such uses of library resources. By 2000, before Congress enacted CIPA, almost 17% of public libraries used such software on at least some of their Internet terminals, and 7% had filters on all of them. A library can set such software to block categories of material, such as "Pornography" or "Violence." When a patron tries to view a site that falls within such a category, a screen appears indicating that the site is blocked. But a filter set to block pornography may sometimes block other sites that present neither obscene nor pornographic material, but that nevertheless trigger the filter. To minimize this problem, a library can set its software to prevent the blocking of material that falls into categories like "Education," "History," and "Medical." A library may also add or delete specific sites from a blocking category, and anyone can ask companies that furnish filtering software to unblock particular sites.

Responding to this information, Congress enacted CIPA. It provides that a library may not receive E-rate or LSTA assistance unless it has "a policy of Internet safety for minors that includes the operation of a technology protection measure . . . that protects against access" by all persons to "visual depictions" that constitute "obscen[ity]" or "child pornography," and that protects against access by minors to "visual depictions" that are "harmful to minors." The statute defines a "[t]echnology protection measure" as "a specific technology that blocks or filters Internet access to material covered by" CIPA. CIPA also permits the library to "disable" the filter "to enable access for bona fide research or other lawful purposes. Under the E-rate program, disabling is permitted "during use by an adult." Under the LSTA program, disabling is permitted during use by any person. . . .

Congress has wide latitude to attach conditions to the receipt of federal assistance in order to further its policy objectives. *South Dakota v. Dole*, (1987). But Congress may not "induce" the recipient "to engage in activities that would themselves be unconstitutional." To determine whether libraries would violate the First Amendment by employing the filtering software that CIPA requires, we must first examine the role of libraries in our society.

Public libraries pursue the worthy missions of facilitating learning and cultural enrichment. Appellee ALA's Library Bill of Rights states that libraries should provide "[b]ooks and other . . . resources . . . for the interest, information, and enlightenment of all people of the community the library serves." To fulfill their traditional missions, public libraries must have broad discretion to decide what material to provide to their patrons. Although they seek to provide a wide array of information, their goal has never been to provide "universal coverage." Instead, public libraries seek to provide materials "that would be of the greatest direct benefit or interest to the community." To this end, libraries collect only those materials deemed to have "requisite and appropriate quality.". . .

We have held in two analogous contexts that the government has broad discretion to make content-based judgments in deciding what private speech to make available to the public. In *Arkansas Ed. Television Comm'n v. Forbes,* (1998), we held that public forum principles do not generally apply to a public television station's editorial judgments regarding the private speech it presents to its viewers.

Similarly, in *National Endowment for Arts v. Finley,* (1998), we upheld an art funding program that required the National Endowment for the Arts (NEA) to use content-based criteria in making funding decisions. We explained that "[a]ny content-based considerations that may be taken into account in the grant-making process are a consequence of the nature of arts funding."

The principles underlying Forbes and Finley also apply to a public library's exercise of judgment in selecting the material it provides to its patrons. Just as forum analysis and heightened judicial scrutiny are incompatible with the role of public television stations and the role of the NEA, they are also incompatible with the discretion that public libraries must have to fulfill their traditional missions. Public library staffs necessarily consider content in making collection decisions and enjoy broad discretion in making them. . . .

. . . A public library does not acquire Internet terminals in order to create a public forum for Web publishers to express themselves, any more than it collects books in order to provide a public forum for the authors of books to speak. It provides Internet access, not to "encourage a diversity of views from private speakers," but for the same reasons it offers other library resources: to facilitate research, learning, and recreational pursuits by furnishing materials of requisite and appropriate quality. . . .

. . . A library's failure to make quality-based judgments about all the material it furnishes from the Web does not somehow taint the judgments it does make. A library's need to exercise judgment in making collection decisions depends on its traditional role in identifying suitable and worthwhile material; it is no less entitled to play that role when it collects material from the Internet than when it collects material from any other source. Most libraries already exclude pornography from their print collections because they deem it inappropriate for inclusion. We do not subject these decisions to heightened scrutiny; it would make little sense to treat libraries' judgments to block online pornography any differently, when these judgments are made for just the same reason.

Moreover, because of the vast quantity of material on the Internet and the rapid pace at which it changes, libraries cannot possibly segregate, item by item, all the Internet material that is appropriate for inclusion from all that is not. While a library could limit its Internet collection to just those sites it found worthwhile, it could do so only at the cost of excluding an enormous amount of valuable information that it lacks the capacity to review. Given that tradeoff, it is entirely reasonable for public libraries to reject that approach and instead exclude certain categories of content, without making individualized judgments that everything they do make available has requisite and appropriate quality. . . .

Because public libraries' use of Internet filtering software does not violate their patrons' First Amendment rights, CIPA does not induce libraries to violate the Constitution, and is a valid exercise of Congress' spending power. Nor does CIPA impose an unconstitutional condition on public libraries. Therefore, the judgment of the District Court for the Eastern District of Pennsylvania is

Reversed.

JUSTICE KENNEDY, concurring in the judgment.

If, on the request of an adult user, a librarian will unblock filtered material or disable the Internet software filter without significant delay, there is little to this case. The Government represents this is indeed the fact.

The District Court, in its "Preliminary Statement," did say that "the unblocking may take days, and may be unavailable, especially in branch libraries, which are often less well staffed than main libraries." That statement, however, does not appear to be a specific finding. It was not the basis for the District Court's decision in any event, as the court assumed that "the disabling provisions permit public libraries to allow a patron access to any speech that is constitutionally protected with respect to that patron."

If some libraries do not have the capacity to unblock specific Web sites or to disable the filter or if it is shown that an adult user's election to view constitutionally protected Internet material is burdened in some other substantial way, that would be the subject for an as-applied challenge, not the facial challenge made in this case.

There are, of course, substantial Government interests at stake here. The interest in protecting young library users from material inappropriate for minors is legitimate, and even compelling, as all Members of the Court appear to agree. Given this interest, and the failure to show that the ability of adult library users to have access to the material is burdened in any significant degree, the statute is not unconstitutional on its face. For these reasons, I concur in the judgment of the Court.

JUSTICE BREYER, concurring in the judgment.
... [T]he Act contains an important exception that limits the speech-related harm that "overblocking" might cause. As the plurality points out, the Act allows libraries to permit any adult patron access to an "overblocked" Web site; the adult patron need only ask a librarian to unblock the specific Web site or, alternatively, ask the librarian, "Please disable the entire filter."

The Act does impose upon the patron the burden of making this request. But it is difficult to see how that burden (or any delay associated with compliance) could prove more onerous than traditional library practices associated with segregating library materials in, say, closed stacks, or with interlibrary lending practices that require patrons to make requests that are not anonymous and to wait while the librarian obtains the desired materials from elsewhere. Perhaps local library rules or practices could further restrict the ability of patrons to obtain "overblocked" Internet material. . . .

Given the comparatively small burden that the Act imposes upon the library patron seeking legitimate Internet materials, I cannot say that any speech-related harm that the Act may cause is disproportionate when considered in relation to the Act's legitimate objectives. I therefore agree with the plurality that the statute does not violate the First Amendment, and I concur in the judgment.

JUSTICE STEVENS, dissenting.
... I agree with the plurality that it is neither inappropriate nor unconstitutional for a local library to experiment with filtering software as a means of curtailing children's access to Internet Web sites displaying sexually explicit images. I also agree with the plurality that the 7% of public libraries that decided to use such software on all of their Internet terminals in 2000 did not act unlawfully. Ante, at 3. Whether it is constitutional for the Congress of the United States to impose that requirement on the other 93%, however, raises a vastly different question. Rather than allowing local decisionmakers to tailor their responses to local problems, the Children's Internet Protection Act (CIPA) operates as a blunt nationwide restraint on adult access to "an enormous amount of valuable information" that individual librarians cannot possibly review. Most of that information is constitutionally protected speech. In my view, this restraint is unconstitutional.

I

The unchallenged findings of fact made by the District Court reveal fundamental defects in the filtering software that is now available or that will be available in the foreseeable future. Because the software relies on key words or phrases to block undesirable sites, it does not have the capacity to exclude a precisely defined category of images. . . .

Given the quantity and ever-changing character of Web sites offering free sexually explicit material, it is inevitable that a substantial amount of such material will never be blocked. Because of this "underblocking," the statute will provide parents with a false sense of security without really solving the problem that motivated its enactment. Conversely, the software's reliance on words to identify undesirable sites necessarily results in the blocking of thousands of pages that "contain content that is completely innocuous for both adults and minors, and that no rational person could conclude matches the filtering companies' category definitions, such as 'pornography' or 'sex.' " In my judgment, a statutory blunderbuss that mandates this vast amount of "overblocking" abridges the freedom of speech protected by the First Amendment.

The effect of the overblocking is the functional equivalent of a host of individual decisions excluding hundreds of thousands of individual constitutionally protected messages from Internet terminals located in public libraries throughout the Nation. Neither the interest in suppressing unlawful speech nor the interest in protecting children from access to harmful materials justifies this overly broad restriction on adult access to protected speech. . . .

Until a blocked site or group of sites is unblocked, a patron is unlikely to know what is being hidden and therefore whether there is any point in asking for the filter to be removed. It is as though the statute required a significant part of every library's reading materials to be kept in unmarked, locked rooms or cabinets, which could be opened only in response to specific requests. Some curious readers would in time obtain access to the hidden materials, but many would not. Inevitably, the interest of the authors of those works in reaching the widest possible audience would be abridged. Moreover, because the procedures that different libraries are likely to adopt to respond to unblocking requests will no doubt vary, it is impossible to measure the aggregate effect of the statute on patrons' access to blocked sites. Unless we assume that the statute is a mere symbolic gesture, we must conclude that it will create a significant prior restraint on adult access to protected speech. A law that prohibits reading without official consent, like a law that prohibits speaking without consent, "constitutes a dramatic departure from our national heritage and constitutional tradition." *Watchtower Bible & Tract Soc. of N. Y., Inc. v. Village of Stratton,* (2002).

II

... In short, the message conveyed by the use of filtering software is not that all speech except that which is prohibited by CIPA is supported by the Government, but rather that all speech that gets through the software is supported by the Government. And the items that get through the software include some visual depictions that are obscene, some that are child pornography, and some that are harmful to minors, while at the same time the software blocks an enormous amount of speech that is not sexually explicit and certainly does not meet CIPA's definitions of prohibited content. . . .

... If a library has 10 computers paid for by nonfederal funds and has Internet service for those computers also paid for by nonfederal funds, the library may choose not to put filtering software on any of those 10 computers. Or a library may decide to put filtering software on the 5 computers in its children's section. Or a library in an elementary school might choose to put filters on every single one of its 10 computers. But under this statute, if a library attempts to provide Internet service for even one computer through an E-rate discount, that library must put filtering software on all of its computers with Internet access, not just the one computer with E-rate discount.

This Court should not permit federal funds to be used to enforce this kind of broad restriction of First Amendment rights, particularly when such a restriction is unnecessary to accomplish Congress' stated goal. See supra, at 4 (discussing less restrictive alternatives). The abridgment of speech is equally obnoxious whether a rule like this one is enforced by a threat of penalties or by a threat to withhold a benefit.

I would affirm the judgment of the District Court.

JUSTICE SOUTER, with whom JUSTICE GINSBURG joins, dissenting.
... The statute could ... have protected children without blocking access for adults or subjecting adults to anything more than minimal inconvenience, just the way (the record shows) many librarians had been dealing with obscenity and indecency before imposition of the federal conditions. Instead, the Government's funding conditions engage in overkill to a degree illustrated by their refusal to trust even a library's staff with an unblocked terminal, one to which the adult public itself has no access.

The question for me, then, is whether a local library could itself constitutionally impose these restrictions on the content otherwise available to an adult patron through an Internet connection, at a library terminal provided for public use. The answer is no. A library that chose to block an adult's Internet access to material harmful to children (and whatever else the undiscriminating filter might interrupt) would be imposing a content-based restriction on communication of material in the library's control that an adult could otherwise lawfully see. This would simply be censorship. True, the censorship would not necessarily extend to every adult, for an intending Internet user might convince a librarian that he was a true researcher or had a "lawful purpose" to obtain everything the library's terminal could provide. But as to those who did not qualify for discretionary unblocking, the censorship would be complete and, like all censorship by an agency of the Government, presumptively invalid owing to strict scrutiny in implementing the Free Speech Clause of the First Amendment. "The policy of the First Amendment favors dissemination of information and opinion, and the guarantees of freedom of speech and press were not designed to prevent the censorship of the press merely, but any action of the government by means of which it might prevent such free and general discussion of public matters as seems absolutely essential.". . .

There is no good reason . . . to treat blocking of adult enquiry as anything different from the censorship it presumptively is. For this reason, I would hold in accordance with conventional strict scrutiny that a library's practice of blocking would violate an adult patron's First and Fourteenth Amendment right to be free of Internet censorship, when unjustified (as here) by any legitimate interest in screening children from harmful material. On that ground, the Act's blocking requirement in its current breadth calls for unconstitutional action by a library recipient, and is itself unconstitutional.

> **Source:** U.S. Supreme Court of the United States. *United States v. American Library Association Inc.* No. 02–361, 539. U.S. ____ (2003), June 23, 2003. http://supct.law.cornell.edu/supct/html/02-361.ZS.html (accessed July 26, 2003).

Supreme Court on Sodomy Laws, Massachusetts Court on Gay Marriage

June 26 and November 18, 2003

INTRODUCTION

Two major court rulings in 2003 significantly advanced the cause of gay rights but touched off a political controversy that was likely to be front and center in the 2004 presidential election. On June 26 the U.S. Supreme Court by a 6–3 vote struck down a Texas law that made sexual relations between people of the same gender a crime. The dissenting justices, among others, warned that the Court was virtually paving the way for legalizing gay marriage. Five months later, on November 18, the Supreme Judicial Court of Massachusetts came close to doing that in a 4–3 decision holding that the state's ban on gay marriage violated the state constitution. The court did not immediately legalize gay marriages but instead gave the Massachusetts legislature 180 days to pass an "appropriate" bill in light of its ruling.

The two rulings were cheered by the gay rights community but denounced by religious and social conservative groups that found homosexuality repugnant for moral or religious reasons. Many of these organizations planned to push for a federal constitutional amendment that defined marriage as the union between a man and a woman. Polls showed that about 60 percent of Americans opposed gay marriage and that the percentage had risen since the Supreme Court ruling on sodomy laws. The public was more evenly split on the acceptability of civil unions, which provided same-sex couples most of the rights, benefits, and obligations of marriage but did not recognize the union as "marriage."

That split in public opinion presented a balancing act for President George W. Bush, who said repeatedly that he opposed gay marriage. Until mid-December, however, he avoided taking a stand on a federal constitutional amendment banning it, and even then his support was tentative and qualified. For Bush the issue appeared to be one of finding a stance that pleased his conservative core enough to keep them from sitting out the 2004 presidential election, while not appearing so intolerant of gays that more moderate voters turned away. Bush also had to be careful not to drive gays out of the Republican party—one-fourth of all gay voters supported Bush in the 2000 election, according to exit polls. Some political analysts said that Bush's December statement supporting a constitutional amendment "if necessary" indicated that his political operatives had decided Bush could use the issue to turn out his core supporters and bash the eventual Democratic nominee.

For Democrats, the issue was one of not appearing out of step with mainstream Americans. Most of the major Democratic presidential candidates in the race at the end of 2003 opposed same-sex marriage, while generally supporting civil unions.

If Massachusetts did legalize gay marriage, it would be the first state to do so. In 2000 Vermont became the first state to allow civil unions. That bill was signed into law by Howard Dean, then Vermont's governor and at the end of 2003 the leading contender for the Democratic presidential nomination. The federal government and thirty-seven states had laws banning same-sex marriages and allowing states to disregard same-sex marriages sanctioned elsewhere. Two of those states, California and Hawaii, provided some spousal rights to same-sex couples. New Jersey was expected to enact legislation early in 2004 that would recognize some same-sex partnerships but that did not establish civil unions. Ten states had no law barring same-sex marriages.

In Canada courts in Ontario and British Columbia ruled that Canada's legal definition of marriage as the union of a man and a woman was unconstitutional, but an effort in the Canadian parliament to change its law to allow marriages by same-sex couples was postponed. Only two other nations—Belgium and the Netherlands—allowed homosexual couples to legally wed, although France, Germany, and several other nations allowed civil unions.

Supreme Court on Sodomy Laws

The Supreme Court last dealt with state sodomy laws in 1986, when it ruled 5–4 that Georgia's sodomy law criminalizing certain kinds of sexual activity was unconstitutional. At the time the Court ruled in *Bowers v. Hardwicke,* half the states had laws that made "deviant" sex, often including anal and oral sex, a crime. The other half had already repealed similar laws as anachronisms that were seldom if ever enforced. Since then, twelve states (including Georgia) had repealed their sodomy laws. Nine of the thirteen states that still had sodomy laws on the books barred consensual sodomy for heterosexual as well as homosexual couples. Four states, including Texas, barred only homosexual sodomy.

Since *Bowers* was handed down, gay activists had looked for a test case that might become the vehicle for overturning the controversial decision. That test case arose in 1998 when law enforcement officers, responding to a neighbor's false report of "an armed man going crazy," entered an apartment in Houston, Texas, and found two men engaged in sex. They were convicted of deviate sexual intercourse under the state law and fined $200 each. (The neighbor was convicted of filing a false report.) The two men challenged the constitutionality of the Texas law, arguing that it violated their constitutional right to privacy as well as their right to equal treatment under the law. Their arguments were rejected by the Texas courts, and the two men appealed to the Supreme Court.

That the Court agreed to hear the case of *Lawrence v. Texas* was an indication that at least four justices wanted to reconsider the *Bowers* decision. So the ruling striking down the Texas law did not come as a surprise. What had not been expected was the breadth of the decision. Five justices signed a sweeping opinion holding that the Constitution's due process guarantee of liberty extended to the right of mutually consenting adults to engage in private sexual activity without fear of government intervention. "Liberty presumes an autonomy of self that includes freedom of thought, belief, expression, and certain intimate conduct," wrote Justice Anthony M. Kennedy. The case did not involved minors, prostitutes, coercion, or public conduct, he continued. It did involve "two adults who, with full and mutual consent from each other, engaged in sexual practices common to a homosexual lifestyle. The petitioners are entitled to respect for their private lives. The State cannot demean their existence or control their destiny by making their private conduct a crime." Kennedy's opinion was joined by Justices John Paul Stevens, David H. Souter, Ruth Bader Ginsburg, and Stephen G. Breyer.

The five justices also explicitly overturned the 1986 *Bowers* case, saying it "was not correct when it was decided, and it is not correct today" and that its "continuance as precedent demeans the lives of homosexual persons." Justice Sandra Day O'Connor agreed with the outcome but disagreed with the majority's reasoning. She argued that the Texas law was a violation of the Constitution's Equal Protection Clause because it outlawed certain types of sexual conduct for homosexuals but not for heterosexuals. O'Connor, who had been in the majority on the *Bowers* decision, said she saw no reason to overturn it now.

Writing for the dissenting justices, Antonin Scalia said the majority had "largely signed onto the homosexual agenda" and invented a "a brand-new constitutional right." Saying that the decision "effectively decrees the end of all morals legislation," Scalia argued that such social issues should be decided upon by state legislatures and not courts. Chief Justice William H. Rehnquist and Justice Clarence Thomas joined the dissent. Thomas also filed his own dissent, noting that he found the Texas law "uncommonly silly" and that if he were a member of the Texas legislature, he would vote to repeal it.

Gay rights activists and their supporters were thrilled with the ruling, likening it to the Court's 1954 ruling in *Brown v. Board of Education* barring racial segregation in public schools. "*Bowers* took away the humanity of gay people, and this decision gives it back," said Suzanne Goldberg, a Rutgers Law School professor who had represented the two men in the Texas courts. She and others said the decision effectively legitimized gay relationships and thus had broad implications for other gay efforts to win legal rights in such areas as marriage, the military, employment, child custody, and adoption. Others said that the Court's decision, by so forcefully endorsing a right to privacy in intimate relations, had strengthened the fundamental basis the Court had used to legalize abortion in *Roe v. Wade.* Efforts to overturn that decision would be much more difficult as a result of *Lawrence,* they predicted.

Massachusetts Ruling on Gay Marriage

The majority opinion in *Lawrence* explicitly said that the case did not "involve whether the government must give formal recognition to any relationship that homosexual persons seek to enter." The 4–3 decision on November 18 by the Supreme Judicial Court ruled that the Massachusetts constitution required the state to recognize same-sex civil marriages. "The question before us," began Chief Justice Margaret H. Marshall in her majority opinion, "is whether, consistent with the Massachusetts Constitution, the Commonwealth may deny the protections, benefits, and obligations conferred by civil marriage to two individuals of the same sex who wish to marry. We conclude that it may not. The Massachusetts Constitution affirms the dignity and equality of all individuals. It forbids the creation of second-class citizens. In reaching our conclusion we have given full deference to the arguments made by the Commonwealth. But it has failed to identify any constitutionally adequate reason for denying civil marriage to same-sex couples." The case, *Goodridge v. Department of Public Health,* was brought by seven same-sex couples who were refused marriage licenses in 2001.

The Massachusetts court did not immediately legalize same-sex marriage but instead gave the state legislature 180 days "to take such action as it may deem appropriate in light of this opinion." In anticipation of the court ruling, the legislature already had three bills before it—one a state constitutional amendment defining marriage as a union between a man and a woman, another providing for civil unions, and a third allowing same-sex marriages. A state constitutional amendment would nullify the court's ruling and was supported by Republican governor Mitt Romney and Attorney General Thomas F. Reilly, a Democrat. Legislators were scheduled to vote on a ban at a constitutional convention in February 2004. The earliest such an amendment could go before the state's voters was 2006.

Opinion varied about whether passage of a law permitting civil unions would satisfy the court. In late December the Massachusetts Senate asked the court for an advisory opinion on whether a civil union bill would comply with the court's ruling. As of year's end, the court had not responded.

Push for Constitutional Amendments

Many political analysts predicted that the Massachusetts ruling would push the polarizing issue of gay marriage to the forefront in the 2004 presidential election. Some social conservatives said that they actually welcomed the Massachusetts decision because it would create a backlash among the public that would make it easier to get constitutional amendments approved at both the state and the federal levels. "We can prevail on this one. That's all the buzz among Christian groups," the cofounder of one evangelist group said. "This is an opportunity to stop the liberal social juggernaut that has been in motion for forty years."

Thirty-four states had already passed measures defining marriage as a union between a man and a woman, while three had amended their state constitutions to incorporate such bans. In 1996 Congress passed and then-president Bill Clinton signed a Defense of Marriage Act that defined marriage as the union between a man and a woman and allowed states to refuse to recognize gay marriages conducted outside their borders. The constitutionality of that law had never been tested, however. *(Defense of Marriage Act, Historic Documents of 1996, p. 687)*

Legislation to amend the federal constitution to ban gay marriages was introduced in both the Senate and the House. Although no action was taken in 2003, its supporters promised to press the issue in 2004. The Family Research Council, one of the most prominent backers of the amendment, sent out blanket e-mail messages to build support for the measure. The group was also asking political candidates to pledge that they would oppose allowing gays to marry.

Although opposed to gay marriage, many legislators, including Republicans, expressed uncertainty about a constitutional amendment. "I firmly believe marriage should be between a man and a woman," one senior Republican on the House Judiciary Committee told Congressional Quarterly. "I'm just not certain how far we should be going legislatively on this, particularly when it involves the Constitution."

President Bush appeared to share that uncertainty. Throughout the summer and fall Bush avoided taking a direct stand on a constitutional amendment, saying when asked that he would do "what is legally necessary to defend the sanctity of marriage." On December 16, however, the president gave tentative support to a constitutional amendment in an interview with ABC television. "If necessary, I will support a constitutional amendment which would honor marriage between a man and woman, codify that," he said. At the same time he made it clear that he preferred to leave the issue of gay marriage up to the states.

> *Following are excerpts from the majority opinion in the case of* Lawrence v. Texas, *in which the Supreme Court, on June 26, 2003, by a 6–3 vote, struck down as unconstitutional state laws that criminalized sex between mutually consenting gay adults; and from the majority in the case of* Goodridge v. Department of Public Health, *in which the Supreme Judicial Court of Massachusetts, ruled 4–3 on November 18, 2003, that the state's ban on gay marriage was a violation of the state's constitution.*

Lawrence v. Texas

No. 02–102

John Geddes Lawrence and Tyron Garner, Petitioners *v.* Texas	On writ of certiorari to the Court of Appeals of Texas, Fourteenth District

[June 26, 2003]

JUSTICE KENNEDY delivered the opinion of the Court.

Liberty protects the person from unwarranted government intrusions into a dwelling or other private places. In our tradition the State is not omnipresent in the home.

And there are other spheres of our lives and existence, outside the home, where the State should not be a dominant presence. Freedom extends beyond spatial bounds. Liberty presumes an autonomy of self that includes freedom of thought, belief, expression, and certain intimate conduct. . . .

I

The question before the Court is the validity of a Texas statute making it a crime for two persons of the same sex to engage in certain intimate sexual conduct. In Houston, Texas, officers of the Harris County Police Department were dispatched to a private residence in response to a reported weapons disturbance. They entered an apartment where one of the petitioners, John Geddes Lawrence, resided. The right of the police to enter does not seem to have been questioned. The officers observed Lawrence and another man, Tyron Garner, engaging in a sexual act. The two petitioners were arrested, held in custody over night, and charged and convicted before a Justice of the Peace. . . .

The petitioners exercised their right to a trial *de novo* in Harris County Criminal Court. They challenged the statute as a violation of the Equal Protection Clause of the Fourteenth Amendment and of a like provision of the Texas Constitution. . . . Those contentions were rejected. The petitioners, having entered a plea of *nolo contendere*, were each fined $200 and assessed court costs of $141.25. . . .

The Court of Appeals for the Texas Fourteenth District considered the petitioners' federal constitutional arguments under both the Equal Protection and Due Process Clauses of the Fourteenth Amendment. After hearing the case en banc the court, in a divided opinion, rejected the constitutional arguments and affirmed the convictions. . . . The majority opinion indicates that the Court of Appeals considered our decision in *Bowers v. Hardwick* [1986], to be controlling on the federal due process aspect of the case. *Bowers* then being authoritative, this was proper.

We granted certiorari . . . to consider three questions:

> "1. Whether Petitioners' criminal convictions under the Texas "Homosexual Conduct" law—which criminalizes sexual intimacy by same-sex couples, but not identical behavior by different-sex couples—violate the Fourteenth Amendment guarantee of equal protection of laws?
> "2. Whether Petitioners' criminal convictions for adult consensual sexual intimacy in the home violate their vital interests in liberty and privacy protected by the Due Process Clause of the Fourteenth Amendment?
> "3. Whether *Bowers* . . . should be overruled?". . .

The petitioners were adults at the time of the alleged offense. Their conduct was in private and consensual.

II

We conclude the case should be resolved by determining whether the petitioners were free as adults to engage in the private conduct in the exercise of their liberty under the Due Process Clause of the Fourteenth Amendment to the Constitution. For this inquiry we deem it necessary to reconsider the Court's holding in *Bowers*.

There are broad statements of the substantive reach of liberty under the Due Process Clause in earlier cases. . . but the most pertinent beginning point is our decision in *Griswold v. Connecticut* [1965].

In *Griswold* the Court invalidated a state law prohibiting the use of drugs or devices of contraception and counseling or aiding and abetting the use of contraceptives. The Court described the protected interest as a right to privacy and placed emphasis on the marriage relation and the protected space of the marital bedroom. . . .

After *Griswold* it was established that the right to make certain decisions regarding sexual conduct extends beyond the marital relationship. In *Eisenstadt v. Baird* [1972], the Court invalidated a law prohibiting the distribution of contraceptives to unmarried persons. The case was decided under the Equal Protection Clause; . . . but with respect to unmarried persons, the Court went on to state the fundamental proposition that the law impaired the exercise of their personal rights. . . . It quoted from the statement of the Court of Appeals finding the law to be in conflict with fundamental human rights, and it followed with this statement of its own:

> "It is true that in *Griswold* the right of privacy in question inhered in the marital relationship. . . . If the right of privacy means anything, it is the right of the individual, married or single, to be free from unwarranted governmental intrusion into matters so fundamentally affecting a person as the decision whether to bear or beget a child.". . .

The opinions in *Griswold* and *Eisenstadt* were part of the background for the decision in *Roe v. Wade* [1973]. As is well known, the case involved a challenge to the Texas law prohibiting abortions, but the laws of other States were affected as well. Although the Court held the woman's rights were not absolute, her right to elect an abortion did have real and substantial protection as an exercise of her liberty under the Due Process Clause. The Court cited cases that protect spatial freedom and cases that go well beyond it. *Roe* recognized the right of a woman to make certain fundamental decisions affecting her destiny and confirmed once more that the protection of liberty under the Due Process Clause has a substantive dimension of fundamental significance in defining the rights of the person. . . .

The facts in *Bowers* had some similarities to the instant case. A police officer, whose right to enter seems not to have been in question, observed Hardwick, in his own bedroom, engaging in intimate sexual conduct with another adult male. The conduct was in violation of a Georgia statute making it a criminal offense to engage in sodomy. One difference between the two cases is that the Georgia statute prohibited the conduct whether or not the participants were of the same sex, while the Texas statute, as we have seen, applies only to participants of the same sex. Hardwick was not prosecuted, but he brought an action in federal court to declare the state statute invalid. He alleged he was a practicing homosexual and that the criminal prohibition violated rights guaranteed to him by the Constitution. The Court, in an opinion by Justice White, sustained the Georgia law [by a 5–4 vote]. . . .

The Court began its substantive discussion in *Bowers* as follows: "The issue presented is whether the Federal Constitution confers a fundamental right upon homosexuals to engage in sodomy and hence invalidates the laws of the many States that still make such conduct illegal and have done so for a very long time.". . . That statement, we now conclude, discloses the Court's own failure to appreciate the extent of the liberty at stake. To say that the issue in *Bowers* was simply the right to engage in certain sexual conduct demeans the claim the individual put forward, just as it would demean a married couple were it to be said marriage is simply about the right to have sexual intercourse. The laws involved in *Bowers* and here are, to be sure, statutes that purport to do no more than prohibit a particular sexual act. Their penalties and purposes, though, have more far-reaching consequences, touching upon the most private human conduct, sexual behavior, and in the most private of places, the home. The statutes do seek to control a personal relationship that, whether or not entitled to formal recognition in the law, is within the liberty of persons to choose without being punished as criminals.

This, as a general rule, should counsel against attempts by the State, or a court, to define the meaning of the relationship or to set its boundaries absent injury to a person or abuse of an institution the law protects. It suffices for us to acknowledge that adults may choose to enter upon this relationship in the confines of their homes and their own private lives and still retain their dignity as free persons. When sexuality finds overt expression in intimate conduct with another person, the conduct can be but one element in a personal bond that is more enduring. The liberty protected by the Constitution allows homosexual persons the right to make this choice. . . .

[A discussion of the history and enforcement of sodomy laws in the United States has been omitted.]

In summary, the historical grounds relied upon in *Bowers* are more complex than the majority opinion and the concurring opinion by Chief Justice Burger indicate. Their historical premises are not without doubt and, at the very least, are overstated.

It must be acknowledged, of course, that the Court in *Bowers* was making the broader point that for centuries there have been powerful voices to condemn homosexual conduct as immoral. The condemnation has been shaped by religious beliefs, conceptions of right and acceptable behavior, and respect for the traditional family. For many persons these are not trivial concerns but profound and deep convictions accepted as ethical and moral principles to which they aspire and which thus determine the course of their lives. These considerations do not answer the question before us, however. The issue is whether the majority may use the power of the State to enforce these views on the whole society through operation of the criminal law. "Our obligation is to define the liberty of all, not to mandate our own moral code.". . .

Chief Justice Burger joined the opinion for the Court in *Bowers* and further explained his views as follows: "Decisions of individuals relating to homosexual conduct have been subject to state intervention throughout the history of Western civilization. Condemnation of those practices is firmly rooted in Judeao-Christian moral and ethical standards.". . . As with Justice White's assumptions about history, scholarship casts some doubt on the sweeping nature of the statement by Chief Justice Burger as it pertains to private homosexual conduct between consenting adults. . . . In all events we think that our laws and traditions in the past half century are of most relevance here. These references show an emerging awareness that liberty gives substantial protection to adult persons in deciding how to conduct their private lives in matters pertaining to sex. . . .

This emerging recognition should have been apparent when *Bowers* was decided. In 1955 the American Law Institute promulgated the Model Penal Code and made clear that it did not recommend or provide for "criminal penalties for consensual sexual relations conducted in private.". . . It justified its decision on three grounds: (1) The prohibitions undermined respect for the law by penalizing conduct many people engaged in; (2) the statutes regulated private conduct not harmful to others; and (3) the laws were arbitrarily enforced and thus invited the danger of blackmail. . . .

In *Bowers* the Court referred to the fact that before 1961 all 50 States had outlawed sodomy, and that at the time of the Court's decision 24 States and the District of Columbia had sodomy laws. . . . Justice Powell pointed out that these prohibitions often were being ignored, however. Georgia, for instance, had not sought to enforce its law for decades. . . .

The sweeping references by Chief Justice Burger to the history of Western civilization and to Judeo-Christian moral and ethical standards did not take account of other authorities pointing in an opposite direction. A committee advising the British Parliament recommended in 1957 repeal of laws punishing homosexual conduct. . . . Parliament enacted the substance of those recommendations 10 years later. . . .

Of even more importance, almost five years before *Bowers* was decided the European Court of Human Rights considered a case with parallels to *Bowers* and to today's case. An adult male resident in Northern Ireland alleged he was a practicing homosexual who desired to engage in consensual homosexual conduct. The laws of Northern Ireland forbade him that right. He alleged that he had been questioned, his home had been searched, and he feared criminal prosecution. The court held that the laws proscribing the conduct were invalid under the European Convention on Human Rights. . . . Authoritative in all countries that are members of the Council of Europe (21 nations then, 45 nations now), the decision is at odds with the premise in *Bowers* that the claim put forward was insubstantial in our Western civilization.

In our own constitutional system the deficiencies in *Bowers* became even more apparent in the years following its announcement. The 25 States with laws prohibiting the relevant conduct referenced in the *Bowers* decision are reduced now to 13, of which 4 enforce their laws only against homosexual conduct. In those States where sodomy is still proscribed, whether for same-sex or heterosexual conduct, there is a pattern of nonenforcement with respect to consenting adults acting in private. The State of Texas admitted in 1994 that as of that date it had not prosecuted anyone under those circumstances. . . .

Two principal cases decided after *Bowers* cast its holding into even more doubt. In *Planned Parenthood of Southeastern Pa. v. Casey* [1992], the Court reaffirmed the substantive force of the liberty protected by the Due Process Clause. The *Casey* decision again confirmed that our laws and tradition afford constitutional protection to personal decisions relating to marriage, procreation, contraception, family relationships, child rearing, and education. . . . In explaining the respect the Constitution demands for the autonomy of the person in making these choices, we stated as follows:

> "These matters, involving the most intimate and personal choices a person may make in a lifetime, choices central to personal dignity and autonomy, are central to the liberty protected by the Fourteenth Amendment. At the heart of liberty is the right to define one's own concept of existence, of meaning, of the universe, and of the mystery of human life. Beliefs about these matters could not define the attributes of personhood were they formed under compulsion of the State.". . .

Persons in a homosexual relationship may seek autonomy for these purposes, just as heterosexual persons do. The decision in *Bowers* would deny them this right.

The second post–*Bowers* case of principal relevance is *Romer v. Evans* [1996]. There the Court struck down class-based legislation directed at homosexuals as a violation of the Equal Protection Clause. *Romer* invalidated an amendment to Colorado's constitution which named as a solitary class persons who were homosexuals, lesbians, or bisexual either by "orientation, conduct, practices or relationships" . . . and deprived them of protection under state antidiscrimination laws. We concluded that the provision was "born of animosity toward the class of persons affected" and further that it had no rational relation to a legitimate governmental purpose. . . .

As an alternative argument in this case, counsel for the petitioners and some *amici* contend that *Romer* provides the basis for declaring the Texas statute invalid under the Equal Protection Clause. That is a tenable argument, but we conclude the instant case requires us to address whether *Bowers* itself has continuing validity. Were we to hold the statute invalid under the Equal Protection Clause some might question whether a prohibition would be valid if drawn differently, say, to prohibit the conduct both between same-sex and different-sex participants.

Equality of treatment and the due process right to demand respect for conduct protected by the substantive guarantee of liberty are linked in important respects, and a decision on the latter point advances both interests. If protected conduct is made criminal and the law which does so remains unexamined for its substantive validity, its stigma might remain even if it were not enforceable as drawn for equal protection reasons. When homosexual conduct is made criminal by the law of the State, that declaration in and of itself is an invitation to subject homosexual persons to discrimination both in the public and in the private spheres. The central holding of *Bowers* has been brought in question by this case, and it should be addressed. Its continuance as precedent demeans the lives of homosexual persons.

The stigma this criminal statute imposes, moreover, is not trivial. The offense, to be sure, is but a class C misdemeanor, a minor offense in the Texas legal system. Still, it remains a criminal offense with all that imports for the dignity of the persons charged. The petitioners will bear on their record the history of their criminal convictions. . . . We are advised that if Texas convicted an adult for private, consensual homosexual conduct under the statute here in question the convicted person would come within the registration laws of a least four States were he or she to be subject to their jurisdiction. . . . This underscores the consequential nature of the punishment and the state-sponsored condemnation attendant to the criminal prohibition. Furthermore, the Texas criminal conviction carries with it the other collateral consequences always following a conviction, such as notations on job application forms, to mention but one example. . . .

The rationale of *Bowers* does not withstand careful analysis. In his dissenting opinion in *Bowers* JUSTICE STEVENS came to these conclusions:

> "Our prior cases make two propositions abundantly clear. First, the fact that the governing majority in a State has traditionally viewed a particular practice as immoral is not a sufficient reason for

upholding a law prohibiting the practice; neither history nor tradition could save a law prohibiting miscegenation from constitutional attack. Second, individual decisions by married persons, concerning the intimacies of their physical relationship, even when not intended to produce offspring, are a form of "liberty" protected by the Due Process Clause of the Fourteenth Amendment. Moreover, this protection extends to intimate choices by unmarried as well as married persons.". . .

JUSTICE STEVENS' analysis, in our view, should have been controlling in *Bowers* and should control here.

Bowers was not correct when it was decided, and it is not correct today. It ought not to remain binding precedent. *Bowers v. Hardwick* should be and now is overruled.

The present case does not involve minors. It does not involve persons who might be injured or coerced or who are situated in relationships where consent might not easily be refused. It does not involve public conduct or prostitution. It does not involve whether the government must give formal recognition to any relationship that homosexual persons seek to enter. The case does involve two adults who, with full and mutual consent from each other, engaged in sexual practices common to a homosexual lifestyle. The petitioners are entitled to respect for their private lives. The State cannot demean their existence or control their destiny by making their private sexual conduct a crime. Their right to liberty under the Due Process Clause gives them the full right to engage in their conduct without intervention of the government. . . . The Texas statute furthers no legitimate state interest which can justify its intrusion into the personal and private life of the individual.

Had those who drew and ratified the Due Process Clauses of the Fifth Amendment or the Fourteenth Amendment known the components of liberty in its manifold possibilities, they might have been more specific. They did not presume to have this insight. They knew times can blind us to certain truths and later generations can see that laws once thought necessary and proper in fact serve only to oppress. As the Constitution endures, persons in every generation can invoke its principles in their own search for greater freedom.

The judgment of the Court of Appeals for the Texas Fourteenth District is reversed, and the case is remanded for further proceedings not inconsistent with this opinion.

It is so ordered.

Source: U.S. Supreme Court of the United States. *Lawrence v. Texas.* No. 02–102, 539 U.S. ___ (2003), June 26, 2003. http://supct.law.cornell.edu/supct/html/02-102.ZO.html (accessed July 23, 2003).

Goodridge et al. v. Department of Public Health

MARSHALL, C.J. Marriage is a vital social institution. The exclusive commitment of two individuals to each other nurtures love and mutual support; it brings stability to our society. For those who choose to marry, and for their children, marriage provides an abundance of legal, financial, and social benefits. In return it imposes weighty legal, financial, and social obligations. The question before us is whether, consistent with the Massachusetts Constitution, the Commonwealth may deny the protections, benefits, and obligations conferred by civil marriage to two individuals of the same sex who wish to marry. We conclude that it may not. The Massachusetts Constitution affirms the dignity and equality of all individuals. It forbids the creation of second-class citizens. In reaching our conclusion we have given full deference to the arguments made by the Commonwealth. But it has failed to identify any constitutionally adequate reason for denying civil marriage to same-sex couples.

We are mindful that our decision marks a change in the history of our marriage law. Many people hold deep-seated religious, moral, and ethical convictions that marriage should be limited to the union of one man and one woman, and that homosexual conduct is immoral. Many hold equally strong religious, moral, and ethical convictions that same-sex couples are entitled to be married, and that homosexual persons should be treated no differently than their heterosexual neighbors. Neither view answers the question before us. Our concern is with the Massachusetts Constitution as a charter of governance for every person properly within its reach. "Our obligation is to define the liberty of all, not to mandate our own moral code.". . .

Whether the Commonwealth may use its formidable regulatory authority to bar same-sex couples from civil marriage is a question not previously addressed by a Massachusetts appellate court. It is a question the United States Supreme Court left open as a matter of Federal law in *Lawrence [v. Texas* (2003)], where it was not an issue. There, the Court affirmed that the core concept of common human dignity protected by the Fourteenth Amendment to the United States Constitution precludes government intrusion into the deeply personal realms of consensual adult expressions of intimacy and one's choice of an intimate partner. The Court also reaffirmed the central role that decisions whether to marry or have children bear in shaping one's identity. . . . The Massachusetts Constitution is, if anything, more protective of individual liberty and equality than the Federal Constitution; it may demand broader protection for fundamental rights; and it is less tolerant of government intrusion into the protected spheres of private life.

Barred access to the protections, benefits, and obligations of civil marriage, a person who enters into an intimate, exclusive union with another of the same sex is arbitrarily deprived of membership in one of our community's most rewarding and cherished institutions. That exclusion is incompatible with the constitutional principles of respect for individual autonomy and equality under law.

I

The plaintiffs are fourteen individuals from five Massachusetts counties. . . .

The plaintiffs include business executives, lawyers, an investment banker, educators, therapists, and a computer engineer. Many are active in church, community, and school groups. They have employed such legal means as are available to them—for example, joint adoption, powers of attorney, and joint ownership of real property—to secure aspects of their relationships. Each plaintiff attests a desire to marry his or her partner in order to affirm publicly their commitment to each other and to secure the legal protections and benefits afforded to married couples and their children.

The Department of Public Health (department) is charged by statute with safeguarding public health. . . . Among its responsibilities, the department oversees the registry of vital records and statistics (registry), which "enforce[s] all laws" relative to the issuance of marriage licenses and the keeping of marriage records. . . , and which promulgates policies and procedures for the issuance of marriage licenses by city and town clerks and registers. . . .

In March and April, 2001, each of the plaintiff couples attempted to obtain a marriage license from a city or town clerk's office. . . . In each case, the clerk either refused to accept the notice of intention to marry or denied a marriage license to the couple on the ground that Massachusetts does not recognize same-sex marriage. Because obtaining a marriage license is a necessary prerequisite to civil marriage in Massachusetts, denying marriage licenses to the plaintiffs was tantamount to denying them access to civil marriage itself, with its appurtenant social and legal protections, benefits, and obligations.

On April 11, 2001, the plaintiffs filed suit in the Superior Court against the department and the commissioner seeking a judgment that "the exclusion of the [p]laintiff couples and other qualified same-sex couples from access to marriage licenses, and the legal and social status of civil marriage, as well as the protections, benefits and obligations of marriage, violates Massachusetts law.". . .

The department, represented by the Attorney General, admitted to a policy and practice of denying marriage licenses to same-sex couples. It denied that its actions violated any law or that the plaintiffs were entitled to relief. The parties filed cross motions for summary judgment.

A Superior Court judge ruled for the department. In a memorandum of decision and order dated May 7, 2002, he dismissed the plaintiffs' claim that the marriage statutes should be construed to permit marriage between persons of the same sex. . . . Turning to the constitutional claims, he held that the marriage exclusion does not offend the liberty, freedom, equality, or due process provisions of the Massachusetts Constitution, and that the Massachusetts Declaration of Rights does not guarantee "the fundamental right to marry a person of the same sex." He concluded that prohibiting same-sex marriage rationally furthers the Legislature's legitimate interest in safeguarding the "primary purpose" of marriage, "procreation." The Legislature may rationally limit marriage to opposite-sex couples, he concluded, because those couples are "theoretically . . . capable of procreation," they do not rely on "inherently more cumbersome" noncoital means of reproduction, and they are more likely than same-sex couples to have children, or more children.

After the complaint was dismissed and summary judgment entered for the defendants, the plaintiffs appealed. Both parties requested direct appellate review, which we granted.

[Part II omitted.]

III

A

The larger question is whether, as the department claims, government action that bars same-sex couples from civil marriage constitutes a legitimate exercise of the State's authority to regulate conduct, or whether, as the plaintiffs claim, this categorical marriage exclusion violates the Massachusetts Constitution. We have recognized the long-standing statutory understanding, derived from the common law, that "marriage" means the lawful union of a woman and a man. But that history cannot and does not foreclose the constitutional question.

The plaintiffs' claim that the marriage restriction violates the Massachusetts Constitution can be analyzed in two ways. Does it offend the Constitution's guarantees of equality before the law? Or do the liberty and due process provisions of the Massachusetts Constitution secure the plaintiffs' right to marry their chosen partner? In matters implicating marriage, family life, and the upbringing of children, the two constitutional concepts frequently overlap, as they do here. . . . We begin by considering the nature of civil marriage itself. Simply put, the government creates civil marriage. In Massachusetts, civil marriage is, and since pre-Colonial days has been, precisely what its name implies: a wholly secular institution. . . . No religious ceremony has ever been required to validate a Massachusetts marriage.

In a real sense, there are three partners to every civil marriage: two willing spouses and an approving State. . . . While only the parties can mutually assent to marriage, the terms of the marriage—who may marry and what obligations, benefits, and liabilities attach to civil marriage—are set by the Commonwealth. Conversely, while only the parties can agree to end the marriage (absent the death of one of them or a marriage void ab initio), the Commonwealth defines the exit terms. . . .

Civil marriage is created and regulated through exercise of the police power. . . . "Police power" (now more commonly termed the State's regulatory authority) is an old-fashioned term for the Commonwealth's lawmaking authority, as bounded by the liberty and equality guarantees of the Massachusetts Constitution and its express delegation of power from the people to their government. In broad terms, it is the Legislature's power to enact rules to regulate conduct, to the extent that such laws are "necessary to secure the health, safety, good order, comfort, or general welfare of the community". . . .

Without question, civil marriage enhances the "welfare of the community." It is a "social institution of the highest importance.". . . Civil marriage anchors an ordered society by encouraging stable relationships over transient ones. It is central to the way the Commonwealth identifies individuals, provides for the orderly distribution of property, ensures that children and adults are cared for and supported whenever possible from private rather than public funds, and tracks important epidemiological and demographic data.

Marriage also bestows enormous private and social advantages on those who choose to marry. Civil marriage is at once a deeply personal commitment to another human being and a highly public celebration of the ideals of mutuality, companionship, intimacy, fidelity, and family. . . . Because it fulfils yearnings for security, safe haven, and connection that express our common humanity, civil marriage is an esteemed institution, and the decision whether and whom to marry is among life's momentous acts of self-definition.

Tangible as well as intangible benefits flow from marriage. The marriage license grants valuable property rights to those who meet the entry requirements, and who agree to what might otherwise be a burdensome degree of government regulation of their activities. . . .

The benefits accessible only by way of a marriage license are enormous, touching nearly every aspect of life and death. The department states that "hundreds of statutes" are related to marriage and to marital benefits. [The opinion then gives several examples touching on property rights and rights associated with parentage.]

It is undoubtedly for these concrete reasons, as well as for its intimately personal significance, that civil marriage has long been termed a "civil right.". . . The United States Supreme Court has described the right to marry as "of fundamental importance for all individuals" and as "part of the fundamental 'right of privacy' implicit in the Fourteenth Amendment's Due Process Clause.". . .

Without the right to marry—or more properly, the right to choose to marry—one is excluded from the full range of human experience and denied full protection of the laws for one's "avowed commitment to an intimate and lasting human relationship." Because civil marriage is central to the lives of individuals and the welfare of the community, our laws assiduously protect the individual's right to marry against undue government incursion. Laws may not "interfere directly and substantially with the right to marry.". . .

Unquestionably, the regulatory power of the Commonwealth over civil marriage is broad, as is the Commonwealth's discretion to award public benefits. . . . Individuals who have the choice to marry each other and nevertheless choose not to may properly be denied the legal benefits of marriage. . . . But that same logic cannot hold for a qualified individual who would marry if she or he only could.

B

For decades, indeed centuries, in much of this country (including Massachusetts) no lawful marriage was possible between white and black Americans. That long history availed not when the Supreme Court of California held in 1948 that a legislative prohibition against interracial marriage violated the due process and equality guarantees of the Fourteenth Amendment [*Perez v. Sharp* (1948)], or when, nineteen years later, the United States Supreme Court also held that a statutory bar to interracial marriage violated the Fourteenth Amendment [*Loving v. Virginia* (1967)]. As both *Perez* and *Loving* make clear, the right to marry means little if it does not include the right to marry the person of one's choice, subject to appropriate government restrictions in the interests of public health, safety, and welfare. . . . In this case, as in *Perez* and *Loving*, a statute deprives individuals of access to an institution of fundamental legal, personal, and social significance—the institution of marriage—because of a single trait: skin color in *Perez* and *Loving*, sexual orientation here. As it did in *Perez* and *Loving*, history must yield to a more fully developed understanding of the invidious quality of the discrimination. . . .

The individual liberty and equality safeguards of the Massachusetts Constitution protect both "freedom from" unwarranted government intrusion into protected spheres of life and "freedom to" partake in benefits created by the State for the common good. . . . Both freedoms are involved here. Whether and whom to marry, how to express sexual intimacy, and whether and how to establish a family—these are among the most basic of every individual's liberty and due process rights. . . . And central to personal freedom and security is the assurance that the laws will apply equally to persons in similar situations. . . . The liberty interest in choosing whether and whom to marry would be hollow if the Commonwealth could, without sufficient justification, foreclose an individual from freely choosing the person with whom to share an exclusive commitment in the unique institution of civil marriage.

The Massachusetts Constitution requires, at a minimum, that the exercise of the State's regulatory authority not be "arbitrary or capricious." . . . Under both the equality and liberty guarantees, regulatory authority must, at very least, serve "a legitimate purpose in a rational way"; a statute must "bear a reasonable relation to a permissible legislative objective." . . . Any law failing to satisfy the basic standards of rationality is void. . . .

The department posits three legislative rationales for prohibiting same-sex couples from marrying: (1) providing a "favorable setting for procreation"; (2) ensuring the optimal setting for child rearing, which the department defines as "a two-parent family with one parent of each sex"; and (3) preserving scarce State and private financial resources. We consider each in turn.

The judge in the Superior Court endorsed the first rationale, holding that "the state's interest in regulating marriage is based on the traditional concept that marriage's primary purpose is procreation." This is incorrect. Our laws of civil marriage do not privilege procreative heterosexual intercourse between married people above every other form of adult intimacy and every other means of creating a family. [Massachusetts law] contains no requirement that the applicants for a marriage license attest to their ability or intention to conceive children by coitus. Fertility is not a condition of marriage, nor is it grounds for divorce. . . . While it is certainly true that many, perhaps most, married couples have children together (assisted or unassisted), it is the exclusive and permanent commitment of the marriage partners to one another, not the begetting of children, that is the sine qua non of civil marriage.

Moreover, the Commonwealth affirmatively facilitates bringing children into a family regardless of whether the intended parent is married or unmarried, whether the child is adopted or born into a family, whether assistive technology was used to conceive the child, and whether the parent or her partner is heterosexual, homosexual, or bisexual. If procreation were a necessary component of civil marriage, our statutes would draw a tighter circle around the permissible bounds of nonmarital child bearing and the creation of families by noncoital means. The [dissent's] attempt to isolate procreation as "the source of a fundamental right to marry" . . . overlooks the integrated way in which courts have examined the complex and overlapping realms of personal autonomy, marriage, family life, and child rearing. Our jurisprudence recognizes that, in these nuanced and fundamentally private areas of life, such a narrow focus is inappropriate.

The "marriage is procreation" argument singles out the one unbridgeable difference between same-sex and opposite-sex couples, and transforms that difference into the essence of legal marriage. . . . In so doing, the State's action confers an official stamp of approval on the destructive stereotype that same-sex relationships are inherently unstable and inferior to opposite-sex relationships and are not worthy of respect.

The department's first stated rationale, equating marriage with unassisted heterosexual procreation, shades imperceptibly into its second: that confining marriage to opposite-sex couples ensures that children are raised in the "optimal" setting. Protecting the welfare of children is a paramount State policy. Restricting marriage to opposite-sex couples, however, cannot plausibly further this policy. "The demographic changes of the past century make it difficult to speak of an average American family. The composition of families varies greatly from household to household.". . . Massachusetts has responded supportively to "the changing realities of the American family" . . . and has moved vigorously to strengthen the modern family in its many variations. . . . Moreover, we have repudiated the common-law power of the State to provide varying levels of protection to children based on the circumstances of birth. . . . The "best interests of the child" standard does not turn on a parent's sexual orientation or marital status. . . .

The department has offered no evidence that forbidding marriage to people of the same sex will increase the number of couples choosing to enter into opposite-sex marriages in order to have and raise children. There is thus no rational relationship between the marriage statute and the Commonwealth's proffered goal of protecting the "optimal" child rearing unit. Moreover, the department readily concedes that people in same-sex couples may be "excellent" parents. These couples (including four of the plaintiff couples) have children for the reasons others do—to love them, to care for them, to nurture them. But the task of child rearing for same-sex couples is made infinitely harder by their status as outliers to the marriage laws. While establishing the parentage of children as soon as possible is crucial to the safety and welfare of children . . . same-sex couples must undergo the sometimes lengthy and intrusive process of second-parent adoption to establish their joint parentage. While the enhanced income provided by marital benefits is an important source of security and stability for married couples and their children, those benefits are denied to families headed by same-sex couples. While the laws of divorce provide clear and reasonably predictable guidelines for child sup-

COURTS ON SODOMY, GAY MARRIAGE   421

port, child custody, and property division on dissolution of a marriage, same-sex couples who dissolve their relationships find themselves and their children in the highly unpredictable terrain of equity jurisdiction. . . . Given the wide range of public benefits reserved only for married couples, we do not credit the department's contention that the absence of access to civil marriage amounts to little more than an inconvenience to same-sex couples and their children. Excluding same-sex couples from civil marriage will not make children of opposite-sex marriages more secure, but it does prevent children of same-sex couples from enjoying the immeasurable advantages that flow from the assurance of "a stable family structure in which children will be reared, educated, and socialized.". . .

No one disputes that the plaintiff couples are families, that many are parents, and that the children they are raising, like all children, need and should have the fullest opportunity to grow up in a secure, protected family unit. Similarly, no one disputes that, under the rubric of marriage, the State provides a cornucopia of substantial benefits to married parents and their children. The preferential treatment of civil marriage reflects the Legislature's conclusion that marriage "is the foremost setting for the education and socialization of children" precisely because it "encourages parents to remain committed to each other and to their children as they grow.". . .

In this case, we are confronted with an entire, sizeable class of parents raising children who have absolutely no access to civil marriage and its protections because they are forbidden from procuring a marriage license. It cannot be rational under our laws, and indeed it is not permitted, to penalize children by depriving them of State benefits because the State disapproves of their parents' sexual orientation.

The third rationale advanced by the department is that limiting marriage to opposite-sex couples furthers the Legislature's interest in conserving scarce State and private financial resources. The marriage restriction is rational, it argues, because the General Court logically could assume that same-sex couples are more financially independent than married couples and thus less needy of public marital benefits, such as tax advantages, or private marital benefits, such as employer-financed health plans that include spouses in their coverage.

An absolute statutory ban on same-sex marriage bears no rational relationship to the goal of economy. . . . Massachusetts marriage laws do not condition receipt of public and private financial benefits to married individuals on a demonstration of financial dependence on each other; the benefits are available to married couples regardless of whether they mingle their finances or actually depend on each other for support.

The department suggests additional rationales for prohibiting same-sex couples from marrying, which are developed by some amici. It argues that broadening civil marriage to include same-sex couples will trivialize or destroy the institution of marriage as it has historically been fashioned.

Certainly our decision today marks a significant change in the definition of marriage as it has been inherited from the common law, and understood by many societies for centuries. But it does not disturb the fundamental value of marriage in our society.

Here, the plaintiffs seek only to be married, not to undermine the institution of civil marriage. They do not want marriage abolished. They do not attack the binary nature of marriage, the consanguinity provisions, or any of the other gate-keeping provisions of the marriage licensing law. Recognizing the right of an individual to marry a person of the same sex will not diminish the validity or dignity of opposite-sex marriage, any more than recognizing the right of an individual to marry a person of a different race devalues the marriage of a person who marries someone of her own race. If anything, extending civil marriage to same-sex couples reinforces the importance of marriage to individuals and communities. That same-sex couples are willing to embrace marriage's solemn obligations of exclusivity, mutual support, and commitment to one another is a testament to the enduring place of marriage in our laws and in the human spirit.

It has been argued that, due to the State's strong interest in the institution of marriage as a stabilizing social structure, only the Legislature can control and define its boundaries. Accordingly, our elected representatives legitimately may choose to exclude same-sex couples from civil marriage in order to assure all citizens of the Commonwealth that (1) the benefits of our marriage laws are available explicitly to create and support a family setting that is, in the Legislature's view, optimal for child rearing, and (2) the State does not endorse gay and lesbian parenthood as the equivalent of being raised by one's married biological parents. These arguments miss the point. The Massachusetts Constitution requires that legislation meet certain criteria and not extend beyond certain limits. It is the function of courts to determine whether these criteria are met and whether these limits are exceeded. In most instances, these limits are defined by whether a rational basis exists to conclude that legislation will bring about a rational result. The Legislature in the first instance, and the courts in the last instance, must ascertain whether such a rational basis exists. To label the court's role as usurping that of the Legislature . . . is to misunderstand the nature and purpose of judicial review. We owe great deference to the Legislature to decide social and policy issues, but it is the traditional and settled role of courts to decide constitutional issues.

The history of constitutional law "is the story of the extension of constitutional rights and protections to people once ignored or excluded.". . . This statement is as true in the area of civil marriage as in any other area of civil rights. . . . As a public institution and a right of fundamental importance, civil marriage is an evolving paradigm. The common law was exceptionally harsh toward women who became wives: a woman's legal identity all but evaporated into that of her husband. . . . But since at least the middle of the Nineteenth Century, both the courts and the Legislature have acted to ameliorate the harshness of the common-law regime. . . . Alarms about the imminent erosion of the "natural" order of marriage were sounded over the demise of antimiscegenation laws, the expansion of the rights of married women, and the introduction of "no-fault" divorce. Marriage has survived all of these transformations, and we have no doubt that marriage will continue to be a vibrant and revered institution.

We also reject the argument suggested by the department, and elaborated by some amici, that expanding the institution of civil marriage in Massa chusetts to include same-sex couples will lead to interstate conflict. We would not presume to dictate how another State should respond to today's decision. But neither should considerations of comity prevent us from according Massachusetts residents the full measure of protection available under the Massachusetts Constitution. The genius of our Federal system is that each State's Constitution has vitality specific to its own traditions, and that, subject to the minimum requirements of the Fourteenth Amendment, each State is free to address difficult issues of individual liberty in the manner its own Constitution demands. . . .

The department has had more than ample opportunity to articulate a constitutionally adequate justification for limiting civil marriage to opposite-sex unions. It has failed to do so. The department has offered purported justifications for the civil marriage restriction that are starkly at odds with the comprehensive network of vigorous, gender-neutral laws promoting stable families and the best interests of children. It has failed to identify any relevant characteristic that would justify shutting the door to civil marriage to a person who wishes to marry someone of the same sex.

The marriage ban works a deep and scarring hardship on a very real segment of the community for no rational reason. The absence of any reasonable relationship between, on the one hand, an absolute disqualification of same-sex couples who wish to enter into civil marriage and, on the other, protection of public health, safety, or general welfare, suggests that the marriage restriction is rooted in persistent prejudices against persons who are (or who are believed to be) homosexual. "The Constitution cannot control such prejudices but neither can it tolerate them. Private biases may be outside the reach of the law, but the law cannot, directly or indirectly, give them effect.". . . Limiting the protections, benefits, and obligations of civil marriage to opposite-sex couples violates the basic premises of individual liberty and equality under law protected by the Massachusetts Constitution.

IV

We consider next the plaintiffs' request for relief. We preserve as much of the statute as may be preserved in the face of the successful constitutional challenge. . . .

Here, no one argues that striking down the marriage laws is an appropriate form of relief. Eliminating civil marriage would be wholly inconsistent with the Legislature's deep commitment to fostering stable families and would dismantle a vital organizing principle of our society. We face a problem similar to one that recently confronted the Court of Appeal for Ontario, the highest court of that Canadian province, when it considered the constitutionality of the same-sex marriage ban under Canada's Federal Constitution, the Charter of Rights and Freedoms (Charter). . . . Canada, like the United States, adopted the common law of England that civil marriage is "the voluntary union for life of one man and one woman, to the exclusion of all others." . . . In holding that the limitation of civil marriage to opposite-sex couples violated the Charter, the Court of Appeal refined the common-law meaning of marriage. We concur with this remedy, which is entirely consonant with established principles of jurisprudence empowering a court to refine a common-law principle in light of evolving constitutional standards. . . .

We construe civil marriage to mean the voluntary union of two persons as spouses, to the exclusion of all others. This reformulation redresses the plaintiffs' constitutional injury and furthers the aim of marriage to promote stable, exclusive relationships. It advances the two legitimate State interests the department has identified: providing a stable setting for child rearing and conserving State resources. It leaves intact the Legislature's broad discretion to regulate marriage. . . .

In their complaint the plaintiffs request only a declaration that their exclusion and the exclusion of other qualified same-sex couples from access to civil marriage violates Massachusetts law. We declare that barring an individual from the protections, benefits, and obligations of civil marriage solely because that person would marry a person of the same sex violates the Massachusetts Constitution. We vacate the summary judgment for the department. We remand this case to the Superior Court for entry of judgment consistent with this opinion. Entry of judgment shall be stayed for 180 days to permit the Legislature to take such action as it may deem appropriate in light of this opinion. . . .

So ordered.

Source: Commonwealth of Massachusetts. Supreme Judicial Court. *Goodridge vs. Department of Public Health.* SJC–08860, November 18, 2003. www.state.ma.us/courts/courtsandjudges/courts/supremejudicial-court/goodridge.html (accessed November 25, 2003).

Democratic Security and Defense Policy of Colombian President Uribe

June 29, 2003

INTRODUCTION

Colombia's new hard-line president had some success during 2003 in combating left-wing guerrillas and right-wing paramilitaries—and the narcotics trade that all these groups ran. But Alvaro Uribe was unable to translate his battlefield success and personal popularity into broad public support for some of the policies he said were needed to curb corruption, stimulate the economy, and win the war against the guerrilla armies.

President Uribe won strong backing from the United States, however. The Bush administration sent Colombia more than $750 million in military aid during the year.

Colombia for decades had been one of the most unstable, violence-plagued countries in Latin America. Leftist guerrilla movements began wars against the government during the early 1960s. They were countered during the 1980s by paramilitary groups that were financed by wealthy landowners and aligned with right-wing elements of the military. The government succeeded during the early 1990s in dismantling criminal cartels that dominated illegal production and trafficking of cocaine and heroin—but then the narcotics industry was taken over by the guerrillas and the right-wing vigilantes.

After a failed effort by President Andres Pastrana to negotiate peace with the guerrillas, Uribe won the presidency in 2002 on a pledge to use a "firm hand" to end the insurgencies and the narcotics trade. Colombia produced an estimated 90 percent of the world's cocaine and was a major producer of heroin, providing about 75 percent of the heroin entering the United States. *(Background, Historic Documents of 2000, p. 840; Historic Documents of 2002, p. 569)*

Violence and Safety

Uribe's pledge of a "firm hand" against rebels represented an explicit statement that military force—not negotiation—was the solution to the decades of violence and turmoil that had plagued Colombia. Uribe stuck to that pledge in terms of the two major leftist guerrilla groups, and the response was an upsurge of bombings in Bogota and other cities, along with hundreds of kidnappings and other forms of guerrilla violence that long had been standard practice in the country. Late in the year Uribe shifted course in the case of the right-wing paramilitaries, agreeing to negotiate with them even though they had not met the conditions he had set for dealing with all such groups. Uribe set forth his tough policy in a document titled "Democratic Security and Defense," made public June 29.

The year's single most violent incident came on February 7, when a car bomb exploded outside an exclusive nightclub in Bogota, killing 36 people and wounding 160 others. The government blamed the attack on the larger of the two leftist guerrilla armies, the Revolutionary Armed Forces of Colombia (FARC, in its Spanish acronym); that group later denied that any of its members had been involved. Colombia sought international support for its condemnation of FARC and on February 12 secured passage of a resolution by the permanent council of the Organization of American States expressing "profound repudiation of the despicable terrorist act" by FARC.

Two back-to-back incidents the following week heightened tension even further. First, on February 13 a U.S. reconnaissance plane carrying anti-narcotics personnel crashed about eighty-five miles south of Bogota. The American pilot and a Colombian intelligence agent, both of whom apparently were injured in the crash, were shot dead; three other U.S. citizens were taken hostage by the FARC guerrillas. News organizations later reported that all four Americans were employees of a subsidiary of Northrop Grumman, a defense contractor hired by the U.S. government to search out and destroy narcotics plantations in rural Colombia. The three hostages were still being held at year's end. On February 14, a bomb exploded in a house beneath the flight path of Uribe's plane. Seventeen people were killed, among them police officers who had been searching the house after being tipped off to an alleged attempt to assassinate the president.

Several other bombings during the year were less deadly but nevertheless damaging to the government's campaign to halt such violence. After one such bombing, on September 28, that killed eleven people in the southern city of Florencia, Uribe declared: "Colombia weeps but doesn't surrender."

Colombia maintained its dubious distinction of being the kidnapping capital of the world, but at a reduced level in 2003. The government claimed nearly a one-third drop, from 2,986 kidnappings in 2002 to 2,043 in 2003. Kidnapping business leaders, government officials, and ordinary citizens for ransom or as political hostages had long been a common practice for the guerrillas and paramilitary forces. The most prominent victim, presidential candidate Ingrid Betancourt, who was taken hostage early in 2002, remained in FARC custody throughout 2003. In May a state governor, a former defense minister, and eight others who had been held hostage for more than a year by FARC in the Antioquia province were killed in a failed rescue attempt by the military.

Despite the continued violence, numerous opinion polls gave Uribe high marks for his campaign against the guerrillas—in large part because many Colombians said they felt safer than at any point in recent years. This perception of relative safety appeared to be bolstered by some statistics collected by the government and private groups. The number of murders declined (although Colombia still had one of the highest murder rates in the world), and "only" 156,000 people were forced from their homes in 2003 because of violence (about half as many as in 2002). Estimates of those who had been permanently displaced ranged from 1 million to 3 million, out of a total population of about 40 million.

The military stepped up its operations against FARC and the much smaller guerrilla force known as the National Liberation Army (ELN, in Spanish). For years Colombia's military had been widely perceived as corrupt and incompetent, but since 2000 an infusion of more than $2.6 billion in U.S. aid appeared to professionalize the army. The newly trained and equipped military forces said they fought more than 2,300 battles with the guerrillas and paramilitary units in 2003, nearly twice as many as the previous year. Most of these "battles" were small engagements, with a handful of fighters on either side.

In addition to ordering more aggressive tactics by the army, Uribe employed two new weapons in the war against the guerrillas: paid civilian informants and small armies of peasants armed and organized by the military. Uribe said the civilians extended the government's reach into territories long controlled by the guerrillas. Several human rights groups expressed deep concern about the use of civilians to combat guerrillas, however, noting that it made civilian populations even more vulnerable than before to retaliation.

Partly in response to the army's increased vigor, the two leftist groups (FARC and ELN) announced in August that they were uniting. Between them, the two groups claimed to have more than 22,000 fighters, and they controlled most of the cocaine- and heroin-producing regions in the south and east of Colombia. In addition to attacking representatives of government authority—mayors, judges, and of course the military—the guerrillas used terror and intimidation to extract support from remote peasant villages.

Another 12,000 or so fighters were aligned with the various right-wing militias, known collectively as the United Self-Defense Forces of Columbia (AUC in Spanish). These groups originally were formed to battle the leftist guerrillas on behalf of wealthy farmers, but by the late 1990s they had become lawless gangs that preyed on civilians and controlled a significant portion of the country's narcotics trade. Many of the paramilitary leaders reportedly were former army officers who maintained close ties to the military. Human Rights Watch said, in a report at year's end, that the government had done little to cut ties between the army and the militias: "Some government commanders promote, encourage, and protect paramilitaries, share intelligence, coordinate military operations, and even share fighters with them."

The AUC announced a cease-fire in December 2002 and in July signed an agreement with the government pledging to demobilize completely by 2005. As part of the agreement, Uribe promised to push legislation through the Colombian Congress granting amnesty to most militia members; the legislation was still pending at year's end. The agreement did not specify what would happen to the AUC's two top leaders, Carlos Castano and Salvatore Mancuso, both of whom had been charged with murders and other crimes and had been indicted in the United States on charges of cocaine trafficking.

Human rights groups in Colombia and the United States opposed the amnesty. Jose Miguel Vivanco, director of the Americas division for Human Rights Watch, said: "This proposal specifically contemplates impunity, not a single day in prison for those who are responsible for atrocities and who have been profiting from narco-trafficking all this time." Criticism on another score came from the International Crisis Group, a think tank based in Brussels, which noted in a November 13 report that the AUC militias had not complied with any of the three conditions Uribe had set for negotiations with groups that fought the government: a cease-fire, a halt to kidnappings and attacks against civilians, and a withdrawal from narcotics trafficking. Despite its claimed cease-fire, the AUC had continued its attacks against government forces and civilians and was still deeply engaged in the drug trade, the group said.

Such criticism did not deter Uribe, who pressed ahead with his plan to demobilize the militias. On November 25 approximately 800 fighters from an AUC unit based in the city of Medellin handed over a relatively small quantity of weapons (one reporter counted fewer than 200), then were bused to a nearby recreation center, where they were to receive job training.

Political Setbacks for Uribe

Uribe's personal popularity apparently did not translate into universal support for his policies. The president suffered electoral setbacks in major votes on October 25–26. In the first vote, a referendum, Uribe had asked the electorate to ratify fifteen complex legal changes he said were required to reform the government, spur the economy, and combat the country's persistent corruption. The key changes Uribe wanted would have reduced the size of the Colombian Congress, frozen the wages and pensions of government workers (except those on the bottom rungs) for two years, and allowed political parties to gain representation in Congress only if they achieved at least a 2 percent threshold of the national vote. All of Uribe's proposals attracted solid majorities (some with more than 90 percent), but voter turnout in the referendum fell just short of the required minimum. Opponents of the changes had urged voters to stay away from the polls or cast blank ballots.

The president suffered his second setback the following day, when voters handed victories to several of his opponents in local elections. The big winner was Lucho Garzon, a former trade union official, who was elected mayor of Bogota. The victory made Garzon the first left-wing candidate ever elected to high public office in Colombia. Garzon was the star candidate of a new center-left alliance called the Democratic Pole. He had finished third in the 2002 presidential election, but his victory appeared to make him a strong candidate for the presidency in 2006.

In addition to undermining key aspects of Uribe's policies, the election results had the unforeseen consequence of blocking—at least temporarily—a drive in Congress to enable the president to serve a second consecutive four-year term. Colombia's constitution limited presidents to a single four-year term in office, but Uribe's early successes had led supporters to offer an amendment setting that provision aside so he could run for a second term in 2006. Before the October 25–26 votes, that proposal seemed certain to pass, but the Senate blocked it on October 28.

The political setback also led Uribe to disregard his campaign pledge to stick with his cabinet throughout his four-year term. During the first two weeks of November Uribe accepted the resignations of three cabinet ministers (including the occupants of the two most important posts, the interior and defense ministries), the commander of the armed forces, and the chief of the national police. The resignation of defense minister Marta Lucia Ramirez was widely seen as a defeat for Uribe's anticorruption campaign. The country's first female defense chief, she had clashed repeatedly with the army's generals by seeking to curb their ability to benefit personally from military contracts. Uribe replaced her with an insurance company executive, Jorge Uribe Echavarria (no relation to the president).

Deeper U.S. Involvement

President Bill Clinton in 2000 convinced U.S. legislators to endorse a major U.S. commitment to a long-term antinarcotics plan developed by Colombia's then-president Pastrana. Under his "Plan Colombia," Pastrana envisioned major infusions of aid from the United States and the European Union to help Colombia fight narcotics trafficking and offer alternative sources of employment for the farmers and peasants who had grown dependent on it. From 2000 to 2003 the United States provided the Colombian army with seventy-two helicopters, radios for command-and-control operations, weapons, and other equipment; annual military aid ranged from about $500 million to $750 million (the fiscal 2003 figure).

Until 2002 Congress stipulated that U.S. aid could be used only to fight narcotics trafficking, which was the highest priority in Washington. But in 2002 the administration of President George W. Bush persuaded Congress to allow Colombia's military to use the U.S.-provided helicopters and other equipment to fight the guerrillas and paramilitaries, who were the major narcotics traffickers. Congress had imposed two other major restrictions on U.S. involvement in Colombia: U.S. troops could not engage in actual combat, and no more than 400 U.S. military personnel and 400 nonmilitary personnel (mostly contract employees) could be stationed in Colombia at any given time. Congress gave the president the right to exceed the troop limits under some circumstances. Congress also had sought to use U.S. aid as a lever to force the Colombian military to cut ties to the paramilitaries and halt its abuse of the human rights of civilians, especially rural peasants. Presidents Clinton and Bush repeatedly told Congress that these human rights conditions were being met, but Human Rights Watch and other advocacy groups said the military had made few of the reforms Congress wanted.

A step toward a possible U.S. combat role was taken in mid-January 2003, when about seventy U.S. special forces troops arrived in the northeastern province of Arauca (bordering Venezuela). The troops were assigned to train several thousand Colombian soldiers in counterinsurgency techniques, including the defense of an oil pipeline operated by the Colombian government and Occidental Petroleum Corporation, of California. FARC guerrillas had attacked the pipeline dozens of times in 2001 and 2002.

Bush told Congress in February that up to 150 additional troops would be sent to Colombia to aid in the search for the three Americans taken hostage after their plane crashed. That deployment briefly put the total of U.S. service personnel in the country over the 400 limit set by Congress; even with the extra troops, the hostages still had not been found by year's end.

Drug Control Program

By 2003 Colombia's intensive U.S.-financed program to reduce the program of cocaine and heroin appeared to be having some success. Although the precise numbers were subject to dispute, most sources agreed that the government had been able to eradicate thousands of acres of coca crops and dismantle hundreds of drug-producing laboratories. The United Nations Office on Drugs and Crime, for example, suggested that cultivation of coca bushes had declined during 2002 from nearly 360,000 acres to about 250,000 acres. During the first six months of 2003 production dropped to about 170,000 acres, the UN office said. The acreage estimates were based on calculations derived from satellite photographs and aerial reconnaissance. Robert B. Charles, U.S. assistant secretary of state for international narcotics and law enforcement affairs, told the Senate Foreign Relations committee on October 29 that more than half of Colombia's 12,000-plus acres of opium poppies had been eradicated through aerial spraying during the 2003 growing season.

The crackdown on drug production in Colombia may have contributed to slight increases in reported production in neighboring Bolivia and Peru. Charles told the Senate committee that the U.S. government was keeping an eye on the "balloon effect"—squeezing the narcotics trade from one country to another.

Following are excerpts from the summary, prepared by the Colombian government, of the "Democratic Security and Defense" policy issued June 29, 2003, by President Alvaro Uribe.

"Democratic Security and Defense"

Democratic Security is a comprehensive long-term State policy for the protection of the population. Its main objective is to strengthen the rule of law in all of Colombia—that is the guarantee of the citizens' rights and liberties.

The rule of law in turn requires the reinforcement of democratic authority. Democratic institutions and elected officials must be able to exercise freely their authority, without being subject to constant threats; the law must apply effectively in all of Colombian territory; and citizens must be able to participate actively in public affairs, without fearing for their security.

Democratic Security does not regard security primarily as the security of the State, as was the case with the old notion of "National Security" in Latin America, nor as the security of the citizen independently of the State, who alone is called upon to protect the population. Rather, security consists in the protection of the citizen and democracy by the State with the solidarity and co-operation of the whole of society. Democratic Security is thus based on three pillars:

- The protection of the rights of all citizens, regardless of gender, race, origin, language, religion or political ideology
- The protection of democratic values, plurality and institutions
- The solidarity and co-operation of all citizens in defence of democratic values

Democratic Security appeals to the fundamental values of democracy: equality and participation. If all citizens are equal before the law, they all deserve the same protection by the State, regardless of whom they may be. When the State protects the peasant, the businessman or the trade unionist, it is fulfilling its most elementary purpose, as stated by the Constitution: *"The authorities of the Republic are instituted to protect all the residents of Colombia."* Equality before the law as an organising principle of democracy not only imposes duties on the State; it also creates opportunities for democratic reaffirmation.

The State's duty to protect the population goes beyond the present security situation or indeed any possible future negotiations with illegal armed groups. Unless the authority of democratic institutions is strengthened throughout Colombia, there will always be organisations, groups or persons who will continue to profit—whether they adduce political motives or not—from the absence of authority in order to wield arbitrary power over the population, extort in return for 'protection' and grow rich from the illegal drugs trade.

There is a direct relationship between the absence of democratic authority and the lack of protection of human rights. Unlike other regions of the hemisphere, where the rights of the citizen were eroded by the excessive use of power on the part of the state, the rights of Colombians have been threatened mainly by the inability of Colombian democracy to assert the authority of its institutions throughout the country. Despite the reinforcement and the extension of the reach of democracy as a result of the 1991 Constitution, there has been a rapid erosion of the authority of democratic institutions, owing to the impact of the illegal armed groups. Together with the drugs traffickers, these organisations destroy the legal framework and thereby open up areas of impunity not only for their own illicit activities, but also for many other forms of crime.

The strengthening of democratic authority is thus the essential prerequisite to guaranteeing a respect for human rights, which are the foundation of the Constitution. If they are to have their full force, democracy must be sovereign over all the territory and the state must be capable of upholding the law. And if they are to take concrete form for the benefit of the population, the political process, too, must be efficient, the State institutions effective, and the citizen must participate actively in public affairs.

The citizen's active participation and his support of democratic institutions is, for that reason, an essential part of the strengthening of the rule of law. Participation and co-operation are not just constitutional duties: they are part of the principle of *solidarity* which is the foundation of asocial and democratic state. If the individual's rights and security depend on the strengthening of the rule of law and the strengthening of the rule of law requires the citizen's participation, it is clear that security is not just the responsibility of the state, but of all citizens. It is the result of the collective effort of the whole of society.

In promoting solidarity the Government will work not only with the citizenry in general but also with all the different sectors of civil society, such as academia, private enterprise, nongovernmental organisations [NGOs] dealing with development and human rights, local civic associations and the Church. The Government supports the co-operation projects and the solidarity promoted by the NGOs in Colombia and will encourage a closer relationship between these organisations and the Colombian State, in the understanding that they operate within the democratic system.

The strengthening of the rule of law requires not only effective institutions, active citizen participation and the prevalence of judicial norms which guarantee rights and liberties; it also requires the government to act according to those norms. The security of Colombians will be re-established within the law and the democratic framework, which will itself become stronger as security improves.

For the rule of law to prevail, the state must first consolidate its control throughout Colombian territory. Without state territorial control it is not possible to guarantee the proper functioning of the judiciary, which is hindered in many areas of the country by the intimidation which prosecutors, judges and local authorities suffer at the hands of illegal armed groups and drugs traffickers.

The consolidation of state control over territory in turn requires the close co-ordination of all state institutions and all branches of government, especially the judiciary, which must discharge their duties within their areas of responsibility, so that the rule of law is consolidated and backed up by development. For true security depends not only on the capacity of the security forces to exercise the coercive powers of the state. The Armed Forces and the National Police will act against all terrorist organisations with absolute determination, in accordance with the principles of efficiency, transparency, economy and legality which guide all Government actions. But their efforts will be in vain if they are not followed by those of all Government ministries and State institutions.

At the same time, the variety of factors which affect security, the disintegration of command structures within the illegal armed groups and their frequent merging with organised crime, as well as the different illicit sources that fund these organisations, mean that different solutions must be found to suit different local conditions. Local authorities will therefore share responsibility with the Government for the design and implementation of action plans tailored to their needs.

Democratic Security also promotes the principle of shared responsibility within the international community in order to address the main security threats of today: terrorism and the international trade in illegal drugs. In the fight against terrorism it is not a single nation's sovereignty that counts, but the joint sovereignty of all democratic nations. For terrorism does not distinguish between borders. In Colombia, the illegal armed groups have made civilians their prime target, in premeditated acts using non-conventional weapons. And they have associated themselves with international terrorist networks to carry out sophisticated and particularly brutal attacks in the cities. Most of these have been thwarted by the security forces, but those that have not have claimed the lives of many. So it is imperative to speed up international co-operation, as Security Council Resolution 1373 mandates, in order to close the loopholes that allow terrorist groups to obtain finance, move around or take action, using third countries as bases. Tolerance with terrorism only breeds terrorism.

Like terrorism, the illegal drugs trade is a transnational problem; the solution does not lie in a single country. It is also well known that illegal drugs traffickers and terrorists use the same channels to obtain supplies and launder money. Often a single organisation is involved in both activities. For that reason, Colombia has been lodging formal requests for more than ten years at the relevant international fora for a greater commitment from the international community to solving the global illicit drugs problem in each and every one of its manifestations. Different countries may and in fact do have different conceptions of how to deal internally with the illegal drugs problem; but these differences must not be allowed to obscure the shared responsibility which comes from involvement in this criminal business.

Terrorism and the illegal drugs trade are two of a number of interrelated threats which often transcend national boundaries and pose an immediate danger to the stability of democratic institutions and the lives of the Colombians. These are:

- Terrorism
- The illegal drugs trade
- Illicit finances
- The traffic of arms, ammunition and explosives
- Kidnapping and extortion
- Homicide

The United Nations Secretary General has said: *"The only common denominator among different variants of terrorism is the calculated use of deadly violence against civilians for political purposes"* (Security Council, 12 November 2001). That is precisely what the illegal armed groups do in Colombia, use of deadly violence against civilians. . . .

Terrorist violence against elected officials is particularly serious. It is not just the integrity of the individual, but the democratic will of the people that is under threat. In 2002, 144 political leaders and government officials were murdered by illegal armed groups (83 by the FARC [Revolutionary Armed Forces of Colombia] and 23 by the AUC [United Self-Defense Forces of Colombia]). In addition, 124 government officials and political leaders, including a female presidential candidate, were kidnapped (82 by the FARC, 30 by the ELN [National Liberation Army] and 6 by the AUC), while more than 600 mayors received death threats.

The economic infrastructure has also suffered at the hands of terrorists. In 2001, a single pipeline was blown up 170 times by the ELN and the FARC, costing the nation US$520 million and depriving it of one of its most important sources of revenue for the funding of the health and education services. Over the last 15 years, pipelines have been blown up more than 950 times by these groups. More than 2.8 million barrels of oil have been spilled into the rivers, fields and woods of Colombia.

The illegal drugs trade threatens the stability of democratic institutions and the cohesion of society by distorting the economy, debilitating institutions and encouraging corruption. It has cost the lives of thousands of judges, journalists, politicians policemen and soldiers. It has also become the main source of funding for the terrorist activities of the illegal armed groups. . . .

Consumption drives the illegal drugs business. Consumers, in particular, should be aware of the ecological damage and loss of life for which they share responsibility. . . .

From these two threats, terrorism and the drugs trade, derive all the rest. The laundering of revenue obtained from the commercialisation of cocaine and heroine—most of which remain in the international banking system, as well as from a whole range of criminal activities, such as kidnapping, extortion, the theft of hydrocarbons and contraband, contributes directly to terrorism, while at the same time upsets financial markets, encourages contraband and the under-invoicing of imports, generally distorts the Colombian economy and leads to corruption. . . .

In order to counter these threats and fulfil the general aim of strengthening the rule of law throughout the country, Democratic Security sets out a series of strategic objectives that must be met:

- Consolidation of State Control throughout Colombia
- Protection of the Population

- Elimination of the Illegal Drugs Trade in Colombia
- Maintenance of a Deterrent Capability
- Transparency, Efficiency and Accountability

Each objective contains a number of specific objectives. For example, the gradual restoration of the presence of the National Police in all municipalities, an increase in judicial action against crimes of high social impact, the reduction of kidnapping and homicide, the prevention of forced displacement, the interdiction of the traffic of illegal drugs and chemical precursors, or the protection of land, sea and river borders. These will serve as a basis for management and impact indicators that will be used to evaluate the achievement of the strategic objectives, so that the necessary adjustments can be made when programmes do not yield the expected results, as well as to establish accountability mechanisms.

Democratic Security has set six courses of action in order to achieve its strategic objectives:

1. *Co-ordinating* State action: a National Defence and Security Council will co-ordinate the implementation of national policies; local security councils, with advisory committees that will include academics, businessmen and members of civil society, will do so within their jurisdiction. At operational level, interinstitutional support structures, composed of the National Police, the Armed Forces, the investigative and control bodies of the State and the judicial authorities, will ensure the co-ordination between different State bodies on the ground and the protection of the judiciary, so that criminals are brought to justice. The Ministry of Defence will co-ordinate the actions of the Armed Forces and the National Police with those of other ministries and State institutions. The Joint Intelligence Committee, for its part, will co-ordinate strategic intelligence.

2. *Strengthening* State institutions: institutional strengthening is a prerequisite to consolidating territorial control and protecting the population. Not only the National Police and the Armed Forces, but in particular the judiciary, the State's capacity to gather intelligence and information and the public finances necessary to support this effort will be strengthened.

3. *Consolidating* control of national territory: a cycle of long term recovery and consolidation of territorial control will be established gradually to restore security throughout the country. It has three phases: recovery, maintenance and consolidation. The Armed Forces and the National Police will begin the recovery process. Once the Armed Forces and the National Police have re-established control over an area, units comprising professional soldiers, rural soldiers (soldiers in rural areas who complete their national service at their

home towns) and National Police carabineros will maintain security and protect the civilian population. This will enable State organisations to carry the consolidation projects of the third phase without being subject to threats and extortion by the illegal armed groups, as has occurred in the past. Democratic Security has also set out courses of action for the maintenance of security in the cities.

The elimination of the illegal drugs trade also depends on the consolidation of territorial control. It is also necessary to dismantle the finances of the drug trafficking and terrorist organisations in order to dismantle their support structures and to weaken their hold over territory. The new laws governing the nullification of property ownership and asset confiscation as well as the controls that have been established on oil royalties, amongst other measures, will reduce the resources which these organisations employ for their criminal activities.

4. *Protecting* the rights of all Colombians and the infrastructure of the nation: the basic mechanism for protecting the lives and rights of Colombian citizens is the strengthening the rule of law throughout Colombian territory. As many Colombians have suffered and continue to suffer directly at the hands of the illegal armed groups, they require special attention. For that reason, Democratic Security has established a series of special policies and programmes, jointly designed by different Government ministries, in order to: (i) protect persons at risk; (ii) protect the victims of forced displacement; (iii) protect against terrorism; (iv) protect against kidnapping and extortion; (v) protect the demobilised and child combatants; (vi) protect against the recruitment of children and adolescents by the illegal armed groups, as well as to (vii) protect the economic infrastructure and (viii) protect the road network.

5. *Co-operating* for the security of all: Democratic Security encourages the voluntary and patriotic co-operation of Colombian citizens, in accordance with the constitutional principle of *solidarity*, in order to help prevent crime and terrorism. A network of citizens has been set up to act as a neighbourhood watch in both urban and rural areas. It will provide the authorities with information which will help in the prevention of a crime or the pursuit of criminals. In addition, a programme has been established to reward those who, as informants of the security forces, provide information which leads to the prevention of a terrorist attack or the arrest of members of any of the illegal armed groups. Democratic Security also seeks to strengthen international co-operation, in accordance with the principle of shared responsibility.

6. *Communicating* State policy and action: as terrorism is a form of political violence which uses communication to spread terror and

confusion, the government will endeavour to keep the public informed of the measures taken and results obtained from the implementation of the Defence and Democratic Security Policy. The Government will also promote debate in the media regarding their role in a democracy under threat. A public diplomacy effort will be made abroad, in order to explain the particular nature of the Colombian situation within the Latin American context and to emphasise the need to strengthen international co-operation, without which it will not possible to guarantee in the long term the security of our citizens.

Security is not the only concern of the Government, but it is the first. There is no greater inequality in Colombia than in the access to security: it is the poor who are the least protected, who are displaced from their land and who suffer at first hand the terror of the illegal armed groups. And it is not just the protection of their rights which depends upon security. Economic development and employment opportunities also require a climate of security to permit investment, trade and local authority spending for the benefit of communities, all of which have suffered constant predation by illegal armed groups. . . .

The Government is just as determined to embrace all those who abandon violence, as it is to defeat terrorism. Those who wish to make peace with the Colombian State have the opportunity to do so speedily by joining the demobilisation programme. The Government is fully prepared to provide all those who demobilise with the necessary security and education opportunities for them to re-enter society.

The Government has also kept the door open to negotiations with those groups which opt for democratic politics, provided they agree to a strictly enforced cease-fire. The Government's position is: an urgent cessation of hostilities, and patient negotiation and disarmament. Those who reintegrate themselves into society and a democratic way of life will be assured the same security guarantees for participating in politics that are the right of all dissidents in a democracy.

Source: Republic of Colombia. Embassy of Colombia in Washington, D.C. *Democratic Security and Defense: Summary.* June 29, 2003. www.colombiaemb.org/download/defense/resumenejecutivopolitica14julio 1.pdf (accessed April 1, 2004).

July

Bureau of Labor Statistics on the U.S. Employment Situation

July 3, 2003

INTRODUCTION

Fears of a lingering "jobless recovery" came true in 2003. Despite steadily improving overall economic growth, job creation in the United States remained stagnant. By the end of August the country had been in the longest hiring slump since 1939, when the government first began tracking such things. Although net new jobs began to pick up in the last four months of the year, they did not grow at anywhere near the pace needed to make a significant dent in the jobless rate, which had hovered around 6 percent all year. Roughly 8.5 million Americans who wanted to work were out of a job at the end of the year; about 25 percent of those had been looking for work for more than six months.

The person whose job was on the line if the job picture did not improve significantly was President George W. Bush, who was up for reelection in 2004. Throughout his presidency, Bush had sought to avoid comparisons to his father, President George H.W. Bush (1989–1993), on economic matters. The senior Bush had lost a reelection bid in 1992, largely because he appeared aloof from the problems created by the lengthy jobless recovery from the recession in 1990–1991. The younger Bush took great pains to show his sympathy to out-of-work voters, saying at every opportunity that he would not be satisfied with the economic recovery until every American who wanted a job had one. But by the end of 2003, with a net loss of about 2.3 million jobs, Bush was in danger of being compared not to his father but to Herbert Hoover (1929–1933), the last president who registered a net job loss during his term of office.

Democrats had faulted the president almost since the recession began in March 2001 for not doing enough to put Americans back to work. Bush insisted that the best way to create jobs was through the massive tax reductions that he proposed and Congress passed in 2001 and 2003 (along with a smaller one in 2002). Tax cuts, Bush said, would stimulate investment, which in turn would stimulate economic growth and job creation. Democrats argued that the tax cuts primarily benefited the wealthy and were doing little to help the unemployed in the short term. Meanwhile, they noted the administration's reluctance to extend federal jobless benefits to the long-term unemployed.

Democrats seeking the party's nomination to run against Bush in 2004 repeatedly blamed the lack of jobs and job growth on Bush's economic policies. A typical remark came from North Carolina senator John Edwards, who said that "a new job is an endangered species" in the Bush economy. These charges found some resonance among manufacturing workers who blamed the administration's trade policies for sending manufacturing jobs overseas where labor was cheaper. Democrats were also hoping to feed off general dissatisfaction with a labor market where wages were stagnant or even falling, where most of the new jobs were service jobs that paid far less than manufacturing jobs, and where executives continued to be paid millions of dollars annually in salaries and bonuses at the same time they were asking their employees to take pay cuts and to pay more for health care and other benefits. *(Retirement, p. 707; health insurance, p. 846)*

Overview of 2003

The year began with the worst hiring slump since the recession of 1982–1983. Between the start of the recession in March 2001 and the end of 2002, the economy had shed more than 2 million jobs. That was a decline of 1.5 percent, which slightly exceeded the 1.3 percent decline recorded at the same point in the jobless recovery from the 1990–1991 recession. Employment grew in January 2003 but then declined again through August. The low point was reached in June when the jobless rate rose to 6.4 percent, its highest rate since April 1994. With the economy racing along at an 8.2 percent growth rate in the third quarter, layoffs began to ease, and in September the economy started to gain more jobs than it lost. By the end of the year the jobless rate had fallen to 5.7 percent. Overall, about 8.4 million workers were counted as unemployed because they were actively looking for work. Another 1.5 million jobless workers wanted to work, according to the Bureau of Labor Statistics, but were discouraged and had not recently looked for a job.

Economic analysts said the job growth was a good sign that the economic recovery under way for some months might in fact be sustainable. The administration said the growth in jobs was evidence that its economic policies were working. Treasury Secretary John W. Snow made news in an October 20 interview with the *Times of London* when he predicted that the

American economy would add 2 million jobs before the 2004 election, or about 200,000 a month. Economists and Democrats alike were skeptical. "We are surprised that Snow would choose to hand the Democratic presidential candidates this optimistic prediction," a senior economist at Goldman Sachs told clients.

Analysts were quick to point out that 200,000 new jobs a month would be enough only to keep the unemployment rate from rising; job creation would have to be even higher to bring down the jobless rate, they said. Democrats noted that so far the Bush economy had come nowhere near producing 200,000 a month; they said the main reason the jobless rate was falling was because so many workers who could not find jobs were dropping out of the labor market and were no longer counted as unemployed. Preliminary figures for 2003 showed that the most new jobs added in a single month was 126,000 in October. Only 1,000 jobs were added in December, while 433,000 unemployed workers stopped looking for work; these were particularly disappointing figures, given six months of economic growth that averaged well above 4 percent.

Causes of the Jobless Recovery

Several reasons helped account for the dismal job growth picture. One was the fast growth in the rate of productivity—the output a worker produced for each hour worked. For the year, productivity was up about 5 percent over 2002 (it grew at a remarkable 9.4 percent annual rate in the third quarter). Analysts said most of the productivity gains resulted from employers figuring out how to use new technologies more efficiently. A high rate of productivity meant that employers that were not experiencing high demand could fulfill their orders without hiring new employees or could even lay off workers, thus improving their labor costs and their overall profitability.

Overcapacity was another reason. Some companies had invested so much in plants and people during the boom years of the 1990s that they were still working off the excess capacity in 2003. Although layoffs and plant closings were slowing, manufacturers, on average, were using only 75 percent of their capacity at the end of the year. Some manufacturers opted to sell off or lease their weaker product lines to companies that were hoping to make profits through more efficient production, not more workers.

About 2.1 million of the 2.3 million lost jobs in the Bush administration were in the manufacturing sector, and workers complained that they were losing jobs to cheaper labor in China and other foreign countries. Estimates of the number of jobs that had migrated overseas were very rough, ranging from a high of 995,000 jobs since the recession began to a low of 500,000, primarily in manufacturing. An increasing number of white collar and high-tech jobs were also going overseas, particularly to India, which had a high number of English speakers and more than 2 million college graduates a year. Indian workers had been performing data entry and low-level programming jobs for American companies for some time. In recent years companies had begun to move more high-skilled jobs to India, ranging from financial analysis and accounting to CAT scan readings and health insurance claim evaluation. The president of one company that used Indian workers to prepare tax returns said his costs could be cut by as much as 50 percent. One study estimated that 3.3 million high-tech and service industry jobs could migrate overseas by 2015, 70 percent of them to India.

Some analysts argued that the jobless rate did not reflect the real employment situation because so many people who had dropped out of the formal economy (or had never been in it the first place) had become part of the informal economy—labor that was "off the books" and thus not subject to income or payroll taxes or employment regulations. The authors of an International Monetary Fund report issued in 2002 estimated that underground economic activity in the United States accounted for 8.6 percent of gross domestic product. Large shares of the informal laborers were immigrants, especially illegal ones. The service sector was a source of jobs for informal workers, particularly those willing to do domestic work such as child care, cleaning, gardening, and painting. Other researchers noted a rise in the number of people who said they were self-employed and therefore not counted in the monthly jobless report that surveyed employers. According to the household survey of employment conducted by Bureau of Labor Statistics every month, more than 9 million people said they were self-employed in 2003. Economists generally considered the household survey to be a less reliable indicator than the employer survey, however.

The Politics of Unemployment

One casualty of Bush's argument that tax cuts would produce jobs was the program of extended unemployment benefits. Despite a last-minute plea from Republicans representing districts with high unemployment, the GOP House leadership adjourned in December without extending the benefit program that was scheduled to expire on December 31. The program provided an additional thirteen weeks of federally funded jobless benefits to those still looking for work after collecting twenty-six weeks of regular state unemployment compensation. The GOP leadership was apparently counting on an improving economy that would get people back to work.

The supplemental benefits, which were first enacted in March 2002, had also lapsed in December 2002, when the Senate and House could not agree on the length of an extension. Democrats, who favored a longer extension, made so much political hay during the holiday season that, when Congress returned in January 2003, Bush urged the Republican leadership to extend the program. Congress complied, extending it first through May 31 and then through the end of the year. Democrats vowed to make the GOP refusal to extend the benefits into 2004 an election-year issue.

Democrats and organized labor also hoped to turn GOP-backed proposals for changes in overtime pay into an election issue. One proposal, by House Republican leaders, would have allowed employers to give certain workers compensatory (or "comp") time off instead of overtime pay. That legislation was withdrawn after organized labor launched an aggressive grass-roots campaign against it. Labor unions came close to blocking a proposed Labor Department regulation that would change eligibility rules for overtime pay. Under the rule, about 1.3 million low-income workers would become eligible for overtime pay, but an estimated 644,000 more highly paid workers would no longer qualify. Labor unions said the actual figure would be as many as 8 million workers. The Senate added language to the appropriations bill for the Labor Department blocking the regulation; similar language proposed in the House fell just three votes shy of passing. After the Bush administration promised a veto, however, the language was dropped from the spending bill.

At the beginning of the year, Bush proposed creation of personal reemployment accounts that would give the unemployed as much as $3,000 for job training, child care, moving costs, and other expenses associated with finding new work. But he did not lobby hard for the proposal, and Congress gave it little consideration. At the same time, the president pushed substantial spending cutbacks in traditional federal job training programs. Manufacturers also noted that the Bush administration had cut back funding for programs that helped manufacturers, such as one that accelerated the commercialization of manufacturing technologies.

Facing increasing pressure to do something about the continuing loss of manufacturing jobs, Bush, at a Labor Day speech to highway construction workers in Richland, Ohio, announced the creation of an assistant secretary of commerce for manufacturing. The announcement was short on details, other than that the post would focus on "the needs of manufacturers." Bush said he understood that "for a full recovery, to make sure people can find work, that manufacturing must do better." The administration followed up that announcement with promises to pursue a level playing field in foreign trade, particularly with China, whose trade and currency practices were putting American exports at a competitive disadvantage. Democrats and others dismissed the announcement as too little too late and a transparent political ploy to appeal to blue-collar voters. A New York Times editorial called Bush's plan "notable for its feebleness."

An early Bush attempt to deal with the unemployment problem in manufacturing—and gain political points at the same time—backfired, leading to an embarrassing reversal for the Bush administration late in 2003. In March 2002 Bush imposed tariffs of as much as 30 percent for three years on steel imports from Europe, Asia, and South America. Despite its support of free trade, the administration justified the duties as a step to help the ailing American steel industry recover from a surge of cheap, imported steel during the late 1990s. The tariffs were widely seen as a political move to win blue-collar voters in key election states such as Ohio, Pennsylvania, and West Virginia.

In July 2003 the World Trade Organization upheld complaints that the U.S. action was unwarranted and violated global trade rules. The European Union (EU) was authorized to impose $2.2 billion in retaliatory sanctions starting on December 15 if the administration did not lift the steel tariffs, and seven other countries were authorized to impose additional sanctions. The EU quickly let it be known that it would put tariffs on products that would raise prices for voters in important election states. The EU targeted citrus from Florida, textile mills in the South, and farm products from California and the Midwest with, as *New York Times* reporter David E. Sanger put it, "a precision that Karl Rove, the president's political adviser, must have grudgingly admired." (Rove was said to have been the chief architect of the higher steel tariffs.)

At home the president was caught between the steel-producing industry, which urged Bush to retain the tariffs, and steel-consuming manufacturers (such as auto and appliance manufacturers in the United States), who said the higher steel prices that resulted from the tariffs were costing them more jobs than the steel industry was saving. Facing a possible trade war with the EU and other allies abroad—as well as a political disaster at home—Bush on December 4 repealed the tariffs, declaring that they had achieved their purpose. Steelmakers, he said, had consolidated, increased productivity, reduced costs, and become more competitive with foreign producers. The fact that the United Steelworkers of America gave an early endorsement to Democratic presidential contender Richard A. Gephardt, a U.S. representative from Missouri, may have influenced Bush's decision. The union represented many of the workers Bush hoped would support him in gratitude for imposing the tariffs.

Following are excerpts from "The Employment Situation: June 2003," a report issued July 3, 2003, by the Bureau of Labor Statistics in the Department of Labor.

"The Employment Situation: June 2003"

Nonfarm payroll employment was essentially unchanged in June, while the unemployment rate rose to 6.4 percent, the Bureau of Labor Statistics of the U.S. Department of Labor reported today. Payroll job losses continued in manufacturing, but were partly offset by employment increases in other industries.

Unemployment (Household Survey Data)

The number of unemployed persons increased by 360,000 in June to 9.4 million, and the unemployment rate rose from 6.1 to 6.4 percent. Since March, unemployment has increased by 913,000. The rate for adult men edged up for the third month in a row; at 6.1 percent, the jobless rate for this group was 0.8 percentage point higher than in March. The teenage unemployment rate, at 19.3 percent, has trended up since the beginning of the year. Over the month, the unemployment rate for blacks increased to 11.8 percent. Jobless rates for the other major worker groups—adult women (5.2 percent), whites (5.5 percent), and Hispanics (8.4 percent)—showed little change from May. The unemployment rate for Asians was 7.8 percent, not seasonally adjusted.

In June, there were 2.0 million unemployed persons who had been looking for work for 27 weeks or longer, an increase of 410,000 over the year. They represented 21.4 percent of the total unemployed, up from 18.8 percent a year earlier.

Total Employment and the Labor Force (Household Survey Data)

The civilian labor force increased by 611,000 over the month to 147.1 million. The labor force participation rate rose by 0.2 percentage point to 66.6 percent in June. The rate is up from its recent low of 66.2 percent in March. Total employment in June was 137.7 million, and the employment-population ratio was unchanged at 62.3 percent.

Persons Not in the Labor Force (Household Survey Data)

In June, 1.5 million persons were marginally attached to the labor force, little changed from a year earlier. These individuals wanted and were available to work and had looked for a job sometime in the prior 12 months. They were not counted as unemployed, however, because they did not actively search for work in the 4 weeks preceding the survey. There were 478,000 discouraged workers in June, up from 342,000 in June 2002. Discouraged workers, a subset of the marginally attached, were not currently looking for work specifically because they believed no jobs were available for them.

Industry Payroll Employment (Establishment Survey Data)

Total nonfarm payroll employment was essentially unchanged (–30,000) in June at 130.0 million. Over the month, job declines continued in manufacturing, but were partially offset by gains in construction and some service-providing industries.

Manufacturing employment decreased by 56,000 in June, in line with the average job loss over the prior 12 months. Losses occurred across most of the component industries. Since its most recent peak in July 2000, manufacturing employment has fallen by more than 2.6 million. In June, primary metals, fabricated metal products, machinery, and plastics and rubber products each lost about 6,000 jobs. Employment in textile mills and leather products manufacturing also declined in June, continuing their long-term downward trends.

Employment in construction edged up in June, the fourth consecutive monthly gain. Construction has added 101,000 jobs since February, reflecting strength in residential building activity.

Employment in health care and social assistance rose by 35,000 over the month and has increased by 306,000 over the year. In June, ambulatory health care services (including offices of physicians, outpatient care centers, and home health care services) added 24,000 jobs; hospital employment increased by 9,000.

Within professional and business services, employment in the temporary help industry rose by 38,000 in June, following a gain of 44,000 in May. This rise was partly offset by an employment decline in accounting and bookkeeping services (–24,000). Accounting and bookkeeping experienced a large seasonal buildup for the tax season followed by even larger layoffs. After seasonal adjustment, employment in this industry is down by 36,000 since last November.

In the leisure and hospitality industry, employment edged up in June following 4 months of declines. The over-the-month gain was largely in the food services industry.

Employment in transportation and warehousing was little changed at 4.1 million in June. Within this sector, air transportation employment continued to decline. This industry has lost 123,000 jobs since its peak in March 2001. Both wholesale and retail trade employment edged lower over the month.

The information sector showed little job change in June. Employment within this industry declined in nearly every month since March 2001, losing a total of 434,000 jobs. The telecommunications industry, which shed 7,000 jobs in June, accounted for nearly half of the losses over that period.

Weekly Hours (Establishment Survey Data)

The average workweek for production or nonsupervisory workers on private nonfarm payrolls was 33.7 hours for the third consecutive month. The manufacturing workweek and manufacturing overtime also were unchanged from May, at 40.2 hours and 4.0 hours, respectively.

The index of aggregate weekly hours of production or nonsupervisory workers on private nonfarm payrolls was unchanged in June at 98.7 (2002 = 100). The manufacturing index fell by 0.4 percent over the month to 94.7.

Hourly and Weekly Earnings (Establishment Survey Data)

Average hourly earnings of production or nonsupervisory workers on private nonfarm payrolls increased by 3 cents in June to $15.38, seasonally adjusted. Average weekly earnings rose by 0.2 percent over the month to $518.31. Over the year, average hourly earnings grew by 3.0 percent, and average weekly earnings increased by 2.1 percent.

Source: United States. Department of Labor. Bureau of Labor Statistics. *The Employment Situation: June* 2003. USDL 03–253, July 3, 2003. ftp://ftp.bls.gov/pub/news.release/History/empsit.07032003.news (accessed October 12, 2003).

UN Secretary General
Annan on Reform in Africa

July 10, 2003

INTRODUCTION

United Nations secretary general Kofi Annan, the first sub-Saharan African to hold that post, continued his crusade on behalf of economic and political reform in Africa. In a toughly worded speech on July 10, 2003, Annan told African leaders that it was their responsibility—not that of Western nations that provided aid to Africa—to take the necessary steps to lift their people out of poverty, end ethnic conflict, and confront the scourge of AIDS.

A career UN diplomat from Ghana, Annan had regularly sought to focus the attention of African leaders on their own responsibilities for overcoming the continent's systemic poverty and chronic wars. In 1998 Annan published a controversial report telling African leaders they could no longer blame their countries' problems on the European colonial powers that had left the continent nearly four decades earlier. In 2001 Annan directly told African leaders they needed to set aside the "ways of the past," including violence, corruption, and dictatorships. *(Background, Historic Documents of 1998, p. 220; Historic Documents of 2001, p. 505)*

Annan's Call for Reform

Since becoming secretary general in 1996, Annan had spent much of his time dealing with the consequences of wars that seemed to sprout like weeds in Africa. In 2003 alone, the UN was involved with diplomatic or peacekeeping missions resulting from wars in Angola, Burundi, the Democratic Republic of the Congo, Ivory Coast, Liberia, Rwanda, Sierra Leone, Somalia, and Sudan. In addition to killing millions of people, driving millions more from their homes, and savaging the economies of these countries and their neighbors, the wars damaged the reputation of Africa worldwide—scaring away potential investors and forcing UN member nations to spend money on peacekeeping operations that otherwise could have gone to build schools or health clinics.

In July 2003 African leaders gathered in Mozambique for their second annual summit of the new African Union, which had formed during the previous two years to replace the ineffective Organization of African Unity. Addressing the leaders, Annan praised recent efforts at political and economic reform in many African countries, and the peace negotiations that seemed to offer hope for ending conflicts in several countries. But he bluntly told the leaders they needed to work harder to end the conflicts and make sure new ones did not arise.

"The United Nations and the rest of the international community can appoint envoys, urge negotiations and spend billions of dollars on peacekeeping missions—but none of this will solve conflicts if the political will and capacity do not exist here, in Africa," he said. "I hope that every one of you, as African leaders, will make it your personal mission to convince the young people of the continent that the lives and safety of their fellow Africans are sacrosanct, and that there can be no substitute for the fruits of peace."

Along with ending wars, African leaders needed to recognize the importance of democracy for their countries. "But democracy means more than holding elections," Annan said. "It requires respect for the rule of law by all, including the government and the party in power. It requires viable institutions to promote respect for all human rights of all people, including minorities. It requires sustained and effective attention from a dynamic and vigilant civil society."

Although Annan named no names and cited no specific cases of the countries most in need of change, examples of the problems he cited were abundant during the year. Peace agreements ending wars had been signed throughout West, Central, and Eastern Africa—but in every case the peace process was fraught with difficulty and the prospects for true peace and prosperity were uncertain at best. Elections had become the rule rather than exception in Africa, but the actual transfer of power through the ballot box still was unusual. According to Harvard University researcher Arthur Goldsmith, only 19 African leaders were voted out of office between 1960 and 2003, all but one of them since 1990; 107 leaders had been overthrown in coups or wars. Typical of the old-style African election was the June 1 ballot in Togo, the tiny West African county whose president, Gnassingbe Eyadema, had seized power in a 1963 military coup and was the world's second longest serving ruler (behind Cuba's Fidel Castro). The government refused to allow opposition parties to monitor the vote count, and Eyadema was declared the winner with 57 percent of the vote; his chief opponent went into hiding, reportedly fearing for his life.

Africa and the G-8

In 2002 the leaders of African and the wealthy industrialized nations entered into a bargain, called the New Partnership for Africa's Development (NEPAD). The Africans agreed to promote democracy and economic liberalization and to work to end the continent's systemic corruption and wars. In turn, the leaders of the Group of Eight (G-8) industrialized nations agreed to reduce their trade practices that hurt African farmers and to increase economic aid to the African countries that carried out promised reforms. Everyone said at the time that putting those plans into practice would be difficult, and subsequent events proved them right. *(Background, Historic Documents of 2002, p. 446)*

A key component of the NEPAD plan was a pledge by African leaders to establish a "peer review" process by which they would monitor each other's reforms. This was a controversial step that was bitterly resented by some leaders as infringing on their nations' independence. Although the process had been under discussion for more than two years, African leaders could not agree on a panel to do the monitoring until May 2003. Among its members were Graca Machel, a human rights activist from Mozambique, who also was the wife of former South African president Nelson Mandela; and Chris Stals, former governor of the South African Reserve Bank. The panel's reports were not to be made public, leaving many observers wondering just how much good its work would do. By July, sixteen African countries had agreed to submit themselves to review by the panel.

For their part, leaders of the G-8 nations seemed reluctant to move ahead with the trade concessions and expanded aid programs they had promised without assurances that the African leaders were actually undertaking the political and economic reforms they had promised. Perhaps the bluntest warning of the year came December 5 from Jean Chrétien, who was just about to step down as Canada's prime minister. Addressing a group of business leaders in Nigeria, Chrétien said: "Africa is very rich, I have no doubt of it in my mind. You need access to markets to sell your products, but you need good administrations if you want people to invest. . . . You need political stability. Stop these bloody conflicts that you have too often in some parts of Africa."

Impact of the Iraq War

At least in the early months of the year, the U.S. war in Iraq appeared to have a dramatic effect in parts of Africa. Leaders and opposition figures in several countries long plagued by internal conflict—notably Somalia and Sudan—expressed concern that the Bush administration might turn its attention to Africa after knocking Iraq leader Saddam Hussein from power. Fears of a possible U.S. invasion helped spur Africans toward the negotiating table in record numbers. Such concerns might have seemed far-fetched to many Americans, who might have forgotten that Osama bin Laden, the leader of the al Qaeda terrorist network (responsible for the September 11, 2001, attacks against the United States) had once operated in Sudan, or that war-torn Somalia exhibited many of the same characteristics of a failed state that had made Afghanistan a sanctuary for bin Laden after he was chased out of Sudan.

Americans might have been more likely to recall that East Africa had been the scene of major terrorist attacks in recent years: the 1998 bombing of the U.S. embassies in Kenya and Tanzania, and the 2002 bombing of a tourist hotel in Kenya patronized by Israelis. *(Embassy bombings, Historic Documents of 1998, p. 555; Kenya hotel bombing, Historic Documents of 2002, p. 1014)*

Other African leaders, including South Africa's Thabo Mbeki, expressed a different fear: that the United States would find it necessary to spend billions of dollars reconstructing Iraq after the war and thus cut back on its aid programs for Africa. James Morris, the head of the UN's World Food program, said he shared this concern. Speaking to the UN Security Council on April 8, Morris noted that the United States and Britain had pledged food aid for Iraq but had fallen short of their pledges for Africa. "As much as I don't like it, I cannot escape the thought that we have a double standard," he said. "How is it we routinely accept a level of suffering and hopelessness in Africa we would never accept in any other part of the world?"

In his usual diplomatic language, Annan voiced a different frustration. At several points during the year he had to warn the Security Council of drastic consequences if it did not pay more attention to Africa. Early in the year, for example, he warned that ethnic fighting in the northeastern region of the Democratic Republic of the Congo might spiral into genocide unless the outside world intervened. After several weeks of diplomatic bargaining, Annan's appeal overcame Washington's resistance to a deeper UN presence in Congo; France led a multinational peacekeeping force that prevented the conflict there from worsening. Annan used a similar warning in a successful appeal for U.S. intervention in Liberia. *(Congo, p. 288; Liberia, p. 767)*

Bush Trip to Africa

President George W. Bush had planned to make his first-ever visit to Africa in January, but the impending war in Iraq forced a delay. The trip was rescheduled for July, with an itinerary that included Botswana, Nigeria, Senegal, South Africa, and Uganda. Bush preceded his trip with speeches in Washington to a group of African American journalists and a council of businesses with interests in Africa. Bush touted several recent proposals for increased U.S. aid to Africa, including a $15 billion fund for AIDS treatment programs (much of it targeted for Africa), and a Millennium Challenge Account to boost development aid to countries in Africa and other regions that made economic and political reforms. Although his two senior foreign policy advisers (Secretary of State Colin Powell and National Security Adviser Condoleezza Rice) were African Americans, Bush was widely perceived in Africa as uninterested in the continent's problems. Bush himself had contributed to this perception with his comments during the 2000 election campaign suggesting that Africa was not of vital national interest to the United States. The U.S. invasion of Iraq also was highly unpopular in the region—a reminder to many Africans of the colonial era when wealthy European countries routinely invaded poorer lands.

Ironically, from the outset of his trip the president found himself pressed to intervene in Africa, with troops, not just money. At his first meetings in Senegal on July 8, Bush heard requests that he dispatch U.S. troops to Liberia, where efforts were under way to end a bloody civil war. Bush said the United States "will participate in the process" of ending the war, but he offered no details on what that participation might be. Ultimately, Bush sent small contingents of Marines to Monrovia to secure the U.S. embassy, as well as a fleet of three navy ships to the Liberian coast as a symbol of U.S. determination that the war should end.

In South Africa and Botswana, Bush touted his AIDS initiative, along with free-trade agreements the United States was negotiating with those countries. The president encountered the only overt hostility of his trip while in South Africa. The ruling African National Congress Party mounted a protest march to the U.S. embassy in Pretoria, and President Mbeki left his country just a half-day after Bush arrived, so he could attend the African Union summit in Mozambique. Mbeki's predecessor, Nelson Mandela, also arranged to be out of the country during Bush's visit; Mandela had harshly criticized the war in Iraq, saying it demonstrated that the U.S. president "cannot think properly." *(AIDS in Africa, p. 780)*

As with nearly all his public statements since the September 11, 2001, terrorist attacks against the United States, Bush devoted much of his remarks to the subject of countering terrorism. One of the initiatives he had announced before the trip was a proposed $100 million fund to help the countries of East Africa root oust Islamic terrorists. "Several African nations face particular danger from terrorists, and the United States is working closely with these nations to fight terror," Bush said in Nigeria on July 12. "We will not allow terrorists to threaten the African peoples, or to use Africa as a base to threaten the world."

While Bush was promising African leaders increased U.S. aid, back in Washington the House Foreign Operations Appropriations subcommittee made major cuts in some of those programs. The panel cut $500 million from Bush's $1.3 billion request for the Millennium Challenge Account program in fiscal year 2004, and it set funding for the president's AIDS initiative at $2 billion—the same amount Bush ultimately requested but $1 billion less than what he originally had said needed to be spent each year.

Following is the text of an address by United Nations Secretary General Kofi Annan, delivered July 10, 2003, to the annual summit meeting of the African Union, held in Maputo, Mozambique.

"Secretary-General's Address to the African Union Summit"

Presidents, Prime Ministers, Excellencies, Ladies and Gentlemen, My fellow Africans,

Let me first thank our hosts, President Joaquim Chissano and the people of Mozambique, for their wonderful welcome and generous hospitality. Equally, let me say a special word of gratitude to President Thabo Mbeki for his hard work and leadership during the first—and highly challenging—year in the life of the African Union.

I should also like to pay tribute to Mr. Amara Essy, First Chairman of the Commission of the African Union, for his dedicated service and for the leadership he has provided in helping lay down foundations for the Commission of the African Union.

One year ago, you, the leaders of Africa, launched this Union with a call on all Africans to redefine their destiny; to build a better life for all the people of this continent; to enable Africa to assume its full role and responsibility in global affairs.

Indeed, the birth of your Union, forty years after the creation of the OAU [Organization of African Unity], reflected an historic reaffirmation that Africa itself bears the primary responsibility for shaping its fate and future; and that the best way—the only way—for Africa to carry out that mission is to unite around the needs and aspirations of your people.

The theme of this Summit—ensuring the implementation of the New Partnership for Africa's Development—shows that you mean to pursue that mission with the seriousness and focus it requires.

It shows you are determined that the African Union must play a central role in the work to achieve the strategic goals of NEPAD [New Partnership for Africa's Development] in the areas of peace and security, democracy, good governance, poverty reduction and sound economic management.

The rest of the world is recognizing your determination to take your own challenges in hand. We can see it in the commitments made by the Group of Eight in their Plan of Action for Africa, as well as in initiatives by the President of the United States and by the European Union to increase funds to fight HIV/AIDS in Africa.

We in the United Nations will keep supporting you as advocates, to convince developed countries to do more—such as provide more official development assistance; lift tariffs and subsidies; offer greater debt relief; provide yet stronger support for the struggle against AIDS.

Indeed, here at this Summit later today, the UN Development Programme is launching its new Human Development Report on the Millennium Development Goals [MDGs]. The Report sets out a number of fresh ideas on how to achieve these critical Goals across Africa and the rest of the world. It calls on donor countries to back reforms in developing countries with more resources and trade opportunities. And it urges rich and poor nations to put the MDGs at the centre of national and global decision-making. Mutual accountability is the key—accountability of Governments to their people; accountability of developed and developing partners towards one another.

The more decisively Africa pursues its commitment to reform, the greater our chances of success in the work to reach the MDGs. In that work, NEPAD, and a truly effective use of its Peer Review Mechanism, have a vital role to play.

As African finance ministers stated at their conference last month, Africa's partnership with the rest of the world must be based on monitoring both donor and recipient performance; on policy coherence, a shared responsibility for making development happen, and a reciprocal sense of trust. I would add that this partnership should also justify the trust that your own peoples have placed in you.

We all now recognize that this sense of African responsibility must be applied to all the challenges facing the continent. Allow me to highlight some of the challenges that I believe are especially important.

Armed conflict continues to take an unconscionable toll on African men, women and children, and on the development of our continent as a whole. Recently, we have seen progress and the promise of peace in some countries, including Burundi, Côte d'Ivoire [Ivory Coast] and Sudan. Let us hope that we will soon witness similar progress in Somalia. And there have been significant achievements in the peace process of the Democratic Republic of Congo, although much remains to be done.

These are heartening examples of conflict management and resolution, where African leadership has been the decisive ingredient. And nowhere can we find a more shining example of the rewards of such leadership than right here in Mozambique.

But we continue to witness heartbreaking events in Liberia, as well as in the beleaguered regions of Ituri and the Kivus in the DRC [Democratic Republic of the Congo]. Unspeakable horrors have been perpetrated which should fill every African, every human being, with a sense of shame. They make it painfully evident that Africa has nowhere near the effective mechanisms it needs to prevent the outbreak of conflict or enforce basic international humanitarian law.

The United Nations and the rest of the international community can appoint envoys, urge negotiations and spend billions of dollars on peace-keeping missions—but none of this will solve conflicts if the political will and capacity do not exist here, in Africa. That is why this Union, and all its Members, must work for an integrated strategy of peaceful settlements. I hope that every one of you, as African leaders, will make it your personal mission to convince the young people of the continent that the lives and safety of their fellow Africans are sacrosanct, and that there can be no substitute for the fruits of peace.

I salute those African leaders who have already shown such energy, imagination and perseverance in dealing with conflicts—especially within ECOWAS, CEMAC and IGAD [regional subgroups in Africa], as well as your outgoing Chair, South Africa.

Lasting peace is far more than the absence of war. It is sustainable only if accompanied by democratic transformation and good governance. We know that democratic countries usually do not declare war on each other. The more we expand the number of countries built on democracy, the greater our chances for sustainable peace in the region as a whole.

Democracy also means alternating government. The value of peaceful and periodic change in government has been proven time and again, in all parts of the world. Democracy is a constant struggle—but a struggle by peaceful means. If term limits are necessary to make this possible, so be it.

So let us press ahead with democratic transformation. Many African countries are making the transition to genuine multi-party democracy, or have already done so. For others, this remains a challenge. But democracy means more than holding elections. It requires respect for the rule of law by all, including the Government and the party in power. It requires viable institutions to promote respect for all human rights of all our people, including minorities. It requires sustained and effective attention from a dynamic and vigilant civil society.

And it must go hand in hand with the work for poverty reduction and development. That means a whole-hearted investment in education and the empowerment of women, the most effective development strategies we know. It also means a focus on employment creation. Work is the source of personal dignity, family stability, peace in the community and ultimately, political credibility.

And while progress in trade depends greatly on developed nations dismantling subsidies and tariffs, Africa still needs to make efforts of its own: by striving for more competitive economies; by promoting intra-regional trade to overcome the constraints of market size; by strengthening its capacity to participate in global trade negotiations.

At the same time, an agricultural transformation is needed to break the pattern of recurring food crises. The latest famine in Ethiopia and Eritrea is a tragic reminder of the desperate need for Africa to develop the capacity to feed itself—to bring about the kind of Green Revolution we have seen take hold elsewhere. Achieving this will require radical approaches on multiple fronts, based on both new and existing technologies, as well as far-sighted land and water management.

And it will require addressing the inextricable link between food insecurity and the biggest threat facing Africa today—the continuing spread of HIV/AIDS.

The lethal impact of AIDS on food security has become devastatingly obvious. But the killing fields of AIDS stretch far further than that. Just as Africa seeks to focus on the future, some parts of it can barely hang on to the present. Africa's efforts are being systematically undermined—by a virus so cruel that it strikes young adults as they are poised to enter their most productive years, and assume the mantle of leadership. A virus which robs children of their parents, or forces them to drop out of school, leaving a generation without care or education—and therefore itself more vulnerable to HIV. A virus that strikes more and more against women—who hold together the African family, who sustain the African continent, who make up Africa's lifeline.

That is why, ladies and gentlemen, the fight against AIDS is vital not only for its own sake. It is vital to all our efforts to build a stronger Africa. Only if we work towards the goal of halting the spread can we hope to make progress toward meeting all the other Millennium Development Goals.

Spending on the fight against HIV/AIDS by African Governments, the US and the EU [European Union] has risen significantly, but it is still not enough. Twice as much is needed, this year, next year, and every year, for the foreseeable future.

Greater efforts are also needed from all of you. As our host, President Chissano, said in advance of this summit: "We as leaders will need to do more to fight and defeat AIDS. We have to show great commitment and significant actions in dealing with a disease that could wipe out our populations and set us back many years in development."

We know from experience that the spread can be turned back. Some African countries have indeed done so. But it cannot be done piecemeal. It requires a coordinated response from all sectors of society. It requires leadership—in Governments, in schools, on the streets, in places of worship, in families, among people living with HIV/AIDS and in the most affected communities. It requires empowering young people to be at the forefront of change—especially through the education of girls—so they have the knowledge, confidence and means to protect themselves against the virus.

It requires all of you to show the way by example: by breaking the deadly wall of silence that continues to surround the pandemic, and by making the fight against AIDS a priority second to none. I have made it mine; I know several among you have made it yours.

Ladies and Gentlemen,

I have outlined a few areas of particular urgency where—in my view—Africa needs to demonstrate ownership through action.

The United Nations family will keep working in close partnership with you across the full range of those challenges: at the country level— from education to governance, from agricultural development to the fight against AIDS; and at the level of the African Union, by supporting the development of key AU institutions. We will keep working with you to strengthen African peace-building and conflict resolution capacities. And we will keep working with you to help ensure that the new peace and security architecture for Africa benefits from enhanced African peacekeeping capabilities as well as active UN engagement.

President Chissano, a while ago you gave a speech about the meaning of the word partnership—a word which seems to have become the catch-all expression of our age. (I confess to having used it five times today!). Mr. President, you admitted in that speech that you did not consult the Oxford English Dictionary for a definition of the word. But you did describe what it took for the developed countries to be true partners of Africa. They would be true partners, you said, when "they care about our gains as they do about theirs". When they "respect, acknowledge and accept that we Africans have a contribution to make to our own development and to the development of all humanity".

Excellencies,

Through this Union, you, the leaders of Africa, have the opportunity, the right and the responsibility to make that contribution plain for all the world to see. If you do, the world will owe you an equal contribution in return.

Thank you very much. *Je vous remercie. Choukran Jazeelan. Muchas Gracias. Muito obrigado.*

Source: United Nations. "Secretary-General's Address to the African Union Summit." Maputo, Mozambique. July 10, 2003. www.un.org/apps/ sg/printsgstats.asp?nid=412 (accessed January 21, 2004).

UN Security Council on International Peacekeeping in Bosnia

July 11, 2003

INTRODUCTION

Bosnia in 2003 continued to stumble along the road to nationhood that was set out by international powers after the end of its war in 1995. The ethnic nationalist parties that had led Bosnia into Europe's worst war since World War II returned to office in Bosnia in February, but this time they were publicly committed to political and economic reforms. By adopting one of the most significant reforms, Bosnia's leaders agreed to the unified command of the two armies that symbolized the postwar division of the country into two parts: one controlled by ethnic Serbs and the other by ethnic Croats and Muslims.

Perhaps most surprising to those who had not been following Bosnian affairs closely, the country by 2003 was making strides toward eventual membership in both the European Union (EU) and the North Atlantic Treaty Organization (NATO) alliance. A committee within the EU suggested that Bosnia might be ready for membership after 2007. Bosnia also was on course for 2004 membership in NATO's Partnership for Peace, a training ground developed in the 1990s for the formerly communist countries of Eastern Europe that hoped to become full members of the alliance. *(EU expansion, p. 492)*

However, progress on institutional reforms had still done little to improve the daily lives of most of Bosnia's nearly 4 million people. Officially, unemployment was at 40 percent, but most estimates put the real percentage of unemployed workers much higher. The country's gross domestic product was less than half the prewar level; corruption and organized crime were among the most successful aspects of the economy.

The effective division of the country into two territories was a constant reminder of the success of those who had used the war to pursue nationalist agendas. Moreover, the two most notorious Bosnian war criminals remained at large: Serb nationalist leader Radovan Karadzic and his military chief Ratko Mladic. NATO peacekeepers had made only intermittent efforts to capture the two men, both of whom had been indicted on multiple charges by the United Nation's war crimes tribunal. Paddy Ashdown, the top UN official in Bosnia, told the Security Council in October that Karadzic "remains a baleful curse over the whole country. We know that peace cannot be described as fully entrenched until the perpetrators of these unspeakable crimes are finally brought to justice."

The 1992–1995 war had dislocated nearly 2 million Bosnians. Many were forced from their homes in campaigns that came to be known as "ethnic cleansing": Serb paramilitary forces (backed by the army of Serb-led Yugoslavia) forced Croats and Muslims from areas that Serbian national-ists claimed, while Croat militias forced Serbs and Muslims from their homes; to a far lesser degree, Muslim militias took similar actions against Croats and Serbs.

By 2003 nearly 1 million people had returned to their former homes in Bosnia, including 390,000 in areas where they were in the minority. Another half-million Bosnian citizens remained refugees as of year's end; the govern-ment hoped to settle most of them in their former home areas within four years.

The UN Security Council on July 11 extended for one year the mandate of NATO peacekeepers in Bosnia. The council reiterated its support for the peace agreement, negotiated near Dayton, Ohio, in 1995, that ended the Bosnia war. *(Background, Historic Documents of 1995, p. 717; Historic Doc-uments of 2000, p. 142)*

Nationalist Parties Return to Power

The 1995 Dayton peace agreement divided Bosnia and Herzegovina (the country's official title) into two parts based on the location of ethnic popula-tions at the end of the war: a Croat-Muslim federation in the central areas of the country, surrounded on three sides by a Serb Republic (the Republika Srpska, in Serbo-Croatian). A weak national government was made up of a multiethnic parliament and a rotating presidency with representatives from each of the three ethnic groups. A "high representative," appointed by the United Nations, had broad authority to impose legislation and fire government officials who violated the peace agreement, the national constitution, or laws.

After the war Bosnia held numerous elections, a process that through repetition proved to disenchant many Bosnians with the concept of democ-racy. In general, the elections pitted moderate, pro-Western political parties against the successors to ethnic-based, nationalist parties whose leaders had held power during the war. Nationalist parties controlled the federal government from 1998 to 2000 and failed to pass any significant pieces of legislation. After parliamentary elections in November 2000, the high representative at the time, Wolfgang Petritsch, used his influence to paste together a coalition of moderate parties under the banner "Alliance for Change." The resulting coalition government managed to enact some reforms but at a pace so slow that most Bosnians could see little improvement in their daily lives.

Mounting dissatisfaction with the moderate coalition—coupled with low turnout resulting from voter fatigue—worked to the advantage of nationalist parties in the subsequent elections, held in October 2002. The winning parties in the Muslim-Croat federation were the Party of Democratic Action and the Croatian Democratic Union—the nationalist parties, respectively, of Bosnian Muslims and Croats. The hard-line Serbian Democratic Party retained its majority in the Serb Republic. Despite these victories for nationalist parties, the election marked something of a turning point: It was the first in which Serbs won any seats in the Muslim-Croat federation, and Muslims and Croats won seats in the Serb republic.

By the time of the 2002 elections, Ashdown, one of Britain's most charismatic politicians, had taken over as high representative and had used his political skills to strike a grand bargain with all the major political parties. Before the campaign got under way, Ashdown convinced all major parties to endorse a reform agenda he had devised emphasizing the rule of law and economic reform—complex ideas that he summarized with the title "Justice and Jobs." Ashdown thus boxed the nationalist parties into a commitment that limited their ability to focus solely on their narrow individual interests and, instead, forced them to pay at least some attention to the needs of the nation as a whole. After more than three months of politicking, the new national parliament took office February 14, 2003.

The chief success of Ashdown's reform program was the establishment of a new legal system for Bosnia. A new criminal code and procedures for enforcing it took effect January 24, and three days later new judges and prosecutors assumed office. "Bosnia's lawless rule was being replaced by the rule of law," Ashdown said.

Ashdown acknowledged in a June 9 speech that the heavy hand that he, and his predecessors, exerted in Bosnian affairs had the unintended consequence of relieving local politicians of responsibility for their actions. When a problem arises, he said, "we tend to intervene, the problem disappears, and life goes on. So the symptoms are relieved, the crisis is averted; but too often the chronic disease remains unaffected."

In an experiment, Ashdown created three "reform commissions" to develop new policies on taxes, defense, and intelligence. Each commission was chaired by an international expert, but its staff and members were Bosnians.

The defense commission, chaired by former U.S. Pentagon official James Locher, helped develop one of the country's most significant reforms since the war: a step toward the creation of a unified military. The 1995 Dayton peace agreement had allowed two Bosnian armies—one for the Muslim-Croat federation and the other for the Serb Republic. The chief author of the Dayton agreement, U.S. diplomat Richard Holbrooke, subsequently bemoaned that provision, arguing that Bosnia could never be a united country if it had two armies. On September 27 the parliament approved draft laws putting the two armies under the command of a united, national defense minister and chief of staff. Although the two armies could continue, for the first time they would wear the same uniform and swear allegiance to the Bosnian nation rather than to a separate ethnic entity.

Peacekeeping Mission Pared Back

When the war ended in late 1995, NATO sent to tiny Bosnia the largest international peacekeeping mission ever mounted: 60,000 troops, one-third of them from the United States. NATO led the mission, rather than the United Nations, because it had the manpower and the UN was still recovering from its previous peacekeeping failures, notably its inability to prevent a genocide in Rwanda in 1994 and the massacre of at least 8,000 at the town of Srebrenica, in Bosnia, in July 1995. *(Rwanda, p. 1069; Srebrenica massacre, Historic Documents of 1999, p. 735)*

In its early years the NATO mission (known as the stabilization force) was needed simply to prevent renewed violence between the warring parties in Bosnia. As peace settled in, the NATO troops were called on to suppress organized crime and—occasionally—to mount searches for elusive war criminals, especially Karadzic and Mladic. NATO gradually reduced the number of troops in Bosnia; in 2003 the mission had 11,900 troops, 1,500 of them from the United States.

The European Union in October offered to take over the peacekeeping mission from NATO; it would be the EU's first major operation since the creation earlier in 2003 of a European defense force that had been in the planning stages for several years. NATO announced on December 19 that it planned to reduce its Bosnia mission to about 7,000 troops by June 2004. By the end of 2003 NATO had not formally decided whether to accept the EU's offer.

Parallel to the peacekeeping mission was a United Nations program to train police officers in Bosnia and help local authorities deal with organized crime. The EU took over that program at the beginning of 2003; the EU Police Mission had 500 police officers and 50 civilian experts.

War Crimes Prosecutions

Overhanging the political process in Bosnia was the continued war crimes trial of Slobodan Milosevic, the Yugoslav leader who unleashed the ethnic conflict that engulfed much of his nation after it collapsed in 1991–1992. The International Criminal Tribunal for the former Yugoslavia, seated at The Hague, Netherlands, had indicted Milosevic on sixty-six charges of genocide and other crimes in those wars. His trial began in 2002 and was expected to last into 2005; the trial was delayed repeatedly because of Milosevic's poor health. *(Background, Historic Documents of 2001, p. 826)*

The year's most dramatic testimony came in mid-December when former NATO commander Wesley Clark told the court that in 1999 he had discussed with Milosevic the most important crime of the war: the Srebrenica massacre. Clark said Milosevic told him that he had warned the Bosnian Serb military commander, Mladic, against the killings but had been ignored. Clark's testimony helped strengthen the case of prosecutors that Milosevic had advance knowledge of the Srebrenica massacre and other mass killings. As NATO commander in the late 1990s, Clark met repeatedly with Milosevic. At the time of his testimony Clark was a candidate for the Democratic presidential nomination. *(Srebrenica background, Historic Documents of 1999, p. 735)*

Prosecutors at the Hague gathered several convictions and guilty pleas among lower-level Serb officials accused of war crimes. Among them was Darko Mrdja, who commanded a special police unit that in 1992 forced more than 200 Muslim men to kneel at the edge of a cliff and then shot them or pushed them over; on July 25 he pleaded guilty to murder and attempted murder. On July 31 the tribunal sentenced a Serb politician to life in prison—its harshest punishment yet—for inciting war crimes. Milomir Stakic had been mayor of the town of Prijedor, where an estimated 1,500 non-Serbs were killed and at least 20,000 were forced from their homes. Former colonel Dragan Obrenovic, the commander of one of two brigades that carried out the Srebrenica massacre, was sentenced to seventeen years in prison. Obrenovic received the relatively light sentence because he had pleaded guilty to one count of "persecution" and had testified against two codefendants; in exchange prosecutors dropped four more serious charges.

While the trials continued at The Hague, the Bosnian government made plans for its own tribunal to hear less serious charges stemming from the war. The War Crimes Chamber within the State Court of Bosnia and Herzegovina was expected to begin operations in 2004; it would ease the burden on The Hague court, which had become overwhelmed with cases of war crimes committed in Bosnia, Croatia, and Kosovo during the 1990s. The new court was financed with $18.4 million in donations from the United States and twenty-nine other countries.

Families of some of the victims of the Srebrenica massacre were able to come to closure with their losses in 2003, when the first 1,000 victims to be identified were buried in a new cemetery and memorial with spaces set aside for 10,000 bodies. Former U.S. president Bill Clinton attended the

September 20 dedication of the cemetery, saying he was there to "pay tribute to the innocent lives, many of them children, snuffed out in what must
be called genocidal madness." The process of locating and identifying the
bodies of an estimated 6,000 to 8,000 other victims was still under way.

Election in Croatia

Croatia—Bosnia's neighbor and fellow participant in the Balkan wars of the
1990s—also installed a new government in 2003 dominated by a wartime
nationalist party. Croatian voters on November 23 returned to office the
Christian Democratic Party, which had been led during and after the
1992–1995 war by hard-line Croatian nationalist Franjo Tudjman. More than
250,000 ethnic Serbs fled or were driven from Croatia during the war, and
the UN tribunal had indicted several prominent Croatian military leaders—
but no political leaders—on war crimes charges.

Tudjman's party was removed from office in 2000 by a center-left coalition that promised economic and political reforms aimed at winning Croatia membership in the European Union. But that government was plagued
by a sagging economy and numerous missteps, and voters in November
turned back to the conservatives. This time, however, the Christian Democratic Party was headed by Ivo Sanader, a former theater director who once
worked for Tudjman. Sanader insisted his party had shed Tudjman's nationalist policies and was now a standard European conservative party determined to lead Croatia into the EU. The party won 66 seats in the 152-mem-
ber parliament and took office on December by assembling a coalition with
other conservative parties.

Try as he might to put the war behind him, Sanader faced the challenge
of the EU's demand that Croatia hand over to the UN tribunal Ante Gotovina, the most prominent Croatian general who had been indicted on war
crimes charges. Many Croatians considered Gotovina a hero because of
his successful attacks against Serbs. The moderate government in power
from 2000 to 2003 claimed it could not arrest him because his whereabouts
were unknown. Sanader was charged with finding Gotovina, however,
because the EU insisted that Croatia's membership application could proceed only if the general was handed over to The Hague tribunal.

*Following is the text of United Nations Resolution 1491,
adopted unanimously July 11, 2003, by the United Nations
Security Council, extending for one year the authorization of a
NATO peacekeeping force in Bosnia and Herzegovina.*

"United Nations Security Council Resolution 1491"

The Security Council,

Recalling all its previous relevant resolutions concerning the conflicts in the former Yugoslavia and relevant statements of its President, including resolutions 1031 (1995) of 15 December 1995, 1088 (1996) of 12 December 1996 and 1423 (2002) of 12 July 2002,

Reaffirming its commitment to the political settlement of the conflicts in the former Yugoslavia, preserving the sovereignty and territorial integrity of all States there within their internationally recognized borders,

Emphasizing its full support for the High Representative's continued role in Bosnia and Herzegovina,

Underlining its commitment to support the implementation of the General Framework Agreement for Peace in Bosnia and Herzegovina and the Annexes thereto (collectively the Peace Agreement, S/1995/999, annex), as well as the relevant decisions of the Peace Implementation Council (PIC),

Emphasizing its appreciation to the High Representative, the Commander and personnel of the multinational stabilization force (SFOR), the Organization for Security and Cooperation in Europe (OSCE), and the personnel of other international organizations and agencies in Bosnia and Herzegovina for their contributions to the implementation of the Peace Agreement,

Emphasizing that a comprehensive and coordinated return of refugees and displaced persons throughout the region continues to be crucial to lasting peace,

Recalling the declarations of the Ministerial meetings of the Peace Implementation Conference,

Noting the reports of the High Representative, including his latest report of 21 October 2002,

Determining that the situation in the region continues to constitute a threat to international peace and security,

Determined to promote the peaceful resolution of the conflicts in accordance with the purposes and principles of the Charter of the United Nations,

Recalling the relevant principles contained in the Convention on the Safety of United Nations and Associated Personnel adopted on 9 December 1994 and the statement of its President of 10 February 2000,

Welcoming and encouraging efforts by the United Nations to sensitize peacekeeping personnel in the prevention and control of HIV/AIDS and other communicable diseases in all its peacekeeping operations,

Acting under Chapter VII of the Charter of the United Nations,

I

1. *Reaffirms* once again its support for the Peace Agreement, as well as for the Dayton Agreement on implementing the Federation of Bosnia and Herzegovina of 10 November 1995, *calls upon* the parties to comply strictly with their obligations under those Agreements, and *expresses* its intention to keep the implementation of the Peace Agreement, and the situation in Bosnia and Herzegovina, under review;

2. *Reiterates* that the primary responsibility for the further successful implementation of the Peace Agreement lies with the authorities in Bosnia and Herzegovina themselves and that the continued willingness of the international community and major donors to assume the political, military and economic burden of implementation and reconstruction efforts will be determined by the compliance and active participation by all the authorities in Bosnia and Herzegovina in implementing the Peace Agreement and rebuilding a civil society, in particular in full cooperation with the International Tribunal for the Former Yugoslavia, in strengthening joint institutions, which foster the building of a fully functioning self-sustaining state, able to integrate itself into the European structures and in facilitating returns of refugees and displaced persons;

3. *Reminds* the parties once again that, in accordance with the Peace Agreement, they have committed themselves to cooperate fully with all entities involved in the implementation of this peace settlement, as described in the Peace Agreement, or which are otherwise authorized by the Security Council, including the International Tribunal for the Former Yugoslavia, as it carries out its responsibilities for dispensing justice impartially, and *underlines* that full cooperation by States and entities with the International Tribunal includes, inter alia, the surrender for trial of all persons indicted by the Tribunal and provision of information to assist in Tribunal investigations;

4. *Emphasizes* its full support for the continued role of the High Representative in monitoring the implementation of the Peace Agreement and giving guidance to and coordinating the activities of the civilian organizations and agencies involved in assisting the parties to implement the Peace Agreement, and *reaffirms* that the High Representative is the final authority in theatre regarding the interpretation of Annex 10 on civilian implementation of the Peace Agreement and

that in case of dispute he may give his interpretation and make recommendations, and make binding decisions as he judges necessary on issues as elaborated by the Peace Implementation Council in Bonn on 9 and 10 December 1997;

5. *Expresses* its support for the declarations of the Ministerial meetings of the Peace Implementation Conference;

6. *Recognizes* that the parties have authorized the multinational force referred to in paragraph 10 below to take such actions as required, including the use of necessary force, to ensure compliance with Annex 1-A of the Peace Agreement;

7. *Reaffirms* its intention to keep the situation in Bosnia and Herzegovina under close review, taking into account the reports submitted pursuant to paragraphs 18 and 20 below, and any recommendations those reports might include, and its readiness to consider the imposition of measures if any party fails significantly to meet its obligations under the Peace Agreement;

II

8. *Pays tribute* to those Member States which participated in the multinational stabilization force established in accordance with its resolution 1088 (1996), and *welcomes* their willingness to assist the parties to the Peace Agreement by continuing to deploy a multinational stabilization force;

9. *Notes* the support of the parties to the Peace Agreement for the continuation of the multinational stabilization force, set out in the declaration of the Ministerial meeting of the Peace Implementation Conference in Madrid on 16 December 1998;

10. *Authorizes* the Member States acting through or in cooperation with the organization referred to in Annex 1-A of the Peace Agreement to continue for a further planned period of 12 months the multinational stabilization force (SFOR) as established in accordance with its resolution 1088 (1996) under unified command and control in order to fulfil the role specified in Annex 1-A and Annex 2 of the Peace Agreement, and *expresses* its intention to review the situation with a view to extending this authorization further as necessary in the light of developments in the implementation of the Peace Agreement and the situation in Bosnia and Herzegovina;

11. *Authorizes* the Member States acting under paragraph 10 above to take all necessary measures to effect the implementation of and to ensure compliance with Annex 1-A of the Peace Agreement, *stresses* that the parties shall continue to be held equally responsible for compliance with that Annex and shall be equally subject to such

enforcement action by SFOR as may be necessary to ensure implementation of that Annex and the protection of SFOR, and *takes note* that the parties have consented to SFOR's taking such measures;

12. *Authorizes* Member States to take all necessary measures, at the request of SFOR, either in defence of SFOR or to assist the force in carrying out its mission, and *recognizes* the right of the force to take all necessary measures to defend itself from attack or threat of attack;

13. *Authorizes* the Member States acting under paragraph 10 above, in accordance with Annex 1-A of the Peace Agreement, to take all necessary measures to ensure compliance with the rules and procedures established by the Commander of SFOR, governing command and control of airspace over Bosnia and Herzegovina with respect to all civilian and military air traffic;

14. *Requests* the authorities in Bosnia and Herzegovina to cooperate with the Commander of SFOR to ensure the effective management of the airports of Bosnia and Herzegovina, in the light of the responsibilities conferred on SFOR by Annex 1-A of the Peace Agreement with regard to the airspace of Bosnia and Herzegovina;

15. *Demands* that the parties respect the security and freedom of movement of SFOR and other international personnel;

16. *Invites* all States, in particular those in the region, to continue to provide appropriate support and facilities, including transit facilities, for the Member States acting under paragraph 10 above;

17. *Recalls* all the agreements concerning the status of forces as referred to in Appendix B to Annex 1-A of the Peace Agreement, and *reminds* the parties of their obligation to continue to comply therewith;

18. *Requests* the Member States acting through or in cooperation with the organization referred to in Annex 1-A of the Peace Agreement to continue to report to the Council, through the appropriate channels and at least at monthly intervals;

19. *Welcomes* the deployment by the European Union (EU) of its Police Mission (EUPM) to Bosnia and Herzegovina since 1 January 2003;

20. *Also requests* the Secretary-General to continue to submit to the Council reports from the High Representative, in accordance with Annex 10 of the Peace Agreement and the conclusions of the Peace Implementation Conference held in London on 4 and 5 December 1996 (S/1996/1012), and later Peace Implementation Conferences, on the implementation of the Peace Agreement and in particular on compliance by the parties with their commitments under that Agreement;

21. *Decides* to remain seized of the matter.

Source: United Nations. Security Council. *Resolution 1491.* S/RES/1491 (2003). July 11, 2003. www.un.org/Docs/sc/unsc_resolutions03.html (accessed September 15, 2003).

Human Rights Watch on Conflict in Northern Uganda

July 15, 2003

INTRODUCTION

A long-running, brutal, yet little-noticed conflict continued to terrorize hundreds of thousands of people in the east African country of Uganda during 2003. The United Nations and international human rights groups were able to focus an unprecedented amount of attention on the fighting, in part because of a dramatic upsurge in the number of young children who were abducted and forced to serve as fighters or slaves for a rebel group that called itself the Lord's Resistance Army (LRA).

A grim reminder of the worst period of Uganda's troubled history passed from the scene in August, when the country's most notorious former dictator, Idi Amin, died in exile in Saudi Arabia. Amin seized power in 1971 and ruled for nearly nine bloody years before he, in turn, was overthrown by a coalition of rebel forces and the army of neighboring Tanzania. Uganda under Amin symbolized the excesses of African's dictatorial rulers in the decades after independence. The government's campaign to suppress the Langi and Acholi groups resulted in the deaths of about 300,000 people, according to widely accepted estimates by international observers. Amin was ousted in 1979 by a previous ruler, Milton Obote, who conducted his own terror campaign before being overthrown in 1985. Amin took up residence in Saudi Arabia, where he reportedly lived in comfort until his death. *(Amin's abuses, Historic Documents of 1977, p. 143)*

Background

As with most of Africa's conflicts, the fighting in Uganda had its roots in ancient differences among ethnic and tribal groups that had been lumped together in the colonies formed by western European nations in the nine-teenth century. At independence in 1962 Uganda was a collection of a half-dozen major groups and dozens of tribes and other subgroups, the largest of which represented only about 20 percent of the total population. A suc-cession of dictators—the most famous of whom was Amin—exploited the nation's differences for their own purposes and blocked any possibility that the resource-rich country could reach its full potential.

One of the groups at the heart of Uganda's conflicts was the Acholi people, who lived in the north of the country and historically had been dominated by other groups based in the south. Since Uganda's indepen-dence, the Acholi had been aligned with some rulers, exploited by some, and ignored by others. In 1985 an Acholi woman calling herself Alice Lak-wena and claiming to be guided by a spiritual messenger created the Holy Spirit Movement, a guerrilla force that was supposed to protect the Acholi people from the government. That group lasted only about a year before it was defeated by the government, and Lakwena and her followers fled into Kenya.

In 1987 Joseph Kony, who said he was Lakwena's nephew and had inherited her spiritual powers, formed a new guerrilla group in Uganda that eventually came to be known as the Lord's Resistance Army. Kony was a recluse who reportedly spent hours each day communing with the Chris-tian and Muslim spirits who, he said, provided the guidance for his cam-paign, which had as its only discernible goal the ousting of the government, headed since 1986 by Yoweri Museveni. Kony's spirits occasionally gave him bits of practical advice, which he passed on to his troops, including a "divine" admonition against riding bicycles.

Kony's LRA quickly developed into a band of thugs that terrorized the populace of northern Uganda by raiding villages for food and other sup-plies, killing or maiming adults, and abducting children. Abducted boys were pressed into service as fighters for the LRA, and girls were forced to do manual labor until they reached puberty, when they became sex-slaves for the fighters or "wives" for guerrilla commanders. Kony himself was said to have numerous wives and dozens of children.

According to Human Rights Watch and other observers, the government of Sudan in 1994 began giving the LRA weapons as well as sanctuary in southeastern Sudan. In turn, the Ugandan government provided support to black African rebels in southern Sudan who were fighting the Arab-dominated government in Khartoum. The governments of Sudan and Uganda agreed in 1999 to stop supporting the rebels in each other's countries. That agreement brought a short period of relative calm, even though cross-border fighting continued. *(Sudan war, p. 835)*

Apparently hoping to shut down Kony's rebellion, Uganda's government in March 2002 launched what it called "Operation Iron Fist": an all-out mil-itary assault on LRA camps in southern Sudan. Instead of destroying the rebels, that operation had the perverse effect of pushing them back into northern Uganda, where they managed to evade the Ugandan army and, beginning in June 2002, stepped up their attacks on the local civilian population. The LRA rebels also attacked camps that housed refugees from Sudan's civil war—one of many indications, according to Human Rights Watch, that the rebels were still aligned with the Sudanese government.

The fighting in northern Uganda raged nonstop from June 2002 to March 2003, when the Ugandan government and the LRA rebels arranged a cease-fire. That respite lasted only a few weeks, however, and by April 2003 gangs of LRA fighters were again rampaging throughout northern Uganda, with elements of the Ugandan army in pursuit.

Statistics gathered by relief workers and other observers on the consequences of the fighting were appalling even by the standards of ethnic conflict in east Africa. By late 2003 United Nations agencies estimated that more than 80 percent of the 900,000 Acholi people in northern Uganda had been displaced from their homes. Another 300,000 or so people in the Teso region of central Uganda had been pushed out of their homes. When added to displacements elsewhere in the country, that brought the total number of Ugandans who had been displaced by the fighting, as of December 2003, to 1.4 million—out of a total population in the country of about 25 million. Tens of thousands of these people lived in overcrowded, poorly serviced camps, where they were subjected to further raids by the LRA. Others took up refuge in schools, hospitals, churches, and other public buildings, or simply on the streets.

After visiting Uganda in November, Jan Egeland, the United Nations undersecretary general in charge of emergency relief, said he had been "shocked" by the extent of the conflict, which he called "the biggest forgotten, neglected humanitarian emergency in the world today." The UN had done "too little," he said, "the donors have done too little. The government has done too little, we have all done to little" to stop the fighting and care for those were afflicted by it.

Abduction of Children

Over the years only one aspect of the conflict in northern Uganda drew any degree of sustained international attention: the LRA's practice of abducting thousands of children, who were then forced to become fighters or sex-slaves. In the twelve months following the upsurge of fighting in June 2002, LRA fighters had kidnapped an estimated 10,000 children, according to estimates by UN and private relief agencies. Only a small percentage of the children escaped or were recovered in counterattacks by the Ugandan army.

The LRA's standard practice called for small groups of armed fighters to raid villages at night, stealing as much food and as many children as they could handle. Adults who resisted were killed or mutilated (most often by having their hands, ears, and even lips chopped off). The children usually were tied together with ropes and forced to carry the food and other supplies the rebels had stolen from the village. The cruel irony of the conflict was that nearly all the LRA fighters had themselves been abducted as children and had then been terrorized into joining the rebellion's ranks. According to numerous reports, the LRA set the age of seven as the minimum for its fighters. While most of the fighters were boys, the LRA reportedly forced many girls to fight, as well.

In many cases, former LRA abductees were returning, as fighters, to their own home areas, where they repeated the cycle of terror against former neighbors or even family members. By 2002 the LRA's abduction of children had become so commonplace that families in remote villages of the Acholi region began sending their children, in groups, to larger towns, where they could sleep at night in relatively more safety. Known locally as "night commuters," thousands of children slept on the streets or in the schools of Gulu, Kitgum, Pader, and other towns, in many cases after walking as much as five miles from their home villages. Each morning, the children would walk home for the day, then repeat the commute at night. The number of "night commuters" varied according to the frequency of LRA attacks in any given area. In June UN aid workers reported that about 14,000 children were spending the nights in the town of Gulu; in December the Norwegian Refugee Council cited reports that some 15,000 children were spending each night in Kitgum.

While blaming the LRA for the vast majority of humanitarian abuses in the war, Human Rights Watch and other organizations also accused the Ugandan army of turning a blind eye to abuses by its own soldiers, notably the raping of civilian women. The government denied these charges.

Ending the Conflict

By 2003 the Ugandan government faced conflicting types of international pressure to bring the conflict with the LRA to an end. Humanitarian organizations, such as Human Rights Watch and the Norwegian Refugee Council, charged that the government was bent on a "military solution" that clearly did not seem to be working. Rather than destroying the LRA in its camps in southern Sudan, the government's Operation Iron Fist merely moved the fighting back into Uganda, which led to more fighting and misery, according to this view. The chief European Union diplomat in Uganda, Sigurd Illing, appeared to endorse that view in November, saying the government needed to "find an alternative" to continuing the conflict.

The government appeared to get some support for its military approach from the United States, which in 2001 declared the LRA to be a "terrorist organization" and gave the Ugandan army weapons and training for its antiguerrilla campaign. President George W. Bush offered praise, but no public criticism, of the Museveni government during a four-hour visit to Uganda on July 10; it was the fourth stop on his five-nation tour of Africa. *(Bush Africa visit, p. 450)*

Perhaps the central dilemma facing Uganda's government was the difficulty of negotiating with the LRA and especially with Kony, its mystical leader. Kony reportedly spurned all forms of contact with the government or outside mediators. Few of his aides would even admit knowing how to get in touch with him. The United Nations news agency quoted one UN official in Uganda as saying the LRA rebels "don't seem to want anything negotiable. Kony consults the spirits on a daily basis to dictate the battle. How do you negotiate with spirits?"

Apparently in response to domestic pressure from opposition leaders and the bishops of several churches, Museveni in 2002 offered to talk to the rebels, but only after they had agreed to a cease-fire. Each side announced a unilateral cease-fire in March 2003, but LRA representatives failed to show up for talks the government offered. Fighting resumed in April. The government also extended, through 2003, an amnesty it had offered to LRA rebels who surrendered. Few fighters took advantage of the offer, however. The government said only low-level fighters—not LRA commanders—would be eligible for the amnesty.

Following is the summary chapter from "Abducted and Abused: Renewed Conflict in Northern Uganda," a report published July 15, 2003, by Human Rights Watch that detailed human rights abuses committed during the conflict in Uganda, notably the abduction of children by a rebel group called the Lord's Resistance Army.

"Abducted and Abused: Renewed Conflict in Northern Uganda"

The seventeen-year war in northern Uganda has been characterized by great brutality by the rebel Lord's Resistance Army (LRA), as documented in Human Rights Watch's 1997 report, *The Scars of Death: Children Abducted by the Lord's Resistance Army in Northern Uganda*, and later publications. The atrocities increased in 2002, but international attention has been distracted by less savage emergencies. A Ugandan peace effort, spearheaded by the Acholi Religious Leaders Peace Initiative (ARLPI), has not broken through the parties' desire for a military solution.

The latest effort to bring the war to a close by military means has failed as well. In March 2002, Uganda's army, the Ugandan People's Defence Force (UPDF), launched Operation Iron Fist, a military campaign intended to wipe out the LRA by attacking its southern Sudanese sanctuaries. Instead the conflict inside northern Uganda intensified. The LRA—which draws its recruits, mostly abducted children, from the Acholi population of northern Uganda—evaded the UPDF in Sudan and moved back into Uganda in June 2002 where it has stepped up its abduction, killing, looting, and destruction aimed at civilians and their property.

The UPDF responded with massive forced displacement and increased arrests. The victimized northern population became more alienated from both sides, and less hopeful about the future, than ever before.

This report, a follow-up to the 1997 study, details the deteriorating situation in northern Uganda today. Dozens of eyewitnesses and civilian victims provided Human Rights Watch detailed accounts of the renewed devastation being wreaked by the conflict, particularly on children. Since June 2002, the LRA has abducted approximately 8,400 children, resumed its despicable practice of mutilating people it believes to be affiliated with the government, and targeted religious leaders, aid providers, and other civilians. It has expanded the war's reach beyond northern Uganda into the Soroti area of eastern Uganda.

One thirteen-year-old boy was abducted together with his four brothers in 2002 and he escaped. Others were less fortunate, if this can be termed "fortunate": he reported that "the LRA explained to us that all five brothers couldn't serve in the LRA because we would not perform well. So they tied up my two younger brothers and invited us to watch. Then they beat them with sticks until the two of them died. They told us it would give us strength to fight. My youngest brother was nine years old."

Although the Ugandan government has an obligation to intervene to end such abuses, government forces themselves have been responsible for human rights violations, including cases of torture and rape, summary execution, and arbitrary detention of suspects. Government investigators have pursued some cases of abuse by UPDF soldiers, but prosecutions have languished and wrongdoers continue to enjoy virtual impunity. Both the UPDF and the Local Defence Force (LDU) have recruited underage boys as soldiers.

The history of the alienation of northern Uganda from the government of Yoweri Museveni, and government forces' abuses in the north, may partly explain why some northern Ugandans tolerate or assist the LRA in their midst, despite its atrocities. This tolerance, and fear of LRA retaliation, is evident from the widespread dispersion of LRA forces and the inability of the UPDF to achieve a military solution.

The Ugandan government's forced displacement policy also has contributed to the suffering of northern Ugandans and their resentment of the heavy-handed and ineffective way the UPDF wages war, at their expense. On October 2, 2002, the government ordered thousands of civilians in the affected areas of Gulu, Kitgum, and Pader districts (Acholiland) to relocate into "protected" camps. This had been tried before, in 1996. In early 2002, there were still more than 500,000 civilians internally displaced in northern Uganda. By the end of 2002 and as a result of the LRA's stepped up attacks and the Ugandan government's October 2 displacement order, this figure had increased substantially, to more than 800,000 internally displaced persons (IDPs), or approximately 70 percent of the population of Acholiland, a staggering proportion of IDPs.

Despite these measures, the government has been unable to provide sufficient security and assistance to the population to offset the economic disruption caused by massive displacement. Insecurity in the form of LRA ambushes and attacks on World Food Programme (WFP) and other relief vehicles hampers the delivery of humanitarian aid, and the WFP is under funded.

Since 1994, the LRA's only known supporter has been the Sudanese government, reportedly in retaliation for the Ugandan government's support of the rebel Sudan People's Liberation Movement/Army (SPLM/A). Both sides deny that they are providing material support to the other's rebels.

After the LRA was declared a terrorist organization by the U.S. Department of State in late 2001, however, the Sudanese government quietly claimed it had cut off supplies to the LRA; it sought to improve Sudanese-U.S. relations. This purported assistance cut-off was short-lived. After the LRA helped the Sudanese government recapture the Sudanese garrison town of Torit from the SPLM/A in October 2002, arms and ammunition—including anti-tank landmines—flowed again from the Sudanese side to the LRA. This happened despite LRA killing and looting of Sudanese civilians in southern Sudan and in refugee camps in Uganda.

Despite the tragic situation the war has created, there is no silver bullet solution for the seventeen-year conflict. But the situation may change soon, as the Sudanese government and the SPLM/A are engaged in serious peace negotiations supported by the U.S., the U.K., and Norway (the "Troika"). If the Sudanese conflict ends, it should no longer be necessary for the Sudanese and Ugandan governments to engage in retaliatory arming of each other's rebels. The Troika must assure that any Sudan peace agreement provides guarantees for cessation of all cross-border rebel assistance.

Although the LRA claims that it has prepared for this eventuality by stockpiling weapons and ammunition, it stands to loose its sanctuaries across the border in Sudan and its main arms and ammunition supplier. The LRA may again become willing to negotiate, as it was in mid-2002 after the Sudanese government reduced or eliminated its assistance.

At this point it will be up to the donors and others in the international community to press the parties to find an end to the conflict. The difficulty then may be to persuade the Ugandan government to abandon its efforts for a military solution, and to improve its relations with its northern citizens by improving its human rights performance.

In the meantime, the U.N. secretary-general should appoint a special envoy to negotiate the release of the abducted children from the LRA. The Sudan peace talks may not succeed, and the 8,400 children abducted from June 2002–May 2003—who have not already been murdered or escaped—require urgent release from captivity, together with the thousands already in LRA hands. The Sudanese government must end all forms of support for the LRA, both directly and indirectly, not on account of any promises by the Ugandan government, but because of the LRA's long record of gross abuses of human rights. The LRA should release all abducted people in its custody and cease abductions and attacks on civilians and civilian infrastructure.

The Ugandan government must put an end to abuses by its armed and security forces. It must promptly and publicly investigate complaints of their abuses and punish those found guilty. Donors should fully fund relief efforts. They should insist that the UPDF provide proper protection for civilians and relief convoys in northern Uganda, and not condition protection on payment for fuel and food, which is all too frequently done. Donors should encourage the Ugandan government to devise creative and attractive solutions to demobilization, and impress upon it the need to end the suffering in northern Uganda, keeping in mind that seventeen years of military solutions have not brought peace.

One major justification for Operation Iron Fist was the rescue of abducted children held by the LRA at its bases in southern Sudan. But during June to December 2002, the number of LRA child abductions (5,000) was two times greater than the number of abducted children rescued by the UPDF (2,227).

The number of civilians—many very young—killed, injured, and abducted by the LRA, and the extensive property destruction, are not the whole story. The LRA's brutality to its victims is shocking. From the beginning of the LRA's activities in northern Uganda, children and adults it abducted frequently have been beaten into submission to serve as LRA soldiers. Many are given weapons training and some are forced to fight against the UPDF and, inside southern Sudan, against the SPLM/A. All have to porter heavy, looted loads over long distances.

Young girls must work long hours fetching water and firewood, gathering food, and performing domestic duties for LRA commanders. After they reach puberty, girls are forced into sexual slavery as "wives" of LRA commanders. They are subjected to rape, forced pregnancy, and the risk of sexually transmitted diseases, including HIV/AIDS.

LRA abductees—adult and child—are threatened with death if they try to escape, and these threats have been carried out in the thousands since 1994. Children are forced to beat, club, or trample to death other children and adults who attempt to escape.

The threat of LRA abduction makes children fear for their safety. Each night, thousands of children pour into Gulu, Kitgum, and Pader towns (Acholiland) from surrounding areas, hoping to avoid abduction. They seek refuge on verandahs, in the bus park, on church grounds and in local factories before returning home again each morning. They receive little assistance, and are vulnerable to theft, sexual assault, and other abuses from other children and adults.

The UPDF and other government-related armed groups have contributed to fear and insecurity in northern Uganda. UPDF soldiers have arrested scores of civilians, with little evidence, on suspicion of rebel collaboration; some of the detainees are supporters of the unarmed political opposition. Suspects of treason or terrorism (death penalty crimes) are kept in detention without bail and without cause shown for up to 360 days. In practice this period is longer. There are also cases of UPDF torture, ill-treatment, and rape: in January 2003, UPDF soldiers severely beat a surrendering sixteen-year-old LRA child soldier so much that he was sure his backbone had been broken. He reported, "I was tied in the three-point way and kicked. I really regretted my decision to surrender. [LRA leader Joseph] Kony told us that the UPDF will kill you and I felt it was true." In another case, two UPDF soldiers captured a girl aged thirteen and a nineteen-year-old woman returning from working in the fields; each soldier raped both the girl and the woman and both contracted the HIV virus from the rapes. Although the soldiers' names were reported to the UPDF, it appears the only government response was to transfer them to another garrison.

Paramilitary groups created and armed by the government or its officials, such as the Kalangala Action Plan (KAP), headed by the senior presidential advisor Kakooza Mutale, engage in harassment and unauthorized arrest, and sometimes kill civilians. All levels of government deny that they control the KAP and other paramilitary groups, making accountability almost impossible.

Since Operation Iron Fist began in March 2002, ceasefires have come and gone. Peace negotiations have broken down. The aims of the LRA, and what it wants in a negotiated settlement, have been impossible to establish.

The brunt of the war is borne by the civilian population, in terms of homes destroyed, goods stolen, children abducted and brutalized, family members killed and raped, all of which has reduced the more than one million Acholi inhabitants of northern Uganda to a state of destitution and despair. Many wonder about their future. Sixteen-year-old John W., a former LRA child soldier abductee made an orphan by the LRA, said, "What disappoints me most is the future. Some seem to have things to do here, and a place to go, but for me, the future is blank. . . ."

Absent a major impetus from outside Uganda, the war in northern Uganda will continue at this heightened pace, cruelly destroying families, schools, lives, and hope—especially affecting the young. The case for international action on behalf of this stricken area could not be stronger.

Source: Human Rights Watch. *Abducted and Abused: Renewed Conflict in Northern Uganda.* Vol. 15, No. 12 (A). New York, N.Y. July 15, 2003. www.hrw.org/reports/2003/uganda0703 (accessed April 1, 2004).

Surgeon General on Countering Obesity

July 16, 2003

INTRODUCTION

As evidence mounted about the dire health consequences of obesity, governments, health and medical organizations, consumer groups, and the food industry all weighed in with plans for helping Americans eat less, eat healthier, and exercise more. Health organizations recommended that both children and adults be monitored annually and offered counseling if their weight was getting out of control. Schools began paying closer attention to the nutritional value of the lunches their students received, and a handful of schools removed snack and soda vending machines. Schools, which had been cutting gym classes to save money, began to reinstitute physical education programs.

The American Cancer Society mounted its first "Great American Weigh In" to focus attention on the links between obesity and several types of cancer. Employers were encouraging their employees to walk rather than take elevators and escalators. Led by McDonald's, several fast-food restaurants began offering and marketing healthier alternatives to their calorie-laden standard fare. A few companies, like Kraft Foods, announced that they planned to modify ingredients to reduce some of the fats and calories in their products.

Although they acknowledged it was a good start, some consumer and health groups said more aggressive steps were necessary. They wanted to see an end to vending machines in schools and curbs on marketing sugar-, salt-, and fat-laden snacks and drinks to children and adolescents. Many groups wanted more nutritional information on food product labels and calorie information on restaurant menus. Some were skeptical that the fast-food restaurants would follow through on their promises. They pointed to McDonald's, which was widely applauded when it promised in 2002 to reduce trans fatty acids, or trans fats, in the oil it used for its fried foods; at the end of 2003 the company was still using the harmful fats, apparently because it was not satisfied with any of the substitutes it had tried.

The Bush administration was also getting mixed reviews on its efforts to deal with obesity. Led by the Department of Health and Human Services, the administration continued its multifaceted campaign to make the public aware of the problem. It also ordered food makers to reveal how much trans fat was in their food products. At the same time, it questioned the global dietary guidelines proposed by the World Health Organization (WHO). The administration argued that the science underlying the proposed guidelines was faulty, but some consumer groups and public health experts said the Bush administration was really trying to protect the sugar and food industries.

Sizing Up the Problem

The alarming increase in obesity, not only in the United States but also throughout the world, had been the subject of intense study for several years. In the United States nearly two of every three adults were overweight or obese. The proportion of overweight children ages six to seventeen nearly quadrupled in forty years, from 4 percent to 15 percent. Worldwide more than 1 billion people were overweight, according to WHO, and 300 million of those were obese or severely obese. (Since 1998 the federal government had used a weight-to-height ratio called body mass index, or BMI, to classify weight. A BMI between 18.5 and 25 was considered a healthy weight. People with a BMI between 25 and 30 were considered overweight, while those with a BMI above 30 were considered obese, and those above 40 severely obese.)

Excess weight was a contributing factor to several chronic diseases and conditions, including heart failure, cancer, stroke, diabetes, asthma, and arthritis, and to psychological disorders such as depression. One of every eight deaths in the United States was caused by an illness directly related to overweight and obesity, according to Surgeon General Richard H. Carmona.

Doctors and others were especially concerned about the high incidence of overweight children. Researchers estimated that as many as four of every five overweight children would be overweight or obese as adults and thus susceptible at an early age to devastating health conditions. Type 2 diabetes, once typically found only in adults, was showing up with increasing frequency in children and adolescents. New research showed that nearly 1 million overweight adolescents might have metabolic syndrome—a group of conditions, including high blood pressure and cholesterol levels, that led to diabetes and heart disease. The stigma associated with being overweight also fostered emotional problems in adolescents that in some cases led to drinking, drug use, depression, and suicide. The American Academy of Pediatrics recommended in August that all children should have their BMI measured and evaluated annually. The academy recommended counseling for children who were overweight or in danger of becoming overweight. In adolescents the BMI varied depending on gender and age.

The Costs of Obesity

Attention was also beginning to focus on the costs of obesity. In addition to the estimated 300,000 deaths a year in the United States from illnesses associated with obesity, a study released May 14 estimated that $93 billion was spent treating such illnesses—as much as was spent on treating smoking-related disease. Obesity and smoking each accounted for 9 percent of all health care expenditures. The study, which was paid for by the U.S. Centers for Disease Control and Prevention (CDC), also found that about half the amount spent on treating obesity-related diseases was paid for by the government through the Medicare and Medicaid programs. An obese elderly person (with a BMI above 30) spent, on average, $1,500 more on medical care every year than did an elderly person who was not overweight. In addition indirect costs associated with obesity, such as lost productivity, were estimated at $56 billion annually.

"Obesity is something as costly to society as smoking, yet the government and private health insurers have done very little to reduce obesity rates," said one of the lead authors on the study. "The fact that the government, and ultimately the taxpayer, is financing half the economic burden of obesity suggests that the government has a clear justification to try to reduce obesity rates."

Expanding Nutritional Labels

Reducing obesity rates, like reducing smoking rates, was easier said than done. Most obesity was preventable. The primary causes were overeating, eating unhealthy foods, and lack of physical exercise. A sedentary lifestyle and the availability of convenient, inexpensive, and calorie-filled meals and snacks were often cited as contributing factors, along with lack of knowledge about nutrition. In December 2001 then surgeon general David Satcher issued a call to action to help bring Americans' weight under control by encouraging them to exercise more, eat less, and consume more fruits and vegetables and less sugar, fat, and salt. In 2002 the federal government followed up with several awareness initiatives. *(Call to action, Historic Documents of 2001, p. 935; awareness campaigns, Historic Documents of 2002, p. 626)*

The Bush administration continued the awareness campaign in 2003, with the president, Surgeon General Carmona, and Health and Human Services

Secretary Tommy G. Thompson all making appearances boosting the benefits of healthy diets and exercise. A typical example was Carmona's testimony before the House Subcommittee of Education Reform on July 16, in which he called on members of Congress, as community leaders and parents, to set a good example by making "healthy personal choices" in their own lives and to work with the administration on improving "health literacy." Thompson also advocated that insurance companies offer premium discounts to people with healthier lifestyles, just as they already did for people who did not smoke.

On July 9 the Food and Drug Administration (FDA) announced that it would require food manufacturers to include the amount of trans fats on nutritional labels. Trans fats were created when hydrogen was added to vegetable oil to solidify it and improve shelf life. Nutritionists generally considered trans fats to be as unhealthy, if not more so, than saturated fats, which were found naturally in red meats and dairy products. As little as two or three grams consumed daily could raise cholesterol levels and thus the risk of heart disease. Trans fats were common in a wide range of prepared foods, from margarine to cookies to fried foods. The FDA estimated that the new requirement would save between $900 million and $1.8 billion a year in medical costs, lost productivity, and pain and suffering.

Although the new labeling requirement would not take effect until 2006, a few food manufacturers were already reducing or eliminating trans fats from their products. Frito-Lay announced that it was eliminating trans fats from its popular Doritos, Tostitos, and Cheetos and began in 2003 to add information on trans fat content to its nutritional labels. Unilever Bestfoods also announced that it would eliminate trans fats from some of its margarine products by 2004. While consumer groups generally applauded the FDA for adding trans fat information to nutritional labels, some said that the agency should have banned trans fat altogether, as Europe had done.

Restaurants could become the next big battleground in the labeling wars. Nutritional experts and consumer groups were pressing the FDA to encourage or even require restaurants to display calorie information alongside their menu offerings. Several state legislatures were also considering laws requiring restaurants to put the equivalent of nutritional labels on their menus. The restaurant industry opposed such requirements, arguing that the choice of where and what to eat was the personal choice of diners. Nonetheless fast-food restaurants, casual restaurants, and others were beginning to offer lighter fare and smaller portions alongside their standard menus, in part to attract diet-conscious customers and in part to avoid lawsuits.

In 2003 a federal district judge in New York dismissed two class-action lawsuits against McDonald's from plaintiffs who argued that the fast-food chain was responsible for their obesity and related health conditions. The judge said the law did not protect people from "personal excess." But the restaurant industry was still nervous about the threat of lawsuits. Several dozen lawyers attended a conference in Boston in the spring of 2003 to discuss legal strategies for making restaurants liable for obesity-related illnesses. Two possible strategies—that the fats and sugars in the foods were addictive and that the restaurants did not warn customers that the foods contained harmful substances such as trans fats—appeared to be modeled after successful lawsuits directed against cigarette manufacturers.

Legislation was introduced in both the House and Senate in 2003 to protect the restaurant and food industries from such lawsuits. At a June hearing on the House bill, the measure's sponsor, Rep. Ric Keller, R-Fla., argued that such suits were frivolous and would not do much to reduce obesity but would fatten attorneys' wallets. But John F. Banzhaf, a law professor who worked on some of the tobacco lawsuits, disagreed. "Note that the smoker lawsuits, the nonsmoker lawsuits, and the lawsuits by the states against the tobacco industry, all were initially called frivolous. But they have all proven their worth and helped to make a significant dent in the public health problem of smoking." *(Tobacco wars, p. 260)*

Global Dietary Guidelines

Two United Nations agencies, WHO and the Food and Agriculture Organization, touched off an international controversy in March when they released recommendations on global dietary guidelines put together by an international panel of experts. The guidelines were to serve as the foundation of WHO's Global Strategy on Diet, Physical Activity and Health, which was aimed at reducing obesity and the chronic diseases associated with it. The expert panel recommended diets that were low in fats, sugars, and salt and high in fresh fruits and vegetables. Although many of the recommendations were in line with prevailing opinion, including U.S. guidelines, the panel recommended that sugar should account for no more than 10 percent of all calories. The federal government's dietary guidelines stipulated only that sugar should be used in moderation.

The U.S. sugar lobby immediately protested, arguing that the expert panel had used "misguided" science. "A thorough review of scientific literature on the subject of obesity shows there is no association between sugar consumption and obesity," said Richard Adamson, a vice president of the National Soft Drink Association. The Sugar Association wrote to WHO general director Gro Harlem Brundtland, pledging to "exercise every avenue available to expose the dubious nature" of the report, "including asking Congress to challenge future funding of the United States' $406 million contribution to the WHO." Brundtland dismissed the criticism. "I haven't seen such strong and misdirected language since I first came to the WHO," she said in April. At the behest of the sugar industry and legislators from sugar-growing states, the Bush administration also questioned the conclusions that panel reached. WHO, however, appeared likely to present the guidelines as recommended for approval by its member states at the World Health Assembly scheduled for May 2004.

Related Developments

Just as many restaurants were beginning to realize there was a market for smaller and lighter meals, other businesses were beginning to cater to oversize Americans, providing everything from scales that could accommodate one thousand pounds to seat-belt extenders and oversize caskets and burial vaults. Retailers were offering an increasing array of larger towels, clothing, jewelry, umbrellas, and furniture. A resort in Cancun, Mexico, marketed itself as the first resort designed for obese people and offered such amenities as walk-in showers rather than bathtubs and large, armless chairs. Ambulances and hospitals were finding they needed bigger stretchers, wheelchairs, even blood pressure cuffs. Hospitals were finding that diagnostic machines such as MRIs and CAT scanners and even hospital bathrooms were too small to accommodate severely obese patients.

On May 12 the Federal Aviation Administration (FAA) increased the assumed average weight of every passenger by ten pounds and the assumed weight for each checked bag by five pounds. The order, which applied to all airplanes with more than nineteen seats, was spurred by the fatal crash in January of a U.S. Airways plane in North Carolina that may have been overloaded even though its load was within the assumed weight tolerances. Although the order said the additional ten pounds were for personal carry-on items, such as laptop computers, briefcases, purses, and diaper bags, an FAA spokeswoman said, "It's really ten pounds per person."

Following are excerpts from "The Obesity Crisis in America," prepared testimony delivered July 16, 2003, by Surgeon General Richard H. Carmona before the House Education Subcommittee on Education Reform.

"The Obesity Crisis in America"

Good morning. . . .

As Surgeon General, I welcome this chance to talk with you about a health crisis affecting every state, every city, every community, and every school across our great nation.

The crisis is obesity. It's the fastest-growing cause of disease and death in America. And it's completely preventable.

- Nearly two out of every three Americans are overweight or obese.
- One out of every eight deaths in America is caused by an illness directly related to overweight and obesity.

Think of it this way: statistics tell us that of the 20 members serving on this subcommittee, at least two will die because of a completely preventable illness related to overweight or obesity. Because of overweight or obesity, two of you will spend less time serving your communities and enjoying your children and grandchildren.

America's children are already seeing the initial consequences of a lack of physical activity and unhealthy eating habits. Fortunately, there is still time to reverse this dangerous trend in our children's lives.

Let's start with the good news: I am pleased to be able to report that most of America's children are healthy.

Overall, 82 percent of our nation's 70 million children are in very good or excellent health. Infant mortality is at an all-time low, childhood immunization is at an all-time high. Our children are less likely to smoke, and less likely to give birth as teenagers.

These are important gains in pediatric health.

But the bad news is that an unprecedented number of children are carrying excess body weight. That excess weight significantly increases our kids' risk factors for a range of health problems, including diabetes, heart disease, asthma, and emotional and mental health problems.

As a father, I work hard to teach my children about the importance of physical activity and healthy eating. Every parent in this room wants the best for their children.

But the fact is that we have an epidemic of childhood obesity. A study conducted in May by the New York City Department of Health and Mental Hygiene and the Department of Education found that, adjusted to National Standards, nearly one in four of the children in New York City's public elementary schools is overweight.

Today I will discuss the three key factors that we must address to reduce and eliminate childhood obesity in America. They are:

1. Increased physical activity;
2. Healthier eating habits; and
3. Improved health literacy. . . .

Looking back 40 years to the 1960s, when many of us in this room were children, just over four percent of 6- to 17-year-olds were overweight. Since then, that rate has more than tripled, to over 15 percent. And the problem doesn't go away when children grow up. Nearly three out of every four overweight teenagers may become overweight adults.

I'm not willing to stand by and let that happen. American children deserve much better than being condemned to a lifetime of serious, costly, and potentially fatal medical complications associated with excess weight. The facts are staggering:

- In the year 2000, the total annual cost of obesity in the United States was $117 billion. While extra value meals may save us some change at the counter, they're costing us billions of dollars in health care and lost productivity. Physical inactivity and super-sized meals are leading to a nation of oversized people.
- This year, more than 300,000 Americans will die from illnesses related to overweight and obesity.
- Obesity contributes to the number-one cause of death in our nation: heart disease.
- Excess weight has also led to an increase in the number of people suffering from Type 2 diabetes. There are at least 17 million Americans with diabetes, and another 16 million have pre-diabetes. Each year, diabetes costs America $132 billion. It can lead to eye diseases, cardiovascular problems, kidney failure, and early death.

Why are we facing this epidemic of overweight and obesity? Over 50 genes associated with obesity have been located in the human gene map. But the ever-increasing problem of overweight among American children cannot be explained away by changes in genetic composition.

Studies conducted by HHS' National Institutes of Health and the Centers for Disease Control and Prevention are already yielding important clues about the multiple factors that contribute to overweight and obesity. Studies are also providing new information about potentially successful interventions.

We know more than ever about the combination of genetic, social, metabolic, and environmental factors that play a role in children's weight.

But the fundamental reason that our children are overweight is this: Too many children are eating too much and moving too little.

In some cases, solving the problem is as easy as turning off the television and keeping the lid on the cookie jar.

Our children did not create this problem. Adults did. Adults increased the portion size of children's meals, developed the games and television that children find spellbinding, and chose the sedentary lifestyles that our children emulate. So adults must take the lead in solving this problem.

I'm pleased that businesses like Kraft Foods, Coca Cola, and Nike are supporting major efforts and making significant changes to help kids make healthier choices.

These and other business leaders, foundations, schools and universities across our nation are starting to make a difference in children's health. I encourage other organizations and every parent in America to join the fight against childhood obesity.

We must teach our children to enjoy healthy foods in healthy portions. As parents, we should never use food as a reward or punishment.

And especially now, during the summer, we need to encourage all children to be physically active for at least 60 minutes a day. Not only sports, but simple things like taking the stairs, riding their bikes, and just getting out and playing.

And as we are getting our kids to make healthy choices, we also need to make them for ourselves. James Baldwin captured the essence of this when he said: "Children have never been good at listening to their elders, but they have never failed to imitate them."

I'll be the first to say it won't be easy. My wife and I have four kids. I know first-hand that families live such busy lives that it's tough to prepare healthy meals and have enough time to get in some physical activity.

But it's so important, because the choices that children make now, the behaviors they learn now, will last a lifetime.

As adults we must lead by example. Personally, I work out every day. I do my best to make healthy choices in all I do. My bosses President Bush and Secretary Thompson also find time to exercise. In fact, Secretary Thompson put the Department of Health and Human Services on a diet and has led by example by losing over 15 pounds.

President Bush, Secretary Thompson, and I have made disease prevention and health promotion a priority in our roles as leaders. As Surgeon General, prevention comes first in everything I do. Prevention is the vision behind the President's *HealthierUS Initiative* and the Secretary's *Steps to a HealthierUS Initiative.*

One of the many challenges is that there are so many more incentives in our current health care system for treatment than for prevention. When I was a practicing physician in a hospital, I made a good living treating people who could have avoided my hospital entirely if they had made better lifestyle choices.

Benjamin Franklin was absolutely right back in the 1700s: an ounce of prevention is worth a pound of cure. But more than 200 years later, prevention is still a radical concept to most Americans.

At the Department of Health and Human Services, we're encouraging healthy habits more than ever through our work to eliminate health disparities; our many initiatives designed to encourage physical activity, healthy eating, and regular checkups; and our nationwide campaigns to discourage smoking and drug and alcohol abuse.

To help promote healthy lifestyles, I am visiting schools across America in my 50 Schools in 50 States Initiative to talk with kids about avoiding drugs and alcohol, avoiding tobacco in every form, being physically active, eating right, and making healthy choices every day.

Each time I'm out on the road, whether at a school or passing through an airport, I meet young people who are making choices that affect their health and well-being. I believe that what they see and hear in the media can have a profound effect on their choices.

Secretary Thompson also appreciates that, and it's why he focused the Youth Media Campaign on getting young people excited about increasing the physical activity in their lives and on showing parents that physical activity and healthy eating are essential to their children's well-being.

This week, the President's Council on Physical Fitness and Sports will launch a brand-new Presidential Champions Award. The award encourages a lifetime of activities for children and their parents or other role models.

We need initiatives like the Youth Media Campaign and the Presidential Champions Awards because the average American child spends more than four hours every day watching television, playing video games, or surfing the web. We are seeing a generation of kids who grew up off the playground and on the PlayStation.

We must all work together to help our children lead healthy lives. I caution people against playing the "blame game." Instead of blaming children for being overweight, we need to encourage them and help them to make healthier choices.

We need physical activity and healthy food choices in every school in America. We need better food choices at affordable prices in every neighborhood in America. And we need community planning that includes neighborhood playgrounds and safe walking paths.

Some people want to blame the food industry for our growing waistlines. The reality is that restaurants, including many fast food restaurants, now offer low-fat, healthy choices.

For the meals we eat at home, and the meals we eat out, it's still our decision what we eat, where we eat, and how much we eat. That concept is part of what I'm talking about with Americans of all ages: increasing our health literacy.

Health literacy is the ability of an individual to access, understand, and use health-related information and services to make appropriate health decisions.

Low health literacy contributes to our nation's epidemic of overweight and obesity. For example, some mothers are unaware that they can promote their baby's health through breastfeeding. Experience with my own patients and students indicates that many Americans don't understand the impact of caloric intake versus expenditure.

Every morning people wake up and, while they're sitting at the kitchen table, they read the newspaper and the cereal box. Throughout the day they read the nutritional information on their meals and on their snacks. But do they really understand the information they're reading?

The labels list grams of fat. But do you know how many grams of fat you should eat in a meal? Or in a day? Or how many is too many? Or too few? These are seemingly simple questions, but we're not giving Americans simple answers.

Parents are hearing about overweight and obesity. So they're trying to figure out how much food they should feed their children. How much is too much? How much is not enough? They're concerned and confused about everything from calories and carbohydrates, to vitamins and portion sizes.

When children are growing and developing, a restrictive diet may not be the best choice for every child. Just as with adults, one diet does not fit every child.

As parents, we know that. But when we see a child gaining weight and not exercising enough, we see the social and psychological pain it causes. When we see a child's self-esteem drop by the day because she's left out of schoolyard games, or because he just can't keep up with the other kids on their bikes, we know that we need to help that child.

I'm pleased to hear from parents and pediatricians that moms and dads are asking about how to establish healthy eating habits for kids.

Parents should always talk to a pediatrician or family physician before putting any child on a diet or beginning any vigorous exercise plan.

The reality is that often, if a child is overweight but still gaining height, the best thing parents can do is maintain the child's weight. Kids come in all shapes and sizes, and sometimes a child just needs a little more physical activity and a little less food intake. Again, it's not about blame—it's about balance.

And to make healthy choices, parents and children need easy-to-understand information that fits into their busy lifestyles. All of us—government, academia, health care professionals, businesses, schools, and communities—need to work together to ensure that straightforward information about healthy eating and physical activity is available.

For example, Secretary Thompson announced last week that food labels will list trans fat content. By putting trans fat information on food labels, we're giving American families information to make smart choices to lower their intake of these unhealthy fats.

The food pyramid is another great example. It's probably the most-recognized nutrition guideline tool in America. HHS is looking forward to working with the Department of Agriculture to evaluate and update the food pyramid based on the latest scientific evidence.

I don't have all the answers today. But we can figure this out together. We can increase health literacy and reduce childhood obesity. Secretary Thompson has been a pioneer in getting prevention into the American mindset. We're starting to see some results, and we need your help. As members of Congress, as members of your communities, and as parents, you are role models and leaders.

As Surgeon General, I charge you to make healthy personal choices in your own lives, and to set good examples for all the children around you.

And I ask you to work with me to support our efforts to improve Americans' health literacy, to put prevention first, and to end our nation's obesity epidemic before it has a chance to reach into another generation of Americans.

Thank you. I would be happy to answer any questions.

Source: U.S. Department of Health and Human Services. U.S. Public Health Service. Office of the Surgeon General. "The Obesity Crisis in America." Testimony by Surgeon General Richard H. Carmona before the Subcommittee on Education Reform of the House Committee on Education and the Workforce, July 16, 2003. www.surgeongeneral.gov/news/testimony/obesity07162003.htm (accessed January 19, 2004).

Report on European Union Draft Constitution

July 18, 2003

INTRODUCTION

Growing pains were painful, indeed, for the European Union (EU) in 2003—one year before the EU intended to expand its membership from fifteen to twenty-five countries. At the beginning of the year, EU leaders engaged in a dispute of unprecedented bitterness over whether to support the United States and its planned war in Iraq. That angry dispute infected nearly everything else the EU did during the year, including its consideration of a complex new constitution. The constitution was supposed to help make the union governable once it got ten new members, all of them poorer than most current EU members. *(Iraq war debate, p. 40)*

The debate over the constitution demonstrated that Europeans remained reluctant to set aside their national interests in the pursuit of a common good. Unable to reconcile their differences, EU leaders in December put the constitution on hold. Some leaders even talked of splitting the union in two, with a small core charging ahead into greater unity while the rest lagged behind.

The EU already was split in one important way: Only twelve of its fifteen current members belonged to the European Monetary Union, the subgrouping of countries that had replaced their national currencies with the euro. The three countries outside the so-called euro zone were Great Britain, Denmark, and Sweden. Voters in Sweden on September 14 rejected, for the second time since 2000, their government's call to adopt the euro. The strong, 56 percent vote against the euro came despite a surge of sympathy resulting from the assassination four days earlier of Foreign Minister Anna Lindh, one of the country's most respected politicians, who had campaigned tirelessly for a yes vote. *(Euro background, Historic Documents of 1999, p. 75)*

Ten Countries Prepare for Membership

The European Union traced its roots to a post–World War II consortium of France, West Germany, and other countries to revitalize the production of coal and steel. These countries established a common market in the 1960s, and the gradual addition of new countries and responsibilities offered the promise of the most unity in the history of a fractured continent. The collapse of communism at the beginning of the 1990s led to the establishment of a formal European Union of fifteen countries that retained their national identities and cultures but shared common economic, trading, and even foreign policies.

The end of communism also offered the opportunity for the EU to expand eastward and encompass more than a dozen countries that once had been under the domination of the Soviet Union. The attraction was mutual. Current EU members would gain new markets and cheap labor, and new member nations would gain access to much-needed capital and a stamp of approval for their efforts to replace communism with democracy and free markets. The EU in 2002 officially invited ten countries into membership by 2004: Cyprus, the Czech Republic, Estonia, Hungary, Latvia, Lithuania, Malta, Poland, Slovakia, and Slovenia. The three Baltic countries (Estonia, Latvia, and Lithuania) had been part of the Soviet Union until its collapse in 1991; all others, except Cyprus and Malta, also had been under communist rule for the half-century following World War II. *(EU expansion, Historic Documents of 2002, p. 679)*

Under rules established in anticipation of expansion, preparing for EU membership was a daunting task, especially for countries that had no experience with democracy and no recent experience with capitalism. Candidate countries had to rewrite nearly all their laws and regulations to comply with the thousands of pages of EU standards known as the *acquis communitaire*. The EU issued annual reports on the progress each candidate country was making; collectively, these reports documented the deep economic and social stresses the candidate countries faced. In several countries, for example, corruption had replaced communism as the glue holding the economy together. Ethnic disputes that had been suppressed by communist leaders suddenly emerged as human rights problems, in such places as the Baltic countries, where the Soviet Union had implanted large Russian minorities to help maintain Moscow's control. Most of the candidate countries were decades behind the rest of Europe in establishing modern regulations on such matters as environment protection and food safety, let alone in modernizing industrial infrastructure. The EU published its final report cards on November 5. The reports identified a total of thirty-nine serious failures among the ten countries; each candidate was cited for failures, but Poland received the most warnings, with nine.

In economic terms, all of the ten candidate countries lagged well behind Europe's richest countries and most ranked behind the poorest current EU members (Greece, Portugal, and Spain). In November Britain's *Economist* magazine projected how many years it would take for the new EU members to reach the average per capita income of the current members, assuming robust economic growth continentwide. Cyprus and Malta were by far the closest, respectively lagging twenty-one and twenty-nine years behind current EU members. Most others were thirty to fifty years behind, with Lithuania (fifty-eight years) and Poland (fifty-nine years) at the rear.

Despite the challenges, leaders and their publics in all the candidate countries remained committed to the goal of EU membership. Polls indicated dwindling support among some specific groups in some countries; for example, many of Poland's farmers had become worried about having to compete with their modernized and government-subsidized counterparts in France and Germany.

Nine of the ten candidate countries (Cyprus was the exception) held referendums in 2003 on EU membership, and voters gave their approval in all nine. Most of the countries voted yes by 2–1 or even 3–1 margins. The exception was Malta, the tiny Mediterranean archipelago that had been aloof from Europe since gaining its independence from Britain in 1964. Maltese voters approved EU membership by a relatively narrow margin of 54 to 46 percent.

Cyprus was the richest of the candidate countries, but its membership in some ways was the most controversial. Physically closer to the Middle East than to Europe, the island had been divided ever since 1974 when Turkey invaded, saying it was protecting the Turkish minority against a supposed plan by the Greek majority to unite Cyprus with Greece. The northern two-fifths of the island remained under Turkish protection and fell behind the rest of the island, which prospered as the Republic of Cyprus—the entity invited to EU membership. Numerous diplomatic attempts to resolve the Cyprus dispute had failed, generally because of opposition by Turkish-Cypriot leader Rauf Denktash and the Turkish military.

In anticipation of EU expansion, United Nations Secretary General Kofi Annan in 2002 and 2003 mounted an aggressive new campaign on behalf of a plan to reunite the island, but with the Greek and Turkish communities retaining their individual identities. Annan had little more success than preceding diplomats who waded into the Cyprus dispute. Denktash remained adamantly opposed, and legislative elections in the Turkish sector of Cyprus resulted in an even split between parties that favored Annan's plan and those opposing it. At year's end, however, Turkey's new prime minister, Recip Erdogan, began pushing for a compromise because he wanted to gain international support for Turkey's own long-stalled application for EU membership.

Turkey was one of several countries in an ever-lengthening queue of potential candidates. Ankara had been rebuffed repeatedly over the previous four decades in its request to join the EU and its predecessors. European leaders often cited the Cyprus dispute as the reason, but Turkey's poverty, its large population (at 68 million, it had more people than any EU country except Germany), and its Muslim identity were the real reasons for Europe's reluctance to extend its union across the Bosporus. EU leaders pledged in 2002 to begin membership talks with Turkey as early as 2005—

if Turkey consolidated its democracy. Ankara's subsequent progress on this score took many European leaders by surprise and stirred new opposition based on claims that Turkey really was not a "European" country. *(Turkish elections, Historic Documents of 2002, p. 906)*

Bulgaria and Romania also had commitments to be considered for EU membership, probably by 2007, and Croatia was considered a possible candidate for inclusion. The other Balkan countries—Albania, Bosnia, Macedonia, and Serbia-Montenegro—also had applied and in June received $249 million in aid to help them take the initial steps to meet the EU's criteria. *(Serbia-Montenegro, p. 55; Bosnia, p. 460)*

A Failed Constitution

EU expansion caused stresses not just within the candidate countries but also between the existing and candidate EU members. These stresses broke out into the open in January and February when European leaders split on whether to support the impending U.S. war in Iraq. French president Jacques Chirac and German chancellor Gerhard Schroeder led the opposition, while British prime minister Tony Blair and Spanish prime minister Jose Maria Aznar led a parade of European members backing the war. U.S. defense secretary Donald H. Rumsfeld characterized the split as one between "old Europe" (meaning France and Germany) and "new Europe" (meaning the formerly communist countries of Eastern Europe whose leaders were eager to align themselves with Washington). The split even produced insults, with Chirac implying that his Eastern European colleagues were badly behaved.

The bitterness of the dispute continued to plague discussions within the EU on matters that, officially, had nothing to do with Iraq. The most important of these was a proposed new constitution to replace the network of treaties on which the EU was based. The most recent of these treaties, negotiated during an EU summit in Nice, France, in December 2000, had attempted to resolve the thorny issue of how the union would govern itself once twenty-five nations of disparate size and wealth were at the table. The Nice treaty established a voting arrangement so complex that it was fully understood by few leaders, let alone ordinary citizens. A year later, EU leaders had second thoughts and established a convention to draft a formal constitution for the union. Former French president Valery Giscard d'Estaing was named chairman.

Giscard d'Estaing's convention published the first draft of its constitution on February 7. Any illusions that the constitutional process would go smoothly were quashed immediately. British politicians raised the most objections, particularly to a proposal to change the name of the EU to *United Europe* and to call it a *federal* structure—words they said implied the union itself was a nation-state. Politicians in several midsize countries, notably Poland and Spain, complained that the constitution would take away some of the voting power they had gained in the Nice treaty. A second draft version was published May 26; it dropped the word *federal* and reverted to the name *European Union* but kept provisions giving the EU some aspects of statehood, including a strong president (two of them, in fact), a foreign minister, and a binding charter of civil and social rights.

The convention completed its work on June 12 and on July 18 published a "final draft" containing more than four hundred articles. Even so, delegates acknowledged that the draft was not perfect and would face further changes. A new arrangement for voting by the twenty-five member states topped the list of controversial issues. Critics, including one of the convention's vice chairmen (former Italian prime minister Giuliano Amato) derided a proposal for two European presidents: one representing the European Council (composed of national leaders), the other representing the European Commission (the EU's executive agency). European leaders endorsed the broad outlines of the constitution on June 20 but disputed matters both large (such as whether the EU would be a federal state) and small (such as whether the document should make an explicit reference to God).

EU leaders again endorsed the constitution in general terms at a summit in Rome on October 5 but failed to resolve fundamental disagreements, most importantly how much voting power each country would have. The meeting was the first at which all twenty-five leaders sat as equals at the same oval table; leaders of the ten candidate countries were invited to participate even though their membership was not yet final. The one hundred minutes allocated for opening speeches (four minutes for each leader) gave a hint of the logistical and political hurdles that would arise when the leaders gathered for a final decision in December.

Even before the December summit, another event sharpened the divisions in Europe. On November 25 European finance ministers essentially scrapped an agreement, known as the "stability and growth pact," that underpinned the European Monetary Union, on which the new euro currency was based. That agreement required sanctions against euro zone countries that repeatedly ran government budget deficits in excess of 3 percent of their gross domestic products. That rule had been controversial for many years. European Commission president Romano Prodi in 2002 caused a stir by calling it "stupid," and most economists agreed. Even so, the rule had been invoked in 2001 to force Portugal to cut its budget deficit. By 2003 France and Germany were facing their third consecutive years of running afoul of the 3 percent limit, and they refused a demand by the European Commission that they cut fiscal 2004 budget spending to come under the limit. Exercising their political and economic muscle, the two countries convinced a majority of other countries to "suspend" the rules—an action that was widely interpreted as gutting the stability pact. Finance ministers from several smaller countries bitterly complained that the rules seemed to apply only to small countries, not big ones.

In that abrasive context, the European leaders gathered in Brussels on December 12 for a final session to wrap up the new convention. The leaders quickly approved a common defense strategy but then fell into dispute about the voting provisions under the new constitution. The central issue was whether the EU would abandon the voting system established by the 2000 Nice treaty, which tended to favor small and medium-size countries at the expense of larger ones. Under that system, for example, Poland and Spain (each with about 40 million people) each would have as many votes as Germany (with 82 million people) and France (with 60 million people).

Polish prime minister Leszek Miller and Spanish prime minister Aznar insisted on retaining the Nice voting system. France, Germany, and several other countries endorsed the system outlined in the new constitution, under which major EU decisions would be approved by a simple majority of the twenty-five member nations—but only if the total population of that majority exceeded 60 percent of the union's total population. This plan, called a "double majority," would have balanced the interests of both large and small nations. The French endorsement of this new plan marked a reversal of position; Chirac had engineered the Nice treaty just three years earlier and warned Germany against trying to undermine it.

Miller and Aznar refused to back down and refused even to consider a compromise under which any change in the voting system would be delayed until 2014. Because unanimous approval was needed, the opposition of the two leaders stymied an agreement on the new constitution.

Failure of the summit was one of the most embarrassing setbacks for the EU in years, and it lead to the inevitable recriminations. Schroeder complained that "one or another country put the European ideal behind the national interest." Chirac unexpectedly suggested that a "pioneer group" of nations might move ahead with its own plan for integration of Europe. "It would be a motor that would set an example," he said. "It would allow Europe to go better, faster." Most other leaders reacted coolly to Chirac's suggestion, which commentators dubbed the "two speed Europe." But simply raising the idea indicated the depth of disagreements within a Europe that claimed to be more united than ever before.

Establishing a European Military Force

Before their summit collapsed, European leaders did approve what they called a "common security strategy" that represented the EU's most extensive statement ever of a unified approach to its role in world affairs. The strategy included a mutual defense guarantee, similar to the 1949 NATO treaty, that called on all EU member states to assist another state victimized by "armed aggression." The document also committed the EU to combat "new" security threats, including terrorism, weapons of mass destruction, and international organized crime, but it also argued that "none of the new threats is purely military, nor can they be tackled by purely military means." Proceeding with a plan first developed in 1999, the EU would maintain a "rapid reaction force" of about 60,000 troops, capable of being deployed within a month or two in response to international crises. *(EU force, Historic Documents of 1999, p. 817)*

Harking back to the earlier dispute over Iraq, the one controversial issue faced by leaders involved the relationship of that new EU force to NATO, which was led and largely funded by the United States. Most EU members also belonged to NATO, and vice versa, but there were exceptions, notably France, which had withdrawn from NATO's military arm in the 1960s even while remaining a member of the NATO political councils. France, Germany, and several other countries had wanted to sharpen the independence of the new EU force by giving it a full-scale headquarters in Brussels—thus separating it from NATO's political headquarters in that city and defense headquarters in nearby Mons. Britain's Blair, echoing concerns of the Bush administration, argued this setup would needlessly duplicate NATO. Blair's objections were heeded, in part because Britain had by far the largest military in Europe. As a compromise, EU leaders agreed to create a military planning staff of about one hundred officers stationed at the NATO offices in Mons.

Following are excerpts from two documents made public July 18, 2003: first, "Report from the Presidency of the Convention to the President of the European Council," a draft version of a constitution for the European Union; second, "Rome Declaration," a statement by Valery Giscard d'Estaing, chairman of the European Convention.

"Report to the President of the European Council"

1. In response to the mandate from the European Council meeting in Laeken on 14 and 15 December 2001, the Convention on the Future of Europe has completed its task, and submits to the President of the European Council the outcome of its work: a draft Treaty establishing a Constitution for Europe.

2. As envisaged in the Laeken Declaration, the President of the Convention gave progress reports to the European Council at its meetings in June 2002 (Seville), October 2002 (Brussels), December 2002

(Copenhagen), and April 2003 (Athens). He presented Parts I and II of the draft Treaty to the European Council in Thessaloniki on 20 June 2003: they have not been subsequently changed. Parts III and IV, interim texts of which were available at Thessaloniki, have since been finalised, and are now added.

3. This concludes seventeen months of work by the Convention whose members, together with their alternates, are listed in Annex I. They met in plenary session on 26 occasions (52 days), hearing over 1800 interventions. The Convention also established eleven Working Groups and three Discussion Circles, each with its own specific mandate, which met to address particular issues (listed at Annex II) and make recommendations to the Convention as a whole. Convention members also provided 386 written contributions to the Convention as a whole, and 773 to Working Groups and Discussion circles.

4. The Praesidium, whose members are listed in Annex I, met on 50 occasions, and submitted 52 papers to the Convention. Members of the Praesidium chaired the Working Groups and Discussion Circles listed at Annex II, and presented their reports to the Convention.

5. The Convention operated in a fully transparent manner: its meetings were open to the public, and all its official documents were available on its website, which received an average of 47,000 visitors per month, rising to 100,000 in June 2003. In addition it took a number of initiatives to ensure wider participation in its work. The Forum established in accordance with the Laeken declaration received 1264 contributions from NGOs, the business community, academia and others. Meetings were organised with a wide range of groups with an interest in the Convention. These included churches and religious organisations, Think tanks, representatives of local and regional organisations, and NGOs. In addition a special plenary session devoted to civil society took place in June 2002. A Youth Convention was organised in July 2002: its elected Chairman became an additional observor of the Convention's continuing work.

6. A key element in the Convention's success was the full role played by its members from candidate countries. In accordance with the Laeken declaration, they participated fully in the Convention's proceedings; the Convention decided to go further, and one of their representatives, elected by them, was invited to participate in all Praesidium discussions. Interpretation arrangements were also made to enable members from candidate countries to address the Convention in their own languages. The decision by the European Council on enlargement in December 2002, and the subsequent ratification process in the candidate countries, underlines the significance of these practical decisions taken early on in the Convention's life.

7. The task given to the Convention was founded on the four issues addressed in the "Nice declaration on the future of the Union", and then developed further in the mandate set out by the European Council in Laeken. During its initial meetings, the Convention addressed issues such as the delimitation of competences and the simplification of the Union's instruments and procedures. These discussions in plenary, together with the outcome of the first wave of working groups, enabled the Convention to define, in October 2002, the most appropriate future treaty structure which would respond in particular to the requirements of clarity and simplification. The outcome of the Convention reflects this: a merge and reorganisation of the existing treaties in the form of a draft Constitution, and hence a single legal personality for the European Union. This approach secured support from a large number of Convention members, and enabled the Convention subsequently to reach broad consensus on the consolidated and complete text of a draft Treaty, in four Parts, which it presents to the European Council.

8. The Convention agreed on a major enhancement of the democratic nature of the Union. The Constitution incorporates it, calling for a significant expansion of the role of the European Parliament, with a doubling of the scope of legislation taken by co-decision, which becomes the normal legislative process of the Union, and a substantial simplification of corresponding procedures. In addition, new mechanisms to ensure improved information flow to national Parliaments, and their closer involvement in the Union's work, in particular on legislation, have been devised. The Union's competences have been clarified, categorised and stabilised, and its range of legal instruments reduced, in the interests of better public understanding, more effective action, and a clear distinction between the roles of the Union and of the Member States.

9. To enable the Union's central Institutions to adapt to the new Enlargement dimension, means of strengthening all three, while retaining the balance between them, have been incorporated in the Constitution. The Convention is convinced that these reforms will substantially improve the Union's effectiveness.

10. The Constitution incorporates, as its Part II, the Charter of Fundamental Rights proclaimed at the Nice European Council. The Convention noted that the "Explanations" drawn up at the instigation of the Praesidium of the Charter Convention, and updated under the authority of this Convention's Praesidium, are one important tool for the interpretation of the Charter.

11. The Convention has prepared the texts of new Protocols on the Role of National Parliaments in the European Union and on the Application of the Principles of Subsidiarity and Proportionality, as well as on the Eurogroup and Euratom. It has not attempted to

review existing Protocols to the current Treaties, nor therefore to prepare the texts of the Protocols mentioned in Articles IV-1 and IV-2: it will fall to the Intergovernmental Conference to undertake the task. Similarly, it will be for the Intergovernmental Conference to conclude the lists, foreseen in Articles III-213 and III-214, of those Member States participating in closer co-operation and on mutual defence; and to ensure a response to the call, set out in the relevant Convention Declaration, for the timely establishment of a European External Action Service.

12. The attention of the European Council is drawn to two further specific issues which it may wish to follow up. Firstly, a large number of members of the Convention argued for a more ambitious approach to the issue of transparency, including specifically the automatic presumption of public right of access to all documents. The proposed Constitution imposes an obligation on the institutions to adopt rules on transparency. The level of ambition of these rules, and so the extent to which demands for access can be met, therefore needs to be addressed within the framework of subsequent legislation.

13. Secondly, although some members wished to re-examine, and perhaps update, the provisions of the Euratom treaty, the Convention did not believe it had either the mandate or the time and competence to do so. The future of Euratom therefore remains an issue which the European Council may wish at some stage to address.

14. Certain members of the Convention, though not seeking to block consensus, were unable to give their support to the draft Constitution. One group of 4 members considered that the Convention had not responded appropriately to the section of the Laeken mandate on increasing democratic legitimacy; their minority alternative report proposing a "Europe of democracies" is attached at Annex III.

15. Some other members of the Convention, whilst joining the broad consensus on the text of the draft Constitution, would have preferred an approach going rather further, particularly as regards the extension of Qualified Majority Voting and the procedures for future Amendment of the Constitution.

16. It is thanks to the high degree of commitment and engagement of all its members that the Convention has been able successfully to complete its work, and to present what the Thessaloniki European Council considered to be a "good basis" for the forthcoming Intergovernmental Conference. It hopes that the momentum which has been generated, and the balance of the synthesis on which it found consensus after long and careful examination, will be maintained by the Intergovernmental Conference.

17. Having fulfilled the mandate given to it by the Laeken European Council, the Convention has ended. In presenting the draft Treaty

establishing a Constitution for Europe, and this report, its Presidency discharges its mission, and steps down.

18. The archives of the Convention will be deposited at the Secretariat of the Council.

> **Source:** European Union. The European Convention. *Report From the Convention Presidency to the President of the European Council.* CONV 851/03. Brussels. July 18, 2003. http://european-convention.eu.int/docs/Treaty/cv00851.en03.pdf (accessed April 1, 2004).

"Rome Declaration"

II. With this Constitution, Europe is taking a decisive step towards political union: a union of citizens and a union of Member States. The Constitution:

- enshrines citizens' rights by incorporating the European Charter of Fundamental Rights;
- turns Europe towards its citizens by holding out new opportunities for them to participate;
- establishes a clear, transparent apportionment of powers between the Union and its Member States, enabling national parliaments to intervene. The Union's powers are extended in areas where that is what its citizens want:
  —implementation of an area of freedom, security and justice, with more effective action to combat major crime, and recognition by Member States of one another's different systems of civil law;
  —gradual development of a common foreign and defence policy, with a European Foreign Minister to act and speak for Europe in the world, and establishment of a European arms agency;
  —improvement of economic coordination between countries using the euro, so as to ensure the stability and success of our common currency;
- provides Europe with stable, democratic and effective
  —*the European Parliament* becomes the Union's main legislature. It will enact laws together with the Council. European legislation will be the product of agreement between citizens' elected representatives and States;
  —*the Council* will have a face and a measure of durability; its President will organise States' work and will be able to plan for the future and think ahead;

—*the Commission,* organised so as to fulfil its European role, will act as a driving force and the main executive. It will embody the common European interest.

III. The draft Constitution is a success because it strikes the necessary balance between peoples, between States new and old, between institutions and between dream and reality.

The draft is a success because it is a finished product, with no loose ends to be tied up, no options left open.

It is in the general interest. With that in mind, the Chairman of the Convention, together with the two Vice-Chairmen, called on the Italian Presidency—and the President of the European Council, Silvio Berlusconi, in person—to have the text left as it stands. Reopening it, even in part, would cause it to unravel. . . .

Source: European Union. The European Convention. *Rome Declaration [by] V. Giscard D'Estaing, Chairman of the European Convention.* Rome. July 18, 2003. http://european-convention.eu.int/docs/Treaty/Rome_EN.pdf (accessed April 1, 2004).

Presidential Commission on Mental Health Care

July 22, 2003

INTRODUCTION

A report released July 22, 2003, by the New Freedom Commission on Mental Health recommended a wholesale transformation of the nation's mental health care system. The presidential commission, created by President George W. Bush in April 2002, called for care to move beyond simply treating symptoms and accepting long-term disability to adopting an approach that helped the mentally ill recover so that they were able to live, work, learn, and participate fully in their communities. The report recommended the creation of an individualized plan of care for each patient, elimination of existing disparities in mental health services, and faster incorporation of promising new treatments into routine care.

Mental health experts and advocates for people with mental illnesses generally praised the report, although some noted that it dealt in generalities instead of providing specific details about how to achieve its goals. They also pointed out that the report did not recommend any new funding for mental health, even though the nation's mental health system was woefully underfunded. The lack of funding was becoming even more acute because a growing number of companies were dropping mental health insurance coverage for their employees as health care costs continued rising. *(Health insurance, p. 846)*

The report was the latest in a series of high-profile government reports on various aspects of mental health and mental health care in the United States. Most recently, David Satcher, who served as surgeon general of the United States in the Clinton administration and the first months of the Bush administration, issued several pathbreaking reports that focused attention on the problems of suicide and mental disorders. *(Suicide prevention, Historic Documents of 1999, p. 436, Historic Documents of 2001, p. 290; Surgeon General's Report on Mental Health, Historic Documents of 1999, p. 836; Surgeon General's Report on Minority Mental Health, Historic Documents of 2001, p. 575)*

The Bush commission report emphasized the need for early intervention, particularly with children. Three months earlier, a study by the General Accounting Office (GAO), the investigative arm of Congress, found that thousands of parents of children with mental illnesses had given up custody to child welfare or criminal justice authorities because it was the only way their children could receive treatment or because the parents could not cope with the illnesses. The GAO said more than 12,700 children were handed over to government authorities in 2001 alone, and that the number might actually be much higher because neither the states nor the federal government maintained complete data on the problem.

On another front, the Food and Drug Administration (FDA) said that new studies found that some antidepressant drugs could trigger suicide or suicidal thoughts in children and adolescents. The FDA warned doctors to use caution in prescribing those drugs.

Transforming Mental Health Care

The commission, a panel of twenty-two experts on mental health and social services, was chaired by Michael F. Hogan, the director of the Ohio Department of Mental Health. In a preliminary report released November 1, 2002, the commission said the existing mental health care system was an inefficient tangle of programs that frustrated not only people trying to obtain treatment but also those trying to give care. Among the barriers the commission said unnecessarily impeded care were: fragmentation and gaps in the care delivery system for both children and adults, high unemployment and disability rates among people with serious mental illness, insufficient attention to older adults, and failure to make mental health and suicide prevention national priorities. *(Bush speech, Historic Documents of 2002, p. 268)*

In its final report, "Achieving the Promise: Transforming Mental Health Care in America," issued July 22, the presidential commission reiterated these shortcomings of the system and emphasized that mental illness was an unrecognized public health burden. In any given year, the commission said, 5 to 7 percent of adults and 5 to 9 percent of children suffered from serious mental and emotional disorders. Rather than reiterate statistics on the condition of mental health in the United States, the commission instead focused much of its final report on its vision for a system in which "recovery will be the common, recognized outcome of mental health services" and every American will have "easy and continuous access to most current treatments [for mental disorders] and best supportive services."

Achieving this goal, the commission said, would require earlier recognition of existing disorders and earlier intervention to treat them, greater knowledge about mental health disorders among general practitioners, and a greater emphasis on mental health care in schools, child welfare programs, and the criminal and juvenile justice systems. The commission called for more aggressive research to promote recovery and faster introduction of effective treatments into routine care. Currently, the panel said it took fifteen to twenty years for effective treatments to become widely used in patient care.

Advocate groups for the mentally ill generally praised the report. "I think it brings us out of the dark ages," said Richard Birkel, national executive director of the National Alliance for the Mentally Ill. "The goals and standards they have set are good ones. Get people into treatment early, have high expectations of recovery. This is the opposite of what we have now. This really envisions a very modern health care system in mental health." But Birkel and others noted that the report did not offer any concrete steps for achieving the goals it outlined, not did it recommend new funding. "The reality is that there needs to be a big structural change" in the mental health care delivery system," said Marcia Goin, president of the American Psychiatric Association, "and you can't do that without funding."

Still, these observers noted, the report gave mental health advocates a useful tool in seeking reform of the system. "I think it's up to us as advocates, and up to our champions in Congress, to move from this platform to the nitty-gritty," Bill Emmet, a project director at the National Association of Sate Mental Health Program Directors told the *New York Times.*

Although the commission did not recommend new funding for mental health care, it did endorse the concept of full mental health insurance parity with other health insurance. Congress at the end of the year extended for one year, through 2004, the 1996 mental health parity bill, which required employer-provided insurance plans to impose the same annual and lifetime limits on mental health benefits that they apply to medical and surgical benefits. But efforts to prohibit health insurance plans from charging higher deductibles, copayments, and out-of-pocket expenses for treatment of a range of mental disorders than they charged for other disorders failed again. Two-thirds of the Senate had cosponsored the legislation, which was named after Paul Wellstone, the late Democratic senator from Minnesota who had championed the legislation for several years along with Sen. Pete V. Domenici, R-N.M. But Republican leaders refused to let the measure come to the floor, saying that they wanted to pass a bill that was likely to be approved by the House. The Senate had passed a version of the Domenici-Wellstone bill in 2001, but it died in the House. *(Parity, Historic Documents of 2002, p. 267)*

According to at least one report, the proportion of employer-provided insurance plans that no longer paid any benefits for mental health treatments was increasing. According to the Society for Human Resource Management, the share of employers offering mental health benefits dropped from 84 percent in 1998 to 76 percent in 2002. "Employers are looking for areas where they can cut [health care] costs, and mental health is one of the areas that's easier to cut," the society's Jennifer Schramm said. "People are less likely to protest because of the stigma around it."

FDA Warning on Antidepressants

At least some of the stigma once attached to depression seemed to be waning. A study of more than nine thousand people found that 57 percent of those with recent major depression sought and received treatment, a 40 percent increase over the rates reported in the early 1980s. That was the good news. The bad news, according to Ronald Kessler, a lead author of the report and a professor of health care policy at Harvard, was that in nearly 80 percent of the cases the treatment they received was inadequate. Kessler said a main reason for inadequate treatment was that people often sought care from family doctors, many of whom were "apparently not up to speed" on providing quality care. That report, along with several others on depression, appeared in special issue of the *Journal of the American Medical Association,* released June 18.

New concerns arose during the year about whether a class of popular drugs for treating depression was in fact increasing the risk of suicide among children and adolescents. In June British health regulators reported findings from unpublished studies on Paxil that showed an elevated risk of causing suicidal thoughts in children and adolescents who had been given the drug to treat depression. The studies also concluded that Paxil, which was made by GlaxoSmithKline, was no more effective than a placebo in treating adolescent depression, and the British authorities therefore recommended that no new Paxil prescription be written for patients under age eighteen and that those young patients taking the drug be carefully monitored. A week after the British authorities acted, the Food and Drug Administration endorsed a similar recommendation for the United States.

The FDA also said it was reviewing studies of eight other selective serotonin reuptake inhibitors, or SSRIs, used to treat depression, and in October the agency warned doctors to use caution in prescribing the drugs to children. The agency said the data available to it did not clearly link the drugs to an increased risk of suicide, but such a link could not be ruled out, either. The only SSRI the FDA had approved for use for adolescent depression was Prozac, but doctors frequently prescribed the others. The FDA said it had scheduled a hearing by an expert advisory subject on the issue for February 2, 2004. The issue was further complicated in December when the British regulators extended their warning about Paxil to five other antidepressants. The only drug whose benefits outweighed the risks of side effects was Prozac, the agency said.

The possible link between SSRIs and suicide in young people had been raised in the late 1980s and early 1990s but was rejected at the time. Since then tens of millions of prescriptions for the SSRIs had been written, although no one knew how many were for patients under age eighteen. After the regulators acted in June, many doctors and psychiatrists suggested that the British and American agencies were overreacting. Several doctors noted that the adolescent suicide rate had been declining during the same years that treatment with the SSRIs had been increasing. Others said a careful look at the evidence was warranted. Both the British and American authorities warned adolescents taking the SSRIs not to discontinue their use without first consulting a doctor.

Following are excerpts from "Achieving the Promise: Transforming Mental Health Care in America," a report released July 22, 2003, in which the President's New Freedom Commission on Mental Health recommended a wholesale overhaul of the nation's mental health care delivery system.

"Achieving the Promise: Transforming Mental Health Care in America"

Vision Statement

We envision a future when everyone with a mental illness will recover, a future when mental illnesses can be prevented or cured, a future when mental illnesses are detected early, and a future when everyone with a mental illness at any stage of life has access to effective treatment and supports—essentials for living, working, learning, and participating fully in the community.

In February 2001, President George W. Bush announced his New Freedom Initiative to promote increased access to educational and employment opportunities for people with disabilities. The Initiative also promotes increased access to assistive and universally designed technologies and full access to community life. Not since the Americans with Disabilities Act (ADA)—the landmark legislation providing protections against discrimination-and the Supreme Court's *Olmstead v. L.C.* decision, which affirmed the right to live in community settings, has there been cause for such promise and opportunity for full community participation for all people with disabilities, including those with psychiatric disabilities.

On April 29, 2002, the President identified three obstacles preventing Americans with mental illnesses from getting the excellent care they deserve:

- Stigma that surrounds mental illnesses,
- Unfair treatment limitations and financial requirements placed on mental health benefits in private health insurance, and
- The fragmented mental health service delivery system.

The President's New Freedom Commission on Mental Health (called the *Commission* in this report) is a key component of the New Freedom Initiative. The President launched the Commission to address the problems in the current mental health service delivery system that allow Americans to fall through the system's cracks.

In his charge to the Commission, the President directed its members to study the problems and gaps in the mental health system and make concrete recommendations for immediate improvements that the Federal government, State governments, local agencies, as well as public and private health care providers, can implement. Executive Order 13263 detailed the instructions to the Commission. . . .

The Commission's findings confirm that there are unmet needs and that many barriers impede care for people with mental illnesses. Mental illnesses are shockingly common; they affect almost every American family. It can happen to a child, a brother, a grandparent, or a co-worker. It can happen to someone from any background—African American, Alaska Native, Asian American, Hispanic American, Native American, Pacific Islander, or White American. It can occur at any stage of life, from childhood to old age. No community is unaffected by mental illnesses; no school or workplace is untouched.

In any given year, about 5% to 7% of adults have a serious mental illness, according to several nationally representative studies. A similar percentage of children—about 5% to 9%—have a serious emotional disturbance. These figures mean that millions of adults and children are disabled by mental illnesses every year.

President Bush said,

"... Americans must understand and send this message: mental disability is not a scandal—it is an illness. And like physical illness, it is treatable, especially when the treatment comes early."

Over the years, science has broadened our knowledge about mental health and illnesses, showing the potential to improve the way in which mental health care is provided. The U.S. Department of Health and Human Services (HHS) released *Mental Health: A Report of the Surgeon General*, which reviewed scientific advances in our understanding of mental health and mental illnesses. However, despite substantial investments that have enormously increased the scientific knowledge base and have led to developing many effective treatments, many Americans are not benefiting from these investments.

Far too often, treatments and services that are based on rigorous clinical research languish for years rather than being used effectively at the earliest opportunity. For instance, according to the Institute of Medicine report, *Crossing the Quality Chasm: A New Health System for the 21st Century*, the lag between discovering effective forms of treatment and incorporating them into routine patient care is unnecessarily long, lasting about 15 to 20 years.

In its report, the Institute of Medicine (IOM) described a strategy to improve the quality of health care during the coming decade, including priority areas for refinement. These documents, along with other recent publications and research findings, provide insight into the importance of mental heath, particularly as it relates to overall health. . . .

Mental Illnesses Present Serious Health Challenges

Mental illnesses rank first among illnesses that cause disability in the United States, Canada, and Western Europe. This serious public health challenge is under-recognized as a public health burden. In addition, one of the most distressing and preventable consequences of undiagnosed, untreated, or under-treated mental illnesses is suicide. The World Health Organization (WHO) recently reported that suicide worldwide causes more deaths every year than homicide or war.

In addition to the tragedy of lost lives, mental illnesses come with a devastatingly high financial cost. In the U.S., the annual economic, indirect cost of mental illnesses is estimated to be $79 billion. Most of that amount-approximately $63 billion—reflects the loss of productivity as a result of illnesses. But indirect costs also include almost $12 billion in mortality costs (lost productivity resulting from premature death) and almost $4 billion in productivity losses for incarcerated individuals and for the time of those who provide family care.

In 1997, the latest year comparable data are available, the United States spent more than $1 trillion on health care, including almost $71 billion on treating mental illnesses. Mental health expenditures are predominantly publicly funded at 57%, compared to 46% of overall health care expenditures. Between 1987 and 1997, mental health spending did not keep pace with general health care because of declines in private health spending under managed care and cutbacks in hospital expenditures.

The Current Mental Health System Is Complex

In its *Interim Report to the President*, the Commission declared, " . . . the mental health delivery system is fragmented and in disarray . . . lead[ing] to unnecessary and costly disability, homelessness, school failure and incarceration." The report described the extent of unmet needs and barriers to care, including:

- Fragmentation and gaps in care for children,
- Fragmentation and gaps in care for adults with serious mental illnesses,
- High unemployment and disability for people with serious mental illnesses,
- Lack of care for older adults with mental illnesses, and
- Lack of national priority for mental health and suicide prevention.

The *Interim Report* concluded that the system is not oriented to the single most important goal of the people it serves—the hope of recovery. State-of-the-art treatments, based on decades of research, are not being transferred from research to community settings. In many communities, access to quality care is poor, resulting in wasted resources and lost opportunities for recovery. More individuals could recover from even the most serious mental illnesses if they had access in their communities to treatment and supports that are tailored to their needs.

The Commission recognizes that thousands of dedicated, caring, skilled providers staff and manage the service delivery system. The Commission does not attribute the shortcomings and failings of the contemporary system to a lack of professionalism or compassion of mental health care workers. Rather, problems derive principally from the manner in which the Nation's community-based mental health system has evolved over the past four to five decades. In short, the Nation must replace unnecessary institutional care with efficient, effective community services that people can count on. It needs to integrate programs that are fragmented across levels of government and among many agencies.

Building on the research literature and comments from more than 2,300 consumers, family members, providers, administrators, researchers, government officials, and others who provided valuable insight into the way mental health care is delivered, after its yearlong study, the Commission concludes that traditional reform measures are not enough to meet the expectations of consumers and families.

To improve access to quality care and services, the Commission recommends fundamentally transforming how mental health care is delivered in America. The goals of this fundamental change are clear and align with the direction that the President established.

The Goal of a Transformed System: Recovery

To achieve the promise of community living for everyone, new service delivery patterns and incentives must ensure that every American has easy and continuous access to the most current treatments and best support services. Advances in research, technology, and our understanding of how to treat mental illnesses provide powerful means to transform the system. In a transformed system, consumers and family members will have access to timely and accurate information that promotes learning, self-monitoring, and accountability. Health care providers will rely on up-to-date knowledge to provide optimum care for the best outcomes.

When a serious mental illness or a serious emotional disturbance is first diagnosed, the health care provider—in full partnership with consumers and families—will develop an individualized plan of care for managing the illness. This partnership of personalized care means basically choosing who, what, and how appropriate health care will be provided:

- Choosing which mental health care professionals are on the team,
- Sharing in decision making, and
- Having the option to agree or disagree with the treatment plan.

The highest quality of care and information will be available to consumers and families, regardless of their race, gender, ethnicity, language, age, or place of residence. Because recovery will be the common, recognized outcome of mental health services, the stigma surrounding mental illnesses will be reduced, reinforcing the hope of recovery for every individual with a mental illness.

As more individuals seek help and share their stories with friends and relatives, compassion will be the response, not ridicule.

Successfully transforming the mental health service delivery system rests on two principles:

- **First, services and treatments must be consumer and family centered,** geared to give consumers real and meaningful choices about treatment options and providers—not oriented to the requirements of bureaucracies.
- **Second, care must focus on increasing consumers' ability to successfully cope with life's challenges, on facilitating recovery, and on building resilience,** not just on managing symptoms.

Built around consumers' needs, the system must be seamless and convenient.

Transforming the system so that it will be both consumer and family centered and recovery-oriented in its care and services presents invigorating challenges. Incentives must change to encourage continuous improvement in agencies that provide care. New, relevant research findings must be systematically conveyed to front-line providers so that they can be applied to practice quickly. Innovative strategies must inform researchers of the unanswered questions of consumers, families, and providers.

Research and treatment must recognize both the commonalities and the differences among Americans and must offer approaches that are sensitive to our diversity. Treatment and services that are based on proven effectiveness and consumer preference—not just on tradition or outmoded regulations—must be the basis for reimbursements.

The Nation must invest in the infrastructure to support emerging technologies and integrate them into the system of care. This new technology will enable consumers to collaborate with service providers, assume an active role in managing their illnesses, and move more quickly toward recovery.

The Commission identified the following six goals as the foundation for transforming mental health care in America. The goals are intertwined. No single step can achieve the fundamental restructuring that is needed to transform the mental health care delivery system.

Goals: In a transformed Mental Health System . . .

Goal 1: Americans Understand that Mental Health Is Essential to Overall Health.

Goal 2: Mental Health Care Is Consumer and Family Driven.

Goal 3: Disparities in Mental Health Services Are Eliminated.

Goal 4: Early Mental Health Screening, Assessment, and Referral to Services Are Common Practice.

Goal 5: Excellent Mental Health Care Is Delivered and Research Is Accelerated.

Goal 6: Technology Is Used to Access Mental Health Care and Information.

Achieving these goals will transform mental health care in America.

The following section of this report gives an overview of each goal of the transformed system, as well as the Commission's recommendations for moving the Nation toward achieving it. In the remainder of this report, the Commission discusses each goal in depth, showcasing model programs to illustrate the goal in practice and providing specific recommendations needed to transform the mental health system in America.

Goal 1—Americans Understand that Mental Health Is Essential to Overall Health

In a transformed mental health system, Americans will seek mental health care when they need it—with the same confidence that they seek treatment for other health problems. As a Nation, we will take action to ensure our health and well being through learning, self-monitoring, and accountability. We will continue to learn how to achieve and sustain our mental health.

The stigma that surrounds mental illnesses and seeking care for mental illnesses will be reduced or eliminated as a barrier. National education initiatives will shatter the misconceptions about mental illnesses, thus helping more Americans understand the facts and making them more willing to seek help for mental health problems. Education campaigns will also target specific audiences, including:

- Rural Americans who may have had little exposure to the mental health service system,
- Racial and ethnic minority groups who may hesitate to seek treatment in the current system, and
- People whose primary language is not English.

When people have a personal understanding of the facts, they will be less likely to stigmatize mental illnesses and more likely to seek help for mental health problems. The actions of reducing stigma, increasing awareness, and encouraging treatment will create a positive cycle that leads to a healthier population. As a Nation, we will also understand that good mental health can have a positive impact on the course of other illnesses, such as cancer, heart disease, and diabetes.

Improving services for individuals with mental illnesses will require paying close attention to how mental health care and general medical care systems work together. While mental health and physical health are clearly connected, the transformed system will provide collaborative care to bridge the gap that now exists.

Effective mental health treatments will be more readily available for most common mental disorders and will be better used in primary care settings. Primary care providers will have the necessary time, training, and resources to appropriately treat mental health problems. Informed consumers of mental health service will learn to recognize and identify their symptoms and will seek care without the fear of being disrespected or stigmatized. Older adults, children and adolescents, individuals from ethnic minority groups, and uninsured or low-income patients who are treated in public health care settings will receive care for mental disorders.

The transformed mental health system will rely on multiple sources of financing with the flexibility to pay for effective mental health treatments and services. This is a basic principle for a recovery-oriented system of care.

To aid in transforming the mental health system, the Commission makes two recommendations:

1.1 Advance and implement a national campaign to reduce the stigma of seeking care and a national strategy for suicide prevention.

1.2 Address mental health with the same urgency as physical health.

Goal 2—Mental Health Care Is Consumer and Family Driven

In a transformed mental health system, a diagnosis of a serious mental illness or a serious emotional disturbance will set in motion a well-planned, coordinated array of services and treatments defined in a single plan of care. This detailed roadmap—a personalized, highly individualized health management program—will help lead the way to appropriate treatment and supports that are oriented toward recovery and resilience. Consumers, along with service providers, will actively participate in designing and developing the systems of care in which they are involved.

An individualized plan of care will give consumers, families of children with serious emotional disturbances, clinicians, and other providers a valid opportunity to construct and maintain meaningful, productive, and healing relationships. Opportunities for updates—based on changing needs across the stages of life and the requirement to review treatment plans regularly—will be an integral part of the approach. The plan of care will be at the core of the consumer-centered, recovery-oriented mental health system. The plan will include treatment, supports, and other assistance to enable consumers to better integrate into their communities; it will allow consumers to realize improved mental health and quality of life.

In partnership with their health care providers, consumers and families will play a larger role in managing the funding for their services, treatments, and supports. Placing financial support increasingly under the management of consumers and families will enhance their choices. By allowing funding to follow consumers, incentives will shift toward a system of learning, self-monitoring, and accountability. This program design will give people a vested economic interest in using resources wisely to obtain and sustain recovery.

The transformed system will ensure that needed resources are available to consumers and families. The burden of coordinating care will rest on the system, not on the families or consumers who are already struggling because of a serious illness. Consumers' needs and preferences will drive the types and mix of services provided, considering the gender, age, language, development, and culture of consumers.

To ensure that needed resources are available to consumers and families in the transformed system, States will develop a comprehensive mental health plan to outline responsibility for coordinating and integrating programs. The State plan will include consumers and families and will create a new partnership among the Federal, State, and local governments. The plan will address the full range of treatment and support service programs that mental health consumers and families need.

In exchange for this accountability, States will have the flexibility to combine Federal, State, and local resources in creative, innovative, and more efficient ways, overcoming the bureaucratic boundaries between health care, employment supports, housing, and the criminal justice systems.

Increased flexibility and stronger accountability will expand the choices and the array of services and supports available to attain the desired outcomes. Creative programs will be developed to respond to the needs and preferences of consumers and families, as reflected in their individualized plans of care.

Giving consumers the ability to participate fully in their communities will require a few essentials:

- Access to health care,
- Gainful employment opportunities,
- Adequate and affordable housing, and
- The assurance of not being unjustly incarcerated.

Strong leadership will need to:

- Align existing programs to deliver services effectively,
- Remove disincentives to employment (such as loss of financial benefits or having to choose between employment and health care), and
- Provide for a safe place to live.

In this transformed system, consumers' rights will be protected and enhanced. Implementing the 1999 *Olmstead v. L.C.* decision in all States will allow services to be delivered in the most integrated setting possible—services in communities rather than in institutions. And services will be readily available so that consumers no longer face unemployment, homelessness, or incarceration because of untreated mental illnesses.

No longer will parents forgo the mental health services that their children desperately need. No longer will loving, responsible American parents face the dilemma of trading custody for care. Families will remain intact. Issues of custody will be separated from issues of care.

In this transformed system, stigma and discrimination against people with mental illnesses will not have an impact on securing health care, productive employment, or safe housing. Our society will not tolerate employment discrimination against people with serious mental illnesses— in either the public or private sector.

Consumers' rights will be protected concerning the use of seclusion and restraint. Seclusion and restraint will be used only as safety interventions of last resort, not as treatment interventions. Only licensed practitioners who are specially trained and qualified to assess and monitor consumers' safety and the significant medical and behavioral risks inherent in using seclusion and restraint will be able to order these interventions.

The hope and the opportunity to regain control of their lives—often vital to recovery—will become real for consumers and families. Consumers will play a significant role in shifting the current system to a recovery-oriented one by participating in planning, evaluation, research, training, and service delivery.

To aid in transforming the mental health system, the Commission makes five recommendations:

2.1 Develop an individualized plan of care for every adult with a serious mental illness and child with a serious emotional disturbance.

2.2 Involve consumers and families fully in orienting the mental health system toward recovery.

2.3 Align relevant Federal programs to improve access and accountability for mental health services.

2.4 Create a Comprehensive State Mental Health Plan.

2.5 Protect and enhance the rights of people with mental illnesses.

Goal 3—Disparities in Mental Health Services Are Eliminated

In a transformed mental health system, all Americans will share equally in the best available services and outcomes, regardless of race, gender, ethnicity, or geographic location. Mental health care will be highly personal, respecting and responding to individual differences and backgrounds. The workforce will include members of ethnic, cultural, and linguistic minorities who are trained and employed as mental health service providers. People who live in rural and remote geographic areas will have access to mental health professionals and other needed resources. Advances in treatments will be available in rural and less populated areas. Research and training will continuously aid clinicians in understanding how to appropriately tailor interventions to the needs of consumers, recognizing factors such as age, gender, race, culture, ethnicity, and locale.

Services will be tailored for culturally diverse populations and will provide access, enhanced quality, and positive outcomes of care. American Indians, Alaska Natives, African Americans, Asian Americans, Pacific Islanders, and Hispanic Americans will not continue to bear a disproportionately high burden of disability from mental health disorders. These populations will have accessible, available mental health services. They will receive the same high quality of care that all Americans receive. To develop culturally competent treatments, services, care, and support, mental health research will include these underserved populations. In addition, providers will include individuals who share and respect the beliefs, norms, values, and patterns of communication of culturally diverse populations.

In rural and remote geographic areas, service providers will be more readily available to help create a consumer-centered system. Using such tools as videoconferencing and telehealth, advances in treatments will be brought to rural and less populated areas of the country. These technologies will be used to provide care at the same time they break down the sense of isolation often experienced by consumers.

Mental health education and training will be provided to general health care providers, emergency room staff, and first responders, such as law enforcement personnel and emergency medical technicians, to overcome the uneven geographic distribution of psychiatrists, psychologists, and psychiatric social workers.

To aid in transforming the mental health system, the Commission makes two recommendations:

3.1 Improve access to quality care that is culturally competent.
3.2 Improve access to quality care in rural and geographically remote areas.

Goal 4—Early Mental Health Screening, Assessment, and Referral to Services Are Common Practice

In a transformed mental health system, the early detection of mental health problems in children and adults—through routine and comprehensive testing and screening—will be an expected and typical occurrence. At the first sign of difficulties, preventive interventions will be started to keep problems from escalating. For example, a child whose serious emotional disturbance is identified early will receive care, preventing the potential onset of a co-occurring substance use disorder and breaking a cycle that otherwise can lead to school failure and other problems.

Quality screening and early intervention will occur in both readily accessible, low-stigma settings, such as primary health care facilities and schools, and in settings in which a high level of risk exists for mental health problems, such as criminal justice, juvenile justice, and child welfare systems. Both children and adults will be screened for mental illnesses during their routine physical exams.

For consumers of all ages, early detection, assessment, and links with treatment and supports will help prevent mental health problems from worsening. Service providers across settings will also routinely screen for co-occurring mental illnesses and substance use disorders. Early intervention and appropriate treatment will also improve outcomes and reduce pain and suffering for children and adults who have or who are at risk for co-occurring mental and addictive disorders.

Early detection of mental disorders will result in substantially shorter and less disabling courses of impairment.

To aid in transforming the mental health system, the Commission makes four recommendations:

4.1 Promote the mental health of young children.
4.2 Improve and expand school mental health programs.
4.3 Screen for co-occurring mental and substance use disorders and link with integrated treatment strategies.
4.4 Screen for mental disorders in primary health care, across the lifespan, and connect to treatment and supports.

Goal 5—Excellent Mental Health Care Is Delivered and Research Is Accelerated

In a transformed mental health system, consistent use of evidence-based, state-of-the art medications and psychotherapies will be standard practice throughout the mental health system. Science will inform the provision of services, and the experience of service providers will guide future research. Every time any American—whether a child or an adult, a member of a majority or a minority, from an urban or rural area—comes into contact with the mental health system, he or she will receive excellent care that is consistent with our scientific understanding of what works. That care will be delivered according to the consumer's individualized plan.

Research has yielded important advances in our knowledge of the brain and behavior, and helped develop effective treatments and service delivery strategies for many mental disorders. In a transformed system, research will be used to develop new evidence-based practices to prevent and treat mental illnesses. These discoveries will be immediately put into practice. Americans with mental illnesses will fully benefit from the enormous increases in the scientific knowledge base and the development of many effective treatments.

Also benefiting from these developments, the workforce will be trained to use the most advanced tools for diagnosis and treatments. Translating research into practice will include adequate training for front-line providers and professionals, resulting in a workforce that is equipped to use the latest breakthroughs in modern medicine. Research discoveries will become routinely available at the community level. To realize the possibilities of advances in treatment, and ultimately in prevention or a cure, the Nation will continue to invest in research at all levels.

Knowledge about evidence-based practices (the range of treatments and services of well-documented effectiveness), as well as emerging best practices (treatments and services with a promising but less thoroughly documented evidentiary base), will be widely circulated and used in a variety of mental health specialties and in general health, school-based, and other settings. Countless people with mental illnesses will benefit from improved consumer outcomes including reduced symptoms, fewer and less severe side effects, and improved functioning. The field of mental health will be encouraged to expand its efforts to develop and test new treatments and practices, to promote awareness of and improve training in evidence-based practices, and to better finance those practices.

The Nation will have a more effective system to identify, disseminate, and apply proven treatments to mental health care delivery. Research and education will play critical roles in the transformed mental health system. Advanced treatments will be available and adapted to individual preferences and needs, including language and other ethnic and cultural considerations. Investments in technology will also enable both consumers and providers to find the most up-to-date resources and knowledge to provide optimum care for the best outcomes. Studies will incorporate the unique needs of cultural, ethnic, and linguistic minorities and will help ensure full access to effective treatment for all Americans.

To aid in transforming the mental health system, the Commission makes four recommendations:

5.1 Accelerate research to promote recovery and resilience, and ultimately to cure and prevent mental illnesses.

5.2 Advance evidence-based practices using dissemination and demonstration projects and create a public-private partnership to guide their implementation.

5.3 Improve and expand the workforce providing evidence-based mental health services and supports.

5.4 Develop the knowledge base in four understudied areas: mental health disparities, long-term effects of medications, trauma, and acute care.

Goal 6—Technology Is Used to Access Mental Health Care and Information

In a transformed mental health system, advanced communication and information technology will empower consumers and families and will be a tool for providers to deliver the best care. Consumers and families will be able to regularly communicate with the agencies and personnel that deliver treatment and support services and that are accountable for achieving the goals outlined in the individual plan of care. Information about illnesses, effective treatments, and the services in their community will be readily available to consumers and families.

Access to information will foster continuous, caring relationships between consumers and providers by providing a medical history, allowing for self-management of care, and electronically linking multiple service systems. Providers will access expert systems that bring to bear the most recent breakthroughs and studies of optimal outcomes to facilitate the best care options. Having agreed to use the same health messaging standards, pharmaceutical codes, imaging standards, and laboratory test names, the Nation's health system will be much closer to speaking a common language and providing superior patient care. Informed consumers and providers will result in better outcomes and will more efficiently use resources.

Electronic health records can improve quality by promoting adoption and adherence to evidence-based practices through inclusion of clinical reminders, clinical practice guidelines, tools for clinical decision support, computer order entry, and patient safety alert systems. For example, prescription medications being taken or specific drug allergies would be known, which could prevent serious injury or death resulting from drug interactions, excessive dosages or allergic reactions.

Access to care will be improved in many underserved rural and urban communities by using health technology, telemedicine care, and consultations. Health technology and telehealth will offer a powerful means to improve access to mental health care in underserved, rural, and remote areas. The privacy of personal health information—especially in the case of mental illnesses—will be strongly protected and controlled by consumers and families. With appropriate privacy protection, electronic records will enable essential medical and mental health information to be shared across the public and private sectors.

Reimbursements will become flexible enough to allow implementing evidence-based practices and coordinating both traditional clinical care and e-health visits. In both the public and private sectors, policies will change to support these innovative approaches.

An integrated information technology and communications infrastructure will be critical to achieving the five preceding goals and transforming mental health care in America. To address this technological need in the mental health care system, this goal envisions two critical technological components:

- A robust telehealth system to improve access to care, and
- An integrated health records system and a personal health information system for providers and patients.

To aid in transforming the mental health system, the Commission makes two recommendations:

6.1 Use health technology and telehealth to improve access and coordination of mental health care, especially for Americans in remote areas or in underserved populations.

6.2 Develop and implement integrated electronic health record and personal health information systems.

Preventing mental illnesses remains a promise of the future. Granted, the best option is to avoid or delay the onset of any illness, but the Executive Order directed the Commission to conduct a comprehensive study of the delivery of mental health services. The Commission recognizes that it is better to prevent an illness than to treat it, but unmet needs and barriers to services must first be identified to reach the millions of Americans with existing mental illnesses who are deterred from seeking help. The barriers may exist for a variety of reasons:

• Stigma,
• Fragmented services,
• Cost,
• Workforce shortages,
• Unavailable services, and
• Not knowing where or how to get care.

These barriers are all discussed in this report.

The Commission—aware of all the limitations on resources—examined realigning Federal financing with a keen awareness of the constraints. As such, the policies and improvements recommended in this *Final Report* reflect policy and program changes that make the most of existing resources by increasing cost effectiveness and reducing unnecessary and burdensome regulatory barriers, coupled with a strong measure of accountability. A transformed mental health system will more wisely invest resources to provide optimal care while making the best use of limited resources.

The process of transforming mental health care in America drives the system toward a delivery structure that will give consumers broader discretion in how care decisions are made. This shift will give consumers more confidence to require that care be sensitive to their needs, that the best available treatments and supports be available, and that demonstrably effective technologies be widely replicated in different settings. This confidence will then enhance cooperative relationships with mental health care professionals who share the hope of recovery. . . .

Source: United States. Department of Health and Human Services. President's New Freedom Commission on Mental Health. "Achieving the Promise: Transforming Mental Health Care in America." DHHS Pub. No. SMA–03–3832, July 22, 2003. http://purl.access.gpo.gov/GPO/LPS36928 (accessed September 2, 2003).

State Attorney General on Child Abuse by Priests

July 23, 2003

INTRODUCTION

Repercussions from the clerical sex abuse scandal in the Roman Catholic Church that broke open in 2002 continued to be felt across the country in 2003. In Boston, where the scandal began, the state attorney general reported that as many as 1,000 children may have been abused between 1940 and 2002. Although the attorney general said that the Boston archbishop, Cardinal Bernard F. Law, and other officials had put children in harm's way by covering up the abuse, the state would not bring criminal charges. A new archbishop, appointed to replace Law, who was forced to resign as a result of the scandal, reached a long-stalled settlement with more than 500 abuse victims. Three other dioceses agreed to unusual legal settlements to avoid criminal charges stemming from abuse allegations, but other dioceses were still fighting lawsuits, denying legal culpability for covering up for abusive priests, and refusing to make public the names of priests accused of abuse.

Frank Keating, chairman of the lay committee appointed by the U.S. Conference of Catholic Bishops to monitor how well dioceses were complying with its new national policy on sexual abuse, resigned his post after accusing unnamed bishops of acting "like La Cosa Nostra" in their zeal to hide and suppress information on child abuse by priests and other church employees. But the president of the conference insisted that its "zero tolerance" policy reforms were "on track." Another bishop working on the abuse crisis said that the church hierarchy had made a "monumental effort" to apply the reforms, remove abusive priests from active ministry, and restore confidence in the church. A victims group agreed that the bishops were making progress but said that some were still protecting abusive priests in contravention of the "zero tolerance" policy. The reforms, which among other things barred the transfer of abusive priests to other dioceses and required church officials to report allegations of abuse to civil authorities, were adopted in November 2002 after months of contentious debate. *(Background, Historic Documents of 2002, p. 867)*

The American church hierarchy put aside its concerns about the sex abuse scandal for a few days in October to celebrate the twenty-fifth anniversary of John Paul II's reign over the Roman Catholic Church. Thousands of church officials and lay Catholics crammed St. Peter's Square in Rome on October 16 for ceremonies honoring the popular but increasingly frail pope. One of only four popes to serve that long, John Paul was widely lauded for his efforts to bring peace to the world; to seek reconciliation among Christians, Jews, and Muslims; and to bridge the divide between rich and poor nations. But he was also criticized for driving Catholics away from the church because of his unbending and conservative stands on social issues such as birth control, abortion, and homosexuality. *(Pope's visit to the Holy Land, Historic documents of 2000, p. 77; Holocaust repentance, Historic Documents of 1998, p. 121)*

A Scathing Report and Settlement

In Boston a new archbishop negotiated a $85 million settlement with abuse victims in September following a scathing report by the Massachusetts attorney general detailing the extent of the abuse in the archdiocese over sixty years. The actions, though not directly related, seemed to clear the air in the city's Catholic community, which had been consumed for more than a year in charges, countercharges, and distrust. The crisis began in Boston in January 2002 when Cardinal Law was forced to admit that he had moved a priest, John J. Geoghan, from parish to parish over a thirty-year period despite knowing that Geoghan had been accused of molesting children. Evidence released later in the year showed that Law had handled several other abuse cases similarly, moving priests to other parishes without notifying either the new parish or law enforcement officials of the suspected abuse.

Law apologized, but for many Catholics in the Boston area, those apologies were too little too late. As the Boston church hierarchy balked both at reaching a settlement with victims and at cooperating with law enforcement investigation, the calls for Law's resignation increased, and he was finally forced to resign in December 2002. Law's departure eased tensions somewhat, but the atmosphere of distrust remained.

On July 23 Massachusetts Attorney General Thomas F. Reilly released the results of his office's eighteen-month investigation of the abuse scandal in the archdiocese, which he said described as "one of the greatest tragedies to befall children in this Commonwealth." The extent of the abuse was so massive that it "borders on the unbelievable," Reilly said. Church records showed that 789 victims had filed sexual abuse complaints with the archdiocese between 1940 and 2002 and that there was sufficient evidence to suggest that the total number of abuse victims exceeded 1,000. Reilly said the records showed complaints were brought against 237 priests and 13 other archdiocese workers. Forty-eight of those had allegedly abused children since 1984, when Law was appointed archbishop.

Reilly also said there was "overwhelming evidence" that Law and other top church officials had known about the abuse for years; any claim otherwise "is simply not credible," he added. "The sexual abuse of children of such staggering magnitude and over several decades is nothing less than a complete failure of leadership. Even after knowing the scope of the abuse, top officials of the Archdiocese chose to protect their own priests and the reputation of the institution rather than protecting children," Reilly said. But, because of the weak child protection laws in effect at the time and the statute of limitations, he could not bring criminal charges against Law and his senior managers. "No one is more disappointed than I and my staff that we cannot bring criminal charges," Reilly said at a news conference. "If we could have, we would have."

Reilly implored the state legislature to tighten child protection laws and the penalties for breaking them. He said there was no evidence of any recent or ongoing sexual abuse by priests in the archdioceses, but he also said church officials had not yet shown "an appropriate sense of urgency for attacking the problem of child sexual abuse or for changing [church] culture to remove the risk to children." Thus he concluded it was too soon to say that the abuse had stopped or would not recur in the future.

A week later, on July 30, the Rev. Sean P. O'Malley, a Capuchin friar, was installed as archbishop of Boston. "The whole Catholic community is ashamed and anguished because of the pain and damage inflicted on so many young people and because of our inability and unwillingness to deal with the crime of sexual abuse of minors," O'Malley said at his installation. O'Malley, who had already dealt with problems of clerical abuse as bishop in Fall River, Massachusetts, and Palm Beach, Florida, moved quickly to reach a settlement with abuse victims. On August 9 the archdiocese offered $55 million to settle 542 abuse claims. That offer was spurned by victims, who said it was woefully inadequate. A month later, on September 9, a settlement was announced. The archdiocese agreed to pay $85 million to settle the claims—the largest settlement to date to resolve church sex abuse cases. Each victim was to receive $80,000 to $300,000 within three months, with the amount determined by a mediator and based on the type and duration of the alleged abuse. The archdiocese also agreed to finance psychiatric counseling for victims, who would be allowed to choose their own therapists.

O'Malley reportedly played a crucial role in reaching the agreement. "If he had not been present . . . these cases would not have settled," said an attorney whose firms represented about half the victims. "He has a way with people, and he was able to make phone calls and arrange the money and several of the other conditions." Most of the funding was expected to come from church insurance policies, and O'Malley was said to be prepared to sue the insurance companies if need be. Many insurance companies had insisted that churches fight the alleged abuse cases in court in an effort to keep down damage costs, which were far in excess of any amounts that insurers had ever contemplated having to pay out. The archdiocese also said it would raise money by selling up to fifteen church properties, including the ornate, Italian-style mansion that Law had lived in and that had become a symbol of the rift between church leaders and their followers. Although not all the victims were pleased with the settlement, several expressed relief that the church was finally being forced to recognize the validity of their claims.

Closure of an entirely different sort came to Geoghan, the defrocked priest who was at the center of the Boston scandal. Geoghan died August 23 in the state prison where he was serving a ten-year sentence for indecent assault and battery after being strangled by a fellow inmate.

Avoiding Accountability

Bishop Wilton D. Gregory, the president of the United States Conference of Catholic Bishops, called the Boston settlement an "important agreement," which "demonstrates that the church is committed to working out just settlements which seek to meet, to the extent possible, the needs of people who have suffered terribly." Several commentators said the settlement could put pressure on church officials in other dioceses to break through the legal standoffs over abuse lawsuits that had prevented both the church and the victims from reaching closure. By year's end, however, several archdioceses and dioceses were still engaged in legal suits and settlement discussions.

Three other dioceses agreed to unusual arrangements to avoid legal accountability. The Roman Catholic diocese in Manchester, New Hampshire, agreed in March to a settlement in which it acknowledged that it had failed to protect children by covering up allegations of clerical sexual abuse for years and that the government had enough evidence to convict the diocese of child endangerment, a misdemeanor. The diocese also agreed to the release of 9,000 pages of documents and a report detailing the abuses and the cover-up. In return, the government agreed not to pursue the criminal misdemeanor charge. In May the diocese agreed to pay $6.5 million to settle 61 lawsuits; it had already settled 176 cases for $15.45 million.

In early June the Roman Catholic bishop of Phoenix agreed to give up some of his authority to escape being prosecuted for obstruction of justice for covering up allegations of abuse levied against at least fifty priests, former priests, and church employees. In return for immunity from prosecution in any criminal cover-up, Bishop Thomas J. O'Brien agreed to delegate day-to-day administrative responsibility for running the diocese to a chief of staff and to appoint an independent special advocate to handle abuse complaints. Two weeks later, on June 18, O'Brien resigned as bishop after being arrested for leaving the scene of an automobile accident in which he was alleged to have struck and killed a pedestrian.

On November 20 the Archdiocese of Cincinnati pleaded no contest to a charge of failing to tell law enforcement authorities about allegations of clerical sexual abuse and agreed to pay a $10,000 fine. The plea saved the archdiocese from facing criminal charges that it had "an institutional knowledge that certain felony sex crimes involving minors occurred."

Other dioceses escaped criminal charges because, as in Boston, the statute of limitations had expired. A report, released by the district attorney's office in Suffolk County, New York, on February 10, said that a special grand jury had concluded that the Diocese of Rockville Center on Long Island had repeatedly protected priests accused of sexual abuse but that the grand jury could not issue any indictments because the statute of limitations had expired. The grand jury recommended that the statute of limitations be eliminated for child abuse cases and that priests be required to report suspected cases of abuse directly to the police.

Controversy over National Survey

In June 2003 Frank Keating, the former governor of Oklahoma and the chairman of the lay panel set up by the U.S. Conference of Catholic Bishops in 2002 to monitor compliance with the new sexual abuse policy, accused several bishops of failing to be forthcoming in providing the panel with information about the clerical abuse in their dioceses. In an interview with the Los Angeles Times, the outspoken Keating pointed to Los Angeles bishop Roger N. Mahoney as an example of this resistance and went on to say that some unnamed bishops went to extremes in their refusal to cooperate fully with the National Review Board. "To act like La Cosa Nostra and hide and suppress, I think, is very unhealthy. Eventually, it will all come out," Keating was quoted as saying.

Mahoney and others were outraged and demanded Keating's removal. Keating submitted his resignation on June 16, saying that he had always intended to step down after a year and refusing to back down from his comments to the *Times*. "My remarks, which some bishops found offensive, were deadly accurate. I make no apology," Keating wrote in his resignation letter to Bishop Gregory. "To resist grand jury subpoenas, to suppress the names of offending clerics, to deny, to obfuscate, to explain away; that is the model of a criminal organization, not my church."

At issue in the controversy was a survey asking every Roman Catholic diocese in the country to provide information on how many priests had been accused of child sexual abuse since 1950, how those cases had been handled, and how much those cases had cost the church in lawsuits, legal fees, and counseling. Although many dioceses supplied the information, some, including Los Angeles, objected on various grounds, including concerns about violating privacy laws. In the wake of the Keating controversy, the lay committee took steps to resolve some of the complaints about the survey and later said it expected full compliance with the survey by the November deadline. The results of the study were expected to be made public in 2004.

In the absence of the National Review Board survey, the most reliable information about the extent of child sexual abuse might have come from a survey conducted by the *New York Times* and released January 12, 2003. That survey, which was based on court records, news reports, church documents, and interviews, found that 1,205 priests had been accused of abusing 4,268 people since 1940. Experts told the *Times* that the actual number was likely to be much higher because many people who were subjected to abuse had probably not publicly revealed it. The survey found that the abuse was widespread, with accusations arising in all but 16 of the 177 Latin rite dioceses in the United States.

In percentage terms, the *Times* study said that 1.8 percent of all priests ordained between 1950 and 2001 had been accused of abuse. Fifty percent of the these priests were accused of molesting more than one minor and 16 percent were accused of abusing five or more. Eighty percent were accused of molesting boys, and 43 percent were accused of molesting children age twelve and under. Most of the abuse occurred in the 1970s and 1980s. The steep decline in clerical abuse cases in the 1990s mirrored an overall decline in the sexual abuse of children. Several reasons might account for that decline, including greater awareness about identifying and reporting sexual abuse, closer supervision of children, and longer imprisonment for offenders. But, as the *Times* suggested, another reason might be that people abused as children in the 1990s had not yet come forward with their accusations.

Following are excerpts from "The Sexual Abuse of Children in the Roman Catholic Archdiocese of Boston," a report issued July 23, 2003, by Thomas F. Reilly, the attorney general of Massachusetts.

"The Sexual Abuse of Children in the Archdiocese of Boston"

To the People of the Commonwealth of Massachusetts

The education, care and protection of our children are among the most important undertakings of our society. In the past one hundred years, we in the United States and the Commonwealth of Massachusetts have made great gains in how we protect our children—and our nation and state have been the better for it. It was with this single motivation—to protect children—that in January 2002, the Office of the Attorney General undertook to address the massive and prolonged mistreatment of children by priests assigned to the Roman Catholic Archdiocese of Boston; and it is with this single motivation that the Office of the Attorney General submits the accompanying report of what it did and learned.

Throughout the history of the United States, the Catholic Church in America has been responsible for countless good works. Outside of government, it is probably the country's foremost social services provider: feeding the hungry, caring for the old, the weak and the dispossessed, and fighting in the name of social justice. Its schools and universities have educated generations of children. And thousands of devout and honorable priests provide the Church's followers with moral and spiritual guidance every day.

But in the past twenty years, events have revealed a dark side to the Church's relationship with its children. In the early 1980's, and again in the early 1990's, the sexual assault of scores of children by individual priests came to light. Then, eighteen months ago, we began to learn of a tragedy of unimaginable dimensions: According to the Archdiocese's own files, 789 victims have complained of sexual abuse by members of the clergy; the actual number of victims is no doubt higher. The evidence to date also reveals that 250 priests and church workers stand accused of acts of rape or sexual assault of children. This widespread assault on children has occurred for at least six decades under the administrations of three successive Archbishops; clearly, this massive assault is the responsibility of no one person or administration. The facts learned over the past eighteen months describe one of the greatest tragedies to befall children in this Commonwealth. Perhaps most tragic of all, much of the harm could have been prevented.

When the Office of the Attorney General undertook to address the widespread sexual abuse of children within the Archdiocese, it set three objectives: to determine whether sexual abuse of children within the Archdiocese was recent or ongoing; to determine whether the Archdiocese or its senior managers had committed crimes under applicable state law; and to use all available means to ensure that children within the Archdiocese would be safe in the future. Concurrently, the Commonwealth's District Attorneys assumed responsibility for investigating and prosecuting individual priests and church workers accused of sexually abusing children.

In pursuit of its objectives, the Office of the Attorney General initiated an extensive investigation, which involved prosecutors, State Police, civilian investigators and the Grand Jury. It worked with the District Attorneys and the Legislature to enact important changes in our laws. And it undertook substantial efforts to have the Archdiocese adopt policies and procedures to protect children from sexual assault. Based on these activities, I report the following:

- The investigation of the Office of the Attorney General did not produce evidence of recent or ongoing sexual abuse of children; but it is far too soon to conclude that the abuse has stopped and will not reoccur in the future.
- The investigation did not produce evidence sufficient to charge the Archdiocese or its senior managers with crimes under applicable state law.
- The investigation did produce evidence that the widespread abuse of children was due to an institutional acceptance of abuse and a massive and pervasive failure of leadership.

I have determined that based on my conclusions and in order to ensure that children will be safe in the future, this report is essential. It is essential to create an official public record of what occurred. The mistreatment of children was so massive and so prolonged that it borders on the unbelievable. This report will confirm to all who may read it, now and in the future, that this tragedy was real.

It is essential to create an official record of what occurred because although this Office is unable to charge crimes, the conduct of the Archdiocese and its senior managers was undeniably wrong. For decades, Cardinals, Bishops and others in positions of authority within the Archdiocese chose to protect the image and reputation of their institution rather than the safety and well-being of children. They acted with a misguided devotion to secrecy and a mistaken belief that they were accountable only to themselves. They must be held to account, if not in a court of law, then before the ultimate arbiter in our democracy: you, the people.

Finally, it is essential to create an official public record of what occurred so that this type of widespread abuse of children might never happen again here or elsewhere. New laws enacted by our Legislature create important tools to prevent widespread and systematic abuse of children, and dedicated prosecutors are ready and willing to enforce those new laws. Nevertheless, the failure of Archdiocese leadership has been too massive and too prolonged; and the Archdiocese has yet to demonstrate a commitment to reform proportional to the tragedy it perpetrated. Until the Archdiocese clearly demonstrates an understanding of what occurred and how to provide a safe environment for its children, there must be a period of vigilance by the public and its officials and by members of the Archdiocese, including priests and the laity.

To assure the safety of children within the Archdiocese and to mark the day when special vigilance is no longer necessary, there must be a continued push for openness by the Archdiocese when it comes to issues related to the protection of children; implementation of rigorous and effective policies and procedures for protecting children; ongoing examination of key indicators that the Archdiocese is doing all it can to keep children safe; compliance and enforcement of the new legal obligations on clergy and other church workers to be mandated reporters of child abuse; and active involvement among the laity in the implementation of all policies and procedures designed to protect children.

This sad chapter reminds us of how precious our children are and of the responsibility we share as a society for their well-being. All that we value and prize depends on preserving the promise of their future.

I respectfully submit the accompanying Report.

Sincerely,
Thomas F. Reilly
Attorney General
Commonwealth of Massachusetts

Background

[Sections A and B on the organizational and management structure of the archdiocese and of its procedures for dealing with claims of sexual abuse omitted.]

C. The Magnitude of Clergy Sexual Abuse of Children in the Archdiocese

For many reasons, including under-reporting by victims of clergy sexual abuse, the understandable desire of many victims for privacy and confidentiality, and the failure of the Archdiocese to keep precise and organized records of abuse complaints over the past fifty or more years, the full magnitude of the Archdiocese's history of clergy sexual abuse of children is difficult, if not impossible, to determine. Nevertheless, whether the magnitude is calculated in terms of numbers of known victims, or numbers of known offenders, the magnitude of the Archdiocese's history of clergy sexual abuse of children is staggering.

Records produced by the Archdiocese reveal that at least 789 victims (or third parties acting on the behalf of victims) have complained directly to the Archdiocese (including complaints filed through the Archdiocese's attorneys). When information from other sources is considered—such as groups representing survivors of clergy abuse, plaintiffs' attorneys, media reports, and records from civil suits—the number of alleged victims who have disclosed their abuse likely exceeds one thousand. And the number increases even further when considering that an unknown number of victims likely have not, and may never disclose their abuse to others. . . .

The magnitude of the Archdiocese's history of clergy sexual abuse is equally shocking if evaluated in terms of the number of priests and other Archdiocese workers alleged to have sexually abused children since 1940. Analysis of relevant documents, including those produced by the Archdiocese, documents filed in civil suits on behalf of alleged victims of clergy sexual abuse, and media reports, reveal that allegations of sexual abuse of children have been made against at least 237 priests and thirteen other Archdiocese workers. Of these 250 priests and other Archdiocese workers, 202 of them allegedly abused children between 1940 and 1984, with the other forty-eight allegedly abusing children during Cardinal Law's tenure as Archbishop of Boston.

Approximately 110 of the 237 priests alleged to have sexually abused children since 1946 graduated from the Archdiocese's principal seminary, St. John's Seminary, located on the grounds of the Chancery in Brighton; two others graduated from another Archdiocesan seminary, Blessed John XXIII National Seminary in Weston. . . . Despite evidence that a large number of abusive priests graduated from St. John's Seminary between 1949 and 1990, there was no evidence that the Archdiocese at any time undertook a comprehensive analysis of possible systemic causes of the abuse and whether there was a causal relationship between the prevalence of abuse, the type of candidates attracted to the priesthood, and the Archdiocese's policies and practices for recruiting and screening applicants to the seminary. While applicants to the Archdiocese's seminaries did not undergo psychiatric screening or testing prior to the late 1960's, the two principal seminaries in the Archdiocese did eventually implement policies concerning screening and testing of applicants.

Findings and Conclusions

Finding No. 1: The Investigation Did Not Produce Evidence of Recent or Ongoing Sexual Abuse of Children in the Archdiocese of Boston, But It Is Too Soon to Conclude That the Archdiocese Has Undertaken the Changes Necessary to Ensure That Abuse Has Stopped and Will Not Occur in the Future

The Attorney General's investigation did not produce evidence of recent or ongoing sexual abuse of children by priests or other Archdiocese workers. Significantly, the investigation also did not produce evidence that would readily explain the lack of recent complaints. Given the magnitude of mistreatment and the fact that the Archdiocese's response over the past eighteen months remains inadequate, it is far too soon to conclude that the abuse has, in fact, stopped or could not reoccur in the future. . . .

The Archdiocese has yet to demonstrate an appropriate sense of urgency for attacking the problem of child sexual abuse or for changing its culture to remove the risk to children. The Archdiocese's response over the past eighteen months to the public disclosure of the long history of clergy sexual abuse of children demonstrates an insufficient commitment to (1) determining the systemic causes of clergy sexual abuse; (2) removing priests and other Archdiocese workers who committed such serious crimes against children and holding them accountable for their actions; (3) addressing its failure to prevent sexual abuse of children; (4) full information sharing and cooperation with state law enforcement authorities concerning suspicions or allegations of clergy sexual abuse of children; or (5) taking adequate steps to ensure that children are not sexually abused in the future.

On May 30, 2003, more than sixteen months after the first disclosures of the full history of the sexual abuse of children in the Archdiocese, the Archdiocese finally promulgated and adopted its new sexual abuse policy, Policies and Procedures for the Protection of Children. This policy followed extensive communications with the Office of the Attorney General as well as the production in October 2002 of recommended policies and procedures by The Cardinal's Commission for the Protection of Children, a commission of lay experts appointed by Cardinal Law. According to the Archdiocese, the policies adopted in May were "consistent with church law and codify the substantial implementation of the Cardinal's Commission," as the Attorney General had recommended. The new document is a marked improvement over the 1993 policy, and recognizes important child protection measures advocated by the Attorney General and the Commission, including age-appropriate sex abuse prevention programs in all Catholic schools and religious education classes; background checks of all current and prospective clergy, archdiocesan personnel and volunteers; screening seminary students; mandatory training on the obligation to report suspected child abuse; establishment of a code of pastoral conduct for clergy, archdiocesan personnel and volunteers; and cooperation with law enforcement. The policy also establishes the role of the Review Board and various other boards and offices, including the Office for Pastoral Support and Outreach created to address the needs of victims.

The May policy is a disappointment, because—faced with both the history of pervasive and prolonged abuse and the willingness of many qualified persons and organizations to help—the Archdiocese needlessly delayed in adopting new policies and procedures and the policy adopted remains deficient in the following critical ways:

Investigation and Discipline Process. The investigation and discipline process does not envision consistent, uniform or mandatory practices, but depends at all stages on the exercise of the Archbishop's discretion as to whether or not to proceed. The process protects priests at the expense of victims and, in the final analysis, is incapable of leading to timely and appropriate responses to sex abuse allegations. It is essential that the Archdiocese provide a rigorous investigation and discipline process that does not favor alleged abusive priests over their victims.

Independent Review Boards. None of the various boards or offices appearing in the Policies and Procedures is "independent" or "independently incorporated," raising doubts about the Archdiocese's commitment to objective oversight and further hampering attempts to rebuild trust in the institution. Under the Policies and Procedures, the Archbishop has complete control over selection of Review Board members who must be "in full communion" with the church. As a result, it is less likely that the Review Board can operate independently and effectively (a problem under the 1993 policy) or make decisions, judgments or recommendations adverse to the Archdiocese as an institution, but still in the public interest.

Independent Victim's Assistance Board. The experts on the Commission and the Attorney General, recognizing the conflict of interest that arose from the Archdiocese's control over the provision of assistance to victims who came forward with allegations of sexual abuse, advocated for an independent board to oversee this function. It is essential that services to victims be arranged or provided by persons financed by, but unaffiliated with, the Archdiocese.

Supervision of Abusive Priests. The Archdiocese still has not committed to supervise, monitor and assess the dangerousness of priests who have been or will be removed from ministry because they sexually abused children, even though the Archdiocese has helped them find housing and, in some cases, employment. These priests have either admitted to sexual abuse, been diagnosed with pedophilia or another sexual disorder, or the

Archdiocese has concluded that the priest committed sexual abuse. Since the Archdiocese refused to hand those priests over to law enforcement for criminal prosecution, many are potentially dangerous to children in the communities where they live and work. The Attorney General has consistently urged the Archdiocese to monitor those priests closely and deems this essential to protect children in the future from sexual abuse.

Accountability. The Attorney General has continued to maintain that the Archdiocese hold accountable and discipline bishops, other clergy, employees and volunteers for committing sexual abuse or permitting it to occur through inaction. The Archdiocese's Policies and Procedures notably exempts bishops from their coverage and does not even require all clergy, employees and volunteers to comply with the Policies and Procedures or set forth penalties for non-compliance. A person who fails to comply with the mandatory requirement to report sexual abuse or a priest who violates the code of pastoral conduct should be subject to discipline. The Archdiocese should also require permanent retention of all records of child sexual abuse.

Anonymous Complaints. The Archdiocese does not affirmatively commit to investigating all anonymous complaints to the fullest extent possible. The Policies and Procedures repeatedly states that the accused has a right to know his accuser and leaves it to the discretion of the Archbishop "to determine how to handle the allegation."

Implementation. The Archdiocese's structure for implementing the various parts of its Policies and Procedures is highly decentralized. It is imperative that the Archdiocese appoint a leader for the Office for Child Advocacy, Implementation and Oversight who has the authority and qualifications to achieve coordination among the various boards, offices, parochial elementary and secondary schools and local parishes, and has the proper staff and appropriate financial resources for the Office's work. The Implementation and Oversight Advisory Committee should consist of persons with relevant expertise who receive appropriate support from the Archdiocese and meaningful input from the other boards and offices. Finally, . . . it is the Archdiocese and its management team who bear ultimate responsibility for assuring compliance with the Policies and Procedures.

Finding No. 2: The Investigation Did Not Produce Evidence Sufficient to Charge the Archdiocese or Its Senior Managers with Crimes Under Applicable State Law

Another objective of the Attorney General's investigation was to determine whether the Archdiocese or its senior managers committed state criminal acts either in their response to allegations that priests and other Archdiocese workers sexually abused children or in their failure to prevent such abuse. . . .The investigative team identified the following state statutory and common law crimes as those most likely applicable to the conduct of the Archdiocese and its senior managers:

- Accessory After the Fact to a Felony—requires proof beyond a reasonable doubt that the defendant rendered aid to a felon with the specific intent to help him avoid or escape detention, arrest, trial or punishment;
- Accessory Before the Fact to a Felony—requires proof beyond a reasonable doubt that the defendant shared the primary felon's state of mind and aided in the commission of the felony by counseling, hiring or encouraging the felony to be committed;
- Conspiracy—requires proof beyond a reasonable doubt that the defendant entered into an agreement with one or more people where the objective was criminal or unlawful, or the means of achieving the objective was criminal or unlawful; and
- Obstruction of Justice (Common Law)—requires proof beyond a reasonable doubt that the defendant knowingly interfered with the testimony or role of a witness in a judicial proceeding.

Additionally, because in certain circumstances state criminal law permits the prosecution of a corporation such as the Archdiocese for crimes committed by its agents, the investigative team identified the possibility of criminally prosecuting the Archdiocese for the sexual assaults committed against children by Archdiocese priests and church workers, or for being an accessory before or after the fact of such assaults. The evidence gathered during the course of the Attorney General's sixteen-month investigation does not provide a basis for bringing criminal charges against the Archdiocese or its senior managers. The investigation did not produce evidence that senior Archdiocese managers encouraged priests to abuse children, intended that priests would abuse children, intended to obstruct justice by helping abusive priests avoid arrest or punishment, interfered with the testimony or role of a witness in a judicial proceeding, or entered into unlawful agreements. Nor is there evidence that the Archdiocese benefited by priests sexually abusing children. . . .

Finding No. 3: The Investigation Did Produce Evidence That Widespread Sexual Abuse of Children Was Due to an Institutional Acceptance of Abuse and a Massive and Pervasive Failure of Leadership

1. Top Archdiocese Officials Knew the Extent of the Clergy Sexual Abuse Problem for Many Years Before It Became Known to the Public

There is overwhelming evidence that for many years Cardinal Law and his senior managers had direct, actual knowledge that substantial numbers of children in the Archdiocese had been sexually abused by substantial numbers of its priests. Members of the Cardinal's senior management team received complaints of abuse; determined the Archdiocese's response to the complaints; reported to the Cardinal and often sought his approval for their actions; and conferred with the Cardinal and sought his approval of their recommendations. Any claim by the Cardinal or the Archdiocese's senior managers that they did not know about the abuse suffered by, or the continuing threat to, children in the Archdiocese is simply not credible.

Although the public did not learn of the magnitude of the clergy sex abuse problem within the Archdiocese until 2002, Cardinal Law was generally aware of instances where priests had sexually abused children even before arriving in Boston, and he and his management team were aware of an ongoing problem in the Archdiocese of clergy sexual abuse of children almost from the time of his installation as Archbishop in 1984. Moreover, the Archdiocese dedicated substantial resources to dealing with abusive priests and their victims throughout Cardinal Law's tenure as Archbishop.

The Archdiocese's own record-keeping also shows the extent of information about the Archdiocese's history of clergy sexual abuse that was available to senior Archdiocese managers had they chosen to examine it. Although the files produced by the Archdiocese often were disorganized and had not been centrally maintained, it was evident that Archdiocese personnel, including senior managers within the Chancery, regularly created contemporaneous records documenting allegations by victims of clergy sexual abuse and the response to the allegations. These documents included handwritten and typed notes and memoranda of interviews of accused priests, victims and others with information relating to allegations; reports prepared by psychiatrists and notes of conversations with psychiatrists detailing their conclusions about accused priests; correspondence to and from victims and their families; notes detailing conversations with attorneys who represented accused priests and victims; and memoranda detailing the rationale for actions taken by senior management with respect to particular priests. . . .

2. The Archdiocese's Response to Reports of Sexual Abuse of Children, Including Maintaining Secrecy of Reports, Placed Children at Risk

Top Archdiocese officials, in response to reports of sexual abuse of children and aware of the magnitude of the sexual abuse problem, decided that they should conceal—from the parishes, the laity, law enforcement and the public—their knowledge of individual complaints of abuse and the long history of such complaints within the Archdiocese. By practice and policy, information concerning the complaints of abuse was shared with only a small number of senior Archdiocese officials, and only these officials were responsible for fashioning a response to the harm to children in the Archdiocese. As a result, the response by the Archdiocese reflected tragically misguided priorities. Top Archdiocese officials regularly addressed and supported the perceived needs of offending priests more than the needs of children who had been, or were at risk of being, abused.

As the chief executive of the Archdiocese, Cardinal Law was responsible for and approved many of the policies, procedures and practices concerning clergy sexual abuse cases in effect during his administration. . . .

Although Cardinal Law delegated responsibility for handling clergy sexual abuse matters, his senior managers kept the Cardinal apprised of such matters either directly or through the Vicar of Administration, who supervised the Secretary of Ministerial Personnel and the Delegate. Moreover, throughout his tenure, Cardinal Law personally participated in decisions concerning the final disposition of clergy sexual abuse cases, including decisions on whether to permit accused priests to return to ministry duties. For the most part, his involvement included the review and approval of recommendations on such matters from his Vicar for Administration or Secretary for Ministerial Personnel, or after adoption of the 1993 policy, from the Review Board.

As Archbishop, and therefore chief executive of the Archdiocese, Cardinal Law bears ultimate responsibility for the tragic treatment of children that occurred during his tenure. His responsibility for this tragedy is not, however, simply that of the person in charge. He had direct knowledge of the scope, duration and severity of the crisis experienced by children in the Archdiocese; he participated directly in crucial decisions concerning the assignment of abusive priests, decisions that typically increased the risk to children; and he knew or should have known that the policies, practices and procedures of the Archdiocese for addressing sexual misconduct were woefully inadequate given the magnitude of the problem.

Cardinal Law by no means bears sole responsibility for the harm done to children in the Archdiocese. With rare exception, none of the Cardinal's senior managers advised him to take any of the steps that might have ended the systemic abuse of children. Rather, they generally preserved the key elements of the culture within the Archdiocese that sustained this crisis.

[Summaries of the roles and conduct of senior Archdiocese officials who served Cardinal Law omitted.]

3. The Archdiocese Did Not Notify Law Enforcement Authorities of Clergy Sexual Abuse Allegations

Throughout the decades that the Archdiocese was dealing with a large and growing problem of clergy sexual abuse of children, it steadfastly maintained a practice of not reporting allegations of sexual abuse of children to law enforcement or child protection authorities. This practice continued even after the Archdiocese created the Office of the Delegate, and even when the Archdiocese was dealing with priests who continued to abuse children after unsuccessful intervention by the Archdiocese. In fact, the Attorney General's investigation revealed only two instances during Cardinal Law's administration when the Archdiocese affirmatively reached out to law enforcement—in 1993 the Archdiocese reported to the Middlesex County District Attorney's Office that a pastor believed he had observed another priest (Father Paul Manning) having sex with a young boy, and in 1997 the Archdiocese notified law enforcement of allegations against Father Paul Mahan.

During the course of the Attorney General's investigation, Archdiocese personnel gave different explanations for why they did not report abuse allegations to public authorities, including:

- State law did not mandate that priests report suspected child abuse to law enforcement or child protection authorities;
- The Archdiocese felt less compelled to report abuse because most clergy sexual abuse was reported years after the abuse had occurred and after the victim had reached adulthood;
- Because most abuse was reported years after it occurred, the Archdiocese managers were less inclined to report the abuse because of their belief that the state's applicable statutes of limitation barred criminal prosecutions;
- The Archdiocese believed that Canon Law—the church's internal policies and procedures—prohibited it from reporting abuse to civil authorities in most instances;
- The Archdiocese was concerned about the impact that reporting to civil authorities would have on the alleged abuser's reputation and well-being;
- The Archdiocese believed that reporting allegations of abuse would violate victims' privacy rights and undermine the relationship between victims and the Archdiocese;
- The Archdiocese believed that reporting allegations of abuse to civil authorities would make other victims more reluctant to come forward;
- The Archdiocese believed that victims, and not the Archdiocese, should make the decision whether to report alleged abuse to civil authorities; and
- The Archdiocese believed that reporting of clergy sexual abuse of children to civil authorities would cause scandal, and the resulting publicity would harm the reputation of the Church.

If the Archdiocese had adopted a policy of reporting abuse allegations to civil authorities, it is likely that the combined effect of the ensuing law enforcement investigations and public scrutiny would have reduced significantly the number of children who ultimately were victimized.

4. Archdiocese Officials Did Not Provide All Relevant Information to Law Enforcement Authorities During Criminal Investigations

In the very few cases where allegations of sexual abuse of children were communicated to law enforcement, senior Archdiocese managers remained committed to their primary objectives—safeguarding the well-being of priests and the institution over the welfare of children and preventing scandal—and often failed to advise law enforcement authorities of all relevant information they possessed, including the full extent of the alleged abuser's history of abusing children. The Archdiocese's practice of providing minimal information and support to law enforcement authorities resulted in investigative and prosecutorial decisions being made on less than complete information. . . .

5. The Archdiocese Failed to Conduct Thorough Investigations of Clergy Sexual Abuse Allegations

Under both Cardinal Law and Cardinal Medeiros before him, the Archdiocese repeatedly failed to thoroughly investigate allegations of clergy sexual abuse of children, including the facts of the alleged abuse and the history of the alleged abuser. While the practices and policies of the Archdiocese for investigating allegations of clergy sexual abuse changed and evolved during Cardinal Law's administration, several remained constant. The Archdiocese did not investigate general, anonymous, vague and third-party complaints. Because secrecy remained a top priority, the Archdiocese did not explore potential sources of information concerning allegations of clergy sexual abuse or accused priests' prior conduct. . . .

6. The Archdiocese Placed Children at Risk by Transferring Abusive Priests to Other Parishes

During Cardinal Medeiros' tenure as Archbishop and during the early years of Cardinal Law's administration, the Archdiocese's response to allegations of clergy sexual abuse of children included at times quietly transferring the alleged abuser to a different parish in the Archdiocese, sometimes without disclosing the abuse to the new parish or restricting the abusive priest's ministry functions. These transfers tended to appease the concerns of victims because the abusive priests no longer were in their communities, and scandal was avoided because there was no public discussion of, or reporting on, the abuse. However, this practice of reassigning abusive priests placed new children at risk and evidenced the Archdiocese's failure to set the protection of children as a higher priority than protecting the well-being of abusive priests.

[Examples of priests being transferred to new parish assignments after the Archdiocese was put on notice of allegations of sexual abuse omitted.]

Conclusion

One of the ways we mark the progress of our society is how we protect our children. In keeping with this essential obligation, the Attorney General sought to address the decisions and practices that led to the massive and prolonged sexual abuse of children by priests assigned to the Roman Catholic Archdiocese of Boston. Based on that effort, the Attorney General has concluded that the widespread abuse of children was due to an institutional acceptance of abuse and a massive and pervasive failure of leadership. For at least six decades, three successive Archbishops, their Bishops and others in positions of authority within the Archdiocese operated with tragically misguided priorities. They chose to protect the image and reputation of their institution rather than the safety and well-being of the children entrusted to their care. They acted with a misguided devotion to secrecy. And they failed to break their code of silence even when the magnitude of what had occurred would have alerted any reasonable, responsible manager that help was needed.

Still, the failure of the Archdiocese leadership has been too massive and too prolonged, and the Archdiocese has yet to demonstrate a commitment to reform proportional to the tragedy it perpetrated. Therefore, the Attorney General has also concluded that it is far too soon to know whether the Archdiocese has undertaken the types of changes necessary to ensure that abuse has stopped and will not reoccur in the future. New laws enacted by our Legislature create important tools to prevent widespread and systematic abuse of children, and dedicated prosecutors are ready and willing to enforce those new laws. However, until the Archdiocese clearly demonstrates an understanding of what occurred and how to provide a safe environment for its children, there must be a period of vigilance. This vigilance must come from the public and its officials as well as from members of the church, including priests and the laity. This vigilance must continue until the end of this tragic episode is clear and unmistakable.

To ensure the safety and well-being of children in the care and custody of the Archdiocese and to mark the day when special vigilance is no longer necessary:

1. The Archdiocese Must Demonstrate Over Time Its Understanding That It Is Criminal to Sexually Abuse a Child

The Archdiocese must recognize the enormous harm that results from the sexual abuse of a child. The child sexual abuse in the Archdiocese has affected untold numbers of lives and caused horrific pain and confusion for the victims and their families. That this rape or abuse occurred at the hands of a religious authority figure has only multiplied the cost to the victims. The Archdiocese must demonstrate that it understands that any person who sexually abuses a child commits a criminal offense by effective training, compliance and enforcement of the new legal obligations on clergy and other church workers to be mandated reporters of child sexual abuse.

2. The Archdiocese Must End the Culture of Secrecy That Has Protected the Institution at the Expense of Children

The Archdiocese must adopt a new spirit of openness when it comes to issues related to the protection of children. That includes active involvement of the laity in the implementation of all policies and procedures designed to protect children; communicating fully with pastors, parishioners, and the public concerning allegations of abuse against priests or church workers; full cooperation with law enforcement in any investigation of alleged abuse; regular public reporting on the progress and implementation of new policies and procedures; and seeking advice and assistance from law enforcement and child protection experts on preventing child sexual abuse and addressing allegations of abuse.

3. The Archdiocese Must Adopt and Implement Comprehensive and Effective Measures to Prevent the Sexual Abuse of Children

Education and training are fundamental aspects of any abuse prevention program. The Archdiocese should direct all necessary resources to create and implement sexual abuse education programs for adolescents, teenagers and religious education students on what constitutes sex abuse and how to respond. The Archdiocese must train all priests, employees, volunteers and adult parishioners to recognize and respond to and report signs of abuse. The Archdiocese must also assure that applicants to the priesthood undergo psychological testing and background checks and must establish a screening and selection process for all other staff, employees or volunteers to identify potential abusers.

4. The Archdiocese Must Appropriately Respond to All Allegations of Child Sexual Abuse

The Archdiocese must respond promptly to allegations of sexual abuse, including anonymous and third-party complaints, quickly and thoroughly resolve those allegations, and then impose appropriate sanctions. The Archdiocese must immediately report all allegations of child sexual abuse to law enforcement and child protection authorities and remove anyone in a position of authority who fails to do so. The Archdiocese must acknowledge that anyone who sexually abuses a child must be removed and establish a structured and clearly defined oversight and monitoring program for those priests removed or restricted from ministry because of sexual abuse.

5. The Archdiocese Must Be Accountable at Every Level of the Institution for Ensuring the Protection of Children

The Archdiocese must establish a code of conduct that sets boundaries and guidelines for appropriate interactions between priests and other Archdiocese personnel and children. With these standards established, the Archdiocese must hold management, priests, employees and volunteers responsible for complying with all policies and set forth a progressive disciplinary process and penalties for failure to comply. The Archdiocese must appoint members of its various boards and offices related to the protection of children who have relevant experience and who are capable of exercising independent judgment and who are perceived as independent. The Archdiocese must undergo regular independent audits to assure institutional compliance with each and every provision of the policies and procedures.

It is not enough for the Archdiocese of Boston simply to declare a commitment to the protection of children. The Archdiocese must live that commitment through its policies and demonstrated practices. Only when the Archdiocese makes all of these child protection practices a part of its everyday dealings will there exist reliable indicators to declare with confidence that the children within the Archdiocese are safe.

For years, deference was afforded to the Archdiocese when it came to the protection of children. In many ways, that climate allowed these abuses to continue unchecked for so long. Should there be any deference in the future, let it be to the notion that the protection of children comes before all else and to the proposition that abuse of this kind against children must never happen again. . . .

Source: Commonwealth of Massachusetts. Office of the Attorney General. *The Sexual Abuse of Children in the Roman Catholic Archdiocese of Boston: A Report by the Attorney General.* Boston: July 23, 2003. www.ago.state.ma.us/archdiocese.pdf (accessed January 22, 2004).

Joint Congressional Panel on September 11 Attacks

July 24, 2003

INTRODUCTION

The final version of a congressional study of the September 11, 2001, terrorist attacks against the United States offered new details of the conspiracy by the al Qaeda terrorist network to hijack commercial airliners and fly them into the World Trade Center buildings in New York and the Pentagon (and possibly the White House). The report was released July 24, 2003, after a seven-month review by the Bush administration of the classified information on which it was based. The administration withheld numerous pieces of information from the public, including a twenty-eight-page section that reportedly discussed possible support for the al Qaeda hijackers by people with ties to the government of Saudi Arabia.

Also during 2003, an independent federal commission began its work on a more broadly focused study of U.S. vulnerabilities that made the attacks possible. That commission, mandated by Congress and reluctantly accepted by the Bush administration in 2002, engaged in running battles with the administration over access to classified information it said was needed for its study.

Among the new facts about the September 11 attacks that emerged during the year was one of symbolic importance. The New York City mayor's office in October said a revised tally showed that 2,752 people had died in the attack on the World Trade Center towers—40 fewer than the number that was officially declared a year earlier. Officials offered several explanations for the reduction of 40 names from the list. Some of the supposed victims had been found alive; some names had been duplicated; no evidence could be found that some of the named victims ever existed; and the names of some "victims" had been fraudulently reported, possibly to secure death benefits.

Another milestone came December 22, when the federal government stopped accepting new applications for a compensation fund for victims of the attacks. Attorney Kenneth R. Feinberg, the fund's administrator, said 95 percent of families eligible to file claims had done so by the deadline. The fund provided payments, averaging $1.5 million for each victim's family.

Some survivors had criticized the fund, in part because the proceeds from life insurance and other death benefits were deducted from the payments, and also because they could receive payment only after waiving the legal right to sue the airlines, government agencies, or others on grounds of negligence. *(Background, Historic Documents of 2001, p. 614)*

The Final "Final" Congressional Report

The congressional report was prepared by a special joint panel of the House and Senate Intelligence committees. The committees had formed the panel to investigate widespread charges that U.S. intelligence and law enforcement agencies had failed to uncover and act on available evidence of the September 11 conspiracy in time to prevent the attacks. The joint panel issued what it called its "final" report on December 11, 2002. That document argued that bureaucratic failures were largely responsible for numerous lapses by U.S. agencies, notably the FBI. The panel recommended nineteen specific changes in U.S. counterterrorism operations, the most controversial of which was requiring all intelligence agencies to report to a single director. *(Background, Historic Documents of 2002, p. 990)*

The report released in December 2002 contained the panel's recommendations and many details of findings from its hearings and its review of government documents. Much of the 800-plus-page report was withheld at that time, however, pending the Bush administration's review of the classified information contained in it. That review reportedly resulted in numerous disputes between the congressional panel and the administration over what information could be made public. The process was completed by mid-July, and on July 24 the panel published what it again called its "final" report that included some of the information that had been deleted seven months earlier. Even so, dozens of pages in the latest version showed blank spaces where classified information had been deleted.

The newly declassified information did not provide definitive answers to the fundamental questions about how and why U.S. intelligence and law enforcement agencies failed to detect the al Qaeda hijacking conspiracy beforehand. The panel had concluded that bureaucratic obstacles, misunderstandings, lack of follow-through, and simple human errors had prevented the agencies from assembling bits of information that had been collected into a coherent analysis. No single piece of information could have alerted the government to the conspiracy in time to prevent the attacks, the panel said: "The joint inquiry did not uncover a smoking gun."

New information in the report offered some tantalizing tidbits about the September 11 conspiracy and what the government knew about it beforehand. The most solid information in the report dealt with the handling—or mishandling—of information about two Saudi men, Khalid al-Mihdhar and

Nawaf al-Hazmi. The CIA had learned that the two men had attended a meeting in Malaysia of al Qaeda operatives early in 2000 and that al-Mihdhar had later entered the United States (al-Hazmi apparently entered the United States undetected by the CIA). In the summer of 2000, the report said, an FBI informant gave the agency information about the two men, who were then living in San Diego. The FBI failed to grasp the significance of this information, however, in part because the CIA had not told the FBI about their al Qaeda connections. The names of the two men were not put on the government's "watch list" of suspected terrorists until August 2001, which was too late to prevent their entry into the United States. At that point the government might have been able to locate the men quickly through their use of credit cards, but the warning about them was not passed on to the Treasury Department and FBI agencies that had the authority and resources to take such steps. The two were among the hijackers whose plane crashed into the Pentagon.

The congressional panel also confirmed, and expanded upon, numerous news reports after the September 11 attacks that intelligence agencies had learned, beginning at least in 1994, of vague plans by terrorists to use airplanes as weapons against U.S. targets, perhaps CIA headquarters outside Washington, an embassy, or an airport. Information about these possible plans was never shared with other government agencies, including the Federal Aviation Administration, which was responsible at the time for aviation security. Intelligence agencies picked up worrisome information in the summer of 2001 that al Qaeda leader Osama bin Laden was planning a major terrorist attack against the United States, the report said. President George Bush was alerted to this threat on August 6, when his daily intelligence summary noted a report that bin Laden supporters were "planning attacks in the United States with explosives." None of the information specifically cited dates or places for the possible attacks, however.

Summarizing its findings, the panel said the U.S. intelligence community "failed to capitalize on both the individual and collective significance of available information that appears relevant to the events of September 11. As a result, the community missed opportunities to disrupt the September 11 plot by denying entry to or detaining would-be hijackers; to at least try to unravel the plot through surveillance or other investigative work within the United States; and, finally, to generate a heightened state of alert and thus harden the homeland against attack."

The joint panel did not attempt to blame individual officials, arguing that the important lesson of its inquiry was that the government needed better coordination, and more cooperation among agencies, in fighting terrorism. Sen. Richard Shelby, R-Ala., vigorously dissented from this approach and directed his anger at several current and former high-level officials, in particular George J. Tenet, the director of the CIA.

Release of the report set off a brief furor because of what was not in the public version: a twenty-eight-page section discussing possible foreign support for the al Qaeda terrorists. News accounts, based on information leaked by administration and congressional sources, said much of the still-classified section dealt with aid that may have been provided by citizens or even officials of Saudi Arabia. Fifteen of the hijackers were Saudi citizens. Congressional investigators—and even the Saudi government—asked the administration to declassify the twenty-eight pages so they could be made public, but President Bush refused. *(Saudi Arabian connection, p. 227)*

Independent Commission Begins Work

The broader inquiry into the September 11 attacks by a federal commission formally began its work on January 26 after a controversy over its leadership. President Bush had appointed former secretary of state Henry A. Kissinger as the commission's chairman, and congressional Democrats had appointed former senator George Mitchell as vice chairman. Both men resigned because of conflicts with their business interests or schedules, and replacements were not named until late December 2002: former New Jersey governor Thomas H. Kean as chairman and former House member Lee H. Hamilton as vice chairman. The commission's formal title was the National Commission on Terrorist Attacks Upon the United States.

The commission held its first public hearings in April and announced plans to present a draft report by May 2004. On July 8 the commission complained about lack of cooperation from the Bush administration, noting that the Pentagon, the Justice Department, and some other agencies had been slow in responding to its requests for information. That complaint apparently got the administration's attention, and on September 23 the panel was able to report "significantly improved" cooperation by government agencies. Even so, the commission later said it continued to find resistance to its requests for information at the White House and the Pentagon. For months, the White House refused to turn over to the commission the full intelligence reports that the president received each day, in particular those given him prior to September 11 dealing with possible terrorist threats against the United States. After the panel went public with its complaints in late October, Bush promised cooperation, and the commission announced on November 12 that it would get access to the material. The Pentagon proved more resistant, refusing to turn over to the commission documents and other information dealing with how the North American Aerospace Defense Command, known as Norad, responded to the attacks on September 11. The commission issued a subpoena for that information on November 11.

One commission member, former senator Max Cleland, a Georgia Democrat, resigned in November, saying he was frustrated by the administration's delay in giving the commission necessary information. He was replaced by another former Democratic senator, Robert Kerrey of Nebraska.

Dirty Air at Ground Zero

Yet another controversy stemming from the September 11 attacks erupted in late August 2003 when the inspector general of the Environmental Protection Agency (EPA) reported that the Bush White House had ordered the agency to issue misleading statements about the air quality in southern Manhattan after the destruction of the World Trade Center towers. The inspector's report, issued August 22, said the EPA had repeatedly told New Yorkers that the air was safe to breathe, even though it had no solid information to back up that statement. The collapse of the trade center towers generated intense levels of smoke and dust that coated large parts of the city. Tens of thousands of offices and apartments remained covered in dust for months, causing respiratory ailments and other diseases in several thousand people, many of them rescue and recovery workers,

In its August 22 report, inspector general Nikki L. Tinsley said the White House "convinced EPA to add reassuring statements and delete cautionary ones" in its news releases. The EPA issued nine statements between September 11 and the end of 2001, all assuring the public that New York City's air was safe, but it lacked "sufficient data and analysis" for its statements, Tinsley said. James Connaughton, chairman of the White House Council on Environmental Quality, defended the administration's statements after the attacks and said the EPA did "an incredible job" under difficult circumstances.

At a hearing in New York on October 29, a House subcommittee learned that 75 percent of the nearly eight thousand recovery workers who were examined by a federal program had shown persistent respiratory problems. Forty percent of the workers also suffered from some form of mental health problems, and many of the workers did not have health insurance, the panel was told.

Following are excerpts from "Joint Inquiry into Intelligence Community Activities Before and After the Terrorist Attacks of September 11, 2001," a report provided to Congress in December 2002 and publicly released July 24, 2003, by the Senate Select Committee on Intelligence and the House Permanent Select Committee on Intelligence. Brackets followed by the word deleted *contained classified material that was deleted before public release, paragraphs that begin and end with brackets identify sections that were rewritten in whole or in part before public release to remove classified information, and double sets of brackets indicate material added by the editors.*

"Intelligence Community Activities Before and After September 11, 2001"

Part One—Findings and Conclusions

I. The Joint Inquiry

In February 2002, the Senate Select Committee on Intelligence and the House Permanent Select Committee on Intelligence agreed to conduct a Joint Inquiry into the activities of the U.S. Intelligence Community in connection with the terrorist attacks perpetrated against our nation on September 11, 2001. Reflecting the magnitude of the events of that day, the Committees' decision was unprecedented in Congressional history: for the first time, two permanent committees, one from the House and one from the Senate, would join together to conduct a single, unified inquiry.

The three principal goals of this Joint Inquiry were to:

- conduct a factual review of what the Intelligence Community knew or should have known prior to September 11, 2001, regarding the international terrorist threat to the United States, to include the scope and nature of any possible international terrorist attacks against the United States and its interests;
- identify and examine any systemic problems that may have impeded the Intelligence Community in learning of or preventing these attacks in advance; and
- make recommendations to improve the Intelligence Community's ability to identify and prevent future international terrorist attacks. . . .

II. The Context

September 11, 2001, while indelible in our collective memory, was by no means America's first confrontation with international terrorism. Although the nature of the threat had evolved considerably over time, the United States and its interests have long been prime terrorist targets. For example, the bombings of the Marine barracks and the U.S. Embassy in Beirut, Lebanon in 1983 should have served as a clear warning that terrorist groups were not reluctant to attack U.S. interests when they believed such attacks would further their ends.

The Intelligence Community also had considerable evidence before September 11 that international terrorists were capable of, and had planned, major terrorist strikes within the United States. The 1993 attack on the World Trade Center confirmed this point, as did the 1993 plots to bomb New York City landmarks and the 1999 arrest at the U.S.-Canadian border of Ahmad Ressam, who intended to bomb the Los Angeles International Airport.

Usama Bin Ladin's role in international terrorism had also been well known for some time before September 11. He initially came to the attention of the Intelligence Community in the early 1990s as a financier of terrorism. However, Bin Ladin's own words soon provided evidence of the steadily escalating threat to the United States he and his organization posed. In August 1996, he issued a *fatwa*—or religious decree—authorizing attacks on Western military targets in the Arabian Peninsula. In February 1998, Bin Ladin issued a second *fatwa* authorizing attacks on U.S. civilians and military personnel anywhere in the world. Bin Ladin's *fatwas* cited the U.S. military presence in Saudi Arabia and the Persian Gulf, the Palestinian issue, and U.S. support for Israel as justification for ordering these attacks.

The gradual emergence of Bin Ladin and others like him marked a change from the type of terrorist threat that had traditionally confronted the Intelligence Community. Throughout the Cold War, radical left and ethno-nationalist groups had carried out most terrorist acts. Many of these groups were state-sponsored. The first bombing of the World Trade Center in February 1993, however, led to a growing recognition in the Intelligence Community of a new type of terrorism that did not conform to the Cold War model: violent radical Islamic cells, not linked to any specific country, but united in anti-American zeal. A July 1995 National Intelligence Estimate noted the danger of this "new breed". By 1996, agencies within the Intelligence Community were aware that Bin Ladin was organizing these kinds of cells, and they began to collect intelligence on him actively. . . .

The August 1998 bombing of two American embassies in East Africa definitively put the U.S. Intelligence Community on notice of the danger that Bin Ladin and his network, al-Qa'ida, posed. The attacks showed that Bin Ladin's network was capable of carrying out very bloody, simultaneous attacks and inflicting mass casualties. In December 1998, George Tenet, the Director of Central Intelligence, gave a chilling direction to his deputies at the CIA:

> "We must now enter a new phase in our effort against Bin Ladin. . . . We are at war. . . . I want no resources or people spared in this effort, either inside the CIA or the [[Intelligence]] Community."

Discovering and disrupting al-Qa'ida's plans proved exceptionally difficult, however. Details of major terrorist plots were not widely shared within the al-Qa'ida organization, making it hard to develop the intelligence necessary to preempt or disrupt attacks. Senior al-Qa'ida officials were sensitive to operational security, and many al-Qa'ida members enjoyed sanctuary in Afghanistan, where they could safely plan and train for their missions. Finally, senior members of al-Qa'ida were skilled and purposeful: they learned from their mistakes and were flexible in organization and planning.

Nonetheless, particularly after the bombings in East Africa, the Intelligence Community amassed a body of information detailing Bin Ladin's ties to terrorist activities against U.S. interests around the world. Armed with that information, prior to September 11, 2001, U.S. Government counterterrorist efforts to identify and disrupt terrorist operations focused to a substantial degree on Bin Ladin and his network. The Intelligence Community achieved some successes—in some cases, major successes—in these operations. In other cases, little came of the Intelligence Community's efforts.

By late 2000 and 2001, the Intelligence Community was engaged in an extensive, shadowy struggle against al-Qa'ida. Despite such efforts, Bin Ladin carried out successful and devastating attacks against Americans and citizens of other nations, including the bombing of USS Cole in Yemen in October 2000 and the attacks on the World Trade Center and the Pentagon on September 11, 2001.

III. Findings and Conclusions

A. Factual Findings

In reviewing the documents, interview reports, and witness testimony gathered during this Inquiry, the Joint Inquiry has sought to determine what information was available to the Intelligence Community prior to September 11, 2001 that was relevant to the attacks that occurred on that day. The record that has been established through this Inquiry leads to the following factual findings and conclusions.

1. *Finding:* While the Intelligence Community had amassed a great deal of valuable intelligence regarding Usama Bin Ladin and his terrorist activities, none of it identified the time, place, and specific nature of the attacks that were planned for September 11, 2001. Nonetheless, the Community did have information that was clearly relevant to the September 11 attacks, particularly when considered for its collective significance.

Discussion: This Inquiry has uncovered no intelligence information in the possession of the Intelligence Community prior to the attacks of September 11 that, if fully considered, would have provided specific, advance warning of the details of those attacks. The task of the Inquiry was not, however, limited to a search for the legendary, and often absent, "smoking gun." The facts surrounding the September 11 attacks demonstrate the importance of strengthening the Intelligence Community's ability to detect and prevent terrorist attacks in what appears to be the more common, but also far more difficult, scenario. Within the huge volume of intelligence reporting that was available prior to September 11, there were various threads and pieces of information that, at least in retrospect, are both relevant and significant. The degree to which the Community was or was not able to build on that information to discern the bigger picture successfully is a critical part of the context for the September 11 attacks and is addressed in the findings that follow.

2. *Finding:* During the spring and summer of 2001, the Intelligence Community experienced a significant increase in information indicating that Bin Ladin and al-Qa'ida intended to strike against U.S. interests in the very near future.

Discussion: The National Security Agency (NSA), for example, reported at least 33 communications indicating a possible, imminent terrorist attack in 2001. Senior U.S. Government officials were advised by the Intelligence Community on June 28 and July 10, 2001, that the attacks were expected, among other things, to "have dramatic consequences on governments or cause major casualties" and that "[a]ttack preparations have been made. Attack will occur with little or no warning."

Some Community personnel described the increase in threat reporting as unprecedented, at least in their own experience. The Intelligence Community advised senior policymakers of the likelihood of an attack but, given the non-specific nature of the reporting, could not identify when, where, and how an attack would take place. Deputy Secretary of State Richard Armitage, in his testimony, described his recollection of the threat and the U.S. Government's response:

> "We issued between January and September nine warnings, five of them global, because of the threat information we were receiving from the intelligence agencies in the summer, when [DCI] George Tenet was around town literally pounding on desks saying, something is happening, this is an unprecedented level of threat information. He didn't know where it was going to happen, but he knew that it was coming."

3. *Finding:* Beginning in 1998 and continuing into the summer of 2001, the Intelligence Community received a modest, but relatively steady, stream of intelligence reporting that indicated the possibility of terrorist attacks within the United States. Nonetheless, testimony and interviews confirm that it was the general view of the Intelligence Community, in the spring and summer of 2001, that

the threatened Bin Ladin attacks would most likely occur against U.S. interests overseas, despite indications of plans and intentions to attack in the domestic United States.

Discussion: Communications intercepts, the arrests of suspected terrorists in the Middle East and Europe, and a credible report of a plan to attack a U.S. Embassy in the Middle East shaped the Community's thinking about where an attack was likely to occur. While former FBI Director Louis Freeh testified that the FBI was "intensely focused" on terrorist targets within the United States, the FBI's Executive Assistant Director for Counterterrorism testified that in 2001 he thought there was a high probability—"98 percent"—that the attack would be overseas. The latter was the clear majority view, despite the fact that the Intelligence Community had information suggesting that Bin Ladin had planned, and was capable of, conducting attacks within the domestic United States.

This stream of reporting began as early as 1998 and continued during the time of heightened threat levels in 2001. For example, the Community received reporting in May 2001 that Bin Ladin supporters were planning to infiltrate the United States to conduct terrorist operations and, in late summer 2001, that an al-Qa'ida associate was considering mounting terrorist attacks within the United States.

[Of particular interest to the Joint Inquiry was whether and to what extent the President received threat-specific warnings during this period. The Joint Inquiry was advised by a representative of the Intelligence Community that, in August 2001, a closely held intelligence report for senior government officials included information that Bin Ladin had wanted to conduct attacks in the United States since 1997. The information included discussion of the arrest of Ahmed Ressam in December 1999 at the U.S.-Canadian border and the 1998 bombings of U.S. embassies in Kenya and Tanzania. It mentioned that members of al-Qa'ida, including some U.S. citizens, had resided in or traveled to the United States for years and that the group apparently maintained a support structure here. The report cited uncorroborated information obtained and disseminated in 1998 that Bin Ladin wanted to hijack airplanes to gain the release of U.S.-held extremists; FBI judgments about patterns of activity consistent with preparations for hijackings or other types of attacks; as well as information acquired in May 2001 that indicated a group of Bin Ladin supporters was planning attacks in the United States with explosives].

4. *Finding:* From at least 1994, and continuing into the summer of 2001, the Intelligence Community received information indicating that terrorists were contemplating, among other means of attack, the use of aircraft as weapons. This information did not stimulate any specific Intelligence Community assessment of, or collective U.S. Government reaction to, this form of threat.

Discussion: [While the credibility of the sources was sometimes questionable and the information often sketchy, the Inquiry confirmed that the Intelligence Community did receive intelligence reporting concerning the potential use of aircraft as weapons. For example, the Community received information in 1998 about a Bin Ladin operation that would involve flying an explosive-laden aircraft into a U.S. airport and, in summer 2001, about a plot to bomb a U.S. embassy from an airplane or crash an airplane into it. The FBI and CIA were also aware that convicted terrorist Abdul Hakim Murad and several others had discussed the possibility of crashing an airplane into CIA Headquarters as part of "the Bojinka Plot" in the Philippines, discussed later in this report. Some, but apparently not all, of these reports were disseminated within the Intelligence Community and to other agencies].

The Transportation Security Administration, for example, advised the Committees that the Federal Aviation Administration (FAA) had not received three of these reports, that two others were received by the FAA but through State Department cables, and that one report was received by the FAA, but only after September 11, 2001. Many policymakers and U.S. Government officials apparently remained unaware of this kind of potential threat and the Intelligence Community did not produce any specific assessments of the likelihood that terrorists would in fact use airplanes as weapons. For example, former National Security Advisor Sandy Berger testified before these Committees that:

> "I don't recall being presented with any specific threat information about an attack of this nature [the use of aircraft as weapons] or any alert highlighting this threat or indicating it was any more likely than any other."

That testimony is consistent with the views publicly expressed by the current National Security Advisor, Condoleeza Rice, shortly after the September 11 attacks. Similarly, Deputy Under Secretary of Defense Paul Wolfowitz testified that he had not been made aware of this type of potential threat:

> "I don't recall any warning of the possibility of a mass casualty attack using civilian airliners or any information that would have led us to contemplate the possibility of our shooting down a civilian airliner."

Even within the Intelligence Community, the possibility of using aircraft as weapons was apparently not widely known. At the FBI, for instance, the FBI Phoenix field office agent who wrote the so-called "Phoenix memo" testified that he was aware of the plot to crash a plane into CIA Headquarters, but not the other reports of terrorist groups considering the use of aircraft as weapons. The Chief of the Radical Fundamentalist Unit in the FBI's Counterterrorism Division also confirmed, in an Joint Inquiry interview, that he was not aware of such reports.

5. *Finding:* **Although relevant information that is significant in retrospect regarding the attacks was available to the Intelligence Community prior to September 11, 2001, the Community too often failed to focus on that information and consider and appreciate its collective significance in terms of a probable terrorist attack. Neither did the Intelligence Community demonstrate sufficient initiative in coming to grips with the new transnational threats. Some significant pieces of information in the vast stream of data being collected were overlooked, some were not recognized as potentially significant at the time and therefore not disseminated, and some required additional action on the part of foreign governments before a direct connection to the hijackers could have been established. For all those reasons, the Intelligence Community failed to capitalize fully on available, and potentially important, information. The sub-findings below identify each category of this information.**

[Terrorist Communications in 1999]

5.a. [During 1999, the National Security Agency obtained a number of communications—none of which included specific detail regarding the time, place or nature of the September 11 attacks—connecting individuals to terrorism who were identified, after September 11, 2001, as participants in the attacks that occurred on that day].

Discussion: [In early 1999, the National Security Agency (NSA) analyzed communications involving a suspected terrorist facility in the Middle East that had previously been linked to al-Qa'ida activities directed against U.S. interests. Information obtained [deleted] included, among other things, the full name of future hijacker Nawaf al-Hazmi. Beyond the fact that the communications involved a suspected terrorist facility in the Middle East, the communications did not, in NSA's view at the time, feature any other terrorist-related information. The information was not published because the individuals mentioned in the communications were unknown to NSA, and, according to NSA, the information did not meet NSA's reporting thresholds. NSA has explained that these thresholds are flexible, sometimes changing daily, and consist of several factors, including: the priority of the intelligence requirement; the apparent intelligence value of the information; the level of customer interest in the topic; the current situation; and the volume of intercept to be analyzed and reported].

[During the summer of 1999, NSA analyzed additional communications involving a suspected terrorist facility in the Middle East that included the name of Khaled. At about the same time, the name Khallad also came to NSA's attention. This information did not meet NSA's reporting thresholds and thus was not disseminated]. [In late 1999, NSA analyzed communications involving a suspected terrorist facility in the

Middle East that included the names of Khaled and Nawaf. At this time, NSA did not associate the latter individual with the Nawaf al-Hazmi it had learned about in early 1999. Later, the two individuals [deleted] were determined to be Khalid al-Mihdhar and Nawaf al-Hazmi, now known to be two of the September 11 hijackers. [deleted]. This information was passed to the CIA as well as the FBI in late 1999. In early 2000, NSA also [deleted] passed additional information about Khalid to the CIA, FBI, FAA, the Departments of State, Treasury, Transportation, and Justice, and others in the U.S. Government].

Malaysia Meeting and Travel of al-Qa'ida Operatives to the United States

5.b. The Intelligence Community acquired additional, and highly significant, information regarding Khalid al-Mihdhar and Nawaf al-Hazmi in early 2000. Critical parts of the information concerning al-Mihdhar and al-Hazmi lay dormant within the Intelligence Community for as long as eighteen months, at the very time when plans for the September 11 attacks were proceeding. The CIA missed repeated opportunities to act based on the information in its possession that these two Bin Ladin-associated terrorists were traveling to the United States, and to add their names to watchlists.

Discussion: [By early January 2000, CIA knew al-Mihdhar's full name and that it was likely Nawaf's last name was al-Hazmi, knew that they had attended what was believed to be a gathering of al-Qa'ida associates in Malaysia, was aware that they had been traveling together, and had documents indicating that al-Mihdhar held a U.S. B-1B-2 multiple entry visa that would allow him to travel to and from the United States until April 6, 2000. CIA arranged surveillance of the meeting and the DCI was kept informed as the operation progressed].

Despite having all this information, and despite the republication of CTC guidance regarding watchlisting procedures in December 1999 (see Appendix, "CTC Watchlisting Guidance—December 1999"), CIA did not add the names of these two individuals to the State Department, INS, and U.S. Customs Service watchlists that are used to deny individuals entry into the United States. The weight of the record also suggests that, despite providing the FBI with other, less critical, information about the Malaysia meeting, the CIA did not advise the FBI about al-Mihdhar's U.S. visa and the very real possibility that he would travel to the United States. The CIA stated its belief that the visa information was sent to the FBI and produced a cable indicating that this had been done.

The FBI, for its part, had no record the visa information was received. Although the facts of the Malaysia meeting were included in several briefings for senior FBI officials, including FBI Director Louis Freeh, no record could be found that the visa information was part of these briefings.

[On March 5, 2000, CIA Headquarters received a cable from an overseas CIA station indicating that Nawaf al-Hazmi had traveled to Los Angeles, California on January 15, 2000. The following day, March 6, CIA Headquarters received a message from another CIA station noting its "interest" in the first cable's "information that a member of this group had traveled to the U.S." The CIA did not act on either message, again did not watchlist al-Hazmi or al-Mihdhar, and, again, did not advise the FBI of their possible presence in the United States. In 2000, these same two individuals had numerous contacts with an active FBI counterterrorism informant while they were living in San Diego, California].

On January 4, 2001, CIA acquired information that Khallad, a principal planner in the bombing of *USS Cole*, had, along with al-Mihdhar and al-Hazmi, attended the January 2000 meeting in Malaysia. Again, the CIA did not watchlist these two individuals. At the time, al-Mihdhar was abroad, but al-Hazmi was still in the United States. FBI Director Robert Mueller testified to the Joint Inquiry that: "al-Mihdhar's role in the September 11 plot . . . before his re-entry into the United States may well have been that of the coordinator and organizer of . . . the non-pilot hijackers."

In May 2001, the CIA provided FBI Headquarters with photographs taken in Malaysia, including one of al-Mihdhar, for purposes of identifying another *Cole* bombing suspect. Although the CIA told FBI Headquarters about the Malaysia meeting and about al-Mihdhar's travel in Southeast Asia at that time, the CIA did not advise the FBI about al-Mihdhar's or al-Hazmi's possible travel to the United States. Again, the CIA did not watchlist the two individuals. While CIA personnel were working closely with the FBI in support of the *USS Cole* bombing investigation, the importance and urgency of information tying suspected terrorists to the domestic United States apparently never registered with them. CIA Director Tenet testified that CIA personnel:

> ". . . in their focus on the [*USS Cole*] investigation, did not recognize the implications of the information about al-Hazmi and al-Mihdhar that they had in their files."

On June 11, 2001, FBI Headquarters and CIA personnel met with the New York FBI field office agents who were handling the *USS Cole* investigation. The New York agents were shown the Malaysia photographs, but were not given copies. Although al-Mihdhar's name was mentioned, the New York agents' requests for more information about al-Mihdhar and the circumstances surrounding the photographs were refused, according to one of the field office agents. The FBI Headquarters analyst recalls that she said at the meeting that she would try to get the information the agents had requested. . . .

Again, in that meeting, the CIA had missed yet another opportunity to advise the FBI about al-Mihdhar's visa and possible travel to the United States and, again, the CIA took no action to watchlist these individuals. Just two days later, al-Mihdhar obtained a new U.S. visa and, on July 4, 2001, he re-entered the United States.

It was not until mid July 2001, that a concerned CIA officer assigned to the FBI triggered a CIA review of its cables regarding the Malaysia meeting, a task that, ironically, fell to an FBI analyst assigned to the CTC. Working with the Immigration and Naturalization Service (INS), the FBI analyst determined that both al-Mihdhar and al-Hazmi had entered the United States. As a result of that effort, on August 23, 2001, the CIA finally notified the FBI and requested of the State Department that the two individuals should be watchlisted.

Even then, there was less than an all-out effort to locate what amounted to two Bin Ladin-associated terrorists in the United States during a period when the terrorist threat level had escalated to a peak level. For example, neither CIA, FBI, nor State Department informed the FAA. On August 21, 2001, coincidentally, FAA had issued a Security Directive, entitled "Threat to U.S. Aircraft Operators." That Directive alerted commercial airlines that nine named terrorism-associated individuals—none of whom were connected to the 19 hijackers—were planning commercial air travel and should receive additional security scrutiny if they attempted to board an aircraft. The Directive was updated on August 24 and August 28, 2001. Had FAA been advised of the presence of al-Hazmi and al-Mihdhar in the United States, a similar directive could have been issued, subjecting the two, their luggage and any carry-on items to detailed, FAA-directed searches.

Further, only the FBI's New York field office received a request from FBI Headquarters to conduct a search for the two prior to September 11, 2001. The Headquarters written instruction to the New York field office only identified al-Mihdhar in its subject line. Nawaf al-Hazmi was mentioned in the text, and it is not clear whether it was intended that he be a subject of the search as well. It was not until September 11, 2001 that the Los Angeles FBI field office was asked to conduct a search. Other FBI offices with potentially useful informants, such as San Diego, were not notified prior to September 11.

A New York FBI field office agent testified that he urged FBI Headquarters on August 28, 2001 to allow New York field office criminal agents to participate in the search with FBI intelligence agents, given the limited resources that are often applied to intelligence investigations. The request was refused by FBI Headquarters because of concerns about the perceived "wall" between criminal and intelligence matters. . . .

Joint Inquiry witnesses testified that other federal agencies with potentially valuable information databases were never asked to assist in FBI's search.

[Terrorist Communications in Spring 2000]

5.c. [In January 2000, after the meeting of al-Qa'ida operatives in Malaysia, Khalid al-Mihdhar and Nawaf al-Hazmi entered the United States [deleted]. Thereafter, the Intelligence Community obtained information indicating that an individual named "Khaled" at an unknown location had contacted a suspected terrorist facility in the Middle East. The Intelligence Community reported some of this information, but did not report all of it. Some of it was not reported because it was deemed not terrorist-related. It was not until after September 11, 2001 that the Intelligence Community determined that these contacts had been made from future hijacker Khalid al-Mihdhar while he was living within the domestic United States].

Discussion: [While the Intelligence Community had information regarding these communications, it did not determine the location from which they had been made [deleted] [deleted]. After September 11, the FBI determined from domestic toll records that it was in fact the hijacker Khalid al-Mihdhar who had made these communications and that he had done so from within the United States. The Intelligence Community did not identify what was critically important information in terms of the domestic threat to the United States: the fact that the communications were between individuals within the United States and suspected terrorist facilities overseas. That kind of information could have provided crucial investigative leads to law enforcement agencies engaged in domestic counterterrorist efforts].

[Two Hijackers Had Numerous Contacts with an Active FBI Informant]

5.d. [This Joint Inquiry confirmed that these same two future hijackers, Khalid al-Mihdhar and Nawaf al-Hazmi, had numerous contacts with a long time FBI counterterrorism informant in California and that a third future hijacker, Hani Hanjour, apparently had more limited contact with the same informant. In mid- to late-2000, the CIA already had information indicating that al-Mihdhar had a multiple entry U.S. visa and that al-Hazmi had in fact traveled to Los Angeles, but the two had not been watchlisted and information suggesting that two suspected terrorists could well be in the United States had not yet been given to the FBI. The San Diego FBI field office, which handled the informant in question, did not receive that information or any of the other intelligence information pertaining to al-Mihdhar and al-Hazmi, prior to September 11, 2001. As a result, the FBI missed the opportunity to task a uniquely well-positioned informant—who denies having any advance knowledge of the plot—to collect information about the hijackers and their plans within the United States.]

Discussion: [Nawaf al-Hazmi and Khalid al-Mihdhar had numerous contacts with a long-time FBI counterterrorism informant while they were living in San Diego, California. There are several indications that hijacker Hani Hanjour may have had more limited contact with the same informant in December 2000.]

[During the summer of 2000, the informant advised the FBI handling agent that the informant had contacts with two individuals named "Nawaf" and "Khalid". The informant described meeting these individuals. The informant described the two to the FBI agent as Saudi Muslim youths who were legally in the United States to visit and attend school. The FBI agent did not, at the time, consider these individuals to be of interest to the FBI. While the agent says he asked the informant for the individuals' last names, the informant never provided that information and the FBI agent did not press for the names because he had no reason to think they were significant until after September 11, 2001.]

[deleted][During one of their last contacts, al-Hazmi advised the informant that he was moving to Arizona to attend flight training, but the informant did not advise the FBI of this information until after the September 11 attacks].

[When the FBI's San Diego field office determined after the attacks that a longtime FBI counterterrorism informant had had numerous contacts in 2000 with two of the September 11 hijackers, personnel there were immediately suspicious about whether the informant was involved in the plot. Subsequently, however, all of the field office personnel, including senior managers and various case agents, concluded that the informant was unwitting of, and had no role in, the September 11 plot].

[Several questions remain, however, with regard to the informant's credibility. First, while there are several indications suggesting that future hijacker Hani Hanjour had contact with the informant in December 2000, the informant has repeatedly advised the FBI that the informant does not recognize photos of Hanjour. Second, the informant told the FBI that the hijackers did nothing to arouse the informant's suspicion, but the informant also acknowledged that al-Hazmi had contacts with at least four individuals the informant knew were of interest to the FBI and about whom the informant had previously reported to the FBI. Third, the informant has made numerous inconsistent statements to the FBI during the course of interviews after September 11, 2001. Fourth, the informant's responses during an FBI polygraph examination to very specific questions about the informant's advance knowledge of the September 11 plot were judged by the FBI to be "inconclusive," although the FBI asserts that this type of result is not unusual for such individuals in such circumstances].

[Finally, there is also information which conflicts with the information provided by the informant concerning the dates of contacts with the hijackers. The Joint Inquiry, for example, brought to the FBI's attention information that is inconsistent with the date of initial contact as provided by the informant. In its November 18, 2002 written response to the Joint Inquiry, the FBI has acknowledged that there are "significant inconsistencies" in the informant's statements about these contacts. The FBI investigation regarding this issue is continuing].

[The Administration has to date objected to the Inquiry's efforts to interview the informant in order to attempt to resolve those inconsistencies. The Administration also would not agree to allow the FBI to serve a Committee subpoena and deposition notice on the informant. Instead, written interrogatories from the Joint Inquiry were, at the suggestion of the FBI, provided to the informant. Through an attorney, the informant has declined to respond to those interrogatories and has indicated that, if subpoenaed, the informant would request a grant of immunity prior to testifying].

[The FBI agent who was responsible for the informant testified before the Joint Inquiry that, had he had access to the intelligence information on al-Mihdhar's and al-Hazmi's significance at the time they were in San Diego:

"It would have made a huge difference. We would have immediately opened [deleted] investigations. We had the predicate for a [deleted] investigation if we had that information. . . . [W]e would immediately go out and canvas the sources and try to find out where these people were. If we locate them, which we probably would have since they were very close—they were nearby—we would have initiated investigations immediately. . . . We would have done everything. We would have used all available investigative techniques. We would have given them the full court press. We would . . . have done everything—physical surveillance, technical surveillance and other assets."

[Whether, as the agent testified he believes, that kind of investigative work would have occurred and would have then uncovered the hijackers' future plans will necessarily remain speculation. What is clear, however, is that the informant's contacts with the hijackers, had they been capitalized on, would have given the San Diego FBI field office perhaps the Intelligence Community's best chance to unravel the September 11 plot. Given the CIA's failure to disseminate, in a timely manner, intelligence information on the significance and location of al-Mihdhar and al-Hazmi, that chance, unfortunately, never materialized].

The Phoenix Electronic Communication
5.e. On July 10, 2001, an FBI Phoenix field office agent sent an "Electronic Communication" to four individuals in the Radical Fundamentalist Unit (RFU) and two individuals in the Usama Bin Ladin Unit (UBLU) at FBI Headquarters, and to two agents on International Terrorism squads in the FBI New York field office. In the communication, the agent expressed his concerns, based on his first-hand

knowledge, that there was a coordinated effort underway by Bin Ladin to send students to the United States for civil aviation-related training. He noted that there was an "inordinate number of individuals of investigative interest" in this type of training in Arizona and expressed his suspicion that this was an effort to establish a cadre of individuals in civil aviation who would conduct future terrorist activity. The Phoenix agent's communication requested that FBI Headquarters consider implementing four recommendations:

- accumulate a list of civil aviation universities/colleges around the country;
- establish liaison with these schools;
- discuss the theories contained in the Phoenix EC with the Intelligence Community; and
- consider seeking authority to obtain visa information concerning individuals seeking to attend flight schools.

However, the FBI Headquarters personnel did not take the action requested by the Phoenix field office agent prior to September 11, 2001. The Phoenix communication generated little or no interest at either FBI Headquarters or the FBI's New York field office. . . .

The FBI Investigation of Zacarias Moussaoui

5.f. In August 2001, the FBI's Minneapolis field office, in conjunction with the INS, detained Zacarias Moussaoui, a French national who had enrolled in flight training in Minnesota. FBI agents there also suspected that Moussaoui was involved in a hijacking plot. FBI Headquarters attorneys determined that there was not probable cause to obtain a court order to search Moussaoui's belongings under the Foreign Intelligence Surveillance Act (FISA). However, personnel at FBI Headquarters, including the Radical Fundamentalist Unit and the National Security Law Unit, as well as agents in the Minneapolis field office, misunderstood the legal standard for obtaining an order under FISA. As a result, FBI Minneapolis field office personnel wasted valuable investigative resources trying to connect the Chechen rebels to al-Qa'ida. Finally, no one at the FBI apparently connected the Moussaoui investigation with the heightened threat environment in the summer of 2001, the Phoenix communication, or the entry of al-Mihdhar and al-Hazmi into the United States. . . .

Hijackers in Contact with Persons of FBI Investigative Interest in the United States

5.g. The Joint Inquiry confirmed that at least some of the hijackers were not as isolated during their time in the United States as has been previously suggested. Rather, they maintained a number of contacts both in the United States and abroad during this time period. Some of those contacts were with individuals who were known to the FBI, through either past or, at the time, ongoing FBI inquiries and investigations. Although it is not known to what extent any of these contacts in the United States were aware of the plot, it is now clear that they did provide at least some of the hijackers with substantial assistance while they were living in this country. . . .

Hijackers' Associates in Germany

5.h. [Since 1995, the CIA had been aware of a radical Islamic presence in Germany, including individuals with connections to Usama Bin Ladin. Prior to September 11, 2001, the CIA had unsuccessfully sought additional information on individuals who have now been identified as associates of some of the hijackers]. . . .

Khalid Shaykh Mohammad

5.i. Prior to September 11, the Intelligence Community had information linking Khalid Shaykh Mohammed (KSM), now recognized by the Intelligence Community as the mastermind of the attacks, to Bin Ladin, to terrorist plans to use aircraft as weapons, and to terrorist activity in the United States. The Intelligence Community, however, relegated KSM to rendition target status following his 1996 indictment in connection with the Bojinka Plot and, as a result, focused primarily on his location, rather than his activities and place in the al-Qa'ida hierarchy. The Community also did not recognize the significance of reporting in June 2001 concerning KSM's active role in sending terrorists to the United States, or the facilitation of their activities upon arriving in the United States. Collection efforts were not targeted on information about KSM that might have helped better understand al-Qa'ida's plans and intentions, and KSM's role in the September 11 attacks was a surprise to the Intelligence Community.

Discussion: [According to information obtained by the Intelligence Community from several sources after September 11, 2001, Khalid Shaykh Mohammed (KSM)—also known as "Mukhtar" (Arabic for "The Brain")—masterminded the September 11 attacks. The information indicates that KSM presented a plan to Usama Bin Ladin to mount an attack using small rental aircraft filled with explosives. Usama Bin Ladin reportedly suggested using even larger planes. Thus, the idea of hijacking commercial airliners took hold. Thereafter, KSM reportedly instructed and trained the hijackers for their mission, including directing them to undergo pilot training].

KSM came to the attention of the Intelligence Community as a terrorist in early 1995 when he was linked to Ramzi Yousef's "Bojinka Plot" in the Philippines. One portion of that plot involved the idea of crashing an airplane into CIA Headquarters. Through additional intelligence and investigative efforts in 1995, KSM was also connected to the first World Trade Center bombing. He was indicted by a U.S. grand jury in January 1996. The indictment was kept under seal until 1998 while the FBI and CIA attempted to locate him and arrange to take him into custody. Subsequently, indications were received that he might have been involved in the East Africa U.S. Embassy bombings.

[In June 2001, [deleted] disseminated a report to all Intelligence Community agencies, [deleted], military commanders, and components in the Treasury and Justice Departments emphasizing KSM's ties to Bin Ladin as well as his continuing travel to the United States. The report explained that KSM appears to be one of Bin Ladin's most trusted lieutenants and was active in recruiting people to travel outside Afghanistan, including to the United States, on behalf of Bin Ladin. According to the report, he traveled frequently to the United States, including as recently as May 2001, and routinely told others that he could arrange their entry into the United States as well. Reportedly, these individuals were expected to establish contact with colleagues already there. The clear implication of his comments, according to the report, was that they would be engaged in planning terrorist related activities].

Although this particular report was sent from the CIA to the FBI, neither agency apparently recognized the significance of a Bin Ladin lieutenant sending terrorists to the United States and asking them to establish contacts with colleagues already there. CTC questioned this report at the time and commented: "We doubt the real [KSM] would do this...because if it is [KSM], we have both a significant threat and an opportunity to pick him up." Neither the CIA nor the FBI has been able to confirm whether KSM had in fact been traveling to the United States or sending recruits here prior to September 11. . . .

B. Conclusion—Factual Findings

In short, for a variety of reasons, the Intelligence Community failed to capitalize on both the individual and collective significance of available information that appears relevant to the events of September 11. As a result, the Community missed opportunities to disrupt the September 11 plot by denying entry to or detaining would-be hijackers; to at least try to unravel the plot through surveillance and other investigative work within the United States; and, finally, to generate a heightened state of alert and thus harden the homeland against attack.

No one will ever know what might have happened had more connections been drawn between these disparate pieces of information. We will never definitively know to what extent the Community would have been able and willing to exploit fully all the opportunities that may have emerged. The important point is that the Intelligence Community, for a variety of reasons, did not bring together and fully appreciate a range of information that could have greatly enhanced its chances of uncovering and preventing Usama Bin Ladin's plan to attack the United States on September 11, 2001.

C. Systemic Findings

Our review of the events surrounding September 11 has revealed a number of systemic weaknesses that hindered the Intelligence Community's counterterrorism efforts before September 11. If not addressed, these weaknesses will continue to undercut U.S. counterterrorist efforts. In order to minimize the possibility of attacks like September 11 in the future, effective solutions to those problems need to be developed and fully implemented as soon as possible.

1. *Finding:* Prior to September 11, the Intelligence Community was neither well organized nor equipped, and did not adequately adapt, to meet the challenge posed by global terrorists focused on targets within the domestic United States. Serious gaps existed between the collection coverage provided by U.S. foreign and U.S. domestic intelligence capabilities. The U.S. foreign intelligence agencies paid inadequate attention to the potential for a domestic attack. The CIA's failure to watchlist suspected terrorists aggressively reflected a lack of emphasis on a process designed to protect the homeland from the terrorist threat. As a result, CIA employees failed to watchlist al-Mihdhar and al-Hazmi. At home, the counterterrorism effort suffered from the lack of an effective domestic intelligence capability. The FBI was unable to identify and monitor effectively the extent of activity by al-Qa'ida and other international terrorist groups operating in the United States. Taken together, these problems greatly exacerbated the nation's vulnerability to an increasingly dangerous and immediate international terrorist threat inside the United States.

Discussion: The United States has a long history of defining internal threats as either foreign or domestic and assigning responsibility to the intelligence and law enforcement agencies accordingly. This division reflects a fundamental policy choice and is codified in law. For example, the National Security Act of 1947 precludes CIA from exercising any internal security or law enforcement powers. The Congressional investigations of the 1970's into the activities of the intelligence agencies, including their efforts to collect information regarding anti-Vietnam War activists and other "radicals," reinforced the importance of this division in the minds of the Congress, the American public, and the agencies.

The emergence, in the 1990s, of a threat posed by international terrorists who operate across national borders demanded huge changes in focus and approach from intelligence agencies traditionally organized and trained to operate primarily in either the United States or abroad. The legal authorities, operational policies and cultures that had molded agencies like CIA, NSA and the FBI for years had not responded to the "globalization" of terrorism that culminated in the September 11 attacks in the United States. While some efforts, such as the creation of the CTC at CIA in 1986, were made to increase collaboration between these agencies, the agencies focused primarily on what remained essentially separate spheres of operations. In the absence of any collective national strategy, they retained significant autonomy in deciding how to attack and array their resources against Usama Bin Ladin and al-Qa'ida. Efforts to develop such a strategy might have exposed the significant counterterrorism gaps that existed between the agencies as well as the increasingly urgent need to compensate for those gaps in the absence of more fundamental changes in organization and legal authority.

Prior to September 11, CIA and NSA continued to focus the bulk of their efforts on the foreign operations of terrorists. While intelligence reporting indicated that al-Qa'ida intended to strike in the United States, these agencies believed that defending against this threat was primarily the responsibility of the FBI. This Joint Inquiry found that both agencies routinely passed a large volume of intelligence to the FBI, but that neither agency followed up to determine what the FBI learned from or did with that information. Neither did the FBI keep NSA and CIA adequately informed of developments within its areas of responsibility.

As noted earlier, the record confirms instances where, despite numerous opportunities, information that was directly relevant to the domestic threat was simply overlooked and not disseminated in a timely manner to the FBI. For example, the CIA analyst who neglected to raise the information concerning al-Mihdhar and al-Hazmi's U.S. travel in a June 2001 meeting with the FBI in New York said in a Joint Inquiry interview that the information he had learned concerning the pair's travel to Los Angeles "did not mean anything to him." He also explained to the Joint Inquiry that the information was operational in nature and he would have needed permission before disclosing it.

The CIA's inconsistent performance regarding the watchlisting of suspected terrorists prior to September 11 also suggests a lack of attention to the domestic threat. Watchlists are a vital link in denying entry to the United States by terrorists and others who threaten the national security, and CTC had reminded personnel of the importance of watchlisting in December 1999. . . . Yet, some CIA officers in CTC indicated they did not put much emphasis on watchlists. The Joint Inquiry confirmed that there was no formal process in place at the CTC prior to September 11 for watchlisting suspected terrorists, even where, as was the case with al-Hazmi and al-Mihdhar, there were indications of travel to the United States.

Other CIA personnel reported that they received no training on watchlisting and that names were added on an ad hoc basis. In the days and weeks following the September 11 attacks, more focused CIA review of over 1,500 Classified Intelligence Reports that had not previously been provided to the State Department for watchlist purposes resulted in the identification of 150 suspected terrorists and the addition of 58 suspected terrorist names to the watchlist. DCI Tenet acknowledged in his testimony before the Joint Inquiry that CIA's watchlisting training had been deficient and that a mistake had been made in the failure to watchlist both al-Mihdhar and al-Hazmi promptly.

[There were also gaps between NSA's coverage of foreign communications and the FBI's coverage of domestic communications that suggest a lack of sufficient attention to the domestic threat. Prior to September 11, neither agency focused on the importance of identifying and then ensuring coverage of communications between the United States and suspected terrorist-associated facilities abroad [deleted]. Consistent with its focus on communications abroad, NSA adopted a policy that avoided intercepting the communications between individuals in the United States and foreign countries].

NSA adopted this policy even though the collection of such communications is within its mission and it would have been possible for NSA to obtain FISA Court authorization for such collection. NSA Director Hayden testified to the Joint Inquiry that NSA did not want to be perceived as targeting individuals in the United States and believed that the FBI was instead responsible for conducting such surveillance. NSA did not, however, develop a plan with the FBI to collect and to ensure the dissemination of any relevant foreign intelligence to appropriate domestic agencies. This further evidences the slow response of the Intelligence Community to the developing transnational threat.

[The Joint Inquiry has learned that one of the future hijackers communicated with a known terrorist facility in the Middle East while he was living in the United States. The Intelligence Community did not identify the domestic origin of those communications prior to September 11, 2001 so that additional FBI investigative efforts could be coordinated. Despite this country's substantial advantages, there was insufficient focus on what many would have thought was among the most critically important kinds of terrorist-related communications, at least in terms of protecting the Homeland].

While most of the Intelligence Community focused on the collection of foreign intelligence, the Joint Inquiry was told repeatedly that the nation lacked an effective domestic intelligence capability prior to September 11. . . .

While the FBI's counterterrorist program had produced successful investigations and major prosecutions of both domestic and international terrorists, numerous witnesses told the Joint Inquiry that the program was, at least prior to September 11, incapable of producing significant intelligence products. The FBI's traditional reliance on an aggressive, case-oriented, law enforcement approach did not encourage the broader collection and analysis efforts that are critical to the intelligence mission. Lacking appropriate personnel, training, and information systems, the FBI primarily gathered intelligence to support specific investigations, not to conduct all-source analysis for dissemination to other intelligence agencies. . . .

Numerous individuals told this Inquiry that the FBI's 56 field offices enjoy a great deal of latitude in managing their work, consistent with the dynamic and reactive nature of its traditional law enforcement mission. In counterterrorism efforts, however, that flexibility apparently served to dilute the FBI's national focus on Bin Ladin and al-Qa'ida. Although the FBI made counterterrorism a "Tier One" priority, not all of its field offices responded consistently to this FBI Headquarters decision. The New York Field Office did make terrorism a high priority and was given substantial responsibility for the al-Qa'ida target following the first attack on the World Trade Center in 1993. However, many other FBI offices were not focused on al-Qa'ida and had little understanding of the extent of the threat it posed within this country prior to September 11.

The combination of these factors seriously handicapped efforts to identify and defend against the foreign terrorist threat to the domestic United States. It is not surprising, in the absence of more focused intelligence, that senior policymakers told this Inquiry that, prior to September 11, they believed the terrorist threat was focused on U.S. interests overseas. Deputy Secretary of State Armitage, for example, testified that ". . . I don't think we really had made the leap in our mind that we are no longer safe behind these two great oceans. . . ." Former Deputy Secretary of Defense John Hamre said in a Joint Inquiry interview that he could not remember ever seeing an intelligence report on the existence of terrorist sleeper cells in the United States. In retrospect, he recalled: ". . . we thought we were dealing in important things, but we missed the domestic threat from international terrorism."

2. *Finding:* **Prior to September 11, 2001, neither the U.S. Government as a whole nor the Intelligence Community had a comprehensive counterterrorist strategy for combating the threat posed by Usama Bin Ladin. Furthermore, the Director of Central Intelligence (DCI) was either unwilling or unable to marshal the full range of Intelligence Community resources necessary to combat the growing threat to the United States.**

Discussion: The Intelligence Community is a large distributed organism. It encompasses 14 agencies and tens of thousands of employees. The number of people employed exclusively in the effort against

Usama Bin Ladin and al-Qa'ida was relatively small. In addition, these people were operating in geographically dispersed locations, often not connected by secure information technologies, and within established bureaucracies that were not culturally or organizationally attuned to one another's requirements. Many of them had limited experience against the target, and did not know one another. To achieve success in such an environment, leadership is a critical factor. The Joint Inquiry found that the Intelligence Community's structure made leadership difficult.

Usama Bin Ladin first came to the attention of the Intelligence Community in the early 1990s, initially as a financier of terrorist activities. In 1996, as Bin Ladin's direct involvement in planning and directing terrorist acts became more evident, the DCI's Counterterrorist Center (CTC) created a special unit to focus specifically on him and the threat he posed to the interests of the United States. Personnel within CTC recognized as early as 1996 and 1997 that Usama Bin Ladin posed a grave danger to the United States.

Following the August 1998 bombings of two U.S. embassies in East Africa, the DCI made combating the threat posed by Usama Bin Ladin one of the Intelligence Community's highest priorities, establishing it as a "Tier 0 priority." The DCI raised the status of the Bin Ladin threat still further when he announced in writing in December 1998 regarding Bin Ladin: "We are at war . . . I want no resources or people spared in this effort, either inside the CIA or the [Intelligence] Community." This declaration appeared in a memorandum from the DCI to CIA senior managers, the Deputy DCI for Community Management and the Assistant DCI for Military Support.

The Intelligence Community as a whole, however, had only a limited awareness of this declaration. For example, some senior managers in the National Security Agency and the Defense Intelligence Agency say they were aware of the declaration. However, it was apparently not well known within the Federal Bureau of Investigation. In fact, the Assistant Director of the FBI's Counterterrorism Division testified to the Joint Inquiry that he "was not specifically aware of that declaration of war."

Furthermore, and even more disturbing, Joint Inquiry interviews of FBI field office personnel indicated that they were not aware of the DCI's declaration, and some had only a passing familiarity with the very existence of Usama Bin Ladin and al-Qa'ida prior to September 11. Neither were the Deputy Secretary of Defense or the Chairman of the Joint Chiefs of Staff aware of the DCI's declaration. This suggests a fragmented Intelligence Community that was operating without a comprehensive strategy for combating the threat posed by Bin Ladin, and a DCI without the ability to enforce consistent priorities at all levels throughout the Community. . . .

The inability to realign Intelligence Community resources to combat the threat posed by Usama Bin Ladin is a relatively direct consequence of the limited authority of the DCI over major portions of the Intelligence Community. As former Senator Warren Rudman noted on October 8, 2002 in his testimony before the Joint Inquiry: "You have a Director of Central Intelligence who is also the Director of CIA; eighty-five percent of [the Intelligence Community's budget] is controlled by the Department of Defense."...

While the FBI devoted considerable resources to the criminal investigations of the terrorist attacks overseas, substantial efforts to prevent similar attacks at home were lacking. Former National Security Advisor Sandy Berger told the Joint Inquiry: "... if there was a flood of intelligence information [on terrorism] from the CIA, there was hardly a trickle from the FBI." In some FBI field offices, there was little focus on, or awareness of, Usama Bin Ladin and al-Qa'ida. This included the San Diego field office where FBI agents would discover, after September 11, that there had been numerous local connections to at least two of the hijackers. . . .

3. *Finding:* Between the end of the Cold War and September 11, 2001, overall Intelligence Community funding fell or remained even in constant dollars, while funding for the Community's counterterrorism efforts increased considerably. Despite those increases, the accumulation of intelligence priorities, a burdensome requirements process, the overall decline in Intelligence Community funding, and reliance on supplemental appropriations made it difficult to allocate Community resources effectively against an evolving terrorist threat. Inefficiencies in the resource and requirements process were compounded by problems in Intelligence Community budgeting practices and procedures. . . .

4. *Finding:* While technology remains one of this nation's greatest advantages, it has not been fully and most effectively applied in support of U.S. counterterrorism efforts. Persistent problems in this area included a lack of collaboration between Intelligence Community agencies, a reluctance to develop and implement new technical capabilities aggressively, the FBI's reliance on outdated and insufficient technical systems, and the absence of a central counterterrorism database. . . .

5. *Finding:* Prior to September 11, the Intelligence Community's understanding of al-Qa'ida was hampered by insufficient analytic focus and quality, particularly in terms of strategic analysis. Analysis and analysts were not always used effectively because of the perception in some quarters of the Intelligence Community that they were less important to agency counterterrorism missions than were opera-

tions personnel. The quality of counterterrorism analysis was inconsistent, and many analysts were inexperienced, unqualified, undertrained, and without access to critical information. As a result, there was a dearth of creative, aggressive analysis targeting Bin Ladin and a persistent inability to comprehend the collective significance of individual pieces of intelligence. These analytic deficiencies seriously undercut the ability of U.S. policymakers to understand the full nature of the threat, and to make fully informed decisions. . . .

6. *Finding:* Prior to September 11, The Intelligence Community was not prepared to handle the challenge it faced in translating the volumes of foreign language counterterrorism intelligence it collected. Agencies within the Intelligence Community experienced backlogs in material awaiting translation, a shortage of language specialists and language-qualified field officers, and a readiness level of only 30% in the most critical terrorism-related languages. . . .

7. *Finding:* [Prior to September 11, the Intelligence Community's ability to produce significant and timely signals intelligence on counterterrorism was limited by NSA's failure to address modern communications technology aggressively, continuing conflict between Intelligence Community agencies, NSA's cautious approach to any collection of intelligence relating to activities in the United States, and insufficient collaboration between NSA and the FBI regarding the potential for terrorist attacks within the United States]. . . .

8. *Finding:* The continuing erosion of NSA's program management expertise and experience has hindered its contribution to the fight against terrorism. NSA continues to have mixed results in providing timely technical solutions to modern intelligence collection, analysis, and information sharing problems. . . .

9. *Finding:* The U.S. Government does not presently bring together in one place all terrorism-related information from all sources. While CTC does manage overseas operations and has access to most Intelligence Community information, it does not collect terrorism-related information from all sources, domestic and foreign. Within the Intelligence Community, agencies did not adequately share relevant counterterrorism information, prior to September 11. This breakdown in communications was the result of a number of factors, including differences in the agencies' missions, legal authorities and cultures. Information was not sufficiently shared, not only between different Intelligence Community agencies, but also within individual agencies, and between the intelligence and the law enforcement agencies. . . .

10. *Finding:* Serious problems in information sharing also persisted, prior to September 11, between the Intelligence Community and relevant non-Intelligence Community agencies. This included other federal agencies as well as state and local authorities. This lack of communication and collaboration deprived those other entities, as well as the Intelligence Community, of access to potentially valuable information in the "war" against Bin Ladin. The Inquiry's focus on the Intelligence Community limited the extent to which it explored these issues, and this is an area that should be reviewed further.

Discussion: This Inquiry confirmed that, prior to September 11, problems in information sharing reached beyond the boundaries of the Intelligence Community to encumber the flow of information to and from various other entities. At each level, communications with potentially valuable partners in the war against terrorism—other federal agencies, state and local authorities—were restricted. Witnesses testified that these restrictions on information flow occurred at great cost to the counterterrorism effort.

Officials in the Departments of Treasury, Transportation, and State told the Joint Inquiry that, although they receive threat information from the Intelligence Community, they do not always receive the information that adds context to the threat warnings. In many instances, officials told the Joint Inquiry, this lack of context prevents them from properly estimating the value of the threat information and taking preventive actions. The Joint Inquiry was also told that not all threat information in the possession of the Intelligence Community is shared with non-Intelligence Community entities that need it the most in order to counter the threats. . . .

11. *Finding:* Prior to September 11, 2001, the Intelligence Community did not effectively develop and use human sources to penetrate the al-Qa'ida inner circle. This lack of reliable and knowledgeable human sources significantly limited the Community's ability to acquire intelligence that could be acted upon before the September 11 attacks. In part, at least, the lack of unilateral (i.e., U.S.-recruited) counterterrorism sources was a product of an excessive reliance on foreign liaison services. . . .

12. *Finding:* During the summer of 2001, when the Intelligence Community was bracing for an imminent al-Qa'ida attack, difficulties with FBI applications for Foreign Intelligence Surveillance Act (FISA) surveillance and the FISA process led to a diminished level of coverage of suspected al-Qa'ida operatives in the United States. The effect of these difficulties was compounded by the perception that spread among FBI personnel at Headquarters and the field offices that the FISA process was lengthy and fraught with peril. . . .

14. *Finding:* [Senior U.S. military officials were reluctant to use U.S. military assets to conduct offensive counterterrorism efforts in Afghanistan, or to support or participate in CIA operations directed against al-Qa'ida prior to September 11. At least part of this reluctance was driven by the military's view that the Intelligence Community was unable to provide the intelligence needed to support military operations. Although the U.S. military did participate in [deleted] counterterrorism efforts to counter Usama Bin Ladin's terrorist network prior to September 11, 2001, most of the military's focus was on force protection]. . . .

15. *Finding:* The Intelligence Community depended heavily on foreign intelligence and law enforcement services for the collection of counterterrorism intelligence and the conduct of other counterterrorism activities. The results were mixed in terms of productive intelligence, reflecting vast differences in the ability and willingness of the various foreign services to target the Bin Ladin and al-Qa'ida network. Intelligence Community agencies sometimes failed to coordinate their relationships with foreign services adequately, either within the Intelligence Community or with broader U.S. Government liaison and foreign policy efforts. This reliance on foreign liaison services also resulted in a lack of focus on the development of unilateral human sources. . . .

16. *Finding:* [The activities of the September 11 hijackers in the United States appear to have been financed, in large part, from monies sent to them from abroad and also brought in on their persons. Prior to September 11, there was no coordinated U.S. Government-wide strategy to track terrorist funding and close down their financial support networks. There was also a reluctance in some parts of the U.S. Government to track terrorist funding and close down their financial support networks. As a result, the U.S. Government was unable to disrupt financial support for Usama Bin Ladin's terrorist activities effectively].

Discussion: [Tracking terrorist funds can be an especially effective means of identifying terrorists and terrorist organizations, unraveling and disrupting terrorist plots, and targeting terrorist financial assets for sanctions, seizures, and account closures. As with organized criminal activity, financial support is critically important to terrorist networks like al-Qa'ida. Prior to September 11, 2001, however, no single U.S. Government agency was responsible for tracking terrorist funds, prioritizing and coordinating government-wide efforts, and seeking international collaboration in that effort. Some tracking of terrorist funds was undertaken before September 11. For the most part, however, these efforts were unorganized and ad-hoc, and there was a reluctance to take actions such as seizures of assets and bank accounts and arrests of those involved in the funding. A U.S. Government official testified before the Joint Inquiry, for example, that this reluctance hindered counterterrorist efforts against Bin Ladin: "Treasury was concerned about any activity that could adversely affect the international financial system . . .]." . . .

D. Related Findings

During the course of this Joint Inquiry, testimony and information were received that pertained to several issues involving broader, policy questions that reach beyond the boundaries of the Intelligence Community. In the three areas described below, the Inquiry finds that policy issues were relevant to our examination of the events of September 11.

17. *Finding:* Despite intelligence reporting from 1998 through the summer of 2001 indicating that Usama Bin Ladin's terrorist network intended to strike inside the United States, the United States Government did not undertake a comprehensive effort to implement defensive measures in the United States.

Discussion: As noted earlier, the Joint Inquiry has established that the Intelligence Community acquired and disseminated from 1998 through the summer of 2001 intelligence reports indicating in broad terms that Usama Bin Ladin's network intended to carry out terrorist attacks inside the United States. This information encompassed, for example, indications of plots for attacks within the United States that would include:

- attacks on civil aviation;
- assassinations of U.S. public officials;
- use of high explosives;
- attacks on Washington, D.C., New York City, and cities on the West Coast;
- crashing aircraft into buildings as weapons; and
- using weapons of mass destruction.

The intelligence that was acquired and shared by the Intelligence Community was not specific as to time and place, but should have been sufficient to prompt action to insure a heightened sense of alert and implementation of additional defensive measures. Such actions could have included: strengthened civil aviation security measures; increased attention to watchlisting suspected terrorists so as to keep them out of the United States; greater collaboration with state and local law enforcement authorities concerning the scope and nature of the potential threat; a sustained national effort to inform and alert the American public to the growing danger; and improved capabilities to deal with the consequences of attacks involving mass destruction and casualties. The U.S. Government did take some steps in regard to detecting and preventing the use of weapons of mass destruction, but did not pursue a broad program of additional domestic defensive measures or public awareness. . . .

18. *Finding:* Between 1996 and September 2001, the counterterrorism strategy adopted by the U. S. Government did not succeed in eliminating Afghanistan as a sanctuary and training ground for Usama Bin Ladin's terrorist network. A range of instruments was used to counter al-Qa'ida, with law enforcement often emerging as a leading tool because other means were deemed not to be feasible or failed to produce results. Although numerous successful prosecutions were generated, law enforcement efforts were not adequate by themselves to target or eliminate Bin Ladin's sanctuary. While the United States persisted in observing the rule of law and accepted norms of international behavior, Bin Ladin and al-Qa'ida recognized no rules and thrived in the safehaven provided by Afghanistan. . . .

19. *Finding:* Prior to September 11, the Intelligence Community and the U.S. Government labored to prevent attacks by Usama Bin Ladin and his terrorist network against the United States, but largely without the benefit of an alert, mobilized and committed American public. Despite intelligence information on the immediacy of the threat level in the spring and summer of 2001, the assumption prevailed in the U.S. Government that attacks of the magnitude of September 11 could not happen here. As a result, there was insufficient effort to alert the American public to the reality and gravity of the threat.

Discussion: The record of this Joint Inquiry indicates that, prior to September 11, 2001, the U.S. Intelligence Community was involved in fighting a "war" against Bin Ladin largely without the benefit of what some would call its most potent weapon in that effort: an alert and committed American public. Senior levels of the Intelligence Community, as well as senior U.S. Government policymakers, were aware of the danger posed by Bin Ladin. Information that was shared with senior U.S. Government officials, but was not made available to the American public because of its national security classification, was explicit about the gravity and immediacy of the threat posed by Bin Ladin. . . .

Source: U.S. Congress. Senate and House. "Joint Inquiry into Intelligence Community Activities Before and After the Terrorist Attacks of September 11, 2001." Report of the U.S. Senate Select Committee on Intelligence and the U.S. House Permanent Select Committee on Intelligence. 107th Cong., 2nd sess., July 24, 2003. S. Rept. 107–351, H. Rept. 107–792. www.gpoaccess.gov/serialset/creports/911.html (July 25, 2003).

Civil Rights Commission on Native Americans

July 25, 2003

INTRODUCTION

The federal government's failure to provide adequate health care, housing, education, law enforcement, and other services to American Indians not only resulted in massive and escalating unmet needs among Native Americans but also constituted a flagrant civil rights violation, the U.S. Commission on Civil Rights charged in a report released July 25, 2003. The commission said that Native Americans were effectively denied equal opportunity because the federal government was not living up to its moral and legal obligations to compensate them for the lands from which they had been displaced during the nation's westward expansion.

The report was issued shortly before a long-running lawsuit alleging that the federal government had cheated American Indians out of billions of dollars in mineral and other royalties entered a new phase. The class-action lawsuit involving hundreds of thousands of American Indians alleged that the Interior Department had mismanaged tens of billions of dollars owed to the Indians for mineral, oil, gas, timber, and grazing royalties dating back to 1887. In 1999 U.S. District Judge Royce Lamberth ruled that the Interior Department had violated its trust responsibility and ordered a full accounting of the money owed to the Indians. In a September 2003 ruling, Lamberth gave the department until September 30, 2007, to complete the accounting. In another case, a federal appeals court ruled in October that the Navajo Nation could continue its suit to prove that the federal government and a coal company conspired to cheat the tribe out of $600 million in mineral royalties.

Meanwhile the Census Bureau began to release findings from the 2000 Census and subsequent updates to paint a portrait of the existing Native American population. As of July 1, 2002, an estimated 4.3 million people in the United States considered themselves to be all or part American Indian and Alaska native. (For the first time, in 2000, the Census Bureau allowed people to categorize themselves as more than one race.) Some

3.1 million Native Americans claimed membership in a specific tribe. Chero-kee was the largest, with a population of nearly 700,000.

Some 538,000 Native Americans lived on reservations, the largest of which was the Navajo Nation, with 175,000 residents on a reservation that spanned parts of Arizona, New Mexico, and Utah. Two-thirds of all Native Americans lived in metropolitan areas, the lowest percentage of any racial group but a major increase since 1990 when more than half of all Indians lived outside metropolitan areas. California had the largest number of Native Americans of any state population, while Alaska had the highest percentage (19 percent), followed by Oklahoma and New Mexico, each with 11 percent.

Native Americans were using their growing numbers to wield some polit-ical influence at both the national and state level. In 2000 Indian voters helped defeat Sen. Slade Gorton, R-Wash., and in 2002 they also influ-enced the outcome of the Senate race in South Dakota and the governor's race in Oklahoma. During the California gubernatorial recall election in 2003 tribes that ran gambling casinos on their property opposed the front-runner and eventual winner Arnold Schwarzenegger, who railed at the tribes for making billions in their gambling operations while failing to pay their fair share to help the state overcome its financial problems. The tribes report-edly made at least $11 million in campaign contributions, much of it to Cruz M. Bustamante, the lieutenant governor and leading Democrat in the race and a staunch supporter of the tribes. In preparation for the 2004 presi-dential election, leaders of the American Indian Congress organized a voter registration drive in 2003, particularly in Arizona, New Mexico, Washington, and Oregon, where the Indian vote might play a pivotal role in the election. *(California recall election, p. 1005)*

Commission Report: A Quiet Crisis

The Civil Rights Commission report, "A Quiet Crisis: Federal Funding and Unmet Needs in Indian Country," reviewed the status of living conditions in what it called Indian country and found that Native Americans ranked at or near the bottom on just about every measure. For example, the report said, Indians had lower life expectancies and higher rates of many diseases, including diabetes, tuberculosis, and alcoholism, than other racial groups. Even so, the federal government spent less per capita on Native American health care than it did for any other group, including Medicaid recipients and prisoners. Most Indians did not have private health insurance and thus relied on the federal Indian Health Service for care.

Housing was often found to be inadequate and substandard. One in five reservation homes lacked complete plumbing. Law enforcement was also often substandard and frequently in conflict with Native American culture. The inadequacy of Indian education was reflected in achievement scores.

Overall, Native Americans scored lower than any other racial or ethnic group in basic reading, math, and history. Insufficient federal funding limited the success of economic development programs, which is turn resulted in food shortages and hunger.

The commission offered eleven recommendations for rectifying the situation, starting with the establishment of a bipartisan task force, made up of elected officials, officials from federal agencies with a responsibility for Indian programs, and Native American advocacy groups, to develop solutions to the existing problems and implement change. It called for feasible objectives that could be achieved quickly. Among the other recommendations was a call for a coordinated approach to developing infrastructure roads, multipurpose buildings, utilities, and communications systems in Indian Country that would make services more accessible and their delivery more efficient.

The executive director of the National Congress of American Indians, the nation's largest Indian advocacy group, said the commission report was the most comprehensive analysis of the unmet needs in Indian country in a decade. Without adequate funding for vital programs, empowerment of tribal institutions, and a genuine commitment on the part of the federal government to the policy of self-determination, tribal governments are ill-equipped to provide for their citizens, and their citizens, in turn, are denied equal access to resources most other citizens enjoy, Jacqueline Johnson wrote in a letter to the commission.

Interior Department Accounting

The class-action lawsuit against the Interior Department was seeking an accounting for the Indian trust fund, which was set up in 1887 when Congress gave the department responsibility for managing the mineral and other royalties from land allocated to the Indians. Government reports and investigations since 1915 had said that the money was mismanaged, but it was not until 1994 that Congress asked the Interior Department to account for the money. In 1996, after the department failed to act, a group of Indians brought suit. In 1999 Lamberth ordered the government to undertake an accounting.

Frustrated by the department's continuing inaction, Lamberth in 2002 held Gale Norton, the secretary of interior, in contempt of court and set a trial to determine whether the department was capable of fulfilling his order. Norton's contempt citation was later overturned, but at the trial, in 2003, attorneys for the Indians argued that the Interior Department had lost or destroyed too many documents to be able to do an accurate accounting and asked Lamberth to appoint an outside receiver to manage the funds. Lamberth declined to do that, but set deadlines for the department to complete phases of the accounting, with a final accounting due by September 30, 2007. He held out few expectations, however, that the department would comply with his deadline. The department said if would cost $335 million and take five years to complete the accounting.

In another long-running lawsuit, the U.S. Court of Appeals for the Federal Circuit ruled October 24 that the Navajo Nation could continue its efforts to prove that an Interior Department official had conspired with the Peabody Coal Company in the mid-1980s to persuade the tribe to accept lower royalties for coal the company mined on the Navajo reservation than other government officials thought the royalties were worth. The suit alleged that the tribe had lost as much as $600 million as a result of the conspiracy and said that the Interior Department had failed in its legal duty under the Indian Mineral Lease Act to protect the tribe's interests.

The appeals court in 2001 had ruled in the tribe's favor, but in March 2003 the Supreme Court said that violations of the minerals act did not entitle the tribe to receive payment. In October the appeals court allowed the case to go forward, saying that the Navajo Nation was entitled to present its argument that the government broke a network of laws not considered by the Supreme Court that entitled the tribe to damages.

Following is an excerpt from "A Quiet Crisis: Federal Funding and Unmet Needs in Indian Country," a report released July 25, 2003, by the U.S. Commission on Civil Rights.

"A Quiet Crisis: Federal Funding and Unmet Needs in Indian Country"

Closing the Gap—Addressing Unmet Needs Through Funding

The magnitude of need for services in Indian Country clearly indicates that the federal government has largely failed [its] responsibility. Tribes fulfilled their promises when they ceded their lands, but the federal government has yet to fulfill its promises. [Quoting from a report by the Friends Committee on National Legislation].

A quiet crisis is occurring in Indian Country. Whether intentional or not, the government is failing to live up to its trust responsibility to

Native peoples. The federal government undertook a legal and moral obligation to make up for what had been taken from Native Americans and to ensure their well-being. This obligation is rooted in the history of displacement of entire tribes and the confiscation of natural resources that they depended upon for their livelihood. Perennial government failure to compensate Native Americans and the residual effects of the nation's long history of mistreatment of Native peoples have increased the need for federal assistance even further. Efforts to bring Native Americans up to the standards of other Americans have failed in part because of a lack of sustained funding. The failure manifests itself in massive and escalating unmet needs in areas documented in this report and numerous others. The disparities in services show evidence of discrimination and denial of equal protection of the laws.

The Growing Crisis: An Expression of Unmet Needs

Health Care

Native Americans have lower life expectancy (nearly six years less) than any other group and higher rates of many diseases, including diabetes, tuberculosis, and alcoholism. Native Americans are also much more likely to suffer accidental death or commit suicide. Yet, health facilities are frequently inaccessible and medically obsolete; preventive care and specialty services are too few; and adequate sanitation facilities are not yet available to everyone. Most Native Americans do not have private health insurance and thus rely exclusively on the Indian Health Service [IHS] for health care.

Despite widely documented health disparities, the federal government spends less per capita on Native American health care than on any other group for which it has this responsibility, including Medicaid recipients, prisoners, veterans, and military personnel. Annually, IHS spends 60 percent less on its beneficiaries than is spent on the average American for health care. Moreover, while other public health programs such as Medicare and Medicaid accrue annual interest to keep pace with inflation, IHS funds do not. The disparity in funding is amplified by the poorer health conditions of Native Americans. By most accounts, IHS has done well to work within its resource limitations and is regarded as an agency focused on the needs of Native Americans. If funded sufficiently, however, it could do more to stem the crisis.

Housing

The availability of safe, sanitary housing in Indian Country is significantly less than the need. Overcrowding and its effects are a persistent problem. It is not uncommon for large extended families to share small one-bedroom houses. In fact, a third of Native homes are overcrowded. The effects of overcrowding on children and adults alike are evident: poor performance in school; increased stress, which heightens the risk for alcoholism and abuse; unsanitary conditions; and higher rates of infectious disease.

Existing housing structures are substandard: approximately 40 percent of on-reservation housing is considered inadequate, compared with 6 percent nationwide. One in five reservation homes lacks complete plumbing, and 16 percent lack telephone service. Native American families wait twice as long as other American families for subsidized housing. They also have less access to homeownership resources, due to limited access to credit, land ownership restrictions, geographic isolation, and harsh environmental conditions that make construction difficult and expensive.

Unequal housing opportunities and standards lower than those available to other low-income individuals is a violation of Native Americans' civil rights. While HUD [Department of Housing and Urban Development] has made efforts to improve housing, lack of funding has hindered progress.

Law Enforcement
All three components of law enforcement—policing, justice, and corrections—are substandard in Indian Country compared with the rest of the nation. Native Americans are twice as likely as any other racial/ethnic group to be the victims of crime. Crimes on reservations are more likely to be violent in nature and racially incongruent (i.e., committed by non-Natives). Yet, per capita spending on law enforcement in Native American communities is roughly 60 percent of the national average, and significantly fewer police officers serve Indian Country than other rural areas. These factors, in addition to the disproportionately higher incarceration rates of Native Americans and unfair police practices, have perpetuated a profound mistrust of the criminal justice system. There is a strong perception of a dual system of justice and a correlation between race and law enforcement outcomes.

The U.S. criminal justice system often conflicts with traditional Native American culture. The divide between "mainstream" and Native justice furthers the mistrust, but efforts to develop and maintain tribal courts have been unsuccessful. Native Americans have long argued that tribal court systems do not have means to operate equal to other court systems, nor have they historically been funded sufficiently or consistently. Likewise, funding for juvenile justice programs and correctional facilities has not met the growing needs of Native communities.

There is consensus among law enforcement professionals that the dire situation in Indian Country is understated. While DOJ [Department of Justice] should be commended for its stated intention to meet its obligations to Native Americans, particularly in the late 1990s, promising projects have suffered from inconsistent or discontinued funding. Lack of adequate law enforcement has created unsafe communities that do not have fair and relevant justice systems.

Education

As a group, Native American students are not afforded educational opportunities equal to other American students. They routinely face deteriorating school facilities, underpaid teachers, weak curricula, discriminatory treatment, and outdated learning tools. In addition, the cultural histories and practices of Native students are rarely incorporated in the learning environment. As a result, achievement gaps persist with Native American students scoring lower than any other racial/ethnic group in basic levels of reading, math, and history. Native American students are also less likely to graduate from high school and more likely to drop out in earlier grades.

The lack of educational opportunities in Native communities also extends to postsecondary and vocational programs, a problem that continues to erode and retard individual economic advancement. Special education programs for Indian adults have not been funded at all for years, and vocational rehabilitation programs that assist individuals with physical and mental challenges are too underfunded to meet the abundant need. Tribal colleges and universities receive 60 percent less federal funding per student than other public community colleges, resulting in increased financial burden for students who are already the most economically disadvantaged.

The substandard schools in Indian Country are products of debilitating poverty and lack of adequate federal funding. Because many states do not provide assistance to Native schools and because there is no local tax base to support education in Indian Country, the federal government has sole responsibility for providing education to these students—an obligation it has failed to meet.

Rural Development and Food Distribution

The USDA [U.S. Department of Agriculture] is largely responsible for rural development and farm and business supplements in rural communities. Native Americans rely on such programs to foster conditions that encourage and sustain economic investments by external sources. However, insufficient funding has limited the success of development programs and perpetuated unstable economies. Moreover, fluctuations in funding have impeded efforts to establish solid markets in Native communities.

Poor economic conditions have resulted in another crisis: food shortages and hunger. For all the prosperity of the United States, there remain communities that resemble developing nations with their prevalence of hunger and food insecurity. Many Native communities fall within this unacceptable category, as Native Americans are more than twice as likely as the general population to face hunger and food insecurity at any given time. High rates of unemployment and poverty render it difficult for many Native families to have regular meals, necessitating reliance on federal food distribution programs.

The inaccessibility of food and economic development programs compromises their usefulness. The isolated and rural situation of Native Americans often makes it difficult for them to meet with program administrators or to access food sources. Transportation and basic communication tools, such as telephones, are not available to Native Americans to the extent they are to other groups. Moreover, programs are less accessible to the Native American population because tribes often do not have the requisite equipment, expertise, or orientation to navigate the complex processes. By its failure to make programs to both tribes and individuals accessible, the federal government has denied Native Americans the opportunity to receive benefits routinely available to other citizens.

In sum, the Commission finds evidence of a crisis in the persistence and growth of unmet needs in the areas reviewed. A cross-cutting and universal problem is the absence of basic infrastructure in Native communities. In fact, much of the unmet need could be fulfilled with adequate funding for infrastructure that supports services, programs, and product delivery. Policymakers appear not to consider this, or the higher costs associated with providing services to geographically isolated Native communities. Following is a list of specific programs that, based on the Commission's analysis, are not funded in accordance with the true costs of delivery or the needs of the people they serve.

Unmet Needs in Indian Country, by Agency.

Department of the Interior
Public safety initiatives
Economic development programs
BIA-funded schools
Tribal priority allocations
Facility construction

Department of Health and Human Services
Health facility construction and renovation
Urban health programs
Contract health services
Preventive health
Sanitation services
Health professional training

Department of Housing and Urban Development
Housing construction, maintenance, and renovation
Loan guarantee programs
Emergency funds for unforeseen disasters
Affordable urban housing

Department of Justice
Police services and public safety programs
Juvenile justice programs
Correctional facilities
Tribal courts

Department of Education
School construction and repair
Grants to local education agencies
Tribal colleges and universities

Department of Agriculture
Rural development for Native communities
Food distribution and nutritional services

The agencies reviewed are responsible for addressing these needs; however, inadequate funding, overall and within specific program areas, has rendered doing so impossible. What is perhaps most revealing is that the conditions in Indian Country could be greatly relieved or remedied if the federal government honored its commitment to funding. Unfortunately, Native Americans living on tribal lands do not have access to the same services and programs available to other Americans, even though the government has a binding trust obligation to provide them. The trust responsibility makes the provision of services to Native Americans a legal entitlement, not just a moral, social, or economic one.

Not all federal agencies make efforts to assess actual needs, much less remedy them. Assessing the actual disparity in spending between Native Americans and other groups is difficult because relatively little comparative data are collected. For example, neither HUD nor any housing organizations collect information on expenditures for Native housing versus public subsidized housing. Analyses must be conducted of construction costs in rural Native areas versus urban centers, expenditures per housing unit and per resident, and remaining unmet needs (waiting lists, length of waiting time, etc.). Similarly, the Department of Education does not collect definitive data that would monitor per student spending in Indian Country compared with spending nationwide.

In reviewing the six agencies that control the largest share of Native American funding, the Commission has given context to the unmet obligations of the federal government. The findings that follow reveal both substantive and administrative problems. Substantively, deficiencies in funding levels have resulted in perpetuation of poor living conditions in Native communities. Administratively, the federal government fails to keep accurate and comprehensive records of its expenditures on Native American programs. Reporting is so fragmented that it renders global analysis of spending nearly impossible. Solutions to these problems are urgent and overdue.

Funding Shortfalls

Over the last 10 years, federal funding for Native American programs has increased significantly, but not to the level needed to eliminate the backlog of unmet needs or to raise the standard of living to that of other Americans. As noted above, the living conditions in Native communities remain unmatched by any other group in the United States, characterized by persistent poverty, poor health, and substandard housing and education. The severity of the situation constitutes a flagrant civil rights violation, as Native Americans are in essence denied equal opportunity by the federal government's failure to live up to its promises.

Federal spending on Native programs is relatively small in comparison to that for other populations. What might be perceived as a minor sum in other areas of federal spending, is significant with respect to Indian funding. A million dollars is a large amount for the Indian Health Service, for example, when one considers the many badly needed services it could fund. Moreover, because so many tribes and communities are forced to compete for a share, decreases in Native American funding, even when small, resonate throughout the population.

In examining the federal government's funding record over the last six years, the Commission accounted for inflation and found that many individual programs have lost spending power. In instances where funding for Native American programs has increased, those increases have been insufficient, and the budgets remain minute proportions of the overall budget authorities of the parent agencies. For examples:

- The Indian Health Service, although the largest source of federal spending on Native Americans, constitutes only 0.5 percent of the entire Department of Health and Human Services [HHS] budget. Moreover, it makes up a smaller proportion of HHS' discretionary budget today than it did five years ago.
- Native American law enforcement funding increased almost 85 percent between 1998 and 2003, but the amount allocated was so small to begin with that its proportion to the Department of Justice's total budget hardly changed.
- Funding for Native American programs in the Department of Housing and Urban Development increased only slightly over the years, significantly less than the agency as a whole, and when deflated, amounted to a loss of spending power.

- Likewise, funding for the Department of Education's Indian Education Program has decreased as a proportion of the department's total discretionary budget for the last two years.
- The Bureau of Indian Affairs [BIA] receives a significant proportion of the Department of the Interior's overall appropriation each year; however, after adjusting for inflation, BIA's budget authority actually grew at a much slower rate than the department's total budget.
- The Food Distribution Program on Indian Reservations within the Department of Agriculture has also lost funding when accounting for inflation, negatively affecting available food resources and number of recipients.

These findings illustrate the federal government's withdrawal from its previous commitments and further demonstrate that Native American programs, as evidenced by their disproportionately small share of agency budgets, are not a high priority. Civil rights concerns are manifest in the fact that Native Americans often receive fewer services and less funding than other populations. Finally, this analysis proves the inversely proportional relationship between federal funding and unmet needs; as funding decreases, unmet needs increase.

The Need for Agency Coordination

It would be easy, and truthful, to simply state that greater resources are needed, and that federal funding for Native American programs should be increased across the board. But careful analysis reveals that the underlying priorities and bureaucratic hurdles of the federal government are massive, imbued, hard to quantify, and thus difficult to change. The problems in Indian Country have been studied extensively, yet no coordinated, comprehensive federal effort has been made to audit spending and develop viable solutions. The result has been a patchwork of assorted programs, not a functioning results-oriented system with appropriate program delivery and tracking. Thoughtful analysis is needed followed by swift and decisive action oriented to a system overhaul, not a tune-up. These problems cannot be resolved through minor modifications to existing mechanisms.

While some agencies are more proficient at managing funds and addressing the needs of Native Americans than others, the government's failure is systemic. Although the purpose of this report was to review appropriations, not to evaluate program administration and effectiveness, the Commission notes several areas of jurisdictional overlap, inadequate collaboration, and a lack of articulation among agencies. The result is inefficiency, service delay, and wasted resources. For example, overlap in housing responsibilities between HUD, HHS, BIA, and USDA, according to some sources, lengthens efforts to build and repair homes in Native communities. Moreover, it is necessary that BIA and HUD maintain open lines of communication with respect to land title, so that individuals wishing to purchase homes and businesses seeking to develop land in Indian Country are not dissuaded by bureaucracy and burdensome paperwork.

Likewise, the responsibility for providing education to Native children is shared between DOEd and BIA. DOEd's role has essentially become one of funding rather than one of coordinating, overseeing, and ensuring equal educational opportunity. Rural and economic development, as broad categories, are shared among USDA, HUD, and BIA, as well as other agencies not discussed here. More sophisticated articulation between HHS and DOJ could eliminate criminal justice problems associated with illness. Fragmented funding and lack of coordination not only complicate the application and distribution processes, but also dilute the benefit potential of the funds.

Inconsistent Reporting and Tracking

As Commission staff discovered during the research phase of this study, tracking Native American expenditures governmentwide and within individual departments is complex, incomplete, and difficult. There is no uniform reporting requirement for Native American program funding. Thus, reviewing the voluminous appropriations legislation for each federal agency—and even then there is no guarantee that actual Indian expenditures are listed—is the only conceivable way to assess how much the government spends in total each year. Even individual agencies could not easily determine how much was budgeted and how much was spent. Commission staff had to contact multiple offices within the departments reviewed to construct the information in this report. This laborious challenge renders monitoring of federal spending too difficult. Moreover, federal funding of Native American services is too fragmented, making it difficult for tribal governments, much less the public, to navigate.

Included in the annual appropriations bills under the Department of Interior and Related Agencies is a table, "Federal Funding of Indian Programs," which lists funding by department. While this list provides a general overview of funding, it does not provide detail about specific allocations. In addition, because agencies self-report their expenditures, information availability varies across agencies. Some agencies include every program from which a Native American benefits, even if the program also benefits the general population. Other agencies only track funding for Native-specific programs; still others track grant programs, but cannot easily determine how much of a grant is actually distributed to tribes.

Recommendations

Recommendation 1: Native Americans have suffered too long from inattention and halfhearted efforts, and the crisis in Indian Country must be addressed with the urgency it demands. The federal government must take immediate steps to resolve the disparate living conditions that plague Indian Country. Enough studies, including this one, have concluded that the existing patchwork of service delivery is not working. The administration should establish a bipartisan, action-oriented initiative at the highest level of accountability in the government, with representatives including elected officials, members of Congress, officials from each federal agency that funds programs in Indian Country, tribes, and Native American advocacy organizations. The action group should be charged with analyzing the current system, developing solutions, and implementing change. This process must begin immediately with feasible objectives that can be accomplished as early as the next fiscal year.

The goals of the action group should include increasing Native American participation in government programs; fostering coordination among federal agencies; improving research and data collection on Native American populations and subpopulations; and involving the public and private sectors in improving the well-being of Native Americans.

Recommendation 2: All agencies that distribute funds for Native American programs should be required to regularly assess unmet needs for both urban and rural Native individuals. Such an assessment would compare community needs with available resources and identify gaps in service delivery. Agencies should establish benchmarks for the elevation of Native American living conditions to those of other Americans, and in doing so create attainable resource-driven goals.

In addition, each federal agency that administers Native American programs should specifically and accurately document Native American participation in its programs and account for all projects and initiatives. This inventory will provide tribal governments and Native individuals with up-to-date information on the services and programs available and will enable agencies to identify and reduce program redundancies.

Recommendation 3: The Commission commends the Indian Health Service for the progress it has made to compare federal spending on Indian health care with that of other populations. The agency's Federal Disparity Index assessment has worthy elements for assessing unmet needs and as such should be replicated by other agencies. Tribal organizations and Native American advocacy groups have consistently monitored funding issues and unmet needs, and as such should be consulted when agencies develop measures so that the true needs of their constituencies are included. The results of such examinations should be used to prepare budget estimates, prioritize spending, and assess the status of programs. Congress should require and review unmet needs analyses annually as a component of each agency's budget justification.

Recommendation 4: All federal agencies that administer Native American programs, including those not addressed here, should be required to set aside money for infrastructure building that, when coordinated, will ensure that funds are spent more wisely. This will benefit both tribes and the agencies that need these basic installations to provide their services. Examples of needed infrastructure include roads, multipurpose buildings, utilities, and communications systems. Such a fund should be jointly managed by the Bureau of Indian Affairs, representatives from each contributing agency, and a coalition of tribal leaders or representatives from existing tribal organizations/councils. The contributing agencies should develop memoranda of understanding and other formal coordination mechanisms that outline precisely how the money will be spent.

Recommendation 5: Federal agencies should avoid instituting across-the-board budget cuts because Native American programs already make up such a small proportion of agencies' budgets. Any decrease magnifies the severity of already underfunded Native American programs. Rather than reduce funding across the board, agencies must honor the government's trust responsibility and the urgent needs of Native Americans. Ignoring unmet needs and legal obligations to tribes undercuts the ability of funds to solve problems. In addition, agencies must prepare budgets that account for the proportionality of Native American funding. As this study demonstrates, an increase in funds to an agency has not always resulted in increased spending power for Native American programs.

Recommendation 6: Native American funding programs should be situated within the federal agencies that have the requisite expertise, but agencies should continually improve processes for redistributing funds as necessary to other agencies or tribal governments. The Commission does not go so far as to recommend that all Native American funding be channeled through one source, such as the BIA, because dispersed budget authority reduces the risk that problems or mismanagement in one agency would adversely affect all services. However, the Commission recommends that funding for a single purpose be consolidated to reduce redundancy and clarify accountability. A system of centralized services, according to function, would reduce the government's redundancy and wasteful spending, and streamline the bureaucratic hurdles that often limit or delay tribal and individual participation in programs.

Consolidation of funds would further enable agencies to draw on all available resources, including those not specifically designated for Native Americans, such as those for rural communities and the operation of existing facilities (schools, health clinics, etc.). However, consolidation would require more vigilant tracking and consistent reporting methods on the part of all agencies.

Recommendation 7: Self-determination ultimately requires that Indian nations govern their own resources. To the extent possible, programs for Native Americans should be managed and controlled by Native Americans. Past experiences reveal that many funds simply are not spent on their intended purpose. Distribution of funds to tribes will require close monitoring by the source agencies to ensure that funds are used as directed. However, the methods of distribution and monitoring must be established in consultation with Native Americans and tribal governments so that the trust fund mismanagement situation does not repeat itself. The federal government must determine the most effective and ethical means of disbursing funds to tribal governments and to directly assist Native peoples.

Recommendation 8: Federal appropriations must account for costs that are unique to Indian tribes, such as those required to build necessary infrastructure, those associated with geographic remoteness, and those required for training and technical assistance. Overall, more money is needed to support independent enterprise, such as through guaranteed loans that facilitate home and business ownership, and to provide incentives for lending institutions, builders, educators, and health management companies to conduct business on Indian lands. The federal government should develop widespread incentives to facilitate education and to promote the return of services to Indian communities. In doing so, it will promote economic development in Indian Country, which will eventually reduce reliance on government services.

In addition, the unique needs of non-reservation and urban Native Americans must be assessed, and adequate funding must be provided for programs to serve these individuals. Native Americans are increasingly leaving reservations, and their way of life, not always by choice but due to economic hardships. Yet, funding for health, education, housing, job training, and other critical needs of urban Native Americans is a low priority.

Recommendation 9: Congress should require that this review be taken further, to include an analysis of the spending patterns of every federal agency that supports Native American programs. Such a review should be done by either the Congressional Research Service, which already conducts regular assessments of selected agencies, or the U.S. General Accounting Office, which has the resources to do full-scale evaluations. In addition, an independent external contractor should audit fund management of all federal agencies distributing Native American appropriations. The audit should be comprehensive, cross-cutting, and include an assessment of program efficiency; an analysis of how agencies test or evaluate programs for effectiveness; solutions for more efficient coordination among agencies; and an action plan with target dates.

Recommendation 10: Each agency should have one central office responsible for oversight and management of Indian funds, and which prepares budgets and analyses that can be compared and aggregated across agencies.

Recommendation 11: The Office of Management and Budget (OMB) should develop governmentwide, uniform standards for tracking and reporting spending on Native American programs. Agencies should be required to include justifications for each Native American project, as well as justifications for discontinuation of projects, in annual budget requests. They should be required to maintain comprehensive spending logs for Indian programs, including actual grant disbursements, numbers of beneficiaries, and unfunded programs. Such information will facilitate future short-term and longitudinal analyses.

Toward Reform

Measured by honor of funding commitments, none of the agencies reviewed has met its obligations to Native American tribes. Plans were made to reinforce the government's commitment in the late 1990s, but lost ground when budgets were cut. The government's failure has resulted in services that are of lower quality than those provided to other Americans and inequitable access to much-needed programs.

Federal law and policy already require tribal self-determination. Thus, new agreements and studies, unless they collect badly needed evaluation data so as to eliminate wasteful and burdensome agency redundancy, are not the priority. Conversely, swift and decisive action oriented to fulfilling existing federal responsibility must be taken. Clearly, Native Americans will achieve greater political empowerment and more influence in the political process when the federal government meets its financial obligations to them. Native Americans must be given the opportunity to be heard.

Insufficiencies have roots that lie deep in the past. Through monitoring of the type that this report provides, the Commission believes that Native people and federal agencies profit. The void that this study has identified, unless filled, renders laws and agreements with Native peoples little more than empty promises. If pursued now, focused federal attention and resolve to remedy the quiet crisis occurring in Indian Country would signal a decisive moment in this nation's history. That moment would constitute America's rededication to live up to its trust responsibility for its Native people. Only through sustained, systemic commitment and action will this massive federal responsibility be realized.

Source: U.S. Commission on Civil Rights. Office of Civil Rights Evaluation. "A Quiet Crisis: Federal Funding and Unmet Needs in Indian Country." July 16, 2003. www.usccr.gov/pubs/na0703/na0731.pdf (September 7, 2003).

State Department Official on the "Dictatorship" in North Korea

July 31, 2003

INTRODUCTION

The United States and North Korea engaged in another war of words during 2003 over North Korea's stated plans to develop nuclear weapons. Despite bellicose rhetoric, the two sides went through two rounds of diplomacy that appeared to offer at least the prospect of an agreement under which North Korea would give up its nuclear weapons in exchange for security guarantees.

Throughout the year, both North Korea and the United States sent mixed signals about their intentions. In North Korea's case, the multiple messages appeared to be consistent with its standard operating procedure of couching threats in inflammatory rhetoric and then backing down once it had gotten at least some of what it demanded.

The conflicting messages emanating from Washington appeared to result not from an intentional strategy but from differing views among the senior aides to President George W. Bush. Some administration officials appeared to want to engage in diplomacy to explore the chance that North Korea could be persuaded to give up its nuclear weapons. Secretary of State Colin Powell and his chief deputy, Richard Armitage, appeared to be among those advocating such an approach. Others in the administration advocated a more hard-line approach and insisted on putting as much pressure as possible on the North Korean regime in hopes that it would collapse. Deputy Secretary of Defense Paul Wolfowitz articulated this viewpoint in a May 31 speech, saying that North Korea "is teetering on the edge of economic collapse," a status that "is a major point of leverage." Bush appeared to waver between these poles; he authorized State Department diplomats to talk to the North Koreans, but until late in the year he appeared unwilling to offer North Korea any incentives in exchange for giving up its weapons. The *New*

York Times on January 12 quoted one Asian diplomat in Washington as saying the Bush administration "sends as many conflicting signals as the North Koreans."

One irony was that the United States continued to be one of the biggest sources of food aid to North Korea even as the two countries traded barbed threats. North Korea had been unable to feed its people since the mid-1990s because of famines and the country's inefficient agricultural system. An estimated 3 million people had died from malnutrition, health experts said, and millions of North Korean children had been physically and mentally stunted by lack of a proper diet. During the course of the year the United States shipped 40,000 tons of wheat, rice, and other food supplies to North Korea, where it was distributed by the World Food Program. Washington announced in December that another 60,000 tons would be sent in 2004. Bush and his aides repeatedly said the United States would not use food as a weapon against the North Korean regime. *(Background, Historic Documents of 2002, p. 731)*

An Escalating War of Words

The communist regime of North Korea had long made clear that it harbored intentions of developing nuclear weapons—for the reason, it said, of deterring a possible attack by the United States. In 1994, under intense international pressure, North Korea agreed to halt a program of building nuclear weapons from the plutonium it was extracting from a small nuclear reactor in Yongbyon, about sixty miles north of the capital, Pyongyang. In turn, the United States, Japan, South Korea, and other countries agreed to build two nuclear reactors to provide electricity for North Korea, and in the meantime to provide the country with fuel oil. In 2002 the Bush administration accused North Korea of violating that agreement by using another method to develop the necessary fuel for nuclear weapons: enriching uranium at a different facility. In the resulting diplomatic spat, North Korea ousted international inspectors who had been monitoring the 1994 agreement and declared its intention to resume work on building nuclear weapons by processing plutonium from some 8,000 spent fuel rods that had been in storage.

In Washington, 2003 opened with a flap over whether the situation with North Korea was a "crisis." The Bush administration, which at the time was preparing for its war in Iraq, insisted North Korea's nuclear ambitions did not yet present a crisis. Some Democrats on Capitol Hill, and many Asian policy experts, said North Korea presented a graver, more imminent threat to U.S. interests than did Iraq. *(Iraq war preparations, p. 40)*

On January 10, as these political discussions were under way in Washington, North Korea declared that it was withdrawing from the Nuclear Non-Proliferation Treaty, effective immediately. The treaty, which North Korea had signed, was the basis under which the United Nations' International Atomic Energy Agency had been monitoring North Korea's nuclear power program since 1994. North Korea's withdrawal of the treaty was widely seen as another indication that it intended to produce nuclear weapons, regardless of what the rest of the world thought about it.

The next four months were taken up in diplomatic maneuvering among the United States and its allies over whether and how to resume negotiations with the North Koreans. The administration of President Bill Clinton had negotiated with North Korea up to its last days in office in 2000, but Bush had cut off all substantive contact with North Korea shortly after he took office in 2001. Bush in January 2002 listed North Korea, along with Iraq and Iran, as an "axis of evil" because of its repressive regime and alleged attempts to develop nuclear bombs and other weapons of mass destruction. Since then, the North Korean government had demanded direct negotiations with the United States, but the Bush administration insisted that any further discussions be held with all six of the countries directly affected by the issue: the two Koreas, China, Japan, Russia, and the United States. *(Axis of evil speech, Historic Documents of 2002, p. 33)*

While the discussions over diplomatic process continued, both North Korea and the United States took provocative steps. On February 5 North Korea said it had restarted its five megawatt experimental nuclear reactor at Yongbyon. U.S. weapons experts said the plant had produced enough plutonium for one or two bombs before it was shut down in 1994. Later in February North Korea fired two short-range missiles into the Sea of Japan; neither missile carried a warhead, but the demonstration clearly was intended as a reminder that North Korea had missiles capable of reaching both Seoul and Tokyo. Possibly in response, the United States early in March publicly announced that Bush had ordered long-range bombers deployed to the island of Guam in the Western Pacific, within easy reach of the Korean peninsula. This deployment clearly was for show because the United States had no intention of waging war against North Korea.

China ultimately settled the diplomatic debate over format by arranging a session in Beijing on April 23–24 involving just three parties: China, North Korea, and the United States. That meeting produced no agreements, but North Korea did use it to ratchet up the tension by announcing, for the first time, that it had nuclear weapons and that it had completed reprocessing all of the spent fuel rods. U.S. officials said it was impossible to verify the truth of either statement. U.S. spy satellites had detected activity in January that seemed to indicate that North Korea was moving the fuel rods, possibly to a reprocessing facility, but it was not until after the meetings in Beijing that the satellites and other sensors detected signs that the reprocessing actually had begun.

The processing of the spent fuel was considered a significant step because North Korea could use the resulting plutonium to produce five or six nuclear bombs, experts said. Added to the one or two bombs the country was assumed to have built in the early 1990s, North Korea would then have a sufficient nuclear arsenal to pose a serious threat to its neighbors— or, more likely, to use as bargaining chips.

According to news reports, North Korea's claim led some officials in the Bush administration to acknowledge that it might be too late to pursue a policy of demanding that North Korea give up all its nuclear weapons. A second-best alternative, according to this view, was to try to prevent North Korea from developing more weapons and from selling weapons-grade material or technology to other countries, such as Iran or Syria.

Once again adopting as provocative a posture as possible, North Korea announced on June 9 that its development of nuclear weapons as a "deterrence force" was necessitated by the "hostile policy" of the United States. On July 1 the *New York Times* reported that U.S. intelligence officials believed that North Korea was developing the technology to put nuclear weapons into warheads on missiles. Such a capability would raise the ante considerably, because much of Asia (including Japan, South Korea, and parts of China) would then be within range of a North Korean nuclear weapon. Intelligence agencies said North Korea also was developing longer-range missiles capable of reaching Hawaii and parts of Alaska, but it was unclear whether these missiles could carry nuclear weapons.

Bush administration officials continued to send mixed signals about the U.S. approach. Perhaps the year's clearest statement of a hard-line position came July 31, from John R. Bolton, the undersecretary of state for arms control and international security affairs. Long considered one of the administration's hawks on issues such as Iraq and North Korea, Bolton used a speech in Seoul to denounce the North Korean government of Kim Jong Il in exceptionally harsh terms. "Kim Jong Il seems to care more about enriching uranium than enriching his own people," Bolton said. "Kim Jong Il, of course, has not had to endure the consequences of his failed policies. While he lives in royalty in Pyongyang, he keeps hundreds of thousands of people locked in prison camps with millions more mired in abject poverty, scrounging the ground for food. For many in North Korea, life is a hellish nightmare." Bolton's remarks apparently struck a nerve in North Korea, where a government spokesman labeled Bolton "human scum and bloodsucker" and said the government would not deal with him.

Six-Nation Talks

The first diplomatic breakthrough in the war of words over what North Korea had, or had not, done to produce nuclear weapons came on August 1, when the two Koreas jointly announced a new round of multilateral talks. In this round, the two Koreas were to be joined by China, Japan, Russia, and the United States.

On August 27, just a few days before the scheduled start of the talks, the internal divisions within the Bush administration once again were on display. Charles Pritchard, the State Department's special envoy for negotiations with North Korea, abruptly resigned on August 22—reportedly under pressure from Republicans on Capitol Hill because he supposedly had told North Korean diplomats that Bolton's hotly worded speech represented his "personal" views and not administration policy. Powell denied that Pritchard had been forced to resign, and he endorsed Bolton's remarks as "official" policy. Three weeks later Pritchard said he disagreed with what he called the administration's reluctance to engage in "sustained" discussions with North Korea. "We've got to get serious about this rather than the drive-by meetings that occur when we roll down the window, wave at the North Koreans, and move on," he said.

The six-party talks in Beijing began, as scheduled, on August 27 and lasted for the better part of three days. Diplomats who attended the talks said they were not formal negotiations, but rather forums at which each of the nations could express its own views. Now that it had the attention of its immediate neighbors plus the United States, North Korea reportedly used the sessions to declare officially that it had nuclear weapons and was considering a test of one of them to erase any doubts about it. Later news reports said the chief U.S. official at the sessions—James Kelly, the assistant secretary of state for East Asian affairs—read from a script prepared by the White House and was under instructions not to deviate from it. Despite the apparent lack of give-and-take in the sessions, the six parties did agree to hold further talks within two months—although they did not issue a formal communiqué, as was customary for such negotiations.

"We knew from the outset that this was going to be a very difficult process with a very difficult interlocutor," one U.S. official told reporters in Beijing. "But we set a policy direction that has proven promising. We intend to stay the course." U.S. officials said one benefit of the talks was that North Korea heard five countries of different viewpoints—including its long-time ally China—declare that its nuclear weapons program was unacceptable. Perhaps for that very reason, North Korea announced on August 30—just as the diplomats were leaving Beijing—that it would not participate in further talks because six-party sessions had been a "trick" to force it to disarm. Instead, the announcement from Pyongyang said, North Korea would strengthen its "nuclear deterrent force." Three days later, for reasons left unexplained, North Korea reversed course again and said it remained willing "to peacefully settle the nuclear issue" between it and the United States "through dialogue."

North Korea came under even more international pressure on September 19 when the 137 member nations of the International Atomic Energy Agency (IAEA) called on it to "completely dismantle" its nuclear weapons program and allow the agency to resume inspections of the country's nuclear facilities. North Korea had ousted IAEA inspectors in December 2002 as part of its claimed effort to resume the production of nuclear weapons.

A North Korean diplomat at the United Nations said on October 2 that his country had finished processing plutonium from the 8,000 spent fuel rods and was building nuclear weapons. But in an apparent response to U.S. warnings, Vice Foreign Minister Choe Su Hon said North Korea had "no intention of transferring any means of that nuclear deterrence to other countries." U.S. officials and nongovernmental weapons experts again said it was impossible to verify any part of the latest North Korean statement.

Attempting to Arrange a Deal

Once the rhetoric following the six-party meetings in Beijing had died down the Bush administration faced the question of whether to pursue further multilateral talks with North Korea and, if so, on what grounds. Once again the ideological split within the administration appeared to hobble decision making, and only in mid-October did a carrot-and-stick consensus appear to emerge. Advocates of continued negotiations, led by Secretary of State Powell, won agreement within the administration on a proposal to offer North Korea an informal "nonaggression" guarantee in exchange for demonstrated action by North Korea to dismantle its nuclear weapons program. Bolton and other hard-liners succeeding in guaranteeing that there would be no other concessions to North Korea.

Bush offered the carrot to North Korea, during a meeting with Asian leaders in Thailand on October 19. The United States would join with other countries in pledging not to attack North Korea, he said, "but we will not have a treaty . . . that's off the table." A few days later, Japanese newspapers reported that a senior North Korean diplomat had accepted the offer and agreed that a "president's letter," rather than a formal treaty, would satisfy North Korea's demand for assurances that it would not be attacked by the United States. North Korean diplomats went even further in mid-November, telling news organizations that as part of a multilateral agreement North Korea would abandon its nuclear weapons program, open its nuclear facilities to international inspections, and stop exporting missiles.

The stick of the latest U.S. policy became clear on November 21, when an international consortium led by Washington said all work would be stopped on construction of two nuclear power plants in North Korea. The United States, Japan, and other countries had financed the plants in 1994, as part of an agreement under which North Korea halted work on its nuclear weapons program. The new plants were to provide electricity for the country, but the construction of them had fallen years behind the 2003 completion date. Moreover, hard-liners in the Bush administration opposed continued work on the plants so long as North Korea violated the agreement under which they were being built. The suspension of work on the power plants offered North Korea yet another opportunity to denounce the United States, but for the moment it merely delayed and did not stop all talk of further negotiations.

U.S. and Asian newspapers reported on December 8 that the United States, Japan, and South Korea had agreed on a new negotiating strategy under which North Korea would be offered a guarantee of security, to be provided only after North Korea had moved to dismantle its nuclear weapons program. North Korea responded with an offer to freeze—not dismantle—its nuclear weapons program in exchange for extensive economic aid, as well as a security guarantee. Bush rejected that offer on December 9, saying he would not accept a "freeze" on North Korea's program but wanted it to be dismantled "in a verifiable and irreversible way."

Those disagreements, over who would do what and when, stymied plans the Chinese had laid for another round of six-party talks in mid-December. At year's end, diplomats in Washington, Beijing, and Pyongyang were talking about the possibility of talks in January or February 2004.

Following is the text of "A Dictatorship at the Crossroads," a speech delivered July 21, 2003, in Seoul, South Korea, by John R. Bolton, undersecretary of state for arms control and international security affairs, denouncing the government of North Korean leader Kim Jong Il.

"A Dictatorship at the Crossroads"

Distinguished guests, it is a pleasure to have the opportunity to speak to you again. Since I last spoke here in Seoul nearly one year ago, the United States and the Republic of Korea have forged ahead in strengthening our alliance and friendship. The foundation for this was made all the stronger by the extremely successful summit last May between President Bush and President Roh [South Korean president Roh Moo Hyun]. At that summit, our two presidents made the firm commitment to move in lock-step to meet our shared challenges and opportunities. I am happy to say that we are taking the shared vision of our presidents and putting it into action.

Indeed, action is needed. As we stand here today having just celebrated the 50th anniversary of the Armistice agreement that ended combat on the peninsula, the threat to the North posed by the Kim Jong Il dictatorship is a constant reminder of a powerful truth—freedom is not free.

In preserving freedom, it is important for all to have a shared understanding of the threats we face. Unfortunately, the last year has seen a dizzying whirlwind of developments on the threat posed by the Kim Jong Il dictatorship. Being so close to North Korea, there is no doubt that the threat posed by Kim Jong Il must weigh heavily on you. While it would be naive and disingenuous for me to dismiss the danger, let me start off by striking a positive note: The world is united in working together to seek a peaceful solution to the threat posed by Kim Jong Il. Rarely have we seen the international community so willing to speak with the same voice and deliver a consistent message on an issue. In addition to consistency, there is a striking clarity to this message as well: The world will not tolerate Kim Jong Il threatening international peace and security with weapons of mass destruction, particularly nuclear weapons.

The brazenness of Kim Jong Il's behavior in the past year is striking. While nuclear blackmail used to be the province of fictional spy movies, Kim Jong Il is forcing us to live that reality as we enter the new millennium. To give in to his extortionist demands would only encourage him, and perhaps more ominously, other would-be tyrants around the world. One needs little reminding that we have tested Kim Jong Il's intentions many times before—a test he has consistently failed. Since 1994, billions of dollars in economic and energy assistance have flowed into the coffers of Pyongyang to buy off their nuclear weapons program. Nine years later, Kim Jong Il has repaid us by threatening the world with not one, but two separate nuclear weapons programs—one based on plutonium, the other highly enriched uranium.

If history is any guide, Kim Jong Il probably expects that his current threats will result in newfound legitimacy and billions of dollars of economic and energy assistance pouring into his failed economy. In this case, however, history is not an especially good guide—a page has been turned. Particularly after September 11, the world is acutely aware of the danger posed to civilian populations by weapons of mass destruction being developed by tyrannical rogue state leaders like Kim Jong Il or falling into the hands of terrorists. Simply put, the world has changed. Consider that in 1994, I could have used the term "WMD" and most audiences would have stared at me blankly. In 2003, we all know it is shorthand for "weapons of mass destruction." Clearly, this is a sad reflection on the dangerous times we live in.

Let us also consider the fact that in 1994, North Korea could have chosen to enter the international community on a new and different footing. While communist dictatorships were collapsing or reforming across the globe, there was even hope that Kim Il Sung's North Korea would follow suit. When power passed to Kim Jong Il, the world hoped he would be more enlightened and recognize the benefits of participating in the global community—as opposed to threatening and blackmailing it.

Unfortunately, this still has not come to pass. Even a cursory glance of the first decade of Kim Jong Il's dictatorial reign suggests that he has done nothing but squander opportunity after opportunity, olive branch after olive branch. Sadly, as an editorial cartoon in *The Economist* recently expressed so well, Kim Jong Il seems to care more about enriching uranium than enriching his own people.

Kim Jong Il, of course, has not had to endure the consequences of his failed policies. While he lives like royalty in Pyongyang, he keeps hundreds of thousands of his people locked in prison camps with millions more mired in abject poverty, scrounging the ground for food. For many in North Korea, life is a hellish nightmare. As reported by the State Department Report on Human Rights, we believe that some 400,000 persons died in prison since 1972 and that starvation and executions were common. Entire families, including children, were imprisoned when only one member of the family was accused of a crime. Consider the testimony of Lee Soon-ok, a woman who spent years in North Korean prison camps. She testified before the U.S. Senate that she witnessed severe beatings and torture involving water forced into a victim's stomach with a rubber hose and pumped out by guards jumping on a board placed across the victim's abdomen. She also reported chemical and biological warfare experiments conducted on inmates by the army.

And while Kim Jong Il is rumored to enjoy the internet so he can observe the outside world, he does not afford that right to his own people who are forced to watch and listen to only government television and radio programs.

Why is Kim Jong Il so scared of letting his people observe the outside world? The answer, of course, is that they will see the freedom enjoyed by much of the world and what they have been denied. They will see their brothers and sisters in Seoul, the capital of a booming vibrant democracy. They will see that there is a world where children stand a good chance to live to adulthood—a dream of every parent. More important, they will see that the excuses for their failed system provided by Kim Jong Il don't stand scrutiny.   It is not natural disasters that are to blame for the deprivation of the North Korean people—but the failed policies of Kim Jong Il. They will see that, unless he changes course, his regime is directly responsible for bringing economic ruin to their country. The world already knows this—which is why we will continue to give humanitarian food aid to the starving people of North Korea. But let there be no doubt about where blame falls for the misery of the North Korean people—it falls squarely on the shoulders of Kim Jong Il and his regime.

There is still hope that Kim Jong Il may change course. All civilized nations and peace-loving people hope this to be true. But Kim Jong Il must make the personal decision to do so and choose a different path.

It is holding out this hope that has prompted the United States, in lock-step with our friends and allies in the region, to pursue the multilateral negotiations track. Let me be clear: the United States seeks a peaceful solution to this situation. President Bush has unambiguously led the way in mobilizing world public opinion to support us in finding a lasting multilateral solution to a problem that threatens the security of the entire world.

The operative term is "multilateral." It would be the height of irresponsibility for the Bush administration to enter into another bilateral agreement with the Kim Jong Il dictatorship. The Clinton administration bravely tried with the Agreed Framework but failed because Kim Jong Il instructed his subordinates to systematically violate it in secret. To enter into a similar type of agreement again would simply postpone the problem for some future administration—something the Bush administration will not do.

Postponing the elimination of Kim Jong Il's nuclear weapons program will only allow him time to amass even more nuclear, chemical and biological weapons and to develop even longer range missiles. Any doubts that Kim Jong Il would peddle nuclear materials or nuclear weapons to any buyer on the international market were dispelled last April when his envoy threatened to do just that.

This will not stand. Some have speculated that the U.S. is resigned to nuclear weapons on the peninsula and we will simply have to learn to live with nuclear weapons in the hands of a tyrannical dictator who has threatened to export them. Nothing could be further from the truth.

This is why we are working so hard on pursuing the multilateral track in Beijing. Having just been in Beijing, I can confirm that we all believe this track is alive and well, but the ball is North Korea's court. The key now is to get South Korea and Japan, and ultimately Russia and others, a seat at the table. We know that as crucial players in the region, and the countries most threatened by Kim Jong Il, the roles of Seoul and Tokyo are vital to finding any permanent solution. Those with a direct stake in the outcome must be part of the process. On this point we will not waver.

While the Beijing track is on course, prudence suggests that we pursue other tracks as well. We have been clear in saying that we seek a peaceful solution to resolve the threat posed by Kim Jong Il, but that all options are on the table. I would like to discuss two complementary tracks that we are pursuing now.

The first is action through the United Nations Security Council. As the UN body charged with protecting international peace and security, it could play an important role in helping to reach a peaceful settlement. Unfortunately, the Council is not playing the part it should. It was 6 months ago that the Board of Governors of the International Atomic Energy Agency voted overwhelmingly to report North Korea's violations to the Security Council.

To date, virtually nothing has happened. We believe that appropriate and timely action by the Security Council would complement our efforts on the multilateral track in Beijing. Just as important, it would send a signal to the rest of the world that the Council takes its responsibilities seriously. I would note that when North Korea withdrew from the Nuclear Nonproliferation Treaty the first time in March 1993, the Council took action within a month. Ignoring this issue will not make it go away—it will only reduce confidence in the Council and suggest to proliferators that they can sell their deadly arsenals with impunity.

The other track we are pursuing now is through the Proliferation Security Initiative, or PSI. When I spoke in Seoul almost a year ago, I detailed at length the WMD programs actively being pursued by Kim Jong Il. The last year has seen Kim Jong Il accelerate these programs, particularly on the nuclear front. Brazenly threatening to demonstrate, even export, nuclear weapons, Kim Jong Il and his supports have defied the unanimous will of the international community.

If Pyongyang thought the international community would simply ignore its threats—it was mistaken. Recently, I attended the second meeting of the PSI, held in Brisbane, Australia and met with officials from 10 other countries on the threats posed by dictators like Kim Jong Il. As the Chairman's Statement underscores, "the PSI is a global initiative with global reach." And we "agreed to move quickly on direct, practical measures to impede the trafficking in weapons of mass destruction, missiles and related items." Specifically, we are working on "defining actions necessary to collectively or individually interdict shipments of WMD or missiles and related items at sea, in the air or on land."

While global in scope, the PSI is cognizant of the reality that different countries pose different degrees of threat. Just as the South Korean Ministry of National Defense recently defined North Korea as the "main enemy," the nations participating in the PSI put North Korea and Iran at the top of the list of proliferant countries. That North Korea has earned this dubious distinction should come as little surprise in light of Pyongyang's trafficking in death and destruction to keep Kim Jong Il in power. It is practically their only source of hard currency earnings, unless of course you add narcotics and other illegal activities.

Hopefully, initiatives such as PSI will send a clear message to dictators like Kim Jong Il. In his specific case, we hope to communicate that while actively pursuing and believing that multilateral talks are a preferable way to find a lasting solution to the situation, we are not going to allow the DPRK regime to peddle its deadly arsenals to rogue states and terrorists throughout the world. Our national security, and our allies, as well as the lives of our citizens are at stake. Already, we are planning operational training exercises on interdiction utilizing both military and civilian assets. Kim Jong Il would be wise to consider diversifying his export base to something besides weapons of mass destruction and ballistic missiles.

The international community's tolerance for actions that defy global norms is fast shrinking. There is growing political will to take concrete steps to prevent dictators such as Kim Jong Il from profiting in ill-gotten gains. We are moving to translate this political will into action.

This choice is Kim Jong Il's and his alone. In coordination with our allies, we are prepared to welcome a reformed North Korea into the world of civilized nations. This would mean, however, that Kim Jong Il makes the political decision to undergo sweeping reforms. A good start would be to respect the human rights of his people and not starve them to death or put them in death camps. He should allow the families of the Japanese abductees to be reunited, and he should provide a full account of the cause of death for the eight deceased abductees.

It would also mean respecting international norms and abiding by international commitments and giving up their extensive chemical and biological weapons programs. And it will certainly require Kim Jong Il to dismantle his nuclear weapons program—completely, verifiably, and irreversibly.

The days of DPRK [Democratic Peoples Republic of Korea] blackmail are over. Kim Jong Il is dead wrong to think that developing nuclear weapons will improve his security. Indeed, the opposite is true. As President Bush has made clear: "A decision to develop a nuclear arsenal is one that will alienate you from the rest of the world." Kim Jong Il has already squandered the first decade of his rule. To continue down the path toward nuclear weapons will squander his legacy as well. The choice is his to make—but whichever path he does choose—the United States and its allies are prepared. Let us hope he makes the right choice.

Source: U.S. Department of State. "A Dictatorship at the Crossroads." Speech by John R. Bolton, Undersecretary for Arms Control and International Security Affairs, before the East Asia Institute in Seoul, South Korea. July 31, 2003. www.state.gov/t/us/rm/23028pf.htm (accessed December 16, 2003).

August

Attorney General Ashcroft and Former Vice President Gore on the Patriot Act

August 19 and November 9, 2003

INTRODUCTION

A national debate gathered steam in 2003 over whether the police actions taken by the Bush administration to hunt down and detain terrorist suspects were infringing on the civil liberties of Americans. Civil liberties advocates said the new powers given to the Federal Bureau of Investigation and other law enforcement agencies were too broad, cloaked in too much secrecy, and not subject to enough checks and balances. The administration countered that the tools and the secrecy were necessary to protect the nation from another terrorist attack like the one on September 11, 2001, that killed nearly 3,000 people, destroyed the World Trade Center towers, and damaged the Pentagon.

At the heart of the controversy was the USA Patriot Act. Enacted within weeks of the terrorist attack, the new law substantially expanded the ability of the FBI and other law enforcement agencies to eavesdrop on the telephone calls of people suspected of aiding terrorism, to conduct secret "sneak-and-peak" searches of property without notifying suspects, to track Internet communications, and to monitor the financial transactions of noncitizens and foreign financial institutions operating in the United States. Subsequent directives issued by Attorney General John D. Ashcroft further loosened restrictions on who and what law enforcement agents could monitor, including removing the wall that had separated criminal investigations from counterintelligence investigations. *(Background, Historic Documents of 2001, p. 641; Historic Documents of 2002, p. 561)*

In the ensuing months the Patriot Act quickly came to symbolize all the government police actions taken in the name of protecting the United States from terrorism—whether covered by the Patriot Act or not. These included detaining hundreds of mostly Muslim citizens as well as foreign nationals for months and tightening scrutiny of foreign visitors coming into the country.

FBI field offices were told to keep mosques under surveillance and record the number of Muslims in attendance. Agents reportedly sought information on individual patrons of several dozen libraries and monitored demonstrators protesting the U.S. invasion of Iraq. In one bizarre event that raised cries of abuse, federal agents were even called upon to help track down the whereabouts of several Democratic Texas state legislators who had fled the state to block a vote on a Republican-backed redistricting bill. *(Border security, p. 218; detainees, p. 310; airline security, p. 720)*

Civil liberties advocates on both the right and the left sharply criticized these tactics, saying the expanded police powers gave the government the authority to delve into personal and private information about individuals in complete secrecy and without having to account for their actions. The Justice Department's refusal to account publicly for the ways in which it used the act helped fuel suspicions. Critics said that the Bush administration was using the Patriot Act and the broader war on terrorism for partisan political advantage and likened the situation to that of the 1950s and 1960s when the FBI under J. Edgar Hoover surreptitiously wiretapped civil rights leaders and others who spoke out against government policies. Several organizations filed lawsuits against various parts of the act. State and local governments began passing resolutions condemning the act. By the end of 2003 three states—Alaska, Hawaii, and Vermont—and more than 200 local governments had passed such resolutions.

The Patriot Act also came under attack in Congress, where opposition from both the left and the right stymied administration plans to seek even wider powers. In an outspoken speech to the American Constitution Society on November 9, former vice president Al Gore challenged the Bush administration's "implicit assumption that we have to give up many of our traditional freedoms in order to be safe from terrorists. Because it is simply not true." Gore, who lost the presidency to George W. Bush in a bitterly contested election in 2000, called the Patriot Act "a terrible mistake" and said the administration was exploiting public fears and anxieties about the threat of terrorism "to consolidate its power and to escape any accountability for its use."

In a unusual move to shore up support for Patriot Act, the administration in August sent Attorney General Ashcroft on a month-long speaking tour to try to correct what it said were misperceptions and misunderstandings about how the law was working. Beginning with a speech on August 19 to the American Enterprise Institute (a conservative think tank in Washington, D.C.), Ashcroft delivered eighteen speeches to law enforcement and other organizations in sixteen states, in which he defended the Justice Department's use of the act. "We have used these tools to prevent terrorists from unleashing more death and destruction on our soil. We have used these tools to save innocent American lives. We have used these tools to provide the security that ensures liberty," Ashcroft declared. "To abandon these tools would senselessly imperil American lives and American liberty, and ignore the lessons of September 11th."

Ashcroft's spirited defense of the Patriot Act in particular and the domestic war on terrorism in general did not appear to have changed many minds. Congress gave scant consideration to administration proposals to add broad new powers under the Patriot Act, although it did expand the FBI's access to financial records. New support appeared to be building to repeal what opponents found to be some of the more objectionable parts of the law.

Looking Over the Shoulders of Readers

Two groups that were outspoken in their opposition to the Patriot Act were librarians and booksellers, who said the new authorities given to FBI agents to look at library records endangered patrons' privacy rights and discouraged patrons from reading certain books for fear of ending up on an FBI watch list. At issue was Section 215 of the law, which allowed the FBI to obtain secret subpoenas to review library and bookstore records for anyone who might have information relevant to a terrorist investigation. The subpoenas contained a gag order forbidding the library or bookstore from telling patrons that their records were being searched.

Librarians recalled when the FBI routinely monitored library reading records in the 1950s and 1960s, sometimes using the information to help label people as "communists." At its January convention the American Library Association urged its members to warn their patrons that the government could be scrutinizing their reading material. Several libraries around the country posted warning signs, and some libraries shredded documentation showing what books their patrons had checked out. The furor helped fuel local opposition to the act and led to passage of dozens of resolutions by towns and counties condemning it.

The controversy was fed by the Justice Department's refusal to provide information on how it was using Section 215. In January FBI director Robert S. Mueller said that recent FBI requests for library searches involved tracking suspects who used public-access library computers to communicate with other conspirators or to send threatening e-mail. He added that he could not recall a case where agents sought library records to see what books patrons were reading. The controversy was heightened in May when Assistant Attorney General Viet Dinh, the main author of the Patriot Act, told a House subcommittee that libraries had been "contacted approximately 50 times" in the last year, often at the invitation of librarians who saw something suspicious and primarily in connection with criminal, rather than terrorism, investigations. He would provide no other details, however. Many librarians said they thought librarians had been contacted much more often.

The issue came to a head on September 15 when Ashcroft, in a pointed and sarcastic speech, said if one listened to the "baseless hysteria" fomented by the American Library Association and other critics one might think that the FBI was more interested in "checking how far you have gotten on the latest Tom Clancy novel" than in fighting the war on terrorism. Ashcroft flatly denied that the Justice Department had any interest in reading habits. "Tracking reading habits would betray our high regard for the First Amendment," he said in a speech that was part of his month-long campaign to build support for the act.

In response, the American Library Association on September 16 issued a direct challenge. Saying it was "deeply concerned that the Attorney General should be so contemptuous of those who seek to defend our Constitution," the association asked Ashcroft to "allay concerns" by divulging the number of libraries searched under the Patriot Act. On September 18 the Justice Department released a memo Ashcroft had written to FBI director Mueller revealing that to date Section 215 had never been used. Ashcroft said he was declassifying this previously secret information because he did not want the public to be "misled about the manner in which the U.S. Department of Justice, and the FBI in particular, have been utilizing the authorities in the USA Patriot Act."

The administration's critics were not to be quelled, however. "If the Justice Department had been more forthcoming with the public," said one library association official, "this high level of suspicion wouldn't have developed. But they've been fighting for two years not to tell people what they were doing, and that's left a lot of people wondering what they had to hide."

Common Criminals and War Protestors

Another charge leveled against the Bush administration was that it used the threat of terrorism to insert several provisions in the Patriot Act that law enforcement had wanted long before September 11 to enhance its abilities to go after "ordinary" criminal suspects such as drug traffickers, blackmailers, white-collar criminals, and child pornographers. In September the Justice Department reported to Congress that it had in fact used the expanded powers in the Patriot Act to investigate and arrest wrong-doers with little or no connection to terrorism. The report cited investigations of Latin American officials thought to be engaged in illegal money-laundering and described more aggressive investigations of cash smuggling that led to the seizure of about $35 million. Details were given of surveillance of e-mail and Internet use that allowed authorities to arrest two suspects who had threatened to kill executives at a foreign corporation unless they were paid a ransom and to investigate a computer hacker who stole a company's trade secrets. In another example, investigators used a provision of the Patriot Act to recover $4.5 million from a group of telemarketers who were accused of swindling elderly Americans by making them think they had won the Canadian lottery.

The Justice Department made no apologies for this use of the law. "There are many provisions in the Patriot Act that can be used in the general criminal law," Mark Corallo, a department spokesman, told the *New York Times*. "And I think any reasonable person would agree that we have an obligation to do everything we can to protect the lives and liberties of Americans from attack, whether it's from terrorists or garden-variety criminals." Ashcroft reinforced this message in his speaking tour, reciting in almost every speech not only the achievements of the Bush administration in stopping terrorist plots in the United States but in reducing the incidence of all kinds of crime against Americans. *(Crime report, p. 979)*

The department's use of the Patriot Act in pursuing ordinary criminals nonetheless troubled at least one lawmaker. Although he said he knew the Patriot Act could be used to conduct investigations unrelated to terrorism, Vermont senator Patrick J. Leahy, the ranking Democrat on the Senate Judiciary Committee, said the Justice Department's refusal to disclose information on its activities even to Congress made him question whether the "government is taking shortcuts around the criminal laws." In passing the Patriot Act, Leahy said, Congress "did not intend for the government to shed the traditional tools of criminal investigations, such as grand jury subpoenas governed by well-established precedent and wiretaps strictly monitored" by the federal courts.

In November the FBI publicly denied that it was using the war on terror as an excuse to monitor the activities of people who were protesting the government's invasion and subsequent occupation of Iraq. Several civil rights organizations and members of Congress had complained about a confidential FBI bulletin sent to state and local law enforcement agencies on October 15 warning about planned antiwar protests and asking them to report suspicious behavior to the FBI. John Pistole, assistant FBI director for counterterrorism, told the Associated Press that allegations the FBI was trying to intimidate protestors by collecting information on them was "flat-out wrong." The FBI said its intelligence-gathering efforts were aimed solely at detecting extremist elements that might be plotting violence. Anthony Romero, executive director of the American Civil Liberties Union (ACLU), was not convinced. "The line between terrorism and legitimate civil disobedience is blurred," he said, "and I have a serious concern about whether we're going back to the days of [J. Edgar] Hoover."

Legal Challenges

Several lawsuits challenging various provisions of the USA Patriot Act were filed in 2003; none of the major cases were resolved by the end of the year. Among the important suits was one by the ACLU that challenged Section 215 on behalf of several Muslim and Arab advocacy and community groups that believed they were targets of investigation under Section 215 because of their ethnicity, religion, and political affiliations. The ACLU said the section violated the Fourth Amendment guarantee against unreasonable search and seizure and First Amendment rights to freedom of speech and association. "Ordinary Americans should not have to worry that the FBI is rifling through their medical records, seizing their personal papers, or forcing charities and advocacy groups to divulge membership lists," said Ann Beeson, associate legal director of the ACLU and the lead attorney in the suit.

The suit was filed in federal district court in Detroit. In December the government argued for dismissal, saying there was no basis to the plaintiff's complaint since section 215 had never been used. The judge's ruling on the dismissal motion was pending at the end of the year.

A group of organizations and individuals in Los Angeles filed suit in federal district court there challenging a section of the Patriot Act that made it illegal to provide "expert advice and assistance to groups thought to be linked to terrorists. The group, which included the Humanitarian Law Project of Los Angeles and the World Tamil Coordinating Committee of New York, said it wanted to be able to support the "lawful humanitarian and political activities" of the Kurdistan Workers Party and the Tamil Tigers in Sri Lanka. The State Department listed both groups as international terrorist organizations.

Congressional Oversight

Undaunted by opposition, the Bush administration continued to push for an expansion of the Patriot Act. At the beginning of the year a Justice Department draft of expansion legislation raised a firestorm of criticism when it was leaked to the press. Among the proposals under consideration were a prohibition on releasing information about detainees under the Freedom of Information Act, authority to collect DNA samples from both convicted and suspected terrorists, and a provision making it easier for the government to strip U.S. citizenship from anyone who served in a foreign army or terrorist group. The draft was quietly shelved after House Judiciary Committee chairman Rep. James F. Sensenbrenner Jr., R-Wis., told Ashcroft that it would be "counterproductive" for the administration to pursue what had quickly been dubbed Patriot II.

On September 10, the eve of the second anniversary of the terrorist attacks, President Bush revived elements of the earlier draft legislation. He asked Congress for legislation that would expand the use of administrative subpoenas, or national security letters, that allowed law enforcement officials to search documents without first seeking approval from a court or grand jury. Bush also asked for authority to deny bail to terrorism suspects and to expand the use of the death penalty to those who finance terrorist operations and to activities such as sabotaging a defense installation or nuclear power facility.

Congress did expand one element of the Patriot Act in a reauthorization of intelligence programs (HR 2419, PL 108–00) that cleared in November. That provision broadened the kinds of financial records the FBI and other law enforcement agencies could demand to inspect without first obtaining a judge's approval. In addition to bank, credit card, and other obvious financial records that the FBI had long been able to search, agents could now also look into financial records of car dealerships, pawnbrokers, casinos, and travel agencies in search of evidence in terrorist cases.

But in a vote that jolted the White House, the Republican-controlled House in May voted overwhelmingly to repeal the act's so-called sneak and peak searches that allowed police to conduct searches and seizures under a judge's order but without first notifying the subjects of the investigations. The language passed on a 309–118 vote but was later dropped from the spending bill to which it was attached. The Senate approved legislation that would have made it easier for agents to monitor so-called lone-wolf terrorists under the Foreign Intelligence Surveillance Act (PL 95–511). The suspect would not have to be linked to a specific terror group or foreign power, as under existing law. The House did not act on the legislation in 2003.

Early in the year Congress put the brakes on one aspect of the war on terrorism: a Defense Department proposal for a giant computer system that could search vast amounts of personal information about Americans and foreigners for clues to potential terrorist attacks. In February Congress prohibited the use of the Total Information Awareness (TIA) project against Americans without congressional approval. Congress did allow the Defense Department to continue to research and develop the program so long as it was not used against U.S. citizens. TIA thus joined the Terrorism Information and Prevention System (TIPS) on the cutting-room floor. TIPS was a proposal by the Justice Department to set up a volunteer corps of citizens informants to help the government collect information about possible terrorist threats. That plan was killed in 2002 when Congress barred "any and all activities" to carry it out. (Data mining, TIPS, Historic Documents of 2002, p. 559)

Still pending when Congress adjourned for the year were bills incorporating the rest of the president's proposals as well as legislation that would curb some portions of the Patriot Act, including making it more difficult for investigators to obtain records from libraries and booksellers and limiting some types of wiretaps.

Following are the texts from two speeches. First, "Preserving Life and Liberty," was delivered August 19, 2003, by Attorney General John D. Ashcroft to the American Enterprise Institute in Washington, D.C.; the speech was the first in a month-long series in which Ashcroft defended the USA Patriot Act and the administration's conduct of the domestic war on terror. The second, "Freedom and Security," was delivered November 9, 2003, by former vice president Al Gore to the American Constitution Society and is excerpted here; Gore called the Patriot Act "a terrible mistake" and urged its repeal.

"Preserving Life and Liberty"

This morning, terrorists struck the United Nations mission in Baghdad, killing at least 13 people and seriously injuring at least 120 others. The victims were innocent people who traveled to Iraq on a mission of peace and human dignity. Let me express sympathy to the victims and their loved ones.

This morning's attack again confirms that the worldwide terrorist threat is real and imminent. Our enemies continue to pursue ways to murder the innocent and the peaceful. They seek to kill us abroad and at home. But we will not be deterred from our responsibility to preserve American life and liberty, nor our duty to build a safer, more secure world.

Nearly two years have now passed since American ground was hallowed by the blood of innocents.

Two years separate us from the day when our nation's stock of consecrated ground grew tragically larger. That day, a familiar list of monuments to American freedom . . . places like Bunker Hill, Antietam, the Argonne, Iwo Jima, and Normandy Beach . . . grew longer by three: 16 acres in lower Manhattan, the Pentagon, a field in Shanksville, Pennsylvania.

For the dead, the hallowed spaces of freedom are memorials, testaments to their sacrifice. For the living, they are a warning. They are a reminder that the first responsibility of government is to provide the security that preserves the lives and liberty of the people.

In 1863, Abraham Lincoln stood on the hallowed ground of freedom at Gettysburg and expressed the sense of resolution familiar to anyone who has looked into the void at Ground Zero, surveyed the wreckage of the Pentagon, or seen the gash in the earth left by Flight 93.

"We cannot dedicate, we cannot consecrate, we cannot hallow this ground," Lincoln said. "The brave men, living and dead, who struggled here have consecrated it far above our poor power to add or detract."

The responsibility of those who remain, said Lincoln, is to honor the dead not with their words but with their actions . . . to be, quote, "dedicated to the unfinished work which they who fought here have thus far so nobly advanced."

It is now as it was then. We should build monuments. We should erect memorials. But our final tribute to the dead of September 11th must be to fulfill our responsibility to defend the living. Our greatest memorial to those who have passed must be to protect the lives and liberties of those yet to come.

The unfinished work of September 11 began before the towers fell, when Americans began to fight back against terror.

It was the work of the passengers on Flight 93, who fought to end the flight in a Pennsylvania field rather than a building on Pennsylvania Avenue.

It was the work of the fire fighters and police officers running up the stairs as others were running down.

It was the work of unknown heroes, whose stories will never be known, but whose spirit is the measure of hope we take from that terrible day.

The cause for which these men and women gave the last full measure of devotion . . . the protection of the lives and liberty of their fellow Americans . . . has become the cause of our time. It has transformed the mission of the Justice Department. In its service, the men and women of justice have given new meaning to sacrifice, and new depth to duty.

Where a culture of law enforcement inhibition prevented communication and coordination, we have built a new ethos of justice, one rooted in cooperation, nurtured by coordination, and focused on a single, overarching goal: the prevention of terrorist attacks. All of this has been done within the safeguards of our Constitution and its guarantees of protection for American freedom.

When terrorists had bested us with technology, communications, and information, we fought for the tools necessary to preserve the lives and liberty of the American people.

In the long winter of 1941, Winston Churchill appealed to the United States for help in defending freedom from Nazism with the phrase, "Give us the tools and we will finish the job." In the days after September 11, we appealed to Congress for help in defending freedom from terrorism with the same refrain: "Give us the tools and we will finish the job."

Congress responded by passing the USA Patriot Act by an overwhelming margin. And while our job is not finished, we have used the tools provided in the Patriot Act to fulfill our first responsibility to protect the American people. We have used these tools to prevent terrorists from unleashing more death and destruction on our soil. We have used these tools to save innocent American lives. We have used these tools to provide the security that ensures liberty.

Today, almost two years from the day of the attack, we know more than ever before about our capacity to defend ourselves from terrorists. We know now that there were fatal flaws in our national defenses prior to September 11. We know now that al Qaeda understood these flaws. And we know now that al Qaeda exploited the flaws in our defenses to murderous effect.

Two years later, the evidence is clear: If we knew then what we know now, we would have passed the Patriot Act six months before September 11th rather than six weeks after the attacks.

For Congress to have done less would have been a failure of government's most basic responsibility to the American people . . . to preserve life and liberty.

For Congress to have done less would have ignored the lethal lessons taught that tragic day in September.

Congress recently completed an 18-month study of the causes of September 11th. Congress's conclusions . . . that there was a need for better communication, a need for better cooperation, a need for prevention . . . read like a preamble to the Patriot Act written two years after the hard lessons of history.

First, the report found that prior to September 11th intelligence agencies and law enforcement failed to communicate with each other about terrorist hijackers . . . even those identified as suspects. This lack of communications had its roots deep in the culture of government. The walls between those who gather intelligence and those who enforce the laws prevented action that could save lives.

Fortunately, in the Patriot Act, Congress began to tear down the walls that cut off communication between intelligence and law enforcement officials. The Patriot Act gave agencies like the FBI and the CIA the ability to integrate their capabilities. It gave government the ability to "connect the dots," revealing the shadowy terrorist network in our midst.

In Portland, Oregon, we have indicted several persons for allegedly conspiring to travel to Afghanistan after the September 11th attacks in an effort to fight against American forces. In an example of excellent information-sharing between local, state, and federal authorities, the investigation began when a local sheriff in another state shared with the Portland Joint Terrorism Task Force information one of his deputies had developed from a traffic stop.

Because the investigation involved both intelligence techniques and law enforcement tools, the Patriot Act's elimination of the "wall" was critical in allowing all of the dots to be connected and the criminal charges to be fully developed. Recently one of the defendants, Maher Hawash, pled guilty to illegally providing support to the Taliban and agreed to cooperate with the government. He faces a sentence of seven to ten years in prison.

Second, the congressional report on September 11th found that U.S. law enforcement had long been forced to rely on outdated and insufficient technology in its efforts to prevent terrorist attacks.

Fortunately, in the Patriot Act, Congress gave law enforcement improved tools to prevent terrorism in the age of high technology. For example, where before investigators were forced to get a different wiretap order every time a suspect changed cell phones, now investigators can get a single wiretap that applies to the suspect and various phones he uses.

Thanks to the Patriot Act, we may deploy technology to track and develop cases against alleged terrorist operatives.

Uzir Paracha was a Pakistani national living in New York, who allegedly met an al Qaeda operative overseas. Paracha allegedly agreed to help procure United States immigration documents, deposit money in a U.S. bank account, and use a post office box, all to allegedly facilitate the al Qaeda operative's clandestine arrival in this country.

Paracha was charged on August 8 with conspiracy to provide material support to al Qaeda.

Third, the congressional report on September 11th determined that there was not enough cooperation among federal, state, and local law enforcement to combat a terrorist threat that found safe haven in the most nondescript of communities.

Fortunately, the Patriot Act expanded the capabilities of our Joint Terrorism Task Forces, which combine federal, state and local law enforcement officers into a seamless anti-terror team with international law enforcement and intelligence agencies.

Hemant Lakhani is an alleged arms dealer in Great Britain, who is charged with attempting to sell shoulder-fired missiles to terrorists for use against American targets. After a long undercover investigation in several countries, Lakhani traveled to Newark, New Jersey, last week, and was arrested, along with two alleged financial facilitators, as he allegedly prepared to finalize the sale of the first missile.

The Lakhani investigation would not have been possible had American, Russian and other foreign intelligence and law enforcement agencies not been able to coordinate and communicate the intelligence they had gained from various investigative tools.

To address all of the issues surrounding the Patriot Act would require more time than we have here. It is critical, however, for everyone to understand what the Patriot Act means for our success in the war against terrorism. I would encourage Americans to take a few minutes and log on to a new web site, www.lifeandliberty.gov. There, you can read about the Patriot Act, read what members of Congress and others have said about the Patriot Act, and find out how it is keeping our nation safe and secure.

Armed with the tools provided by the Patriot Act, the men and women of justice and law enforcement have dedicated themselves to the unfinished work of those who resisted, those who assisted, and those who sacrificed on September 11th.

We have neutralized alleged terrorist cells in Buffalo, Detroit, Seattle and Portland.

To date, we have brought 255 criminal charges. One hundred thirty two individuals have been convicted or pled guilty.

All told, more than 3,000 suspected terrorists have been arrested in many countries. Many more have met a different fate.

We have worked hard, but we have not labored alone:

Our efforts have been supported by Republicans and Democrats in Congress.

Our efforts have been ratified by the courts in legal challenge after legal challenge.

Our efforts have been rewarded by the trust of the American people. A two to one majority of Americans believe the Patriot Act is a necessary and effective tool that protects liberty, because it targets terrorists. Ninety one percent of Americans understand that the Patriot Act has not affected their civil rights or the civil rights of their families.

The painful lessons of September 11th remain touchstones, reminding us of government's responsibility to its people. Those lessons have directed us down a path that preserves life and liberty.

Almost two years after Americans fought in the skies over Shanksville, we know that communication works. The Patriot Act opened opportunities for information sharing. To abandon this tool would disconnect the dots, risk American lives and liberty, and reject September 11th's lessons.

Almost two years after Americans died at the Pentagon, we know that cooperation works. The Patriot Act creates teamwork at every level of law enforcement and intelligence. To block cooperation against terrorists would make our nation more vulnerable to attack and reject the teachings of September 11th.

Almost two years after Americans and the citizens of more than 80 other nations died at the World Trade Center we know that prevention works. The Patriot Act gives us the technological tools to anticipate, adapt and out-think our terrorist enemy. To abandon these tools would senselessly imperil American lives and American liberty, and ignore the lessons of September 11th.

The cause we have chosen is just. The course we have chosen is constitutional. The course we have chosen is preserving lives. For two years Americans have been safe. Because we are safer, our liberties are more secure.

During the long days of Operation Enduring Freedom, the struggle against the Taliban in Afghanistan, it was reported that every morning military commanders read a list to their troops . . . the names of men and women who died on September 11.

By reciting the names of the dead, the commanders paid tribute to the words of Lincoln, spoken on another battlefield 140 years and half a world away. They are words of hope, and words of resolution. "That from these honored dead," said Lincoln, "we take increased devotion to that cause for which they gave the last full measure of devotion."

That cause is liberty; given a new birth at Gettysburg, and reborn once again in the struggle which history places before us today. We did not seek this struggle, but we embrace this cause.

Providence, which has bestowed on America the responsibility to lead the world in liberty, has also handed America a great trust: to provide the security that ensures liberty.

We accept this trust not with anger or arrogance but with belief. Belief that liberty is the greatest gift of our Creator. Belief that such liberty is the universal endowment of all humanity. Belief that as long as there is an America, liberty must not, will not, shall not perish from the earth.

Thank you. God bless you and God bless America.

Source: U.S. Department of Justice. Office of the Attorney General. "Preserving Life and Liberty." Prepared Remarks of Attorney General John Ashcroft [before the] American Enterprise Institute, Washington, D.C. August 19, 2003. www.usdoj.gov/ag/speeches/2003/081903remark-sataeifinal.htm (accessed February 2, 2004).

"Freedom and Security"

For my part, I'm just a "recovering politician"—but I truly believe that some of the issues most important to America's future are ones that all of us should be dealing with.

And perhaps the most important of these issues is the one I want to talk about today: the true relationship between Freedom and Security.

So it seems to me that the logical place to start the discussion is with an accounting of exactly what has happened to civil liberties and security since the vicious attacks against America of September 11, 2001—and it's important to note at the outset that the Administration and the Congress have brought about many beneficial and needed improvements to make law enforcement and intelligence community efforts more effective against potential terrorists.

But a lot of other changes have taken place that a lot of people don't know about and that come as unwelcome surprises. For example, for the first time in our history, American citizens have been seized by the executive branch of government and put in prison without being charged with a crime, without having the right to a trial, without being able to see a lawyer, and without even being able to contact their families.

President Bush is claiming the unilateral right to do that to any American citizen he believes is an "enemy combatant." Those are the magic words. If the President alone decides that those two words accurately describe someone, then that person can be immediately locked up and held incommunicado for as long as the President wants, with no court having the right to determine whether the facts actually justify his imprisonment.

Now if the President makes a mistake, or is given faulty information by somebody working for him, and locks up the wrong person, then it's almost impossible for that person to prove his innocence—because he can't talk to a lawyer or his family or anyone else and he doesn't even have the right to know what specific crime he is accused of committing. So a constitutional right to liberty and the pursuit of happiness that we used to think of in an old-fashioned way as "inalienable" can now be instantly stripped from any American by the President with no meaningful review by any other branch of government.

How do we feel about that? Is that OK?

Here's another recent change in our civil liberties: Now, if it wants to, the federal government has the right to monitor every website you go to on the internet, keep a list of everyone you send email to or receive email from and everyone who you call on the telephone or who calls you—and they don't even have to show probable cause that you've done anything wrong. Nor do they ever have to report to any court on what they're doing with the information. Moreover, there are precious few safeguards to keep them from reading the content of all your email.

Everybody fine with that?

If so, what about this next change?

For America's first 212 years, it used to be that if the police wanted to search your house, they had to be able to convince an independent judge to give them a search warrant and then (with rare exceptions) they had to go bang on your door and yell, "Open up!" Then, if you didn't quickly open up, they could knock the door down. Also, if they seized anything, they had to leave a list explaining what they had taken. That way, if it was all a terrible mistake (as it sometimes is) you could go and get your stuff back.

But that's all changed now. Starting two years ago, federal agents were given broad new statutory authority by the Patriot Act to "sneak and peak" in non-terrorism cases. They can secretly enter your home with no warning—whether you are there or not—and they can wait for months before telling you they were there. And it doesn't have to have any relationship to terrorism whatsoever. It applies to any garden-variety crime. And the new law makes it very easy to get around the need for a traditional warrant—simply by saying that searching your house might have some connection (even a remote one) to the investigation of some agent of a foreign power. Then they can go to another court, a secret court, that more or less has to give them a warrant whenever they ask.

Three weeks ago, in a speech at FBI Headquarters, President Bush went even further and formally proposed that the Attorney General be allowed to authorize subpoenas by administrative order, without the need for a warrant from any court.

What about the right to consult a lawyer if you're arrested? Is that important?

Attorney General [John] Ashcroft has issued regulations authorizing the secret monitoring of attorney-client conversations on his say-so alone; bypassing procedures for obtaining prior judicial review for such monitoring in the rare instances when it was permitted in the past. Now, whoever is in custody has to assume that the government is always listening to consultations between them and their lawyers.

Does it matter if the government listens in on everything you say to your lawyer? Is that Ok?

Or, to take another change—and thanks to the librarians, more people know about this one—the FBI now has the right to go into any library and ask for the records of everybody who has used the library and get a list of who is reading what. Similarly, the FBI can demand all the records of banks, colleges, hotels, hospitals, credit-card companies, and many more kinds of companies. And these changes are only the beginning. Just last week, Attorney General Ashcroft issued brand new guidelines permitting FBI agents to run credit checks and background checks and gather other information about anyone who is "of investigatory interest"—meaning anyone the agent thinks is suspicious—without any evidence of criminal behavior.

So, is that fine with everyone? . . .

I want to challenge the Bush Administration's implicit assumption that we have to give up many of our traditional freedoms in order to be safe from terrorists.

Because it is simply not true.

In fact, in my opinion, it makes no more sense to launch an assault on our civil liberties as the best way to get at terrorists than it did to launch an invasion of Iraq as the best way to get at Osama Bin Laden.

In both cases, the Administration has attacked the wrong target.

In both cases they have recklessly put our country in grave and unnecessary danger, while avoiding and neglecting obvious and much more important challenges that would actually help to protect the country.

In both cases, the administration has fostered false impressions and misled the nation with superficial, emotional and manipulative presentations that are not worthy of American Democracy.

In both cases they have exploited public fears for partisan political gain and postured themselves as bold defenders of our country while actually weakening not strengthening America.

In both cases, they have used unprecedented secrecy and deception in order to avoid accountability to the Congress, the Courts, the press and the people. Indeed, this Administration has turned the fundamental presumption of our democracy on its head. A government of and for the people is supposed to be generally open to public scrutiny by the people—while the private information of the people themselves should be routinely protected from government intrusion.

But instead, this Administration is seeking to conduct its work in secret even as it demands broad unfettered access to personal information about American citizens. Under the rubric of protecting national security, they have obtained new powers to gather information from citizens and to keep it secret. Yet at the same time they themselves refuse to disclose information that is highly relevant to the war against terrorism.

They are even arrogantly refusing to provide information about 9/11 that is in their possession to the 9/11 Commission—the lawful investigative body charged with examining not only the performance of the Bush Administration, but also the actions of the prior Administration in which I served. The whole point is to learn all we can about preventing future terrorist attacks,

Two days ago, the Commission was forced to issue a subpoena to the Pentagon, which has—disgracefully—put [Defense] Secretary [Donald] Rumsfeld's desire to avoid embarrassment ahead of the nation's need to learn how we can best avoid future terrorist attacks. The Commission also served notice that it will issue a subpoena to the White House if the President continues to withhold information essential to the investigation.

And the White House is also refusing to respond to repeated bipartisan Congressional requests for information about 9/11—even though the Congress is simply exercising its Constitutional oversight authority. In the words of Senator [John] McCain [R-Ariz.], "Excessive administration secrecy on issues related to the September 11 attacks feeds conspiracy theories and reduces the public's confidence in government."

In a revealing move, just three days ago, the White House asked the Republican leadership of the Senate to shut down the Intelligence Committee's investigation of 9/11 based on a trivial political dispute. Apparently the President is anxious to keep the Congress from seeing what are said to have been clear, strong and explicit warnings directly to him a few weeks before 9/11 that terrorists were planning to hijack commercial airliners and use them to attack us.

Astonishingly, the Republican Senate leadership quickly complied with the President's request. Such obedience and complicity in what looks like a cover-up from the majority party in a separate and supposedly co-equal branch of government makes it seem like a very long time ago when a Republican Attorney General and his deputy resigned rather than comply with an order to fire the special prosecutor investigating Richard Nixon.

In an even more brazen move, more than two years after they rounded up over 1,200 individuals of Arab descent, they still refuse to release the names of the individuals they detained, even though virtually every one of those arrested has been "cleared" by the FBI of any connection to terrorism and there is absolutely no national security justification for keeping the names secret. Yet at the same time, White House officials themselves leaked the name of a CIA operative serving the country, in clear violation of the law, in an effort to get at her husband, who had angered them by disclosing that the President had relied on forged evidence in his state of the union address as part of his effort to convince the country that Saddam Hussein was on the verge of building nuclear weapons.

And even as they claim the right to see the private bank records of every American, they are adopting a new policy on the Freedom of Information Act that actively encourages federal agencies to fully consider all potential reasons for non-disclosure regardless of whether the disclosure would be harmful. In other words, the federal government will now actively resist complying with *any* request for information.

Moreover, they have established a new exemption that enables them to refuse the release to the press and the public of important health, safety and environmental information submitted to the government by businesses—merely by calling it "critical infrastructure."

By closely guarding information about their own behavior, they are dismantling a fundamental element of our system of checks and balances. Because so long as the government's actions are secret, they cannot be held accountable. A government for the people and by the people must be transparent to the people.

The administration is justifying the collection of all this information by saying in effect that it will make us safer to have it. But it is not the kind of information that would have been of much help in preventing 9/11. However, there was in fact a great deal of specific information that *was* available prior to 9/11 that probably could have been used to prevent the tragedy. . . .

Not to put too fine a point on it, but what is needed is better and more timely analysis. Simply piling up more raw data that is almost entirely irrelevant is not only not going to help. It may actually hurt the cause. As one FBI agent said privately of Ashcroft: "We're looking for a needle in a haystack here and he (Ashcroft) is just piling on more hay."

In other words, the mass collecting of personal data on hundreds of millions of people actually makes it more difficult to protect the nation against terrorists, so they ought to cut most of it out.

And meanwhile, the real story is that while the administration manages to convey the impression that it is doing everything possible to protect America, in reality it has seriously neglected most of the measures that it could have taken to really make our country safer.

For example, there is still no serious strategy for domestic security that protects critical infrastructure such as electric power lines, gas pipelines, nuclear facilities, ports, chemical plants and the like.

They're still not checking incoming cargo carriers for radiation. They're still skimping on protection of certain nuclear weapons storage facilities. They're still not hardening critical facilities that must never be soft targets for terrorists. They're still not investing in the translators and analysts we need to counter the growing terror threat.

The administration is still not investing in local government training and infrastructures where they could make the biggest difference. The first responder community is still being shortchanged. In many cases, fire and police still don't have the communications equipment to talk to each other. The CDC [Centers for Disease Control and Prevention] and local hospitals are still nowhere close to being ready for a biological weapons attack.

The administration has still failed to address the fundamental disorganization and rivalries of our law enforcement, intelligence and investigative agencies. In particular, the critical FBI-CIA coordination, while finally improved at the top, still remains dysfunctional in the trenches.

The constant violations of civil liberties promote the false impression that these violations are necessary in order to take every precaution against another terrorist attack. But the simple truth is that the vast majority of the violations have not benefited our security at all; to the contrary, they hurt our security.

And the treatment of immigrants was probably the worst example. This mass mistreatment actually hurt our security in a number of important ways.

But first, let's be clear about what happened: this was little more than a cheap and cruel political stunt by John Ashcroft. More than 99% of the mostly Arab-background men who were rounded up had merely overstayed their visas or committed some other minor offense as they tried to pursue the American dream just like most immigrants. But they were used as extras in the Administration's effort to give the impression that they had caught a large number of bad guys. And many of them were treated horribly and abusively.

Consider this example reported in depth by Anthony Lewis:

> Anser Mehmood, a Pakistani who had overstayed his visa, was arrested in New York on October 3, 2001. The next day he was briefly questioned by FBI agents, who said they had no further interest in him. Then he was shackled in handcuffs, leg irons, and a belly chain and taken to the Metropolitan Detention Center in Brooklyn. Guards there put two more sets of handcuffs on him and another set of leg irons. One threw Mehmood against a wall. The guards forced him to run down a long ramp, the irons cutting into his wrists and ankles. The physical abuse was mixed with verbal taunts.
>
> After two weeks Mehmood was allowed to make a telephone call to his wife. She was not at home and Mehmood was told that he would have to wait six weeks to try again. He first saw her, on a

visit, three months after his arrest. All that time he was kept in a windowless cell, in solitary confinement, with two overhead fluorescent lights on all the time. In the end he was charged with using an invalid Social Security card. He was deported in May 2002, nearly eight months after his arrest.

The faith tradition I share with Ashcroft includes this teaching from Jesus: "whatsoever you do unto the least of these, you do unto me."

And make no mistake: the disgraceful treatment suffered by many of these vulnerable immigrants at the hands of the administration has created deep resentments and hurt the cooperation desperately needed from immigrant communities in the U.S. and from the Security Services of other countries.

Second, these gross violations of their rights have seriously damaged U.S. moral authority and goodwill around the world, and delegitimized U.S. efforts to continue promoting Human Rights around the world. As one analyst put it, "We used to set the standard; now we have lowered the bar." And our moral authority is, after all, our greatest source of enduring strength in the world.

And the handling of prisoners at Guantanamo has been particularly harmful to America's image. Even England and Australia have criticized our departure from international law and the Geneva Convention. Secretary Rumsfeld's handling of the captives there has been about as thoughtful as his "postwar" plan for Iraq.

So the mass violations of civil liberties have hurt rather than helped. But there is yet another reason for urgency in stopping what this administration is doing. Where Civil Liberties are concerned, they have taken us much farther down the road toward an intrusive, "Big Brother"-style government—toward the dangers prophesized by George Orwell in his book *1984*—than anyone ever thought would be possible in the United States of America.

And they have done it primarily by heightening and exploiting public anxieties and apprehensions. Rather than leading with a call to courage, this Administration has chosen to lead us by inciting fear. . . .

Rather than defending our freedoms, this Administration has sought to abandon them. Rather than accepting our traditions of openness and accountability, this Administration has opted to rule by secrecy and unquestioned authority. Instead, its assaults on our core democratic principles have only left us less free and less secure. . . .

It is important to remember that throughout history, the loss of civil liberties by individuals and the aggregation of too much unchecked power in the executive go hand in hand. They are two sides of the same coin.

A second reason to worry that what we are witnessing is a discontinuity and not another turn of the recurring cycle is that the new technologies of surveillance—long anticipated by novelists like Orwell and other prophets of the "Police State"—are now more widespread than they have ever been.

And they do have the potential for shifting the balance of power between the apparatus of the state and the freedom of the individual in ways both subtle and profound.

Moreover, these technologies are being widely used not only by the government but also by corporations and other private entities. And that is relevant to an assessment of the new requirements in the Patriot Act for so many corporations—especially in the finance industries—to prepare millions of reports annually for the government on suspicious activities by their customers. It is also relevant to the new flexibility corporations have been given to share information with one another about their customers.

The third reason for concern is that the threat of more terror strikes is all too real. And the potential use of weapons of mass destruction by terrorist groups does create a new practical imperative for the speedy exercise of discretionary power by the executive branch—just as the emergence of nuclear weapons and ICBMs [intercontinental ballistic missiles] created a new practical imperative in the Cold War that altered the balance of war-making responsibility between Congress and the President.

But President Bush has stretched this new practical imperative beyond what is healthy for our democracy. Indeed, one of the ways he has tried to maximize his power within the American system has been by constantly emphasizing his role as Commander-in-Chief, far more than any previous President—assuming it as often and as visibly as he can, and bringing it into the domestic arena and conflating it with his other roles: as head of government and head of state—and especially with his political role as head of the Republican Party.

Indeed, the most worrisome new factor, in my view, is the aggressive ideological approach of the current administration, which seems determined to use fear as a political tool to consolidate its power and to escape any accountability for its use. Just as unilateralism and dominance are the guiding principles of their disastrous approach to international relations, they are also the guiding impulses of the administration's approach to domestic politics. They are impatient with any constraints on the exercise of power overseas—whether from our allies, the UN, or international law. And in the same way, they are impatient with any obstacles to their use of power at home—whether from Congress, the Courts, the press, or the rule of law.

Ashcroft has also authorized FBI agents to attend church meetings, rallies, political meetings and any other citizen activity open to the public simply on the agents' own initiative, reversing a decades old policy that required justification to supervisors that such infiltrations has a provable connection to a legitimate investigation.

They have even taken steps that seem to be clearly aimed at stifling dissent. The Bush Justice Department has recently begun a highly disturbing criminal prosecution of the environmental group Greenpeace because of a non-violent direct action protest against what Greenpeace claimed was the illegal importation of endangered mahogany from the Amazon. Independent legal experts and historians have said that the prosecution—under an obscure and bizarre 1872 law against "sailor-mongering"—appears to be aimed at inhibiting Greenpeace's First Amendment activities.

And at the same time they are breaking new ground by prosecuting Greenpeace, the Bush Administration announced just a few days ago that it is dropping the investigations of 50 power plants for violating the Clean Air Act—a move that Senator Chuck Schumer [D-N.Y.] said, "basically announced to the power industry that it can now pollute with impunity."

The politicization of law enforcement in this administration is part of their larger agenda to roll back the changes in government policy brought about by the New Deal and the Progressive Movement. Toward that end, they are cutting back on Civil Rights enforcement, Women's Rights, progressive taxation, the estate tax, access to the courts, Medicare, and much more. And they approach every issue as a partisan fight to the finish, even in the areas of national security and terror.

Instead of trying to make the "War on Terrorism" a bipartisan cause, the Bush White House has consistently tried to exploit it for partisan advantage. The President goes to war verbally against terrorists in virtually every campaign speech and fundraising dinner for his political party. It is his main political theme. Democratic candidates like Max Cleland in Georgia were labeled unpatriotic for voting differently from the White House on obscure amendments to the Homeland Security Bill.

When the Republican leader in the House of Representatives, Tom DeLay [R-Texas], was embroiled in an effort to pick up more congressional seats in Texas by forcing a highly unusual redistricting vote in the state senate, he was able to track down Democratic legislators who fled the state to prevent a quorum (and thus prevent the vote) by enlisting the help of President Bush's new Department of Homeland Security—as many as 13 employees of the Federal Aviation Administration conducted an eight-hour search and at least one FBI agent (though several other agents who were asked to help refused to do so).

By locating the Democrats quickly with the technology put in place for tracking terrorists, the Republicans were able to succeed in focusing public pressure on the weakest of the Senators and forced passage of their new political redistricting plan. Now, thanks in part to the efforts of three different federal agencies, Bush and DeLay are celebrating the gain of up to seven new Republican congressional seats in the next Congress.

The White House timing for its big push for a vote in Congress on going to war with Iraq also happened to coincide exactly with the start of the fall election campaign in September a year ago. The President's chief of staff said the timing was chosen because "from a marketing point of view, you don't introduce new products in August."

White House political advisor Karl Rove advised Republican candidates that their best political strategy was to "run on the war." And as soon as the troops began to mobilize, the Republican National Committee distributed yard signs throughout America saying, "I support President Bush and the troops"—as if they were one and the same.

This persistent effort to politicize the war in Iraq and the war against terrorism for partisan advantage is obviously harmful to the prospects for bipartisan support of the nation's security policies. By sharp contrast, consider the different approach that was taken by Prime Minister Winston Churchill during the terrible days of October 1943 when, in the midst of World War II, he faced a controversy with the potential to divide his bipartisan coalition. He said, "What holds us together is the prosecution of the war. No man has been asked to give up his convictions. That would be indecent and improper. We are held together by something outside, which rivets our attention. The principle that we work on is, 'Everything for the war, whether controversial or not, and nothing controversial that is not bona fide for the war.' That is our position. We must also be careful that a pretext is not made of war needs to introduce far-reaching social or political changes by a side wind."

Yet that is exactly what the Bush Administration is attempting to do—to use the war against terrorism for partisan advantage and to introduce far reaching controversial changes in social policy by a "side wind," in an effort to consolidate its political power.

It is an approach that is deeply antithetical to the American spirit. Respect for our President is important. But so is respect for our people. Our founders knew—and our history has proven—that freedom is best guaranteed by a separation of powers into co-equal branches of government within a system of checks and balances—to prevent the unhealthy concentration of too much power in the hands of any one person or group. . . .

This Administration simply does not seem to agree that the challenge of preserving democratic freedom cannot be met by surrendering core American values. Incredibly, this Administration has attempted to compromise the most precious rights that America has stood for all over the world for more than 200 years: due process, equal treatment under the law, the dignity of the individual, freedom from unreasonable search and seizure, freedom from promiscuous government surveillance. And in the name of security, this Administration has attempted to relegate the Congress and the Courts to the sidelines and replace our democratic system of checks and balances with an unaccountable Executive. And all the while, it has constantly angled for new ways to exploit the sense of crisis for partisan gain and political dominance. How dare they!

. . . So what should be done? Well, to begin with, our country ought to find a way to immediately stop its policy of indefinitely detaining American citizens without charges and without a judicial determination that their detention is proper.

Such a course of conduct is incompatible with American traditions and values, with sacred principles of due process of law and separation of powers.

It is no accident that our Constitution requires in criminal prosecutions a "speedy and public trial." The principles of liberty and the accountability of government, at the heart of what makes America unique, require no less. The Bush Administration's treatment of American citizens it calls "enemy combatants" is nothing short of un-American.

Second, foreign citizens held in Guantanamo should be given hearings to determine their status provided for under Article V of the Geneva Convention, a hearing that the United States has given those captured in every war until this one, including Vietnam and the Gulf War.

If we don't provide this, how can we expect American soldiers captured overseas to be treated with equal respect? We owe this to our sons and daughters who fight to defend freedom in Iraq, in Afghanistan and elsewhere in the world.

Third, the President should seek congressional authorization for the military commissions he says he intends to use instead of civilian courts to try some of those who are charged with violating the laws of war. Military commissions are exceptional in American law and they present unique dangers. The prosecutor and the judge both work for the same man, the President of the United States. Such commissions may be appropriate in time of war, but they must be authorized by Congress, as they were in World War II, and Congress must delineate the scope of their authority. Review of their decisions must be available in a civilian court, at least the Supreme Court, as it was in World War II.

Next, our nation's greatness is measured by how we treat those who are the most vulnerable. Noncitizens who the government seeks to detain should be entitled to some basic rights. The administration must stop abusing the material witness statute. That statute was designed to hold witnesses briefly before they are called to testify before a grand jury. It has been misused by this administration as a pretext for indefinite detention without charge. That is simply not right.

Finally, I have studied the Patriot Act and have found that along with its many excesses, it contains a few needed changes in the law. And it is certainly true that many of the worst abuses of due process and civil liberties that are now occurring are taking place under the color of laws and executive orders other than the Patriot Act.

Nevertheless, I believe the Patriot Act has turned out to be, on balance, a terrible mistake, and that it became a kind of Tonkin Gulf Resolution conferring Congress' blessing for this President's assault on civil liberties. Therefore, I believe strongly that the few good features of this law should be passed again in a new, smaller law—but that the Patriot Act must be repealed.

As John Adams wrote in 1780, ours is a government of laws and not of men. What is at stake today is that defining principle of our nation, and thus the very nature of America. As the Supreme Court has written, "Our Constitution is a covenant running from the first generation of Americans to us and then to future generations." The Constitution includes no wartime exception, though its Framers knew well the reality of war. And, as Justice Holmes reminded us shortly after World War I, the Constitution's principles only have value if we apply them in the difficult times as well as those where it matters less.

The question before us could be of no greater moment: will we continue to live as a people under the rule of law as embodied in our Constitution? Or will we fail future generations, by leaving them a Constitution far diminished from the charter of liberty we have inherited from our forebears? Our choice is clear.

Source: Gore, Al. "Freedom and Security." Remarks as prepared for delivery [at an event cosponsored by MoveOn.org and the American Constitution Society], Washington, D.C. November 9, 2003. www.moveon.org/gore/speech.html (accessed November 10, 2003).

Investigating Board on the *Columbia* Space Shuttle Disaster

August 26, 2003

INTRODUCTION

The space shuttle *Columbia* disintegrated as it returned to Earth on February 1, 2003, from a sixteen-day mission, killing all seven astronauts on board. It was the second deadly disaster in the twenty-two-year history of the space shuttle program; the *Challenger* shuttle had exploded shortly after lift-off in 1986, killing all seven of its astronauts. A special commission appointed by the National Aeronautics and Space Administration (NASA) to investigate the *Columbia* accident found disturbing "echoes" from the disaster seventeen years earlier. In a damning report made public August 26, the panel said the space agency had failed to learn vital safety lessons from the *Challenger* accident and had developed an institutional "culture" that enabled mistakes to occur. Systemic failures at NASA were just as responsible for the *Columbia* tragedy as were technical ones, the panel said.

NASA administrator Sean O'Keefe reassigned key managers of the shuttle program and said the agency already had begun to carry out all of the twenty-nine recommendations made by the investigating panel. "We get it," he said in response to the report. "We clearly got the point." President George W. Bush also promised to support the space agency as it implemented required changes, including reforms in the shuttle program. At year's end, however, Bush reportedly was considering a fundamental redirection of the nation's space program that eventually would eliminate the space shuttle program along with some of the space initiatives it supported, notably the Hubble space telescope. Bush was expected to announce his plans early in 2004.

As a new agency during the 1960s, responsible for putting humans in space and eventually on the moon, NASA was the most glamorous arm of the federal government. NASA astronauts became national heroes, and space program inventions were put to daily use in millions of homes and offices. The space agency boasted of a "can do" spirit that inspired public confidence in the government even during the troubled times of the cold war, racial divisions in the civil rights era, and protests against the Vietnam War. But a series of accidents and missteps gradually ate away at NASA's public credibility: a January 1967 fire that killed three astronauts aboard their *Apollo* space craft during a test at the Kennedy Space Center; the *Challenger* explosion; the discovery in 1990 of flaws in the Hubble telescope after it was orbiting in space; and the losses in 1999 of two missions to Mars, one resulting from a simple engineering miscalculation. Over the years Congress and several presidents starved NASA of funding for basic organizational and safety missions, and during the 1990s the agency was driven by a "faster, better, cheaper" philosophy that critics said emphasized speed and cost savings over quality. More than a dozen commissions and investigating panels reported that NASA had allowed routine mistakes, taken too many safety matters for granted, and generally lost its edge. These same problems, and more, seemed to contribute to the loss of the *Columbia*. (Challenger *disaster, Historic Documents of 1986, p. 515; Hubble flaws, Historic Documents of 1990, p. 753; failed Mars missions, Historic Documents of 2000, p. 88)*

Breakup of the *Columbia*

It was a clear, sunny Saturday morning on February 1 as the *Columbia* descended from outer space into the Earth's upper atmosphere in preparation for its scheduled 9:16 A.M. landing at the Kennedy Space Center in Florida. *Columbia,* the oldest of the four remaining shuttles in NASA's fleet, had been launched on January 16 to conduct an intense schedule of scientific experiments. At about 8:50 A.M. eastern standard time—as *Columbia* was approaching the California coast—technicians at mission control at the Johnson Space Center in Houston noticed unusual pressure and temperature readings on the shuttle's left wing, but it did not cause deep concern. Moments later people on the ground in California noticed the first signs that pieces of the wing had burst into flame. Seconds before 9 A.M., contact with the shuttle was lost; the last words from *Columbia* commander Rick D. Husband before sudden silence were: "Roger, uh." At about the same time, observers on the ground in Texas saw the shuttle burst into flames and then break apart. Dramatic video footage made the shuttle's fiery chunks resemble an extraordinary meteor shower.

Within minutes, NASA lowered its flags. A shaken O'Keefe, who had been waiting at the Kennedy Space Center to greet the returning astronauts, told a news conference: "This is a tragic day for the NASA family but also for the American people." Five hours after the shuttle's destruction, a tearful Bush spoke to the nation from the White House and made the first formal announcement of the fate of the astronauts: "There are no survivors." Along with Husband, the dead astronauts were William C. McCool, the pilot; Michael P. Anderson, the payload commander; mission specialists David M. Brown, Kalpana Chawla, and Laurel Blair Salton Clark; and Ilan Ramon, a payload specialist. Ramon was the first Israeli ever to fly in space. Bush said the disaster had not shaken his confidence in human space flight: "Mankind is led into the darkness beyond our world by the inspiration of discovery and the longing to understand. Our journey into space will go on."

Law enforcement authorities, followed within a day by NASA search teams, move quickly to secure pieces of the shuttle that had landed over thousands of square miles in east Texas and well into Louisiana. Eventually, about 25,000 people were to be involved in tracking down more than 84,000 pieces of debris. The search itself resulted in one tragedy: a helicopter looking for debris in East Texas crashed, killing two men and injuring three others.

The Investigation

Following standard protocol, O'Keefe ordered all documents related to the *Columbia* mission impounded, and he announced the appointment of a seven-member panel to investigate the accident. The chairman was retired navy admiral Harold W. Gehman Jr., who just two years earlier had been cochairman of the navy's investigation into the terrorist bombing of a destroyer, the U.S.S. *Cole*, in Yemen. *(Cole bombing, Historic Documents of 2001, p. 3)*

Attention immediately focused on an incident that had occurred just eighty-one seconds after the *Columbia's* liftoff on January 16: A piece of foam insulation broke off the shuttle's fuel tank and struck the leading edge of the left wing. Ron Dittemore, project manager for the space shuttle, said NASA would look into the possibility that the foam had caused damage that triggered the eventual breakup of the shuttle, but he quickly cautioned reporters against jumping to conclusions: "There are a lot of things in this business that look like the smoking gun but turn out not even to be close." Dittemore reinforced that point on February 5, after the first rounds of analysis of data collected by NASA: "It just does not make sense to us that a piece of debris would be the root cause," he said. "There's got to be another reason." Dittemore retracted his statement the following day, but by then it appeared that senior NASA officials were determined to find another cause.

Some members of Congress and experts in the space program quickly raised concerns about the investigation and demanded a greater degree of independence from NASA than O'Keefe's charter provided Gehman's panel. On February 12 O'Keefe provided a new set of instructions that, he said, made clear the panel had complete freedom to conduct the investigation as it saw fit.

In subsequent weeks, news reports and testimony before Gehman's panel revealed that midlevel engineers and other officials at NASA had raised concerns—starting the second day of *Columbia's* mission—about possible damage to the left wing from the impact of the foam insulation. A "debris assessment team" within NASA had suggested asking the Pentagon to use its spy satellites and long-range telescopes to examine the shuttle wing for possible damage, but this suggestion was never pursued vigorously and top managers blocked it. NASA officials never seriously considered a possible mission to rescue the *Columbia* astronauts.

As the investigation was proceeding, the NASA officials directly involved with the shuttle were replaced one by one. First to go was Dittemore, who announced his resignation April 2. Dittemore's successor at the helm of the shuttle program, William Parsons, on July 2 removed two of the key officials whose actions had come under criticism during the investigating commission's hearings: Linda Ham, the chairman of the *Columbia's* mission management team, and Ralph R. Roe Jr., manager of the shuttle's vehicle engineering office. Another engineer, Lambert Austin, also was replaced. Ham, Roe, and Austin all had been involved in blocking the request for Pentagon help in examining possible damage to the shuttle while it was in space.

Much of the Gehman panel's investigation consisted of hearings and reviews of dry technical details. In late June, however, the panel began a series of experiments to test its theory that the collision of the piece of foam into the wing was the "probable cause" of the accident. In the experiment, pieces of foam were fired at a mock-up of the shuttle wing—an attempt to recreate what happened at lift-off. Six of these impact tests failed to provide any conclusive evidence, but the seventh, on July 7, cracked the heat-resistant tiles on the wing and created a sixteen-inch hole. "We have found the smoking gun," investigating board member Scott Hubbard (a former astronaut) said.

Cause of the Accident

In its report, released August 26, the panel left no uncertainty about its basic conclusion: A piece of foam weighing less than two pounds broke from the fuel tank eighty-one seconds after lift-off and struck one of the reinforced carbon tiles on the shuttle's left wing. When the shuttle reentered the Earth's atmosphere sixteen days later, the resulting crack, or "breach," in the tile allowed hot air into the wing. This air melted the aluminum structure of the wing, causing it to collapse. With the shuttle traveling at more than 10,000 miles an hour, the failure of the wing produced aerodynamic forces that literally ripped the shuttle apart.

The board found no serious cases of negligence in preparations of the shuttle, and it ruled out terrorism or deliberate sabotage. Wild rumors had circulated for weeks that international terrorists had somehow penetrated the NASA organization or the private contractors that performed most of the actual work of preparing the shuttle. The rumors were fueled, in large part, by the presence of an Israeli astronaut on the *Columbia*.

The panel said it had found seven previous cases in which foam had fallen from fuel tanks and struck shuttles. These included several cases that NASA had not noticed at the time, indicating that the space agency did not have an adequate system for detecting damage to shuttles upon launch, the board said. One important question probably never would be answered, the board said: Why did the foam fall off the fuel tank? The board's best explanation of a cause was a combination of factors, including "imperfect" application of the foam. NASA needed to develop a new system for preventing such losses of foam and protecting shuttles against the damage they caused, the board said.

In its step-by-step review of the events leading to the shuttle's demise, the board focused particular attention on NASA's failure to take decisive action after it learned, on the second day of *Columbia's* mission, that the foam had struck the wing. Midlevel officials made three requests to have the Pentagon photograph *Columbia* in space to determine the extent of the damage, but none of the requests were pursued vigorously enough, the panel said. Further, the board found what it called eight "missed opportunities" in which steps to examine the damage could have been taken but were not. The first of these missed opportunities came on the fourth day of the mission and the last on the fourteenth day. In essence, the board said, NASA managers concluded that because foam panels had never caused fatal damage to a shuttle in the past, they would not do so in the future. This failure to reexamine assumptions prevented the agency from understanding what had happened to *Columbia,* the panel said. Summarizing the failures, the panel said: "Management decisions made during *Columbia's* final flight reflect missed opportunities, blocked or ineffective communication channels, flawed analysis, and ineffective leadership."

NASA's Organizational Flaws

While the decisions made—or not made—and the actions taken—or not taken—during *Columbia's* flight were important, the panel said the fundamental lesson from the disaster was that NASA needed to be fixed. Over the years the agency had been deprived of funding to carry out essential tasks, including safety; had focused more attention on meeting schedules than on maintaining quality and safety; had developed a "culture of invincibility" that led managers at all levels to accept too many risks and ignore warnings of possible trouble; and had developed institutional barriers that prevented the concerns of low- and midlevel employees from reaching the top.

Nearly all these shortcomings had been identified in a shelf-full of previous reports and studies, the panel said, but NASA had failed to reform itself. Perhaps most disturbing, the panel said, was that the particular institutional flaws that had led to the *Challenger* disaster in 1986 were still present when *Columbia* went into orbit in 2003. "These repeating patterns mean that flawed practices embedded in NASA's organization system continued for twenty years and made substantial contributions to both accidents," the board said.

The board made clear that NASA's top leaders ultimately were responsible for the failures within the organization. "Leaders create culture," the board said. "It is their responsibility to change it." In particular, the board left no doubt that it was skeptical of the strategies and actions of Daniel Goldin, NASA's hard-charging administrator from early 1993 through late 2001. Goldin had pressed the agency to do more with less money, summarized by his "faster, better, cheaper" philosophy. The board said Goldin had made many positive contributions to NASA, but it also said the cutbacks he had imposed—with the full cooperation of both parties in Congress—had "starved" the agency of necessary funding and had forced managers to focus on the "faster" and "cheaper" components of Goldin's mandate at the expense of "better." The board did not directly criticize O'Keefe, who had been in his job for little more than a year and whose background was in finance and administration, not space science. However, the board did suggest that O'Keefe had established an arbitrary, unrealistic schedule for shuttle missions, leading to the completion of U.S. contributions to the international space station by February 2004. The schedule did not allow "margin to accommodate unforeseen problems" and may have led NASA managers to cut too many corners, the panel said.

The board's twenty-nine recommendations included technical steps to ensure that future shuttle missions were safer than the *Challenger* and *Columbia* ones had been. The board also recommended specific steps for reforming NASA's organization to give more prominence to safety issues. More broadly, however, the panel demanded that NASA's top leadership "rid the system of practices and patterns that have been validated simply because they have been around so long." Reforms of the agency's basic practices "will be difficult to initiate, and they will encounter some degree of institutional resistance," the board said. But the reforms "are so critical to safe operations of the shuttle's fleet that they must be carried out completely," the board said, and both Congress and the White House had the "ultimate responsibility" to see that this was done.

Moving to an even broader plane, the board called for a "national debate" on the future of the space program. The panel did not offer specific suggestions for what the results should be, except to argue that the United States should "maintain a human presence in space, but with enhanced safety of flight." The three remaining shuttles could, and should, be made safe for future missions into the following ten or even twenty years, the board said. But, it added, the country needed to give more serious consideration than it had to whether to develop a "second generation" vehicle for getting people and equipment into space.

Reaction

O'Keefe and other administration officials said they accepted the board's report in full and would ensure that the recommendations were carried out. In one early sign of his acceptance of the report, O'Keefe said NASA was rethinking its schedules that called for resumption of shuttle flights as early as March 2004. Instead, the shuttles would remain grounded until NASA was certain that they were safe, he said. O'Keefe announced a new scheduled on October 3; it called for the resumption of shuttle flights in September or October 2004. NASA on November 24 sent Congress a report detailing $280 million in planned safety improvements for the shuttle, most of it to be spent in the fiscal 2004 budget year.

Members of Congress, who would have to provide the money and political support for NASA to make the required changes, generally endorsed the specific recommendations and the call for a broader debate about the future of the space program. John McCain, R-Ariz., who chaired the Senate Commerce Committee, said: "We are going to have to examine the whole issue of the future of manned space travel, where the emphasis should be, what our priorities are." One question that quickly leapt to the center of attention was whether NASA should develop a vehicle to succeed the shuttle, known tentatively as a "space plane." O'Keefe told Congress in late October that NASA was considering speeding up work on such a plane. Key House members objected, but O'Keefe appeared to win important support in the Senate. Congress took no action to resolve the issue by year's end. However, news reports late in the year indicated that the administration was working on a new plan for space exploration, one that might suggest a dramatic change of direction that would scrap the shuttles by 2010 and some of the programs they serviced (including the still-incomplete international space station) and focus instead on a return of manned missions to the Moon and possibly even Mars.

Space policy experts outside the government generally said the investigating board had correctly identified the technical and organizational flaws that had contributed to the *Columbia* disaster. Some experts said the panel had not gone far enough and should have demanded a wholesale replacement of NASA's top managers, including O'Keefe. Others said the agency could change, with its current managers in place, if Congress and the White House applied consistent pressure. Even some members of the investigating board expressed skepticism about NASA's ability to change its organizational culture, as the board had demanded. Duane Deal, an air force brigadier general and board member, submitted a "supplement" to the report detailing numerous technical items he said had been left out of, or "buried," in the overall report. Asked if a turnaround at NASA was likely, board member Douglas Osheroff, a professor of physics at Stanford University, responded this way: "If I were betting, I would probably bet no."

Following are excerpts made public August 26, 2003, from the report of the Columbia Accident Investigation Board, which had been appointed by the National Aeronautics and Space Administration to examine the causes of the February 1, 2003, destruction of the space shuttle Columbia.

Report of the Columbia Accident Investigation Board

Part One: The Accident

Chapter 1: The Evolution of the Space Shuttle Program

More than two decades after its first flight, the Space Shuttle remains the only reusable spacecraft in the world capable of simultaneously putting multiple-person crews and heavy cargo into orbit, of deploying, servicing, and retrieving satellites, and of returning the products of on-orbit research to Earth. These capabilities are an important asset for the United States and its international partners in space. Current plans call for the Space Shuttle to play a central role in the U.S. human space flight program for years to come.

The Space Shuttle Program's remarkable successes, however, come with high costs and tremendous risks. The February 1 disintegration of *Columbia* during re-entry, 17 years after *Challenger* was destroyed on ascent, is the most recent reminder that sending people into orbit and returning them safely to Earth remains a difficult and perilous endeavor.

It is the view of the Columbia Accident Investigation Board that the *Columbia* accident is not a random event, but rather a product of the Space Shuttle Program's history and current management processes. Fully understanding how it happened requires an exploration of that history and management. This chapter charts how the Shuttle emerged from a series of political compromises that produced unreasonable expectations—even myths—about its performance, how the *Challenger* accident shattered those myths several years after NASA began acting upon them as fact, and how, in retrospect, the Shuttle's technically ambitious design resulted in an inherently vulnerable vehicle, the safe operation of which exceeded NASA's organizational capabilities as they existed at the time of the *Columbia* accident. The Board's investigation of what caused the *Columbia* accident thus begins in the fields of East Texas but reaches more than 30 years into the past, to a series of economically and politically driven decisions that cast the Shuttle program in a role that its nascent technology could not support. To understand the cause of the *Columbia* accident is to understand how a program promising reliability and cost efficiency resulted instead in a developmental vehicle that never achieved the fully operational status NASA and the nation accorded it. . . .

Concluding Thoughts

The Orbiter that carried the STS-107 [Space Transportation System flight 107: NASA's formulation for the *Columbia* mission] crew to orbit 22 years after its first flight reflects the history of the Space Shuttle Program. When *Columbia* lifted off from Launch Complex 39-A at Kennedy Space Center on January 16, 2003, it superficially resembled the Orbiter that had first flown in 1981, and indeed many elements of its airframe dated back to its first flight. More than 44 percent of its tiles, and 41 of the 44 wing leading edge Reinforced Carbon-Carbon (RCC) panels were original equipment. But there were also many new systems in *Columbia*, from a modern "glass" cockpit to second-generation main engines.

Although an engineering marvel that enables a wide-variety of on-orbit operations, including the assembly of the International Space Station, the Shuttle has few of the mission capabilities that NASA originally promised. It cannot be launched on demand, does not recoup its costs, no longer carries national security payloads, and is not cost-effective enough, nor allowed by law, to carry commercial satellites. Despite efforts to improve its safety, the Shuttle remains a complex and risky system that remains central to U.S. ambitions in space. *Columbia*'s failure to return home is a harsh reminder that the Space Shuttle is a developmental vehicle that operates not in routine flight but in the realm of dangerous exploration. . . .

Chapter 3: Accident Analysis

One of the central purposes of this investigation, like those for other kinds of accidents, was to identify the chain of circumstances that caused the *Columbia* accident. In this case the task was particularly challenging, because the breakup of the Orbiter occurred at hypersonic velocities and extremely high altitudes, and the debris was scattered over a wide area. Moreover, the initiating event preceded the accident by more than two weeks. In pursuit of the sequence of the cause, investigators developed a broad array of information sources. Evidence was derived from film and video of the launch, radar images of *Columbia* on orbit, and amateur video of debris shedding during the in-flight breakup. Data was obtained from sensors onboard the Orbiter—some of this data was downlinked during the flight, and some came from an on-board recorder that was recovered during the debris search. Analysis of the debris was particularly valuable to the investigation. Clues were to be found not only in the condition of the pieces, but also in their location—both where they had been on the Orbiter and where they were found on the ground. The investigation also included extensive computer modeling, impact tests, wind tunnel studies, and other analytical techniques. . . .

The Physical Cause
The physical cause of the loss of *Columbia* and its crew was a breach in the Thermal Protection System on the leading edge of the left wing. The breach was initiated by a piece of insulating foam that separated from the left bipod ramp of the External Tank and struck the wing in the vicinity of the lower half of Reinforced Carbon-Carbon panel 8 at 81.9 seconds after launch. During re-entry, this breach in the Thermal Protection System allowed superheated air to penetrate the leading-edge insulation and progressively melt the aluminum structure of the left wing, resulting in a weakening of the structure until increasing aerodynamic forces caused loss of control, failure of the wing, and breakup of the Orbiter. . . .

Foam loss has occurred on more than 80 percent of the 79 missions for which imagery is available, and foam was lost from the left bipod ramp on nearly 10 percent of missions where the left bipod ramp was visible following External Tank separation. For about 30 percent of all missions, there is no way to determine if foam was lost; these were either night launches, or the External Tank bipod ramp areas were not in view when the images were taken. The External Tank was not designed to be instrumented or recovered after separation, which deprives NASA of physical evidence that could help pinpoint why foam separates from it.

The precise reasons why the left bipod foam ramp was lost from the External Tank during STS-107 may never be known. The specific initiating event may likewise remain a mystery. However, it is evident that a combination of variable and pre-existing factors, such as insufficient testing and analysis in the early design stages, resulted in a highly variable and complex foam material, defects induced by an imperfect and variable application, and the results of that imperfect process, as well as severe load, thermal, pressure, vibration, acoustic, and structural launch and ascent conditions.

Findings:

- NASA does not fully understand the mechanisms that cause foam loss on almost all flights from larger areas of foam coverage and from areas that are sculpted by hand.
- There are no qualified non-destructive evaluation techniques for the as-installed foam to determine the characteristics of the foam before flight.
- Foam loss from an External Tank is unrelated to the tank's age and to its total pre-launch exposure to the elements. Therefore, the foam loss on STS-107 is unrelated to either the age or exposure of External Tank 93 before launch.
- The Board found no indications of negligence in the application of the External Tank Thermal Protection System.
- The Board found instances of left bipod ramp shedding on launch that NASA was not aware of, bringing the total known left bipod ramp shedding events to 7 out of 72 missions for which imagery of the launch or External Tank separation is available.
- Subsurface defects were found during the dissection of three bipod foam ramps, suggesting that similar defects were likely present in the left bipod ramp of External Tank 93 used on STS-107.
- Foam loss occurred on more than 80 percent of the 79 missions for which imagery was available to confirm or rule out foam loss.
- Thirty percent of all missions lacked sufficient imagery to determine if foam had been lost.
- Analysis of numerous separate variables indicated that none could be identified as the sole initiating factor of bipod foam loss. The Board therefore concludes that a combination of several factors resulted in bipod foam loss.

Recommendation:

- Initiate an aggressive program to eliminate all External Tank Thermal Protection System debris-shedding at the source with particular emphasis on the region where the bipod struts attach to the External Tank. . . .

Chapter 4: Other Factors Considered

During its investigation, the Board evaluated every known factor that could have caused or contributed to the *Columbia* accident, such as the effects of space weather on the Orbiter during re-entry and the specters of sabotage and terrorism. In addition to the analysis/scenario investigations, the Board oversaw a NASA "fault tree" investigation, which accounts for every chain of events that could possibly cause a system to fail. Most of these factors were conclusively eliminated as having nothing to do with the accident; however, several factors have yet to be ruled out. Although deemed by the Board as unlikely to have contributed to the accident, these are still open and are being investigated further by NASA. In a few other cases, there is insufficient evidence to completely eliminate a factor, though most evidence indicates that it did not play a role in the accident. In the course of investigating these factors, the Board identified several serious problems that were not part of the accident's causal chain but nonetheless have major implications for future missions. . . .

Part Two: Why the Accident Occurred

Many accident investigations do not go far enough. They identify the technical cause of the accident, and then connect it to a variant of "operator error"—the line worker who forgot to insert the bolt, the engineer who miscalculated the stress, or the manager who made the wrong decision. But this is seldom the entire issue. When the determinations of the causal chain are limited to the technical flaw and individual failure, typically the actions taken to prevent a similar event in the future are also limited: fix the technical problem and replace or retrain the individual responsible. Putting these corrections in place leads to another mistake—the belief that the problem is solved. The Board did not want to make these errors.

Attempting to manage high-risk technologies while minimizing failures is an extraordinary challenge. By their nature, these complex technologies are intricate, with many interrelated parts. Standing alone, the components may be well understood and have failure modes that can be anticipated. Yet when these components are integrated into a larger system, unanticipated interactions can occur that lead to catastrophic outcomes. The risk of these complex systems is increased when they are produced and operated by complex organizations that also break down in unanticipated ways.

In our view, the NASA organizational culture had as much to do with this accident as the foam. Organizational culture refers to the basic values, norms, beliefs, and practices that characterize the functioning of an institution. At the most basic level, organizational culture defines the assumptions that employees make as they carry out their work. It is a powerful force that can persist through reorganizations and the change of key personnel. It can be a positive or a negative force.

In a report dealing with nuclear wastes, the National Research Council quoted Alvin Weinberg's classic statement about the "Faustian bargain" that nuclear scientists made with society. "The price that we demand of society for this magical energy source is both a vigilance and a longevity of our social institutions that we are quite unaccustomed to." This is also true of the space program. At NASA's urging, the nation committed to building an amazing, if compromised, vehicle called the Space Shuttle. When the agency did this, it accepted the bargain to operate and maintain the vehicle in the safest possible way. The Board is not convinced that NASA has completely lived up to the bargain, or that Congress and the Administration has provided the funding and support necessary for NASA to do so. This situation needs to be addressed—if the nation intends to keep conducting human space flight, it needs to live up to its part of the bargain. . . .

Chapter 5: From *Challenger* to *Columbia*

The Board is convinced that the factors that led to the *Columbia* accident go well beyond the physical mechanisms discussed in Chapter 3. The causal roots of the accident can also be traced, in part, to the turbulent post–Cold War policy environment in which NASA functioned during most of the years between the destruction of *Challenger* and the loss of *Columbia*. The end of the Cold War in the late 1980s meant that the most important political underpinning of NASA's Human Space Flight Program—U.S.-Soviet space competition—was lost, with no equally strong political objective to replace it. No longer able to justify its projects with the kind of urgency that the superpower struggle had provided, the agency could not obtain budget increases through the 1990s. Rather than adjust its ambitions to this new state of affairs, NASA continued to push an ambitious agenda of space science and exploration, including a costly Space Station Program.

If NASA wanted to carry out that agenda, its only recourse, given its budget allocation, was to become more efficient, accomplishing more at less cost. The search for cost reductions led top NASA leaders over the past decade to downsize the Shuttle workforce, outsource various Shuttle Program responsibilities—including safety oversight—and consider eventual privatization of the Space Shuttle Program. The program's budget was reduced by 40 percent in purchasing power over the past decade and repeatedly raided to make up for Space Station cost overruns, even as the Program maintained a launch schedule in which the Shuttle, a developmental vehicle, was used in an operational mode. In addition, the uncertainty of top policymakers in the White House, Congress, and NASA as to how long the Shuttle would fly before being replaced resulted in the delay of upgrades needed to make the Shuttle safer and to extend its service life.

The Space Shuttle Program has been transformed since the late 1980s implementation of post–*Challenger* management changes in ways that raise questions, addressed here and [later], about NASA's ability to safely operate the Space Shuttle. While it would be inaccurate to say that NASA managed the Space Shuttle Program at the time of the *Columbia* accident in the same manner it did prior to *Challenger*, there are unfortunate similarities between the agency's performance and safety practices in both periods. . . .

The NASA Human Space Flight Culture

Though NASA underwent many management reforms in the wake of the *Challenger* accident and appointed new directors at the Johnson, Marshall, and Kennedy centers, the agency's powerful human space flight culture remained intact, as did many institutional practices, even if in a modified form. As a close observer of NASA's organizational culture has observed, "Cultural norms tend to be fairly resilient . . . The norms bounce back into shape after being stretched or bent. Beliefs held in common throughout the organization resist alteration." This culture . . . acted over time to resist externally imposed change. By the eve of the *Columbia* accident, institutional practices that were in effect at the time of the *Challenger* accident— such as inadequate concern over deviations from expected performance, a silent safety program, and schedule pressure—had returned to NASA.

The human space flight culture within NASA originated in the Cold War environment. The space agency itself was created in 1958 as a response to the Soviet launch of Sputnik, the first artificial Earth satellite. In 1961, President John F. Kennedy charged the new space agency with the task of reaching the moon before the end of the decade, and asked Congress and the American people to commit the immense resources for doing so, even though at the time NASA had only accumulated 15 minutes of human space flight experience. With its efforts linked to U.S.-Soviet competition for global leadership, there was a sense in the NASA workforce that the agency was engaged in a historic struggle central to the nation's agenda.

The Apollo era created at NASA an exceptional "can-do" culture marked by tenacity in the face of seemingly impossible challenges. This culture valued the interaction among research and testing, hands-on engineering experience, and a dependence on the exceptional quality of the its workforce and leadership that provided in-house technical capability to oversee the work of contractors. The culture also accepted risk and failure as inevitable aspects of operating in space, even as it held as its highest value attention to detail in order to lower the chances of failure.

The dramatic Apollo 11 lunar landing in July 1969 fixed NASA's achievements in the national consciousness, and in history. However, the numerous accolades in the wake of the moon landing also helped reinforce the NASA staff's faith in their organizational culture. Apollo successes created the powerful image of the space agency as a "perfect place," as "the best organization that human beings could create to accomplish selected goals." During Apollo, NASA was in many respects a highly successful organization capable of achieving seemingly impossible feats. The continuing image of NASA as a "perfect place" in the years after Apollo left NASA employees unable to recognize that NASA never had been, and still was not, perfect, nor was it as symbolically important in the continuing Cold War struggle as it had been for its first decade of existence. NASA personnel maintained a vision of their agency that was rooted in the glories of an earlier time, even as the world, and thus the context within which the space agency operated, changed around them.

As a result, NASA's human space flight culture never fully adapted to the Space Shuttle Program, with its goal of routine access to space rather than further exploration beyond low-Earth orbit. The Apollo-era organizational culture came to be in tension with the more bureaucratic space agency of the 1970s, whose focus turned from designing new spacecraft at any expense to repetitively flying a reusable vehicle on an ever-tightening budget. This trend toward bureaucracy and the associated increased reliance on contracting necessitated more effective communications and more extensive safety oversight processes than had been in place during the Apollo era, but the Rogers Commission [the commission, headed by former secretary of state William Rogers, that investigated the 1986 *Challenger* disaster] found that such features were lacking.

In the aftermath of the *Challenger* accident, these contradictory forces prompted a resistance to externally imposed changes and an attempt to maintain the internal belief that NASA was still a "perfect place," alone in its ability to execute a program of human space flight. Within NASA centers, as Human Space Flight Program managers strove to maintain their view of the organization, they lost their ability to accept criticism, leading them to reject the recommendations of many boards and blue-ribbon panels, the Rogers Commission among them.

External criticism and doubt, rather than spurring NASA to change for the better, instead reinforced the will to "impose the party line vision on the environment, not to reconsider it," according to one authority on organizational behavior. This in turn led to "flawed decision making, self deception, introversion and a diminished curiosity about the world outside the perfect place." The NASA human space flight culture the Board found during its investigation manifested many of these characteristics, in particular a self-confidence about NASA possessing unique knowledge about how to safely launch people into space. As will be discussed later . . . the Board views this cultural resistance as a fundamental impediment to NASA's effective organizational performance. . . .

Space Shuttle Progam Budget Patterns. For the past 30 years, the Space Shuttle Program has been NASA's single most expensive activity, and of all NASA's efforts, that program has been hardest hit by the budget constraints of the past decade. Given the high priority assigned after 1993 to completing the costly International Space Station, NASA managers have had little choice but to attempt to reduce the costs of operating the Space Shuttle. This left little funding for Shuttle improvements. The squeeze on the Shuttle budget was even more severe after the Office of Management and Budget in 1994 insisted that any cost overruns in the International Space Station budget be made up from within the budget allocation for human space flight, rather than from the agency's budget as a whole. The Shuttle was the only other large program within that budget category. . . .

Conclusion

Over the last decade, the Space Shuttle Program has operated in a challenging and often turbulent environment.

As discussed in this chapter, there were at least three major contributing factors to that environment:

- Throughout the decade, the Shuttle Program has had to function within an increasingly constrained budget. Both the Shuttle budget and workforce have been reduced by over 40 percent during the past decade. The White House, Congress, and NASA leadership exerted constant pressure to reduce or at least freeze operating costs. As a result, there was little margin in the budget to deal with unexpected technical problems or make Shuttle improvements.
- The Shuttle was mischaracterized by the 1995 Kraft Report [issued by an advisory panel headed by space veteran Christopher Kraft] as "a mature and reliable system . . . about as safe as today's technology will provide." Based on this mischaracterization, NASA believed that it could turn increased responsibilities for Shuttle operations over to a single prime contractor and reduce its direct involvement in ensuring safe Shuttle operations, instead monitoring contractor performance from a more detached position. NASA also believed that it could use the "mature" Shuttle to carry out operational missions without continually focusing engineering attention on understanding the mission-by-mission anomalies inherent in a developmental vehicle.
- In the 1990s, the planned date for replacing the Shuttle shifted from 2006 to 2012 and then to 2015 or later. Given the uncertainty regarding the Shuttle's service life, there has been policy and budgetary

ambivalence on investing in the vehicle. Only in the past year has NASA begun to provide the resources needed to sustain extended Shuttle operations. Previously, safety and support upgrades were delayed or deferred, and Shuttle infrastructure was allowed to deteriorate.

The Board observes that this is hardly an environment in which those responsible for safe operation of the Shuttle can function without being influenced by external pressures. It is to the credit of Space Shuttle managers and the Shuttle workforce that the vehicle was able to achieve its program objectives for as long as it did.

An examination of the Shuttle Program's history from *Challenger* to *Columbia* raises the question: Did the Space Shuttle Program budgets constrained by the White House and Congress threaten safe Shuttle operations? There is no straightforward answer. In 1994, an analysis of the Shuttle budget concluded that reductions made in the early 1990s represented a "healthy tightening up" of the program. Certainly those in the Office of Management and Budget and in NASA's congressional authorization and appropriations subcommittees thought they were providing enough resources to operate the Shuttle safely, while also taking into account the expected Shuttle lifetime and the many other demands on the Federal budget. NASA Headquarters agreed, at least until Administrator [NASA administrator Daniel] Goldin declared a "space launch crisis" in June 1999 and asked that additional resources for safety upgrades be added to the NASA budget. By 2001, however, one experienced observer of the space program described the Shuttle workforce as "The Few, the Tired," and suggested that "a decade of downsizing and budget tightening has left NASA exploring the universe with a less experienced staff and older equipment."

It is the Board's view that this latter statement is an accurate depiction of the Space Shuttle Program at the time of STS-107. The Program was operating too close to too many margins. The Board also finds that recent modest increases in the Shuttle Program's budget are necessary and overdue steps toward providing the resources to sustain the program for its now-extended lifetime. Similarly, NASA has recently recognized that providing an adequately sized and appropriately trained workforce is critical to the agency's future success.

An examination of the Program's management changes also leads to the question: Did turmoil in the management structure contribute to the accident? The Board found no evidence that the transition from many Space Shuttle contractors to a partial consolidation of contracts under a single firm has by itself introduced additional technical risk into the Space Shuttle Program. The transfer of responsibilities that has accompanied the Space Flight Operations Contract has, however, complicated an already complex Program structure and created barriers to effective communication. Designating the Johnson Space Center as the "lead center" for the Space Shuttle Program did resurrect some of the Center rivalries and communication difficulties that existed before the *Challenger* accident. The specific ways in which this complexity and lack of an integrated approach to Shuttle management impinged on NASA's performance during and before the flight of STS-107 are discussed [later].

As the 21st century began, NASA's deeply ingrained human space flight culture—one that has evolved over 30 years as the basis for a more conservative, less technically and organizationally capable organization than the Apollo-era NASA—remained strong enough to resist external pressures for adaptation and change. At the time of the launch of STS-107, NASA retained too many negative (and also many positive) aspects of its traditional culture: "flawed decision making, self deception, introversion and a diminished curiosity about the world outside the perfect place" [quotation from Garry D. Brewer in "Perfect Places: NASA as an Idealized Institution]. . . .

Chapter 6: Decision Making at NASA

The dwindling post—Cold War Shuttle budget that launched NASA leadership on a crusade for efficiency in the decade before *Columbia*'s final flight powerfully shaped the environment in which Shuttle managers worked. . . .

A History of Foam Anomalies

The shedding of External Tank foam—the physical cause of the *Columbia* accident—had a long history. . . .

Conclusion. Despite original design requirements that the External Tank not shed debris, and the corresponding design requirement that the Orbiter not receive debris hits exceeding a trivial amount of force, debris has impacted the Shuttle on each flight. Over the course of 113 missions, foam-shedding and other debris impacts came to be regarded more as a turnaround or maintenance issue, and less as a hazard to the vehicle and crew.

Assessments of foam-shedding and strikes were not thoroughly substantiated by engineering analysis, and the process for closing In-Flight Anomalies is not well-documented and appears to vary. Shuttle Program managers appear to have confused the notion of foam posing an "accepted risk" with foam not being a "safety-of-flight issue." At times, the pressure to meet the flight schedule appeared to cut short engineering efforts to resolve the foam-shedding problem.

NASA's lack of understanding of foam properties and behavior must also be questioned. Although tests were conducted to develop and qualify foam for use on the External Tank, it appears there were large gaps in NASA's knowledge about this complex and variable material. Recent testing conducted at Marshall Space Flight Center and under the auspices of the Board indicate that mechanisms previously considered a prime source of foam loss, cryopumping and cryoingestion, are not feasible in the conditions experienced during tanking, launch, and ascent. Also, dissections of foam bipod ramps on External Tanks yet to be launched reveal subsurface flaws and defects that only now are being discovered and identified as contributing to the loss of foam from the bipod ramps.

While NASA properly designated key debris events as In-Flight Anomalies in the past, more recent events indicate that NASA engineers and management did not appreciate the scope, or lack of scope, of the Hazard Reports involving foam shedding. Ultimately, NASA's hazard analyses, which were based on reducing or eliminating foam-shedding, were not succeeding. Shuttle Program management made no adjustments to the analyses to recognize this fact. The acceptance of events that are not supposed to happen has been described by sociologist Diane Vaughan as the "normalization of deviance." The history of foam-problem decisions shows how NASA first began and then continued flying with foam losses, so that flying with these deviations from design specifications was viewed as normal and acceptable. Dr. Richard Feynman, a member of the Presidential Commission on the Space Shuttle Challenger Accident, discusses this phenomena in the context of the *Challenger* accident. The parallels are striking:

> "The phenomenon of accepting . . . flight seals that had shown erosion and blow-by in previous flights is very clear. The *Challenger* flight is an excellent example. There are several references to flights that had gone before. The acceptance and success of these flights is taken as evidence of safety. But erosions and blow-by are not what the design expected. They are warnings that something is wrong. . . . The O-rings of the Solid Rocket Boosters were not designed to erode. Erosion was a clue that something was wrong. Erosion was not something from which safety can be inferred. . . . If a reasonable launch schedule is to be maintained, engineering often cannot be done fast enough to keep up with the expectations of originally conservative certification criteria designed to guarantee a very safe vehicle. In these situations, subtly, and often with apparently logical arguments, the criteria are altered so that flights may still be certified in time. They therefore fly in a relatively unsafe condition, with a chance of failure of the order of a percent (it is difficult to be more accurate)."

Findings:

- NASA has not followed its own rules and requirements on foam-shedding. Although the agency continuously worked on the foam-shedding problem, the debris impact requirements have not been met on any mission.

- Foam-shedding, which had initially raised serious safety concerns, evolved into "in-family" or "no safety-of-flight" events or were deemed an "accepted risk."
- Five of the seven bipod ramp events occurred on missions flown by *Columbia*, a seemingly high number. This observation is likely due to *Columbia* having been equipped with umbilical cameras earlier than other Orbiters.
- There is lack of effective processes for feedback or integration among project elements in the resolution of In-Flight Anomalies.
- Foam bipod debris-shedding incidents on STS-52 and STS-62 [previous Shuttle missions] were undetected at the time they occurred, and were not discovered until the Board directed NASA to examine External Tank separation images more closely.
- Foam bipod debris-shedding events were classified as In-Flight Anomalies up until STS-112, which was the first known bipod foam-shedding event not classified as an In-Flight Anomaly.
- The STS-112 assignment for the External Tank Project to "identify the cause and corrective action of the bipod ramp foam loss event" was not due until after the planned launch of STS-113, and then slipped to after the launch of STS-107.
- No External Tank configuration changes were made after the bipod foam loss on STS-112.
- Although it is sometimes possible to obtain imagery of night launches because of light provided by the Solid Rocket Motor plume, no imagery was obtained for STS-113.
- NASA failed to adequately perform trend analysis on foam losses. This greatly hampered the agency's ability to make informed decisions about foam losses.
- Despite the constant shedding of foam, the Shuttle Program did little to harden the Orbiter against foam impacts through upgrades to the Thermal Protection System. Without impact resistance and strength requirements that are calibrated to the energy of debris likely to impact the Orbiter, certification of new Thermal Protection System tile will not adequately address the threat posed by debris. . . .

Schedule Pressure

Countdown to Space Station "Core Complete": A Workforce Under Pressure. During the course of this investigation, the Board received several unsolicited comments from NASA personnel regarding pressure to meet a schedule. These comments all concerned a date, more than a year after the launch of *Columbia*, that seemed etched in stone: February 19, 2004, the scheduled launch date of STS-120. This flight was a milestone in the minds of NASA management since it would carry a section of the International Space Station called "Node 2." This would configure the International Space Station to its "U.S. Core Complete" status. . . .

Conclusion

The agency's commitment to hold firm to a February 19, 2004, launch date for Node 2 influenced many of decisions in the months leading up to the launch of STS-107, and may well have subtly influenced the way managers handled the STS-112 foam strike and *Columbia's* as well.

When a program agrees to spend less money or accelerate a schedule beyond what the engineers and program managers think is reasonable, a small amount of overall risk is added. These little pieces of risk add up until managers are no longer aware of the total program risk, and are, in fact, gambling. Little by little, NASA was accepting more and more risk in order to stay on schedule.

Findings:

- NASA Headquarters' focus was on the Node 2 launch date, February 19, 2004.
- The intertwined nature of the Space Shuttle and Space Station programs significantly increased the complexity of the schedule and made meeting the schedule far more challenging.
- The capabilities of the system were being stretched to the limit to support the schedule. Projections into 2003 showed stress on vehicle processing at the Kennedy Space Center, on flight controller training at Johnson Space Center, and on Space Station crew rotation schedules. Effects of this stress included neglecting flight controller recertification requirements, extending crew rotation schedules, and adding incremental risk by scheduling additional Orbiter movements at Kennedy.
- The four flights scheduled in the five months from October 2003, to February 2004, would have required a processing effort comparable to the effort immediately before the *Challenger* accident.
- There was no schedule margin to accommodate unforeseen problems. When flights come in rapid succession, there is no assurance that anomalies on one flight will be identified and appropriately addressed before the next flight.
- The environment of the countdown to Node 2 and the importance of maintaining the schedule may have begun to influence managers' decisions, including those made about the STS-112 foam strike.
- During STS-107, Shuttle Program managers were concerned with the foam strike's possible effect on the launch schedule.

Recommendation:

- Adopt and maintain a Shuttle flight schedule that is consistent with available resources. Although schedule deadlines are an important management tool, those deadlines must be regularly evaluated to ensure that any additional risk incurred to meet the schedule is recognized, understood, and acceptable.

Decision-Making During the Flight of STS-107

Summary. Management decisions made during *Columbia*'s final flight reflect missed opportunities, blocked or ineffective communications channels, flawed analysis, and ineffective leadership. Perhaps most striking is the fact that management—including Shuttle Program, Mission Management Team, Mission Evaluation Room, and Flight Director and Mission Control—displayed no interest in understanding a problem and its implications. Because managers failed to avail themselves of the wide range of expertise and opinion necessary to achieve the best answer to the debris strike question—"Was this a safety-of-flight concern?"—some Space Shuttle Program managers failed to fulfill the implicit contract to do whatever is possible to ensure the safety of the crew. In fact, their management techniques unknowingly imposed barriers that kept at bay both engineering concerns and dissenting views, and ultimately helped create "blind spots" that prevented them from seeing the danger the foam strike posed.

Because this chapter has focused on key personnel who participated in STS-107 bipod foam debris strike decisions, it is tempting to conclude that replacing them will solve all NASA's problems. However, solving NASA's problems is not quite so easily achieved. Peoples' actions are influenced by the organizations in which they work, shaping their choices in directions that even they may not realize. . . .

Findings: Intercenter Photo Working Group

- The foam strike was first seen by the Intercenter Photo Working Group on the morning of Flight Day Two during the standard review of launch video and high-speed photography. The strike was larger than any seen in the past, and the group was concerned about possible damage to the Orbiter. No conclusive images of the strike existed. One camera that may have provided an additional view was out of focus because of an improperly maintained lens.
- The Chair of the Intercenter Photo Working Group asked management to begin the process of getting outside imagery to help in damage assessment. This request, the first of three, began its journey through the management hierarchy on Flight Day Two.

- The Intercenter Photo Working Group distributed its first report, including a digitized video clip and initial assessment of the strike, on Flight Day Two. This information was widely disseminated to NASA and contractor engineers, Shuttle Program managers, and Mission Operations Directorate personnel.
- Initial estimates of debris size, speed, and origin were remarkably accurate. Initial information available to managers stated that the debris originated in the left bipod area of the External Tank, was quite large, had a high velocity, and struck the underside of the left wing near its leading edge. The report stated that the debris could have hit the RCC or tile.

The Debris Assessment Team:

- A Debris Assessment Team began forming on Flight Day two to analyze the impact. Once the debris strike was categorized as "out of family" by United Space Alliance, contractual obligations led to the Team being Co-Chaired by the cognizant contractor sub-system manager and her NASA counterpart. The team was not designated a Tiger Team by the Mission Evaluation Room or Mission Management Team.
- Though the Team was clearly reporting its plans (and final results) through the Mission Evaluation Room to the Mission Management Team, no Mission manager appeared to "own" the Team's actions. The Mission Management Team, through the Mission Evaluation Room, provided no direction for team activities, and Shuttle managers did not formally consult the Team's leaders about their progress or interim results.
- During an organizational meeting, the Team discussed the uncertainty of the data and the value of on-orbit imagery to "bound" their analysis. In its first official meeting the next day, the Team gave its NASA Co-Chair the action to request imagery of *Columbia* on-orbit.
- The Team routed its request for imagery through Johnson Space Center's Engineering Directorate rather than through the Mission Evaluation Room to the Mission Management Team to the Flight Dynamics Officer, the channel used during a mission. This routing diluted the urgency of their request. Managers viewed it as a non-critical engineering desire rather than a critical operational need.
- Team members never realized that management's decision against seeking imagery was not intended as a direct or final response to their request.
- The Team's assessment of possible tile damage was performed using an impact simulation that was well outside Crater's test database. The Boeing analyst was inexperienced in the use of Crater and the interpretation of its results. Engineers with extensive Thermal Protection

System expertise at Huntington Beach were not actively involved in determining if the Crater results were properly interpreted.

- Crater initially predicted tile damage deeper than the actual tile depth, but engineers used their judgment to conclude that damage would not penetrate the densified layer of tile. Similarly, RCC damage conclusions were based primarily on judgment and experience rather than analysis.
- For a variety of reasons, including management failures, communication breakdowns, inadequate imagery, inappropriate use of assessment tools, and flawed engineering judgments, the damage assessments contained substantial uncertainties.
- The assumptions (and their uncertainties) used in the analysis were never presented or discussed in full to either the Mission Evaluation Room or the Mission Management Team.
- While engineers and managers knew the foam could have struck RCC panels; the briefings on the analysis to the Mission Evaluation Room and Mission Management Team did not address RCC damage, and neither Mission Evaluation Room nor Mission Management Team managers asked about it.

Space Shuttle Program Management:

- There were lapses in leadership and communication that made it difficult for engineers to raise concerns or understand decisions. Management failed to actively engage in the analysis of potential damage caused by the foam strike.
- Mission Management Team meetings occurred infrequently (five times during a 16 day mission), not every day, as specified in Shuttle Program management rules.
- Shuttle Program Managers entered the mission with the belief, recently reinforced by the STS-113 Flight Readiness Review, that a foam strike is not a safety-of-flight issue.
- After Program managers learned about the foam strike, their belief that it would not be a problem was confirmed (early, and without analysis) by a trusted expert who was readily accessible and spoke from "experience." No one in management questioned this conclusion.
- Managers asked "Who's requesting the photos?" instead of assessing the merits of the request. Management seemed more concerned about the staff following proper channels (even while they were themselves taking informal advice) than they were about the analysis.
- No one in the operational chain of command for STS-107 held a security clearance that would enable them to understand the capabilities and limitations of National imagery resources.

- Managers associated with STS-107 began investigating the implications of the foam strike on the launch schedule, and took steps to expedite post-flight analysis.
- Program managers required engineers to prove that the debris strike created a safety-of-flight issue: that is, engineers had to produce evidence that the system was unsafe rather than prove that it was safe.
- In both the Mission Evaluation Room and Mission Management Team meetings over the Debris Assessment Team's results, the focus was on the bottom line—was there a safety-of-flight issue, or not? There was little discussion of analysis, assumptions, issues, or ramifications.

Communication:

- Communication did not flow effectively up to or down from Program managers.
- Three independent requests for imagery were initiated.
- Much of Program managers' information came through informal channels, which prevented relevant opinion and analysis from reaching decision makers.
- Program Managers did not actively communicate with the Debris Assessment Team. Partly as a result of this, the Team went through institutional, not mission-related, channels with its request for imagery, and confusion surrounded the origin of imagery requests and their subsequent denial.
- Communication was stifled by the Shuttle Program attempts to find out who had a "mandatory requirement" for imagery.

Safety Representative's Role:

- Safety representatives from the appropriate organizations attended meetings of the Debris Assessment Team, Mission Evaluation Room, and Mission Management Team, but were passive, and therefore were not a channel through which to voice concerns or dissenting views.

Recommendation:

- Implement an expanded training program in which the Mission Management Team faces potential crew and vehicle safety contingences beyond launch and ascent. These contingences should involve potential loss of Shuttle or crew, contain numerous uncertainties and unknowns, and require the Mission Management Team to assemble and interact with support organizations across NASA/Contractor lines and in various locations.

- Modify the Memorandum of Agreement with the National Imagery and Mapping Agency (NIMA) to make the imaging of each Shuttle flight while on orbit a standard requirement.

Possibility of Rescue or Repair

To put the decisions made during the flight of STS-107 into perspective, the Board asked NASA to determine if there were options for the safe return of the STS-107 crew. In this study, NASA was to assume that the extent of damage to the leading edge of the left wing was determined by national imaging assets or by a spacewalk. NASA was then asked to evaluate the possibility of:

1. Rescuing the STS-107 crew by launching *Atlantis*. *Atlantis* would be hurried to the pad, launched, rendezvous with *Columbia*, and take on *Columbia*'s crew for a return. It was assumed that NASA would be willing to expose *Atlantis* and its crew to the same possibility of External Tank bipod foam loss that damaged *Columbia*.
2. Repairing damage to *Columbia*'s wing on orbit. In the repair scenario, astronauts would use onboard materials to rig a temporary fix. Some of *Columbia*'s cargo might be jettisoned and a different re-entry profile would be flown to lessen heating on the left wing leading edge. The crew would be prepared to bail out if the wing structure was predicted to fail on landing. . . .

Findings:

- The repair option, while logistically viable using existing materials onboard *Columbia*, relied on so many uncertainties that NASA rated this option "high risk."
- If Program managers were able to unequivocally determine before Flight Day Seven that there was potentially catastrophic damage to the left wing, accelerated processing of *Atlantis* might have provided a window in which *Atlantis* could rendezvous with *Columbia* before *Columbia*'s limited consumables ran out.

Recommendation:

- For missions to the International Space Station, develop a practicable capability to inspect and effect emergency repairs to the widest possible range of damage to the Thermal Protection System, including both tile and Reinforced Carbon-Carbon, taking advantage of the additional capabilities available when near to or docked at the International Space Station.

For non-Station missions, develop a comprehensive autonomous (independent of Station) inspection and repair capability to cover the widest possible range of damage scenarios.

Accomplish an on-orbit Thermal Protection System inspection, using appropriate assets and capabilities, early in all missions.

The ultimate objective should be a fully autonomous capability for all missions to address the possibility that an International Space Station mission fails to achieve the correct orbit, fails to dock successfully, or is damaged during or after undocking. . . .

Chapter 7: The Accident's Organizational Causes

Many accident investigations make the same mistake in defining causes. They identify the widget that broke or malfunctioned, then locate the person most closely connected with the technical failure: the engineer who miscalculated an analysis, the operator who missed signals or pulled the wrong switches, the supervisor who failed to listen, or the manager who made bad decisions. When causal chains are limited to technical flaws and individual failures, the ensuing responses aimed at preventing a similar event in the future are equally limited: they aim to fix the technical problem and replace or retrain the individual responsible. Such corrections lead to a misguided and potentially disastrous belief that the underlying problem has been solved. The Board did not want to make these errors. A central piece of our expanded cause model involves NASA as an organizational whole.

Organizational Cause Statement

The organizational causes of this accident are rooted in the Space Shuttle Program's history and culture, including the original compromises that were required to gain approval for the Shuttle Program, subsequent years of resource constraints, fluctuating priorities, schedule pressures, mischaracterizations of the Shuttle as operational rather than developmental, and lack of an agreed national vision. Cultural traits and organizational practices detrimental to safety and reliability were allowed to develop, including: reliance on past success as a substitute for sound engineering practices (such as testing to understand why systems were not performing in accordance with requirements/specifications); organizational barriers which prevented effective communication of critical safety information and stifled professional differences of opinion; lack of integrated management across program elements; and the evolution of an informal chain of command and decision-making processes that operated outside the organization's rules.

Understanding Causes

In the Board's view, NASA's organizational culture and structure had as much to do with this accident as the External Tank foam. Organizational culture refers to the values, norms, beliefs, and practices that govern how an institution functions. At the most basic level, organizational culture defines the assumptions that employees make as they carry out their work. It is a powerful force that can persist through reorganizations and the reassignment of key personnel.

Given that today's risks in human space flight are as high and the safety margins as razor thin as they have ever been, there is little room for overconfidence. Yet the attitudes and decision-making of Shuttle Program managers and engineers during the events leading up to this accident were clearly overconfident and often bureaucratic in nature. They deferred to layered and cumbersome regulations rather than the fundamentals of safety. The Shuttle Program's safety culture is straining to hold together the vestiges of a once robust systems safety program.

As the Board investigated the *Columbia* accident, it expected to find a vigorous safety organization, process, and culture at NASA, bearing little resemblance to what the Rogers Commission identified as the ineffective "silent safety" system in which budget cuts resulted in a lack of resources, personnel, independence, and authority. NASA's initial briefings to the Board on its safety programs espoused a risk-averse philosophy that empowered any employee to stop an operation at the mere glimmer of a problem. Unfortunately, NASA's views of its safety culture in those briefings did not reflect reality. Shuttle Program safety personnel failed to adequately assess anomalies and frequently accepted critical risks without qualitative or quantitative support, even when the tools to provide more comprehensive assessments were available.

Similarly, the Board expected to find NASA's Safety and Mission Assurance organization deeply engaged at every level of Shuttle management: the Flight Readiness Review, the Mission Management Team, the Debris Assessment Team, the Mission Evaluation Room, and so forth. This was not the case. In briefing after briefing, interview after interview, NASA remained in denial: in the agency's eyes, "there were no safety-of-flight issues," and no safety compromises in the long history of debris strikes on the Thermal Protection System. The silence of Program-level safety processes undermined oversight; when they did not speak up, safety personnel could not fulfill their stated mission to provide "checks and balances." A pattern of acceptance prevailed throughout the organization that tolerated foam problems without sufficient engineering justification for doing so. . . .

Organizational Causes: Insights from Theory
To develop a thorough understanding of accident causes and risk, and to better interpret the chain of events that led to the *Columbia* accident,

the Board turned to the contemporary social science literature on accidents and risk and sought insight from experts in High Reliability, Normal Accident, and Organizational Theory. Additionally, the Board held a forum, organized by the National Safety Council, to define the essential characteristics of a sound safety program. . . .

The Board selected certain well-known traits from these models to use as a yardstick to assess the Space Shuttle Program, and found them particularly useful in shaping its views on whether NASA's current organization of its Human Space Flight Program is appropriate for the remaining years of Shuttle operation and beyond. Additionally, organizational theory, which encompasses organizational culture, structure, history, and hierarchy, is used to explain the *Columbia* accident, and . . . to produce an expanded explanation of the accident's causes. The Board believes the following considerations are critical to understand what went wrong during STS-107. . . .

- **Commitment to a Safety Culture:** NASA's safety culture has become reactive, complacent, and dominated by unjustified optimism. Over time, slowly and unintentionally, independent checks and balances intended to increase safety have been eroded in favor of detailed processes that produce massive amounts of data and unwarranted consensus, but little effective communication. Organizations that successfully deal with high-risk technologies create and sustain a disciplined safety system capable of identifying, analyzing, and controlling hazards throughout a technology's life cycle.
- **Ability to Operate in Both a Centralized and Decentralized Manner:** The ability to operate in a centralized manner when appropriate, and to operate in a decentralized manner when appropriate, is the hallmark of a high-reliability organization. On the operational side, the Space Shuttle Program has a highly centralized structure. Launch commit criteria and flight rules govern every imaginable contingency. The Mission Control Center and the Mission Management Team have very capable decentralized processes to solve problems that are not covered by such rules. The process is so highly regarded that it is considered one of the best problem-solving organizations of its type. In these situations, mature processes anchor rules, procedures, and routines to make the Shuttle Program's matrixed workforce seamless, at least on the surface.

  Nevertheless, it is evident that the position one occupies in this structure makes a difference. When supporting organizations try to "push back" against centralized Program direction—like the Debris Assessment Team did during STS-107—independent analysis generated by a decentralized decision-making process can be stifled. The Debris Assessment Team, working in an essentially decentralized format, was well-led and had the right expertise to work the problem, but their charter was "fuzzy," and the team had little direct connection to the Mission Management Team. This lack of connection to the Mission Management Team and the Mission Evaluation Room is the single most compelling reason why communications were so poor during the debris assessment. In this case, the Shuttle Program was unable to simultaneously manage both the centralized and decentralized systems.

- **Importance of Communication:** At every juncture of STS-107, the Shuttle Program's structure and processes, and therefore the managers in charge, resisted new information. Early in the mission, it became clear that the Program was not going to authorize imaging of the Orbiter because, in the Program's opinion, images were not needed. Overwhelming evidence indicates that Program leaders decided the foam strike was merely a maintenance problem long before any analysis had begun. Every manager knew the party line: "we'll wait for the analysis—no safety-of-flight issue expected." Program leaders spent at least as much time making sure hierarchical rules and processes were followed as they did trying to establish why anyone would want a picture of the Orbiter. These attitudes are incompatible with an organization that deals with high-risk technology.

- **Avoiding Oversimplification:** The *Columbia* accident is an unfortunate illustration of how NASA's strong cultural bias and its optimistic organizational thinking undermined effective decision-making. Over the course of 22 years, foam strikes were normalized to the point where they were simply a "maintenance" issue—a concern that did not threaten a mission's success. This oversimplification of the threat posed by foam debris rendered the issue a low-level concern in the minds of Shuttle managers. Ascent risk, so evident in *Challenger*, biased leaders to focus on strong signals from the Shuttle System Main Engine and the Solid Rocket Boosters. Foam strikes, by comparison, were a weak and consequently overlooked signal, although they turned out to be no less dangerous.

- **Conditioned by Success:** Even after it was clear from the launch videos that foam had struck the Orbiter in a manner never before seen, Space Shuttle Program managers were not unduly alarmed. They could not imagine why anyone would want a photo of something that could be fixed after landing. More importantly, learned attitudes about foam strikes diminished management's wariness of their danger. The Shuttle Program turned "the experience of failure into the memory of success." Managers also failed to develop simple contingency plans for a re-entry emergency. They were convinced, without study, that nothing could be done about such an emergency. The intellectual curiosity and skepticism that a solid safety culture requires was almost entirely absent. Shuttle managers did not embrace safety-conscious attitudes. Instead, their attitudes were shaped and reinforced by an organization that, in this instance, was incapable of stepping back and gauging its biases. Bureaucracy and process trumped thoroughness and reason.

- **Significance of Redundancy:** The Human Space Flight Program has compromised the many redundant processes, checks, and balances that should identify and correct small errors. Redundant systems essential to every high-risk enterprise have fallen victim to bureaucratic efficiency. Years of workforce reductions and outsourcing have culled from NASA's workforce the layers of experience and hands-on systems knowledge that once provided a capacity for safety oversight. Safety and Mission Assurance personnel have been eliminated, careers in safety have lost organizational prestige, and the Program now decides on its own how much safety and engineering oversight it needs. Aiming to align its inspection regime with the International Organization for Standardization 9000/9001 protocol, commonly used in industrial environments—environments very different than the Shuttle Program—the Human Space Flight Program shifted from a comprehensive "oversight" inspection process to a more limited "insight" process, cutting mandatory inspection points by more than half and leaving even fewer workers to make "second" or "third" Shuttle systems checks. . . .

Organizational Causes: A Broken Safety Culture

Perhaps the most perplexing question the Board faced during its seven-month investigation into the *Columbia* accident was "How could NASA have missed the signals the foam was sending?" Answering this question was a challenge. The investigation revealed that in most cases, the Human Space Flight Program is extremely aggressive in reducing threats to safety. But we also know—in hindsight—that detection of the dangers posed by foam was impeded by "blind spots" in NASA's safety culture.

From the beginning, the Board witnessed a consistent lack of concern about the debris strike on *Columbia*. NASA managers told the Board "there was no safety-of-flight issue" and "we couldn't have done anything about it anyway." The investigation uncovered a troubling pattern in which Shuttle Program management made erroneous assumptions about the robustness of a system based on prior success rather than on dependable engineering data and rigorous testing.

The Shuttle Program's complex structure erected barriers to effective communication and its safety culture no longer asks enough hard questions about risk. (Safety culture refers to an organization's characteristics and attitudes—promoted by its leaders and internalized by its members—that serve to make safety the top priority.) In this context, the Board believes the mistakes that were made on STS-107 are not isolated failures, but are indicative of systemic flaws that existed prior to the accident. Had the Shuttle Program observed the principles discussed in the previous two sections, the threat that foam posed to the Orbiter, particularly after the STS-112 and STS-107 foam strikes, might have been more fully appreciated by Shuttle Program management. . . .

Findings and Recommendations

The evidence that supports the organizational causes also led the Board to conclude that NASA's current organization, which combines in the Shuttle Program all authority and responsibility for schedule, cost, manifest, safety, technical requirements, and waivers to technical requirements, is not an effective check and balance to achieve safety and mission assurance. Further, NASA's Office of Safety and Mission Assurance does not have the independence and authority that the Board and many outside reviews believe is necessary. Consequently, the Space Shuttle Program does not consistently demonstrate the characteristics of organizations that effectively manage high risk. Therefore, the Board offers the following Findings and Recommendations.

Findings:

- Throughout its history, NASA has consistently struggled to achieve viable safety programs and adjust them to the constraints and vagaries of changing budgets. Yet, according to multiple high level independent reviews, NASA's safety system has fallen short of the mark.
- The Associate Administrator for Safety and Mission Assurance is not responsible for safety and mission assurance execution, as intended by the Rogers Commission, but is responsible for Safety and Mission Assurance policy, advice, coordination, and budgets. This view is consistent with NASA's recent philosophy of management at a strategic level at NASA Headquarters but contrary to the Rogers' Commission recommendation.
- Safety and Mission Assurance organizations supporting the Shuttle Program are largely dependent upon the Program for funding, which hampers their status as independent advisors.
- Over the last two decades, little to no progress has been made toward attaining integrated, independent, and detailed analyses of risk to the Space Shuttle system.
- System safety engineering and management is separated from mainstream engineering, is not vigorous enough to have an impact on system design, and is hidden in the other safety disciplines at NASA Headquarters.

- Risk information and data from hazard analyses are not communicated effectively to the risk assessment and mission assurance processes. The Board could not find adequate application of a process, database, or metric analysis tool that took an integrated, systemic view of the entire Space Shuttle system.
- The Space Shuttle Systems Integration Office handles all Shuttle systems except the Orbiter. Therefore, it is not a true integration office.
- When the Integration Office convenes the Integration Control Board, the Orbiter Office usually does not send a representative, and its staff makes verbal inputs only when requested.
- The Integration office did not have continuous responsibility to integrate responses to bipod foam shedding from various offices. Sometimes the Orbiter Office had responsibility, sometimes the External Tank Office at Marshall Space Flight Center had responsibility, and sometime the bipod shedding did not result in any designation of an In-Flight Anomaly. Integration did not occur.
- NASA information databases such as The Problem Reporting and Corrective Action and the Web Program Compliance Assurance and Status System are marginally effective decision tools.
- Senior Safety, Reliability & Quality Assurance and element managers do not use the Lessons Learned Information System when making decisions. NASA subsequently does not have a constructive program to use past lessons to educate engineers, managers, astronauts, or safety personnel.
- The Space Shuttle Program has a wealth of data tucked away in multiple databases without a convenient way to integrate and use the data for management, engineering, or safety decisions.
- The dependence of Safety, Reliability & Quality Assurance personnel on Shuttle Program support limits their ability to oversee operations and communicate potential problems throughout the organization.
- There are conflicting roles, responsibilities, and guidance in the Space Shuttle safety programs. The Safety & Mission Assurance Pre-Launch Assessment Review process is not recognized by the Space Shuttle Program as a requirement that must be followed (NSTS 22778). Failure to consistently apply the Pre-Launch Assessment Review as a requirements document creates confusion about roles and responsibilities in the NASA safety organization.

Recommendations:

- Establish an independent Technical Engineering Authority that is responsible for technical requirements and all waivers to them, and will build a disciplined, systematic approach to identifying, analyzing, and controlling hazards throughout the life cycle of the Shuttle System. The independent technical authority does the following as a minimum:

— Develop and maintain technical standards for all Space Shuttle Program projects and elements

— Be the sole waiver-granting authority for all technical standards

— Conduct trend and risk analysis at the sub-system, system, and enterprise levels

— Own the failure mode, effects analysis and hazard reporting systems

— Conduct integrated hazard analysis

— Decide what is and is not an anomalous event

— Independently verify launch readiness

— Approve the provisions of the recertification program. . . .

The Technical Engineering Authority should be funded directly from NASA Headquarters, and should have no connection to or responsibility for schedule or program cost.

- NASA Headquarters Office of Safety and Mission Assurance should have direct line authority over the entire Space Shuttle Program safety organization and should be independently resourced.

- Reorganize the Space Shuttle Integration Office to make it capable of integrating all elements of the Space Shuttle Program, including the Orbiter.

Chapter 8: History as a Cause: *Columbia* and *Challenger*

The Board began its investigation with two central questions about NASA decisions. Why did NASA continue to fly with known foam debris problems in the years preceding the *Columbia* launch, and why did NASA managers conclude that the foam debris strike 81.9 seconds into *Columbia*'s flight was not a threat to the safety of the mission, despite the concerns of their engineers?

Echoes of Challenger

As the investigation progressed, Board member Dr. Sally Ride, who also served on the Rogers Commission, observed that there were "echoes" of *Challenger* in *Columbia*. Ironically, the Rogers Commission investigation into *Challenger* started with two remarkably similar central questions: Why did NASA continue to fly with known O-ring erosion problems in the years before the *Challenger* launch, and why, on the eve of the *Challenger* launch, did NASA managers decide that launching the mission in such cold temperatures was an acceptable risk, despite the concerns of their engineers?

The echoes did not stop there. The foam debris hit was not the single cause of the *Columbia* accident, just as the failure of the joint seal that permitted O-ring erosion was not the single cause of *Challenger*. Both

Columbia and *Challenger* were lost also because of the failure of NASA's organizational system. . . .

This chapter shows that both accidents were "failures of foresight" in which history played a prominent role. First, the history of engineering decisions on foam and O-ring incidents had identical trajectories that "normalized" these anomalies, so that flying with these flaws became routine and acceptable. Second, NASA history had an effect. In response to White House and Congressional mandates, NASA leaders took actions that created systemic organizational flaws at the time of *Challenger* that were also present for *Columbia*. The final section compares the two critical decision sequences immediately before the loss of both Orbiters—the pre-launch teleconference for *Challenger* and the post-launch foam strike discussions for *Columbia*. It shows history again at work: how past definitions of risk combined with systemic problems in the NASA organization caused both accidents.

Connecting the parts of NASA's organizational system and drawing the parallels with *Challenger* demonstrate three things. First, despite all the post–*Challenger* changes at NASA and the agency's notable achievements since, the causes of the institutional failure responsible for *Challenger* have not been fixed. Second, the Board strongly believes that if these persistent, systemic flaws are not resolved, the scene is set for another accident. Therefore, the recommendations for change are not only for fixing the Shuttle's technical system, but also for fixing each part of the organizational system that produced *Columbia*'s failure. Third, the Board's focus on the context in which decision making occurred does not mean that individuals are not responsible and accountable. To the contrary, individuals always must assume responsibility for their actions. What it does mean is that NASA's problems cannot be solved simply by retirements, resignations, or transferring personnel.

The constraints under which the agency has operated throughout the Shuttle Program have contributed to both Shuttle accidents. Although NASA leaders have played an important role, these constraints were not entirely of NASA's own making. The White House and Congress must recognize the role of their decisions in this accident and take responsibility for safety in the future. . . .

Changing NASA's Organizational System

The echoes of *Challenger* in *Columbia* identified in this chapter have serious implications. These repeating patterns mean that flawed practices embedded in NASA's organizational system continued for 20 years and made substantial contributions to both accidents. The Columbia Accident Investigation Board noted the same problems as the Rogers Commission. An organization system failure calls for corrective measures that address all relevant levels of the organization, but the Board's investigation shows that for all its cutting-edge technologies, "diving-catch" rescues, and imaginative plans for the technology and the future of space exploration, NASA has shown very little understanding of the inner workings of its own organization.

NASA managers believed that the agency had a strong safety culture, but the Board found that the agency had the same conflicting goals that it did before *Challenger*, when schedule concerns, production pressure, cost-cutting and a drive for ever-greater efficiency—all the signs of an "operational" enterprise—had eroded NASA's ability to assure mission safety. The belief in a safety culture has even less credibility in light of repeated cuts of safety personnel and budgets—also conditions that existed before *Challenger*. NASA managers stated confidently that everyone was encouraged to speak up about safety issues and that the agency was responsive to those concerns, but the Board found evidence to the contrary in the responses to the Debris Assessment Team's request for imagery, to the initiation of the imagery request from Kennedy Space Center, and to the "we were just 'what-iffing'" e-mail concerns that did not reach the Mission Management Team. NASA's bureaucratic structure kept important information from reaching engineers and managers alike. The same NASA whose engineers showed initiative and a solid working knowledge of how to get things done fast had a managerial culture with an allegiance to bureaucracy and cost-efficiency that squelched the engineers' efforts. When it came to managers' own actions, however, a different set of rules prevailed. The Board found that Mission Management Team decision-making operated outside the rules even as it held its engineers to a stifling protocol. Management was not able to recognize that in unprecedented conditions, when lives are on the line, flexibility and democratic process should take priority over bureaucratic response.

During the *Columbia* investigation, the Board consistently searched for causal principles that would explain both the technical and organizational system failures. These principles were needed to explain *Columbia* and its echoes of *Challenger*. They were also necessary to provide guidance for NASA. The Board's analysis of organizational causes . . . supports the following principles that should govern the changes in the agency's organizational system. . . .

Leaders create culture. It is their responsibility to change it. Top administrators must take responsibility for risk, failure, and safety by remaining alert to the effects their decisions have on the system. Leaders are responsible for establishing the conditions that lead to their subordinates' successes or failures. The past decisions of national leaders—the White House, Congress, and NASA Headquarters—set the *Columbia* accident in motion by creating resource and schedule strains that compromised the principles of a high-risk technology organization. The measure of NASA's success became how much costs were reduced and how efficiently the schedule was met. But the Space Shuttle is not now, nor has it ever been, an operational vehicle. We cannot explore space on a fixed-cost basis. Nevertheless, due to International Space Station needs and scientific experiments that require particular timing and orbits, the Space Shuttle Program seems likely to continue to be schedule-driven. National leadership needs to recognize that NASA must fly only when it is ready. As the White House, Congress, and NASA Headquarters plan the future of human space flight, the goals and the resources required to achieve them safely must be aligned.

Changes in organizational structure should be made only with careful consideration of their effect on the system and their possible unintended consequences. Changes that make the organization more complex may create new ways that it can fail. When changes are put in place, the risk of error initially increases, as old ways of doing things compete with new. Institutional memory is lost as personnel and records are moved and replaced. Changing the structure of organizations is complicated by external political and budgetary constraints, the inability of leaders to conceive of the full ramifications of their actions, the vested interests of insiders, and the failure to learn from the past.

Nonetheless, changes must be made. The Shuttle Program's structure is a source of problems, not just because of the way it impedes the flow of information, but because it has had effects on the culture that contradict safety goals. NASA's blind spot is it believes it has a strong safety culture. Program history shows that the loss of a truly independent, robust capability to protect the system's fundamental requirements and specifications inevitably compromised those requirements, and therefore increased risk. The Shuttle Program's structure created power distributions that need new structuring, rules, and management training to restore deference to technical experts, empower engineers to get resources they need, and allow safety concerns to be freely aired.

Strategies must increase the clarity, strength, and presence of signals that challenge assumptions about risk. Twice in NASA history, the agency embarked on a slippery slope that resulted in catastrophe. Each decision, taken by itself, seemed correct, routine, and indeed, insignificant and unremarkable. Yet in retrospect, the cumulative effect was stunning. In both pre-accident periods, events unfolded over a long time and in small increments rather than in sudden and dramatic occurrences. NASA's challenge is to design systems that maximize the clarity of signals, amplify weak signals so they can be tracked, and account for missing signals. For both accidents there were moments when management definitions of risk might have been reversed were it not for the many missing signals—an absence of trend analysis, imagery data not obtained, concerns not voiced, information overlooked or dropped from briefings. A safety team must have equal and independent representation so that managers are not again lulled into complacency by shifting definitions of risk. It is obvious but worth acknowledging that people who are marginal and powerless in organizations may have useful information or opinions that they don't express. Even when these people are encouraged to speak, they find it intimidating to contradict a leader's strategy or a group consensus. Extra effort must be made to contribute all relevant information to discussions of risk. These strategies are important for all safety aspects, but especially necessary for ill-structured problems like O-rings and foam debris. Because ill-structured problems are less visible and therefore invite the normalization of deviance, they may be the most risky of all. . . .

Part Three: A Look Ahead

Chapter 9: Implications for the Future of Human Space Flight

The report up to this point has been a look backward: a single accident with multiple causes, both physical and organizational. In this chapter, the Board looks to the future. We take the insights gained in investigating the loss of *Columbia* and her crew and seek to apply them to this nation's continuing journey into space. We divide our discussion into three timeframes: 1) short-term, NASA's return to flight after the *Columbia* accident; 2) mid-term, what is needed to continue flying the Shuttle fleet until a replacement means for human access to space and for other Shuttle capabilities is available; and 3) long-term, future directions for the U.S. in space. The objective in each case is for this country to maintain a human presence in space, but with enhanced safety of flight.

In this report we have documented numerous indications that NASA's safety performance has been lacking. But even correcting all those shortcomings, it should be understood, will not eliminate risk. All flight entails some measure of risk, and this has been the case since before the days of the Wright Brothers. Furthermore, the risk is not distributed evenly over the course of the flight. It is greater by far at the beginning and end than during the middle.

This concentration of risk at the endpoints of flight is particularly true for crew-carrying space missions. The Shuttle Program has now suffered two accidents, one just over a minute after takeoff and the other about 16 minutes before landing. The laws of physics make it extraordinarily difficult to reach Earth orbit and return safely. Using existing technology, orbital flight is accomplished only by harnessing a chemical reaction that converts vast amounts of stored energy into speed. There is great risk in placing human beings atop a machine that stores and then burns millions of pounds of dangerous propellants. Equally risky is having humans then ride the machine back to Earth while it dissipates the orbital speed by converting the energy into heat, much like a meteor entering Earth's atmosphere. No alternatives to this pathway to space are available or even on the horizon, so we must set our sights on managing this risky process using the most advanced and versatile techniques at our disposal.

Because of the dangers of ascent and re-entry, because of the hostility of the space environment, and because we are still relative newcomers to this realm, operation of the Shuttle and indeed all human spaceflight must be viewed as a developmental activity. It is still far from a routine, operational undertaking. Throughout the *Columbia* accident investigation, the Board has commented on the widespread but erroneous perception of the Space Shuttle as somehow comparable to civil or military air transport. They are not comparable; the inherent risks of spaceflight are vastly higher, and our experience level with spaceflight is vastly lower. If Shuttle operations came to be viewed as routine, it was, at least in part, thanks to the skill and dedication of those involved in the program. They have made it look easy, though in fact it never was. The Board urges NASA leadership, the architects of U.S. space policy, and the American people to adopt a realistic understanding of the risks and rewards of venturing into space.

Near-Term: Return to Flight

The Board supports return to flight for the Space Shuttle at the earliest date consistent with an overriding consideration: safety. The recognition of human spaceflight as a developmental activity requires a shift in focus from operations and meeting schedules to a concern for the risks involved. Necessary measures include:

- Identifying risks by looking relentlessly for the next eroding O-ring, the next falling foam; obtaining better data, analyzing and spotting trends.
- Mitigating risks by stopping the failure at its source; when a failure does occur, improving the ability to tolerate it; repairing the damage on a timely basis.
- Decoupling unforeseen events from the loss of crew and vehicle.
- Exploring all options for survival, such as provisions for crew escape systems and safe havens.
- Barring unwarranted departures from design standards, and adjusting standards only under the most rigorous, safety-driven process.

The Board has recommended improvements that are needed before the Shuttle Program returns to flight, as well as other measures to be adopted over the longer term—what might be considered "continuing to fly" recommendations. To ensure implementation of these longer-term recommendations, the Board makes the following recommendation, which should be included in the requirements for return-to-flight:

- Prepare a detailed plan for defining, establishing, transitioning, and implementing an independent Technical Engineering Authority, independent safety program, and a reorganized Space Shuttle Integration Office. . . . In addition, NASA should submit annual reports to Congress, as part of the budget review process, on its implementation activities. . . .

Mid-Term: Continuing to Fly

It is the view of the Board that the present Shuttle is not inherently unsafe. However, the observations and recommendations in this report are needed to make the vehicle safe enough to operate in the coming years. In order to continue operating the Shuttle for another decade or even more, which the Human Space Flight Program may find necessary, these significant measures must be taken:

- Implement all the recommendations listed in Part One of this report that were not already accomplished as part of the return-to-flight reforms.
- Institute all the organizational and cultural changes called for in Part Two of this report.
- Undertake complete recertification of the Shuttle, as detailed in the discussion and recommendation below.

The urgency of these recommendations derives, at least in part, from the likely pattern of what is to come. In the near term, the recent memory of the *Columbia* accident will motivate the entire NASA organization to scrupulous attention to detail and vigorous efforts to resolve elusive technical problems. That energy will inevitably dissipate over time. This decline in vigilance is a characteristic of many large organizations, and it has been demonstrated in NASA's own history. As reported in Part Two of this report, the Human Space Flight Program has at times compromised safety because of its organizational problems and cultural traits. That is the reason, in order to prevent the return of bad habits over time, that the Board makes the recommendations in Part Two calling for changes in the organization and culture of the Human Space Flight Program. These changes will take more time and effort than would be reasonable to expect prior to return to flight.

Through its recommendations in Part Two, the Board has urged that NASA's Human Space Flight Program adopt the characteristics observed in high-reliability organizations. One is separating technical authority from the functions of managing schedules and cost. Another is an independent Safety and Mission Assurance organization. The third is the capability for effective systems integration. Perhaps even more challenging than these organizational changes are the cultural changes required. Within NASA, the cultural impediments to safe and effective Shuttle operations are real and substantial, as documented extensively in this report. The Board's view is that cultural problems are unlikely to be corrected without top-level leadership. Such leadership will have to rid the system of practices and patterns that have been validated simply because they have been around so long. Examples include: the tendency to keep knowledge of problems contained within a Center or program; making technical decisions without in-depth, peer-reviewed technical analysis; and an unofficial hierarchy or caste system created by placing excessive power in one office. Such factors interfere with open communication, impede the sharing of lessons learned, cause duplication and unnecessary expenditure of resources, prompt resistance to external advice, and create a burden for managers, among other undesirable outcomes. Collectively, these undesirable characteristics threaten safety.

Unlike return-to-flight recommendations, the Board's management and cultural recommendations will take longer to implement, and the responses must be fine-tuned and adjusted during implementation. The question of how to follow up on NASA's implementation of these more subtle, but equally important recommendations remains unanswered. The Board is aware that response to these recommendations will be difficult to initiate, and they will encounter some degree of institutional resistance. Nevertheless, in the Board's view, they are so critical to safer operation of the Shuttle fleet that they must be carried out completely. Since NASA is an independent agency answerable only to the White House and Congress, the ultimate responsibility for enforcement of the recommended corrective actions must reside with those governmental authorities.

Recertification. Recertification is a process to ensure flight safety when a vehicle's actual utilization exceeds its original design life; such a baseline examination is essential to certify that vehicle for continued use, in the case of the Shuttle to 2020 and possibly beyond. This report addresses recertification as a mid-term issue.

Measured by their 20 or more missions per Orbiter, the Shuttle fleet is young, but by chronological age—10 to 20 years each—it is old. The Board's discovery of mass loss in RCC panels, the deferral of investigation into signs of metal corrosion, and the deferral of upgrades all strongly suggest that a policy is needed requiring a complete recertification of the Space Shuttle. This recertification must be rigorous and comprehensive at every level (i.e., material, component, subsystem, and system); the higher the level, the more critical the integration of lower-level components. A post–*Challenger*, 10-year review was conducted, but it lacked this kind of rigor, comprehensiveness and, most importantly, integration at the subsystem and system levels.

Aviation industry standards offer ample measurable criteria for gauging specific aging characteristics, such as stress and corrosion. The Shuttle Program, by contrast, lacks a closed-loop feedback system and consequently does not take full advantage of all available data to adjust its certification process and maintenance practices. Data sources can include experience with material and component failures, non-conformances (deviations from original specifications) discovered during Orbiter Maintenance Down Periods, Analytical Condition Inspections, and Aging Aircraft studies. Several of the recommendations in this report constitute the basis for a recertification program (such as the call for nondestructive evaluation of RCC components). [Previous chapters] cite instances of waivers and certification of components for flight based on analysis rather than testing. The recertification program should correct all those deficiencies.

Finally, recertification is but one aspect of a Service Life Extension Program that is essential if the Shuttle is to continue operating for another 10 to 20 years. While NASA has such a program, it is in its infancy and needs to be pursued with vigor. The Service Life Extension Program goes beyond the Shuttle itself and addresses critical associated components in equipment, infrastructure, and other areas. . . .

The Board makes the following recommendation regarding recertification:

- Prior to operating the Shuttle beyond 2010, develop and conduct a vehicle recertification at the material, component, subsystem, and system levels. Recertification requirements should be included in the Service Life Extension Program.

Long-Term: Future Directions for the U.S. in Space
The Board in its investigation has focused on the physical and organizational causes of the *Columbia* accident and the recommended actions required for future safe Shuttle operation. In the course of that investigation, however, two realities affecting those recommendations have become evident to the Board. One is the lack, over the past three decades, of any national mandate providing NASA a compelling mission requiring human presence in space. President John Kennedy's 1961 charge to send Americans to the moon and return them safely to Earth "before this decade is out" linked NASA's efforts to core Cold War national interests. Since the 1970s, NASA has not been charged with carrying out a similar high priority mission that would justify the expenditure of resources on

a scale equivalent to those allocated for Project Apollo. The result is the agency has found it necessary to gain the support of diverse constituencies. NASA has had to participate in the give and take of the normal political process in order to obtain the resources needed to carry out its programs. NASA has usually failed to receive budgetary support consistent with its ambitions. The result, as noted throughout Part Two of the report, is an organization straining to do too much with too little.

A second reality, following from the lack of a clearly defined long-term space mission, is the lack of sustained government commitment over the past decade to improving U.S. access to space by developing a second-generation space transportation system. Without a compelling reason to do so, successive Administrations and Congresses have not been willing to commit the billions of dollars required to develop such a vehicle. In addition, the space community has proposed to the government the development of vehicles such as the National Aerospace Plane and X-33, which required "leapfrog" advances in technology; those advances have proven to be unachievable. As Apollo 11 Astronaut Buzz Aldrin, one of the members of the recent Commission on the Future of the United States Aerospace Industry, commented in the Commission's November 2002 report, "Attempts at developing breakthrough space transportation systems have proved illusory." The Board believes that the country should plan for future space transportation capabilities without making them dependent on technological breakthroughs. . . .

Chapter 11: Recommendations

It is the Board's opinion that good leadership can direct a culture to adapt to new realities. NASA's culture must change, and the Board intends the following recommendations to be steps toward effecting this change. Recommendations have been put forth in many of the chapters. In this chapter, the recommendations are grouped by subject area with the Return-to-Flight [RTF] tasks listed first within the subject area. . . . These recommendations are not listed in priority order.

Part One—The Accident
Thermal Protection System

- Initiate an aggressive program to eliminate all External Tank Thermal Protection System debris-shedding at the source with particular emphasis on the region where the bipod struts attach to the External Tank. [RTF]
- Initiate a program designed to increase the Orbiter's ability to sustain minor debris damage by measures such as improved impact-

resistant Reinforced Carbon-Carbon and acreage tiles. This program should determine the actual impact resistance of current materials and the effect of likely debris strikes. [RTF]

- Develop and implement a comprehensive inspection plan to determine the structural integrity of all Reinforced Carbon-Carbon system components. This inspection plan should take advantage of advanced non-destructive inspection technology. [RTF]

- For missions to the International Space Station, develop a practicable capability to inspect and effect emergency repairs to the widest possible range of damage to the Thermal Protection System, including both tile and Reinforced Carbon-Carbon, taking advantage of the additional capabilities available when near to or docked at the International Space Station.

  For non-Station missions, develop a comprehensive autonomous (independent of Station) inspection and repair capability to cover the widest possible range of damage scenarios.

  Accomplish an on-orbit Thermal Protection System inspection, using appropriate assets and capabilities, early in all missions. The ultimate objective should be a fully autonomous capability for all missions to address the possibility that an International Space Station mission fails to achieve the correct orbit, fails to dock successfully, or is damaged during or after undocking. [RTF]

- To the extent possible, increase the Orbiter's ability to successfully re-enter Earth's atmosphere with minor leading edge structural subsystem damage.

- In order to understand the true material characteristics of Reinforced Carbon-Carbon components, develop a comprehensive database of flown Reinforced Carbon-Carbon material characteristics by destructive testing and evaluation.

- Improve the maintenance of launch pad structures to minimize the leaching of zinc primer onto Reinforced Carbon-Carbon components.

- Obtain sufficient spare Reinforced Carbon-Carbon panel assemblies and associated support components to ensure that decisions on Reinforced Carbon-Carbon maintenance are made on the basis of component specifications, free of external pressures relating to schedules, costs, or other considerations.

- Develop, validate, and maintain physics-based computer models to evaluate Thermal Protection System damage from debris impacts. These tools should provide realistic and timely estimates of any impact damage from possible debris from any source that may ultimately impact the Orbiter. Establish impact damage thresholds that trigger responsive corrective action, such as on-orbit inspection and repair, when indicated.

Imaging:

- Upgrade the imaging system to be capable of providing a minimum of three useful views of the Space Shuttle from liftoff to at least Solid Rocket Booster separation, along any expected ascent azimuth. The operational status of these assets should be included in the Launch Commit Criteria for future launches. Consider using ships or aircraft to provide additional views of the Shuttle during ascent. [RTF]
- Provide a capability to obtain and downlink high-resolution images of the External Tank after it separates. [RTF]
- Provide a capability to obtain and downlink high-resolution images of the underside of the Orbiter wing leading edge and forward section of both wings' Thermal Protection System. [RTF]
- Modify the Memorandum of Agreement with the National Imagery and Mapping Agency to make the imaging of each Shuttle flight while on orbit a standard requirement. [RTF]

Orbiter Sensor Data:

- The Modular Auxiliary Data System instrumentation and sensor suite on each Orbiter should be maintained and updated to include current sensor and data acquisition technologies.
- The Modular Auxiliary Data System should be redesigned to include engineering performance and vehicle health information, and have the ability to be reconfigured during flight in order to allow certain data to be recorded, telemetered, or both as needs change.

Wiring:

- As part of the Shuttle Service Life Extension Program and potential 40-year service life, develop a state-of-the-art means to inspect all Orbiter wiring, including that which is inaccessible.

Bolt Catchers:

- Test and qualify the flight hardware bolt catchers. [RTF]

Closeouts:

- Require that at least two employees attend all final closeouts and intertank area hand-spraying procedures. [RTF]

Micrometeoroid and Orbital Debris:

- Require the Space Shuttle to be operated with the same degree of safety for micrometeoroid and orbital debris as the degree of safety calculated for the International Space Station. Change the micrometeoroid and orbital debris safety criteria from guidelines to requirements.

Foreign Object Debris:

• Kennedy Space Center Quality Assurance and United Space Alliance must return to the straightforward, industry-standard definition of "Foreign Object Debris" and eliminate any alternate or statistically deceptive definitions like "processing debris." [RTF]

Part Two—Why the Accident Occurred
Scheduling:

• Adopt and maintain a Shuttle flight schedule that is consistent with available resources. Although schedule deadlines are an important management tool, those deadlines must be regularly evaluated to ensure that any additional risk incurred to meet the schedule is recognized, understood, and acceptable. [RTF]

Training:

• Implement an expanded training program in which the Mission Management Team faces potential crew and vehicle safety contingencies beyond launch and ascent. These contingencies should involve potential loss of Shuttle or crew, contain numerous uncertainties and unknowns, and require the Mission Management Team to assemble and interact with support organizations across NASA/Contractor lines and in various locations. [RTF]

Organization:

• Establish an independent Technical Engineering Authority that is responsible for technical requirements and all waivers to them, and will build a disciplined, systematic approach to identifying, analyzing, and controlling hazards throughout the life cycle of the Shuttle System. The independent technical authority does the following as a minimum:
  — Develop and maintain technical standards for all Space Shuttle Program projects and elements. Be the sole wemer-granting authority for all technical standards
  — Conduct trend and risk analysis at the sub-system, system, and enterprise levels
  — Own the failure mode, effects analysis and hazard reporting systems
  — Conduct integrated hazard analysis
  — Decide what is and is not an anomalous event
  — Independently verify launch readiness
  — Approve the provisions of the recertification program. . . .

The Technical Engineering Authority should be funded directly from NASA Headquarters, and should have no connection to or responsibility for schedule or program cost.

- NASA Headquarters Office of Safety and Mission Assurance should have direct line authority over the entire Space Shuttle Program safety organization and should be independently resourced.
- Reorganize the Space Shuttle Integration Office to make it capable of integrating all elements of the Space Shuttle Program, including the Orbiter.

Part Three—A Look Ahead
Organization:

- Prepare a detailed plan for defining, establishing, transitioning, and implementing an independent Technical Engineering Authority, independent safety program, and a reorganized Space Shuttle Integration Office. . . . In addition, NASA should submit annual reports to Congress, as part of the budget review process, on its implementation activities.[RTF]

Recertification:

- Prior to operating the Shuttle beyond 2010, develop and conduct a vehicle recertification at the material, component, subsystem, and system levels. Recertification requirements should be included in the Service Life Extension Program.

Closeout Photos/Drawing System:

- Develop an interim program of closeout photographs for all critical sub-systems that differ from engineering drawings. Digitize the closeout photograph system so that images are immediately available for on-orbit troubleshooting. [RTF]
- Provide adequate resources for a long-term program to upgrade the Shuttle engineering drawing system including:

  — Reviewing drawings for accuracy
  — Converting all drawings to a computer-aided drafting system
  — Incorporating engineering changes

Source: United States. National Aeronautics and Space Administration. Columbia Accident Investigation Board. *Final Report.* Vol. 1. August 2003. www.caib.us/news/report/volume1/default.html (accessed June 12, 2004).

Congressional Budget Office on the Federal Deficit

August 26, 2003

INTRODUCTION

The hangover from the recession of 2001, lost revenue from massive tax cuts, and increased spending to finance the war on terror and the invasion of Iraq conspired to push the federal budget deficit to its highest dollar level in history in 2003. Figures at the end of the fiscal year showed that the budget deficit had ballooned to $374 billion in 2003 and was projected to reach at least $500 billion in 2004. It was a remarkable reversal from 2000, when the federal budget ran a surplus of $236 billion.

Although the deficit's dollar amount was at an all-time high, it was within historical levels in relation to the overall economy. The deficit represented only 3.4 percent of the nation's gross domestic product (GDP), the value of all goods and services produced in the United States—about $11 trillion in 2003. The Republican administration of George W. Bush called that a manageable level, justifiable in the face of a slow economic recovery and the heightened need for spending on national security. Democrats in Congress and on the presidential campaign trail, as well as some Republicans, disagreed, portraying the administration as fiscally reckless in pursuing tax cuts as the deficit spiraled out of control. That was a role reversal from the 1980s and early 1990s, when it was congressional Republicans who called for a balanced-budget constitutional amendment to stop the "tax and spend" Democrats who they accused of driving the federal deficit to unacceptably high limits.

Most economists agreed that a short-term deficit was acceptable, even needed, to smooth the economic rough edges caused by recession and war. They were more concerned about the long-term effects if the president and Congress proved unable to bring the deficit under control quickly. The retirement of the baby boom generation, starting in 2008, was going to increase Social Security and Medicare costs dramatically. The need for the government to borrow to cover those costs, added to an already large budget deficit, could stifle economic growth by raising interest rates, economists cautioned. Some warned that without changes in tax and benefit policy, the children and grandchildren of the baby boomers could be saddled with unsustainably high national debt.

The public did not appear to be particularly concerned about the mounting debt. A Gallup poll conducted in December found that only 2.8 percent of those surveyed identified the federal deficit as the most important problem facing the nation. The economy in general, unemployment, the war in Iraq, and terrorism were the leading concerns. People were also more concerned about poor health care, poverty, moral decline, and corruption than about the federal deficit.

The Return of Deficits

Until the late 1960s, the federal government had followed a fairly predictable cycle of deficits during times of war or economic crisis, followed by surpluses during peacetime. The deficits that accompanied World War I and its immediate aftermath, for example, disappeared in 1920 and were followed by eleven years of surpluses during the "roaring" 1920s. As the Great Depression took hold, President Franklin D. Roosevelt (1933–1945) sought to spur the economy and put people back to work through his brand of Keynesian economics, which held that activist government intervention in the free market was the only sure route to economic prosperity and stability. Under Roosevelt, Congress began a long-term expansion of the federal government. Yet even with the cost of World War II, the federal ledger quickly returned to surplus in 1947. Similarly, deficits caused by the Korean War turned to surpluses soon after the war ended.

Things soon began to change, however, giving way in 1961 to what would become a thirty-eight year run of deficits, interrupted by one year of black ink: a $3.2 billion surplus in fiscal 1969. The end of the Vietnam War did not yield the "peace dividend" in the 1970s to parallel the postwar surpluses of the1940s and 1950s. The difference, in large part, was the creation and expansion of entitlement programs, such as Medicare and Social Security during the presidency of Lyndon B. Johnson (1963–1969). Expenses for such programs increased so rapidly that the reduction in defense spending accompanying the U.S. pullout from Vietnam did not balance the federal ledger.

The annual deficit reached an all-time high of 6 percent of GDP in fiscal 1983, after a massive tax cut and the cold war defense budget championed by President Ronald Reagan (1983–1989) took hold. The highest deficit in terms of dollars before 2003 was $290 billion, racked up in 1992. That deficit, and the tax increase imposed in an effort to control it, helped turn the current president's father, George H. W. Bush, out of office after only one term.

Beginning in the mid-1980s presidents and Congress engaged in strenuous deficit-fighting efforts that seemed to produce relatively few benefits.

In 1998, however, a booming economy began to produce surpluses far in excess of what most analysts had expected. The remarkable reversal of the government's fiscal situation—going from a $290 billion deficit in fiscal 1992 to a $236 billion surplus in fiscal 2000—was attributed to economic growth and gains from the stock market boom that produced an unanticipated windfall of new tax revenue. The economy grew at an annual average pace of 3.6 percent between 1993 and 2000, while tax receipts doubled to $2.03 trillion. At the end of fiscal 2002 the $236 billion surplus had become a $158 billion deficit, after the deepest tax cut in two decades (PL 107–16) coincided with a slumping economy and the terrorist attacks of September 11, 2001. A small tax cut in 2002 further reduced government revenues. *(2001 tax cut, Historic Documents of 2001, p. 400)*

Developments in 2003

Driven primarily by a boost in defense spending and a drop in revenue collections, the deficit more than doubled in 2003, jumping from $158 billion in 2002 to $379 billion a year later. Although that was higher than the Bush administration had originally projected, it was lower than virtually anyone thought it would be at midyear.

In the president's fiscal 2004 budget request, sent to Congress in early February 2003, the Office of Management and Budget (OMB) projected budget deficits of $304 billion in fiscal 2003 and $307 billion in 2004; the deficit would then shrink through fiscal 2007 and begin climbing again in 2008, when some of the major costs of the 2001 tax cut would begin to kick in and the baby boom generation would begin to retire. The projections included the costs of Bush's proposed ten-year $1.5 trillion tax cut and his reform of Medicare but not the billions he was sure to request for the pending invasion of Iraq. Bush refused to say how much would be spent on the war on terror and in Iraq, arguing that those numbers were impossible to predict. *(2003 tax cut, p. 68; Iraq invasion and occupation, p. 135)*

In July OMB revised its projections upward, saying the deficit could hit $455 billion in 2003 and $475 billion in 2004, roughly half again as much as predicted in February, before falling back to $226 billion by fiscal 2008. OMB director Joshua B. Bolten acknowledged on July 15 that the deficit figures were "a legitimate subject of concern" but insisted they were manageable. "Restoring a balanced budget is an important priority for this administration," Bolten said, "but a balanced budget is not a higher priority than winning the global war on terror, protecting the American homeland, or restoring economic growth and job creation."

The nonpartisan Congressional Budget Office (CBO) projected similar deficits in its updated budget outlook, released August 26. By law, the CBO baseline was predicated on the assumption that there would be no changes in existing law, clearly an unlikely scenario. Including just two of the most likely changes—extending the tax cuts, rather than letting them expire as scheduled, and providing a Medicare prescription drug benefit—would turn the projected surplus of $211 billion in fiscal 2013 into a deficit of $324 billion, CBO said. Instead of totaling $1.4 trillion over the fiscal 2004–2013 period, the deficit would total $3.7 trillion. If Congress continued to approve discretionary spending (the spending it has control over) at the same pace that it had since 1998, the deficit in 2013 could total $5 trillion, the CBO said. *(Medicare reform, p. 1119)*

As it turned out, both the White House and the CBO overestimated the fiscal 2003 deficit. An unexpected increase in corporate tax revenues helped bring it down to $374 billion. But the administration was warning that the fiscal 2004 deficit could exceed $500 billion.

The size of the projected deficits over the long term was beginning to make some politicians, economists, and corporate executives uneasy. The major concern was the retirement of the baby boom generation—76 million Americans—beginning in 2008. Instead of paying into Social Security and Medicare, they would begin drawing benefits. At the same time, the number of workers paying into the two systems was expected to decline from 3.4 workers for each retiree in 2003 to 2.1 in 2030. Without major tax increases or reductions in benefits, the government would have to borrow heavily to meet its obligations. Many economists said such huge deficits could induce foreign investors to withdraw, undermine the value of the dollar, and cause prices and interest rates to soar and the stock market to crash,

A report issued by the CBO in December suggested that both tax increases and benefit reductions "will probably be necessary to provide a significant likelihood of fiscal stability in the coming decades." Simply limiting spending on defense, education, and other discretionary programs would not be sufficient to produce a sound federal budget, the report said. The CBO added that even letting the trillions of dollars in tax cuts enacted since Bush took office expire as currently scheduled—a move that would dramatically increase federal revenues—would not be enough to ensure fiscal stability. Similar warnings by other government agencies and outside organizations had been made for years, but so far few politicians had been willing to risk their political future by pushing for what were sure to be extremely unpopular policy changes.

Gathering Criticisms

Bush rejected criticisms that the growing deficit was a cause for alarm and denied that his tax cuts were making the deficit worse by lowering revenue. Rather, he said, the tax cuts would stimulate economic growth that would produce the necessary revenue to cut the deficit in half within five years, so long as Congress held down spending. "The deficit, we've got a plan to cut it in half over the next five years. It means Congress is going to have to toe the line when it comes to spending," Bush said during a December 16 television interview. "They can't, particularly in campaign years, try to be all things to all people and overspend. But I think we're making good progress. I'm satisfied with the progress we've made."

Some analysts questioned whether the economy was capable of growing out of the deficit. They calculated that, to do so, the economy would need to grow at an annual average pace of 4 percent or more for as long as ten years. The economy had never grown that fast for that long, although growth averaged more than 4 percent for seven years between 1983 and 1989. Even in the boom years of the 1990s, growth averaged under 4 percent.

Others questioned whether Congress could hold down spending enough to make a difference in the deficit. Ignoring Bush's request that discretionary spending be capped at 4 percent, Congress in 2003 approved a 12.5 percent increase in discretionary spending in 2003, according to preliminary data. The figures included emergency spending for one-time events such as natural disasters and war, but even when those items were removed, discretionary spending increased 7.9 percent in 2003, according to one set of calculations.

Deficit hawks in and out of Congress, many of them conservative Republicans, deplored the rising deficits and Congress's failure to hold down spending. "Republicans used to believe in fiscal responsibility, limited international entanglements, and limited government. We have lost our way. We have come loose from our moorings," Sen. Chuck Hegel, R-Neb., wrote in November. Brian Reidl, a budget analyst with the Heritage Foundation (a conservative think tank), said conservatives were "showing an astonishing willingness to spend now and dump all the cost in our children's laps, and an amazing unwillingness to reconcile the size of government with the amount of taxes needed to fund it."

Others said Bush shared some of the blame for Congress's failure to act. "It's very hard for Congress to show fiscal restraint when the White House hasn't raised the deficit as a primary issue," said Robert D. Reischauer, a former CBO director and the head of the Urban League. "Spending restraint and tax increases are unnatural acts on Capitol Hill. It takes some political leadership from the White House, some external motivation, to get Congress to focus on the deficit, and there doesn't seem to be any of those forces at work." Rudolph G. Penner, another former CBO director and a Republican, agreed. "The most interesting thing is Bush has not vetoed anything, let alone a spending bill," he said. "One wonders how serious the White House is about holding the line."

Most observers were not expecting much to change in 2004, a presidential election year. Bush had already indicated that he would ask Congress to make the tax cuts permanent, although Democrats in the Senate were likely to try to block that request. It was also questionable whether Bush could control spending, particularly on popular programs and pet projects of legislators, including those in his own party. An early test was likely to be the reauthorization of the highway bill, scheduled to be taken up early in 2004; it was a traditional vehicle for pork-barrel projects, especially in an election year.

Following are excerpts from "The Budget and Economic Outlook: An Update," a report released August 26, 2003, by the Congressional Budget Office, projecting that federal budget deficits would reach $401 billion in fiscal 2003 and $480 billion in 2004, absent any changes in current law.

"The Budget and Economic Outlook: An Update"

Chapter 1: The Budget Outlook

If current laws and policies do not change, the federal government will incur a total budget deficit of $401 billion this year and $480 billion in 2004, the Congressional Budget Office (CBO) projects. . . . Although those deficits represent record levels in dollar terms, at about 4 percent of the nation's gross domestic product (GDP) they are smaller than the deficits of the mid-1980s. . . . In the absence of further legislative changes, the recent surge in deficits will peak in 2004, CBO estimates; after that, annual deficits will decline steadily before giving way to surpluses early in the next decade. Deficits are projected to total $1.4 trillion over the next five years. The five years after that show a small net surplus (less than $50 billion) in CBO's latest projections.

Actual budget totals, however, will almost certainly differ from those baseline projections. By statute, CBO's baseline must estimate the future paths of federal revenues and spending under current laws and policies. The baseline is therefore not intended to be a prediction of future budgetary outcomes; instead, it is meant to serve as a neutral benchmark that lawmakers can use to measure the effects of proposed changes to taxes and spending.

Such changes can significantly affect the budget outlook. For example, legislation enacted since CBO's previous baseline projections were published in March has increased the deficits and reduced the surpluses projected for the next 10 years by a total of $1.6 trillion. Nearly all of that amount stems from two laws enacted this spring: the Emergency Wartime Supplemental Appropriations Act, 2003 (Public Law 108–11), and the Jobs and Growth Tax Relief Reconciliation Act (P.L. 108–27). In addition to policy changes, factors beyond lawmakers' direct control—such as unexpected economic developments—can affect the budget outlook positively or negatively. . . .

In 2002, the federal government recorded a deficit of $158 billion. This year, its finances have deteriorated sharply because of declining revenues—for the third year in a row—combined with double-digit growth in discretionary spending. (Such spending was accelerating even before $79 billion in supplemental appropriations for 2003 were enacted in April.) CBO estimates that current tax and spending policies would produce steadily declining deficits after 2004, which would change to surpluses for 2012 and 2013—largely because of increases in revenues from the scheduled expiration of the major tax-cut provisions enacted in 2001.

Although anticipated policy changes cannot be incorporated in the baseline projections, this report shows how some alternative policy assumptions would affect the budget over the next 10 years. For example, if all expiring tax provisions (except some related to the alternative minimum tax) were extended and a Medicare prescription drug benefit was provided at the cost assumed in the Congressional budget resolution, the baseline budget outlook projected for 2013 would change from a surplus of $211 billion to a deficit of $324 billion. Debt held by the public at the end of that year would climb to 44 percent of GDP from the baseline projection of 31 percent of GDP, and the deficit over the 2004-2013 period would total $3.7 trillion instead of $1.4 trillion. In the other direction, if the 2003 supplemental appropriations enacted in April were not extended throughout the projection period, the 10-year deficit would shrink to $0.4 trillion, and debt held by the public at the end of 2013 would drop to 25 percent of GDP.

Over the longer term, the federal budget faces significant strains, which will begin within the current 10-year budget window and intensify as more of the baby-boom generation reaches retirement age. The number of people of retirement age is projected to surge by about 80 percent over the next 30 years, raising costs for federal health and retirement programs. Meanwhile, the number of workers whose taxes help pay for those benefits is expected to grow by only 15 percent. In addition to that demographic situation, costs per enrollee in federal health care programs are likely to grow much faster than inflation. As a result, spending on Medicare, Medicaid, and Social Security as a share of GDP will rise sharply. In the absence of changes to federal programs, that rise could lead to unsustainable levels of debt.

A Look at 2003

CBO expects the budget deficit to more than double this year as a percentage of GDP: from 1.5 percent last year to 3.7 percent in 2003. . . . That sharp rise in the deficit results from a continuing decline in revenues coupled with a large increase in spending.

Revenues

CBO anticipates that revenues will fall in 2003 for the third consecutive year. After peaking at 20.8 percent of GDP in 2000, revenues are expected to slide to 16.5 percent of GDP this year—their lowest level since 1959. In all, CBO expects revenues in 2003 to fall by $83 billion, or 4.5 percent, from last year's total. . . .

Receipts from withheld income and payroll taxes are expected to decline by about $10 billion, or 0.7 percent, in 2003. Withholding has been held down by weak income growth and the tax cuts enacted in 2001 and 2003. If the effects of those cuts in individual taxes were excluded, withholding would grow by just over 1 percent this year, CBO estimates—more than the 0.5 percent growth recorded last year (also excluding the effects of tax cuts) but far below the 8 percent annual growth averaged from 1995 through 2000.

Nonwithheld payments of individual income taxes (net of refunds) will fall by about $50 billion this year, CBO estimates. Much of that projected drop relates to taxpayers' liabilities for tax year 2002, either from tax returns filed by April 15 or from estimated payments made earlier in the year. (The effects of recent tax cuts on nonwithheld receipts are very difficult to identify.)

Corporate income tax receipts are expected to decline by $23 billion, or about 16 percent, in 2003. Recent changes in tax laws make determining the sources of that decline more difficult than usual. However, CBO estimates that corporate receipts would have risen slightly this year in the absence of the tax-law changes enacted after 2000.

The revenue estimates for 2003 are based largely on actual tax collections so far this year, without complete information about either the status of the economy during that period or the details of tax liabilities and payments. Consequently, the underlying economic behavior that has led to the drop in receipts cannot be fully understood. For tax year 2002, summary information from individual income tax returns will not be available until late in calendar year 2003. And a sample of those returns—which is required for a full examination of the sources of receipts—will not be available for inspection until next summer. Information from corporate tax returns is available on a similar schedule. Current collections also reflect economic activity in 2003, and tax returns for that year will not be available until 2005.

Outlays

At the same time that revenues are expected to diminish, total outlays will rise in 2003 by $160 billion (7.9 percent) from last year's level, CBO estimates. Outlays for discretionary programs—the part of the budget whose spending levels are set anew each year in appropriation acts—are projected to jump by $91 billion (12.4 percent) this year. Outlays for entitlements and other mandatory programs—whose spending levels are usually governed by eligibility rules and benefit levels set forth in existing laws—are projected to increase by $83 billion (7.5 percent). Those rises will be partially offset by a decline in net interest costs, which are expected to fall by $14 billion (8.4 percent), largely because of lower interest rates. Excluding net interest, spending will increase by about 9.5 percent this year, CBO estimates.

The fastest growing component of discretionary spending is defense, which is projected to rise by $58 billion (about 17 percent) in 2003, reaching $407 billion. Roughly half of that increase stems from funds provided for the war in Iraq and continuing operations for the war on terrorism. As a result, discretionary defense spending will total about 3.8 percent of GDP this year—the highest level since 1994, but well below the levels recorded during the mid-1980s and early 1990s (which were generally between 4.5 percent and 6 percent of GDP).

Nondefense discretionary spending is expected to grow by $33 billion (8.5 percent) in 2003, reaching a total of $419 billion. The largest increases occur for education, health, and transportation programs. That overall growth will raise nondefense discretionary spending to about 3.9 percent of GDP—its highest level since 1985.

Mandatory spending is expected to rise by 7.5 percent in 2003—down from the nearly 10 percent growth recorded last year. Among the large programs in that category, only Medicare is forecast to grow at a faster rate than it did last year (nearly 8 percent in 2003 compared with 6.4 percent in 2002). Medicare spending continues to rise primarily because of automatic updates to payment rates and increases in caseloads. Social Security spending is expected to grow by about 4 percent this year, a rate dampened by last December's cost-of-living adjustment of 1.4 percent, which was the lowest in several years. Spending for Medicaid will rise by 9.8 percent in 2003, CBO estimates, a slowdown from last year's growth rate of 13.2 percent. That slowdown results mainly from slower growth in enrollment and the implementation of constraints on certain payments to public health care providers. Medicaid's growth rate this year would be even lower had the Jobs and Growth Tax Relief Reconciliation Act of 2003 (JGTRRA) not allotted states nearly $4 billion in additional funds through an increase in the federal share of Medicaid costs.

Two other legislative changes will boost mandatory spending in 2003. The first is another provision of JGTRRA, which provides $10 billion in temporary fiscal aid to states, half to be disbursed in 2003. The second involves extensions of temporary emergency unemployment compensation, which will increase spending by almost $11 billion in 2003. Including that temporary aid, spending for unemployment benefits will rise from $51 billion last year to about $56 billion in 2003, CBO estimates.

For most of the past decade, mandatory spending (net of offsetting receipts) has hovered around 10 percent of GDP. In 2003, such spending will grow to 11.1 percent of GDP—higher than in any other year in U.S. history.

Baseline Budget Projections for 2004 Through 2013

CBO projects that if current laws and policies remain the same, the budget deficit will peak at 4.3 percent of GDP in 2004 and diminish each year thereafter, reaching 0.9 percent in 2010. . . . After that, primarily because of increased revenues from the scheduled expiration of the tax cuts enacted in the 2001 Economic Growth and Tax Relief Reconciliation Act (EGTRRA), the baseline deficit is projected to drop almost to zero in 2011 and then turn to surplus, rising to 1.2 percent of GDP in 2013.

Revenues
Under current law, total revenues are projected to fall slightly as a percentage of GDP next year—from 16.5 percent in 2003 to 16.2 percent—and then rise throughout the projection period, reaching 17.4 percent of GDP in 2005 and 18.7 percent in 2010. Revenues are projected to rise more rapidly thereafter because of the expiration of EGTRRA, equaling 20.5 percent of GDP by 2013. (The average level for the post-World War II period is 17.9 percent of GDP.)

Most of the change in projected revenues relative to GDP over the next decade results from individual and corporate income taxes. Other sources of revenue, such as social insurance taxes, are projected to grow at about the same rate as GDP. . . .

Outlays
Under current laws and policies, total outlays as a share of GDP are projected to decline gradually over the next 10 years—from 20.5 percent in 2004 to 19.3 percent in 2013. . . . Although mandatory spending grows at roughly the same rate as GDP in the baseline, discretionary spending is assumed to grow at the rate of inflation and thus more slowly than GDP. Net interest spending is projected to rise in response to continued deficits—growing from 1.4 percent of GDP in 2004 to a peak of 2.1 percent in 2009. As baseline deficits turn into surpluses at the end of the projection period, net interest declines to 1.7 percent of GDP by 2013. . . .

Budget Projections Under Alternative Scenarios

Just as legislation enacted in the past few years has had a major impact on the paths of federal spending and revenues, future legislation will undoubtedly affect the budget outlook in significant ways. . . .

CBO's baseline projection of revenues rests on the assumption that current tax laws remain unaltered. Therefore, CBO assumes that tax provisions scheduled to expire will actually do so. For example, CBO's baseline envisions that major provisions of EGTRRA—such as the introduction of the 10 percent tax bracket, decreases in previously existing tax rates for individuals, increases in the child tax credit, and the repeal of the estate tax—will expire as scheduled at the end of 2010. Since most expiring tax provisions reduce receipts, projections that assume the extension of those provisions show lower revenues than the baseline does. If all expiring tax provisions (except those related to the exemption amount for the alternative minimum tax) were extended, revenues would be a total of nearly $1.6 trillion lower during the 2004–2013 period.

Another potential impact on revenues involves modifying the alternative minimum tax. As noted earlier, the impact of the AMT will grow in coming years as more taxpayers become subject to it (many of whom were not the intended target of the tax when it was enacted). If the AMT was indexed for inflation after 2004, federal revenues would be $400 billion lower over the next 10 years, according to the Joint Committee on Taxation (JCT).

On the spending side of the budget, legislation that has passed both Houses of Congress would make a number of changes to the Medicare program, including providing a prescription drug benefit for most enrollees. If legislation is enacted that matches the amount allocated in this year's budget resolution, the initiative will cost $400 billion over the next decade.

Assumptions about the future path of discretionary spending can also have a significant effect on the budget outlook. In CBO's baseline, budget authority for discretionary programs is inflated from the level appropriated for the current year, as specified by the Deficit Control Act. For comparison, CBO estimated the budgetary impact of four other assumptions about future discretionary spending, two of which would worsen the budget outlook and two of which would improve it. Assuming that appropriations will increase at the same rate as nominal GDP through 2013 adds $1.4 trillion to projected discretionary spending. Assuming that appropriations will rise by 7.7 percent a year—the average growth rate from 1998 through 2003 (excluding $79 billion in supplemental appropriations for 2003)—boosts discretionary spending by $2.8 trillion.

In the other direction, excluding $79 billion in supplemental appropriations for 2003 from projections for future years reduces discretionary outlays by $0.8 trillion over 10 years. Assuming that appropriations are frozen at the current level through 2013, with no adjustment for inflation, has a larger effect: reducing cumulative discretionary spending by $1.2 trillion.

In addition to policy changes, the budget is highly sensitive to the state of the economy and to technical assumptions about the impact of tax and spending policies. Consequently, the outlook for the budget can best be described not as a single row of numbers but as a large range of possible outcomes centered around those numbers, with the range widening as the projection period extends. . . . Projections that are very different from the baseline also have a significant probability of coming to pass because of the uncertainty surrounding CBO's economic and technical assumptions.

Changes to the Budget Outlook Since March

The budget outlook has deteriorated substantially since CBO issued its previous baseline projections in March. In that baseline, CBO estimated that under the laws and policies then in force, the deficit would total $246 billion this year and $200 billion in 2004 but that the 2004–2013 period would show a cumulative surplus of $891 billion.

Today, under the laws and policies now in effect (and using updated economic and technical assumptions), CBO's estimate of this year's deficit has risen by $155 billion, and its estimate of next year's deficit has grown by $280 billion. For the 10-year period, the baseline budget outlook has worsened by a total of almost $2.3 trillion. . . .

When CBO revises its baseline projections, it divides the changes into three categories based on their cause: recently enacted legislation, changes to CBO's outlook for the economy, and other, so-called technical factors that affect the budget. More than two-thirds of the total change in this baseline is attributable to legislation (a cumulative $1.6 trillion between 2004 and 2013). Technical changes worsen the bottom line by another $0.7 trillion, and, on net, economic revisions have a relatively minor effect (totaling $72 billion from 2004 through 2013).

CBO now anticipates $122 billion less in revenues for 2003 than it did last March. Total revenues projected for the 2004-2013 period have fallen by $878 billion, with the largest changes in 2004 and 2005. The effects of recent legislation, notably the Jobs and Growth Tax Relief Reconciliation Act of 2003, account for the majority of revisions to CBO's revenue projections for the next few years. After 2005, technical changes explain most of the drop in revenues relative to the March baseline.

Spending this year is projected to be $33 billion higher than CBO anticipated in March, and outlay projections for the 10-year period are a total of $1.4 trillion higher, largely because of laws enacted since March.

However, the requirement to extend both of the recent supplemental appropriation acts over the 2004-2013 period in the baseline accounts for $873 billion of that total. Additional debt-service costs resulting from both tax and spending legislation account for most of the rest. . . .

The Long-Term Outlook

Without changes to federal programs for the elderly, the aging of the baby-boom generation will cause a historic shift in the United States' fiscal position in coming decades. The number of people at retirement age is expected to jump by about 80 percent over the next three decades while the number of workers grows by just 15 percent. All of those future retirees are alive today, as are most of the people who will be working 30 years from now (although an increase in immigration and labor force participation over that period could ease some of the pressure by adding to the U.S. workforce). In addition to those demographic changes, costs per enrollee in federal health care programs are likely to grow much faster than inflation.

As a result of those forces, federal spending on the major health and retirement programs—Social Security, Medicare, and Medicaid—is projected to grow by more than two-thirds as a share of the economy by 2030, rising from 8 percent of GDP today to 14 percent. Consequently, either taxes will need to rise dramatically, spending on other federal programs will have to be cut severely, or federal borrowing will soar.

Beyond 2030, those fiscal pressures will intensify as longevity continues to increase and health costs continue to grow. Only reforming programs for the elderly before the baby boomers retire and enacting policies to enhance economic growth could alleviate the demands on future generations.

Source: U.S. Congress. Congressional Budget Office. *The Budget and Economic Outlook: An Update.* August 26, 2003.http://purl.access.gpo. gov/GPO/LPS5076 (accessed October 26, 2003).

September

2003 HISTORIC DOCUMENTS

New York State Court on Mutual Funds

September 3, 2003

INTRODUCTION

Scandal tainted the mutual funds industry in 2003, bringing home to millions of Americans the costs of financial improprieties that for two years had plagued major corporations and financial houses on Wall Street. Investigations initiated by New York state attorney general Eliot Spitzer—and followed up by the Securities and Exchange Commission (SEC) and other regulators—disclosed that several of the country's largest mutual funds had engaged in obscure practices that enriched a few investors, including managers at the funds, at the expense of the vast majority of shareholders.

The New York Stock Exchange also slipped into the morass of financial scandal after it was revealed that the board had awarded Chairman Richard Grasso nearly $140 million in deferred payments. Grasso was forced to resign, and the stock exchange was pressured into adopting major reforms to protect its dual role as a financial institution and as one of the country's most important regulators of the securities industry.

These revelations further damaged the reputation of Wall Street, which had come under extraordinary scrutiny in 2002 because of charges that major investment banks had given the public biased advice about new stock offerings. A "global settlement" of legal cases against the big banks, tentatively reached in late 2002, was finalized October 2003. *(Corporate scandals of 2003, p. 332; background, Historic Documents of 2002, p. 397)*

Investigations into Mutual Funds

By 2003 mutual funds had become the most popular form of long-term investment for most Americans. According to some studies, more than 90 million Americans held shares in mutual funds, with most of it in pension-related investments. More than 8,000 funds held total assets of nearly $7 trillion—nearly half of it in stocks and the rest in bonds, money-market funds, and other types of investments. Until 2003 the mutual fund industry had escaped the waves of scandal that had hit Wall Street and major corporations. Americans assumed that their life savings were secure with mutual funds, which were obliged by law to operate solely in the interests of investors.

That assumption came under challenge in the last half of 2003, when investigations appeared to show that some—but not all—of the largest mutual funds had shown favoritism to a tiny fraction of investors and thereby undercut the interests of the vast majority of their clients. For the most part, these mutual funds engaged in practices that cost the majority of investors only pennies apiece on each transaction but enriched the few. In other words, the funds had allowed favored investors to get away with the age-old practice of stealing small amounts from a large number of people in hopes that the losses would not be noticed.

The public did not notice until July 14, when New York attorney general Spitzer announced that he was launching an investigation into the sale of investments in mutual funds by large banks. Spitzer disclosed the first details of his investigation on September 3 when he announced a $40 million settlement with Canary Capital Partners and two related firms. Spitzer said the companies had engaged in two complex financial maneuvers known as "late trading" and "market timing" of shares in mutual funds. Canary Capital was a "hedge fund"—a business that made investments based on speculation about future changes in share prices. Canary Capital's manager and main investor was Edward J. Stern.

Late trading involved the buying and selling of securities after the markets had closed for the day, but only if the closing prices of the securities had risen or fallen to a level enabling the trader to make money. Late trading was illegal in the United States, but a SEC survey later in 2003 found that 25 percent of the nation's large brokerage firms allowed some clients to engage in it. Market timing was a legal practice in which investors bought and sold securities very rapidly to take advantage of fluctuations in market prices; most mutual funds, however, had rules prohibiting or severely restricting the practice. The SEC said it found that nearly 70 percent of firms were aware that some customers engaged in market timing, and 30 percent of firms admitted having helped those customers do it.

Both late trading and market timing could produce dramatic short-term profits. But when practiced at mutual funds, these maneuvers damaged the overall financial picture of the funds, which were supposed to be havens for long-term investors.

Spitzer said his investigation of Canary Capital had revealed evidence of "widespread illegal trading schemes" in the mutual fund industry. Based on the information gathered in that case, plus tips provided by whistle-blowers, Spitzer already had launched investigations into several large mutual funds. On September 4 the Securities and Exchange Commission—

which had primary national authority for regulating the funds—sent letters demanding information from the country's largest funds and brokerage houses, then launched several investigations based on the responses. Speaking to the Securities Industry Association on November 7, SEC chairman William Donaldson said: "If there is more wrongdoing, we will find it and will punish the perpetrators."

The last three months of the year brought almost daily disclosures of illegal or improper dealings by some of the nation's biggest mutual funds. Spitzer, the SEC, or in some cases both filed lawsuits that forced the resignations of fund managers and forced companies to change their operating policies. A few companies took action before charges were brought against them—apparently in hopes that preemptive steps would lessen the bad publicity. None of the major fund companies that faced public charges denied all wrongdoing; some acknowledged all the complaints that were brought against them and others admitted to at least some improprieties. Many large mutual funds were not named as targets of the investigations, however.

Putnam Investments, based in Boston, which had been the nation's fifth-largest mutual fund, suffered the biggest fall. On October 28 the SEC and the state of Massachusetts charged Putnam with failing to halt instances of improper personal trading by two of its fund managers and market timing by favored investors. The SEC settled the suit on November 13, after Putnam's chairman, Lawrence Lasser, was forced to resign and the company promised to institute the types of financial controls (including an independent board of directors) that it had previously claimed to have in place. The SEC announced no fines or other penalties against Putnam, leading critics to charge that the firm had been given no more than a slap on the wrist. William F. Galvin, Massachusetts secretary of the commonwealth, told the *New York Times* the settlement showed that the SEC was "not interested in exposing wrongdoing; they're interested in giving comfort to the industry." Even if it escaped tough action by regulators, Putnam did suffer direct consequences. Pension funds in a dozen states, including its home state, and the giant public employee fund in California pulled more than $20 billion—nearly 10 percent of the fund's primary holdings—out of Putnam in a few weeks.

Putnam's problems ultimately caused some trouble at the SEC, which forced the head of the SEC's Boston office, Juan M. Marcelino, to resign in November. News organizations reported that Marcelino had failed to follow up on a tip given him the previous March by a whistle-blower at Putnam.

Other mutual funds hit in the scandal included:

- *Strong Mutual Funds,* based in Wisconsin. Spitzer on October 30 accused founder Richard Strong of engaging in improper trading activities. Strong resigned two days later and in December gave up control of a related company, Strong Financial.

- *Morgan Stanley.* The large investment bank on December 15 agreed to pay a $50 million civil penalty to settle charges brought by the SEC concerning improper trades by a mutual fund it controlled.
- *Pilgrim Baxter and Associates,* based in Wayne, Pennsylvania. Its founders, Gary Pilgrim and Harold Baxter, were forced out after regulators filed charges in October that Pilgrim had engaged in market timing.
- *Charles Schwab,* the nation's largest discount stockbroker, acknowledged in November that it had allowed market timing by five institutional investors in its mutual fund operation called U.S. Trust.
- *Alliance Capital Management* on December 18 settled charges brought by the SEC and Spitzer's office that it had allowed some clients to engage in market timing. Alliance was one of the country's largest money managers, with $456 billion in its various funds as of the end of November. The company agreed to pay its customers $250 million in restitution, and in a separate agreement with Spitzer agreed to reduce its fees by $70 million annually over a five-year period. The $600 million total was the largest settlement to date by a mutual fund company. The company also fired two of its top officials, including John D. Carifa, board chairman of its mutual funds division.
- *Ivesco Funds Group Inc.* The SEC and Spitzer on December 2 filed civil fraud charges against the Denver-based company and its chief executive, Raymond R. Cunningham. The charges said the firm had encouraged market timing by large investors.

As of year's end, only one senior pension fund official had been sentenced to prison as a result of the scandal. On December 17 James Patrick Connelly Jr., a former sales director at Fred Alger Management, was sentenced to one to three years in prison. He had pleaded guilty in October to charges of tampering with evidence—e-mail messages that Spitzer's office had sought for its inquiry into the fund.

In addition to late trading and market timing, investigations unearthed other common practices in the mutual fund industry that cost investors millions of dollars. Some funds were found to have charged investors fees and commissions without telling them or to have failed to give investors credit for volume discounts to which they were entitled. Merrill Lynch on December 3 said it had engaged in the latter practice; the company said it would reimburse more than 20,000 customers of its mutual funds about $11 million that they should have received in volume discounts.

Critics and some industry insiders agreed that the questionable or illegal practices had arisen because of an industrywide drive toward growth at any cost. "Amassing assets under management became the industry's primary goal, and our focus shifted from stewardship to salesmanship," John Bogle, founder of the Vanguard family of mutual funds told the *Economist* magazine in November. Bogle had long advocated tougher regulations of his industry. The practices had escaped notice because regulators had paid little attention to the operations of mutual funds, and the law allowed the funds to file public reports that disguised many of their practices. Spitzer went further, charging that the SEC—which had ultimate responsibility for monitoring mutual funds—was "asleep at the switch."

Battered by the surge of bad publicity about its practices, the mutual fund industry produced a sudden battery of reforms in late October. The industry's trade group, the Investment Company Institute, said it supported rules that would curb the practices of late trading and market timing. The industry lobbied on Capitol Hill against new legislation, however, saying it could clean up its own mess, with the cooperation of the SEC. The House on November 19 passed legislation (HR 2420) requiring mutual funds to tell investors about their fees and policies, and it established rules intended to make the boards of directors of fund companies more independent from the managers. The Senate took no action on the issue during the year.

The SEC on December 3 gave tentative approval to its first new regulations arising from the scandal. One rule attempted to ban late trading by establishing a "hard cutoff" of 4 P.M., Eastern time, for the pricing of shares on mutual funds. Another rule required the funds to disclose to investors their policies on market timing. The rules "will go a long way toward restoring investor confidence in these important investment vehicles," SEC chairman Donaldson said.

Although the scandal severely damaged the credibility of the mutual fund industry, it had only a modest impact—at least short-term—on the amount of money Americans kept in the funds. Several of the funds that were early targets of investigators lost billions of dollars in holdings in September and October as a small number of individual investors and some state pension funds withdrew their holdings. The rate of withdrawals slowed later in the year, however. Aside from leading to tougher regulations, perhaps the greatest impact of the scandal was that some Americans began paying more attention to the quarterly statements from the mutual funds and to the ratings given those funds by independent monitors.

Upheaval at New York Stock Exchange

The scandals at mutual funds were based on complex financial transactions that were only dimly understood by the vast majority of ordinary investors. By contrast, the New York Stock Exchange was hit by a major scandal resulting from an action that anyone could understand. On August 27 the exchange disclosed that its board chairman, Grasso, would receive $139.5 million in compensation that had been deferred over the previous eight years. The pay had been set by a compensation committee whose members

Grasso had chosen; most of them represented firms that the stock exchange regulated.

The revelation of Grasso's pay package—which was huge even by Wall Street standards—brought cries of outrage from groups representing investors. SEC chairman Donaldson, who himself had been the exchange's chairman two decades earlier, sent the board a letter saying the pay package raised "serious questions" about how the exchange was run. For more than two weeks board members defended both Grasso and his pay, noting that he had been a long-time employee who had modernized the exchange and headed off threats from competitors. Apparently hoping to calm dissent, the board on September 9 announced that Grasso had agreed not to take an additional $48 million he had been promised for pay incentives in the future. But that announcement—revealing that Grasso's pay package actually was close to $190 million—merely fanned the flames of outrage and brought calls for his resignation from politicians and the heads of several major institutional investors. To cut its losses, the exchange board voted, 13–7, on September 17 to ask Grasso to resign.

Grasso's resignation ended the furor over his pay but failed to satisfy critics who said the incident exposed underlying conflicts of interest between the two roles of the stock exchange: one as a financial services company that listed the stocks of some 2,800 publicly traded companies, the other as a regulator of those companies. To restore confidence, the exchange's board chose John S. Reed as its interim chairman. A retired former executive of Citigroup, Reed had been one of the country's most respected financial leaders.

Reed on November 5 unveiled a plan for major changes, including replacing the entire twenty-seven-member board of directors with a new, independent board of eight members from outside the securities industry. Reed also proposed splitting the roles of the board chairman and chief executive officer—a move to keep a single person from holding too much power. However, Reed did not call for separating the exchange's stock-listing and regulatory functions. The exchange could handle both tasks, without conflict, if it was well managed and controlled by an attentive, independent board, he said. Reed also proposed a twenty-member "advisory" board for the exchange that would include industry representatives.

The SEC approved Reed's reorganization plan on December 17. Donaldson said the plan would put in place "every possible safeguard" to prevent conflicts between the exchange's two functions.

Investment Banks and Stock Analysts

Investigations in 2002 had uncovered numerous other abuses in the securities industry—the most important of which appeared to be widespread conflicts of interests at some of Wall Street's biggest investment banks. Spitzer, the SEC, and other regulators had found that banks had deceived investors by providing them with supposedly unbiased financial "research" that came from analysts who had financial relationships with the firms they were researching. During the 1990s some Wall Street analysts had gained fame and huge fortunes because of their ability to "pick" up-and-coming stocks ahead of time. Many of those favored companies, especially in the Internet and technology sectors, collapsed when the country's high-tech bubble burst in late 1999 and early 2000.

In December 2002 Spitzer and the SEC reached what they called a "global settlement" with ten investment banks, settling charges that they had misled investors. Among the banks were most of the large Wall Street firms: Bear Sterns, Citigroup, Credit Suisse First Boston, Goldman Sachs, J.P. Morgan Chase, Lehman Brothers, Merrill Lynch, Morgan Stanley, Piper Jaffray, and UBS Warburg. Under the settlement, the banks agreed to pay a total of $894 million in penalties and refunds to investors, $432.5 million to fund independent investment research for investors, and $80 million for programs to educate investors about how to judge the advice they received.

Spitzer and Donaldson said the settlement was a major victory for investors, but some critics noted that the $1.4 billion total paid by the banks was only a small fraction of what investors had lost because of the bad advice they had received. Testifying before the Senate Banking Committee on May 7, 2003, Donaldson said investors still had the option to sue the banks on their own, but he acknowledge that "they can never fully be repaid."

The settlement won final approval on October 31, 2003, from U.S. District Court Judge William H. Pauley III, in New York. Pauley, who had handled Spitzer's lawsuits that had led to the settlement, had demanded several changes in the procedures for refunding an estimated $399 million to investors.

The only investment banker to be charged with a crime as a result of the stock market collapse escaped conviction in October—at least for the time being. A jury deadlocked on October 24 in the case of Frank P. Quattrone, a former investment banker for Credit Suisse First Boston who had arranged the stock offerings for some of the major high-tech firms that appeared on the scene in the 1990s. Prosecutors and critics alleged that Quattrone abused his influence by persuading investors to sink billions of dollars into companies that had little inherent value and collapsed along with the stock market bubble. Despite an extensive investigation, prosecutors were unable to charge Quattrone with securities-related fraud and instead charged him only with two counts of obstruction of justice and one count of witness tampering. A Manhattan jury deliberated for five days but was unable to reach a unanimous verdict. Federal prosecutors said they would try again in 2004.

Following are excerpts from a complaint filed September 3, 2003, with a New York state court by Attorney General Eliot Spitzer alleging that from 1999 to 2003 Canary Capitol Partners, LLC; Canary Investment Management, LLC; Canary Capital Partners, LTD; and Edward J. Stern engaged in fraudulent schemes, known as late trading and market timing, that shortchanged investors in several mutual funds. The complaint was accompanied by a settlement in which the firms and Stern agreed to make restitution of $30 million in profits and pay a $10 million penalty.

State of New York v. Canary Capital Partners

Preliminary Statement

8. From 1999 to 2003, Canary engaged in two fraudulent schemes and benefitted to the extent of tens of millions of dollars at the expense of mutual fund investors. Both schemes involved the complicity of mutual fund management companies that violated their fiduciary duties to their customers in return for substantial fees and other income for themselves and their affiliates.

9. The first scheme was Canary's "late trading" of mutual fund shares. As described in greater detail below, the daily price of mutual fund shares is generally calculated as of 4:00 p.m. EST. Orders to buy, sell or exchange mutual fund shares placed at or before 4:00 p.m. EST on a given day receive that day's price. Conversely, orders placed after 4:00 p.m. EST are supposed to be priced using the following day's price. Canary agreed with certain financial institutions (including the Bank of America) that orders Canary placed after 4 p.m. on a given day would illegally receive that day's price (as opposed to the next day's price, which the order would have received had it been processed lawfully). This allowed Canary to capitalize on post-4:00 p.m. information while those who bought their mutual fund shares lawfully could not.

10. Late trading can be analogized to betting today on yesterday's horse races.

11. The second scheme involved "timing" of mutual funds. "Timing" is an investment technique involving short-term, "in and out" trad-

ing of mutual fund shares. The technique is designed to exploit inefficiencies in the way mutual fund companies price their shares. This practice is by no means limited to Canary. Indeed: (1) it is widely acknowledged that timing inures to the detriment of long-term shareholders; (2) because of this detrimental effect, mutual fund prospectuses typically state that timing is monitored and the funds work to prevent it; and (3) nonetheless, in return for investments that will increase fund managers' fees, fund managers enter into undisclosed agreements to allow timing.

12. In fact, certain mutual fund companies have employees (generally referred to as the "timing police") who are supposed to ferret out "timers" and put a stop to their short-term trading activity. Nonetheless, the mutual fund managers arranged to give Canary and other market timers a "pass" with the timing police, who would look the other way rather than attempt to shut down their short-term trading.

13. The mutual fund prospectuses created the misleading impression that mutual funds were vigilantly protecting investors against the negative effects of timing. In fact, the opposite was true: managers sold the right to time their funds to Canary and other hedge fund investors. The prospectuses were silent about these arrangements.

14. As a result of "late trading" and "timing" of mutual funds, Canary, the mutual fund companies and their intermediaries profited handsomely. The losers were unsuspecting long-term mutual fund investors. Canary's excess profits came dollar-for-dollar out of their pockets.

A. Late Trading

15. Canary's practice of late trading exploited the unique way in which mutual funds set their prices. Mutual funds are valued once a day, usually at 4:00 p.m. EST, when the New York market closes. The price, known as the Net Asset Value or "NAV," generally reflects the closing prices of the securities that comprise a given fund's portfolio, plus the value of any cash that the fund manager maintains for the fund. A mutual fund stands ready to buy or sell (the mutual fund industry refers to sales as "redemptions") its shares at the NAV with the public all day, any day—but unlike a stock, the price of a mutual fund does not change during the course of the day. Accordingly, orders placed at any time during the trading day up to the 4:00 p.m. cutoff get that day's NAV, but an order placed at 4:01 p.m. or thereafter receives the next day's NAV. This is the rule of "forward pricing", which became law in 1968.

1. *The Purpose of "Forward Pricing"*

16. This system assures a level playing field for investors. Mutual fund investors do not know the exact price at which their mutual fund orders will be executed at the time they place the orders (unlike stock investors), because NAVs are calculated after the market closes. Orders placed on or before 4 P.M. on a given day are filled at the NAV determined that day while orders placed after 4 p.m. are filled at the NAV calculated the next day. Thus, all investors have the same opportunity to assemble "pre-4:00 p.m. information" before they buy or sell. And no investor has (or at least is supposed to have) the benefit of "post-4:00 information" prior to making an investment decision. The importance of this protection becomes clear when, for example, there is an event after 4:00 p.m. (like an unexpectedly positive corporate earnings announcement) that makes it highly probable that the market for the stocks in a given fund will open sharply higher the next day. Forward pricing ensures fairness: those who bought the fund during the day, before the information came out, will enjoy a gain. Those who buy shares in the fund after the announcement are not supposed to share in this profit. Their purchase order should receive the NAV set at the end of the next day, when the market will have digested the news and reflected its impact in (1) higher prices for the stock held by the fund and therefore (2) a higher NAV for the fund.

17. An investor who has the ability to avoid forward pricing and buy at the prior NAV enjoys a significant trading edge. He or she can wait until after the market closes for significant news such as the above-earnings announcement to come out, and then buy the fund at the old, low NAV that does not reflect the impact of the new information. When the market goes up the next day, the lucky investor would be able to sell and realize an arbitrage profit based solely on the privilege of trading on the "stale" NAV.

18. Where does the late trader's arbitrage profit come from? Dollar for dollar, it comes out of the mutual fund that the late trader buys. In essence, the late trader is being allowed into the fund after it is closed for the day to participate in a profit that would otherwise have gone completely to the fund's buy-and-hold investors. When the late trader redeems his shares and claims his profit, the mutual fund manager has either to sell stock or use cash on hand—stock and cash that used to belong to the long-term investors—to give the late trader his gain. This makes late trading basically a zero-sum game. Putting to one side the investment results of the mutual fund for the brief time that the late trader actually holds it, the late trader's gain is the long-term investors' loss. The forward pricing rule was enacted to prevent this kind of abuse.

2. Summary of Canary's Late Trading

19. Canary engaged in late trading on a daily basis from in or about March 2000 until this office began its investigation in July of 2003. It targeted dozens of mutual funds and extracted tens of millions of dollars from them. During the declining market of 2001 and 2002, it used late trading to, in effect, sell mutual fund shares short. This caused the mutual funds to overpay for their shares as the market went down, serving to magnify long-term investors' losses.

20. Canary obtained some of its late trading "capacity" (the opportunity to engage in late trading) directly from one mutual fund manager, the Bank of America. Bank of America installed special computer equipment in Canary's office that allowed it to buy and sell Bank of America's own mutual funds—the Nations Funds—and hundreds of other mutual funds at the 4:00 p.m. price until 6:30 p.m. New York time. In return, Canary agreed to leave millions of dollars in Bank of America bond funds on a long-term basis. These parked funds are known in the trade as "sticky assets."

21. Canary obtained additional late trading capacity from intermediaries, including Security Trust Company ("STC"), an Arizona company providing trust administrative services (including access to mutual funds) to retirement plans. STC gave Canary the ability to trade hundreds of additional mutual funds as late as 9:00 p.m. New York time. So profitable was this opportunity that STC ultimately demanded, and received, a percentage of Canary's winnings.

B. Timing

22. Mutual funds are meant to be long-term investments. They are designed for buy-and-hold investors, and are therefore the favored homes for Americans' retirement and college savings accounts. Nevertheless, quick-turnaround traders routinely try to trade in and out of certain mutual funds in order to exploit inefficiencies in the way they set their NAVs.

23. This strategy works only because some funds use "stale" prices to calculate the value of securities held in the fund's portfolio. These prices are "stale" because they do not necessarily reflect the "fair value" of such securities as of the time the NAV is calculated. A typical example is a U.S. mutual fund that holds Japanese shares. Because of the time zone difference, the Japanese market may close at 2:00 a.m. New York time. If the U.S. mutual fund manager uses the closing prices of the Japanese shares in his or her fund to arrive at an NAV at 4:00 p.m. in New York, he or she is relying on market information that is fourteen hours old. If there have been positive market moves

during the New York trading day that will cause the Japanese market to rise when it later opens, the stale Japanese prices will not reflect them, and the fund's NAV will be artificially low. Put another way, the NAV does not reflect the true current market value of the stocks the fund holds. On such a day, a trader who buys the Japanese fund at the "stale" price is virtually assured of a profit that can be realized the next day by selling. This and similar strategies are known as "time zone arbitrage." Taking advantage of this kind of short-term arbitrage repeatedly in a single mutual fund is called "timing" the fund.

24. A similar type of timing is possible in mutual funds that contain illiquid securities such as high-yield bonds or small capitalization stocks. Here, the fact that some of the fund's securities may not have traded for hours before the New York closing time can render the fund's NAV stale, and thus open it to being timed. This is sometimes known as "liquidity arbitrage."

1. The Effect on Long Term Shareholders

25. Like late trading, effective timing captures an arbitrage profit. And like late trading, the arbitrage profit from timing comes dollar-for-dollar out of the pockets of the long-term investors: the timer steps in at the last moment and takes part of the buy-and-hold investors' upside when the market goes up, so the next day's NAV is reduced for those who are still in the fund. If the timer sells short on bad days—as Canary did—the arbitrage has the effect of making the next day's NAV lower than it would otherwise have been, thus magnifying the losses that investors are experiencing in a declining market.

26. Timing is not entirely risk free, however. For example, the timer has to keep his or her money in the target fund for at least a day, so he or she may enjoy additional gains or incur losses, depending on the market. But such gains and losses are distinct from the timer's arbitrage profit, which is essentially crystallized at the moment of purchase.

27. Besides the wealth transfer of arbitrage (called "dilution"), timers also harm their target funds in a number of other ways. They impose their transaction costs on the long-term investors. Indeed, trades necessitated by timer redemptions can also lead to realization of taxable capital gains at an undesirable time, or may result in managers having to sell stock into a falling market. Accordingly, fund managers often seek to minimize the disruptive impact of timers by keeping cash on hand to pay out the timers' profits without having to sell stock. This "strategy" does not eliminate the transfer of wealth out of the mutual fund caused by timing; it only reduces the administrative cost of those transfers. However, at the same time it can also reduce the overall performance of the fund by requiring the fund manager to keep a certain amount of the funds' assets in cash at all times, thus depriving

the investors of the advantages of being fully invested in a rising market. Some fund managers even enter into special investments as an attempt to "hedge" against timing activity (instead of just refusing to allow it), thus deviating altogether from the ostensible investment strategy of their funds, and incurring further transaction costs.

2. Tools to Combat Market Timing

28. Mutual fund managers are aware of the damaging effect that timers have on their funds. And while the effects on individual shareholders may be small once they are spread out over all the investors in a fund, their aggregate impact is not: for example, one recent study estimates that U.S. mutual funds lose $4 billion each year to timers. While it is virtually impossible for fund managers to identify every timing trade, large movements in and out of funds—like those made by Canary—are easy for managers to spot. And mutual fund managers have tools to fight back against timers.

29. Fund managers typically have the power simply to reject timers' purchases. Many funds have also instituted short-term trading fees ("early redemption fees") that effectively wipe out the arbitrage that timers exploit. Generally, these fees go directly into the affected fund to reimburse it for the costs of short term trading. In addition, fund managers are required to update NAVs at the end of the day in New York when there have been market moves that might render the NAV stale. This is called giving the fund a "fair value." It eliminates the timer's arbitrage. As fiduciaries for their investors, mutual fund managers are obliged to do their best to use these weapons to protect their customers from the dilution that timing causes.

3. Incentives for Allowing Market Timing

30. Given the harm that timing causes, and the tools available to put a stop to it, why would a mutual fund manager allow his fund to be timed? The answer lies in the way that mutual funds are organized. Typically a single management company sets up a number of mutual funds to form a family. For example, Banc of America Capital Management, LLC is the manager for the Nations Funds family, including Nations International Equity fund, Nations Small Cap fund and so on. While each mutual fund is in fact its own company, as a practical matter the management company runs it. The portfolio managers who make the investment decisions for the funds and the executives to whom they report are all typically employees of the management company, not the mutual funds themselves. Still, the management company owes fiduciary duties to each fund and each investor.

31. The management company makes its profit from fees it charges the funds for financial advice and other services. These fees are typically

a percentage of the assets in the fund, so the more assets in the family of funds, the more money the manager makes. The timer understands this perfectly, and frequently offers the manager more assets in exchange for the right to time. Fund managers have succumbed to temptation and allowed investors in the target funds to be hurt in exchange for additional money in their own pockets in the form of higher management fees.

32. Canary found many mutual fund managers willing to take that deal. In the period from 2000 to 2003, Canary entered into agreements with dozens of mutual fund families allowing it to time many different mutual funds. Typically, Canary would agree with the fund manager on target funds to be timed–often international and equity funds offering time zone or liquidity arbitrage—and then move the timing money quickly between those funds and a resting place in a money market or similar fund in the same fund family. By keeping the money—often many million dollars—in the family, Canary assured the manager that he or she would collect management and other fees on the amount whether it was in the target fund, the resting fund, or moving in between. In addition, sometimes the manager would waive any applicable early redemption fees. By doing so, the manager would directly deprive the fund of money that would have partially reimbursed the fund for the impact of timing.

33. As an additional inducement for allowing the timing, fund managers often received "sticky assets." These were typically long-term investments made not in the mutual fund in which the timing activity was permitted, but in one of the fund manager's financial vehicles (e.g., a bond fund or a hedge fund run by the manager) that assured a steady flow of fees to the manager.

4. Failure to Disclose Timing Arrangements

34. These arrangements were never disclosed to mutual fund investors. On the contrary, many of the relevant mutual fund prospectuses contained materially misleading statements assuring investors that the fund managers discouraged and worked to prevent mutual fund timing. . . .

35. Canary realized tens of millions of dollars in profits as a result of these timing arrangements. In many cases these profits also reflect late trading, as Canary would frequently negotiate a timing agreement with a mutual fund management company, and then proceed to late trade the target funds through Bank of America, STC or another intermediary. . . .

Source: U.S. New York. Supreme Court of the State of New York, County of New York. *State of New York v. Canary Capital Partners.* Complaint. September 3, 2003. www.oag.state.ny.us/press/2003/sep/canary_complaint.pdf (accessed January 13, 2004).

Pension Benefit Guaranty Corporation on Underfunded Pensions

September 4, 2003

Concerns over the financial health of the nation's retirement system heightened in 2003 with revelations that traditional defined benefit plans were underfunded by an estimated $350 billion and that the quasi-government agency that insured the plans was itself running an $11.2 billion deficit. The underfunding was largely attributed to the stock market slump and declining interest rates, which lowered returns on retirement fund investments generally and thus increased the contributions that some employers had to make to ensure that their plans were "fully funded" as defined by federal law. In the event that an underfunded company went bankrupt, the Pension Benefit Guaranty Corporation (PBGC) continued paying benefits to current and future retirees but generally at a reduced rate. Although the head of the PBGC said there was no immediate cause for worry, he warned of a potential need for a taxpayer bailout if the agency ran out of money.

About 44 million American workers and retirees participated in traditional defined benefit plans, which guaranteed them a fixed benefit upon retirement. Most traditional retirement plans were offered by firms in the manufacturing industry, which was having difficulty coping with foreign competition and the economic downturn that began in 2001. Most of the plans were not in jeopardy, although employers might have preferred to use the money necessary to ensure that the plans were fully funded for other purposes. The plans that were in danger of being unable to meet their funding obligations tended to be those offered by large corporations with unionized workers, such as auto makers and their suppliers, and declining industries with many retirees, such as the steel industry. Some airlines were also having trouble meeting their obligations to fully fund their pension plan. (Employment, p. 441)

Both chambers of Congress weighed measures that would give short-term relief to employers who offered defined benefit plans, temporarily lowering the amount the companies would have to devote to their pension funds. Although the House passed two bills aimed at reducing costs to corporations, the Senate did not act before Congress adjourned for the session. Senate leaders promised to take up the legislation early in the 2004 session.

Two other changes in pension plans were also threatening workers' well-being in 2003. One was a switch by many employers from traditional defined benefit plans to so-called cash balance plans. Such plans usually benefited younger and mobile workers, who would take their cash balances with them from job to job. But the plans often cut benefits for workers nearing retirement age. In July a federal district court ruled that IBM had illegally discriminated against its older workers when it converted its pension plans. The ruling was certain to be appealed. In the interim, Congress moved to block finalization of proposed regulations making it harder for other workers to bring similar age discrimination suits, while it worked on legislation to ensure that conversions were fair to older workers.

The second change was the decision by many companies to cut back or eliminate health insurance plans for retired workers. Companies said that the soaring costs of health care made such plans unaffordable. Elimination of such plans meant that affected retirees would pay more for private insurance to cover gaps in Medicare coverage. *(Health insurance, p. 846)*

The Underfunding Problem

The underfunding problem for defined benefit plans had three interrelated components—the way pension contributions and liabilities were calculated, the additional problems caused by companies that were bankrupt or verging on bankruptcy, and the strain that the underfunding was placing on the Pension Benefit Guaranty Corporation. In testimony September 4 before the House Education and Workforce Committee, Steven A. Kandarian, executive director of the PBGC, estimated that the total underfunding of defined benefit plan pension liabilities exceeded $400 billion as of December 31, 2002. "Financially weak" companies accounted for about $35 billion of that total, an amount that he said could rise to $80 billion by the end of the year. Airline and steel company plans accounted for about half of the shortfall for financially troubled companies. (By the end of the year the overall shortfall had fallen back to an estimated $350 billion, in large part because of improvement in the stock market.)

Under federal law, each company with a defined benefit plan was required to ensure that the plan's assets—the company's contributions and the return on those contributions—equaled 90 percent of the plan's liabilities. Companies typically invested their pension contributions in a mix of stocks, bonds, and other financial instruments. During the heady days of the stock market boom in the 1990s, many companies did not need to make any contributions to their pension plans because soaring stock prices and rising interest rates fattened their holdings. But the market decline and low interest rates that followed the 2001 recession dramatically altered corporate pension balance sheets; by 2003, several major companies were facing the need to make big pension contributions just as they were battling huge operating losses.

General Motors (GM), for example, reported in January that for 2002 it had a $19.3 billion deficit in its U.S. pension plans, despite a contribution of $50 billion over the last decade. Analysts calculated that GM's pension obligations added $1,700 to the cost of every car the company built. IBM, Honeywell International, and Ford were among the other companies that had to make hefty contributions to meet liabilities. A company without enough cash to make its pension obligations could be forced into bankruptcy. Companies were expected to put $83 billion into pension funds in 2003, nearly double the amount contributed in 2002 and six times what they paid in 2001,when pension funds were still reaping high returns on their investments.

In addition, a temporary change in the rules for calculating how much money companies had to put into their pension funds was set to expire at the end of 2003. Unless Congress acted, companies would be required, as early as April 2004, to put aside billions of additional dollars to cover their pension obligations. Both companies and labor unions appealed to Congress to change the rules to make it easier for corporations to fund pension plans, saying that without such changes companies might be forced to cut pension benefits or terminate plans altogether.

At the same time, financially strapped airline and steel companies appealed for temporary exemptions from requirements that called for larger pension contributions from companies with chronically underfunded pension funds—those funds whose assets fell below 90 percent of liabilities for two out of three years. Airlines were able to fully fund their pensions as recently as 2000, but the decline in air travel following the September 11, 2001, terrorist attacks, a rise in oil prices, and a surge in competition had hurt many of them. United Airlines, the second largest carrier in the United States, sought bankruptcy protection, while U.S Airways had already defaulted on its pilots' pension plan. Steel companies were also financially pressed; the PBGC had already taken over the pension plans of a number of steel manufacturers, including Bethlehem Steel, LTV, and National Steel.

Whatever relief Congress granted could, however, further exacerbate the deficit of the PBGC. The agency was created in 1974 to ensure that workers continued to receive benefits when their companies went bankrupt or out of business. Using premiums paid by companies participating in the plan and returns on investments, PBGC paid a maximum benefit in 2003 of $3,664 a month or $43,977 a year. On average retirees received 94 percent of the benefits they had earned. In fiscal 2003 the agency expected to pay out nearly $2.5 billion in benefits to nearly 1 million retirees.

Because of the failure of a large number of underfunded companies, the PBGC program had dropped from a surplus of $7.7 billion at the beginning of fiscal 2002 to a deficit of $3.6 billion at the end of the fiscal year. By the end of fiscal 2003 the deficit had grown to $11.2 billion. The agency had more than $30 billion in assets, so it was in no immediate danger of running out of money. The $2.5 billion the agency expected to pay out to retirees in 2003 was three times more than it collected in premiums, however, and a persistent imbalance of that magnitude or larger could eventually pose a funding problem that might require a taxpayer bailout.

Although most lawmakers and the Bush administration seemed prepared to grant overall temporary relief to companies, the administration and others warned that too much relief, especially for financially troubled companies, could mean that they would not set enough money aside to meet their pension obligations, further increasing the fiscal demands on the PBGC. "If the company can get away with putting in less money and things go badly, that is going to come out of the government's pocket," said Jeremy Bulow, a Stanford University economist.

Although the House passed two measures giving temporary relief to all companies with defined benefit plans and special relief to airlines, procedural issues over competing Senate measures were not resolved before the end of the year. Senate leaders promised to act quickly when Congress reconvened in January 2004.

Shaky Retirement System

The underfunding of traditional pension plans was just one of a multitude of problems affecting the retirement system. The bursting of the stock market bubble that began at the turn of the century also affected holders of 401(k) and other plans known as defined contribution plans. Under these retirement plans, which covered about 55 million people, an employee saved a certain percentage of wages, often matched by the employer, which typically was invested; the size of the retirement benefit depended upon the return on the investment. Most 401(k) funds were invested in stocks and bonds, and workers were horrified as they watched the value of their retirement portfolio fall by 25 percent or more.

The collapse of the giant energy trading company Enron in 2001 exposed another problem affecting some 401(k) plans. Enron employees had heavily invested their retirement funds in Enron stock; when the company went bankrupt, their retirement savings also disappeared. Although reforms were introduced in Congress, legislators were unable to agree on a measure that would limit the amount of employer stock that an employee could hold in a 401(k) or other defined contribution plan. *(Enron and 401[k] plans, Historic Documents of 2002, p. 101)*

A third element of the nation's retirement system was the government-run Social Security system, which paid minimal benefits to retirees out of a fund financed by taxes shared equally between employer and employee. Social Security was expected to come under heavy pressure starting around 2008, when the baby boom generation (those born between 1946 and 1964) would begin reaching retirement age, while the number of workers paying into the system for each retiree would begin to decline from more than three to about two. Economists and others were already warning that to avoid running up unsustainable federal deficits, Congress might have to raise taxes, reduce benefits, or do both—politically unpalatable steps that few legislators were willing to take. *(Federal deficit, p. 678)*

The last element of the retirement system was personal saving. Yet there was some question whether Americans were saving sufficient money to ensure that, together with Social Security and private pension benefits, they would have enough money to retire when they wanted to and to live comfortably thereafter. A report released by the Congressional Budget Office in December that surveyed recent academic studies on retirement and the baby boomer generation concluded that the typical baby boomer had more current income and wealth than his or her parents had at the same age, was accumulating wealth at about the same rate, and was therefore likely to have more resources in retirement. However, the report cautioned, several uncertainties, including the rate of return on investments and possible changes in the Social Security benefits, could mean that some boomers would fare less well in retirement than their parents.

Following are excerpts from testimony given September 4, 2003, by Steven A. Kandarian, executive director of the federal Pension Benefit Guaranty Corporation, before the House Committee on Education and the Workforce.

"Statement Before the House by Steven A. Kandarian"

Introduction

[The Pension Benefit Guaranty Corporation] protects the pensions of nearly 44 million workers and retirees in more than 32,000 private defined benefit pension plans. . . .

PBGC insures pension benefits worth $1.5 trillion and is responsible for paying current and future benefits to 783,000 people in over 3,000 terminated defined benefit plans. As a result of the recent terminations of several very large plans, PBGC will be responsible for paying benefits to nearly 1 million people in FY 2003. Similarly, benefit payments that exceeded $1.5 billion dollars in FY 2002 will rise to nearly $2.5 billion in FY 2003.

Defined benefit pension plans continue to be an important source of retirement security for 44 million American workers. But there has been a sharp deterioration in the funded status of pension plans, and the PBGC now has a record deficit as the result of the recent terminations of large underfunded plans.

When underfunded pension plans terminate, three groups can lose: participants can see their benefits reduced, other businesses can see their PBGC premiums go up, and ultimately Congress could call on taxpayers to support the PBGC.

Recently, the Administration issued our initial set of proposals to deal with the problem of pension underfunding. It has four parts:

- First, as the necessary initial step toward comprehensive reform of the funding rules, it improves the accuracy of pension liability measurement to reflect the time structure of each pension plan's benefit payments. This would be accomplished by measuring a plan's liabilities using a yield curve of highly-rated corporate bonds to calculate the present value of those future payments.
- Second, it requires better disclosure to workers, retirees, investors and creditors about the funded status of pension plans, which will improve incentives for adequate funding.
- Third, it provides new safeguards against underfunding by requiring financially troubled companies with highly underfunded plans to immediately fund or secure additional benefits and lump sum payments. Similarly, it prohibits unfunded benefit increases by those severely underfunded plans sponsored by corporations with below investment-grade debt.
- And fourth, it calls for additional reforms to protect workers' retirement security by improving the funded status of defined benefit plans. . . .

PBGC estimates that the total underfunding in the single-employer defined benefit system exceeded $400 billion as of December 31, 2002, the largest number ever recorded. When the PBGC is forced to take over underfunded pension plans, the burden often falls heavily on workers and retirees. In some cases, participants lose benefits that were earned but not guaranteed by the pension insurance system. In all cases, workers lose the opportunity to earn additional benefits under the terminated pension plan.

PBGC's premium payers—employers that sponsor defined benefit plans—also pay a price when an underfunded plan terminates. Although PBGC is a government corporation, it is not backed by the full faith and credit of the U.S. government and receives no federal tax dollars. When PBGC takes over underfunded pension plans, financially healthy companies with better-funded pension plans end up making transfers to financially weak companies with chronically underfunded pension plans. If these transfers from strong to weak plans become too large, then over time strong companies with well-funded plans may elect to leave the system.

In the worst case, PBGC's deficit could grow so large that the size of the premium increase necessary to close the gap would be unacceptable to responsible premium payers. If this were to occur, Congress could call upon U.S. taxpayers to pick up the cost of underfunded pension plans through a Federal bailout of PBGC. In essence, all taxpayers would shoulder the burden of paying benefits to the 20 percent of private-sector workers who still enjoy the security of a defined benefit plan.

PBGC's Deteriorating Financial Condition

As a result of record pension underfunding and the failure of a number of plan sponsors in mature industries, PBGC's financial position has deteriorated sharply in the last two years. During FY 2002, PBGC's single-employer insurance program went from a surplus of $7.7 billion to a deficit of $3.6 billion—a loss of $11.3 billion in just one year. The $11.3 billion loss is more than five times larger than any previous one-year loss in the agency's 28-year history. Moreover, based on our latest unaudited financial report, the deficit had grown to $5.7 billion as of July 31, 2003.

Because of this extraordinary one-year loss, the dramatic increase in pension underfunding, and the risk of additional large claims on the insurance program, the General Accounting Office (GAO) recently placed PBGC's single-employer program on its "high risk" list. In its report to Congress, GAO points to systemic problems in the private-sector defined benefit system that pose serious risks to PBGC. For example, the insured participant base continues to shift away from active workers, falling from 78% of all participants in 1980 to only 53% in 2000. In addition, GAO's report notes that the insurance risk pool has become concentrated in industries affected by global competition and the movement from an industrial to a knowledge-based economy. My hope is that GAO's "high risk" designation will spur reforms to better protect the stakeholders in the pension insurance system—participants and premium payers.

Reasons for PBGC's Current Financial Condition

PBGC's record deficit has been caused by the failure of a significant number of highly underfunded plans of financially troubled and bankrupt companies. These include the plans of retailers Bradlees, Caldor, Grand Union, and Payless Cashways; steel makers including Bethlehem, LTV, National, Acme, Empire, Geneva, and RTI; other manufacturers such as Singer, Polaroid, Harvard Industries, and Durango; and airlines such as TWA. In addition, PBGC has taken over the failed US Airways pilots plan. Mr. Chairman, pension claims against PBGC for 2002 alone were greater than the total claims for all previous years combined. At current premium levels, it would take about 12 years of premiums to cover just the claims from 2002.

During the last economic downturn in the early 1990s, the pension insurance program absorbed what were then the largest claims in its history—$600 million for the Eastern Airlines plans and $800 million for the Pan American Airlines plans. Those claims seem modest in comparison to the steel plans we have taken in lately: $1.3 billion for National Steel, $1.9 billion for LTV Steel, and $3.9 billion for Bethlehem Steel. Underfunding in the financially troubled airline sector is larger still, totaling $26 billion.

PBGC premiums have not kept pace with the growth in pension claims or in pension underfunding. Premium income, in 2002 dollars, has fallen every year since 1996, even though Congress lifted the cap on variable-rate premiums that year. The premium has two parts: a flat-rate charge of $19 per participant, and a variable-rate premium of 0.9 percent of the dollar amount of a plan's underfunding, measured on a "current liability" basis. As long as plans are at the "full funding limit," which generally means 90 percent of current liability, they do not have to pay the variable-rate premium. That is why Bethlehem Steel, the largest claim in the history of the PBGC, paid no variable-rate premium for five years prior to termination.

Challenges Facing the Defined Benefit Pension System

The funding of America's private pension plans has become a serious public policy issue. Recent financial market trends—falling interest rates and equity returns—have exposed underlying weaknesses in the pension system, weaknesses that must be corrected if that system is to remain viable in the long run. In addition to falling interest rates and equity returns, there are serious challenges facing the defined benefit system: substantial underfunding, adverse demographic trends, and weaknesses in the pension funding rules.

Concurrent Falling Interest Rates and Stock Market Returns

The unprecedented, concurrent drops in both equity values and interest rates have caused the unfunded liabilities of most defined benefit pension plans to increase dramatically over the last three years. Some argue that the current problems are cyclical and that they will disappear as the stock market recovers, but it is not reasonable to base pension funding on the expectation that the stock market gains of the 1990s will repeat themselves.

In order to understand how pension plans got so underfunded, it is important to consider how mismatching assets and liabilities affects pension plan funding levels. Pension plan liabilities tend to be bond-like in nature. For example, both the value of bonds and the value of pension liabilities have risen in recent years as interest rates fell. Were interest rates to rise, both the value of bonds and the value of pension liabilities would fall. The value of equity investments is more volatile than the value of bonds and less correlated with interest rates. Most companies prefer equity investments because they have historically produced a higher rate of return than bonds. These companies are willing to accept the increased risk of equities and interest rate changes in exchange for expected lower pension costs over the long term. Similarly, labor unions support investing in equities because they believe it results in larger pensions for workers. Investing in equities rather than bonds shifts some of these [risks] to the PBGC.

Pension Underfunding

Pension liabilities represent financial obligations of plan sponsors to their workers and retirees. Thus, any pension underfunding is a matter of concern and may pose risks to plan participants and the PBGC. In ongoing, healthy companies, an increase in the amount of underfunding can affect how secure workers feel about their pension benefits, even though the actual risk of loss maybe low, at least in the near-term. Of immediate concern is chronic underfunding in companies with debt below investment-grade or otherwise financially troubled, where the risk of loss is much greater. Some of these financially troubled companies have pension underfunding significantly greater than their market capitalization.

As detailed in our most recent annual report, plans that are sponsored by financially weak companies had $35 billion in unfunded vested benefits. Of this $35 billion, about half represented underfunding in airline and steel plans. By the end of this fiscal year, the amount of underfunding in financially troubled companies could exceed $80 billion. As I previously noted, the Administration has already made specific legislative recommendations to limit the PBGC's growing exposure to such plans.

Demographic Trends

Demographic trends are another structural factor adversely affecting defined benefit plans. Many defined benefit plans are in our oldest and most capital intensive industries. These industries face growing pension and health care costs due to an increasing number of older and retired workers.

Retirees already outnumber active workers in some industries. In some of the plans we have trusteed in the steel industry, only one out of every eight pension participants was an active worker. *The Detroit Free Press* recently reported that pension, retiree health and other retiree benefits account for $631 of every Chrysler vehicle's cost, $734 per Ford vehicle, and $1,360 for every GM car or truck. In contrast, pension and retiree benefit costs per vehicle for the U.S. plants of Honda and Toyota are estimated to be $107 and $180 respectively. In a low-margin business, retiree costs can have a serious impact on a company's competitiveness.

Demographic trends have also made defined benefit plans more expensive. Americans are living longer in retirement as a result of earlier retirement and longer life spans. Today, an average male worker spends 18.1 years in retirement compared to 11.5 in 1950, an additional seven years of retirement that must be funded. Medical advances are expected to increase life spans even further in the coming years.

Weaknesses in the Funding Rules

When PBGC trustees underfunded plans, participants often complain that companies should be legally required to fund their pension plans. The fact is, current law is simply inadequate to fully protect the pensions of America's workers when their plans terminate. There are many weaknesses with the current funding rules. I would like to focus on six:

First, the funding targets are set too low. Employers can stop making contributions when the plan is funded at 90 percent of "current liability." The definition of current liability is a creature of past legislative compromises, and has no obvious relationship to the amount of money needed to pay all benefit liabilities if the plan terminates. As a result, employers can stop making contributions before a plan is sufficiently funded to protect participants, premium payers and taxpayers. . . .

For example, in its last filing prior to termination, Bethlehem Steel reported that it was 84 percent funded on a current liability basis. At termination, however, the plan was only 45 percent funded on a termination basis—with total underfunding of $4.3 billion. Similarly, in its last filing prior to termination, the US Airways pilots plan reported that it was 94 percent funded on a current liability basis. At termination, however, it was only 33 percent funded on a termination basis—with total underfunding of $2.5 billion. It is no wonder that the US Airways pilots were shocked to learn just how much of their promised benefits would be lost. In practice, a terminated plan's underfunded status can influence the actual benefit levels. Under the Administration's already-announced transparency proposal, participants would have been aware of the lower funding level on a termination basis.

Second, the funding rules often allow "contribution holidays" even for seriously underfunded plans. Bethlehem Steel, for example, made no cash contributions to its plan for three years prior to plan termination, and US Airways made no cash contributions to its pilots plan for four years before the plan was terminated. When a company contributes more than the minimum required contribution, it builds up a "credit balance" for minimum funding. It can then treat the credit balance as a payment of future required contributions, even if the assets in which the extra contributions were invested have lost some or all of their value.

Third, the funding rules do not reflect the risk of loss to participants and premium payers. The same funding rules apply regardless of a company's financial health, but a PBGC analysis found that nearly 90 percent of the companies representing large claims against the insurance system had junk-bond credit ratings for 10 years prior to termination.

Fourth, the minimum funding rules and the limits on maximum deductible contributions require companies to make pension contributions within a narrow range. Under these minimum and maximum limits, it is difficult for companies to build up an adequate surplus in good economic times to provide a cushion for bad times.

Fifth, current liability does not include reasonable estimates of expected future lump sum payments. Liabilities must be calculated as if a plan will pay benefits only as annuities. Even if it is clear that most participants will choose lump sums, and that these lump sums may be more expensive for the plan than the comparable annuity, the minimum funding rules do not account for lump sums because they are not part of how current liability is calculated.

Sixth, because of the structure of the funding rules under ERISA and the Internal Revenue Code, defined benefit plan contributions can be extremely volatile. After years of the funding rules allowing companies to make little or no contributions, many companies are suddenly required to make contributions of hundreds of millions of dollars to their plans at a time when they are facing other economic pressures. Although the law's complicated funding rules were designed, in part, to minimize the volatility of funding contributions, the current rules clearly have failed to achieve this goal. Masking market conditions is neither a good nor a necessary way to avoid volatility in funding contributions.

PBGC Premiums

As I noted earlier, because PBGC is not backed by the full faith and credit of the federal government and receives no federal tax dollars, it is the premium payers—employers that sponsor defined benefit plans—who bear the cost when underfunded plans terminate. Well-funded plans represent the best solution for participants and premium payers. However, PBGC's premiums should be re-examined to see whether they can better reflect the risk posed by various plans to the pension system as a whole.

Reforms Needed To Protect the Defined Benefit System

Mr. Chairman, we must make fundamental changes in the funding rules that will put underfunded plans on a predictable, steady path to better funding. Improvements in the funding rules should set stronger funding targets, foster more consistent contributions, mitigate volatility, and increase flexibility for companies to fund up their plans in good economic times.

At the same time, we must not create any new disincentives for companies to maintain their pension plans. Pension insurance creates moral hazard, tempting management and labor at financially troubled companies to make promises that they cannot or will not fund. The cost of wage increases is immediate, while the cost of pension increases can be deferred for up to 30 years and shutdown benefits may never be pre-funded. In exchange for smaller wage increases today, companies often offer more generous pension benefits tomorrow, knowing that if the company fails the plan will be handed over to the PBGC. This unfairly shifts the cost of unfunded pension promises to responsible companies and their workers. At some point, these financially strong companies may exit the defined benefit system, leaving only those companies that pose the greatest risk of claims.

In addition to the proposals the Administration has already introduced to accurately measure pension liabilities, improve pension disclosure, and protect against underfunding, the Departments of Labor, Treasury, and Commerce, and the PBGC are actively working on comprehensive reform. We are examining how to eliminate some of the risk shifting and moral hazard in the current system. We are crafting proposals to get pension plans better funded, especially those at risk of becoming unable to meet their benefit promises. And we are re-evaluating statutory amortization periods and actuarial assumptions regarding mortality, retirement, and the frequency and value of lump sum payments to ensure they are consistent with the goal of improved funding.

Conclusion

Mr. Chairman, we should not pass off the cost of today's pension problems to future generations. If companies do not fund the pension promises they make, someone else will have to pay—either workers in the form of reduced benefits, other companies in the form of higher PBGC premiums, or taxpayers in the form of a PBGC bailout. . . .

Source: U.S. Pension Benefit Guarantee Corporation. *Statement of Steven A. Kandarian Before the House Committee on Education and the Workforce.* September 4, 2003. www.pbgc.gov/news/speeches/testimony_090403.htm (accessed September 10, 2003).

General Accounting Office on Aviation Security

September 9, 2003

INTRODUCTION

The federal government made significant progress during 2003 in its crash program to protect air travel in the United States from terrorists and other security threats. But investigations by government watchdog agencies and the news media indicated that major gaps remained in the country's aviation security system.

Congress and the administration of President George W. Bush rushed to make improvements in aviation security following the September 11, 2001, terrorist attacks in which nineteen men hijacked four passenger airliners and flew two of them into the World Trade Center towers in New York City and one into the Pentagon outside Washington; the fourth plane crashed in a field in rural Pennsylvania. The hijackers had used simple knives to commandeer the planes.

In late 2001 Congress established a new Transportation Security Administration (TSA) to manage security programs for all forms of transportation in the United States, including air travel. That agency was ordered to hire tens of thousands of government employees to take over the job of screening passengers and their carry-on luggage at airports; previously, private security firms hired by the airlines had done that job. In 2002 Congress incorporated the TSA into another new agency, the Department of Homeland Security, which assumed broader responsibility for protecting the United States against terrorism and similar threats. (Background, Historic Documents of 2001, p. 650; Historic documents of 2002, p. 746)

Passenger Screening

For airline passengers and the general public, by far the most visible aspect of the government's new aviation security system was the TSA's rapid hiring in 2002 of about 50,000 people to screen all passengers and carry-on luggage at the nation's 429 commercial airports. Congress intended that the TSA's new screeners would be highly trained, closely supervised, and well-paid—in contrast to the previous, privately funded system in which employee turnover was high and performance was poor because of low wages and inadequate training. The first new TSA-employed screeners began work at Baltimore-Washington International Airport in April 2002, and by the end of that year federal screeners were working at all commercial airports. Their jobs were to check passengers as they walked through metal detectors and carry-on luggage as X-ray machines screened it. TSA gradually reduced its screener workforce to about 45,000 during 2003, citing tight budgets and a reassessment of how many screeners were actually needed.

Most news reports and investigative studies indicated that the new system of government screeners was remarkably efficient and effective, given how fast the screeners had been hired, trained, and put to work. Some problems did appear, however. The General Accounting Office (GAO), the investigative arm of Congress, issued several reports detailing those problems. An overview report given to Congress on September 9 said the TSA was not adequately monitoring the performance of airport screeners and their supervisors. The agency conducted too-few covert tests of its employees and was failing to use a computer software program that checked the ability of screeners to identify weapons that showed up in X-rays of passenger luggage, the GAO said.

The Homeland Security Department—TSA's parent agency—said in October that five agents posing as passengers had been able to sneak weapons past screeners at Boston's Logan International Airport. That airport had come under special scrutiny because it was the departure point for two of the planes hijacked on September 11, 2001. Also in October, Southwest Airlines employees found bags containing knives and suspicious notes on board planes in Houston and New Orleans. Nathaniel Heatwole, a college student from Damascus, Maryland, later was charged with taking the items onto the planes; he had sent TSA e-mail messages saying what he had done and reporting "security breaches" at two airports.

One of the most important remaining weak points in the screening system was that airport metal detectors and X-ray machines could not identify explosives taken by passengers onto airplanes in their clothing or carry-on luggage. Airport screeners could check baggage for explosives by running a swab over the handle and then testing the swab with a computer program; this time-consuming procedure was not done routinely, however. The TSA had budgeted $60 million in fiscal year 2003 to develop bomb-detection equipment for passenger checkpoints but diverted it to other programs because of cutbacks.

Another—far more controversial—element of passenger screening involved checking the identities of individual passengers to locate people suspected of posing security threats. Developed in the mid-1990s, this system used the airlines' computerized reservation programs to compare the names of passengers with the government's terrorism "watch list" and lists of suspicious behavioral characteristics (such as using cash to buy a one-way ticket at the last minute).

The government was developing a second-generation database, called Computer Assisted Passenger Prescreening System (CAPPS II), that would use broader sets of information, including commercial databases (such as credit files) and government files (such as arrest records), to identify passengers who might pose a security risk. Under the new system, passengers buying airline tickets would be required to provide personal information (including date of birth, home address, and telephone number); that information would be submitted to the TSA, which would check it against criminal records, lists of outstanding arrest warrants, and credit databases. Government computers would then categorize each passenger according to the potential threat he or she might pose: "green," for those who appeared to pose no risk; "yellow," for those whose records raised questions and would then be pulled aside for extra screening at the airport; and "red," for those flagged as potential security threats (these people might be denied permission to board an aircraft or might even be arrested at the airport).

The proposed new system generated strong opposition from groups across the political spectrum—including the American Civil Liberties Union, Americans for Tax Reform, the American Conservative Union, and the NAACP. At a news conference on August 26, Grover Norquist, president of Americans for Tax Reform—a conservative group with close ties to the Bush administration—said the CAPPS II proposal was part of "a series of police power and informational privacy power grabs that flowed from September 11." These groups got the attention of Congress, which in its fiscal 2004 appropriations bill for the Homeland Security Department (PL 108–90) temporarily barred the TSA from using the new CAPPS II system. Congress asked the GAO to study the system's potential impact on passenger privacy and whether it posed a danger of producing an excessive number of "false positives" flagging innocent passengers as potential terrorists. The GAO study of these questions was under way at year's end.

Another program being developed in 2003 would free some travelers from some of the hassles of airport security checks. Under this "registered traveler program," frequent travelers could volunteer to undergo criminal background checks; if cleared, their names would be put on a priority list entitling them to face less scrutiny at airports.

Checked Baggage and Cargo Screening

As part of its aviation security bill passed in November 2001, Congress required that all baggage checked by passengers be screened for explosives by the end of 2002. When it became clear that not all airports could meet that deadline, Congress allowed one-year extensions. TSA administrator James Loy told Congress in October that only 5 of the 429 commercial airports in the United States would not meet the final December 31, 2003, deadline for the electronic screening of all baggage; he refused to identify those airports. Airports were supposed to install machines—similar to the CAT scanners used at hospitals—capable of detecting explosives in checked baggage. At some airports, however, the screening consisted of airlines matching each piece of luggage to the passenger who checked it. Critics said this process would not deter a terrorist who was willing to commit suicide, as were the September 11 hijackers.

The biggest remaining gap in the country's aviation system, the GAO said, was the fact that commercial cargo was not routinely screened. Commercial cargo was bulk freight shipped by airlines and specialty carriers—as distinct from the personal luggage that passengers carried on planes or checked with the airlines. Congress in 2001 had required the screening of air cargo but set no deadlines and provided little funding to reach that goal. The GAO report quoted figures showing that about 12.5 million tons of cargo were shipped on airlines in the United States each year; most of the cargo (9.7 million tons) was shipped on all-cargo planes, and the rest (2.8 million tons) was carried on passenger planes. According to a report in September by the Congressional Research Service, only about 5 percent of the cargo carried on passenger planes was physically screened.

The Transportation Security Administration developed a system called the "known shipper program" under which well-known shipping companies could place cargo on passenger planes without submitting it to security checks. The GAO report said this program had "weaknesses," including "possible tampering with freight at various handoff points before it is loaded into an aircraft." The House of Representatives in 2003 passed legislation requiring security inspection of all cargo carried in passenger planes, but that measure was rejected in conference committee. Instead, Congress added $85 million to the fiscal 2004 Homeland Security Department spending bill (PL 108–90) for research into improved cargo security programs.

Airport Perimeter and General Aviation Security

Two other weak points in the country's aviation security system, the GAO report said, were lax controls over the perimeters of many airports and the near-total lack of security in the country's noncommercial "general aviation" industry. By 2003 all commercial airports in the United States were protected by fencing, but the GAO said many airports had not installed motion sensors, closed-circuit television systems, or other devices to detect intruders. Most airports also were located near highways and other public areas where a terrorist could use a shoulder-mounted antiaircraft missile to attack an airplane at its most vulnerable stages—takeoff and landing.

General aviation posed another security challenge, the GAO said. More than 200,000 privately owned airplanes were registered in the United States, ranging from two-seat, single engine planes to corporate jets as large as commercial airliners. Most general aviation airplanes flew out of the nation's 19,000 noncommercial airports, only about one-fourth of which were publicly owned. Very few of the passengers or pilots flying on general aviation planes had to go through metal detectors or any other form of security screening. The GAO said organizations representing the general aviation interests were opposed to mandating security requirements for their industry, arguing that small airplanes "do not pose a significant risk to the country." Even so, the industry was a "vulnerable" one, the GAO said, and the Transportation Security Administration was working on ways to reduce risks to the public.

Paying for Increased Security

Congress in 2001 imposed a $2.50 per-passenger fee to pay for improved screening of passengers and their luggage, but the GAO said the fee "has not generated enough money to do so." GAO quoted the transportation department's inspector general as estimating the fee would generate only about $1.7 billion in fiscal 2004; airlines were expected to contribute another $300 million. Congress in 2003 suspended the fee for the busiest travel season of the year—June through September—in its legislation paying for the war in Iraq and its aftermath. The rationale was that lowering travel costs might help the airline industry, which was still struggling financially from the aftermath of the September 11 attacks and then public nervousness about traveling during the Iraq war.

The Department of Homeland Security had asked for $4.8 billion for aviation security operations in fiscal 2004. The White House pared that request down to $4.2 billion, but Congress ultimately appropriated $4.6 billion.

One major question still unanswered in 2003 was how airports and the government would pay the estimated $3 billion cost of installing high-technology equipment to screen checked baggage. Some of the cost could be paid through an existing Federal Aviation Administration program for upgrading airports, but doing so would reduce the amount available for other needed improvements, GAO said.

In its report, the GAO also said the Transportation Security Administration was having trouble controlling costs. The agency relied heavily on private contractors for major services, such as developing and manufacturing equipment to screen checked baggage. A February 5 report by the Transportation Department's inspector general detailed several cases in which spending by contractors ballooned well past initial estimates, in part because the TSA failed to exercise effective control over the contractors' work. For example, a contract issued to the NCS Pearson company to recruit and hire about 40,000 airport screeners during 2002 was estimated at $104 million but grew to about $700 million—or about $17,000 per screener. One of that company's subcontractors was paid $18 million, of which an estimated $6 million to $9 million appeared to result from "wasteful and abusive spending practices" that NCS Pearson had failed to control, the inspector general said, without revealing the name of the subcontractor. Airport managers also complained to TSA and Congress about the quality of work done by a joint venture of Boeing and the German company Siemens AG under a $500 million contract to install baggage screening equipment.

Screening Airport Personnel

News organizations and government watchdog agencies continued to report that people with criminal records, or who posed some sort of potential security risk, had been hired at airports despite increased security precautions. In July officials at Los Angeles International Airport said 29 screeners had been fired because they were found to have criminal histories; another 256 screeners had been put on leave because they failed to have their fingerprints taken by a June 20 deadline. At least 50 screeners at New York's John F. Kennedy International Airport had been found to have criminal records, news reports said in May. TSA administrator Loy told a House subcommittee on June 3 that the agency had fired more than 1,200 screeners, most for falsifying job applications. Of that total, 85 had been convicted of felonies, he said. People with criminal records were barred from many jobs at airports because of concern that they might pose security risks.

At least one other news report, however, suggested that some airport employees might have been targeted because of faulty record keeping or administrative errors. The *New York Times* reported on March 7 that judges and juries had acquitted some of the several dozen workers and job applicants at New York area airports who had been arrested the previous November on charges of lying about criminal records. Some people had been arrested because of simple mistakes on their job applications, the *Times* reported.

Following are excerpts from "Aviation Security: Progress Since September 11, 2001, and the Challenges Ahead," testimony given September 9, 2003, by Gerald L. Dillingham, director of civil aviation issues for the General Accounting Office, before the Senate Committee on Commerce, Science, and Transportation.

"Aviation Security: Progress Since September 11, 2001"

In the 2 years since the terrorist attacks of September 11, 2001, the security of our nation's civil aviation system has assumed renewed urgency, and efforts to strengthen aviation security have received a great deal of congressional attention. On November 19, 2001, the Congress enacted the Aviation and Transportation Security Act (ATSA), which created the Transportation Security Administration (TSA) within the Department of Transportation (DOT) and defined its primary responsibility as ensuring security in aviation as well as in other modes of transportation. The act set forth specific improvements to aviation security for TSA to implement and established deadlines for completing many of them. The Homeland Security Act, passed on November 25, 2002, transferred TSA to the new Department of Homeland Security, which assumed overall responsibility for aviation security.

My testimony today addresses the (1) progress that has been made since September 11 to strengthen aviation security, (2) potential vulnerabilities that remain, and (3) longer-term management and organizational challenges to sustaining enhanced aviation security. The testimony is based on our prior work, our review of recent literature, and discussions with aviation industry representatives and TSA.

In summary:

Since September 2001, TSA has made considerable progress in meeting congressional mandates related to aviation security, thereby increasing aviation security. For example, by the end of December 2002, the agency had hired and deployed a workforce of about 65,000, including passenger and baggage screeners and federal air marshals, and it was using explosives detection equipment to screen about 90 percent of all checked baggage. In addition, TSA has initiated several programs and research and development efforts that focus on the use of technology and information to advance security. For example, the agency is developing the Transportation Workers Identification Card program to provide a nationwide standard credential for airport workers that is issued after a background check has been completed and biometric indicators have been incorporated so that each worker can be positively matched to his or her credential. TSA is also developing the next-generation Computer Assisted Passenger Prescreening System (CAPPS II), which would use national security and commercial databases to assess the risk posed by passengers and identify some passengers for additional screening before they board their flights. These uses of technology and information—particularly CAPPS II—have raised some concerns about privacy rights that will need to be addressed as these programs move toward implementation.

Although TSA has focused much effort and funding on ensuring that bombs and other threat items are not carried onto planes by passengers or in their luggage, vulnerabilities remain in areas such as air cargo security, general aviation security, and airport perimeter security. For example, air cargo is vulnerable because very little of the estimated 12.5 million tons transported each year on all-cargo and passenger planes is physically screened for explosives. As a result, a potential security risk is the introduction of explosive and incendiary devices in cargo placed aboard aircraft. . . .

TSA faces longer-term management and organizational challenges to sustaining enhanced aviation security that include (1) developing and implementing a comprehensive risk management approach, (2) paying for increased aviation security needs and controlling costs, (3) establishing effective coordination among the many public and private entities involved in aviation security, (4) strategically managing its workforce and ensuring appropriate staffing levels, and (5) building a results-oriented culture as it shifts its aviation security and other functions to the Department of Homeland Security. . . .

Background

Before September 2001, we and others had demonstrated significant, long-standing vulnerabilities in aviation security. These included weaknesses in screening passengers and baggage, controlling access to secure areas at airports, and protecting air traffic control computer systems and facilities. To address these and other weaknesses, ATSA created the Transportation Security Administration and established security requirements for the new agency with mandated deadlines.

Civil Aviation Was Vulnerable Before September 11, 2001

Before September 2001, screeners, who were then hired by the airlines, often failed to detect threat objects located on passengers or in their carry-on luggage. Principal causes of screeners' performance problems were rapid turnover and insufficient training. As we previously reported, turnover rates exceeded 100 percent a year at most large airports, leaving few skilled and experienced screeners, primarily because of low wages, limited benefits, and repetitive, monotonous work.

In addition, before September 2001, controls for limiting access to secure areas of airports, including aircraft, did not always work as intended. As we reported in May 2000, our special agents used fictitious law enforcement badges and credentials to gain access to secure areas, bypass security checkpoints at two airports, and walk unescorted to aircraft departure gates. The agents, who had been issued tickets and boarding passes, could have carried weapons, explosives, or other dangerous objects onto aircraft. DOT's Inspector General also documented numerous problems with airport access controls, and in one series of tests, nearly 7 out of every 10 attempts by the Inspector General's staff to gain access to secure areas were successful. Upon entering the secure areas, the Inspector General's staff boarded aircraft 117 times. The Inspector General further reported that the majority of the aircraft boardings would not have occurred if employees had taken the prescribed steps, such as making sure doors closed behind them.

Our reviews also found that the security of the air traffic control computer systems and of the facilities that house them had not been ensured. The vulnerabilities we identified, such as not ensuring that contractors who had access to the air traffic control computer systems had undergone background checks, made the air traffic control system susceptible to intrusion and malicious attacks. The air traffic control computer systems provide information to air traffic controllers and aircraft flight crews to help ensure the safe and expeditious movement of aircraft. Failure to protect these systems and their facilities could cause a nationwide disruption of air traffic or even collisions and loss of life.

Over the years, we made numerous recommendations to the Federal Aviation Administration (FAA), which, until ATSA's enactment, was responsible for aviation security. These recommendations were designed to improve screeners' performance, strengthen airport access controls, and better protect air traffic control computer systems and facilities. As of September 2001, FAA had implemented some of these recommendations and was addressing others, but its progress was often slow. In addition, many initiatives were not linked to specific deadlines, making it difficult to monitor and oversee their implementation.

Legislation Transferred Most Aviation Security Responsibilities to TSA

ATSA defined TSA's primary responsibility as ensuring security in all modes of transportation. The act also shifted security-screening responsibilities from the airlines to TSA and established a series of requirements to strengthen aviation security, many of them with mandated implementations. For example, the act required the deployment of federal screeners at 429 commercial airports across the nation by November 19, 2002, and the use of explosives detection technology at these airports to screen every piece of checked baggage for explosives not later than December 31, 2002. However, the Homeland Security Act subsequently allowed TSA to grant waivers of up to 1 year to airports that would not be able to meet the December deadline.

Some aviation security responsibilities remained with FAA. For example, FAA is responsible for the security of its air traffic control and other computer systems and of its air traffic control facilities. FAA also administers the Airport Improvement Program (AIP) trust fund, which is used to fund capital improvements to airports, including some security enhancements, such as terminal modifications to accommodate explosives detection equipment.

Since September 2001, Multiple Initiatives Have Increased Aviation Security

Over the past 2 years, TSA and FAA have taken major steps to increase aviation security. TSA has implemented congressional mandates and explored options for increasing the use of technology and information to control access to secure areas of airports and to improve passenger screening. FAA has focused its efforts on enhancing the security of the nation's air traffic control systems and facilities. . . .

TSA Met Many Aviation Security Mandates but Encountered Some Difficulties

In its first year, TSA worked to establish its organization and focused primarily on meeting the aviation security deadlines set forth in ATSA, accomplishing a large number of tasks under a very ambitious schedule. In January 2002, TSA had 13 employees—1 year later, the agency had about 65,000 employees. TSA reported that it met over 30 deadlines during 2002 to improve aviation security. For example, according to TSA, it:

- met the November 2002 deadline to deploy federal passenger screeners at airports across the nation by hiring, training, and deploying over 40,000 individuals to screen passengers at 429 commercial airports;
- hired and deployed more than 20,000 individuals to screen all checked baggage;
- has been using explosives detection systems or explosives trace detection equipment to screen about 90 percent of all checked baggage as of December 31, 2002;

- has been using alternative means such as canine teams, hand searches, and passenger-bag matching to screen the remaining checked baggage;
- confiscated more than 4.8 million prohibited items (including firearms, knives, and incendiary or flammable objects) from passengers; and
- has made substantial progress in expanding the Federal Air Marshal Service.

In addition, according to FAA, U.S. and foreign airlines met the April 2003 deadline to harden cockpit doors on aircraft flying in the United States.

Not unexpectedly, TSA experienced some difficulties in meeting these deadlines and achieving these goals. For example, operational and management control problems, cited later in this testimony, emerged with the rapid expansion of the Federal Air Marshal Service, and TSA's deployment of some explosives detection systems was delayed. As a result, TSA had to grant waivers of up to a year (until Dec. 31, 2003) to a few airports, authorizing them to use alternative means to screen all checked baggage. Recently, airport representatives with whom we spoke expressed concern that not all of these airports would meet the new December 2003 deadline established in their waivers because, according to the airport representatives, there has not been enough time to produce, install, and integrate all of the systems required to meet the deadline.

TSA Is Making Greater Use of Technology and Information to Enhance Aviation Security

To strengthen control over access to secure areas of airports and other transportation facilities, TSA is pursuing initiatives that make greater use of technology and information. For example, the agency is investigating the establishment of a Transportation Workers Identification Card (TWIC) program. TWIC is intended to establish a uniform, nationwide standard for the secure identification of 12 million workers who require unescorted physical or cyber access to secure areas at airports and other transportation facilities. Specifically, TWIC will combine standard background checks and biometrics so that a worker can be positively matched to his or her credential. Once the program is fully operational, the TWIC card will be the standard credential for airport workers and will be accepted by all modes of transportation. According to TSA, developing a uniform, nationwide standard for identification will minimize redundant credentialing and background checks. Currently, each airport is required, as part of its security program, to issue credentials to workers who need access to secure, nonpublic areas, such as baggage loading areas. Airport representatives have told us that they think a number of operational issues need to be resolved for the TWIC card to be feasible. For example, the TWIC card would have to be compatible with the many types of card readers used at airports around the country, or new card readers would have to be installed. At large airports, this could entail replacing hundreds of card readers, and airport representatives have expressed concerns about how this effort would be funded. In April 2003, TSA awarded a contract to test and evaluate various technologies at three pilot sites.

In addition, TSA has continued to develop the next-generation Computer Assisted Passenger Prescreening System (CAPPS II)—an automated passenger screening system that takes personal information, such as a passenger's name, date of birth, home address, and home telephone number, to confirm the passenger's identity and assess a risk level. The identifying information will be run against national security information and commercial databases, and a "risk" score will be assigned to the passenger. The risk score will determine any further screening that the passenger will undergo before boarding. TSA expects to implement CAPPS II throughout the United States by the fall of 2004. However, TSA's plans have raised concerns about travelers' privacy rights. It has been suggested, for example, that TSA is violating privacy laws by not explaining how the risk assessment data will be scored and used and how a TSA decision can be appealed. These concerns about the system will need to be addressed as it moves toward implementation. . . .

Additionally, TSA has begun to develop initiatives that could enable it to use its passenger screening resources more efficiently. For example, TSA has requested funding for fiscal year 2004 to begin developing a registered traveler program that would prescreen low-risk travelers. Under a registered traveler program, those who voluntarily apply to participate in the program and successfully pass background checks would receive a unique identifier or card that would enable them to be screened more quickly and would promote greater focus on those passengers who require more extensive screening at airport security checkpoints. In prior work, we identified key policy and implementation issues that would need to be resolved before a registered traveler program could be implemented. Such issues include the (1) criteria that should be established to determine eligibility to apply for the program, (2) kinds of background checks that should be used to certify applicants' eligibility to enroll in the program and the entity who should perform these checks, (3) security-screening procedures that registered travelers should undergo and the differences between these procedures and those for unregistered travelers, and (4) concerns that the traveling public or others may have about equity, privacy, and liability.

FAA Is Strengthening Air Traffic Control Security

Since September 2001, FAA has continued to strengthen the security of the nation's air traffic control computer systems and facilities in response to 39 recommendations we made between May 1998 and December 2000. For example, FAA has established an information systems security management structure under its Chief Information Officer, whose office has developed an information systems security strategy, security architecture (that is, an overall blueprint), security policies and directives, and a security awareness training campaign. This office has also managed FAA's incident response center and implemented a certification and accreditation process to ensure that vulnerabilities in current and future air traffic control systems are identified and weaknesses addressed. Nevertheless, the office faces continued challenges in increasing its intrusion detection capabilities, obtaining accreditation for systems that are already operational, and managing information systems security throughout the agency. In addition, according to senior security officials, FAA has completed assessments of the physical security of its staffed facilities, but it has not yet accredited all of these air traffic control facilities as secure in compliance with its own policy. Finally, FAA has worked aggressively over the past 2 years to complete background investigations of numerous contractor employees. However, ensuring that all new contractors are assessed to determine which employees require background checks, and that those checks are completed in a timely manner, will be a continuing challenge for the agency.

Potential Vulnerabilities Remain in Several Aviation Sectors

Although TSA has focused much effort and funding on ensuring that bombs and other threat items are not carried onto commercial aircraft by passengers or in their luggage, vulnerabilities remain, according to aviation experts, TSA officials, and others. In particular, these vulnerabilities affect air cargo, general aviation, and airport perimeter security.

Air Cargo Security

As we and DOT's Inspector General have reported, vulnerabilities exist in securing the cargo carried aboard commercial passenger and all-cargo aircraft. TSA has reported that an estimated 12.5 million tons of cargo are transported each year—9.7 million tons on all-cargo planes and 2.8 million tons on passenger planes. Some potential security risks associated with air cargo include the introduction of undetected explosive and incendiary devices in cargo placed aboard aircraft; the shipment of undeclared or undetected hazardous materials aboard aircraft; and aircraft hijackings and sabotage by individuals with access to cargo aircraft. To address some of the risks associated with air cargo, ATSA requires that all cargo carried aboard commercial passenger aircraft be screened and that TSA have a system in place as soon as practicable to screen, inspect, or otherwise ensure the security of cargo on all-cargo aircraft. In August 2003, the Congressional Research Service reported that less than 5 percent of cargo placed on passenger airplanes is physically screened. TSA's primary approach to ensuring air cargo security and safety and to complying with the cargo-screening requirement in the act is the "known shipper" program—which allows shippers that have established business histories with air carriers or freight forwarders to ship cargo on planes. However, we and DOT's Inspector General have identified weaknesses in the known shipper program and in TSA's procedures for approving freight forwarders.

Since September 2001, TSA has taken a number of actions to enhance cargo security, such as implementing a database of known shippers in October 2002. The database is the first phase in developing a cargo-profiling system similar to the Computer-Assisted Passenger Prescreening System. However, in December 2002, we reported that additional operational and technological measures, such as checking the identity of individuals making cargo deliveries, have the potential to improve air cargo security in the near term. We further reported that TSA lacks a comprehensive plan with long-term goals and performance targets for cargo security, time frames for completing security improvements, and risk-based criteria for prioritizing actions to achieve those goals. Accordingly, we recommended that TSA develop a comprehensive plan for air cargo security that incorporates a risk management approach, includes a list of security priorities, and sets deadlines for completing actions. TSA agreed with this recommendation and expects to develop such a plan by the fall of 2003. It will be important that this plan include a timetable for implementation and that TSA expeditiously reduce the vulnerabilities in this area.

General Aviation Security

Since September 2001, TSA has taken limited action to improve general aviation security, leaving it far more open and potentially vulnerable than commercial aviation. General aviation is vulnerable because general aviation pilots are not screened before takeoff and the contents of general aviation planes are not screened at any point. General aviation includes more than 200,000 privately owned airplanes, which are located in every state at more than 19,000 airports. Over 550 of these airports also provide commercial service. In the last 5 years, about 70 aircraft have been stolen from general aviation airports, indicating a potential weakness that could be exploited by terrorists. Moreover, it was reported that the September 11 hijackers researched the use of crop dusters to spread biological or chemical agents. General aviation's vulnerability was revealed in January 2002, when a Florida teenage flight student crashed a single-engine Cessna airplane into a Tampa skyscraper.

FAA has since issued a notice with voluntary guidance for flight schools and businesses that provide services for aircraft and pilots at general aviation airports. The suggestions include using different keys to gain access to an aircraft and start the ignition, not giving students access to aircraft keys, ensuring positive identification of flight students, and training employees and pilots to report suspicious activities. However, because the guidance is voluntary, it is unknown how many general aviation airports have implemented these measures. . . .

Airport Perimeter Security

Airport perimeters present a potential vulnerability by providing a route for individuals to gain unauthorized access to aircraft and secure areas of airports. For example, in August 2003, the national media reported that three boaters wandered the tarmac at Kennedy International Airport after their boat became beached near a runway. In addition, terrorists could launch an attack using a shoulder-fired missile from the perimeter of an airport, as well as from locations just outside the perimeter. For example, in separate incidents in the late 1970s, guerrillas with shoulder-fired missiles shot down two Air Rhodesia planes. More recently, the national media have reported that since September 2001, al Qaeda has twice tried to down planes outside the United States with shoulder-fired missiles.

We reported in June 2003 that airport operators have increased their patrols of airport perimeters since September 2001, but industry officials stated that they do not have enough resources to completely protect against missile attacks. A number of technologies could be used to secure and monitor airport perimeters, including barriers, motion sensors, and closed-circuit television. Airport representatives have cautioned that as security enhancements are made to airport perimeters, it will be important for TSA to coordinate with FAA and the airport operators to ensure that any enhancements do not pose safety risks for aircraft. . . .

Aviation Security Poses Longer-Term Management and Organizational Challenges

TSA's efforts to strengthen and sustain aviation security face several longer-term challenges in the areas of risk management, funding, coordination, strategic human capital management, and building a results-oriented organization.

Risk Management

As aviation security is viewed in the larger context of transportation and homeland security, it will be important to set strategic priorities so that national resources can be directed to the greatest needs. Although TSA initially focused on increasing aviation security, it has more recently begun to address security in the other transportation modes. However, the size and diversity of the national transportation system make it difficult to adequately secure, and TSA and the Congress are faced with demands for additional federal funding for transportation security that far exceed the additional amounts made available. . . .

Funding

Two key funding and accountability challenges will be (1) paying for increased aviation security and (2) ensuring that these costs are controlled. The costs associated with the equipment and personnel needed to screen passengers and their baggage alone are huge. The administration requested $4.2 billion for aviation security for fiscal year 2004, which included about $1.8 billion for passenger screening and $944 million for baggage screening. ATSA created a passenger security fee to pay for the costs of aviation security, but the fee has not generated enough money to do so. DOT's Inspector General reported that the security fees are estimated to generate only about $1.7 billion in fiscal year 2004.

A major funding issue is paying for the purchase and installation of the remaining explosives detection systems for the airports that received waivers, as well as for the reinstallation of the systems that were placed in airport lobbies last year and now need to be integrated into airport baggage-handling systems. Integrating the equipment with the baggage handling systems is expected to be costly because it will require major facility modifications. For example, modifications needed to integrate the equipment at Boston's Logan International Airport are estimated to cost $146 million. Estimates for Dallas/Fort Worth International Airport are $193 million. DOT's Inspector General has reported that the cost of integrating the equipment nationwide could be as high as $3 billion. . . .

An additional funding issue is how to ensure continued investment in transportation research and development. For fiscal year 2003, TSA was appropriated about $110 million for research and development, of which $75 million was designated for the next-generation explosives detection systems. However, TSA has proposed to reprogram $61.2 million of these funds to be used for other purposes, leaving about $12.7 million to be spent on research and development this year. This proposed reprogramming could limit TSA's ability to sustain and strengthen aviation security by continuing to invest in research and development for more effective equipment to screen passengers, their carry-on and checked baggage, and cargo. . . .

By reprogramming funds and making acknowledged use of certain funds for purposes other than those intended, TSA has raised congressional concerns about accountability. According to TSA, it has proposed to reprogram a total of $849.3 million during fiscal year 2003, including the $61.2 million that would be cut from research and development and $104 million that would be taken from the federal air marshal program and used for unintended purposes. . . .

In July 2002, we reported that long-term attention to cost and accountability controls for acquisition and related business processes will be critical for TSA, both to ensure its success and to maintain its integrity and accountability. According to DOT's Inspector General, although TSA has made progress in addressing certain cost-related issues, it has not established an infrastructure that provides effective controls to monitor contractors' costs and performance. For example, in February 2003, the Inspector General reported that TSA's $1 billion hiring effort cost more than most people expected and that TSA's contract with NCS Pearson to recruit, assess, and hire the screener workforce contained no safeguards to prevent cost increases. The Inspector General found that TSA provided limited oversight for the management of the contract expenses and, in one case, between $6 million and $9 million of the $18 million paid to a subcontractor appeared to be a result of wasteful and abusive spending practices. As the Inspector General recommended, TSA has since hired the Defense Contract Audit Agency to audit its major contracts. To ensure control over TSA contracts, the Inspector General has further recommended that the Congress set aside a specific amount of TSA's contracting budget for overseeing contractors' performance with respect to cost, schedule, and quality.

Coordination

Sustaining the aviation security advancements of the past 2 years also depends on TSA's ability to form effective partnerships with federal, state, and local agencies and with the aviation community. Effective, well-coordinated partnerships at the local level require identifying roles and responsibilities; developing effective, collaborative relationships with local and regional airports and emergency management and law enforcement agencies; agreeing on performance-based standards that describe desired outcomes; and sharing intelligence information. The lynchpin in TSA's efforts to coordinate with airports and local law enforcement and emergency response agencies is, according to the agency, the 158 federal security directors and staff that TSA has deployed nationwide. The security directors' responsibilities include ensuring that standardized security procedures are implemented at the nation's airports; working with state and local law enforcement personnel, when appropriate, to ensure airport and passenger security; and communicating threat information to airport operators and others. Airport representatives, however, have indicated that the relationships between federal security directors and airport operators are still evolving and that better communication is needed at some airports.

Key to improving the coordination between TSA and local partners is establishing clearly defined roles. In some cases, concerns have arisen about conflicts between the roles of TSA, as the manager of security functions at airports, and of airport officials, as the managers of other airport operations. Industry representatives viewed such conflicts as leading to confusion in areas such as communicating with local entities. According to airport representatives, for example, TSA has developed guidance or rules for airports without involving them, and time-consuming changes have then had to be made to accommodate operational factors. The representatives maintain that it would be more efficient and effective to consider such operational factors earlier in the process. Ultimately, inadequate coordination and unclear roles result in inefficient uses of limited resources.

TSA also has to ensure that the terrorist and threat information gathered and maintained by law enforcement and other agencies—including the Federal Bureau of Investigation, the Immigration and Naturalization Service, the Central Intelligence Agency, and the Department of State—is quickly and efficiently communicated among federal agencies and to state and local authorities, as needed. Disseminating such information is important to allow those who are involved in protecting the nation's aviation system to address potential threats rather than simply react to known threats.

In aviation security, timely information sharing among agencies has been hampered by the agencies' reluctance to share sensitive information and by outdated, incompatible computer systems. As we found in reviewing watch lists maintained by nine federal agencies, information was being shared among some of them but not among others. Moreover, even when sharing was occurring, costly and overly complex measures had to be taken to facilitate it. To promote better integration and sharing of terrorist and criminal watch lists, we have recommended that the Department of Homeland Security, in collaboration with the other departments and agencies that have and use watch lists, lead an effort to consolidate and standardize the federal government's watch list structures and policies.

In addition, as we found earlier this year, representatives of numerous state and local governments and transportation industry associations indicated that the general threat warnings received by government agencies are not helpful. Rather, they said, transportation operators, including airport operators, want more specific intelligence information so that they can understand the true nature of a potential threat and implement appropriate security measures.

Strategic Human Capital Management

As it organizes itself to protect the nation's transportation system, TSA faces the challenge of strategically managing its workforce of more than 60,000 people, most of whom are deployed at airports or on aircraft to detect weapons and explosives and to prevent them from being taken aboard and used on aircraft. Additionally, over the next several years, TSA faces the challenge of "right-sizing" this workforce as efficiency is improved with new security-enhancing technologies, processes, and procedures. . . .

In January 2003, we reported that TSA was addressing some critical human capital success factors by hiring personnel, using a wide range of tools available for hiring, and beginning to link individual performance to organizational goals. However, concerns remain about the size and training of that workforce, the adequacy of the initial background checks for screeners, and TSA's progress in setting up a performance management system. As noted earlier in this testimony, TSA now plans to reduce its screener workforce by 6,000 by September 30, 2003, and it has proposed cutting the workforce by an additional 3,000 in fiscal year 2004. This planned reduction has raised concerns about passenger delays at airports and has led TSA to begin hiring part-time screeners to make more flexible and efficient use of its workforce. In addition, TSA used an abbreviated background check process to hire and deploy enough screeners to meet ATSA's screening deadlines in 2002. After obtaining additional background information, TSA terminated the employment of some of these screeners. TSA reported 1,208 terminations as of May 31, 2003, that it ascribed to a variety of reasons, including criminal offenses and failures to pass alcohol and drug tests. Furthermore, the national media have reported allegations of operational and management control problems that emerged with the expansion of the Federal Air Marshal Service, including inadequate background checks and training, uneven scheduling, and inadequate policies and procedures. . . .

Concluding Observations

After spending billions of dollars over the past 2 years on people, policies, and procedures to improve aviation security, we have much more security now than we had before September 2001, but it has not been determined how much more secure we are. The vast number of guns, knives, and other potential threat items that screeners have confiscated suggests that security is working, but it also suggests that improved public awareness of prohibited items could help focus resources where they are most needed and reduce delays and inconvenience to the public. Faced with vast and competing demands for security resources, TSA should continue its efforts to identify technologies, such as CAPPS II, that will leverage its resources and potentially improve its capabilities. Improving the efficiency and effectiveness of aviation security will also require risk assessments and plans that help maintain a balance between security and customer service.

Source: U.S. Congress. General Accounting Office. "Aviation Security: Progress Since September 11, 2001, and the Challenges Ahead." Statement by Gerald L. Dillingham Before the Senate Committee on Commerce, Science and Transportation. September 9, 2003. GAO–03–1150T. www.gao.gov/new.items/d031150t.pdf (accessed September 10, 2003).

World Trade Organization on Collapse of Trade Talks

September 14 and December 15, 2003

INTRODUCTION

Talks aimed at breaking down barriers to global trade collapsed on September 14, 2003, when trade delegates from Africa, Asia, Latin America, and the Caribbean walked out of World Trade Organization (WTO) negotiations in Cancún, Mexico. The delegates said they would rather go away empty handed than accept the modest compromises the United States, European Union (EU), and other wealthy nations were willing to offer on agriculture and other issues that had long been stumbling blocks in global trade negotiations. "They were not generous enough; there was just not enough on the table for developing countries," said Richard L. Bernal, a delegate from Jamaica.

Although the WTO was set up in 1995 in part to harmonize trade rules in an increasingly interconnected world, negotiations on trade rules since then had increasingly exposed a deep rift between rich and poor nations. Led by the United States and Europe, the wealthy countries had advocated free trade as a means of creating wealth and jobs throughout the world. The World Bank, for example, estimated that if agreement were reached in this latest round of trade talks, the resulting expansion in trade could increase global incomes by $520 billion by 2015 and lift 144 million people out of poverty. Developing countries argued, however, that many of the trade rules, especially those dealing with agriculture, were stacked against them and in some cases left poor countries even farther behind.

In 1999 similar frustrations, combined with massive and violent demonstrations by antiglobalization protestors, had led to the collapse of talks in Seattle, Washington, which were intended to kick off a new round of negotiations. Delegates from developing countries insisted then that their voices be heard in the WTO decision-making process, which until the 1990s had largely been the domain of the United States and other industrialized countries. But the Cancún talks represented the first time that the developing countries had been so assertive in confronting the wealthy nations, and many delegates and their supporters saw it as a moral victory. "This is the best thing that has happened to developing nations in a long time. I mean, for heaven's sake, if Africans have to compete with rich nations on the price of exporting a mango or rice or cotton or yogurt, how can we ever work our way out of poverty," one observer from Ghana told the *Washington Post.*

U.S. Trade Representative Robert B. Zoellick said that rhetoric got in the way of negotiation and warned that the big losers from the failed talks were likely to be the poorer countries. That view was widely shared by other delegates and observers alike, who said that even the modest concessions the wealthy nations were willing to make could have gone some way in correcting the acknowledged imbalance in the trade rules.

The collapse of the talks was also seen as a significant setback for the World Trade Organization, which now seemed unlikely to be able to complete negotiations by its January 1, 2005, deadline. Several commentators noted that decision making by consensus in a 148-member organization could prove to be a fatal flaw, undermining the ability of the WTO to make meaningful or timely decisions.

Delegates from both wealthy and developing countries said they expected the multilateral negotiations to resume once things had calmed down. "The pieces will be picked up again, and the negotiation will go on," said Celso Amorim, the foreign minister of Brazil, which was a key leader for the developing countries. Talks continued at lower levels of government later in the year, but the chairman overseeing the talks at the WTO said on December 15 that there had been "little real negotiation, or movement towards accommodation among positions" and that delegations were not displaying a "sense of urgency" about resolving their differences.

Although Zoellick said he would move ahead on several pending bilateral and regional trade talks while waiting to see what would happen with multilateral talks, the Bush administration was likely to face a domestic political controversy over free trade in general. The disappearance of about 2.5 million U.S. manufacturing jobs, many of which had been shifted to developing countries where labor costs were cheaper, had sparked a wave of protectionist sentiment around the country that was being fanned by Democrats seeking the nomination to run against President George W. Bush in 2004.

Prelude to the Talks

The United States and its key trading partners had been negotiating regularly since the 1930s about the principles underlying global trade. For most of those years, talks centered on tariffs, the taxes that each country imposed on goods imported from other countries. Following World War II the global trade talks were conducted under a system known as the General Agreement on Tariffs and Trade (GATT). The last round of negotiations under GATT (known as the Uruguay Round because the negotiations began there in 1986) was concluded in 1994. A principle outcome of the Uruguay Round was the formation of the WTO, a global agency based in Geneva with significant power to enforce trading standards and to mediate disputes between countries. *(Uruguay Round, Historic Documents of 1994, p. 555)*

In 1998 key European countries began pressing for another round of trade talks to deal with the many complex issues that were arising because of the increasing importance of worldwide trade—a key component of globalization. Plans were made for a meeting in Seattle in December 1999 to establish an agenda for the negotiations, which were expected to last for at least three years. But the launch of a "Millennium Round" of talks collapsed during a stormy four-day session in Seattle—punctuated by massive street demonstrations that erupted into a day of unexpected violence. Negotiators attempted to take up dozens of trade matters, but little progress was made on any. In the end, three major underlying issues blocked agreement on scheduling a formal round of negotiations: a rash of disputes over agricultural trade policy, demands by developing nations for a greater say in WTO decisions, and making labor and environmental standards a central part of future trade deals. *(Seattle talks, Historic documents of 1999, p. 797)*

Spurred by a global economic slowdown and the terrorist attacks in the United States on September 11, 2001, momentum picked up for another attempt to start a new round of trade liberalizing talks. As one U.S. trade official put it, an increasing number of countries were coming around to believing that "we're better off with a round than without it." Meeting in Doha, Qatar, for six days in November 2001, WTO trade ministers approved an agenda for a new round of trade talks with a specific emphasis on helping developing countries, including the least-developed countries. January 1, 2005, was set as the target date for concluding the negotiations, known as the Doha Development Agenda.

Over the next two years, trade negotiators made little progress on the issues before them, other than to agree to put aside direct talks on environmental and labor issues for the time being. Then, in August 2003, the United States made a major concession, agreeing to ease some patent rules, thus making it easier for developing countries to gain access to cheaper versions of some drugs critical in fighting malaria, tuberculosis, and HIV/AIDS. The United States also indicated that it was prepared to make sizable cuts in farm subsidies and to make its agricultural markets more accessible to both developed and developing countries in return for reciprocal treatment. *(AIDS, p. 780)*

Disagreement and Discouragement

Those developments gave rise to modest hope that trade ministers might be able to reach some accommodation on agriculture at Cancún. The joint proposal for liberalization of farm trade made by the United States and the EU, however, was not as generous as the original U.S. proposal. It was rejected by a group of developing countries led by Brazil, China, and India. They demanded even larger cuts in the $300 billion in government subsidies paid to farmers annually in the United States and Europe. These subsidies resulted in overproduction of many crops, including cotton, that were then dumped on the global markets, thereby depressing prices and hurting developing countries, especially those that relied on agriculture as their main trading commodities. Developing countries also wanted reductions in the tariffs wealthy countries placed on agricultural goods, especially those from poor countries. They demanded reductions on the export subsidies that wealthy economies, particularly the EU, placed on agricultural products. At the same time, many of the developing countries were unwilling to reduce their own tariffs on agricultural imports, many of which were considerably higher than the 12 percent imposed in the United States. India, for example, had tariffs of 112 percent on farm products, while Brazil's tariffs were 37 percent.

Anger with the developed countries came to a head when Benin, Burkina Faso, Chad, and Mali, four of the poorest nations in Africa, asked that the subsidies given to American and European cotton farmers be eliminated or reduced and that cotton growers in Africa be paid $300 million in compensation for losses they sustained as a result of the unfair competition. About 10 million cotton farmers in western and central Africa grew high-quality cotton at low cost but lost about $1 billion a year in export earnings. The EU, which subsidized cotton growers in Greece and Spain, said it was willing to make some concessions in this area. But the United States, which paid some $3 billion annually to 25,000 cotton farmers, rejected the proposal to deal with cotton separately from other agricultural issues. The U.S. delegation instead proposed that the issue be studied. The delegation also promised some aid to help the countries diversify their crops—a proposal that the African countries and their supporters construed as condescending and dismissive.

At the same time, developing countries were upset by the insistence of the EU, Japan, and South Korea that trade talks begin on the four "Singapore issues" involving trade and foreign investment, competition policy, transparency in government procurement, and trade facilitation. Developing countries argued that they had not yet developed the technical capacity to deal with these issues, and they feared that trade rules in these areas could also limit their ability to take policy steps they deemed necessary for their economic development. Although Pascal Lamy, the chief

EU negotiator, finally backed down and agreed to set aside negotiations on investment and trade policy, it was too late. Key developing countries in those talks, including India, Kenya, Malaysia, and South Africa, refused to negotiate any of the Singapore issues. With talks at an apparent impasse, the chairman of the conference, Mexican foreign minister Luis Ernesto Derbez, ended the talks.

Finger-Pointing and Follow-Up

In the immediate aftermath of the failed talks, participants traded charges over who was at fault. U.S. Trade Representative Zoellick complained that "the harsh rhetoric of the 'won't do' overwhelmed the concerted efforts of the 'can do,' " and said the United States would pursue its trade objectives through bilateral and regional talks. The United States was already engaged in talks on a regional free trade zone with all the countries of Latin American and the Caribbean except Cuba. But those talks ran into similar disagreements over agriculture and other issues at meetings in Miami in mid-November. In any event, given rising protectionist sentiment in the United States, it seemed unlikely that the Bush administration would pursue tough trade negotiations at any level during the 2004 election year. The European Union, which was admitting ten new members in 2004, was also seen as unlikely to take on the additional challenge of renewed trade negotiations in the near future. *(Free trade talks, p. 8; EU membership expansion, p. 492)*

Nongovernmental organizations that supported developing countries on trade issues placed the blame on wealthy countries. Phil Bloomer with the British advocacy and relief organization Oxfam, for example, said that the United States and the European Union "were not prepared to listen and take the necessary steps to make global trade rules work for the poor as well as the rich."

Yet many participants, as well as others, predicted that despite the rancor and disagreements, multilateral trade talks would resume, in large part because there was no real alternative available for liberalizing global trade. That point was made in a November 20 letter to member governments by World Bank president James D. Wolfensohn and International Monetary Fund managing director Horst Köhler calling on them to resume the talks. "Successive rounds of multilateral trade liberalization have been central to the unprecedented rise in global prosperity over the past half century . . . bilateral and regional arrangements are no substitutes," they wrote. Moreover, they said, "collectively reducing trade barriers is the single most powerful tool that countries working together can deploy to reduce poverty and raise living standards." In remarks aimed at both developing and developed countries, the two said that trade liberalization was "not a 'concession,' but a step towards helping promote opportunity and productivity that benefits the society taking it."

Talks continued throughout the remainder of 2003 between WTO officials, trade representatives, and others. On December 15 the chairman of the WTO General Council, Carlos Perez del Castillo, reported that WTO members had made a commitment to a multilateral trading system and a willingness to move forward. But, he said, gaps remained "wide" not only between negotiating positions but also between statements professing a willingness to engage and be flexible on one hand and actually acting on those statements on the other hand.

Following is the text of the ministerial statement, issued September 14, 2003, in Cancún, Mexico, after talks sponsored by the World Trade Organization to liberalize global trade ended in failure. Following that are excerpts from a statement issued December 15 by Carlos Pérez del Castillo, chairman of the WTO General Council, reporting on the status of talks to get the negotiations back on track.

"Ministerial Statement"

1. As we conclude our Fifth Ministerial Conference in Cancún, we would like to express our deep appreciation to the Government and people of Mexico for the excellent organization and warm hospitality we have received in Cancún.
2. At this meeting we have welcomed Cambodia and Nepal as the first least-developed countries to accede to the WTO since its establishment.
3. All participants have worked hard and constructively to make progress as required under the Doha mandates. We have, indeed, made considerable progress. However, more work needs to be done in some key areas to enable us to proceed towards the conclusion of the negotiations in fulfilment of the commitments we took at Doha.
4. We therefore instruct our officials to continue working on outstanding issues with a renewed sense of urgency and purpose and taking fully into account all the views we have expressed in this Conference. We ask the Chairman of the General Council, working in close co-operation with the Director-General, to coordinate this work and to convene a meeting of the General Council

at Senior Officials level no later than 15 December 2003 to take the action necessary at that stage to enable us to move towards a successful and timely conclusion of the negotiations. We shall continue to exercise close personal supervision of this process.

5. We will bring with us into this new phase all the valuable work that has been done at this Conference. In those areas where we have reached a high level of convergence on texts, we undertake to maintain this convergence while working for an acceptable overall outcome.

6. Notwithstanding this setback, we reaffirm all our Doha Declarations and Decisions and recommit ourselves to working to implement them fully and faithfully.

Source: World Trade Organization. Ministerial Conference, fifth session. "Ministerial Statement." Cancún, Mexico. September 14, 2003. www.wto.org/english/thewto_e/minist_e/min03_e/min03_20_e.doc (accessed December 12, 2003).

"Statement by the Chairperson of the General Council"

I would now like to make a report on behalf of both myself and the Director-General on the consultations we have been conducting since early October pursuant to the Statement adopted by Ministers at Cancún. . . .

Firstly, let me briefly review the evolution of the consultative process. After our return to Geneva, the Director-General and I conducted an intensive round of consultations with Member Governments, both in Geneva as well as in capitals. In the course of these consultations, as also in our subsequent intensive rounds of consultations on substance, we met with the widest possible range of the membership. As you know, our overall approach to our initial consultations focussed on how to move the process forward and delegations provided us with constructive advice and orientation.

At an informal meeting at the level of Heads of Delegation on 14 October, we reported on these consultations. As you will recall, our assessment was encouraging. We had sensed that there was a willingness on all sides to get back to work in line with the mandate agreed by Ministers at Cancún. Similarly, all delegations continued to support a strong and reinforced multilateral trading system and expressed willingness to engage and show the necessary flexibility in order to get the process back on track. . . .

Following the October meeting, we proceeded on the basis of the Ministerial mandate, and the understanding reached at that Heads of Delegation meeting, to take up in turn each of the four key outstanding issues, namely Agriculture, Cotton, Non-Agricultural Market Access and the Singapore Issues. This was done through an intensive series of consultations with individual delegations, regional groupings and other groups, and with non-resident Members during Geneva Week. Throughout this process, a special effort was made to keep everyone informed, in pursuit of the commitment to transparency and inclusiveness that we all share. We made a particular effort to consult regularly with the co-ordinators of various groups so that they in turn could report to their constituencies.

We undertook two intensive rounds of consultations on these four key issues over the past eight weeks. In the first round, our aim was to test the flexibilities of Members and the possibilities for reaching common ground on an appropriate approach to each of the four issues addressed. This was part of a horizontal and integrated process whereby progress on specific issues could contribute to progress across the board. These consultations were positive and showed that there was a sense of engagement on all sides.

At a second informal Heads of Delegation meeting on 18 November, I reported that there had been positive steps in rebuilding the necessary trust and confidence among Members, which were essential ingredients to move the process forward. I suggested that the continuing sense of engagement on all sides would allow us to move on to a second round of consultations on the four issues, which would be more substantive and detailed in order to test the commitment and flexibility of each and every delegation so as to be able to determine whether there were any genuine possibilities for reaching common ground. . . .

On 9 December, we convened a further informal Heads of Delegation meeting to report on the second round of consultations. On that occasion, I also outlined my intentions for my report to this meeting of the General Council and the Director-General offered his observations on recent developments. . . .

To sum up the consultations overall, I would say that both rounds were conducted in a constructive spirit and a good atmosphere. Delegations largely avoided general statements and we explored key issues on the four subjects. However, as we went deeper into substance in the second round, the persisting difficulties became more apparent.

On the positive side, much effort has been put in and we have come a long way from Cancún in a short time. Members have been prepared to enter into substance and we have had interactive exchanges on substantive issues. I have put to delegations a number of key questions as well as some proposals, which have been addressed seriously. There has been progress in a number of areas, and clarification on some important aspects, which for me as Chair has given a clearer sense of possible ways forward. There is a strong sense of commitment to the multilateral trading system and the Doha Development Agenda (DDA), and also of willingness to move forward. I understand that this feeling has also come through very clearly in the Director-General's recent contacts with Ministers.

On the negative side, we have witnessed little real negotiation, or movement towards accommodation among positions, or searching for common ground, with some limited but welcome exceptions. Gaps remain wide, not only among positions but also, and this must be cause for concern, between generalized statements of commitment, engagement and flexibility on the one hand, and any concrete manifestation of those statements in negotiating positions on the other. Many delegations have noted that there does not seem to be a sense of urgency, and I would agree with them. . . .

Let me now turn to Agriculture. In this area, as in all others, it is clear that we are working to fully implement the Doha mandate for these negotiations, which is in fact what the Ministers reaffirmed in their Cancún Statement. Our consultations underlined both the important central role this issue has in the DDA and the large amount of work we will have to do in order to bridge positions here. We are all aware that positive results on agriculture will have positive implications in other areas. . . .

In the consultations, we have identified the key issues in this area of work and I sincerely believe that we can make progress here in the early part of next year, if Members focus and give priority attention to them, and show the necessary flexibility to accommodate other Members' views and look for common ground. . . .

With regard to domestic support there is recognition that one of the aims of multilateral negotiations should be to support and provide incentives for the expansion of domestic reforms that move from more distorting to less distorting forms of support and which result in lower levels of overall support. It follows therefore that . . . the more trade-distorting measures should be the focus of greater reductions. . . .

On market access, the notion of a common approach for both developed and developing countries seems now to be gaining ground, while acknowledging of course, that the formula would have to incorporate a clear differentiation through special and differential treatment, in order to take care of the development, food security and/or livelihood security needs of developing countries. The blended formula suggested in the Derbez text has been the subject of concerns by a number of developing countries and further work is obviously needed on this or other formulas, in order to ensure that all Members will have to share the burden of tariff reductions, but that developing countries will not be called upon to assume a disproportionate part. Providing we make progress on the other two pillars, I am hopeful that common ground will also be found with regard to market access.

On export competition, my reading of the situation is that there is general acceptance that the commitments regarding reductions or elimination will apply to all forms of unfair export competition, and the Derbez text seems to be an acceptable basis for an eventual agreement, at the framework stage. The key outstanding issue is the end date for the phasing out of export subsidies for all agricultural products. . . . I have stated it before and I repeat it today, that I feel this commitment to the elimination of all forms of export subsidies is a must for these negotiations to be successful, although I am aware of the difficulties that some Members may have at present to make definitive commitments to that effect.

The process of consultations has been useful and I sense that progress has been made. What we need is to find some wording that will imply an agreed sense of commitment towards that goal, although at the framework stage, we do not need to specify an end date. This could remain in brackets to be negotiated as part of the modalities for agricultural negotiations. . . .

Moving on now to Cotton. . . .

Although there are outstanding issues to be addressed, I believe we have made progress. We now have more clarity on the outlines for a meaningful direction that needs to be further pursued in subsequent consultations. We now know that further work will need to be pursued along three inter-related tracks, namely procedure; trade-related substance; and, development-related issues, including financial and technical assistance. In all three areas, we have had some good discussions and have identified the main issues.

I am sure that everyone is committed to finding a positive response to the Cotton Initiative and to develop a collective sense of the way forward. In view of the divergent positions on the procedural issue of whether to take up Cotton on a stand-alone basis or within the broader agricultural negotiations, I suggest we should try to avoid getting bogged down now on this question. I believe if we can make progress on substance, the procedural issue will tend to resolve itself at an appropriate time. In continuing work on this issue, I urge delegations to focus on practical responses, since this is what counts in the final analysis. . . .

Finally, let me report on our work on the Singapore Issues. During our consultations, a number of different proposals on how to deal with them were put forward, including one by myself. These were the subject of debate but not consensus. Looking ahead, I believe we can build on the general acceptance of unbundling these issues—that is to say, treating each of them on its own merits. On this basis, I suggest that it seems appropriate to continue with the work we have already started on exploring possible modalities for two of these issues, Trade Facilitation and Transparency in Government Procurement, without prejudice to the eventual outcome. What treatment, if any, the other two issues might receive in the future is a matter for further reflection at some appropriate time.

To conclude, in my view we have reached a point where the key issues are much clearer and where possible solutions are also becoming visible. However, moving on to grasp those solutions will require intensive negotiations backed by political determination and willingness to make the necessary compromises. This is what has been lacking in this process so far, and what is urgently needed in the weeks and months ahead.

From my perspective, the message is that we have made progress towards getting the Round back on track, and there is a firm commitment to do so by all Members. However, we are not yet there. There is unfinished business that must be taken care of. I believe we still have before us a window of opportunity early next year which could allow us to move further forward. We need to use it to the fullest.

Source: World Trade Organization. "Statement by the Chairperson of the General Council." *WTO News.* Geneva, Switzerland. December 15, 2003. www.wto.org/english/news_e/news03_e/stat_gc_chair_15dec03_e.htm (accessed January 15, 2004).

International Monetary
Fund on the 2003 World
Economic Outlook

September 18, 2003

INTRODUCTION

Pessimism about the condition of the global economy turned to cautious optimism in the second half of 2003, as the U.S. economy showed signs of entering a sustained recovery and as fears spawned by the U.S.-led invasion of Iraq and the outbreak of the deadly and mysterious Severe Acute Respiratory Syndrome (SARS) virus began to abate. In its annual *World Economic Outlook,* released September 18, 2003, the International Monetary Fund (IMF) projected that the global economy would grow 3.2 percent in 2003, up from 3.0 percent in 2002, and would rise 4.1 percent—close to the norm—in 2004. "There is now good cause to be reasonably optimistic that the global economy is digging itself out of a very deep hole," said Kenneth Rogoff, the IMF's chief economist. "But it is certainly no time for complacency."

While most international organizations, economists, financial analysts, and government officials who monitored the world economy agreed that it was positioned to grow, they were nonetheless concerned that any one of a number of factors, or a combination, could derail a recovery either globally or regionally. Among these factors were record high budget and trade deficits in the United States, high public indebtedness throughout the world, the high value of the dollar as measured against other currencies, the persistent slow growth in Europe, deflation in Japan, the slowing growth of international trade, and continuing deadlocks over liberalizing agricultural and other key areas of trade. Overhanging the global economy like a dark cloud was the threat of another terrorist attack like the one on September 11, 2001, that destroyed the World Trade Center towers in New York and tipped an already faltering world economy into near recession.

United States: High Deficits, Strong Dollar

Whether global economic growth would pick up, and how fast, depended to a great extent on how events unfolded in the United States, at $11 trillion by far the world's largest economy. Consumer demand remained high, as it had throughout the 2001 recession and recovery, fueled by low interest rates and low inflation. Two massive tax cuts, in 2001 and 2003, supplied additional stimulus. High productivity also continued, tamping down job creation, but as 2003 ended there were increasing signs that businesses had worked through some of their overinvestment and excess capacity. Business investment, which had collapsed along with the stock market in 1999–2000, began to pick up at the end of the year. Investors also began to return to the stock market, although many analysts said stocks were still overvalued. The slow pace of job creation remained worrisome, holding down consumer confidence and giving rise to new calls for protectionism. Several of the factors that allowed for economic recovery in the near term were also creating what many analysts worried could become serious global economic problems in the not-so-distant future—record-high domestic and international deficits. *(Status of U.S. economy, p. 68)*

The federal budget deficit, projected at nearly $500 billion for 2004, was largely the result of lost revenue from the tax cuts, which together totaled more than $1.6 trillion over ten years, as well as sharply stepped-up military spending to support the invasion of Iraq and the ongoing war on terrorism. Although agreement on the harmful effects of the federal budget deficit was far from unanimous, many economists said that continued high deficits would eventually push up interest rates and could choke off growth. *(Iraq invasion, p. 135; Federal budget deficit, p. 678)*

The onset of huge budget deficits, after several years of surplus, exacerbated concerns about the U.S. current account deficit (a broad measure of goods and services entering and leaving the country), which accounted for more than 5 percent of U.S. gross domestic product (GDP). Concerns that the United States could not continue to sustain such huge debt led to a weakening of the dollar in 2003, particularly against the euro, the currency unit for the twelve countries of the European Monetary Union, or eurozone. Depending on the measure used, the value of dollar dropped between about 8 and 14 percent in 2003, its steepest decline since the late 1980s. Still, most experts thought that it needed to fall even more but hoped that it would not fall too fast or collapse, and that the exchange rate adjustment would be spread broadly through other economies. They called particularly for more exchange rate flexibility in Asian currencies, particularly the yuan in China, which was pegged to the dollar and moved up or down in with the dollar. Even an orderly adjustment of the value of the dollar downward was likely to slow growth in the United States and possibly the rest of the world as well.

Europe: Weak Growth

So far the devaluation of the dollar had been absorbed largely by the euro. At year's end 1 dollar equaled about 1.26 euros, and demand for European exports had weakened as a consequence. The European Union (EU, the twelve countries of the eurozone plus Denmark, Sweden, and the United Kingdom) was the second-largest economy in the world, but its growth had been stagnant for years, as governments struggled under high labor and social welfare costs as well as with the strains of integrating the economies of fifteen rich and poorer countries into an economic union. Those strains were likely to grow even worse in 2004 when ten countries, eight of which had been under communist rule, joined the union. *(EU expansion, p. 492)*

The combination of weak consumer and export demand helped push Germany, the Netherlands, and Italy into recession, and the French economy also contracted. Fearful of inflation, the European Central Bank kept interest rates relatively high (and higher than many analysts thought they should be), thus dampening both consumer demand and business investment. An EU agreement, known as the Stability and Growth Pact, prohibited members from running budget deficits over 3 percent of GDP for more than three years, making it difficult for governments to use fiscal policy to stimulate their economies. Several analysts revised their estimates for future growth downward during the year. In September the IMF said, for example, that it expected Germany to record zero growth for 2003 and an increase of only 1.5 percent in 2004. For the eurozone, it predicted growth of 0.5 percent in 2003 and 1.9 percent in 2004.

By the end of the year, however, prospects for an upturn in growth had brightened. Despite occasionally noisy public protests, Germany and France (the two largest economies after the United States and Japan) had both taken steps toward structural reform. German chancellor Gerhard Schroeder pushed through some tax cuts and won crucial support for cuts in unemployment, health, and pension benefits, while the French parliament voted to bring the pension system for public employees in line with the less generous private pension system. Germany and France also rebelled against a European Commission demand that they cut their fiscal 2004 budgets to come under the 3 percent deficit limit. In November the two countries persuaded a majority of EU members to "suspend the rules." Both countries argued that the limit should be relaxed until their economies were on the mend, although the suspension was widely viewed as the death knell for the Stability and Growth Pact.

Japan: Growing Out of Deflation?

Analysts were more optimistic about another problem country, Japan, where exports and new investment seemed poise to lead growth, at least in the short term. Japan's economy had been in crisis since 1990, when its over-heated securities and real estate markets collapsed, sending thousands of speculators into bankruptcy and creating mountains of bad debt based on loans that were no longer worth anywhere near their face value. With the government unwilling to undertake painful economic reforms, especially of the debt-ridden banking system, Japan slid into deflation, a period of continuing falling prices that often led to cuts in wages, which in turn could lead to higher debt, lower demand, and even lower prices. Since 1995 prices in Japan had fallen by about 7 percent. *(Background, Historic Documents of 1998, p. 532; Historic Documents of 2001, p. 304)*

By the end of 2003 Japan had enjoyed nearly two straight years of economic growth. Business confidence was at its highest level in years, and domestic demand was beginning to pick up. But deflation was expected to continue, as Japan's central bank kept short-term interest rates low for fear that raising them would damage corporations and banks still grappling with their debt and bad-loan problems and worsen the country's growing public debt. Forecasters generally predicted that Japan's growth would continue for at least a few more months; they were less optimistic about the longer-term picture. The IMF outlook forecast growth of 2.0 percent in 2003 and 1.4 percent in 2004.

Emerging Economies

Apart from Japan, Asia was the fastest growing economic region in the world, with China—now the world's sixth largest economy—leading the way. China's booming economy had been growing at an average rate of 9 percent for two decades and was not expected to slow much in the near future. The IMF forecast growth at 7.5 percent for both 2003 and 2004; other forecasters pegged growth even higher. China was now the world's largest recipient of foreign direct investment. Although its $125 billion trade surplus with the United States was a sore point between the two countries, China was running a trade deficit with several Asian states, and its imports were rising faster than its exports. India, the world's second most populous country after China, was also growing strongly. The IMF projected growth of 5.6 percent in 2003 and 5.9 percent in 2004. *(China-U.S trade, pp. 441, 1173)*

The outbreak of SARS, first in China and then in several other Asian countries, dealt a harsh blow to the tourism and travel industries in the region in the first half of the year. But by year's end, most of these countries had recovered and begun growing again. Only Hong Kong and Singapore appeared to be suffering lingering economics effects from the deadly virus. *(SARS outbreak, p. 121)*

The economic picture in Latin America also appeared relatively bright, as exports there picked up. Argentina and Brazil both inaugurated new presidents in 2003 who took steps to revive faltering economies. However, high debt and political uncertainty in several countries, notably oil-rich Venezuela, had the potential to undermine the fragile emerging recovery in the region. *(Brazil, p. 3; Venezuela, p. 279; Argentina, p. 824)*

Economic Growth and Development Goals

While signs of growing economic recovery were welcome news, the IMF and other forecasters warned that recovery might not be sustainable. Continuing geopolitical uncertainties such as terrorism and civil conflicts could inhibit investment, while a spike in worldwide prices for oil and other fuels could slow the pace of recovery. In late September the Organization of Petroleum Exporting Countries unexpectedly announced that it was cutting back production of crude oil as of November 1 to keep prices at their current levels. Critics said the move might instead have the effect of increasing oil prices due to competing demands for oil from growing economies and to the onset of the winter heating season in the Northern Hemisphere. The United States and several European countries had relatively low supplies of oil and natural gas on hand.

International development organizations were also growing increasingly pessimistic that the world economy was growing fast enough to meet the UN-sponsored Millennium Development Goals—a set of goals agreed upon by industrial and developing countries in 2000 for reducing poverty and its effects. For example, in 2003–2004, the IMF expected economic growth to range between 3 and 5 percent in Sub-Saharan Africa, which had some of the poorest countries in the world. That was a healthy pace for a region ravaged by HIV/AIDS, hunger, civil wars, and widespread corruption. But it was far from the 7 percent or so rate needed to begin to reduce poverty in the region. *(Millennium Development Goals, Historic Documents of 2000, p. 700)*

Developing countries were largely dependent on international trade and investment to help build their economies. Yet the growth of international trade had slowed since 2001 as a result of the global economic downturn, and negotiations within the World Trade Organization aimed at liberalizing trade had collapsed. In September delegates from developing countries walked out of negotiations in Cancún, Mexico, rather than accept what they described as only modest compromises offered by the wealthy industrial countries. Developing countries, many of which relied on agricultural exports, said they could not compete against the flood of heavily subsidized agricultural products exported by the United States and Europe. At his September 18 news conference, IMF's Rogoff called the collapse of the talks "a tragedy, not least because without stronger trade, global growth will eventually slow significantly and global poverty will rise." *(Trade talks, p. 740)*

Foreign investment in developing countries was another source of growth for those countries, providing money, jobs, and technology that a developing country could build upon to strengthen its domestic economy. But the economic weakness and noneconomic shocks were having a negative effect in this area as well. Net foreign direct investment flows into developing countries fell from their high of $145.3 billion in 2001 to $110.0 billion in 2002. Taking into consideration trade balances, foreign investment, official development assistance, and foreign debt, developing countries transferred a net of $192.5 billion to industrialized countries in 2002. In a speech to a meeting of high-level development finance officials on October 30, UN Secretary General Kofi Annan said that "even taking all subtlety and nuance into account, the overall result defies common sense. Funds should be moving from developed countries into developing countries, but these numbers tell us the opposite is happening. Funds that should be promoting investment and growth in developing countries, or building schools and hospitals, or sponsoring other steps towards the Millennium Development Goals, are instead being transferred abroad. Despite promising investment opportunities in the developing world, and improved economic policies, fear and uncertainty are keeping resources from being deployed where they are most needed."

Meanwhile, development agencies reported a raft of grim statistics about the debilitating effects of poverty. In its annual development report, the World Bank examined the provision of basic services, such as education, health care, clean water, and sanitation. The report found, for example, that 2.5 billion people worldwide did not have access to improved sanitation. But it also found that the quality of the services provided could be improved significantly with a little effort. Mexico, for example, reduced childhood illness and increased secondary school enrollment by giving cash to poor families who attended health clinics regularly and who sent their children to school.

One measure of poverty, hunger, appeared to be on the rise again after falling steadily during the last half of the 1990s. According to the UN's Food and Agriculture Organization (FAO), nearly 850 million people—roughly one-seventh of the world's population—were undernourished, the report said, and the number was increasing by about 5 million a year. The reversal made achieving the UN goal of cutting the number of malnourished people in half by 2015 "increasingly remote," the report said.

FAO found that nineteen countries had reduced the number of hungry people by 80 million since 1990–1992. Among these countries was China, which cut its number of hungry people by 58 million. India reduced hunger in the first half of the 1990s by 20 million but then lost ground later in the decade, when 19 million people were added to the roles of the hungry. Hunger also increased over the decade in several countries involved in wars or civil conflicts, including Afghanistan, Congo, Burundi, Liberia, and Sierra

Leone. In North Korea, famine and economic mismanagement had caused a decade-long food emergency. An estimated 2 million people—about 10 percent of the population—had starved to death in North Korea in the 1990s. In parts of Sub-Saharan Africa, food production had been severely reduced not only by drought and other natural disaster but also by the loss of workers to HIV/AIDS. In testimony before the U.S. Senate Foreign Relations Committee, James T. Morris, executive director of the U.N. World Food Programme, said there was "more than enough food worldwide" to end hunger. "People are hungry because governments have made the wrong political choices," he said. *(Congo, p. 288; North Korea, p. 592; Liberia, p. 767; Burundi, p. 922; Afghanistan, p. 1089)*

Following are excerpts from the International Monetary Fund's annual World Economic Outlook, *released to the public September 18, 2003.*

"The IMF *World Economic Outlook*"

When the last *World Economic Outlook* was published in April 2003, the IMF [International Monetary Fund] staff expected—provided the war in Iraq was short and contained—that the global recovery would resume in the second half of the year, with global growth picking up to about 4 percent in 2004. In the event, with major hostilities in Iraq indeed ending quickly, forward-looking indicators generally turned up, with equity markets strengthening markedly, accompanied by some pickup in business and consumer confidence, particularly in the United States.

Concurrent data initially remained weak, with industrial production and trade growth slowing markedly in the second quarter, reflecting continued geopolitical uncertainties, the continued aftereffects of the bursting of the equity price bubble, and—particularly in Asia—the impact of Severe Acute Respiratory Syndrome (SARS). Most recently, however, there have been growing signs of a pickup in activity—including investment—particularly in the United States, Japan, and some emerging market countries, notably in Asia. With inflationary pressures very subdued, macroeconomic policies have been eased further across the globe. Interest rates have been reduced in Europe and the United States, as well as in a number of other industrial and emerging market countries; and fiscal policy has been further relaxed in the United States and a number of Asian countries. That said, the degree of macroeconomic stimulus among the major industrial countries continues to vary widely, with significant stimulus in the pipeline in the United States and the United Kingdom and relatively little in the euro area and Japan.

In mature financial markets, the combination of ample liquidity, monetary easing, and the expectation that low policy interest rates will be maintained for longer than earlier thought drove long-run interest rates down to 40-year lows by mid-June. Since that time, long-run interest rates have rebounded, most sharply in the United States, apparently reflecting growing expectations of recovery, higher inflationary expectations, and the continuing strong supply of government paper. Even so, the recent rebound has had only a limited effect on equity markets, which have retained their substantial gains since March, and on corporate spreads, which have benefited from actual and anticipated progress in corporate restructuring and continued positive risk appetite. In currency markets, the U.S. dollar continued to depreciate through mid-May, reflecting a combination of relatively low interest rates and continued investor concerns about the large U.S. current account deficit, though since then it has strengthened somewhat. Overall, since its peak in early 2002, the U.S. dollar has fallen by some 12 percent in nominal effective terms, matched by a substantial appreciation of the euro, the Canadian dollar, and some other industrial country currencies.

In emerging markets, financing conditions eased significantly through June, aided by low industrial country interest rates and improved sentiment toward a number of key markets, notably Brazil. Financing costs have risen since then, reflecting higher U.S. interest rates, but spreads have continued to decline; and while primary issuance has slowed, this appears to have been largely discretionary, with little evidence of an underlying tightening of market access. With capital outflows from many countries slowing, net private capital inflows to emerging markets are projected to rise to over $110 billion in 2003, the highest level since the mid-1990s. Emerging market currencies have in general been little affected by the fall in the U.S. dollar—indeed, most have depreciated in nominal effective terms since the dollar peak. In Asia, which has continued to run large surpluses on both current and capital accounts, this has been accompanied by a very large increase in reserves. . . .

Commodity markets have continued to be heavily influenced by geopolitical developments, the cyclical situation, and supply shocks. After peaking at over $34 a barrel before the war, oil prices fell back sharply in April, but by end-August had returned to $30 a barrel, reflecting a slower-than-expected recovery in Iraq's oil production, persisting tight industrial country inventories, and concerns about the sustainability of current production levels in Nigeria and Venezuela. In early September, oil prices fell back, and—while they are expected to remain elevated during the remainder of 2003—they are projected to drop to an average $25.50 a barrel in 2004 in the face of rising supply, including from Iraq; indeed, many oil market analysts see a possibility of a significantly larger price decline. In contrast, nonfuel commodity prices are projected to rise moderately, aided by rising global activity and the fading of earlier supply shocks. At the current conjuncture, several issues remain important in assessing the speed and nature of the recovery, including:

- *How long will the aftereffects of the bubble—defined broadly as discussed below—persist?* As stressed at the time of the last *World Economic Outlook*, the recent weakness of the world economy has not just been due to the war. The equity boom in the late 1990s was the largest in modern history: the unwinding of its effects is uncharted territory, and it is perhaps not surprising that most observers, including the *World Economic Outlook*, have found it difficult to gauge the aftermath. While the direct impact of equity market losses on household consumption growth should now have peaked, household balance sheets in some countries, notably the United States, remain stretched and housing markets—boosted in part by the aggressive easing of monetary policy in the last three years—are unlikely to provide the same support to the recovery going forward as they did in the past. In addition, the adjustment process in the corporate sector and, to a lesser extent, in the financial sector—eliminating excess capacity, restructuring of balance sheets, and rebuilding defined benefit pension funds—still has some way to go, particularly in Europe; and recent accounting scandals may continue to weigh on corporate confidence.
- *Will the U.S. dollar experience a renewed depreciation, and, if so, will the euro continue to bear the brunt of the offsetting adjustment?* To date, the decline in the U.S. dollar has been relatively orderly and— given the large U.S. current account deficit—generally welcome, and the resulting tightening in financial conditions in the euro area has been largely offset by European Central Bank (ECB) interest rate cuts. . . . While the World Economic Outlook projections are, as usual, based on the assumption that real effective exchange rates remain constant, further substantial dollar depreciation cannot be ruled out and would have significant implications for the outlook, especially if the offsetting appreciation continued to be focused on the euro area rather than spread more widely. Consistent with the signs of renewed recovery discussed above, the IMF staff's baseline forecast continues to project an upturn from the second half of 2003. Global GDP growth is expected at 3.2 percent in 2003,

rising to 4.1 percent—close to trend—in 2004, underpinned by reduced geopolitical uncertainties, policy stimulus in the pipeline, a pickup in inventories, the projected decline in oil prices, and a gradual diminution of the aftereffects of the bubble. Monetary policies are expected to remain accommodative, with a gradual withdrawal of stimulus unlikely to begin until 2004; in Japan, the quantitative easing policy is expected to continue. Looking across individual countries and regions:

- Among the *industrial countries*, recovery will continue to be led by the United States where—despite a weak labor market and considerable excess capacity—current data have shown greatest signs of improvement, forward-looking indicators are strongest, and there is the most policy stimulus in the pipeline. In the euro area, the forecast has once again been significantly reduced, reflecting continued disappointing private domestic demand and the appreciation of the euro. With the overall policy stance less supportive and the region-wide outlook adversely affected by the continuing difficulties in Germany, the projected pickup is expected to be relatively gradual, supported mainly by a gradual pickup in private consumption (underpinned by lower interest rates and the automatic stabilizers) and inventories, and the expected improvement in external demand. In Japan, given the stronger-than-expected second quarter outturn, the stock market pickup, and heightened optimism about the U.S. recovery, the forecast has been revised upward significantly for both 2003 and 2004. However, with the outlook still clouded by deflation and corporate and banking system weaknesses, the pace of recovery is still expected to remain moderate.

- The outlook for *emerging markets* continues to be driven—to differing extents—by developments in industrial countries, external financing conditions, geopolitical factors, and country-specific developments. In emerging markets in Asia, with the effects of SARS now waning, growth is expected to pick up in the second half of 2003 and remain strong in 2004, aided by timely additional policy easing and continued robust growth in China. However, much will depend on a prompt rebound in domestic demand, as well as the pace of the global recovery and a continuation of the nascent recovery in the information technology (IT) sector. Activity in much of Latin America appears to be stabilizing and external confidence in the region—particularly Brazil—has improved markedly. Nonetheless, the recovery remains fragile and, with a number of countries facing significant debt problems and political uncertainties, the region remains vulnerable to a reversal in financial market sentiment. In the Middle East, while the quick end to the conflict in Iraq has boosted confidence, the fragile security situation remains a major source of uncertainty; GDP growth forecasts for the region have been revised upward in 2003 owing to higher oil production, but lower oil prices will adversely affect the outlook in 2004. Reduced geopolitical concerns also benefit Turkey although, to maintain investor confidence, the authorities need to firmly maintain the sustainability of the fiscal position. Growth in the transition countries remains solid, led by Russia and Ukraine; European Union (EU) accession countries continue to benefit from strong direct investment inflows, although weak euro area demand remains an important risk.

- Among the *poorest countries*, GDP growth in sub-Saharan Africa (excluding South Africa) is projected to rise to 3.6 percent in 2003, with the positive effects of improved macroeconomic policies, rising commodity prices, and debt relief under the Heavily Indebted Poor Countries (HIPC) initiative partly offset by continued political instability and adverse weather conditions (the latter—together with the high incidence of HIV/AIDS—contributing to serious food shortages in the Horn of Africa and Southern Africa). GDP growth is expected to pick up markedly in 2004 but, as in the past, this baseline outcome critically depends on a significant improvement in political stability and favorable weather conditions.

Inflationary pressures remain very low. In advanced countries, inflation is projected to be below 2 percent in 2003 for the second year in succession and to fall to 1.3 percent in 2004, the lowest level for 30 years; inflation in developing countries is expected to fall to 5 percent, also a historical low. Against this background, and given the weakness of the global recovery, the possibility of deflation has attracted increased attention. Recently, there has been overt deflation in only a few countries, most importantly Japan; however, inflation in a number of advanced countries is projected at below 1 percent in 2004, uncomfortably close to zero (especially given the general upward bias to measured inflation). The risk of a global deflationary spiral appears remote, and inflationary expectations have recently edged up, reflecting increasing expectations of recovery and recent policy measures. However, in an environment of low inflation, the possibility of a temporary period of price declines in the event of an adverse shock remains significant in a number of countries, most importantly Germany, adding to arguments for maintaining a relatively accommodative monetary stance.

While the baseline forecast for global growth is little changed from a few months ago, the balance of risks has improved significantly. Given the quick end to the war, the likelihood of worst-case scenarios has been much reduced since the last *World Economic Outlook*, while policies have been further eased. Indeed, as recent developments in financial markets underscore, it is possible that growth may pick up more quickly than currently expected, particularly in the United States, where productivity growth has been most robust, corporate balance sheet restructuring appears most advanced, and the policy stimulus in the pipeline is particularly large (and, given the expected supplementary budget to finance expenditures in Iraq and Afghanistan, is likely to increase further). While stronger U.S. growth would, of course, benefit the rest of the world, it would come at the cost of exacerbating the already large U.S. current account deficit, underscoring the need to accelerate implementation of measures to reduce the associated medium-term risks, as discussed below. The possibility that oil prices could be lower than expected in 2004 and beyond is also a potential upside risk to global activity.

At the same time, however, downside risks remain, particularly in 2004 and beyond. While geopolitical risks have declined since April they are far from eliminated, as recent tragic events in a number of countries underscore. In addition, beyond the specific risks in Japan, and to a lesser extent Germany, key concerns include the following:

- *The current account imbalances in the global economy and, associated with that, the continued dependence of the world on the outlook for the United States remain a serious concern.* Despite the depreciation of the U.S. dollar, the U.S. current account deficit is projected at 5 percent of GDP in 2003, falling only to 4 percent of GDP by 2008, suggesting that further adjustment will be needed to achieve medium-term sustainability. While the extent, nature, and timing of further dollar adjustment is impossible to predict, history suggests that even an orderly adjustment is likely to be associated with a slowdown in U.S. growth—and, if growth in the rest of the world remains weak, in global growth as well. In addition, a disorderly adjustment—or overshooting—remains an important risk, particularly if the offsetting appreciation continues to be concentrated on a few currencies. Volatility among the major currencies—often associated with currency misalignment—could also be a cause for concern, particularly for developing countries with fixed exchange rates or significant mismatches between the currency structure of trade and external debt.
- *The recent pickup in investment may not prove enduring, depending in part on the extent to which aftereffects of the bubble persist.* Apart from the direct costs, a more prolonged period of slower growth would make the global economy more vulnerable to new adverse shocks, especially given the still heavy dependence on developments in the United States, the relatively low level of inflation in some countries, and the increasingly limited room for policy maneuver in many countries.
- *In financial markets, as noted in the September* Global Financial Stability Report, *a further sharp rise in bond yields could adversely affect*

the recovery, particularly if that were not driven by expectations of higher growth. This would be especially so in countries where house prices have risen sharply in recent years (notably the United Kingdom, Australia, Ireland, the Netherlands, and to a lesser extent the United States), where such an eventuality would reduce the support that is presently being provided to demand in most of these countries and could increase the risk of a housing bust. In addition, if growth and corporate earnings were to disappoint, the recent rise in equity markets could prove ephemeral, putting renewed pressure on household, corporate, and financial balance sheets.

- *In emerging markets, the recent improvement in financing conditions owes much to temporary cyclical factors and could be reversed if industrial country interest rates were to rise rapidly.* This underscores the need to use the current relatively benign financing conditions to press ahead with measures to address significant medium-term vulnerabilities. In this connection, public sector debt in emerging markets, on average now higher as a percentage of GDP than in industrial countries, is a serious concern, and in many cases is well above the level that would be sustainable if countries do not improve on historical growth and budgetary performance. Overall, there are increasing signs that the expected pickup in global activity is developing, although it is as yet unclear how broad-based and robust it will be. Against this background, and with inflationary pressures very moderate, macroeconomic policies need to remain supportive. At the same time, policymakers face major medium-term challenges: to reduce the dependence of global growth on the United States; to foster an orderly reduction in global imbalances; and to strengthen medium-term fiscal positions, especially in view of future pressures from aging populations. In general, monetary policy remains the short-term instrument of choice, and while sustained low policy interest rates run some risk of exacerbating some imbalances—notably in the housing market—these must be balanced against the need to support the recovery and reduce potential deflationary risks. On the fiscal side, with many countries facing substantial medium-term pressures, difficult trade-offs need to be made. In general, the automatic stabilizers should be allowed to operate; beyond that, much depends on country-specific circumstances and constraints, as well as the conjunctural situation. A slower pace of short-term consolidation—or even underlying budgetary deterioration—is clearly of less concern if accompanied by credible plans for future consolidation, by structural reforms to boost future growth, or—perhaps most importantly—by measures to address the future costs of aging populations (the latter having the advantage of having only a limited short-term impact on demand).

Against this background, the main policy priorities would appear to be the following.

- *In industrial countries, monetary policies need to remain accommodative.* In the United States, the federal funds rate is now at the lowest level in 40 years. Even so, given the continued sluggishness of activity, and the potential risks of deflation, the Federal Reserve has appropriately indicated that rates could remain low for a considerable period. Fiscal policy has provided support to demand, but at the cost of a serious deterioration in the long-run outlook; consequently, there is now a pressing need for a credible medium-term framework to restore balance (excluding Social Security) and put Social Security and Medicare on a sound footing. In the euro area, where inflationary pressures have declined amid weak activity and the appreciation of the euro, the ECB's [European Central Bank] 50-basis-point reduction in interest rates in June was welcome. Further easing will be needed if inflation threatens to undershoot significantly: for instance, if activity fails to pick up quickly or the euro appreciates significantly. In the larger European countries, medium-term fiscal consolidation remains a priority. In these cases, underlying adjustment of 0.5 percent of GDP a year or, where underpinned by tangible and credible quality consolidation measures and structural reform efforts, cumulative adjustment of 1.5 percent of GDP over 2004–06 would appear to provide scope for a reasonable compromise between short- and medium-term policy trade-offs. Automatic stabilizers should be allowed to operate fully around the consolidation path, even if that results in breaches of the 3 percent of GDP deficit limit. In Japan, despite stronger-than-expected recent data, a much more aggressive monetary policy—accompanied by a clear communication strategy and a commitment to end deflation in a short period—remains essential to turn around deflationary expectations. Given the very high public deficit and debt, modest structural fiscal consolidation appears appropriate. In almost all industrial countries, additional pension and health sector reform is essential to address the future pressures from aging populations.
- *In emerging markets, the policy priorities vary widely across regions.* In Latin America, recent currency appreciation has increased the room for monetary easing in some countries, but—notwithstanding the improvement in financing conditions—it will be critical to ensure that the pace of fiscal consolidation and structural reform is sustained. In Asia, the scope for policy maneuver is greater, and macroeconomic policies have appropriately been eased in a number of countries, in part to offset the impact of SARS. . . . [I]n many emerging and developing countries a broad-based effort to improve medium-term public debt sustainability—encompassing tax reforms,

improved expenditure control, institutional strengthening, and structural reforms to boost growth—is a central priority.

- *Given the continued need to reduce global dependence on growth in the United States and address global imbalances, the case for structural reform takes on new urgency.* As has been discussed many times in the *World Economic Outlook,* the priorities include labor and product market reforms to boost potential growth in Europe; corporate and financial restructuring in Japan; a greater reliance on domestic demand in emerging markets in Asia, again supported by continued corporate and financial sector reform; and in the United States, measures to boost national savings, particularly through strengthening the medium-term fiscal position. Over the past several years, progress has unfortunately been limited, and in some aspects—notably the U.S. fiscal outlook—the situation has deteriorated. In marked contrast to the situation in the mid-1980s, when the United States last ran a current account deficit of this size, neither Japan nor, to a lesser extent, Europe is well placed to pick up the slack if growth in the United States were to slow. This underscores the need for accelerated efforts to address the issues listed above. In this connection, the recent initiatives in Europe—especially Agenda 2010 in Germany and the recent pension reform in France—are encouraging, although there is much further to go. In many countries, continued efforts to strengthen corporate governance are also required.

- *Policymakers will need to stand ready to manage the effects of a further depreciation in the U.S. dollar, if it were to occur.* To date, the brunt of the adjustment to the depreciation of the dollar has been borne by the euro, the Canadian dollar, and a number of smaller industrial country currencies. . . . [T]his has been broadly in line with medium-term fundamentals, and in most cases there has been scope for offsetting monetary easing. Were the U.S. dollar to depreciate significantly further, most of these countries still have some room for policy action; however, with the degree of undervaluation much less than before, it would be desirable for the necessary currency appreciation to be spread more broadly. The critical need for a more aggressive monetary policy to address deflation in Japan implies, if anything, some downward pressure on the yen. In these circumstances, greater upward exchange rate flexibility in emerging markets in Asia—which is relatively well placed from a cyclical perspective—would significantly facilitate the global adjustment process, given the region's importance in global trade, as well as being desirable for domestic reasons. In those countries where poverty remains a major concern, GDP growth has remained relatively resilient despite the weakness of the global economy. However, substantial differences across countries remain. In China and, to a lesser extent, India, per capita GDP growth is quite robust; but in sub-Saharan Africa it remains below 1 percent, far from sufficient to meet poverty reduction targets under the Millennium Development Goals. In this connection, it is notable that per capita GDP growth has been significantly stronger in those African countries where political stability has been achieved and where the most progress has been made toward macroeconomic stability and structural and institutional reform. This underscores the need to press forward with the region-wide implementation of the New Partnership for Africa's Development (NEPAD), which fully embodies these objectives.

But while improved domestic policies in Africa are crucial, they are not enough: additional financial assistance from the international community is also essential and—provided appropriate domestic policies are followed—can be effectively absorbed. Following the Monterrey Summit, progress has been made, including the establishment of the Millennium Challenge Account and additional funding to address the AIDS pandemic by the United States; and the United Kingdom has put forward innovative proposals for an International Financing Facility to finance the achievement of the Millennium Development Goals. While the impact of aid and other key macroeconomic policies in industrialized countries is difficult to measure precisely, recent analysis by the Center for Global Development suggests that in most cases they are far from supportive of development, underscoring the need for further progress to help developing countries meet the Millennium Development Goals. A central and immediate challenge for the global community is to achieve further multilateral trade liberalization under the Doha Round. This would clearly be of enormous benefit to the globe as a whole: as the IMF's Managing Director has stressed, ". . . lowering barriers to trade . . . has been the foundation of the tremendous expansion in global trade and prosperity in the second half of the twentieth century." Moreover, with nearly three-fourths of the world's poor working in the rural sector, competing with industrial country farmers who receive a third of their income in subsidies and other forms of protection, it is clearly also critical for poverty reduction. The developing countries themselves have much to do—and much to gain—from reducing their own trade barriers. But progress in the Doha Round requires leadership from the largest industrial countries, as well as a clear commitment by the developing countries to trade integration as a core element of their development strategy. Regrettably, progress to date has generally been disappointing, although recent steps by the European Union toward agricultural reforms are welcome, if still somewhat partial. At the Evian G-7 Summit in May, industrial country leaders renewed their commitment to ensure a successful Doha Round; the WTO Cancun Ministerial meeting in September—which was under way as the *World Economic Outlook* went to press—must be the occasion to match words with action. . . .

UN Security Council on Peacekeeping in Liberia

September 19, 2003

INTRODUCTION

The civil wars of the Mano River basin in West Africa engulfed Liberia in 2003, resulting in the ouster of President Charles Taylor, who had been largely responsible for conflict in the region. A brief U.S. military intervention, and a broader peacekeeping effort led by Nigeria, were among the key elements that quieted the conflict and led to establishment of a new interim government. But at year's end the situation in Liberia was far from stable, and United Nations Secretary General Kofi Annan urgently appealed for more peacekeeping troops and humanitarian aid.

Under Taylor, himself a former guerrilla leader, Liberia for several years had been the focal point of civil wars that swept through the countries in the Mano River region. Taylor supported guerrillas who terrorized Sierra Leone for a decade until international peacekeepers brought the fighting to a conclusive end in 2002. Taylor's government also contributed to civil conflict and political chaos in Ivory Coast, which for decades had been one of Africa's most prosperous and stable countries. The wash of refugees and movements of guerrilla groups endangered Guinea, which bounded all three countries in turmoil and had supported some of the rebels in Liberia. *(Ivory Coast, p. 237; Sierra Leone background, Historic Documents of 2002, p. 247)*

Liberia Descends into Civil War, Again

Liberia was founded in 1847 by freed slaves from the United States, and it managed to retain its independence throughout the colonial era, the only African country to do so except for Ethiopia (which came under Italian rule just before World War II). Liberia started to fall apart in 1981 when president

William Tolbert Jr. was assassinated during a coup led by army master sergeant Samuel Doe. Doe won fraudulent elections in 1985 and developed what many observers called one of the most corrupt and inefficient governments in Africa. By all accounts, one of Doe's most corrupt aides was Charles Taylor, who had been educated in the United States. When Doe accused him of embezzling nearly $1 million, Taylor fled to the United States, where he was briefly imprisoned under a Liberian extradition warrant. After escaping from a Boston-area jail under never-explained circumstances, Taylor returned to his native Liberia in 1989 and launched his guerrilla campaign. The leader of an offshoot of Taylor's group killed Doe in 1990, sparking a fierce civil war between three rival guerrilla movements that lasted, on and off, for more than five years.

Taylor ultimately prevailed in the war and won the presidency in a widely criticized election arranged by West African countries in 1997. By that time Liberia's economy and infrastructure had been decimated by years of war. The once-bustling capital city, Monrovia, lay in ruins, its surviving buildings pockmarked by bullet holes and most of its people reduced to begging or bartering for whatever food and staple goods they could find. Hundreds of outlying villages had been destroyed and largely abandoned as people fled one or another of the guerrilla armies. According to most international estimates, about 200,000 Liberians died in the decade of fighting.

Reverting to his guerrilla mode, Taylor in 1999 began supplying weapons to rebels in Sierra Leone in exchange for diamonds looted from that country's mines. The United Nations attempted to block this trade in 2001 by imposing an arms embargo against Liberia, but by then the region had been flooded with weapons, and Taylor reportedly had amassed a fortune from the illicit diamonds. UN investigators reported that Taylor received a large shipment of weapons in 2002 from Serbia via Burkina Faso, in defiance of the embargo.

In 1999, even as Taylor was dabbling in Sierra Leone's war, his government came under attack from a guerrilla group called Liberians United for Reconciliation and Democracy (LURD). Based in northern Liberia, LURD was dominated by the guerrilla leaders whom Taylor had defeated years earlier; UN reports showed the guerrillas received weapons through Guinea. Taylor launched offensives in 2000 and 2001 but failed to suppress the guerrillas, who gained control over much of the country's northeast.

The civil war entered a new phase early in 2003 when LURD stepped up its attacks and a new guerrilla group, called the Movement for Democracy, emerged and quickly pushed government forces from southeastern Liberia. On April 25 UN Secretary General Annan said the rebel groups, between them, controlled about 60 percent of the country. Relief agencies estimated that about half of the country's 3 million people had been driven from their homes by the fighting; tens of thousands took refuge in neighboring countries, including Ivory Coast, itself beset by civil war. The fighting was so severe that the U.N. World Food Programme and other aid agencies were forced, in April and May, to suspend their relief work on behalf of the refugees. Guerrillas had raided villages and refugee camps on the days food and medical supplies were delivered; rebels even attacked convoys of aid workers as they tried to deliver their humanitarian supplies.

Like Taylor, both sets of rebels appeared to be driven not by ideological, political, or tribal concerns but by desire to control Liberia's natural resources, principally timber and diamonds. The UN Security Council on May 6 extended, for one year, its sanctions and arms embargo against Liberia; stepping up its pressure, the council added a ban on international trade in timber products from Liberia. Yet more international pressure on Taylor came on June 4, when a UN-sponsored war crimes tribunal indicted him on war crimes charges stemming from his aid to the rebels there. That panel said Taylor bore "the greatest responsibility" for the widespread killings, rapes, amputations, and other assaults on civilians during the Sierra Leone war. The indictment was announced just as Taylor gave in to pressure by African leaders and said he would step down as president at the end of 2003.

The indictment appeared to reinforce Taylor's determination to fight on, if only because it was no longer safe for him to travel outside Liberia, or even inside most of it. By June 8 the LURD guerrillas advanced to Monrovia's northern suburbs and gave Taylor an ultimatum to step down within three days. The siege of the capital prompted the first intervention in Liberia's war by a Western power—not the United States, which had deep historic links to the country, but France, which had been the colonial power in much of West Africa. French special forces troops flew to Monrovia by helicopter on June 9 and rescued several dozen foreigners, even as thousands of Liberian civilians sought refuge from the fighting.

Under pressure from all sides, Taylor on June 17 agreed to resign as president in exchange for a cease-fire agreement negotiated by diplomats from West Africa, the European Union, and the United States. Taylor renounced that promise just three days later, and the guerrillas intensified their assault, seizing control of nearly half of Monrovia.

Pressure on Bush to Intervene

The renewed fighting led to international calls for intervention in Liberia by the United States. On June 26 families of war victims took seven bodies to the U.S. embassy in Monrovia, leading to a large demonstration in support of an American intervention. Britain's ambassador to the United Nations, Jeremy Greenstock, said the United States was the "natural candidate" to lead an international force to back up the cease-fire Taylor had signed then renounced. In Washington, President George W. Bush responded by calling on Taylor to step down, but his aides said the United States had no plans to intervene militarily.

In a letter to the Security Council on June 28, Secretary General Annan warned that Liberia faced a "major humanitarian catastrophe." Using diplomatic language, he commended West African nations for their efforts to end the conflict, but said "broader international action is urgently needed to reverse Liberia's drift towards total disintegration." While Annan did not say so directly, he clearly was calling on the United States to lead a peacekeeping force in Liberia. Annan repeated his call two days later and, this time referring to U.S. officials, said "all eyes are on them." West African leaders said they would be willing to contribute 3,000 troops to a peacekeeping force in Liberia if Washington would send 2,000 troops and lead it. Bush said on July 2 that he was "looking at all options" for action in Liberia, but aides suggested the most likely course was that Washington could send a small contingent of troops only after Taylor had quit and a cease-fire was in place. By coincidence, Bush was about to head to Africa for his first-ever visit, and he was aware that African leaders would appeal for U.S. action in Liberia.

Taylor took a step toward the first condition on July 6, announcing that he would resign as president and go into exile in Nigeria. But after meeting with Nigerian president Olusegun Obasanjo at the Monrovia airport, Taylor gave no indication as to when he might give up power. The next day, the advance team of a small unit of U.S. troops arrived in Monrovia for what was called an "assessment mission." As the soldiers moved about the city they were mobbed by thousands of people calling for more U.S. troops and denouncing Taylor. "No more Taylor," people in one crowd cried out. "We want George Bush." Bush himself was just a few hundred miles away, in Senegal, at the beginning of his visit to Africa. He said on July 8 that he had not yet decided whether to send more American troops to Liberia.

A brief lull in the fighting came to an end with another rebel attack on Monrovia starting July 18. By then, a new United Nations special envoy for Liberia—veteran U.S. diplomat Jacques Klein—said he understood that the United States would not contribute to a peacekeeping mission until after West African countries had put soldiers on the ground in Liberia. As fighting escalated around the capital, another contingent of three dozen U.S. Marines arrived July 21, with the assignments of evacuating American citizens and securing the U.S. embassy grounds.

After Bush's return to Washington, administration officials said a decision on a larger U.S. troop commitment still had not been made, in part because of a disagreement among Bush's aides about the next step. Secretary of State Colin Powell on July 22 became the highest-level U.S. official to endorse action, saying the United States had an interest "in making sure that West Africa doesn't simply come apart." But General Richard B. Myers, chairman of the Joint Chiefs of Staff, cautioned against viewing a U.S. deployment as an "instant fix" of Liberia's problems. Most news reports said the Pentagon was the main source of U.S. reluctance to intervene; the U.S. military already was stretched thin with large deployments in Iraq and

Afghanistan. But in an August 3 column, Douglas Farah, the former West Africa correspondent for the *Washington Post,* suggested another explanation for what he called the Bush administration's "dithering" was the backing given Taylor by Rev. Pat Robertson, head of the Christian Broadcasting Network and a strong supporter of Bush. Farah quoted Robertson as calling the war crimes indictment of Taylor "nonsense" and endorsing the Liberian leader as "a fine Christian." Robertson told CBS News he had invested $8 million in a Liberian gold mine—at Taylor's suggestion—but had "written off" that investment because of the fighting there.

Whatever the reason for his hesitation, Bush did announce a limited action on July 25. In an apparent compromise, the president ordered the deployment of U.S. naval ships carrying about 2,000 marines to the Liberian coast. U.S. officials said the troops would "support," but not participate in, a peacekeeping mission of troops from Nigeria and other African countries. At a news conference on July 30, Bush renewed his call for Taylor to leave Liberia. "I also want to remind you, the [U.S.] troop strength will be limited and the time frame will be limited, and we're working on that," he said.

Bush's long-delayed decision set off a chain of events that quickly led to at least a short-term resolution of the Liberian crisis. The UN Security Council on August 1 authorized an interim multinational force to help stabilize Liberia after Taylor gave up power. The first contingent of Nigerian peacekeepers arrived in Monrovia on August 4; they were joined two days later by seven U.S. Marines, whose mission was to help ensure the delivery of humanitarian supplies. Taylor on August 7 announced that he would resign and appoint vice president Moses Blah as his successor. Taylor attributed the pressure for him to step down to a "broad-based international conspiracy." Taylor kept the rest of the world guessing about his actual departure from Liberia, however, and hinted that he might not leave. Taylor finally ended the guessing game on August 11, staging an elaborate ceremony at which he resigned and Blah was sworn in as president. As Taylor spoke, calling himself the "whipping boy" for international powers, the three U.S. warships that had been off the Liberian coast suddenly came into view—an action U.S. officials said was intended to help calm the city. Taylor then flew into exile in Nigeria, where he was installed in a mansion in the coastal city of Calabar. UN officials later told reporters that Taylor had stolen about $100 million from Liberia, some in government funds and the rest through his control of corrupt enterprises, such as illegal diamond trading.

Post-Taylor Liberia

The departure of Charles Taylor did not end Liberia's problems. Two guerrilla armies still controlled much of the country and remained on the outskirts of Monrovia, and acting president Blah had no domestic or international support.

The first step toward a longer-term resolution of the situation came August 18, when Blah's government and the guerrillas signed a peace agreement calling for a joint interim government, with elections to be held by 2005 or 2006. Liberian leaders quickly named Gyude Bryant, a businessman, as head of the interim government. A vocal opponent of all Liberia's warring factions, Bryant described himself as a "neutralist" who could help unite the country after two decades of civil war. He took office October 14. Most of the U.S. Marines withdrew from Monrovia on August 24, leaving only small contingents guarding the embassy and providing logistical support to the peacekeeping troops from other West African nations. The U.S. warships departed in late September.

Sporadic fighting continued in Liberia despite the cease-fire and the peace agreement. On September 5, UN envoy Klein called for a giant peacekeeping force of 15,000 troops, saying that yet another failure to bring peace in Liberia "potentially destabilizes West Africa." Annan endorsed Klein's proposal, and on September 19 the Security Council authorized a Nigerian-led mission, the United Nations Mission in Liberia (UNMIL). If it reached its full authorized strength of 15,000 troops and 1,000 civilian police officers, the Liberia mission would be the largest current UN peacekeeping force—and the second largest since the early days of the UN operation in neighboring Sierra Leone, where 17,000 troops had enforced a peace agreement. The UN mission was formally launched on October 1, when 3,500 West African troops already in Liberia put on the UN's blue helmets and came under UN command.

Even with the UN mission on the ground, Taylor's presence was still felt in Liberia. Reports by diplomats and journalists early in October indicated that Taylor was communicating with his supporters and attempting to generate enthusiasm for his return. In response, the Security Council on October 9 issued a statement demanding that Taylor "respect the commitment" he had made to keep out of Liberian affairs. The council took even stronger action on November 7, voting to maintain sanctions against Liberia in hopes of blocking Taylor's sale of ill-gotten gains. Nigerian president Obasanjo said in late November that he was willing to turn Taylor over to the war crimes tribunal in Sierra Leone—if Liberia requested that step. Most observers considered such a request unlikely because interim leader Bryant said he feared that putting Taylor on trial might again destabilize Liberia.

In a report to the Security Council on December 18, Annan expressed cautious optimism about the situation in Liberia but called on UN member nations to step up their contributions to the peacekeeping force. Fewer than 6,000 peacekeeping troops were on the ground in Liberia, far short of the 15,000 authorized strength, and Annan said more troops were "sorely needed" to make sure the fragile peace was maintained. Noting that skirmishes continued in several parts of the country, and that rebel leaders had demanded "lucrative posts" in exchange for their continued cooperation,

Annan said Liberia's armed groups "have yet to demonstrate their full commitment to the peace process." On December 29 UN peacekeepers moved for the first time into an area controlled by the LURD rebels. The guerrillas had tried to delay the deployment of peacekeepers, but they relented when UN commanders said they would not negotiate.

Following is the text of United Nations Security Council Resolution 1509, adopted September 19, 2003, authorizing the UN mission in Liberia, a peacekeeping force of 15,000 troops and 1,000 civilian police officers, with a mandate to help the country's interim government implement a peace agreement ending a civil war.

"United Nations Security Council Resolution 1509"

The Security Council,

Recalling its previous resolutions and statements by its President on Liberia, including its resolution 1497 (2003) of 1 August 2003, and the 27 August 2003 Statement by its President, and other relevant resolutions and statements,

Expressing its utmost concern at the dire consequences of the prolonged conflict for the civilian population throughout Liberia, in particular the increase in the number of refugees and internally displaced persons,

Stressing the urgent need for substantial humanitarian assistance to the Liberian population,

Deploring all violations of human rights, particularly atrocities against civilian populations, including widespread sexual violence against women and children,

Expressing also its deep concern at the limited access of humanitarian workers to populations in need, including refugees and internally displaced persons, and stressing the need for the continued operation of United Nations and other agencies' relief operations, as well as promotion and monitoring of human rights,

Emphasizing the need for all parties to safeguard the welfare and security of humanitarian workers and United Nations personnel in accordance with applicable rules and principles of international law, and recalling in this regard its resolution 1502 (2003),

Mindful of the need for accountability for violations of international humanitarian law and urging the transitional government once established to ensure that the protection of human rights and the establishment of a state based on the rule of law and of an independent judiciary are among its highest priorities,

Reiterating its support for the efforts of the Economic Community of West African States (ECOWAS), particularly organization Chairman and President of Ghana John Kufuor, Executive Secretary Mohammed Ibn Chambas, and mediator General Abdulsalami Abubakar, as well as those of Nigerian President Olusegun Obasanjo, to bring peace to Liberia, and *recognizing* the critically important role they continue to play in the Liberia peace process,

Welcoming the continued support of the African Union (AU) for the leadership role of ECOWAS in the peace process in Liberia, in particular the appointment of an AU Special Envoy for Liberia, and further encouraging the AU to continue to support the peace process through close collaboration and coordination with ECOWAS and the United Nations,

Commending the rapid and professional deployment of the ECOWAS Mission in Liberia (ECOMIL) forces to Liberia, pursuant to its resolution 1497 (2003), as well as Member States which have assisted ECOWAS in its efforts, and stressing the responsibilities of all parties to cooperate with ECOMIL forces in Liberia,

Noting that lasting stability in Liberia will depend on peace in the subregion, and emphasizing the importance of cooperation among the countries of the subregion to this end, as well as the need for coordination of United Nations efforts to contribute to the consolidation of peace and security in the subregion,

Gravely concerned by the use of child soldiers by armed rebel militias, government forces, and other militias,

Reaffirming its support, as stated in its Statement by its President on 27 August 2003, for the Comprehensive Peace Agreement reached by Liberia's Government, rebel groups, political parties, and civil society leaders in Accra, Ghana on 18 August 2003, and the Liberian ceasefire agreement, signed in Accra, 17 June 2003,

Reaffirming that the primary responsibility for implementing the Comprehensive Peace Agreement and the ceasefire agreement rests with the parties, and urging the parties to move forward with implementation of these agreements immediately in order to ensure the peaceful formation of a transitional government by 14 October 2003,

Welcoming the 11 August 2003 resignation and departure of former Liberian President Charles Taylor from Liberia, and the peaceful transfer of power from Mr. Taylor,

Stressing the importance of the Joint Monitoring Committee (JMC), as provided for by the 17 June ceasefire agreement, to ensuring peace in Liberia, and urging all parties to establish this body as quickly as possible,

Recalling the framework for establishment of a longer-term United Nations stabilization force to relieve the ECOMIL forces, as set out in resolution 1497 (2003),

Welcoming the Secretary-General's report of 11 September 2003 (S/2003/875) and its recommendations,

Taking note also of the intention of the Secretary-General to terminate the mandate of the United Nations Office in Liberia (UNOL), as indicated in his letter dated 16 September 2003 addressed to the President of the Security Council (S/2003/899),

Taking note also of the intention of the Secretary-General to transfer the major functions performed by UNOL to the United Nations Mission in Liberia (UNMIL), together with staff of UNOL, as appropriate,

Determining that the situation in Liberia continues to constitute a threat to international peace and security in the region, to stability in the West Africa subregion, and to the peace process for Liberia,

Acting under Chapter VII of the Charter of the United Nations,

1. *Decides* to establish the United Nations Mission in Liberia (UNMIL), the stabilization force called for in resolution 1497 (2003), for a period of 12 months, and requests the Secretary-General to transfer authority from the ECOWAS-led ECOMIL forces to UNMIL on 1 October 2003, and further decides that UNMIL will consist of up to 15,000 United Nations military personnel, including up to 250 military observers and 160 staff officers, and up to 1,115 civilian police officers, including formed units to assist in the maintenance of law and order throughout Liberia, and the appropriate civilian component;

2. *Welcomes* the appointment by the Secretary-General of his Special Representative for Liberia to direct the operations of UNMIL and coordinate all United Nations activities in Liberia;

3. *Decides* that UNMIL shall have the following mandate:

Support for Implementation of the Ceasefire Agreement:

(a) to observe and monitor the implementation of the ceasefire agreement and investigate violations of the ceasefire;

(b) to establish and maintain continuous liaison with the field headquarters of all the parties' military forces;

(c) to assist in the development of cantonment sites and to provide security at these sites;

(d) to observe and monitor disengagement and cantonment of military forces of all the parties;

(e) to support the work of the JMC;

(f) to develop, as soon as possible, preferably within 30 days of the adoption of this resolution, in cooperation with the JMC, relevant international financial institutions, international development organizations, and donor nations, an action plan for the overall implementation of a disarmament, demobilization, reintegration, and repatriation (DDRR) programme for all armed parties; with particular attention to the special needs of child combatants and women; and addressing the inclusion of non-Liberian combatants;

(g) to carry out voluntary disarmament and to collect and destroy weapons and ammunition as part of an organized DDRR programme;

(h) to liase with the JMC and to advise on the implementation of its functions under the Comprehensive Peace Agreement and the ceasefire agreement;

(i) to provide security at key government installations, in particular ports, airports, and other vital infrastructure;

Protection of United Nations Staff, Facilities and Civilians:

(j) to protect United Nations personnel, facilities, installations and equipment, ensure the security and freedom of movement of its personnel and, without prejudice to the efforts of the government, to protect civilians under imminent threat of physical violence, within its capabilities;

Support for Humanitarian and Human Rights Assistance:

(k) to facilitate the provision of humanitarian assistance, including by helping to establish the necessary security conditions;

(l) to contribute towards international efforts to protect and promote human rights in Liberia, with particular attention to vulnerable groups including refugees, returning refugees and internally displaced persons, women, children, and demobilized child soldiers, within UNMIL's capabilities and under acceptable security conditions, in close cooperation with other United Nations agencies, related organizations, governmental organizations, and non-governmental organizations;

(m) to ensure an adequate human rights presence, capacity and expertise within UNMIL to carry out human rights promotion, protection, and monitoring activities;

Support for Security Reform:

(n) to assist the transitional government of Liberia in monitoring and restructuring the police force of Liberia, consistent with democratic policing, to develop a civilian police training programme, and to otherwise assist in the training of civilian police, in cooperation with ECOWAS, international organizations, and interested States;

(o) to assist the transitional government in the formation of a new and restructured Liberian military in cooperation with ECOWAS, international organizations and interested States;

Support for Implementation of the Peace Process:

(p) to assist the transitional Government, in conjunction with ECOWAS and other international partners, in reestablishment of national authority throughout the country, including the establishment of a functioning administrative structure at both the national and local levels;

(q) to assist the transitional government in conjunction with ECOWAS and other international partners in developing a strategy to consolidate governmental institutions, including a national legal framework and judicial and correctional institutions;

(r) to assist the transitional government in restoring proper administration of natural resources;

(s) to assist the transitional government, in conjunction with ECOWAS and other international partners, in preparing for national elections scheduled for no later than the end of 2005;

4. *Demands* that the Liberian parties cease hostilities throughout Liberia and fulfil their obligations under the Comprehensive Peace Agreement and the ceasefire agreement, including cooperation in the formation of the JMC as established under the ceasefire agreement;

5. *Calls upon* all parties to cooperate fully in the deployment and operations of UNMIL, including through ensuring the safety, security and freedom of movement of United Nations personnel, together with associated personnel, throughout Liberia;

6. *Encourages* UNMIL, within its capabilities and areas of deployment, to support the voluntary return of refugees and internally displaced persons;

7. *Requests* the Liberian Government to conclude a status-of-force agreement with the Secretary-General within 30 days of adoption of this resolution, and notes that pending the conclusion of such an agreement

the model status-of-force agreement dated 9 October 1990 shall apply provisionally;

8. *Calls upon* all parties to ensure, in accordance with relevant provisions of international law, the full, safe and unhindered access of relief personnel to all those in need and delivery of humanitarian assistance, in particular to internally displaced persons and refugees;

9. *Recognizes* the importance of the protection of children in armed conflict, in accordance with its resolution 1379 (2001) and related resolutions;

10. *Demands* that all parties cease all use of child soldiers, that all parties cease all human rights violations and atrocities against the Liberia population, and stresses the need to bring to justice those responsible;

11. *Reaffirms* the importance of a gender perspective in peacekeeping operations and post-conflict peace-building in accordance with resolution 1325 (2000), recalls the need to address violence against women and girls as a tool of warfare, and encourages UNMIL as well as the Liberian parties to actively address these issues;

12. *Decides* that the measures imposed by paragraphs 5 (a) and 5 (b) of resolution 1343 (2001) shall not apply to supplies of arms and related materiel and technical training and assistance intended solely for support of or use by UNMIL;

13. *Reiterates* its demand that all States in the region cease military support for armed groups in neighbouring countries, take action to prevent armed individuals and groups from using their territory to prepare and commit attacks on neighbouring countries and refrain from any actions that might contribute to further destabilization of the situation in the region, and declares its readiness to consider, if necessary, ways of promoting compliance with this demand;

14. *Calls upon* the transitional government to restore fully Liberia's relations with its neighbours and to normalize Liberia's relations with the international community;

15. *Calls on* the international community to consider how it might help future economic development in Liberia aimed at achieving long-term stability in Liberia and improving the welfare of its people;

16. *Stresses* the need for an effective public information capacity, including the establishment as necessary of United Nations radio stations to promote understanding of the peace process and the role of UNMIL among local communities and the parties;

17. *Calls on* the Liberian parties to engage for the purpose of addressing the question of DDRR on an urgent basis and urges the parties, in particular the transitional government of Liberia, and rebel groups Liberians United for Reconciliation and Democracy (LURD) and the Movement for Democracy in Liberia (MODEL), to work closely with UNMIL, the JMC, relevant assistance organizations, and donor nations, in the implementation of a DDRR programme;

18. *Calls on* the international donor community to provide assistance for the implementation of a DDRR programme, and sustained international assistance to the peace process, and to contribute to consolidated humanitarian appeals;

19. *Requests* the Secretary-General to provide regular updates, including a formal report every 90 days to the Council on the progress in the implementation of the Comprehensive Peace Agreement and this resolution, including the implementation of UNMIL's mandate;

20. *Decides* to remain actively seized of the matter.

Source: United Nations. Security Council. *Resolution* 1509. S/RES/1509 (2003). September 19, 2003. http://daccess-ods.un.org/access.nsf/ Get?Open&DS=S/RES/1509%20(2003)&Lang=E&Area=UNDOC (accessed September 28, 2003).

UN Envoy on HIV/AIDS in Africa

September 21, 2003

INTRODUCTION

New pledges of greater funding, cheaper drugs, and enhanced prevention and treatment programs were committed to the war on HIV/AIDS in 2003. In a surprise announcement, President George W. Bush said he would seek $15 billion over five years to help fight the AIDS epidemic overseas—three times as much as the United States had previously committed. Former president Bill Clinton announced in October that his private foundation had reached agreement with four generic drug manufacturers to reduce the costs of their AIDS drugs to victims in Africa and the Caribbean. China, India, and South Africa were among the countries that said they would make drugs available free to at least some AIDS patients. The World Health Organization (WHO) announced that it was starting a program to work with hard-struck countries to deliver drug treatment to 3 million AIDS patients by 2005.

United Nations officials coordinating the war against AIDS welcomed the stepped-up aid but said it still fell far short of what was needed. "We are not on track to begin reducing the scale and impact of the epidemic by 2005," United Nations Secretary General Kofi Annan said September 22 at a special General Assembly meeting on AIDS. Referring to several goals for reducing AIDS that UN member countries had set in 2001, Annan noted that one-third of all countries still had no policies guaranteeing women access to prevention and care, even though women now accounted for more than half of all new cases of HIV; more than one-third of the heavily affected countries still had no plans in place for caring for the millions of AIDS orphans; and two-thirds of the countries provided no antidiscrimination protections for people with AIDS. According to the goals, Annan said, the number of young people and infants with HIV should be sharply reduced by 2005 and comprehensive health care programs should be in place. "At the current rate of progress," Annan said, "we will not achieve any of those targets by 2005."

At a separate AIDS conference in Kenya on September 21, Stephen Lewis, Annan's special envoy on AIDS in Africa, spoke more bluntly, taking the rich countries of the world to task for their failure to do more to stem the pandemic that had already killed 28 million people worldwide, wiped out an entire generation in some parts of Africa, and left more than 13 million children orphaned and largely on their own. Speaking specifically of the plight of orphans, Lewis asked: "How can this be happening, in the year 2003, when we can find over $200 billion to fight a war on terrorism, but we can't find the money to prevent children from living in terror? And we can't find the money to provide the antiretroviral treatment for all of those who need such treatment in Africa? This double standard is the grotesque obscenity of the modern world."

In their annual report, the Joint United Nations Programme on HIV/AIDS (UNAIDS) and WHO said the pandemic "remains rampant," with 3 million people dead of acquired immunodeficiency syndrome in 2003, and 5 million newly infected with human immunodeficiency virus, which caused the incurable AIDS. Those were the highest numbers of annual deaths and new infections recorded since the epidemic began in Africa in the early 1980s. (UNAIDS reported 3 million deaths and 5 million new infections in 2002, but said in its 2003 report that more precise measurements put the figures for 2002 at 2.7 million deaths and 4.8 million infections.) Using those more precise measurements, UNAIDS and WHO estimated that 40 million people were living with HIV/AIDS, adding that the number could range as high as 46 million and as low as 34 million. Most of the cases were in sub-Saharan Africa, where 26.6 million people had the disease. UNAIDS said it was closely monitoring emerging epidemics elsewhere, including in China, India, and Indonesia—three of the four most populous countries in the world.

In the United States, the federal Centers for Disease Control and Prevention (CDC) reported in July that the number of Americans developing AIDS had gone up 2.2 percent in 2002, the first increase since 1993. Experts attributed the increase to several causes, including an increase in the number of HIV-infected people who were not responding to drug treatment and state budget cuts that limited access to care among poor people. Many experts focused on the increase in infections among gay and bisexual men, which rose for the third year in a row. New HIV diagnoses among gay men rose 17.7 percent from their low point in 1999 through 2002, according to the CDC data. Altogether, there were 42,136 cases of AIDS in the United States in 2002. An estimated 850,000 to 950,000 people in the United States were infected with HIV, but the CDC said that only about one-quarter of them were aware they carried the virus.

New Commitment from Bush

Bush had not devoted much time earlier in this presidency to the AIDS pandemic, so his announcement in his annual State of the Union address on January 28 that he would seek $15 billion over the next five years to prevent and treat AIDS in fourteen countries in Africa and the Caribbean came as a welcome surprise to AIDS activists. The commitment, if fully funded, would make the United States by far the largest single contributor to the global fight against AIDS. The initiative also represented a significant change of policy in that the administration said it would devote a substantial portion of the new money to providing antiretroviral drug therapies to extend the lives of HIV/AIDS patients. Previously, the administration had provided such drugs only in limited pilot programs, but now, Bush implied in his State of the Union speech, the availability of low-priced generic drug therapies made drug treatment programs possible in poor countries. "Seldom has history offered a greater opportunity to do so much for so many," Bush said. *(2003 State of the Union address, p. 18)*

Bush and his initiative were widely praised both at home and abroad. "We think it's an extraordinary development; we're thrilled," said Paul Zeitz of the Global AIDS Alliance, a nonprofit organization in Washington. UN special envoy Lewis said the announcement "opens the floodgates of hope." In May Congress passed legislation (PL 108–25) in May authorizing $3 billion for international AIDS programs for each of the next five years. Bush used the authorizing legislation to put pressure on leaders of other industrial countries to step up their contributions to the AIDS fight at a June meeting of the Group of 8 industrial countries. He also touted his AIDS program on a trip to Africa—his first—in July.

In the following weeks and months, it became apparent that the president was not prepared to support as much spending on international AIDS programs as his earlier declarations had implied. Arguing that international AIDS programs were not yet equipped to handle a greater infusion of cash, Bush requested only $2 billion for fiscal 2004, including just $200,000 for the UN-coordinated Global Fund to Fight AIDS, Tuberculosis, and Malaria. AIDS workers and some Democrats disagreed, saying that the money was urgently needed right away. They were also concerned that the steeply rising budget deficit would force Congress and the president to cut back even more on AIDS funding in future years. Congress ultimately appropriated $2.4 billion for international AIDS programs in fiscal 2004, including more money than Bush requested for the global fund.

AIDS workers were also concerned about the implementation of the initiative itself. At least one-third of the prevention money was to be spent on programs advocating sexual abstinence as the best way to prevent the spread of AIDS and other sexually transmitted diseases. Administration officials said the initiative was being modeled on Uganda's ABC plan—Abstain, Be Faithful, Use a Condom—which had been highly successful in bringing that country's epidemic under control. But some experts warned that an approach that worked well in one country might not be as successful in others with different social mores and conditions. Some AIDS activists also questioned language in the authorizing legislation that channeled half the money earmarked for helping AIDS orphans through religious and other faith-based organizations. Although faith-based groups were often the main providers of health and welfare care in African villages, these activists worried that money could go to groups that had no experience working with AIDS/HIV victims overseas and that some groups would proselytize or give help only to those who adhered to their religion.

Bush's choice of Randall Tobias, a former chairman and chief executive of Eli Lilly & Company, to run the new program further worried some AIDS workers, who questioned his close ties to the pharmaceutical company. "We're concerned about whether or not he can be an honest broker," Zeitz of the Global AIDS Alliance told the *New York Times* on July 2, the day Tobias's appointment was announced. "He'll be protecting the interests of the pharmaceutical industry versus cost-effective generically manufactured drugs."

Pushing Drug Prices Down

In recent years much attention had been focused on supplying HIV/AIDS patients in Africa with life-saving drug therapies. Two issues stood in the way. The first was their price and availability. The most effective therapies, "cocktails" of three different antiretroviral drugs (ARVs), cost between $10,000 and $15,000 a year in Western countries. That put the drugs out of reach to all but the wealthiest people in Africa and the Caribbean, where families often lived on only a few dollars a day and where health insurance was uncommon. Under a great deal of pressure, major drug companies had agreed in 2001 to drop some of their ARV drug prices for poor countries in Africa, and even cheaper generic drugs had become available in a few countries. But the cheapest drugs still cost $300 or more a year. As a result only about 50,000 people in Africa were receiving the drugs out of the 4 million who could benefit from them. Worldwide, an estimated 6 million patients could benefit from ARV therapy.

Several important developments that could increase the availability of cheaper generics were announced in 2003. In August the World Trade Organization (WTO) announced that a compromise had been reached on a complicated licensing scheme that would allow countries facing public health emergencies to import generic drugs from countries whose domestic patent laws prohibited such licensing agreements. Under heavy pressure from its pharmaceutical industry, the United States had long blocked the provision, arguing that it covered more medicines than was necessary. At the end of the year Canada was on the verge of passing legislation that would have allowed its pharmaceutical companies to supply generics under the new WTO agreement. If the legislation passed, Canadian generics could help ensure that there would not be a shortage of the drugs. *(Background, Historic Documents of 2002, p. 472)*

On October 23 former president Bill Clinton announced that his Clinton Foundation had negotiated a deal with four generic drug manufacturers to bring the per-patient cost of their ARVs drugs down to about $140 a year, or thirty-seven cents a day. Three Indian companies and one South African company agreed to increase their production of their generic ARVs in return for a guaranteed customer base. The drugs were to be available in Rwanda, Mozambique, South Africa, Tanzania, and several Caribbean countries.

In another significant development, the governments of China, India, and South Africa announced plans to start providing free ARV treatment to AIDS patients. The announcements were seen as long-overdue acknowledgments by all three governments of the need to deal more fully and more openly with the AIDS epidemic. India, for example, was estimated to have at least 4.6 million people with HIV. While that represented less than 1 percent of India's population, it was the second highest number of HIV cases outside South Africa.

The Chinese announcement was remarkable because the government for several years had been publicly denying that the country faced an AIDS problem. About 1 million Chinese were thought to have HIV/AIDS, and experts warned there could be 10 million cases by 2010. In a campaign apparently planned to coincide with World AIDS Day on December 1, Chinese television ran ads to raise public awareness of the disease and the ways it was transmitted. In one dramatic appearance designed to reduce the stigma surrounding the disease, Prime Minister Wen Jiabao was shown comforting AIDS patients and pledging support. It was the first time a senior Chinese official had publicly shown sympathy for victims of the disease. Government openness about the AIDS epidemic also coincided with new openness about the appearance of possible new cases of Severe Acute Respiratory Syndrome (SARS) in Guangdong province. Attempts by the Chinese government earlier in the year to cover up a SARS epidemic resulted in worldwide criticism as the sometimes fatal disease spread to several neighboring nations and Canada. *(SARS outbreak, p. 121)*

Perhaps the biggest turnabout came in South Africa, where an estimated 5.3 million South Africans had HIV/AIDS at the end of 2002. The government of President Thabo Mbeki had long resisted widespread distribution of AIDS drugs. Mbeki himself had publicly questioned whether HIV caused AIDS and argued that HIV was just one factor, along with poverty and malnutrition, that caused the disease. He also questioned the safety, cost, and efficacy of the ARV drugs and said that South Africa lacked the health care infrastructure necessary to ensure that the drugs were used properly. Under intense pressure, both from inside and outside South Africa, the government finally relented. On November 19 the government announced that it would distribute free ARV drugs within five years to everyone who needed them. *(Mbeki position on AIDS, Historic Documents of 2000, p. 410)*

WHO's "3 by 5" Plan

The other issue in supplying ARV drugs to AIDS patients was how to deliver them safely and effectively. Studies showed that ARV drugs had been extremely effective in lengthening survival rates for persons with HIV and for restoring them to nearly normal health. But the ARV therapies used in the western world involved multiple pills taken every day along with careful monitoring to measure the effectiveness and side effects in each patient. Some experts were also concerned that patients who were not carefully monitored might not follow the complicated regimen, consistently, allowing the HIV virus to become drug resistant. Yet most countries in the developing world had only rudimentary health care delivery systems and comparatively few doctors or trained health care workers.

On December 1 WHO announced a plan it had been developing for some time to deliver ARV drugs to 3 million AIDS patients by the end of 2005. The plan, dubbed "3 by 5," was expected to cost $5.5 billion. Several other international organizations, government agencies, and private groups were working with WHO on the program.

The cornerstone of the plan was a call for affected countries to organize and train 100,000 health care and nonprofessional workers to deliver the drugs. "We will say, you don't need to get care only from doctors; let's train nurses, community organizations, and families," said Paulo Teixeira, the director of WHO's HIV/AIDS program, in October when the plan was still in development. Teixeira was widely credited for having rapidly and successfully increased access to treatment for HIV patients in Brazil, his native country.

To make the job easier, WHO said it would simplify the drug treatments by using just four combinations of drugs out of thirty-five possible combinations and by combining them into a single "fixed-dose" pill where possible. WHO said it also planned to simplify monitoring by using easy-to-administer tests like body weight checks and color-scale blood exams instead of the more complicated and costly exams typically used in western countries. WHO and UN officials acknowledged that the program would require countries to make difficult ethical choices about who to treat and the treatment itself, but they argued that the program was necessary if progress was to be made in stopping AIDS. "We firmly believe that we stand no chance of halting this epidemic unless we dramatically scale up access to HIV care," said Peter Piot, director of the UNAIDS program. "Treatment and prevention are the two pillars of a truly effective, comprehensive AIDS strategy."

Work continued in 2003 on developing a vaccine for the disease, with several experiments being conducted on humans. Many researchers said reliable vaccines were the only effective means of controlling the spread of AIDS. Although several researchers were optimistic that biotechnology breakthroughs had put scientists on the right track, few were predicting that a vaccine would be ready in the near future. In February VaxGen Inc.

reported that its human vaccine experiment—thought to be the most advanced at the time—had failed.

Following is the text of remarks made by Stephen Lewis, the United Nations secretary general's special envoy for HIV/AIDS in Africa, on September 21, 2003, at the opening ceremonies of the thirteenth International Conference on AIDS and STIs in Africa. A widely quoted phrase that was omitted from the official transcript of Lewis's speech is inserted in double brackets.

Address by Stephen Lewis at the Opening of the Conference on AIDS and STIs in Africa

Your Excellency, Mr. President; Madam the First Lady of Gabon, Honourable Ministers (including the Minister of Health, who just yesterday joined the ranks of Kenya's famous long-distance runners), Distinguished Guests, Ladies and Gentlemen.

I am obviously delighted to have the privilege of participating in this opening session of ICASA [International conference on AIDS and STIs (Sexually Transmitted Infections) in Africa]. But I'm also aware that the speaking list is lengthy. So quite frankly, I'm going to scrap the remarks I intended to make—primarily on financial resources and treatment—which would have required elaboration and time, and I will use this opportunity instead to pursue the theme of Access to Care in the context of children orphaned by AIDS, and other vulnerable children. I choose to focus on orphaned children because they remain perhaps the most intractable of all issues related to care and support We've obviously been dealing with legions of orphaned children—sometimes adequately, mostly inadequately—for well over a decade But something startling is happening: the increased spiral of adult deaths in so many countries means that the numbers of children orphaned each day is expanding exponentially. Africa is staggering under the load.

In late July, early August I made a trip to Uganda and Zambia with Mrs. Graça Machel. Graça Machel is, as you know, the former Minister of Education of Mozambique, the former First Lady of Mozambique, and is now married to Nelson Mandela. Graça knows every corner of Africa intimately.

The trip left us both with an overwhelming sense of dismay, anxiety, even dread at the situation of orphans. Uganda and Zambia aren't unique; they are mirrors of the continent.

Let me attempt to illustrate some of what we experienced with four brief anecdotes.

First, in Kampala, Graça and I visited Mulago Hospital and the clinic running "Prevention of Mother to Child Transmission Plus". The 'Plus' as you're surely aware, represents overall care for the family—not only the treatment of the mother, but where necessary, her partner and any children who are HIV-positive. It's a new initiative in Africa, with pilots in a number of countries, overseen by the Columbia University School of Public Health working in conjunction with governments, UNICEF and the Elizabeth Glazer Pediatric AIDS Foundation.

The principle here—and it's the most powerful principle that could be invoked—is that the one foolproof way to reduce the orphan population is to keep the mothers alive. At Mulago, we met with a number of women enrolled in the programme who were on antiretroviral treatment. You will know that in most countries, eligibility for treatment requires a CD4 [blood] count below 250 or 200. We met a woman whose CD4 count had dropped to 'one'—yes, '1'—when she was given drugs. It was unheard of. When we saw her, she was a month into treatment, looking good, feeling good, and equally important, her two lovely children played at her feet while their mother laughed with us.

If ever the skyrocketing orphan population—already pushing 13 million— is to be brought under control, then treatment is absolutely imperative to success. When WHO [World Health Organization] says three million people will be treated with anti-retrovirals by 2005, the world must make it happen. Anything less is an ethical abomination.

Second, this time in Zambia, Graça and I were taken to a village where the orphan population was described as out of control. As a vivid example of that, we entered a home and encountered the following: to the immediate left of the door sat the 84-year-old patriarch, entirely blind. Inside the hut sat his two wives, visibly frail, one 76, the other 78. Between them they had given birth to nine children; eight were now dead and the ninth, alas, was clearly dying. On the floor of the hut, jammed together with barely room to move or breathe, were 32-orphaned children ranging in age from two to sixteen. Graça and I looked at each other, and wordlessly communicated the inevitable fear: What in God's name is the future for these youngsters?

It is now commonplace that grandmothers are the caregivers for orphans—I've certainly seen it in every country without exception—but that is no solution. The grandmothers are impoverished, their days are numbered, and the decimation of families is so complete that there's often no one left in the generation coming up behind. We're all struggling to find a viable response, and there are, of course, some superb projects and initiatives in all countries, but we can't seem to take them to scale. In the meantime, millions of children live traumatized, unstable lives, robbed not just of their parents, but of their childhoods and futures. How can this be happening, in the year 2003, when we can find over $200 billion to fight a war on terrorism, but we can't find the money to prevent children from living in terror? [[And when we can't find the money to provide the anti-retroviral treatment for all of those who need such treatment in Africa? This double standard is the grotesque obscenity of the modern world.]]

Third, towards the end of the trip to Zambia, I visited an unplanned community of approximately five thousand people in a tiny settlement just outside Lusaka. The people were bursting with pride: they had graded a rough road and built a community centre, with two of the rooms used as a makeshift school—albeit without benches, desks, black-boards, chalk, paper or pencils. They showed me around and then asked me to say a few words as they gathered in their hundreds on some rocky ground in front of the community centre.

I looked out at the crowd, and was suddenly jolted by a shock of rec-ognition. In the front row were a handful of young mothers, their babies at their breasts. And then, as far as the eye could see into the crowd, made up mostly of women, everyone else was elderly. I asked: "how many of you are grandmothers?" and a forest of hands shot up. I asked: "how many of you are caring for children?" and the same hands shot up.

And I suddenly realized, in a vivid momentary photograph of life, that the entire middle generation seemed to be missing: there were chil-dren, very young women, old women, and a handful of older men—and almost nothing in between. We all know that that's the way the pan-demic works. But there comes a moment when the statistics on paper, the intellectual abstractions suddenly hit home. And at that moment, they hit home for me with an almost visceral force.

Thus it is that orphaned children are the most vexing issue related to care, because there are not enough adults left to do the caregiving—no one to hand down knowledge or experience, or—perhaps most impor-tant of all—values—from one generation to another. It's appalling that so many children are growing up without the kind of emotional anchor that leads to a life of stability.

The final anecdote takes place in Uganda, in Masaka Distrist, at what is known as "ground zero" in the pandemic. It was there that the first case of HIV/AIDS was diagnosed in 1982. The villagers were anxious that we visit one of the many child-headed households, in this instance headed by a fourteen-year-old girl, with two sisters, 12 and 10, and two brothers, aged 11 and 8. Theirs was not a dramatic story of sexual violence or property theft. The injustice of their young lives was much more straightforward, but as deeply compelling.

We went into the children's hut, and Graça told everyone to leave: media, UN staff, hangers-on. The only people who remained behind were a translator and the local World Vision staff woman who helped tend to the village. We sat down side by side with the children, our backs to the wall, the two boys on my left, and the three girls on Graça's right. I had no idea what to expect.

Graça turned to the young girls, and very gently asked: "Have you started to menstruate yet?" Very shyly, the 14-year-old and the 12-year-old girls said they had. "Do you know what it means?" said Graça. "What did you think was happening to you? Do you talk about it with other girls at school? Do you talk about it with your teacher?" And as the two girls answered, in whispered voices, I suddenly realized that they were experiencing their first act of 'parenting' around one of the most anxious moments of a young girl's life. I couldn't get over it. I thought to myself: this is the gap that women all over Africa are trying to fill, but the ratio of children to adults is completely out of whack. (In both Uganda and Zambia, orphaned children constitute 10% or more of the population.) The depth of psychological distress that plagues an entire generation of children numbering in the millions is simply overwhelming, and the struggle to cope is complicated fiercely by a lack of resources at the grass roots.

There are emerging, internationally, strong plans for dealing with orphaned children, plans focusing on the removal of school fees, on school feeding programmes, on the cultivation of school gardens, on health care for vulnerable children, on protection from sexual violence, on significant and lasting community support. Here in Kenya, there's reason for optimism. When you removed primary school fees, Mr. President [referring to Kenyan president Mwai Kibaki], and nearly one and a half million new children turned up at school, you set a precedent for the entire continent. Everyone is talking about it, and a campaign to abolish school fees in Africa is now in the works. What is more, just yesterday, the Women's AIDS Run showed the astonishing solidarity that exists at community level amongst women across this country, in providing access to care and support. Despite their disproportionate levels of infection, and the poisonous absence of any semblance of gender equality, African women are incredibly strong.

But the women can't do it alone. That's how I want to end. You can't do it alone. The women of Africa, all the people of Africa, the governments of

Africa: they can't do it alone. This is a full-blown emergency; in every emergency there is a division of labour. Africa is struggling to hold up its end; the west is not.

I have to say that what's happening to the continent makes me extremely angry. And I don't feel I have to apologize for being angry. The job of an Envoy isn't merely to observe and to report back, but also to identify with those he serves. And I serve Africa. And I'm enraged by the behaviour of the rich powers . . . how much more grievous, by their neglect, they have made the situation in Africa. That isn't to take Africa off the hook: the behaviour of many former African leaders was indefensible. But Africa has moved mountains in the last couple of years, while the western world remains mired in the foothills.

Africa needs no instructions from the west; Africa needs no arrogance from the west; Africa needs no churlish lectures from the west. Africans know HIV/AIDS in all its manifestations and requirements. Admittedly, no one in the world has yet developed a plan for coping with this new phenomenon of millions of orphaned children, but Africa has vastly more experience of orphans than the rest of us, and we should simply stop barracking, and provide the resources for Africa to find solutions. The knowledge and human resources are there: organizations of People Living With AIDS, the inspired youth peer counselors, the political leadership, the religious leadership, the activist women's groups, the community-based and faith-based organizations: there is overwhelming sophistication and strength on this continent. What's missing are the tools and support to do the job. Provide those to Africa, and we can break the back of this pandemic.

But that requires money. Money, for example, for the Global Fund— and the money is not there. Africa is unrelievedly poor. In the straitjacket of poverty, whole countries are fighting for survival. And that, my friends, is morally unconscionable. There's just no time for debate: the crisis has gone on for so long that those who were once orphaned children are now young adults having children of their own. How do you bring up a child, when you've had no parenting to fall back on? It's a blessed thing that against all odds, there remains such tremendous determination and spirit among Africans to save this continent. The world need only feed that spirit, and Africa will prevail.

Source: United Nations. UNAIDS: The Joint United Nations Programme on HIV/AIDS. "Address by Stephen Lewis, the UN Secretary-General's Special Envoy for HIV/AIDS in Africa, at the Official Opening of the XIIIth International Conference on AIDS and STIs in Africa." Nairobi, Kenya. September 21, 2003. www.unaids.org/html/pub/media/speeches01/lewis_speech_icasa_21sep03_en_doc.htm (accessed January 21, 2004).

Report on Allegations of Sexual Misconduct at the U.S. Air Force Academy

September 22, 2003

INTRODUCTION

Numerous allegations of sexual abuse and misconduct among cadets at the U.S. Air Force Academy, together with charges that school officials had failed to respond adequately to those allegations, led in 2003 to multiple investigations, the demotion of one official, the firing of several others, and a hold-up in the Senate on confirming the nomination of the top-ranking civilian official in the air force to be secretary of the army. As the year drew to a close, officials at the academy and in the air force were in the process of implementing several changes at the school designed to reduce the incidence of sexual misconduct and to ensure that future cases were dealt with properly.

The 2003 incidents were the latest in a series of sexual scandals that had dogged the military, beginning with the 1991 Tailhook scandal in which more than eighty women were found to have been groped or assaulted by drunken navy and marine pilots at a convention in Las Vegas. In 1997 allegations of sexual harassment, discrimination, misconduct, and marital infidelity embarrassed the military throughout the year. In highly publicized episodes, a candidate for the nation's top military post was forced to withdraw his name from consideration, the army's senior enlisted man faced a court-martial, and the first female pilot of the B-52 bomber accepted a general discharge from the air force—all because of alleged sexual misconduct. *(Tailhook convention, Historic Documents of 1994, p. 107; 1997 scandals, Historic Documents of 1997, p. 654)*

The Air Force Academy scandal was all the more embarrassing because it unfolded while women in the military were engaged in combat and other dangerous military operations during the U.S. invasion of Iraq, which began on March 20. Several female soldiers were killed during the hostilities, including Lori Ann Piestewa, a Hopi Indian, whose body was recovered during the rescue of her fellow soldier and friend, Jessica Lynch. *(Lynch rescue, p. 142)*

Unfolding Scandal

The scandal at the prestigious school in Colorado Springs, Colorado, came to public attention late in 2002 after Colorado senator Wayne Allard asked the air force to investigate several complaints he had received from female cadets who said they had been disciplined or "hounded out" of the academy after reporting sexual assaults by male cadets. By early 2003, Allard said, his office had heard from twenty-five current and former cadets complaining about the way academy officials had mishandled their reports of sexual assault.

Some of the women later discussed their complaints publicly. Most described a campus climate in which men dominated and women were made to feel weak and unwelcome. Such messages were conveyed in the motto "Bring Me Men," which was prominently displayed in a campus entrance arch, and the letters "LCWB"—shorthand for the vulgar phrase "last class with balls," celebrating the class of 1979, the last all-male class at the academy—were frequently seen on license plates, pep rally signs, and baseball caps. The women said sexual assault was commonplace and victims were warned not to report it for fear of being exposed to shame, retribution, punishment, and even dismissal. Older cadets "tell you to expect getting raped, and if it doesn't happen to you, you're one of the rare ones," one cadet, who left the academy rather than report her assault, told the *New York Times.* "They say if you want a chance to stay here, if you want to graduate, you don't tell. You just deal with it."

Secretary of the Air Force James G. Roche, the service's top civilian officer, ordered an internal investigation of the complaints in January 2003 after he receiving an anonymous e-mail message from a female cadet who said she had been sexually assaulted and warned other female cadets that assaults were "one of the things they don't deal with properly" at the academy. At a hearing on March 6 before Allard and other members of the Senate Armed Services Committee, Roche said the investigation had so far identified fifty-four complaints of rape or sexual assault involving academy cadets in recent years. He said he was turning several of the complaints over to the Defense Department's inspector general for follow-up. Roche also said that changes would be made. "We're learning enough to realize that change must occur—change in the climate, change in how we manage" the academy, he told the panel.

A few days later the air force announced that the academy would separate male and female cadets in different wings of the school's dormitories and provide victims with counselors who could help them with their complaints. In an *Agenda for Change,* released March 16, Roche and Gen. John P. Jumper, the air force chief of staff, ordered several more changes designed to ensure that charges of sexual assault were reported promptly through the chain of command and that the complaints were dealt with thoroughly. Students who reported misconduct were to be granted amnesty for breaking relatively minor infractions such as drinking in the dormitories. The agenda also called for more effective training to deter sexual misconduct, better controls to reduce misuse of alcohol and underage drinking among cadets, and aggressive steps to eliminate sexual harassment and gender bias on campus. The agenda also stressed the importance of leadership training and female role models for the benefit of both male and female cadets.

The first, and by the end of the year only, Air Force Academy cadet to be court-martialed in connection with the scandal was Douglas Meester. The cadet was charged with raping and sodomizing a freshman female cadet in a dorm room in October 2002. Meester maintained his innocence, saying the sex was consensual. His request to resign from the air force rather than face court-martial was denied on October 10, and his case was still pending at the end of the year. If convicted, he faced a maximum sentence of life in prison. Meester's lawyers maintained that the cadet was being made a scapegoat. The academy had also disciplined the woman who made the accusation against Meester for drinking and fraternization with older cadets.

Searching for Accountability

Roche initially refused to hold any academy officials personally accountable for the scandal, placing all the blame on cadets who had committed the assaults and on a climate that had evolved over time. Under increasing pressure from members of Congress, Roche in early April announced the retirement of Lt. Gen. John R. Dallager, superintendent of the academy, and the reassignment of three other high-ranking officials at the academy. Roche subsequently demoted Dallager, stripping him of one of his three stars, which reduced his retirement pay by about $800 a month.

In June the controversy over accountability was heightened when the air force's internal investigation—known as the Working Group—issued a report that minimized not only the scope of the problem, but also the need for leadership accountability. At a June 19 news conference releasing the findings of the internal investigation, Mary Walker, general counsel of the air force, acknowledged problematic "process and cultural factors" at the academy that required correction and added that "less active involvement" from some members of the academy's leadership produced a "less than optimal environment in which to respond to reports of sexual assault." But she denied that academy leadership had avoided or ignored the problem. "We did not find any systematic ignorance of the issue, any systematic avoidance by leadership, and we did not find any wholesale maltreatment of cadets who brought forward allegations," she said. "Instead, we found a fairly comprehensive program to deter sexual assaults. . . ."

Three months later an independent panel created by Congress in April reached the opposite conclusion. In its final report, released September 22, the panel said that the "failure of the Academy and Air Force Headquarters leadership to respond aggressively and in a timely and committed way to eliminate serious causes of problems was a failure of leadership. Those responsible should be held accountable."

Secretary of Defense Donald H. Rumsfeld commissioned the seven-member panel of private citizens, which was chaired by Tillie K. Fowler, a former Republican member of the House from Florida. It reviewed much the same data available to the air force's Working Group. Between January 1, 1993, when the current procedures for dealing with sexual assault were put in place at the academy, and December 31, 2002, there were 142 allegations of sexual assault. Little was known about most of these allegations, the panel said, including whether they were true. Nonetheless, the panel said, leadership "knew or should have known that this data was an unmistakable warning sign and quite possibly signaled an even larger crisis." The report singled out for criticism the four academy officials that Roche had retired or reassigned as well as the new superintendent, Brigadier General David A. Wagie, who had previously served as dean of faculty.

The panel reserved its harshest criticism for the work of the air force's working group and its head, general counsel Walker. The panel said the working group "attempted to shield Air Force Headquarters from public criticism by focusing exclusively on events at the Academy." The panel then listed several instances since 1993 in which air force headquarters had failed to fully investigate sexual misconduct allegations at the academy or to ensure that policy changes were implemented. These matters, the panel, said, were known to Walker and other members of the working group but were not included or only "obliquely referenced" in its report. That failure, the panel said "undermined" the working group's "own credibility and conclusion."

The panel said that Roche and Jumper had made a good start on correcting problems but had not gone far enough in some important respects. The most important shortcomings were the failure of the new policies to ensure "enduring changes in the culture and gender climate" at the Air Force Academy, the failure to provide for permanent and consistent oversight by air force leadership, and the failure to improve the external oversight provided by the academy's Board of Visitors.

The independent panel also said it was troubled by the air force decision to eliminate the policy that allowed sexual misconduct at the academy to be reported in confidence. That change, the panel said, removed "critical options" for victims to receive confidential treatment and counseling and could result in underreporting of sexual assault. To support its call for confidentiality, the panel cited a May 2003 survey of women who graduated from the academy in 2003. The survey found that 81 percent of the female cadets who said they were victims of sexual assault did not report the incident. Nearly one-fifth of female cadets said they had been victims of at least one incident of sexual assault or attempted assault, and more than 7 percent said they were victims of rape or attempted rape. Over the objections of some academy personnel, Roche subsequently announced that the air force would change the policy and give confidentiality to cadets who reported sexual assaults.

In a cover letter Fowler emphasized that the "common failure" in all past efforts to solve the problem of sexual assault at the Air Force Academy was "the absence of sustained attention to the problem and follow-up on the effectiveness of the solution." Whatever steps are taken by the academy, the air force, the Defense Department, or Congress in this case, Fowler said, "it is absolutely critical that those actions be reviewed sometime after their implementation by those in a position to objectively evaluate their effectiveness. The women of the U.S. Air Force Academy deserve no less."

Sen. John Warner, R-Va., chairman of the Armed Services Committee, carried the matter one step further on September 30. During a hearing on the independent panel's report, Warner told Roche that his committee would not vote on Roche's nomination to be secretary of the army until the inspector generals of the air force and the Defense Department included their separate investigations of the way current and former air force officials handled the sexual assault allegations. Those investigations were still pending at the end of the year.

Following are excerpts from the "Report of the Panel to Review Sexual Misconduct Allegations at the U.S. Air Force Academy," released September 22, 2003.

Report on Sexual Misconduct Allegations at the U.S. Air Force Academy

Executive Summary

The United States Air Force Academy is an institution with a proud tradition of service to our nation. The Academy is responsible for the education and training of future officers who will lead our military forces. The Academy's mission is to "inspire and develop young men and women to become Air Force officers with knowledge, character and discipline; motivated to lead the world's greatest aerospace-force in service to the nation". This national interest requires the Academy and its governing leaders to be held to the highest of standards.

The first class of women cadets arrived at the Academy 27 years ago and helped to begin an era of men and women standing together to defend our nation and its freedom. Today, women comprise about one-fifth of our Armed Forces, and their admirable performance and dedication allows our nation to maintain an all-volunteer force.

Sadly, this Panel found a chasm in leadership during the most critical time in the Academy's history—a chasm which extended far beyond its campus in Colorado Springs. It is the Panel's belief that this helped create an environment in which sexual assault became a part of life at the Academy.

The Air Force has known for many years that sexual assault was a serious problem at the Academy. Despite that knowledge and periodic attempts at intervention, the problem has continued to plague the Academy to this day. The regular turnover of Air Force and Academy leadership, together with inconsistent command supervision and a lack of meaningful and effective external oversight, undermined efforts to alter the culture of the Academy. During the ten-year period from January 1, 1993 through December 31, 2002, there were 142 allegations of sexual assault at the Academy, for an average of more than 14 allegations per year. Academy and Air Force leaders knew or should have known that this data was an unmistakable warning sign and quite possibly signaled an even larger crisis.

For example, a February 14, 1997 presentation by the Academy to the Air Force Inspector General ("Air Force IG"), Air Force Surgeon General and the Judge Advocate General of the Air Force acknowledged that statistically, as few as one in ten rapes is reported to authorities. Recently, the Department of Defense Inspector General ("DoD IG") disclosed that a May 2003 survey of Academy cadets showed that 80.8% of females who said they have been victims of sexual assault at the Academy did not report the incident.

Over the past decade, the Academy and Air Force leadership had increasing cause for alarm, and should have aggressively changed the culture that allowed abuses to occur. Unfortunately, Academy leadership acted inconsistently and without a long-term plan. As a result, female cadets entrusted to the Academy have suffered, sexual offenders may have been commissioned as Air Force officers and the reputation of a fine institution has been tarnished.

The sexual assault problems at the Academy are real and continue to this day. According to the May 2003 DoD IG survey of female cadets (Classes 2003–2006), 18.8% reported they have been victims of at least one instance of sexual assault or attempted sexual assault in their time at the Academy. Included in this number are 7.4% of female cadets who said they were victims of at least one rape or attempted rape while at the Academy.

Other recent indicators of problems in the institutional culture are found in the Academy's own survey data, which showed that one in five responding male cadets do not believe that women belong at the Academy. Clearly, the Academy's gender climate has changed little in the past ten years.

Recent widespread media attention caused the Air Force to address the problem of sexual assault at the Academy. In March 2003, Air Force Secretary James G. Roche and Air Force Chief of Staff General John P. Jumper announced a series of directives and policy improvements at the Academy known as the *Agenda for Change*. The new policy corrects many of the conditions contributing to an environment that tolerates sexual misconduct. However, the *Agenda for Change* is only a blueprint, and should be viewed as the initial step in reversing years of institutional ineffectiveness.

In April 2003, Secretary Roche made a step towards serious reform when he replaced the Academy's leadership with a new leadership team comprised of Lieutenant General John W. Rosa, Superintendent; Brigadier General Johnny A. Weida, Commandant of Cadets; and Colonel Debra D. Gray, Vice Commandant of Cadets. Subsequently, General Rosa and his staff have begun implementing changes in the Academy's institutional culture, military training, living environment and sexual assault reporting processes.

The *Agenda for Change* is evidence that the Air Force, under Secretary Roche's leadership, is serious about taking long-overdue steps to correct the problems at the Academy, but in certain respects it does not go far enough to institutionalize permanent change. The most important of these shortcomings are:

- **Culture and Climate of the Academy.** The *Agenda for Change* recognizes that the sexual assault problems at the Academy are related to the culture of the institution, yet it does not go far enough to institute enduring changes in the culture and gender climate at the Academy.
- **Command Supervision.** The *Agenda for Change* does not address the need for permanent, consistent oversight by Air Force Headquarters leadership.
- **External Oversight.** The *Agenda for Change* does not address the need to improve the external oversight provided by the Academy's Board of Visitors.
- **Confidentiality Policy.** The *Agenda for Change* effectively eliminates the Academy's confidential reporting policy for sexual misconduct. In doing so, however, it removes critical options for sexual assault victims to receive confidential counseling and treatment, and may result in the unintended consequence of reducing sexual assault reporting.

The *Agenda for Change* provides several positive changes to the Academy's institutional culture, living environment, and education and training programs. These measures include establishing policies and procedures for: improving the selection and training of Air Officers Commanding to ensure highly-qualified role models and leadership for male and female cadets; promulgating new rules and procedures to maintain dormitory safety and security; setting clearer mandates for cadets to conduct themselves according to the spirit of the Honor Code; requiring academic courses in leadership and character development as part of the core academic curriculum; and improving Basic Cadet Training to reemphasize fair treatment and mutual respect.

The Panel understands that recently implemented policy changes represent significant progress, but concluded that they do not go far enough to institute enduring changes in the institutional culture and gender climate at the Academy.

As far as the Academy's response today to sexual assaults, the *Agenda for Change* established several progressive changes to ensure the Academy is proactive and meaningful when responding. The most noteworthy of these changes is the establishment of an Academy Response Team ("ART") which provides a victim of sexual assault immediate assistance and ensures appropriate command actions. The Panel conducted an extensive review of the ART and is impressed that it presents a significant step toward achieving a consistent, appropriate response to reports of sexual assault, and to restoring trust and confidence in the Academy's handling of them. The Panel is confident that the ART has the necessary foundations to endure beyond the short-term implementation of the *Agenda for Change* and will be available to future generations of cadets.

The Panel is also encouraged that, while not required by the *Agenda for Change*, the Air Force Office of Special Investigations ("AFOSI") has taken the initiative to develop advanced training in sexual assault investigations which shall be provided to its Academy agents.

The Panel is concerned that the *Agenda for Change* essentially eliminates the Academy's confidential reporting policy for sexual misconduct, which removes critical options for sexual assault victims to receive confidential counseling and treatment. Additionally, the Panel believes the new policy overlooks an established form of privileged communication, the psychotherapist-patient privilege, and may have the unintended consequence of reducing sexual assault reporting.

The Panel also reviewed the *Agenda for Change* provision that essentially provides for blanket amnesty to victims of sexual assault. This could have the unintended consequence of creating the misperception that amnesty has been used as a sword, rather than as a shield, by some cadets to avoid accountability for their own misconduct.

In June 2003, after completing her investigation of sexual assault at the Academy, Air Force General Counsel Mary L. Walker released *The Report of the Working Group Concerning Deterrence of and Response to Incidents of Sexual Assault at the U.S. Air Force Academy ("Working Group Report")*. The *Working Group Report* covers many aspects of cadet life, Academy policies and sexual assault reporting procedures in place at the Academy during the last ten years. However, it avoids any reference to the responsibility of Air Force Headquarters for the failure of leadership which occurred at the Academy.

Any credible assessment of sexual misconduct problems over the last ten years must include an examination of the responsibility of both Academy and Air Force Headquarters leadership. The *Working Group Report* failed to do that even though the Air Force General Counsel had access to considerably more information, resources and time for study than did the Panel. The Panel believes that the Air Force General Counsel attempted to shield Air Force Headquarters from public criticism by focusing exclusively on events at the Academy.

The matters listed below are among those known to the members and staff of the Working Group, but not included or only obliquely referenced in its report:

- Since at least 1993, the highest levels of Air Force leadership have known of serious sexual misconduct problems at the Academy;

- Air Force Headquarters knew that over the objections of the AFOSI the Academy maintained unique confidential reporting procedures for sexual assaults deviating from the procedures of the Air Force. Air Force Headquarters failed to monitor how the procedures affected the ability to investigate and prosecute sexual assault offenders;
- In 1996, the Air Force Surgeon General notified the Air Force Chief of Staff of serious sexual misconduct at the Academy, but there is no evidence that the Air Force fully investigated the matter. The Office of the Air Force Surgeon General participated in the General Counsel's Working Group, but the *Working Group Report* omits any reference to this apparently unheeded warning;
- In 1996–1997, a team of lawyers at Air Force Headquarters recommended changes in the Academy's sexual assault reporting procedures. The Academy rejected the changes, and Air Force Headquarters deferred, but failed to monitor whether the procedures were working;
- In 2000–2001, after AFOSI again complained that the Academy's unique sexual assault reporting procedures interfered with its ability to investigate sexual assaults, Air Force Headquarters formed another team to review the procedures. After the Academy and AFOSI reached an agreement to resolve their competing concerns, Air Force Headquarters failed to monitor whether it was ever implemented;
- The 2000–2001 working group was chaired by the Air Force's Deputy General Counsel (National Security & Military Affairs). Three years later, that same attorney led the 2003 Working Group. Nevertheless, the *Working Group Report* makes only a brief reference to the earlier review and fails to disclose the lead attorney's substantial involvement; and
- In 2000, the Senate Armed Services Committee requested an investigation of allegations by the former Air Force Surgeon General that sexual misconduct at the Academy in 1996 had not been investigated or had been covered up. The Air Force Inspector General conducted a limited 30-day review, but did not investigate serious institutional problems after 1996. The *Working Group Report* does not mention the 2000–2001 review, even though the Air Force IG was a member of the Working Group.

The *Working Group Report* failed to chronicle these significant matters and events, undermining its own credibility and conclusion that there was "no systemic acceptance of sexual assault at the Academy [or] institutional avoidance of responsibility." The Panel cannot agree with that conclusion given the substantial amount of information regarding the sexual assaults and the Academy's institutional culture available to leaders at the Academy, Air Force Headquarters and the Office of the Air Force General Counsel. The failure of the Academy and Air Force Headquarters leadership to respond aggressively and in a timely and committed way to eliminate causes of serious problems was a failure of leadership. Those responsible should be held accountable.

The Panel is well aware of the difficulty in holding accountable those who long ago left their positions of responsibility and now are beyond the reach of meaningful action by the Department of Defense. We do believe, however, that to make clear the exceptional level of leadership performance expected of future leaders in these positions and to put the failures of the recently removed Academy leadership in perspective, there must be some further accounting. To the extent possible, the failures of the Academy and Air Force Headquarters leaders over the past ten years should be made a matter of official record.

During the last decade, attention to the Academy's sexual assault problems depended on the interest of the leadership in place and on other competing demands for time and resources. This shortcoming in consistent and effective command supervision co-existed with an absence of meaningful external oversight from entities such as the Academy's Board of Visitors. This resulted in depriving the Academy of long-term solutions to the complex problem of sexual assault.

The Panel examined and reviewed the culture and environment at the Academy. It found an atmosphere that helped foster a breakdown in values which led to the pervasiveness of sexual assaults and is perhaps the most difficult element of the problem to solve.

The American people expect the highest integrity of officers serving in our Armed Forces. This expectation is a strong obligation at the Air Force Academy and was discarded by perpetrators of these crimes over the past decade. The Panel has found deficiencies in the Honor Code System and in the Academy's character development programs that helped contribute to this intolerable environment.

The Panel recognizes that the overwhelming majority of cadets are honorable and strive to live by the core values of integrity, service and excellence. Yet, these core values need to be more effectively interjected into real life situations for cadets.

Through its investigation and examination of this crisis, the Panel has determined the reasons this trusted institution failed many of its students. The Panel offers substantive recommendations to repair the Academy's foundation in hopes of restoring trust in its leadership and its mission. The situation demands institutional changes, including cultural changes. These changes are incremental and cannot be made overnight. Members of this Panel collectively agree it is in our nation's interest to ensure the vitality of this Academy for future generations. . . .

VII. Recommendations

After performing the study required by H.R. 1559 and reviewing the policy changes being implemented by the *Agenda for Change*, the Panel has made various recommendations throughout this report. Those recommendations, organized according to the major area of this report to which they apply, are summarized below.

Awareness and Accountability—Section III

1. The Panel recommends that the DoD IG conduct a thorough review of the accountability of Academy and Air Force Headquarters leadership for the sexual assault problems at the Academy over the last decade. This review should include an assessment of the actions taken by leaders at Air Force Headquarters as well as those at the Academy, including General Gilbert, General Wagie and Colonel Slavec. The review should also consider the adequacy of personnel actions taken, the accuracy of individual performance evaluations, the validity of decorations awarded and the appropriateness of follow-on assignments. The Panel further recommends that the DoD IG provide the results of the review to the House and Senate Armed Services Committees and to the Secretary of Defense.

Command Supervision and Oversight at the Academy— Section IV

2. The Panel recommends that the Secretary of the Air Force adopt the management plan announced on August 14, 2003, including the creation of an Executive Steering Group, as the permanent organizational structure by which the senior Air Force leadership will exercise effective oversight of the Academy's deterrence of and response to incidents of sexual assault and sexual harassment.
3. The Panel recommends that the Air Force extend the tour length of the Superintendent to four years and the tour length of the Commandant of Cadets to three years in order to provide for greater continuity and stability in Academy leadership.
4. The Panel recommends that the Air Force prepare a legislative proposal to revise 10 U.S.C. § 9335(a) to expand the available pool of potential candidates for the position of Dean of Faculty beyond the current limitation to permanent professors.

5. The Panel recommends that the Academy Board of Visitors:
   - Operate more like a corporate board of directors with regularly organized committees charged with distinctive responsibilities (e.g., academic affairs, student life, athletics, etc.). The Board should meet not less than four times per year, with at least two of those meetings at the Academy. To the extent practical, meetings should include at least one full day of meaningful participation and should be scheduled so as to provide the fullest participation by Congressional members. Board members must have unfettered access to Academy grounds and cadets, to include attending classes and meeting with cadets informally and privately; and
   - Receive candid and complete disclosure by the Secretary of the Air Force and the Academy Superintendent of all institutional problems, including but not limited to, all gender related matters, cadet surveys and information related to culture and climate and incidents of sexual harassment and sexual assaults.
6. The Panel recommends that the Air Force prepare a legislative proposal to revise 10 U.S.C. § 9355. The suggested revisions should include both the foregoing and following recommendations:
   - Changing the composition of the Board to include fewer Congressional (and, therefore, more Presidential-appointed) members, more women and minority individuals and at least two Academy graduates;
   - Requiring that any individual who accepts an appointment as a Board member does, thereby, pledge full commitment to attend each meeting of the Board, and to carry out all of the duties and responsibilities of a Board member, to the fullest extent practical;
   - Terminating any Board member's appointment who fails to attend or fully participate in two successive Board meetings, unless granted prior excusal for good cause by the Board Chairman;
   - Providing clear oversight authority of the Board over the Academy, and direct that, in addition to the reports of its annual meetings required to be furnished to the President, it shall submit those reports and such other reports it prepares, to the Chairmen of the Senate and House Armed Services Committees, the Secretary of Defense and the Secretary of the Air Force, in order to identify all matters of the Board's concerns with or about the Air Force Academy and to recommend appropriate action thereon; and
   - Eliminating the current requirement for Secretarial approval for the Board to visit the Academy for other than annual visits.

Organizational Culture & Character Development— Section V

7. The Panel recommends that the Air Force conduct the same review of Non-Commissioned Officer assignment policies and tour lengths at the Academy as it is conducting for officer assignments policies.

8. The Panel recommends that the Academy draw upon climate survey resources at the Air Force Personnel Center Survey Branch for assistance in creating and administering the social climate surveys. Further, the Panel recommends that the Academy keep centralized records of all surveys, responses and reports and keep typed records of all written comments (not abbreviated or paraphrased)—to be provided as an appendix to any report. All such reports must be provided to Academy leadership.

9. The Panel recommends that the Academy place a renewed emphasis on education and encouragement of responsible consumption of alcohol for all cadets.

10. To ensure the safety of every cadet, the Panel recommends that the Academy implement a policy permitting unrestricted (i.e., no explanation required at any time) private access to telephones for the use by any cadet, including Fourth-Class cadets, in an emergency.

11. The Panel recommends that the Center for Character Development education instruction be mandatory for all cadets. The Panel further recommends the cadet curriculum require completion of at least one course per year that emphasizes character values, for which cadets shall receive a grade and academic credit.

12. While the Panel appreciates that the demands on the time of new cadets are significant, we recommend reassessing the training calendar to place prevention and awareness training at a time of day in which cadets will be most receptive to the training session.

13. The Panel recommends that the Academy focus on providing better training to the trainers of prevention and awareness classes including enlisting the aid of faculty members who are well-skilled in group presentation techniques that are effective and energize the cadets, developing small group training sessions which will be more effective than large audience presentations, developing training sessions that educate the students on the reporting process and Air Force Office of Special Investigations investigatory practices and procedures, and establishing a review process for training session materials that includes the use of the Academy Response Team and cadet cadre or some other multi-disciplinary group of experts.

Intervention and Response to Sexual Assault—Section VI

14. The Panel recommends that the Air Force establish a policy that achieves a better balance of interests and properly employs psychotherapist-patient counseling, and its associated privilege, for the benefit of cadet victims. The Panel recommends that the Academy's policy for sexual assault reporting clearly recognize the applicability of the psychotherapist-patient privilege and that the Academy staff the Cadet Counseling Center with at least one Victim Advocate provider who meets the legal definition of "psychotherapist." Further, the Panel recommends that the individual assigned to serve as the initial point of reporting, whether by "hotline" or in person, be a qualified psychotherapist who has completed a recognized rape crisis certification program. Optimally, the Victim Advocate psychotherapist should be in charge of the sexual assault program within the Cadet Counseling Center and will provide direction and supervision to those assistants supporting the assigned psychotherapists.

15. The Panel recommends that the Academy establish a program that combines the existing CASIE [Cadet Advocating Sexual Integrity and Education] program with a Victim Advocate psychotherapist managing the program, and which offers cadets a choice in reporting either to the psychotherapist or to a cadet peer. If reports to CASIE representatives continue to be considered non-confidential, then the Panel recommends that cadets be clearly advised of this fact and further advised that a confidential reporting option is available through the Victim Advocate psychotherapist. As an alternative, it is possible for CASIE cadet representatives to come within the protective umbrella of the psychotherapist-patient privilege if they meet the definition of being an "assistant to a psychotherapist."

16. The Panel recommends that once the psychotherapist reporting option is fully implemented, the Air Force Academy conduct a thorough review of the CASIE program with a view toward either reducing the size of the program or eliminating it entirely. As an interim measure, the Panel recommends that the Academy consider modeling the CASIE program after the Respect Program at West Point, and expand the program to include assisting cadets with issues such as homesickness, respect for fellow cadets and academic difficulties.

17. The Panel recommends that the Academy create a web site devoted to educating cadets about sexual assault.

18. The Panel recommends that the Air Force review the West Point and Naval Academy policies to encourage reporting of sexual assault and adopt its own clear policy to encourage reporting.

19. The Panel recommends that the Academy ensure that the Academy Response Team is always proactively involved in cases in which the victim and potential witnesses are also alleged to have committed misconduct. The Panel also recommends that the Academy Response Team continue to remain involved in a case, in the event that a particular allegation is suspected to be false.

20. The Panel recommends that the Air Force Office of Special Investigations Academy detachment participate fully in the recently established Academy Response Team and use it for informing and educating Academy leadership, victim advocates and CASIE representatives of their responsibilities and limitations. AFOSI's educational efforts should include programs that provide a basic understanding of how and why it takes certain investigative actions, and the benefits of timely reporting and investigation of all sexual assault incidents.

21. The Panel recommends that the Academy take measures to ensure that transportation to the hospital, and any other necessary logistical support, is always available to a cadet who chooses to receive a rape kit examination. In particular, transportation must be provided by an appropriate individual, such as the psychotherapist or Academy Response Team member, who will be discreet and can address the victim's emotional needs during the long car trip to the hospital.

VIII. Conclusion

For nearly fifty years the United States Air Force Academy has been a model academic institution whose mission is to train and educate future leaders of our nation's armed forces.

The institution's mission remains, yet its reputation has lost some of its luster as the school grapples with an institutional crisis that goes beyond its campus in the Rocky Mountains and extends to the halls of Congress and the Pentagon.

The Congress tasked this Panel to examine and investigate this misconduct whose roots, the Panel has found, have gradually grown to the foundation of the Academy and the Air Force. Though the magnitude of this crisis cannot be diminished, the Panel is confident the institution and its principled mission will survive for future generations.

The Panel has sought to help restore the institution's commitment to its cadets and the American people through substantive and constructive recommendations. This is an opportunity to strengthen an institution and help ensure it will have a safe and secure learning environment for all of its cadets.

The *Agenda for Change* is evidence that the Air Force, under the leadership of Secretary Roche and General Jumper, is serious about correcting the sexual assault problems that have plagued the Academy for a decade. The Academy's new leadership team already has implemented many changes to improve the immediate physical security of female cadets and more effectively respond to the needs of victims.

Despite these efforts, and those intended to address the underlying conditions that contributed to an environment in which sexual assaults occurred, the Academy and the Air Force must do much more. In addition to holding accountable those leaders who failed the Academy and its cadets, the Air Force must permanently change the Academy's institutional culture and implement command and oversight improvements that will identify and correct problems before they become engrained in the fabric of the institution.

Change will not happen overnight; nor will it truly be effective without a sustained, dedicated focus by Academy officials and senior Air Force leadership to alter the very culture of the Academy. The reputation of the institution, and by extension the Air Force it serves, depends on finding a lasting solution to this problem. Only then will the Academy restore its reputation and meet the high standards expected by the Air Force and our nation.

Through its work, the Panel found one thing to be certain: it is and should always be an honor to call oneself a cadet at the United States Air Force Academy.

Source: United States. Department of Defense. "Report of the Panel to Review Sexual Misconduct Allegations at the U.S. Air Force Academy." Arlington, Va. September 22, 2003. www.defenselink.mil/news/Sep2003/ d20030922usafareport.pdf (accessed December 12, 2003).

Secretary General Annan on Reform of the United Nations

September 23, 2003

INTRODUCTION

The United Nations in 2003 faced some of the greatest challenges ever in its nearly six decades in existence, and it responded by opening the door to the prospect of radical reform. The U.S.-led war in Iraq, pursued without an explicit authorization from the UN Security Council, forced the world body to confront the question of its relevance to some of the major international issues of the day. A terrorist bombing in Baghdad then forced the UN into a hasty withdrawal of a high-profile mission it had undertaken at U.S. insistence.

Secretary General Kofi Annan on September 23 told the General Assembly that these events, among others, had led the United Nations to "a fork in the road," where the choice was between continuing to struggle or making "radical changes" so it could match the dreams of its founders in 1945. Annan appointed a committee of sixteen "eminent personalities" to reexamine the fundamental assumptions and structure of the United Nations. The panel was to report its findings by the time the General Assembly began its fifty-ninth annual session in September 2004.

The Role of the UN

As the year opened, the UN Security Council tried, and failed, to reach consensus on a United States demand for support for its planned war against Iraq. The UN then watched from the sidelines as Washington went to war, ousted the regime of Saddam Hussein, and began writing its own plan for a political transformation of the country. At Washington's insistence, the UN sent an aid mission to Iraq, headed by Sergio Vieira de Mello, one of the

UN's most successful diplomats. The UN headquarters in Baghdad was bombed on August 19, killing 22 people, including Vieira de Mello, and wounding more than 150 others. A suicide bombing outside the same UN building in Baghdad on September 22 killed 5 Iraqi police officers (but no UN workers) and prompted Annan to withdraw all the UN's non-Iraqi personnel from the country. That step amounted to a humiliating concession that the UN could not protect its own people. That humiliation was compounded on October 22,when a commission appointed by Annan reported that the UN's security apparatus was "dysfunctional." *(Iraq prewar debate, pp. 40, 135; postwar developments in Iraq, p. 933)*

These events prompted a series of steps in which the United Nations began the process of examining its basic operations and working assumptions. The Security Council began its own reassessment on May 13, less than two weeks after President George W. Bush declared the end of major combat in Iraq. Annan, diplomats, and others offered numerous suggestions for ways in which the council could be more successful in dealing with wars, terrorism, and other security challenges. Brian Urquhart, a former head of UN peacekeeping operations, revived an often-discussed but never-adopted proposal for the world body to have its own "rapid reaction force" that could be sent to deal with short-term crises. The Security Council needed to be able to respond with action, not just high-sounding words, he said.

In his September 23 speech to the General Assembly, Annan directly challenged the intellectual justification the Bush administration had offered for its war in Iraq: a new doctrine of preemption, which held that the United States was obliged to confront potential threats to its security, such as Saddam's regime in Iraq, even if it had to do so without UN authorization. "This logic represents a fundamental challenge to the principles on which, however imperfectly, world peace and stability have rested for the last fifty-eight years," Annan said. "My concern is that, if it were to be adopted, it could set precedents that resulted in a proliferation of the unilateral and lawless use of force, with or without justification." *(Bush's preemption strategy, Historic Documents of 2002, p. 633)*

Annan said the preemption doctrine, and its implementation by the United States in the Iraq war, had brought the United Nations "to a fork in the road. This may be a moment no less decisive than 1945 itself, when the United Nations was founded."

To point the way down the correct fork, Annan on November 4 appointed a sixteen-member panel to examine how the United Nations, and its member nations, could better address threats facing the world, including terrorism. Although Annan had promised that such a panel would look for unconventional solutions, all the members were former government or UN officials or well-known international experts. Its chairman was Anand Panyarachun, a former prime minister of Thailand who had also served as that country's ambassador to the United States. The only American on the panel was

Brent Scowcroft, a former air force general and national security adviser to presidents Gerald R. Ford and George H. W. Bush.

Washington and the UN

Perhaps to a greater degree than any other event in recent times, the Iraq debate exposed fundamental disagreements among world leaders about the relationship between the United Nations and the United States, its host and most powerful member. Bush administration officials, from the president on down, said the United States strongly supported the UN as an essential tool to promote peace and prosperity in the world. Administration officials pointed to recent UN successes, such as the rebuilding of East Timor, the World Health Organization's quick action against the Severe Acute Respiratory Syndrome (SARS) epidemic, and the U.N. World Food Programme's response to famines in Africa and parts of Asia. *(SARS epidemic, p. 121)*

The administration said its commitment to the UN also was illustrated by the U.S. return, on October 1, to membership in the United Nations Educational, Scientific, and Cultural Organization (UNESCO). President Ronald Reagan had pulled the United States out of UNESCO in 1984, arguing that the agency was mismanaged and had become a tool for left-wing propaganda attacks against Washington. Bush said on September 12 that he would send U.S. delegates back to UNESCO because it "has been reformed."

Other world leaders, especially in developing countries, said the United States was willing to use the UN to deal with unpleasant situations of no particular interest to Washington—notably famines and wars in Africa. But when it came to matters of deep concern to U.S. interests, such as Iraq, Washington merely wanted the UN to ratify decisions it had already made or to stay out of the way, according to this line of argument.

The fate of the UN mission in Iraq illustrated the differing views of the relationship between Washington and the UN. The Bush administration made it clear that it saw no role for the UN after the war in devising a framework for a new Iraqi government, but it did want UN relief agencies to help with emergency humanitarian needs there. A reluctant Annan responded by sending the mission headed by Vieira de Mello—his most trusted deputy and a man widely considered a leading candidate to succeed Annan as secretary general. The UN mission quickly became a target for attacks by rebels, most of them aligned with Saddam's old regime, who sought to drive the United States out of Iraq. United Nations workers later said many Iraqis viewed the UN mission merely as a component of the massive U.S. presence in their country.

In a December 2 speech in Los Angeles, Annan directly addressed international perceptions of the United States, saying he sensed "a widespread international acceptance of American leadership." But he quickly added that

U.S. leadership "will be more admired than resented, and indeed it will be most effective, when it is exercised within a multilateral framework, when it is based on dialogue and the patient building of alliances through diplomacy, and when it is aimed at strengthening the rule of law in international affairs."

Revising the UN Security Council

Annan offered few hints about his ideas for possible radical changes in the United Nations, but one of them involved perhaps the most contentious issue of all: revising the membership of the Security Council. Under the UN charter, that council was the only United Nations body with any real power to take action against member governments. The Security Council could impose a variety of sanctions and could authorize the use of military force by member nations to back up its decisions. Fifteen nations were represented on the council at any given time: five permanent members (the victors in World War II: Britain, China, France, Russia, and the United States), and ten members representing world regions (each of whom served two-year terms). Each of the permanent members had the power to veto any action by the council as a whole.

During the cold war, the Security Council rarely took effective action in response to world crises because of disputes between the United States and the Soviet Union (which held one of the five permanent seats until its collapse in late 1991, after which Russia assumed the role). The council worked more cooperatively during much of the 1990s, although it was slow to respond to the 1992–1995 wars in Bosnia and Croatia and the 1994 genocide in Rwanda. *(Bosnia, p. 460; Rwanda, p. 1069)*

The Security Council's inability, early in 2003, to come to an agreement on Iraq seemed to threaten a new period of gridlock. The Bush administration had strong support for its war stance from only two other council members at the time (Britain and Spain), while several members were vehemently opposed, including permanent members France and Russia. Later in the year the council gave unanimous support to U.S. requests for authority to manage the affairs of Iraq temporarily, but the council had little choice in the matter since the United States already had some 130,000 troops in Iraq.

The Iraq dispute revived long-dormant interest in expanding the Security Council, and possibly even revising its authority. In his September 23 address, Annan noted that the question of expanding the council had been discussed for more than a decade, and that "virtually all member states agree" that the council should be enlarged. But, he said, "there is no agreement on the details."

Brazil, India, and Japan for years had claimed the right to permanent representation on the council: Brazil because it was the largest country in South America, India because it was the world's second-most populous country (after China), and Japan because it had the world's second largest economy (after the United States). Germany, with the third largest economy, also wanted a permanent seat but hesitated to make the claim directly because of its World War II history. Many African leaders also argued for a regional presence on the council, probably through South Africa.

Expanding the council, especially by expanding the number of permanent members, raised a host of questions, including whether gridlock would become even more likely than in the past. Kim R. Holmes, the U.S. assistant secretary of state for international organizations, raised this issue in an October 21 speech, warning against making the council "oversized and even more unwieldy than it already is."

The Security Council itself engaged in no public debate on the expansion issue during the year. It was widely assumed, however, that Annan's panel on the future of the United Nations would discuss the makeup of Security Council in its 2004 report, perhaps forcing the world body to consider its most important institutional change since its founding in 1945.

Following is the text of a speech by United Nations Secretary General Kofi Annan, delivered September 23, 2003, to the opening session of the United Nations General Assembly.

"Address to the General Assembly"

The last twelve months have been very painful for those of us who believe in collective answers to our common problems and challenges.

In many countries, terrorism has once again brought death and suffering to innocent people.

In the Middle East, and in certain parts of Africa, violence has continued to escalate. In the Korean peninsula, and elsewhere, the threat of nuclear proliferation casts an ominous shadow across the landscape.

And barely one month ago, in Baghdad, the United Nations itself suffered a brutal and deliberate assault, in which the international community lost some of its most talented servants. Yesterday it was attacked again. Another major disaster was averted only by the prompt action of the Iraqi police, one of whom paid with his life.

I extend my most sincere condolences to the family of that brave policeman. And my thoughts go also to the nineteen injured, including two Iraqi

UN staff members. I wish them all a rapid recovery. Indeed, we should pray for all those who have lost their lives or been injured in this war—innocent civilians and soldiers alike. In that context I deplore—as I am sure you all do—the brutal attempt on the life of Dr. Akila al-Hashemi, a member of the Governing Council, and I pray for her full recovery, too.

Excellencies, you are the United Nations. The staff who were killed and injured in the attack on our Baghdad headquarters were your staff. You had given them a mandate to assist the suffering Iraqi people, and to help Iraq recover their sovereignty.

In future, not only in Iraq but wherever the United Nations is engaged, we must take more effective measures to protect the security of our staff. I count on your full support—legal, political and financial.

Meanwhile, let me reaffirm the great importance I attach to a successful outcome in Iraq. Whatever view each of us may take of the events of recent months, it is vital to all of us that the outcome is a stable and democratic Iraq—at peace with itself and with its neighbours, and contributing to stability in the region.

Subject to security considerations, the United Nations system is prepared to play its full role in working for a satisfactory outcome in Iraq, and to do so as part of an international effort, an effort by the whole international community, pulling together on the basis of a sound and viable policy. If it takes extra time and patience to forge that policy, a policy that is collective, coherent and workable, then I for one would regard that time as well spent. Indeed, this is how we must approach all the many pressing crises that confront us today.

Excellencies,

Three years ago, when you came here for the Millennium Summit, we shared a vision, a vision of global solidarity and collective security, expressed in the Millennium Declaration.

But recent events have called that consensus in question.

All of us know there are new threats that must be faced—or, perhaps, old threats in new and dangerous combinations: new forms of terrorism, and the proliferation of weapons of mass destruction.

But, while some consider these threats as self-evidently the main challenge to world peace and security, others feel more immediately menaced by small arms employed in civil conflict, or by so-called "soft threats" such as the persistence of extreme poverty, the disparity of income between and within societies, and the spread of infectious diseases, or climate change and environmental degradation.

In truth, we do not have to choose. The United Nations must confront all these threats and challenges—new and old, "hard" and "soft". It must be fully engaged in the struggle for development and poverty eradication, starting with the achievement of the Millennium Development Goals; in the common struggle to protect our common environment; and in the struggle for human rights, democracy and good governance.

In fact, all these struggles are linked. We now see, with chilling clarity, that a world where many millions of people endure brutal oppression and extreme misery will never be fully secure, even for its most privileged inhabitants.

Yet the "hard" threats, such as terrorism and weapons of mass destruction, are real, and cannot be ignored.

Terrorism is not a problem only for rich countries. Ask the people of Bali, or Bombay, Nairobi, or Casablanca.

Weapons of mass destruction do not threaten only the western or northern world. Ask the people of Iran, or of Halabja in Iraq.

Where we disagree, it seems, is on how to respond to these threats.

Since this Organisation was founded, States have generally sought to deal with threats to the peace through containment and deterrence, by a system based on collective security and the United Nations Charter.

Article 51 of the Charter prescribes that all States, if attacked, retain the inherent right of self-defence. But until now it has been understood that when States go beyond that, and decide to use force to deal with broader threats to international peace and security, they need the unique legitimacy provided by the United Nations.

Now, some say this understanding is no longer tenable, since an "armed attack" with weapons of mass destruction could be launched at any time, without warning, or by a clandestine group.

Rather than wait for that to happen, they argue, States have the right and obligation to use force pre-emptively, even on the territory of other States, and even while weapons systems that might be used to attack them are still being developed.

According to this argument, States are not obliged to wait until there is agreement in the Security Council. Instead, they reserve the right to act unilaterally, or in ad hoc coalitions. This logic represents a fundamental challenge to the principles on which, however imperfectly, world peace and stability have rested for the last fifty-eight years.

My concern is that, if it were to be adopted, it could set precedents that resulted in a proliferation of the unilateral and lawless use of force, with or without justification.

But it is not enough to denounce unilateralism, unless we also face up squarely to the concerns that make some States feel uniquely vulnerable, since it is those concerns that drive them to take unilateral action. We must show that those concerns can, and will, be addressed effectively through collective action.

Excellencies, we have come to a fork in the road. This may be a moment no less decisive than 1945 itself, when the United Nations was founded.

At that time, a group of far-sighted leaders, led and inspired by President Franklin D. Roosevelt, were determined to make the second half of the twentieth century different from the first half. They saw that the human race had only one world to live in, and that unless it managed its affairs prudently, all human beings may perish.

So they drew up rules to govern international behaviour, and founded a network of institutions, with the United Nations at its centre, in which the peoples of the world could work together for the common good.

Now we must decide whether it is possible to continue on the basis agreed then, or whether radical changes are needed.

And we must not shy away from questions about the adequacy, and effectiveness, of the rules and instruments at our disposal.

Among those instruments, none is more important than the Security Council itself.

In my recent report on the implementation of the Millennium Declaration, I drew attention to the urgent need for the Council to regain the confidence of States, and of world public opinion—both by demonstrating its ability to deal effectively with the most difficult issues, and by becoming more broadly representative of the international community as a whole, as well as the geopolitical realities of today.

The Council needs to consider how it will deal with the possibility that individual States may use force "pre-emptively" against perceived threats.

Its members may need to begin a discussion on the criteria for an early authorisation of coercive measures to address certain types of threats—for instance, terrorist groups armed with weapons of mass destruction.

And they still need to engage in serious discussions of the best way to respond to threats of genocide or other comparable massive violations of human rights—an issue which I raised myself from this podium in 1999. Once again this year, our collective response to events of this type—in the Democratic Republic of the Congo, and in Liberia—has been hesitant and tardy.

As for the composition of the Council, that has been on the agenda of this Assembly for over a decade. Virtually all Member States agree that the Council should be enlarged, but there is no agreement on the details.

I respectfully suggest to you, Excellencies, that in the eyes of your peoples the difficulty of reaching agreement does not excuse your failure to do so. If you want the Council's decisions to command greater respect, particularly in the developing world, you need to address the issue of its composition with greater urgency.

But the Security Council is not the only institution that needs strengthening. As you know, I am doing my best to make the Secretariat more effective—and I look to this Assembly to support my efforts.

Indeed, in my report I also suggested that this Assembly itself needs to be strengthened, and that the role of the Economic and Social Council—

and the role of the United Nations as a whole in economic and social affairs, including its relationship to the Bretton Woods institutions— needs to be re-thought and reinvigorated.

I even suggested that the role of the Trusteeship Council could be reviewed, in light of new kinds of responsibility that you have given to the United Nations in recent years. In short, Excellencies, I believe the time is ripe for a hard look at fundamental policy issues, and at the structural changes that may be needed in order to strengthen them.

History is a harsh judge: it will not forgive us if we let this moment pass.

For my part, I intend to establish a High-Level Panel of eminent personalities, to which I will assign four tasks:

First, to examine the current challenges to peace and security;

Second, to consider the contribution which collective action can make in addressing these challenges;

Third, to review the functioning of the major organs of the United Nations and the relationship between them; and

Fourth, to recommend ways of strengthening the United Nations, through reform of its institutions and processes.

The Panel will focus primarily on threats to peace and security. But it will also need to examine other global challenges, in so far as these may influence or connect with those threats.

I will ask the Panel to report back to me before the beginning of the next session of this General Assembly, so that I can make recommendations to you at that session. But only you can take the firm and clear decisions that will be needed.

Those decisions might include far-reaching institutional reforms. Indeed, I hope they will.

But institutional reforms alone will not suffice. Even the most perfect instrument will fail, unless people put it to good use.

The United Nations is by no means a perfect instrument, but it is a precious one. I urge you to seek agreement on ways of improving it, but above all of using it as its founders intended—to save succeeding generations from the scourge of war, to reaffirm faith in fundamental human rights, to reestablish the basic conditions for justice and the rule of law, and to promote social progress and better standards of life in larger freedom.

The world may have changed, Excellencies, but those aims are as valid and urgent as ever. We must keep them firmly in our sights.

Thank you very much.

Source: United Nations. "The Secretary-General Address to the General Assembly." New York. September 23, 2003. www.un.org/webcast/ga/58/statements/sg2eng030923.htm (accessed October 6, 2003).

General Accounting Office
on U.S. Missile Defense

September 23, 2003

INTRODUCTION

The Bush administration pushed ahead with its plan to deploy parts of a missile defense system by late September 2004 despite technical problems that would leave key components of the system inoperable for at least a year or two. Critics said the administration was rushing the system so President George W. Bush would be able to claim it as an important achievement just weeks before the November 2004 elections. Administration officials insisted that protecting the country, rather than politics, was the driving force behind the target date.

For more than five decades, political leaders and defense officials had talked about a system to protect the United States against attacks by missiles carrying nuclear, biological, or chemical weapons. A system called Safeguard, intended to protect U.S. long-range nuclear missiles against an attack by the Soviet Union, was deployed in 1975 but quickly dismantled because it was found to be obsolete. Presidents Ronald Reagan (1981–1989), George H.W. Bush (1989–1993), and Bill Clinton (1993–2001) all proposed systems to protect at least some parts of the United States from missile attacks. The Reagan and Bush proposals resulted in large, expensive research projects but no workable missile defense systems. Clinton's more modest proposal was under development at the time of the 2000 elections; he delayed a decision to deploy the system so his successor could choose the next step. Between fiscal years 1997 and 2001, the Pentagon spent about $6.2 billion developing that system. *(Clinton decision, Historic Documents of 2000, p. 677)*

During his first two years in office, George W. Bush considered a range of missile defense options but ultimately settled on a series of systems, to be phased into service as the technology became available. The first phase would use ground-based missiles—guided by radar and satellites—to attack and destroy incoming missiles as they sped toward the United States. Among the systems to be deployed later were missiles based on ships at sea and lasers mounted on airplanes to attack incoming missiles. In

December 2002 Bush announced that he had ordered the Pentagon to deploy the ground-based antimissile system by September 30, 2004, at the end of the 2004 fiscal year. Work also would continue on the other systems, he said. *(Background, Historic Documents of 2002, p. 1026)*

All the proposals for missile defense systems had generated controversy. For many years, opponents—including some Democrats in Congress and proponents of arms control treaties—argued that building missile defenses merely would fuel an arms race. According to this view, countries that might want to attack the United States would build more and more missiles in hopes of overwhelming the new U.S. defenses. Opponents also criticized missile defense plans because of the high costs and the lack of certainty about whether they would work as advertised.

The opponents lost some of their leverage after the September 11, 2001, terrorist attacks against the United States. Bush used those attacks to argue that the United States needed to step up its defenses against all types of attacks and enemies. Backed by Republican majorities in both chambers of Congress, Bush in 2003 overcame residual opposition to most of his program. Congress approved nearly all the $9 billion he requested for missile defense work in fiscal year 2004. By then, Democratic critics had taken to suggesting that Bush was rushing work on the system so he could claim success during his reelection campaign. "The president's decision to deploy an untested national missile defense system still seems to be motivated more by politics than effective military strategy," Sen. Jack Reed, D-R.I., said. Administration officials rejected that contention and insisted the presidential election had not determined the schedule for deploying the system. Lt. Gen. Ronald T. Kadish, head of the Pentagon's Missile Defense Agency, told the *Washington Post* in late November that he had not been pressured by the administration to rush the schedule for political reasons.

Developing a Ground-Based System

The initial system announced by Bush was to be similar in many respects to what the Pentagon had been working on during the Clinton years. At least in its early phases, the system was aimed almost exclusively at detecting and destroying missiles from North Korea. As of 2003, U.S. intelligence agencies estimated that North Korea had developed a long-range missile capable of hitting Hawaii and parts of Alaska. North Korea had not successfully tested that missile as of 2003, however, and many U.S. experts said it probably would be many years before North Korea would be capable of attacking the United States with a missile powerful enough to carry a nuclear warhead. *(North Korean weapons, p. 592)*

Under Bush's proposed system, ten missiles (called "interceptors) would be deployed: six at Fort Greeley in Alaska and four at Vandenberg Air Force Base in California. Attacking missiles from north Asia would be detected by satellites, which would alert both the missile defense command headquarters in Colorado and an existing early-warning radar, known as Cobra Dane, on Shemya Island at the western extreme of the Aleutian Islands. Once an attacking missile had been detected, at least one of the interceptor missiles would be launched, powered by a three-stage rocket known as a booster. When the interceptor missile reached space, its booster would fall away and a warhead called a exoatmospheric kill vehicle (EKV, in Pentagon terms) would speed toward the enemy missile, guided by updated information sent to it by the Alaskan radar and by data gathered by its own infrared sensors. If all went as planned, the EKV warhead would collide with, and thereby destroy, the enemy missile—a process the Pentagon called "hit to kill." Some experts compared this process—lasting no more than a few minutes altogether—to hitting one bullet with another bullet.

Every aspect of this proposed system was fraught with technical challenges. The Alaska radar was essentially a stop-gap measure, taking the place temporarily of a more sophisticated sea-based radar (called an X-band) that was not scheduled for completion until mid-2005. Development of the booster rocket, needed to get the EKV interceptors into space, had fallen more than two years behind schedule. Two different partnerships of defense contractors were competing for the contract to produce the booster rocket; as of December 2003 neither of the partnerships had successfuly tested a prototype. One of the partnerships, headed by Lockheed Martin Corp., experienced two accidental explosions of rocket fuel, one of which killed an employee in September. Lockheed Martin did not plan a full test of its booster rocket until 2005.

The Pentagon conducted eight tests of the EKV interceptor, five of which it claimed as successes. In the latest test, in December 2002, the interceptor failed to hit its target because of a broken metal pin; no further tests were scheduled until 2004. The Pentagon said the tests had proved that the system would work as planned. Critics, however, said none of the tests had been realistic ones mimicking the conditions an interceptor would face in an actual attack. For example, Philip Coyle, who had monitored all Pentagon testing during the Clinton administration, said the tests of the EKV had been conducted at "unrealistically low speeds and altitudes."

GAO Report

On September 23, the General Accounting Office (GAO), the investigative arm of Congress, published a report suggesting that the Bush administration was pushing deployment of this missile defense system too fast, risking technical failures that would prove more costly in the long run. The GAO noted that the system depended on ten new technologies, only two of which had been proven to work as of mid-2003. The Pentagon expected to complete work on five other technologies in the first three months of 2004, the GAO said.

According to the GAO, the most problematic element of the system involved the radars that were supposed to guide the interceptor missile to its target. The Cobra Dane radar in western Alaska had been used for years to detect test launches of long-range missiles in Russia, but it did not have the ability to process and transmit the information it received instantaneously—or in "real time," in Pentagon terms. The Pentagon was developing new software to give the radar this capability, the GAO said, but the new software would not be completed until early 2004. Moreover, the GAO said, the Pentagon had no plans, during the next three years, to subject the upgraded radar to realistic tests using simulated launches of "enemy" missiles.

Two other radar components of the missile defense system—an existing radar at Beale Air Force Base in California and the proposed X-band radar to be built on a platform in the Pacific Ocean—also were not yet ready for deployment, the GAO said. The Beale radar, which was to help track enemy missiles, might be ready in late 2004. The sea-based radar would not be available for testing until the summer of 2005, at the earliest. Even then, the GAO said, the effectiveness of the sea-based radar would be known only after it was subjected to Pacific Ocean weather.

The GAO recommended that the Defense Department consider "real-world" testing of the Cobra Dane radar in Alaska before deploying the overall system. In response, the Pentagon agreed, and said it was exploring options for such a test. The Pentagon said it was studying another GAO recommendation involving complex changes in the procedures used to verify that private contractors were doing the work they claimed to be doing.

The GAO put the total anticipated cost of the ground-based missile defense system at $21.8 billion through fiscal year 2009. Nearly one-third of that amount, $6.2 billion, was the "sunk cost" of work done during the Clinton administration. Spending would average just under $3 billion annually in fiscal years 2002 through 2005, then tail off to less than $1 billion toward the end of the decade, the GAO said.

Other System Components

Barring last-minute delays, the ground-based missile defense system appeared headed for deployment before the 2004 election, but other aspects of Bush's vision for a comprehensive defense against missile attacks were years away from reality. The Pentagon estimated that these other components would cost about $26 billion between fiscal years 2004 and 2009. Perhaps the most hotly debated part of Bush's long-range plan called for a new panoply of weapons that would destroy enemy missiles right after they were launched—during the first three to five minutes of flight, known as the boost phase.

At Bush's direction, the Pentagon was studying ways of using interceptor missiles and lasers, based on land, at sea, and in space, to attack enemy missiles in the boost phase. One of the technologies, called the Airborne Laser, would use high-intensity lasers mounted in seven Boeing 747 airliners that would patrol the skies near potential enemies; when U.S. satellites detected the launch of an enemy missile, the nearest Airborne Laser would attack the missile and destroy it. This Airborne Laser technology originally was intended to be used against short- and medium- range missiles, such as those fired by armies in conventional battle. The Bush administration decided to adapt the technology for use against longer-range missiles aimed at the United States. The Pentagon had planned to have an experimental version of this laser system ready in 2004 but later pushed the earliest deployment back to 2005.

Another proposed system would use ground-based interceptor missiles to attack enemy missiles in the boost phase. The Pentagon in December awarded a $4.5 billion contract to Northrop Grumman for work on this system, called the Kinetic Energy Interceptor. It was scheduled for deployment in 2010.

On July 15, a panel of twelve scientists assembled by the American Physical Society—a professional association of physicists—issued a report suggesting that the boost phase missile defense proposals stretched the bounds of what might be physically and technologically possible. The scientists noted that detecting and analyzing the launch of an enemy missile would take nearly a minute, leaving only two to four minutes (at most) for a U.S. laser or other device to be fired and reach the missile while it was still in its boost phase. This might work in the case of relatively slow-moving, liquid-fueled missiles, the scientists said. But Iran and North Korea—the two countries that the United States in 2003 considered to be its most likely foes—reportedly were developing much faster solid-fuel missiles that probably would push out of their boost phase before being attacked by a U.S. interceptor.

The physicists noted one other potential problem with the boost phase proposals: In all likelihood, the U.S. interceptor laser or missile would destroy the enemy rocket but not the warhead carrying a nuclear, biological, or chemical bomb. The warhead would then fall back to Earth, hundreds or even thousands of miles from where it was launched.

Following are the "results in brief" from "Missile Defense: Additional Knowledge Needed in Developing System for Intercepting Long-Range Missiles," a report released September 23, 2003, by the General Accounting Office. The report was submitted to Sen. Daniel K. Akaka, D-Hawaii, in his capacity as ranking Democratic member of the Governmental Affairs Subcommittee on Financial Management, the Budget, and International Security. The report raised questions about the Pentagon's plans for deployment of the ground-based component of the missile defense system proposed by President George W. Bush.

"Missile Defense: Developing a System for Intercepting Long-Range Missiles"

MDA [the Missile Defense Agency of the Department of Defense] expects to demonstrate the maturity of most of the ten technologies critical to GMD's [Ground-Based Midcourse Defense] initial performance before fielding of the element begins in September 2004. However, the agency has accepted a higher risk of cost growth and schedule slips by beginning the integration of the element's components before these technologies have been demonstrated. So far, MDA has matured two critical GMD technologies—the infrared sensors of the kill vehicle and the fire control software of the battle management component. But if development and testing progress as planned, MDA expects to demonstrate the maturity of five others—resident in the kill vehicle, interceptor boosters, and the battle management component—by the second quarter of fiscal year 2004 [January to March 2003]. MDA intends to demonstrate the maturity of an upgraded early warning radar—located at Beale Air Force Base, California—in the first quarter of fiscal year 2005 [October to December 2004] and a sea-based X-band radar, located in the Pacific Ocean, in the fourth quarter of that year [July to September 2005]. MDA does not plan to demonstrate through its own integrated flight tests the maturity of a technology resident in the Cobra Dane radar located in Alaska, which will serve as the element's primary radar when GMD is first fielded. Agency officials told us that they may be able to test the radar through the anticipated launch of foreign test missiles. However, it is not clear that testing Cobra Dane in this manner will provide all of the information that a dedicated test provides because MDA will not control the configuration of the target or the flight environment.

MDA estimates that it will spend about $21.8 billion between 1997 and 2009 to develop the GMD element. This estimate includes $7.8 billion to develop and field the GMD Block 2004 [the first phase of the program] capability and to develop the GMD portion of the test bed between 2002 and 2005. For example, the funds will be used to install interceptors at Fort Greely, Alaska, and Vandenberg Air Force Base, California; upgrade existing radars and the test bed infrastructure; and develop the sea-based X-band radar.

MDA has incurred a greater risk of cost growth because for more than a year the agency was not able to rely fully on the data from its primary tool for monitoring whether the GMD contractor was performing work within cost and on schedule—the prime contractor's Earned Value Management (EVM) system. In February 2002, MDA modified GMD's contract to bring it into line with the agency's new capabilities-based acquisition strategy. It took several months to establish an interim cost baseline against which to measure the contractor's performance and 13 months to complete revisions to the baseline. Also, MDA and the contractor did not complete a review until July 2003 to ensure that the revised baseline was accurate and that contractor personnel were correctly using it to measure performance.

This review was of particular importance because an earlier review revealed significant deficiencies in the contractor's development and use of the initial contract baseline. Until this review was completed, MDA did not know for sure whether it could rely fully on the data from its EVM system to recognize and correct potential problems in time to prevent significant cost increases and schedule delays.

We are making recommendations that MDA (1) consider adding a test of the effectiveness of the radar in Alaska; and (2) ensure that procedures are in place that will increase MDA's confidence in data from its EVM system. DOD concurred with our first recommendation and partially concurred with the second. In commenting on the draft report, DOD stated that the feasibility of these procedures will be determined and that a portion of the work is already being accomplished.

Source: U.S. General Accounting Office. "Missile Defense: Additional Knowledge Needed in Developing System for Intercepting Long-Range Missiles." GAO–03–600, September 23, 2003. www.gao.gov/docdblite/-summary.phprecflag=&accno=A08177&rptno=GAO-03-600 (accessed October 14, 2003).

President of Argentina on Economic Recovery

September 25, 2003

INTRODUCTION

Argentina elected a new president in 2003 and made significant progress in recovering from an economic crisis that had thrown the country into a deep depression during the previous two years. The recovery was far from complete, however, and international lenders were demanding difficult reforms as the price of pouring in new money that Argentina would need for long-term economic growth.

An estimated one-half of Argentina's 36 million people had been thrown into poverty by the depression of 2001–2002, but the government had little money or borrowing power to help them. Pot-banging demonstrators took to the streets during the year to demand jobs; the official unemployment rate remained higher than 20 percent, and many experts said the real jobless rate was much higher. Economic reforms demanded by international lenders might improve the economy over the long run and thus help lift many Argentines out of poverty, but they might also make life more difficult for many in the short term. During his first months in office, President Nestor Kirchner appeared to be maneuvering skillfully between these competing demands and interests. *(Background, Historic Documents of 2002, p. 80)*

Kirchner Elected, by Default

Argentina's default on its more than $100 billion in public debt at the end of 2001 set off a series of events that rapidly dragged the country into economic and political instability. The country went through five presidents in two weeks before Eduardo Duhalde, a leader of the Peronist Party who had run unsuccessfully for the presidency in 1999, was given the office and began implementing budget and economic policies that offered some hope for recovery. Duhalde announced in 2002 that he would not seek the presidency in elections scheduled for 2003.

Duhalde's withdrawal from the race immediately gave the front-runner status to Carlos Menem, who had been president during much of the 1990s. Duhalde had been Menem's vice president, but the two men quarreled and had become bitter enemies. Menem had promoted the free-market, free-trade economic policies that at first made the country's economy an international model but that—following the crash of late 2001—Duhalde and many other Argentines said made the country vulnerable to the whims of international investors. Menem's presidency also was known for its corruption—extensive even by Latin American standards—and unbridled spending. Menem had been charged in 2001 with illegal arms smuggling while president but had managed to escape prison when the charges were dropped.

Hoping to keep Menem from gaining back the presidency, Duhalde nominated Kirchner as his favored successor. Also a member of the long-dominant Peronist Party, Kirchner was governor of the Patagonian province of Santa Cruz, known for its sheep farms and oil wells. Although he had served as governor for three terms, Kirchner was not widely known nationally and was unknown on the international stage.

The first round of voting was held April 27, with Argentines able to choose from nineteen candidates that spanned the broad range of the country's political spectrum. Menem, by far the best known candidate, finished first with 24 percent of the vote, and Kirchner was close behind with 22 percent. The two men could not have been more of a contrast in style. The flamboyant Menem portrayed himself as a latter day version of Argentina's notorious populist leader Juan Peron. The sedate Kirchner appealed to voters on the basis of his left-of-center policy prescriptions and his reputation for running a clean government. Buenos Aires political commentators described Kirchner as a colorless country bumpkin, someone who might be taken in by the sharp-elbowed politicians who had long dominated Argentina at the national level.

Menem's first-place finish appeared to make him the favorite for the runoff scheduled three weeks later. He quickly found, however, that only a minority of voters yearned for the days of his high-flying presidency, and a large majority could find nothing kind to say about him. Plummeting rapidly in the polls, Menem unexpectedly announced on May 14 that he was pulling out of the race, leaving the presidency to Kirchner. That move spared voters the task of trudging back to the polls, but it also denied Kirchner the mandate he would have received from an overwhelming electoral victory. Kirchner denounced Menem for "running away" from the voters in hopes of weakening the new government.

Kirchner may have been denied his formal mandate, but when he took office on May 25 public opinion polls gave him an approval rating of 70 percent. Voters said they had high hopes and expectations that he would turn around the economy and end the political infighting that had contributed to the depression. As he had during the campaign, Kirchner adopted a populist tone in his inaugural speech, saying Argentina would repay its debts but foreign lenders "will only get their money if Argentina does well."

Kirchner quickly moved to make Argentines feel better about their troubled country. He launched a campaign promoting what he called "Argentina: Un Pais en Serio" (Argentina: A Serious Country) and ousted judges, military officers, and police officials whose corruption had long been considered a public disgrace. Kirchner's actions against these holdovers from previous governments were widely popular, but opposition leaders and some political commentators also expressed concern that he was attempting to replace the country's old political establishment with a new one beholden to him.

Kirchner's standing was bolstered in November by legislative and municipal elections that gave the Peronist Party a majority in both houses of Congress and a strong majority of provincial governorships. Even so, continuing splits within the party made it likely that Kirchner would have to struggle to win passage of any proposals that might be highly controversial.

Agreement with the IMF

Breaking with symbols of the past helped establish Kirchner's leadership style and enhance his popularity, but the real test of his presidency would be his ability to contribute to a lasting economic revival. His central tasks included dealing with the country's gigantic public debt, which had grown to about $185 billion; ensuring that fiscal and monetary policies would stimulate economic growth; and finding ways to ease the immediate pain of the millions of Argentines thrown into poverty. Dealing with the last problem meant spending money, which Argentina did not have and which foreign lenders were no longer willing to provide.

A little more than three months after taking office, Kirchner struck a bold deal with the International Monetary Fund (IMF) that offered at least a promise of helping Argentina find its way out of its economic malaise. On September 10, in the midst of negotiations with the IMF, Kirchner's government defaulted on a $2.9 billion interest payment. The default signaled that Kirchner was unafraid to damage Argentina's already poor credit rating if, by doing so, he could win better terms on future lending. His gamble paid off, and the next day the IMF agreed to refinance about $21 billion in lending to Argentina on generous terms requiring the government to pay only interest for the next three years. That deal covered $12.5 billion that Argentina owed the IMF directly, plus $5.6 billion owed the World Bank and the Inter-American Development Bank, and about $3 billion owed European and other international lenders. By lowering Argentina's debt service, the agreement helped postpone cuts in domestic spending that might have slowed short-term economic recovery. One day after the IMF approved the new loan terms, Argentina made the $2.9 billion payment on which it had defaulted.

To get that debt relief, Kirchner promised to make important long-term economic reforms the IMF had been demanding—but he was given until 2005 to make some of most painful changes. The chief items included reforming the tax system to reduce favoritism and encourage investment; raising utility prices, which had been frozen since January 2002, so the country's utilities industries would not go bankrupt; recapitalizing the banking system, which was awash with bad loans; and revising the basic system of government finance, which gave provinces near total freedom to spend the federal government's tax dollars.

The IMF's board of governors approved the new lending package on September 20. Anne Krueger, the IMF's deputy managing director, acknowledged that the deal posed "risks" for the IMF and other lenders because some reforms "that are crucial to sustainability will only be formulated at a later stage." In particular, she noted that the government had until 2004 to propose, and until 2005 to enact, tax reforms and proposed controls over spending by the provinces.

Argentina also promised to negotiate with private lenders—primarily international commercial banks and pension funds—who held bonds and other debt originally valued at nearly $100 billion. The government began negotiations with those lenders in September and made an initial offer that would pay back a net of only about 10 cents on the dollar. A group of Argentina's largest creditors countered in December with a demand for payment of about 65 cents on the dollar. Negotiations to narrow the 55-cent difference were expected to be difficult and last well into 2004. Even if an agreement could be reached, Argentina faced a tough sell in getting private lenders to reopen their pocketbooks for new loans anytime soon.

In an address to the United Nations General Assembly on September 25, Kirchner sought to emphasize that international creditors shared the blame for Argentina's troubles. Kirchner noted that the IMF, the World Bank, the United States, and other international powers had pressured Argentina to adopt free-market economic policies that, he said, "led us to such heavy indebtedness." Those institutions, he said, "should accept their own share of responsibility" for getting Argentina ought of debt. Repeating the populist rhetoric that had bolstered his standing at home, Kirchner also lashed out at economic models "in which the prosperity of some is based on the poverty of others."

Some economists said Argentina's best hope for a quick infusion of cash was among its own people. According to some estimates, Argentines had stashed $100 billion or more in overseas bank accounts and investments during the economic crisis and might have another $20 billion in cash at home—outside the troubled banking system. If Kirchner managed to stimulate enough confidence among Argentines that the economy was on the mend, some of their own money would help speed the cure.

By year's end the initial signs of a recovery were promising. The IMF and other economic forecasters said Argentina's gross domestic product grew by 8 percent in 2003 and was on a pace to grow by about 5–7 percent in 2004. At that rate, the economy would return to its previous peak, reached in 1998, by 2005.

The Legacy of the Dirty War

Kirchner may not have been as flamboyant as Menem, his election rival, but he proved to be a master of political symbolism. This skill was particularly noticeable in his insistence that Argentina confront some of the demons of its past, including the "dirty war" against dissenters during the military's 1976–1983 dictatorship.

During their seven-plus years in power, Argentina's right-wing generals had brutally suppressed dissent, especially by those on the left. Regime opponents were kidnapped and killed; they became known as "the disappeared"— people who simply vanished and were never heard from again. International human rights groups estimated that 20,000 to 30,000 people were killed this way. The military gave up power, in disgrace, after losing a brief war with Britain over the Falkland Islands. *(Disappeared persons, Historic Documents of 1983, p. 455, 1984, p. 789; Falkland war, Historic Documents of 1982, p. 283)*

The dirty war had been the one aspect of Argentina's past that subsequent political leaders had been most reluctant to confront. The first post-dictatorship civilian government—headed by Raul Alfonsin, a lawyer who had become famous representing victims of the dictatorship—prosecuted and jailed some generals but then enacted two amnesty laws for others. Menem in 1990 pardoned the generals who had been imprisoned.

In his inaugural address, Kirchner signaled that he intended to revisit the consequences of the dirty war. "I am part of a decimated generation, and I do not believe in the axiom that when you govern you trade convictions for pragmatism," he said. Kirchner himself had been a student radical who was imprisoned twice during the dirty war.

Responding to Kirchner's pressure, both chambers of Congress in August voted to repeal the two amnesty laws from the mid-1980s. Conservatives hotly resisted the move, arguing that it violated the constitution and threatened to reopen old wounds that should remain closed. Families of victims of the dirty war celebrated the end to what they called "impunity" for the generals. "Justice is finally coming to life in this country after a long struggle," Berta Schuboroff, a member of one group pushing for trials of the generals said. At year's end the amnesty repeal legislation was under review by the Supreme Court.

Kirchner also took steps during the year to reopen investigations into two bombings that had raised charges of anti-Semitism in Argentina, which had a sizable and vibrant Jewish minority. In 1992 a bomb destroyed the Israeli embassy in Buenos Aires, killing twenty-eight people. A bomb in 1994 destroyed a Jewish community center in the city, killing eighty-five people. Menem, who had been president at the time, blamed the 1994 bombing on Iranian terrorists, and the government issued arrest warrants for four Iranian officials it said had planned the attack. But the government provided little support for that claim, and key evidence disappeared. After taking office, Kirchner signed an executive order that gave prosecutors access to secret intelligence files about the bombing. Kirchner called the government's failure to find those responsible for the bombings a "national disgrace."

Following are excerpts from an address delivered September 23, 2003, by Nestor Kirchner, president of Argentina, to the United Nations General Assembly in which he called for international support for his program to revitalize Argentina's economy.

Statement by the President of the Argentine Republic to the United Nations

Mr. President:

I would first like to congratulate you on your appointment to preside over these sessions and, in doing so, I would also like to congratulate the outgoing president, Mr. Jan Kavan, on his work in conducting this Assembly.

On behalf of our government, I would also like to reiterate our recognition towards the action for peace and multilateralism carried out by the Secretary General, Mr. Annan, and to express our solidarity in the face of the criminal attack, which cost the lives of several members of this organization.

We have come from the South to attend this General Assembly, in the firm belief that revitalizing this global representation forum is essential in order for international law to become once again the rational instrument enabling us to resolve conflicts and face threats. Giving back to this Assembly the major political role it played in the early days of the

United Nations Organization is key to strengthening the value of security for all citizens of the world.

It is a fact that multilateralism was the foundation on which this organization was created. But it is also an undeniable fact that the Cold War and bipolarity that became the hallmark of the world from Yalta to the fall of the Berlin Wall, undoubtedly conditioned the instruments and legislation that were adopted within its framework.

An objective look at the situation—beyond any individual assessment that may be made by the members of this organization—evidences technological, military and economic supremacy of one country over the rest, which is the hallmark of the world's current situation.

We therefore consider it necessary to reaffirm our deep support for the purposes and principles inspiring the United Nations, both in order to have an organization actively participating to further peace as well as to promote mankind's social and economic development.

However, reaffirming multilateralism cannot be limited to a mere exercise in rhetoric, but requires a twofold strategy: on the one hand, intellectual openness, in order to understand the full extent of the new scenario, which is an objective one. On the other hand, a rethinking of instruments and rules making it possible to deal with this new reality using the same approach taken during bipolarity in order to prevent the world from going up in flames.

Multilateralism and security are inseparable elements, but they are not the only ones in this new equation.

The world is going through times of change, against the backdrop of globalization, which creates unprecedented opportunities as well as risks.

The greatest risk is the widening of the gap between the rich and the poor. Central and peripheral countries are not mere nuances in an intellectual exercise, nor are they a matter of ideology. Quite on the contrary, they reflect a grim reality in terms of unprecedented poverty and social exclusion. Our priority must be to ensure that globalization works for all and not for just a few.

This is because taking steps to improve the development of peripheral countries must no longer be only a matter of social sensibility for central countries, but also because it is a matter that has an impact on their own situation and on their own security.

Hunger, illiteracy, exclusion and ignorance are some of the basic ingredients that breed conditions for the proliferation of international terrorism or for the development of dramatic mass processes of true national migration, which have a resulting cultural, social and economic impact and, as an inevitable consequence, the impairment of the value of security for central countries.

Economic integration and political multilateralism hold the key to a future in which the world is a safer place. We need to build global institutions and effective partnerships, within the framework of fair and open trade, in addition to bolstering support for the development of those most relegated.

Encouraging collective progress and security in an intelligent way requires an understanding of the fact that the value of security is not only a military concept but one which stems from a preexisting political, economic, social and cultural scenario. Those are the central tasks for the main players on the international agenda.

In this framework, the relations of countries such as ours, and others, with the rest of the world are marked by a crushing, gigantic debt owed to both multilateral financial institutions as well as private creditors.

As a country, we recognize our responsibility for having adopted the policies of others, which led us to such heavy indebtedness. But we also urge the international financial institutions, which in dictating such policies, contributed to, encouraged and favoured the growth of debt, to accept their own share of responsibility. It is almost a truism to point out that when a debt grows to such an extent, it is not only the debtor that is responsible, but also the creditor.

It is therefore necessary to acknowledge an actual, verifiable and, to a certain extent, common sense fact: the terrible difficulties involved in paying such a debt. Without concrete international assistance aimed at enabling indebted countries to rebuild their economic solvency and, consequently, their payment capacity, and without measures to promote their growth and sustainable development by taking concrete steps to promote their market access and the growth of their exports, debt repayment becomes an impossible dream.

Developing exports which add value to the natural resources that most indebted countries have, can lay the foundations for the first steps towards sustainable development, without which creditors will have to face their losses without any other realistic options. No one is known to have succeeded in getting their money back from the dead.

In furtherance of this objective, i.e. of making a country viable in order for it to be able to pay its debts, it would be of great help to intensify multilateral negotiations for elimination of tariff and nontariff barriers hindering access of our exports to the markets of developed countries, which have larger purchasing capacity.

The fact is that in international trade in food products, for example, which is Argentina's main export item, export and production subsidies continue, as well as tariff quotas, unjustified phytosanitary measures and tariff ladders, which distort the terms of exchange for primary products and seriously hamper market access for products with higher added value.

The failure of the WTO [World Trade Organization] negotiations at Cancun should serve as a reminder to us in this regard, and should be remedied by achieving the sort of link we are highlighting as desirable between new business opportunities in international trade, growth of indebted countries and their debt repayment capacity. It is a paradox, and almost ridiculous, that we should be expected to pay our debt while at the same time we are prevented from trading and selling our products.

On the other hand, although it is true that the objectives of multilateral institutions such as the International Monetary Fund [IMF] include "shortening the duration and lessening the degree of imbalance in the balance of payments of member countries", as well as to "instill confidence in them through resources in order to create the opportunity for correction without the need to resort to measures that are detrimental to national or international prosperity", it is also necessary to redesign institutions such as the IMF.

Redesigning multilateral lending agencies should include changing their paradigms, so that the success or failure of economic policies is measured in terms of success or failure in the fight for growth, equitable distribution, the fight against poverty and in ensuring adequate employment levels.

This new millennium should put an end to adjustment models in which the prosperity of some is based on the poverty of others. The dawn of the 21st century should signal the end of an age and the beginning of a new cooperation between creditors and debtors.

In a nutshell, it is essential to note the close connection between security, multilateralism and economics.

The defense of human rights is a central element of Argentina's new agenda and we therefore insist on permanently supporting the strengthening of the international system for protection of human rights and the trial and sentencing of violators, all of this based on the view that respect for persons and their dignity arises out of principles preceding the development of positive law and whose origins can be traced back to the beginning of human history.

Respecting diversity and plurality and relentlessly fighting against impunity are principles that have been unwaveringly pursued in our country ever since the tragedy of recent decades.

We strongly advocate a peaceful settlement of international disputes, particularly in a matter as dear to our feelings and interests as our sovereignty dispute with regard to the Malvinas, South Georgias and South Sandwich Islands and their surrounding maritime space.

The United Nations has recognized that this is a colonial situation maintained by the United Kingdom and that it must be settled through bilateral negotiations between the Argentine Republic and the UK.

We value the role of the United Nations Special Committee on Decolonialization and express our full willingness to negotiate in order to conclusively settle this long-standing dispute, a permanent objective for Argentina. We urge the United Kingdom to agree to resume bilateral negotiations to resolve this major issue [referring to the dispute between Argentina and the United Kingdom over the Falkland Islands].

As long as we are talking about the southern reaches, we undertake to protect the interests of the international community in Antarctica, ensuring that the activities carried out there are consistent with the Antarctic Treaty and with the Madrid Protocol on environmental conservation.

We shall take steps at the relevant fora to enable the installation of the authorities and the operation of the Antarctic Treaty Secretariat at its designated seat, the City of Buenos Aires.

We express our support and wish for stable and lasting peace in the Middle East, based on the inalienable right to self-determination of the Palestinian people to an independent and viable State, while at the same time recognizing the right of Israel to live at peace with its neighbors, within safe and internationally recognized borders.

We have mentioned progress and collective security as the global challenges of our time. We have highlighted the very close link there is today between economic problems and security. We firmly condemn all terrorist actions.

And we know what we are talking about. In 1992 and 1994 we suffered firsthand our own Twin Towers [a reference to the September 11, 2001, attacks against the World Trade Center towers in New York City]. The attacks against the Israeli Embassy and the Jewish community centre AMIA [in Buenos Aires] took the lives of over one hundred of our compatriots. We can bear witness to the need to fight effectively against the new threats posed by international terrorism.

The vulnerability of all countries in the international community to this scourge can only be reduced through intelligent concerted and multilateral action sustained over time. The fight against terrorism requires a new rationality. We face an enemy whose logic is to trigger reactions in symmetry with its actions. The worse the better is the scenario it longs for, and that logic partly accounts for the growing, almost cinematographic, spectacularity of its operations. Legitimacy in the response and the support of international public opinion are two basic assumptions to deal with these new forms of violence.

This view places the problem of terrorism in a dimension exceeding a unilateral view or military solution. On the contrary, merely responding through the use of force, however impressive such force may be or appear to be often ends up with the perpetrators being presented as victims. This means closing in a perfect circle the sort of perverse mindset to which we have referred.

As can be seen, in view of the complexity of the situation, it is no longer useful to take shelter in old alignments, anachronistic ways of thinking or dated structures. The new challenges call for different and creative solutions, in order not to be left behind by the changes in the world, in the technological, economic, social and, undoubtedly, in the cultural field.

Let us rise to the challenge of "thinking new" for a new world. Combining different ideas and creating practical means for them to be put to the service of the peoples we represent is our duty.

Thank you very much.

Source: Argentine Republic. Permanent Mission of Argentina to the United Nations. *Statement by Dr. Nestor Carlos Kirchner, President of the Argentine Republic to the United Nations General Assembly.* September 25, 2003. www.un.int/argentina/english/statements/ miscelaneous/ President%202003.htm (accessed January 15, 2004).

Agreement on Interim
Security for Sudan

September 25, 2003

INTRODUCTION

The twenty-year civil war in Sudan edged closer than ever to a final settlement during 2003. The conflict—over religion, political power, territory, and oil wealth—had long proven resistant to international mediation. But leaders of the warring parties—the Islamist Arab-dominated government based in northern Sudan and black African rebels from the south—negotiated directly with each other during the year and made significant progress in resolving some of their core differences. International diplomats expressed hope that a final peace agreement could be reached in 2004. If successful, a peace agreement negotiated primarily by the warring parties—who would have the greatest stake in carrying it out—might set an example for other African countries beset by civil war. Many of the continent's other wars in recent years had been settled with peace agreements that essentially were imposed by a combination of other African countries, Western powers, and the United Nations; those peace agreements tended to be fragile ones.

One dark cloud hanging over the peace process was an upsurge of fighting, indirectly related to the main war, in the Darfur region of western Sudan. That fighting displaced an estimated 500,000 people from their homes and sent another 70,000 refugees streaming into neighboring Chad between April and September 2003. Darfur was home to about one-fifth of Sudan's population and represented a mix of about eighty tribes and ethnic groups. Relief workers were unable to reach most of the displaced civilians because of the fighting; nine Sudanese relief workers employed by the U.S. Agency for International Development were killed in clashes in October. The UN's Office for the Coordination of Humanitarian Affairs in December called the situation "one of the worst in the world."

An estimated 2 million people had died during Sudan's main civil war, most as a result of famines that were made worse by the conflict. The United Nations said Sudan in 2003 had about 4 million "internally displaced" people (those forced from their homes but remaining within the country), the greatest number anywhere in the world. Another half-million had taken refuge in neighboring countries.

Background

Sudan was the largest country in Africa in terms of land area—about one-fourth as big as the United States. Its population of about 30 million was split along a north-south divide resulting from the country's tumultuous history. The northern three-fourths of Sudan was dominated by Arabs whose ancestors had conquered the region during the rapid growth of the Islamic world in the seventh and eighth centuries. Southern Sudan, by contrast, had remained part of black Africa; most of the people there adhered to indigenous religious beliefs, and a powerful minority had adopted Christianity. Britain and Egypt, which had jointly controlled the country since 1899, granted independence in 1956 and drew a boundary dividing Sudan into north and south "administrative" areas. Sudan's first civil war, between the north and the south, erupted right after independence and raged until 1972, when a left-wing military dictatorship ceded some aspects of autonomy to the southern provinces. That arrangement calmed the fighting temporarily but did not resolve the underlying disputes over ethnicity and power.

Conflict again broke out into the open in 1983 when the government in Khartoum moved to enforce Islamic law, known as *Shariah,* nationwide. Several rebel groups, most based in the south, began fighting the government, with a demand for complete independence. Sudan in the meantime endured several famines that were caused by drought but intensified by the fighting, which stymied cultivation of crops and relief efforts. Some rebel factions in the south reached a peace accord with the government in 1997, but the largest guerrilla force, the Sudan People's Liberation Movement and Army (best known as SPLA), refused to lay down its arms. Its leader was John Garang, a charismatic Christian who had won strong political backing from some evangelical groups in the United States and Europe. Garang was educated in the United States and received a doctorate from Iowa State University. The influence of Christian groups reinforced pressure that the U.S. government had placed on Khartoum because of its alleged support for, or at least tolerance of, Islamist terrorists. Garang's SPLA controlled most of southern Sudan except for seven cities that remained in the hands of the national army or militias associated with it.

During the late 1990s the conflict took on an important economic dimension, with the exploitation of Sudan's substantial oil resources. Oil had been discovered in 1978, but the country's wars and political instability made it an unattractive place for international oil companies to invest. That changed in 1998 when Talisman Energy, of Canada, began developing oilfields in southern Sudan and was quickly joined by a Swedish-Austrian partnership.

During the next four years the government evicted hundreds of thousands of people—some estimates put the figure as high as 600,000—to make way for the oilfields. Pressured by international human rights organizations to pull out of Sudan, the three Western companies in 2002–2003 sold their stakes to the state-owned oil firms of China, India, and Malaysia. The Sudanese government reportedly earned about $1 billion annually in oil revenues, on production of about 250,000 barrels a day.

Sudan's war alarmed all its neighbors in central and east Africa, several of whom had experienced their own internal conflicts based on tribal or territorial disputes. Neighboring countries were especially concerned that a breakup of Sudan along ethnic lines might encourage even more conflict in the region. Colonial powers had drawn the boundaries of African countries for their own convenience, without regard to the local populations. Even so, African leaders since independence had come to regard the boundaries as offering a form of protection against the breakup of the continent into hundreds of ethnic-based ministates.

In 1994 Kenya—Sudan's neighbor to the southeast—launched an attempt to mediate peace between the warring Sudanese parties. The talks were sponsored by a regional group called the Intergovernmental Authority on Development (IGAD) and moderated by Kenyan general Lazaro K. Sumbeiywo. The United States, Britain, and Norway participated in the talks, and France and the Arab League sent observers. The negotiations continued all through the 1990s but made little headway until 2002, when former Sen. John S. Danforth, R-Mo., acting as a special envoy for the president, persuaded both sides that ending the war would bring substantial economic benefits to Sudan, in the form of trade and aid for economic development.

On July 20, 2002, the government and rebels reached their first significant agreement on the political issues between them. Signed after weeks of negotiations in the Kenyan city of Machakos, the agreement called for a six-year "interim" period of joint government between the north and the south, after which the south would hold a referendum to decide whether to remain part of Sudan or secede. The government won its key demand—a right to retain Islamic law throughout the north of the country. This agreement was followed on October 15, 2002, by a formal cease-fire.

More Steps Toward Peace in 2003

All through 2003 both sides expressed high hopes that the political accord would lead to a resolution of all other outstanding issues. The hopes were especially high after April, when Sudan's president, Omar Hassan al-Bashir, met in Nairobi for the first time with Garang, the southern rebel leader. Those hopes crashed in May, however, when the international mediators tried to get the two sides to consider a bundle of compromises that dealt with all the remaining points in dispute. The government rejected that comprehensive approach, and further talks were put on hold.

The deadlock was broken by the first direct involvement of Sudan's vice president, Ali Osman Taha, whom diplomats had considered a hard-line opponent of concessions to the south. Encouraged by Kenyan diplomats, Taha agreed to participate directly in negotiations and, in midyear, reportedly won a power struggle within the Khartoum government over his role.

On September 5 Taha held his first meeting with Garang in the Kenyan town of Naivasha. By September 23 the two sides had reached agreement on one of the most contentious issues between them: how to manage the two separate armies that had been fighting each other for two decades. Signed formally on September 25, the ageement allowed each side to keep its army for the time being, but an "integrated" force of 24,000 soldiers (half from each side) would be created to patrol the south. Another merged force of 3,000 troops would be responsible for security in Khartoum, and two integrated armies of 6,000 troops each would take over two disputed areas, the Nuba Mountains and the Southern Blue Nile. The government was to withdraw its 100,000 troops from the south within two-and-a-half years.

The first formal peacekeeping under the security arrangement began in November. Joint patrols, consisting of former combatants from both sides plus representatives from African and Western countries, worked out of a base in the southern town of Leer, with the assignment of ensuring that the two armies avoided combat. Patrols were planned for other places in the south during 2004.

Another round of negotiations opened early in October but quickly became bogged down in the details of remaining issues, which went to the heart of what the conflict was all about. Those issues included:

- *Interim government.* The July 2002 power-sharing agreement provided for the southern rebels to join the government but left important specifics unresolved, including the precise roles to be played by the current leaders, al-Bashir, Taha, and Garang.
- *Khartoum.* The government insisted on its right to impose Islamic law in the capital, but the rebels pressed for the city to be governed by secular law, in recognition of its status as the capital of a country with a diverse population. Although it had an Arab majority, Khartoum was home to thousands of non-Arabs who did not want to be subjected to Islamic law.
- *Oil wealth.* Oil production was the country's main source of foreign currency earnings, and it would become even more important once peace took hold and foreign oil companies developed new fields. Dividing the revenue from the southern oilfields remained a key point of contention.

The "three areas." Also on the negotiating table was the status of three regions in south-central Sudan claimed by both sides: the Nuba Mountains,

Abyei, and South Blue Nile. The Nuba Mountains and South Blue Nile were important sources of water for the entire country; oil was discovered in Abyei in 2001. All three areas had mixed populations of Arabs and blacks.

Another important step in the peace process came on December 6, when Garang arrived in Khartoum for more talks with Vice President Taha. It was his first visit to the capital since the war began twenty years earlier, and he was greeted by enormous, enthusiastic crowds.

On December 20 the two sides announced that they had agreed, in principle, on a formula for sharing oil wealth. It closely reflected a plan that had been on the table for more than a year, providing for the SPLA to receive half of the income from oil generated in the south, with the other half going to the government. The SPLA would turn 2 percent of its share over to state governments in the southern region.

After a break for Christmas, the negotiations resumed on December 26, and both sides said they hoped to reach a final deal resolving all other issues by the end of the year. But on December 29 a government official told reporters that the status of the "three areas" in dispute was proving to be a negotiating "nightmare" that made meeting the year-end deadline impossible. The negotiations were still under way at year's end, and they continued into January 2004.

Humanitarian Issues

The war had made Sudan a humanitarian disaster zone, extreme even by the standards of civil conflict in Africa. The human wreckage left by the fighting and repeated famines were made worse by a long-term lack of investment in the education, health care, and basic infrastructure necessary for economic development.

The United Nations and international human rights organizations catalogued human rights violations by both the government and the SPLA rebels—but most observers placed the majority of the blame on the succession of governments in Khartoum. Over the years a shelf-full of reports documented cases in which the army, and Arab militias aligned with it, had bombed villages and towns, withheld food aid from civilians in areas sympathetic toward the rebels, forced hundreds of thousands of civilians out of their homes to make way for oilfields and military operations, and abducted thousands of people who were forced into slavery.

Many of these tactics had become standard fare in Africa's civil conflicts since the late twentieth century. The specifics of what was happening in Sudan received little attention in the outside world, in large part because the abuses had become cruelly routine and occurred in remote war zones out of sight of international observers.

The word *slavery* brought some international scrutiny, however. For nearly twenty years there had been rumors and reports that militias aligned with the government had kidnapped thousands of young men and women in the south and put them into slavery—the men as laborers, the women as sex-slaves. The government acknowledged that militias had abducted some people, but it denied the numbers were large or that the abductees had been forced to become slaves. The first real evidence came May 28, when the Rift Valley Institute, based in Kenya, said it had documented the cases of 10,380 southern Sudanese youths and young adults who had been abducted and likely pressed into slave labor since 1983. The institute based its findings on an eight-month investigation during which dozens of researchers interviewed thousands of families in towns and villages in the south. Institute officials said the 10,380 figure almost certainly was a "minimum" count of those who had been abducted. The majority of those kidnapped were young men under the age of eighteen, the institute said.

The tragedy of the war in southern Sudan was compounded by the fact that for years the governments of Sudan and neighboring Uganda had supported rebel groups in each other's countries. The Sudanese government had provided weapons to a terroristic rebel group from Uganda known as the Lord's Resistance Army. That group used southern Sudan as a base from which to conduct raids back in Uganda, where it terrorized villages by stealing food and enslaving children. Uganda, in turn, had provided weapons and some logistical support for the Sudanese rebels. The governments of Sudan and Uganda agreed in 1999 to stop supporting the rebel groups on both sides of the border, but most observers said that agreement was never fully carried out. *(Uganda war, p. 470)*

Sudan and Terrorism

The United States never had good relations with the various governments of Sudan, especially after a leftist leader, Gen. Muhammed Nimeiri, seized power in 1969. Relations deteriorated further in the 1990s when a new government moved aggressively to turn Sudan into an Islamist state. Washington in 1993 put Sudan on its list of countries that supported terrorism because Khartoum was providing refuge to international terrorists, including Saudi Arabian exile Osama bin Laden, who headed the al Qaeda terrorist network. Blaming al Qaeda for the 1993 bombing of the World Trade Center in New York, the administration of President Bill Clinton in 1996 successfully pressured the Sudanese government to expel him, whereupon bin Laden moved his operations to Afghanistan. Also in 1996, the United Nations Security Council imposed international diplomatic sanctions against Sudan for its alleged role in a plot by Islamist extremists to kill Egyptian president Hosni Mubarak; those sanctions were lifted in 2001. *(Al Qaeda, p. 1050)*

The Clinton administration tightened the noose on Sudan in 1997, imposing extensive economic and diplomatic sanctions against Sudan. The sanctions barred Sudan from getting U.S. economic or military aid and effectively prohibited it from obtaining loans from the World Bank and other international financial institutions, where the United States wielded considerable influence. The terrorist bombings in August 1998 of the U.S. embassies in Kenya and Tanzania plunged U.S.-Sudanese relations to a low point. Clinton charged that the Khartoum government continued to support the al Qaeda network, which he blamed for the bombings. He ordered a missile attack against a chemical plant near Khartoum, which he said had been producing material for the poison gas VX (a charge the factory's owner and the government denied), and he withdrew the U.S. ambassador from Sudan. *(Sudan attack, Historic Documents of 1998, p. 586)*

After the September 11, 2001, terrorist attacks against the United States, Sudan's government shifted course and sought to align itself with the antiterrorism war mounted by the administration of President George W. Bush. Sudan gave diplomatic support to the U.S. war against the al Qaeda network and the Islamist Taliban regime in Afghanistan, including allowing the use of its airspace by U.S. planes headed to and from Afghanistan. *(Afghanistan war, Historic Documents of 2001, p. 686)*

Secretary of State Colin Powell intervened in the Sudan peace negotiations twice in 2003. On May 21 he met with Sudan's foreign minister, Mustafa Osman Ismail, and pressed for additional steps Khartoum could take to get off the U.S. list of countries supporting terrorism. State Department spokesman Richard Boucher said Sudan had made progress: "I think it's safe to say that Sudan is not the kind of haven for terrorism that it used to be." Boucher also suggested that Khartoum's negotiation of a final peace agreement with the SPLA might win the lifting of some or all U.S. sanctions.

On October 21 Powell met in Nairobi with Sudan's president, al-Bashir, and suggested again that sanctions could be lifted and Washington could restore diplomatic relations once a final peace agreement was in place. State Department officials said Powell pressed the government to close the offices in Khartoum of two Palestinian extremist groups: the Islamic Resistance Movement (Hamas) and Islamic Jihad, both of which had claimed responsibility for suicide bombings and other attacks against Israel. Al-Bashir later denied that Powell had made such demands; he said Islamic Jihad did not have offices in Sudan and claimed his country had only "political" relationship with Hamas.

> *Following is the text of the "Framework Agreement on Security Arrangements During the Interim Period Between the Government of the Sudan and The Sudan People's Liberation Movement/Sudan People's Liberation Army," signed September 25, 2003, in Naivasha, Kenya. The agreement allowed the rebel movement in southern Sudan to keep its military force during a six-year interim period and provided for joint units, composed of troops from both the army and the rebels, in four sections of the country.*

"Framework Agreement on Security Arrangements During the Interim Period"

WHEREAS the Government of the Republic of the Sudan and the Sudan People's Liberation Movement/Sudan People's Liberation Army (the Parties) have been conducting negotiations in Naivasha, Kenya, since 2nd September, 2003 under the auspices of the IGAD [Intergovernmental Authority on Development] Peace Process; and

WHEREAS the Parties reiterated their commitment to a negotiated, peaceful, comprehensive resolution to the Sudan Conflict within the Unity of Sudan as set forth in the Machakos Protocol of 20th July 2002 [a power-sharing agreement, negotiated in Machakos, Kenya]; and

NOW RECORD THAT within the above context, the Parties have reached specific agreement on Security Arrangements during the Interim Period, the initialed text of which is annexed hereto and which will be subsequently incorporated into the final Peace Agreement; and

IT IS AGREED AND CONFIRMED THAT the Parties shall immediately resume negotiations on the remaining outstanding issues and subsequently negotiate a comprehensive ceasefire agreement in order to achieve a final, comprehensive Peace Agreement in the Sudan. . . .

1. Status of the Two Armed Forces:

    a. In the context of a united Sudan, and should the result of the referendum on self-determination confirm unity, the Parties (the Government of the Sudan and the Sudan People's Liberation Movement and Army) agree to the formation of the future army of Sudan that shall be composed from the Sudanese Armed Forces (SAF) and the Sudan People's Liberation Army (SPLA).

    b. As part of a peace agreement and in order to end the war, the Parties agree that the two forces, the SAF and the SPLA shall remain separate during the Interim Period, and further agree that both forces shall be considered and treated equally as Sudan's National Armed Forces during the Interim Period taking into consideration 1 (c) below.

    c. The parties agree to the principles of proportional downsizing of the forces on both sides, at a suitable time, following the completion of the comprehensive ceasefire arrangements.

d. The national Armed Forces shall have no internal law and order mandate except in constitutionally specified emergencies.

2. Ceasefire:

The parties agree to an internationally monitored ceasefire which shall come into effect from the date of signature of a Comprehensive Peace Agreement. Details of the Ceasefire Agreement shall be worked out by the two parties together with the IGAD mediators and international experts.

3. Redeployment:

a. The two forces shall be disengaged, separated, encamped and redeployed as will be detailed in the Comprehensive Ceasefire Agreement.
b. Except for those deployed in the joint/Integrated Units, the rest of the forces of SAF currently deployed in the South shall be redeployed North of the South/North border of 1/1/1956 [the date of Sudan's independence] under international monitoring and assistance within and up to two and one half years (2 1/2) from the beginning of the pre-Interim Period.
c. Except for those deployed in the Joint/Integrated Units, the rest of the SPLA forces currently deployed in Nuba Mountains and Southern Blue Nile shall be redeployed South of the South/North border of 1/1/1956 as soon as the Joint/Integrated Units are formed and deployed under international monitoring and assistance.
d. The SPLM/A undertakes that the demobilized Southern Sudanese from those currently serving in SAF in Southern Sudan shall be absorbed into various institutions of the Government of Southern Sudan along with demobilized SPLA soldiers.
e. The parties agree to implement with the assistance of the international community DDR programmes for the benefit of all those who will be affected by the reduction, demobilization and downsizing of the forces as agreed in 1(c), 3(d) and 7(b).

4. Joint/Integrated Units:

There shall be formed joint/integrated Units consisting of equal numbers from the Sudanese Armed Forces (SAF) and the Sudan People's Liberation Army (SPLA) during the Interim Period. The Joint/Integrated Units shall constitute a nucleus of a post referendum army of Sudan, should the result of the referendum confirm unity, otherwise they would be dissolved and the component parts integrated into their respective forces.

4.1 Elaboration on Joint/Integrated Units:-

a. Their Character:-
They should have a new character based on a common doctrine.
b. *Their Functions:-*
I. They will be a symbol of national unity during the Interim Period.
II. They will be a symbol of sovereignty during the Interim Period.
III. They will participate in the defense of the country together with the two forces.
IV. They will provide a nucleus of a post Interim Period future army of the Sudan should the vote of referendum confirm unity.
V. They shall be involved in the reconstruction of the country.
c. *Size and Deployment:*
The size and deployment of the Joint/Integrated Units throughout the Interim Period shall be as indicated below:-
I. Southern Sudan: twenty four thousands (24,000)
II. Nuba Mountains: six thousands (6,000)
III. Southern Blue Nile: six thousands (6,000)
IV. Khartoum: three thousands (3,000)
V. Eastern Sudan:-
a. The redeployment of SPLA forces from Eastern Sudan to South of the South/North border of 1/1/1956 shall be completed within one (1) year from the beginning of the pre-Interim period.
b. The parties shall discuss the issue of establishing Joint/Integrated Units.

5. Command and Control of the Two Forces:-

1. The Parties agree to establish a Joint Defence Board (JDB) under the Presidency, and shall be comprised of the chiefs of staff of the two forces, their deputies and any number of senior officers to be agreed to by the parties. It shall take its decisions by consensus and it shall be chaired alternately by the respective Chiefs of Staff.
2. Functions of JDB:
The JDB shall perform the following functions:
a. Co-ordination between the two forces.
b. Command of the Joint Integrated Units.

6. Common Military Doctrine:-

The parties shall develop a common military doctrine as a basis for the Joint/integrated Units as well as a basis for a post Interim Period army of the Sudan, if the referendum vote is in favour of unity. The parties shall develop this common doctrine within one year from the beginning of the Interim Period. During the Interim Period, the training of the SPLA (in the South), the SAF (in the North) and the joint units (in both North and South) will be based on this common doctrine.

7. Status of Other Armed Groups in the Country:

a. No armed group allied to either party shall be allowed to operate outside the two forces.
b. The Parties agree that those mentioned in 7(a) who have the desire and qualify shall be incorporated into the organized forces of either Party (Army, Police, Prisons and Wildlife forces), while the rest shall be reintegrated into the civil service and civil society institutions.
c. The parties agree to address the status of other armed groups in the country with the view of achieving comprehensive peace and stability in the country and to realize full inclusiveness in the transition process.

8. National Security Organs and Police Forces:

Structures and arrangements affecting all law enforcement organs, especially the Police, and National Security Organs shall be dealt with as part of the power sharing arrangements, and tied where is necessary to the appropriate level of the executive.

Source: Republic of Sudan. Government of the Republic of Sudan and the Sudan People's Liberation Movement/Army. *Framework Agreement on Security Arrangements During the Interim Period.* Naivasha, Kenya. September 25, 2003. www.reliefweb.int/w/rwb.nsf/f303799b16d2074285256830007fb33f/2b48a 3a02e5cb440c1256db90059506d?OpenDocument (accessed January 12, 2004).

Census Bureau Report on Health Insurance Coverage

September 30, 2003

INTRODUCTION

A fitful economy, high unemployment, and soaring health care costs in 2003 conspired to increase the number of Americans without health insurance for the second year in a row. According to the U.S. Census Bureau, a total of 43.6 million people—15.2 percent of the population—were without coverage for all of 2002. That was an increase of 2.4 million over 2001, when 14.6 percent were uninsured. It was the largest annual increase in a decade.

The bureau said most of the increase was attributable to a decrease in the number of people who were covered under private employer-sponsored plans. That in turn reflected a combination of workers losing their jobs (and thus their insurance) as well as employer decisions in the face of skyrocketing premium costs to eliminate their insurance programs or sharply increase the share of the costs that workers paid. *(Insurance coverage in 2001, Historic Documents of 2002, p. 666)*

The number of uninsured might have been even higher had it not been for government health insurance programs. The Census Bureau reported that participation in those programs increased from 25.3 percent of the total population in 2001 to 25.7 percent in 2002. Most of that increase came from increased enrollments in Medicaid, the federal-state program that provided health care to the poor. The faltering economy, however, was forcing many states to cut back on Medicaid payments. A report by the Kaiser Commission on Medicaid and the Uninsured, released in September, said all fifty states imposed tighter controls on their Medicaid programs in 2003 and planned more for 2004. The most frequent restrictions either froze or reduced payments for doctors and hospitals and curbed payments for prescription drugs. Seventeen states increased the copayments beneficiaries were required to pay.

The increase in the number of uninsured sparked new calls for federal measures to extend coverage to the uninsured, but the proposals differed greatly in both their approach to solving the problem and in their cost.

Congress, caught up for much of the year in a difficult partisan fight over amending Medicare to extend prescription drug coverage to the elderly, took no action on the proposals. The Bush administration and leaders of the Republican-led Congress said they were planning a major initiative to provide coverage for the uninsured. "For my next three years, that will be the overriding issue. That's the next big challenge," said Senate majority leader Bill Frist of Tennessee after President George W. Bush signed the prescription drug bill.

The Medicare reform law (PL 108–173) contained two sets of provisions that supporters said might keep the uninsurance problem from growing larger. The first set of provisions established tax-free health savings accounts allowing any taxpayers with a high-deductible health insurance plan to save and withdraw money tax-free to pay for medical expenses. The second set of provisions authorized $70 billion in subsidies and tax breaks for ten years starting in 2006 to encourage companies to continuing offering health care to their retirees. *(Pension coverage, p. 707; Medicare reform, p. 1119)*

In a related development, Congress failed to pass legislation, backed by Republicans, that would have set limits on the amount of damages that could be awarded in medical malpractice suits. Supporters argued that high awards were pushing up the cost of malpractice insurance and pushing out many doctors who opted to abandon their practices rather than pay exorbitant premiums. Opponents said caps would unfairly penalize some patients who had suffered serious injury or even death at the hands of negligent doctors. Opponents also charged that the premium increases were designed by insurance companies to cover stock market losses and bad business decisions.

Rising Numbers of Uninsured

According to the Census Bureau report, the percentage of Americans who received coverage under employer-sponsored plans fell to 61.3 percent in 2002, down from 62.6 percent in 2001. Much of the decrease was due to layoffs, but the number of full-time workers without health insurance increased by 897,000 to 19.9 million. Most of these workers were employed by small firms that never offered health insurance plans, but some larger employees were also canceling their insurance plans in the face of falling profits and rising premium costs. Premiums increased on average by around 15 percent in 2003, the third year in a row that the increases had been in the double digits. A similar increase was expected for 2004. Substantially more companies were asking their employees to pick up a larger share of the tab. A study by the Kaiser Family Foundation and the Health Research and Educational Trust, released in early September, found that covered workers were paying 48 percent more out of their own pockets for care in 2003 than they had paid in 2000. In California, Ohio, and elsewhere, unionized workers struck grocery stores chains to protest the benefit cuts.

Two other studies released in 2003 said the number of uninsured was actually much higher than the Census Bureau reported. A study prepared by Families USA, a liberal consumer advocacy group, for the Robert Wood Johnson Foundation looked at health care coverage over a two-year period and estimated that 75 million Americans were without health insurance coverage for at least part of the time. The study found that nearly 25 percent were without insurance for the full two-year period, while only 10 percent were uninsured for two months or less. The Census Bureau reported only on people who were without insurance coverage for a full calendar year, thus missing those who may have been uncovered for only part of a year or even part of two years. The study was released on March 4 as part of a campaign by a coalition of health foundations, business organizations, and labor groups to draw attention to the problem.

In May the Congressional Budget Office (CBO) released a report showing that the Census Bureau data overestimated the number of people who went without insurance for a full year, while underestimating those who were uncovered for part of a year. The report said for 1998, the most recent year for which CBO had reliable data, as many as 59 million were without coverage for part of the year, while the number without coverage for the entire year ranged between 21 million and 31 million. CBO, noting that the Census Bureau based its estimates on responses to the annual Current Population Survey, said that many of those surveyed report their insurance status at the time of the interview, rather than for the previous calendar year, as requested. "Far from being a static group, the uninsured population is constantly changing," CBO director Douglas J. Holtz-Eakin said. "While many people are chronically uninsured, many more are uninsured for shorter periods of time." Holtz-Eakin urged Congress to distinguish between the long-term and short-term uninsured in any legislation to expand coverage.

Consequences of Lacking Insurance

The Institute of Medicine, an arm of the National Academy of Sciences, issued two more reports in its series on the problems stemming from lack of health insurance. The first study, issued March 6, concluded that a large number of uninsured in any given community could adversely affect the availability of health care that even the insured received in that community. Providing uncompensated care to the uninsured strained hospital emergency rooms as well as community health care facilities. Some hospitals had closed or threatened to close their emergency facilities in part because of the expenses they incurred in treating uninsured patients.

In the second study, released June 17, the institute estimated that the poor health and premature deaths of the uninsured cost the nation as much as $130 billion every year. The study used a "health capital" index that measured earnings potential, children's physical and mental development, and the subjective value of being alive and healthy to estimate the value of improved health the uninsured would have if they had insurance coverage. The estimates ranged between $1,645 and $3,280 a year for each individual, or from $65 billion to $130 billion, assuming 41 million Americans were uninsured in any one year. By contrast, the study estimated that it would cost from $34 billion to $69 billion to provide the uninsured with the health services equivalent to the services used by the insured. The final report in the series, expected in 2004, was expected to offer recommendations for resolving the uninsured problem. *(Earlier institute reports, Historic Documents of 2002, p. 669; Historic Documents of 2001, p. 710)*

Little Consensus on a Solution

Although support was growing for some sort of universal health insurance that would cover the uninsured, there was little agreement among the interested parties about either the approach or the funding of such programs. At the national level, the Bush administration favored tax credits for people who bought their own insurance, the health savings account included in the Medicare reform bill that allowed people to put aside tax-free money to pay for medical expenses, and "association health plans" that would allow groups of small employers to band together to bargain for lower insurance rates. Bills introduced in Congress took different approaches. Sen. John Breaux, D-La., offered a measure that would guarantee all Americans basic coverage, financed through tax credits for low- and middle-income families and state-operated insurance pools. Other Democrats called for financing expanded health insurance coverage by repealing some of the tax cuts that Congress had enacted in 2001–2003. Some also suggested that funds could be raised by taxing employers who did not already pay basic benefits for their employees. It seemed likely that these proposals would be debated extensively in Congress and on the campaign trail in 2004.

Some states were not waiting for the federal government to act. In June 2003 Maine became the first state to extend coverage to the uninsured. The measure required that all Maine residents who could not otherwise afford health insurance have access to low-cost coverage by 2009. Premiums would be subsidized; the subsidy would vary depending on each person's ability to pay and the type of coverage bought. The coverage was to be financed through a tax on insurers and $80 million the state expected to save in unreimbursed health care costs.

On October 5, two days before voters threw him out of office in a recall election, California governor Gray Davis signed a bill requiring companies with two hundred or more workers to offer health benefits to their employees by 2006. Smaller companies would have to provide benefits starting in 2007. Employers could either buy insurance on their own or pay into a state purchasing pool that would be used to buy insurance. The measure was expected to cover 1.1 million people, about one-third of the state's uninsured. The California Chamber of Commerce and other business organizations opposed the measure, saying it was too expensive and would inhibit economic and job growth. Three other states, Hawaii, Oregon, and Washington, had similar laws. *(California recall, p. 1005)*

Several other states allowed health insurers to offer lower-cost policies that did not provide coverage for some or all of the so-called state mandates—requirements by the state that health insurance policies include certain coverages, such as chiropractic care. Insurers wanted to see even more of the mandates lifted, but critics of this approach warned that basic coverage could still leave many health care needs uncovered.

Medical Malpractice

Republicans in Congress had been trying to cap medical malpractice awards since the mid-1990s but had little success. The issue gained new urgency at the beginning of the year, however, after doctors in New Jersey, Pennsylvania, and West Virginia walked off the job to protest the high malpractice premiums they had to pay. The strikes, most of them either very brief or involving only a handful of doctors, came on top of numerous reports of doctors who abandoned their practices or switched to other medical specialties that were not so prone to malpractice suits. According to the American Hospital Association, 20 percent of hospitals had curtailed services because of rising malpractice insurance premiums and 6 percent had closed or discontinued certain services.

Doctors and their insurance companies argued that the premiums were a direct result of high jury awards in malpractice suits. Trial lawyers countered that insurers were increasing their premiums to compensate for money they would have earned if the stock market had remained robust. Siding with the doctors, a majority of Republicans in the U.S. House passed a bill in March setting ceilings on noneconomic damages for pain and suffering and punitive damages in malpractice suits. It was the seventh time the House had passed such a bill since 1995. Once again it fell victim to Democratic opposition in the Senate. When Senate majority leader Frist tried to bring a Republican bill to the floor without it first having gone through committee, Democrats objected, and Frist fell eleven votes short of the sixty he needed to break the filibuster.

Arthur Caplan, a bioethicist at the University of Pennsylvania, suggested that the issue could largely be resolved if state legislators and medical licensing boards were more aggressive about reducing medical errors by prohibiting bad doctors from practicing. "The doctors want their premiums reduced and malpractice lawyers want their incomes maintained," he said. "Neither is paying attention to the public issue, which is making medicine safer and compensating those who are injured."

Following are excerpts from "Health Insurance Coverage in the United States: 2002," a report released September 30, 2003, by the U.S. Census Bureau giving data on the number of Americans estimated to have been without health insurance in 2002.

"Health Insurance Coverage in the United States: 2002"

Highlights

- The share of the population without health insurance rose in 2002, the second consecutive annual increase. An estimated 15.2 percent of the population or 43.6 million people were without health insurance coverage during the entire year in 2002, up from 14.6 percent in 2001, an increase of 2.4 million people.
- The number and percentage of people covered by employment-based health insurance dropped in 2002, from 62.6 percent to 61.3 percent, driving the overall decrease in health insurance coverage.
- The number and percentage of people covered by government health insurance programs rose in 2002, from 25.3 percent to 25.7 percent, largely from an increase in the number and percentage of people covered by medicaid (from 11.2 percent to 11.6 percent).
- The proportion of children who were uninsured did not change, remaining at 11.6 percent of all children, or 8.5 million, in 2002.
- Although medicaid insured 14.0 million people in poverty, 10.5 million other people in poverty had no health insurance in 2002; the latter group represented 30.4 percent of the poverty population, unchanged from 2001.

- Hispanics (67.6 percent) were less likely to be covered by health insurance than non-Hispanic Whites who reported a single race (89.3 percent), Blacks who reported a single race (79.8 percent), and Asians who reported a single race (81.6 percent).
- Among the entire population 18 to 64 years old, workers were more likely to have health insurance (82.0 percent) than nonworkers (74.3 percent). Among those in poverty, workers were less likely to be covered (52.6 percent) than nonworkers (61.9 percent).
- Compared with 2001, the proportion who had employment-based policies in their own name decreased from 56.3 percent to 55.2 percent in 2002.
- Young adults (18 to 24 years old) were less likely than other age groups to have health insurance coverage—70.4 percent in 2002, compared with 82.0 percent of those 25 to 64 and, reflecting widespread medicare coverage, 99.2 percent of those 65 and over.
- Spells without health insurance, measured on a monthly basis, tend to be short in duration—about three-quarters (74.7 percent) were over within 1 year.

More people did not have health insurance in 2002 than in 2001.

The number of people without health insurance coverage rose to 43.6 million (15.2 percent of the population) in 2002, up 2.4 million from the previous year, when 14.6 percent of the population lacked coverage. However, the number of people covered by health insurance also increased in 2002, up 1.5 million to 242.4 million (84.8 percent of the population). Both increases can be attributed largely to an overall population growth from 2001 to 2002.

A decline in employment-based insurance prompted the decrease in insurance coverage rates.

Most people (61.3 percent) were covered by a health insurance plan related to employment for some or all of 2002, a decline of 1.3 percentage points from the previous year. This decline essentially explains the drop in total private health insurance coverage, to 69.6 percent in 2002.

Health insurance coverage provided by the government increased between 2001 and 2002, but not enough to offset the decline in private coverage. Medicaid coverage rose by 0.4 percentage points to 11.6 percent in 2002. Among the entire population, 25.7 percent had government insurance, including medicare (13.4 percent), medicaid (11.6 percent), and military health care (3.5 percent). Many people carried coverage from more than one plan during the year; for example, 7.4 percent of people were covered by both private health insurance and medicare.

The uninsured rates for people in or close to poverty did not change between 2001 and 2002.

Despite the medicaid program, 10.5 million poor people, or 30.4 percent of people in poverty, had no health insurance of any kind during 2002. This percentage—double the rate for the total population—did not change from the previous year. About 24.1 percent of all uninsured people were in poverty.

Medicaid was the most widespread type of health insurance among people in poverty, with 40.5 percent (14.0 million) of them covered by medicaid for some or all of 2002. This percentage did not change from the previous year.

Among the near poor (whose family incomes were at least 100 percent, but less than 125 percent, of their poverty thresholds), 27.9 percent (3.5 million people) lacked health insurance in 2002, unchanged from 2001.

Key demographic factors affect health insurance coverage.

Age
People 18 to 24 years old were less likely than other age groups to have health insurance coverage, with 70.4 percent covered for some or all of 2002. Because of medicare, almost all people 65 and over (99.2 percent) had health insurance in 2002. For other age groups, health insurance coverage ranged from 75.1 percent to 88.4 percent.

Among people in poverty, those 18 to 64 years old had a markedly lower health insurance coverage rate (57.6 percent) in 2002 than people under 18 (79.9 percent) or 65 and over (98.1 percent).

Race and Hispanic Origin
The uninsured rate for non-Hispanic Whites who reported only one race was 10.7 percent in 2002—higher than the uninsured rate of 10.0 percent for non-Hispanic Whites in 2001. Similarly, the uninsured rate for Blacks who reported a single race was 20.2 percent in 2002 and it was 19.9 percent for Blacks who reported one or more races in 2002—both higher than the uninsured rate of 19.0 percent for Blacks in 2001. The uninsured rate for people who reported Asian and/or Native Hawaiian

and Other Pacific Islander ranged from 18.1 percent to 18.7 percent in 2002, not statistically different from the rate for Asians and Pacific Islanders in 2001 (18.2 percent). The uninsured rate among Hispanics (32.4 percent in 2002) did not change from 2001 to 2002 and was higher than any other racial or ethnic group.

Nativity

In 2002, the proportion of the foreign-born population without health insurance (33.4 percent) was more than double that of the native population (12.8 percent). Among the foreign born, noncitizens were much more likely than naturalized citizens to lack coverage—43.3 percent compared with 17.5 percent.

Educational Attainment

Among all adults, the likelihood of being insured increases as the level of education rises. Compared with the previous year, coverage rates decreased both for those who were high school graduates only and for those with more education. Coverage rates did not change for adults with no high school diploma.

Economic status affects health insurance coverage.

Income

The likelihood of being covered by health insurance rises with income. Among households with annual incomes of less than $25,000, 76.5 percent had health insurance; the level rises to 91.8 percent for those with incomes of $75,000 or more.

Compared with the previous year, the coverage rate remained the same for those with household incomes less than $25,000, whereas rates dropped for those in each higher category of household income. For those with household incomes of $25,000 to $50,000, the coverage rate decreased 1.5 percentage points to 80.7 percent, while for those with incomes of $50,000 to $75,000, it dropped by 0.4 percentage points to 88.2 percent, and for households with incomes of $75,000 or more, it decreased by 0.5 percentage points to 91.8 percent.

Work experience

Of those 18 to 64 years old in 2002, full-time workers were more likely to be covered by health insurance (83.2 percent) than part-time workers (76.5 percent), who in turn were more likely to be insured than nonworkers (74.3 percent). However, among people in poverty, nonworkers (61.9 percent) were more likely to be insured than part-time workers (55.6 percent), who were more likely to be insured than full-time workers (50.7 percent).

Firm Size

Of the 142.9 million workers in the United States who were 18 to 64 years old, 55.2 percent had employment-based health insurance policies in their own name. The proportion increased with the size of the employing firm from 30.8 percent for firms with fewer than 25 employees to 68.7 percent for firms with 1,000 or more employees. (These estimates do not reflect the fact that some workers were covered by another family member's employment-based policy). Compared with the previous year, the proportion of workers who had employment-based policies in their own name in 2002 decreased from 56.3 percent to 55.2 percent.

The uninsured rate for children did not change between 2001 and 2002.

The number and percentage of children (people under 18 years old) without health insurance did not change in 2002, remaining at 8.5 million or 11.6 percent. A decline in employment-based health insurance coverage of children was offset by an increase in coverage by medicaid or the State Children's Health Insurance Program.

Among children in poverty, 20.1 percent (2.4 million children) had no health insurance during 2002, unchanged from the previous year. For this group, government health insurance coverage increased from 63.3 percent to 64.8 percent in 2002, while employment-based coverage (17.4 percent) did not change. Children in poverty made up 28.5 percent of all uninsured children in 2002.

Among near-poor children (those in families whose incomes were at least 100 percent, but less than 125 percent, of their poverty thresholds), 22.2 percent (0.9 million children) were without health insurance in 2002, unchanged from 2001. For this group, neither private health insurance coverage nor government health insurance coverage changed from the previous year.

The likelihood of health insurance coverage varies among children.

- Children 12 to 17 years old were more likely to be uninsured than those under 12—12.9 percent compared with 11.0 percent.
- Whereas 22.7 percent of Hispanic children did not have any kind of health insurance in 2002, the comparable rates among children reporting a single race were 7.8 percent for non-Hispanic White children, 13.9 percent for Black children, and 11.5 percent for Asian children.

- Most children (67.5 percent) were covered by an employment-based or privately purchased health insurance plan in 2002, but nearly 1 in 4 (23.9 percent) was covered by medicaid.
- Black children with no other race reported had a higher rate of medicaid coverage in 2002 than children of any other racial or ethnic group examined here—41.2 percent, compared with 37.3 percent of Hispanic children, 18.1 percent of Asian children with no other race reported, and 15.5 percent of non-Hispanic White children with no other race reported.
- Children living in single-parent families in 2002 were less likely to be insured than children living in married-couple families—84.7 percent compared with 90.3 percent.

Uninsured rates vary among the states.

The proportion of people without health insurance ranged from 8.0 percent in Minnesota to 24.1 percent in Texas, based on 3-year averages for 2000, 2001, and 2002. Although the data may appear to suggest that Minnesota had the lowest uninsured rate, its rate was not statistically different from the rates for Rhode Island, Wisconsin, and Iowa.

Comparisons of 2-year moving averages (2000–2001 to 2001–2002) show that the proportion of people without coverage rose in eighteen states: Colorado, Idaho, Indiana, Maryland, Michigan, Mississippi, Missouri, Nevada, New Hampshire, New Jersey, North Carolina, Oregon, Pennsylvania, Rhode Island, Texas, Vermont, Virginia, and Wisconsin. The proportion of people without coverage fell in only one state, New Mexico.

Spells Without Health Insurance

The CPS [Current Population Survey] ASEC [Annual Social and Economic Supplement] provides good estimates of the net change in the number of uninsured people from one year to the next, but it does not show how long a given person remains uninsured, what percentage of the uninsured population remains uninsured in the following year, how many people obtain coverage, or any changes in a person's coverage within a given year.

These more dynamic measures of health insurance coverage are available from the Survey of Income and Program Participation (SIPP). Unlike the CPS ASEC, which is not designed to follow the same respondents in consecutive years, the SIPP is a longitudinal survey which interviews the same respondents three times a year over the course of 3 to 4 years.

The latest longitudinal data available from the SIPP come from the 1996 panel, which covered January 1996 to December 1999. . . . A spell without insurance is the number of consecutive months a person is not covered. To be considered in a spell, the person must be uninsured for at least 2 months. . . .

Spells without health insurance tend to be short in duration—about three-quarters (74.7 percent) were over within 1 year and only 2.5 percent lasted more than 36 months. Some people, such as full-time workers and non-Hispanic Whites, regained health insurance sooner than others after losing it. Although some people had only one spell without insurance, others had several during the 4-year period. The median duration of spells was 5.6 months for all people who experienced at least one, excluding spells underway during the first month of the SIPP survey.

Technical Notes

National Surveys and Health Insurance Coverage

Health insurance coverage is likely to be underreported on the ASEC. While under reporting affects most, if not all, surveys, under reporting of health insurance coverage on the CPS appears to be a larger problem than in other national surveys that ask about insurance. Some reasons for the disparity may include he fact that income, not health insurance, is the main focus of the ASEC questionnaire. In addition, we collect health insurance information in the ASEC by asking about the previous year's coverage in February-April of the subsequent year. Asking annual retrospective questions appears not to be a problem when collecting income data (possibly because our interview period is close to when people pay their taxes), but is probably less than ideal when asking about health insurance coverage. . . .

Source: Mills, Robert J., and Shailesh Bhandari. U.S. Census Bureau. "Health Insurance Coverage in the United States: 2002." *Current Population Reports,* P60–223. Washington, D.C. September 30, 2003. www.census.gov/prod/2003pubs/p60-223.pdf (accessed October 20, 2003).

October

2003 HISTORIC DOCUMENTS	

General Accounting Office on Global Warming Policy

October 1, 2003

INTRODUCTION

On July 24, 2003, the administration of President George W. Bush launched its long-discussed project to research the causes and consequences of climate change, better known as global warming. The ambitious research effort came after a scientific panel said the administration appeared to be too focused on answering questions that most scientists believed were already settled—most important, the extent to which global warming was caused by the burning of fossil fuels. Another key aspect of the administration's global warming policy came under fire from the General Accounting Office (GAO), the investigative arm of Congress, which issued a report in October that questioned the assumptions the administration had used in its policy to slow the increase in emissions of so-called greenhouse gases by 2012.

Numerous scientific studies over the previous twenty years had said that the gradual but steady warming of the Earth's surface since the mid-nineteenth century was largely a result of human actions, principally the burning of coal, gas, and oil, which produced carbon dioxide and other gases that trapped heat in the upper atmosphere. Unless the trend was reversed, these studies warned, the Earth could experience major changes in climate and the environment during the twenty-first century. Most studies predicted that the oceans would rise because of melting glaciers and polar ice (flooding low-lying islands and coastal areas); rising temperatures would affect agriculture and the ability of humans, animals, and plants to cope with increasingly extreme variations in weather; and many areas of the world would experience prolonged droughts. Some scientists—along with many business leaders—rejected these conclusions. They argued that the perceived warming of the Earth's surface resulted primarily from natural, not man-made causes, and would pose no major problems for the foreseeable future.

The most extensive international effort to head off global warming—a United Nations treaty negotiated in Kyoto, Japan, in 1997—appeared to be on the verge of collapse at the close of 2003. The United States had refused to ratify the treaty, leaving Russia as the one country whose participation was essential if it was to enter into legal force. A top aide to Russian president Vladimir Putin suggested in early December that Moscow would not ratify the treaty. *(Global warming background, Historic Documents of 2002, p. 298)*

Bush Administration Policy

The White House in February 2002 announced the centerpiece of its global warming policy: a plan calling for voluntary actions by businesses and individuals. On its surface, the plan appeared to call for lower U.S. greenhouse gas emissions by 2012. The details of the plan, however, assumed that total U.S. emissions would continue to increase—just at a slightly lower rate of increase than in the past.

This plan was based not on the actual emissions of greenhouse gases but on the relationship of those emissions to the overall economy. The administration used a measure it called greenhouse gas emissions "intensity"; this measure divided the country's gross domestic product (GDP) by the annual emissions of greenhouse gases (in metric tons). In 2002, for example, the White House said the United States was expected to produce 183 metric tons of greenhouse gases for each $1 million in GDP. The administration set a goal of reducing emissions to 151 metric tons for each $1 million of GDP by 2012—a reduction of 18 percent (after rounding). The 18 percent figure was 4 percentage points greater than what the administration estimated the reduction in greenhouse intensity would be during the ten-year period if the economy grew and there were no government policy changes during that period; in other words, the administration assumed that the intensity level would be 158 metric tons in 2012 without any policy changes, the GAO reported.

Most other scientific studies measured greenhouse gas emissions by the actual amount of gases that were sent into the atmosphere from each country, regardless of any relationship to the economy. Under this measure, actual U.S. emissions were expected to continue to increase during the ten-year period that Bush cited—by as little as 12 percent according to some estimates and by as much as 14 percent according to others.

In a report to Congress on October 1, the GAO said the Bush administration had been unable to provide full and convincing explanations for the major assumptions in its policy. The GAO said the administration cited thirty factors (such as regulations, tax credits, and other incentives for voluntary actions) as contributing to the planned 18 percent reduction in greenhouse gas intensity. But, the GAO reported, the administration could not explain how these factors would combine to produce the reduction it projected, nor could it explain why that percentage goal was chosen rather than some other goal. Of the thirty factors, the administration gave some specific information about possible reductions in greenhouse gas emissions that would result from only eleven, the GAO said. Eight of those were policies or programs that already were under way at the time the White House made its announcement, the GAO said, and the other three were announced later. Overall, the GAO said, it was "unclear to what extent the thirty elements will contribute to the goal of reducing emissions, and thus, lowering emissions intensity, by 2012."

The GAO also noted that the administration had no plans to assess the progress of its initiative before 2012—four years after the end of Bush's presidency, assuming he won a second term in office. Unless the administration conducted interim assessments, the GAO said, "it will not be in a position to determine, until a decade after announcing the initiative, whether its efforts are having the intended effect or whether additional efforts may be warranted."

Conducting Further Studies

A second major aspect of Bush's policy was an emphasis on what he called the need for stronger scientific evidence about the causes and consequences of climate change. Bush, a former oil company executive, had repeatedly expressed his skepticism about the validity of numerous scientific studies that had pointed to the burning of fossil fuels—along with other human actions, such as cutting down forests—as being among the major contributors to the perceived warming of the Earth's surface over the past century. Bush said he wanted better research as the basis for determining future government policy. Critics said he merely wanted to study a problem that already had been studied intensively for two decades, rather than taking actions that might discomfort the oil, gas, and coal industries.

The Bush administration in November 2002 unveiled a "draft plan" for the scientific research it intended to fund and promised a final research plan for 2003. The draft plan was itself the subject of a study made public on February 25 by the National Academy of Sciences. The study, titled "Planning Climate and Global Change Research: A Review of the Draft U.S. Climate Change Science Program Strategic Plan," was conducted by a panel of seventeen environmental and atmospheric specialists.

The scientists generally praised Bush's call for more scientific research into climate change and acknowledged numerous "uncertainties" about climate change. They said additional research could help decision makers, both in government and the private sector, take steps to reduce the consequences.

The scientists also offered two major criticisms of the administration's plan. First, they said the administration appeared to disregard numerous previous scientific studies that had concluded that human activities were a major cause of climate change. The administration focused on the scientific uncertainties but made no effort to determine which uncertainties were truly important for policy makers to understand, the panel said. Second, the scientists called for more focused research on how humans could deal with the consequences of climate change—by adapting to changes and taking steps to try to minimize the impact. In short, the panel wrote that the administration's plan "lacks most of the basic elements of a strategic plan: a guiding vision, executable goals, clear timetables and criteria for measuring progress."

The administration's final version of its plan for climate study, released July 24, was given a budget of $103 million over two years. It called for an emphasis on studying five major areas: the extent of "natural variability" of the Earth's climate and environment in the past, the forces that caused changes in the Earth's climate and "related systems," how to reduce the uncertainty in projections of how the Earth's climate and environment may change in the future, the "sensitivity and adaptability" of natural and human-influenced systems to climate change, and how mankind can "manage risks and opportunities" resulting from climate change. None of these topics appeared to be specifically directed at studying what could be done to forestall or minimize climate change.

James Mahoney, the assistant secretary of commerce who directed U.S. scientific studies on climate change, said the new plan took into account the criticisms and recommendations offered by the National Academy of Sciences panel five months earlier. "The greatest focus is on what we can deliver in the shortest period," he told the Associated Press. The academy's panel held meetings in August and October to review the administration's new study plan, but it had made no public comment on it as of year's end.

Kyoto Treaty

By late 2003 the Kyoto treaty on global warming had become little more than a symbol of the debate between those who demanded action to head off further climate change and those who doubted the urgency of the matter. The treaty was known formally as the Kyoto Protocol to the United Nations Framework Convention on Climate Change. The framework convention was negotiated in 1992; it called for voluntary actions by every country to reduce emissions of greenhouse gases. The Kyoto Protocol called for mandatory actions by the industrialized countries to reduce their emissions by 2012 to levels below what they produced in 1990. The administration of President Bill Clinton (1993–2001) signed the treaty but never submitted it for approval to the Senate, where opposition to it was strong. Bush renounced the treaty in 2001 but did not formally withdraw the Clinton administration's signature from it. A chief complaint of Bush and other treaty opponents was that it did not mandate actions by China, India, and other developing countries—which were rapidly increasing their consumption of fossil fuels as their economies grew. *(Kyoto treaty background, Historic Documents of 1997, p. 859; Historic Documents of 2001, p. 112)*

Under its provisions, the Kyoto treaty would not come into legal force until it had been ratified by countries that were responsible for 55 percent of global emissions of greenhouse gases. Because the United States produced about more than 30 percent of the world's greenhouse gases, its refusal to ratify meant the treaty would become law only if all other major industrialized countries ratified it. Most European countries had done so by 2001, and Canada added its ratification in December 2002, putting the total number of countries supporting the treaty at 120. That left Russia as the last major country whose ratification could put the treaty into effect. President Putin himself was vague about the matter during the year, but in December his top economics adviser, Andrei N. Illarionov, said flatly that Russia would not ratify the treaty because it would damage the country's economy. Although other Kremlin officials said no decisions had been made, Illarionov's statement was the clearest sign, since Bush's comparable statement in 2001, that the Kyoto treaty might never become law.

Even if it eventually suffered the same fate as many other unfulfilled UN agreements, supporters and opponents both said the Kyoto treaty had influenced government decisions around the world. The European Union had enacted legislation requiring its member nations to reduce greenhouse gas emissions to comply with the treaty. British prime minister Tony Blair went even further than his European colleagues, committing Britain to a goal of cutting greenhouse gas emissions by 60 percent by 2050. Japan had adopted its first legislation intended to curb emissions of greenhouse gases. More than a dozen state governments in the United States had taken various steps to encourage businesses and individuals to curb the burning of fossil fuels, for example by using more energy from "renewable" sources (such as wind- and solar-power). A dozen states also filed suit in federal court in Washington, D.C., in October, attempting to force the Environmental Protection Agency to regulate industrial emissions of carbon dioxide, the principal greenhouse gas. The Bush administration had opposed mandatory curbs on carbon dioxide (produced mainly by the burning of oil and coal) and had weakened other regulations under the Clean Air Act. *(Clean air issues, p. 173)*

Years of debate about climate change might also have begun to change the atmosphere on Capitol Hill, where climate change issues had rarely been discussed since the Senate in 1997 put itself on record as opposing the Kyoto treaty. Advocates of tougher U.S. action against global warming mounted a major push in the Senate during 2003; although their effort failed, it gained more support than most observers had expected. On October 30 senators John McCain, R-Ariz., and Joseph I. Lieberman, D-Conn., offered a proposal that would have required industrial plants to restrain their emissions of carbon dioxide by 2010 to a level no higher than they had been in 2000. In effect, that proposal would have required most businesses to cut their consumption of fossil fuels during the decade. The proposal was defeated on a 55–43 vote, a much closer margin than the sponsors had expected when they began work on it several months earlier.

Another Warm Year

The global warming aspect of climate change appeared to be in evidence again during 2003, which the United Nation's World Meteorological Organization described as the third-warmest in more than 140 years of modern record keeping. In a report issued December 17, the organization estimated that the Earth's average surface temperature was 0.81 degrees Fahrenheit higher than the long-term "normal" of 57 degrees. The warmest year on record was 1998, when the average temperature was nearly 1 degree above normal. (Historic Documents of 1998, p. 945)

Extreme heat waves hit several areas around the world during 2003, including Europe, where several thousand people died during one of the warmest summers on record; the Indian subcontinent, which suffered a heat wave that saw temperatures rise to 120 degrees Fahrenheit; and Australia, which had record spring-time temperatures (in September). Both the Arctic Sea and Antarctica continued to experience significant melting of their ice caps. Most of North America recorded unusually low snowfall, and the western United States again experienced serious drought conditions that caused major wildfires, particularly in southern California.

Following are excerpts from "Climate Change: Preliminary Observations on the Administration's February 2002 Climate Initiative," a statement delivered October 1, 2003, to the Senate Committee on Commerce, Science, and Technology, by John B. Stephenson, director of the Natural Resources and Environment Division of the General Accounting Office.

"Climate Change: Observations on the Administration's 2002 Climate Initiative"

We are pleased to be here today to discuss our preliminary observations on certain aspects of the Administration's February 2002 Global Climate Change Initiative. This Initiative included, among other things, a goal related to domestic emissions of carbon dioxide and other greenhouse gases.

Specifically, the Initiative established the goal of reducing U.S. emissions intensity 18-percent by 2012, which is 4 percentage points more than the 14-percent reduction that was otherwise expected to occur. In 2012, this 4-percent reduction in emissions intensity is expected to translate into a 100 million ton reduction in carbon emissions below levels that would be expected in the absence of the Initiative. The Initiative is comprised of 30 elements, including partnerships with industry and tax credits, designed to achieve the reduction in emissions intensity.

It is important to note that the Administration's goal is to reduce emissions intensity, not total emissions. Emissions intensity measures the amount of greenhouse gases emitted per unit of economic output. For example, in 1990, U.S. emissions totaled 1,909 million metric tons of carbon equivalent and economic output (or Gross Domestic Product) totaled $9,216 billion. Dividing these numbers yields an emission intensity ratio of 207 tons of emissions per million dollars of economic output. Emissions intensity changes in response to variations in either emissions or economic output. For example, if emissions increase more slowly than economic output increases, the ratio decreases. If emissions increase more quickly than economic output increases, the ratio increases. If emissions and economic output increase by the same proportion, emissions intensity does not change.

Our testimony, which is based on ongoing work, discusses the extent to which the Administration's public documents (1) explain the basis for its general goal of reducing emissions and its specific goal of reducing emissions intensity 18 percent by 2012, (2) explain how the elements included in the Administration's Initiative are expected to reduce emissions and contribute to the goal of reducing emissions intensity 18 percent, and (3) discuss the Administration's plans to track progress toward meeting the goal. We expect to issue a final report on the results of our work later this year.

Our testimony is based on our analysis of the Administration's February 2002 Global Climate Change Policy Book and subsequent White House fact sheets, as well as congressional testimony by administration officials, an August 2003 report on federal climate change spending, and related documents. Because of time constraints, we limited our work to reviewing these documents. We performed our work between July and September 2003 in accordance with generally accepted government auditing standards.

Background

Carbon dioxide and certain other gases trap some of the sun's heat in the earth's atmosphere and prevent it from returning to space. The trapped energy warms the earth's climate, much as glass in a greenhouse. Hence, the gases that cause this effect are often referred to as greenhouse gases. In the United States, the most prevalent greenhouse gas is carbon dioxide, which results from the combustion of coal and other fossil fuels in power plants, the burning of gasoline in vehicles, and other sources. The other gases are methane, nitrous oxide, and three synthetic gases. In recent decades, concentrations of these gases have built up in the atmosphere, raising concerns that continuing increases might interfere with the earth's climate, for example, by increasing temperatures or changing precipitation patterns.

In 1997, the United States participated in drafting the Kyoto Protocol, an international agreement to limit greenhouse gas emissions, and in 1998 it signed the Protocol. However, the previous administration did not submit it to the Senate for advice and consent, which are required for ratification. In March 2001, President Bush announced that he opposed the Protocol.

In addition to the emissions intensity goal and domestic elements intended to help achieve it, the President's February 2002 climate initiative includes (1) new and expanded international policies, such as increasing funding for tropical forests, which sequester carbon dioxide, (2) enhanced science and technology, such as developing and deploying advanced energy and sequestration technologies, and (3) an improved registry of reductions in greenhouse gas emissions. According to testimony by the Chairman of the White House Council on Environmental Quality, the President's climate change strategy was produced by a combined working group of the Domestic Policy Council, National Economic Council, and National Security Council.

While U.S. greenhouse gas emissions have increased significantly, the Energy Information Administration reports that U.S. emissions intensity has generally been falling steadily for 50 years. This decline occurred, in part, because the U.S. energy supply became less carbon-intensive in the last half-century, as nuclear, hydropower, and natural gas were increasingly substituted for more carbon-intensive coal and oil to generate electricity.

Administration's Public Documents Provide a Context But Not a Specific Basis for the 18-percent Goal

The Administration explained that the Initiative's general goal is to slow the growth of U.S. greenhouse gas emissions, but it did not explain the basis for its specific goal of reducing emissions intensity 18 percent by 2012 or what a 4-percent reduction is specifically designed to accomplish. Reducing emissions growth by 4 percentage points more than is currently expected would achieve the general goal, but—on the basis of our review of the fact sheets and other documents—we found no specific basis for establishing a 4-percentage-point change, as opposed to a 2- or 6-percentage-point change, for example, relative to the already anticipated reductions.

According to the Administration's analysis, emissions under its Initiative will increase between 2002 and 2012, but at a slower rate than otherwise expected. Specifically, according to Energy Information Administration (EIA) projections cited by the Administration, without the Initiative emissions will increase from 1,917 million metric tons in 2002 to 2,279 million metric tons in 2012. Under the Initiative, emissions will increase to 2,173 million metric tons in 2012, which is 106 million metric tons less than otherwise expected. We calculated that under the Initiative, emissions would be reduced from 23,162 million metric tons to 22,662 million metric tons cumulatively for the period 2002–12. This difference of 500 million metric tons represents a 2-percent decrease for the 11-year period.

Because economic output will increase faster than emissions between 2002 and 2012, according to EIA's projections, emissions intensity is estimated to decline from 183 tons per million dollars of output in 2002 to 158 tons per million dollars in 2012 (a 14-percent decline) without the initiative, and to 150 tons per million dollars under the Initiative (an 18-percent decline).

Administration's Public Documents Estimated Contributions for Some, but Not All, of the Initiative's Elements

The Administration identified 30 elements (26 in February 2002 and another 4 later) that it expected would help reduce U.S. emissions by

2012 and, thus, contribute to meeting its 18-percent goal. These 30 elements include regulations, research and development, tax incentives, and other activities. The Administration groups them into four broad categories, as described below.

Providing incentives and programs for renewable energy and certain industrial power systems. Six tax credits and seven other elements are expected to increase the use of wind and other renewable resources, combined heat-and-power systems, and other activities. The tax credits cover electricity from wind and new hybrid or fuel-cell vehicles, among other things. Other elements would provide funding for geothermal energy, primarily in the western United States, and advancing the use of hydropower, wind, and other resources on public lands. Still other elements involve research and development on fusion energy and other sources.

Improving fuel economy. Three efforts relating to automotive technology and two other elements are expected to improve fuel economy. The technology efforts include advances in hydrogen-based fuel cells and low-cost fuel cells. Two of the five elements are mandatory. First, a regulation requiring the installation of tire pressure monitoring systems in cars and certain other vehicles was finalized in June 2002 and will be phased in between 2003 and 2006. Properly inflated tires improve fuel efficiency. Second, a regulation requiring an increase in the fuel economy of light trucks, from the current 20.7 miles per gallon to 22.2 miles per gallon in 2007, was finalized in April 2003.

Promoting domestic carbon sequestration. Four U.S. Department of Agriculture programs were identified as promoting carbon sequestration on farms, forests, and wetlands. Among other things, these programs are intended to accelerate tree planting and converting cropland to grassland or forests.

Challenging business to reduce emissions. Voluntary initiatives to reduce greenhouse gases were proposed for U.S. businesses. For major companies that agreed to establish individual goals for reducing their emissions, the Environmental Protection Agency (EPA) launched a new Climate Leaders Program. In addition, certain companies in the aluminum, natural gas, semiconductor, and underground coal mining sectors have joined voluntary partnerships with EPA to reduce their emissions. Finally, certain agricultural companies have joined two voluntary partnerships with EPA and the Department of Agriculture to reduce their emissions.

The Administration provided some information for all 30 of the Initiative's elements, including, in some cases, estimates of previous or anticipated emission reductions. However, inconsistencies in the nature of this information make it difficult to determine how contributions from the individual elements would achieve the total reduction of about 100 million metric tons in 2012. First, estimates were not provided for

19 [of] the Initiative's elements. Second, for the 11 elements for which estimates were provided, we found that 8 were not clearly attributable to the Initiative because the reductions (1) were related to an activity already included in ongoing programs or (2) were not above previous or current levels. We did find, however, that the estimated reductions for the remaining 3 elements appear attributable to the Initiative.

We have concerns about some of the 19 emission reduction elements for which the Administration did not provide savings estimates. At least two of these elements seem unlikely to yield emissions savings by 2012. For example, the April 2003 fact sheet listed hydrogen energy as an additional measure, even though it also stated a goal of commercializing hydrogen vehicles by 2020, beyond the scope of the Initiative. Similarly, the same fact sheet listed a coal-fired, zero-emissions power plant as an additional measure, but described the project as a 10-year demonstration; this means that the power plant would not finish its demonstration phase until the last year of the Initiative, much less be commercialized by then.

Of the 11 elements for which estimates were provided, we found that the estimated reductions for 8 were not clearly attributable to the Initiative. In five cases, an estimate is provided for a current or recent savings level, but no information is provided about the expected additional savings to be achieved by 2012. For example, the Administration states that aluminum producers reduced their emissions by 1.8 million metric tons to meet a goal in 2000, but it does not identify future savings, if any. Similarly, it states that Agriculture's Environmental Quality Incentives Program, which provides assistance to farmers for planning and implementing soil and water conservation practices, reduced emissions by 12 million metric tons in 2002. However, while the Administration sought more funding for the program in fiscal year 2003, it did not project any additional emissions reductions from the program.

In two cases, it is not clear how much of the claimed savings will occur by the end of the Initiative in 2012. The requirement that cars and certain other vehicles have tire pressure monitoring systems is expected to yield savings of between 0.3 and 1.3 million metric tons a year when applied to the entire vehicle fleet. However, it will take years for such systems to be incorporated in the entire fleet and it is not clear how much of these savings will be achieved by 2012. Similarly, the required increase in light truck fuel economy is expected to result in savings of 9.4 million metric tons over the lifetime of the vehicles covered. Again, because these vehicles have an estimated lifetime of 25 years, it is not clear how much savings will be achieved by 2012.

In one case, savings are counted for an activity that does not appear to be directly attributable to the Initiative. Specifically, in March 2001 (nearly a year before the Initiative was announced), EPA and the Semiconductor Industry Association signed a voluntary agreement to reduce emissions by an estimated 13.7 million metric tons by 2010. Because this agreement was signed before the Initiative was announced, it is not clear that the estimated reductions should be considered as additions to the already anticipated amount.

Estimates for the remaining 3 of the 11 elements appear to be attributable to the Initiative in that they represent reductions beyond previous or current levels and are associated with expanded program activities. These are:

- Agriculture's Conservation Reserve Program was credited with additional savings of 4 million metric tons a year. This program assists farm owners and operators to conserve and improve soil, water, air, and wildlife resources and results in carbon sequestration.
- Agriculture's Wetland Reserve Program was credited with additional savings of 2 million metric tons a year. This program helps convert cropland on wetland soils to grassland or forest and also sequesters carbon emissions.
- The Environmental Protection Agency's Natural Gas STAR Program was credited with additional savings of 2 million metric tons a year. This program works with companies in the natural gas industry to reduce losses of methane during production, transmission, distribution, and processing.

More current information about certain of these elements and their expected contributions has been made public, but has not been consolidated with earlier information about the Initiative. For example, the Department of Agriculture's web site includes a June 2003 fact sheet on that agency's programs that contribute to carbon sequestration. Among other things, the fact sheet estimated that the Environmental Quality Incentives Program, cited above, will reduce emissions 7.1 million metric tons in 2012. However, we did not find that such information had been consolidated with the earlier information, and there appears to be no comprehensive source for information about all of the elements intended to help achieve the Initiative's goal and their expected contributions. The lack of consistent and comprehensive information makes it difficult for relevant stakeholders and members of the general public to assess the merits of the Initiative.

Administration's Public Documents Do Not Discuss Plans for Monitoring Interim Progress

According to the February 2002 fact sheet, progress in meeting the 18-percent goal will be assessed in 2012, the final year of the Initiative. At that point, the fact sheet states that if progress is not sufficient and if science justifies additional action, the United States will respond with further policies; these policies may include additional incentives and voluntary programs. The fact sheets did not indicate whether the Administration plans to check its progress before 2012. Such an interim assessment, for example, after 5 years, would help the Administration determine whether it is on course to meet the goal in 2012 and, if not, whether it should consider additional elements to help meet the goal.

Source: U.S. Congress. General Accounting Office. "Climate Change: Preliminary Observations on the Administration's February 2002 Climate Initiative." Statement by John B. Stephenson, director of natural resources and environment, before the Senate Committee on Commerce, Science, and Transportation. GAO–04–131T. October 1, 2003. www.gao.gov/new.items/d04131t.pdf (accessed April 21, 2004).

U.S. Inspector on Weapons of Mass Destruction in Iraq

October 2, 2003

INTRODUCTION

After ousting the regime of Iraqi leader Saddam Hussein, the United States was unable to find any of the "thousands" of weapons of mass destruction (WMDs) that President George W. Bush said Saddam had accumulated. The U.S. failure to uncover the weapons led critics to question both the rationale that Bush had used to justify the war and the intelligence information that had underpinned that rationale.

In particular, questions were raised about a September 2002 intelligence report (called a National Intelligence Estimate) that had expressed much more certainty than had previous U.S. reports about Iraq's WMDs. Bush and his aides repeatedly cited that report to bolster their charges against Saddam's regime. By late 2003 many of the statements in that report appeared to have been wrong, and administration critics were beginning to question whether U.S. intelligence agencies had tailored their reporting to fit the administration's preconceived notions about Iraq.

Several investigations of prewar intelligence already were under way, and others were certain to follow. In December the CIA appointed a former deputy director, Richard Kerr, to analyze the quality of prewar intelligence. The Senate Intelligence Committee was examining the same issue. In Britain, Prime Minister Tony Blair had given wide latitude to a senior judge to investigate a report by the BBC that his government had "sexed up" intelligence reports to justify the war. *(Iraq War, p. 135; Background, Historic Documents of 2001, p. 612; Historic Documents of 2002, pp. 33, 612)*

The Prewar Allegations

After the Persian Gulf War of 1991, the United Nations Security Council passed resolutions demanding that Iraq give up all the unconventional weapons it was assumed to have developed or had tried to develop:

biological and chemical weapons, a nuclear weapons program, and medium-range missiles capable of hitting targets throughout the Middle East. Teams of UN inspectors monitored Iraq's compliance with that demand during the 1990s. The inspectors successfully dismantled many of Iraq's missiles and destroyed large quantities of biological chemical weapons after Baghdad acknowledged their existence in 1995. UN inspectors also dismantled all apparent components of Iraq's program to develop nuclear weapons.

The inspections process was a difficult one. Baghdad attempted to block or hinder the inspectors' work at every turn. The last of several crisis points came in late 1998, when President Bill Clinton (1993–2001) accused Iraq of refusing to cooperate. The UN withdrew its inspectors and Clinton sent U.S. bombers and cruise missiles to attack Baghdad and some of Iraq's weapons installations. In a final report to the UN, which was never officially made public, the inspectors said Iraq still had the equipment and technology to produce several forms of biological and chemical weapons and might still have large quantities of those weapons in hiding. The inspectors noted, however, that some of the biological and chemical weapons that Iraq produced before the Gulf war might have deteriorated and become almost useless because the country lacked the technology to manufacture and store long-life weapons. After the UN inspectors left, Western intelligence services no longer had any direct access to Iraq's weapons infrastructure, forcing them to use electronic intelligence gathering and old-fashioned human espionage to try to find out what weapons Iraq still had or might be trying to build.

After the September 11 terrorist attacks in the United States, Bush suddenly stepped up his rhetoric against Iraq, warning of a connection between Iraq and terrorism. Then, in his January 2002 State of the Union speech, Bush said Iraq was part of an "axis of evil" along with Iran and North Korea—all of whom, he said, possessed or were trying to build weapons of mass destruction. From that point on, the Bush administration, and the intelligence agencies that gave it information, appeared to become increasingly certain that Iraq still had weapons from the Persian Gulf War era and was working intently to build more of them.

In September 2002, as Congress was preparing to debate Bush's request for authorization to wage a war in Iraq, U.S. intelligence agencies prepared an updated report on Iraq's weapons, called a National Intelligence Estimate. Top congressional leaders received a classified version of the report; the administration in October made public an unclassified version that contained the same conclusions but left out most of the details, including dissenting opinions by some intelligence experts. Much of the classified version later was leaked to the news media. That intelligence report dramatically changed previous U.S. estimates of Iraq's WMD programs, stating as a near certainty several major assumptions that earlier had been listed in the "possible" or "probable" categories.

The Bush administration's claims starting in late 2002 and continuing through much of 2003 about Iraq's nuclear, biological, and chemical weapons are summarized below.

Nuclear weapons. Iraq had restarted, and was making substantial progress on, its program to build and develop nuclear weapons. The only uncertainty, the administration said, was whether Iraq had been able to acquire the weapons-grade material (plutonium or highly enriched uranium) needed to create a bomb. In a nationally televised speech on October 7, 2002, Bush said that if Iraq could "buy or steal" a quantity of uranium "a little larger than a single softball, it could have a nuclear weapon in less than a year."

The administration offered two specific pieces of evidence to bolster its contention that Baghdad had revived its nuclear weapons program. One claim was that Iraq had attempted to buy about 100,000 high-strength, calibrated aluminum tubes to be used in the process of enriching uranium. This claim was a central item in the U.S. intelligence community's September 2002 report on Iraq. That report contained a significant dissent, however; Energy Department experts said the tubes more likely were intended for use in making rocket engines. UN weapons inspectors reached the same conclusion, which they reported to the Security Council on January 27, 2003. In his January 2003 State of the Union speech the next day, however, Bush said the tubes were "suitable for nuclear weapons production"—but he did not mention the differing views on that point.

Another reference in that speech came back to haunt Bush, but not until weeks after the war had ended. Bush said the British government "has learned that Saddam Hussein recently sought significant quantities of uranium from Africa." In subsequent weeks, it emerged that Bush was referring to a report that Iraq had attempted to buy uranium in Niger—and that the CIA had investigated the report and had been unable to verify it. UN inspectors said on March 7 that the British report was based on inexpertly forged documents. CIA director George Tenet and top White House officials later apologized for allowing the unfounded allegation to appear in Bush's speech. *(Details, p. 33)*

Biological weapons. Perhaps the most alarming reports from Iraq during the 1990s involved that country's program to develop biological weapons. Starting in 1995, UN inspectors found evidence that Iraq had produced material that could have been developed into nearly 10 billion doses of anthrax and versions of the plague. The UN inspectors dismantled three biological weapons plants, but in their final report the inspectors said they could not account for most of the weapons those plants could have produced. Subsequent U.S. intelligence reports that were made public between 1998 and 2001 said it was unclear whether Iraq had been able to restart its biological weapons program or what the status was of the anthrax and other biological agents it had produced earlier.

The administration's September 2002 intelligence report contained no ambiguity, stating that "all key aspects" of Iraq's biological weapons program were "active" and that some elements "are larger and more advanced" than before the Gulf war. In particular, the report said Iraq could "quickly" produce a variety of biological weapons, including anthrax, that could be delivered by bombs, missiles, aerial sprayers, or covert operatives. The report did not give estimates of the quantities of biological weapons remaining in Iraq's arsenal.

The report introduced a new charge: that Iraq had built "mobile facilities" to produce biological weapons and that "within three to six months" these facilities probably could produce "an amount of [biological] agent equal to the total that Iraq produced in the years prior to the Gulf war." Bush and his aides cited the estimates from this report in nearly all their speeches prior to the 2003 Iraq War, drawing particular attention to the mobile laboratories. In a detailed presentation to the UN Security Council on February 5, Powell said Iraq had "at least seven" of the laboratories and showed satellite photographs of some of them. "There can be no doubt that Saddam Hussein has biological weapons and the capability to rapidly produce many, many more," Powell told the council.

Chemical weapons. Iraq produced several kinds of chemical weapons before the Persian Gulf War. As with biological weapons, UN inspectors during the 1990s dismantled several chemical weapons plants, but their final report suggested that Iraq might have hidden sizable quantities of the weapons. The inspectors noted that any chemical weapons left over from before the Gulf war probably had deteriorated because Iraq lacked the technical skills to produce weapons with a long shelf-life.

By late 2002 the Bush administration had become certain that Iraq had chemical weapons and was making more of them. In his October 7, 2002, speech, Bush said: "We know that the regime has produced thousands of tons of chemical agents, including mustard gas, sarin nerve gas, and VX nerve gas." This assertion, which he and other officials repeated in various forms until after the Iraq War, appeared to be based on elements of the September 2002 intelligence report, which hardened the government's previous assessments about the extent of the Iraqi chemical weapons arsenal. The president counted many more weapons than had his intelligence agencies, however. Rather than the "thousands of tons" he cited, the intelligence assessment said Iraq "probably has stocked at least 100 metric tons and possibly as much as 500 [metric tons]" of chemical weapons agents. The intelligence assessment added that "much" of those weapons had been "added in the last year," indicating that Iraq's program remained active.

Iraq and Terrorists

In every speech on Iraq, Bush said that confronting Saddam Hussein was a central component of the war against terrorism, which he had launched following the September 11 attacks in the United States. The key link between Iraq and terrorism, he said, was that Saddam might turn his mass weapons over to terrorist groups, which would then use them against U.S. allies in the Middle East (Israel and moderate Arab states such as Jordan, Egypt, or Saudi Arabia), against U.S. military forces in the region, or even against the United States directly. Bush was careful not to charge that Iraq already had given its weapons to terrorists, but nearly all his statements—and those of his aides—suggested that it was only a matter of time before Baghdad would do so. In his March 17 speech setting a forty-eight-hour ultimatum for Saddam Hussein to give up power or face war, Bush gave this rationale for the war he was about to launch: "The danger is clear: Using chemical, biological or, one day, nuclear weapons obtained with the help of Iraq, the terrorists could fulfill their stated ambitions and kill thousands or hundreds of thousands of innocent people in our country or any other."

Despite its centrality to Bush's political case for the war, this alleged link between Iraq and terrorist use of mass weapons was disputed at the time by many experts outside the U.S. and British governments. Most experts said there was no evidence that Baghdad had given weapons to terrorists or that it had any inclination to do so. In its September 2002 report, the U.S. intelligence community said Saddam was likely to turn some of its weapons over to terrorists only if he feared an attack by the United States. Doing so, the report said, "would be his last chance to exact vengeance by taking a large number of victims with him."

The UN's Weapons Search

UN weapons inspectors returned to Iraq, for the first time since 1998, on November 27, 2002, and began their work in earnest the following month. There were two groups of inspectors. A UN mission of about 100 inspectors, headed by Swedish diplomat Hans Blix, checked for biological and chemical weapons, plus missiles that had a range of more than ninety miles (which were prohibited by the Security Council in 1991). The other inspectors, from the International Atomic Energy Agency (IAEA), looked for signs that Iraq had revived its nuclear weapons program; this team was headed by IAEA director Mohamed El Baradei.

Blix and El Baradei reported five times to the UN Security Council: on December 19, 2002, and January 9, January 27, February 14, and March 7, 2003. A cautious man known for his understatement, Blix generally gave the council evenhanded assessments, noting shortcomings in Iraq's cooperation but generally expressing at least some optimism that his inspectors would be able to discover the truth, if given the time to do so. Blix spoke out forcefully just once, in his January 27 appearance before the council.

"Iraq appears not to have come to genuine acceptance—not even today—of the disarmament which was demanded of it and which it needs to carry out to win the confidence of the world and live in peace," he said. The Bush administration seized on that statement as justifying its hard-line approach toward Baghdad. Powell said the United States had "made it very clear from the beginning that we would not allow the process of inspections to string out forever." Such rhetoric apparently alarmed Blix, who thereafter reverted to his mode of caution—enraging Bush administration officials who implied that he was not trying hard enough to find Iraq's weapons.

The inspector's January 27 report to the Security Council was an important moment in another way: El Baradei used the occasion to challenge the Bush administration's assertions about Iraq's nuclear weapons program. "We have to date found no evidence that Iraq has revived its nuclear weapons program since the elimination of the program in the 1990s," he told the Security Council. El Baradei said IAEA inspectors had examined all the buildings identified by U.S. spy satellites as likely locations for Iraq's nuclear arms industry but had found "no prohibited nuclear activities." He acknowledged that the IAEA's work in Iraq was not yet complete and that a final assessment would not be possible for several months.

In his February 5 presentation to the Security Council, Powell said Iraq had taken elaborate steps to trick the UN inspectors, including issuing a fake death certificate for a scientists the inspectors had asked to interview. Powell also said the government had hidden rocket warheads, filled with biological weapons, in palm groves in remote regions of western Iraq—and was moving them every few weeks to keep the inspectors from discovering them. Powell also showed satellite photographs that appeared to depict the movement of weapons from some facilities just before the inspectors arrived. Intelligence officials had detected "this kind of housecleaning" at thirty sites in Iraq, he said.

The UN inspectors continued their work in Iraq all through February and into March. They located some items left over from Iraq's pre-Gulf war weapons program, including eleven empty rocket warheads that could have been used to deliver chemical weapons. The inspectors' one major surprise find was a new missile, the al Samoud 2, which had an estimated range of 108 miles—about 18 miles more than a maximum set by the UN Security Council in 1991. Starting on March 1, Iraq destroyed seventy-two of these missiles, under UN supervision. On March 7 Blix told the council that inspectors had located a document that gave the impression Iraq might still have "about 10,000 liters of anthrax," but the material itself had not been found.

The inspectors began leaving Iraq on March 17, when Bush set his ultimatum for Saddam to give up power. All the inspectors had pulled out by the time the war began two days later. Blix gave a final written report to the UN on May 30. That report noted that the inspectors had been unable to complete their work, because of the war. The inspectors "did not find evidence of the continuation or resumption of programs of weapons of mass destruction or significant quantities of proscribed items," Blix said. In interviews with reporters before he left his UN post at the end of June, Blix said he had concluded that Iraq still had only the "debris" of its pre-Gulf war weapons program. Blix said he also was puzzled that the United States had been unable to give him solid intelligence information to back up its claims about Iraq's weapons.

The U.S. Weapons Search

As the war got under way, U.S. intelligence agents and Army special forces units entered Iraq and began looking for the country's hidden weapons. Administration officials said they had no doubt that U.S. teams would be able to locate the weapons that the UN inspectors had missed. In June, after the main fighting of the war was over, the administration assembled a team called the Iraq Survey Group, composed of up to 1,400 civilian and military specialists from the United States, Australia, and Britain. This team reported to the CIA. David Kay, a former UN inspector who then headed a mid-sized U.S. defense contractor in California, was named coordinator of the group. In addition to looking for weapons, the survey group searched for ties between Iraq and terrorists and attempted to document human rights abuses by the Iraqi regime.

After just a month on the job, the U.S. inspectors began expressing doubts that Iraq's weapons would be as easy to find as top administration officials had implied. The *Washington Post* reported on April 22 that the administration was "losing confidence" in its prewar assumptions about where the weapons were located. The inspectors had not yet completed searching all the eighty-seven priority sites identified by U.S. intelligence agencies, the *Post* reported. Even so, some teams of inspectors already were being taken off the weapons hunt and were assigned instead to search for terrorists and prisoners of war.

On May 10 the *New York Times* quoted inspectors as saying they had found a trailer, near the northern Iraq city of Mosul, that was a "mobile biological weapons laboratory." This was the first apparently solid report of a weapons discovery by the inspectors, and it cheered the Bush administration. The CIA issued a report on May 28 saying U.S. forces had discovered two trucks that also appeared to be related to production of biological weapons. The next day, Bush referred to those units in saying, "We found the weapons of mass destruction" in Iraq. By October, however, U.S. officials acknowledged that the trailer and trucks probably were not intended for use in building biological weapons; most likely, experts said, the units were used to produce hydrogen for weather balloons.

By mid-May, as the weapons hunt continued without noticeable success, some Washington policy experts who had advocated the war shifted to a new line of argument. Iraq might have destroyed its weapons during the 1990s but, for political reasons, still wanted the rest of the world to think it had them, these experts said. Secretary of Defense Donald Rumsfeld was the first senior administration to raise this possibility, saying on May 27 that Iraq might have gotten rid of its weapons before the war. Rumsfeld and other officials also began arguing that Iraq had mass weapons "programs," even if it no longer had the actual weapons.

In June the House and Senate intelligence committees both announced inquiries into the prewar intelligence gathering about Iraq's weapons. "The situation is becoming one where the credibility of the administration and Congress is being challenged," Sen. John Warner, R-Va., chairman of the Armed Services Committee, said. The Republican leaders of both chambers rejected calls by Democrats for a formal investigation, however.

By late summer several major U.S. news organizations were reporting that key aspects of the Bush administration's prewar arguments about Iraq had proven to be exaggerated or false. The *Washington Post* offered one of the most extensive of these reports, on August 10. It cited a "pattern" in which Bush, Vice President Dick Cheney, and other top officials "made allegations depicting Iraq's nuclear weapons program as more active, more certain, and more imminent in its threat than the data they had would support."

Kay's Report to Congress

In late September U.S. chief weapons inspector Kay began briefing administration officials and congressional committees about what had been found—or not found—during the nearly six months since U.S. forces took control of most of Iraq. Kay offered a formal "interim" report to Congress on October 2. In essence, Kay said his inspectors had not yet found any evidence to support the administration's prewar assertions about Iraq's weapons. The inspectors had found no biological, chemical, or nuclear weapons, nor any of the longer-range missiles that would have been needed to deliver such weapons far beyond Iraq's borders. The inspectors had found evidence that Iraq had the "intent" to develop prohibited weapons, Kay said, based on the fact that it had built, and then hidden, "dozens of WMD-related program activities and significant amounts of equipment." As examples, he cited a "clandestine network of laboratories and safe houses" that contained equipment "suitable for continuing CBW [chemical and biological warfare] research." Iraq also had conducted "new research" on some biological warfare agents, including ricin (a highly toxic poison), that had not been reported to UN inspectors, he said.

Saddam clearly wanted to develop nuclear weapons, and his government had tried to preserve some of the nuclear weapons program it had developed before the Persian Gulf War, Kay said. But inspections so far had not turned up any evidence that Iraq had taken "significant" steps since UN inspectors left in 1998 to actually build those weapons, he reported.

"It clearly does not look like a massive, resurgent program, based on what we've discovered," Kay told reporters. Kay's report left congressional leaders searching for explanations for why a detailed investigation on the ground in Iraq had not verified the claims of the government's prewar intelligence. "I'm not pleased by what I heard today," said Sen. Pat Roberts, R-Kan., chairman of the Senate Intelligence Committee. Some of the prewar assessments were "sloppy," he added.

In the wake of Kay's report, the Bush administration sought to shift attention from Iraq's weapons to the overall utility of the Iraq War. Defending his decision to launch the war, Bush said on October 3: "I can't think of any people who think that the world would be a safe place with Saddam Hussein in power." Bush also pointed to the line in Kay's report saying that inspectors had found "WMD-program related activities." That finding proved that "Saddam Hussein was a danger to the world," he said.

In interviews with reporters following his report to Congress, Kay said he had been personally surprised by the lack of prohibited weapons in Iraq. In particular, he said it was surprising that Iraq appeared not to have any chemical weapons—by far the easiest kinds of weapons of mass destruction to manufacture. "Most of us thought there was little doubt" about Iraq's chemical weapons, he said. Kay said the investigators would continue their work. He added that his team was considering several theories about what had happened to Iraq's weapons: that Saddam did not have them but wanted the world to think he did so he would be seen as a major actor in the Middle East; that Iraq had buried its weapons, had sent them to other countries, or had destroyed them; or that Iraqi scientists had lied to Saddam about their ability to produce weapons for him.

Newspapers reported on October 24 that the Senate Intelligence Committee was preparing a toughly worded report criticizing Tenet and other intelligence officials for overstating the case that Iraq had weapons. The committee had not completed its work as of the end of the year.

Anthony Cordesman, a military expert at the Center for Strategic and International Studies in Washington, said on November 16 that the government had found no evidence that Iraq had tried to give weapons of mass destruction to al Qaeda or other terrorist groups. After spending two weeks in Iraq, where he interviewed top U.S. officials, Cordesman said there had been "talk" among some Iraqis about aiding terrorists, but nothing came of it. Cordesman later submitted a detailed report saying he had found "major gaps" in U.S. and British intelligence about Iraq's weapons.

Under continuing pressure to defend the work of intelligence agencies, Tenet on November 28 released a statement defending the September 2002 intelligence estimate of Iraq's weapons. Tenet cited what he called ten "myths" on which the criticism was based. The intelligence estimate was based on the best available evidence, he said, and it was not skewed "to meet the needs of the Bush administration." Tenet also said he worried that criticism had forced senior intelligence officials "to spend much of their time looking backwards" and might discourage analysts from making judgments "that go beyond ironclad evidence."

British Role in the Weapons Issue

The postwar failure of inspectors to find any weapons of mass destruction in Iraq was a major political embarrassment to President Bush and his administration—but it posed a much greater danger to British prime minister Blair. Blair had been Bush's most loyal ally in the run-up to the war, promoting support for it among fellow European leaders and at home, where many of his constituents were ambivalent, at best.

The British intelligence services also had been in the forefront of making the case that Iraq's weapons of mass destruction posed an imminent danger to the rest of the world. In September 2002 British intelligence services produced—and Blair's government publicized—a dossier that contained alarming statements about Iraq's weapons. It was titled "Iraq's Weapons of Mass Destruction: The Assessment of the British Government." Most attention focused on a claim, which was stated four times in the dossier, that the Iraqi government could deploy some biological or chemical weapons within forty-five minutes. On February 3, 2003, Blair's government followed that publication with another report, "Iraq: Its Infrastructure of Concealment, Deception, and Intimidation," which detailed Iraq's alleged efforts to hide its weapons from the UN inspectors. Five days after its publication, the government acknowledged that most of the report was copied from various magazines.

It was the earlier, September 2002 dossier that ended up causing a major political storm in Britain during 2003. On May 29 BBC Radio reporter Andrew Gilligan aired a report charging that British intelligence had "sexed up" the report on orders from Blair's office. Gilligan quoted a "senior intelligence official" as saying the claim about Iraq's forty-five minute weapons capability was included in the dossier "against our wishes."

Blair heatedly denied the allegation. "The idea that we authorized, or made, our intelligence agencies invent some piece of evidence is completely absurd, and what is happening here is that people who have opposed this action [the war] throughout are now trying to find a fresh reason of saying why it wasn't the right thing to do," he said.

On July 7 a parliamentary investigating committee said Blair's government mishandled the Iraq weapons dossier, especially by giving such prominence to the forty-five minute claim. But the panel said Blair had not misled Parliament when he presented his overall case for the Iraq War.

That report might have ended the matter, but eleven days later, on July 18, David Kelly, a Defense Ministry weapons scientist, was found dead near his home in Oxfordshire—an apparent suicide. The BBC later confirmed rumors that Kelly had been the source of Gilligan's controversial report.

His government suddenly shaken by a potential scandal, Blair called for an independent inquiry, headed by one of the country's senior appellate judges, Lord Hutton. Hutton opened his inquiry on August 11 and within a few weeks had collected numerous bits of evidence embarrassing to the government—notably a chaotic approach to its compilation of the dossier. Alastair Campbell, Blair's communications director, who had been at the center of the dispute over the dossier, resigned on August 29, a week after testifying before Hutton's inquiry. The inquiry also raised questions about journalistic standards at the BBC. Three reporters who had interviewed Kelly had different recollections about what he had said, and an editor for the company testified that Gilligan had demonstrated a "a lack of judgment" in his report.

Blair testified to the Hutton inquiry on August 28 and strongly denied that anyone in his government had ordered the Iraq document to be exaggerated. "It is one thing to say we disagree with the government, we should not have gone to war; people can have a disagreement about that," he said. "But if the allegation had been true, it would have merited my resignation."

Hutton ended his inquiry on September 25 and suggested he would file a final report in November or December. By year's end he was still working on it, however. Even before the report was filed, the inquiry had damaged Blair's standing. By the time Hutton's hearings ended, opinion surveys showed that 60 percent of Britons were dissatisfied with Blair's performance, and an even stronger majority said he was too concerned about public relations.

What Went Wrong?

Bush administration officials, other political leaders, intelligence experts, and public policy analysts offered numerous explanations for the apparent discrepancies between what U.S. and British intelligence agencies thought Iraq had, and what it apparently did not have, in terms of weapons of mass destruction. The most obvious explanation was that after UN inspectors left Iraq in late 1998, Western intelligence agencies had no reliable, direct access to Iraq's weapons facilities or the engineers and scientists who worked in them. Nearly all the direct, inside information gathered after that point came from defectors or sources inside the Iraqi government—two types of sources with their own agendas. News reports during the year revealed that U.S. intelligence agencies relied heavily on information provided by Iraqi exiles, some of whom were of questionable reliability and all of whom bore a grudge against Saddam's regime. Much of the U.S. information came through the Iraqi National Congress, a group of exiles who had lobbied Congress during the 1990s and subsequently gained millions of dollars in U.S. funding because of its opposition to Saddam. In his State of the Union speech Bush cited "three defectors" as the source of information about Iraq's alleged mobile laboratories to produce biological weapons; once found, the laboratories turned out to have a different purpose.

Intelligence agencies also relied heavily on what they euphemistically called "national technical means"—spy satellites that took overhead pictures and reconnaissance planes that were able to intercept telephone and radio conversations among Iraqi officials. Aerial photographs and intercepted communications were subject to interpretation. Some of the interpretation given by the intelligence agencies turned out to be wrong or misleading, possibly because the agencies strained to match their observations with their expectations.

In addition, some aspects of the standard procedures for the consideration of intelligence information by the highest levels of the U.S. government appeared to have been side-stepped in the Iraq case. The September-October 2002 intelligence assessment was produced in a rush to bolster the administration's case before Congress took its votes authorizing war and the UN Security Council acted on a resolution demanding that Iraq give up its weapons. That report also contained an exceptionally high number of dissents, some of them lodged by the government agencies with the greatest expertise in the subject at hand. Another procedural issue noted by some critics was the Pentagon's use of a new bureau, the Office of Special Plans, to funnel raw, unevaluated intelligence information to top policy makers. Rumsfeld said he had been so impressed with this information that he asked the Pentagon aides to brief CIA director Tenet.

In a letter to Tenet on September 25, the top leaders of the House Intelligence committee—Porter J. Goss, R-Fla., and Jane Harman, D-Calif., respectively—cited "significant deficiencies" in the intelligence community's gathering of prewar information about Iraq. Key judgments in the October 2002 intelligence assessment about Iraq's weapons were "based on too many uncertainties," Goss and Harman said.

By far the most sensitive allegation was that the Bush and Blair governments imposed a political agenda upon their nations' intelligence services; in other words, they pressured the intelligence experts to draw the conclusions that political leaders demanded of them. The *New York Times* on March 22 quoted unnamed intelligence officials as saying they felt pressured by the administration to produce evidence backing the case against Iraq. In particular, the newspaper said CIA officials complained that the administration had pressured the agency to substantiate the claim that Iraq was cooperating with al Qaeda. "A lot of analysts have been upset about the way the al Qaeda case has been handled," the *Times* quoted one intelligence official as saying. CIA director Tenet repeatedly rejected this argument and said it was "simply wrong" for anyone to argue that prewar intelligence had been tailored to suit the administration. Even so, the issue was certain to be the subject of further investigations during 2004 and possibly beyond.

Whatever the combination of reasons, it was clear by year's end that before the war top officials in the United States and Britain had convinced themselves—and many in the public—that the state of knowledge about Iraq's weapons programs was more certain than it was. On March 30, for example, Rumsfeld said of Iraq's weapons: "We know where they are." Nine months later, hundreds of U.S. agents, with complete access to Iraq, had found none of those weapons.

Following is the text of an unclassified version of prepared testimony by David Kay, the chief U.S. weapons inspector in Iraq, that the Central Intelligence Agency released after he testified October 2, 2003, in closed hearings before several congressional committees.

Testimony by U.S. Weapons Inspector on Iraq's WMD Programs

Thank you, Mr. Chairman. I welcome this opportunity to discuss with the Committee the progress that the Iraq Survey Group has made in its initial three months of its investigation into Iraq's Weapons of Mass Destruction (WMD) programs.

I cannot emphasize too strongly that the Interim Progress Report, which has been made available to you, is a snapshot, in the context of an on-going investigation, of where we are after our first three months of work. The report does not represent a final reckoning of Iraq's WMD programs, nor are we at the point where we are prepared to close the file on any of these programs. While solid progress—I would say even remarkable progress considering the conditions that the ISG [Iraq Study Group] has had to work under—has been made in this initial period of operations, much remains to be done. We are still very much in the collection and analysis mode, still seeking the information and evidence that will allow us to confidently draw comprehensive conclusions to the actual objectives, scope, and dimensions of Iraq's WMD activities at the time of Operation Iraqi Freedom [OIF, the 2003 war in Iraq]. Iraq's WMD programs spanned more than two decades, involved thousands of people, billions of dollars, and were elaborately shielded by security and deception operations that continued even beyond the end of Operation Iraqi Freedom. The very scale of this program when coupled with the conditions in Iraq that have prevailed since the end of Operation Iraqi Freedom dictate the speed at which we can move to a comprehensive understanding of Iraq's WMD activities.

We need to recall that in the 1991–2003 period the intelligence community and the UN/IAEA [United Nations/International Atomic Energy Administration] inspectors had to draw conclusions as to the status of Iraq's WMD program in the face of incomplete, and often false, data supplied by Iraq or data collected either by UN/IAEA inspectors operating within the severe constraints that Iraqi security and deception actions imposed or by national intelligence collection systems with their own inherent limitations. The result was that our understanding of the status of Iraq's WMD program was always bounded by large uncertainties and had to be heavily caveated. With the regime of Saddam Husayn at an end, ISG has the opportunity for the first time of drawing together all the evidence that can still be found in Iraq—much evidence is irretrievably lost—to reach definitive conclusions concerning the true state of Iraq's WMD program. It is far too early to reach any definitive conclusions and, in some areas, we may never reach that goal. The unique nature of this opportunity, however, requires that we take great care to ensure that the conclusions we draw reflect the truth to the maximum extent possible given the conditions in post-conflict Iraq.

We have not yet found stocks of weapons, but we are not yet at the point where we can say definitively either that such weapon stocks do not exist or that they existed before the war and our only task is to find where they have gone. We are actively engaged in searching for such weapons based on information being supplied to us by Iraqis.

Why are we having such difficulty in finding weapons or in reaching a confident conclusion that they do not exist or that they once existed but have been removed? Our search efforts are being hindered by six principal factors:

1. From birth all of Iraq's WMD activities were highly compartmentalized within a regime that ruled and kept its secrets through fear and terror and with deception and denial built into each program;
2. Deliberate dispersal and destruction of material and documentation related to weapons programs began pre-conflict and ran trans-to-post conflict;
3. Post-OIF looting destroyed or dispersed important and easily collectable material and forensic evidence concerning Iraq's WMD program. As the report covers in detail, significant elements of this looting were carried out in a systematic and deliberate manner, with the clear aim of concealing pre-OIF activities of Saddam's regime;
4. Some WMD personnel crossed borders in the pre/trans conflict period and may have taken evidence and even weapons-related materials with them;
5. Any actual WMD weapons or material is likely to be small in relation to the total conventional armaments footprint and difficult to near impossible to identify with normal search procedures. It is important to keep in mind that even the bulkiest materials we are searching for, in the quantities we would expect to find, can be concealed in spaces not much larger than a two car garage;
6. The environment in Iraq remains far from permissive for our activities, with many Iraqis that we talk to reporting threats and overt acts of intimidation and our own personnel being the subject of threats and attacks. In September alone we have had three attacks on ISG facilities or teams: The ISG base in Irbil was bombed and four staff injured, two very seriously; a two person team had their vehicle blocked by gunmen and only escaped by firing back through their own windshield; and on Wednesday, 24 September, the ISG Headquarters in Baghdad again was subject to mortar attack.

What have we found and what have we not found in the first 3 months of our work?

We have discovered dozens of WMD-related program activities and significant amounts of equipment that Iraq concealed from the United Nations during the inspections that began in late 2002. The discovery of these deliberate concealment efforts have come about both through the admissions of Iraqi scientists and officials concerning information they deliberately withheld and through physical evidence of equipment and activities that ISG has discovered that should have been declared to the UN. Let me just give you a few examples of these concealment efforts, some of which I will elaborate on later:

- A clandestine network of laboratories and safehouses within the Iraqi Intelligence Service that contained equipment subject to UN monitoring and suitable for continuing CBW research.
- A prison laboratory complex, possibly used in human testing of BW agents, that Iraqi officials working to prepare for UN inspections were explicitly ordered not to declare to the UN.
- Reference strains of biological organisms concealed in a scientist's home, one of which can be used to produce biological weapons.
- New research on BW-applicable agents, Brucella and Congo Crimean Hemorrhagic Fever (CCHF), and continuing work on ricin and aflatoxin were not declared to the UN.
- Documents and equipment, hidden in scientists' homes, that would have been useful in resuming uranium enrichment by centrifuge and electromagnetic isotope separation (EMIS).
- A line of UAVs [unmanned aerial vehicles] not fully declared at an undeclared production facility and an admission that they had tested one of their declared UAVs out to a range of 500 km, 350 km beyond the permissible limit.
- Continuing covert capability to manufacture fuel propellant useful only for prohibited SCUD variant missiles, a capability that was maintained at least until the end of 2001 and that cooperating Iraqi scientists have said they were told to conceal from the UN.
- Plans and advanced design work for new long-range missiles with ranges up to at least 1000 km—well beyond the 150 km range limit imposed by the UN. Missiles of a 1000 km range would have allowed Iraq to threaten targets through out the Middle East, including Ankara, Cairo, and Abu Dhabi.
- Clandestine attempts between late-1999 and 2002 to obtain from North Korea technology related to 1,300 km range ballistic missiles—probably the No Dong—300 km range anti-ship cruise missiles, and other prohibited military equipment.

In addition to the discovery of extensive concealment efforts, we have been faced with a systematic sanitization of documentary and computer evidence in a wide range of offices, laboratories, and companies suspected of WMD work. The pattern of these efforts to erase evidence—hard drives destroyed, specific files burned, equipment cleaned of all traces of use—are ones of deliberate, rather than random, acts. For example,

- On 10 July 2003 an ISG team exploited the Revolutionary Command Council (RCC) Headquarters in Baghdad. The basement of the main building contained an archive of documents situated on well-organized rows of metal shelving. The basement suffered no fire damage despite the total destruction of the upper floors from coalition air strikes. Upon arrival the exploitation team encountered small piles of ash where individual documents or binders of documents were intentionally destroyed. Computer hard drives had been deliberately destroyed. Computers would have had financial value to a random looter; their destruction, rather than removal for resale or reuse, indicates a targeted effort to prevent Coalition forces from gaining access to their contents.

- All IIS [Iraqi Intelligence Service] laboratories visited by IIS exploitation teams have been clearly sanitized, including removal of much equipment, shredding and burning of documents, and even the removal of nameplates from office doors.

- Although much of the deliberate destruction and sanitization of documents and records probably occurred during the height of OIF combat operations, indications of significant continuing destruction efforts have been found after the end of major combat operations, including entry in May 2003 of the locked gated vaults of the Ba'ath party intelligence building in Baghdad and highly selective destruction of computer hard drives and data storage equipment along with the burning of a small number of specific binders that appear to have contained financial and intelligence records, and in July 2003 a site exploitation team at the Abu Ghurayb Prison found one pile of the smoldering ashes from documents that was still warm to the touch.

I would now like to review our efforts in each of the major lines of enquiry that ISG has pursued during this initial phase of its work.

With regard to biological warfare activities, which has been one of our two initial areas of focus, ISG teams are uncovering significant information—including research and development of BW-applicable organisms, the involvement of Iraqi Intelligence Service (IIS) in possible BW activities, and deliberate concealment activities. All of this suggests Iraq after 1996 further compartmentalized its program and focused on maintaining smaller, covert capabilities that could be activated quickly to surge the production of BW agents.

Debriefings of IIS officials and site visits have begun to unravel a clandestine network of laboratories and facilities within the security service apparatus. This network was never declared to the UN and was previously unknown. We are still working on determining the extent to which this network was tied to large-scale military efforts or BW [biological warfare] terror weapons, but this clandestine capability was suitable for preserving BW expertise, BW capable facilities and continuing R&D [research and development]—all key elements for maintaining a capability for resuming BW production. The IIS also played a prominent role in sponsoring students for overseas graduate studies in the biological sciences, according to Iraqi scientists and IIS sources, providing an important avenue for furthering BW-applicable research. This was the only area of graduate work that the IIS appeared to sponsor.

Discussions with Iraqi scientists uncovered agent R&D work that paired overt work with nonpathogenic organisms serving as surrogates for prohibited investigation with pathogenic agents. Examples include: *B. Thurengiensis* (Bt) with *B. anthracis* (anthrax), and medicinal plants with ricin. In a similar vein, two key former BW scientists confirmed that Iraq under the guise of legitimate activity developed refinements of processes and products relevant to BW agents. The scientists discussed the development of improved, simplified fermentation and spray drying capabilities for the simulant Bt that would have been directly applicable to anthrax, and one scientist confirmed that the production line for Bt could be switched to produce anthrax in one week if the seed stock were available.

A very large body of information has been developed through debriefings, site visits, and exploitation of captured Iraqi documents that confirms that Iraq concealed equipment and materials from UN inspectors when they returned in 2002. One noteworthy example is a collection of reference strains that ought to have been declared to the UN. Among them was a vial of live C. botulinum Okra B. from which a biological agent can be produced. This discovery—hidden in the home of a BW scientist—illustrates the point I made earlier about the difficulty of locating small stocks of material that can be used to covertly surge production of deadly weapons. The scientist who concealed the vials containing this agent has identified a large cache of agents that he was asked, but refused, to conceal. ISG is actively searching for this second cache.

Additional information is beginning to corroborate reporting since 1996 about human testing activities using chemical and biological substances, but progress in this area is slow given the concern of knowledgeable Iraqi personnel about their being prosecuted for crimes against humanity.

We have not yet been able to corroborate the existence of a mobile BW production effort. Investigation into the origin of and intended use for the two trailers found in northern Iraq in April has yielded a number of explanations, including hydrogen, missile propellant, and BW production, but technical limitations would prevent any of these processes from being ideally suited to these trailers. That said, nothing we have discovered rules out their potential use in BW production.

We have made significant progress in identifying and locating individuals who were reportedly involved in a mobile program, and we are confident that we will be able to get an answer to the questions as to whether there was a mobile program and whether the trailers that have been discovered so far were part of such a program.

Let me turn now to chemical weapons (CW). In searching for retained stocks of chemical munitions, ISG has had to contend with the almost unbelievable scale of Iraq's conventional weapons armory, which dwarfs by orders of magnitude the physical size of any conceivable stock of chemical weapons. For example, there are approximately 130 known Iraqi Ammunition Storage Points (ASP), many of which exceed 50 square miles in size and hold an estimated 600,000 tons of artillery shells, rockets, aviation bombs and other ordinance. Of these 130 ASPs, approximately 120 still remain unexamined. As Iraqi practice was not to mark much of their chemical ordinance and to store it at the same ASPs that held conventional rounds, the size of the required search effort is enormous.

While searching for retained weapons, ISG teams have developed multiple sources that indicate that Iraq explored the possibility of CW production in recent years, possibly as late as 2003. When Saddam had asked a senior military official in either 2001 or 2002 how long it would take to produce new chemical agent and weapons, he told ISG that after he consulted with CW experts in OMI he responded it would take six months for mustard. Another senior Iraqi chemical weapons expert in responding to a request in mid-2002 from Uday Husayn for CW for the Fedayeen Saddam estimated that it would take two months to produce mustard and two years for Sarin.

We are starting to survey parts of Iraq's chemical industry to determine if suitable equipment and bulk chemicals were available for chemical weapons production. We have been struck that two senior Iraqi officials volunteered that if they had been ordered to resume CW production Iraq would have been willing to use stainless steel systems that would be disposed of after a few production runs, in place of corrosive-resistant equipment which they did not have.

We continue to follow leads on Iraq's acquisition of equipment and bulk precursors suitable for a CW program. Several possibilities have emerged and are now being exploited. One example involves a foreign company with offices in Baghdad that imported in the past into Iraq dual-use equipment and maintained active contracts through 2002. Its Baghdad office was found looted in August 2003, but we are pursuing other locations and associates of the company.

Information obtained since OIF has identified several key areas in which Iraq may have engaged in proscribed or undeclared activity since 1991, including research on a possible VX stabilizer, research and development for CW-capable munitions, and procurement/concealment of dual-use materials and equipment.

Multiple sources with varied access and reliability have told ISG that Iraq did not have a large, ongoing, centrally controlled CW program after 1991. Information found to date suggests that Iraq's large-scale capability to develop, produce, and fill new CW munitions was reduced—if not entirely destroyed—during Operations Desert Storm [the 1991 Persian Gulf war] and Desert Fox [U.S. attacks on Iraq in 1998], 13 years of UN sanctions and UN inspections. We are carefully examining dual-use, commercial chemical facilities to determine whether these were used or planned as alternative production sites.

We have also acquired information related to Iraq's CW doctrine and Iraq's war plans for OIF, but we have not yet found evidence to confirm pre-war reporting that Iraqi military units were prepared to use CW against Coalition forces. Our efforts to collect and exploit intelligence on Iraq's chemical weapons program have thus far yielded little reliable information on post-1991 CW stocks and CW agent production, although we continue to receive and follow leads related to such stocks. We have multiple reports that Iraq retained CW munitions made prior to 1991, possibly including mustard—a long-lasting chemical agent—but we have to date been unable to locate any such munitions.

With regard to Iraq's nuclear program, the testimony we have obtained from Iraqi scientists and senior government officials should clear up any doubts about whether Saddam still wanted to obtain nuclear weapons. They have told ISG that Saddam Husayn remained firmly committed to acquiring nuclear weapons. These officials assert that Saddam would have resumed nuclear weapons development at some future point. Some indicated a resumption after Iraq was free of sanctions. At least one senior Iraqi official believed that by 2000 Saddam had run out of patience with waiting for sanctions to end and wanted to restart the nuclear program. The Iraqi Atomic Energy Commission (IAEC) beginning around 1999 expanded its laboratories and research activities and increased its overall funding levels. This expansion may have been in initial preparation for renewed nuclear weapons research, although documentary evidence of this has not been found, and this is the subject of continuing investigation by ISG.

Starting around 2000, the senior Iraqi Atomic Energy Commission (IAEC) and high-level Ba'ath Party official Dr. Khalid Ibrahim Sa'id began several small and relatively unsophisticated research initiatives that could be applied to nuclear weapons development. These initiatives did not in-and-of themselves constitute a resumption of the nuclear weapons program, but could have been useful in developing a weapons-relevant science base for the long-term. We do not yet have information indicating whether a higher government authority directed Sa'id to initiate this research and, regretfully, Dr. Said was killed on April 8th during the fall of Baghdad when the car he was riding in attempted to run a Coalition roadblock.

Despite evidence of Saddam's continued ambition to acquire nuclear weapons, to date we have not uncovered evidence that Iraq undertook significant post-1998 steps to actually build nuclear weapons or produce fissile material. However, Iraq did take steps to preserve some technological capability from the pre-1991 nuclear weapons program.

- According to documents and testimony of Iraqi scientists, some of the key technical groups from the pre-1991 nuclear weapons program remained largely intact, performing work on nuclear-relevant dual-use technologies within the Military Industrial Commission (MIC). Some scientists from the pre-1991 nuclear weapons program have told ISG that they believed that these working groups were preserved in order to allow a reconstitution of the nuclear weapons program, but none of the scientists could produce official orders or plans to support their belief.
- In some cases, these groups performed work which could help preserve the science base and core skills that would be needed for any future fissile material production or nuclear weapons development.
- Several scientists—at the direction of senior Iraqi government officials—preserved documents and equipment from their pre-1991 nuclear weapon-related research and did not reveal this to the UN/IAEA. One Iraqi scientist recently stated in an interview with ISG that it was a "common understanding" among the scientists that material was being preserved for reconstitution of nuclear weapons-related work.

The ISG nuclear team has found indications that there was interest, beginning in 2002, in reconstituting a centrifuge enrichment program. Most of this activity centered on activities of Dr. Sa'id that caused some of his former colleagues in the pre-1991 nuclear program to suspect that Dr. Sa'id, at least, was considering a restart of the centrifuge program. We do not yet fully understand Iraqi intentions, and the evidence does not tie any activity directly to centrifuge research or development.

Exploitation of additional documents may shed light on the projects and program plans of Dr. Khalid Ibrahim Sa'id. There may be more projects to be discovered in research placed at universities and private companies. Iraqi interest in reconstitution of a uranium enrichment program needs to be better understood through the analysis of procurement records and additional interviews.

With regard to delivery systems, the ISG team has discovered sufficient evidence to date to conclude that the Iraqi regime was committed to delivery system improvements that would have, if OIF had not occurred, dramatically breached UN restrictions placed on Iraq after the 1991 Gulf War.

Detainees and co-operative sources indicate that beginning in 2000 Saddam ordered the development of ballistic missiles with ranges of at least 400km and up to 1000km and that measures to conceal these projects from UNMOVIC [United Nations Monitoring, Verification and Inspection Commission in Iraq] were initiated in late-2002, ahead of the arrival of inspectors. Work was also underway for a clustered engine liquid propellant missile, and it appears the work had progressed to a point to support initial prototype production of some parts and assemblies. According to a cooperating senior detainee, Saddam concluded that the proposals from both the liquid-propellant and solid-propellant missile design centers would take too long. For instance, the liquid-propellant missile project team forecast first delivery in six years. Saddam countered in 2000 that he wanted the missile designed and built inside of six months. On the other hand several sources contend that Saddam's range requirements for the missiles grew from 400–500km in 2000 to 600–1000km in 2002.

ISG has gathered testimony from missile designers at Al Kindi State Company that Iraq has reinitiated work on converting SA-2 Surface-to-Air Missiles into ballistic missiles with a range goal of about 250km. Engineering work was reportedly underway in early 2003, despite the presence of UNMOVIC. This program was not declared to the UN. ISG is presently seeking additional confirmation and details on this project. A second cooperative source has stated that the program actually began in 2001, but that it received added impetus in the run-up to OIF, and that missiles from this project were transferred to a facility north of Baghdad. This source also provided documentary evidence of instructions to convert SA-2s into surface-to-surface missiles.

ISG has obtained testimony from both detainees and cooperative sources that indicate that proscribed-range solid-propellant missile design studies were initiated, or already underway, at the time when work on the clustered liquid-propellant missile designs began. The motor diameter was to be 800 to 1000mm, i.e. much greater than the 500-mm Ababil-100. The range goals cited for this system vary from over 400km up to 1000km, depending on the source and the payload mass.

A cooperative source, involved in the 2001–2002 deliberations on the long-range solid propellant project, provided ISG with a set of concept designs for a launcher designed to accommodate a 1m diameter by 9m length missile. The limited detail in the drawings suggest there was some way to go before launcher fabrication. The source believes that these drawings would not have been requested until the missile progress was relatively advanced, normally beyond the design state. The drawings are in CAD [computer-assisted design] format, with files dated 09/01/02.

While we have obtained enough information to make us confident that this design effort was underway, we are not yet confident which accounts of the timeline and project progress are accurate and are now seeking to better understand this program and its actual progress at the time of OIF.

One cooperative source has said that he suspected that the new large-diameter solid-propellant missile was intended to have a CW-filled warhead, but no detainee has admitted any actual knowledge of plans for unconventional warheads for any current or planned ballistic missile. The suspicion expressed by the one source about a CW warhead was based on his assessment of the unavailability of nuclear warheads and potential survivability problems of biological warfare agent in ballistic missile warheads. This is an area of great interest and we are seeking additional information on warhead designs.

While I have spoken so far of planned missile systems, one high-level detainee has recently claimed that Iraq retained a small quantity of Scud-variant missiles until at least 2001. Although he subsequently recanted these claims, work continues to determine the truth. Two other sources contend that Iraq continued to produce until 2001 liquid fuel and oxidizer specific to Scud-type systems. The cooperating source claims that the al Tariq Factory was used to manufacture Scud oxidizer (IRFNA) from 1996 to 2001, and that nitrogen tetroxide, a chief ingredient of IRFNA was collected from a bleed port on the production equipment, was reserved, and then mixed with highly concentrated nitric acid plus an inhibitor to produce Scud oxidizer. Iraq never declared its pre-Gulf War capability to manufacture Scud IRFNA out of fear, multiple sources have stated, that the al Tariq Factory would be destroyed, leaving Baghdad without the ability to produce highly concentrated nitric acid, explosives and munitions. To date we have not discovered documentary or material evidence to corroborate these claims, but continued efforts are underway to clarify and confirm this information with additional Iraqi sources and to locate corroborating physical evidence. If we can confirm that the fuel was produced as late as 2001, and given that Scud fuel can only be used in Scud-variant missiles, we will have strong evidence that the missiles must have been retained until that date. This would, of course, be yet another example of a failure to declare prohibited activities to the UN.

Iraq was continuing to develop a variety of UAV platforms and maintained two UAV programs that were working in parallel, one at Ibn Fernas and one at al-Rashid Air Force Base. Ibn Fernas worked on the development of smaller, more traditional types of UAVs in addition to the conversion of manned aircraft into UAVs. This program was not declared to the UN until the 2002 CAFCD in which Iraq declared the RPV-20, RPV-30 and Pigeon RPV systems to the UN. All these systems had declared ranges of less than 150km. Several Iraqi officials stated that the RPV-20 flew over 500km on autopilot in 2002, contradicting Iraq's declaration on the system's range. The al-Rashid group was developing a competing line of UAVs. This program was never fully declared to the UN and is the subject of on-going work by ISG. Additional work is also focusing on the payloads and intended use for these UAVs. Surveillance and use as decoys are uses mentioned by some of those interviewed. Given Iraq's interest before the Gulf War in attempting to convert a

MIG-21 into an unmanned aerial vehicle to carry spray tanks capable of dispensing chemical or biological agents, attention is being paid to whether any of the newer generation of UAVs were intended to have a similar purpose. This remains an open question.

ISG has discovered evidence of two primary cruise missile programs. The first appears to have been successfully implemented, whereas the second had not yet reached maturity at the time of OIF.

The first involved upgrades to the HY-2 coastal-defense cruise missile. ISG has developed multiple sources of testimony, which is corroborated in part by a captured document, that Iraq undertook a program aimed at increasing the HY-2's range and permitting its use as a land-attack missile. These efforts extended the HY-2's range from its original 100km to 150–180km. Ten modified missiles were delivered to the military prior to OIF and two of these were fired from Umm Qasr during OIF—one was shot down and one hit Kuwait.

The second program, called the Jenin, was a much more ambitious effort to convert the HY-2 into a 1000km range land-attack cruise missile. The Jenin concept was presented to Saddam on 23 November 2001 and received what cooperative sources called an "unusually quick response" in little more than a week. The essence of the concept was to take an HY-2, strip it of its liquid rocket engine, and put in its place a turbine engine from a Russian helicopter—the TV-2-117 or TV3-117 from a Mi-8 or Mi-17 helicopter. To prevent discovery by the UN, Iraq halted engine development and testing and disassembled the test stand in late 2002 before the design criteria had been met.

In addition to the activities detailed here on Iraq's attempts to develop delivery systems beyond the permitted UN 150km, ISG has also developed information on Iraqi attempts to purchase proscribed missiles and missile technology. Documents found by ISG describe a high level dialogue between Iraq and North Korea that began in December 1999 and included an October 2000 meeting in Baghdad. These documents indicate Iraqi interest in the transfer of technology for surface-to-surface missiles with a range of 1300km (probably No Dong) and land-to-sea missiles with a range of 300km. The document quotes the North Koreans as understanding the limitations imposed by the UN, but being prepared "to cooperate with Iraq on the items it specified". At the time of OIF, these discussions had not led to any missiles being transferred to Iraq. A high level cooperating source has reported that in late 2002 at Saddam's behest a delegation of Iraqi officials was sent to meet with foreign export companies, including one that dealt with missiles. Iraq was interested in buying an advanced ballistic missile with 270km and 500km ranges.

The ISG has also identified a large volume of material and testimony by cooperating Iraq officials on Iraq's effort to illicitly procure parts and foreign assistance for its missile program. These include:

- Significant level of assistance from a foreign company and its network of affiliates in supplying and supporting the development of production capabilities for solid rocket propellant and dual-use chemicals.
- Entities from another foreign country were involved in supplying guidance and control systems for use in the Al-Fat'h (Ababil-100). The contract was incomplete by the time of OIF due to technical problems with the few systems delivered and a financial dispute.
- A group of foreign experts operating in a private capacity were helping to develop Iraq's liquid propellant ballistic missile RDT&E and production infrastructure. They worked in Baghdad for about three months in late 1998 and subsequently continued work on the project from abroad. An actual contract valued at $10 million for machinery and equipment was signed in June 2001, initially for 18 months, but later extended. This cooperation continued right up until the war.
- A different group of foreign experts traveled to Iraq in 1999 to conduct a technical review that resulted in what became the Al Samoud 2 design, and a contract was signed in 2001 for the provision of rigs, fixtures and control equipment for the redesigned missile.
- Detainees and cooperative sources have described the role of a foreign expert in negotiations on the development of Iraq's liquid and solid propellant production infrastructure. This could have had applications in existing and planned longer range systems, although it is reported that nothing had actually been implemented before OIF.

Uncertainty remains about the full extent of foreign assistance to Iraq's planned expansion of its missile systems and work is continuing to gain a full resolution of this issue. However, there is little doubt from the evidence already gathered that there was substantial illegal procurement for all aspects of the missile programs.

I have covered a lot of ground today, much of it highly technical. Although we are resisting drawing conclusions in this first interim report, a number of things have become clearer already as a result of our investigation, among them:

1. Saddam, at least as judged by those scientists and other insiders who worked in his military-industrial programs, had not given up his aspirations and intentions to continue to acquire weapons of mass destruction. Even those senior officials we have interviewed who claim no direct knowledge of any on-going prohibited activities readily acknowledge that Saddam intended to resume these programs whenever the external restrictions were removed. Several of these officials acknowledge receiving inquiries since 2000 from Saddam or his sons about how long it would take to either restart CW production or make available chemical weapons.

2. In the delivery systems area there were already well advanced, but undeclared, on-going activities that, if OIF had not intervened, would have resulted in the production of missiles with ranges at least up to 1000 km, well in excess of the UN permitted range of 150 km. These missile activities were supported by a serious clandestine procurement program about which we have much still to learn.

3. In the chemical and biological weapons area we have confidence that there were at a minimum clandestine on-going research and development activities that were embedded in the Iraqi Intelligence Service. While we have much yet to learn about the exact work programs and capabilities of these activities, it is already apparent that these undeclared activities would have at a minimum facilitated chemical and biological weapons activities and provided a technically trained cadre.

Let me conclude by returning to something I began with today. We face a unique but challenging opportunity in our efforts to unravel the exact status of Iraq's WMD program. The good news is that we do not have to rely for the first time in over a decade on

- the incomplete, and often false, data that Iraq supplied the UN/IAEA;
- data collected by UN inspectors operating with the severe constraints that Iraqi security and deception actions imposed;
- information supplied by defectors, some of whom certainly fabricated much that they supplied and perhaps were under the direct control of the IIS;
- data collected by national technical collections systems with their own limitations.

The bad news is that we have to do this under conditions that ensure that our work will take time and impose serious physical dangers on those who are asked to carry it out.

Why should we take the time and run the risk to ensure that our conclusions reflect the truth to the maximum extent that is possible given the conditions in post-conflict Iraq? For those of us that are carrying out this search, there are two reasons that drive us to want to complete this effort.

First, whatever we find will probably differ from pre-war intelligence. Empirical reality on the ground is, and has always been, different from intelligence judgments that must be made under serious constraints of time, distance and information. It is, however, only by understanding precisely what those differences are that the quality of future intelligence and investment decisions concerning future intelligence systems can be improved. Proliferation of weapons of mass destruction is such a continuing threat to global society that learning those lessons has a high imperative.

Second, we have found people, technical information and illicit procurement networks that if allowed to flow to other countries and regions could accelerate global proliferation. Even in the area of actual weapons there is no doubt that Iraq had at one time chemical and biological weapons. Even if there were only a remote possibility that these pre-1991 weapons still exist, we have an obligation to American troops who are now there and the Iraqi population to ensure that none of these remain to be used against them in the ongoing insurgency activity.

Mr. Chairman and Members I appreciate this opportunity to share with you the initial results of the first 3 months of the activities of the Iraqi Survey Group. I am certain that I speak for Major General Keith Dayton, who commands the Iraqi Survey Group, when I say how proud we are of the men and women from across the Government and from our Coalition partners, Australia and the United Kingdom, who have gone to Iraq and are carrying out this important mission.

Thank you.

Source: U.S. Central Intelligence Agency. "Statement by David Kay on the Interim Progress Report on the Activities of the Iraq Survey Group before the House Permanent Select Committee on Intelligence, the House Committee on Appropriations, Subcommittee on Defense, and the Senate Select Committee on Intelligence." October 2, 2003. www.cia.gov/cia/public_affairs/speeches/2003/david_kay_10022003.html (accessed October 2, 2003).

GAO, Homeland Security Department on Weapons of Mass Destruction

October 7 and December 19, 2003

INTRODUCTION

The term "weapons of mass destruction" (WMDs)—once familiar only to diplomats and a handful of experts—entered the popular lexicon during 2003 because of the high-profile search for them in Iraq and the Bush administration's focus on the alleged efforts by Iran, North Korea, and terrorist groups to acquire them. At year's end, Libya unexpectedly acknowledged that it, too, had worked to develop these weapons but was renouncing that effort. *(Iraq, p. 135; North Korea, p. 592; Iran, p. 1025; Libya, p. 1218)*

Three types of weapons were generally considered to be weapons of mass destruction: biological, chemical, and nuclear. The "mass destruction" title signified the fact that a single such weapon, if used properly, could kill hundreds or thousands of people.

For decades diplomats had negotiated treaties intended to slow or even halt the spread of these weapons around the world. The success of these treaties was subject to intense debate, and that debate became even hotter following the September 11, 2001, terrorist attacks against the United States.

President George W. Bush and his aides argued that terrorists, including the al Qaeda network that sponsored those attacks, were intent on acquiring WMDs. Bush said the United States would take preemptive action, if necessary, to protect itself from being attacked by those weapons. He followed through on that pledge in 2003 with a war in Iraq, charging that the regime of Saddam Hussein might give its weapons to terrorists. Back at home, government agencies from the national to the local level were struggling to establish procedures to deal with a WMD attack, should one occur.

Loose Controls on U.S. Weapon Materials

Congressional investigations, reports by independent agencies, and news reports during the year indicated that some of the equipment and material needed to fashion WMDs still lacked adequate protection in the United States. Perhaps the most startling revelation came in a report given Congress on October 7 by the General Accounting Office (GAO), the investigative arm of Congress. Gregory D. Kutz, director of GAO's Financial Management And Assurance Division, told a House subcommittee that investigators had used a fictitious company to buy surplus equipment that could be used to manufacture biological weapons. The purchases were all made over the Internet from a private contractor hired by the Pentagon to dispose of surplus equipment. Among other things, the GAO bought a bacteriological incubator, a laboratory centrifuge, an evaporator, a biological safety cabinet, and clothing and other gear to protect against exposure to biological or chemical weapons. Kutz sad the GAO bought this equipment for a total of $4,000; the Pentagon's original cost to buy it was $46,960.

In addition to disclosing how easy it was to buy such equipment, the GAO report demonstrated that the Pentagon made no effort to determine who was buying the surplus equipment. Kutz said the GAO identified 176 Internet buyers of similar biological laboratory equipment. The agency contacted 42 of those buyers and discovered that 15 of them had exported the equipment to secondary buyers in other countries, including Canada, Dubai, Egypt, Malaysia, and the Philippines. These sales appeared to circumvent U.S. law, which barred exports of similar items to those countries, Kutz said. The Pentagon in January 2003 had restricted the sale of biological and chemical weapons protective gear to the public, but the GAO said that Pentagon units "did not always follow the policy." Fred Baillie, an executive with the Defense Logistics Agency, said the Pentagon was taking steps to correct the problems identified by the GAO report.

Another GAO report, released June 24, uncovered security lapses at the nation's three nuclear weapons laboratories. The report said that staffing shortages, bureaucratic obstacles, and "confusion about roles and responsibilities" had hampered the Energy Department's management of security at the laboratories. Investigators had uncovered specific lapses, such as a the theft of computers, guards found to be asleep, and the unreported loss of two vials of plutonium oxide.

In November the Agriculture Department's inspector general reported that laboratories at some universities failed to provide adequate security for pathogens that could be used to make biological weapons. In one case, a biological agent for a form of the plague was kept in an unlocked freezer. Many college laboratories lacked such basic security measures as alarm systems and surveillance cameras.

Preparing for Attacks in the United States

Long before the September 11 terrorist attacks experts had warned that the United States was ill-prepared to deal with the consequences of a significant attack by biological, chemical, or nuclear weapons. Among other things, numerous reports said that first responders (fire, police, and emergency medical personnel) lacked proper equipment and training to help the victims of such weapons, and a single attack in any metropolitan area would overwhelm local hospitals with victims. After the September 11 attacks demonstrated some of these problems in real life, the federal government stepped up aid to local and state governments to improve their response to major emergencies, including terrorist attacks. Even so, the federal money was slow in reaching many localities, and reports continued to suggest that the country was only marginally better prepared than it had been. *(Background, Historic Documents of 2000, p. 281; Historic Documents of 2001, p. 672)*

To test preparedness at the federal, state, and local level, the Department of Homeland Security conducted an elaborate exercise from May 12 to May 16 in the Seattle and Chicago areas. In Seattle a "terrorist organization" supposedly detonated a so-called dirty bomb (known officially as a radiological dispersal device), which combined radioactive nuclear material with a conventional explosive. In Chicago the same "terrorist" group released material containing the pneumonic plague, one of the most dangerous biological agents. This exercise, called Top Officials Exercise Series (or TOPOFF), was a follow-up to a smaller one conducted in 2000.

In a report released December 19, the Department of Homeland Security said the exercise had uncovered numerous communications and logistical problems in both locations. In Seattle, for example, emergency personnel could not determine for many hours where the radiation from the pretend dirty bomb had spread—causing delays, which could be fatal, in evacuating and treating people who had been exposed. Chicago's drill jammed telephone lines, which made it difficult for emergency personnel to communicate with each other. That drill also uncovered a severe shortage of medical supplies, along with a widespread uncertainty among medical personnel about how to treat victims of the plague.

Homeland security officials said the exercise involved more than 8,500 people from about 100 federal, state, and local agencies, as well as the Canadian government. The department called the exercise a success because it identified both emergency procedures that worked and those that did not. In particular, officials said they were pleased by the results from having sixty-four hospitals in the Chicago area participate in the exercise.

On December 28 the *New York Times* reported that the Bush administration had conducted another high-level exercise, in November, that simulated the release of anthrax, in aerosol form, in several cities. The exercise was intended to determine the country's ability to deal with a larger-scale version of the isolated anthrax attack that occurred in late 2001, which appeared to be aimed at members of Congress and well-known news media personnel. Five people died as a result of the 2001 attack, and the perpetrator had not been found as of the end of 2003. *(Anthrax attack, Historic Documents of 2001, p. 674)*

The November exercise, code named Scarlet Cloud, showed that the government had improved its ability to detect an anthrax attack since 2001, the *Times* reported. Even so, the drill demonstrated that a simultaneous anthrax attack could kill thousands of people, panic the public, and overwhelm the ability of medical personnel to deliver and administer antibiotics to victims. The *Times* and other news organizations reported during the year that the al Qaeda terrorist network—the sponsor of the September 11 attacks—had been seeking biological and chemical weapons, including anthrax.

A broad analysis of the ability of hospitals to deal with the consequences of biological terrorism attacks ("bioterrorism") was conducted during the year by the GAO. In a report to Congress on August 6, the agency said it had sent surveys to 2,041 urban hospitals and received responses from 1,482. Most hospitals reported that they had emergency plans and had provided at least some training to their personnel for dealing with biological agents. Fewer than half the hospitals had conducted any emergency drills for a bioterrorism attack, and most hospitals did not have enough equipment or supplies (such as ventilators) to deal with a large influx of patients from a terrorist attack.

New U.S. Nuclear Weapons

The Bush administration in 2003 won approval from Congress for work to develop a new generation of "low-yield" nuclear weapons—the first expansion of the U.S. arsenal since the collapse of the Soviet Union a dozen years earlier. The weapons were called low yield because they would produce an explosive force of less than 5,000 tons of TNT (which is less than one-third the force of the bomb the United States dropped on Hiroshima in 1945). The United States long had possessed such weapons, but Congress in 1993 banned the development of new ones because of an assumption that the end of the cold war made them unnecessary. Some weapons researchers and advocates of modernizing the U.S. nuclear arsenal pushed throughout the 1990s to repeal the 1993 ban but had no success. The Bush administration signaled in 2002 that it was interested in developing new low-yield weapons that could be affixed to earth-boring missiles to destroy underground bunkers. Bush in 2003 formally asked Congress to repeal the 1993 ban so research could begin on those weapons.

Bush's request generated significant controversy, especially in the Senate, which debated it twice. Opponents, most of them Democrats, said a move by the United States to develop new weapons might trigger a new worldwide nuclear arms race; advocates said lifting the ban merely gave the administration flexibility to upgrade the U.S. arsenal. The administration won both votes in the Senate on the issue, by a 59–38 margin on May 21 and by a 53–41 margin on September 16. Both votes came on the fiscal 2004 Defense Department authorization bill, which Bush signed into law (PL 108–136) on November 24. That law allowed the administration to perform engineering work on the new weapons but barred actual development or deployment of them; the latter restriction merely postponed further action on the new weapon until after it had been designed. In a separate Energy Department spending bill, Congress allocated $6 million for the research.

Congress also gave the administration $7.5 million to continue research on a "Nuclear Earth Penetrator": a nuclear-tipped missile that would be able to dive deep beneath the Earth's surface to destroy buried targets, such as WMDs that an enemy had stored in underground bunkers. Yet another administration request approved by Congress was for $25 million to upgrade the U.S. nuclear testing grounds in Nevada to reduce the amount of time that would be needed to resume the testing of nuclear weapons. Bush's father, President George H. W. Bush, had halted U.S. nuclear testing in 1992, and the policy had been in place ever since, although the government had the stated capability of resuming tests within two to three years of a presidential order to do so. Bush said he needed $25 million for programs that would enable testing to be resumed within eighteen months. Congress approved both of these requests in the fiscal 2005 appropriations bill for the Energy Department (PL 108–137).

Updating Nuclear Nonproliferation Controls

The U.S. war against terrorism following the September 11 attacks—coupled with renewed allegations that Iran, Iraq, and North Korea had attempted to develop nuclear weapons—drew heightened attention during 2003 to the longstanding international system to control the spread of technology needed to make nuclear weapons. Since taking office in 2001 the Bush administration had argued that treaties and diplomacy had failed to prevent determined countries from obtaining bomb-making materials on the black market. Terrorist groups, notably al Qaeda, also were trying to acquire these weapons, the administration said. As a consequence, the administration had argued, in various strategy documents released in 2002, that the United States had the right and duty to take preemptive action to protect itself against possible attacks. The U.S. war against Iraq in 2003 was the first use of this theory of preemption. *(Preemption doctrine, Historic Documents of 2002, p. 633)*

The administration added another component to its policy after the start of the Iraq War, unveiling what it called a Proliferation Security Initiative on May 31. That initiative, which included several NATO allies plus Australia and Japan, called for a series of joint exercises in 2003 and 2004 to train military and law enforcement personnel to detect and interdict illegal trading in components for WMDs, as well as missiles.

Yet another component of administration policy emerged September 23, when Bush called on the United Nations to ban all forms of international trafficking in biological, chemical, and nuclear weapons or material. For decades UN treaties had aimed to control the weapons trade among nations but did not specifically ban the sale of mass weapons to individuals or groups, such as the al Qaeda terrorist network. U.S. diplomats gave the Security Council a draft proposal on December 16 that would require countries to make trafficking in mass weapons a criminal offense and prevent transfers of those weapons, or materials needed to make them, to all "non-state" entities. The proposal did not include a mechanism for the United Nations to enforce this weapon ban—in effect leaving that responsibility to individual countries. The Security Council had not acted on the proposal by year's end.

One other proposal for containing the spread of nuclear weapons came on November 3 from Mohamed El Baradei, head of the International Atomic Energy Agency. In a speech to the UN General Assembly, El Baradei said all facilities capable of producing weapons-grade material (plutonium and highly enriched uranium) should be placed under "multinational control"—in other words, under the supervision of his agency.

Controlling Former Soviet Weapons

A host of U.S.-funded programs to dismantle and protect biological, chemical, and nuclear weapons in Russia continued to operate in 2003, but at a slower pace than officials in both countries had promised. Since 1992 the United States had spent more than $6 billion to help the Russian government destroy thousands of missiles, submarines, and other weapons that had been built by the Soviet Union during the cold war. U.S. funding also helped Russia upgrade security at weapons-storage facilities, which were able to install fencing, alarms, and surveillance cameras, among other precautions. (Background, Historic Documents of 2002, p. 437)

In a report issued March 5, the GAO said that after ten years Russia was still not cooperating fully with the United States on these programs, even though Russian president Vladimir Putin had personally pledged full cooperation to Bush. The Russian government had failed to pay its share for several major projects, including the $275 million it had promised for construction of a major nuclear-weapons storage warehouse, the GAO said. In addition, Moscow was continuing to deny U.S. officials access to important weapons facilities, including some that the two countries had agreed to renovate with U.S. funds.

In 2002 leaders of the Group of Eight industrialized nations agreed to match a $10 billion, ten-year U.S. commitment to secure Russia's vast weapons arsenal. As of late 2003, however, the other nations had provided virtually none of the money they promised, according to the Nuclear Threat Institute, a Washington think tank that studied the issue.

A U.S.-Russian treaty intended to reduce both countries' arsenals of long-range nuclear weapons became law on June 1. Signed by Bush and Putin in 2002, the treaty required each country to reduce its deployed arsenal to fewer than 2,200 warheads by 2012; that level was less than one-third of each country's existing arsenal, and about one-fifth as many as the United States deployed at the height of the cold war. Despite the cutbacks, the Bush administration said the United States would retain several thousand warheads in storage. Critics said that provision made the treaty almost meaningless. The U.S. Senate approved the treaty by a 95–0 vote on March 6, even though some members in both parties expressed deep concerns about the lack of details in its three pages. Both chambers of Russia's legislature approved the treaty in May, shortly before Bush and Putin exchanged ratification documents during a summit meeting in St. Petersburg. *(Background, Historic Documents of 2002, p. 275)*

Following are excerpts from two reports: first, "DOD Excess Property: Risk Assessment Needed on Public Sales of Equipment that Could be Used to Make Biological Weapons," a report to Congress released October 7, 2003, by the General Accounting Office and delivered to the Subcommittee on National Security, Emerging Threats, and International Relations of the House Committee on Government Reform by Gregory D. Kutz, GAO's director of financial management and assurance; second, "Top Officials (TOPOFF) Exercise Series: TOPOFF 2, After Action Summary Report for Public Release," a report by the Department of Homeland Security, issued December 19, 2003.

"DOD Excess Property"

Conflicting statements have been made before the Congress on how difficult it would be for terrorists or a lone scientist to effectively produce and disseminate anthrax to cause mass casualties. As we previously reported, terrorists face serious technical and operational challenges at different stages of the process for producing and delivering biological agents. Experts represented to us that the production of biological agents as a weapon of mass destruction would require substantial expertise and sophisticated equipment, and that several other obstacles would need to be overcome. For example, terrorists who may lack access to an effective vaccine or antibiotic/antiviral treatment for biological agents would be exposed to a significant risk. In addition, terrorists would risk capture and personal safety in acquiring and processing source materials, disposing of byproducts, and releasing the anthrax. Further, outdoor delivery of anthrax can be disrupted by pollution and meteorological conditions. Once released, an aerosol cloud gradually dissipates over time as a result of exposure to oxygen, pollutants, and ultraviolet rays. If wind conditions are too erratic or strong, the agent might dissipate too rapidly or fail to reach the desired area. Indoor dissemination of anthrax could be affected by the air exchange rate of the building. Given the difficulty involved in producing and releasing high-quality agents that could cause mass casualties, experts told us it is more likely that terrorists could produce and disseminate a crude form of anthrax or biological agent. The dissemination of even a crude form of anthrax, particularly with simultaneous dissemination at multiple locations, could result in widespread shutdowns, panic, possibly some infections and deaths, and major national security concerns.

Further, as previously reported by GAO and six other federal agencies, there is a lack of assurance that biological source agents have not fallen into the wrong hands due to poor controls at laboratories handling biological source agents through at least 2002. The DOD Inspector General (IG) has reviewed 26 federal agency investigative reports on security over biological source agents prepared by the Department of Agriculture, the Army, DOD, the Department of Energy, the Department of Health and Human Services (HHS), and the Department of Veterans Affairs. The DOD IG review identified nine systemic areas of weaknesses that were reported for more than one agency, including management oversight, policy and procedures, physical security, personnel access, inventory control, emergency plans, the Centers for Disease Control and Prevention (CDC) registration, training, and transfer controls. According to a DOD IG official, at the time of the 2001 anthrax attacks, it was determined that the federal government did not have a complete inventory of biological source agents. Moreover, laboratories did not have a complete inventory of the source agents they handled, and they had not performed risk assessments as a means of identifying and reducing or eliminating vulnerabilities. The possibility that anthrax and other biological source agents could have fallen into the wrong hands due to poor controls at laboratories handling biological agents, as previously reported by GAO and other federal investigators, calls for an assessment of the national security risk posed by public sales of excess DOD biological laboratory equipment and protective clothing.

While our audit and investigation focused on DOD sales of laboratory equipment, laboratory equipment is available from other sources, including General Services Administration (GSA) sales of federal agency excess property, medical industry supplies, manufacturers, and others— indicating a much broader problem. Our DOD work covered excess property inventory activity related to five case study items, including four pieces of biological laboratory equipment and chemical and biological protective suits (coats and trousers), for fiscal year 2000 through the first 6 months of fiscal year 2003. We obtained and analyzed DOD's excess property database and its Internet sales database, except that we did not audit the general operating system or application system controls over the electronic data processing of DOD excess property transactions or verify the accuracy of the databases. In performing our work, we discussed the production, weaponization, and dissemination of biological agents with experts formerly with U.S. and foreign biological warfare and public health programs. We conducted our audit work and our investigative work from December 2002 through September 2003. . . .

My remarks today will focus on (1) the extent to which DOD is selling biological equipment and protective clothing that can be used to make and disseminate biological agents, such as anthrax, and (2) whether existing federal regulations and guidance in DOD policies and procedures address the risk of public sales of these items.

Summary

In summary, we found that DOD was selling excess biological laboratory equipment and chemical and biological protective clothing over the Internet to the public from its excess property inventory for pennies on the dollar, making them both easy and economical to obtain. The possibility that anthrax and other biological source agents could have fallen into the wrong hands combined with the ability to easily and economically obtain excess DOD biological equipment and protective clothing over the Internet increase the risk that this equipment could be used to produce and disseminate a biological warfare agent, such as a crude form of anthrax. Although the production of biological warfare agents requires a high degree of expertise, public sales of these DOD excess items increase the risk that terrorists could obtain and use them to produce and deliver biological agents within the United States.

In total, we spent about $4,100 using a fictitious company and fictitious individual identities to purchase over the Internet a large number of new and usable items, including a biological safety cabinet, a bacteriological incubator, a centrifuge, and an evaporator. We also purchased excess DOD chemical and biological protective suits (jackets and trousers) and related gear, such as a mask, hood, gloves, and boot covers that could be used to protect terrorists during the later stages of production of biological agents when particles may become aerosolized as well as during the handling and dissemination of biological warfare agents. The total original acquisition value of the items we purchased as $46,960. We submitted End Use Certificates [a form used by DOD to document the intended destination and disposition of sensitive, controlled items released from the department] in the name of a fictitious individual for our purchases of chemical and biological protective clothing. DOD approved our End Use Certificates because there were no suspicious activity or export violations associated with the fictitious individual and our fictitious address was not detected.

Further, our investigation of numerous buyers of the DOD case study items identified a large secondary market for used biological equipment and protective clothing in good condition. We found that some buyers of excess DOD biological equipment resold these items to buyers in Canada, the Philippines, Malaysia, Egypt, and Dubai in the United Arab Emirates (UAE) for transit to India, Pakistan, and other countries. Once these items are in the secondary market, controls are not adequate to prevent their sale to countries that are prohibited from receiving exports of certain U.S. technological items that are subject to trade security control.

In reviewing federal regulations issued by other agencies with various authorities over the sale, control, or export of biological equipment and related DOD policies, we found that these requirements do not generally restrict DOD from selling the case study biological equipment to the general public. Further, DOD units did not always follow the department policy issued in January 2003 to restrict chemical and biological protective clothing to DOD use only. The Department of Homeland Security's Bureau of Customers and Border Protection has a program— Operation Shield American—to monitor sales and exports of about 100 nuclear, biological, and chemical items sought by terrorists, including all five of the types of items in our biological equipment and protective clothing case studies. Although Customs officials briefed DOD policy and investigating officials in December 2002, DOD has not reassessed its policy of selling excess biological equipment to the public. . . .

Source: U.S. Congress. General Accounting Office. "DOD Excess Property: Risk Assessment Needed on Public Sales of Equipment That Could Be Used to Make Biological Agents." Statement of Gregory D. Kutz, Keith A. Rhodes, and John Ryan before the Subcommittee on National Security, Emerging Threats and International Relations, House Committee on Government Reform. GAO–04–81TNI. October 7, 2003. [Not posted online for security reasons].

"TOPOFF 2, After Action Summary Report"

Introduction

Top Officials 2 (TOPOFF 2) was a Congressionally-mandated, national terrorism exercise that was designed to identify vulnerabilities in the nation's domestic incident management capability by exercising the plans, policies, procedures, systems, and facilities of federal, state, and local response organizations against a series of integrated terrorist threats and acts in separate regions of the country.

TOPOFF 2 was the largest and most comprehensive terrorism response exercise ever conducted in the United States. The exercise scenario, which was played out from May 12 to May 16, 2003, depicted a fictitious, foreign terrorist organization that detonated a simulated radiological dispersal device (RDD) in Seattle, Washington, and released the Pneumonic Plague (*Yersinia pestis*) in several Chicago metropolitan area locations. There was also significant pre-exercise intelligence play, a cyber-attack, and credible terrorism threats against other locations. The exercise brought together top government officials from 25 federal, state, and local agencies and departments, and the Canadian Government to test the domestic incident management in response to WMD terrorist attacks in the United States.

The first TOPOFF exercise, TOPOFF 2000, was a single, no-notice, exercise co-chaired by the Department of Justice and the Federal Emergency Management Agency (FEMA) in May 2000. Unlike TOPOFF 2000, TOPOFF 2 was designed as an "open" exercise in which participants were introduced to the exercise scenario prior to the exercise through a cycle of activity of increasing complexity that included:

- a series of seminars that explored emergency public information, RDD response, bioterrorism, and national direction and control issues; and
- the *Top Officials Seminar* that brought together top government officials from 25 FSL agencies and departments, and the Canadian Government, in a roundtable discussion to explore inter-governmental domestic incident management in response to WMD terrorist attacks on the United States.

The purpose of the open exercise design was to enhance the learning and preparedness value of the exercise through a "building-block" approach, and to enable participants to develop and strengthen relationships in the national response community. Participants at all levels stated that this approach has been of enormous value to their domestic preparedness strategies. . . .

Summary Findings

1. Alerts and Alerting: The Elevation of the Homeland Security Advisory System Threat Condition to Red

The TOPOFF 2 Exercise provided several opportunities to test the Homeland Security Advisory System (HSAS): it was the first time (real or notional) that the HSAS Threat Condition was raised to Red; it represented the first time for agencies to experiment with the actions associated with the Threat Condition of "Severe," or Red; and it allowed for examination of the implications of raising specific regions or localities to Red. In addition, local jurisdictions raised their own threat levels to Red. The exercise highlighted that additional refinement of this advisory system is needed. Findings from the exercise include the following:

- Following the local threat level elevations of Seattle and King County early in the exercise, there was uncertainty as to the status of the HSAS Threat Condition of other jurisdictions. This situation was caused in part by a) a lack of awareness of local threat advisory systems; b) inconsistent or non-existent formal notification protocols of threat elevations; and c) a lack of language clarity—elevations of the HSAS are referred to as elevations of the "national threat level," even if applied to regions or localities.
- There was also uncertainty regarding specific protective actions to be taken by specific agencies under a HSAS Severe Threat Condition Red. Many agencies lack a consistent and comprehensive understanding of the protective actions that might be taken by other agencies or jurisdictions under various threat levels.
- The federal, state, and local response to elevations of the HSAS needs to be further developed and synchronized. Participants in the TOPOFF 2 suggested the development of a tiered, operational response linked to the HSAS levels and based upon the nature of the threat. This system would be defined by a coalition of federal, state, and local agencies and would offer a comprehensive operational response framework that jurisdictions at all levels could use to help define their response plans at each HSAS Threat Condition.

2. Declarations and Proclamation of Disaster and Emergency

During the exercise, several declarations of emergencies and disasters were issued. Local and state jurisdictions in both exercise venues invoked their authorities to declare emergencies, and requested federal assistance under the Stafford Act. These requests ultimately led to a Presidential Declaration of Major Disaster in Washington and a Presidential Declaration of Emergency in Illinois. The bioterrorism attack in Illinois was especially challenging as its impact involved multiple counties, the city of Chicago and the state of Illinois. In addition, the Secretary of Health and Human Services declared a Public Health Emergency in the state of Illinois under the authorities of the Public Health Service Act. This occurred before the Presidential Declaration of Emergency, enabling the activation of several response assets. Findings from the exercise include the following:

- Officials in Illinois requested a Major Disaster Declaration to obtain maximum federal assistance for the growing bioterrorism disaster. The emergency declaration in Illinois led to concerns about whether some individual assistance programs, which are specifically authorized for a disaster but not for an emergency, would be authorized.
- It is worth noting that during the exercise, the large-scale bioterrorism attack did not qualify as a Major Disaster under the Stafford Act; biological disasters are not specifically cited in the Act. It is not clear from the exercise whether the difference in declaring a major disaster would result in substantive real-world issues given the exception clauses under declarations of emergency as previously described.
- The relationships between the authorities and resources brought to bear under the Public Health Act and the Stafford Act should continue to be exercised. The exercise did not indicate confusion with activation of the Public Health Act or the declaration by the HHS Secretary of a Public Health Emergency, but additional clarity, especially regarding the authorities and resources brought to bear under both Acts, would be valuable.

3. Department of Homeland Security Play in TOPOFF 2: The Role of the Principal Federal Official

The exercise was the first opportunity for the newly created DHS to exercise and experiment with its organization, functions, and assets. For example, the DHS Principal Federal Official (PFO) concept was first implemented during the exercise, which provided the opportunity to examine the role of the PFO during an emergency response. During the exercise, the PFOs in both venues facilitated integrated communications and coordinated action planning. Findings from the exercise include the following:

- The PFO was well-received and successfully integrated into the unified command structure in both venues. In Seattle, the PFO quickly instituted a unified command to manage the overall federal response and coordinate integrated communications and action planning. The PFO in Seattle also helped to prioritize and adjudicate between the often-competing needs of the crisis and consequence management sides of the response phase. In Illinois, the PFO worked within the framework of a unified command to ensure that integrated communications were achieved and that action plans were coordinated.
- Both PFOs required additional technical support beyond their deployed administrative and security details. The exercise highlighted the need for the PFO to have a dedicated staff with the flexibility and expertise to support all emergencies, natural and terrorist-related. If the Domestic Emergency Support Team is expected to support the PFO and the federal response, DHS should consider providing additional resources to staff at least one additional team in the event that more than one federal emergency occurs at the same time, as was exercised during TOPOFF 2.

4. Data Collection and Coordination: Radiological Dispersal Device Plume Modeling and Deposition Assessment in Washington

During TOPOFF 2, there were multiple federal, state, and local agencies that had responsibilities for collecting data. The data were then sent to one or more locations to be compiled and analyzed. Once the analyses were complete, information was provided to top officials to assist in their decision-making. However, there were critical data collection and coordination challenges that had significant impacts on the response to the RDD attack in Seattle and impacted the ability to get timely, consistent, and valid information to top officials. Findings from the exercise include the following:

- The coordination of on-site and off-site data collection by multiple agencies at federal, state, and local levels of government needs improvement. The exercise highlighted the many radiological data collection assets that exist at all levels of government. Federal, state, and local agencies and departments, therefore, need to be educated about the importance of coordinating the data collection process, and to work with the Federal Radiological Monitoring and Assessment Center to ensure that coordination takes place during radiological emergencies. The development of the National Response Plan and the National Incident Management Plan may help to facilitate the data collection and coordination processes in the future.

- There is a need for additional education among both responders and decision-makers as to the timing and value of the different types of information following a radiological incident. The value and limitations of plume models and other analysis products are not widely understood. Plume models provide a prediction of where the material in the explosion will travel. Once actual data from the incident are collected and evaluated, the value of plume models diminishes. Once responders learn what really is out there and where it is, predictions alone become less important.

5. Play Involving the Strategic National Stockpile

The activation, requests for and deployment and distribution of the Strategic National Stockpile (SNS) were extensively played during TOPOFF 2. The exercise tested the ability of all levels of government to make decisions, allocate resources, coordinate and communicate, and inform the public regarding this critical SNS resource. The state of Illinois tested its ability to break down and secure the antibiotic stocks. Local jurisdictions tested their abilities to distribute supplies of antibiotics to their first responders and citizens. Overall, the request, receipt, breakdown, distribution, and dispensing of the SNS during the exercise were completed successfully. Findings from the exercise include the following:

- Determining a prophylaxis distribution policy for first responders and citizenry across local jurisdictions was challenging. This was due, in part, to the enormous logistical challenges of distributing medications to a large metropolitan area, as well as the very real limitation of the amount of medication that was immediately available.
- Inconsistent information was given by different jurisdictions as to who should seek prophylaxis and when, as well as the locations of the suspected plague release sites.
- The Homeland Security Council is leading an interagency effort to remedy the plume modeling process deficiencies noted during the exercise.

6. Hospital Play in the Illinois Venue: Resources, Communications, and Information Sharing during a Public Health Emergency

During TOPOFF 2, 64 hospitals in the Illinois venue participated in the exercise, making it one of the largest mass casualty exercises ever undertaken. This aspect of the exercise presented an unprecedented opportunity to examine the coordinated efforts of the medical and public health communities to react to and control the spread of a disease outbreak, specifically an outbreak initiated by a bioterrorism attack. Because of the large number of participating hospitals, challenges regarding communication and the management of resource requirements were significant. Findings from the exercise include the following:

- During the exercise, the lack of a robust and efficient emergency communications infrastructure was apparent. Communications heavily relied upon telephones and faxes for data transmission. The unanticipated large call volume was the greatest problem. The phone system in at least one location was overwhelmed, requiring three HAM radio operators to maintain communications connectivity. Facsimile communications were also subject to transmission and receipt problems due to call volumes. "Blast fax transmissions" took up to two hours to complete. In addition, information was often copied manually to a form. The form was then faxed (in some cases degrading its readability) to a collection point, where it was then manually tabulated on another form, and then entered into an information system for transmission. This process increases potential errors.
- Resource demands challenged hospitals throughout the exercise. These included short supplies of isolation and negative pressure rooms, as well as staff shortages. Hospitals employed a number of solutions to these problems including activating staff phone trees to recall medical personnel; using extra conference rooms, lobbies, and Clinical Decision Units (closed units) as isolation wards; and using same day surgery, radiology, and endoscopy labs, as well as an off-site tent, as negative pressure (i.e., disease containment) rooms.

7. Balancing the Safety of First Responders and the Rescue of Victims

In incidents when victim survival is dependent upon the timeliness of medical treatment, first responders typically initiate victim rescue and removal as rapidly as possible, while incident commanders manage responder safety with an ongoing risk-benefit analysis. However, when faced with an emergency that potentially involves a WMD, first responders face a greater potential of becoming casualties themselves. Given the uncertainty surrounding the simulated RDD explosion during the exercise, many of the responders artificially had the knowledge that it was a radiological incident and the incident commander had to take precautions to ensure that the responders were safe. Findings from the exercise include the following:

- Rescue operations at the RDD incident site highlighted the need for more frequent, informational communication between incident command and hospital control. Incident commanders may need to be more proactive in providing information. While hospital control was aware that radiation had been detected at the incident site, there is no indication in the data analyzed that incident command or the medical group at the incident site communicated with hospital control to explain the need to conduct a more detailed risk-benefit analysis before rescue operations could commence. In addition, hospital control was not always aware of the periodic halts to rescue operations that occurred during the initial hours of the exercise response due to both the suspected and real presence of secondary explosive devices.

- The public health and medical communities, the media, and the general public should be educated on the unique considerations that must be factored into rescue operations following a terrorist WMD attack. Considerations non-responder communities should be aware of include the need to balance responder safety and rescue efforts and the specific practices rescuers employ when responding to critical situations, such as the potential for secondary explosive devices in or around an incident scene. The public health and medical communities should be made aware of the need for incident command to conduct a detailed risk-benefit analysis prior to the start of rescue operations. Finally, a consistent message to the public from incident command, public health, and medical communities is critical.

Conclusions

TOPOFF 2 was an innovative, useful, and successful exercise and was the first national combating terrorism exercise conducted since DHS was established. As a result, TOPOFF 2 provided a tremendous learning experience for both the new DHS and the federal agencies now working with DHS during a response to domestic incidents. In addition, the experience in Washington and Illinois provided important lessons regarding federal, state, and local integration. These lessons are valuable to other states and localities as they work to train, exercise, and improve their own response capabilities.

TOPOFF 2 involved the play of new agencies and entities within DHS (e.g., the Transportation Security Administration, the PFO, and the Crisis Action Team).

- The PFO concept was tested in both exercise venues. While this position has the potential to assist greatly with the coordination of federal activities across the spectrum of the response, TOPOFF 2 results also indicated that the roles and responsibilities of the PFO need to be clarified with respect to those of the FBI Special Agent in Charge, the FEMA RD, and the FCO. In addition, the PFO requires an emergency support team with the flexibility and expertise to provide support across the full range of homeland security operations.

TOPOFF 2 represented the first time (real or notional) in which the HSAS Threat Condition was raised to Red.

- Valuable experience was gained as the Secretary of DHS, in concert with the Homeland Security Council, first raised selected areas of the country and then the whole country to Threat Condition Red. In addition, local jurisdictions raised their own threat levels to Red.

TOPOFF 2 involved an extraordinary sequence of two Presidential Declarations wrapped around a Public Health Emergency declaration by the Secretary of HHS.

- The Presidential declarations were for a major disaster in the Washington venue and an emergency in the Illinois venue. These two declarations illustrated some of the subtleties of the Stafford Act that may not have been fully appreciated before the exercise; for instance, a bioterrorism attack does not clearly fit the existing definition of disaster as defined by the Act. The Secretary of Department of Health and Human Services (HHS), acting on authorities through the Public Health Service Act and in consultation with the region, declared a Public Health Emergency. This permitted HHS to authorize the use of federal assets (with costs covered by HHS). It appeared to lead to some uncertainty about where authority to deploy certain assets really lay, with HHS or DHS.

Planning and development of the National Incident Management System (NIMS) should take advantage of the TOPOFF Exercise Series.

- This comment from the TOPOFF 2000 report bears repeating: "Multiple direction and control nodes, numerous liaisons, and an increasing number of response teams complicated coordination, communications, and unity of effort." If anything, TOPOFF 2 may have been characterized by even more teams and communication nodes.
- Communication and coordination issues drove the course and outcome of critical public policy decisions, from raising the threat level to the various disaster/emergency declarations, from the determination of exclusion zones to the re-opening of transportation systems. To the extent that there were problems in these areas, communication issues were likely the primary cause.
- TOPOFF 2 showed that how people believe communications and coordination is supposed to work based on policy is often not how they work in reality. What may appear to be clearly defined processes—such as requesting the SNS—in practice become much more difficult.

With the active participation of 64 hospitals in the Chicago metropolitan area responding to the notional bioterrorism attack, TOPOFF 2 represented one of the largest hospital mass casualty exercises ever conducted.

- TOPOFF 2 represented a significant experiment in communications and coordination for the public health and medical communities. In particular, the massive amounts of communication required to track resource status (beds, specialized spaces, medical equipment), and the cumbersome procedures and insufficient electronic means to do so in many cases, taxed hospital staff.
- TOPOFF 2 did not last long enough to fully explore the impacts of mass casualties on the medical system. Much less than half of the infected population was visible to the medical system at the conclusion of the exercise.
- While there were a number of attempts to estimate the potential scope of the outbreak, the focus of most activities appeared to be on the cases that were presented to the health care system. It should be noted that HHS was working actively during the exercise to identify the resources that would be required to deal with the infected population.

TOPOFF 2 Illinois play also involved an extensive SNS request and distribution component.

- Although the actual distribution process appeared to go quite well, there was some confusion over the procedures and processes for requesting and receiving the SNS. The SNS Operations Center coordinated the stockpile deployment through the FEMA EP&R Director. Additionally, senior-level consultation occurred between DHS and HHS via video teleconference and direct communication.

- The jurisdictions in the Chicago metropolitan area were forced to confront important decisions about how the stockpile (and local assets) would be divided and who would be among the first population groups to receive prophylaxis. The discussions and decision-making involved, as well as the challenges in coordinating public information, are worthy of study by other metropolitan areas for the lessons they provide.

DHS should consider the integration of existing response policies and plans into the NRP.

- States are familiar with and have built their response plans to coincide with federal assets and plans using similar agency and department structures and language. Federal agencies are satisfied with the language, authorities, and relationships outlined in existing plans such as the FRERP and the NRP. As the NRP undergoes development, the integration of response plans and policies merit consideration—particularly where existing plans are considered effective for emergency response.

TOPOFF 2 involved more sustained play by top officials than TOPOFF 2000.

- Of particular note was the involvement of DHS (which had been in existence for only a little more than ten weeks prior to the exercise), the DHS Secretary, and other senior civilians.
- HHS operated the Secretary's Command Center for 24 hours-a-day throughout the exercise with extensive play at the Assistant Secretary- and Operating Division Director levels. The Secretary was actively involved, and since one venue involved substantial public health play, the participation of HHS was critical to the success of the exercise.
- In both Washington and Illinois, the offices of the mayors, county executives, and governors were well-represented throughout the exercise by either the elected officials themselves or high-level policy-makers in respective administrations.

TOPOFF 2 represents a foundational experience to guide the future development of the TOPOFF Exercise Series.

- Because of the extensive data collection process and the effort to make TOPOFF 2 findings both well-documented and traceable through a detailed reconstruction of the exercise events, TOPOFF 2 represents a baseline upon which subsequent TOPOFF exercises can build and to which they can be rigorously compared.

- TOPOFF 2 demonstrated the value of the international, private sector, and non-profit perspectives and roles in response to WMD terrorism. Future exercises will, no doubt, expand on these elements by broadening the participation of all these sectors.

- The success of the Video News Network and widespread participant feedback regarding the desire for additional challenges in the area of public information suggest that future exercises should include a more aggressive mock-media element with a more aggressive news-gathering function that includes mock-press conferences.

Source: U.S. Department of Homeland Security. "Top Officials (TOPOFF) Exercise Series: TOPOFF 2. After Action Summary Report for Public Release." December 19, 2003. www.dhs.gov/interweb/assetlibrary/ T2_Report_Final_Public.doc (accessed January 20, 2004).

Peace Agreement Between Government and Rebels in Burundi

October 8, 2003

INTRODUCTION

A decade-long war in the tiny East African country of Burundi appeared close to an end in 2003, when the government and the largest of several rebel groups signed a formal peace agreement. If successful over the long haul, the peace accord could close out a long period of conflict in both Burundi and its neighbor, Rwanda. Previous peace agreements in Burundi had proven fragile, however, and at the end of 2003 one rebel group was continuing to fight the government.

The United Nations estimated that 250,000 to 300,000 people had died since the current round of fighting broke out in Burundi in 1993. Of the country's total population of about 6.8 million, at least 1.3 million had been forced from their homes during the conflict; of those, about 500,000 remained in Burundi as "internally displaced" people and another 800,000 had fled to neighboring countries. Some 200,000 Burundians had been living in Tanzania, the neighbor to the south and east, ever since an earlier conflict in 1972.

Background

Before the colonial era began in the nineteenth century, both Burundi and Rwanda had been feudal monarchies, in which most of the power was held by a minority group, the Tutsi, whose relative wealth came from raising cattle. The much larger majority population in both countries were the Hutu, who were traditional sedentary farmers. In both countries, colonial rulers (first Germany, then Belgium) exploited differences between these two groups by using the Tutsi to maintain local control. After independence in 1962, the Tutsi continued to dominate political affairs in both countries.

Both Burundi and Rwanda experienced waves of violence between the Hutu and Tutsi—and between factions within each group—in the decades after independence. Conflict was more frequent in Burundi than in Rwanda. Violent uprisings occurred in Burundi in 1965, 1969, 1972, 1988, and 1993. The fighting between the Hutu and Tutsi that began in 1972 and lasted into 1973 was by far the most intense in Burundi's recent history; an estimated 250,000 people died, most of them Hutus. The intensity of that conflict was exceeded in the region only by the 1994 genocide in Rwanda, during which Hutu extremists killed an estimated 800,000 Tutsis and moderate Hutus in about three months. *(Rwanda background, p. 1069)*

The current conflict in Burundi began in October 1993 after Tutsi soldiers assassinated the president, Melchior Ndadaye, a Hutu, who had taken office that June as the first democratically elected president in Burundi's history. The assassination led to a new period of severe internal conflict, during which tens of thousands were killed and several hundred thousand people fled their homes into Tanzania and neighboring Zaire (later called the Democratic Republic of the Congo). After several weak governments, Major Pierre Buyoya—a Tutsi who as president in 1993 had allowed the elections won by Ndadaye—returned to power in a coup in 1996. Fighting continued among various factions, however.

Starting in 1998, former Tanzanian president Julius Nyerere led negotiations aimed at settling the conflict; after Nyerere's death in October 1999, former South African president Nelson Mandela took over. On August 28, 2000, Mandela and then-U.S. president Bill Clinton witnessed the signing in Arusha, Tanzania, of a peace agreement among nineteen political parties in Burundi. Guerrilla leaders refused to sign the accord, however, and were harshly condemned by Mandela and Clinton. Under strong pressure from Mandela and other international leaders, the government closed what it called "regroupment camps" near the capital, Bujumbura. The government had forced an estimated 300,000 Hutu civilians into these overcrowded camps, saying it was for their own protection. *(Historic Documents of 2000, p. 65)*

The Arusha peace accord collapsed a half-year later, in February 2001, when Hutu rebels captured Bujumbura. The Burundi army retook the capital in March, and Mandela arranged another peace agreement that also was signed by most political parties—but not the armed rebel groups—in July 2001. That accord provided for power sharing among the Hutu and Tutsi parties, and a new joint government took office in November 2001. A key provision was that Buyoya would remain in office for eighteen months, after which a Hutu leader, Domitien Ndayizeye, would assume the presidency. That political arrangement gained a measure of stability a year later, in December 2002, when three of the four guerrilla groups signed a formal cease-fire with the government. Among the groups signing the accord was the largest one, the Forces for the Defense of Democracy (FDD, in French).

A much smaller Hutu rebel group, the National Liberation Front (NLF), refused to negotiate with the government.

A New Peace Accord

Despite the December 2002 cease-fire, fighting continued in Burundi throughout 2003. In the early months, units of the FDD were involved, as was the hold-out NLF. Human Rights Watch, based in New York, on February 28 accused the national army and rebel groups of continuing to commit atrocities, including killing civilians, raping women, and looting villages. In particular, Human Rights Watch said the army had killed dozens of civilians in several villages in eastern Burundi. Rebel groups, Human Rights Watch said, "deliberately kill civilians who refuse their demands for support or who are thought to support the government." The army and a spokesman for the FDD both denied the Human Rights Watch report.

The first contingents of an African peacekeeping force, comprised of about 3,000 troops from Ethiopia, Mozambique, and South Africa, began arriving in Burundi in late March to monitor the cease-fire. The force did not have a mandate from the United Nations, which was not a party to Burundi's peace process.

Another major step came on April 30, when Ndayizeye, leader of the largest Hutu political party, took over as president from Tutsi leader Buyoya. This was the political transition promised by the previous peace agreements, and it was the second time that Buyoya had given up power peacefully. However, the transition failed to satisfy the Hutu rebels, who claimed Ndayizeye was a figurehead who would exercise no real power so long as the army remained dominated by Tutsis.

Once again, fighting continued despite the cease-fire between the government and the FDD rebels. Beginning in early July the other rebel group—the NLF—attacked the capital with mortars and raided upper-class neighborhoods, killing several dozen civilians and displacing several thousand people from their homes. According to some reports, the NLF guerrillas were aided in their attack by the FDD. Denouncing the attack, the United Nations said sixteen of Burundi's seventeen provinces were afflicted with some sort of violence, more than twice as many provinces as were in conflict a year earlier.

As the fighting continued into September, mediators from South Africa and Tanzania worked to get a new peace agreement between the government and the FDD. In these talks, the leaders of both sides were Hutus: interim president Ndayizeye and the leader of the FDD rebels, Pierre Nkurunziza. The negotiations finally produced a substantial peace agreement, signed by the two leaders at an October 8 ceremony in South Africa, presided over by that country's president, Thabo Mbeki. Both sides said they would again order their forces to stop fighting. The agreement provided for the FDD rebels to enter into the government: rebel leaders as members of the cabinet and the parliament, and fighters as members of the army and police force. Four rebel leaders were to become members of the cabinet, one of whom had to be consulted by the president "on all key matters."

The October 8 agreement left unsettled several major issues, including the granting of immunity to rebel fighters for their actions during the war and the exact status of the FDD as a political party. Those matters were settled by a follow-up agreement, announced in South Africa on November 2. A key provision giving the rebels temporary immunity from prosecution subsequently was denounced by Human Rights Watch and other groups as condoning the many atrocities committed during the war. The agreement was formally signed in Tanzania on November 16.

On December 7 FDD leader Nkurunziza arrived in Bujumbura to take his cabinet position as minister for good governance—a post that, under the October 8 peace accord, gave him a virtual veto over major government decisions. "We take this opportunity to ask forgiveness from the people of Burundi for all the harm we have done to them because of a war that was forced upon us," he told reporters. "For our part, we forgive those who imposed this war on us." Also during December FDD rebel fighters began turning in their weapons and applying for positions with the army. Under the peace agreements, the next major step in Burundi's peace process was to be the holding of democratic elections in late 2004—the country's first since just before the war began in 1993.

Most observers said the 2003 peace agreements appeared to have a greater chance of success than previous ones because it gave the FDD rebel leaders potentially powerful positions within the government, and thus a stake in keeping the peace. The accord also isolated the National Liberation Front as the only rebel group that had not made peace with the government. Several military analysts said that group could continue to make trouble but had no realistic chance of gaining power if the other rebels kept their bargain with the government. At year's end there were reports that some NLF leaders had met secretly with the government. Early in January 2004 that group announced plans to hold formal peace talks with the government.

Additional peacekeepers from other African countries began arriving in Burundi later in October. The first new contingent, from Mozambique, was funded by the British government. The United States also provided money for peacekeepers. South Africa's vice president, Jacob Zuma, appealed to the UN Security Council on December 4 to take over responsibility for the peacekeeping mission in Burundi. The council on December 22 agreed to consider that request and asked Secretary General Kofi Annan to develop recommendations for its review early in 2004.

The final major event in Burundi in 2003 was yet another tragic one. On December 29 gunmen attacked and killed the Vatican's papal nuncio (ambassador) to Burundi, Archbishop Michael Courtney, an Irishman. The gunmen opened fire on Courtney's car as he was traveling in a town about thirty miles north of the capital; he died at a hospital. The attack occurred in an area where the NLF had many fighters, but a spokesman for that group denied responsibility.

Humanitarian Situation

The long war caused vast devastation. According to the UN's Office for the Coordination of Humanitarian Affairs, about one in six Burundians lived away from their homes at the end of 2003, including nearly 300,000 in camps for internally displaced people. The UN estimated that nearly three-fourths of those people lacked access to the minimum daily requirement of drinking water. In late 2003 the UN's World Food Programme estimated that 965,000 people in Burundi needed food aid; nearly 600,000 of these faced what the agency called "serious food insecurity"—in other words, they had no reliable supply of even the minimum daily calorie requirements.

Burundi lacked the natural resources, such as diamonds and gold, that made some of its neighbors potentially wealthy. Its economy was based almost exclusively on agriculture, with coffee as its principal export crop. During the war the country's estimated gross domestic product fell by half, from about $1.2 billion in 1991 to about $600 million in 2002. On a per capita basis, that made Burundi one of the three or four poorest countries in the world.

In a report to the UN Security Council on December 15, Annan warned of an "urgent" need for donor nations to help with both the short-term humanitarian needs and the long-term economic reconstruction of Burundi. "There is a risk that the hopeful signs of peace which have now begun to appear could be lost unless they are accompanied by improvements in the living conditions of the population as a 'peace dividend,' " Annan said. A conference of donor nations was to be held in Belgium in January 2004.

Following are excerpts from the "Pretoria Protocol on Political, Defense, and Security Power Sharing in Burundi," signed in South Africa on October 8, 2003, by the president of Burundi, Domitien Ndayizeye, and the head of the Forces for the Defense of Democracy rebel movement, Pierre Nkurunziza.

"Pretoria Protocol on Political, Defense, and Security Power Sharing in Burundi"

Preamble

The Transitional Government of Burundi (hereafter referred to as "TGoB") and the National Council for the Defence of Democracy-Forces for Defence of Democracy (hereafter referred to as "CNDD-FDD") both hereafter referred to as "the Parties", hereby;

Take note of the commitments of the TGoB and the CNDD-FDD to reach an all embracing agreement for the achievement of lasting peace, security and stability in Burundi;

Acknowledge the principles and objectives of the Arusha Peace and Reconciliation Agreement for Burundi and the Transitional Constitution of the Republic of Burundi;

Reaffirm their commitment to the Ceasefire Agreement between the Parties signed in Arusha on 2 December 2002 as well as the Joint Declaration of Agreement addressing the practical implementation of the December 2002 Ceasefire Agreement, signed in Pretoria on 27 January 2003;

Acknowledge further the Dar es Salaam Communique of the Regional Summit of 20 July 2003 recommitting the parties to a negotiated framework to resolve all outstanding issues related to Political Power Sharing and Technical Forces Agreement;

Recognise that the conflict in Burundi requires an inclusive dialogue and participation of all political groups and movements;

Conscious of the need to give impetus to the Implementation of the content and spirit of the various agreements reached on the Burundi Peace Process;

Hereby agree to engage in the following process in order to effect the power sharing agreement in terms of paragraphs 1.1.12 and 1.1.15 of the December 2002 Ceasefire Agreement between the CNDD-FDD and the Transitional Government of Burundi.

Political Power Issues

Executive

The CNDD-FDD will have four ministries including a Minister of State. The Presidency will consult the Minister of State on all key matters.

The Legislature

National Assembly

1. CNDD-FDD will participate in the Bureau as follows:
   - Second-Vice President.
   - Deputy Secretary-General.
   The Bureau will be increased to six.
   Two advisors will be appointed in the Staff of the National Assembly.
2. CNDD-FDD will also have 15 members of the Assembly.
3. Measures will be taken to respect the balance among the political families as reflected in the Arusha Agreement.

Senate

The question of the participation of the CNDD-FDD will be discussed at the next meeting, prior to the Regional Summit. (See Article VII below.)

Governors of Provinces

CND-FDD will have:

- Three Governors.
- Five Advisors.

Diplomatic Corps

CNDD-FDD will have:

- Two ambassadors.
- Six secretaries and/or advisors.

Local Government

CNDD-FDD will have 30 Administrators.

Public Enterprizes [sic]

CNDD-FDD will lead 20% of these. The exact distribution will be negotiated later.

Defence and Security Issues:

The power sharing process in terms of defence and security issues shall consist of the following phases;

I. The Burundi National Defence Force

1.1 Cantonment

The combatants of the CNDD-FDD will move to areas designated by the Joint Ceasefire Commission (JCC) under the supervision of the African Mission. The Burundi Armed Forces (FAB) will be confined to areas agreed upon under supervision of the African Mission, with certain elements being exempted in accordance with par 1.1.7 of the December 2002 Ceasefire Agreement.

1.2 Verification

1.2.1 Once members have been cantoned and confined, a verification exercise will be undertaken to determine the size of the respective forces by the Joint Ceasefire Commission. The suitability of personnel submitted by both parties will be determined on the basis of the Forces Technical Agreement (FTA), to be finalized, under the guidance/leaders of the JCC.

1.2.2 Those determined to be suitable will form the new Defence and Security Forces of Burundi.

1.3 Formation of the Burundi National Defence Force (BNDF)

1.3.1 The integrated General Staff and the Officer Corps, shall be composed of 60% officers selected from the governmental army and 40% officers from the FDD.

1.3.2 The composition of the non commissioned officers and the rank and file shall be determined by the integrated General Staff according to the size of each party and of the agreed balance.

1.3.3 On proposal of the integrated General Staff, the government shall determine;
The structure of the Burundi National Defence Force
The size of the army and
Composition of the officer corps.

1.3.4 The allocation of command posts shall be on the basis of ethnic balance (50-50) as stipulated in the Arusha Peace and Reconciliation Agreement.

1.3.5 The President of the Republic of Burundi undertakes to give expression to this arrangement through a Presidential decree.

1.4. Demobilisation

1.4.1 Combatants of the CNDD-FDD or FAB who have been found not to be eligible to join the Burundi National Defence Force terms of the Forces Technical Agreement, will be demobilized, taking into consideration paragraph 1.1.14 of the December 2002 Ceasefire Agreement.

1.4.2 The demobilization and integration of these combatants will be progressive, bearing In mind social stability and affordability. The Government shall oversee this process through the Minister of State and the Minister of Defence.

1.4.3 The final phase of demobilization will take place once the elected government is in place, guided by the required size of the Burundi National Defence Force and taking into consideration the work undertaken by the Transitional Government of Burundi. The Government of Burundi shall oversee this process.

II. Burundi Police Force

2.1 The parties agreed on the establishment of a new police force in Burundi.

2.2 The structure of the new Police Force will be guided by the following principles:
- Inclusivity and integration.
- General Staff structure based on the principle of 65% TGoB and 35% CNDD-FDD;
- The principle of 50-50 ethnic balance.

2.3 Composition of junior structures of the Police Force shall also be guided by the principles of inclusivity

2.4 The decisions will be taken on the basis of consensus

III. Gendarmerie

3.1 The Gendarmerie will be treated as part of the FAB;

3.2 Elements of the Gendarmerie may be deployed to both the new Defence and Police Forces,

3.3 Equally, elements of the CNDD-FDD will also be deployed into the Burundi Police Force.

IV. Militia

Militia will be disarmed according to the December 2002 Ceasefire Agreement under the supervision of the African Mission at the beginning of cantonment and barracking exercises.

V. Intelligence

5.1 The parties agreed on the establishment of a Ministry of Intelligence under the President;

5.2 Parties will submit names for the General Staff of Intelligence to the President.
The agreed criteria for the composition will be as follows;
- 65% -TGoB
- 35% -CNDD-FDD
- The principle of 50-50 ethnic balance.

5.3 The President informed by the capacity/suitability of persons proposed and guided by the principles of integration and inclusivity shall retain the discretion to determine the final composition of his General Staff of Intelligence.

VI. Palipehutu/FNL

6.1 To address the current security situation in Burundi certain elements of the FAB will be exempted from confinement, as per the provisions of the December 2002 Ceasefire Agreement.

6.2 Prior to the establishment of a National Defence Force and in terms of the December 2002 Ceasefire Agreement, joint military units will be constituted to perform certain tasks:

VII. Outstanding Matters:

Temporary Immunity,
CNDD-FDD as a political party.
Forces Technical Agreement.
The question of the participation of CNDD-FDD in the Senate.

These matters will be finalized at the next meeting that will be convened as a matter of urgency.

Source: Republic of South Africa. Department of Foreign Affairs. *The Pretoria Protocol on Political, Defence and Security Power Sharing in Burundi.* Pretoria, South Africa. October 8, 2003. www.usip.org/library/pa/burundi_10082003.hml (accessed December 13, 2003).

United Nations Security Council on Postwar Iraq

October 16, 2003

INTRODUCTION

The Bush administration's stated expectation that its occupation of Iraq would go as smoothly as the brief war to oust Iraqi leader Saddam Hussein ran up against grim reality in the second half of 2003. The United States faced determined resistance that undermined its plans for a rapid transformation of Iraq into a stable democracy. The administration was forced repeatedly to change its plans to catch up with events on the ground, and it faced a prolonged military occupation even after it handed sovereignty back to Iraqis in 2004.

Very little in Iraq after the war went according to expectations that the Bush administration had expressed in the year or so before the war. Except for brief celebrations after Saddam's fall from power, Iraqis did not greet U.S. troops as liberators. Iraqi soldiers did not immediately flock by the thousands to help the occupying forces establish security. Iraqi civilians did not embrace the U.S.-backed exiles who returned, in the war's wake, to take up political leadership in the country. Iraq's oil industry turned out to be much more deteriorated than U.S. officials expected, and therefore less capable of gushing the export dollars that Washington had counted on to finance the country's reconstruction. Other elements of Iraq's infrastructure—electrical grids, water and sewer plants, roads, schools, and hospitals—all were in much worse shape than U.S. planners had expected. Most important, Saddam and his loyalists did not quietly fade away. A host of guerrilla attacks throughout the year—car bombings, suicide bombings, roadside bombings, missile attacks, and drive-by shootings—killed hundreds of people, kept occupation forces and ordinary Iraqis on edge, and thwarted Washington's plans for a short, triumphal occupation.

Some things did go right in Iraq after the war. The removal of Saddam from power gave Iraqis an opportunity to experience political freedoms for the first time in more than two generations. People could speak their minds freely and hold political meetings without fearing a midnight raid by the secret police. That feeling of relief was heightened in December, when U.S. forces captured Saddam, ensuring that he was no longer a threat. Iraq's Shi'ites, who had been repressed for hundreds of years, suddenly realized they might gain real power for the first time. The Kurdish minority now had a chance to consolidate the broad autonomy it had enjoyed in northern Iraq for a dozen years. Slowly but steadily, Iraq was put back together again. United Nations sanctions, which had throttled the country since 1991, were lifted; the United States poured in billions of dollars to renovate the oil industry and public infrastructure; and Iraqis went to work at whatever jobs they could find. Iraq was a basket case of a country when the war ended in April. By year's end it had the potential, if not yet the reality, for the stability and democracy that President George W. Bush said were his goals when he started the war. *(Iraq War, p. 135; capture of Saddam, p. 1189)*

Bush himself made a quick visit to Baghdad on November 27 to have Thanksgiving dinner with U.S. troops. He thanked them for their work in a "difficult mission" and told the Iraqi people: "You have an opportunity to seize the moment and rebuild your great country, based on human dignity and freedom. The regime of Saddam Hussein is gone forever."

Changing Plans

Before the Iraq war got under way, Bush and his chief aides expressed great confidence that the ouster of Saddam would be followed quickly by stability and a peaceful transfer of power to new, democratic leaders. The administration said it had developed detailed plans to achieve its postwar goals. Some elements of the administration's plans survived the bruising confrontation with reality, but the broad political and security components had to be changed repeatedly.

On the political side, Washington established two different U.S. administrations and tried three different formulas during the year for sharing at least some of the governing responsibility with Iraqis. At year's end the third political formula was under attack and was almost certain to be revised. The Bush administration also had to shuffle its plans for keeping Iraq secure. The initial plan called for maintaining a large U.S. force in Iraq for a few weeks, then rapidly pulling out the vast majority of U.S. troops once the country calmed down and Iraqi police forces took over responsibility for security. Much of Iraq did calm down in 2003—but not enough to enable the quick withdrawal Pentagon planners had assumed. As a result, the United States was forced to keep about 130,000 troops on duty in Iraq (and thousands more in neighboring Kuwait for logistical support) throughout the year. The army drew up plans to keep about 100,000 troops there until early in 2006. The administration also appealed to its allies to send troops to Iraq.

The underlying problem appeared to be that Iraqis were not nearly as grateful to the United States for Saddam's removal as Bush and his aides thought they would be. The expectation that U.S. troops would be welcomed as liberators was overtaken by deep suspicions about Washington's motives and intentions. Even those Iraqis who had been most abused by the dictator—the Kurds in the north and the Shi'ites in the south—made it clear that they wanted to decide their own futures without mandates from Washington. Many Iraqis also were convinced that the United States invaded simply to gain control over the country's oil. This suspicion was fed by the large contracts that were given to U.S. businesses to renovate the oil industry.

Bush on July 1 acknowledged for the first time that Iraq presented the United States with a "massive and long-term undertaking." That undertaking proved costly to U.S. taxpayers. Congress in April approved $79 billion to pay for the war and the early months of the occupation. Bush returned to Congress in September with a request for another $87 billion for Iraq, Afghanistan, and other missions; of that total, $51 billion was for U.S. military operations in Iraq, $15 billion was for reconstruction projects (such as restoring public utilities), and $5 billion was to hire and train Iraqi police, border guards, and a new Iraqi army. Congress approved nearly all of Bush's request on November 4. *(Afghanistan, p. 1089)*

Immediate Aftermath of the War

Under the Bush administration's initial plan for Iraq, a tiny U.S. agency headed by a retired army lieutenant general, Jay M. Garner, would administer humanitarian and reconstruction aid while keeping a watchful eye on the blossoming of democracy. Iraqis would form a national assembly and an interim government by the end of May, just a month after the major fighting ended. The plan assumed this government would be run by, or at least dominated by, longtime exiles who had returned to Iraq, with U.S. support, in the expectation that Washington would put them in charge.

Nearly every element of that plan had to be scrapped. Garner and his handful of aides had trouble grappling with the immensity of the task they faced. After little more than a month on the job, they were replaced in May by a new administration, headed by L. Paul Bremer III, a former State Department counterterrorism official who had close ties to many of the administration's staunchest advocates of the Iraq War. Bremer quickly formed a new, larger entity to govern the country: the Coalition Provisional Authority.

The administration's plans to put an Iraqi face on the occupation—in the form of several exiles who had gained political favor in Washington—failed to survive Garner's brief tenure. The exiles bickered among themselves and generated little political support on their own. By far the most controversial of the exiles was Ahmad Chalabi, who had left Iraq in 1958 and later helped form the Iraqi National Congress. That exile group lobbied the U.S. Congress during the 1990s on behalf of legislation calling for Saddam's overthrow, and it received $15 million in U.S. funding from 1999 to 2001. Chalabi returned to Iraq in April aboard a U.S. military transport plane; he was accompanied by about seven hundred paramilitary troops, called the Free Iraqi Forces, who had been trained by the U.S. military. According to news reports, the Iraqis who knew of him considered him to be "America's man" or even "the Pentagon's man" because he had more visible support in Washington than in his home country.

After conducting negotiations among Western diplomats and a wide range of Iraqi political and religious leaders, Bremer on July 13 appointed a twenty-five-member Iraqi Governing Council, the duties of which were only vaguely defined. The council included Chalabi and several other exiles, as well as leaders who had remained in Iraq. The council also was carefully balanced to represent the country's major religious and ethnic groups: thirteen were Shi'ites, five were Kurds, five were Sunnis, one was an Assyrian Christian, and one was a Turkoman. Three were women. At the time of the appointment, Bremer's aides said the council would appoint members of a constitutional convention by September; that body would draft a constitution, which would be submitted to a referendum, followed by elections for a new government. That plan, the second of the year, later was scrapped.

The governing council had little visibility in Iraq during the summer. Its members reportedly spent days locked in debate over procedural matters. Pressured by Bremer to take more responsibility, the council on September 1 appointed a twenty-five member cabinet that was supposed to assume daily management of the government.

Also by September it was clear that one of the greatest political challenges facing both the United States and the Iraqi council was an insistent demand by the country's most senior Shi'ite cleric, Grand Ayatollah Ali al-Sistani, for early elections. Sistani proposed a national census, which he said would confirm that Shi'ites constituted at least 60 percent of the population, to be followed by elections for an assembly to draft a new constitution. The United States rejected this plan as unrealistic.

Political developments at the national level lagged well behind those at the local level. In many areas, local forces took the initiative and established what they called councils or governments. U.S. authorities were deeply involved in the creation of some of these local units but had no role in creating many others. One of the most widely reported cases was that of Muhammad al-Zobeidi, who proclaimed himself "mayor" of Baghdad in mid-April and held court in a social club for more than a week before U.S. officials hustled him off the scene. Kurds already had effective control over the territory they called Kurdistan in northern Iraq, and they moved to assert authority in areas they said were historically Kurdish, most importantly the city of Kirkuk—the center of the oil industry in northern Iraq. In the south, Shi'ite clerics dominated the drive for political power, although they were divided into factions and did not always share a unified agenda. By late summer nearly every major town in Iraq was governed on a day-to-day basis by a locally established council.

Continuing Security Challenges

As if creating a democratic political process in a country of 25 million people used to dictatorship was not difficult enough, the United States faced a security situation that worsened as the year went on. From May 1, when Bush declared an end to "major combat" in Iraq, through the end of the year, few days passed without at least a handful of attacks on the occupying military forces, other international symbols (including the United Nations and the International Committee of the Red Cross), and troops from other countries that supported the U.S. occupation. Two hundred twelve U.S. soldiers died as a result of hostilities in Iraq in those seven months, generally at the rate of one or two a day. Nearly twice as many U.S. troops were killed in hostile action after the war than during it.

The continuing violence forced the Bush administration into a drastic revision of its plans for providing security. Under the original plan, all but about 30,000 of the 130,000-some U.S. troops in Iraq following the war were to be sent home by late summer. But stability did not come as soon as Pentagon planners had assumed. In late May the Pentagon announced that it would keep a larger US. force in Iraq than had been planned, starting by keeping in place the Third Infantry Division, which had led the drive on Baghdad. On July 23 the Pentagon announced a plan for rotating active duty and National Guard units in and out of Iraq to maintain more than 130,000 U.S. soldiers there well into 2004. The plan involved year-long tours of duty for many troops.

The continuing presence of about 20,000 troops from other countries enabled the United States to call its occupying force a "coalition." Britain had played a major supporting role in the war, by taking control of the region of Basra, Iraq's main city in the south, and it continued that role after the war. About 12,000 British troops remained in the Basra area through the rest of the year. Other countries that had supported the war, notably Poland and Spain, contributed small units as well.

A major problem for the coalition was that the number of soldiers on the ground was tiny when compared to the task at hand. For a country the size of California, the coalition had a total of about 150,000 troops assigned to it. For much of the year security in Baghdad, a city with nearly 5 million people, was provided by only about 12,000 U.S. troops and a ragtag Iraqi police force that had little training or equipment.

As they had before the war, politicians back in Washington confronted the problem with tough rhetoric. Bush on July 2 said the United States would have no trouble dealing with those who were causing the violence in Iraq. "There are some who feel that the conditions are such that they can attack us there," he said. "My answer is: bring 'em on. We've got the force necessary to deal with the security situation." Such statements brought complaints from some Democrats that Bush appeared to be inviting attacks on U.S. soldiers.

An Escalation of Attacks

In the first weeks after Saddam's regime fell on April 9, U.S. and British forces faced numerous small-scale attacks: bombs placed alongside roads used by military convoys, night-time raids by gunmen, and sniper fire. Gaining control of the so-called Sunni triangle was the most difficult assignment. This was the area of central Iraq—encompassing Baghdad, Tikrit (Saddam's home region), and several towns to the west of Baghdad, notably Falluja—that was home to most of Iraq's Sunnis, who had long dominated the country's politics and military. With Saddam gone, Sunnis had the most to fear in a new Iraq because they constituted only about 20 percent of the total population, and they assumed the majority Shi'ites would seek revenge for Saddam's repression of them.

Foreign troops were not the only objects of violence. Iraqi civilians faced repeated assaults by common criminals, as well as by former soldiers and members of Saddam's Ba'ath political party. A wave of looting and vandalism that engulfed Baghdad immediately after Saddam's fall did not subside until well into May. Iraqis who cooperated with the United States—especially those who joined the new police and guard forces—were the most frequent target of attacks. The first of several major attacks came on July 5, when a bomb exploded near a police station in the western town of Ramadi, killing seven new police officers who had just graduated from a U.S. training course.

U.S. officials assumed that much of the violence was coordinated by key leaders of Saddam's former regime, possibly including the dictator himself and his two sons, Qusay and Uday, all of whom were in hiding. Dozens of U.S. special forces troops combed through central Iraq looking for this trio, along with Saddam's chief military and political aides. To help with the search, the U.S. military put the names and pictures of the fifty-five "most wanted" former Iraqi leaders on playing cards; these became popular items in Iraq, and private companies made copies for sale over the Internet worldwide. A major break came in July, when U.S. officials received a tip that Qusay and Uday were in Mosul, Iraq's northernmost city. U.S. troops surrounded the house where the two men were said to be in hiding and killed them during a lengthy gun battle. Photographs of their bodies were shown on Iraqi television to convince a skeptical public that they were no longer a threat. Saddam himself remained at large for nearly five more months.

Any hope that the deaths of Qusay and Uday would halt or reduce the violence was short-lived. As the summer wore on, the small-scale violence escalated into large-scale bombings and other attacks against foreigners and Iraqis that created the impression that the United States and its allies were unable to provide security in the country. No one claimed responsibility for these attacks, so it was difficult to know exactly who was behind them. It was certain that the attacks were pushing back the day when Iraq could be considered a stable place.

The Attacks Escalate

The first major attack came on August 7 when a truck bomb exploded outside the Jordanian embassy in Baghdad, killing seventeen Iraqis and wounding more than forty others. That was followed twelve days later by the highest profile attack of the year. On August 19 a cement mixer filled with an estimated 1,500 pounds of explosives blew up outside UN headquarters in Baghdad, killing twenty-three people and injuring more than one hundred-sixty others. Nineteen UN staffers were among the dead, including Sergio Vieira de Mello, the chief UN representative in Iraq, who appeared to be the principal target. The attack was the deadliest ever against the United Nations, which had lost many diplomats and aid workers to violence over the previous five decades but never so many at one time. Under pressure from UN staffers, Secretary General Kofi Annan subsequently commissioned an investigation by a panel of experts. In a report made public on October 22, they called the UN's security management "dysfunctional." Annan promised to adopt major recommendations offered by the experts, the most important being a new emphasis on accountability for those responsible for protecting UN employees in dangerous locations.

As much as any other postwar event in Iraq, the attack symbolized the fragility of the country's political and security situation. Many Iraqis interviewed by Western news organizations expressed puzzlement and fear about the chaos that had gripped their country, replacing the lightly controlled police state of the Saddam era. "Day after day, there is something terrible in our lives," Raed Ramadani, a shoe salesman in Baghdad told the *Washington Post* three days after the UN bombing. "We thought the Americans were capable of so much, and now we see they are stumbling like drunkards."

If it was intended to force international personnel out of Iraq, the attack was at least a partial success. The World Bank, the International Monetary Fund, and several aid organizations pulled some or all of their staff members out of Iraq in the days after the bombing. Annan defiantly said the UN would stay, to complete the work that Vieira de Mello and his colleagues had started. He changed his mind two weeks later, however, and moved most of the UN's non-Iraqi staff elsewhere in the Middle East until he could determine how to ensure the security of his personnel in Iraq.

Ten days after the UN bombing, an enormous car bomb exploded outside a mosque in the southern city of Najaf, killing more than eighty people. The main target appeared to be Ayatollah Mohammed Bakir al-Hakim, one of Iraq's leading Shi'ite clerics who led a political movement, the Supreme Council for the Islamic Revolution in Iraq. Hakim was killed instantly; the force of the explosion was so great that his family could find none of his body to bury. Hakim was the most important of several older clerics who appeared to view the United States as a possible ally as the majority Shi'ites sought power for the first time in Iraq's eight decades of independence. His death removed from the scene an important moderating force and sent a warning to other leaders that cooperating with the United States could prove deadly.

Najaf, one of the holiest locations for the world's Shi'ites, had been the center of a clash between clerics with opposing agendas. Many young clerics sought to confront the United States. Chief among them was Moqtada Sadr, the thirty-year-old son of a revered Shi'ite ayatollah who had been assassinated in 1999. Sadr mounted numerous demonstrations demanding that the United States leave Iraq immediately and insisting that Iraq be transformed into an Islamic state. He did not, however, call for acts of violence against the occupation.

Other attacks were aimed at ordinary Iraqis, as well as their leaders. On September 2 a truck bomb exploded outside the office of the Baghdad police chief. The explosion killed one officer and wounded two dozen others. Similar attacks later in the year killed more policemen and Iraqis who were cooperating with the occupation. Akila al-Hashemi, one of the three women on the Iraqi Governing Council, died on September 25, five days after she was attacked by gunmen. A car bomber drove into a crowd of Iraqi policemen in Baghdad on October 9, killing eight of them, plus himself. Another car bomb on October 12 killed six people outside a hotel used by the Governing Council.

The UN was targeted a second time, on September 22, when a suicide bomber detonated his explosives in the parking lot outside the UN compound, killing himself and an Iraqi police officer. Another wave of attacks came in late October, at the start of the Muslim holy month of Ramadan. On October 26 an improvised rocket was fired at the al-Rashid Hotel in Baghdad, where Paul D. Wolfowitz, the U.S. deputy defense secretary, was staying and meeting with U.S. officials. Wolfowitz was unharmed, but one U.S. officer was killed. The next day, bombers struck the Baghdad office of the International Committee of the Red Cross, killing two Iraqi staffers and about ten civilians nearby, and at four Iraqi police stations, killing eight officers, at least a dozen civilians, and one U.S. soldier. Like the previous attacks against the UN, the bombing of the Red Cross appeared to be a desperate attempt to force foreigners out of Iraq. As had the UN, the Red Cross cut back its international staff, saying their security could not be guaranteed.

The latest wave of bombings again shook international confidence in the U.S. claims of progress in Iraq, but Bush said he would not change course. In a news conference on October 28, Bush insisted progress was being made in Iraq. "The strategy remains the same," he said.

Two days later the U.S. military passed a milestone it had not wanted to see. The number of U.S. soldiers killed in hostile action since May 1—when Bush declared that "major combat" had ended in Iraq—exceeded the 115 who had been killed during the war. In late October the military reported that the number of attacks against U.S. forces was averaging about thirty a day, more than double the average in July.

The single deadliest attack against U.S. forces since the beginning of the war came on November 2, when a portable surface-to-air missile downed a Chinook helicopter in central Iraq, killing sixteen soldiers and wounding twenty others. The troops had been headed out of Iraq for short furloughs the Pentagon had recently introduced to reduce the strain on its forces there. That attack helped make November the deadliest one yet for U.S. forces in Iraq; seventy-seven U.S. personnel were killed during the month, exceeding the total for the previous two months combined.

The 20,000-some troops from other countries also were targets of attacks, but less frequently. A unit of Italian military police suffered the most. A car bomb exploded at a compound in Nasiriyah, in southern Iraq, on November 12, killing seventeen soldiers and two Italian civilians, plus thirteen Iraqis. The bombing was unusual not only in its target but also because it took place in the Shi'ite-dominated section of Iraq, which had been relatively peaceful since the war, except for the August bombing that killed Ayatollah Hakim. Three coordinated attacks on December 27 in Karbala, another city holy to Shi'ites, killed nineteen people, including fifteen Iraqis, three Bulgarian soldiers, and one soldier from Thailand.

All through the year Iraqis complained that U.S. soldiers seemed more concerned about their own security than providing security for the locals. The military imposed exceptionally tight security restrictions around all U.S. facilities, and there were numerous cases in which hair-trigger responses by frightened U.S. soldiers led to tragedy. One of the most widely reported was a pair of incidents on April 28 and 30 in Falluja, west of Baghdad, during which U.S. troops opened fire on demonstrators, killing twenty Iraqis. After an investigation, Human Rights Watch said it found no evidence to support the U.S. soldiers' assertions that they were returning fire against gunmen who fired first. Another of the many cases that appeared to demonstrate the coalition's difficulty in understanding the locals occurred in the southern town of Umm Qasr early in May, when Spanish troops broke up a demonstration and then discovered that it was a funeral procession.

By early December Defense Secretary Donald H. Rumsfeld said that nearly 160,000 Iraqis had been recruited for various security positions, most of them as policemen or guards at important installations (such as oil pipelines). Lower-level U.S. officials in Iraq questioned that number, however, saying the number of Iraqis actually working in security-related jobs was well under 100,000.

One of the occupation's most difficult tasks was to create a new army to replace the Iraqi military Bremer had disbanded in May. Bremer on June 23 set a target of establishing a 40,000-man force by 2005, to guard Iraq's borders, government offices, military bases, and oil pipelines. The first battalion of 700 soldiers completed a nine-week basic training course in October. In mid-December U.S. officials acknowledged that more than one-third of the soldiers had resigned, apparently because of low pay and threats that had been made against Iraqis who cooperated with the U.S. occupation.

Identifying the Insurgents

During the first months after the war, U.S. officials said the bulk of the attacks appeared to be carried out by the remnants of Saddam's regime. Defense Secretary Rumsfeld called them "dead enders": former military personnel, Ba'ath Party functionaries, and members of a paramilitary force known as "Saddam's fedayeen" (volunteers willing to die for a cause). U.S. officials said many of these Saddam loyalists appeared to have organized themselves into cells for the sole purpose of resisting the occupation. During or right after the war these resisters must have taken some weapons and ammunition from the Iraqi army's giant arsenals because military components were used in many of the subsequent attacks.

Officials in Washington also charged during the aftermath of the war that Syria and Iran were allowing large numbers of foreign terrorists to infiltrate into Iraq, where they either joined up with Saddam's supporters or operated on their own. The primary evidence for this assertion was that some of the attacks—notably the wave of car- and truck-bombings in late summer and early fall—reflected the tactics of Middle East terrorist groups such as al Qaeda and the Iranian-backed Hezbollah (which was based in Lebanon). Military commanders on the ground appeared to be skeptical of Washington's focus on outside terrorists, however. They said they had identified only a few dozen suspect foreigners and had seen no surge of terrorists across the border. "The primary problem is not foreign fighters," Gen. John Abizaid, the head of the U.S. Central Command in the Middle East, said in late November. "It remains former regime loyalists." Abizaid and other

generals said it also appeared that Saddam loyalists used common criminals and Islamic radicals (who he called "angry young men") to carry out
some of the attacks.

As the months passed and the attacks continued, administration officials
increasingly pointed to an Islamist extremist group, Ansar al-Islam, as a
likely sponsor of some of the violence. Before the war the group was based
in a small section of northern Iraq that was not under Baghdad's control.
The United States bombed the group's headquarters in late March, forcing
many of its fighters into Iran. But U.S. officials said many of the fighters
apparently returned to Iraq during the summer. The administration said the
group had ties to al Qaeda, and before the war said that its presence in
Iraq constituted a connection between Saddam's regime and al Qaeda.
Most terrorism experts outside the government said they doubted that the
presence in Iraq of the Ansar group proved any such connection.

One of the most disturbing aspects of the violence was the emergence
of what U.S. officials called "homegrown" terrorists and resisters. These
appeared to be Iraqis who had no links to Saddam's regime but were so
angered by the "infidel" occupation of their land that they resorted to violence. The exact extent of this type of resistance was not clear by year's
end, but its appearance on the scene contributed to the ongoing violence
and instability in Iraq.

The UN Role in Iraq

The failure of the United Nations Security Council to endorse the Iraq War
had hardened the negative attitude of many officials in the Bush administration toward the United Nations. Especially in the Pentagon, which had
control over U.S. policy in Iraq, officials had no interest in giving the United
Nations any serious responsibility for the occupation. Even so, Washington
wanted at least some kind of UN endorsement of the occupation.

After several weeks of negotiations on the details, the UN Security Council on May 22 adopted the first of two resolutions during the year on postwar Iraq. Resolution 1483 lifted international economic sanctions that had
been in place against Iraq since 1991 and recognized the United States
and Britain as the occupying powers "until an internationally recognized,
representative government is established." The UN's own role was limited
to humanitarian assistance, reconstruction, and help in creation of an Iraqi
government. The resolution gave the UN more of a role than the Bush
administration had originally envisioned, but less of a role than many other
countries had wanted.

The Bush administration had asked Annan to name Vieira de Mello as
the head of the UN mission. The Brazilian diplomat had won wide praise
for his work in other postconflict situations (most recently Kosovo and East

Timor), and U.S. officials believed his participation would lend credibility to the occupation of Iraq. Vieira de Mello arrived in Baghdad on June 2 and then spent much of his time working behind the scenes to smooth relations between Bremer's office and Iraqi leaders. For example, Vieira de Mello was able to meet with Ayatollah Sistani, who had refused to meet with Bremer or other U.S. representatives. Vieira de Mello reportedly had a major hand in the selection of the twenty-five members of the Iraqi Governing Council.

Appearing before the Security Council on July 22—a month before his death—Vieira de Mello called on the United States to lay out a timetable "for the earliest possible restoration of sovereignty." Iraqis, he said, "need to know that the current state of affairs will come to an end soon. They need to know that stability will return and that the occupation will end." Politically, one of Vieira de Mello's most important statements was to endorse the Iraqi Governing Council, which he said was "broadly representative of the various constituencies in Iraq" and had "the credibility and authority" to represent Iraqis in the transition period.

Back to the UN

Vieira de Mello's death in the August 19 bombing of the UN headquarters, the assassination of Ayatollah Hakim, the daily attacks on American forces and Iraqis who worked with them, and a growing recognition that the U.S. military was being stretched thin by the occupation gradually led the Bush administration to admit that it had to go back to the UN for help. Bush signaled a change in perspective when he addressed the nation on September 7 to announce his request to Congress for $87 billion to finance the occupation and reconstruction of Iraq. Acknowledging that "not all our friends agreed" with the war, Bush said that UN member nations "now have an opportunity, and the responsibility, to assume a broader role in assuring that Iraq becomes a free and democratic nation."

Bush's speech set in motion a five-week period of negotiations among the same UN Security Council members that had been unable to agree just six months earlier on whether to launch the war in Iraq. The Bush administration sought a new resolution calling on other nations to contribute troops to the peacekeeping mission in Iraq, along with more money for reconstruction. The United States would retain overall control of the international troops and would continue to have the final say in all major governing decisions. But the administration, for the first time, offered the UN more of a substantial role in guiding Iraq's transition to restored sovereignty. The administration's main hope was that a new resolution would encourage countries with large armies—notably India, Pakistan, and Turkey—to send sizable contingents to help maintain order in Iraq.

Bush made a personal appeal to the UN on September 23, in his annual address to the General Assembly. The United Nations, he said, "can contribute greatly to the cause of Iraqi self-government."

Negotiations over a new resolution quickly ran up against a disagreement over the timing of the handover of Iraqi sovereignty. Annan pressed for a faster timetable than the Bush administration had in mind, and he was supported by some of the countries that had opposed the Iraq war. Diplomats also haggled over the exact nature of the UN's possible return to Iraq. Final agreement came in mid-October. It gave the United States most of what it wanted: a renewed mandate for its occupation of Iraq, a pledge that the United Nations would return to help in the political transition and reconstruction "as circumstances permit," and a call on nations to contribute assistance to Iraq, including military forces. The resolution authorized, but did not automatically set up, a "multinational force under unified command" to provide security in Iraq. In effect, this provision gave the United States the option of converting the occupying force into a UN force, if doing so would bring broader international participation.

The resolution said that the Iraqi Governing Council and its cabinet members constituted an administration that "embodies the sovereignty of the state of Iraq" during the transition. Annan called this a "nice phrase" that failed to disguise the fact that the United States, as the occupying power, had the ultimate authority, and thus the real sovereignty. The Security Council approved the resolution, number 1511, on a unanimous vote October 16. It was the most important action the council had taken on Iraq since its adoption a year earlier of Resolution 1441, which demanded that Iraq comply with previous resolutions requiring it to disarm.

While it represented a major diplomatic victory for the Bush administration, Resolution 1511 failed to accomplish the administration's original purpose of encouraging other countries to send large military contingents to Iraq. By the time the council acted, most of the large countries that had been approached by the administration had declined the invitation. "Don't see this resolution as opening the door to troops," Secretary of State Colin Powell said after it was adopted. Only Turkey still held out the prospect of sending troops, but it backed out later in October, after a series of public protests at home. The prospect of Turkish troops also prompted objections from Iraqi leaders, who feared a return of the country that, as the Ottoman empire, had occupied Iraq for centuries.

A New Political Arrangement

The UN resolution set the stage for the Bush administration's third try at establishing a political formula for Iraq. After meeting with administration officials in Washington early in November, Bremer returned to Iraq and negotiated an agreement with the Iraqi Governing Council calling for the United States to hand over sovereignty to a "transitional" Iraqi government by July 1, 2004. Bremer signed the plan on November 15, along with Kurdish leader Jalal Talabani, who was that month's chairman of the council.

The plan called for the council to draft, by the end of February 2004, a "fundamental law" establishing the structure for an interim government and providing a bill of rights. Bremer would have the power to veto or demand major changes in this law. Then a complex series of caucuses would be held around the country to select the members of a transitional national assembly. That assembly would appoint an interim government, which would take office on June 30, 2004, and assume Iraqi sovereignty from the U.S. administration. Elections for a constitutional convention would be held on March 15, 2005, a constitution would be drafted, and elections for a permanent government would be held by December 31, 2005.

Signatures were barely dry on the November 15 plan before it began to unravel. Several members of the council objected to provisions of the plan, saying they had not been consulted in its formulation. Among them was one of the Shi'ite representatives, Abdul Aziz al-Hakim (younger brother of assassinated Ayatollah Hakim), who assumed the council chairmanship for December. One criticism was that the plan failed to provide for a continuing role for the council after the handover of power.

A more serious problem emerged on November 26 when Ayatollah Sistani rejected the plan outright, saying that it "does not guarantee the formation of an assembly that truly represents the people of Iraq." The country's senior Shi'ite cleric repeated his demand for any new government to be chosen by elections—not through the caucus system that officials in Washington had devised. U.S. officials responded that elections—while desirable in theory—could not be held as early as the first half of 2004, given the country's total inexperience with genuine democracy and the absence of such prerequisites as a reliable census and list of eligible voters. Yet another factor, which U.S. officials were reluctant to acknowledge, was that elections would be inviting targets for those who used violence to promote their own agendas.

Sistani's objection put the November 15 plan in serious jeopardy because members of the Iraqi Governing Council were reluctant to be seen as opposing his insistence on an early move toward democracy. Negotiations on the matter were still under way at year's end. It appeared almost certain that key elements of the November 15 plan, especially the cumbersome procedure for caucuses, would be revised and Iraq would get its first elections much sooner than late 2005.

However it was chosen, the new Iraqi government faced a host of difficult issues that were bound to cause major stresses in a society unaccustomed to genuine public debate. Major questions that would have to be addressed in the constitutional process included the role of Islam and whether there would be guarantees of religious freedom, the type of government (presidential, parliamentary, or a combination of both), the relationship between the central government and the regions, and the status of the autonomous Kurdish area in the north.

Rebuilding Iraq

The cycle of violence and the repeated debates over a new government diverted international attention from the equally difficult task of rebuilding a country that over the previous quarter century had suffered three major wars, a brutal dictatorship, and international economic sanctions. Saddam had devoted much of Iraq's oil wealth to maintaining a gigantic military establishment and to building palaces and monuments honoring his own glory. Public services of all kinds were allowed to deteriorate, and the economy crumbled under the weight of sanctions and the inability of the tattered oil industry to produce anything close to its potential. U.S. officials said they knew before the war that Iraq's infrastructure had deteriorated, but they were not prepared for the extent of the problem. Explaining Bush's request for $20 billion to jump-start the rebuilding, Bremer told Congress in October that Iraq was in "a lot worse shape than we thought" before the war.

After surveying Iraq's needs, the World Bank and the United Nations suggested in October that rebuilding essential services in the country would cost about $55 billion over a four-year period. That total included about $19 billion for short-term needs (such as providing security and reviving the oil industry) that had already been identified by the United States, plus $36 billion for longer-term reconstruction through 2007. Delegates at a donor's conference in Madrid in late October pledged $3 billion in aid to Iraq during 2004, in addition to the $19 billion in U.S. aid that Congress was in the process of approving. Before most of them left Iraq in the wake of the UN bombing, international humanitarian organizations provided much of the emergency food, clothing, and limited medical care to Iraqis.

The bulk of the U.S.-financed reconstruction was carried out by large U.S. corporations under contracts written by the Pentagon. The biggest contractor was by far the most controversial one: Halliburton Corporation, a Texas firm that during the 1990s had been headed by Vice President Dick Cheney. The Pentagon in 2002 gave Halliburton a no-bid contract to protect and restore some parts of Iraq's oil industry. That contract later was broadened to include a wide range of services, including supplying U.S. forces in Iraq with food and gasoline. Critics, especially Democrats in Congress, charged that Halliburton won its contracts because of its political ties to the Bush White House and that the firm was gouging U.S.

taxpayers by charging too much money for its services. Halliburton and the administration denied those charges, which were under investigation at year's end.

Another controversy arose in December when the Pentagon announced that countries that had not supported the Iraq War would not be eligible to bid on reconstruction contracts. That announcement threatened to reopen the international political and diplomatic wounds from the prewar period that had just begun to heal. Bush later stepped back from that hard-nosed approach by authorizing former secretary of state James A. Baker III to negotiate exceptions to the ban. Bush had sent Baker to world capitals to seek a reduction of Iraq's estimated $100 billion to $120 billion external debt, some of it held by France, Germany, and Russia, which had been among the staunchest opponents of the war. Those three countries, along with Japan, agreed to waive some of the money they were owed by Iraq, but the exact amounts were still under discussion at year's end.

In one of his most sweeping actions as Iraq's overseer, Bremer on September 20 ordered the total transformation of the country's economy. All the state-owned enterprises that had dominated the economy under Saddam's regime were to be scrapped and replaced with a free-market economy open to foreign investment. Bremer's rules allowed foreign companies to buy total control of Iraqi enterprises. The one exception was the oil industry, which would remain controlled by the government for the time being.

Bush Administration Planning

Even before the war had ended the Bush administration faced widespread criticism that it had meticulously planned the combat but not the aftermath. U.S. officials at first rejected the criticism, but the numerous changes of plans in reaction to unanticipated events undermined their arguments. By late July Paul Wolfowitz, one of the chief architects of U.S. policy, acknowledged that some key assumptions had been invalid, leading the administration "to underestimate the problem" it would face in Iraq.

One assumption was that the majority of Iraqis would be so glad to see Saddam ousted that they would joyfully rush to help the United States restore order. Thomas E. White, who was the secretary of the army until he was dumped by the administration in April, said in September that this rosy view had predominated in the administration's prewar planning.

The administration also appeared to overestimate the political support that Chalabi and other exiles had, or would be able to develop, in Iraq. Much of the Pentagon's prewar planning was based around Chalabi's contention that he and other exiles could quickly establish a legitimate government atop elements of the existing civil service, thus allowing the United States to hand over power quickly and withdraw the bulk of its troops. Once in place, however, the exiles generated little popular enthusiasm, leading Bremer to surround them in the governing council with local leaders who had more credibility among Iraqis.

By mid-summer U.S. officials said they had seriously underestimated the potential for lawlessness following the collapse of Saddam's regime. The signs of trouble emerged in mid-April, when looters ransacked the Iraqi national library and museum in Baghdad because the United States had failed to mount guards there. The Pentagon had few military police officers in Iraq and had not planned any outside aid to help Iraq's civil police get up and running again. As the looting continued into May, even some Republicans on Capitol Hill began saying that the administration, in its desire to avoid "nation building," was ignoring the lessons of recent postconflict situations in the Balkans, Africa, and Afghanistan.

Among the administration's first major decisions was the dismantling of the Iraqi army and the Ba'ath Party—the key structural supports of Saddam's regime. Arguing that Saddam's loyalists had no place in a democratic Iraq, Bremer in May banned some 30,000 Ba'ath Party members from "future employment in the public sector" and cut off the pay for the estimated 350,000 members of Iraq's army. He kept the ban on Ba'ath Party members in place throughout 2003 despite criticism that it deprived Iraq of the people who had administrative skills to run a government. Bremer later modified his decision not to pay the military when it became clear that some of the angry, unpaid former soldiers with guns were taking revenge against Americans.

Before the war, and as it got under way, administration officials confidently predicted that Iraq's oil revenue could pay much of the cost of the occupation and reconstruction. Wolfowitz told a House subcommittee on March 27 that Iraq's oil industry would generate $50 billion to $100 billion over the next two or three years. As a result, Iraq "can really finance its own reconstruction, and relatively soon," he said. Bremer acknowledged in late September that Iraq's oil industry was so dilapidated that it could generate only about $4 billion in 2003 and no more than $14 billion annually in the following two years—well below even the low end of Wolfowitz's earlier assessment.

Finally, a broad issue the administration faced throughout the year was the role of the United Nations. Rumsfeld and other officials insisted that the UN's failure to endorse the war demonstrated that its usefulness in Iraq was marginal, at best. Critics argued that the Bush administration's anger at the UN led it to underestimate the legitimacy the world body could provide, plus the expertise of UN officials who had been involved in postwar operations around the world. The administration implicitly acknowledged some of this criticism by returning to the UN Security Council twice during the year for resolutions blessing the occupation of Iraq. By year's end administration officials also appeared to have discovered the possible utility of the United Nations for political purposes: Getting the UN to endorse the handover of political power to a new Iraqi government by mid-2004—just four months before the U.S. presidential elections—might insulate Bush against charges that he had gotten the United States bogged down in Iraq.

Following is the text of United Nations Security Council Resolution 1511, adopted October 16, 2003, endorsing the interim Iraqi Governing Council of Iraq, which operated under the U.S.-led occupation of the country, and calling on other countries to contribute troops to help stabilize Iraq.

"United Nations Security Council Resolution 1151"

The Security Council,

Reaffirming its previous resolutions on Iraq, including resolution 1483 (2003) of 22 May 2003 and 1500 (2003) of 14 August 2003, and on threats to peace and security caused by terrorist acts, including resolution 1373 (2001) of 28 September 2001, and other relevant resolutions,

Underscoring that the sovereignty of Iraq resides in the State of Iraq, *reaffirming* the right of the Iraqi people freely to determine their own political future and control their own natural resources, *reiterating* its resolve that the day when Iraqis govern themselves must come quickly, and *recognizing* the importance of international support, particularly that of countries in the region, Iraq's neighbours, and regional organizations, in taking forward this process expeditiously,

Recognizing that international support for restoration of conditions of stability and security is essential to the well-being of the people of Iraq as well as to the ability of all concerned to carry out their work on behalf of the people of Iraq, and *welcoming* Member State contributions in this regard under resolution 1483 (2003),

Welcoming the decision of the Governing Council of Iraq to form a preparatory constitutional committee to prepare for a constitutional conference that will draft a constitution to embody the aspirations of the Iraqi people, and *urging* it to complete this process quickly,

Affirming that the terrorist bombings of the Embassy of Jordan on 7 August 2003, of the United Nations headquarters in Baghdad on 19 August 2003, of the Imam Ali Mosque in Najaf on 29 August 2003, and of the Embassy of Turkey on 14 October 2003, and the murder of a Spanish diplomat on 9 October 2003 are attacks on the people of Iraq, the United Nations, and the international community, and *deploring* the assassination of Dr. Akila al-Hashimi, who died on 25 September 2003, as an attack directed against the future of Iraq,

In that context, *recalling* and *reaffirming* the statement of its President of 20 August 2003 and resolution 1502 (2003) of 26 August 2003,

Determining that the situation in Iraq, although improved, continues to constitute a threat to international peace and security,

Acting under Chapter VII of the Charter of the United Nations,

1. *Reaffirms* the sovereignty and territorial integrity of Iraq, and *underscores*, in that context, the temporary nature of the exercise by the Coalition Provisional Authority (Authority) of the specific responsibilities, authorities, and obligations under applicable international law recognized and set forth in resolution 1483 (2003), which will cease when an internationally recognized, representative government established by the people of Iraq is sworn in and assumes the responsibilities of the Authority, inter alia through steps envisaged in paragraphs 4 through 7 and 10 below;

2. *Welcomes* the positive response of the international community, in fora such as the Arab League, the Organization of the Islamic Conference, the United Nations General Assembly, and the United Nations Educational, Scientific and Cultural Organization, to the establishment of the broadly representative Governing Council as an important step towards an internationally recognized, representative government;

3. *Supports* the Governing Council's efforts to mobilize the people of Iraq, including by the appointment of a cabinet of ministers and a preparatory constitutional committee to lead a process in which the Iraqi people will progressively take control of their own affairs;

4. *Determines* that the Governing Council and its ministers are the principal bodies of the Iraqi interim administration, which, without prejudice to its further evolution, embodies the sovereignty of the State of Iraq during the transitional period until an internationally recognized, representative government is established and assumes the responsibilities of the Authority;

5. *Affirms* that the administration of Iraq will be progressively undertaken by the evolving structures of the Iraqi interim administration;

6. *Calls upon* the Authority, in this context, to return governing responsibilities and authorities to the people of Iraq as soon as practicable and *requests* the Authority, in cooperation as appropriate with the Governing Council and the Secretary-General, to report to the Council on the progress being made;

7. *Invites* the Governing Council to provide to the Security Council, for its review, no later than 15 December 2003, in cooperation with the Authority and, as circumstances permit, the Special Representative of the Secretary-General, a timetable and a programme for the drafting of a new constitution for Iraq and for the holding of democratic elections under that constitution;

8. *Resolves* that the United Nations, acting through the Secretary-General, his Special Representative, and the United Nations Assistance Mission in Iraq, should strengthen its vital role in Iraq, including by providing humanitarian relief, promoting the economic reconstruction of and conditions for sustainable development in Iraq, and advancing efforts to restore and establish national and local institutions for representative government;

9. *Requests* that, as circumstances permit, the Secretary-General pursue the course of action outlined in paragraphs 98 and 99 of the report of the Secretary-General of 17 July 2003;

10. *Takes note* of the intention of the Governing Council to hold a constitutional conference and, recognizing that the convening of the conference will be a milestone in the movement to the full exercise of sovereignty, *calls for* its preparation through national dialogue and consensus-building as soon as practicable and *requests* the Special Representative of the Secretary-General, at the time of the convening of the conference or, as circumstances permit, to lend the unique expertise of the United Nations to the Iraqi people in this process of political transition, including the establishment of electoral processes;

11. *Requests* the Secretary-General to ensure that the resources of the United Nations and associated organizations are available, if requested by the Iraqi Governing Council and, as circumstances permit, to assist in furtherance of the programme provided by the Governing Council in paragraph 7 above, and encourages other organizations with expertise in this area to support the Iraqi Governing Council, if requested;

12. *Requests* the Secretary-General to report to the Security Council on his responsibilities under this resolution and the development and implementation of a timetable and programme under paragraph 7 above;

13. *Determines* that the provision of security and stability is essential to the successful completion of the political process as outlined in paragraph 7 above and to the ability of the United Nations to contribute effectively to that process and the implementation of resolution 1483 (2003), and *authorizes* a multinational force under unified command to take all necessary measures to contribute to the maintenance of security and stability in Iraq,

including for the purpose of ensuring necessary conditions for the implementation of the timetable and programme as well as to contribute to the security of the United Nations Assistance Mission for Iraq, the Governing Council of Iraq and other institutions of the Iraqi interim administration, and key humanitarian and economic infrastructure;

14. *Urges* Member States to contribute assistance under this United Nations mandate, including military forces, to the multinational force referred to in paragraph 13 above;

15. *Decides* that the Council shall review the requirements and mission of the multinational force referred to in paragraph 13 above not later than one year from the date of this resolution, and that in any case the mandate of the force shall expire upon the completion of the political process as described in paragraphs 4 through 7 and 10 above, and *expresses* readiness to consider on that occasion any future need for the continuation of the multinational force, taking into account the views of an internationally recognized, representative government of Iraq;

16. *Emphasizes* the importance of establishing effective Iraqi police and security forces in maintaining law, order, and security and combating terrorism consistent with paragraph 4 of resolution 1483 (2003), and *calls upon* Member States and international and regional organizations to contribute to the training and equipping of Iraqi police and security forces;

17. *Expresses* deep sympathy and condolences for the personal losses suffered by the Iraqi people and by the United Nations and the families of those United Nations personnel and other innocent victims who were killed or injured in these tragic attacks;

18. *Unequivocally condemns* the terrorist bombings of the Embassy of Jordan on 7 August 2003, of the United Nations headquarters in Baghdad on 19 August 2003, and of the Imam Ali Mosque in Najaf on 29 August 2003, and of the Embassy of Turkey on 14 October 2003, the murder of a Spanish diplomat on 9 October 2003, and the assassination of Dr. Akila al-Hashimi, who died on 25 September 2003, and *emphasizes* that those responsible must be brought to justice;

19. *Calls upon* Member States to prevent the transit of terrorists to Iraq, arms for terrorists, and financing that would support terrorists, and *emphasizes* the importance of strengthening the cooperation of the countries of the region, particularly neighbours of Iraq, in this regard;

20. *Appeals* to Member States and the international financial institutions to strengthen their efforts to assist the people of Iraq in the reconstruction and development of their economy, and *urges* those

institutions to take immediate steps to provide their full range of loans and other financial assistance to Iraq, working with the Governing Council and appropriate Iraqi ministries;

21. *Urges* Member States and international and regional organizations to support the Iraq reconstruction effort initiated at the 24 June 2003 United Nations Technical Consultations, including through substantial pledges at the 23-24 October 2003 International Donors Conference in Madrid;

22. *Calls upon* Member States and concerned organizations to help meet the needs of the Iraqi people by providing resources necessary for the rehabilitation and reconstruction of Iraq's economic infrastructure;

23. *Emphasizes* that the International Advisory and Monitoring Board (IAMB) referred to in paragraph 12 of resolution 1483 (2003) should be established as a priority, and *reiterates* that the Development Fund for Iraq shall be used in a transparent manner as set out in paragraph 14 of resolution 1483 (2003);

24. *Reminds* all Member States of their obligations under paragraphs 19 and 23 of resolution 1483 (2003) in particular the obligation to immediately cause the transfer of funds, other financial assets and economic resources to the Development Fund for Iraq for the benefit of the Iraqi people;

25. *Requests* that the United States, on behalf of the multinational force as outlined in paragraph 13 above, report to the Security Council on the efforts and progress of this force as appropriate and not less than every six months;

26. *Decides* to remain seized of the matter.

Source: United Nations. Security Council. *Resolution 1511.* S/RES/1511 (2003). October 16, 2003. http://daccess-ods.un.org/access.nsf/ Get?Open&DS=S/RES/1511%20(2003)&Lang=E&Area=UNDOC (accessed October 20, 2003).

UN Report on Intellectual Freedom in the Arab World

October 20, 2003

INTRODUCTION

The U.S. ousting of Iraqi leader Saddam Hussein helped crystallize an emerging debate in the Arab world about the region's instability, lack of democracy, and economic stagnation. Many Arabs continued to blame the United States and other Western countries for the woes of their region. This viewpoint hardened and became even more prevalent in 2003 because of Washington's occupation of Iraq and the failure of diplomacy to end the conflict between Israel and the Palestinians. Some Arab opinion makers, however, were beginning to look inward for the root causes and possible solutions to the region's problems. The Bush administration sought to foster this process by calling for reforms that would slowly lead the Arab world toward democracy. Even so, the administration and some of the Arabs appeared to be talking past each other—especially on the question of whether the war in Iraq and Washington's ongoing war against terrorism opened or closed new avenues to progress.

One of the primary vehicles for the new debate about the Arab world was a series of reports cosponsored by the UN Development Program and the Arab Fund for Economic and Social Development. A widely read report issued in 2002 suggested that the lack of freedom was one of the major factors that had kept much of the Arab world stuck in the equivalent of medieval times.

A follow-up report, released October 20, 2003, detailed the "knowledge gap" between Arab countries and much of the rest of the world. The new report said that a widespread lack of intellectual curiosity and a fear of outside ideas had perpetuated authoritarianism in Arab lands and prevented them from reaching their full potential. *(U.S. occupation of Iraq, p. 135; Israel-Palestinian conflict, p. 191; previous report, Historic Documents of 2002, p. 483)*

UN Report

The 2002 report on Arab Human Development had generated wide comment, in both Arab and non-Arab countries, because it discussed issues that had long been suppressed in much of the Arab world. Perhaps the most important of these matters were the causes of the region's long decline since the height of Islamic intellectual and economic achievement during the early Middle Ages. Among other things, the report detailed a closing of Arab societies to outside information and influences.

The 2003 report took the discussion a step further, documenting how the knowledge gap had developed between Arab lands and the rest of the world and offering suggestions for what could be done about it. As with its predecessor, the report was compiled by a group of several dozen Arab scholars, some of whom lived in Western countries. The report naturally reflected the views of Arab intellectuals who had been exposed to Western culture, but it also cited surveys to capture public opinion in the twenty-two Arab countries, with a total population of about 270 million.

In general, the report said that all areas of intellectual life in Arab societies had stagnated over the centuries, partly because of a resistance to ideas from outside the region. The education curricula in most Arab countries bred "submission, obedience, subordination, and compliance rather than free critical thinking," the report said. Most universities were used for political purposes by governments, libraries were poor, laboratories lacked modern equipment, and scientific and technical research was minimal. Literature had declined to insignificance: very few books were translated into Arabic from other languages, and the publication of books of any kind lagged well behind that of most other cultures. In most Arab countries censorship of the news was a major factor in limiting public access to critical information. And Arab countries, along with Africa, were the parts of the world left behind in the information age. The report estimated that only 1.6 percent of Arabs had access to the Internet.

The report's general prescription for Arab societies was a renewed openness to ideas and information, including that from outside the region. "The truth is that Arab culture has no choice but to engage again in a new global experiment," the report said. "It cannot close itself off, contented with living on history, the past and inherited culture alone in a world whose victorious powers reach into all corners of the earth, dominating all forms of knowledge, life, manufactured goods, and innovation."

This tension between the Arab world and the "victorious powers"— a clear reference in particular to the United States—was a thread that ran throughout the report. Even while saying that Arabs needed to take advantage of the knowledge and skills offered by the rest of the world, the report's authors said the impetus for change needed to come from within the Arab world and could not be imposed from the outside.

The report had harsh words for the United States, arguing that its policies in the Middle East "have heightened political tensions within Arab states and have become in themselves obstacles to open interchange with the United States and its allies." In particular, the report condemned the invasion of Iraq, rejecting the contention of President George W. Bush that the toppling of Saddam Hussein would lead to democracy there. Washington's reluctance to force Israel to make concessions to Palestinians also posed barriers to acceptance of its views in the Arab world, the report said. In addition, the authors said the Bush administration's war against terrorism, since the September 11, 2001, attacks against the United States, had been counterproductive in some respects. New U.S. immigration policies that made it difficult for Arabs to study in the United States had cut off "knowledge acquisition opportunities for young Arabs," they said. Antiterrorism legislation in the United States and other countries also had given authorities in many Arab countries "another excuse to enact new laws limiting civil and political freedoms." *(U.S. immigration restrictions, p. 218)*

As had the previous report, the 2003 report treaded gingerly on the question of Islam's role in Arab society. Noting that Arab intellectual activity flourished in the early centuries of Islam (from the seventh through about the fourteenth centuries), the authors said Islam itself provided "great incentives for knowledge acquisition." It was the misuse of Islam by extreme political movements and authoritarian governments that had deprived Arab countries of the benefits of their shared religion, the authors said.

Although the report talked in general terms about opening Arab societies to new ideas and information and called on Arab governments to allow greater intellectual and political freedoms, it offered few concrete steps to achieve those goals. As a result, some Arab analysts said the report was missing an essential ingredient. "These are problems we in the Arab world have been talking about for decades," Rami Khouri, editor of Beirut's *Daily Star* English-language newspaper told the *Christian Science Monitor.* "We need a plan of political action to address the problem and make it better." Some critics also said the report should have condemned specific authoritarian Arab leaders by name, rather than challenging their practices in general.

Bush Middle East Initiative

President Bush described the war in Iraq to the American people primarily as a security imperative: Saddam Hussein, he said, had built an arsenal of dangerous weapons that might be used against the United States or its allies unless he was ousted from power. But Bush also portrayed the toppling of Saddam as an opportunity to foster democracy throughout the Middle East, starting with Iraq. By embracing democracy, he said, Iraqis would set an example that would unleash an unstoppable, regionwide movement for change.

Bush articulated this view most directly in a November 6 speech marking the twentieth anniversary of the founding of the National Endowment for Democracy, a U.S. government agency that provided grants and technical expertise to groups in countries attempting to move from authoritarianism to democracy. Bush focused on the Middle East as a region where dictatorial regimes had suppressed freedom and created socialist economies that stifled individual initiative. "There are governments that still fear and repress independent thought and creative and private enterprise: human qualities that make for strong and successful societies," he said. "Even when these nations have vast natural resources, they do not respect or develop their great resources, the talent and energy of men and women working and living in freedom."

In his indictment of authoritarianism in the Middle East, the president named only a few specific countries, most of which had long been at odds with Washington, including Syria and Iran. He stirred some interest by citing Egypt, one of the closest U.S. allies in the region. "The great and proud nation of Egypt has shown the way toward peace in the Middle East, and now should show the way toward democracy in the Middle East," Bush declared.

Bush rejected the charge raised by many in the Middle East that the United States wanted to impose a Western concept of democracy in the region. "As we watch and encourage reforms in the region, we are mindful that modernization is not the same as Westernization," he said. "Representative governments in the Middle East will reflect their own cultures. They will not, and should not, look like us. Democratic nations may be constitutional monarchies, federal republics, or parliamentary systems." Bush also acknowledged that political reform likely would be slow in the Middle East, and so he said the West needed to be "patient and understanding."

Bush in this speech offered no new U.S. programs to encourage democracy in the Middle East, but he did affirm his commitment to a program he had launched in 2002 called the Middle East Initiative. That plan included U.S. aid to encourage economic, educational, and political reform in the region, including literacy programs for women and training for judges and parliamentarians. Another component, which Bush announced May 9, was a Middle East Free Trade Area—an expansion during the rest of the decade of free trade agreements the United States already had in place with Israel and Jordan.

As could be expected, Bush's speech prompted a wide range of reaction. Many Arab analysts praised the speech for focusing on the need for democracy, while others said he failed to understand the depth of anti-Americanism even in countries, such as Morocco and Jordan, whose leaders were trying to promote modernization. The reactive view from the "Arab street" was expressed by a young worker in Jordan, Samer Hussein, who told the Associated Press: "With the justification of democracy, Bush and the Americans plan to occupy Arab and Muslim lands. We tell him, we do not want this democracy."

Many U.S. analysts said Bush had to be careful about demanding democracy for the Middle East because of the popularity in many Arab lands of hard-line Islamist movements, which could win elections and then create theocratic states—such as the Islamic dictatorship in Iran (which was a Muslim country but not an Arab one). Among the litany of U.S. sins cited by many Arabs, for example, was Washington's failure in 1991 to condemn the government of Algeria, which cancelled the results of legislative elections after an Islamist party won a clear majority.

U.S. "Public Diplomacy" in the Arab World

In 2002, as part of its run-up to the Iraq war, the Bush administration launched a major public relations program to explain and promote U.S. policies in the Arab and Muslim worlds. The U.S. program included a new Arab language radio station, Radio Sawa ("together"), which began broadcasting to the Middle East in 2002, and a new Arab-language television station, Al Hurra ("free one"), which went on the air in late 2003. Both stations were intended to counter state-run broadcasts in the region, as well as newly popular satellite television networks that were dominated by an anti-American viewpoint; the most important of these networks was Al Jazeera.

The State Department commissioned a study, by American experts, of the effectiveness of the government's efforts to promote the U.S. viewpoint among Arabs and Muslims. Made public on October 1, "Changing Minds, Winning Peace: A New Strategic Direction for U.S. Public Diplomacy in the Arab and Muslim World" lambasted those efforts as inadequate and ineffective. The report was written by a panel chaired by Edward P. Djerejian, a former State Department specialist in Arab affairs. Djerejian and twelve other experts commissioned public opinion polls in Arab and Muslim countries and visited the regions, meeting with opinion leaders and ordinary citizens.

The panel said it found that "a process of unilateral disarmament in the weapons of advocacy over the past decade has contributed to widespread hostility toward Americans and left us vulnerable to lethal threats to our interests and our safety. In this time of peril, public diplomacy is absurdly and dangerously under funded, and simply restoring it to its cold war status is not enough."

Much of what the panel said was unwelcome—if unsurprising—to policy makers in Washington. "Surveys show much of the resentment toward America stems from our policies," the report said. "It is clear, for example, that the Arab-Israeli conflict remains a visible and significant point of contention between the United States and many Arab and Muslim countries, and that peace in the region, as well as the transformation of Iraq, would reduce tensions."

The panel described what it called a "cycle of animosity" between Americans and people in Arab and Muslim lands. "Arabs and Muslims respond in anger to what they perceive as U.S. denigration of their societies and cultures, and to this Arab and Muslim response Americans react with bewilderment and resentment, provoking a further negative response from Arabs and Muslims," the report said.

The panel advocated a "complete transformation" of Washington's efforts to explain itself to Arabs and Muslims, starting with a frank dialogue that acknowledged the deep differences of opinion. " 'Spin' and manipulative public relations and propaganda are not the answer," the panel said.

Djerejian said one of the panel's principal findings was that articulate, Arab-speaking representatives of the American point of view simply were absent from the news media and other forums for public discussion in Arab and Muslim lands. Even the poorest people in many countries had access to satellite television—and more often than not their televisions were tuned to stations that broadcasted a steady stream of anti-American propaganda. "You know, Woody Allen said 90 percent of life is just showing up," Djerejian said. "In the Arab world, the United States just doesn't show up."

Djerejian's report noted surveys in forty-four countries conducted in late 2002 by the Pew Center for the People and the Press. The surveys found that approval of the United States, and its foreign policies, had dropped in most countries, and by substantial margins in many of them. Among the countries where strong majorities of those surveyed expressed unfavorable views of the United States were key U.S. allies in the Arab and Muslim world: Egypt, Jordan, Pakistan, and Turkey.

Halting Progress During 2003

Because of the U.S. invasion, Iraq was the only Middle Eastern country that experienced a dramatic transfer of power during the year. But slower, and more subtle, changes were under way in several other countries.

Perhaps the most attention-getting was the talk—so far just that—of modest reform in Saudi Arabia. Crown Prince Abdullah, the country's day-to-day ruler, proposed reforms early in the year, and plans were announced for the country's first-ever municipal elections, although no dates were set. Saudi Arabia was the richest country in the Arab world, by virtue of its oil resources, but it also was one of the most authoritarian; all power was held by the ruling Saud family, and women were deprived of most basic civil rights. *(Saudi Arabia, p. 227)*

Two of the tiny principalities in the Persian Gulf region appeared to be moving much faster than Saudi Arabia toward political reform. The most advanced was Qatar, the small thumb-shaped peninsula that jutted out into the gulf. Qatar held municipal elections in 1999, even allowing women to vote; women also were allowed to drive cars, a radical step that was prohibited in Saudi Arabia and several other conservative Arab states. In an April 2003 referendum, Qatar's voters approved a plan calling for a new constitution. Bahrain also began to liberalize its political system, announcing a plan to allow political parties.

Jordan held elections in June for the lower chamber of its parliament, the first since 1997. The parliament could enact laws, but only with the approval of the hereditary monarch, King Abdullah, who had the power to dissolve parliament and had done so in 2001. The restoration of parliament did not prove to be an immediate benefit for women, however. The parliament in June rejected proposals to give more rights to women; deputies said doing so would contradict Islam. King Abdullah on October 22 called for unspecified political reforms; three days later he swore in a new government that included three women.

One of the year's clearest signs that moderates and liberals would not necessarily benefit from increased democracy came in Kuwait, which held elections in July for a fifty-seat parliament that could propose laws. Liberals—meaning those who favored giving women the right to vote—were soundly rejected in the election, losing all but three of the fourteen seats they had held in the previous parliament. Conservative factions, including those aligned with the ruling Sabah family, won all the other seats.

There were few signs of serious political change in two of the largest and most authoritarian Arab countries: Egypt and Syria. Egyptian president Hosni Mubarak retained a firm grip on power. He had been elected to office repeatedly (by the parliament), but no serious opposition was allowed. A one-chamber legislature, the People's Assembly, was elected but had no real political power. In September Mubarak promised political reforms and said he would cancel "emergency" decrees that had been in effect for two decades; no action followed, however. On October 20 police prohibited a march to Mubarak's office by prodemocracy activists. Syria's leader, Bashar al-Assad, had succeeded to the presidency when his father died in 2000. Although he gave the impression that he planned significant changes in what had long been a one-party dictatorship, he had not followed through by 2003.

Following are excerpts from the "Arab Human Development Report 2003: Building a Knowledge Society," issued October 20, 2003, by the United Nations Development Program and the Arab Fund for Economic and Social Development.

"Arab Human Development Report 2003"

Executive Summary

The first Arab Human Development Report addressed the most important development challenges facing the Arab world at the beginning of the third millennium. This second Report continues the process by examining in depth one of these challenges: the building of a knowledge society in Arab countries. . . .

A One-Year Overview of Human Development:

Two Setbacks and the Start of Reform

A review of global and regional developments since the publication of AHDR 2002 underlines that the development challenges represented by the three deficits in knowledge, freedom and women's empowerment remain serious. Those challenges may have become even graver in the area of freedoms, as a result of these developments.

Following the bloody events of September 11 and the loss of innocent lives in violation of all man-made and divine laws, a number of countries have adopted extreme security measures and policies as part of the "war on terrorism". These measures and policies, however, exceeded their original goals and led to the erosion of civil and political liberties in many countries in the world, notably the United States, often diminishing the welfare of Arabs and Muslims living, studying or travelling abroad, interrupting cultural exchanges between the Arab world and the West and cutting off knowledge acquisition opportunities for young Arabs.

Among the first effects of these measures was the significant drop in the number of Arab students studying in the United States. Figures available from a number of Arab missions indicate that Arab student numbers in America dropped between 1999 and 2002 by an average of 30 per cent.

One of the worst consequences of freedom-constraining measures in developed countries is that they gave authorities in some Arab countries another excuse to enact new laws limiting civil and political freedoms. The Arab countries as a group adopted an expanded definition of terrorism, which assumed institutional expression at the regional level in "The Arab Charter against Terrorism". This charter was criticised in Arab and international human rights circles, because its expanded definition opens the door to abuse. It allows censorship, restricts access to the Internet, and restricts printing and publication. Moreover, the Charter neither explicitly prohibits detention or torture, nor provides for questioning the legality of detentions. Furthermore, it does not protect personal freedom, since it does not require a prior judicial order authorising the wire-tapping of individuals or groups (Amnesty International).

Israel reoccupied Palestinian territories, inflicting horrifying human casualties and material destruction, thereby committing what one well-respected human rights organization called "war crimes". From September 2000 to April 2003, Israeli occupation forces killed 2,405 Palestinian citizens and injured 41,000 others. Most of those killed (85%) were civilians. A large proportion (20%) of them were children. UNICEF estimates that 7,000 children were injured and that 2,500 persons, of whom 500 were children, suffered permanent handicaps.

A coalition led by the United States and Britain invaded and occupied Iraq, introducing a new challenge to the people of Iraq and the region. The only way to meet that challenge is to enable the Iraqi people to exercise their basic rights in accordance with international law, free themselves from occupation, recover their wealth, under a system of good governance representing the Iraqi people and take charge of rebuilding their country from a human development perspective.

In contrast to efforts to restructure the region from outside, the AHDR series aims to crystallise a strategic vision by Arab elites through a societal innovation process that envisages the restructuring of the region from within, and in service to Arab human development. Such reform from within, based on rigorous self-criticism, is a far more proper and sustainable alternative.

On the level of internal development in the Arab countries, progress was achieved in the advancement of women and in some aspects of popular participation. Women's representation in some parliaments and in senior positions in Executive Authorities increased. A number of Arab countries witnessed parliamentary elections, some of them for the first time in decades. Yet these bright spots, accompanied briefly by dawning awareness of the need for reform, were partly eclipsed by new setbacks in the areas of freedom of opinion, expression and association.

Assessing the present state of regional cooperation, the Report finds that Arab integration continues to fall far behind in achieving what the first Arab Human Development Report called "An Arab Free Citizenship Zone".

Building the Knowledge Society in Arab Countries

The Status of Knowledge in the Arab World
A knowledge-based society is one where knowledge diffusion, production and application become the organising principle in all aspects of human

activity: culture, society, the economy, politics, and private life. Knowledge nowadays can provide the means to expand the scope of human freedoms, enhance the capacity to guarantee those freedoms through good governance and achieve the higher moral human goals of justice and human dignity Contrasting this type of society with the state of knowledge in Arab countries, the Report looks carefully at the characteristics of the two main components of the knowledge acquisition system: diffusion and production.

Knowledge Diffusion: Blocks in Education, Bright Spots in the Media

Key knowledge dissemination processes in Arab countries (socialisation and upbringing, education, the media and translation), face deep-seated social, institutional, economic and political impediments. Notable among these are the meagre resources available to individuals, families and institutions and the restrictions imposed upon them. As a result, these processes often falter and fall short of preparing the epistemological and societal environment necessary for knowledge production.

Studies indicate that the most widespread style of child rearing in Arab families is the authoritarian mode accompanied by the overprotective. This reduces children's independence, self-confidence and social efficiency, and fosters passive attitudes and hesitant decision-making skills. Most of all, it affects how the child thinks by suppressing questioning, exploration and initiative.

Impressive gains in the quantitative expansion of education in Arab countries in the last half of the 20th century are still modest in comparison with other developing countries or with the requirements of human development. High rates of illiteracy among women persist, particularly in some of the less developed Arab countries. Many children still do not have access to basic education. Higher education is characterized by decreasing enrolment, and public spending on education has actually declined since 1985.

In all cases, nevertheless, the most important challenge facing Arab education is its declining quality.

The mass media are the most important agents for the public diffusion of knowledge yet Arab countries have lower information media to population ratios (number of newspapers, radio and televisions per 1000 people) compared to the world average. There are less than 53 newspapers per 1000 Arab citizens, compared to 285 papers per 1000 people in developed countries.

In most Arab countries, the media operate in an environment that sharply restricts freedom of the press and freedom of expression and opinion. Journalists face illegal harassment, intimidation and even physical threats, censorship is rife and newspapers and television channels are sometimes arbitrarily closed down. Most media institutions are stateowned, particularly radio and television.

The last two years, however, have seen some improvements in the Arab information environment, brought about by dawning competition. More independent-minded newspapers have appeared, challenging the iron grip of the older, state-supported press on political opinion, news and information. With bases abroad, these papers can escape state censorship. Some private satellite channels have started to contest the monopoly of state channels over the broadcast media. The most important characteristic of this new information movement is that it broadcasts in Arabic, thereby addressing the largest segment of the Arab audience.

In terms of infrastructure, the newer information channels benefit from the considerable groundwork that a number of Arab countries have laid. However, the general trend gravitates towards the lowest indicators in world standards. The number of telephone lines in the Arab countries is barely one fifth of that in developed countries. Access to digital media is also among the lowest in the world. There are just 18 computers per 1000 people in the region, compared to the global average of 78.3 percent per 1000 persons and only 1.6 per cent of the population has Internet access. These indicators scarcely reflect a sufficient level of preparedness for applying information technology for knowledge diffusion.

Translation is one of the important channels for the dissemination of information and communication with the rest of the world. The translation movement in the Arab world, however, remains static and chaotic. On average, only 4.4 translated books per million people were published in the first five years of the 1980s (less than one book per million people per year), while the corresponding rate in Hungary was 519 books per one million people and in Spain 920 books.

Knowledge Production: Meagre Output, Glimmers of Creativity

Turning knowledge assets into knowledge capital requires the production of new knowledge in all areas: in the physical and social sciences, arts, humanities and all other forms of social activity.

Data in the Report tell a story of stagnation in certain areas of knowledge production, especially in the field of scientific research. In addition to thin production, scientific research in Arab countries is held back by weak basic research and the almost total absence of advanced research in fields such as information technology and molecular biology. It also suffers from miserly R&D expenditure (currently state spending on R&D does not exceed 0.2 percent of GNP, most of which pays only for salaries), poor institutional support and a political and social context inimical to the development and promotion of science. The region's corps of qualified knowledge workers is relatively small. The number of scientists and engineers working in R&D in Arab countries is not more than 371 per million citizens. This is much lower that the global rate of 979 per million. The number of students enrolling in scientific disciplines in higher education in all Arab countries is also generally low, in comparison to countries that have used knowledge to take off, such as Korea, although among Arab countries, Jordan, followed by Algeria have distinguished themselves in this field.

In contrast to their weak production in science and technology, and beleaguered output in the humanities, Arab societies can boast a wealth of distinguished literary and artistic work that stands up to the highest standards of evaluation. One reason is that while science and technology require substantial social and economic investment, Arab artists can, and usually do, produce high-quality work without significant institutional or material support. Innovation in literature and art works under different conditions from those that foster creativity in research and development An Arab scientist would be highly unlikely to win a Nobel Prize in physics without societal and institutional support whereas an Arab novelist might achieve that distinction in literature in the absence of such support. There does not seem to be a conditional correlation between literary creativity and affluence, although financial independence can strengthen an author's intellectual freedom. Difficult conditions may sometimes provide incentives and intellectual and political stimuli for creative literature. Yet while artistic creativity itself defies societal restrictions, the absence of freedoms blocks public access to books and other forms of artistic expression.

Literary production faces other major challenges. These include the small number of readers owing to high rates of illiteracy in some Arab countries and the weak purchasing power of the Arab reader. This limited readership is clearly reflected in the number of books published in the Arab world, which does not exceed 1.1% of world production, although Arabs constitute 5% of the world population. The production of literary and artistic books in Arab countries is lower than the general level. In 1996 it did not exceed 1,945 books, representing only 0.8% of world production, i.e., less than the production of a country such as Turkey, with a population one quarter of that of Arab countries. An abundance of religious books and a relative paucity of books in other fields characterize the Arab book market. Religious books account for 17% of the total number of books published in Arab countries, compared to 5% of the total number of books produced in other parts of the world.

The Report's analysis of the status of knowledge in Arab countries indicates the presence of significant human capital that finds refuge in creativity from a restrictive societal and political environment and that could, under favourable circumstances, provide a solid structural foundation for a knowledge renaissance.

Cumulative Knowledge Outcomes: Ends and Means

The Report Team polled a sample of Arab university faculty members about knowledge acquisition in the region. Respondents expressed dissatisfaction in general with the status of knowledge acquisition in their countries (the average degree of satisfaction was 38%). Their satisfaction with the extent to which Arab knowledge serves human development was slightly less (the average rating was 35%). The survey confirmed that incentives for knowledge acquisition in Arab countries need to be much stronger, while freedom to acquire knowledge is subject to many constraints.

Rating the various aspects of the knowledge system, respondents argued that the lack of a reasonable measure of freedom in radio and television (30%) was one of the largest disincentives to knowledge acquisition. The same assessment applied to research and development in the public sector although, in the view of respondents, the latter area enjoys a higher level of freedom, thus suggesting that its problems have more to do with matters of organisation and financing. . . .

Imported Technology: Consumption Versus Adoption

Arab countries' experiments with the transfer and adoption of technology have neither achieved the desired technological advancement nor yielded attractive returns on investments. Importing technology has not led to its adoption and internalisation in the host country, let alone to its diffusion and production.

The two biggest gaps accounting for this failure have been the absence of effective innovation and knowledge production systems in Arab countries, and the lack of rational policies that ingrain those essential values and institutional frameworks that support a knowledge society. These problems have been aggravated by the mistaken belief that a knowledge society can be built through the importation of scientific products without investing in the local production of knowledge, and through depending on cooperation with universities and research centres in advanced countries for training Arab scientific cadres without creating the local scientific traditions conducive to knowledge acquisition in the region.

The lack of national innovation systems in Arab countries represented, in effect, a waste of investment in industrial infrastructure and fixed capital (buildings, factories, machinery and equipment). Such investments did not bring the wealth that Arab societies had sought through means other than the depletion of raw materials, nor expected social returns. Investment in the means of production does not lead to the real transfer and ownership of technology but rather to an increase in production capacity. Moreover, this is a timebound gain, one that starts to erode as the acquired technology becomes obsolete. The products and services generated by imported technology become economically unfeasible and uncompetitive in local markets, while at the same time technology and production in the advanced countries are perpetually renewed by their own renovation and innovation systems. This does not take place in Arab countries which, with their aging technologies, are stuck at the wrong end of the technology ladder. They must keep purchasing new production capabilities as and when the technologies of the capabilities they own become outmoded.

At the same time, Arab countries have not succeeded in becoming important poles of attraction for foreign direct investment (FDI). None of them figures among the top ten FDI attracting countries in the developing world.

The transfer, embedding and production of knowledge that can generate new technologies require an organisational context that provides incentives for knowledge production. Such a context would consolidate linkages between R&D institutions and the production and service sectors and promote national capabilities for innovation.

The Societal Context for Knowledge Acquisition in Arab Countries

Pillars of the Knowledge-Based Society: Culture

The knowledge system is influenced by societal, cultural, economic and political determinants. Among the most important of these determinants is culture in both of its aspects: the scholarly culture and the popular culture. Within Arabic culture, intellectual heritage constitutes an essential component. Language is the instrumental carrier of this culture and religion is the main and comprehensive belief system that guides its life. Moral, social and political values govern and direct action in the Arabic cultural system.

Religion urges people to seek knowledge, despite some anti-development interpretations: Undoubtedly, the relationship between religion and knowledge and its production is organically associated with concepts determined by the nature of religion and its overall position towards worldly life. Islamic religious texts uphold a balance between religion and worldly life, or between temporal life and the hereafter. The predominant tendency in Arab-Islamic civilization is a robust interest in worldly life and its sciences and in encouraging knowledge and sciences of various forms.

Developments in the contemporary Arab world and the national political, social and economic problems that appeared following the years of independence did, however, leave deep impacts on the intellectual, scholarly and cultural life of Arab countries. Religion—and its associated concepts and teleology—were among the basic aspects influenced by these developments. An alliance between some oppressive regimes and certain types of conservative religious scholars led to interpretations of Islam, which serve the government, but are inimical to human development, particularly with respect to freedom of thought, the interpretation of judgements, the accountability of regimes to the people and women's participation in public life. Constraints on political action in many Arab countries pushed some movements with an Islamic mark underground while causing others to don Islamic garb. Without peaceful and effective political channels for dealing with injustices in the Arab world, at the country, regional and global levels, some political movements identifying themselves as Islamic have resorted to restrictive interpretations and violence as means of political activism. They have fanned the embers of animosity towards both opposing political forces in Arab countries and "the others", accusing them of being enemies of Islam itself. This has heightened the tempo of conflict and friction with society, the state and "the others". This state of "opposition" to and "confrontation" with the West, in particular, reached its peak following the events of September 11, 2001. In this context, the Islamic religion itself was exposed to a harsh wave of libel, slander, provocation and criticism, which at times betrayed total ignorance and at other times, explicit fabrication.

Far from being opposed to knowledge, pure religion unquestionably urges people to seek knowledge and to establish knowledge societies. Perhaps the best evidence of that is the era when Arab science flowered and prospered, a time that was characterised by a strong synergy between religion, represented by Islam, on the one hand and science, on the other.

The Arabic language: a heritage, a resource and a crisis: The role of language in a knowledge society is seminal, because language is an essential basis of culture and because culture is the key axis around which the process of development revolves. Language has a central position in the cultural system because of its association with a number of its components: intellect, creativity, education, information, heritage, values and beliefs. Today, at the gates of the knowledge society and the future, the Arabic language is, however, facing severe challenges and a real crisis in theorization, grammar, vocabulary, usage, documentation, creativity and criticism. To these aspects of the crisis, one must add the new challenges raised by information technologies, which relate to the computerised automation of the language.

The relation between the Arabic language and the transfer and absorption of technology involves many issues. Chief among them are two central and closely inter-related matters, namely, the arabicisation of university education and the teaching of the Arabic language. The arabicisation of university education has become vital in order to enable young minds to develop firm critical and creative faculties in their own language and to assimilate the rising volume of scientific knowledge. In addition, failure to arabicise science creates obstacles to communication between different scientific disciplines and slows knowledge exchange. The authors underline that language is one of the cornerstones in the human development system while emphasising that arabicisation efforts should be accompanied by greater efforts to teach foreign languages to all.

The teaching of Arabic is also undergoing a severe crisis in terms of both methodology and curricula. The most apparent aspect of this crisis is the growing neglect of the functional aspects of (Arabic) language use. Arabic language skills in everyday life have deteriorated and Arabic language classes are often restricted to writing at the expense of reading. The situation of Arabic language teaching cannot be separated from that of classical Arabic in general, which has in effect ceased to be a spoken language. It is only the language of reading and writing; the formal language of intellectuals and academics, often used to display knowledge in lectures. Classical Arabic is not the language of cordial, spontaneous expression, emotions, daily encounters and ordinary communication. It is not a vehicle for discovering one's inner self or outer surroundings.

The Report thus underlines that it has become necessary to work determinedly on strengthening the linguistic shields of Arabic and on sharpening its practical attributes, which emphasise its universal character and its ability to assimilate new informational and technological developments. This is in addition to consolidating its relationship with world languages and providing the necessary economic, social and technical conditions for enhancing the language and its creative products.

Popular culture, between conformity and creativity: Communal and oral folk culture is a vast repository of experiences and creative efforts that have enriched, and continue to enrich, the intellectual, emotional and behavioural life of people in all societies. Folk culture is generally very rich in its constructions, encompassing knowledge, beliefs, arts, morals, law, customs and early industrial knowledge.

Arab folk culture shares all these qualities. Its particular feature is that it expresses two voices: one, a conformist voice, which urges adherence to familiar patterns, the other a creative voice, which questions received wisdom and urges the pursuit of knowledge. Arab popular culture is however not devoid of knowledge. Biographies, a common form of story telling, are often full of historical and geographical knowledge, as well as human insight. Romantic tales depicting imaginary ideal worlds express popular yearnings, dreams and ambitions. These and other forms of oral culture are recurrently recited at group evening gatherings and meetings, and are a means of sharing historical knowledge and rules related to customs. Many popular stories extol the value of information, showing it to be more valuable than wealth. The high respect commonly shown for a written text by folk communities indicates the value they accord to learning and knowledge.

Cultural openness, from imitation to creative interaction: Historically, Arab culture did not constitute a closed system, but rather displayed, at major historical junctures, a profound ability to open up, develop and transcend itself. It welcomed the experiences of other nations and incorporated them in its knowledge systems and way of life, regardless of the differences and variations that distinguished Arab societies from those nations and their experiences.

The first of the two major external influences which this culture embraced dates back to the age of scientific codification and the encounter with Greek civilization and sciences—indeed the demand for and importation of these sciences—in the third and fourth centuries A.H. (on the Islamic calendar)—9th and 10th centuries A.D.

The second major experience came when the modern Arab world encountered Western civilization and opened up to science, literature and other aspects of Western culture at the beginning of the 19th century. The outcome of this encounter was a renovation and modernization of the Arab cultural heritage, descending from the past, opening wide to the future and drawing abundantly on the sinews of modernization and the rich crop of Western production in all fields of knowledge, science, the arts, literature and technology.

Arabic culture, however, like other cultures, finds itself facing the challenges of an emerging global cultural homogeneity and related questions about cultural multiplicity, cultural personalities, the issue of the "self" and the "other", and its own cultural character. These and similar questions raise apprehensions, fears and risks in the minds of its people. Concerns about the extinction of the language and culture and the diminution and dissipation of identity have become omnipresent in Arab thought and culture.

The truth is that Arab culture has no choice but to engage again in a new global experiment. It cannot enclose itself, contented with living on history, the past and inherited culture alone in a world whose victorious powers reach into all corners of the earth, dominating all forms of knowledge, behaviour, life, manufactured goods and innovation. Undoubtedly, some currents embedded in this culture would prefer a policy of withdrawal, of rejection and hostility to all values, ideas, and practices brought about by this global culture. This may appear justified in some ways, but a negative policy of "non-interaction" can only lead to the weakening and diminution of Arab cultural structures rather than their reinforcement and development.

Moreover, the global culture has its own dimensions of knowledge, science, and technology, which countries neglect at their own risk. Openness, interaction, assimilation, absorption, revision, criticism and examination cannot but stimulate creative knowledge production in Arab societies. This is already noticeable in many sectors of contemporary

Arabic culture where various creative developments reveal the beneficial role played by global and human cultural interaction. This process continues to take place despite all local deterrents and external obstacles and notwithstanding the difficulties of national and international politics, where some powers pursue total hegemony or choose the path of collision and conflict, rather than of understanding, dialogue, cooperation and alternation in power.

An analysis of the components of Arabic culture indicates that its essence, extending over three millennia, is capable of supporting the creation of a knowledge society in the third millennium as ably as it did towards the end of the first millennium and in the beginning of the second. Furthermore, the strength and richness of Arabic culture may reinforce the capacity of Arab societies to deal effectively with the torrential currents of globalisation.

Economic Structure: From Depleting Resources to Creating Knowledge

One of the main features of the production pattern prevailing in Arab countries, which influences knowledge acquisition, is a high dependence on the depletion of raw materials, chiefly oil, and reliance on external rents. This rentier economic pattern entices societies to import expertise from outside because this is a quick and easy resort that however ends up weakening local demand for knowledge and forfeiting opportunities to produce it locally and employ it effectively in economic activity. A large part of Arab economic activity is concentrated on primary commodities, as in agriculture, which remains largely traditional, and in industries specializing in the production of consumer goods, which depend heavily on production licences obtained from foreign companies. At the same time, the share of the capital goods industry and of industries embodying higher technology continues to shrink. Demand for industrial products is negatively influenced by the small size of Arab markets, the weak competitiveness of Arab economies and the absence of transparency and accountability, which encourages overlap, and sometimes collusion, between political and business elites. Lack of competition reduces productivity and therefore demand for knowledge in economic activity. Instead, competitive advantage and the ability to maximize profits derive from favouritism in power structures, manifested in money and politics. Resistance to opening up to the outside world by Arab economies and their lack of exposure to foreign competition, coupled with at times excessive protection for local products through import substitution policies, have also slowed the advancement of productivity and the employment of knowledge to that end.

Demand for knowledge has been weakened not only by faltering economic growth and productivity in Arab countries during the last quarter-century but also by the over-concentration of wealth in a few hands.

Although some economies of the world have succeeded in the past in achieving economic growth while their income and wealth distribution patterns were skewed, this occurred in a different global context, characterized by a large number of closed economies throughout the world. The opening up of capital markets promoted by globalisation reduces the chances of local growth through concentration. The vast amount of Arab capital invested in industrialized countries and, therefore, denied to the Arab world, is strong evidence that, in human development terms, it is not the possession of money and wealth that matters but how productively such wealth is invested.

Recovery of economic growth in the Arab world and its main driver—increased productivity—are two prerequisites for the advancement of knowledge, but they are not enough. They will be enough only when decision-makers in Arab societies, the business sector, the civil society and the household sector put the goal of building the knowledge society at the head of their priorities and reflect that in all their decisions to spend and to invest.

Societal Incentives: Power and Wealth Weaken the Ethics of Knowledge

Political, social and economic conditions play a decisive role in orienting systems of values and societal incentives. After independence, most Arab countries came under national political regimes that represented little advance on the autocratic style of ancient and more recent history. Social and individual freedoms were restricted in some areas and were totally absent in others, thus affecting the morals and practical values of people.

In Arab countries, the distribution of power, which sometimes coincided with the distribution of wealth, has had an effect on the morals of societies and individuals. The pursuit of personal gain, the preference for the private over the public good, social and moral corruption, the absence of honesty and accountability and many other illnesses, were all related in one way or another to a skewed distribution of power and the resulting social disparities. Justice, before all else, has been the victim of this state of affairs.

The oil boom also played its role in eroding a number of values and societal incentives that would have been helpful in enhancing creativity and the acquisition and diffusion of knowledge. With the spread of negative values during that period, creative abilities were neglected, and knowledge lost its significance for human development. The social standing of scientists, educated people and intellectuals fell. Social value was measured by the criteria of money and fortune, regardless of how those fortunes were gained. Proprietorship and possession replaced knowledge and intellectualism. Perhaps worst of all, the values of independence, freedom and the importance of a critical mind were also buried.

Repression and marginalisation contributed to blunt the desire for achievement, happiness and commitment. As a result, indifference, political apathy and a sense of futility are becoming dangerously common among broad segments of the populace. Arab citizens are increasingly pushed away from effecting changes in their countries.

The Report calls on the state, civil society, cultural and mass media institutions, enlightened intellectuals and the public at large to plant those values that encourage action and innovation in the political, social and economic spheres. "Reforming the mind" is indeed a significant requirement for Arab culture, yet "reforming action" is equally urgent.

A centrifugal economic, social and political environment in the region, coupled with centripetal factors in other countries led to the growing phenomenon of an Arab brain drain. The emigration of qualified Arabs constitutes a form of reverse development aid since receiving countries evidently benefit from Arab investments in training and educating their citizens. More significant, however, is the opportunity cost of high levels of skilled outflows: the lost potential contribution of emigrants to knowledge and development in their countries of origin. This double loss calls for serious action to minimise its dangers: firstly by tapping the expertise and knowledge of the Arab Diaspora abroad, and secondly by providing Arab expatriates with incentives to return, either on temporary assignments or for good, to their countries of origin, carrying a human capital much larger than that they had migrated with. This can be achieved only by launching a serious project for human development that would attract highly qualified migrants back temporarily or permanently on productive and personally fulfilling assignments to serve their countries.

Unlike the case of Arab culture, the analysis of Arab social and economic structures reveals ingrained obstacles to knowledge acquisition in the Arab world. Only by overcoming those obstacles through reform can a knowledge society be developed.

The Political Context:

Oppression, Knowledge and Development: Political obstacles to knowledge acquisition, as the Report argues, are even more severe in Arab countries than those posed by their socio-economic structures, which are in turn seen to be more obstructive than any features of culture.

Political power plays a key role in directing knowledge and influencing its development. It fosters knowledge that is favourable to its goals and suppresses opposing patterns. Political instability and fierce struggles for access to political positions in the absence of an established rule for the peaceful rotation of power—in short, democracy—impede the growth of knowledge in Arab soil. One of the main results of that unstable political situation has been the subjection of scientific institutions to political strategies and power conflicts. In managing these institutions, political loyalties take precedence over efficiency and knowledge. Power shackles active minds, extinguishes the flame of learning and kills the drive for innovation.

The Report calls for the establishment of an independent knowledge sphere that produces and promotes knowledge free from political coercion. This is possible only by democratising political life and knowledge and ensuring that knowledge can be freely acquired and produced.

Laws are needed to guarantee Arab citizens the essential rights of knowledge—the freedom of thought and expression that are a precondition for knowledge to flourish. The international human rights conventions have been signed by most Arab states, but they have neither entered the legal culture nor been incorporated into substantive domestic legislation. Yet the problem of freedom in the Arab world is not related to the implementation of laws as much as to the violation of these laws. Oppression, the arbitrary application of laws, selective censorship and other politically motivated restrictions are widespread. They often take the form of legal constraints on publications, associations, general assemblies and electronic media, which prevent these from carrying out their communication and cultural roles. Such restrictions also obstruct the diffusion of knowledge and the education of public opinion.

Yet the more dangerous restrictions are those imposed by security authorities when they confiscate publications or ban people from entering a country or prevent the sale of certain books during fairs while promoting other kinds of books. In committing these acts, these authorities reach above the constitutional institutions and the law, citing the pretext of "national security" or public order. Other forms of restriction come from narrowminded, self-appointed custodians of public morality, and from the censorship of books, articles and media events. Creativity, innovation and knowledge are the first victims of the suppression or denial of freedoms.

A global context that poses a challenge: Globalisation in its current form and existing institutions is often weighted towards securing the interests of the rich and powerful nations and their dominance over the world economy, knowledge flows and, by extension, opportunities for development. Without changes that tip the balance of global governance more towards the needs and aspirations of developing countries, including Arab countries, globalisation cannot help these nations to achieve human progress.

Perhaps the most important example from a knowledge perspective is the insistence by industrialised countries, the main producers of knowledge at the global level, that knowledge should be converted from a public good to a private commodity through the instrument of intellectual property rights, which are largely owned by the industrialised West.

This is now happening even in cases where the knowledge originated in developing countries and was later acquired by institutions in the industrialised world. This trend threatens to cut down developing country opportunities to acquire new knowledge and it especially jeopardises productive sectors such as medicine and pharmacology.

In the case of Arab countries in particular, a qualitative jump in the effectiveness of the knowledge acquisition system requires closer and more efficient forms of cooperation at the Pan-Arab level.

A Strategic Vision for Establishing a Knowledge Society in the Arab World

The Report pulls together the various threads of its analysis of the status of Arab knowledge in a concluding strategic vision of the Arab knowledge society, supported by five pillars:

1. ***Guaranteeing the key freedoms of opinion, speech and assembly through good governance bounded by the law.*** A climate of freedom is an essential prerequisite for the knowledge society. These freedoms are the thresholds to knowledge production, to creativity and innovation, and to invigorating scientific research, technical development and artistic and literary expression. Constitutions, laws and administrative procedures need to be refined to remove all restrictions on essential freedoms, particularly administrative censorship, and regulatory restrictions by security apparatuses on the production and diffusion of knowledge and all kinds of creative expression.

2. ***Disseminating high quality education for all.*** The detailed proposals for reform in education include: giving priority to early childhood learning; ensuring universal basic education for all and extending it to at least 10th grade; developing an adult education system for lifelong learning; improving the quality of education at all stages; giving particular attention to promoting higher education, and instituting independent periodic evaluations of quality at all stages of education.

3. ***Embedding and ingraining science, and building and broadening the capacity for research and development in all societal activities.*** This can be achieved through promoting basic research, and establishing a centrally coordinated regional creativity and innovation network that permeates the entire fabric of society and enjoys supportive and complementary linkages in the regional and international spheres.

4. ***Shifting rapidly towards knowledge-based production in Arab socioeconomic structures.*** This calls for a decisive move towards developing renewable resources through knowledge and technological capabilities and towards diversifying economic structures and markets. It also requires upgrading the Arab presence in the "new economy" and the consolidation of a societal incentives system that upholds the acquisition and application of knowledge for human development in contrast to the current mode in which values are centred on material possessions and in seeking access and favour from the two sources of power: money and authority.

5. ***Developing an authentic, broadminded and enlightened Arab knowledge model.*** This would entail:

   • Delivering true religion from political exploitation and respecting critical scholarship. The components of this reform include returning to the civilised, moral and humanitarian vision of pure religion; restoring to religious institutions their independence from political authorities, governments, states and radical religious-political movements; recognising intellectual freedom; activating interpretative jurisprudence, preserving the right to differ in doctrines, religious schools and interpretations.

   • Advancing the Arabic language by undertaking serious research and linguistic reform for translating scientific terms and coining simple linguistic usages. This also includes compiling specialised, functional dictionaries and other reference works that monitor common classical-colloquial words for use in children's programmes and written and audio publications. This must be matched by other persistent efforts to facilitate the acquisition of Arabic through formal and informal learning channels, and to produce creative and innovative writing for young children.

   • Reclaiming some of the myriad bright spots in the Arab cultural heritage. These must be incorporated in the core of the Arab knowledge model in a manner far above and beyond the self-centred singing of one's own praises. This legacy must be assimilated and understood as part of the structure of motivation for developing and nurturing an Arab knowledge system in Arab minds and institutions.

   • Enriching, promoting and celebrating cultural diversity within Arab countries. This calls for providing safeguards for the protection of all sub-cultures and for encouraging them to interact, intermingle, grow and flourish.

   • Opening up to other cultures. Such interaction would be strengthened by translation into other languages; promoting an intelligent and generous exchange with non-Arab cultures and civilisations; maximising benefits from regional and international organisations and initiating reform in the world order through stronger inter-Arab cooperation.

As the Report affirms in closing, knowledge closely approaches a religious obligation that Arabs ought to honour and exercise. It points out the way on the Arab journey to a dignified and prosperous future. The pursuit of knowledge is prompted by religion, culture, history and the human will to succeed. Obstructions on the road are the work of mortals: the defective structures of the past and present—social, economic and, above all, political. Arabs must remove or reform these structures in order to take the place they deserve in the world of knowledge at the beginning of the knowledge millennium.

Source: United Nations. United Nations Development Programme. "Arab Human Development Report 2003: Building a Knowledge Society." Amman, Jordan. October 20, 2003. www.undp.org/rbas/ahdr (accessed December 22, 2003).

FBI Report on Crime in the United States

October 27, 2003

INTRODUCTION

Federal statistics on crime and incarceration for 2002 differed from levels many experts had expected. According to the Federal Bureau of Investigation, the rate of serious crime in the United States fell by 1.1 percent. That was a welcome reversal of direction from 2001, when major crime increased 2.1 percent. But the decline surprised many law enforcement officials and criminologists who had predicted that a poor job market, a diversion of police resources to fight terrorism, and an increase in the number of young people in the prime age for committing crime would combine to push rates up. Overall, the serious crime rate, which remained relatively stable between 2000 and 2002, was down nearly 25 percent from its 1993 level. Preliminary figures for the first six months of 2003 showed that serious crime was continuing to fall. In a report released December 15, the FBI said violent crime had fallen 3.1 percent between January and June 2003, while property crime had dropped 0.8 percent.

At the same time, some experts expressed surprise at the 2.6 percent increase in the prison population in 2002. Nearly 2.2 million men, women, and juveniles were behind bars or in detention centers, according to the Bureau of Justice Statistics. Some experts had predicted that the number of Americans incarcerated would remain relatively stable, given the declining crime rate over the decade and moves by several states facing budget shortfalls to ease sentencing laws and take other steps to reduce their prison populations. Those efforts apparently were not enough to offset several years of tough sentencing policies.

Sentencing policies were the focus of controversy throughout the year as Attorney General John Ashcroft moved on several fronts to ensure that convicted criminals would do jail time. One Ashcroft initiative directed that many white-collar criminals could no longer serve their time in halfway houses but would have to go to prison. Another, more controversial policy directed federal prosecutors to pursue maximum criminal charges and reduce their use of plea bargains. In March the Supreme Court upheld California's "three strikes" law, which required stiff mandatory sentences for repeat offenders. In April, at Ashcroft's behest, Congress passed a law reducing federal judges' discretion in sentencing. Federal judges, backed by Chief Justice William H. Rehnquist and other members of the Supreme Court, were urging Congress to repeal that law.

Crime Rate Remains Stable

According to the FBI's annual report, *Crime in the United States, 2002,* 1.4 million violent crimes (murder, rape, robbery, and aggravated assault) were committed in 2002, down 0.9 percent from 2001. Aggravated assaults and robberies, the two most frequent violent crimes, both declined in 2002, but the number of murders (16,204) represented a 1 percent increase over 2001, while the number of forcible rapes (95,136) represented a 4.7 percent increase. Firearms were used in 71 percent of the murders.

Of the three serious property crimes reported by the FBI, burglary and auto theft both increased slightly in 2002 over 2001, but larceny, which accounted for nearly 60 percent of all serious crime, was down 1.6 percent. The FBI reported that losses from robberies totaled $539 million (for an average of $1,281 per incident), losses from burglaries totaled $3.3 billion, and losses from larceny amounted to $4.9 billion. The estimated value of motor vehicles reported stolen in 2002 came to $8.4 billion.

The South continued to experience the highest crime rate, at 4,722 serious crimes per 100,000 inhabitants, while the Northeast had the lowest rate, at 2,889 serious crimes per 100,000 population. The nation's cities experienced a slight decline in both violent and property crimes, while suburban areas recorded a slight increase in both. Violent crime dropped overall in rural counties, but property crime increased.

Another annual report on crime, released August 24 by the Justice Department, also found that serious crime had dropped in 2002 and was at its lowest level since the Bureau of Justice Statistics began conducting the survey in 1973. According to the report there were 23 violent crimes per 1,000 people in 2002, compared with 25 per 1,000 in 2001. The victimization rate dropped more than 50 percent between 1993 and 2002.

Unlike the FBI report, which was based on crimes reported to federal, state, and local law enforcement agencies, the National Crime Victimization Survey was based on a survey of victims of rape, sexual assault, robberies, assault, and theft, including motor vehicle theft and household burglaries. For that reason it did not count murder. But it covered a far larger number of crimes because so many crimes went unreported to police. For example, the survey recorded 5.3 million violent crimes in 2002, while the FBI report recorded 1.4 million. A separate report released by the Bureau of Justice

Statistics in March found that slightly more than half of all violent crimes in 2000 went unreported to police. Victims often chose not to report crimes when they felt the matter was personal, when their injuries were minor, when they felt partly responsible for the incident, or when they had been intimidated by the aggressor.

Some experts were at a loss to explain the continuing downward trend in crime. "Everyone thought the numbers would bottom out and then go back up, but it hasn't happened," James Lynch, a law professor at the American University Center for Justice, Law, and Society told the Associated Press in August. Others attributed the continuing decline to tougher prison sentences, which kept criminals off the streets longer; a drop in gang membership; a lessening of violence surrounding drug trafficking; and better locks and alarms on homes and offices. Whatever the explanation, the attorney general, criminologists, and others warned against complacency. "We must continue our vigilance and renew our firm commitment to protect all Americans, bringing swift and certain justice to all those who would inflict pain and harm," Ashcroft said in August. The reduction in the crime rate was a "reason for celebration, yet not a reason to give up working on the problem," said James Fox, a criminologist at Northeastern University in Boston.

Incarceration Rate Increase

Because the crime rate had dropped so significantly during the past ten years, some experts were surprised when the Justice Department reported that the nation's prison population had increased 2.6 percent in 2002. That was the largest increase since 1999. Nearly 2.2 million people were in local jails, state or federal prison, or juvenile detention facilities at the end of 2002. Allen J. Beck, the chief prison demographer for the Bureau of Justice Statistics and an author of the report, said the size of the growth was "somewhat surprising . . . after several years of relative stability in the prison population."

Another report released by the Justice Department in August reported that more than 5.6 million Americans were in prison at the end of 2001 or had served time in prison in the past. That number represented 2.7 percent of the adult population of 210 million at the end of 2001. The study, produced by the Bureau of Justice Statistics, represented the first time that the department had released estimates on the prevalence of incarceration rates among adults. The study found that if current imprisonment trends continued, black males in America would have a one-in-three chance of going to prison during their lifetimes. Hispanic men had a one-in-seven chance, while white men had a one-in-seventeen chance. Overall, the study said, the number of people sent to prison for the first time tripled between 1974 and 2001, largely because of tougher sentencing policies aimed at curbing drug and drug-related crimes and mandatory minimum sentencing laws.

"These new numbers are shocking enough, but what we don't see are the ripple effects of what they mean," Marc Mauer, assistant director the Sentencing Project told the *Christian Science Monitor.* Mauer and others noted that ex-felons found it hard to find jobs, were barred from receiving many kinds of public assistance, and were prohibited from voting in many states. "We have the wealthiest society in human history," Mauer said, "and we maintain the highest level of imprisonment. It's striking what that says about our approach to social problems and inequality."

Controversy over Sentencing

Several states, strapped for ways to balance their budgets during the economic downturn, shortened some mandatory minimum sentencing laws, adopted or reinstituted early release programs, offered treatment rather than incarceration for some drug offenders, and took other steps to hold down the costs of supporting their prison populations. To some extent, those efforts were countered in 2003 by Congress and the Justice Department. In April, at the request of Attorney General Ashcroft, Congress added a provision to an unrelated law that reduced the sentencing discretion of federal judges in some circumstances. Chief Justice Rehnquist warned at the time that the restrictions "would seriously impair the ability of the courts to impose just and responsible sentences." In June a federal judge in New York quit the bench in protest. "I no longer want to be part of our unjust criminal justice system," U.S. District Judge John S. Martin wrote in an op-ed column published in the *New York Times.* Later in the summer, Justices Anthony M. Kennedy and Stephen G. Breyer both expressed opposition to mandatory minimum sentences set by Congress, saying that in some cases they were unfair and that judges had to have the discretion to weigh the individual circumstances of each case in making sentencing determinations.

In July the controversy grew even more heated after Ashcroft issued a memo to federal prosecutors asking them to report to the Washington office the names of federal judges who issued "downward departures," or lighter sentences than the mandatory minimum specified in guidelines drawn up by the U.S. Sentencing Commission. Under the new rules, the Justice Department would pass the names of those judges to the judiciary committees in Congress, which could ask the judges to justify their sentencing decision. Mark Corallo, a Justice Department spokesman, said the purpose of Ashcroft's memo was "to make sure that all of our U.S. attorneys understand that we intend to apply U.S. law evenly across all jurisdictions. They should be aware of excessive downward departures and, if necessary, appeal those decisions." Using that same reasoning, Ashcroft in September told federal prosecutors to seek the maximum charges possible and to limit their use of plea bargains. "Federal prosecutors must charge and pursue the most serious, readily provable offenses that are supported by the facts," the attorney general said in a September 22 memo. Asked about the policy later that day, Ashcroft said: "It's important that when the law is broken in Milwaukee, it's attended by the same consequences as when it's broken in Denver."

The following day, September 23, the Judicial Conference of the United States voted unanimously at its semiannual meeting in Washington to ask Congress to repeal the April law. The conference, which was headed by Rehnquist and was the policy-making body for the federal judiciary, noted that Congress had not consulted with the judicial community before passing the law. "We're not at all clear that there was any need for the bill," Chief Judge Carolyn Dineen King of the United States Court of Appeal for the Fifth Circuit said. She estimated that about 10 percent of all downward departures were "judge-initiated," which she said was not "an extraordinarily high" proportion. Most judges, she said, felt it necessary to have a "safety valve for situations in which you would otherwise produce a sentence which is unjust."

According to the U.S. Sentencing Commission, 35 percent of the sentences handed down in federal court in fiscal 2001 were "downward departures" from the guidelines. About half of those represented plea bargains or other sentencing arrangements agreed to by federal prosecutors. Three-fifths of the rest were so-called fast-track procedures for dealing with drug and immigration cases in the southwestern portion of the United States. A considerable portion of the remaining downward departures represented an exercise of discretion by the judge hearing the case. Federal judges imposed sentences that exceeded the sentencing guidelines in only 1 percent of the cases.

Rehnquist used his annual year-end report on the state of the federal judiciary to object again to the April amendment to the sentencing guidelines. That amendment, the chief justice wrote, "could appear to be an unwarranted and ill-considered effort to intimidate individual judges in the performance of their judicial duties." It seemed unlikely, however, that the current Republican-led Congress would repeal the amendment. James Sensenbrenner Jr., the chairman of the House Judiciary Committee, responded to Rehnquist's criticism by saying that Congress had acted because the "growing problem of downward departures" was "undermining sentencing fairness throughout the federal system."

California's Three-Strikes Law Upheld

By a pair of 5–4 votes, the Supreme Court on March 5 upheld the right of states to impose long sentences on repeat offenders, even if the crimes involved were relatively minor. The decisions specifically upheld California's "three-strikes" law, which was considered the harshest in the country because it allowed judges to sentence people who already had two prior convictions, or strikes, to at least twenty-five years in prison, even if the third crime was comparatively insignificant. In an opinion endorsed only by Chief Justice Rehnquist and Justice Kennedy, Justice Sandra Day O'Connor wrote that the lengthy sentences (twenty-five years in one case, fifty in the other) were not a form of "cruel and unusual punishment" prohibited by the Eighth Amendment to the Constitution. She suggested that criticism of the law be directed at the state legislature "which has primary responsibility for making the difficult policy choices that underlie any sentencing scheme." She added that the Court did "not sit as a 'superlegislature' to second-guess these policy choices."

Justices Antonin Scalia and Clarence Thomas agreed with the outcome but offered different reasoning for reaching that conclusion. The four dissenters, John Paul Stevens, David H. Souter, Ruth Bader Ginsburg, and Breyer, argued that the punishment in both cases was "grossly disproportionate to the crime" and thus a violation of the Eighth Amendment.

The case of *Ewing v. California* involved a man who had been convicted several times in the past for crimes including theft, burglary, and threatening a man with a knife. On his "third strike" he was convicted of trying to seal $1,200 worth of golf clubs and was sentenced to twenty-five years. The second case, *Lockyer v. Andrade,* concerned a man who had been in and out of prison over two decades, convicted of such crimes as petty theft, burglary, and marijuana trafficking. He was sentenced to fifty years in prison after being convicted of stealing $150 worth of videos from two separate stores two weeks apart.

Following are excerpts from a news release issued October 27, 2003, by the Federal Bureau of Investigation summarizing the findings of its annual report, Crime in the United States, 2002.

News Release on FBI's Annual *Crime in the United States, 2002*

Nationally, the volume of crime reported to law enforcement in 2002 (estimated at 11.9 million offenses) increased by less than one-tenth of one percent when compared to the 2001 volume, the Federal Bureau of

Investigation reported today. Five- and 10-year trend data showed that the 2002 estimated volume was 4.9 percent lower than the 1998 volume and 16.0 percent lower than the 1993 volume. . . .

In 2002, more than 17,000 city, county, and state law enforcement agencies voluntarily provided data on serious crime: 4 violent crimes (murder and nonnegligent manslaughter, forcible rape, robbery, and aggravated assault) and 3 property crimes (burglary, larceny-theft, and motor vehicle theft) to the UCR Program. These agencies represented 93.4 percent of the total U.S. population as established by the U.S. Bureau of the Census.

Violent Crime

In the United States, the estimated volume of violent crime reported to law enforcement decreased 0.9 percent in 2002, with 1.4 million estimated offenses. Five- and 10-year trend data revealed the estimated number of violent crimes was 7.0 percent lower than the 1998 number and 25.9 percent less than the 1993 number.

Cumulatively, the Nation's cities experienced a 1.9-percent decrease in the volume of violent crime. Rural counties in the United States had a collective decline of 1.2 percent in violent crime, and suburban counties experienced a 1.0-percent increase in violent crime.

The rate for violent crime, an estimated 494.6 offenses per 100,000 in population, decreased 2.0 percent when compared to the 2001 rate.

The weapon data collected for murder, robbery, and aggravated assault showed that offenders used personal weapons, such as hands, fists, and feet, in 31.2 percent of these crimes. Firearms were involved in 26.8 percent of murders, robberies, and aggravated assaults, and knives or cutting instruments were used in 14.9 percent. Other types of weapons were used in 27.1 percent of murders, robberies, and aggravated assaults.

Nationally, law enforcement cleared 46.8 percent of reported violent crime in 2002. Murders were cleared at a rate of 64.0 percent, aggravated assaults had a clearance rate of 56.5 percent, forcible rapes were cleared at a rate of 44.5 percent, and robberies had a clearance rate of 25.7 percent.

During 2002, 11.9 percent of all clearances involved juveniles only. Juveniles were involved in 12.3 percent of clearances in suburban counties, they were a part of 12.1 percent of clearances in cities, and juveniles were involved in 9.6 percent of clearances in rural counties.

Law enforcement made an estimated 620,510 arrests for violent crimes during 2002. Females comprised 17.4 percent of all violent crime arrestees. Individuals under the age of 25 made up 43.7 percent of all violent crime arrestees.

Property Crime

The estimated volume of reported property crime increased 0.1 percent in 2002 when compared to the 2001 number. Trend data for 5 and 10 years showed that the volume was 4.6 percent lower than the 1998 volume and 14.5 percent lower than the 1993 volume.

A breakdown of the data by population group showed that property crime decreased 0.3 percent in the Nation's cities collectively. Rural counties experienced an increase of 0.7 percent, and suburban counties had a collective increase of 1.0 percent in the volume of property crime in 2002.

The 2002 property crime rate estimated at 3,624.1 offenses per 100,000 inhabitants decreased 0.9 percent from the 2001 number.

In 2002, the estimated dollar loss associated with property crime (excluding arson) was $16.6 billion, an increase of less than 0.3 percent from the 2001 estimate. Motor vehicle theft caused a loss of $8.4 billion, larceny-theft accounted for a loss of $4.9 billion, and burglary resulted in a loss of $3.3 billion.

Nationally, in 2002, law enforcement cleared 16.5 percent of all reported property crime. Juveniles were involved in 20.3 percent of clearances for property crime.

Law enforcement made an estimated 1.6 million arrests for property crime offenses during 2002. Females made up 30.7 percent of all property crime arrestees, and adults comprised 70.2 percent of all property crime arrestees.

Crime Rate

The crime rate standardizes the volume of crime by measuring it per 100,000 U.S. resident population. In 2002, the estimated volume of the reported serious crime per 100,000 was 4,118.8, which reflected a 1.1-percent decrease when compared to the 2001 rate, a 10.9-percent decrease when compared to the 1998 rate, and a 24.9-percent decrease when compared to the 1993 rate.

Regionally, the South had a crime rate of 4,721.9 serious crimes per 100,000 inhabitants, the West a rate of 4,418.8, the Midwest a rate of 3,883.1, and the Northeast a rate of 2,889.0 serious crimes per 100,000 in population in 2002. A comparison of this year's crime rate with the 2001 rate showed that the Northeast had a decrease of 3.7 percent, the Midwest experienced a decrease of 2.4 percent, the South had a decrease of 1.2 percent, and the West had an increase of 1.6 percent.

A breakdown of the data by community type showed that Metropolitan Statistical Areas (MSAs) had an estimated rate of 4,409.1 reported offenses per 100,000 inhabitants. Cities outside the Nation's MSAs had a rate of 4,524.0, and rural counties had a rate of 1,908.7 reported offenses per 100,000 in population.

Crime Clearances

Nationwide, law enforcement agencies reported that 20.0 percent of serious crimes were cleared by arrest or exceptional means in 2002. Agencies collectively cleared 46.8 percent of violent crimes, with murder having the highest percentage of clearances at 64.0 percent. They also cleared 16.5 percent of property crimes, with larceny-theft having the highest percentage (18.0) of clearances among the property crimes.

Of the serious crimes cleared by law enforcement in 2002, 18.0 percent involved only juveniles. Juvenile offenders accounted for 11.9 percent of violent crime clearances and 20.3 percent of property crime clearances.

Arrests

In 2002, law enforcement agencies nationwide made an estimated 13.7 million arrests (excluding traffic violations).

In relation to the total U.S. population, the Nation's arrest rate was estimated at 4,783.4 arrests per 100,000 inhabitants.

The violent crime arrest rate was 217.9 arrests per 100,000 inhabitants, and the property crime arrest rate was 570.5 arrests per 100,000 inhabitants.

During 2002, the Nation's cities collectively had an arrest rate of 5,170.2 per 100,000 in population. Suburban counties had an arrest rate of 3,841.5, and rural counties had an arrest rate of 4,025.6 arrests per 100,000 inhabitants.

The total number of arrests increased 0.5 percent from 2001 to 2002.

Arrests for violent crimes decreased 0.8 percent from the 2001 number, and arrests for property crimes increased 0.6 percent.

Arrests for drug abuse violations and driving under the influence accounted for an estimated 21.8 percent of all arrests.

Nationwide, adults accounted for 83.5 percent of persons arrested in 2002. Juveniles were most often arrested for larceny-theft, and adults were most often arrested for driving under the influence.

Overall, when compared to the number of arrests during 2001, arrests of adults increased 1.2 percent, and arrests of juveniles decreased 3.0 percent.

In 2002, males comprised 77.0 percent of all arrestees. Males also accounted for 82.6 percent of those arrested for violent crimes and 69.3 percent of those arrested for property crimes. The offenses for which males were most often arrested were drug abuse violations and driving under the influence.

The number of females arrested in 2002 increased 2.1 percent from the 2001 number. The offense for which females were most often arrested was larceny-theft.

By race, 70.7 percent of all arrestees in 2002 were white. The offense for which whites were arrested most often was driving under the influence. The offense for which blacks were arrested most often was drug abuse violations.

Murder

The violent crime of murder is the most serious crime in the UCR hierarchy. An estimated 16,204 murders took place in 2002, a 1.0-percent increase over the 2001 estimate. A comparison of the data from 5 and 10 years ago showed that the 2002 estimate decreased 4.5 percent from the 1998 estimate and 33.9 percent from the 1993 estimate.

During 2002, law enforcement agencies provided supplemental homicide data for 14,054 homicides. In 2002, 90.1 percent of murder victims were adults. Males accounted for 76.8 percent of murder victims. Juveniles accounted for 8.2 percent of all male victims and 15.3 percent of all female victims. By race, 48.7 percent of murder victims were white, 48.5 percent were black, and 2.7 percent were of other races.

During 2002, the relationship between the victim and the offender was unknown for 42.8 percent of the victims. Among the incidents for which the victims' relationship to their killers was known, 22.2 percent were related to their murderers, 53.4 percent were acquainted with their offenders, and 24.4 percent did not know their killers.

Husbands and boyfriends killed 32.1 percent of female victims, and wives and girlfriends murdered 2.7 percent of male victims.

Data from single victim/single offender incidents indicated that 92.3 percent of black victims were slain by black offenders, and 84.7 percent of white victims were slain by white offenders.

In 2002, 71.1 percent of reported murders involved a firearm. Offenders used knives or cutting instruments in 13.4 percent of the murders, personal weapons (hands, fist, feet, etc.) in 7.1 percent, and blunt objects in 5.1 percent of incidents. Other weapon types (poison, arson, etc.) accounted for the remainder.

Felonious acts (forcible rape, robbery, arson, etc.) were the circumstances surrounding 16.5 percent of the murder offenses in 2002. Another 0.5 percent of murders involved circumstances suspected of being felonious in nature. Arguments were the cause of 27.5 percent of the murders, and 23.0 percent involved other types of circumstances (brawls, sniper attacks, etc.). Circumstances were unknown in 32.6 percent of the incidents.

Forcible Rape

There were an estimated 95,136 forcible rapes in 2002, an increase of 4.7 percent when compared to the 2001 estimate.

During 2002, an estimated 64.8 of every 100,000 females in the country were victims of forcible rape, an increase of 3.5 percent from the 2001 rate of 62.6. In comparison with rates of 5 and 10 years ago, the 2002 rate of forcible rapes of females was 3.9 percent below the 1998 rate and 19.4 percent below the 1993 rate.

By community type, cities outside MSAs had the highest rate of forcible rape, estimated at 75.9 forcible rapes for every 100,000 females. MSAs had a rate of 66.5 forcible rapes per 100,000 females, and rural counties had a rate of 46.8 forcible rapes for every 100,000 females.

Law enforcement cleared 44.5 percent of forcible rapes nationwide.

Robbery

There were an estimated 420,637 robberies in 2002, a 0.7-percent decrease from the 2001 number. The robbery rate nationwide was 145.9 per 100,000 inhabitants, a decrease of 1.7 percent from the 2001 rate.

Robbery accounted for 3.5 percent of reported serious crime in 2002 and comprised an estimated 29.5 percent of the violent crimes.

Robbery resulted in an estimated $539 million loss, or an average loss of $1,281 per incident. Bank robberies resulted in the highest average loss at $4,763 per incident.

In 2002, offenders used firearms in 42.1 percent of the robberies reported by law enforcement. Another 39.9 percent of robberies involved strong-arm tactics, and offenders used knives or cutting instruments in 8.7 percent of robbery offenses. Other weapons were used in 9.3 percent of robberies.

Aggravated Assault

The estimated 894,348 aggravated assaults that occurred in 2002 marked the ninth consecutive year of decline for that offense, a decrease of 1.6 percent from the 2001 estimate. The 2002 figure reflected a decrease of 8.4 percent from the 1998 number and a decrease of 21.2 percent from the 1993 number.

Aggravated assaults accounted for 62.7 percent of the violent crimes in 2002. There were an estimated 310.1 reported victims of aggravated assault per 100,000 inhabitants. This rate was 2.7 percent lower than in 2001, 14.2 percent lower than in 1998, and 29.6 percent lower than in 1993.

Personal weapons, such as hands, fist, and feet, were used in 27.7 percent of reported aggravated assaults in 2002. Law enforcement reported that firearms were used in 19.0 percent of aggravated assaults, and knives or other cutting instruments were used in 17.8 percent. Other weapon types were used in 35.4 percent of the aggravated assaults in 2002.

Burglary

There were an estimated 2.2 million burglaries in 2002, a 1.7-percent increase over the 2001 number. The burglary rate was estimated at 746.2 per 100,000 in population, an increase of 0.6 percent over the 2001 rate.

Losses due to burglary totaled an estimated $3.3 billion in 2002, with an average value of $1,549 per offense. The majority of burglaries, 65.8 percent, were residential in nature, and 61.7 percent of these occurred during daytime hours.

Forcible entry burglaries accounted for 62.8 percent of all burglary offenses, unlawful entry comprised 30.8 percent, and attempted forcible entry accounted for approximately 6.5 percent.

Among the 7 serious crimes for which law enforcement report data, burglary had the lowest percentage of clearances at 13.0 percent.

Larceny-Theft

Law enforcement reported an estimated 7.1 million larceny-theft offenses in 2002, a decrease of 0.6 percent from the 2001 number. The rate for larceny-theft was estimated as 2,445.8 per 100,000 inhabitants, a decrease of 1.6 percent from the 2001 rate.

Larceny-theft accounted for 59.4 percent of the reported serious crime in 2002 and 67.5 percent of the property crime.

The monetary loss due to larceny-theft offenses in 2002 was estimated at $4.9 billion, with an average value of $699 per offense.

Motor Vehicle Theft

There were an estimated 1.2 million reported motor vehicle thefts in 2002, which represented a 1.4-percent increase in volume when compared to the 2001 number. The rate for motor vehicle theft was estimated at 432.1 per 100,000 inhabitants, a 0.4-percent increase over last year's rate.

Automobiles were stolen at a rate of 337.5 cars per 100,000 inhabitants. Trucks and buses (commercial vehicles) were stolen at a rate of

85.2 per 100,000 in population, and other types of vehicles were stolen at a rate of 35.9 per 100,000 in population.

The estimated value of all motor vehicles stolen was $8.4 billion in 2002. The average value of motor vehicles reported stolen was $6,701.

Hate Crime

A total of 12,073 law enforcement agencies contributed hate crime data to the UCR Program in 2002. Of these agencies, 1,868 agencies (15.5 percent) submitted 7,462 hate crime incident reports that involved 8,832 separate offenses, 9,222 victims, and 7,314 known offenders.

Of the total number of single-bias crime incidents reported in 2002, 48.8 percent were motivated by racial bias, 19.1 percent were driven by religious bias, 16.7 percent were motivated by sexual-orientation bias, 14.8 percent resulted from an ethnicity/national origin bias, and 0.6 percent were motivated by disability bias.

During 2002, a total of 5,960 (67.5 percent) of reported hate crime offenses were crimes against persons, and 2,823 (32.0 percent) were crimes against property. Crimes against society comprised 0.6 percent of the reported offenses.

Intimidation continued to be the most frequently reported hate crime against individuals and accounted for 52.1 percent of all crimes against persons.

Destruction/damage/vandalism was the most frequently reported hate crime against property and accounted for 83.1 percent of the total hate crimes against property.

Arson

During 2002, a total of 12,454 law enforcement agencies reported 74,921 arson offenses to the UCR Program.

For the 66,308 arson offenses for which law enforcement supplied supplemental data, the average dollar loss was $11,253.

By property type, the average dollar loss for structural property destroyed by arson was $20,818, the average dollar loss for mobile property was $6,073, and the average dollar loss for other property types was $2,536. . . .

Special Study—Bank Robbery in the United States

Bank robberies account for millions of dollars in losses in the United States each year. In a special study included in Crime in the United

States, 2002, the FBI examined information about bank robberies from three of its criminal justice databases: the UCR Program's Summary system, the UCR Program's National Incident-Based Reporting System (NIBRS), and data from the Bank Robbery and Incidental Crimes Statute (BCS). The study updates part of a previous study, Crime Indicators System, Fourth Semiannual Briefing on Crime, published by the FBI in 1983.

An examination of the NIBRS data showed that in the years 1996 through 2000, the average amount of money taken in a bank robbery was less than $5,000.

Additionally, during that same time period, only 20.0 percent of the money stolen in bank robberies was recovered.

The 1996-2000 NIBRS data also revealed that violence and injury occurred during 2.3 percent of bank robberies.

Special Report—Reported Sniper Attacks, 1982–2001

The FBI examined data taken from the 1982–2001 Supplementary Homicide Reports to compile a report, which is also published in Crime in the United States, 2002, on the incidence of sniper attacks using firearms as reported by law enforcement.

The report showed that in this 20-year period there were 327 murder incidents that law enforcement classified as sniper attacks with firearms and 379 victims of these attacks.

An examination of the weapons data revealed that handguns were used in the commission of 63.6 percent of these attacks; rifles in 22.9 percent; shotguns in 7.0 percent; and other types of firearms, unknown firearms, and firearms type not stated in 6.7 percent of these sniper murders.

The data also showed that the majority of the victims and offenders of these sniper attacks were between 25 and 49 years old, male, white, and strangers to each other.

Source: U.S. Federal Bureau of Investigation. FBI National Press Office. "Uniform Crime Reporting Program Releases Crime Statistics for 2002." October 27, 2003. www.fbi.gov/pressrel/pressrel03/ucr2002.htm (accessed November 17, 2003).

November

2003 HISTORIC DOCUMENTS

President, Federal Courts on Partial Birth Abortion

November 5 and 6, 2003

INTRODUCTION

Thirty years after the U.S. Supreme Court's historic *Roe v. Wade* decision legalized abortion, President George W. Bush signed the first federal law that would limit it. Whether the law would ever take effect was in question, however. Less than an hour after Bush signed the Partial Birth Abortion Ban Act (PL 108–105) on November 5, 2003, a federal judge in Nebraska issued a temporary restraining order prohibiting its enforcement. Federal judges in New York and California issued similar orders the next day. Between them the three orders effectively blocked government action against most abortion providers in the United States, pending the outcome of lawsuits that contended the law was unconstitutional.

Abortion opponents had tried for eight years to make illegal what the medical community called intact dilation and extraction, a procedure used to end late-term pregnancies that involved partially extracting the live fetus from the uterus, killing it, and then fully extracting it from the mother's body. Dubbing the procedure partial birth abortion, the antiabortion forces likened the procedure to infanticide and used graphic pictures and descriptions to reinforce their opposition to the ban. Twice before, in 1996 and 1997, Congress had passed laws prohibiting use of the controversial procedure but was unable to override President Bill Clinton's veto. In 2003, with Bush promising to sign the ban and Republicans in control of both chambers of Congress, there was little doubt that the ban would be enacted.

There was also little doubt that the act's constitutionality would be challenged. In 2000 the Supreme Court ruled in the case of *Stenberg v. Carhart* that a Nebraska ban similar to the one passed by Congress was unconstitutional, both because its language was too broad and because it did not contain an exception to protect the health of the mother. Although PL 108–105 provided an exception to protect a mother's life, it did not provide one to protect a mother's health. Abortion rights advocates said that omission, together with the broad language in the law, infected the federal ban with the same fatal flaws as the unconstitutional Nebraska ban and immediately moved to stop its enforcement while legal challenges proceeded. In issuing their restraining orders, all three courts observed that the federal ban appeared to run counter to the Supreme Court's ruling in the Nebraska case. *(Supreme Court decision, Historic Documents of 2000, p. 429)*

Despite the legal challenges to the federal ban, its enactment was seen by both sides in the debate as a clear victory for abortion opponents. So far unsuccessful in their efforts to have *Roe v. Wade* repealed or reversed outright, antiabortion advocates were pushing legislation to push through incremental changes in both federal and state laws that would make it harder for women to get an abortion. Three-fifths of the states required girls under age eighteen to have parental consent before getting an abortion or to seek a consent waiver from a judge. About half the states required that women receive mandatory counseling about abortion, and most of those states required a twenty-four-hour waiting between the counseling and the abortion.

At the federal level, the next "to-do" legislation was likely to be what was known as the "unborn victims" bill, which would make it a separate offense to harm or kill a fetus during the commission of a federal crime. Its supporters said that the legislation had been narrowly drawn to exempt pregnant women and doctors who performed abortions and simply recognized that attacks on pregnant women could result in harm to two victims, the mother and the fetus. Abortion rights advocates opposed the legislation, arguing that it would give legal standing to a fetus for the first time, thereby undermining the constitutional right to an abortion. The House had passed the legislation in 1999 and 2001 and was widely expected to pass it again in 2004. The outcome in the Senate was uncertain. Democrats in 2003 blocked an attempt by the Republican leadership to bring the measure to the Senate floor without allowing amendments.

The Incidence of Abortion

According to a study by the Alan Guttmacher Institute, a research organization respected by both sides of the abortion debate for the accuracy of its data, the number of abortions in the United States was at its lowest level since 1974, the year after the *Roe v. Wade* decision. The institute reported 1.3 million abortions in 2000, or 21.3 for every 1,000 women ages fifteen to forty-four. The peak abortion years were 1980 and 1981, when the rate was 29.3 abortions for every 1,000 women. According to the institute, only 2,200 of the 1.3 million abortions in 2000 were partial birth abortions. But the number of such abortions had tripled since 1996, an increase that the pro-life lobby used to buttress its opposition to the procedure.

Most of the women who got abortions in 2000 were in their twenties and unmarried. Nearly half who had abortions had not used contraception at all; most of the rest had used contraception but not correctly. The study also estimated that about 37,000 women had used the "abortion pill"—RU-486, or mifepristone—in the first six months of 2001. The drug, which would abort a pregnancy in the first seven weeks, was approved for use in the United States in September 2000. A disproportionate share of women having abortions were black or Hispanic. They were also poor. The abortion rate went up 25 percent for women below the poverty line and 23 percent for women just above the poverty line. For the most well-off women in the survey, the abortion rate dropped 39 percent. (RU-486 approval, Historic Documents of 2000, p. 781)

Passage of Partial Birth Abortion Ban

In many ways, the debate on the partial birth abortion ban was almost anticlimactic. The arguments had all been made in the past, and the only real difference was the shift of control in the Senate from Democratic to Republican.The Senate took up the ban first, passing the legislation in March by a 64–33 vote but only after adding language reaffirming the ruling in Roe v. Wade. The House easily passed its version of the bill in June, which was identical to the Senate bill except for the language reaffirming Roe.

For several months Senate abortion rights supporters, led by Democrat Barbara Boxer of California, refused to send the bill to a House-Senate conference to resolve the one outstanding difference until the Senate voted a second time to reaffirm Roe. The impasse in the Senate was broken on September 17, when Republicans joined Democrats in sending the measure to conference. "Everybody knows that the conference committee will convene for the sole purpose of dropping the Roe language," a spokesman for the National Right to Life Committee said, explaining the apparent Republican capitulation on Roe. Boxer "knows it, we know it, everybody in the press gallery knows it. She's suffering a big defeat." As predicted, the conference quickly agreed to drop the Senate language reaffirming Roe, and both the Senate and House cleared the final measure by substantial votes.

The final legislation banned the procedure in all instances, except when a pregnant woman's life was endangered "by a physical disorder, physical illness, or physical injury." It did not include an exception for cases in which a woman's health, but not her life, was at risk. Instead it relied on more than a dozen pages of congressional "findings" showing that a partial birth abortion was never medically necessary. Doctors who performed the procedure were subject to fines and up to two years in prison.

Opponents of the ban had argued that in some cases the dilation and extraction procedure was safer for the pregnant woman than other procedures. They also argued that the definition of partial birth abortion in the bill was so vague that it could be construed to cover the much more common abortion procedure known as dilation and evacuation. It was similar vague language that led the Supreme Court to strike down the Nebraska law. At least one medical group objected to the ban on the grounds that legislatures should not tell doctors how to practice medicine. Doctors and patients, not legislators, "are the appropriate parties to determine the best method of treatment," said the American College of Obstetricians and Gynecologists.

At the bill signing ceremony on November 5, Bush repeated many of the graphic arguments that proponents of the ban had used to gather support. "The best case against partial birth abortion is a simple description of what happens and to whom it happens," the president said. "It involves the partial delivery of a live boy or girl, and a sudden violent end of that life. Our nation owes its children a different and better welcome." As several commentators noted afterward, no women participated in the bill-signing ceremony.

The three federal court injunctions barring enforcement of the ban were issued within hours of its enactment. One injunction was issued by the same district court judge in Nebraska who first declared the state's ban unconstitutional. That temporary restraining order applied only to four doctors named in a lawsuit brought by the Center for Reproductive Rights. One of the doctors was Leroy Carhart, who had successfully challenged the constitutionality of the original Nebraska ban. A second restraining order was issued in New York in response to a challenge by the American Civil Liberties Union on behalf of the National Abortion Federation, which represented most doctors that performed abortions in the United States. The third temporary restraining order was issued in San Francisco in response to a petition filed by Planned Parenthood Federation of America asking that enforcement of the ban be blocked in all clinics across the nation that were affiliated with Planned Parenthood.

Related Developments

In another potentially significant development, two expert advisory committees to the Food and Drug Administration (FDA) recommended on December 16 that a so-called morning-after pill designed to prevent unwanted pregnancies be made available through pharmacies without prescription. The final decision, to be made by FDA commissioner Mark B. McClellan, was expected early in 2004. The drug, called Plan B by its manufacturer, Barr Laboratories, was an emergency contraceptive that a woman could take within seventy-two hours of unprotected sexual intercourse. The company said it could prevent up to 89 percent of unplanned and unwanted pregnancies. Five states—Alaska, California, Hawaii, New Mexico, and Washington—already made the drug available without prescription through a limited number of pharmacies.

Supporters of widespread availability of the drug without prescription said it could prevent as many as half the 3 million unintended pregnancies in the United States every year. "There is a public health imperative to increase access to emergency contraception," said Vivian Dickerson, president-elect of the American College of Obstetricians and Gynecologists. "If we are truly dedicated to lowering the number of unintended pregnancies and abortion in this country, then let's prove it by making emergency contraception available over the counter."

But religious and pro-life groups opposed the recommendation, saying widespread availability would increase both irresponsible sex, particularly among adolescents, and the incidence of sexually transmitted diseases. Some also argued that women might not realize that in some cases they were aborting a baby. The pill worked in most cases by preventing ovulation, but in some cases it prevented a fertilized egg from implanting in the uterus. Although implantation was the medical definition of pregnancy, those who believed that pregnancy began with fertilization equated the morning-after drugs with abortion.

In still other action related to the abortion debate, a federal district court in Dallas on June 20 rejected a bid from Norma McCorvey, the "Jane Roe" of *Roe v. Wade,* to reconsider the Supreme Court's decision in that landmark 1973 case. McCorvey joined the pro-life movement in the early 1990s. In dismissing McCorvey's "motion for relief from judgment," the court said that petitions to reopen cases had to be filed within weeks or months of the judgment, not decades later.

A week later, on June 27, the Supreme Court declined to hear arguments in a case appealing a lower court ruling holding that abortion clinic protesters were in violation of a federal law that made it illegal to incite violence and threaten doctors. At issue were "wanted" posters listing the names of doctors who performed abortions. Protesters carried the posters outside abortion clinics and also put them on the Internet along with personal information about the doctors. Three doctors who had been featured on the posters were subsequently murdered. The suit was brought by the American Coalition of Life Activists, who argued that the posters were a form of free speech protected under the Constitution. A federal district judge disagreed and ordered the activists to pay $108 million in punitive damages and $12 million in compensatory damages. The U.S. Circuit Court of Appeals for the Ninth District told the lower court judge to reduce the punitive damages but otherwise left the ruling in place.

On September 3 the state of Florida executed Paul Hill, a former Presbyterian minister who had been convicted of shooting to death an abortion doctor and his unarmed security escort in 1994. Hill became the first American to be executed for committing antiabortion violence. Speaking to reporters before his execution, Hill said he had no regret for the killings. "I don't feel remorse because I think it [the killing] was a good thing, and instead of being shocked, more people should do what I did."

Following are three documents: first, excerpts of remarks made by President George W. Bush on November 5, 2003, upon signing legislation banning partial birth abortion unless necessary to save the life of the mother; second, the text of the temporary restraining order issued November 5 by U.S. District Judge Richard G. Kopf, the District of Nebraska, in Leroy Carhart et al. v. John Ashcroft, *blocking enforcement of the ban for four doctors in Nebraska; and third, the text of the temporary restraining order issued November 6 by U.S. District Court Judge Richard Conway Casey, the Southern District of New York, in* National Abortion Federation v. John Ashcroft, *suspending enforcement of the ban for members of the federation, which represented most doctors that performed abortions in the United States.*

Remarks by President Bush on Signing the Partial Birth Abortion Ban Act

Thank you very much. Good afternoon. I'm pleased that all of you have joined us as the Partial Birth Abortion Ban Act of 2003 becomes the law of the land. For years, a terrible form of violence has been directed against children who are inches from birth, while the law looked the other way. Today, at last, the American people and our government have confronted the violence and come to the defense of the innocent child.

I want to thank you all for coming. Many of you have worked long and hard to see this bill come to fruition, and we thank you for your efforts. . . .

In passing this legislation, members of the House and Senate made a studied decision based upon compelling evidence. The best case against partial birth abortion is a simple description of what happens and to whom it happens. It involves the partial delivery of a live boy or girl, and a sudden, violent end of that life. Our nation owes its children a different and better welcome. The bill I am about to sign protecting innocent new life from this practice reflects the compassion and humanity of America.

In the course of the congressional debate, the facts became clear. Each year, thousands of partial birth abortions are committed. As Doctor C. Everett Koop, the pediatrician and former Surgeon General has pointed out, the majority of partial birth abortions are not required by medical emergency. As Congress has found, the practice is widely regarded within the medical profession as unnecessary, not only cruel to the child, but harmful to the mother, and a violation of medical ethics.

The facts about partial birth abortion are troubling and tragic, and no lawyer's brief can make them seem otherwise. By acting to prevent this practice, the elected branches of our government have affirmed a basic standard of humanity, the duty of the strong to protect the weak. The wide agreement amongst men and women on this issue, regardless of political party, shows that bitterness in political debate can be overcome by compassion and the power of conscience. And the executive branch will vigorously defend this law against any who would try to overturn it in the courts.

America stands for liberty, for the pursuit of happiness and for the unalienable right of life. And the most basic duty of government is to defend the life of the innocent. Every person, however frail or vulnerable, has a place and a purpose in this world. Every person has a special dignity. This right to life cannot be granted or denied by government, because it does not come from government, it comes from the Creator of life.

In the debate about the rights of the unborn, we are asked to broaden the circle of our moral concern. We're asked to live out our calling as Americans. We're asked to honor our own standards, announced on the day of our founding in the Declaration of Independence. We're asked by our convictions and tradition and compassion to build a culture of life, and make this a more just and welcoming society. And today, we welcome vulnerable children into the care and protection of Americans.

The late Pennsylvania governor Robert Casey once said that: when we look to the unborn child, the real issue is not when life begins, but when love begins. This is the generous and merciful spirit of our country at its best. This spirit is reflected in the Partial Birth Abortion Ban Act of 2003, which I am now honored to sign into law. God bless.

Source: U.S. The White House. "Remarks on Signing the Partial-Birth Abortion Ban Act of 2003." November 5, 2003. *Weekly Compilation of Presidential Documents,* 39, no. 45 (November 10, 2003): 1540–1541. Washington, D.C.: National Archives and Records Administration. www.gpoaccess.gov/wcomp/v39no45.html (accessed April 21, 2004).

Carhart et al. v. Ashcroft

Memorandum and Order

Congress has passed the "Partial-Birth Abortion Ban Act of 2003." The President has signed it. After hearing the views of the parties and considering the evidence offered by them, I now temporarily restrain enforcement of the Act.

The Supreme court, citing the factual findings of eight different federal trial judges (appointed by four different Presidents) and the considered opinion of the American College of Obstetricians and Gynecologists, has found a very similar law unconstitutional because it banned "partial-birth abortions" without the requisite exception for the preservation of the health of the woman. *Stenberg v. Carhart* [2000]. The law challenged here appears to suffer from a similar vice. While it is also true that Congress found a health exception is not needed, it is, at the very least, problematic whether I should defer to such a conclusion when the Supreme Court has found otherwise. . . . Therefore, applying the familiar *Dataphase* factors, and especially given the fact that the health of women may be harmed if I do otherwise,

IT IS ORDERED that:

1. The request for a temporary restraining order . . . is granted. That is, John Ashcroft, in his official capacity as Attorney General of the United States, and his employees, agents, and successors in office, are temporarily restrained from enforcing the "Partial Birth Abortion Ban Act of 2003" . . . against the plaintiffs and their officers, agents, servants, and employees, including those individual and entities (both medical and non-medical) with whom plaintiffs work, teach, supervise, or refer. This temporary restraining order shall remain in effect until further order of the court.

2. Plaintiffs' counsel shall arrange and schedule a telephone conference ca;; between counsel of record and the undersigned United States district judge to occur on Wednesday, November 12, 2003, to discuss scheduling of the preliminary injunction hearing, other progression-related issues, and whether the court should retain its own experts.

    DATED this 5th day of November, 2003. . . .

Source: U.S. United States District Court for the District of Nebraska. *Leroy Carhart et al. v. John Ashcroft. Memorandum and Order.* November 5, 2003. www.crlp.org/pdf/110503_memo_carhart_ashcroft.pdf (accessed April 21, 2004).

National Abortion Federation v. John Ashcroft

Memorandum and Order

Before the Court is Plaintiffs' Application for a Temporary Restraining Order, requesting that the Court enjoin the Attorney General of the United States from enforcing the Partial-Birth Abortion Ban Act of 2003 ("the Act"). The Act was signed on November 5, 2003, and took effect at 12:01 A.M. on November 6, 2003. Having considered the parties' written submissions and oral arguments, the Court hereby GRANTS Plaintiffs' Application.

To obtain a temporary restraining order, Plaintiffs must show irreparable harm and a likelihood of success on the merits. Plaintiffs have met this standard.

First, Plaintiffs have made an adequate showing as to the requisite risk of harm. Second, Plaintiffs have shown a likelihood of success on the merits. Plaintiffs argue that the Act is unconstitutional because, among other things, it does not contain an exception to protect women's health. In *Stenberg v. Carhart,* 530 U.S. 914 (2000), the Supreme Court declared unconstitutional a Nebraska statute banning partial-birth abortions based, in part, on the fact that the statute did not contain such an exception. In so holding, the *Stenberg* Court determined that a "division of medical opinion . . . at most means uncertainty, a factor that signals the presence of risk . . . [w]here a significant body of medical opinion believes a procedure may bring with it greater safety for some patients and explains the medial reasons supporting the view," then a health exception is constitutionally required. At oral argument, Defendant took the position that there remains a disagreement in the medical community as to whether the abortion procedures covered by the Act are ever necessary to protect a woman's health, and that Congress did not find a consensus on the matter. Given the Defendant's position, the Court is constrained, at this time, to conclude that it is substantially likely that Plaintiffs will succeed on the merits.

Therefore, it is ORDERED that:

1. The Application for a Temporary Restraining Order is granted. Defendant John Ashcroft, in his official capacity as Attorney General of the United States, and his employees, agents, and successors in office, are temporarily restrained from enforcing the Partial-Birth

Abortion Ban Act of 2003, against Plaintiffs, their members, officers, agents, servants, and employees.

2. Pursuant to Rule 65(b), this Temporary Restraining Order shall be in force for ten days from its issuance. Under the computation of time set forth in Rule 6(a), the Temporary Restraining Order shall remain in effect through November 21, 2003.

3. The parties are directed to submit briefs to the Court on the issues of whether the Court must hold an evidentiary hearing on Plaintiffs' Application for a Preliminary Injunction, whether a decision can be made as a legal matter without an evidentiary hearing, and whether the Court should retain its own medical experts. The parties shall service their briefs on one another and with the Court by 5:00 P.M. on November 10, 2003.

So Ordered.

Source: U.S. District Court. Southern District of New York. *National Abortion Federation v. John Ashcroft. Memorandum and Order.* 03 CIV, 8695 (RCC). November 6, 2003. www.prochoice.org/legal/legislation/hr760/tro.pdf (accessed November 10, 2003).

Schwarzenegger on His Inauguration as Governor of California

November 17, 2003

INTRODUCTION

California's penchant for governing through voter referendums took an unusual—some said bizarre—turn in 2003 when the state's voters ousted their recently reelected Democratic governor, Gray Davis, in a recall election on October 7 and replaced him with the action actor and body-builder Arnold Schwarzenegger. A Republican and a political neophyte, Schwarzenegger was elected to fill the remaining three years of Davis's term. The Austrian-born celebrity, who emigrated to the United States in 1968 and obtained American citizenship in 1983, was sworn in as governor of the nation's most populous state on November 17. Schwarzenegger was the second Hollywood star to become governor of California. The first was Ronald Reagan, who served the state as governor from 1967 to 1975 before going on to win two terms as president (1981–1989).

Lingering public anger over the state's energy crisis in 2000–2001, combined with distress over a $38 billion budget deficit, had risen to fever pitch in mid-2003 after Davis and Republican legislators deadlocked over the best way to reduce the deficit. Republicans argued that Davis's recall was the result of a popular uprising against the "tax-and-spend" policies and "special interests" that the governor represented. Democrats argued that the recall, financed largely by multimillionaire Rep. Darrell Issa, R-Calif., amounted to a "right-wing coup d'etat," aided by Republican legislators who blocked Davis on the budget issue not out of principle but in an effort to weaken him in the recall campaign.

The recall itself was deplored by many commentators as a threat to the orderly democratic election process that could lead to political instability if voters turned to it every time they became frustrated with the actions of their elected government officials. They noted California's long history of exercising direct democracy, with voters passing hundreds of initiatives—ranging from tax limits to spending mandates to social policies at the ballot box—and rejecting hundreds of others. Economist and columnist Paul Krugman derided the recall as turning California from a democracy into a "banana republic." Others were less concerned. They pointed out that of thirty-two attempts to initiate a recall of a California governor, the Davis recall was the first to reach the state ballot. Moreover, Davis was only the second governor in U.S. history to be recalled by the voters. The first was North Dakota's Lynn Frazier, a Republican, who was recalled in 1921 amid allegations that he and other state officials had abused their power and misused state funds. The chances of recalls succeeding in the sixteen other states that permitted them seemed even less likely than in California, largely because the rules for mounting such campaigns were much tougher than were those in California.

It was unclear what effect the recall might have on the 2004 presidential election. In recent years the state had voted solidly in the Democratic column. Republican George W. Bush lost California to Democrat Al Gore by eleven percentage points in 2000, and before the recall most political commentators had given Bush only an outside chance of winning the state's fifty-five electoral votes in 2004. Schwarzenegger ran seventeen percentage points ahead of his nearest challenger, the Democratic lieutenant governor, Cruz Bustamante, and Schwarzenegger's election was clearly a psychological boost for Republicans. But whether it would change the odds in the presidential election depended on numerous unknowables, including how the actor performed in his new role as governor.

Background: Energy Crisis and Budget Crunch

A lifelong politician, Gray Davis served as a state assemblyman, state controller, and lieutenant governor before being elected in 1998 to succeed Republican Pete Wilson. Described as rigid, detached, and more comfortable fund raising than dealing with state legislators and policy issues, Davis was not particularly popular with voters. He won the governorship largely because he ran against weak candidates, often conservative Republicans whose views were out of step with the majority of Californians. Davis narrowly won reelection in 2002, and only after running a series of negative TV ads sharply attacking the main Republican contender, Los Angeles mayor Richard Riordan. Riordan lost the Republican primary to conservative businessman Bill Simon, a political novice who then lost the general election to Davis in November.

Davis's problems were not entirely of his own making. The California economy, particularly its crucial technology sector, was hit early and hard by the collapse of the stock market and the recession that followed. The situation was worsened when California fell into a temporary but deep energy crisis that cost residents of the state an estimated $45 billion in higher electricity costs, lost business due to rolling blackouts, and forced a slowdown in production. Although Davis took steps to curb the crisis, including declaring a state of emergency, voters said he was slow to act and blamed him for their higher electricity bills. *(California energy crisis, Historic Documents of 2001, p. 332)*

By early 2003 California was running a $38 billion deficit and two Republican conservative groups announced plans to mount a recall campaign against Davis. The campaign gained traction in May, when Representative Issa announced that he would run to replace Davis and contributed nearly $445,000 to the anti-Davis campaign. By June the governor and the Republican minority in the state legislature were in complete deadlock over a budget, with Davis blaming Republicans for refusing to consider tax increases and Republicans insisting that that the state cut spending rather than tax its way out of the crisis. Although Republicans denied it, Democrats said the Republican refusal to negotiate on the budget was an intentional strategy designed to make Davis more vulnerable to a recall. The GOP minority had this leverage because of a constitutional provision that state budgets must be approved by a two-thirds majority vote in both houses of the legislature.

On July 23 the secretary of state announced that more than enough valid petition signatures had been filed to qualify the recall for the ballot. On July 24 Lt. Gov. Bustamante announced that the election would take place October 7. On the same day, Standard and Poor's downgraded California's bond rating to BBB, the lowest of any state and just two points above junk-bond status. Later in the day Senate leaders announced they had broken the legislative deadlock and reached agreement on a budget plan that contained no new taxes but relied instead on spending cuts and borrowing, as well as funds transfers and other accounting gimmickry, to balance the state budget. Davis signed the package into law on August 4.

The Race to Replace Davis

The announcement that a recall election would be held touched off a mad scramble in both parties. Democrats were in a dilemma because of the two-part ballot that would be presented to California voters. On the first part they would be asked to vote yes or no on recalling Davis. On the second part they could vote for a candidate to replace Davis in the event he lost the recall vote. Initially Democrats agreed not to enter any candidate in the replacement race, reasoning that the appearance of other Democratic names on the ballot would only confuse voters and undermine Davis's chances of defeating the recall vote. Despite the apparent unity, the names of several prominent Democrats, such as U.S. senator Dianne Feinstein and former U.S. representative Leon E. Panetta, kept cropping up, indicating that Davis's support was fragile at best. On the Republican side Issa and another conservative, state senator Tom McClintock, both filed to run, while Riordan and Simon both said they were considering the race. Although his name was frequently mentioned as a potential candidate, Schwarzenegger remained in the background. Many political pundits expected him to stay out of the race and endorse Riordan.

Instead, in a surprise announcement on August 6, Schwarzenegger threw his hat into the ring. Appearing on NBC's *The Tonight Show with Jay Leno,* the former Mr. Universe, known around the world for his role in the "Terminator" movies, told a national audience that he was aware of his vulnerabilities as a political candidate. "I know they're going to throw everything at me, that I have no experience and I'm a womanizer and a terrible guy," Schwarzenegger said in his heavily accented English. But he said he could provide the leadership that the state currently lacked. "You all know that Gray Davis knows how to run a dirty campaign better than anyone, but he doesn't know how to run a state," Schwarzenegger said.

Schwarzenegger became the immediate frontrunner and his entry into the race changed the calculus for both Republicans and Democrats. On the Republican side, Riordan opted to stay out of the race, and Issa, who spent a total of $1.7 million on the recall campaign, dropped out. Simon entered, but then dropped out later in the campaign. On the Democratic side, Lt. Gov. Bustamante, whose relations with Davis were said to be frosty, and the state insurance commissioner, John Garamendi, both announced they would run, destroying the fragile Democratic solidarity that had offered some protection to Davis. Once Bustamante and other Democrats entered the race, Davis was fighting the perception that his recall was inevitable.

Meanwhile, literally dozens of other candidates had plunked down the required sixty-five signatures and $3,500 to qualify for the ballot, adding to the circus-like atmosphere of the election. Among them were Peter V. Ueberroth, the former baseball commissioner; Arianna Huffington, a Republican-turned-independent columnist; actor Gary Coleman; skin-magazine publisher Larry Flynt; and adult film actress Mary Carey. "This is America," Carey said when she filed her papers. "I am just as dignified as Arnold Schwarzenegger, and I can speak English." Of the 247 candidates who filed for the election, 135 were certified as qualified and placed on the ballot.

In addition to sorting through dozens of candidates, California voters did not know for several weeks whether the recall would actually take place as scheduled. Davis and the American Civil Liberties Union sued to postpone the election on the grounds that some polling places in the state were still using punch-card ballots like those that disenfranchised thousands of voters in the disputed Florida presidential race in 2000. On September 15, just three weeks before the scheduled election, a three-judge panel of the Ninth U.S. Circuit Court of Appeals agreed that the election should be postponed. A week later, after rehearing the case, the full appeals court said the election should go forward. *(2000 election dispute, Historic Documents of 2000, p. 999)*

Although Davis tried valiantly to portray the recall as a blatant attempt by Republicans to steal back the governorship that they could not win through regular means, that appeal appeared to have little resonance with the state's voters. He also lost ground when he did an about-face on the controversial issue of allowing illegal immigrants to obtain drivers' licenses. Davis had vetoed such a bill in 2002, but he reversed course and signed a similar measure in August. Opponents immediately accused him of pandering to the Hispanic vote. Davis further angered voters when he signed unpopular legislation that tripled the car sales tax. Two of the few campaign promises Schwarzenegger made were to repeal both new laws as soon as he took office.

Schwarzenegger also called for a constitutional cap on state spending, opposed new taxes, and promised not to cut spending on education. He won endorsements from billionaire investor Warren Buffett and former secretary of state George P. Shultz. He also was aided by his marriage to Kennedy cousin and NBC journalist Maria Shriver, who campaigned tirelessly in her husband's behalf. But he offered few other specifics about policy positions he might take once in office, and with one exception, he refused to be drawn into any public debates with other candidates. At one point he said he would not offer specifics on possible budget cuts because "the public doesn't care about figures. What the people want to hear is, are you willing to make the changes? Are you tough enough to go in there and provide leadership?"

In the end, Schwarzenegger's analysis proved to be correct. Whether voters were enamored with his celebrity or simply tired of the usual politicians, polls taken before October 7 showed that Republicans, Democrats, and independents, both women and men, were prepared to vote for the actor even though few thought he had "the best experience for the job" or "seemed more knowledgeable than his opponents" in the one debate in which he participated. Even last-minute revelations that Schwarzenegger had indulged in group sex before his marriage and allegations that he had groped several women seemed to have little negative effect on the voters. On October 7 Gray Davis lost the recall, 55 percent to 45 percent. Schwarzenegger won the right to replace him with 48 percent of the vote— sixteen percentage points ahead of his closest rival, Cruz Bustamante. McClintock, the conservative Republican, picked up 13 percent of the vote, and the remaining votes were scattered among the dozens of other names that appeared on the ballot.

First Weeks in Office

Surrounded by his wife and four children, Schwarzenegger took the oath of office on November 17 in a brief ceremony. Schwarzenegger said his election was not about "replacing one man or one party" but about "changing the entire political climate of the state." Acknowledging again that he was a newcomer to politics, he said he realized that "I was elected on faith and hope. And I feel a great responsibility not to let the people down." Within an hour of the ceremony, he had repealed the 300 percent car tax that had gone into effect on October 1 and convened a special session of the legislature to deal with the budget deficit.

The Democratic-led legislature handed the new governor an initial setback on December 6 when it refused to endorse his plan for borrowing money and limiting spending to resolve the budget crisis. A week later, after Schwarzenegger personally participated in negotiations, both the Senate and the Assembly agreed to a compromise budget plan. The governor praised the Democrats for being willing to compromise and won praise in return. "I applaud him that he chose to govern and decided he was going to put politics aside," said one local Democratic leader. "He got it. He got it fast."

Less than a week later, the governor blamed Democratic legislators when he invoked emergency procedures to deal with a $2.5 billion shortfall for local governments that was caused by his repeal of the car tax. "Since the legislative leadership refuses to act," the governor said, "I will act without them." Democrats deplored Schwarzenegger's action. "I think he's trying to figure out how he's going to govern and what he's going to be when he grows up," said one Democratic assemblywoman.

Following is the text of the inaugural speech delivered November 17, 2003, by Republican Arnold Schwarzenegger on being sworn in as governor of California to serve the remaining three years of the term of Democratic governor Gray Davis, who was recalled by the voters on October 7.

Swearing-In Remarks of Gov. Arnold Schwarzenegger

Mr. Chief Justice, Governor and Mrs. Davis, Governor and Mrs. Wilson, Governor and Mrs. Deukmejian, Governor Brown, legislative leadership, constitutional officers, my fellow Californians:

I am humbled, I am moved—and I am honored beyond words to be your Governor.

To the thousands of you who came here today—I took this oath to serve you.

To others all across this state—Democrats, Republicans, Independents—it makes no difference—I took this oath to serve you.

To those who have no power, to those who've dropped out—too weary or disappointed with politics as usual—I took this oath to serve you.

I say to everyone here today and to all Californians, I will not forget my oath and I will not forget you.

Let me first thank Governor Davis and Mrs. Davis and their entire administration for a smooth transition. There's been a spirit of mutual respect and cooperation, and I thank you for that.

My fellow citizens: Today is a new day in California. I did not seek this office to do things the way they've always been done. What I care about is restoring your trust in your government.

When I became a citizen 20 years ago, I had to take a citizenship test. I had to learn about the history and the principles of our republic. What I learned—and what I've never forgotten is that in a republic, sovereignty rests with the people—not the government.

In recent years, Californians have lost confidence. They've felt that the actions of their government did not represent the will of the people.

This election was not about replacing one man or one party. It was about changing the entire political climate of our state.

Everywhere I went during my campaign, I could feel the public hunger for our elected officials to work together, to work openly, and to work for the greater good.

The election was the people's veto—of politics as usual.

With the eyes of the world upon us, we did the dramatic. Now we must put the rancor of the past behind us—and do the extraordinary.

It's no secret I'm a newcomer to politics. I realize I was elected on faith and hope. And I feel a great responsibility—not to let the people down.

As soon as I go inside the Capitol behind me, I will sign my first order as Governor.

I will sign Executive Order Number 1—which will repeal the 300 percent increase in the car tax.

I will issue a proclamation convening a Special Session of the Legislature to address California's fiscal crisis.

I will issue a proclamation convening a Special Session to reform our workers' compensation system.

I will call on the legislature to repeal SB-60 and I will work to reform government by bringing openness and full disclosure to public business.

I enter this office beholden to no one except you, my fellow citizens. I pledge my governorship to your interests, not to special interests.

So I've appointed to my cabinet Republicans, Democrats and Independents—because I want people to know that my administration is not about politics. It is about saving California.

The State of California is in crisis.

As I've said many times, we spent ourselves into the largest budget deficit in the nation.

We have the worst credit rating in the nation.

We have the highest worker compensation costs in the nation.

Next year we will have the highest unemployment insurance costs in the nation.

And we have the worst business climate in the nation.

But even though these problems are staggering, they do not compare to what Californians have overcome in the past.

Our state has endured earthquakes, floods and fires. The latest fires destroyed lives, homes, businesses, and devastated hundreds of thousands of acres of the land we love.

On behalf of my fellow citizens, I salute all those who served on the front lines of the battle: firefighters, emergency workers, National Guard, law enforcement officials, and thousands of volunteers. As we watched the firestorms raging—we saw bravery that never faltered and determination that never wavered in a fight that never flagged.

To the families of those who gave their lives and those who lost their lives—your loss is ours. As Californians, we mourn together, we fight together, and we will rebuild together.

And just as California will come back from the fires, we will also come back from fiscal adversity.

I know there are some who say that the Legislature and I will never agree on solutions to our problems. But I've found in my life that people often respond in remarkable ways to remarkable challenges.

In the words of President Kennedy, "I am an idealist without illusions."

I know it will be hard to put aside years of partisan bitterness.

I know it will be hard to overcome the political habits of the past.

But for guidance, let's look back in history to a period I studied when I became a citizen: the summer of 1787. Delegates of the original 13 states were meeting in Philadelphia.

The dream of a new nation was falling apart. Events were spiraling downward. Divisions were deep: merchant against farmer, big states against small, North against South.

Our Founding Fathers knew that the fate of the union was in their hands—just as the fate of California is in our hands.

What happened in that summer of 1787 is that they put their differences aside—and produced the blueprint for our government, our constitution. Their coming together has been called "the Miracle of Philadelphia."

Now, the members of the Legislature and I must bring about the "Miracle of Sacramento"—a miracle based on cooperation, good will, new ideas, and devotion to the long-term good of California.

What we face may look insurmountable. But I learned something from all those years of training and competing. I learned something from all those sets and reps when I didn't think I could lift another ounce of weight.

What I learned is that we are always stronger than we know. California is like that, too.

We are stronger than we know.

There's a massive weight we must lift off our state.

Alone, I cannot lift it. But together, we can.

It's true: things may get harder before they get better. But I've never been afraid of the struggle. I've never been afraid of the fight and I've never been afraid of the hard work.

I will not rest until out fiscal house is in order.

I will not rest until California is a competitive job-creating machine.

And I will not rest until the people of California come to see their government as a partner in their lives, not a roadblock to their dreams.

Today I ask all of you to join me in a new "Partnership" for California. One that is civil and respectful of our diverse population. One that challenges each and every one of us to serve our state in a joyful, productive and creative way.

Ladies and gentlemen, I have an immigrant's optimism—that what I learned in citizenship class is true: the system does work.

I believe that with all of my heart.

I have big hopes for California. President Reagan spoke of America as "the shining city on the hill." I see California as the golden dream by the sea.

Perhaps some think this is fanciful or poetic, but to an immigrant like me—who, as a boy, saw Soviet tanks rolling through the streets of Austria; to someone like me who came here with absolutely nothing and gained absolutely everything, it is not fanciful to see this state as a Golden Dream.

For millions of people around the world, California has always glimmered with hope and glowed with opportunity. Millions of people around the world send their dreams to California with the hope their lives will follow.

My fellow citizens,

I have taken the oath to uphold the Constitution of California. Now, with your help and God's, I will also uphold the dream that is California.

God bless you—and may God bless California.

Source: State of California. Office of the Governor. "Swearing-In Remarks (as prepared) of Gov. Arnold Schwarzenegger." November 17, 2003. www.governor.ca.gov/state/newgov/govsite/gov_htmldisplay.jsp?BV_SessionID=@@@@1365907523.1069265635@@@@&BV_EngineID=eadcildffhgmbemgcfkmchcog.0&sCatTitle=Speeches&sFilePath=/govsite/selected_speeches/20031117_SwearingIn.html&sTitle=2003 (accessed November 19, 2003).

Report on Causes of
Massive Power Blackout

November 19, 2003

INTRODUCTION

A massive power outage cascaded through parts of eight eastern and mid-western states and two Canadian provinces on August 14, 2003, leaving as many as 50 million customers in the dark. The largest power failure in U.S. history closed down water systems, air and ground transportation, and businesses in a swath that stretched from western New England across the Great Lakes region, including New York City, Cleveland, Detroit, and Toronto. Although the lights came on in most places within twenty-four hours, full power was not restored in several areas for days. Estimates of the economic losses caused by the outage ranged into the billions of dollars.

Initial fears that the blackout had been caused by terrorists or computer hackers sabotaging the system were quickly allayed, and attention began to focus on several failed transmission lines operated by FirstEnergy Corporation near Akron, Ohio, south of Cleveland. A report issued November 19 by a joint task force composed of government energy officials in the United States and Canada confirmed that the outage began with those downed lines and then quickly spread through the system as a result of a series of computer malfunctions and human errors. "This blackout was largely preventable," Spencer Abraham, secretary of the U.S. Department of Energy, said at a news conference releasing the report. "A number of small problems combined to create a very big one."

The power failure renewed questions about the reliability of nation's electricity grid and the deregulation of the electricity industry. It also pumped new life into congressional efforts to pass an omnibus energy bill that was a top legislative priority for President George W. Bush. By the end of the year, however, congressional leaders had been unable to break several impasses that prevented passage of the measure. When Congress adjourned for the year in December, Senate Republicans were two votes shy of defeating a Democrat-led filibuster of the omnibus bill.

Deregulation of the power industry had already contributed to an earlier energy crisis in California, where the state's efforts to deal with high wholesale prices for electric power in 2001 led to a fiscal crisis in the state. That in turn contributed to the recall in October 2003 of Democratic Governor Gray Davis and his replacement with actor and bodybuilder Arnold Schwarzenegger. *(Recall election, p. 1005; California energy crisis, Historic Documents of 2001, p. 332)*

The Immediate Causes of the Blackout

On August 15, the day after the power failure, President Bush and Canadian prime minister Jean Chrétien announced the formation of the U.S.-Canada Power System Outage Task Force to investigate the blackout. The joint task force, chaired by U.S. Secretary Abraham and Canadian minister of natural resources Herb Dhaliwal, was expected to deliver a final report sometime in 2004 making recommendations to reduce the potential for future outages. Meanwhile, on November 19 the task force issued a 124-page interim report on the immediate causes of the blackout. The report essentially confirmed earlier news stories and filled in some of the details.

The problem began, Abraham said at a news conference, when three high-voltage transmission lines operated by FirstEnergy Corporation, an Ohio utility, short-circuited and went out of commission because they sagged into trees that the utility had failed to trim away from the lines. The loss of the three transmission lines caused too much electricity to pile up on other lines. But a computer-driven alarm system that should have warned operators in FirstEnergy's main control room that the transmission lines failed had also malfunctioned. Because operators were unaware of the transmission failures, they took no action to prevent overloading on other transmission lines. Nor did they warn neighboring utilities of the problem.

Meanwhile the regional energy coordinator, Midwest Independent System Operator (MISO) was having its own problems. Its computer tools for monitoring trouble on the grid were ineffective. MISO was also unable to identify the location and significance of transmission line breaks reported by its monitoring system and so could not properly analyze what steps should be taken to resolve the problem. Human error was also a problem. At one point a technician turned off a key monitoring tool to repair it and then went to lunch forgetting to turn the monitor back on. Another serious transmission problem by another utility earlier in the day may have diverted the attention of some MISO operators. Moreover, MISO and its neighboring coordinator, PJM Interconnection, which coordinated transmission in Pennsylvania, New Jersey, Maryland and parts of other states, did not have joint procedures for responding to problems near their common border. Overall, Abraham said, the task force found that poor communications, human error, lack of accurate information, and inadequate training all prevented either the utility or MISO from seeing the big picture and taking appropriate and timely steps to avoid the blackout.

As a result, electricity built up in the system, creating voltage and frequency fluctuations that pushed their way through the grid. These surges were intensified as more and more transmission lines sensed trouble and automatic circuit-breakers "tripped" to avoid overloading and damage to equipment from surging electricity. The instability was soon too great for the remaining lines to withstand, and they also tripped. Just seven minutes elapsed between the time the cascade began and the time the system collapsed.

A Broader Problem with Deregulation?

Although the joint task force identified the immediate causes of the blackout, many power experts and policy makers said it had not looked at the underlying causes of the problem, which they said stemmed from the deregulation and restructuring of the power industry. As some noted, such a widespread outage probably could not physically have occurred before the 1990s, when federal- and state-regulated utilities typically generated and transmitted power within a relatively confined geographic area. Beginning in 1992, however, electricity generation was deregulated, and dozens of private companies began to generate and sell wholesale power across regions and across the country using transmission lines mostly owned by traditional public utilities. In several areas of the country, utilities belonged to independent operating systems, which typically monitored the supply of power from generating plants and managed the moment-by-moment flow of electricity through the system to its final destination. In the Midwest, the situation was even more complicated because the flow of power was controlled by individual utilities like EnergyFirst rather than by the independent operator MISO.

After a blackout in New York City in 1965, the power industry formed the North American Electric Reliability Council (NERC) to monitor the system. It set standards to ensure that electricity was transmitted safely and reliably, but compliance with the standards was voluntary. Aware that its transmission rules were being pushed to the limits and perhaps beyond by generators and utilities competing for the best wholesale power prices, NERC had long sought power to levy sanctions against companies that did not comply with the standards.

A federal agency, the Federal Energy Regulatory Commission (FERC), proposed a broader approach. It wanted to create a "standard market design" for selling electricity on the wholesale market and to require public utilities to turn over control of transmission lines to regional operators that would coordinate traffic on the lines and enforce reliability rules. Although national lawmakers agreed that something had to be done to improve the reliability of the system, they could not agree on what that should be. Legislators from the Northeast supported the FERC proposal, but legislators from the South and Northwest, where power was plentiful and relatively inexpensive, objected for fear federal regulation would result in higher prices for customers in their states. The final version of the omnibus energy bill, which was still pending at the end of 2003, postponed implementation of the FERC plan until 2007. Absent any other action, that decision meant that little could be done to improve overall coordination of the nation's power grid.

Impasse on Omnibus Energy Bill

The disagreement on electrical power was only one of several controversies that stalled final action on an omnibus energy bill that had been in the works since President Bush entered the White House in 2001. In 2002 negotiations between the Republican-controlled House and the Democratic-controlled Senate on an omnibus energy measure collapsed in conference. When Republicans gained control of the Senate after the 2002 elections, the administration thought the odds of enacting an energy policy bill had improved. The House quickly passed the measure. In March, however, the Senate dealt a blow to the core of the president's energy plan when it voted against opening Alaska's Arctic National Wildlife Refuse to drilling for oil and gas. Unable to resolve a bipartisan deadlock over other elements of the package, the Senate finally agreed to repass the bill it had passed in the previous Congress. Republican leaders closed negotiations between the House- and Senate-passed bills to Democrats only to find that their own forces were far from unified. Intervention by Vice President Dick Cheney and the top Republican leaders in the House and Senate finally settled the disputes. The House passed the conference version on November 18, but Democrats in the Senate, supported by a handful of Republicans, mounted a filibuster. Two votes shy of the sixty needed to cut off the filibuster, Republicans gave up for the year.

Opponents of the measure said it did nothing to address rising energy consumption and that its nearly $26 billion in tax subsidies to the oil, gas, coal, nuclear, and ethanol industries was excessive. Several senators were also distressed by the decision to postpone action on the FERC plan until 2007. But the issue that most galvanized opposition was a liability waiver for producers of methyl tertiary butyl ether, a fuel additive that was designed to make gasoline burn more cleanly but that had been found to contaminate groundwater.

Energy Task Force Inquiry

Almost as controversial as the bill containing the president's national energy policy was the process the administration used to develop that policy early in 2001. A task force, headed by Vice President Cheney, wrote the policy in close consultation with representatives from the energy industry and with minimal input from environmental and consumer groups. The drafting of the policy became a political issue in part because both Bush and Cheney had close ties with the oil industry and received significant financial backing from the energy industry. Opponents also said the policy included much of the industry's long-standing legislative "wish list."

The issue became even more politicized later in 2001 when the administration repeatedly denied requests from the news media and Congress for a list of those whose views had been solicited during work on the report. In 2002 the General Accounting Office (GAO), Congress's watchdog agency, sued the vice president to force him to release the list. That lawsuit was dismissed in December 2002, when a U.S. district judge ruled that the GAO had no legal standing to sue the vice president.

GAO decided not to appeal that ruling in part because a similar suit had been filed by the Sierra Club, an environmental group, and Judicial Watch, a conservative watchdog organization, who argued that the close association of the energy industry lobbyists with the task force might have violated a federal law. A federal district court in 2002 ordered the administration to turn over documents that would help prove or disprove that claim. But while the administration agreed to turn over thousands of pages of documents from federal agencies, it refused to turn over any material involving the Cheney task force and asked the U.S. Court of Appeals for the D.C. Circuit to throw out the lower court's order regarding the vice president's office. That court ruled in July that it did not have jurisdiction in the case, which left the lower court ruling in place. Cheney then appealed the appeals court ruling to the Supreme Court, which on December 15 agreed to review the issue. A decision in the case was expected before the court adjourned in summer 2004.

In withholding the documents, Cheney argued that the separation of powers meant that neither Congress nor the courts had the authority to second-guess the executive branch in its decision-making process. The administration deliberately did not invoke "executive privilege"—a prerogative allowing presidents to shield conversation with their close aides from public scrutiny—because it said the doctrine of separation of powers should provide enough protection.

Following is the text of remarks made by Spencer Abraham, the U.S. secretary of energy, on November 19, 2003, as he released the "Interim Report: Causes of the August 14th Blackout in the United States and Canada," prepared by the U.S.-Canada Power System Outage Task Force, headed by Abraham and Herb Dhaliwal, the Canadian minister of natural resources.

"Remarks by Secretary of Energy Spencer Abraham"

Three months ago today, large sections of the United States and Canada were still recovering from one of the largest power blackouts in our nations' histories.

Since the blackout, a U.S-Canadian Task Force has been working to determine how and why it occurred. Today, we are releasing an Interim Report that marks our progress to date.

August 14, 2003, started out as a fairly normal summer afternoon for most people in areas of Ontario and sections of the Northeast and Midwestern United States. But all that changed when the electricity suddenly went out in city after city across the region.

Communications were disrupted, traffic was snarled, elevators stopped, air-conditioners quit, stores and businesses were forced to close, factories shut down, and hospitals and other vital facilities went to emergency power.

Millions of people were inconvenienced—some were even endangered—and everybody wanted answers about what caused such a widespread power blackout. For the past three months, hundreds of technical experts and energy specialists from both the United States and Canada have been working to find those answers.

The investigation into the August 14th blackout by the U.S.-Canada Task Force has made impressive progress in collecting and analyzing enormous amounts of complex data related to this power outage.

The Task Force investigation is being conducted by three Working Groups that are focused on specific aspects of the outage:

- the Electric System Working Group, which has the immense task of looking at the thousands of working parts of the power grid and its operations to determine exactly what happened on August 14th and why;
- the Nuclear Working Group, which has examined how nuclear power stations performed in the affected areas;
- and the Security Working Group, which is looking at whether any intentional actions were among the causes and whether any security issues were involved.

These three Working Groups have submitted their Interim Report to me and Canadian Minister of Natural Resources Herb Dhaliwal, and the other members of our Task Force. And yesterday, the Task Force voted unanimously to accept the Working Groups' findings to date and move ahead to the next phase of our process.

This Interim Report focuses on the events, actions, failures, and conditions that led to the blackout and allowed it to cascade over such a large region. It also focuses on questions relating to nuclear power operations during the blackout and to the security of the grid itself and the control systems that make it work.

The release of the Interim Report also marks the beginning of Phase Two of the Task Force investigation. During Phase Two, we will hold a series of public forums in the affected areas of both countries. These forums will give the public an opportunity to comment on the Interim Report's findings and present ideas for improving the reliability of our electric infrastructure and preventing future blackouts.

After this process, the Task Force will issue a final report containing our recommendations for improving the electric system and for any appropriate follow-up.

When the Task Force began its work three months ago, we said that we would not speculate on potential causes or make any judgments until we had studied the facts. We also said we would conduct a fair and thorough investigation. And, we said we would follow the facts wherever they lead.

We now have progressed far enough in the investigation that the public should see the results to date.

In addition to exploring the basic questions of what caused the blackout and why it spread, this Interim Report reminds us of the complexity of our power grid and the tremendous responsibility of those who are charged with ensuring its reliability.

One major conclusion of the Interim Report is that this blackout was largely preventable. However, the report also tells us that once the problem grew to a certain magnitude, nothing could have been done to prevent it from cascading out of control.

The electric grid is a complex and sensitive infrastructure that can only work properly when a delicate balance of electric supply and demand is maintained across the system. To accomplish this constant balancing act, hundreds of people are at work 24 hours a day all across North America to keep the grid operating.

Their job is to monitor the state of the power system, to identify and stay ahead of any problems, and to take steps to remedy any situations or conditions that might upset the delicate balance of electric supply and demand.

Grid operators must also deal every day with the unexpected. They watch for mechanical failures in equipment that keeps electricity flowing at the proper voltage. They must know where power is being consumed and at what rate, where it's being produced, and where more can be obtained if it's needed. And they must be prepared to shed load or take other necessary actions to offset any lost generation or transmission capacity. They must monitor the power lines to make sure they are working properly, and that the right amount of power is flowing to keep everything in balance.

And when something goes wrong, their job is to quickly find alternatives and activate backup plans, and take action to compensate for the imbalance, so the grid can still operate in a stable manner.

Electricity transmission experts know that the best way to keep a blackout from spreading over a wide area is to never let it get started. That's what the policies and procedures of organizations like the North American Electric Reliability Council are all about. NERC and its affiliated organizations set the voluntary reliability standards that govern the operations of our power grids.

When the procedures are followed and equipment works properly, the grid's delicate balance is maintained—even when things go wrong. But when something does go wrong—and very important procedures aren't followed and critical transmission monitoring and control equipment fails—the likelihood of major problems intensifies.

And that's what our Electric System Working Group has determined happened on August 14th. And, because of that, a number of relatively small problems combined to became a very big one.

The Electric System Working Group found that the initial events that led to the cascading blackout occurred in Ohio.

- The blackout was initiated when three high-voltage transmission lines operated by FirstEnergy Corporation short-circuited and went out of service when they came into contact with trees that were too close to the lines.
- The report tells us that FirstEnergy's control-room alarm system wasn't working properly—and the control-room operators were unaware it was not working properly—which meant they were also unaware that transmission lines had gone down.
- And because FirstEnergy's monitoring equipment wasn't telling them about the downed lines, the control room operators took no action—such as shedding load—which could have kept the problem from growing, and becoming too large to control.
- Moreover, because FirstEnergy operators did not know their monitoring equipment had failed and were unaware of the growing problems, they did not inform neighboring utilities and reliability coordinators, who also could have helped address the problem.
- The loss of the three lines resulted in too much electricity flowing onto other nearby lines, which caused them to overload.
- While all this was happening, there were also problems at the Midwest Independent System Operator—also called the MISO—which is the entity that coordinates power transmission in the region that includes FirstEnergy.

- The Interim Report found that MISO's system analysis tools weren't performing effectively on the afternoon of August 14th. This prevented MISO from becoming aware of FirstEnergy's problems earlier and taking action.
- The Working Group also found that MISO's reliability coordinators were using outdated data to support real-time monitoring, which hindered them in detecting further problems on the FirstEnergy system and assisting in relief actions.
- Furthermore, the investigators found that MISO also lacked an effective means to identify the location and significance of transmission line breaker operations reported by its monitoring systems. Having that information would have enabled MISO operators to become aware of important line outages much earlier.
- The report shows that MISO and the PJM Interconnection—which is the reliability control area that includes Pennsylvania, Maryland, New Jersey and parts of other states—lacked joint procedures to coordinate their reactions to transmission problems near their common boundary.
- And the report identifies other factors that contributed to the conditions that led to the blackout, including poor communications, human error, mechanical breakdowns, inadequate training, software glitches, and insufficient attention to things ranging from the performance of sophisticated computer modeling systems to simple tree-trimming.

The Electric System Working Group has concluded that at least four reliability standards established by NERC were not observed by FirstEnergy on August 14th, and two were not followed by MISO. These failures helped create a problem of such magnitude as to be insurmountable.

In addition to determining what started the blackout, the Working Group also attempted to determine how the blackout spread so far.

If several major power lines suddenly go out of service in close proximity, like they did in Ohio on August 14th, it can disrupt the area's balance between production and consumption of electricity. It can also cause fluctuations in reactive power or voltage levels, which can likewise destabilize the system. As discussed earlier, when this occurs, grid operators must restore that balance—either by adjusting the output of certain power plants, or taking certain customers temporarily off-line, or by adjusting equipment to stabilize the power flows.

If they don't, as was the case on August 14, the electricity being produced quickly moves on to other lines. But if those other lines are unprepared to receive the additional power, this extra electricity can overload them and shut them down. If that happens, the power keeps moving to other lines, and the problem builds.

If a power imbalance is allowed to reach a certain magnitude, it can spread over a wide area in an uncontrollable cascading blackout—which is what happened on August 14th as transmission line after line went out and generators disconnected from the grid.

The reason the blackout spread where it did has to do with physics and geography—including how many power lines are in an area, how large they are, how close they are to major power plants and load centers, what sort of protective equipment they have, and how much electricity is already moving across them.

We know, though, that the blackout did not reach every part of the Eastern Interconnect, and that some areas were still receiving power. The report outlines three principal factors that—working alone, or, in some cases, together—appear to have allowed this to happen.

- First, because of line trips, some areas were isolated from the portions of the grid experiencing instability, yet they retained sufficient on-line generation or the capacity to import power from other, unaffected, parts of the grid. This enabled them to balance their system and keep the power on.
- Second, other areas were sufficiently distant from the central source of the cascade that they received smaller current and voltage fluctuations than areas closer to the source. Consequently, the instability encountered by relays and other circuit breakers in these areas did not cause additional plants and lines to trip.
- Finally, some areas possess more robust transmission lines and were better able to absorb more of the power and voltage surges. Certain areas also are interconnected by direct current—or D.C.—tie-lines, which kept the alternating-current power disturbance from getting through.

In addition to the findings of the Electric System Working Group, our Nuclear Working Group determined that all the affected nuclear plants in the United States and Canada functioned properly.

- Procedures at the nuclear plants were followed, and the procedures and equipment both worked well on August 14th.
- The nuclear plants all shut down safely when they detected a disturbance.
- And they were restarted safely when the grid was restored.

The Security Working Group has found no evidence to date of terrorist activities or any sort of foul play or sabotage on August 14th.

- No deliberate damage or tampering has been found in any equipment in affected areas of the grid.
- And no computer viruses or any sort of illicit cyber activities have been identified as factors.

While the Interim Report identifies a significant number of problems and shortcomings, it also shows us something very positive.

In the 100-plus years that the grid system has been in operation, massive power outages have occurred only a few times. But smaller outages occur every day. These minor outages are inevitable on such a vast and complex array of interconnected and interrelated machinery that is so vulnerable to internal malfunctions and external forces. Things go wrong. But it is the responsibility of the people who operate the system to keep the small problems from getting bigger.

So despite the potential for a major blackout, it hardly ever happens. That's a credit to the design of the system and the people who run and maintain it. It's a good record, overall. But even one major blackout is too many, and we intend to use what we've learned from our investigation of August 14th to make the system even stronger and even more reliable.

Phase One of our Task Force investigation has given us a wealth of information that will be the basis for Phase Two of the process—formulating recommendations on ways to make our electric system stronger, more efficient, and better able to withstand and adapt to all the things that can hinder its safe and reliable operation.

On behalf of the U.S.-Canada Task Force, I would like to thank the dozens of highly skilled men and women who have spent so much time and effort producing this report today—and who continue to work on this project. I would also like to thank the regulators, utility employees, political leaders and technical experts who have cooperated with this investigation, and helped us make such excellent progress.

And I would like to thank the people of the United States and Canada for their patience and support as we have worked to answer your questions about the blackout—and as we move forward to improve this infrastructure that is so vital to our economy and our way of life.

Source: U.S. Department of Energy. Press Office. "U.S.-Canada Power System Outage Task Force: Remarks by Secretary of Energy Spencer Abraham." November 19, 2003. www.energy.gov/engine/content.do?PUBLIC_ID=14475&BT_CODE=PR_SPEECHES&TT_CODE=PRESSSPEECH (accessed April 21, 2004).

IAEA Resolution on Iran's Nuclear Program

November 26, 2003

INTRODUCTION

Longtime suspicions by the United States and other Western countries that Iran was attempting to develop nuclear weapons appeared to be confirmed in 2003. Under intense international pressure, the Iranian government revealed that during the previous two decades it had secretly built several nuclear facilities. The government claimed the facilities were intended to produce electricity, not weapons. But U.S. officials charged, and most experts agreed, that the secrecy of Iran's program and the nature of the facilities involved indicated that Iran had been on track to develop nuclear weapons within a few years. Israel was the only country in the Middle East to possess nuclear weapons, and Pakistan was the only Islamic country to have them. Libya acknowledged in December that it also had attempted to build nuclear weapons, and it agreed to have its weapons program dismantled. *(Libya, p. 1218)*

By late 2003 Iran's nuclear program was being subjected to intense scrutiny by the International Atomic Energy Agency (IAEA), a unit of the United Nations. IAEA inspectors were combing through records of Iran's purchases from other countries of nuclear material and equipment and were examining a more than a half-dozen facilities throughout Iran, looking for evidence of a program to build weapons.

Along with Iraq and North Korea, Iran was one of three countries labeled by U.S. President George W. Bush in 2002 as part of an "axis of evil." The governments of all three countries were attempting to develop biological, chemical, and nuclear weapons, he said. *(Iraq, pp. 135, 874; North Korea, p. 592; "axis of evil" speech, Historic Documents of 2002, p. 33)*

Background

With help from German firms, Iran began work on a nuclear power program in 1976, leading to reports at the time that it also was intending to develop nuclear weapons. As a signatory to the 1970 Nuclear Nonproliferation

Treaty, Iran had the right to develop nuclear power—so long as the program was subject to IAEA inspections—but it was barred from building nuclear weapons. The country's nuclear program was halted for five years after the 1979 revolution that brought Islamic clerics to power. In 1995 Russia signed a contract to help Iran complete the work that German firms had started two decades earlier on a light-water nuclear reactor at Bushehr, a port city on the Persian Gulf. In addition to finishing the plant, Russia agreed to provide the necessary fuel for it. The United States vigorously protested that deal, arguing that Iran—with its extensive oil resources—did not need nuclear energy and that Tehran was using the Bushehr program as a cover for its nuclear weapons ambitions. Experts said the plant could produce plutonium for use in a small number of nuclear weapons. Washington's objections failed to halt the Iran-Russia deal, however, and the Bushehr reactor was expected to be completed in 2005, at a cost estimated by the U.S. government at $800 million. The plant would have a production capacity of 1,000 megawatts of electricity.

New allegations about Iran's alleged nuclear weapons program emerged in August 2002. An Iranian opposition group, the National Council of Resistance of Iran, said it had learned that the government was building two secret nuclear sites: one, a plant with underground components near the city of Natanz south of Tehran, was intended to produce enriched uranium (a fuel normally used for nuclear weapons but not for electrical power); the other, near the city of Arak in central Iran, was to produce heavy water, which was necessary for the development of plutonium for use in weapons. Both plants were being funded by front companies, the Iranian opposition group said. The group was the political arm of a guerrilla force, the Mujaheddin-e Kalq, which claimed to be fighting to overthrow the Iranian government.

President Mohammad Khatami said on February 9, 2003, that Iran was mining uranium and building facilities—including the plant near Natanz and another one near the city of Isfahan—to process it. But, he insisted, "Iran's efforts in the field of nuclear technology are focused on civilian application and nothing else." The National Council of Resistance of Iran rejected that assertion and offered a new allegation that the plant near Isfahan was intended to produce uranium hexafluoride, a gas that could be converted into enriched uranium for weapons.

IAEA inspectors visited three Iranian nuclear facilities between February 21 and 23: the Bushehr reactor, the plant at Arak, and the facility at Natanz. The inspection of the Natanz plant was especially revealing; it showed that Iran was in the process of building several thousand centrifuges—the devices that were necessary to turn uranium hexafluoride into weapons-grade highly enriched uranium. The IAEA urged Iran to sign a document known as the "Additional Protocol" to the nonproliferation treaty; that protocol would allow the agency to conduct surprise inspections of Iran's nuclear facilities. The government rejected that request at the time but pledged to tell the IAEA in advance about any new nuclear facilities it planned to build.

IAEA director general Mohamed El Baradei reported to his board of governors on June 16 that Iran had "failed to report certain nuclear material and activities," as it was required to do under the nonproliferation treaty. El Baradei called on Iran to sign the Additional Protocol and to allow the IAEA to conduct environmental sampling at the Natanz facility to determine whether uranium was being enriched.

On June 18, as the IAEA Board of Governors was meeting in Vienna to discuss El Baradei's report, President Bush stepped up the level of U.S. rhetoric on the issue. Responding to a reporter's question, Bush said: "The international community must come together to make it very clear to Iran that we will not tolerate the construction of a nuclear weapon. Iran would be dangerous if they have a nuclear weapon."

The Bush administration had hoped to use El Baradei's report as the basis for a formal resolution by the IAEA Board of Governors declaring that Iran was in "noncompliance" with the nonproliferation treaty. That step would have put the issue before the United Nations Security Council, which then could have threatened to impose sanctions unless Iran improved its cooperation on the matter. But the United States lacked support among other nations represented on the IAEA board for such a tough stance. Instead, the board on June 19 adopted a milder statement noting El Baradei's concerns and calling on Iraq to "resolve questions that remain open" and to sign the Additional Protocol.

European Intervention

Countries other than the United States began to take a tougher stance after IAEA inspectors found traces of highly enriched uranium at the Natanz facility during several visits between June and August. The Iranian government said the uranium was on the centrifuges it had purchased from another country—reportedly Pakistan—and had not been produced in Iran. In late August European officials demanded that Iran sign the Additional Protocol as a means of proving that it had no intention of building nuclear weapons. During a visit to Tehran on August 30, Javier Solana, the foreign policy spokesman for the European Union, said Iran needed to sign the protocol to remove international suspicions and should not expect any reward for doing so. "The issue is not for bargaining," he said. "It is a matter of a friend advising another friend, and Iranian authorities are politically mature to hear a friend's advice."

An immediate result of Solana's visit was the unanimous adoption by the IAEA Board of Governors, on September 12, of an explicit warning to Tehran. Adopting a resolution sponsored by Washington, the agency's board set an October 31 deadline for Iran to provide a "full declaration" of the material and components for its uranium enrichment program, to provide "unrestricted access" by IAEA inspectors to its nuclear facilities, and to "resolve all outstanding issues" that had been raised by previous inspections.

The IAEA ultimatum put unprecedented international pressure on Tehran, forcing the country's sharply divided rulers—hard-line clerics and reformist politicians alike—to confront a difficult choice on its nuclear weapons ambitions. Refusing the IAEA's demands almost certainly would have led to increased international pressure and given the Bush administration ammunition for a drive to impose economic sanctions against Iran. Accepting the demands—and fully complying with the subsequent inspections—likely would cause at least a temporary halt to Iran's nuclear weapons program, which had wide public support in the country.

As the deadline approached, El Baradei visited Tehran on October 16 and said Iranian officials promised increased cooperation. More pressure came the next week, when the foreign ministers of Britain, France, and Germany arrived with a demand that Iran comply with the IAEA directives and sign the Additional Protocol authorizing snap inspections by that agency. The European pressure appeared to bear fruit. On October 21, the Iranian government and the European diplomats issued a joint statement saying Iran would sign the Additional Protocol, would "engage in full cooperation" with the IAEA, and would suspend work on its uranium enrichment program. The statement also said that "the Iranian authorities reaffirmed that nuclear weapons have no place in Iran's defense doctrine and that its nuclear program and activities have been exclusively in the peaceful domain." In turn, the European diplomats said Iran "could expect easier access to modern technology and supplies in a number of areas" once it had "fully resolved" international concerns about its nuclear program.

Some representatives of hard-line factions in Tehran denounced the October 21 statement as a forced concession or even a "disgrace" for Iran. But Iran's decision to sign the accord appeared to have resulted from a long and contentious debate among the country's various factions—a debate that produced a general consensus that the country could not afford the sanctions and other costs that would result from continuing to defy the IAEA demands. Western observers noted that the decision to sign the accord appeared to have broad support among key actors on both sides of the country's political and social divide. One important sign was that the accord was negotiated by Hassan Rohani, secretary of the Supreme National Security Council, which was composed of representatives from all factions of government. Rohani was appointed by Iran's ultimate leader, Ayatollah Ali Khamenei, who himself publicly endorsed the agreement on November 3 as a "correct and wise decision."

Two days after signing that agreement, Iran provided the IAEA with a secret "dossier" that, Tehran officials said, proved that it did not have a program to build nuclear weapons. Among other things, the dossier acknowledged that Iran had used centrifuges, at a facility known as the Kalaye Electric Company in Tehran, to enrich uranium secretly imported from China in 1991; had developed another program to enrich uranium using lasers; and had extracted "small quantities" of plutonium from uranium dioxide between 1988 and 1992. All these activities had been kept secret from the IAEA, and experts said all were typical of steps a country would take to develop nuclear weapons rather than electricity.

Iran waited until November 10 to formally declare to the IAEA that it would sign the Additional Protocol and suspend the enrichment of uranium. That declaration came just in time to be included in El Baradei's formal report to the IAEA Board of Governors. That report, made public November 20, detailed a pattern, stretching over at least eighteen years, in which Iran had imported nuclear materials and technology and built major nuclear facilities without notifying the IAEA, as it was required to do under the Nonproliferation Treaty. In general, El Baradei's report painted a picture of a much broader, and more sophisticated, nuclear program in Iran than most Western analysts had believed existed. But the report also stopped short of declaring that Iran actually was trying to develop nuclear weapons.

"Iran's policy of concealment continued until last month, with cooperation being limited and reactive, and information being slow in coming, changing, and contradictory," El Baradei said. "While most of the breaches identified to date have involved limited quantities of nuclear material, they have dealt with the most sensitive aspects of the nuclear fuel cycle, including enrichment [of uranium] and reprocessing [of plutonium]. And although materials would require further processing before being suitable for weapons purposes, the number of failures by Iran to report in a timely manner the material, facilities, and activities in question as it is obliged to do pursuant to its Safeguards Agreement [under the Nonproliferation Treaty] has given rise to serious concerns."

Since its October 21 agreement with the European diplomats, Iran had adopted a policy of "full disclosure" and had promised to give the IAEA a "full picture of all its nuclear activities," El Baradei said. He called that a "welcome development" but noted that the agency still had to verify the new information Iran was providing. While there yet was "no evidence" that Iran's secret activities were related to building weapons, he said, "given Iran's past pattern of concealment, it will take some time before the agency [IAEA] is able to conclude that Iran's nuclear program is exclusively for peaceful purposes."

U.S. officials rejected El Baradei's assertion that there was no evidence of a nuclear weapons program in Iran and said the cumulative evidence in his report pointed exactly in that direction. Iran's representative to the IAEA, Ali Akbar Salehi, said his country's failures to disclose information to the agency had been "minor" and that "the matter is closed" because Tehran now was cooperating fully.

El Baradei did not say where Iran had obtained the nuclear materials and technology for its covert program. In subsequent weeks, however, diplomats from the United States and other countries said China, Pakistan, and Russia had been the main sources: China had provided large quantities of natural uranium, Pakistan had provided the centrifuges and other equipment used to enrich that uranium, and Russia had provided equipment and material that could be diverted to weapons production at the Bushehr reactor.

El Baradei's report set off a contentious debate within the IAEA Board of Governors about the next steps in dealing with Iran's nuclear programs. The board began its deliberations on November 20 and took four days to reach an agreement. The United States demanded a tough statement chastising Iran for its past failures and threatening to take the issue to the UN Security Council. Representatives from most other countries said the IAEA already had denounced Iran's obstructions and should now take a different tack of encouraging Tehran to continue its new policy of cooperating with the inspections. European diplomats said they agreed with El Baradei that condemning Iran at that stage would be counterproductive because Tehran would then walk away from further negotiations and resume its nuclear activities.

Much of the debate within the board reportedly centered around a charge by the U.S. representative, Kenneth Brill, that the IAEA's credibility had been called into question because of El Baradei's statement that there was "no evidence" that Iran was building nuclear weapons. El Baradei rejected Brill's comment and noted that the agency long had used that phrase to describe cases in which it did not have technical proof of a country's intention to build such weapons.

The debate within the IAEA board was resolved November 24 with an agreement on a resolution that deplored Iran's past failures and suggested that Tehran would face some form of punishment unless it cooperated even more than it had. The board adopted the compromise resolution on November 26. In it, the board said it "strongly deplores Iran's past failures" to disclose its nuclear activities, called for a "robust verification system" to ensure that Iran was disclosing its future activities, and warned that "any further serious Iranian failures" would lead the board to consider "all options at its disposal." The latter statement was the reference, demanded by the United States, to the possibility of sending the matter to the UN Security Council.

Diplomats on all sides praised the resolution. Brill, the U.S. representative, said the resolution showed that the IAEA board "will not countenance further evasive actions by Iran." El Baradei reinforced that message, saying that "the board is sending a very serious and ominous message that failure in the future will not be tolerated."

Iran on December 18 formally signed the Additional Protocol giving the IAEA increased powers to inspect the country's nuclear facilities. Among other things, the protocol allowed the agency to inspect any facility with little or no advance warning and required Iran to notify the IAEA of all major developments in its nuclear program, including when it imported uranium or equipment that could be used to make weapons. The Iranian parliament had not ratified the protocol as of the end of 2003.

A surprise revelation on December 19 by the United States and Britain that Libya had agreed to dismantle its nuclear weapons program was expected to lead to further revelations about Iran's program, as well. News reports late in the year indicated that both Iran and Libya had imported key components for their nuclear programs from Pakistan. In its February inspections of the plant at Natanz, Iran, the IAEA had found 160 working centrifuges that reportedly were similar to those used by Pakistan when it produced its first nuclear bombs in 1998. Pakistan's centrifuges were based on designs reportedly stolen in the 1970s from a Dutch firm by Abdul Qadeer Kahn, known as the father of Pakistan's bomb. The Pakistani government acknowledged on December 25 that some of its nuclear scientists provided technology to Iran but denied that the government had authorized the action.

Iran's Missiles

One of the reasons for international concern about Iran's apparent plans to build nuclear weapons was the country's parallel program to develop medium-range missiles. The Central Intelligence Agency and independent weapons experts had said for years that Iran had one of the most advanced missile development programs in the Middle East outside of Israel. Using designs and technology reportedly acquired from North Korea, Iran in 2003 had two short-range missiles, the Shehab-1 and Shehab-2 (*Shehab* means "meteor" in Farsi). Iran also had flight-tested its Shehab-3 missile, which Western experts said was capable of carrying a one-ton warhead (such as a small nuclear bomb) about 800 miles.

There were conflicting reports during 2003 about Iran's plans for a longer-range missile, the Shehab-4. Early in the year some Western weapons analysts said Iran appeared to be working on such a missile, able to carry a small nuclear bomb about 1,200 miles—putting Israel within range. On November 6, however, Iranian news services quoted the defense ministry as saying that Iran had no plans to manufacture the missile because of "certain expressions in society." That announcement came just about two weeks after Iran signed the agreement with European diplomats to reveal details of its nuclear programs.

Political Developments in Iran

Internationally, the dispute over Iran's nuclear programs overshadowed continuing domestic political tensions. The reformist government, headed by President Khatami, kept up efforts begun in previous years to shake off the domination by hard-line Islamist clerics—but Khatami lost nearly every important battle of the year. The political conflict was almost certain to worsen in 2004, when elections were due for a new national parliament.

Khatami had been elected in 1997, and reelected in 2001, on a platform of modernizing Iran and easing Islamic restrictions on everyday life. Reformist parties allied with Khatami took control of parliament in 2001. Khatami's grip on real power was severely constrained, however, because all government decisions were subject to a veto by the conservative Guardian Council, which reported to Ayatollah Khamenei. *(Background, Historic Documents of 2001, p. 793)*

Late in 2002 Khatami called on parliament to adopt a series of bills giving the elected government increased power, at the expense of the clerics. One by one, the legislature approved key elements of Khatami's reforms early in 2003—and, one by one, the Guardian Council rejected them. The first confrontation came on a bill, approved April 8 by the parliament, that was intended to allow Khatami to overturn actions by courts and other agencies dominated by the hard-line clerics. The Guardian Council vetoed that bill on May 9. Later in May, 127 members of parliament signed an open letter to Ayatollah Khamenei denouncing the Guardian Council and calling for a referendum to affirm the rule of democracy. Conservative authorities immediately suppressed the letter. On June 3 the Guardian Council vetoed another element of President Khatami's reform plan—a bill allowing him to call a referendum on reforms, including eliminating the Guardian Council's authority to screen political candidates.

A series of student protests swept through Tehran in mid-June, resulting in the largest demonstrations in Iran since similar protests in 1999. The protests started on June 10, apparently in reaction to a government plan to privatize universities. Within days thousands of students and other demonstrators were clogging the streets of Tehran and several other large cities, demanding reforms and denouncing the hard-line clerics. Some demonstrators also denounced Khatami and other reformist politicians, saying they had failed to follow through on their promises to improve the economy and reduce the power of the clerics. An estimated 4,000 people were arrested during the protests, which lasted about a week but had no visible impact on the actions of the conservative authorities.

On August 12 Khatami acknowledged that his reform program had stalled. "Lately, speaking for me has become difficult because I feel many of the ideas and programs I sincerely offered, and the people voted for, have not materialized," he was quoted as saying. The very next day brought yet more evidence of Khatami's inability to overcome the opposition of conservative powers. The parliament approved three reform bills, all of which were vetoed within hours by the Guardian Council. Two of the bills would have adopted United Nations conventions eliminating discrimination against women and torture; the third bill was another attempt to eliminate the

Guardian Council's power to determine which candidates could run for public office. Some international attention to Iran's domestic political struggle resulted from the awarding of the 2003 Nobel Peace Prize to Shirin Ebadi, a female lawyer who had fought for human rights and political reform in Iran. *(Nobel prize, p. 1129)*

By year's end most analysts inside and outside Iran were declaring Khatami's reform movement dead, or nearly so, because of his inability to enact legislation and a resulting drop in his personal popularity. Khatami repeatedly threatened to resign the presidency if he did not get his way, and then repeatedly backed down when the Guardian Council and other agents of clerical power rejected his reforms. "The reform process has been emasculated," Davoud Hermidas Bavand, a law professor at the Supreme National Defense University in Tehran told the *Christian Science Monitor.* "The mood in Iran now is angry, but above all pessimistic."

Earthquake in Iran

A major earthquake hit central Iran on December 26, killing at least 30,000 people. The trembler was centered in the city of Bam, 610 miles southeast of Tehran. Relief workers said about three-fourths of the buildings in the city of 80,000 people were destroyed, including a famous fort that was more than 2,000 years old. The twelve-second earthquake hit at 5:28 A.M. local time, catching most people in bed. Most of the city's one- or two-story buildings, constructed of brick, clay tile, or concrete block, crumbled under the force of the earthquake and several aftershocks and trapped thousands of people in the rubble. It was the worst earthquake in the country since one in 1990 killed about 50,000 people.

Two dozen countries, including the United States, sent relief workers and supplies. Twelve U.S. humanitarian workers reached Bam on December 30; it was the largest official group of Americans in Iran since January 1981, when four dozen diplomats and other hostages were released from the U.S. embassy in Tehran after fourteen months of confinement. *(Iran hostages, Historic Documents of 1981, p. 137)*

Following is the text of "Implementation of the NPT Safeguards Agreement in the Islamic Republic of Iran," the resolution adopted November 26, 2003, by the International Atomic Energy Agency Board of Governors in Vienna, Austria, concerning nuclear programs in Iran.

"Implementation of the NPT Safeguards Agreement in Iran"

The Board of Governors,

(a) *Recalling* the Resolution adopted by the Board on 12 September 2003. in which the Board, inter alia:
  - expressed concern over failures by the Islamic Republic of Iran to report material, facilities and activities that Iran is obliged to report pursuant to its Safeguards Agreement;
  - decided it was essential and urgent, in order to ensure IAEA verification of non-diversion of nuclear material, that Iran remedy all failures identified by the Agency and cooperate fully with the Agency by taking all necessary actions by the end of October 2003;
  - requested Iran to work with the Secretariat to promptly and unconditionally sign, ratify and fully implement the Additional Protocol, and, as a confidence-building measure, to act thenceforth in accordance with the Additional Protocol; and
  - called on Iran to suspend all further uranium enrichment-related activities, including the further introduction of nuclear material into Natanz, and any reprocessing activities,

(b) *Welcoming* the Agreed Statement between the Foreign Ministers of France, Germany and the United Kingdom and the Secretary of the Iranian Supreme National Security Council issued in Tehran on 21 October,

(c) *Noting with appreciation* the Director General's report of 10 November 2003, on the implementation of safeguards in Iran,

(d) *Commending* the Director General and the Secretariat for their professional and impartial efforts to implement the Safeguards Agreement with Iran and to resolve all outstanding safeguards issues in Iran, in pursuance of the Agency's mandate and of the implementation, inter alia, of the Resolution adopted by the Board on 12 September 2003,

(e) *Acknowledging* that Vice-President Aghazadeh of the Islamic Republic of Iran has reaffirmed his country's decision to provide a full picture of its nuclear activities and has also reaffirmed his country's decision to implement a policy of cooperation and full transparency,

(f) *Noting with deep concern* that Iran has failed in a number of instances over an extended period of time to meet its obligations under its Safeguards Agreement with respect to the reporting of nuclear material, and its processing and use, as well as the declaration of facilities where such material has been processed and stored, as set out in paragraph 48 of the Director General's report,

(g) *Noting* in particular, *with the gravest concern,* that Iran enriched uranium and separated plutonium in undeclared facilities, in the absence of IAEA safeguards,

(h) *Noting* also, *with equal concern,* that there has been in the past a pattern of concealment resulting in breaches of safeguard obligations and that the new information disclosed by Iran and reported by the Director General includes much more that is contradictory to information previously provided by Iran,

(i) *Noting* that the Director General, in his opening statement, indicated that Iran has begun cooperating more actively with the IAEA and has given assurances that it is committed to a policy of full disclosure,

(j) *Recognising* that, in addition to the corrective actions already taken, Iran has undertaken to present all nuclear material for Agency verification during its forthcoming inspections,

(k) *Emphasising* that, in order to restore confidence, Iranian cooperation and transparency will need to be complete and sustained so that the Agency can resolve all outstanding issues and, over time, provide and maintain the assurances required by Member States,

(l) *Noting with satisfaction* that Iran has indicated that it is prepared to sign the Additional Protocol, and that, pending its entry into force, Iran will act in accordance with the provisions of that Protocol,

(m) *Noting* that the Director General, in his opening statement, reported that Iran has decided to suspend enrichment-related and reprocessing activities,

(n) *Stressing* that the voluntary suspension by Iran of all its uranium enrichment-related activities and reprocessing activities remains of key importance to rebuilding international confidence,

(o) *Recognising* the inalienable right of States to the development and practical application of atomic energy for peaceful purposes, including the production of electric power, with due consideration for the needs of developing countries,

(p) *Stressing* the need for effective safeguards in order to prevent the use of nuclear material for prohibited purposes in contravention of safeguards agreements, and *underlining* the vital importance of effective safeguards for facilitating cooperation in the field of peaceful uses of nuclear energy,

1. *Welcomes* Iran's offer of active cooperation and openness and its positive response to the demands of the Board in the resolution adopted by Governors on 12 September 2003 and *underlines* that, in proceeding, the Board considers it essential that the declarations that have now been made by Iran amount to the correct, complete and final picture of Iran's past and present nuclear programme, to be verified by the Agency;

2. *Strongly deplores* Iran's past failures and breaches of its obligation to comply with the provisions of its Safeguards Agreement, as reported by the Director General; and *urges* Iran to adhere strictly to its obligations under its Safeguards Agreement in both letter and spirit;

3. *Notes* the statement by the Director General that Iran has taken the specific actions deemed essential and urgent and requested of it

in paragraph 4 of the Resolution adopted by the Board on 12 September 2003;

4. *Requests* the Director General to take all steps necessary to confirm that the information provided by Iran on its past and present nuclear activities is correct and complete as well as to resolve such issues as remain outstanding;

5. *Endorses* the view of the Director General that, to achieve this, the Agency must have a particularly robust verification system in place: an Additional Protocol, coupled with a policy of full transparency and openness on the part of Iran, is indispensable;

6. *Reiterates* that the urgent, full and close co-operation with the Agency of all third countries is essential in the clarification of out-standing questions concerning Iran's nuclear programme;

7. *Calls on* Iran to undertake and complete the taking of all necessary corrective measures on an urgent basis, to sustain full cooperation with the Agency in implementing Iran's commitment to full disclosure and unrestricted access, and thus to provide the transparency and openness that are indispensable for the Agency to complete the considerable work necessary to provide and maintain the assurances required by Member States;

8. *Decides* that, should any further serious Iranian failures come to light, the Board of Governors would meet immediately to consider, in the light of the circumstances and of advice from the Director General, all options at its disposal, in accordance with the IAEA Statute and Iran's Safeguards Agreement;

9. *Notes with satisfaction* the decision of Iran to conclude an Additional Protocol to its Safeguards Agreement, and *re-emphasises* the importance of Iran moving swiftly to ratification and also of Iran acting as if the Protocol were in force in the interim, including by making all declarations required within the required timeframe;

10. *Welcomes* Iran's decision voluntarily to suspend all enrichment-related and reprocessing activities and *requests* Iran to adhere to it, in a complete and verifiable manner; and also *endorses* the Director General's acceptance of Iran's invitation to verify implementation of that decision and report thereon;

11. *Requests* the Director General to submit a comprehensive report on the implementation of this resolution by mid-February 2004, for consideration by the March Board of Governors, or to report earlier if appropriate; and

12. *Decides* to remain seized of the matter.

Source: International Atomic Energy Agency. Board of Governors. *Implementation of the NPT Safeguards Agreement in the Islamic Republic of Iran.* GOV/2003/81. November 26, 2003. www.iaea.org/Publications/Documents/Board/2003/gov2003-81.pdf (accessed December 2, 2003).

December

2003 HISTORIC DOCUMENTS

Acting President of Georgia on Political Change

December 1, 2003

INTRODUCTION

Eduard Shevardnadze—once one of the most respected figures in international affairs—found himself pushed in disgrace from the world stage in 2003. Shevardnadze was overthrown as president of Georgia on November 23, just three weeks after he attempted to rig parliamentary elections. He was succeeded as acting president by the parliament's speaker, Nino Burdzhanadze, who herself stepped aside so fellow opposition leader Mikhail Saakashvili could present a united front in a rushed presidential election held in January 2004. Saakashvili won that election in a landslide and promised to tackle corruption and work to restore the sagging economy of the former Soviet republic in the Caucuses region.

The overthrow of Shevardnadze was one of the most dramatic pro-democracy developments anywhere in the former Soviet Union since the communist empire collapsed at the end of 1991. It was all the more remarkable that Shevardnadze should be the victim of his own failure to make necessary reforms. As the last Soviet foreign minister, Shevardnadze had worked closely with reformer Mikhail Gorbachev, the last Soviet leader. Together, the two men had eased the Soviet grip on Eastern Europe and allowed the Berlin Wall to fall in 1989, a momentous event that brought a rapid end to communism in the region. They also promoted mild democratic reforms that exposed the decay of Soviet society and led to the collapse of the Soviet Union. Shevardnadze's return to his Georgian homeland in 1992 raised hopes that he would be able to use his world fame and connections to restore order and prosperity to a once-proud country, with just 5 million people, that had been harshly repressed in Soviet times and then torn by separatist conflicts. The hopes were soon dashed, however, as Shevardnadze failed to revive the economy or to bring peace to the warring regions. Corruption became the hallmark of his government as favored friends took over state-owned businesses. By 2003 his domestic popularity had plummeted and most Georgians were looking forward to his planned retirement in two years.

To many observers, the ouster of Shevardnadze was strikingly similar to the peaceful revolution almost exactly three years earlier in Yugoslavia. In both cases, a president who was widely seen as having lost touch with public opinion attempted to rig an election, only to be overthrown in mass protests that were carefully organized by opposition groups that had received some support and encouragement from the United States. *(Milosevic ouster, Historic Documents of 2000, p. 833)*

Internationally, the year's events in Georgia were of more than historical interest. Georgia was located at the heart of the long-troubled Caucuses region, which had gained new prominence in recent years because of the development of the vast oil resources of the Caspian Sea. Moreover, both Russia and the United States claimed that Islamic terrorists had taken over a small corner of eastern Georgia known as the Pankisi Valley. Washington poured large quantities of military aid into Georgia to combat the guerrillas, unnerving Russia, which had historically viewed Georgia as within its sphere of influence.

Velvet, or Rose, Revolution

The parliamentary election scheduled for November was widely expected to be one of the most important political events in Georgia's post-Soviet history. The election would demonstrate how far Georgia had come, or not come, in responding to international criticism about the mechanics of its democracy. It also was considered a run-up to the planned 2005 election to choose Shevardnadze's successor.

Events leading up to the election were not encouraging. Georgia had never held an election that was deemed credible by international observers, and it was widely assumed that the 2003 election would fall into that pattern unless Shevardnadze could be pressed into making reforms. European and U.S. diplomats intervened in hopes of winning approval for procedures that would at least approximate a fair election. Among those involved in the international diplomatic push was James A. Baker III, who had been U.S. secretary of state during Shevardnadze's last years as Soviet foreign minister. The Bush administration asked Baker to go to Tbilisi to appeal to his old friend to allow an honest election. During his visit in early July, Baker made public a set of recommendations for free elections, such as the posting of voter registration lists two months ahead of time. Shevardnadze accepted Baker's plan, but then did not act on it. Other high-profile U.S. representatives arrived in Tbilisi in October with the same call for an honest election, among them Sen. John McCain, R-Ariz.; John M. Shalikashvili, a former chairman of the U.S. Joint Chiefs of Staff (who was of Georgian heritage); and Strobe Talbott, a deputy secretary of state during the Clinton administration. Talbott later said Shevardnadze pretended to accept the advice but then ignored it.

Opposition leaders and representatives of Shevardnadze's governing party haggled over election procedures right up to election day, November 2. In a December 3 report, the International Crisis Group—an international affairs think tank based in Brussels—said the pre-election wrangling demonstrated that Georgia's political system was "more like a medieval kingdom than a modern European democracy."

The voting was chaotic, marred by numerous irregularities. Some polling stations did not open, voter lists were incomplete, the names of opposition candidates did not appear on some ballots, and soldiers and policemen were observed voting at multiple polling places. In an apparent effort to intimidate the opposition, riot police were deployed in towns considered to be opposition strongholds. The day after the election international observers from the Organization for Security and Cooperation in Europe (OSCE) said the voting irregularities "contributed to a climate of uncertainty and mistrust, and raised questions about the willingness and capacity of the Georgian governmental and parliamentary authorities to conduct a credible election process."

Election rules called for the results to be announced within four days after the voting, but opposition leaders immediately declared themselves the victors, citing exit polls. The opposition mounted a mass protest in front of Tbilisi city hall on November 4. Saakashvili—a former justice minister who had broken with Shevardnadze in 2001 and formed an opposition party called the National Movement—said the demonstrations would continue until the government recognized what he said was a victory by the opposition. Another protest was held November 6 when the government produced partial returns indicating a lead for parties that supported Shevardnadze. The president's response to the protests was to forge an alliance with Aslan Abashidze, the leader of the Adzharia region, which long had been seeking autonomy from the central government. Abashidze then met with Russian officials to seek Russia's support for Shevardnadze. Shevardnadze met with a group of protesters outside parliament on November 9 but rejected their demands that he resign. He said he could not "allow people who would destroy and devastate everything to come to power."

By then it was clear that the opposition's strategy was to continue the protests as long as possible to demonstrate Shevardnadze's lack of popular support. He responded with increasingly harsh language, announcing on television November 14 that the "civil confrontation may develop into civil war." On that day about 20,000 demonstrators surrounded his office building, chanting "Go away." The first and only pro-government demonstration was held November 17. Many of the 10,000-some demonstrators were bussed to the capital from Adzharia—apparently in keeping with the deal Shevardnadze had struck with that region's leader.

The first sign that the president's support might be crumbling came November 19, when several senior officials resigned, including the head of the state broadcasting service, an old friend. Shevardnadze's chief of security services also acknowledged that the election was marred by fraud, and he called for new voting; Shevardnadze fired him.

The government finally produced official election results on November 20. The results put the bloc supporting Shevardnadze in the lead, with 38 of the 150 seats in parliament. Other parties likely to support the government won enough seats to ensure its control. Opposition leaders called the results a sham.

Shevardnadze summoned the new parliament into session on November 22. Tens of thousands of protesters massed around the parliament building. As Shevardnadze began addressing the parliament, demonstrators swarmed into the building, with Saakashvili in the lead. They carried red roses—a symbol, they said, of the birth of democracy. The protesters forced out pro-government parliamentarians, and Shevardnadze was escorted by his bodyguards out a side door, declaring "I will not resign."

Burdzhanadze, who had been speaker of the previous parliament, declared that she was acting president and said new elections would be held within forty-five days. Saakashvili had this warning for Shevardnadze and the security services: "The Georgian people are here. We will trample and run over this regime tomorrow. They had better flee right now." Shevardnadze responded by declaring a state of emergency, which he said was necessary to head off a "civil war." The security forces did not move against the protestors, however—a sign, one opposition leader said, that the military officers had "switched sides."

The key event at this point was the arrival in Tbilisi of Russian foreign minister Igor Ivanov, who immediately went into meetings, first with Shevardnadze and then with opposition leaders. He then brought the two sides together for a final session on November 23. According to witnesses, Shevardnadze said he would resign for the good of the country, would not flee into exile, and would offer whatever help he could to the new government. "It wasn't the gesture of an angry person, but it was the gesture of a president who realized he had failed, failed very badly," said Zurb Zhvania, one of the opposition leaders who was present. The seventy-five-year-old Shevardnadze later claimed to be relieved. "To tell you the truth, for me personally it's happiness, because I need time to catch up and write something while I am still alive." Shevardnadze rejected an offer of asylum in Germany, saying he wanted to remain in Georgia. Saakashvili said he would personally guarantee the safety of the former president.

The announcement of Shevardnadze's resignation touched off celebrations on the streets of Tbilisi. Some demonstrators called the ousting of the president the "velvet revolution," echoing the term used to describe the sudden collapse of communism in Czechoslovakia in 1990. Others called it the "rose revolution," in honor of the flowers that Saakashvili and other antigovernment leaders carried as they swept into the parliament. "There was no blood, no killing, everything was peaceful," remarked Nona Ushuilidze, a university teacher as she watched the celebrations. By coincidence, Shevardnadze fell from power on a national holiday, St. George's Day, honoring the legendary knight who slew a dragon to rescue a maiden, and whose name was adopted by the republic.

An Interim Government

All three of the young opposition leaders who had led the drive for Shevardnadze's ouster had once been his protégés. Burdzhanadze was a thirty-nine-year-old lawyer who had served in parliament as a member of the president's party, then broke with him and established a party with her own name: the Burdzhanadze-Democratic Party. As the speaker of the former parliament—which technically had not yet been replaced—she had a legitimate claim as acting president. Zhvania had been groomed as Shevardnadze's successor, serving as parliament speaker during the latter 1990s. But he also split from the president and, in 2003, sided with Burdzhanadze. He became minister of state, the equivalent of prime minister, in the post-Shevardnadze government.

Most of the attention centered on Saakashvili, by far the most dynamic of the opposition figures. Just thirty-five years old, he had attended George Washington University in Washington, D.C., received a law degree from Columbia University, and briefly worked for a New York City law firm. Shortly after his return to Georgia in 1995, he joined Shevardnadze's party and, in 2000, became justice minister—a post he used to wage an aggressive campaign against the country's endemic corruption. He lasted just about a year before Shevardnadze fired him (in 2001) and denounced elements of his anticorruption crusade. Saakashvili formed his own political party and emerged as the most assertive of a handful of key opposition politicians. Never afraid to speak his mind, Saakashvili was prone to wild claims and hot rhetoric—a tendency that got him attention as an opposition leader but, critics said, had gotten him in trouble as justice minister and could do so again once he returned to public office.

Burdzhanadze on November 24 pledged to hold new elections, and she brought back into office the old parliament that she had headed. She also repealed the state of emergency Shevardnadze had announced two days earlier in his desperate bid to hold onto power. Parliament the next day set presidential elections for January 4, and on November 26 Burdzhanadze said she would support Saakashvili as the unified opposition candidate. Saakashvili handily won the election, with 96 percent of the vote. Even Shevardnadze said he voted for the one-time protégé, who had led the demonstrations that forced him from power. New parliamentary elections were scheduled for March 2004.

Once he took office, Saakashvili would confront a Georgia in deep trouble, with very little prospect for immediate improvement. The corruption he had denounced, first as justice minister and then as an opposition leader, in many ways was the glue that held much of the country's economy together. According to news accounts, nearly every major element of the economy was controlled by, or at least influenced by, shady businessmen who were associated with Shevardnadze's government or with friends and family members of the former president. Shevardnadze had sold several major state-owned businesses, some to personal associates and some to foreign investors. A U.S. firm, American Energy Systems, bought Georgia's natural gas supplier only to discover that its equipment was dilapidated and few customers bothered to pay their bills. After losing millions of dollars, the company pulled out and sold its interests to Russian firms.

With its rich agricultural lands, Georgia once was known as the "fruit basket" of the Soviet Union, and its economy had been among the most prosperous of the fifteen Soviet republics. The collapse of the Soviet Union and subsequent economic turmoil in Russia meant the closing of Russian markets and, more ominously, the cut-off of subsidized gas and oil from Russia's huge energy industries. Economic output in Georgia plummeted in the early 1990s—by about 70 percent, according to one estimate—and crept back only slowly during the rest of the decade. The official unemployment rate was above 30 percent, but even those who had jobs were ill-paid; the average monthly salary in 2003 was about $40. School teachers, policemen, soldiers, and most other public employees regularly went weeks or even months without being paid. Burdzhanadze said in December that the country's treasury was down to "zero" and she could not say when the next paychecks would be issued.

Many observers said another challenge facing Saakashvili would be to keep intact the opposition coalition. He and his colleagues had been united mainly in their youth and their desire for change. Maintaining unity and public support, in the face of difficult decisions that would have to be made, was likely to prove more daunting than facing down the former president.

U.S. Interests and Role in Georgia

Despite Washington's long-standing support for Shevardnadze—and contrasting cool ties between Shevardnadze and Moscow—Russian officials were quick to blame the United States for the ouster of the Georgian leader. "I think there are enough facts proving that what happened in those days wasn't spontaneous, it didn't arise suddenly," Russian foreign minister Ivanov said December 6. "Of course, there were preparations and the U.S. ambassador was involved, as Shevardnadze himself admitted." This was a reference to a claim by the ousted president that U.S. ambassador Richard Miles had encouraged the opposition. Shevardnadze was among many who insisted that Miles represented a link between the events in Tbilisi and the earlier ouster of Milosevic. Miles had been posted to the U.S. embassy in Belgrade until a year before Milosevic fell.

There was no question that Washington was involved in both the run-up to the election and the events afterward. The visits of Baker and other U.S. representatives were clear signs that the Bush administration was concerned about the potential for political chaos. The United States provided $2.4 million in various programs to help organize the election, some of which went to opposition parties. Ambassador Miles had been a busy man during the climactic days of November 22 and 23, meeting frequently with both Shevardnadze and opposition leaders. Secretary of State Colin Powell also called Shevardnadze on both days. Powell did not urge Shevardnadze to resign but did encourage him "to make decisions that would lead Georgia forward in a peaceful manner within the constitution of Georgia," State Department spokesman Richard Boucher said later.

Defense Secretary Donald H. Rumsfeld on December 5 became the first high-ranking U.S. official to visit Georgia after the ouster of Shevardnadze. He said his visit was intended to "underscore America's very strong support for stability and security and the territorial integrity here in Georgia."

The United States had multiple interests in Georgia, the foremost of which was maintaining a degree of stability in a region that might become increasingly important as a source of oil. U.S. diplomacy had been a key factor in winning agreement in 2000 on the route for a pipeline that would carry oil from the Caspian Sea waters of Azerbaijan, through Georgia, and then to the Mediterranean coast of Turkey. British Petroleum and Norway's Statoil were the major investors in the $3 billion Baku-Tbilisi-Ceyhan pipeline, which was to be finished in 2005. The pipeline would bring Georgia millions of dollars annually in transit fees, making it one of the country's few sources of hard earnings.

Washington also saw Georgia as an important ally in the war against terrorism, particularly after fighters for the al Qaeda network were said to have taken up residence in the Pankisi Valley. The Bush administration sent U.S. troops to train Georgian security forces in counterinsurgency techniques. At the same time, Shevardnadze refused to allow the Russian military into the Pankisi region to battle rebels from the breakaway province of Chechnya, who also were said to be operating there. The heightened U.S. involvement in Georgia naturally annoyed Moscow, which considered the republic as within its sphere of influence. *(Chechnya conflict, p. 245)*

The Separatist Regions

In addition to economic decline and embedded corruption, Georgia faced real threats to its existence as a unified state. Two regions had rebelled against Tbilisi in the early 1990s and had essentially gained de facto independence; a third was controlled by a leader who refused to recognize the new government. All three regions had much closer links to Russia than to Georgia.

The two rebel regions were Abkhazia in the northwest and South Ossetia in north central Georgia. Abkhazia declared itself independent of Georgia shortly after the collapse of the Soviet Union. A bloody civil war there during the early 1990s killed as many as 10,000 people and was a major factor leading to Georgia's decline. Its leader, Raul Khadzhimba, refused to recognize any formal links with Georgia, and his government was heavily dependent on Russia, which maintained a military base there. South Ossetia, as the name implied, was the southern portion of a region in the Caucuses mountains known as Ossetia. During the Soviet era the northern portion was made part of Russia, and the southern portion was put into Georgia; the majority of people in both regions were Russian. After the collapse of the Soviet Union, the leaders in South Ossetia refused to recognize Georgian rule.

The third restive region was Adzharia, along the Black Sea in southwest Georgia. Abashidze, a former Soviet official who took control of the region in 1991, had long called Adzharia "autonomous" but had never formally declared independence. He threw his support behind Shevardnadze before and after the November 2 elections and then refused to acknowledge the new government. Like Abkhazia, Adzharia was home to a Russian military base, and a sizable percentage of its population considered themselves to be Russians, not Georgians.

The leaders of all three regions met with Russian officials in Moscow in late November and early December, raising concerns in Tbilisi that Russia was attempting to annex them. In a December 1 speech in the Netherlands, Burdzhanadze denounced Russian actions that she said were "undermining Georgian sovereignty and territorial integrity" and putting the two countries in a "confrontational position." Burdzhanadze's speech, to a meeting of the OSCE, was the first major international statement by the new government. She used it to assure European officials that Georgia was committed to democracy.

The tensions between Georgia and Russia calmed at least temporarily in late December, when Burdzhanadze met in Moscow with Russian president Vladimir Putin. Burdzhanadze called the two days of talks, on December 24–25, a "breakthrough," and a Russian official said steps had been taken to eliminate "negative developments" between the two countries.

Following are excerpts from a speech delivered December 1, 2003, by Nino Burdzhanadze, the acting president of Georgia, to the eleventh meeting of the ministerial council of the Organization of Security and Cooperation in Europe, held in Maastricht, the Netherlands.

"Statement of H.E. Nino Burjanadze to the Ministerial Council of the OSCE"

It is my pleasure to address the distinguished representatives of the OSCE [Organization of Security and Cooperation in Europe] participant and partner states, as well as the invited guests from different International and Non-Governmental Organizations.

Let me start with a few comments on events which have been taking place in Georgia since the November 2nd parliamentary elections and have been widely recognized as a truly democratic revolution. These events prove that Georgian nation has irreversibly chosen the way of democratic development. People, who—for the sake of stability—had patiently endured economic problems, hardship, corruption, lack of electricity, delay in salaries and pensions, have voiced their protest immediately as soon as democracy was endangered, national dignity was injured and the basic constitutional right—the right to vote was disregarded.

With the November revolution Georgian people obtained the right to live in a democratic state. Most importantly, this right was obtained absolutely peacefully, without violence and blood, without breaking the constitutional order, through the nationwide protests. November events have proved that Georgian nation deserves to be a part of the new, wider, democratic Europe.

Large-scale peaceful protests eventually resulted in the resignation of President Shevardnadze—a well-known political figure who has seriously contributed to the turn of the century international politics. He made a courageous decision on November 23rd as he stepped down to avoid interruption of constitutional processes and further escalation of the tension.

In this respect I would like to express our appreciation to all those who facilitated the dialogue between the political leaders and, therefore, significantly contributed to the peaceful resolution of this political crisis. We are especially grateful to the Russian Federation and personally Minister Igor Ivanov, the OSCE Chairman-in-Office and the United States Administration, who closely monitored the situation and supported the non-violent changes in the leadership of the country.

In the light of the recent political developments in my country, I have to openly declare that the foreign policy priorities, of which Georgia's full integration in European and Euro-Atlantic structures is the most important, remain unchanged. Georgia also remains committed to all international obligations and agreements, including the OSCE Istanbul decisions on foreign military bases in Georgian territory. Full and unconditional implementation of these decisions, followed by the eventual withdrawal of all Russian military bases from Georgia is a serious contribution to the lasting peace in South Caucasus.

Together with this, we firmly believe that one of our top priorities is an improvement of the relationships with neighboring states—in this regard let me specifically underline the importance of Russia for the stability of Georgia and entire South Caucasus, Russian intervention in recent political crisis in Georgia, which I've already mentioned, became a pleasant exception in a recent list of events and proved that in case of mutual willingness, relations between Georgia and Russia can be and must be based on respect and good will—we are ready to step out of a box of historical prejudices and start our relations from a clean paper. At the same time, this is supposed, and even should be a two-way street and our Russian colleagues should also understand that actions undermining Georgian sovereignty and territorial integrity, similar to those we witnessed during the last week in Moscow, ruin all positive messages and put us in an unavoidable confrontational position.

Georgia will continue close and fruitful cooperation with its strategic partner nations, remaining a faithful member of the anti-terrorist alliance. We will not deviate from the course of democratic development, fighting against corruption, economic reforms and continue to show full respect to humanistic values and principles of the International law. At the same time let me underline that our policy will be more dynamic, vigorous and consistent in achieving the above-mentioned strategic goals.

Taking into account the specific geo-political location of Georgia, being on the cross-roads between Europe and Asia and, thus, representing a pivotal element in the entire system of the East-West energy corridor, also given Georgia's crucial role in providing peace and security in the Caucasus region, we fully realize our responsibility for our domestic situation. I mean the quickest possible return to full institutional normalcy within the framework of the Constitution. As you may already know the Supreme Court of Georgia has annulled the results of the November 2nd parliamentary elections. The new presidential elections have already been scheduled for January 4, 2004; parliamentary elections will be held as soon as we are technically ready to organize them in a proper way. We will do our best to keep both the elections in full compliance with OSCE principles and international standards. We regard these immediate tasks as key priorities of Georgia at present, despite the persistence of the horrific economic and financial problems, unresolved conflicts, and serious drawbacks in the protection of human rights in the conflict zones.

Since I have touched upon the issue of the conflicts let me remind you that there are two conflict zones in my country awaiting for more than a decade their due political solution and seriously threatening the territorial integrity of my country as well as the stability of the whole region. I do not intend to go into details, but I find it necessary to underscore the key negative aspect common to all efforts at conflict resolution. This is the lack of political negotiations on the issues of status, that the separatist leaderships deliberately ignore. In this regard we strongly believe that all projects for economic rehabilitation and humanitarian assistance ought to be viewed as facilitators in the achievement of the central goal. Regrettably the process of the conflict settlement in Georgia has long been at a standstill. Though that with concerted common efforts of all countries and international organizations involved we shall be able to cope with the current stalemate.

Mr. Chairman,

I wish to express my sincere thanks for inviting me to this remarkable forum of the OSCE, the organization I would like to thank for its active role and in advancing democratic developments in my country. Almost in every part of Georgia we can see the OSCE presence. We boast one of the biggest missions in the OSCE area, which is actively involved in conflict resolution and preventive diplomacy, in the issues of the Human Rights, Democratization, Rule of Law, as well as in the monitoring of the Georgian Russian State boarder, thus significantly contributing to the security and stability in the region.

Besides, I would like to use this opportunity and address all distinguished representatives of the countries present, that Georgia, standing at the turning point of its history, relies on your active assistance and support to overcome with dignity the existing difficulties in due time and prove that the country is firmly moving along the path of democracy. I am fully aware how much the international community has done to support democratic developments in Georgia. It is deeply regrettable that these efforts had been ignored. However, Georgian people rehabilitated itself through the nationwide Peaceful protests and now, as never before, deserves encouragement. I can assure you on our part that the current Georgian leadership fully acknowledges its responsibility not only to the people of Georgia, but also to the international community. We stand ready to fulfill all democratic commitments so that my country to become an esteemed member of the European Family of nations, a reliable partner in the formation of the 21st century European Security architecture.

In closing, on behalf of Georgians let me express our deep gratitude to all nations represented here and their governments for backing and understanding us at this most significant moment of Georgia's history.

Thank you for your attention.

Source: Georgia. Embassy of Georgia [in the United States]. "Statement of the Acting President of Georgia H.E. Nino Burjanadze at the 11th Meeting of the Ministerial Council of the OSCE in Maastricht." Maastricht, Netherlands. December 1, 2003. www.georgiaemb.org/Print.asp?id=244 (accessed January 24, 2004).

United Nations on the al Qaeda Terrorist Network

December 2, 2003

INTRODUCTION

Terrorism by extreme Islamist groups continued to plague much of the world during 2003, most importantly in the Middle East, North Africa, and parts of Asia. The greatest number of terrorist attacks occurred in Iraq—all of them after the United States and some of its allies invaded the country and toppled the government of Saddam Hussein. Terrorists did not carry out any attacks in the United States during the year, but U.S. officials said some attacks had been planned and foiled, and they warned that the United States remained vulnerable to terrorism despite massive efforts against it.

The world's most feared terrorist group—the al Qaeda network headed by Saudi Arabian exile Osama bin Laden—almost certainly sponsored or promoted some of the year's bombings and other forms of terrorism. The United States blamed al Qaeda for the September 11, 2001, terrorist attacks that destroyed the World Trade Center towers in New York and damaged the Pentagon. However, groups that were only loosely affiliated with al Qaeda, or that may only have been inspired by it, were said to have carried out most of the attacks during 2003. Bin Laden himself remained at large, along with some of his top aides, presumably in a remote mountainous area of Pakistan. *(Background, Historic Documents of 2001, pp. 614, 802; Historic Documents of 2002, p. 1014)*

During the year U.S. officials offered two fundamentally different—and seemingly conflicting—assessments of the status of al Qaeda. President George W. Bush, his chief aides, and senior intelligence officers frequently claimed that al Qaeda had been "weakened," "hobbled," or even "dismantled" since late 2001 because of the loss of its bases in Afghanistan, the capture of several top leaders, and the rounding up of hundreds of supporters around the world. In congressional testimony and other public statements, administration officials proudly recited the damage that had been done to al Qaeda's infrastructure since September 11 and said dozens of potential attacks had been disrupted.

Administration officials also warned that al Qaeda remained a significant threat worldwide, and they urged Americans and U.S. allies not to let up their guard against terrorism. CIA director George Tenet told congressional committees on February 11 that "it will take years of determined effort to unravel this and other terrorist networks and stamp them out."

Most terrorism experts outside the government said both of those assessments were correct: al Qaeda undoubtedly had been damaged by the U.S.-led war against terrorism, but it remained dangerous—and possibly even more dangerous to the interests of the United States and its allies than before September 11. As evidence for the latter contention, analysts said al Qaeda had decentralized its operations into cells in more than ninety countries, making the network more difficult for law enforcement agencies to target.

Some experts said al Qaeda was becoming more important as a symbol for Islamist extremists than as an organization with an identifiable command structure. Among the experts sharing that view were the members of a United Nations committee that monitored al Qaeda and similar groups. In a report published December 2, the committee said al Qaeda "has to be seen as an ideology, to which many young Muslims are being drawn." In that case, the committee and other experts said, the arrests of al Qaeda operatives—and even the potential capture or death of bin Laden—might have only a marginal impact on the overall level of Islamist terrorism.

Moreover, the U.S.-led war in Iraq, and the subsequent military occupation of that country, gave al Qaeda a new recruiting incentive for the young, disaffected men in Islamic lands believed that the United States was intent on world domination. Mohammed Salah, an Egyptian journalist who wrote about al Qaeda for the pan-Arab newspaper *Al-Hayat,* told the Associated Press early in April that the 2001 war in Afghanistan had temporarily disrupted al Qaeda's ability to attract new volunteers. "But now it is much easier," he said. "The war in Iraq has made every angry Muslim man with nothing to do want to join anything that's against America." Bin Laden himself attempted to encourage an anti-U.S. reaction, saying in an audiotape aired by Arab television networks on February 11 that Washington's planned war in Iraq was part of a goal "to divide and conquer the Middle East [that] is not just a passing fancy." *(Iraq war, pp. 40, 135, 933)*

Major Terrorist Attacks in 2003

Terrorist organizations carried out a greater number of significant attacks during 2003 than in any other recent year, killing hundreds of people—most of them in the Middle East and Asia. None of the attacks was as spectacular as the September 11, 2001, airplane hijackings that killed nearly 3,000 people in the United States. But, cumulatively, the bombings and other attacks in

2003 demonstrated that al Qaeda and other terrorist organizations were still functioning. Moreover, most of the attacks—outside of those in Iraq—were against non-U.S. targets, indicating that Washington and its Middle East policies were not the only targets of extremist groups.

The year's major terrorist attacks included:

- Two waves of bombings in Saudi Arabia on May 12 and November 9, which killed a total of fifty-three people and forced the kingdom to confront its vulnerability to attacks by terrorists associated with al Qaeda. *(Saudi bombings, p. 227)*
- A series of bombings in Casablanca, Morocco, on May 17, killing a total of forty-one people, including twelve suicide bombers. The targets included a luxury hotel, a Spanish club, a Jewish community center and cemetery, and a street adjacent to the Belgian consulate.
- Dozens of bombings and shootings in Iraq following the U.S.-led war there. In addition to the military forces of the United States and its allies, important targets included the headquarters of the United Nations mission in Baghdad (which was bombed twice), the Jordanian embassy, one of the nation's key Shi'ite religious figures and many of his followers, the offices of the International Committee of the Red Cross, numerous Iraqi police units, and ordinary Iraqi citizens. *(Postwar Iraq, p. 933)*
- A series of bombings that appeared to be related to the ongoing conflict in Chechnya, a province of Russia. Bombings in Chechnya and Russia proper, including in Moscow, killed several dozen civilians and Russian military personnel. Russian authorities blamed all the bombings on Islamist rebels who sought independence for Chechnya. *(Russia, p. 245)*
- The August 5 bombing of the J.W. Marriott Hotel in Jakarta, Indonesia, killing twelve people. Indonesian authorities attributed the attack to Jemaah Islamiyah, a Southeast Asian terrorist network that some experts said was an arm of al Qaeda. Several days later a statement attributed to al Qaeda claimed responsibility for the attack, saying it had been ordered by the network's number-two official, Ayman al-Zawahiri. On August 14 the White House announced the arrest of Riduan Isamuddin, better known as Hambali, who was said to be the link between Jemaah Islamiyah and al Qaeda. He had been wanted in connection with a series of terrorist attacks in Southeast Asia, including the bombing in 2002 of a nightclub in Bali, Indonesia, that killed 202 people. *(Bali bombing, Historic Documents of 2002, p. 702)*
- A series of bombings in Istanbul, Turkey, in November. On November 18 a suicide bomber crashed a pickup truck laden with explosives into the gate of the British consulate in Istanbul, killing sixteen people, including consul-general Roger Short; another bomber attacked the

local headquarters of HSBC, a major British bank, killing a dozen people and wounding several hundred others. Two days later two synagogues were bombed, killing twenty-three people. Some international experts said the attacks likely were carried out by local affiliates of al Qaeda, rather than the network itself, but Turkish officials in mid-December said they had collected evidence suggesting that al Qaeda was responsible. The coordinated nature of the attacks was a hallmark of previous al Qaeda operations.

- Two attempted assassination attempts against Pakistan president Pervez Musharraf in December. In both cases, bombs were placed along roadsides and timed to go off as Musharraf's motorcade passed by; both attempts failed. *(Pakistan attacks, p. 209)*
- More than a dozen major suicide bombings and other attacks against Israeli civilian and military targets, both inside Israel and in the Palestinian territories occupied by Israel. Nearly all the attacks were carried out by three Palestinian extremist groups: Hamas (the Islamic Resistance Movement), Islamic Jihad, and the Al-Aqsa Martyr's Brigade, an offshoot of the Fatah movement of Palestinian leader Yasir Arafat. Israel responded with targeted assassinations of Palestinian militants and broad military operations in Palestinian civilian areas. *(Middle East violence, p. 1200)*
- Numerous terrorist attacks in Afghanistan, where the United Nations and a U.S.-led peacekeeping force were attempting to shore up a new, multiparty government that took office following the U.S. invasion in late 2001. The single bloodiest attack was the August 13 bombing of a bus in southwest Afghanistan, in which fifteen passengers died. Officials blamed the bombing on remnants from the former Taliban regime. Eleven international aid workers also were killed during the year. *(Afghanistan, p. 1089)*

Some analysts noted that the expanded U.S. presence in the Middle East offered al Qaeda and like-minded groups a host of new targets. "The deployment of American military forces from Djibouti to the border of Iran may now be seen by al Qaeda strategists as presenting the movement with a 'target-rich environment' alongside multiple new operational opportunities and, as such, simply the next phase in a long struggle," RAND Corporation terrorism expert Bruce Hoffman wrote in a study published by the think tank on May 5.

Even as it was building up its overall military presence in the Middle East, the United States during 2003 withdrew nearly all its forces from Saudi Arabia. The United States had built several large military bases and stationed thousands of air force personnel in that country in the years following the 1991 Persian Gulf War. In all his proclamations, bin Laden had cited the U.S. presence in the kingdom—the birthplace of Islam—as his major grievance against the United States. Defense Secretary Donald H. Rumsfeld said in April that all but a few hundred of U.S. service personnel would be relocated from Saudi Arabia to other facilities in East Africa and the Middle East, including a new air base that had been built in Qatar. Although Rumsfeld insisted the decision was based on military needs, the U.S. withdrawal was widely viewed in the Middle East as an implicit acknowledgement by Washington of the power of bin Laden's argument. Many commentators in the region said bin Laden could brag that terrorism had achieved his foremost goal.

Bin Laden's Whereabouts

At least from a public relations point of view, the single greatest failure of the U.S.-led war against terrorism, as of 2003, was bin Laden's ability to elude his pursuers. The United States, with some cooperation from Pakistan, launched two major operations during the year to capture bin Laden, who was presumed to be hiding in a mountainous region along the Afghanistan-Pakistan border. U.S. officials said these operations resulted in the capture of several dozen fighters for al Qaeda and the former Taliban regime of Afghanistan, but bin Laden was not among them. Also eluding capture as of the end of 2003 was bin Laden's alleged number two, al-Zawahiri, an Egyptian doctor who founded the Islamic Jihad organization in that country and then merged it with al Qaeda in 1998. Likewise, U.S. manhunts had failed to locate Mullah Mohammad Omar, the leader of the former Taliban regime.

Several audiotapes and statements attributed to bin Laden surfaced during the year. All these statements encouraged Muslims around the world to engage in *jihad,* or holy war, against the United States, Britain, other Western powers, and the governments of Islamic countries that bin Laden called "lackeys" of the West. The al Jazeera television channel on February 11 broadcast an audiotape, said to be the voice of bin Laden, urging Muslims to help Iraq fight invasion by the United States. "We stress the importance of martyrdom operations against the enemy, these attacks that have scared Americans and Israelis like never before," bin Laden was reported to have said. On September 10 al Jazeera broadcast a videotape showing bin Laden and al-Zawahiri together, along with voiceovers reportedly by each of them. Another audiotape, broadcast October 18, also contained what the network said was bin Laden's voice, calling for renewed attacks against the United States and all countries that cooperated with its occupation of Iraq.

U.S. officials and Western experts on terrorism said it was unclear how much direct control bin Laden retained over the al Qaeda network. They noted that, because of intense surveillance by U.S. intelligence agencies, he no longer used radio or satellite telephones to communicate with his subordinates and instead appeared to rely on handwritten notes delivered by trusted couriers. Some experts said bin Laden's personal involvement was no longer essential because he had established a decentralized network capable of generating new fighters to replace those who died in suicide attacks or were killed or captured by law enforcement agencies. "The movement has metastasized well beyond the organizational boundaries of al Qaeda," Steven Simon, a White House terrorism expert during the 1990s told the Associated Press in late December. "Innumerable local groups now subscribe to the bin Laden agenda."

Attacking the al Qaeda Network

In a television broadcast commemorating the second anniversary of the September 11 attacks, President Bush said the United States had made "great progress" against terrorism. "We have exposed terrorist front groups, seized terrorist [bank] accounts, taken new measures to protect our homeland, and uncovered sleeper cells inside the United States," he said. In particular, Bush said nearly two-thirds of the top al Qaeda leadership had been captured or killed.

By far the most important strike against al Qaeda during the year was the March 1 arrest in Pakistan of Khalid Shaykh Mohammed, who U.S. officials said had been the mastermind of the September 11, 2001, attacks against the United States. Also known as Muktar Balucci, Mohammed was a Kuwait-born citizen of Pakistan who had received an engineering degree from a college in North Carolina in 1986. U.S. authorities began pursuing him in the mid-1990s because of his alleged role in several terrorism plots, including the 1993 bombing of a World Trade Center building in New York. His nephew, Ramzi Yousef, was convicted on charges related to that bombing. After the September 11 attacks U.S. officials described Mohammed as al Qaeda's senior operations official and said he was involved in several other attacks, including the bombing in April 2002 of a synagogue in Tunisia that killed nearly two dozen tourists.

Pakistani authorities captured Mohammed in an early morning raid of a house in Rawalpindi. Also captured in the raid was Mustafa Ahmed Hawsawi, a Saudi native who U.S. officials had said was the paymaster for the nineteen men who hijacked the four airplanes used in the September 11 attacks. FBI director Robert S. Mueller III said Hawsawi had opened a bank account in Dubai that was used by the hijackers. Pakistan turned both men over to the United States, which held and interrogated them for the rest of the year at a secret location. U.S. officials later said documents found in Mohammed's possession provided vital information about the internal operations of al Qaeda. However, there were conflicting reports about Mohammed's role in al Qaeda at the time of his capture. U.S. officials at first said the documents appeared to show that Mohammed had met with bin Laden in Pakistan less than a month before he was captured. Other terrorism experts expressed doubt about that claim and said there was evidence that Mohammed had not been in contact with bin Laden for about one year and that he might not have been as key a figure in al Qaeda as U.S. officials had said.

The capture of Mohammed and Hawsawi was a major public relations coup for the U.S.-led war against al Qaeda, but it also focused new attention on apparent links between al Qaeda and an Islamic political party that was gaining strength in Pakistan—Jamaat-e Islami. Jamaat was the largest of five fundamentalist parties in a coalition, known as the United Front, that made major gains in Pakistan's October 2002 elections. The coalition took control of the Northwest Frontier province and held the third-largest bloc of seats in the national parliament. The two men were captured at the home of a local official of the Jamaat Party, and a relative of that official was arrested along with them.

On March 4 the Justice Department announced the arrest of Mohammed al Hasan al-Moayad, a Yemeni cleric who was alleged to have helped finance al Qaeda. He was arrested in Frankfurt, Germany, on January 10, under a U.S. warrant. U.S. officials charged that al-Mouyad had raised about $20 million to help finance al Qaeda activities.

The United States and Iran engaged in a diplomatic war of words in August over Tehran's announcement that it had arrested several senior al Qaeda officials, including Saif al-Adel, described as one of bin Laden's top aides. The United States had said he played a leading role in organizing the August 1998 bombings of the U.S. embassies in Kenya and Tanzania. There were conflicting reports about whether Iran also was holding Abu Musab al-Zarqawi, a Jordanian who U.S. officials said had at least informal connections to al Qaeda. Secretary of State Colin Powell had told the UN Security Council in February that Zarqawi's presence in Iraq, during 2002, constituted evidence of a link between al Qaeda and the regime of Saddam Hussein. Bush administration officials demanded that Iran turn al-Adel and Zarqawi over to the United States for prosecution, but Tehran refused. *(Embassy bombings, Historic Documents of 1998, p. 555)*

Disrupting Terrorism Plots

One aspect of the international war against terrorism took place almost entirely outside of public view: the disruption by intelligence and law enforcement agencies of terrorism plots before they could be carried out. Bush administration officials said the United States and its allies had become increasingly successful in learning about potential terrorist plots and using that information to disrupt the plans. It was difficult to judge the merit of those claims, however, because officials revealed details for only a few of them.

Among the examples cited by the Bush administration was the reported disruption early in 2003 of a plan by al Qaeda to crash a small airplane, loaded with explosives, into the U.S. consulate in Karachi, Pakistan. That plot was discovered after the arrest in Karachi of six suspected al Qaeda members, including Waleed bin Attash, who U.S. officials had said was involved in planning both the September 11 attacks and the October 2000 bombing of the USS *Cole* in Yemen. The alleged plot against the consulate appeared to be similar to a reported al Qaeda plan, foiled in 2002, to fly a small plane carrying explosives into a U.S. warship in the Persian Gulf. The discovery of the 2003 plot led the Department of Homeland Security to warn airport and law enforcement personnel in the United States to be alert for a possible domestic attack using small planes. Another case cited by administration was the disruption in 2002, by the United States and Morocco, of al Qaeda's plans to attack U.S. and British warships in the strait of Gibraltar. *(Cole bombing, Historic Documents of 2001, p. 3)*

A series of warnings and international police actions at the end of 2003 might also have disrupted possible attacks by al Qaeda or related organizations. In late December officials in the United States, Britain, and other countries that terrorists affiliated with al Qaeda were determined to carry out new attacks. The warnings prompted the U.S. Department of Homeland Security to raise the terrorist threat level to "Code Orange" (the second-highest level) on December 21. Air France cancelled flights from Paris to Los Angeles on December 24 and 25 in response to U.S. intelligence warnings, and other flights between the United States and Britain and Mexico were cancelled in the four-day period around New Years Eve. U.S. officials also suspended oil shipments from the port of Valdez, Alaska, between December 30 and January 1 because of concerns about possible terrorism. The extent of the actual terrorist threats that prompted these warnings was unclear at year's end.

Terrorism Financing

In the two-plus years after the September 11 attacks, the United States, other countries, and the United Nations made some progress in cutting off funding for al Qaeda and related terrorist organizations. The Bush administration said it had seized more than $130 million in bank accounts and other assets from al Qaeda, for example. However, the December 2 report by the UN's terrorism monitoring committee said these organizations still had ready access to money because many countries were failing to take adequate steps against their funding sources.

Estimates of al Qaeda's potential financial resources ranged from several hundred million dollars to several billion dollars, depending on who was doing the estimating and what was included. It was clear in 2003 that the organization still had plenty of money to sustain its operations for many years to come. This was in part because al Qaeda's type of terrorism was extremely cost-effective. U.S. officials had estimated, for example, that the total cost of the September 11 attacks was less than $500,000. A member of a wealthy Saudi Arabian family, bin Laden was said to be worth several hundred million dollars. He also had built several profitable businesses in Sudan during the early 1990s.

In its report, the UN committee documented financial support for al Qaeda and related organizations by several Islamic charities and businesses. Among the most important charities were two based in Saudi Arabia: the International Islamic Relief Organization and the Al-Haramain Islamic Foundation. Both groups operated in dozens of countries and had financed numerous al Qaeda operations, the UN panel said. Under U.S. pressure, the Saudi Arabian government in 2003 ordered Al-Haramain to suspend operations outside of Saudi Arabia. Despite this order, the UN panel said, the group was "still active" in at least several other countries and had recently opened a new Islamic school near Jakarta.

The UN committee also traced some of the activities of two businessmen, Youssef Nada and Idris Nasreddin, who had been widely reported by law enforcement agencies and news organizations as major financiers for al Qaeda. Nada, an Egyptian, and Nasreddin, an Eritrean, had been headquartered at an Italian enclave near Lugano, Switzerland, and had extensive business interests in numerous countries, including the Bahamas, Italy, Liechtenstein, Switzerland, and Turkey. The United Nations had listed them as terrorist financiers, ordered their assets frozen, and imposed a ban on international travel by them. Even so, the men continued to run their businesses, the committee said, although their current whereabouts were unknown. The ability of these men—and others like them—to operate both legally and illegally, and to continue generating support for al Qaeda, demonstrated "continuing serious weaknesses regarding the control of business activities and assets other than bank accounts," the UN panel said. The panel called for greater international cooperation against terrorist-related groups and businesses, including an increased willingness by countries to give the UN information about them.

Following are excerpts from Second Report of the Monitoring Group, Pursuant to Resolution 1363 (2001) and as Extended by Resolutions 1390 (2002) and 1455 (2003) on Sanctions Against al-Qaida, the Taliban and Their Associates and Associated Entities, *made public December 2, 2003, by the group established by the United Nations Security Council to examine the implementation of sanctions the council had imposed against the al Qaeda terrorist network, the Taliban regime of Afghanistan (which was deposed in 2001), and individuals and entities associated with them.*

"Second Report of the Group Monitoring Sanctions Against al-Qaida and Their Associates"

Summary

The Security Council, on 17 January 2003, acting under Chapter VII of the Charter of the United Nations, adopted resolution 1455 (2003), in which it decided to improve the implementation of measures imposed under its resolutions 1267 (1999), 1333 (2000) and 1390 (2002) against Osama bin Laden, Al-Qaida, the Taliban and individuals or entities associated with them. Those measures include a freeze of financial and economic assets, a travel ban, and an arms embargo. They are to be applied by all States against individuals and entities designated by the Al-Qaida and Taliban sanctions Committee.

A Monitoring Group of experts was reappointed in accordance with paragraph 8 of resolution 1455 (2003), and instructed to monitor and report on the implementation of the measures by States and to follow up on leads relating to any incomplete implementation. This is the second report of the Monitoring Group. It supplements information provided in the Group's previous report and provides a more in-depth analysis of specific problems associated with the implementation. The report also contains an assessment of reports submitted by States pursuant to paragraph 6 of resolution 1455 (2003). Some 83 such reports have been submitted so far. . . .

Al-Qaida ideology has continued to spread, raising the spectre of further terrorist attacks and further threats to international peace and security. A synopsis of the terrorist attacks, allegedly linked to Al-Qaida network, carried out since the Group's last report is included in this report. More and more of these attacks are being perpetrated by suicide bombers. No region has been spared from such terrorist activities.

Iraq has become a fertile ground for Al-Qaida. It is readily accessible to Al-Qaida followers anxious to take up the battle against the coalition forces and other "Crusaders". The attack on the United Nations headquarters in Baghdad on 19 August 2003, followed a month later by one against the headquarters of the International Committee of the Red Cross, also in Baghdad, were yet further signs of the appalling lengths to which the terrorists are prepared to go in their indiscriminate war.

Progress is being made, worldwide, by law enforcement agencies, and military and security forces, in dealing with Al-Qaida and in hunting down and neutralizing its operatives and supporters. In South-East Asia, the arrest in Thailand of one of the principal leaders of the Jemaah Islamiyah, Nurjaman Riduan Isamuddin, also known as Hambali, and the death of Fathur al-Ghozi following a shoot-out with security forces in the southern Philippines highlight the ongoing successes in this global operation.

The Group has reiterated in each of its reports the importance the United Nations consolidated list [a list of individuals and groups that supported al Qaeda, the Taliban, and related terrorist organizations] plays in the implementation of the measures provided for in the resolutions. While the list has grown in numbers, it has not kept pace with the actions taken, or the increased intelligence and other information available, concerning Al-Qaida, the Taliban and associated individuals and entities. The current list contains a total of 371 names of individuals and entities. This represents only a small subset of individuals and entities associated with Al-Qaida network. It reflects a continuing reluctance on the part of many States to provide such names to the Al-Qaida and Taliban sanctions Committee. In many cases States have preferred to communicate such information only through bilateral channels. The Group continues to believe that further action is needed to encourage all States to provide the Committee with the names of all the individuals and entities known by them to be associated with Al-Qaida network. More effort is also required to ensure that border control authorities in each State are provided with, and apply, the most recently updated version of the list.

Important progress has been made towards cutting off Al-Qaida financing. A large part of its funds have been located and frozen, and many of the key financial managers have been incarcerated. The international financial community is devoting significantly increased resources to this effort. Yet many Al-Qaida sources of funding have not been uncovered, and Al-Qaida continues to receive funds it needs from charities, deep-pocket donors, and business and criminal activities, including the drug trade. Extensive use is still being made of alternative remittance systems, and Al-Qaida has shifted much of its financial activity to areas in Africa, the Middle East and South-East Asia where the authorities lack the resources or the resolve to closely regulate such activity. The Counter-Terrorism Action Group sponsored by the Group of Eight is beginning to address this issue.

Controlling charities used, or abused, for purposes that support terrorism is proving extremely difficult. The close association of such charities with both religious and humanitarian relief purposes has made government regulation and oversight very sensitive. One important example of the use by Al-Qaida of charities and the difficulty of dealing therewith, touches directly on the activities of one of the largest Islamic charities, the International Islamic Relief Organization. Most of that organization's activities relate to religious, educational, social and humanitarian programmes, but it and some of its constituent organizations have also been used to assist in Al-Qaida financing. Concern has also surfaced regarding the activities of the Al-Haramain Islamic Foundation. The Somalia and Bosnia branches of Al-Haramain have already been designated for their Al-Qaida funding activities. Questions have now also arisen concerning the activities of other Al-Haramain branches.

Even when charities have been designated, it has proved difficult to shut them down. Al-Haramain offices continue to function in Somalia. Other designated charities, including the Global Relief Foundation, the Rabita Trust, Al-Rashid Trust and Lajnat al-Daawa al-Islamiya continue in operation. A number of the charities implicated in Al-Qaida funding are also engaged in business ventures to supplement their revenues. Little is yet known concerning those assets and activities.

The use of shell companies and offshore trusts to hide the identity of individuals or entities engaged in the financing of terrorism is also a difficult problem. Such arrangements serve to mask potential terrorist-financing activities, and make it difficult to locate and deal with terrorist-related financial assets other than bank accounts. The issue is complicated further by a reluctance on the part of States to freeze tangible assets such as business or property. The Group has looked closely at the activities of two designated individuals, Youssef Nada and Idris Nasreddin, in this respect, and concluded that shell companies, offshore trusts and other beneficial ownership arrangements have allowed them to circumvent the full application of the measures set out in the resolutions.

While great importance has been put on limiting the mobility of individuals linked to Al-Qaida, there have been no reports yet from any State that a designated individual has sought entry into or has been stopped from entering or transiting their country. Almost a third of the countries that have submitted the required "90-day" reports to the Committee have indicated that they have not yet incorporated all the names on the United Nations consolidated list in their "national stop lists". Only about a half of the States report that they regularly transmit updated lists to their border services. The continuing lack of identifiers has also been sited as a major obstacle to the inclusion of names in national stop lists.

The Group is also concerned that the whereabouts of many designated individuals remain unknown. Of the 272 designated individuals, only a few have been accounted for. This calls for more proactive measures by States to enforce the objectives of the travel ban. The arms embargo is another area of concern. The Group continues to encounter serious difficulties in monitoring and reporting on the implementation of the embargo. Countries are reluctant to provide information concerning their seizures of illegal weapons and explosives believed destined for Al-Qaida, the Taliban and their associates.

During this reporting period the Group visited several countries in the Middle East. Many were aware that weapons were crossing their borders, but indicated that they had great difficulties in controlling such illegal traffic. Both Saudi Arabia and Yemen, for example, confirmed that weapons and explosives used in the recent terrorist attacks in Saudi Arabia had been smuggled across their 1,100-mile common border. Yemeni officials informed the Group that most of the illegal weapons entering the country were coming from Somalia. The Group is also concerned about reports indicating that weapons are being smuggled out of Iraq, including shoulder-fired missiles.

The international community must remain alert also to the increasing availability of man-portable air-defence systems to non-State actors. The Group considers it important that measures be initiated by the United Nations to harmonize the various controls necessary to ensure that such missiles cannot be acquired by Al-Qaida or its associates.

The scope of the Security Council resolutions and their incomplete implementation appear unable to stop Al-Qaida, the Taliban and their associates from obtaining whatever weapons and explosives they need, where and whenever they need them, to effect attacks, many of which have devastating results.

The risk of Al-Qaida members acquiring and using weapons of mass destruction also continues to grow. They have already taken the decision to use chemical and biological weapons in their forthcoming attacks. The only restraint they are facing is the technical complexity of operating them properly and effectively. Their possible use of a dirty bomb is also of great concern.

Following its intensive review of the implementation of the measures provided for in the resolutions, the Group has concluded that further steps are required to strengthen the measures and their application. **Without a tougher and more comprehensive resolution—a resolution which obligates States to take the mandated measures—the role played by the United Nations in this important battle risks becoming marginalized. . . .**

VII. Findings and Conclusions

157. The submission by States, as at 30 October 2003, of a total of 83 reports, six and half months after the requested submission date, is disappointing.

158. Eighty-three States account for less than half of the membership of the United Nations! When considered against the fact some

4,000 members, supporters and associates of Al-Qaida have been arrested in no less than 102 countries, there is a serious question about the extent to which States are looking to the United Nations resolution in this regard.

159. Of the 108 States that have not yet submitted a report, the Group has a particular interest in 25 of them, because of information that would suggest that Al-Qaida or their associates may, in some way or another, be active within their borders.

160. The Group found that, in a number of countries it visited during the reporting period, few, if any, officials were aware of the measures called for in resolution 1455 (2003) and its provisions regarding the submission of names, and the listing and delisting procedures associated with the list.

161. Many States that were aware of the listing requirements relied heavily on the exemption clause in paragraphs 4 and 5 of the resolution, referring to the possibility of compromising investigations or enforcement actions, as the reason for not listing individuals or entities. This appeared to the Group to be more in the nature of an excuse than an actual impediment to providing such names.

162. Recent visits by the Group to certain States indicated that there appeared to be little, or no, knowledge regarding the work of the Committee or the Monitoring Group and the availability of information about the Committee and its United Nations web site. This included a lack of knowledge concerning the posting of the list. This has significantly impeded and delayed the application of updated lists.

163. The Group also observed a serious lack of coordination between a number of the Permanent Missions to the United Nations in New York and the capitals regarding the work of the Committee and the Monitoring Group. Unfortunately this lack of coordination often jeopardizes the implementation of the relevant Security Council resolutions.

164. The Group has concluded, from its research, review of reports, visits and discussions with government officials and experts that, despite the significant progress that has been made in the United Nations effort to combat Al-Qaida, the Taliban and their associates, some serious problems and systemic weaknesses remain with regard to the resolutions.

165. Many of the sources of funding for Al-Qaida have not yet been uncovered or blocked. Al-Qaida continues to have access to sufficient funds to recruit, train and mount operations.

166. Since 17 January 2002, when resolution 1390 (2002) was adopted, few if any assets of designated individuals or entities

have reportedly been frozen, despite the increase in the numbers of both on the list.

167. Those assets that have been frozen are limited to bank accounts. A serious problem exists, which appears to be widespread, namely, that States either lack the authority or are unwilling to freeze or seize tangible assets such as businesses or property.

168. Although a number of entities, be they extremist groups, charities or businesses, have been designated on the list, only a very small number of the individuals responsible for leading or managing the operations of those entities have themselves been designated, leaving them free to set up new entities and/or continue with activities in breach of the resolution.

169. Charitable foundations continue to provide a conduit for funding the activities of Al-Qaida network and its many associates around the world.

170. To date there have been no reports submitted to the Committee of any designated individuals being stopped from entering or transiting as a result of their names being on the list, and no reports of arms being seized en route to any designated individuals or entities. Together with the fact that few additional assets have reportedly been frozen in connection with resolutions 1390 (2002) or 1455 (2003), this would clearly indicate that the resolutions in their present form are much less effective than was intended.

171. There is a reluctance on the part of many States to recognize the presence of Al-Qaida or elements of the network within their territory. There is also a reluctance to propose individuals and entities to the Committee to be listed. A lack of awareness of the resolutions and the obligation they impose further complicates the implementation of the measures. This contributes to the continuing resilience of Al-Qaida.

172. This being said, the Group has noted the many successes, around the world, of law enforcement agencies and security forces in the capture or killing of key individuals connected with Al-Qaida network and the foiling of possible attacks by elements of the network before they can be mounted. For the most part, however, these would appear to be the result of bilateral cooperation rather than the measures called for in the resolutions.

173. **The Group considers that, without a much tougher and more comprehensive resolution, in which the Security Council requests States to take the mandated measures and obliges them to cooperate fully with the Committee and its Monitoring Group, little or no progress will be achieved with regard to the sanctions regime imposed on Osama bin Laden, Al-Qaida, the Taliban and associated individuals and entities under the auspices of the Security Council.**

VIII. Recommendations

174. The following recommendations are based on the findings and conclusions of the Group and are intended to complement, not supersede or replace, but in some cases reinforce, the recommendations made in its four previous reports to the Committee under resolutions 1390 (2002) and 1455 (2003).

Consolidated list

175. States should be further encouraged to become proactive in proposing the names of individuals and entities known to be associated with Al-Qaida network, including persons who have been recruited and trained by Al-Qaida and its associated groups for terrorist purposes. The Group considers this an important adjunct to further disrupting the ability of the network to operate and of its members to move freely between countries.
176. States should also be encouraged further to provide additional information concerning individuals and entities already included in the list. This information should include, inter alia, a description of their current location.
177. When proposals are made to designate entities associated with Al-Qaida network, they should be accompanied by requests to list the principal individuals involved with such entities, including all managers and directors implicated in the activities motivating the request for listing.

Financial and economic asset freeze

178. Language should be introduced into the resolutions to clarify the obligations on States to block assets other than bank accounts and other intangible financial assets. This should include direct reference to businesses or property owned or controlled by designated individuals and entities.
179. States should be encouraged further to ensure that adequate penalties are imposed for violations of any of the sanctions measures set out in the resolutions.
180. States should be encouraged further to adopt the Eight Special Recommendations on Terrorist Financing issued by FATF [the UN's Financial Action Task Force], and to adopt the measures recommended in its various "best practices" papers.

181. Special requirements should be imposed by States to ensure, to the extent possible, that charities route their transactions through established banking systems. In such cases the recipient organization should be required to maintain bank accounts, and to transact business as much as possible through verifiable means such as cheques and electronic transfers.

182. An increased international cooperative effort is necessary to compile and publish usable information concerning the conduct and reputation of charities, including information relating to questionable activities, such as links to terrorist financing.

183. The Security Council should consider measures requiring all States to take follow-up action to update and report at regular intervals to the Committee the status and activities of designated entities within their countries. This should include a description of the actions States are taking to ensure that such activities, if any, conform to the requirements of the measures in resolutions 1390 (2002) and 1455 (2003).

184. The Security Council may wish to consider the adoption of steps to ensure that all United Nations bodies are apprised of each designation against an entity. All United Nations bodies should terminate any association with such entities.

185. The Security Council may wish to consider establishing a data bank on charities to which information, favourable and unfavourable, could be provided by government agencies or recognized and established international charities. Such a database could serve as a due diligence reference point for concerned charities.

186. The Group believes that several proactive requirements or measures should be considered by the Security Council to stop the circumvention of the measures concerning the freezing of economic assets and resources currently in the resolutions. The measures should include:

    (a) Strengthening and clarifying asset freezing requirements to cover mingled assets, shared assets, and jointly owned assets which may continue to benefit, or are subject to manipulation by, designated individuals or entities;

    (b) Placing specific obligations on States to ensure that designated entities do not have access to offshore financial centres, and that their assets in such centres are frozen. This should include a required accounting of their assets and holdings in third countries;

    (c) Calling upon States to enact stiff penalties for the violation of laws and regulations relating to the implementation of the measures in the resolutions, including possible forfeiture of any economic resources made available to designated individuals or entities in violation of such laws;

    (d) Requiring States to identify and catalogue, wherever possible, all assets, tangible and intangible, wholly or jointly, directly or indirectly owned and controlled by a designated individual or entity that are subject to freezing under the resolutions;

(e) Providing States with a mechanism by which they can enquire concerning the identity of assets that may be related to a designated individual or entity;

(f) Prohibiting designated individuals from altering the status of assets subject to freezing under the resolutions. This should include a prohibition against altering business registrations, or changing business names, addresses or administering parties, without the consent of the Committee.

Travel ban

187. To render the list more effective, the Group recommends the extensive use by border control authorities of electronic means for sharing and searching data related to designated individuals.

188. Recognizing the importance of adequate identifiers, States should not set the standards for including names in national stop lists so high as to bar the inclusion of persons who might still be identified using the information available.

189. The Security Council may wish to call upon States to report regularly on the status or whereabouts of nationals or residents who are designated on the list. This should include any indication as to whether they have been arrested or detained, had warrants issued against them, or are deceased. States should also indicate the whereabouts of the individual, if known.

190. The information listed above should be available for distribution by the Committee and included, where possible, in the list.

191. Individuals with outstanding warrants of arrest who are stopped or detained at border entry points should be sent back to their country of origin or extradited to the country where the warrant was issued.

192. Government authorities in all countries should inform their nationals or their residents about their inclusion in the list and their obligation to strictly respect the ban on their travel. Any violation of the travel ban by the designated individual should be subject to tough penalties.

193. The Group recommends that the designated individuals should be considered as holding only one citizenship or nationality for the purpose of applying the travel ban.

Arms embargo

194. The arms embargo should not be limited only to the individuals and entities designated on the list but should be applied to all Al-Qaida followers and their associates.

195. Regional approaches to implementing the arms embargo should be encouraged.
196. Full cooperation should be given by all States to the Monitoring Group with respect to the discharge of its mandate regarding the implementation of the arms embargo.
197. Consideration should be given to expanding the mandate of the Monitoring Group to include some investigative powers and the authority to issue letters rogatory regarding its work.
198. All States should be encouraged to adopt, without delay, the measures incorporated in the Programme of Action to Prevent, Combat and Eradicate the Illicit Trade in Small Arms and Light Weapons in All Its Aspects.
199. All States which have not yet ratified and/or implemented the following international instruments should be encouraged to do so as soon as possible. Those instruments include:
    • Convention on the Physical Protection of Nuclear Material
    • Treaty on the Non-Proliferation of Nuclear Weapons
    • Convention on the Prohibition of the Development, Production, Stockpiling and Use of Chemical Weapons and on Their Destruction
    • Convention on the Prohibition of the Development, Production and Stockpiling of Bacteriological (Biological) and Toxin Weapons and on Their Destruction
    • Convention on the Marking of Plastic Explosives for the Purpose of Detection
    • International Convention for the Suppression of Terrorist Bombings.
200. The United Nations may wish to consider approving measures to harmonize the various controls necessary to ensure that man-portable air-defence systems do not fall into the hands of non-State actors and terrorist groups, particularly Al-Qaida or its associates or other elements of Al-Qaida network.

Source: United Nations. Security Council. Security Council Committee Established Pursuant to Resolution 1267 (1999) Concerning Al-Qaida and the Taliban and Associated Individuals and Entities. *Second Report of the Monitoring Group, Pursuant to Resolution 1363 (2001) and as Extended by Resolutions 1390 (2002) and 1455 (2003) on Sanctions Against al-Qaida, the Taliban and Their Associates and Associated Entities.* S/2003/1070, December 1, 2003. www.un.org/Docs/sc/committees/1267/126/SelectedEng.htm (accessed January14, 2004).

UN Criminal Tribunal on Rwanda Genocide Verdicts

December 3, 2003

INTRODUCTION

Rwanda during 2003 took significant steps into the next phase of the country's life, which for nine years had been dominated by the consequences and memories of the 1994 genocide. More than 40,000 people who had been charged with crimes related to the genocide were released from prison; most were sent to "re-education" camps and then allowed to return to their home communities. Voters adopted a new constitution in May and then participated in Rwanda's first-ever multicandidate elections for president (in August) and for parliament (in October). A United Nations tribunal that was hearing the most serious genocide cases handed down several convictions, including those of three journalists who had helped fuel the genocide with vitriolic calls for hatred and violence. The tribunal itself underwent major changes, as the UN appointed a new chief prosecutor in response to complaints that the court's work was taking too long.

The Rwandan genocide was the most intense slaughter of human beings anywhere in the world since World War II. In just three months, between April and June 1994, extremist elements of the Hutu majority in Rwanda killed 500,000 to 1 million people. Most of the victims were Tutsi, the main minority group in the country, but a significant number were moderate Hutus. Despite their minority status, the Tutsi had dominated Rwanda's economic and political life prior to independence from Belgium in 1962. The Hutu gained control after independence, but subsequent decades saw repeated conflicts between the two factions.

The 1994 genocide ended when a guerrilla army led by Tutsi exiles, who had been living in neighboring Uganda, gained control of Rwanda and drove off the Hutu extremists, many of whom fled into the Democratic Republic of the Congo (then known as Zaire). The guerrillas, called the Rwandan Patriotic Army, installed a new "transitional" government in Kigali, headed by a moderate Hutu politician, Pasteur Bizimungu. However, the real power was held by the army's leader, Paul Kagame, the son of Tutsis who had fled fighting between Hutus and Tutsis in 1959. Complaining of Tutsi domination, Bizimungu resigned in 2000 and was succeeded by Kagame. *(Rwanda background, Historic Documents of 1994, p. 541; Historic Documents of 1999, p. 860; Historic Documents of 2000, p. 449)*

Presidential and Parliamentary Elections

As a member of the Tutsi minority—which after the genocide constituted only about 15 percent of Rwanda's 7.8 million people—Kagame preached reconciliation and urged people to think of themselves as Rwandans, rather than as Hutus or Tutsis. Despite occasional problems, such as Bizimungu's angry departure from government in 2000, Kagame's approach appeared to be generally effective in soothing the wounds of an intensely troubled country. Domestic and international critics said Kagame was merely consolidating personal power while pretending to bridge the nation's historic differences.

Rwanda held its first local elections in 2001. A year later the government held several hundred meetings in local communities as it drafted a new constitution that, Kagame said, was intended to introduce genuine democracy. The result was a constitution providing for an elected president, an appointed prime minister, and a two-chamber parliament, which was to represent all major ethnic and political factions. Among its provisions, the constitution prohibited one party from controlling more than one-half of the posts in the cabinet or all three of the top government posts: president, prime minister, and head of the lower house of parliament. Voters overwhelmingly approved that constitution in a referendum held May 27, 2003.

The constitution called for multiparty presidential elections, and Kagame vowed to uphold that provision. However, the election held on August 26 turned out to be more of a coronation of Kagame than an exercise in rough-and-tumble democracy. The government banned the nation's second-largest party, the Democratic Republican Movement, because of its alleged "divisionism"—a code word for fueling ethnic hatred. The party had been a member of Kagame's coalition since 1994, but with elections looming the government apparently decided not to risk allowing the formation of a credible opposition. That left Kagame's Rwandan Patriotic Front as the only well-organized political party.

The names of three candidates were on the ballot, in addition to Kagame, but only one had any degree of national support: Faustin Twagiramungu, a Hutu moderate and former prime minister who had returned to Rwanda early in 2003 after living in exile in Belgium for several years. Without the active support of a political party, and with some of his campaign rallies cancelled by the government, Twagiramungu was unable to mount an effective campaign. Another opposition candidate abandoned the race just days before the election and endorsed Kagame—reportedly under pressure from Kagame's party.

As the election approached, the only question was the extent of Kagame's victory. "Not everyone likes him," Laurence Riansofa, a woman attending a Kagame rally told the British *Guardian* newspaper the day before the election. "But nearly everyone will vote for him. He put out the fires in 1994, and nobody wants to return to those terrible times."

That prediction was correct, according to the official results announced on the evening of election day. Kagame won election with just over 95 percent of the vote. Twagiramungu received just under 4 percent, and a third candidate received the remaining votes. International observers offered a mixed verdict on the election. The European Union said the campaign was "not entirely" free and fair but nevertheless called the election "an important step in the democratic process." A group of observers from South Africa offered no major criticism of the election. Twagiramungu registered a complaint about the electoral process with the country's supreme court but did not pursue it after judges said he had offered no evidence that the voting had been rigged.

Kagame was sworn into office for a seven-year term on September 12, pledging to "work with my whole heart for the unity of Rwandans." Addressing complaints about the election, he said: "There are those who have been saying that some things were not right in the recent elections. However, Rwandans say that nothing is perfect throughout the world."

Kagame's ruling party scored a major victory in legislative elections held from September 30 through October 2—although not as sweeping a victory as that of Kagame himself. A five-party coalition led by Kagame's Rwandan Patriotic Front captured about 74 percent of the total vote, giving it a strong majority of seats in both the eight-seat lower house, the Chamber of Deputies, and the twenty-seat upper house, the Senate. The legislature took office October 10, and Kagame reappointed his previous prime minister, Bernard Makuza.

Genocide Trials

Tens of thousands of people had participated in the 1994 genocide. Egged on by government and military authorities, newspapers, a Hutu radio station, and even by religious leaders, Hutus had used guns, machetes, and any other weapons they could find to kill Tutsis and any Hutus who objected to the killings or were identified with the Tutsis. Many of the killers participated voluntarily, even eagerly; some participated only after they were threatened with death if they did not turn against friends, neighbors, or even family members who happened to be Tutsi.

The United Nations in 1994 established a court, the International Criminal Tribunal for Rwanda, to hear the most serious cases arising from the Rwandan genocide. The court was seated at Arusha, Tanzania. The court entered its first conviction in 1998. *(Historic Documents of 1998, p. 614)*

The postgenocide Rwandan government also arrested more than 100,000 people on charges related to the genocide; in most cases, those people were charged with killing "only" one or two people, or with aiding the killings in some fashion. Lacking a modern court system, the government was overwhelmed by the case load. In 2001 the government announced that most cases would be handled by a community-based system of traditional justice known as *gacaca*. Even this system proved unable to deal with the thousands of people who had been accused of crimes; as of 2003 about 6,000 people had been convicted, meaning that more than 100,000 still remained in jail.

In January, Kagame called for the "conditional" release of about 40,000 genocide prisoners, including those who were elderly or seriously ill, as well as healthy prisoners who were willing to confess their roles in the killing. The first prisoners were released January 31, and subsequent releases were held through May. Most of the released prisoners were first sent to what the government called "solidarity camps," where they received education on proper behavior in a civil society, and were then sent home. However, they were supposed to face justice at some point, most like in *gacaca* proceedings. In June the government announced that about 5,800 of the released prisoners had been re-arrested. Most of them had been accused of new allegations by a genocide survivors' group known as Ibuka ("remember" in the local language, Kinyarwanda). Ibuka on December 16 said genocide suspects had killed several witnesses, and harassed others, to prevent them from testifying in the *gacaca* proceedings.

The United Nations tribunal—which was funded by the international community and staffed for the most part by Western-trained lawyers and judges—also had problems dealing with its load of cases. Between 1995, when it began work, and the start of 2003, the tribunal completed work on only nine cases; eight defendants had been convicted and one was acquitted. The court was considering cases involving a total of fifty-six persons, twenty of whom had gone on trial as of early 2003.

Much of the criticism of the tribunal focused on the chief prosecutor, former Swiss judge Carla Del Ponte. She also was the chief prosecutor for the UN tribunal that handled cases of genocide and other war crimes stemming from the 1992–1995 wars in the former Yugoslavia. The Rwandan government and other critics alleged that Del Ponte focused on the Yugoslav tribunal, especially the long-running case involving former Yugoslav president Slobodan Milosevic, at the expense of the Rwandan tribunal. Del Ponte rejected that complaint as unwarranted and said Kagame's government sought to have her removed from the Rwandan tribunal after she launched an investigation of charges that his Tutsi-led army had killed nearly 30,000 Hutus in the final stages of the 1994 genocide. *(Milosevic case, Historic Documents of 2001, p. 826)*

After much diplomatic maneuvering among major world capitals, UN Secretary General Kofi Annan announced July 28 that he was removing Del Ponte as chief prosecutor for the Rwandan tribunal but retaining her as prosecutor at the Yugoslav court for another four years. "There has been some discussion as to whether the tribunals would not be [more] effective if each had a separate prosecutor," Annan said, in a diplomatically worded summary of the dispute. The UN Security Council accepted Annan's recommendation on August 29, and the same day Annan said Hassan Jallow, a former supreme court judge and solicitor general in Gambia, would take over Del Ponte's post at the Rwanda court.

Despite this controversy, the UN tribunal finished several important cases in 2003, including the first-ever conviction of journalists on genocide charges. After a trial that lasted nearly three years, the tribunal on December 3 convicted three men on charges of inciting Hutus to participate in the genocide. Two of the men were given sentences of life in prison (the most severe penalty the court could impose): Ferdinand Nahimana, a founder of a Hutu-extremist radio station, Radio Television Libres des Mille Collines (known as RTLM); and Hassan Ngeze, owner and editor of a Hutu-extremist newspaper, *Kangura* ("wake it up" in Kinyarwanda). A third defendant, Jean-Bosco Barayagwiza, was sentenced to thirty-five years in prison, reduced to twenty-seven years for time already served. He helped found the RTLM station and a Hutu extremist political party and was public affairs director of the Rwandan foreign affairs ministry at the time of the genocide. Barayagwiza had boycotted the trial, which he called unfair.

During the trial of the three men, prosecutors played tape recordings of RTLM broadcasts and displayed articles from the *Kangura* newspaper, calling on Hutus to attack Tutsis and suggesting the use of such weapons as machetes. Some of the incitements suggested that Tutsis would be easy to identify because of their height (most Tutsis were taller than most Hutus) and their relatively small noses. Many of the incitements specifically targeted Tutsi women, arguing that they had deliberately attempted to seduce Hutu men.

Summing up the case, presiding judge Navanethem Pillay told Nahimana: "You chose a path of genocide and betrayed the trust placed in you as an intellectual leader. Without a firearm, machete, or any physical weapon, you caused the deaths of thousands of innocent civilians."

In their ruling, the three judges addressed the question of freedom of the press and argued that the defendants had violated the law, as well as journalistic standards, by advocating mass murder. "The power of the media to create and destroy fundamental human values comes with great responsibility," the judges wrote. "Those who control such media are accountable for its consequences."

The conviction of the three men was the first of news media officials in such a case since the trials of Germany Nazi leaders following World War II. In 1946 the Nuremberg tribunal convicted Nazi newspaper publisher Julius Streicher of war crimes because of his writings against the Jews; he was hung.

Speeding up its work, the UN tribunal handed down decisions in several other cases during the year, including:

- The conviction, on February 19, of a pastor and his son—a medical doctor—on charges of participating in the killing of a large number of people who had taken refugee in a church complex. Elizaphan Ntakiru- timana, a pastor of the Seventh Day Adventist Church in the town of Mugonero, was convicted of aiding and abetting genocide. His son, Gerard Ntakirutimana, a doctor who was practicing at the church's hos- pital, was convicted of genocide and murder as a crime against human- ity. The court found that Ntakirutimana senior had transported attack- ers to various locations, including churches, where Tutsis were in hiding. Ntakirutimana had been the leading figure in one of the most notorious incidents of the entire genocide: After a group of several hun- dred Tutsis took shelter in his church, one sent Ntakirutimana a letter saying: "We wish to inform you that tomorrow we will be killed with our families." The next day Ntakirutimana and his son accompanied the Hutu militias as they attacked the Tutsis and killed all but a few of them. He was the first religious leader to be found guilty of taking part in the genocide; he was sentenced to only ten years in prison because of his age (seventy-eight) and his frail health. Ntakirutimana's son was found guilty of personally murdering two people and participating in several attacks on groups of people; he was sentenced to twenty-five years in prison. However, the court said there was insufficient evidence to con- vict the two men on several other charges.
- The conviction, on May 15, of Eliezer Niyitegeka, who had been Rwanda's information minister at the time of the genocide. He was found guilty of six counts of genocide and crimes against humanity and was sentenced to life in prison. The court said Niyitegeka had given speeches provoking hatred of the Tutsis and had done nothing to stop massacres by his subordinates. On the same day, the court also con- victed Laurent Semanza, the former mayor of the town of Bicumbi, on five counts of complicity to commit genocide and crimes against humanity; he was sentenced to twenty-five years in prison.

- The affirmation, by the tribunal's appeals chamber on May 26, of a 1999 conviction of George Rutaganda, political leader of the Hutu extremist group, the Interahawme, that had carried out most of the killings. The appeals chamber upheld the conviction of Rutaganda on charges of genocide and extermination as a crime against humanity, but overturned his conviction on one charge of murder as a crime against humanity because of "inconsistencies" in testimony by witnesses. However, the appeals chamber entered two new convictions of Rutaganda on charges of murder as a violation of the Geneva Convention protecting refugees. These charges were considered to be war crimes, and the finding against Rutaganda marked the tribunal's first war crimes conviction. He was sentenced to life in prison.
- The conviction, on December 1, of Juvenal Kajelijeli, who had been the mayor of a town north of Kigali during the genocide. Kajelijeli was convicted of genocide, public incitement, and extermination for his role in helping organize killings in his town and in other areas of the country. Judge William Sekule cited, in particular, Kajelijeli's participation in an attack at a courthouse in the town of Ruhengeri, where about three hundred Tutsis were killed. Kajelijeli was sentenced to life in prison.

Also in 2003, the head of the United Nations peacekeeping force that had been unable to prevent the genocide broke his long silence, publishing a book that gave graphic details of the killings and harshly denounced Western nations for refusing to intervene. Retired Canadian Lt. Gen. Romeo Dellaire had unsuccessfully appealed to the UN for more support for his small, ill-equipped peacekeeping force. "We had sent a deluge of paper [reports on the killings] and received nothing in return; no supplies, no reinforcement, no decisions," Dellaire wrote in his book, *Shake Hands with the Devil: The Failure of Humanity in Rwanda.* Dellaire recounted one incident in which the United States gave him detailed intelligence information indicating that he was being targeted for assassination. At the same time, U.S. diplomats in Washington and at UN headquarters claimed not to know what was happening in Rwanda, he said.

Following are excerpts from the summary of the judgment, handed down December 3, 2003, by the United Nations International Criminal Tribunal for Rwanda, in the cases of Jean-Bosco Barayagwiza, Ferdinand Nahimana, and Hassan Ngeze—all of whom were convicted of charges related to the 1994 genocide in Rwanda.

The Prosecutor v. Nahimana, Barayagwiza, and Ngeze

I. Introduction

1. Trial Chamber I today delivers its judgement in the trial of three Accused persons: Ferdinand Nahimana, Jean-Bosco Barayagwiza, and Hassan Ngeze. . . .

2. Ferdinand Nahimana was born on 15 June 1950, in Gatonde commune, Ruhengeri prefecture, Rwanda. He was a professor of history and Dean of the Faculty of Letters at the National University of Rwanda. In 1990, he was appointed Director of ORINFOR (Rwandan Office of Information) and remained in that post until 1992. He was a founder of RTLM [Radio Television Libres des Mille Collines] and a member of its *comité d'initiative,* or Steering Committee.

3. Jean-Bosco Barayagwiza was born in 1950 in Mutura commune, Gisenyi prefecture, Rwanda. A lawyer by training, he held the post of Director of Political Affairs in the Ministry of Foreign Affairs. He was a founder of the CDR [Coalition for the Defense of the Republic, a Hutu political party] and of RTLM and a member of the Steering Committee of RTLM.

4. Hassan Ngeze was born on 25 December 1957 in Rubavu commune, Gisenyi prefecture, Rwanda. From 1978, he worked as a journalist, and in 1990, he founded the newspaper *Kangura* and held the post of Editor-in-Chief.

5. The three Accused are charged in separate Indictments; they were tried jointly. The Accused are all charged on counts of genocide, conspiracy to commit genocide, direct and public incitement to commit genocide, complicity in genocide, and crimes against humanity (persecution and extermination). Additionally, Hassan Ngeze is charged with crimes against humanity (murder). The Accused are charged with individual criminal responsibility under Article 6(1) of the Statute for these crimes. Nahimana is additionally charged with superior responsibility under Article 6(3) in respect of direct and public incitement to commit genocide and the crime against humanity of persecution. Barayagwiza and Ngeze are additionally charged with superior responsibility under Article 6(3) in respect of all the counts except conspiracy to commit genocide.

6. In the Indictments, Ferdinand Nahimana and Jean-Bosco Barayagwiza were also charged with the crime against humanity of murder, and Barayagwiza was charged on counts of serious violations of Article 3 common to the Geneva Conventions and of Additional Protocol II. On 25 September 2002, the Chamber granted the Defence motion for acquittal in respect of these counts.

7. The Accused, Jean-Bosco Barayagwiza, elected not to attend his trial, giving as his reasons that he did not have confidence that he would be afforded a fair trial in light of the Appeal Chamber's reversal of its decision ordering his release before the trial.

8. This case raises important principles concerning the role of the media, which have not been addressed at the level of international criminal justice since Nuremberg. The power of the media to create and destroy fundamental human values comes with great responsibility. Those who control such media are accountable for its consequences.

II. Factual Findings

Violence in Rwanda in 1994

9. The Chamber finds that within the context of hostilities between the RPF and the Rwandan Government, which began when the RPF [Rwandan Patriotic Front, a guerrilla army led by Tutsis] attacked Rwanda on 1 October 1990, the Tutsi population within the country was systematically targeted as suspected RPF accomplices. This targeting included a number of violent attacks that resulted in the killing of Tutsi civilians. The RPF also engaged in attacks on civilians during this period. Following the shooting of the plane and the death of President Habyarimana on 6 April 1994, widespread and systematic killing of Tutsi civilians, a genocide, commenced in Rwanda. . . .

[The remaining factual findings described specific incidents in which they accused were said to have incited hatred of Tutsis and encouraged fellow Hutus to kill them.]

III. Legal Findings

Genocide

The Accused are charged with genocide.

Acts of RTLM

63. The Chamber has found that RTLM broadcasts engaged in ethnic stereotyping in a manner that promoted contempt and hatred for the Tutsi population and called on listeners to seek out and take up arms against the enemy. The enemy was defined to be the Tutsi ethnic group and Hutu opponents. These broadcasts called explicitly for the extermination of the Tutsi ethnic group. In 1994, both before and after 6 April, RTLM broadcast the names of Tutsi individuals and their families, as well as Hutu political opponents who supported the Tutsi ethnic group. In some cases these persons were subsequently killed. A specific causal connection between the RTLM broadcasts and the killing of these individuals—either by publicly naming them or by manipulating their movements and directing that they, as a group, be killed—has been established.

Acts of Kangura

64. The Chamber has found that articles and editorials in *Kangura,* such as *The Appeal to the Conscience of the Hutu,* conveyed contempt and hatred for the Tutsi ethnic group, and for Tutsi women in particular as enemy agents, and called on readers to take all necessary measures to stop the enemy, defined to be the Tutsi population. The cover of *Kangura* No. 26 promoted violence by conveying the message that the machete should be used to eliminate the Tutsi, once and for all. This was a call for the destruction of the Tutsi ethnic group as such. Through fear-mongering and hate propaganda, *Kangura* paved the way for genocide in Rwanda, whipping the Hutu population into a killing frenzy.

65. The nature of media is such that causation of killing and other acts of genocide will necessarily be effected by an immediately proximate cause in addition to the communication itself. In the Chamber's view, this does not diminish the causation to be attributed to the media, or the criminal accountability of those responsible for the communication.

Acts of CDR

66. The Hutu Power movement, spearheaded by CDR, created a political framework for the killing of Tutsi and Hutu political opponents. The CDR and its youth wing, the *Impuzamugambi,* convened meetings and demonstrations, established roadblocks, distributed weapons, and systematically organized and carried out

the killing of Tutsi civilians. As well as orchestrating particular acts of killing, the CDR promoted a Hutu mindset in which ethnic hatred was normalized as a political ideology. The division of Hutu and Tutsi entrenched fear and suspicion of the Tutsi and fabricated the perception that the Tutsi population had to be destroyed in order to safeguard the political gains that had been made by the Hutu majority.

67. The Defence contends that the downing of the President's plane and the death of Habyarimana precipitated the killing of innocent Tutsi civilians [Rwandan president Habyarimana was killed early in April 1994 when his airplane was shot down, under circumstances that never were fully explained]. The Chamber accepts that this moment in time served as a trigger for the events that followed. That is evident. But if the downing of the plane was the trigger, then RTLM, *Kangura* and CDR were the bullets in the gun. The trigger had such a deadly impact because the gun was loaded. The Chamber therefore considers the killing of Tutsi civilians and Hutu political opponents can be said to have resulted, at least in part, from the message of ethnic targeting for death that was clearly and effectively disseminated through RTLM, *Kangura* and CDR, before and after 6 April 1994.

Acts of Barayagwiza

Barayagwiza distributed a truckload of weapons to the local population, which were used to kill individuals of Tutsi ethnicity. At least thirty Tutsi civilians were killed, including children and older people. Barayagwiza played a leadership role in the distribution of these weapons, which formed part of a predefined and structured plan to kill Tutsi civilians. From Barayagwiza's critical role in this plan, orchestrating the delivery of the weapons to be used for destruction, the Chamber finds that Barayagwiza was involved in planning these acts.

Acts of Ngeze

68. Hassan Ngeze on the morning of 7 April 1994 ordered the *Interahamwe* [a militia group of Hutu extremists] in Gisenyi to kill Tutsi civilians and prepare for their burial at the *Commune Rouge*. Many were killed in the attacks that happened immediately thereafter and later on the same day. Ngeze helped secure and distribute, stored, and transported weapons to be used against the Tutsi population. He set up, manned and supervised roadblocks in Gisenyi in 1994 that identified targeted Tutsi civilians who were subsequently taken to and killed at the *Commune Rouge*. Ngeze often drove around with a megaphone in his vehicle, mobilizing the population to

come to CDR meetings and spreading the message that the *Inyenzi* would be exterminated, *Inyenzi* meaning, and being understood to mean, the Tutsi ethnic minority. In this manner, Ngeze instigated the killing of Tutsi civilians.

Genocidal Intent

69. In ascertaining the intent of the Accused, the Chamber has considered their individual statements and acts, as well as the message they conveyed through the media they controlled. On 15 May 1994, the Editor-in-Chief of RTLM, Gaspard Gahigi, told listeners:

> ... they say the Tutsi are being exterminated, they are being decimated by the Hutu, and other things. I would like to tell you, dear listeners of RTLM, that the war we are waging is actually between these two ethnic groups, the Hutu and the Tutsi.

70. Even before 6 April 1994, RTLM was equating the Tutsi with the enemy, as evidenced by its broadcast of 6 January 1994, with Kantano Habimana asking, "Why should I hate the Tutsi? Why should I hate the Inkotanyi?"

71. With regard to *Kangura,* in perhaps its most graphic expression of genocidal intent, the cover of *Kangura* No. 26 answered the question "What Weapons Shall We Use To Conquer The *Inyenzi* Once And For All?" with the depiction of a machete. That the Tutsi ethnic group was the target of the machete was clear.

72. The newspaper and the radio explicitly and repeatedly, in fact relentlessly, targeted the Tutsi population for destruction. Demonizing the Tutsi as having inherently evil qualities, equating the ethnic group with "the enemy" and portraying its women as seductive enemy agents, the media called for the extermination of the Tutsi ethnic group as a response to the political threat that they associated with Tutsi ethnicity.

73. The genocidal intent in the activities of the CDR was expressed through the phrase "*tubatsembasembe*" or "let's exterminate them", a slogan chanted repeatedly at CDR rallies and demonstrations. At a policy level, CDR communiques called on the Hutu population to "neutralize by all means possible" the enemy, defined to be the Tutsi ethnic group.

74. The editorial policies evidenced by the writings of *Kangura* and the broadcasts of RTLM, and the organizational policy evidenced by the activity of CDR, constitute, in the Chamber's view, conclusive evidence of genocidal intent. Individually, each of the Accused made statements that further evidence this intent.

75. Ferdinand Nahimana, in a Radio Rwanda broadcast on 25 April 1994, said he was happy that RTLM had been instrumental in awakening the majority people, meaning the Hutu population, and that the population had stood up with a view to halting the enemy. Nahimana associated the enemy with the Tutsi ethnic group. As the mastermind of RTLM, Nahimana set in motion the communications weaponry that fought the "war of media, words, newspapers and radio stations" he described in his Radio Rwanda broadcast of 25 April as a complement to bullets.

76. Jean-Bosco Barayagwiza himself said in public meetings, "let's exterminate them" with "them" being understood by those who heard it as a reference to the Tutsi population. After separating the Tutsi from the Hutu and humiliating the Tutsi by forcing them to perform the *Ikinyemera,* a traditional dance, at several public meetings, Barayagwiza threatened to kill them and said it would not be difficult. From his words and deeds, Barayagwiza's ruthless commitment to the destruction of the Tutsi population as a means by which to protect the political gains secured by the Hutu majority from 1959 is evident.

77. Hassan Ngeze wrote many articles and editorials, and made many statements that openly evidence his genocidal intent. In one such article he stated that the Tutsi "no longer conceal the fact that this war pits the Hutus against the Tutsis." His radio broadcast of 12 June 1994 called on listeners not to mistakenly kill Hutu rather than Tutsi. Crass references to the physical and personal traits of Tutsi ethnicity permeate *Kangura* and his own writings in *Kangura.* Ngeze harped on the broad nose of the Hutu as contrasted with the aquiline nose of the Tutsi, and he incessantly described the Tutsi as evil. His role in saving Tutsi individuals whom he knew does not, in the Chamber's view, negate his intent to destroy the ethnic group as such. Witness LAG heard him say, "[I]f Habyarimana were also to die, we would not be able to spare the Tutsi". Witness AEU heard Ngeze on a megaphone, saying that he was going to kill and exterminate all the *Inyenzi,* by which he meant the Tutsi, and Ngeze himself ordered an attack on Tutsi civilians in Gisenyi, evidencing his intent to destroy the Tutsi population.

78. Based on this evidence, the Chamber finds that Ferdinand Nahimana, Jean Bosco Barayagwiza and Hassan Ngeze acted with intent to destroy, in whole or in part, the Tutsi ethnic group. The identification of Tutsi individuals as enemies of the state associated with political opposition, simply by virtue of their Tutsi ethnicity, underscores the fact that their membership in the ethnic group, as such, was the sole basis on which they were targeted.

Individual Criminal Responsibility

79. The Chamber has considered the individual criminal responsibility of Ferdinand Nahimana and Jean-Bosco Barayagwiza for RTLM broadcasts, by virtue of their respective roles in the creation and control of RTLM. Nahimana and Barayagwiza were, respectively, "number one" and "number two" in the top management of the radio. They represented the radio at the highest level in meetings with the Ministry of Information; they controlled the finances of the company; and they were both members of the Steering Committee, which functioned in effect as a board of directors for RTLM. Nahimana chaired the Program Committee of this board, and Barayagwiza chaired its Legal Committee.

80. While recognizing that Nahimana and Barayagwiza did not make decisions in the first instance with regard to each particular broadcast of RTLM, these decisions reflected an editorial policy for which they were responsible. The broadcasts collectively conveyed a message of ethnic hatred and a call for violence against the Tutsi population. This message was heard around the world. "Stop that radio" was the cry Alison Des Forges heard from Rwanda during the killings, and it was the cry conveyed to the United Nations by Reporters Without Borders in May 1994. As board members responsible for RTLM, including its programming, Nahimana and Barayagwiza were responsible for this message. Both Barayagwiza and Nahimana knew that RTLM programming was generating concern, even before 6 April 1994. Yet RTLM programming followed its trajectory, steadily increasing in vehemence and reaching a pitched frenzy after 6 April. Nahimana and Barayagwiza knew that the hate being spewed by these programs was of concern and failed to take effective measures to stop their evolution into the deadly weapon of war and genocide that was unleashed in full force after 6 April 1994.

81. After 6 April 1994, although the evidence does not establish the same level of active support, it is nevertheless clear that Nahimana and Barayagwiza knew what was happening at RTLM and failed to exercise the authority vested in them as office-holding members of the governing body of RTLM, to prevent the genocidal harm that was caused by RTLM programming. That they had the *de facto* authority to prevent this harm is evidenced by the one documented and successful intervention of Nahimana to stop RTLM attacks on UNAMIR and General Dallaire. The Chamber notes that Nahimana has not been charged for genocide pursuant to Article 6(3) of its Statute. For his active engagement in the management of RTLM prior to 6 April, and his failure to take necessary and rea-

sonable measures to prevent the acts of genocide caused by RTLM that occurred after 6 April, the Chamber finds Barayagwiza guilty of genocide pursuant to Article 6(3) of its Statute.

82. The Chamber notes Nahimana's particular role as the founder and principal ideologist of RTLM. RTLM was his initiative and his design, which grew out of his experience as Director of ORINFOR and his understanding of the power of the media. Although Nahimana disclaimed responsibility for RTLM broadcasting after 6 April, the Chamber considers this disclaimer too facile. Nahimana's interview on Radio Rwanda, in which he said he was very happy with RTLM's instrumental role in awakening the Hutu population, took place while the genocide was underway; the massacre of the Tutsi population was ongoing. Nahimana may have been less actively involved in the daily affairs of RTLM after 6 April 1994, but RTLM did not deviate from the course he had set for it before 6 April 1994. The programming of RTLM after 6 April built on the foundations created for it before 6 April. RTLM was Nahimana's weapon of choice, which he used to instigate the acts of genocide that occurred. For this reason the Chamber finds Nahimana guilty of genocide pursuant to Article 6(1) of its statute.

83. Jean-Bosco Barayagwiza was one of the principal founders of CDR and played a leading role in its formation and development. He was a decision-maker for the party. The killing of Tutsi civilians was promoted by Barayagwiza himself and by CDR members in his presence at public meetings and demonstrations. Barayagwiza supervised roadblocks manned by the *Impuzamugambi,* established to stop and kill Tutsi. Barayagwiza was at the organizational helm of CDR. He was also on site at the meetings, demonstrations and roadblocks that created an infrastructure for the killing of Tutsi civilians. For this reason, the Chamber finds him guilty of instigating acts of genocide committed by CDR members and *Impuzamugambi,* pursuant to Article 6(1) of its Statute. For his individual acts in planning the killing of Tutsi civilians, the Chamber finds him guilty of genocide, pursuant to Article 6(1) of its Statute.

84. The Chamber further finds that Barayagwiza had superior responsibility over members of the CDR and its militia, the *Impuzamugambi,* as President of CDR at Gisenyi Prefecture and from February 1994 as President of CDR at the national level. He promoted the policy of CDR for the extermination of the Tutsi population and supervised his subordinates, the CDR members and *Impuzamugambi* militia, in carrying out killings and other violent acts. For his active engagement in CDR, and his failure to take necessary and reasonable measures to prevent the acts of genocide caused by CDR members, the Chamber

finds Barayagwiza guilty of genocide pursuant to Article 6(3) of its Statute.

85. The Chamber finds Hassan Ngeze, as founder, owner and editor of *Kangura,* a publication that instigated the killing of Tutsi civilians, as well as for his acts of ordering, inciting and aiding and abetting the killing of Tutsi civilians, guilty of genocide, pursuant to Article 6(1) of its Statute.

Direct and Public Incitement to Genocide

86. The Chamber examined the central principles that emerge from the international jurisprudence on incitement to discrimination and violence that serve as a useful guide to the factors to be considered in defining elements of "direct and public incitement to genocide" as applied to mass media.

87. Editors and publishers have generally been held responsible for the media they control. In determining the scope of this responsibility, the importance of intent, that is the purpose of the communications they channel, emerges from the jurisprudence. The actual language used in the media has often been cited as an indicator of intent. Critical distance is a key factor in evaluating the purpose of the publication.

88. The jurisprudence on incitement also highlights the importance of taking context into account when considering the potential impact of expression. Other factors relating to context that emerge from the jurisprudence, particularly that of the European Court of Human Rights, include the importance of protecting political expression, particularly the expression of opposition views and criticism of the government.

89. In considering whether particular expression constitutes a form of incitement on which restrictions would be justified, the international jurisprudence does not include any specific causation requirement linking the expression at issue with the demonstration of a direct effect. In the well-known Nuremburg case of *Julius Streicher,* there was no allegation that Streicher's publication *Der Stürmer* was tied to any particular violence. Much more generally, it was found to have "injected into the minds of thousands of Germans" a "poison" that caused them to support the National Socialist policy of Jewish persecution and extermination.

90. Counsel for Ngeze has argued that United States law, as the most speech-protective, should be used as a standard, to ensure the universal acceptance and legitimacy of the Tribunal's jurisprudence. The Chamber considers international law, which has been well developed

in the areas of freedom from discrimination and freedom of expression, to be the point of reference for its consideration of these issues, noting that domestic law varies widely while international law codifies evolving universal standards. The Chamber notes that the jurisprudence of the United States also accepts the fundamental principles set forth in international law and has recognized in its domestic law that incitement to violence, threats, libel, false advertising, obscenity, and child pornography are among those forms of expression that fall outside the scope of freedom of speech protection.

Charges Against the Accused

91. The Accused are charged with direct and public incitement to genocide.
92. The crime of incitement is an inchoate offence that continues in time until the completion of the acts contemplated. The Chamber accordingly considers that the publication of *Kangura,* from its first issue in May 1990 through its March 1994 issue, the alleged impact of which culminated in events that took place in 1994, falls within the temporal jurisdiction of the Tribunal. Similarly, the Chamber considers that the entirety of RTLM broadcasting, from July 1993 through July 1994, the alleged impact of which culminated in events that took place in 1994, falls within the temporal jurisdiction of the Tribunal.
93. In its review of *Kangura* and RTLM, the Chamber notes that some of the articles and broadcasts highlighted by the Prosecution convey historical information, political analysis, or advocacy of an ethnic consciousness regarding the inequitable distribution of privilege in Rwanda. Barayagwiza's RTLM broadcast of 12 December 1993, for example, is a moving personal account of his experience of discrimination as a Hutu. The Chamber considers that it is critical to distinguish between the discussion of ethnic consciousness and the promotion of ethnic hatred. This broadcast by Barayagwiza is the former but not the latter. A communication such as this broadcast does not constitute incitement. In fact, it falls squarely within the scope of speech that is protected by the right to freedom of expression. Similarly, public discussion of the merits of the Arusha Accords, however critical, constitutes a legitimate exercise of free speech.
94. The Chamber considers that speech constituting ethnic hatred results from the stereotyping of ethnicity combined with its denigration. In the Chamber's view, the accuracy of a generalization is only one factor to be considered in the determination of whether it is intended to provoke rather than to educate those who receive it.

The tone of the statement is as relevant to this determination as is its content. The Chamber also considers the context in which the statement is made to be important. A statement of ethnic generalization provoking resentment against members of that ethnicity would have a heightened impact in the context of a genocidal environment. It would be more likely to lead to violence. At the same time the environment would be an indicator that incitement to violence was the intent of the statement.

95. The Accused have cited in their defence the need for vigilance against the enemy, the enemy being armed and dangerous RPF forces who attacked the Hutu population and were fighting to destroy democracy and reconquer power in Rwanda. The Chamber accepts that the media has a role to play in the protection of democracy and if necessary the mobilization of civil defence for the protection of the nation and its people. What distinguishes both *Kangura* and RTLM from an initiative to this end is the consistent identification made by the publication and the radio broadcasts of the enemy as the Tutsi population. Readers and listeners were not directed against individuals who were clearly defined to be armed and dangerous. Instead, Tutsi civilians and in fact the Tutsi population as a whole were targeted as the threat.

96. Both *Kangura* and RTLM, as well as CDR in its communiqués, named and listed individuals suspected of being RPF or RPF accomplices. In their defence, the Accused stated that these individuals were, at least in some cases, RPF members. The Chamber accepts that the publication of official information is a legitimate function of the media. Not all lists and names published or broadcast were associated with such sources, however. To the contrary, the evidence reviewed by the Chamber indicates a pattern of naming people on vague suspicion, without articulated grounds, or in those cases where the grounds were articulated they were highly speculative or in some cases entirely unfounded. In these cases, the only common element is the Tutsi ethnicity of the persons named, and the evidence in some cases clearly indicates that their ethnicity was in fact the reason they were named.

97. Also, the names published and broadcast were generally done so in the context of a message, that was at times more or less explicit. An official list of 123 names of suspects was published in *Kangura* No. 40 with an express warning to readers that the government was not effectively protecting them from these people and that they needed to organize their own self-defence to prevent their own extermination. This message classically illustrates the incitement of *Kangura* readers to violence—by instilling fear in them, giving them names to associate with this fear, and mobilizing them

to take independent measures to protect themselves. In some instances, names were mentioned by *Kangura* without such an explicit call to action. The message was nevertheless direct. That it was clearly understood is overwhelmingly evidenced by the testimony of witnesses that being named in *Kangura* would bring dire consequences. Similarly, RTLM broadcast a message of fear, provided listeners with names, and encouraged them to defend and protect themselves, incessantly telling them to "be vigilant".

98. With regard to causation, the Chamber recalls that incitement is a crime regardless of whether it has the effect it intends to have. In determining whether communications represent a risk of causing genocide and thereby constitute incitement, the Chamber considers it significant that in fact genocide occurred. One witness described what RTLM did as "to spread petrol throughout the country little by little, so that one day it would be able to set fire to the whole country". . . .

[The remaining legal findings dealt with the actions of RTLM, CDR, and *Kangura* in relation to the charge of direct and public incitement to genocide; with the charges against the accused of conspiracy to commit genocide, of crimes against humanity (extermination), crimes against humanity (persecution), and crimes against humanity (murder).]

IV. Verdict

FOR THE FOREGOING REASONS, having considered all of the evidence and the arguments:
    THE CHAMBER unanimously finds Ferdinand Nahimana:

    Count 1: Guilty of Conspiracy to Commit Genocide
    Count 2: Guilty of Genocide
    Count 3: Guilty of Direct and Public Incitement to Commit Genocide
    Count 4: Not Guilty of Complicity in Genocide
    Count 5: Guilty of Crimes Against Humanity (Persecution)
    Count 6: Guilty of Crimes Against Humanity (Extermination)
    Count 7: Not Guilty of Crimes Against Humanity (Murder)

    THE CHAMBER unanimously finds Jean-Bosco Barayagwiza:

    Count 1: Guilty of Conspiracy to Commit Genocide
    Count 2: Guilty of Genocide
    Count 3: Not Guilty of Complicity in Genocide
    Count 4: Guilty of Direct and Public Incitement to Commit Genocide

Count 5: Guilty of Crimes Against Humanity (Extermination)
Count 6: Not Guilty of Crimes Against Humanity (Murder)
Count 7: Guilty of Crimes Against Humanity (Persecution)
Count 8: Not Guilty of Serious Violations of Article 3 Common to the
Geneva Conventions and of Additional Protocol II
Count 9: Not Guilty of Serious Violations of Article 3 Common to the
Geneva Conventions and of Additional Protocol II

THE CHAMBER unanimously finds Hassan Ngeze:

Count 1: Guilty of Conspiracy to Commit Genocide
Count 2: Guilty of Genocide
Count 3: Not Guilty of Complicity in Genocide
Count 4: Guilty of Direct and Public Incitement to Commit Genocide
Count 5: Not Guilty of Crimes Against Humanity (Murder)
Count 6: Guilty of Crimes Against Humanity (Persecution)
Count 7: Guilty of Crimes Against Humanity (Extermination)

Source: United Nations. International Criminal Tribunal for Rwanda. *Summary of Judgement and Sentence: The Prosecutor v. Ferdinand Nahimana, Jean-Bosco Barayagwiza, and Hassan Ngeze.* Case No. ICTR-9952-T, December 3, 2003. www.ictr.org/ENGLISH/cases/Nahimana/index.htm.

UN Secretary General on
Situation in Afghanistan

December 3 and 30, 2003

INTRODUCTION

The people of Afghanistan in 2003 got a small taste of what it was like to live in a normal country. After nearly a quarter-century of uninterrupted conflict, much of the country was relatively quiet much of the time, but a dramatic increase in violence late in the year gave rise to serious new concerns about security. The interim government, led by Hamid Karzai, struggled to gain its footing during its second year in office and made modest progress in asserting control outside the capital, Kabul. The United Nations and international aid agencies continued what was certain to be a lengthy process of building an entirely new infrastructure for Afghanistan to replace the roads, schools, power plants, and other necessities destroyed in the years of war.

Security, or the lack of it, was the overriding problem facing Afghanistan, and the danger posed by bombings, shootings, and other terrorist attacks seemed to grow as the year wore on. The United States and other countries, which had planned to begin a slow withdrawal of their peacekeeping troops from Afghanistan by late 2003, instead found themselves under pressure to send in more soldiers to make the country safe. Much of the pressure came from the United Nations, which was responsible both for rebuilding the country and nurturing its new government. UN Secretary General Kofi Annan, who for nearly two years had voiced deep concerns about the lack of security, warned on December 18 that the entire attempt to rebuild Afghanistan was still in jeopardy. "We need to deal with the security issue, and if we do not deal with that, we may lose Afghanistan," he said.

In Washington, Afghanistan clearly took a back seat during the year to the Bush administration's new priority: gaining stability in Iraq following the U.S.-led war to oust Saddam Hussein. Some foreign policy experts and news organizations even referred to the continuing Afghan conflict as the "forgotten war." President George W. Bush and his aides insisted they had not forgotten Afghanistan, and they pointed to dozens of U.S.-funded aid projects and the continued presence of some 10,000 U.S. troops in the country. Even so, the administration's priorities were evident in the funding Bush persuaded Congress to provide for the two troubled countries, each with a population of about 25 million. By year's end the United States had committed nearly $20 billion to help rebuild oil-rich Iraq over a two-year period, five times the level of U.S. spending in Afghanistan. In both countries, the United States was spending much more money on military operations than on reconstruction. *(Background, Historic Documents of 2001, pp. 691, 880; Historic Documents of 2002, p. 15)*

Security Still Lacking

Visiting Kabul on May 1, U.S. defense secretary Donald H. Rumsfeld declared that "major combat activity" had ended in Afghanistan. Rumsfeld's visit, and statement, coincided with President Bush's announcement the same day that major combat had ended in Iraq. In each case, the announcement proved premature. In the last half of the year, more than 400 people died in conflict in Afghanistan, making it the greatest period of conflict since the United States and its allies overthrew the Taliban regime there at the end of 2001. Iraq also was wracked by violence all through the rest of the year. *(Postwar Iraq, p. 933)*

Afghanistan during 2003 was still torn by ethnic disputes and regional battles for power. Most Afghans clearly were ready for peace. But some regional warlords and the forces who had lost the short war in late 2001 still had scores to settle and, more ominously, they nurtured hopes for a return to power once the international community had grown tired of Afghanistan and left.

UN and U.S. officials said the main sources of instability remained the fighters for the al Qaeda terrorist network and the former Taliban government. Thousands of fighters for those related groups had dispersed into the countryside after the U.S.-led invasion in 2001, and most remained at large—and armed—two years later. The United States and its allies captured hundreds of these fighters between 2001 and 2003, but many were replaced by new recruits from the ranks of angry young men fired by Islamist fervor and hatred of the United States.

The UN's chief representative in Afghanistan, Lakhdar Brahimi, noted in December that the former Taliban regime "never accepted defeat" and was "taking full advantage of the popular disaffection" with the new government's inability to provide security and revive the economy. The al Qaeda network, which had trained thousands of fighters in Afghanistan during the 1990s, appeared to be responsible for several terrorist attacks in the country during the year. The U.S. military conducted major offensives against the Taliban and al Qaeda in June and December, killing or capturing several dozen fighters, a small portion of those believed to be still at large in Afghanistan and neighboring Pakistan. *(al Qaeda, p. 1050)*

Also posing a serious threat were fighters loyal to Gulbuddin Hekmatyar, one of the Islamist *mujahideen* who had fought the Soviet occupation of Afghanistan in the 1980s. He had served as an Afghan prime minister after the Soviet forces retreated but was bitterly opposed to Karzai's new government. Hekmatyar issued several statements during the year calling for a holy war against Karzai and U.S. forces in Afghanistan.

The rejectionist forces were especially active in the south and southeast of Afghanistan, the areas that had been the base of the Taliban's support and al Qaeda operations. For the most part, these forces mounted hit-and-run attacks, such as mortar and rocket strikes against international troops and aid workers. The year also saw the first suicide bombings in Afghanistan since the 2001 war. By year's end perhaps the most unsettling developments, for Karzai's government and its international backers, were that the Taliban had recreated a command structure and had been able to capture and hold several remote districts for extended periods.

Many of the bombings, rocket strikes, shootings, and other attacks were directed against the international presence in Afghanistan—clearly part of an effort to drive foreigners out of the country so the leaders of local factions could resume their battles for control. International peacekeepers suffered their biggest loss on June 7, when a suicide bomber set off a car full of explosives next to a bus carrying soldiers in Kabul. Four German soldiers were killed and twenty-nine others were injured; the troops had been on the way to the airport for a flight home, having completed their tours of duty in Afghanistan. Eight U.S. soldiers and two CIA operatives died in hostile incidents in Afghanistan during the year—a tiny number compared to the much heavier toll in Iraq.

UN employees and workers for international aid agencies also were targeted, particularly in the last part of the year when they faced an average of one attack every two days. In March an employee of the International Committee of the Red Cross became the first aid worker killed in Afghanistan since the 2001 war; by year's end a total of thirteen aid workers had died there. The UN itself was among the targets. On November 11 a bomb exploded outside the headquarters in Kandahar of the UN's High Commissioner for Refugees (UNHCR) injuring three people. Five days later Bettina Goislard, a French employee of UNHCR, was killed by two gunmen on motorcycles as she drove to work in the city of Ghazni, south of Kabul. These attacks, which came just three months after the bombing of the UN mission headquarters in Iraq, graphically illustrated the world body's inability to ensure the safety of its staff in conflict zones. As a result, the UN refugee agency withdrew about thirty foreign staff members from Afghanistan, curtailed travel by staff outside of Kabul, and temporarily stopped helping Afghan refugees return from camps in neighboring Pakistan. *(UN bombing in Iraq, p. 939)*

UN officials in December stepped up their calls for heightened security, which they said could only be provided by the United States and other countries able to send more troops to Afghanistan. In a toughly worded statement, as part of a December 8 report to the General Assembly, Annan denounced attacks on UN workers, who, he said, were working to improve the lives of Afghans "who have already suffered far too much. Whoever the perpetrators of these acts may be, they are the enemies of the people of Afghanistan itself and the enemies of peace in Afghanistan and in the whole region." Brahimi threatened on December 12 to recommend that the entire UN mission be withdrawn from Afghanistan because of the continued violence.

Many attacks were directed against the Afghan government's new army and police forces. On July 15, for example, about a dozen suspected Taliban fighters attacked a police station near Kandahar, killing the police chief and four officers. Three days later, eight Afghan soldiers on patrol in southeastern Khost province were killed when a remote-controlled mine destroyed their van.

Ordinary Afghan citizens also were killed or wounded in dozens of attacks during the year. The single bloodiest incident was the August 13 bombing of a civilian bus in the southern province of Helmand, killing fifteen people. Officials blamed the Taliban for the bombing. Apparently by coincidence, that day also was the bloodiest one of the year for the country. About two dozen fighters were killed in a factional dispute in the central Urugan province, and about twenty Taliban, al Qaeda, and Afghan army troops were killed in a battle in Khost province.

U.S. forces were responsible for two other deadly incidents early in December. During a major offensive against the Taliban, called Operation Avalanche, U.S. troops inadvertently killed fifteen children. Nine of them were killed on December 6, when two U.S. A-10 jets fired rockets and machine guns at the village of Hutala in the southern province of Ghazni. U.S. officials said the intended target was a suspected Taliban fighter who, they said, was responsible for attacks on foreign aid workers. That man apparently was not in the village at the time, but the rockets and gunfire killed seven boys and two girls, ages eight to twelve years, along with a young man. The killings angered local villagers and government officials who said they could not understand why the United States military did not have better information about who it was attacking. An investigation into the killing of the children was still under way at year's end. Another incident in July 2002—a U.S. air attack that killed forty-eight civilians at a wedding party—had caused widespread outrage and led the military to restrict the use of air assaults.

Yusuf Pashtoon, the newly appointed governor of troubled Kandahar province, told the *Washington Post* in November that the attackers were succeeding in turning some people in his area against the Kabul government and its international supporters, which had failed to provide security or make much improvement in the daily lives of average citizens. "Where people do not see governance, it creates apathy and grounds for insurgency," he said. "If we are to fight against terrorism, we have to win our people back first, and now that has become more difficult, because it is not easy to provide the proper security for services."

U.S. officials acknowledged the continuing security problems but insisted they did not pose a fundamental danger to the process of giving Afghanistan a democratic government. During an early December visit to Afghanistan, Defense Secretary Rumsfeld brushed aside suggestions that security concerns might force a postponement of Afghan presidential election planned for mid-2004. "I can't imagine that there will be any type of delay," he said. A few weeks later UN officials suggested a delay was inevitable unless more action was taken to guarantee security for voters.

Providing Security Outside Kabul

After the Taliban were pushed from power, the United States and its allies kept two distinct military forces in Afghanistan: a "coalition" army of nearly 12,000 troops (about 10,000 of whom were U.S. soldiers) that concentrated on fighting the Taliban and al Qaeda resisters but provided some security in the provinces; and a peacekeeping force, called the International Security Assistance Force (ISAF), which was authorized by, but did not report to, the United Nations. ISAF in 2003 had about 5,500 troops from about a dozen countries (most from Canada and Germany). Since 2001 it had been confined to Kabul and its immediate area at the insistence of the Pentagon, which had not wanted a larger peacekeeping presence to interfere with its military operations elsewhere in Afghanistan.

For all practical purposes, this arrangement meant that most of Afghanistan during 2002 and well into 2003 was left in the hands of regional warlords, each with his own army. Some warlords were heavily armed with tanks and missiles; others had lightly armed militias. Implicitly recognizing the importance of the warlords, the U.S. military turned over to them much of the weapons and equipment that had been captured from the Taliban. According to most estimates, the warlords had a total of about 400,000 fighters.

Because no single country wanted to have long-term responsibility for running ISAF, its leadership was changed every six months, first from Britain to Turkey, then to the joint command of Germany and the Netherlands. After much debate NATO agreed early in 2003 to assume command as of August 11. It was the first time the U.S.-led alliance had commanded a peacekeeping mission outside Europe (its other current missions were in Bosnia and Kosovo). That change of command, however, did not instantly increase the willingness of countries to provide the large number of troops and quantities of military equipment that were needed to provide security in Afghanistan.

Karzai since January 2002 had pressed for peacekeepers to take up positions outside Kabul, particularly in the dangerous provinces where his government had little security presence. He had support from the UN but little backing from the United States, which had the real power to convert talk into action. Officials in Washington finally acted early in 2003 when they established what they called provincial reconstruction teams to provide security for civil rebuilding efforts in the provinces. By year's end seven teams, of sixty to one hundred soldiers each, were operating around the country, with plans for another ten teams in 2004. Most of the teams were to operate in the southern and eastern provinces, the centers of instability. These teams were controversial, however, because they blurred the distinction between soldiers and reconstruction workers—leading aid agencies to fear that their employees would become even more inviting targets for extremist forces. The new U.S. commander in Afghanistan, Lt. Gen. David Baron, said in December the teams would focus their efforts on providing security, leaving aid groups and the Afghan government to handle the bulk of relief and reconstruction work.

Another potentially important step came on October 13 when the UN Security Council adopted Resolution 1510 authorizing ISAF to take up positions outside Kabul for the first time. The first consequence of this action was NATO's agreement, in December, to have ISAF assume command of a German-led provincial reconstruction team in the northern city of Kunduz as of December 31. Even so, NATO countries were still reluctant to send additional troops to Afghanistan. ISAF was not expected to beef up the peacekeeping presence in other areas outside of Kabul until the summer of 2004, nearly two-and-a-half years after Karzai first asked for the additional security.

Ultimately, Afghanistan would have to take responsibility for its own security. As a first step toward that future, Karzai in December 2002 signed a decree creating an Afghanistan army, with an eventual force of 70,000 troops; it would be the country's first real national army in decades. The United States, Germany, and other countries began recruiting and training recruits for the new army at the beginning of 2003, with a goal of having 13,000 soldiers trained, or in training, at year's end. The vast majority of the first recruits came from the militias of warlords. By December this effort was about half-way toward its initial goal: about 6,500 soldiers had been trained and another 2,000-some were in training. In its first major operations, the army in August participated in U.S.-led raids against suspected Taliban forces in the southeastern region. However, several thousand troops—one-half of the total, recruited in the year, according to some estimates—had quit after only a few weeks or months in service. Many were unable to adjust to the discipline of a conventional army, while others were dissatisfied by the low pay or the fact that they were expected to serve far away from home.

A parallel effort was to disarm and demobilize at least 100,000 of the fighters in militias run by warlords and regional governors. The government planned to incorporate about 5,000 of these fighters into the army and convince the rest to find work in the civilian sector. The latter was certain to be a difficult task, given that many of Afghanistan's fighters had never had a civilian job and the only new jobs being created in Afghanistan were with the military and international aid agencies. Japan provided $41 million for an initial project to disarm fighters and give them training for civilian jobs.

As always in Afghanistan, ethnic differences played a major role in the security situation. Most Afghans in the troubled south and east sections were ethnic Pashtuns, the country's single largest group, which also had provided the base of support for the Taliban. Karzai himself was a Pashtun, but men from the Panjshir Valley in the north dominated many of his government ministries. Chief among them was the defense ministry, headed by Mohammed Qasim Fahim, an ethnic Tajik warlord who had his own militia. The Panjshir Valley was home to Tajiks, Uzbeks, and other minorities who had been prominent in the Northern Alliance, the army that had fought the Taliban during the 1990s. Annan said in December that many Afghans still believed "that real [government] power remains in the hands of a single faction"—the warlords from the Panjshir Valley.

Building a Government

Karzai, a worldly member of a prominent family in southern Afghanistan, became the country's interim leader at the end of 2001. His job, and his government, were both created by an agreement among leaders of major Afghan factions during negotiations in Bonn, Germany, just as the Taliban government was falling in November and December 2001. That agreement envisioned a two-step process toward a permanent government: first, a "transitional" government that officially entered office in June 2002 with the approval of another assembly of Afghan leaders; then the negotiation of a permanent constitution, leading to the country's first-ever elections for president and a parliament.

Karzai's chief task during 2002 had been to create a semblance of a functioning government that was confined to Kabul, since that was the only place where it could be protected by the ISAF peacekeepers. During 2003 Karzai began what was certain to be a longer-term process of extending the government's reach into the other twenty-five provinces. Some of these regions were still controlled by warlords, and some of those warlords had considerably more power locally than Karzai's government could hope to exercise in the foreseeable future. A notable example was western Herat province, where warlord Ismael Kahn held the title of governor and technically reported to Karzai but had his own army and collected his own taxes, a small portion of which, reportedly, he forwarded to Kabul. The government gradually gained a modest degree of control over some other provinces during 2003, but parts of provinces in the south, east, and northeast were still lawless frontiers or even fell under the renewed control of the Taliban.

In the opening shot of his campaign to gain more control over outlying areas, Karzai on May 20 brought ten powerful provincial governors and two regional commanders to Kabul and demanded that they comply with a thirteen-point plan to centralize authority. When some resisted, Karzai on August 13 replaced the governors of three provinces, including the warlord Gul Agha Sherzai, who controlled the important province of Kandahar. Karzai also fired security chiefs in six provinces and stripped Herat governor Kahn of his post as a regional military commander. Moving to bolster the finances of his shaky government, Karzai managed in midyear to confiscate about $65 million in customs revenues that had been hoarded by Kahn and other governors; while significant, UN officials said this amount was only a fraction of what the governors had collected. Karzai's campaign to rein in the warlords appeared to have the support of the U.S. military, which previously had relied on the provincial chieftains to maintain some stability.

After an outburst of conflict between two rival armies in northern Afghanistan during October, Karzai demanded that the region's two powerful rival warlords—Abdul Rashid Dostum and Atta Mohammad—disarm their forces and merge them under neutral leadership. The two men began that process November 21 with the handing over to the government of some tanks and other heavy weapons. Dostum, an ethnic Uzbek, cooperated only grudgingly and turned over far fewer weapons than did his enemy, an ethnic Tajik. As of year's end, however, Karzai had been unable to gain real control over his defense minister, Fahim, whose personal militia of Tajik fighters still ran much of Kabul.

Karzai had been under increasing international pressure to exert more authority. Some of the pressure came from behind-the-scenes warnings by international diplomats, but other pressure came in public declarations by human rights groups and international relief agencies. The U.S.-based Human Rights Watch issued perhaps the strongest warning of the year, saying in a July 28 report that regional warlords—many of whom held government posts—had used kidnapping, extortion, death threats, and other tactics to create a "climate of fear" in much of the country. "If allowed to continue with impunity, these abuses will make it impossible for Afghans to create a modern, democratic state," the report said.

Karzai had even less control over the actions of international governments and agencies in Afghanistan than he did over powerful warlords. Although the government offered some input, it had little real power over the rebuilding of Afghanistan. Brahimi's UN mission supervised most international aid that was funded by donor nations and nongovernmental relief groups. The U.S. military ran its own relief and reconstruction projects, subject to the approval of the Pentagon, not of Karzai or his aides. The simple truth was that Karzai's government lacked the technical resources and bookkeeping skills to satisfy the accountants where the money came from—Washington, Tokyo, London, and other capitals.

One of the most important symbols of the new government was a new currency. Introduced in April, it replaced a crazy-quilt of currencies that warlords and regional governors used.

Drafting a New Constitution

The final and most difficult task of the year proved to be the writing of a new constitution, which was to lead to elections for a permanent government. A working group began writing a constitution in late 2002 and presented a draft in April to Karzai, who turned it over to a thirty-five member commission representing the country's major groups. The commission held public meetings throughout the country and came up with a revised draft on November 3. That document called for a strong president, a bicameral legislature, guaranteed civil rights (including for women), and a legal system that did not contradict Islam but did not necessarily enshrine Islamic law, known as *Shariah*. That document was then turned over to a traditional national assembly, known as a *Loya Jirga,* which began meeting at Kabul University on December 14.

The *Loya Jirga* had five hundred delegates, nearly all of whom had been chosen at the provincial level or by special constituencies, such as women's groups or religious minorities. Karzai himself appointed fifty-two delegates. The vast majority of the delegates were aligned with the Islamist *mujahideen* factions and were committed to ensuring the primacy of Islamic law, rather than the secular legal and political concepts that UN officials had promoted.

Leaders had hoped the *Loya Jirga* could finish its work quickly so that a final constitution could be ready by the end of the year. The debate within the assembly quickly centered on two key issues: the role of Islamic law and the basic type of government to be created by the constitution. Karzai was the focus of the latter question. He had demanded a strong presidency, saying the country needed a firm hand to create unity from the chaos that had reigned for decades. His conservative opponents wanted instead a parliamentary system, with a figurehead president offset by a strong prime minister beholden to the parliament. Some delegates also wanted to restore the power of the former king, Zahir Shah, who had ruled for four decades before he was deposed in 1973. Karzai announced at the outset of the assembly that he would not run for the presidency if the parliamentary system was adopted.

By late December it was clear that Karzai had beaten back the drive for a strong parliament, but continued haggling pushed the conclusion of the constitution past the end of the year. Work was suspended on December 30 because northern warlords were demanding more power for the Tajik, Uzbek, and other minorities.

Final agreement came January 4, 2004, on a constitution that preserved the strong presidency that Karzai wanted but also gave the parliament additional powers. Some observers said wording in the final document also could be interpreted as opening the door to imposition of Islamic law. Praising the document, Karzai told delegates: "The constitution cannot be just on paper. The constitution will be law when it is practiced. And I will implement this law. And if I don't, remove me."

Even before the delay in finishing the constitution, the UN and the Afghan government faced a potentially significant delay in the plans to prepare to the country's first-ever presidential election in June 2004, to be followed at some later point by elections for the parliament. The UN administration on July 26 appointed a commission to prepare for the elections, but a voter registration drive was delayed for six weeks in October and November because donors were slow in committing money for the $78 million election budget. The explosion of a car bomb outside the UN office in Kandahar in November also forced the UN to reduce the number of teams it planned to send into the provinces to register voters. By year's end only about 275,000 of an estimated 10 million potential voters had been registered. Because of this slow process and the uncertain security situation, many observers, and even government officials, expressed doubt at year's end about whether the elections could be held on schedule.

Helping Refugees and Displaced People

At the end of the 2001 war, more than 4 million Afghans were refugees in other countries (most in Pakistan and Iran), and more than 1 million were "internally displaced"—forced from their homes but still living within the country. In 2002 about 1.8 million refugees returned to Afghanistan (although not necessarily to their original homes) and nearly 450,000 of the displaced people returned to their homes. The returns continued in 2003, although at a slower pace than in the previous year because of continuing security problems and because those most anxious to return home already had done so. The UNHCR said in late October that about 700,000 refugees had returned from Iran and Pakistan during the year, bringing the two-year total of returns to about 2.5 million. The murder in November of the UNHCR worker in Ghazni, southwest of Kabul, led the agency to suspend its work of repatriating refugees from Pakistan.

Some reports suggested potential problems with the estimated 1 million or so refugees who remained in Pakistan. Many of them told UN officials they did not want to return to Afghanistan because it was unsafe or they had become relatively comfortable in Pakistan. The Pakistan government appeared equally determined to rid itself of the Afghan refugees and was demanding faster repatriation of them by the UN.

Another 80,000 internally displaced people returned to their homes during 2003, about half of whom received international aid. Most of these people had been living in displacement camps in the southern and western provinces of Afghanistan. The UNHCR estimated at year's end that about 180,000 Afghans remained displaced inside the country, most of them in the two southern provinces of Helmand and Kandahar. The Norwegian Refugee Council and other private agencies gave higher estimates ranging up to 300,000.

Most refugees and displaced people were able to return to their own homes, or to those of relatives, but thousands of returning families discovered that their former homes had been destroyed. By the end of 2003 UNHCR had provided housing for about 250,000 of those homeless returnees. In most cases, families were given four walls for a house on a plot of land, materials for roofing and windows, and a small cash stipend to finish the construction work.

Reconstruction

Afghanistan always had been poor, but more than two decades of war had left it a shambles. Kabul, once a relatively cosmopolitan city for Central Asia, had been wrecked by years of bombing; few buildings were wholly intact, and they had been pockmarked by gunfire. Housing and public buildings in most other cities were in equally bad shape. Rural areas, where most of the conflict had taken place, had been largely depopulated. Thousands of acres of orchards had been destroyed, and millions of land mines had been planted in the countryside, making fields too dangerous for farmers to sow their crops.

The United Nations estimated in January 2002 that restoring just the basic elements of civil society in Afghanistan would cost at least $10 billion over five years. The United States and other donor nations promised to provide that money, but the promises came quicker than did the checks. For 2003, donors had pledged $1.8 billion for UN-supervised reconstruction work. As of late December less than $800 million had actually been delivered to Afghanistan.

The reconstruction that did take place in Afghanistan included several hundred schools that were built or rebuilt—the first in Afghanistan since 1975. The United Nations Children's Fund announced in October that 1 million Afghan girls had entered school in the two years since the fall of the Taliban, who had barred education for girls. Health clinics were created in several cities and rural areas, power stations serving the cities were made to function most of the time, and important public buildings were repaired in Kabul and a handful of other locations.

The pace was slow, however, and many Afghans complained that the piecemeal nature of reconstruction had fallen well behind public expectations of what the United States could do for the country. Among those voicing such complaints was Ahmed Wali Karzai, who represented his brother, the president, in the city of Kandahar. "There have been no significant changes for the people," he told the Associated Press in mid-April. "People are tired of seeing small, small projects. I don't know what to say to people anymore."

In terms of both symbolism and hard reality, one of the key accomplishments of the year was the completion of the first phase of rebuilding Afghanistan's most important road: a two-lane highway that circled the country, starting at Kabul in the east. The United States had built the road in the 1950s, but decades of war and neglect had left it little more than a sand-and-dirt path. Karzai's priority was to rebuild the 300-mile section of the road between Kabul and Kandahar (in south-central Afghanistan), but his efforts to secure international financing were stalled until he convinced Bush to make a personal commitment that the United States would ensure that the entire southern half of the road was rebuilt. Bush pledged that the Kabul to Kandahar section would be finished by December 31, and on December 18 Karzai and U.S. officials staged a ceremony to mark the completion of one layer of asphalt. Additional work was planned for 2004, including rebuilding the rest of the road northwest toward the city of Herat, near the border with Iran. Iran already had rebuilt the road from its border to Herat, one of many reconstruction projects it financed in western Afghanistan.

The United States focused its other aid efforts on building primary schools and health clinics, especially for women in rural areas. According to UN statistics, more than three-fourths of Afghan women were illiterate and the country had the highest rate of maternal mortality in the world because of the near-total lack of health care services in most of the country. UN, U.S., and European agencies established initial goals of building or rebuilding hundreds of schools and making basic health services available, within a four-hour walk or drive, to every woman in Afghanistan. These programs offered new opportunities for women, but numerous reports said Afghan women continued to suffer abuse at the hands of men who believed Islam accorded women no rights.

Afghanistan finally had a good year for agriculture in 2003. After years of drought, the rains came to much of the country, helping produce a bumper crop for many grains, including wheat, the harvest of which reportedly was the best in twenty-five years. Relief agencies continued to provide food for some remote areas, but for the first time in two decades starvation and malnutrition were not serious problems in the country.

The one area of the economy that needed no assistance from the UN and other official agencies was the narcotics trade. Before the Taliban cracked down on production in the late 1990s, Afghanistan was the world's leading source of opium poppies, used to make heroin and morphine. The departure of the Taliban, and the collapse of central authority, enabled poppy farmers in the western and northeastern regions to resume production with the 2002 harvest. By 2003 Afghanistan once again had the dubious distinction of leading the world in the growth of opium; the UN in October estimated that the narcotics trade generated $2.3 billion for Afghan farmers and traffickers, equal to half the country's official gross domestic product.

Following are excerpts from two reports by United Nations Secretary General Kofi Annan on the situation in Afghanistan: first, "Emergency International Assistance for Peace, Normalcy and Reconstruction of War-Stricken Afghanistan," submitted December 3, 2003, to the UN General Assembly; second, "The Situation in Afghanistan and Its Implications for International Peace and Security," submitted December 30, 2003, to the UN Security Council.

"Emergency Assistance for Peace and Reconstruction of War-Stricken Afghanistan"

V. Observations

77. It has been more than 12 months since the establishment of the Transitional Administration [the interim government of Afghanistan]. In this time, the initial euphoria of peace has been replaced by the complex legacies of two and a half decades of armed conflict. As a result, critical political processes have had to be or are at risk of being delayed. Strong political will on the part of the Government of Afghanistan and Member States will be required, in particular to redress insecurity and promote the reform of key government institutions.

78. As the Transitional Administration struggles to consolidate its authority and to extend the mantle of security to the provinces, the same factional politics that destabilize much of the country undermine its effectiveness as a national Government. There has been an increasing sense among key constituencies that certain institutions of government are neither accountable for their actions nor reflective of national aspirations. In this climate, ensuring a secure environment for the Constitutional Loya Jirga and 2004 national elections envisioned by the Bonn Agreement [an agreement among Afghan factions signed in Bonn, Germany, in December 2001] takes on greater importance. If the outcomes of these processes are to lay the foundation for reconciliation and stability, then the processes themselves must be perceived as legitimate and public participation must be free of intimidation and political violence.

79. The success of the upcoming political undertakings therefore depends first and foremost on the commitment of the major factions that have established a military presence extending over various parts of the country. Every day that key Government ministries remain dominated by factional interests is another day in which Afghan confidence in the central Government is further eroded. First among the ministries that must be reformed are those responsible for the security of the nation: Defence, Interior and Intelligence. Continued reform should send an important signal to the country of the Government's commitment to the creation of truly national security forces and should build the trust necessary for a successful disarmament, demobilization and reintegration programme. Additional time-specific benchmarks that should help ensure that the Government and the international community are able to conduct a credible election must be identified and met.

80. Security is needed not only to create the environment for political activities, but for reconstruction as well. The restriction of development activities in the most unstable parts of the country has not been without consequence. The denial of both security and basic social services to populations in these areas serves to further undermine public confidence in the peace process. Providing social sector reconstruction—in terms of schools, clinics, roads, and economic opportunities—attributable to the central Government will build not only political support, but also loyalty to national institutions. Such development opportunities are also likely to minimize entry into the illegal drug economy, which, if unchecked, has the potential to undermine much of the institution-building effort and the rule of law in Afghanistan. In this context, the recently proposed injection of up to $1.5 billion in aid from the United States of America would likely have a major impact on the rebuilding of

Afghanistan, particularly as a portion of the money would finance projects that could be completed within a year, thereby having maximum effect before the elections in 2004.

81. The disarmament, demobilization and reintegration of armed groups and their replacement by a national army; the training of a new, professional police force; the rehabilitation of the justice system; and stemming the threat posed by illicit drugs are all essential for security, prosperity and the restoration of rule of law in Afghanistan. The international community has demonstrated its commitment to help with the establishment of the new security and legal institutions. Yet, while progress in any one of these areas is a step towards peace in Afghanistan, the full benefit of these combined projects will be felt only in the years to come.

82. Clearly, there are grave challenges to the Bonn process, and the commitment of the international community and the Afghan Government must not waver now. To ensure that the Bonn process succeeds in consolidating peace and stability, it is indispensable that international support be significantly increased and sustained. Above all, the international community needs to strengthen its commitment to provide security. The best way to fill the security gap is for Member States to give meaning to [Security Council] resolution 1510 (2003) and contribute the necessary resources to enable ISAF [International Security Assistance Force, the peacekeeping force in Afghanistan] to expand to the areas where it is most needed.

83. The United Nations remains committed to fulfilling the mandate set by Bonn, but it can do so only if the present deterioration in security is halted and reversed, and if the programmes and staff, both national and international, of the United Nations, non-governmental organizations and others assisting the Afghans are provided adequate protection. The increase in attacks on United Nations staff and other international and Afghan civilians engaged in providing assistance and furthering the peace process is a matter of the utmost concern. Their work is aimed only at improving the lives of Afghans, who have already suffered far too much. Whoever the perpetrators of these acts may be, they are the enemies of the people of Afghanistan itself and the enemies of peace in Afghanistan and in the whole region. Such despicable acts must be condemned in the strongest possible terms by everyone, and the criminal elements behind them must be made to understand that they will be resolutely opposed by all Afghan authorities, as well as by all regional and international actors whose interests and duty is to protect and promote the peace process in Afghanistan.

84. Finally, taking note of the invitation made to me by the Security Council mission to Afghanistan to study the possibilities for a second

international conference to ensure the necessary financial support and political momentum for peace and stability in Afghanistan, I have begun a process of consultations on a follow-up to the Bonn process. In broad terms, I believe that such a conference would bring together a representative spectrum of the Afghan population in partnership with the international community. These stakeholders would review what has been achieved so far and assess what must be improved. The second conference would provide an opportunity to revise priorities for Afghanistan and define an agenda beyond the life of the Bonn Agreement. The conference should therefore serve to regenerate the political and financial support necessary for a full political and economic transition, as envisaged by the Bonn Agreement.

Source: United Nations. General Assembly. "The Situation in Afghanistan and Its Implications for International Peace and Security: Emergency International Assistance for Peace, Normalcy and Reconstruction of War-Stricken Afghanistan." Report of the Secretary-General, A/58/616. December 3, 2003. www.un.org/Docs/journal/asp/ws.asp?m=A/58/616 (accessed January 7, 2004).

"Situation in Afghanistan and Its Implications for International Peace"

II. Implementation of the Bonn Agreement

A. Overall security situation

5. Afghanistan has experienced a deterioration in security at precisely the point where the peace process demands the opposite. The reporting period saw an increase in terrorist activity, factional fighting, activities associated with the illegal narcotics trade and unchecked criminality. In the last 90 days, the number of reported incidents targeting civilians exceeded the total of those that occurred in the first 20 months following the signing of the Bonn Agreement. At their height during the reporting period, attacks against the humanitarian community escalated from a rate of one per month to one almost every two days. This rate has subsided over the past several weeks, though threats

against the international community remain and a number of steps have been taken to minimize exposure to them.

6. Attacks on international and national staff of the assistance community and officials of the central Government have been concentrated in the south and the south-east. Previously, such acts were largely conducted in relatively remote or isolated areas, but in recent months they have expanded to city centres. On 16 November an international staff member of the Office of the United Nations High Commissioner for Refugees, Bettina Goislard, was assassinated in broad daylight in the centre of Ghazni. This closely followed a car-bomb attack on United Nations offices in Kandahar on 13 November, which damaged the premises but fortunately did not result in loss of life.

7. In the affected areas, in the absence of sufficient forces to provide security, unarmed civilians cannot be asked to shoulder unreasonable risks and continue activities that make them targets. Accordingly, much of the south and south-east of the country is now effectively off limits to the United Nations, the assistance community and central Government officials, except under special escort. Lack of access to assistance or structures of the State risks further alienating the population, which is predominantly Pashtun, and may increase their willingness to tolerate, if not support, the presence of those among them who have an agenda that is at odds with the peace process.

8. In response to the increased threat against the United Nations and the aid community, on 26 November President Karzai established two national task forces, bringing together the Afghan security ministries, the International Security Assistance Force (ISAF), the coalition forces and the United Nations. One task force is working on short-term measures to ensure the necessary security for the Bonn processes and for aid and reconstruction efforts, while the second is to work on responses to security threats over the longer term. UNAMA presented the former with a list of urgent requests, including requests for increased resources needed by the Ministry of Interior units deployed to protect United Nations and aid community premises and Bonn processes, for greater coordination in security planning, for increased protection support from ISAF and the coalition and for information sharing. The task force structure has been replicated at the regional level, where national and international security actors have worked with UNAMA to prepare local security plans.

9. The arbitrary rule of local commanders and the presence of factional forces in significant portions of the country continued to be another source of insecurity. Allegations continued that communities under

their control are often deprived of their basic rights and are victims of serious human rights abuses. The north, in particular, has suffered the effects of factional fighting. In October, just weeks before the planned start of the pilot phase of the disarmament, demobilization and reintegration programme, the population of Mazar-i-Sharif (Balkh province) was subjected to intense interfactional fighting—6 people were reportedly killed and 30 injured. The Minister of Interior negotiated a ceasefire and heavy weapons disarmament agreement with General Atta Mohammed and General Dostum, the implementation of which is being supervised by the Joint Security Commission, with the participation of the Mazar-i-Sharif provincial reconstruction team and UNAMA.

10. Some 280 Kabul-based police were deployed to Mazar-i-Sharif on 18 October. Despite the insufficiency of equipment, including weapons and ammunition, the police have dismantled illegal checkpoints, are manning official checkpoints with the local police and are doing foot patrols in the city. A battalion of the Afghan National Army (and its trainers from the coalition forces) was also dispatched to the north to provide security to the heavy weapons cantonment site, in accordance with the ceasefire agreement. The troops are also patrolling Chimtal and Charbolok districts (Balkh province), where the sites are located.

11. Thus far, the forces of General Atta Mohammed [a regional warlord] have demonstrated compliance with the agreement; the forces of General [Rashid] Dostum [another regional warlord] have shown some resistance, as reflected in the fact that they have handed over fewer weapons. Some observers have suggested that this resistance to disarmament may be intended to maintain a point of leverage in the ongoing discussions with the Government relating to General Dostum's future position. . . .

VII. Observations

60. The ultimate aim of the Bonn process is of course to ensure Afghanistan's transition from the war and instability of the past 23 years to a degree of peace and stability that is irreversible, with a constitutionally empowered and democratically elected Government and the necessary security and financial resources to provide a sound basis for the country's continued development. Over the past two years, much progress has been made towards that end. However, critical challenges now face the process, and Afghanistan and the international community will need to take further steps, expeditiously, if the process is to be successfully concluded.

61. Chief among these challenges is the problem of insecurity created by factional misrule in the provinces, and by the efforts of "spoilers", including Taliban elements, loyalists of Gulbuddin Hekmatyar and possibly Al-Qaida to disrupt the peace process and the reconstruction effort using tactics of terror and insurgency. With currently limited national army, police and international security resources to provide protection, insecurity in the south and south-east, particularly, has had the effect of shrinking the area in which the Government, the United Nations and the international community can effectively operate. This has negative implications for both the reconstruction effort and the political processes of Bonn. The Government, ISAF, the coalition forces and the United Nations are working hard to better coordinate and increase the resources available on the ground to address the problem, but, as yet, these are too limited to ensure the completion of the Bonn process.

62. To date, the political elements of the Bonn process have been successfully carried forward by concentrating activities in city and regional centres, thereby mitigating threats that predominated in rural areas. Thus, for example, the public consultations on the Constitution, which would preferably have been conducted right down to the district level, were held in provincial capitals. Likewise, the registration and election of Constitutional Loya Jirga delegates drew on the process used for Emergency Loya Jirga district delegates and took place at protected provincial and regional centres, since a new series of elections beginning at the district level was no longer possible in all areas. The recent attacks on the United Nations in the cities of Kandahar and Ghazni, and threats by people claiming to speak on behalf of the Taliban, have highlighted that security threats for international personnel and for the Bonn process now exist in city centres.

63. With the start of electoral registration, the Bonn process has now arrived at the point where such mitigation strategies cannot suffice. The number of registration centres currently open is too low to meet the target rate of registration. Direct access to each of up to 10 million eligible voters must be available, and lack of access due to insecurity will result in the disenfranchisement of voters. Given that inaccessible areas are concentrated in the south, this disenfranchisement would have most damaging ethnic undertones. Also, while presidential elections based on a single national constituency might still credibly be held if a few small areas were left out, (although there would be risks if the winner had only a small margin of victory), legislative elections would not be possible. It is therefore urgently important that the Afghan Government, ISAF and the coalition forces take every measure possible to resolve the security problems facing the electoral process.

64. Security for elections must involve more than the protection of electoral stations and staff. There must also be an environment enabling free political organization and expression. To limit the constraints on political freedom currently maintained by factional leaders through their military dominance in the regions, it is critical that the disarmament, demobilization and reintegration process also move forward. The planned expansion of international security assistance beyond Kabul can accelerate the disarmament, demobilization and reintegration process in a number of ways, including by monitoring the process, encouraging the factional commanders to participate and accelerating the build-up of national army and police forces in the regions to replace demobilized units. Here too, time is of the essence, as the expansion currently planned by NATO is not expected to take effect for some months. I urge NATO and the coalition forces to take every measure possible to speed the deployment of security assistance in the provinces.

65. The Afghan Transitional Administration and the international community have been partners in the Bonn process, a partnership characterized by a high degree of mutual cooperation and support, which is to be commended. Others, who wish to stop the process, have shown that they are reorganizing. It may be said that now there is a race between those who support the Bonn process and those who wish to see it fail.

66. I believe that this race certainly can be won, but complacency is not an option, and we must resolutely take the steps necessary to ensure success. I believe the time has come for the international community, the Afghan Government and, indeed, all Afghans committed to peace in their country to come together, assess the progress made and make the necessary commitments to complete the transition in Afghanistan. President Karzai and Minister for Foreign Affairs Abdullah discussed with the Security Council mission that visited Afghanistan the possibility of a second international conference on Afghanistan. In line with the Council's request to me to further explore that possibility, my Special Representative for Afghanistan has circulated a non-paper to the Afghan Government and diplomatic corps in Kabul. The non-paper acknowledges gains made under the Bonn process so far, but points out that to ensure success, further reforms are needed to broaden the representativeness of the Government, improvements in the security situation must be made to end the misrule of factions and counter at all levels the threat from terrorists, and more progress in reconstruction must be made. The non-paper further argues that donor commitments are needed, beyond the timelines of the Bonn Agreement, to consolidate Government authority,

entrench the rule of law, counter the threat of the narcotics econ-omy and carry Afghanistan's peace process to the point of irreversibility.

67. One way of addressing the issues raised in that non-paper might be the convening of a new political and donor conference, in the first months of 2004, to chart the way forward. Its aim should be to strengthen the gains made and accelerate the implementation of the Bonn Agreement. Such a conference would also help ensure the success of presidential elections in mid-2004, as it would help address some of the challenges that now lie in the path of the Bonn process. A clear plan, coupled with finances conditional on its implementation, will provide a strong signal that the resolve of the Afghan leadership and the international community remains firm.

68. The outcome of the ongoing Constitutional Loya Jirga remains to be seen. Afghans listening to and watching the live broadcasts are observing open political debate of a kind that has been absent in their country for many years. They hope the delegates to the Loya Jirga will undertake their historic responsibility in a spirit of com-promise and with the aim of consensus, so that the new Constitu-tion can be a foundation for a new Afghanistan, at peace with itself and its neighbours.

69. Finally, on the occasion of his departure, I wish to pay a special tribute to Lakhdar Brahimi, my Special Representative, for his exceptional leadership and commitment, and to all the men and women of UNAMA and its partner organizations for their out-standing efforts on behalf of Afghanistan.

Source: United Nations. Security Council. "The Situation in Afghanistan and its Implications for International Peace and Security." Report of the Secretary-General, S/2003/1212. December 30, 2003. http://daccess-ods.un.org/TMP/5959867.html (accessed March 12, 2004).

British Commonwealth
Leaders on Zimbabwe

December 7, 2003

INTRODUCTION

Zimbabwe remained mired in political and economic turmoil during 2003—battered by rising domestic and international dissent over the authoritarian tactics of its longtime leader, Robert Mugabe. Opposition groups mounted numerous protests, which Mugabe's government attempted to suppress with mass arrests and curbs on the news media. Opposition leader Morgan Tsvangirai, who claimed to have defeated Mugabe in a disputed presidential election in March 2002, was put on trial on charges of treason. Mugabe came under strong international pressure, most notably from the fifty-four-nation British Commonwealth, which acted twice during 2003 to isolate him diplomatically until he agreed to negotiate with his opposition.

These pressures, coupled with the rapid implosion of Zimbabwe's economy, appeared to have little immediate impact, however. Mugabe, a leader of the successful movement in the 1960s and 1970s to take control of the country from the country's tiny white minority, remained defiant. He insisted that Tsvangirai and other domestic opponents were merely doing the bidding of Britain, the former colonial ruler. As the aging Mugabe clung to power, his country sank into an economic depression, with an estimated one-half of the population dependent on foreign food aid for survival. (*Background, Historic Documents of 2002, p. 133*)

A Food Crisis and Economic Collapse

During the middle part of the twentieth century Zimbabwe was known as the second richest country in southern Africa (after South Africa) and as the breadbasket of the region because of its relatively vibrant economy, rich farmlands, and productive farmers. That had changed by the early part of the twenty-first century, when an extended drought, the government's confiscation of land from nearly all white farmers, and inefficient government policies had sharply curtailed agricultural production. By January 2003 the UN's World Food Program said that 7.2 million of the 12.5 million Zimbabweans depended on food aid. Production of corn, the staple food in Zimbabwe, dropped by about 70 percent during 2002, according to UN estimates. Zimbabwe was the hardest hit of several southern African countries that suffered a prolonged drought.

By far the most controversial aspect of Zimbabwe's trouble was the role played by a "land reform" program Mugabe initiated in 2000. Arguing that a tiny minority of whites continued to own most of the country's prime farmland, Mugabe pushed through legislation confiscating most white-owned farms and giving them to blacks. According to government records, in 2000 about 4,000 white farmers owned about 27 million acres of prime farmland, while an estimated 1 million blacks owned 40 million acres, much of it unproductive or located in drought-prone areas. By 2003 only 600 white farmers remained on their lands, the rest having been driven off by government seizures or by mass takeovers by black squatters. An estimated 300,000 blacks who worked on the farms were evicted, along with the white owners; most were unable to find new jobs. Opposition groups, including an association of white farmers, said that many farms had been taken over by government officials or friends and family members of Mugabe's—including the president's wife. Mugabe announced in February that the "land reform" program was complete, apparently indicating that he planned no more seizures of the remaining white-owned farms. White farmers, and Western critics of Mugabe's policies, said the land seizures sharply cut Zimbabwe's agricultural production because farms had been broken into small plots that were inadequately managed or even left fallow. Mugabe rejected this argument, saying white farmers had mostly grown crops for export—such as tobacco—that had made money for them but not provided food for Zimbabweans.

Rather than attempting to stimulate production, Mugabe's government responded to the crisis by imposing price controls on food and barring everyone except the government from importing essential grains. Visiting Zimbabwe on January 25, World Food Program director James Morris said these steps made the situation worse by eliminating incentives for the production and distribution of food. "The free market needs to work," he said. Agricultural production did not improve during the year, and the World Food Program announced on December 23 that Western governments had provided only half of the aid that was needed to respond to the drought in the region. The UN agency said it had been forced to cut in half the daily ration of corn meal for about 3 million needy Zimbabweans.

The food crisis was a major factor in the decline of Zimbabwe's overall economy. Between 2000 and 2003, total economic output had fallen by about one-third, according to the International Monetary Fund. An estimated two-thirds of the working-age population was unemployed. Inflation reached astronomical levels—zooming from an annual rate of about 200 percent at the beginning of 2003 to more than 600 percent at year's end, in large part because the government tripled fuel prices. Zimbabwe also was one of the African countries most affected by the AIDS pandemic; as of 2003 an estimated 25 percent of the total population was infected with the HIV virus that caused AIDS. *(AIDS, p. 780)*

A Domestic Political Stalemate

After the 2002 elections Mugabe's government moved to crush the opposition by brushing aside all legal challenges to the outcome, banning public meetings, arresting protesters, curbing the news media, and filing criminal charges against Tsvangirai. The government used similar tactics all through 2003 despite growing international pressure for a negotiated compromise that would enable Mugabe to step aside peacefully. Rumors surfaced repeatedly that Mugabe, age seventy-nine, was planning to retire to a multimillion-dollar palace he was building north of Harare, the capital. The rumors were fueled by some of his own statements hinting that his life's work was near completion. However, his actions indicated a willingness to retire anytime soon.

The year's political developments took place in courtrooms and on the street, but none had come to a final conclusion as of year's end. Legal maneuverings took place on two fronts: a government charge of treason against opposition leader Tsvangirai, and Tsvangirai's counterclaim demanding that the 2002 election be nullified because of vote-rigging. The treason charge stemmed from the government's claim that Tsvangirai had plotted to kill Mugabe. The trial of Tsvangirai and two associates opened February 3 and initially was expected to last three weeks but dragged on, intermittently, through the rest of the year. The government's principal evidence was a videotape showing Tsvangirai discussing Mugabe with a political consultant. Prosecutors said the tape showed that Tsvangirai proposed killing Mugabe when he discussed "eliminating" him. Tsvangirai and his lawyer said the tape had been edited to create the impression the government sought. No decision had been rendered as of year's end.

More than a year after he filed his complaint against the 2002 election, Tsvangirai won a brief hearing before the nation's high court on November 6. His lawyers gave the court more than two hundred pages of documents describing what they said were abuses of the election process. The court had not ruled on the case as of the end of the year.

The Zimbabwe Human Rights Forum, a coalition of churches and human rights groups, on February 1 issued a stinging rebuke of the government, saying that corruption and violence had become commonplace. "Organized violence and torture is taking place on an unremitting basis," the group said.

Political forces aligned with the government routinely attacked leaders and supporters of opposition groups but had little to fear from police, the forum said.

Opposition groups called a series of national strikes, beginning in mid-March, to protest government repression and demand that Mugabe enter into unconditional negotiations with the opposition. Mugabe had said he would talk only after Tsvangirai recognized the legitimacy of the 2002 election. The first work stoppage shut down many factories, offices, and stores, and the government retaliated by arresting several hundred strikers and officials of Tsvangirai's party, the Movement for Democratic Change (MDC), including its vice president. Amnesty International denounced the repression, saying "the alarming escalation in political violence is a clear indication that the Zimbabwe authorities are determined to suppress dissent by any means necessary, regardless of the terrible consequences."

A second three-day strike, organized jointly by the MDC and the Zimbabwe Congress of Trade Unions, began April 23 and successfully shut down much of the economy but had no more effect than the first in budging Mugabe. An even longer strike took place June 2–6; again, most businesses closed, but a massive crackdown by government security forces (including the arrests of more than five hundred opposition supporters) prevented mass demonstrations. Among those arrested was Tsvangirai, who on the last day of the strike was charged with two additional counts of treason because he had advocated mass protests against Mugabe. Tsvangirai was held in jail for two weeks until a judge overruled the government's attempt to deny his release on bail.

Stifling the News Media

Mugabe's government, which during the 1980s and 1990s had taken over nearly all the nation's news media outlets, engaged in running battles throughout 2003 with the last remaining independent newspaper, the *Daily News*. The newspaper for months refused to register with the government, as required by a law Mugabe introduced in 2002 imposing tight conditions on reporting by the news media. Early in 2003 the government arrested more than a dozen journalists, including employees of the *Daily News,* and charged them with defaming political leaders or failing to comply with various registration requirements. The government also barred foreign journalists from working in Zimbabwe, although some U.S. and European reporters were able to enter the country surreptitiously.

On September 11 the chief justice of Zimbabwe's High Court ruled that the *Daily News* had violated the law by failing to register. Two days later police raided the newspaper's office in Harare and ordered it closed. Editor Francis Mdlongwa told the *New York Times* the action was "an unprecedented assault on media freedom by a government that is terrified of media that offers alternative news." Another High Court judge on September 18 ordered the government to allow the *Daily News* to resume publishing; this step occurred after police removed more than one hundred computers from the newspaper and arrested dozens of demonstrators protesting its closing. The government defied the judge's order, however, and on September 20 a government commission rejected the newspaper's belated registration application, saying the owners had missed a deadline. Yet another court on October 24 ordered the government to issue a license to the *Daily News.* The newspaper promptly printed its first edition in nearly six weeks, proclaiming in a defiant editorial that government authorities "were and are still obsessed with muzzling the independent media." Police immediately raided the newspaper, shutting it down again on October 25.

Mugabe's International Isolation

In 2002 a pattern emerged in which most Western leaders sought to pressure Mugabe by isolating him, while many African leaders sought to engage him in a process they called quiet diplomacy. That pattern continued throughout 2003. The reluctance of African leaders to confront Mugabe directly stemmed from a long-standing policy of noninterference in each other's affairs. The leaders of South Africa, the one country with the most ability to influence Mugabe, were reluctant to act against him, at least in part because he had supported their own drive to overcome white minority rule in the 1980s. South African president Thabo Mbeki also faced his own internal political pressures, largely because of his government's inability to improve living standards for millions of poor people. Tsvangirai, Zimbabwe's opposition leader, also acknowledged the limited effectiveness of outside pressure. He told the *New York Times* on June 27 that "there must be a balance in how outside pressures are applied in order to bring results."

The diplomatic events of 2003 were played out in several international forums, most importantly the Commonwealth. That organization of nations that had once been part of the British empire was primarily of symbolic significance; it was a forum where leaders from Africa, Asia, and the Caribbean discussed common problems on an equal footing with leaders of industrialized nations, including Britain, Canada, and Australia. In March 2002, to protest Mugabe's handling of the disputed elections, the Commonwealth suspended Zimbabwe's membership for one year.

As the one-year anniversary of that step approached, Commonwealth leaders appeared to be split on a next step. Australian prime minister John Howard, the current Commonwealth chairman, called in February for a one-year renewal of Zimbabwe's suspension. Two key African leaders—Nigerian president Olusegun Obasanjo and South African president Mbeki—resisted that call, however. They said Mugabe had taken action to ease his country's troubles, including his stated willingness to negotiate with the opposition. On March 16 Commonwealth secretary general Don McKinnon said he had surveyed the leaders of member nations. McKinnon said some leaders had favored lifting the suspension, and others had favored imposing even "stronger measures" against Zimbabwe, but there was a "broadly held view" in favor of maintaining the suspension of Zimbabwe until the scheduled meeting of Commonwealth heads of government in December.

Obasanjo, Mbeki, and Malawi president Bakili Muluzi traveled to Harare early in May for separate talks with Mugabe and Tsvangirai. That mission generated widespread publicity and high hopes for change within Zimbabwe but had no evident success in negotiating an end to the political stalemate.

The Commonwealth took up the issue of Zimbabwe again at its December meetings in Abuja, Nigeria. At the opening sessions on December 5, British prime minister Tony Blair said he was determined to uphold Zimbabwe's suspension "until such time that they have complied with what the Commonwealth set out in terms of human rights, democracy, and proper governance." Mugabe's continuing crackdown on opposition figures and the news media had not helped his case among fellow African leaders who wanted to lift the suspension of Zimbabwe. On December 7 Commonwealth leaders said Zimbabwe would remain suspended. The leaders appointed a six-member committee to monitor developments in Zimbabwe; its members included the leaders of Australia, Canada, India, Jamaica, Mozambique, and South Africa. Nigerian president Obasanjo was assigned to visit Zimbabwe "at an early opportunity" and report back to the committee when he determined that "sufficient progress" had been made toward "national reconciliation." Obasanjo told reporters that, based on internal developments in Zimbabwe, "We will be talking in terms of months rather than years." Mugabe responded angrily to the continued Commonwealth suspension by saying he was withdrawing Zimbabwe from the organization. "Anything that you agreed to on Zimbabwe which is short of [ending the suspension], no matter how sweetly worded, means Zimbabwe is still the subject of the Commonwealth," he said. "It is unacceptable."

Diplomats disclosed that the crucial vote in the closed Commonwealth deliberations came on a motion by some African leaders to oust McKinnon as secretary general. A former prime minister of New Zealand, McKinnon had lobbied both publicly and privately to retain the suspension, angering South Africa's Mbeki, Mozambique's president Joaquin Chissano, and other African leaders who said they—not white officials—had the best understanding of what was needed in Zimbabwe. McKinnon was retained on a 40–11 vote, reportedly the same margin by which Commonwealth leaders maintained the suspension of Zimbabwe.

Mbeki denounced the Commonwealth action several days later in a letter to members of his own African National Congress, saying some Commonwealth officials appeared most concerned about the fate of "former white landowners" in Zimbabwe. Mbeki flew to Zimbabwe on December 18 and stressed the "common problems" shared by his own country and Zimbabwe. In what many observers called a significant step, however, Mbeki also met with leaders of Tsvangirai's party and won promises from them, as well as Mugabe, to resume informal talks that had stalled during the year's upheaval. However, there were no indications that any such talks had taken place as of year's end.

Pressure on Mugabe also came from the European Union (EU) and the United States, but the economic power represented by those forces appeared to have little immediate influence. The EU on February 12 voted to renew diplomatic sanctions it had imposed against Zimbabwe for another year. The sanctions included a ban on visas for officials of Zimbabwe's government, a ban on arms sales to the country, and a freezing of some Zimbabwe government assets held by European banks. The EU watered down the effect of its action, however, by allowing Mugabe to attend a summit meeting in Paris between French and African leaders

President George W. Bush on March 7 ordered U.S. sanctions against Mugabe and seventy-six senior government officials. In an executive order, Bush froze all financial and property holdings in the United States of Mugabe and his aides, and barred U.S. citizens and companies from having any financial dealings with them. Bush's order represented a tightening of restrictions he had imposed in 2002; among the earlier steps had been a denial of visas for travel to the United States by Mugabe and his aides. Bush offered a string of complaints about Mugabe's actions: "To add to the desperation of the besieged Zimbabwean people, the current government has engaged in a violent assault on the rule of law that has thrown the economy into chaos, devastated the nation's agricultural economy and triggered a potentially catastrophic food crisis."

The Bush administration made several attempts during the year—both in public and behind the scenes—to pressure African leaders into taking a tougher stance against Mugabe. One of the public moves was a column by Secretary of State Colin Powell in the June 24 edition of the *New York Times*. Powell said South Africa and other countries "can and should play a stronger role that fully reflects the urgency of Zimbabwe's crisis." Powell called on Mugabe to resign and make way for a negotiated transitional government prior to new elections.

Following is the text of a statement, issued December 7, 2003, in Abuja, Nigeria, by the heads of government of the British Commonwealth, declaring that the suspension of Zimbabwe's membership in the organization would remain in effect.

"CHOGM Statement on Zimbabwe"

Commonwealth Heads of Government [CHOGM] discussed the situation in Zimbabwe. They agreed to establish a Committee consisting of the Heads of Government of Australia, Canada, India, Jamaica, Mozambique and South Africa to examine the issue of Zimbabwe and make recommendations to leaders at their retreat on the way forward. It was agreed that the Prime Minister of Jamaica would be the Chairman of the Committee.

In discussing the issue the Committee was guided by the following considerations:

- The commitment of all Commonwealth countries to adhere to the Principles embodied in the Harare Declaration and the need to address the issues raised in the Marlborough House Statement of 19 March 2002 [a statement announcing the suspension of Zimbabwe's membership in the Commonwealth].
- The earnest desire to facilitate the early return of Zimbabwe to the Councils of the Commonwealth.
- The determination to promote national reconciliation in Zimbabwe.
- Deep concern for the people of Zimbabwe and the desire to assist towards a return to normalcy and economic prosperity.

The Committee also welcomed the tireless efforts of President [Olusegun] Obasanjo [of Nigeria], President [Thabo] Mbeki [of South Africa], President [Joachim] Chissano [of Mozambique] and others to encourage and assist the process of national reconciliation and urged them not to relent.

It re-affirmed the importance of supporting and consolidating democracy, ensuring peace and harmony, and promoting development and growth in Zimbabwe.

Heads of Government endorsed the Committee's recommendations and decided as follows:

- Heads of Government affirmed the Commonwealth's commitment to encourage and assist the process of national reconciliation.
- Heads of Government mandated the Chairperson-in-Office, assisted by the Commonwealth Secretary-General, to engage with the parties concerned to encourage and facilitate continued progress and the

return of Zimbabwe to the Councils of the Commonwealth and, in this regard, express support for the intention of the Chairperson-in-Office to visit Zimbabwe at an early opportunity.

- At an appropriate time when the Chairperson-in-Office believed sufficient progress had been made, he would consult the Committee.
- Provided there were consensus in the Committee that sufficient progress had been made on the issues of concern, the Chairperson-in-Office would consult with Commonwealth leaders on the return of Zimbabwe to the Councils of the Commonwealth.

Source: The Commonwealth Secretariat. *CHOGM Statement on Zimbabwe.* Abuja, Nigeria. Dec. 7, 2003. http://www.thecommonwealth.org/dynamic/press_office/display.asp?id=742&type=press&cat=53

President Bush on Signing
Medicare Reform Law

December 8, 2003

Fulfilling a central promise of his 2000 presidential campaign, President George W. Bush on December 8, 2003, signed into law a major overhaul of the Medicare program that for the first time provided a prescription drug benefit for retirees. Starting in 2006 the 40 million Americans over age sixty-five who were enrolled in Medicare would be able to buy government-subsidized prescription drug insurance that would cover at least some of their drug costs. As passed, the measure (PL 108–173) moved the program toward another long-held goal of the Republican Party—greater reliance on the private sector for delivering social services.

"We kept our promise and found a way to get the job done," Bush said as he signed the ten-year, $395 billion bill in an elaborate ceremony at DAR Constitution Hall in Washington designed to showcase the president's fulfillment of his campaign pledge. Seniors—a critical segment of the electorate—accounted for about half of all spending on prescriptions drugs, which was fast approaching $200 billion a year. About two-thirds of all Medicare recipients had drug coverage under supplemental insurance policies, although many living on fixed incomes found it difficult to meet the required copayments. Roughly 11 million Medicare recipients had no drug coverage and either had to pay for the medicines out of pocket or, as many reportedly did, go without.

Controversy swirled around the new law, with critics on both sides of the political spectrum raising questions about its cost, its subsidies to insurers and employers, and whether it would actually provide seniors with the help they thought they were being promised. Many critics said that politics had once again won out over principle. Fiscally conservative Republicans said the bill created a new entitlement program that taxpayers could not afford. Democratic opponents said the final version of the measure did far more for the insurance and pharmaceutical companies than for seniors, and that it threatened the future of Medicare. Sen. Edward M. Kennedy, D-Mass., called the legislation "a partisan document that embodies the administration's right-wing ideology and its desire to fuel the profits of the wealthy and powerful. It cynically uses the elderly's need for prescription drugs as a Trojan horse to reshape Medicare. This bill is a calculated program to unravel Medicare, to privatize it, and to force senior citizens into the cold arms of HMOs [health maintenance organizations]." Even before Bush signed the measure, Senate Democrats had introduced legislation seeking to repeal five of the most contentious parts of the measure, including language prohibiting the government from negotiating lower drug prices for Medicare.

In the end, however, enough Democrats supported the bill to enable its passage. Like the Republicans, Democrats had also campaigned on enacting a drug benefit for seniors, and neither party wanted to go into the 2004 election campaign empty-handed on that issue. The stakes were raised even higher for Democrats when their erstwhile ally, the AARP, a powerful advocacy group for the nation's seniors, decided to support the compromise version of the measure. AARP argued that it was better to enact legislation that, while imperfect, offered some help to seniors having trouble paying their drug bills than to risk not passing any legislation at all. Opponents of the legislation protested AARP's turnaround, noting that the group was closely associated with one of the insurance companies that was well-positioned to gain financially from the subsidies offered in the new law. Thousands of irate AARP members destroyed their membership cards.

For Bush, passage of the reform was a crucial victory for his impending run for reelection—allowing him to claim credit for expanding a popular social program championed by Democrats and for strengthening "compassionate government," a reformulation of "compassionate conservatism," a key theme of Bush's 2000 campaign. Voters consistently told pollsters that health care and cost issues were among their key concerns. With the parties in even greater disagreement about how best to provide help to the estimated 44 million Americans without any health insurance, offering at least some help to elderly Americans, especially those living on fixed incomes, was a politically necessity for the president. Moreover, in the same week that Medicare reform won final approval in Congress, Senate Democrats blocked action on Bush's highly controversial national energy policy legislation, leaving in doubt whether Congress could enact the president's other top domestic legislation priority before the 2004 election. *(Health insurance, p. 846; energy bill, p. 1014)*

What the voters would make of the new law was still up in the air. About a third of those responding to a *Washington Post*/NBC poll in early December said they had paid little attention to the legislation. Of those who did have an opinion, Republicans favored the measure by a two -to-one margin, while Democrats opposed it by roughly the same margin. Among those over age sixty-five, the margin was also roughly two-to-one—against the legislation.

What the Bill Does

The most far-reaching revision of Medicare since it was enacted in 1965 as part of President Lyndon Johnson's "Great Society." PL 108–173 was a massive, complicated, and expensive measure. At its core was a new program of government subsidies that would cover some of the costs of outpatient prescription drugs for Medicare recipients. (The existing Medicare program paid only for drugs used when recipients were in the hospital.) Starting in 2006, the government would pay $1,500 of the first $5,100 that a senior spent each year on prescription drugs; the senior would pick up the other $3,600 (including a $250 deductible) plus premiums, estimated at about $35 a month. The government would pay for 95 percent of drug costs above $5,100. Seniors whose annual drug costs were in the $3,000 to $5,000 range could find that the new law did not provide as much help as they might have hoped.

Medicare recipients would have to purchase the new drug coverage through private insurers, which could offer a drug-only plan or a more comprehensive health care plan that would include drug benefits. Medicare recipients who elected to purchase the drug-only plans would be barred from buying "gap" insurance to cover their out-of-pocket expenses. The measure set aside about $12 billion in subsidies to private health insurers to encourage them to set up the new programs. If private plans did not step forward to offer coverage, the government would be required to provide a "fallback" plan. The measure also set aside about $70 billion in subsidies and tax breaks over ten years to encourage those companies that provided their retirees with drug benefits to continue providing those benefits.

For 2004 and 2005 the federal government would coordinate a program that would allow Medicare beneficiaries to buy drug discount cards from companies that managed pharmaceutical benefits. The cards were expected to cost about $30. The measure's supporters said the cards might save as much as 15–25 percent on drug costs. Low-income seniors would be eligible for up to $600 to help pay for prescription drugs.

Several other elements of the new law had nothing to do with drug coverage. In one major change set to start in 2007, Medicare for the first time would require high-income seniors to pay higher premiums for doctors and other outpatient services (high income was defined as incomes above $80,000 for individuals and $160,000 for couples). In the past all Medicare recipients paid the same premiums. The reform measure also established a new program of health savings accounts, which would allow any taxpayer with a high-deductible health insurance plan to save and withdraw money tax-free to pay for medical expenses. The measure also made several changes in the rates that it reimbursed doctors, hospitals, and medical laboratories, and it provided for higher payments to rural and small urban hospitals that had disproportionately high numbers of low-income patients.

Criticisms of the Reform

The criticisms of the measure revolved around three interconnected issues—its costs, its failure to do more to hold down the price of drugs, and its shift of the Medicare program toward greater reliance on the private sector.

The Bush administration estimated that the measure would cost $395 billion over ten years. Fiscal conservatives in the Republican Party warned that costs of the new entitlement would balloon well beyond that amount, especially after the baby boomers began reaching age sixty-five, starting in 2011. "This is the largest tax increase that one generation has put on another generation in the history of this country," said Sen. Judd Gregg, R-N.H., who added that the drug benefit had been designed to "get us through the next election." So opposed were conservative Republicans in the House that they nearly blocked passage of the bill twice, first in June, when the House passed its version of the bill by a vote of 216–215, and again in November, when the House passed the final version of the measure by a 220–215 vote. That victory came only after GOP leaders held the roll-call vote open for nearly three hours while they worked to persuade Republicans who voted against the bill to change their votes. It was the longest recorded tally in the thirty-year history of electronic voting; normally a roll-call vote lasted fifteen minutes.

Another issue was whether the billions of dollars in incentives and tax breaks would achieve the stated purpose of inducing employers that already gave their retirees drug benefits to continue that coverage. Some observers warned that despite the incentives, employers might still find it cheaper to abandon their retiree drug benefit plans, shifting the costs of drug coverage to the government. The Congressional Budget Office, for example, estimated that 2.7 million retirees who were receiving drug benefits from their employers would lose those benefits once the program took effect in 2006. "That means a lot of retirees with great drug coverage now will get worse coverage in the future," Richard Evans of Bernstein Research told the *New York Times*. Representatives of employer groups said it was unlikely their members would rush to drop drug benefit coverage. Nonetheless, employers had been cutting back on retiree health care benefits for some time. According to one study the percentage of young retirees with drug coverage dropped from 46 percent in 1996 to 39 percent in 2000, the last year for which data were available at the time of the study.

On the other side of the cost issue were Democrats and their supporters, who said that many seniors would be surprised at how much they still had to pay for their drugs and at how fast their out-of-pocket costs were likely to rise in future years as insurers raised premiums, deductibles, and copayments. Some consumer advocates were also nervous about the decision to prohibit seniors from buying insurance to cover their share of drug costs, noting that many seniors would face a huge gap in coverage. "In a bill that's marketed as providing choice to consumers, comprehensive drug coverage is not really an option. That's a disappointment," said Gail Shearer, a health policy analyst for Consumers Union, an advocacy group that opposed the measure as passed. Supporters of the provision said it was intended to prevent duplication of the drug benefit and also to ensure that beneficiaries shouldered some of the costs of their care. Requiring the patient to pay some of the costs of prescription drugs tended to cut over-use of expensive drugs, these supporters said.

Democrats and some Republicans were irate over two provisions of the final bill that they said prevented the government from taking any meaningful steps to bring drug prices under control. One provision prevented Medicare from negotiating drug price reductions with pharmaceutical companies. Sen. John McCain, R-Ariz., called that provision "outrageous." But administration officials and their supporters said allowing the government to negotiate prices would be tantamount to federal price controls. Instead, they said, it would be preferable for private insurers to rely on pharmacy benefit managers to negotiate discounts from the pharmaceutical companies, just as they already did on behalf of health maintenance organizations and other insurers. The second provision effectively continued to bar importation of cheaper drugs from Canada, including many that were manufactured by American companies. That was a significant turnaround since July, when the House passed drug-import legislation by a surprisingly large margin, with eighty-seven Republicans breaking with their GOP leadership to vote for passage.

Both provisions were avidly sought by the pharmaceutical industry, which had made $60 million in political contributions since the 2000 elections and spent at least that much on lobbying in 2003. The industry had long argued against price controls and drug imports, saying that reduced drug prices would inhibit future research and development of new drugs. The drug lobby may have won the battle but lost the war. Democrats promised to try to repeal both provisions in 2004, when election-year pressures would be strong.

The issue that most sharply divided the two political parties was a Republican insistence that the drug benefit program be structured to give private insurers and health care organizations a greater role in caring for the elderly. The Bush administration and GOP congressional leaders argued that competition to provide drug coverage would help hold down drug prices both for the seniors and the government. In addition to requiring that the new drug coverage be purchased through private companies, conservatives also pushed a plan to force traditional Medicare to compete on price against subsidized private health insurance plans. They wanted the so-called premium support plan to start nationwide in 2010 but eventually agreed to a much smaller six-year, six-city demonstration plan in the face of fierce criticism from Democrats.

Most Democrats opposed privatization of the Medicare program. Kennedy reminded his colleagues that Medicare had been created in 1965 because the private insurance industry had failed the elderly. Others noted that an attempt in the late 1990s to encourage more Medicare beneficiaries to join private health plans fell flat, after private plans began to drop out of the program because they said the Medicare reimbursement rates were too low. The withdrawals forced millions of senior citizens to find another private plan or return to traditional Medicare. The insurance lobby warned lawmakers that the same thing could happen if the Medicare reform bill did not provide financial stability to insurers.

Virtually all parties to the debate were agreed on one thing: The success of the new system boiled down to how beneficiaries responded to the changes and how insurers and health providers calculated risk and profitability. The answers to those questions would not be known until after the main provisions of the law took effect in 2006.

Following are excerpts of remarks made by President George W. Bush on December 8, 2003, as he signed into law an overhaul of the Medicare program that provided a new drug benefit to seniors and shifted some of the responsibility for running the program from the federal government to the private sector.

Bush's Remarks at Signing of the Medicare Prescription Drug Act of 2003

Good morning, thanks for the warm welcome. In a few moments I will have the honor of signing an historic act of Congress into law. I'm pleased that all of you are here to witness the greatest advance in health care coverage for America's seniors since the founding of Medicare.

With the Medicare Act of 2003, our government is finally bringing prescription drug coverage to the seniors of America. With this law, we're giving older Americans better choices and more control over their health care, so they can receive the modern medical care they deserve. With this law, we are providing more access to comprehensive exams, disease screenings, and other preventative care, so that seniors across this land can live better and healthier lives. With this law, we are creating Health Savings Accounts—we do so, so that all Americans can put money away for their health care tax-free.

Our nation has the best health care system in the world. And we want our seniors to share in the benefits of that system. Our nation has made a promise, a solemn promise to America's seniors. We have pledged to help our citizens find affordable medical care in the later years of life. Lyndon Johnson established that commitment by signing the Medicare Act of 1965. And today, by reforming and modernizing this vital program, we are honoring the commitments of Medicare to all our seniors. . . .

Medicare is a great achievement of a compassionate government and it is a basic trust we honor. Medicare has spared millions of seniors from needless hardship. Each generation benefits from Medicare. Each generation has a duty to strengthen Medicare. And this generation is fulfilling our duty.

First and foremost, this new law will provide Medicare coverage for prescription drugs. Medicare was enacted to provide seniors with the latest in modern medicine. In 1965, that usually meant house calls, or operations, or long hospital stays. Today, modern medicine includes outpatient care, disease screenings, and prescription drugs.

Medicine has changed, but Medicare has not—until today. Medicare today will pay for extended hospital stays for ulcer surgery. That's at a cost of about $28,000 per patient. Yet Medicare will not pay for the drugs that eliminate the cause of most ulcers, drugs that cost about $500 a year. It's a good thing that Medicare pays when seniors get sick. Now, you see, we're taking this a step further—Medicare will pay for prescription drugs, so that fewer seniors will get sick in the first place.

Drug coverage under Medicare will allow seniors to replace more expensive surgeries and hospitalizations with less expensive prescription medicine. And even more important, drug coverage under Medicare will save our seniors from a lot of worry. Some older Americans spend much of their Social Security checks just on their medications. Some cut down on the dosage, to make a bottle of pills last longer. Elderly Americans should not have to live with those kinds of fears and hard choices. This new law will ease the burden on seniors and will give them the extra help they need.

Seniors will start seeing help quickly. During the transition to the full prescription benefit, seniors will receive a drug discount card. This Medicare-approved card will deliver savings of 10 to 25 percent off the retail price of most medicines. Low-income seniors will receive the same savings, plus a $600 credit on their cards to help them pay for the medications they need.

In about two years, full prescription coverage under Medicare will begin. In return for a monthly premium of about $35, most seniors without any prescription drug coverage can now expect to see their current drug bills cut roughly in half. This new law will provide 95 percent coverage for out-of-pocket drug spending that exceeds $3,600 a year. For the first time, we're giving seniors peace of mind that they will not have to face unlimited expenses for their medicine.

The new law offers special help to one-third of older Americans will low incomes, such as a senior couple with low savings and an annual income of about $18,000 or less. These seniors will pay little or no premium for full drug coverage. Their deductible will be no higher than $50 per year, and their co-payment on each prescription will be as little as $1. Seniors in the greatest need will have the greatest help under the modernized Medicare system.

I visited with seniors around the country and heard many of their stories. I'm proud that this legislation will give them practical and much needed help. Mary Jane Jones from Midlothian, Virginia, has a modest income. Her drug bills total nearly $500 a month. Things got so tight for a while she had to use needles twice or three times for her insulin shots. With this law, Mary Jane won't have to go to such extremes. In exchange for a monthly premium of about $35, Mary Jane Jones would save nearly $2,700 in annual prescription drug spending.

Hugh Iverson from West Des Moines, Iowa, just got his Medicare membership. And that's a good thing, because he hasn't had health insurance for more than three years. His drug bills total at least $400 a month. Within two years, with the $35 a month coverage, he will be able to cut those bills nearly in half, saving him about $2,400 a year.

Neil LeGrow from Culpepper, Virginia, takes 15 medications, costing him at least $700 a month. To afford all those medications, Neil has to stay working. And thanks to this law, once he is enrolled in the drug benefit, he will be able to cut back his work hours and enjoy his retirement more because he'll have coverage that saves him about $4,700 a year. . . .

In addition to providing coverage for prescription drugs, this legislation achieves a second great goal. We're giving our seniors more health care choices so they can get the coverage and care that meets their needs. Every senior needs to know if you don't want to change your current coverage, you don't have to change. You're the one in charge. If you want to keep your Medicare the way it is, along with the new prescription benefit, that is your right. If you want to improve benefits—maybe dental coverage, or eyeglass coverage, or managed care plans that reduce out-of-pocket costs—you'll be free to make those choices, as well.

And when seniors have the ability to make choices, health care plans within Medicare will have to compete for their business by offering higher quality service. For the seniors of America, more choices and more control will mean better health care. These are the kinds of health care options we give to the members of Congress and federal employees. They have the ability to pick plans to—that are right for their own needs. What's good for members of Congress is also good for seniors. Our seniors are fully capable of making health care choices, and this bill allows them to do just that.

A third purpose achieved by this legislation is smarter medicine within the Medicare system. For years, our seniors have been denied Medicare coverage—have been denied Medicare coverage for a basic physical exam. Beginning in 2005, all newly-enrolled Medicare beneficiaries will be covered for a complete physical.

The Medicare system will now help seniors and their doctors diagnose health problems early, so they can treat them early and our seniors can have a better quality life. For example, starting next year, all people on Medicare will be covered for blood tests that can diagnose heart diseases. Those at high risk for diabetes will be covered for blood sugar screening tests. Modern health care is not complete without prevention—so we are expanding preventive services under Medicare.

Fourth, the new law will help all Americans pay for out-of-pocket health costs. This legislation will create health savings accounts, effective January 1, 2004, so Americans can set aside up to $4,500 every year, tax free, to save for medical expenses. Depending on your tax bracket, that means you'll save between 10 to 35 percent on any costs covered by money in your account. Our laws encourage people to plan for retirement and to save for education. Now the law will make it easier for Americans to save for their future health care, as well.

A health savings account is a good deal, and all Americans should consider it. Every year, the money not spent would stay in the account and gain interest tax-free, just like an IRA. And people will have an incentive to live more healthy lifestyles because they want to see their health savings account grow. These accounts will be good for small business owners, and employees. More businesses can focus on covering workers for major medical problems, such as hospitalization for an injury or illness. And at the same time, employees and their families will use these accounts to cover doctor's visits or lab tests or other smaller costs. Some employers will contribute to employee health accounts. This will help more American families get the health care they need at the price they can afford.

The legislation I'm about to sign will set in motion a series of improvements in the care available to all America's senior citizens. And as we begin, it is important for seniors and those approaching retirement to understand their new benefits.

This coming spring, seniors will receive a letter to explain the drug discount card. In June, these cards, including the $600 annual drug credit for low-income seniors, will be activated. This drug card can be used until the end of 2005. In the fall of that year, seniors will receive an information booklet giving simple guidance on changes in the program and the new choices they will have. Then in January of 2006, seniors will have their new coverage, including permanent coverage for prescription drugs.

These reforms are the act of a vibrant and compassionate government. We show are concern for the dignity of our seniors by giving them quality health care. We show our respect for seniors by giving them more choices and more control over their decision-making. We're putting individuals in charge of their health care decisions. And as we move to modernize and reform other programs of this government, we will always trust individuals and their decisions, and put personal choice at the heart of our efforts.

The challenges facing seniors on Medicare were apparent for many years. And those years passed with much debate and a lot of politics, and little reform to show for it. And that changed with the 108th Congress. This year we met our challenge with focus and perseverance. We confronted problems, instead of passing them along to future administrations and future Congresses. We overcame old partisan differences. We kept our promise, and found a way to get the job done. This legislation is the achievement of members in both political parties. And this legislation is a victory for all of America's seniors.

Now I'm honored and pleased to sign this historic piece of legislation: the Medicare Prescription Drug Improvement and Modernization Act of 2003.

Source: U.S. White House. Office of the Press Secretary. *President Signs Medicare Legislation: Remarks by the President at Signing of the Medicare Prescription Drug, Improvement and Modernization Act of 2003.* December 8, 2003. www.whitehouse.gov/news/releases/2003/12/20031208-2.html (accessed January 14, 2004).

Shirin Ebadi on Receiving the Nobel Peace Prize

December 10, 2003

INTRODUCTION

Human rights activist Shirin Ebadi, a fifty-six-year-old Muslim attorney little known outside her native Iran, was named the recipient of the 2003 Nobel Peace Prize. Citing her work for democracy and human rights, particularly her focus on the rights of women and children, the Norwegian Nobel Committee said Ebadi had "spoken out clearly and strongly in her country, Iran, and far beyond its border" with courage and without regard for the threats to her own safety. At a news conference in Paris, where she was attending a meeting on women, Ebadi said the prize was "good for me, it's very good for human rights in Iran, it's very good for democracy in Iran; this prize gives me energy to pursue my combat for a better future."

An attorney who also taught at the University of Tehran, Ebadi was the founder of associations to promote children's rights and to free political detainees in Iran. She was the author of several books and articles dealing with human rights. In recent years she legally represented political dissidents and their families, seeking to call public attention to the harsh policies enforced by Iran's conservative Islamic government. When she was tapped for the Nobel, Ebadi was representing the family of a Canadian-Iranian freelance photographer who was beaten to death, reportedly by government intelligence interrogators, while she was in jail for taking some pictures during a protest outside a Tehran prison.

The biography of Ebadi released by the Nobel committee said that she was known for working within the system to promote "peaceful democratic solutions" and that she argued "for a new interpretation of Islamic law that was is in harmony with vital human rights, such as democracy, equality before the law, religious freedom, and freedom of speech." The committee emphasized that in choosing Ebadi as the winner of the peace prize, it was making a deliberate statement about the importance of human rights in the world. "We hope that the prize will be an inspiration for all those who struggle for human rights and democracy in her country, in the Muslim world, and in all countries where the fight for human rights needs inspiration and support," the committee said in its formal announcement.

Iran, with a population of 66 million, primarily Muslims, was caught in a power struggle between a reform-minded president, Mohammad Khatami, and conservative Islamic clerics, who had held the real power in Iran since the religious revolution in 1979 and who had imposed a fundamentalist form of Islam on all facets of Iranian society. Women in particular were treated as second-class citizens, required to cover their heads in public, forbidden from holding certain jobs, and denied equal rights with their husbands over legal matters involving children and divorce. The extremist views of the ruling clerics, together with Iran's long history of supporting terrorist movements that targeted Israel and U.S. interests in the Middle East and its pursuit of nuclear weapons, led to President George W. Bush naming Iran as one of the three countries in an "axis of evil." *(Iran and nuclear weapons, p. 1025; background on Iranian reform movement, Historic Documents of 2001, p. 793)*

Ebadi's award was applauded by human rights activists and organizations around the world, including former U.S. president Jimmy Carter, who won the prize in 2002. Ebadi "proves that one person, standing on principle, can make a positive difference in the lives of many," Carter said. A spokesman for Human Rights Watch, which gave Ebadi its highest award in 1996, called her "a brave advocate for human rights in a very hostile environment."

The response from the Iranian government was tepid at best. Iranian state media did not report the award for several hours, and then the item was buried among other news items. President Khatami did not personally respond until four days after the announcement was made, when he told reporters in Iran that he was happy to see an Iranian achieve success, but then added that the peace prize was "not very important" in comparison with the other Nobel awards for achievements in areas such as literature and medicine. He also said Ebadi received the award "totally on the basis of political considerations."

Hard-line Iranian religious conservatives condemned both the award and Ebadi, calling her a "Western mercenary" and a "mentally retarded woman with secular thinking." Numerous death threats to Ebadi in the weeks after she returned home to Tehran from Paris led the police to provide bodyguards for her. Hard-line conservative protestors showed up at all her public appearances after she won the award and even managed to prevent her from speaking at a women's university. At the other political extreme, many Iranian exiles who favored a return to the secular government that existed before the religious revolution of 1979 criticized her for supporting an Islamic government. Representatives of these groups protested in Oslo at the award ceremony. *(Carter and peace prize, Historic Documents of 2002, p. 981)*

Ebadi was the first Iranian and the third Muslim to win the Nobel Peace Prize. The other Muslims were Palestinian leader Yasir Arafat, who shared the prize in 1994 with Israeli leaders Yitzhak Rabin and Shimon Peres, and Egyptian president Anwar Sadat, who shared the prize in 1978 with

Prime Minister Menachem Begin of Israel. Ten other women had won the peace prize.

Ebadi was one of 165 nominees, a record number. Her selection by the notoriously secretive Nobel committee came as a surprise both to Ebadi, who did not even know she had been nominated, and to most of the rest of the world. The short odds had been placed on Pope John Paul II, who had devoted his papacy to reconciliation among religions. Another popular candidate was Vaclav Havel, the anticommunist leader and former president of the Czech Republic. Both the pope and Havel were in frail health, and supporters had hoped they would get the award before they died. Some observers speculated, however, that the two men represented the past, while the committee might have wanted to look forward. Others said that the pope's opposition to birth control and his conservative stance on the role of women may not have settled well with the committee. Whatever the reason, the committee's failure to recognize the Polish pope angered former Polish president Lech Walesa. "I have nothing against this lady," he said, "but if there is anyone alive who deserves this year's Nobel Peace Prize, it is the Holy Father."

Working Within to Effect Change

Born in 1947 in a town about 180 miles southwest of Tehran, Shirin Ebadi received a law degree from the University of Tehran in 1971. She was appointed one of the first female judges in Tehran, serving as president of the city court of Tehran in the 1970s, but was forced to resign in 1979 when Islamic extremists overthrew the monarchy of Shah Mohammad Reza Pahlavi and placed new limits on women's role.

A mother with two daughters, Ebadi nonetheless remained active as a teacher, lecturer, author, and lawyer, soon becoming one of Iran's most outspoken advocates for human rights. Among her books that were translated into English were *The Rights of the Child: A Study of Legal Aspects of Children's Rights in Iran,* published in 1994, and *History and Documentation of Human Rights in Iran,* published in 2000. As an activist attorney, Ebadi represented domestically abused women, street children, and the families of several writers, intellectuals, and other dissidents murdered in 1999 and 2000. She also worked to identify the people who orchestrated attacks on university students demonstrating for political reform in 1999. Several of the students were killed. In 2000 Ebadi and a colleague were arrested for circulating a videotape damaging to government officials. After three weeks in jail, she was sentenced in a closed court to fifteen months in prison and barred from practicing law for five years. The sentence was later suspended, and she was required only to pay a small fine.

In an interview with the Associated Press upon her return to Tehran from Paris, Ebadi reaffirmed her belief in working to make change within the system. "The time for overthrowing a government through violence has ended all over the world. It belongs to the past century," she said. Ebadi also said that she would "never" seek elective office, as some supporters had encouraged her to do. "A defender of human rights must always be among the people and be the voice of those who cannot be heard," she said. "The targets of human rights reform are governments. If a rights defender enters the government, then they are part of the system they are criticizing."

At the same time, she used the occasion of her award to step up pressure for reforms. At her Paris news conference, she called for the release of political prisoners in Iran, including several journalists. In a gesture that might have been missed by most of the Western world but that virtually screamed defiance in Iran, Ebadi appeared at the press conference in modern Western clothes and with nothing covering her hair. In a speech to about a thousand students at Amir Kabir University on October 29, Ebadi wore the head covering required by Iranian law. But she defied two other rules—mentioning the name of Cyrus the Great (the monarch of ancient Persia five hundred years before the birth of Christ who proclaimed a charter of human rights) and shaking hands publicly with two men after the speech. After the 1979 revolution, Islamic clerics outlawed the name Cyrus. Public physical contact between unrelated men and women was a crime under Iranian law punishable by imprisonment or flogging. The day after the speech it was reported that Ebadi had been banned from speaking at the university for a year.

In her speech at Amir Kabir University, Ebadi repeated earlier warnings to avoid militant action, which she said would only result in students being jailed or even killed. She acknowledged that the pace of reform was slow, but asked the students not to lose hope. "If we compare the situation now to twenty years ago, we have made some little progress," she said. "This, although little, was because of your efforts. So, insist on your demands and don't get disappointed." Although the speech was well received, students were among those who criticized Ebadi for being too cautious and unwilling to confront directly the ruling clerics.

Ebadi's Acceptance Speech

In her acceptance speech in Oslo, Norway, on December 10, Ebadi reprised many of the themes that had led the Nobel committee to award her the prize. Again wearing Western clothing and no head covering, Ebadi said that "some Muslims, under the pretext that democracy and human rights are not compatible with Islamic teachings and the traditional structure of Islamic societies, have justified despotic governments, and continue to do so." However, she said, referring to the demand for political reforms in Iran and elsewhere in the Muslim world, "it is not so easy to rule over a people who are aware of their rights, using traditional, patriarchal and paternalistic methods." Ebadi also pointed out that "the discriminatory plight of women in Islamic states . . . has its roots in the patriarchal and male-dominated cultures prevailing in those societies, not in Islam."

For the international audience gathered in Oslo, however, Ebadi reserved her harshest criticisms for Western governments, and especially the United States, that she said used the war on international terrorism as a pretext to deny basic human rights. She specifically cited the American military detention center at Guantanamo Bay, Cuba, where the United States was holding hundreds of prisoners suspected of having ties to Al Qaeda "without the benefit of rights" guaranteed by international human rights treaties to which the United States was a signatory. She also asked a question that she said millions of people around the world had been asking: "Why is it that in the past 35 years, dozens of UN resolutions concerning the occupation of the Palestinian territories by the state of Israel have not been implemented promptly, yet in the past 12 years, the state and people of Iraq, once on the recommendation of the Security Council, and the second time, in spite of UN Security Council opposition, were subjected to attack. Military assault, economic sanctions, and, ultimately, military occupation?" *(Guantanamo detainees, p. 105; Israel-Palestinian conflict, p. 191)*

At a news conference before the speech, Ebadi said she would use the $1.3 million in prize money to help continue her reform work in Iran.

Following is the text of the speech delivered December 10, 2003, by Shirin Ebadi, a human rights activist in Iran, as she accepted the 2003 Nobel Peace Prize.

"Lecture Given by Nobel Peace Prize Laureate 2003, Shirin Ebadi"

In the name of the God of Creation and Wisdom

Your Majesty, Your Royal Highneses, Honourable Members of the Norwegian Nobel Committee, Excellencies, Ladies and Gentlemen,

I feel extremely honoured that today my voice is reaching the people of the world from this distinguished venue. This great honour has been bestowed upon me by the Norwegian Nobel Committee. I salute the spirit of Alfred Nobel and hail all true followers of his path.

This year, the Nobel Peace Prize has been awarded to a woman from Iran, a Muslim country in the Middle East.

Undoubtedly, my selection will be an inspiration to the masses of women who are striving to realize their rights, not only in Iran but throughout the region—rights taken away from them through the passage of history. This selection will make women in Iran, and much further afield, believe in themselves. Women constitute half of the population of every country. To disregard women and bar them from active participation in political, social, economic and cultural life would in fact be tantamount to depriving the entire population of every society of half its capability. The patriarchal culture and the discrimination against women, particularly in the Islamic countries, cannot continue for ever.

Honourable members of the Norwegian Nobel Committee!

As you are aware, the honour and blessing of this prize will have a positive and far-reaching impact on the humanitarian and genuine endeavours of the people of Iran and the region. The magnitude of this blessing will embrace every freedom-loving and peace-seeking individual, whether they are women or men.

I thank the Norwegian Nobel Committee for this honour that has been bestowed upon me and for the blessing of this honour for the peace-loving people of my country.

Today coincides with the 55th anniversary of the adoption of the Universal Declaration of Human Rights; a declaration which begins with the recognition of the inherent dignity and the equal and inalienable rights of all members of the human family, as the guarantor of freedom, justice and peace. And it promises a world in which human beings shall enjoy freedom of expression and opinion, and be safeguarded and protected against fear and poverty.

Unfortunately, however, this year's report by the United Nations Development Programme (UNDP), as in the previous years, spells out the rise of a disaster which distances mankind from the idealistic world of the authors of the Universal Declaration of Human Rights. In 2002, almost 1.2 billion human beings lived in glaring poverty, earning less than one dollar a day. Over 50 countries were caught up in war or natural disasters. AIDS has so far claimed the lives of 22 million individuals, and turned 13 million children into orphans.

At the same time, in the past two years, some states have violated the universal principles and laws of human rights by using the events of 11 September and the war on international terrorism as a pretext. The United Nations General Assembly Resolution 57/219, of 18 December 2002, the United Nations Security Council Resolution 1456, of 20 January

2003, and the United Nations Commission on Human Rights Resolution 2003/68, of 25 April 2003, set out and underline that all states must ensure that any measures taken to combat terrorism must comply with all their obligations under international law, in particular international human rights and humanitarian law. However, regulations restricting human rights and basic freedoms, special bodies and extraordinary courts, which make fair adjudication difficult and at times impossible, have been justified and given legitimacy under the cloak of the war on terrorism.

The concerns of human rights' advocates increase when they observe that international human rights laws are breached not only by their recognized opponents under the pretext of cultural relativity, but that these principles are also violated in Western democracies, in other words countries which were themselves among the initial codifiers of the United Nations Charter and the Universal Declaration of Human Rights. It is in this framework that, for months, hundreds of individuals who were arrested in the course of military conflicts have been imprisoned in Guantanamo, without the benefit of the rights stipulated under the international Geneva conventions, the Universal Declaration of Human Rights and the [United Nations] International Covenant on Civil and Political Rights.

Moreover, a question which millions of citizens in the international civil society have been asking themselves for the past few years, particularly in recent months, and continue to ask, is this: why is it that some decisions and resolutions of the UN Security Council are binding, while some other resolutions of the council have no binding force? Why is it that in the past 35 years, dozens of UN resolutions concerning the occupation of the Palestinian territories by the state of Israel have not been implemented promptly, yet, in the past 12 years, the state and people of Iraq, once on the recommendation of the Security Council, and the second time, in spite of UN Security Council opposition, were subjected to attack, military assault, economic sanctions, and, ultimately, military occupation?

Ladies and Gentlemen,

Allow me to say a little about my country, region, culture and faith.

I am an Iranian. A descendent of Cyrus The Great. The very emperor who proclaimed at the pinnacle of power 2500 years ago that " . . . he would not reign over the people if they did not wish it. And [he] promised not to force any person to change his religion and faith and guaranteed freedom for all". The Charter of Cyrus The Great is one of the most important documents that should be studied in the history of human rights.

I am a Muslim. In the Koran the Prophet of Islam has been cited as saying: "Thou shalt believe in thine faith and I in my religion". That same divine book sees the mission of all prophets as that of inviting all human beings to uphold justice. Since the advent of Islam, too, Iran's civilization and culture has become imbued and infused with humanitarianism, respect for the life, belief and faith of others, propagation of tolerance and compromise and avoidance of violence, bloodshed and war. The luminaries of Iranian literature, in particular our Gnostic literature, from Hafiz, Mowlavi [better known in the West as Rumi] and Attar to Saadi, Sanaei, Naser Khosrow and Nezami, are emissaries of this humanitarian culture. Their message manifests itself in this poem by Saadi:

> The sons of Adam are limbs of one another
> Having been created of one essence.
> When the calamity of time afflicts one limb
> The other limbs cannot remain at rest.

The people of Iran have been battling against consecutive conflicts between tradition and modernity for over 100 years. By resorting to ancient traditions, some have tried and are trying to see the world through the eyes of their predecessors and to deal with the problems and difficulties of the existing world by virtue of the values of the ancients. But, many others, while respecting their historical and cultural past and their religion and faith, seek to go forth in step with world developments and not lag behind the caravan of civilization, development and progress. The people of Iran, particularly in the recent years, have shown that they deem participation in public affairs to be their right, and that they want to be masters of their own destiny.

This conflict is observed not merely in Iran, but also in many Muslim states. Some Muslims, under the pretext that democracy and human rights are not compatible with Islamic teachings and the traditional structure of Islamic societies, have justified despotic governments, and continue to do so. In fact, it is not so easy to rule over a people who are aware of their rights, using traditional, patriarchal and paternalistic methods.

Islam is a religion whose first sermon to the Prophet begins with the word "Recite!" The Koran swears by the pen and what it writes. Such a sermon and message cannot be in conflict with awareness, knowledge, wisdom, freedom of opinion and expression and cultural pluralism.

The discriminatory plight of women in Islamic states, too, whether in the sphere of civil law or in the realm of social, political and cultural justice, has its roots in the patriarchal and male-dominated culture prevailing in these societies, not in Islam. This culture does not tolerate freedom and democracy, just as it does not believe in the equal rights of men and women, and the liberation of women from male domination (fathers, husbands, brothers . . .), because it would threaten the historical and traditional position of the rulers and guardians of that culture.

One has to say to those who have mooted the idea of a clash of civilizations, or prescribed war and military intervention for this region, and resorted to social, cultural, economic and political sluggishness of the South in a bid to justify their actions and opinions, that if you consider international human rights laws, including the nations' right to determine their own destinies, to be universal, and if you believe in the priority and superiority of parliamentary democracy over other political systems, then you cannot think only of your own security and comfort, selfishly and contemptuously. A quest for new means and ideas to enable the countries of the South, too, to enjoy human rights and democracy, while maintaining their political independence and territorial integrity of their respective countries, must be given top priority by the United Nations in respect of future developments and international relations.

The decision by the Nobel Peace Committee to award the 2003 prize to me, as the first Iranian and the first woman from a Muslim country, inspires me and millions of Iranians and nationals of Islamic states with the hope that our efforts, endeavours and struggles toward the realization of human rights and the establishment of democracy in our respective countries enjoy the support, backing and solidarity of international civil society. This prize belongs to the people of Iran. It belongs to the people of the Islamic states, and the people of the South for establishing human rights and democracy.

Ladies and Gentlemen

In the introduction to my speech, I spoke of human rights as a guarantor of freedom, justice and peace. If human rights fail to be manifested in codified laws or put into effect by states, then, as rendered in the preamble of the Universal Declaration of Human Rights, human beings will be left with no choice other than staging a "rebellion against tyranny and oppression". A human being divested of all dignity, a human being deprived of human rights, a human being gripped by starvation, a human being beaten by famine, war and illness, a humiliated human being and a plundered human being is not in any position or state to recover the rights he or she has lost.

If the 21st century wishes to free itself from the cycle of violence, acts of terror and war, and avoid repetition of the experience of the 20th century—that most disaster-ridden century of humankind, there is no other way except by understanding and putting into practice every human righ for all mankind, irrespective of race, gender, faith, nationality or social status.

In anticipation of that day.
With much gratitude
Shirin Ebadi

Source: The Norwegian Nobel Institute. "The Nobel Lecture Given by The Nobel Peace Prize Laureate 2003, Shirin Ebadi." Oslo, Norway. December 10, 2003. www.nobel.no/eng_lect_2003b.html (accessed December 10, 2003).

UN Mission on Building Democracy in Kosovo

December 10, 2003

INTRODUCTION

The United Nations handed significant responsibilities over to the interim government of Kosovo in late 2003, marking an important step toward a still-to-be-defined future for the troubled province in southeastern Europe. Tension continued to be high between the two main ethnic groups, the majority ethnic Albanians (known generally as Kosovars) and the minority ethnic Serbs. Albanians had dominated the interim government since elections in 2001, and Serbs refused to participate in some government functions.

As of the end of 2003 it appeared that negotiations on Kosovo's future—its "final status" in UN terminology—could begin as early as mid-2005. Technically, Kosovo was still a province of Serbia, and Serbs in both Kosovo and Serbia proper insisted on keeping that status. Albanians demanded formal independence for Kosovo. International observers generally agreed that neither side would get exactly what it wanted and that a compromise would have to be found giving the Albanians autonomy while guaranteeing the rights of Serbs and other minorities. In the foreseeable future, international peacekeepers would remain in Kosovo to prevent the two sides from going back to war. A NATO-led peacekeeping force was cutting back its commitment and might be replaced by one sponsored by the European Union.

Kosovo was the scene of the last major ethnic war that engulfed the Balkans during the 1990s as a result of the collapse of Yugoslavia. Kosovar Albanian guerrillas began fighting for independence from Belgrade in 1998, and the Yugoslav government of Slobodan Milosevic responded with brutal suppression. In the spring of 1999 NATO launched an intense air war against Yugoslavia that, after seventy-eight days, forced Milosevic to withdraw his security forces from Kosovo, effectively ending Serbian control of the province. Serb forces drove hundreds of thousands of ethnic Albanians from Kosovo during the war; most of the refugees returned afterwards to find their cities and villages largely destroyed. More than 200,000 ethnic

Serbs fled at the end of the war, but only a few thousand had returned as of 2003. *(Background, Historic Documents of 1999, pp. 134, 285, 802; Historic Documents of 2000, p. 143; Historic Documents of 2001, p. 819)*

The UN and the Kosovar Government

The war left Kosovo without a functioning government and with few public or private resources for reconstruction. The UN Security Council in June 1999 created a United Nations Mission in Kosovo (UNMIK) that had ultimate authority over the province until its final status was determined. NATO had the ultimate responsibility for security. The United States and European governments poured in billions of aid dollars to rebuild Kosovo and establish government institutions that could take over once the UN left.

General elections in November 2001 resulted in formation in March 2002 of an interim Kosovo government. Ibrahim Rugova, a veteran ethnic Albanian political leader who had opposed the guerrilla war against Belgrade, was named president. Bajram Rexhepi, a doctor who had been a member of the Albanian guerrilla group, the Kosovo Liberation Army (KLA), was named prime minister; he represented the Democratic Party of Kosovo, an offshoot of the KLA. Serbs had won a small minority of seats in the elected legislature, the Kosovo Assembly.

The formation of the government coincided with the arrival in Kosovo of a new head of the UN mission: Michael Steiner, who had been the senior foreign policy aid to German chancellor Gerhard Schroeder. Steiner engaged in a series of conflicts with the Kosovo Assembly, the most serious of which came in May 2003 when the assembly passed a resolution insisting that Kosovo become an independent state. Calling the resolution "divisive," Steiner retaliated by excluding Kosovo representatives from three international meetings later in May. UN Secretary General Kofi Annan said a month later that the incident demonstrated the assembly's "tendency to go beyond its prescribed institutional role as a legislative body."

Steiner's term as UN administrator ended in July, and Annan replaced him with Harri Holkeri, a former prime minister of Norway. Holkeri appeared to take a lower-key approach to his dealings with the interim government. Even so, the assembly continued to adopt extreme positions, including passage on December 11 of a bill to repeal all legislation affecting Kosovo that had been adopted by Serbia after March 1989—the date when Milosevic stripped the province of the autonomy it had long enjoyed. Holkeri immediately rejected the assembly's bill.

In addition to these difficult political issues, the UN and the Kosovo government faced daily problems of getting the province running again. The war and years of neglect by Belgrade had left Kosovo's infrastructure in tatters; power stations, sewer and water services, housing, roads, and telecommunications had all been severely damaged. Even in mid-2003, four years after the war, many parts of Kosovo could not count on regular electrical service or garbage collection.

Holkeri told the Security Council on October 30 that unemployment averaged 57 percent; other officials said the jobless rate approached 70 percent in some areas, especially those where Serbs and other minorities lived. As was the case in many other parts of Eastern Europe following the collapse of communism, criminal gangs flourished in Kosovo. The NATO peace-keeping unit, the Kosovo Force (KFOR), reported at year's end that "the most robust part of Kosovo's economy is its illegal side."

The Serb Minority

Kosovo government statistics put the population of the province in 2003 at about 1.9 million. This was a rough estimate, because no official census had been taken for more than two decades. Ethnic Albanians made up about 88 percent of the population, the government said, while 7 percent were ethnic Serbs and 5 percent were ethnic Turks, Roma (Gypsies), Bosniaks (ethnic Muslims from Bosnia), and other minorities.

Most of Kosovo's remaining ethnic Serbs lived in the northern part of the province, along the border with Serbia proper. These estimated 100,000 to 150,000 Serbs continued to struggle with their status as a minority that no longer controlled the affairs of the province. In the decade before the 1999 war, the minority Serbs dominated virtually every aspect of government and society in Kosovo because of Belgrade's tight control. The Serbs who remained in Kosovo after the war found themselves a powerless minority subjected to the Kosovar Albanians' desire for revenge—and independence from Serbia. The UN administration actively sought to discourage revenge-seeking and to encourage Serbs to take part in the new interim government, but these appeals had only limited success in overcoming emotional responses that were still raw.

Serb representatives sat in the assembly, and several towns had Serb majority councils. But, with support and encouragement from Belgrade, Serb leaders refused to participate in some provincewide institutions, and in northern Kosovo established their own governments and courts, which the UN referred to as "parallel structures."

For their part, many Kosovar Albanians appeared to be grudging, at best, in accepting a role for the Serbs. Cooperation was best in the central government in Pristina, where international pressure from the UN was greatest. Even there, Albanians acted in ways that had the effect of exacerbating tensions, such as issuing most government statements in the Albanian language but not in Serbo-Croatian, which was the legal second language of the province.

In local towns and villages, daily life between Serbs and Albanians continued to be dominated by old grievances and the consequences of the shift of power between the two communities. Ethnic conflict remained most intense in northern Kosovo, where the majority of Serbs lived. This was especially true in the city of Mitrovica, where Serbs and Albanians lived on opposite sides of the Ibar River. Many Serbs complained that they did not feel safe traveling in areas dominated by the Kosovars. "I am in prison," Verica Istic, a resident of a small village told the Associated Press in May. "That's what's hard. That I am not free."

The vast majority of the 200,000-some Serbs who had fled into Serbia remained reluctant to return to Kosovo, despite constant encouragement by the UN mission. The few who did return often found an unpleasant welcome. Among them were eleven Serbs who sought on December 10 to return to their homes in Klina, in west-central Kosovo. They were turned back by 250 stone-throwing Kosovar protesters.

Security Issues

Despite a sizable international presence, security remained a serious problem in Kosovo. Criminal gangs and paramilitary forces operated throughout the province, and nearly every household appeared to be armed. A study commissioned by the UN's Development Program estimated in July that Kosovo civilians had 330,000 to 460,000 firearms, most of them unregistered. Many of the guns entered Kosovo when ethnic conflict broke wide open in 1998. The Albanian guerrillas obtained thousands of weapons that were stolen from a military armory in neighboring Albania, and Belgrade security forces gave thousands of guns to Serbs in the province. NATO's KFOR said at year's end that "ethnic-related crime and intimidation remain high."

KFOR remained the principal force for stability in Kosovo, but NATO continued to reduce its presence because of pressures from member governments—most importantly the United States—to reduce their peacekeeping commitments. At the end of the 1999 war NATO had 50,000 troops in Kosovo. That number had dropped to about 25,000 at the beginning of 2003 and was reduced to about 19,200 at year's end. About 2,000 KFOR troops came from the United States, a sharp reduction from the original U.S. presence of 7,500. KFOR troops were supposed to be peacekeepers, not police, but they often found themselves engaging in police work, such as tracking down extremists who attacked civilians or government authorities. For the most part, the peacekeepers protected the Serbs from Albanian reprisals.

The UN in 2000 established a Kosovo Police Service to replace the Serbian police force, whose members had fled to Serbia proper after the war. The service had 5,700 trained personnel as of December 31; nearly 10 percent were ethnic Serbs, and another 6 percent were other ethnic minorities. These local policemen worked alongside 3,700 police officers the UN had recruited temporarily from other countries, often mounting joint patrols. Of the international police, 466 came from the United States, as of year's end.

Yet another official security organization was the Kosovo Protection Corps (KPC), a paramilitary organization the UN established in 1999 to employ guerrillas who had been part of the Kosovo Liberation Army. Guerrillas were supposed to give up their weapons and undergo training for civilian jobs, such as responding to forest fires and floods. As of 2003 the corps had about 3,000 members, all but 131 of whom were ethnic Albanians. In reality, the UN acknowledged that many criminals and Kosovar extremists remained in the ranks of the KPC. The danger posed by these people became evident in April, when a bomb destroyed a railway bridge in the northern town of Zvecan. A police investigation turned up evidence that twelve KPC officers had carried out the bombing. Holkeri on December 3 ordered them suspended, with pay, pending further investigation.

Getting to a "Final Status"

The United Nations Security Council resolution establishing the UN mandate in Kosovo deliberately left vague the single most important question involving the province: What would be its status in the future? In the meantime, Kosovo was left in limbo, neither a fully independent country nor, in reality, a part of Serbia, to which it still technically belonged. The new government was not even a government in name, having been given the unwieldy title of Provisional Institutions of Self-Government. It could pass laws and present a budget, but the UN, through its administrator, had the ultimate decision-making power.

As a preliminary step toward answering the big question, UN administrator Steiner in April 2002 set out eight benchmarks, which he called "standards before status," by which the UN would judge Kosovo's progress before sponsoring negotiations on the province's final status. The benchmarks included such matters as "functioning democratic institutions," "rule of law," and "freedom movement." Steiner drew up these standards himself, without any real input from Kosovo's new leaders—a move that led to some resistance on their part.

Much of the action at the political level during 2003 revolved around the need to put some substance into the eight benchmarks. After taking over from Steiner in August, Holkeri worked out a system in which he would issue quarterly reports on the government's progress toward those standards. Under that system, announced November 5, it was possible that a final determination could be made by mid-2005 on whether the standards had been met; if the answer that time was yes, negotiations toward Kosovo's final status could then get under way. The exact nature of those negotiations had not been resolved as of the end of 2003.

Holkeri also met with representatives of all of Kosovo's ethnic communities to develop specific details for Steiner's eight standards. The result, announced in Pristina and Belgrade on December 10, laid out an idealistic vision of a democratic Kosovo where elections were fair, government operated openly on behalf of the citizens, law enforcement was effective and the court system was impartial, people felt safe to move about their communities, human rights were respected, ethnic minorities were able to return to their homes and get jobs without discrimination, state-owned industries were being privatized, taxes were being collected, property rights were respected, the Kosovo government was engaged in a "constructive and continuing dialogue" with Belgrade, and the Kosovo Protection Corps had become a fully professional agency responding to civil emergencies.

"Kosovo has made enormous progress over the last four years," Holkeri said in announcing the document. "It is a more peaceful place, there is less violence. The government, led by Bajram Rexhepi, comprises all communities and is tackling the problems that Kosovo faces. But the standards are not yet achieved. To achieve them means change." The UN Security Council endorsed the document on December 12 and called on the Kosovo government "and all concerned" (meaning the minority groups in Kosovo and the Serbian government in Belgrade) to cooperate with Holkeri as he worked to ensure the standards were being met. The difficulty of getting that cooperation was made immediately obvious. The Belgrade government denounced Holkeri's document as "unacceptable" because it undermined Serbia's rights in Kosovo, and some leaders among both the Albanian and Serb communities in Kosovo said they were unhappy with it. The document also was likely to be a political issue in Kosovo Assembly elections scheduled for 2004.

Another important step came on December 30, when Holkeri announced that he was turning over to the Kosovo government responsibility for twenty-five tasks that had been handled by the UN administration. These tasks— called "competencies" in UN jargon—were specific powers in the areas of agriculture, culture, the environment, and the media. These were the last in a series of powers that the UN had turned over to the Kosovo government in a gradual process that began in 2002. In a statement, Holkeri said the idea was "to establish progressively greater autonomy and more effective self-government in Kosovo." The UN retained control over several major areas normally handled by a government, including energy, foreign relations, protection of minority rights, and security. Those tasks were to be handed over to whatever government was established when Kosovo's final status was determined.

In anticipation of the negotiations toward final status, each of the two main contenders for eventual power in Kosovo continued to espouse maximalist positions during 2003. The Albanian majority in the Kosovo assembly had adopted several statements demanding immediate independence, and both president Rugova and prime minister Rexhepi made similar statements during the year. The Serbian government in Belgrade in August demanded the right to retake control of Kosovo, although it said it would give the province "substantial autonomy." The first internationally mediated talks between officials from Belgrade and the Kosovo government were held in Vienna on October 14 but accomplished little as each side portrayed its position as nonnegotiable. Rexhepi boycotted those talks, as did some Kosovo Serb leaders.

The situation in Kosovo was complicated enough on its own terms, and it became even more complicated in December, when Serbian nationalists won a parliamentary election in Serbia. That election set off what was expected to be a scramble for control of the government in Belgrade; whatever the outcome, the new government was likely to take an even harder-line position than the previous government when the final negotiations on Kosovo got under way. *(Serbia elections, p. 55)*

Prosecutions from the 1999 War

Among the many unfinished pieces of business from the 1999 war was the prosecution of both Serbs and Albanians who had committed atrocities. By far the most important prosecution was that of former Yugoslav president Milosevic, whose lengthy trial on genocide and war crimes charges was still under way at the UN International Criminal Tribunal at the Hague. A special UN-run court in Pristina heard cases involving other individuals accused of war crimes. On July 16 a three-judge panel of that court convicted four former commanders of the Kosovo Liberation Army for ordering violent acts against fellow ethnic Albanians suspected of collaborating with the Yugoslav government. The court sentenced the men to prison terms of five to seventeen years, with the longest sentence imposed on Rustem Mustafa, who headed KLA in northern Kosovo; he was found guilty of ordering the killings of five Albanians. The convictions were the first by the UN court of any rebel leaders. *(Milosevic case, Historic Documents of 2001, p. 826)*

Following is the text of "Standards for Kosovo," a document issued December 10, 2003, by Harri Holkeri, the United Nations special representative for Kosovo and head of the UN Mission in Kosovo. The document set out the standards for determining when negotiations would begin toward resolving the "final status" of the province.

"Standards for Kosovo"

I. Functioning Democratic Institutions

The Provisional Institutions of Self-Government (PISG) are freely, fairly and democratically elected. The PISG governs in an impartial, transparent and accountable manner, consistent with UNSCR [United Nations Security Council resolution] 1244 and the Constitutional Framework. The interests and needs of all Kosovo communities are fully and fairly represented in all branches and institutions of government. Those communities participate fully in government. The laws and functions of the PISG approach European standards. The PISG provides services for all people of Kosovo throughout the territory of Kosovo; parallel structures have been dismantled.

Elections

- Elections are regular, transparent, free and fair, conforming to international standards, allowing the full and peaceful participation of all communities and ethnic groups.
- Internally-displaced persons and refugees continue to be fully included in the Kosovo election process and their ability to vote is facilitated.
- An independent, representative and multi-ethnic Central Election Commission administers elections.
- A range of democratic political parties contests elections.
- A comprehensive legal framework covering political party operation and finances is adopted and enforced.

Provisional Institutions of Self-Government (PISG)

- All communities are proportionately represented at all levels of the PISG, in accordance with applicable legislation. The PISG and local municipal government decide and enact legislation in an open, accountable and democratic manner.
- All official languages are respected throughout the institutions of government.
- The PISG and municipalities ensure the availability of basic public services, such as health care, utilities and education, without discrimination, to all communities in Kosovo.

- The civil service is professional, impartial and accountable, representative of all communities in Kosovo and includes a significant proportion of women.
- All communities have fair access to employment in public institutions.
- Codes of conduct and enforcement procedures exist to provide for transparent and accountable government; recommendations of the Ombudsperson are given full weight.
- Regular and independent audits of the KCB [Kosovo Central Bank], Assembly, government ministries and municipalities.
- Allegations of misconduct are thoroughly investigated, elected officials and public servants responsible for unethical, fraudulent, or corrupt behavior are effectively disciplined.
- Proposed Assembly legislation is reviewed and cleared by the Assembly Committee on Rights and Interests of Communities prior to adoption by the Assembly.
- Women participate in the institutions of the PISG at rates that equal or exceed rates in the region and the interests of women are fully reflected in its policies and legislation.
- The proposals on decentralization of the Council of Europe have been examined and considered with the aim to create functional structures of local government.
- Parallel structures for the provision of services have been dismantled or integrated into PISG structures.

Media and Civil Society

- A range of private, independent print and broadcast media exists, providing access to information for all communities throughout Kosovo.
- There is an independent and effective media regulatory authority, aspiring to European standards, recruited without discrimination and according to merit.
- Hate speech or any form of incitement, is condemned by political leaders, the media regulatory authority and media commentators.
- Publicly-funded media devotes a full and proportionate share of its resources and output to all ethnic communities.
- Non-governmental organizations, in particular those representing minorities, are able to operate freely within the law and individuals are free to join them without discrimination.

II. Rule of Law

There exists a sound legal framework and effective law enforcement, compliant with European standards. Police, judicial and penal systems act impartially and fully respect human rights. There is equal access to justice and no one is above the law: there is no impunity for violators. There are strong measures in place to fight ethnically-motivated crime, as well as economic and financial crime.

Equal Access to Justice

- All crime is thoroughly investigated, regardless of the ethnic background of the victim or perpetrator.
- The prosecution and conviction of perpetrators of crime is consistent and effective, regardless of the ethnic background of victim or perpetrator.
- Substantial progress has been made in solving the most serious murders and assaults against members of ethnic minorities.
- Witnesses are effectively protected from intimidation and retribution.
- Crime clearance rates for crimes of violence against persons of all communities are roughly equivalent.
- Misconduct by judges, prosecutors, attorneys, police, and penal system employees is routinely investigated and appropriately punished.
- There are professional codes of conduct for judges, prosecutors, lawyers and other members of the police and penal system, including a Bar Association representative of all Kosovo communities.
- Acts of retribution against individuals involved in disciplinary processes are rare and such individuals are adequately protected.
- All communities are fully and fairly represented amongst judges, prosecutors and in the Kosovo Police Service (KPS) and Kosovo Corrections Service (KCS).
- Institutions are functioning to train and educate the police, judges, lawyers, and penal system managers.
- An effective and impartial system of justice in the civil law sector is accessible to members of all communities in Kosovo.
- The backlog of civil law cases in courts is steadily being reduced.
- Judgments in civil law matters are being enforced, court execution officers are functioning, and court fines are routinely being paid.
- Legislation in civil law matters is reviewed and developed to ensure greater conformity with European standards.

- Alternatives to litigation for resolving civil disputes are expeditiously developed and effectively used.
- There is effective action to eliminate violence against women and children, trafficking and other forms of exploitation, including preventative education and provision of legal and social services to victims.

No One Is Above the Law

- All crimes, especially those of violence that promote inter-ethnic hatred and fear are thoroughly investigated and resolved, and perpetrators are brought to justice and punished.
- Incidents of organized crime, trafficking, crime rooted in extremism, terrorism, and economic crime are vigorously investigated and local judges and prosecutors effectively prosecute and try perpetrators. The percentage of unsolved cases of crime rooted in extremism or terrorism is steadily declining.
- Perpetrators of assaults on judges, prosecutors, KPS officers and witnesses are fairly tried in local courts and are sentenced appropriately.
- Mechanisms of regional and international cooperation are functioning for police and judicial authorities, including transfer of suspects and sentenced persons, , and mutual legal assistance to jurisdictions.
- There is full cooperation with the International Criminal Tribunal for the former Yugoslavia (ICTY), including arrest of indictees and provision of witnesses and information.
- Those war crimes not addressed by the ICTY are prosecuted fairly in Kosovo.

Economic and Financial Crime

- Effective legal, financial and administrative mechanisms that conform to EU standards are in place to tackle economic crime in both the public and private sectors, including seizure of illegally-acquired assets.
- There is a clear understanding amongst the vast majority of public sector employees of ethical conduct requirements, especially regarding conflict of interest.
- Adequate investigative mechanisms have been created and are functioning effectively.
- Money laundering legislation is effectively implemented and suspicious financial transaction reporting is in place.

III. Freedom of Movement

All people in Kosovo are able to travel, work and live in safety and without threat or fear of attack, harassment or intimidation, regardless of their ethnic background. They are able to use their own language freely anywhere in Kosovo, including in public places, and enjoy unimpeded access to places of employment, markets, public and social services, and utilities.

Freedom of Movement

- All communities are able freely to exercise rights to social, cultural and religious expression, including attending ceremonies and access to relevant sites.
- Military and police escorts are no longer needed; members of all ethnic communities have access to safe and public transportation.
- Public employees from minority communities are able to work in majority areas without difficulties.
- The number of crimes specifically related to movement by minorities (e.g. stoning incidents) is significantly reduced and infrequent.
- Political leaders, without prompting, condemn and take action against acts of violence against ethnic communities and their members.

Free use of language

- Meetings of the Assembly and its committees are conducted in all official languages.
- Official municipal and ministry documents are translated in a timely manner into all official languages.
- Personal documents are issued in the native language of the recipient.
- Official signs inside and outside municipal and ministerial buildings are expressed in all official languages.
- Names of streets, cities, towns, villages, roads and public places are expressed in Albanian, Serbian and any other language of a community that lives there in a significant number.
- Municipalities and ministries provide adequate interpretation and translation services for all communities, including translation of all official documents and interpretation for all official meetings in relevant languages.

IV. Sustainable Returns and the Rights of Communities and Their Members

Members of all communities must be able to participate fully in the economic, political and social life of Kosovo, and must not face threats to their security and well-being based on their ethnicity. All refugees and displaced persons who wish to return to Kosovo must be able to do so in safety and dignity.

Rights

- The laws of Kosovo provide a full range of protection for human rights and the rights of communities and their members, consistent with European standards.
- A comprehensive and effective structure is in place within the PISG to monitor compliance with human and community rights and to respond to violations.
- Existing mechanisms within municipalities responsible for protection of human and community rights (Municipal Community Offices, Municipal Assembly Communities and Mediation Committees) have adequate resources and staff, and are functioning effectively.
- Kosovo participates in the Council of Europe implementation process for the Framework Convention for the Protection of National Minorities and fully implements recommendations resulting from that process.
- There is fair distribution of municipal and ministerial resources to all communities.
- The educational curriculum encourages tolerance and respect of the contributions of all communities to the history of Kosovo.

Returns

- The number of municipalities with sustainable returns increases, including an increase in returns to urban areas, the pace of returns overall accelerates, and the level of unmet demand for return has been substantially reduced.
- Returnees to Kosovo are able to participate in the economy and job market without discrimination and limitations based on the freedom of movement.
- Health care, social services, education and public utilities are available to returnees on a level equal to that of the rest of the population.

- Returnees face no greater risk of violence than the population as a whole, and police and the judiciary respond promptly and without discrimination to crimes, irrespective of the ethnic background of the victim.
- Municipalities and ministries are able to assume responsibility for returns within all communities in a manner consistent with European standards.
- Funding is allocated from the KCB to support returns projects and smaller communities.
- Visible support of the returns process by community leaders and public information and education efforts supported by the PISG create a climate of tolerance and support for the right to return.
- PISG support for returns, including financial assistance, is distributed equitably to all communities.

V. Economy

The legal framework for a sustainable, competitive market economy is in place and implemented. The minimum essential conditions are a legal and institutional base which act without discrimination against any individual or company; a regulatory system conducive to business that is capable of holding governmental officials and the private sector accountable; a tax regime that sustains the essential functions of government and an infrastructure that provides basic services and facilitates investment. The goal is to move Kosovo towards the achievement of European standards.

- Basic economic legislation is in place and enforced.
- Relevant government institutions and services are functioning.
- The budget process is functioning and meeting all legal requirements.
- Economic statistics are available and regularly published, including on GDP, inflation, trade and unemployment.
- Privatization and liquidation of Socially Owned Enterprises are well advanced; Municipal Authorities and relevant governmental structures support a smooth and reliable transfer of ownership rights.
- Restructuring of Publicly Owned Enterprises, based on independent audits, is progressing and fully backed by the PISG.
- Supervision over commercial banking, insurance and pension scheme is reliable and effective.
- Kosovo wide billings approach 100% of services provided by KEK, PTK and water sector utilities, and collections approach at least the levels of neighbours.

- Tax revenue fully funds the recurrent budget, and an increasing share of the public investment.
- Tax compliance indicators are substantially improving.
- Revenue raising is free from political influence.

VI. Property Rights

The fair enforcement of property rights is essential to encourage returns and the equal treatment of all ethnic communities. This requires that there is effective legislation in place, that there are effective property dispute resolution mechanisms; that rightful owners of residential, commercial and agricultural lands are able to take effective possession of their property and that there is an accurate system for transfer, encumbrance and registration of property as well as the prevention of coerced property sales.

Property Rights

- Legislation is in place that is consistent with European standards.
- Illegal occupants have been evicted from properties and the property returned to its rightful owners.
- Municipal courts resolve property issues without discrimination against minority communities and do so at a rate comparable to European court systems.
- The Police enforce these decisions routinely and without discrimination.
- The Housing and Property Directorate and the Housing and Property Claims Commission have effectively resolved their backlog of cases.
- There is an effective system to remedy disputes over agricultural and commercial property.
- A property rights registry has been established and is functioning and municipal cadastral surveys have been completed.
- Municipal authorities cease unlawful or unjustified attempts to develop public lands that have long-established informal settlements by minority communities or other vulnerable groups.
- Informal settlements of vulnerable minority groups have been legalized and regularized.

Preservation of Cultural Heritage

- Kosovo's cultural heritage is respected as the common patrimony of all of Kosovo's ethnic, religious and linguistic communities.

- All communities are entitled to preserve, restore and protect sites important to their cultural, historical and religious heritage with the assistance of relevant authorities (PISG), in accordance with European standards.
- There shall be neither discrimination nor preferential treatment of cultural heritage properties of any community.

VII. Dialogue

There is a constructive and continuing dialogue between the PISG and their counterparts in Belgrade over practical issues. Kosovo's cooperation within the region is developed.

Belgrade-Pristina dialogue

- There are regular meetings of the working groups (initially four: missing persons, returns, energy and transport & communications) and all working groups are multi-ethnic.
- Meetings take place in atmosphere of constructive cooperation, respecting the rules of procedure and utilizing available international expertise.
- The working groups make progress in resolving practical issues of mutual concern.

Regional

- Working arrangements are in place to provide advanced cooperation in the fields of: freedom of movement (including border crossings), trade and economy, police and justice, public administration, and regional parliamentary exchanges.
- There is participation in bilateral and multilateral arrangements to benefit stability in the region.

VIII. Kosovo Protection Corps

The Kosovo Protection Corps (KPC) thoroughly complies with its mandate, as stated in the Constitutional Framework, as "a civilian emergency organization, which carries out in Kosovo rapid disaster response tasks for public safety in times of emergency and humanitarian assistance."

The KPC operates in a transparent, accountable, disciplined, and professional manner and is representative of the entire population of Kosovo. The KPC is capable of enforcing discipline and is fully funded in a transparent way.

- The KPC performs its mandated functions in full compliance with the rule of law.
- All Kosovo communities are fully and fairly represented in the KPC without being subject to discrimination.
- Funding is transparent and independently audited.
- The number of KPC installations has been reduced by at least one-third; contingent size is reduced to 3,052 active members and 2,000 reserve members.
- All misconduct is punished, under a rigorous Disciplinary Code and Performance Review System.
- The KPC has engaged in a comprehensive campaign to recruit in ethnic minority communities.
- The KPC has devoted a proportionate share of reconstruction activities to ethnic minority communities.
- A Terms of Service Law for active and reserve members has been adopted and implemented.

Source: United Nations. United Nations Mission in Kosovo. Press Office. *Standards for Kosovo.* UNMIK/PR/1078, December 10, 2003. www.unmikonline.org/press/2003/pressr/pr1078.pdf (accessed December 10, 2003).

Supreme Court on Federal Campaign Finance Law

December 10, 2003

In considering the constitutionality of a new federal law aimed at curbing the influence of big money in federal elections campaigns, the Supreme Court was asked to weigh two competing interests. One, at the heart of the new law, was the government's interest in safeguarding campaigns from corruption or the appearance of corruption. The other was the public's right to speak out and participate in the political process. Upholding the key elements of the law on December 10, 2003, the Court came down strongly on the side of preserving the integrity of the political process. By a 5–4 vote, the Court said that the law's ban on "soft money" contributions to the political parties and its restrictions on issue ads did not violate the First Amendment guarantees of free speech and free association.

The ruling was a victory for Sen. John McCain. R-Ariz., who had been fighting since 1996 to close several loopholes in existing campaign finance regulations. The biggest loophole was soft money—unlimited and largely unregulated contributions to political parties from corporations, unions, and wealthy individuals that were not spent directly on candidates' campaigns. In recent election cycles, the two parties between them had raised about $500 million in soft money. Much of the soft money was spent to exploit another loophole in existing law, so-called issue ads, which clearly supported or attacked specific candidates but escaped regulation by not explicitly telling viewers to vote for or against them.

McCain and his chief cosponsors—Sen. Russell D. Feingold, D-Wis., and House members Christopher Shays, R-Conn., and Martin T. Meehan, D-Mass.—won a major victory in 2002, when President George W. Bush signed into law the Bipartisan Campaign Reform Act, more commonly known as McCain-Feingold. But it was clear even before the measure passed that its opponents would challenge its constitutionality and that McCain and his supporters could not celebrate until the Supreme Court had acted—and perhaps not even then if the Court decided that the restrictions in McCain-Feingold, particularly those regarding issue ads, infringed on free speech guarantees.

The majority's unequivocal endorsement of Congress's authority "to anticipate and respond to concerns about circumvention of [campaign finance] regulations" came as a surprise to both proponents and opponents of McCain-Feingold. "This is a very strong opinion—much stronger than people expected," said Don Simon, counsel for Common Cause, which helped shape the law. "There's kind of the words and the music. The words are that this law is constitutional. The music is a very broad acceptance by a majority of the court of the world view of those who have argued that this kind of regulation of money in politics is necessary to keep the democratic process healthy."

Sen. Mitch McConnell, R-Ken., who was the chief opponent of the law and who brought the main suit challenging its constitutionality, said that the Court had sacrificed the guarantee of free speech to preserve a law that would not achieve its intended purpose. Big money would continue to flow, he said, particularly to interest groups, which would cut the political parties out of the picture and make the cash raised and spent even more difficult for the public to track. "This law will not remove one dime from politics," McConnell said in a prepared statement. "Soft money is not gone. It has just changed its address." Floyd Abrams, a noted expert on the First Amendment and one of McConnell's principal lawyers, said of the ruling: "There will be less speech, less debate, and a less-informed electorate."

The ruling was not expected to have much impact on party fund raising for the 2004 federal elections. The McCain-Feingold law had been in effect since November 6, 2002, the day after the 2002 general elections. Ironically, perhaps, the Democratic Party, which had been the primary backer of the law, was most likely to be hurt by it because Democrats had been more reliant on soft money than the Republican Party and were less adept at raising "hard money" (limited contributions that were regulated).

Brief History of Campaign Finance Laws

The role of private money in politics had always been hotly disputed, with some viewing campaign donations as ultimately corrupting and others seeing such funding as a source of vigorous competition. Private donations to support or oppose candidates went back at least as far as the 1830s when urban financiers contributed funds to counter President Andrew Jackson's opposition to the U.S. Bank. The political parties attracted large donors long before the Civil War, and the industrialism that followed that war fed the campaign cost spiral. In the late 1800s concerns began to arise about the power of the trusts and the role of campaign professionals, such as Mark Hanna, an Ohio mining magnate. Hanna raised money for the Republican Party through a systematic assessment of banks and corporations and then used the money to influence potential delegates and pay for a mass propaganda campaign in support of presidential candidate William McKinley. The McKinley campaign spent $16 million on his winning election in 1896—an enormous sum at the time.

The first campaign finance reform law was passed in 1907, when Congress banned bank and corporate gifts to candidates in federal elections. Three years later Congress enacted the Federal Corrupt Practices Act of 1910, which required candidates for the U.S. House of Representatives to disclose names of their major contributors. In 1911 Congress extended the disclosure requirement to Senate candidates, required all candidates for Congress to submit campaign expense reports, and set limits on spending by candidates. The Federal Corrupt Practices Act of 1925 tightened the earlier laws, and in 1942 Congress also barred labor unions from making contributions to political campaigns. In 1971 Congress passed another major reform intended to curb not only the influence of private contributors but also the amounts candidates could spend on television and radio ads.

The Watergate scandal revealed the excesses of the fund-raising campaign orchestrated on behalf of President Richard Nixon's 1972 reelection effort and led to the passage of the Federal Election Campaign Act Amendments of 1974. Among other things the law set limits on individual donations as well as on donations made by political action committees; created an agency, the Federal Election Commission (FEC), to monitor and enforce the contribution and spending limits; and set limits on spending. In the landmark case of *Buckley v. Valeo* (1976), the Supreme Court upheld the contribution limits and disclosure requirements of the 1974 law but ruled that the spending limits were unconstitutional violations of the First Amendment guarantee of freedom of expression.

Ironically, the strict limits on campaign contributions led to the rise of soft money. In 1978 the FEC said state and local political party organizations could use the unregulated contributions for such activities as get-out-the-vote and voter registration drives. That move was endorsed and expanded by Congress in 1979. In 1995 the FEC ruled that political parties could also use soft money to pay for "legislative advocacy media advertisements," or issue ads. Outside groups could also use their own money to run issue ads. These ads could mention a federal candidate by name so long as the ad did not expressly advocate the candidate's election or defeat. In the 1996 elections, Republican Party organizations spent nearly $150 million in soft money; Democratic Party organizations spent nearly $122 million. By one estimate the parties and outside groups spent between $135 million and $150 million on issue ads during the 1995–1996 election cycle.

Congress had been trying to pass campaign financing reform for several years, but partisan strife blocked those efforts. After the 1996 campaign, with its high levels of soft money and issue ad spending, highlighted by a scandal surrounding the Democrats' campaign fund-raising techniques, McCain began a new quest to pass reform legislation. In 2000 McCain had a modest success when Congress passed legislation requiring public disclosure of large contributions to and spending by Section 527 groups (named after the section of the tax code regulating them); many of these tax-exempt political organizations had spent millions on issue ads. Finally, in 2002 Congress passed the Bipartisan Campaign Reform Act of 2002.

The McCain-Feingold Law

The McCain-Feingold act (PL 107–155) was signed into law on March 27, 2002, by President Bush, who had reluctantly supported the bill after questions were raised about the influence of large corporate donors to his 2000 campaign. One of the donors was Enron, the Texas energy trading company that went bankrupt in 2001 amid allegations of fraud and corporate wrongdoing. The law barred national party committees, federal officeholders, and candidates for federal office from accepting or spending soft money contributions. State parties could still raise soft money but could not spend it on federal election activities. To compensate in part for the loss of soft money, the law raised the cap on individual contributions from $1,000 to $2,000 per election. It also raised the contribution limits for House and Senate candidates facing wealthy, self-financed opponents. To prevent wealthy individuals from circumventing contribution limits, the law prohibited donations from children under age eighteen. Finally, to curb abuses of issue ads, McCain-Feingold barred labor unions and corporations from directly funding "electioneering communications"—defined as ads that "refer to a clearly identified" federal candidate—that were targeted to the candidate's state or district within sixty days of a general election or thirty days of a primary. The law took effect November 6, 2002, directly after the 2002 general elections.

Senator McConnell immediately filed suit challenging the constitutionality of the law. Eventually more than eighty plaintiffs filed suits challenging various aspects of the new law; among them were the National Rifle Association, the Republican National Committee, the American Civil Liberties Union, the AFL-CIO, and the California Democratic Party. Anticipating such legal challenges, the law's authors had included provisions that would speed up judicial review so that the constitutionality of the law might be settled before the 2004 campaign season began. But a special three-judge panel, composed of two federal district court judges and an appellate court judge in Washington, D.C., did not issue its opinion until May 2, 2003, five months after it heard arguments in December 2002. Its ruling did little to clarify the situation. Although the net effect of the ruling was to uphold most of the new law, the Court was badly divided, issuing three separate opinions that totaled nearly 1,700 pages.

Following the procedure laid out in the law itself, appeals of the ruling were filed directly with the Supreme Court, which announced on June 5, 2003, that it would hear arguments in the case at a special session on September 8—nearly a month before its regular term began. It was the first special session of the Court since the summer of 1974, when the Court heard arguments on whether President Nixon could be required to turn over tape recordings of his conversations with aides regarding the Watergate break-in and subsequent cover-up. The campaign finance case, known as *McConnell v. the FEC,* was actually a consolidation of twelve appeals of the special court ruling. The Supreme Court agreed to hear four hours of arguments; typically arguments lasted no more than an hour. Arguing in support of the law and its authors were Solicitor General Theodore B. Olson and former solicitor general Seth P. Waxman. Arguing the unconstitutionality of the soft money ban were Kenneth W. Starr, another former solicitor general and the former independent counsel whose investigation of President Bill Clinton led to his impeachment in 1998. Starr was representing McConnell. Four other lawyers also argued for striking down various parts of the law.

A Constitutional Plug for the Loopholes

Writing for the five-justice majority that upheld the soft money ban and issue ad restrictions, Justices John Paul Stevens and Sandra Day O'Connor closely followed the arguments of the law's supporters and dismissed those from opponents that the regulations infringed on First Amendment freedoms. Stevens and O'Connor said "proper deference" was owed to Congress's "ability to weigh competing constitutional interests in an area in which it enjoys particular experience" and that Congress needed "sufficient room to anticipate and respond to concerns about circumvention of regulations designed to protect the political process's integrity." The majority said those concerns extended beyond quid pro quo corruption—directly exchanging favors in return for money—to the appearance of corruption and indicated that the record showed ample evidence that soft money contributions, at a minimum, gave rise to the appearance of corruption. "It is not only plausible, but likely, that candidates would feel grateful for such donations and that donors would seek to exploit that gratitude," Stevens and O'Connor wrote.

The majority also rejected the argument that restrictions on issue ads were a violation of the First Amendment. "The provision is a regulation of, not a ban on, expression," they wrote. In regulating campaign ads, the Court held that Congress could stretch beyond a "magic words" test first laid out in *Buckley v. Valeo,* which allowed the government to regulate only those ads that contained words of "express advocacy" for a candidate. Lawmakers had the latitude to adapt and rewrite campaign finance regulations as politicians opened new loopholes in the law, Stevens and O'Connor wrote. Buckley and later cases "in no way drew a constitutional boundary that forever fixed the permissible scope of provisions regulating campaign-related speech."

Joining Stevens and O'Connor in the opinion on these two matters were Justices David H. Souter, Ruth Bader Ginsburg, and Stephen G. Breyer.

The remaining justices, Chief Justice William H. Rehnquist and Justices Anthony M. Kennedy, Antonin Scalia, and Clarence Thomas, dissented in equally forceful terms. Scalia said it was "a sad day for the freedom of speech." The McCain-Feingold law, Scalia said, "prohibits the criticism of Members of Congress by those entities most capable of giving such criticism loud voice: national political parties and corporations, both the commercial and the not-for-profit sorts." Kennedy agreed with others in the minority that the law amounted to an incumbent protection act: "To the majority, all this is not only valid under the First Amendment but also is part of Congress' 'steady improvement of the elections law.' We should make no mistake. It is neither. . . . It is an effort by Congress to ensure that civic discourse takes place only through the modes of its choosing. . . ."

The Court split multiple ways on some secondary issues. It unanimously struck down the ban on anyone younger than eighteen contributing to campaigns. It also struck down language requiring political parties, when spending money on behalf of a candidate, to choose between making those expenditures in coordination with the candidate or independently. The Court did not rule on two important issues because the majority, led by Chief Justice Rehnquist, said the plaintiffs did not have standing to challenge them. That left in place provisions of the law that increased limits on hard money contributions and that set higher hard money contribution limits for candidates facing wealthy opponents who were bankrolling their own campaign.

A New Loophole?

Even before the Supreme Court ruling, attention was beginning to focus on activities of outside advocacy groups that could still raise and spend unlimited amounts of soft money. Known as "527s," these groups could use soft money for a variety of federal election activities. Provided they did not accept money directly from unions or corporations, such groups could also avoid the new law's restrictions on financing campaign ads that mentioned a candidate close to election day. Attorney Bobby Burchfield, who represented the Republican National Committee in its losing challenge to the law, predicted that outside groups on both ends of the political spectrum would raise and spend $1 billion in the 2004 election season. He said the rise of such groups was bad for democracy. "Interest grounds tend to advocate more extreme and uncompromising views than the political parties," he said. "The speech that we will be hearing will be from a more narrow cross-section of the public."

Fred Wertheimer of the public watchdog group Democracy 21, which helped write McCain-Feingold, disagreed that outside groups would raise so much money. He said big donors who once lavished money on the political parties would not have the same incentive to give to interest groups because such organizations were not perceived to have the same influence with law-makers as the parties had. Nonetheless, Wertheimer and others acknowl-edged that 527s might serve as conduits for circumventing the law's limits. "We're going to take a hard look at the 527 groups in terms of the rules that apply to them and whether more regulations are necessary," Wertheimer said.

Whether it was 527s or some other loophole in the law, at least five jus-tices were certain that the Congress and the Court would be dealing with campaign financing issues in the future. "Money, like water, will always find an outlet," Stevens and O'Connor wrote. "What problems will arise, and how Congress will respond, are concerns for another day."

> *Following are excerpts from the Supreme Court's majority opinion, written by Justices John Paul Stevens and Sandra Day O'Connor, and from dissenting opinions by Justices Antonin Scalia and Anthony M. Kennedy in the case of* McConnell v. Federal Election Commission, *in which the Court on December 10, 2003, upheld provisions of the Bipartisan Campaign Finance Reform Act that barred political parties from accepting soft money contributions and placed restrictions on campaign issue ads.*

McConnell v. Federal Election Commission

Nos. 02–1674, 02–1675, 02–1676, 02–1702, 02–1727, 02–1733, 02–1734, 02–1740, 02–1747, 02–1753, 02–1755, and 02–1756

Mitch McConnell et al., appellants
v.
Federal Election Commission, et al.
}
On Appeals from the
United States District Court for
the District of Columbia

[December 10, 2003]

JUSTICE STEVENS and JUSTICE O'CONNOR delivered the opinion of the Court with respect to BCRA [Bipartisan Campaign Reform Act of 2002] Titles I and II. . . .

[Parts I, II, and beginning of III omitted.]

1. Governmental Interests Underlying New FECA § 323(a)

The Government defends § 323(a)'s ban on national parties' involvement with soft money as necessary to prevent the actual and apparent corruption of federal candidates and officeholders. Our cases have made clear that the prevention of corruption or its appearance constitutes a sufficiently important interest to justify political contribution limits. We have not limited that interest to the elimination of cash-for-votes exchanges. . . .

Of "almost equal" importance has been the Government's interest in combating the appearance or perception of corruption engendered by large campaign contributions. . . . Take away Congress' authority to regulate the appearance of undue influence and "the cynical assumption that large donors call the tune could jeopardize the willingness of voters to take part in democratic governance.". . . And because the First Amendment does not require Congress to ignore the fact that "candidates, donors, and parties test the limits of the current law,". . . these interests have been sufficient to justify not only contribution limits themselves, but laws preventing the circumvention of such limits. . . .

The idea that large contributions to a national party can corrupt or, at the very least, create the appearance of corruption of federal candidates and officeholders is neither novel nor implausible. For nearly 30 years, FECA [Federal Election Campaign Act] has placed strict dollar limits and source restrictions on contributions that individuals and other entities can give to national, state, and local party committees for the purpose of influencing a federal election. The premise behind these restrictions has been, and continues to be, that contributions to a federal candidate's party in aid of that candidate's campaign threaten to create— no less than would a direct contribution to the candidate—a sense of obligation. . . .

This is particularly true of contributions to national parties, with which federal candidates and officeholders enjoy a special relationship and unity of interest. . . .

The question for present purposes is whether large *soft-money* contributions to national party committees have a corrupting influence or give rise to the appearance of corruption. Both common sense and the ample record in these cases confirm Congress' belief that they do. . . . [C]orporate, union, and wealthy individual donors have been free to contribute substantial sums of soft money to the national parties, which the parties can spend for the specific purpose of influencing a particular candidate's federal election. It is not only plausible, but likely, that candidates would feel grateful for such donations and that donors would seek to exploit that gratitude.

The evidence in the record shows that candidates and donors alike have in fact exploited the soft-money loophole, the former to increase their prospects of election and the latter to create debt on the part of officeholders, with the national parties serving as willing intermediaries. Thus, despite FECA's hard-money limits on direct contributions to candidates, federal officeholders have commonly asked donors to make soft-money donations to national and state committees "solely in order to assist federal campaigns," including the officeholder's own. . . . Parties kept tallies of the amounts of soft money raised by each officeholder, and "the amount of money a Member of Congress raise[d] for the national political committees often affect[ed] the amount the committees g[a]ve to assist the Member's campaign.". . . Donors often asked that their contributions be credited to particular candidates, and the parties obliged, irrespective of whether the funds were hard or soft. . . . National party committees often teamed with individual candidates' campaign committees to create joint fundraising committees, which enabled the candidates to take advantage of the party's higher contribution limits while still allowing donors to give to their preferred candidate. . . . Even when not participating directly in the fundraising, federal officeholders were well aware of the identities of the donors: National party committees would distribute lists of potential or actual donors, or donors themselves would report their generosity to officeholders. . . .

For their part, lobbyists, CEOs, and wealthy individuals alike all have candidly admitted donating substantial sums of soft money to national committees not on ideological grounds, but for the express purpose of securing influence over federal officials. For example, a former lobbyist and partner at a lobbying firm in Washington, D.C., stated in his declaration:

> " 'You are doing a favor for somebody by making a large [soft-money] donation and they appreciate it. Ordinarily, people feel inclined to reciprocate favors. Do a bigger favor for someone—that is, write a larger check—and they feel even more compelled to reciprocate. In my experience, overt words are rarely exchanged about contributions, but people do have understandings.'". . .

Particularly telling is the fact that, in 1996 and 2000, more than half of the top 50 soft-money donors gave substantial sums to *both* major national parties, leaving room for no other conclusion but that these donors were seeking influence, or avoiding retaliation, rather than promoting any particular ideology. . . .

The evidence from the federal officeholders' perspective is similar. For example, one former Senator described the influence purchased by non-federal donations as follows:

> " 'Too often, Members' first thought is not what is right or what they believe, but how it will affect fundraising. Who, after all, can

seriously contend that a $100,000 donation does not alter the way one thinks about—and quite possibly votes on—an issue? . . . When you don't pay the piper that finances your campaigns, you will never get any more money from that piper. Since money is the mother's milk of politics, you never want to be in that situation.'. . . (quoting declaration of former Sen. Alan Simpson). . . ."

Plaintiffs argue that without concrete evidence of an instance in which a federal officeholder has actually switched a vote (or, presumably, evidence of a specific instance where the public believes a vote was switched), Congress has not shown that there exists real or apparent corruption. But the record is to the contrary. The evidence connects soft money to manipulations of the legislative calendar, leading to Congress' failure to enact, among other things, generic drug legislation, tort reform, and tobacco legislation. . . . To claim that such actions do not change legislative outcomes surely misunderstands the legislative process. More importantly, plaintiffs conceive of corruption too narrowly. Our cases have firmly established that Congress' legitimate interest extends beyond preventing simple cash-for-votes corruption to curbing "undue influence on an officeholder's judgment, and the appearance of such influence.". . . Many of the "deeply disturbing examples" of corruption cited by this Court in *Buckley* [*v. Valeo* (1976)] to justify FECA's contribution limits were not episodes of vote buying, but evidence that various corporate interests had given substantial donations to gain access to high-level government officials. . . .

The record in the present case is replete with similar examples of national party committees peddling access to federal candidates and officeholders in exchange for large soft-money donations. . . . As one former Senator put it:

"'Special interests who give large amounts of soft money to political parties do in fact achieve their objectives. They do get special access. Sitting Senators and House Members have limited amounts of time, but they make time available in their schedules to meet with representatives of business and unions and wealthy individuals who gave large sums to their parties. These are not idle chit-chats about the philosophy of democracy. . . . Senators are pressed by their benefactors to introduce legislation, to amend legislation, to block legislation, and to vote on legislation in a certain way.'". . .

So pervasive is this practice that the six national party committees actually furnish their own menus of opportunities for access to would-be soft-money donors, with increased prices reflecting an increased level of access. For example, the DCCC [Democratic Congressional Campaign

Committee] offers a range of donor options, starting with the $10,000-per-year Business Forum program, and going up to the $100,000-per-year National Finance Board program. The latter entitles the donor to bimonthly conference calls with the Democratic House leadership and chair of the DCCC, complimentary invitations to all DCCC fundraising events, two private dinners with the Democratic House leadership and ranking members, and two retreats with the Democratic House leader and DCCC chair in Telluride, Colorado, and Hyannisport, Massachusetts. . . .

Despite this evidence and the close ties that candidates and officeholders have with their parties, JUSTICE KENNEDY would limit Congress' regulatory interest *only* to the prevention of the actual or apparent *quid pro quo* corruption "inherent in" contributions made directly to, contributions made at the express behest of, and expenditures made in coordination with, a federal officeholder or candidate. . . . Regulation of any other donation or expenditure—regardless of its size, the recipient's relationship to the candidate or officeholder, its potential impact on a candidate's election, its value to the candidate, or its unabashed and explicit intent to purchase influence—would, according to JUSTICE KENNEDY, simply be out of bounds. This crabbed view of corruption, and particularly of the appearance of corruption, ignores precedent, common sense, and the realities of political fundraising exposed by the record in this litigation.

JUSTICE KENNEDY'S interpretation of the First Amendment would render Congress powerless to address more subtle but equally dispiriting forms of corruption. Just as troubling to a functioning democracy as classic *quid pro quo* corruption is the danger that officeholders will decide issues not on the merits or the desires of their constituencies, but according to the wishes of those who have made large financial contributions valued by the officeholder. Even if it occurs only occasionally, the potential for such undue influence is manifest. And unlike straight cash-for-votes transactions, such corruption is neither easily detected nor practical to criminalize. The best means of prevention is to identify and to remove the temptation. The evidence set forth above, which is but a sampling of the reams of disquieting evidence contained in the record, convincingly demonstrates that soft-money contributions to political parties carry with them just such temptation.

JUSTICE KENNEDY likewise takes too narrow a view of the appearance of corruption. He asserts that only those transactions with "inherent corruption potential," which he again limits to contributions directly to candidates, justify the inference "that regulating the conduct will stem the appearance of real corruption." . . . In our view, however, Congress is not required to ignore historical evidence regarding a particular practice or to view conduct in isolation from its context. To be sure, mere political favoritism or opportunity for influence alone is insufficient to justify regulation. . . . As the record demonstrates, it is the manner in which parties have *sold* access to federal candidates and officeholders that has given rise to the appearance of undue influence. Implicit (and, as the record shows, sometimes explicit) in the sale of access is the suggestion that money buys influence. It is no surprise then that purchasers of such access unabashedly admit that they are seeking to purchase just such influence. It was not unwarranted for Congress to conclude that the selling of access gives rise to the appearance of corruption.

In sum, there is substantial evidence to support Congress' determination that large soft-money contributions to national political parties give rise to corruption and the appearance of corruption. . . .

[Remainder of Part III omitted.]

IV

Title II of BCRA, entitled "Noncandidate Campaign Expenditures," is divided into two subtitles: "Electioneering Communications" and "Independent and Coordinated Expenditures." We consider each challenged section of these subtitles in turn.

BCRA § 201's Definition of "Electioneering Communication"

The first section of Title II, § 201, comprehensively amends FECA 304, which requires political committees to file detailed periodic financial reports with the FEC. The amendment coins a new term, "electioneering communication," to replace the narrowing construction of FECA's disclosure provisions adopted by this Court in *Buckley*. As discussed further below, that construction limited the coverage of FECA's disclosure requirement to communications expressly advocating the election or defeat of particular candidates. By contrast, the term "electioneering communication" is not so limited, but is defined to encompass any "broadcast, cable, or satellite communication" that

"(I) refers to a clearly identified candidate for Federal office;
"(II) is made within—
"(aa) 60 days before a general, special, or runoff election for the office sought by the candidate; or
"(bb) 30 days before a primary or preference election, or a convention or caucus of a political party that has authority to nominate a candidate, for the office sought by the candidate; and

"(III) in the case of a communication which refers to a candidate other than President or Vice President, is targeted to the relevant electorate."...

In addition to setting forth this definition, BCRA's amendments to FECA § 304 specify significant disclosure requirements for persons who fund electioneering communications. BCRA's use of this new term is not, however, limited to the disclosure context: A later section of the Act . . . restricts corporations' and labor unions' funding of electioneering communications. Plaintiffs challenge the constitutionality of the new term as it applies in both the disclosure and the expenditure contexts.

The major premise of plaintiffs' challenge to BCRA's use of the term "electioneering communication" is that *Buckley* drew a constitutionally mandated line between express advocacy and so-called issue advocacy, and that speakers possess an inviolable First Amendment right to engage in the latter category of speech. Thus, plaintiffs maintain, Congress cannot constitutionally require disclosure of, or regulate expenditures for, "electioneering communications" without making an exception for those "communications" that do not meet *Buckley's* definition of express advocacy.

That position misapprehends our prior decisions, for the express advocacy restriction was an endpoint of statutory interpretation, not a first principle of constitutional law. In *Buckley* we began by examining then-18 U.S.C. § 608(e)(1) . . . , which restricted expenditures "'relative to a clearly identified candidate,'" and we found that the phrase "'relative to'" was impermissibly vague. . . . We concluded that the vagueness deficiencies could "be avoided only by reading § 608(e)(1) as limited to communications that include explicit words of advocacy of election or defeat of a candidate.". . . We provided examples of words of express advocacy, such as "'vote for,' 'elect,' 'support,' . . . 'defeat,' [and] 'reject,'" . . . and those examples eventually gave rise to what is now known as the "magic words" requirement.

We then considered FECA's disclosure provisions, . . . which defined "'expenditur[e]'" to include the use of money or other assets "'for the purpose of . . . influencing'" a federal election. . . . Finding that the "ambiguity of this phrase" posed "constitutional problems," we noted our "obligation to construe the statute, if that can be done consistent with the legislature's purpose, to avoid the shoals of vagueness,". . . "To insure that the reach" of the disclosure requirement was "not impermissibly broad, we construe[d] 'expenditure' for purposes of that section in the same way we construed the terms of § 608(e)—to reach only funds used for communications that expressly advocate the election or defeat of a clearly identified candidate.". . .

Thus, a plain reading of *Buckley* makes clear that the express advocacy limitation, in both the expenditure and the disclosure contexts, was the product of statutory interpretation rather than a constitutional command. In narrowly reading the FECA provisions in *Buckley* to avoid problems of vagueness and overbreadth, we nowhere suggested that a statute that was neither vague nor overbroad would be required to toe the same express advocacy line. . . .

In short, the concept of express advocacy and the concomitant class of magic words were born of an effort to avoid constitutional infirmities. . . . [O]ur decisions in *Buckley* and *MCFL* were specific to the statutory language before us; they in no way drew a constitutional boundary that forever fixed the permissible scope of provisions regulating campaign-related speech.

Nor are we persuaded, independent of our precedents, that the First Amendment erects a rigid barrier between express advocacy and so-called issue advocacy. That notion cannot be squared with our longstanding recognition that the presence or absence of magic words cannot meaningfully distinguish electioneering speech from a true issue ad. . . . Indeed, the unmistakable lesson from the record in this litigation, as all three judges on the District Court agreed, is that *Buckley's* magic-words requirement is functionally meaningless. . . . Not only can advertisers easily evade the line by eschewing the use of magic words, but they would seldom choose to use such words even if permitted. And although the resulting advertisements do not urge the viewer to vote for or against a candidate in so many words, they are no less clearly intended to influence the election. *Buckley's* express advocacy line, in short, has not aided the legislative effort to combat real or apparent corruption, and Congress enacted BCRA to correct the flaws it found in the existing system. . . .

BCRA § 203's Prohibition of Corporate and Labor Disbursements for Electioneering Communications

Since our decision in *Buckley*, Congress' power to prohibit corporations and unions from using funds in their treasuries to finance advertisements expressly advocating the election or defeat of candidates in federal elections has been firmly embedded in our law. The ability to form and administer separate segregated funds authorized by FECA § 316 . . . has provided corporations and unions with a constitutionally sufficient opportunity to engage in express advocacy. That has been this Court's unanimous view, and it is not challenged in this litigation.

Section 203 of BCRA amends FECA § 316(b)(2) to extend this rule, which previously applied only to express advocacy, to all "electioneering communications" covered by the definition of that term in amended FECA § 304(f)(3), discussed above. . . . Thus, under BCRA, corporations and unions may not use their general treasury funds to finance electioneering communications, but they remain free to organize and administer segregated funds, or PACs, for that purpose. Because corporations can still fund electioneering communications with PAC money, it is "simply wrong" to view the provision as a "complete ban" on expression rather than a regulation. . . .

V

Many years ago we observed that "[t]o say that Congress is without power to pass appropriate legislation to safeguard . . . an election from the improper use of money to influence the result is to deny to the nation in a vital particular the power of self protection.". . . We abide by that conviction in considering Congress' most recent effort to confine the ill effects of aggregated wealth on our political system. We are under no illusion that BCRA will be the last congressional statement on the matter. Money, like water, will always find an outlet. What problems will arise, and how Congress will respond, are concerns for another day. In the main we uphold BCRA's two principal, complementary features: the control of soft money and the regulation of electioneering communications. Accordingly, we affirm in part and reverse in part the District Court's judgment with respect to Titles I and II.

It is so ordered.

JUSTICE SCALIA, concurring with respect to BCRA Titles III and IV, dissenting with respect to BCRA Titles I and V, and concurring in the judgment in part and dissenting in part with respect to BCRA Title II. . . .

This is a sad day for the freedom of speech. Who could have imagined that the same Court which, within the past four years, has sternly disapproved of restrictions upon such inconsequential forms of expression as virtual child pornography, . . . tobacco advertising, . . . dissemination of illegally intercepted communications, . . . and sexually explicit cable programming . . . would smile with favor upon a law that cuts to the heart of what the First Amendment is meant to protect: the right to criticize the government. For that is what the most offensive provisions of this legislation are all about. We are governed by Congress, and this legislation prohibits the criticism of Members of Congress by those entities most capable of giving such criticism loud voice: national political parties and corporations, both of the commercial and the not-for-profit sort. It forbids pre-election criticism of incumbents by corporations, even not-for-profit corporations, by use of their general funds; and forbids national-party use of "soft" money to fund "issue ads" that incumbents find so offensive.

To be sure, the legislation is evenhanded: It similarly prohibits criticism of the candidates who oppose Members of Congress in their reelection bids. But as everyone knows, this is an area in which evenhandedness is not fairness. If *all* electioneering were evenhandedly prohibited, incumbents would have an enormous advantage. Likewise, if incumbents and challengers are limited to the same quantity of electioneering, incumbents are favored. In other words, *any* restriction upon a type of campaign speech that is equally available to challengers and incumbents tends to favor incumbents.

Beyond that, however, the present legislation *targets* for prohibition certain categories of campaign speech that are particularly harmful to incumbents. Is it accidental, do you think, that incumbents raise about three times as much "hard money"—the sort of funding generally *not* restricted by this legislation—as do their challengers? . . . Or that lobbyists (who seek the favor of incumbents) give 92 percent of their money in "hard" contributions? . . . Is it an oversight, do you suppose, that the so-called "millionaire provisions" raise the contribution limit for a candidate running against an individual who devotes to the campaign (as challengers often do) great personal wealth, but do not raise the limit for a candidate running against an individual who devotes to the campaign (as incumbents often do) a massive election "war chest"? . . . And is it mere happenstance, do you estimate, that national-party funding, which is severely limited by the Act, is more likely to assist cash-strapped challengers than flush-with-hard-money incumbents? . . . Was it unintended, by any chance, that incumbents are free personally to receive some soft money and even to solicit it for other organizations, while national parties are not? . . .

This litigation is about preventing criticism of the government. I cannot say for certain that many, or some, or even any, of the Members of Congress who voted for this legislation did so not to produce "fairer" campaigns, but to mute criticism of their records and facilitate reelection. Indeed, I will stipulate that all those who voted for the Act believed they were acting for the good of the country. There remains the problem of the Charlie Wilson Phenomenon, named after Charles Wilson, former president of General Motors, who is supposed to have said during the Senate hearing on his nomination as Secretary of Defense that "what's good for General Motors is good for the country." Those in power, even giving them the benefit of the greatest good will, are inclined to believe that what is good for them is good for the country. Whether in prescient recognition of the Charlie Wilson Phenomenon, or out of fear of good old-fashioned, malicious, self-interested manipulation, "[t]he fundamental approach of the First Amendment . . . was to assume the worst, and to rule the regulation of political speech 'for fairness' sake' simply out of bounds."... Having abandoned that approach to a limited extent in *Buckley*, we abandon it much further today.

We will unquestionably be called upon to abandon it further still in the future. The most frightening passage in the lengthy floor debates on this legislation is the following assurance given by one of the cosponsoring Senators to his colleagues:

> "This is a modest step, it is a first step, it is an essential step, but it does not even begin to address, in some ways, the fundamental problems that exist with the hard money aspect of the system.". . . (statement of Sen. Feingold).

The system indeed. The first instinct of power is the retention of power, and, under a Constitution that requires periodic elections, that is best achieved by the suppression of election-time speech. We have witnessed merely the second scene of Act I of what promises to be a lengthy tragedy. In scene 3 the Court, having abandoned most of the First Amendment weaponry that *Buckley* left intact, will be even less equipped to resist the incumbents' writing of the rules of political debate. The federal election campaign laws, which are already (as today's opinions show) so voluminous, so detailed, so complex, that no ordinary citizen dare run for office, or even contribute a significant sum, without hiring an expert advisor in the field, can be expected to grow more voluminous, more detailed, and more complex in the years to come—and always, always, with the objective of reducing the excessive amount of speech.

JUSTICE KENNEDY, concurring in the judgment in part and dissenting in part with respect to BCRA Titles I and II.

The First Amendment guarantees our citizens the right to judge for themselves the most effective means for the expression of political views and to decide for themselves which entities to trust as reliable speakers. Significant portions of Titles I and II of the Bipartisan Campaign Reform Act of 2002 (BCRA or Act) constrain that freedom. These new laws force speakers to abandon their own preference for speaking through parties and organizations. And they provide safe harbor to the mainstream press, suggesting that the corporate media alone suffice to alleviate the burdens the Act places on the rights and freedoms of ordinary citizens.

Today's decision upholding these laws purports simply to follow *Buckley* v. *Valeo* (1976) . . . but the majority, to make its decision work, must abridge free speech where *Buckley* did not. *Buckley* did not authorize Congress to decide what shapes and forms the national political dialogue is to take. To reach today's decision, the Court surpasses *Buckley*'s limits and expands Congress' regulatory power. In so doing, it replaces discrete and respected First Amendment principles with new, amorphous, and unsound rules, rules which dismantle basic protections for speech.

A few examples show how BCRA reorders speech rights and codifies the Government's own preferences for certain speakers. BCRA would have imposed felony punishment on Ross Perot's 1996 efforts to build the Reform Party. . . . BCRA makes it a felony for an environmental group to broadcast an ad, within 60 days of an election, exhorting the public to protest a Congressman's impending vote to permit logging in national forests. . . . BCRA escalates Congress' discrimination in favor of the speech rights of giant media corporations and against the speech rights of other corporations, both profit and nonprofit. . . .

To the majority, all this is not only valid under the First Amendment but also is part of Congress' "steady improvement of the national election laws." We should make no mistake. It is neither. It is the codification of an assumption that the mainstream media alone can protect freedom of speech. It is an effort by Congress to ensure that civic discourse takes place only through the modes of its choosing. . . .

Our precedents teach, above all, that Government cannot be trusted to moderate its own rules for suppression of speech. The dangers posed by speech regulations have led the Court to insist upon principled constitutional lines and a rigorous standard of review. The majority now abandons these distinctions and limitations. With respect, I dissent from the majority opinion upholding BCRA Titles I and II. . . .

Source: U.S. Supreme Court of the United States. *McConnell v. FEC.* 540 U.S. ___ (2003). Docket No. 02–1674. December 10, 2003. www.supremecourtus.gov/opinions/03pdf/02-1674.pdf (accessed December 15, 2003).

Chinese Premier on
Reforms in China

December 10, 2003

China's new generation of leadership—the fourth generation since the communist revolution of 1949—spent a hectic first year in power during 2003 by acting to accelerate the already fast pace of reform in all facets of society except the political system. Hu Jintao, who for a decade had been groomed for the nation's leadership and had become head of the Communist Party in late 2002, formally became China's president in March. The new leadership under Hu and Prime Minister Wen Jiabao successfully confronted a major health crisis (an epidemic of Severe Acute Respiratory Syndrome, known as SARS) and moved to deal with another (AIDS); celebrated China's first manned space flight; won Communist Party approval for reforms to reshape the country's super-hot economy; began to emphasize the plight of 800 million rural poor people; stepped up China's role in Asian affairs; and maintained remarkably good relations with the United States on potentially difficult issues. Even in domestic politics, the new leaders appeared to launch a national discussion about introducing a tiny bit of democracy, possibly even within the ruling Communist Party.

President George W. Bush in December accorded Prime Minister Wen five-star treatment during his first visit to the United States. Wen became the first foreign head of government (as opposed to head of state) to be given a nineteen-gun salute upon his arrival at the White House since Bush took office in 2001. On a matter of greater substance, Bush used a news conference with Wen to support China in the latest iteration of its half-century-old dispute with Taiwan, which the United States long had protected. *(Background, Historic Documents of 2002, p. 850)*

New Leaders Take Charge

The second stage of what was expected to be a three-stage succession process among the Chinese leadership was completed in 2003. The first step occurred at a Communist Party Congress in November 2002 when

Jiang Zemin, who had been China's leader for a dozen years, handed over the party leadership to Hu Jintao, a sixty-year-old hydraulic engineer who had worked his way up through the bureaucracy. Then, in March, when the legislature, the National People's Congress, convened in Beijing for its annual session, Jiang stepped down as president of China and Hu took his place. Other senior leaders of Jiang's generation (most in their late seventies) also stepped aside, including Prime Minister Zhu Rongji, who was succeeded by Wen Jiabao, and legislative speaker Li Peng, a former prime minister best known in the West as the man who carried out the 1989 crackdown on pro-democracy protestors in Beijing's Tiananmen Square. Li was replaced by a vice premier, Wu Bangguo. The new government officially took office on March 19. *(Tiananmen Square protests, Historic Documents of 1989, p. 275)*

Despite this leadership shuffle, Jiang remained an important official— some said the real power behind the scenes—by virtue of his chairmanship of the Central Military Commission, a post that also had been held by his predecessor as China's ultimate leader, Deng Xiaoping. Jiang's closest aide, longtime Communist Party official Jia Qinglin, also was appointed to important posts and was seen by some observers as a potential rival to President Hu should he falter. The third stage of China's leadership transition was expected to occur some time in the future when Jiang gave up his military post and allowed the younger generation to take over full responsibility.

Hu and Wen had no time to settle into their new government posts before they confronted their first major crisis: an outbreak of a new infectious disease known as SARS. The viral disease had originated in rural China in November 2002 but was covered up by midlevel government officials who apparently feared its impact on the economy. The government first acknowledged the disease on February 11, 2003. By mid-March the disease had spread through much of East Asia and begun to damage the region's economy. The disease also posed a major leadership test for the new Beijing government. Hu and Wen acted on April 20, forcing the release of the first significant details about the crisis and firing the health minister and the mayor of Beijing, both of whom had participated in the cover-up. *(SARS epidemic, p. 121)*

The government's initial reactive stance of hiding bad news was typical of the old way of doing business in China, and for a time it severely undercut the new leaders' attempt to press ahead with an agenda for change. But Hu and Wen eventually took actions that would have been unthinkable for most of their predecessors. They traveled around China giving speeches and meeting with health care workers; they appointed top-level officials to deal specifically with the epidemic; and on May 8 they announced emergency spending plans to prevent further damage to the economy—in short, they acted like politicians in a democratic country. By June domestic and foreign analysts were saying Hu and Wen appeared to have consolidated their control of the Communist Party and government bureaucracies. Subsequent reports, however, hinted at tensions between Hu and Jiang because of the new leader's rapid attempts to assert his authority. One cause of the tension appeared to have been the government's firing during the SARS crisis of the health minister, a Jiang protégé.

The new government also took a more proactive stance on the danger of AIDS, the lethal viral disease. The previous government for several years had refused to acknowledge AIDS as a problem in China, despite growing evidence that hundreds of thousands of people had been infected with the human immunodeficiency virus (HIV), which causes it. That attitude had slowly changed, and by late 2003 the new government took further steps to deal with the epidemic. Prime Minister Wen visited a clinic and had his photograph taken with an AIDS patient, and on November 7 the government announced that it had begun giving free antiretroviral drugs to people in Henan Province, where the disease was especially prevalent. A deputy health minister, Gao Qiang, said 840,000 Chinese were infected with HIV, the highest figure ever given by the government. Some doctors said the actual number might be much higher. *(AIDS, p. 780)*

Caution, But Reform As Well

Known for his remarkable memory, Hu was a cautious man who was widely expected to build a consensus within the Communist Party leadership before launching significant policy changes. Indeed, most experts had expected Hu to fix isolated problems rather than seek to redesign the political structure that had been in place since the 1949 revolution or the newer capitalist policies that for two decades had given China the fastest-growing economy in the world. The new government's quick action to stem the SARS crisis raised expectations that faster changes might be in the works, and Hu appeared to reinforce the impression that he was ready to push reforms more rapidly than most observers had expected.

Through his own speeches, reports in the government-controlled media, and statements by intellectuals close to the new government, Hu laid out an impressive agenda of reforms across most elements of Chinese society. In May he called for a modernization of the People's Liberation Army, and later reports said the military might cut several hundred thousand jobs and sell off many of the ancillary enterprises (such as hospitals, factories, and stores) that it owned. In August official newspapers reported work was under way on amendments to the constitution, including guarantees for property rights, a significant change from traditional Communist Party ideology.

On September 30 Hu delivered a speech to fellow party leaders that offered a hint of future political reforms: "We must enrich the forms of democracy, make democratic procedures complete, expand citizens' orderly political participation, and ensure that the people can exercise democratic elections, democratic decision-making, and democratic administration and democratic scrutiny." Despite the multiple references to democracy, this speech was not a clarion call for a Jeffersonian political system based on multiparty elections. Instead, most domestic and foreign experts said Hu merely was suggesting a somewhat greater openness within the Communist Party, perhaps by allowing the 62 million party members a greater role in selecting their leaders. "Hu is focusing on improving the operation of the existing system, not changing the system itself," Chinese political analyst Wu Jiaxiang told the *New York Times.* "But he is making very clear that he is in favor of political reform. People's hopes will be raised that he intends to do some significant things."

As far as outsiders could tell, no action was taken during the year to follow up on Hu's rhetoric. However, the new government did take several steps that eased the state's intrusions into the lives of the Chinese people. It repealed a vagrancy law that police had used to prevent people from traveling within China; it allowed people in large cities to apply for passports without getting advance approval from their employers; and it repealed a law that had required couples to get approval from their employers before they could wed or get divorced. This last law had been one of the most despised manifestations of Communist Party ideology that made workers subservient to employers in many aspects of their daily lives. After the law was repealed on October 1, the most important national holiday, China experienced a sudden surge in weddings.

Hu and Wen also sought to identify with the needs and aspirations of common Chinese, especially the hundreds of millions of people who had not yet benefited from the booming economy resulting from China's embrace of capitalism. Hu's first trips around the country as leader were to remote provinces, where he emphasized the role of the rural masses and called on his own government to do more for them. As had all Chinese leaders, Hu and Wen articulated policies in slogans, and the slogan for this new campaign was "people first." Party theoreticians said the slogan was meant to demonstrate that the primary goal of all government policy was to promote the well-being of the people rather than specific groups, such as the party leadership.

Hu's main opportunity to put his stamp on future policy came at the annual meeting, called a plenum, of the top Communist Party leadership. The four-day meeting ended October 14 after party leaders endorsed three important changes that had been under discussion for years: a legal guarantee for private property rights; the legalization of private financing for some public facilities, such as hospitals and schools, that traditionally had been built and controlled exclusively by the state; and a decision to sell majority stakes in hundreds, and possibly thousands, of state-owned companies to private investors, both domestic and foreign. Taken together, these changes amounted to the most significant legal ratification of China's turn toward capitalism since 1979, when foreign companies were first allowed to do business in China.

Following its endorsement by party leaders, the proposed legalization of private property rights was approved by the National People's Congress in December and was expected to be included in a series of constitutional amendments planned for adoption in 2004. Communist theory, and Chinese law, stated that all property was owned by the state. As a practical matter, this had long ceased to be the case in China: millions of people had been able to own homes, and domestic and foreign businesses had built their own factories and stores. A legal guarantee of private property rights would help assure foreign investors and the Chinese themselves that their stakes in China would be protected.

The two other changes endorsed by party leaders had the potential to speed up the privatization of the Chinese economy. Governments in China, from the national level on down to cities and towns, owned tens of thousands of businesses: banks, factories, stores, public utilities, and other enterprises. Many of these businesses long had been unprofitable because government officials viewed them primarily as places of employment for ordinary Chinese and as sources of power for themselves. As part of a privatization process that began in the 1990s, local and provincial governments had sold minority stakes in hundreds of their businesses, but private owners in theory had been prohibited from owning controlling shares. The changes adopted by party leaders in October but not announced until November would allow private investors, including foreign companies, to take majority control of all but a few Chinese enterprises. Officials said the exceptions to the new policy would include industries critical to the economy and national security, such as factories that produced weapons for the military.

Chinese leaders in 2003 also began developing plans to reform the country's faltering banking system. The first step in that process was a still-developing plan to recapitalize, over several years, four large state-owned banks that were on the brink of insolvency because they held tens of billions of dollars in bad loans. Other major changes planned for subsequent years included reforms in taxes and investment laws. Once in place, these reforms were expected to draw even more capital to China, which in 2003 was the world's leading recipient of foreign direct investment. China's gross domestic product for two decades had been growing at an average annual rate of about 9 percent, by far the fastest of any sizable world economy.

Also under way in 2003 were plans for the gradual transfer of several hundred million Chinese peasants from rural areas, where jobs were scarce and agricultural production was inefficient by modern standards, to cities, where new factories were being built every day. Current plans called for nearly one-half the rural population—or at least 300 million people—to move into cities by 2020. Government officials portrayed this social transfer as a voluntary one; for example, Prime Minister Wen, in a speech at Harvard University on December 10, said that "hundreds of millions of farmers are now able to leave their old villages and move into towns and cities, especially in the coastal areas." Even so, there was no doubt that population transfers had become government policy and that China was in the process of being transformed from a largely rural to a predominantly urban society.

Much more attention in China was focused during the year on the temporary relocation of just one man: Army Lt. Col. Yang Lwei, who on October 15 became the first Chinese astronaut in space. Yang spent twenty-one hours circling the Earth in the *Shenzhou 5* ("Divine Vessel") space capsule before landing in Inner Mongolia. Yang instantly became a Chinese hero, and the government began talking about establishing a permanent space station and sending unmanned probes to the Moon.

China and Asia

Hu's new government made tentative but significant moves during 2003 to assert China's role as a major power in Asia. Despite its enormous size and potential influence, China in modern times had only modest political impact in its own region, having been overshadowed by Japan, the United States, and for many years by the Soviet Union. Beijing was a patron of the communist regime in North Korea and supported communist insurgencies in Southeast Asia between the 1950s and 1970s, but most of China's attention long had been directed internally. Only rarely did China use its main point of leverage over international diplomacy: its role since 1971 as one of five veto-wielding powers on the United Nations Security Council.

The crisis in 2003 over North Korea's declared determination to build nuclear weapons gave China an opportunity to play an important role in a matter of intense interest to the United States. China joined a U.S.-led suspension of oil exports to North Korea, sent diplomats to Pyongyang, and even bolstered its military positions along its border with North Korea— signs that it had grown weary of North Korea's habitually provocative actions. China also took the bold diplomatic step of arranging six-party diplomatic discussions in April about North Korea's weapons. The six parties were China, Japan, North Korea, South Korea, Russia, and the United States. Neither those talks, nor follow-up negotiations in August, produced any firm agreements on what to do about North Korea's weapons. Even so, China's indispensable role in arranging them, and acting as a mediator between North Korea and the United States, was widely seen as an indication that Beijing finally was determined to exercise greater influence in its own back yard. *(North Korea, p. 592)*

Hu made important appearances on the world stage, including his attendance in France at a June meeting of leaders of the Group of Eight industrialized nations. Hu thus became the first Chinese leader to meet with the G-8 leaders. Jiang had derided the group as a "rich man's club" and spurned at least one invitation. Hu addressed the Australian parliament on October 24 and attracted significantly more attention and favorable comment than had President Bush, who preceded him on that platform by one day.

Bush's Changed View of China

At the outset of Bush's presidency, it appeared that relations between the United States and China were in for a period of renewed tension, if not outright hostility. Bush had been in office less than three months when an angry dispute over China's forcing-down of a U.S. spy plane drove relations to the lowest point in more than a decade. Then came the September 11, 2001, terrorist attacks against the United States, which changed Bush's world view and put terrorism at the top of all his foreign policy concerns. China offered immediate support for the president's new worldwide war against terrorism, saying that it, too, had been victimized by terrorism. This was a reference to an insurgency by an Islamic minority, the Uighurs in western Xingjian province, who were seeking independence from China. *(Spy plane incident, Historic Documents of 2001, p. 247)*

China in 2002 voted for the U.S.-sponsored United Nations Security Council resolution (1441) that pressured Iraq to give up its weapons of mass destruction, and it remained conspicuously in the background (thus causing no serious trouble for Washington) during the subsequent debate over Bush's planned war against Iraq. China's intervention in the North Korea dispute in 2003 was another help to the United States. *(Iraq prewar debate, pp. 40, 135)*

Despite these convergences of diplomatic interests, the two countries still had different viewpoints on important economic matters, notably the growing concern in the United States that at least some of China's economic prosperity was coming at U.S. expense. American labor unions, and workers in general, were becoming increasingly concerned about the loss of U.S. manufacturing and service jobs, tens of thousands of which had been shifted to low-wage countries, including China. China was a major exporter to the United States, running up a trade surplus of about $125 billion in 2003. In a symbolic protest against what he called unfair trading practices, Bush in November imposed $500 million worth of protective tariffs against Chinese textiles, including bras, dressing gowns, and knitted fabrics. The Bush administration was preparing broader complaints—expected to be lodged in 2004—about China's domestic subsidies and other activities that U.S. officials said violated Beijing's commitments as a new member of the

World Trade Organization. The president's Treasury secretary, John Snow, also went to Beijing early in September to protest China's policy of deliberately holding down the value of its currency, the Yuan, to encourage exports. *(China WTO membership, Historic Documents of 2000, p. 213)*

Harsh Words Across the Taiwan Strait

Just as China's attitude toward its international responsibilities appeared to have changed in the early years of the twenty-first century, so, too, had Bush's views of China—and of the issue that had been at the heart of U.S.-Chinese tension for two generations. This was the matter of Taiwan, the island about one hundred miles from southeastern China that still claimed to be the Republic of China, the name of the government that had ruled China until the communists took power on the mainland in 1949. Ever since 1949 China's communist rulers had claimed Taiwan to be part of China and frequently had threatened to invade the island but had been thwarted, at least in part by a vague U.S. promise to protect Taiwan. Congress put that promise into U.S. law in 1979 when it approved a move by President Jimmy Carter (1977–1981) withdrawing U.S. diplomatic recognition from Taiwan in the course of establishing relations with mainland China. Since then only a handful of countries officially recognized the Taiwan government. *(Historic Documents of 1979, p. 135)*

In 2000 Taiwan's voters elected a new president, Chen Shui-bian, who had advocated formal independence for the island, a stance that Beijing declared was unacceptable. Once in office Chen made several provocative statements about independence but took no formal action until August 2002, when he proposed a referendum on the independence question; even then, Chen said he would not actually call a referendum unless China made an attempt to take over Taiwan. *(Taiwan election, Historic Documents of 2000, p. 190)*

Chen took additional steps in 2003 that China considered provocative, including adding the word *Taiwan* to the Republic of China passports that were issued to the island's citizens. Chinese officials complained that Chen was fanning the flames of independence to bolster his own political fortunes in advance of elections in 2004. After much political maneuvering, Taiwan's legislature on November 27 passed a bill allowing referendums, including one on the question of independence; however, the bill contained several provisions that posed obstacles to actual independence. Beijing's first response to the legislation was a relatively mild rebuke, but on December 3 Chinese news organizations carried harsh warnings by senior military officers that Taiwan was risking war. Chen responded with a threat to call a referendum asking voters to demand that China stop threatening Taiwan with an estimated 400 missiles that were aimed across the Taiwan Strait. He said such a referendum would be held on March 20, 2004—the same day as presidential elections, when he would be seeking office again.

With the temperature rising in this dispute, China's prime minister, Wen, arrived at the White House on December 9 as part of a long-scheduled visit to the United States. Bush had previously expressed opposition to Chen's proposed referendum, but he used a joint "photo opportunity" with Wen to reinforce the message in a way that put a wide grin on the prime minister's face. "We oppose any unilateral decision, by either China or Taiwan, to change the status quo," Bush said. "The comments and actions made by the leader of Taiwan indicate that he may be willing to make decisions unilaterally that change the status quo, which we oppose." Wen immediately thanked Bush for his position "towards the latest news and developments in Taiwan—that is, the attempt to resort to referendum of various kinds as an excuse to pursue Taiwan independence." Wen repeated China's long-standing policy of favoring "peaceful reunification and one country, two systems"—a reference to the different political systems in China and Taiwan.

Bush's aides insisted his statement was intended as a warning to both China and Taiwan, but the tone of the remarks and the circumstances under which they were made left no doubt in anyone's mind that Chen was the intended recipient of the rebuke. The stern nature of the president's warning was all the more remarkable because it came from a representative of the conservative wing of the Republican Party—for decades the center of American political support for Taiwan. Even so, Bush's warning did not appear to have the desired effect. Chen on December 31 signed into law the bill authorizing referendums, calling it a "truly historical moment," and he seemed determined to hold the missile referendum on the same day as the presidential election in March 2004.

Growing Dissent in Hong Kong

China's problems with Taiwan—which it did not control but wanted to—were reflected in its difficulties with Hong Kong, which it had controlled since 1997. When it assumed sovereignty over the prosperous city-state from Britain, China promised not to interfere with Hong Kong's vibrant capitalism and to accord its citizens an undefined degree of democracy. Accepting capitalism posed no problem, but dealing with the aspirations of many of Hong Kong's citizens for democracy gave the leaders in Beijing constant headaches. Since 1997 Hong Kong had been governed by an executive, Tung Chee-hwa, who had been appointed by a committee of local leaders subservient to Beijing, and a legislative council that Tung controlled. *(Hong Kong handover, Historic Documents of 1997, p. 501)*

The controversy in 2003 began with Tung's plan to enact sweeping security legislation that, among other things, gave the government strong powers to curb "subversion" and allowed the banning of groups that were disapproved by Beijing, notably the Falun Gong, a religious organization. On July 1, the sixth anniversary of Hong Kong's coming under Chinese rule, thousands of people marched in downtown Hong Kong to protest the legislation. Police estimated that about 350,000 people participated in the seven-hour protest, while organizers claimed a participation of 500,000. The protest was by far the largest pro-democracy demonstration anywhere in China since the 1989 Tiananmen Square rallies.

Tung deleted the most controversial provisions from the pending security bill on July 5, but that concession failed to satisfy critics, who forced him to postpone action on it indefinitely and then staged more demonstrations, on July 9 and 13, calling for all of Hong Kong's leaders to be subjected to democratic elections. The sudden blossoming of a pro-democracy movement in Hong Kong posed a dilemma for the Beijing government, which in 1997 had promised substantial autonomy for Hong Kong but had no desire to encourage real democracy anywhere in the country.

Two senior Hong Kong government officials, including the unpopular security chief, resigned following the July 13 protest, and on September 5 Tung postponed further action on the proposed security bill. Pro-democracy parties demonstrated their continuing clout on November 23, scoring a major victory in elections for eighteen local advisory councils. These elections were widely seen as a run-up to elections planned for 2008 for the legislative council, the equivalent of a city council for Hong Kong. However, some observers said the opposition's strong showing raised the possibility that Beijing might delay or somehow undermine any future elections.

Following are excerpts from "Turning Your Eyes to China," a speech delivered December 10, 2003, at Harvard University by Wen Jiabao, the prime minister of China.

"Turning Your Eyes to China"

It is my great pleasure today to stand on your rostrum and have this face-to-face exchange with you. I am an ordinary Chinese, the son of a school teacher. I experienced hardships in my childhood and for long years worked in areas under harsh conditions in China. I have been to 1,800 Chinese counties out of a total of 2,500. I deeply love my country and my people.

The title of my speech today is "Turning Your Eyes to China".

China and the United States are far apart, and they differ greatly in the level of economic development and cultural background. I hope my speech will help increase our mutual understanding.

In order to understand the true China- a changing society full of promises—it is necessary to get to know her yesterday, her today, and her tomorrow.

China yesterday was a big ancient country that created a splendid civilization.

As we all know, in the history of mankind, there appeared the Mesopotamian civilization in West Asia, the ancient Egyptian civilization along the Nile in North Africa, the ancient Greek-Roman civilization along the northern bank of the Mediterranean, the ancient Indian civilization in the Indus River Valley in South Asia, and the Chinese civilization originating in the Yellow and Yangtze river valleys. Owing to earthquake, flood, plague or famine, or to alien invasion or internal turmoil, some of these ancient civilizations withered away, some were destroyed and others became assimilated into other civilizations. Only the Chinese civilization, thanks to its strong cohesive power and inexhaustible appeal, has survived many vicissitudes intact. The 5,000-year-long civilization is the source of pride of every Chinese. . . .

China today is a country in reform and opening-up and a rising power dedicated to peace.

The late Dr. John King Fairbank used the following words to describe China's over population and land scarcity. On the land owned by one farmer in the U.S., there might live hundreds of people forming a village in China. He went on to say that although the Americans were mostly farmers in the past, they never felt such pressure of population density.

A large population and underdevelopment are the two facts China has to face. Since China has 1.3 billion people, any small individual shortage, multiplied by 1.3 billion, becomes a big, big problem. And any considerable amount of financial and material resources, divided by 1.3 billion, becomes a very low per capita level. This is a reality the Chinese leaders have to keep firmly in mind at all times.

We can rely on no one except ourselves to resolve the problems facing our 1.3 billion people. Since the founding of the People's Republic, we have achieved much in our national reconstruction; at the same time we have made a few detours and missed some opportunities. By 1978, with the adoption of the reform and opening-up policies, we had ultimately found the right path of development—the Chinese people's path of independently building socialism with Chinese characteristics.

The essence of this path is to mobilize all positive factors, emancipate and develop the productive forces, and respect and protect the freedom of the Chinese people to pursue happiness.

China's reform and opening-up have spread from rural areas to the cities, from the economic field to the political, cultural and social arenas. Each and every step forward is designed, in the final analysis, to release the gushing vitality of labor, knowledge, technology, managerial expertise and capital, and allow all sources of social wealth to flow to the fullest extent.

For quite some time in the past, China had a structure of highly-centralized planned economy. With deepening restructuring toward the socialist market economy and progress in the development of democratic politics, there was gradual lifting of the former improper restrictions, visible and invisible, on people's freedom in choice of occupation, mobility, enterprise, investment, information, travel, faith and lifestyles. This has brought extensive and profound changes never seen before in China's history. On the one hand, the enthusiasm of the work force in both city and countryside has been set free. In particular, hundreds of millions of farmers are now able to leave their old villages and move into towns and cities, especially in the coastal areas, and tens of millions of intellectuals are now able to bring their talent and creativity into full play. On the other hand, the massive assets owned by the state can now be revitalized, the private capital pool in the amount of trillions of Yuancan take shape, and more than 500 billion US dollars worth of overseas capital can flow in. This combination of capital and labor results in a drama of industrialization and urbanization of a size unprecedented in human history being staged on the 9.6 million square kilometers of land called China. Here lies the secret of the 9.4% annual growth rate that China's economy has been able to attain in the past 25 years.

The tremendous wealth created by China in the past quarter of a century has not only enabled our 1.3 billion countrymen to meet their basic needs for food, clothing and shelter, and basically realize a well-off standard of living, but also contributed to world development. China owes all this progress to the policy of reform and opening-up and, in the final analysis, to the freedom-inspired creativity of the Chinese people.

It has become so clear to me that at the current stage China has an abundant supply of labor in proportion to her limited natural resources and short capital. If no effective measures are taken to protect the fundamental rights of our massive labor force, and in particular the farmer-workers coming to the cities, they may end up in a miserable plight as described in the novels by Charles Dickens and Theodore Dreiser. Without effective protection of the citizens' right to property, it will be difficult to attract and accumulate valuable capital.

Therefore, the Chinese Government is committed to protecting (1) the fundamental rights of all workers and (2) the right to property, both public and private. This has been explicitly provided for in China's law and put into practice.

China's reform and opening-up aims at promoting human rights in China. The two are mutually dependent and reinforcing. Reform and opening-up creates conditions for the advancement of human rights, and the latter invigorates the former. If one separates the two and thinks that China only goes after economic growth and ignores the protection of human rights, such a view does not square with the facts. Just as your former President Franklin Roosevelt said, "True individual freedom cannot exist without economic security and independence," and "Necessitous men are not free men."

I am not suggesting that China's human rights situation is impeccable. The Chinese Government has all along been making earnest efforts to correct the malpractices and negative factors of one kind or another in the human rights field. It is extremely important and difficult in China to combine development, reform and stability. Seeing is believing. If our friends come to China and see for themselves, they will be able to judge objectively and appreciate the progress made there in human rights and the Chinese Government's hard work in upholding human rights since the beginning of reform and opening-up.

China is a large developing country. It is neither proper nor possible for us to rely on foreign countries for development. We must, and we can only, rely on our own efforts. In other words, while opening still wider to the outside world, we must more fully and more consciously depend on our own structural innovation, on constantly expanding the domestic market, on converting the huge savings of the citizens into investment, and on improving the quality of the population and scientific and technological progress to solve the problems of resources and the environment. Here lies the essence of China's road of peaceful rise and development.

Of course, China is still a developing country. There is an obvious gap between its urban and rural areas and between its eastern and western regions. If you travel to the coastal cities in China's southeast, you will see modern sights of skyscrapers, busy traffic and brightly-lit streets. But in rural China, especially in the central and western rural parts, there are still many backward places. In the poor and remote mountain villages, folks still use manual labor and animals to till the land. They live in houses made of sun-dried mud bricks. In times of severe drought, there will be scarcity of drinking water for people and animals. A Chinese poet-magistrate of the 18th century wrote:

"The rustling of bamboo outside my door.
Sounds like the moaning of the needy poor."

As China's Premier, I am often torn with anxiety and unable to eat or sleep with ease when I think of the fact that there are still 30 million farmers lacking food and clothing, 23 million city-dwellers living on subsistence allowances and 60 million disabled and handicapped people in need of social security aid. For China to reach the level of the developed countries, it will still take the sustained hard work of several generations, a dozen generations or even dozens of generations.

China tomorrow will continue to be a major country that loves peace and has a great deal to look forward to.

Peace-loving has been a time-honored quality of the Chinese nation. The First Emperor of Qin Dynasty commanded the building of the Great Wall two thousand years ago for defensive purposes. The Tang Dynasty opened up the Silk Road one thousand years ago in order to sell silk, tea and porcelain to other parts of the world. Five hundred years ago Zheng He, the famous diplomat-navigator of the Ming Dynasty, led seven maritime expeditions to seek friendly ties with other countries, taking along China's exquisite products, advanced farming and handicraft skills. The great Russian writer Leo Tolstoy was right when he called the Chinese nation "the oldest and largest nation" and "the most peace-loving nation in the world".

As the modern times began, the ignorance, corruption and self-imposed seclusion of the feudal dynasties led Chinato prolonged social stagnation, declining national strength and repeated invasions by the foreign powers. Despite compounded disasters and humiliation, the Chinese nation never gave up and managed to emerge from each setback stronger than before. A nation learns a lot more in times of disaster and setback than in normal times.

Now, China has laid down her three-step strategy toward modernization. From now to 2020, China will complete the building of a well-off society in an all-round way. By 2049, the year the People's Republic will celebrate its centenary, we will have reached the level of a medium-developed country. We have no illusions but believe that on our way forward, we shall encounter many foreseeable and unpredictable difficulties and face all kinds of tough challenges. We cannot afford to lose such a sense of crisis. Of course, the Chinese Government and people are confident enough to overcome all the difficulties and achieve our ambitious goals through our vigorous efforts. This is because:

- The overriding trend of the present-day world is towards peace and development. China's development is blessed with a rare period of strategic opportunities. We are determined to secure a peaceful international environment and a stable domestic environment in which to concentrate on our own development and, with it, to help promote world peace and development.
- The socialism China adheres to is brimming with vigor and vitality. Socialism is like an ocean that takes in all the rivers and will never go dry. While planting our feet solidly on our national conditions, we will boldly press ahead with reform and opening-up and boldly

absorb all fine achievements of human civilizations. There is no limit to the life and exuberance of a socialism that is good at self-readjustment and self-improvement.

- Twenty-five years of reform and opening-up has given China a considerable material accumulation, and her economy has gained a foothold in the world. The motivation of China's millions to pursue happiness and create wealth is an inexhaustible reservoir of drive for the country's modernization.

- The Chinese nation has rich and profound cultural reserves. "Harmony without uniformity" is a great idea put forth by ancient Chinese thinkers. It means harmony without sameness, and difference without conflict. Harmony entails co-existence and co-prosperity, while difference conduces to mutual complementation and mutual support. To approach and address issues from such a perspective will not only help enhance relations with friendly countries, but also serve to resolve contradictions in the international community.

Ladies and Gentlemen,

A deeper mutual understanding is a two-way process. I hope American young people will turn their eyes to China. I also trust our young people will turn their eyes more to the U.S.

The United States is a great country. Since the days of the early settlers, the Americans, with their toughness, frontier spirit, pragmatism, innovation, their respect for knowledge, admission of talents, their scientific tradition and rule of law, have forged the prosperity of their country. The composure, courage and readiness to help one another shown by the American people in face of the 9.11 terrorist attacks are truly admirable.

Entering the 21st century, mankind is confronted with more complicated economic and social problems. The cultural element will have a more important role to play in the new century. Different nations may speak different languages, but their hearts and feelings are interlinked. Different cultures present manifold features, yet they often share the same rational core elements that can always be passed on by people. The civilizations of different nations are all fruits of human wisdom and contribution to human progress; they call for mutual respect. Conflicts triggered by ignorance or prejudice are sometimes more dreadful than those caused by contradictory interests. We propose to seek common ground in the spirit of equality and tolerance, and carry on extensive inter-civilization dialogue and closer cultural exchanges.

In his poem, Malvern Hill, the famous American poet Herman Melville wrote:

"Wag the world how it will,
Leaves must be green in Spring."

The youth represents the future of the nation and the world. Faced with the bright prospect of China-US relations in the new century, I hope the young people of China and the US will join their hands more closely.

Ladies and Gentlemen,

Chinese forefathers formulated their goals as follows:

To ordain conscience for Heaven and Earth,
To secure life and fortune for the people,
To continue lost teachings for past sages,
To establish peace for all future generations.

Today, mankind is in the middle of a period of drastic social change. It would be a wise approach for all countries to carry forward their fine cultural heritages by tracing back their origin, passing on the essentials, learning from one another and breaking new grounds. My appeal is that we work together with our wisdom and strength for the progress and development of human civilization. Our success will do credit to our forbears and bring benefit to our posterity. In this way, our children and their children will be able to live in a more peaceful, more tranquil and more prosperous world. I am convinced that such an immensely bright and beautiful tomorrow will arrive!

Thank you.

Source: People's Republic of China. Permanent Mission of the People's Republic of China to the United Nations. "Turning Your Eyes to China." Speech by Premier Wen Jiabao at Harvard University. December 10, 2003. www.china-un.org/eng/zt/wfm/t56090.htm (accessed January 15, 2004).

United States on the Capture of Saddam Hussein

December 14, 2003

INTRODUCTION

Two hands stretching up from a hole in the ground north of Baghdad on December 13 gave the first indication that Saddam Hussein had been captured by the U.S. Army. The long-time Iraqi dictator, who had been pushed from power eight months earlier by a U.S.-led invasion, was found hiding underground, far removed from the palaces he had built in his own honor and without the protection of the feared military regime he had headed for a quarter-century.

"Ladies and gentlemen, we got him!" Those were all the words that L. Paul Bremer, the head of the U.S.-led Coalition Provisional Authority, needed the next day to announce Saddam's capture. Iraqis cheered—most of them—and the 150,000-some soldiers in Iraq from the United States, Britain, and other countries had reason to celebrate as well, in the hope that Saddam's capture might somehow reduce the violence that had seized Iraq in the months since he fell from power. The capture of Saddam closed a troubled chapter in the history of Iraq and the Middle East and marked the beginning of a new era, one that as of the end of 2003 was full of new uncertainties and real dangers. President George W. Bush had announced his determination to give Iraqis back their sovereignty by the middle of 2004, but the shape of a new government, much less the identities of those who would lead it, still had not been made clear.

By the time of his capture, Saddam had become almost incidental to the situation in Iraq. U.S. military officials said there was no evidence that Saddam had been coordinating, or even directly involved in, an unending cycle of bombings, shootings, and other violent attacks that targeted the U.S. occupation, international agencies, and Iraqis themselves. Saddam's power centers—the Iraqi military and the Ba'ath socialist party—had been dismantled, and most of their key leaders had been captured since the war. Most important, by mid-December Saddam appeared to have little remaining support of any kind in Iraq. Even if the U.S. military had pulled up stakes and left Iraq before he was captured, Saddam would have been hard-pressed to return to power, if only because the Shi'ites, Kurds, and others who had been repressed by his rule were determined to pursue their own visions of a post-Saddam Iraq. *(Iraq war, p. 135; postwar Iraq, pp. 874, 933)*

Saddam's Rule

Saddam Hussein had been a dominant presence in Iraq and the Middle East since 1968, when he was a leading figure in a coup that brought the Ba'ath Party to power. For the next eleven years he served as second-in-command to a cousin, Ahmed Hassan al-Bakr. During the oil boom of the 1970s Iraq prospered and built modern cities and highways. Saddam shoved al-Bakr aside in 1979 and took over as president, quickly establishing himself as the country's undisputed ruler.

Having consolidated his power in Iraq, Saddam launched what proved to be a bloody and fruitless quest for power throughout the Middle East. Saddam encouraged portrayals of himself as one of the great figures in Middle East history, indeed as a modern-day Saladin, the twelfth-century Muslim leader, born in what later became Iraq, who drove the European Crusaders from Jerusalem.

In 1980 Saddam sent the Iraqi army into Iran to assert control of the Shatt al-Arab waterway at the head of the Persian Gulf. The resulting war between the two countries dragged on until 1988. The war settled nothing but ruined both countries' economies and killed hundreds of thousands of soldiers and civilians. From a historical perspective, one irony of the war was that Saddam received support from Western powers, including the United States, because his ultimate objective was to topple the new Islamist regime of Iran, headed by Ayatollah Ruhollah Khomeini, which at that point was feared by the West even more than was Iraq. *(Iran-Iraq war, Historic Documents of 1988, p. 529)*

Having failed in one costly venture, Saddam in 1990 tried another, sending his army into Kuwait and declaring the tiny but oil-rich neighbor to be Iraq's nineteenth province. That step proved to be an even more costly mistake for Saddam. The United States in 1991 led a multinational coalition that quickly forced Iraq out of Kuwait and destroyed much of Iraq's military and industrial infrastructure. The United Nations Security Council imposed tough economic sanctions against Iraq and ordered it to give up its programs to develop biological, chemical, and nuclear weapons. Saddam refused to comply with the UN demands and with multiple repetitions of them throughout the 1990s. The sanctions stayed in place, Iraq's economy deteriorated even further, and President Bill Clinton (1993–2001) ordered Baghdad bombed again in 1998. *(Iraq and the UN, Historic Documents of 1991, p. 191; Historic Documents of 1998, p. 935)*

In 2002 Bush took the step that ultimately would lead to Saddam's ouster—pressing the UN Security Council to demand that Saddam finally comply with all the previous resolutions demanding that he disarm. In March 2003 Bush declared that Saddam had once again refused to comply, and on March 19 the United States, Britain, and a handful of allies launched a giant invasion that in just three weeks toppled Saddam from power. *(Background, Historic Documents of 2002, pp. 612, 713)*

The Search for Saddam

Saddam—or at least a televised videotape of him—was last seen publicly on April 10, the day after U.S. Marines had helped Iraqis pull down a giant statue of him in central Baghdad, symbolically ending his regime. The tape showed Saddam standing on the roof of a car in a Baghdad neighborhood, waving to his supporters. Saddam then disappeared from view, along with most of his top aides and his two sons, Qusay and Uday. The U.S. military mounted a countrywide manhunt for Saddam and all other senior officials of his regime and put the names, titles, and pictures of fifty-five of the "most wanted" of them on packs of playing cards, which were handed out to U.S. troops. Saddam was shown as the ace of spades. The military had another term for him: HVT 1—"high-value target number one." To encourage Iraqis to help with the search, the United States offered a $25 million reward for information leading to Saddam's capture or death.

On July 22 Qusay and Uday were killed in a gun battle with U.S. troops in the northern Iraq city of Mosul. U.S. forces also raided a house in Mosul where Saddam was said to be in hiding, but the former dictator appeared to have left just hours earlier.

As far as the public could tell, the only evidence that Saddam was still alive consisted of a series of nine audiotapes, said to be of his voice, that were aired by Arab television stations over a period of several months. The tapes denounced the United States and urged Iraqis to resist the occupation of their country. The last of the tapes was aired on November 16.

In late November the U.S. military searchers began focusing on distant relatives of Saddam—members of his own large clan who lived in small villages near the city of Tikrit in central Iraq, north of Baghdad. These inquiries eventually led the searchers to a farm in the village of Dawr, alongside the Tigris River.

On the evening of December 13 soldiers pushed aside a rug and a pile of dirt covering a hatch over a narrow hole in the ground next to a two-room hut. Once the hatch was removed, two hands appeared, and the soldiers pulled out a grubby, disoriented man with long hair and a beard. "I am Saddam Hussein, president of Iraq," he said in English. "I am willing to negotiate."

Maj. Gen. Raymond Odierno, commander of the Army's Fourth Infantry Division and head of the massive manhunt, later said the man claiming to be Saddam offered no resistance when he was caught, and it would have been futile in any event. "He was in the bottom of a hole, so there was no way he could fight back," Odierno said. "So he was just caught like a rat." Aside from a few clothes and food items found in the adjacent hut, the man's only significant possession at the time of his capture was a bag containing $750,000 in cash, U.S. officials later said.

The soldiers gave the man the same treatment as all other military prisoners, binding his hands with plastic ties, covering his head with a loose hood, and then taking him away for an inspection and interrogation. The man was taken to an undisclosed location in Baghdad where he was examined by a military doctor. DNA tests appeared to confirm that he was, in fact, Saddam Hussein.

Early the next day, December 14, four of the Iraqis who had been appointed by the United States to the country's temporary leadership, the Governing Council, were taken to visit Saddam to help confirm his identify. All had been driven into exile by Saddam's regime and then returned during or after the 2003 war. The four men later told reporters that the former Iraqi leader at first seemed tired but then responded defiantly to their questions about why he had unleashed waves of repression on his own people. "He was arrogant and hateful," recalled Adel Abdel-Mehdi, a leader of a Shi'ite Party, the Supreme Council for the Islamic Revolution in Iraq.

After President Bush was notified that Saddam indeed was in custody, the U.S.-led Coalition Provisional Authority in Baghdad called a news conference, where Bremer announced the news. Iraqi journalists and politicians in the room broke into cheers. "This is a great day in your history," Bremer said, addressing himself to the Iraqi people. "For decades hundreds of thousands of you suffered at the hands of this cruel man. For decades Saddam Hussein divided you citizens against each other. For decades he threatened and attacked your neighbors. Those days are over forever."

Bush then made a televised speech from the White House, saying that "a dark and painful era is over" for Iraq. "A hopeful day has arrived," he said. "All Iraqis can now come together and reject violence and build a new Iraq."

To convince the world, most importantly Iraqis, that Saddam indeed had been caught, the U.S. military released a videotape showing a medical technician examining his mouth with a flashlight and tongue depressor and checking his hair, apparently for lice. The footage also captured a bushy-haired Saddam scratching his head, tugging on his beard, and looking somewhat bewildered. These were the last images the public saw of Saddam in 2003. He remained in U.S. custody at an undisclosed location in Iraq.

Reaction to the Capture

The capture of Saddam was greeted with widespread jubilation in Iraq. Except in Tikrit and other areas that had been strongholds of Saddam's Ba'ath Party, Iraqis by the thousands swept out of their homes when the news was announced, many dancing in the streets and firing rifles into the air. The celebration was greatest among Shi'ites and Kurds, the two groups that had borne the brunt of Saddam's internal repression. "I am very happy, because Saddam was a bad leader," a young man in a Shi'ite neighborhood of Baghdad said. Some Iraqis, notably his remaining supporters among fellow Sunni Muslims, at first refused to believe Saddam actually had been captured, but the televised images of his medical examination appeared to convince all but the most skeptical.

Amid the cheering, there also were signs that many Iraqis were expecting much more from their new, if temporary, American rulers than the ousting of Saddam and his eventual capture. "We need salaries, tell the Americans that," Amar Jabbar, a young man in Baghdad told a *New York Times* reporter. "If there are no jobs soon, we will hate them just as much as we love them today."

News of Saddam's capture produced a wide spectrum of reactions elsewhere in the Arab world. While in power Saddam had inspired a full-scale of reactions among Arabs. Many, most notably Palestinians, had long seen him as an Arab hero who stood up to the West and to Israel; others had considered him to be a power-hungry villain who posed a danger to fellow Arabs as well as the wider Islamic world. Some Arabs said they felt humiliated by the pictures of Saddam being examined, "like a gorilla that has come out of the forest," Moroccan journalist Khalid Jamai said. Others expressed outrage, or confusion, that Saddam had given up without a fight. "I was expecting a more honorable end for him, like shooting himself," Lebanese student Salam Derri told Reuters news service.

Perhaps the most widely expressed sentiment in the region was regret that it was Americans, not Iraqis or even other Arabs, who had brought the former dictator low. "There is a surreptitious embarrassment that this fellow who was a problem for so many years was allowed to be a leader for so long, and that his downfall had to come from the outside," said Clovis Maksoud, a former Egyptian diplomat who was teaching in the United States.

On a broader plane, many Arab commentators and leaders were cautious in addressing the question of how the year's events in Iraq would affect their region. Most Arab governments were silent or offered noncommittal comments. Commentary from newspapers and officials associated with governments in several Arab countries focused not on Saddam's past but on the future of Iraq—in particular on the urgency of ending the U.S. occupancy as soon as possible. Many Arab commentators said the fate of Saddam should serve as a lesson for other autocrats in the region. "Saddam has fallen because of what his wooden mind produced, and similar, what their minds produce will lead to their fall," wrote Ahmed al-Jarrallah, editor of the Kuwaiti daily *Al-Siysassah*. Others focused on how the Arab world would respond to a United States presence in the region that seemed to grow more embedded by the day. "Like a force of nature, an emboldened America is now bearing down on the Middle East, whose habitual status is somnolence," the Lebanese English-language *Daily Star* editorialized. "If the countries of the region continue to let others decide the pace and direction of events, the storm will be a highly destructive one."

Saddam's capture also produced some unexpected reactions from world leaders, including two European leaders who had staunchly opposed Bush's war in Iraq—French president Jacques Chirac and German chancellor Gerhard Schroeder. In a statement, Chirac called the capture "a major event which should strongly contribute to the democratization and stabilization of Iraq." Schroeder sent Bush a telegram expressing "great delight" at the news. "I congratulate you on this successful operation," he said. "Saddam Hussein caused horrible suffering to his people and the region."

Saddam's Role in the Insurgency

The most pressing question in Iraq was whether the capture of Saddam would have any impact on the level of violence that had wracked the country ever since the war had ended in May. The general consensus among U.S. civilian and military officials was that violence would continue, and might even escalate temporarily as angry Saddam loyalists attempted to exact revenge against the occupation. "I don't think we will see an immediate end to the violence here," the U.S. commander in Iraq, Lt. Gen. Ricardo Sanchez told the CNN network December 15.

In the early weeks after the war, U.S. officials had assumed that Saddam and his sons were playing some role in the resistance, perhaps by coordinating attacks that appeared to be mounted by former military personnel or Ba'ath Party loyalists. As the year wore on, however, U.S. officials became convinced that the attacks were carried out by small groups without any kind of an overall plan. General Odierno, whose Fourth Infantry Division had responsibility for central Iraq, was among those who said Saddam had been a symbol for the resistance but not a leader of it. "I believe he was there more for moral support," Odierno told reporters on December 14. "I don't believe he was coordinating the effort because I don't believe there's any national coordination."

Saddam himself told his interrogators that he had played no direct role in the attacks during the year, U.S. officials said December 15. Even so, the officials expressed skepticism about the truth of Saddam's answers to all questions during the early stages of his interrogation.

Putting Saddam on Trial

Once Saddam's capture was announced, there was little question that eventually he would be put on trial. There were many questions, however, about who would judge him, what the charges against him would be, and what kind of a penalty he might face. Legal experts, human rights advocates, and others suggested it might be years before Saddam finally was held to account. As a precedent, former Yugoslav president Slobodan Milosevic at the end of 2003 was still on trial on genocide and war crimes charges, two years after he had been handed over to a United Nations tribunal. Many Iraqis, however, demanded swift justice and called for a trial starting in 2004. *(Milosevic case, Historic Documents of 2001, p. 826)*

On December 16 UN Secretary General Kofi Annan endorsed legal action against Saddam but without specifying details. "Mr. Hussein should be held to account for past deeds, through a procedure that meets the highest international standards of due process," Annan told the Security Council. "Accounting for the past will be an important part of bringing about national reconciliation—a process that is vital to Iraq and to all Iraqis."

Saddam's government had been accused of some of the most horrific and widespread crimes of any regime in recent decades. In the weeks after his fall, Kurds, Shi'ites, and other victims of his repression worked frantically to uncover mass graves that were said to hold the bodies of many of the 200,000 to 300,000 people who had "disappeared" in Iraq since he came to power. This digging into the past yielded many bodies that enabled people to confirm the executions of family members, but it also destroyed evidence that would be crucial in any trial that sought to hold Saddam responsible for mass killings.

Much of the repression by Saddam's government had escaped wide notice at the time it was under way. By 2003 opposition groups, journalists, and international human rights organizations had documented systematic attacks by Baghdad since the late 1970s. Among the best-documented cases were:

- Repression of Iraq's Kurds, most of whom lived in the northern part of the country. Between 1977 and 1987, according to Human Rights Watch, more than 4,500 Kurdish villages were destroyed and their inhabitants forced into camps. Between February and September 1988 the Iraqi military conducted what was called the "Anfal" campaign, moving thousands of Kurdish civilians out of areas the government had declared off-limits. An investigation conducted by Human Rights Watch in 1995 produced evidence that more than 100,000 Kurds, most of them men and boys, were trucked to remote sites and executed. According to investigations by the U.S. government and others, the

Iraqi army used chemical weapons against the Kurds in both 1987 and 1988; the single most serious incident was in March 1988, when at least 3,000 Kurds in the town of Halabja, near the border with Iran, died as a result of poison gas.

• Repression of Shi'ite Muslims, most of whom lived in southern Iraq, during and after the 1980–1988 Iran-Iraq War, and again following the 1991 Persian Gulf War. In the early 1980s, according to numerous reports, Iraq forced an estimated 500,000 or more Shi'ites across the border into Iran but also imprisoned at least 50,000 Shi'ite men and boys, most of whom were never seen again. After the 1991 war, then-U.S. President George H. W. Bush (1989–1993) encouraged Iraqis to rebel against Saddam. When Shi'ites did so, the Iraqi military responded with a terror campaign that included destruction of Shi'ite shrines and the arrest, and likely execution, of hundreds of clerics, students, and Shi'ite community leaders. The government also attacked Shi'ites known as "marsh Arabs" who lived in the once-vast marshes along the Iran-Iraq border.

U.S. officials said in late December that Saddam would be turned over to Iraqi authorities at some point so he could face whatever charges the new government chose to press against him. However, Saddam's capture provoked an international debate over how he should be judged, since many of his actions had involved countries other than Iraq, most notably Iran and Kuwait.

On December 11, three days before Saddam was captured, Iraq's Governing Council approved a law establishing an Iraqi court to judge criminal cases involving leaders of the deposed government. The law called for a five-judge panel to hear cases involving international human rights and war crimes statutes as well as Iraqi law—including a 1958 law that made it a capital offense to destabilize or threaten Iraq.

The new Iraqi law came under immediate criticism from some international human rights groups, which said it would not ensure justice in a way that would satisfy Iraqis or the rest of the world. In a statement on December 11, Human Rights Watch noted that Iraq's legal system had never handled a case of the magnitude that would be involved in the prosecution of Saddam and other officials on war crimes and similar charges. Richard Dicker, director of the International Justice Program at Human Rights Watch, noted for example that the law made no provision for non-Iraqi prosecutors with experience in similar cases to help conduct the investigations. Human Rights Watch and other organizations suggested creation of a UN tribunal, or at least a quasi-international court in which Iraq and international legal experts would work together, as was happening in Sierra Leone following that country's civil war. *(Sierra Leone, Historic Documents of 2002, p. 249)*

Following are the texts of two documents, both dated December 14, 2003: first, a statement by L. Paul Bremer, the U.S. administrator of the Coalition Provisional Authority in Iraq, announcing the capture of former Iraqi president Saddam Hussein; second, a statement by President George W. Bush, speaking from the White House, commenting on that event.

Remarks on the Capture of Saddam Hussein

Ladies and Gentlemen,

We got him!

Saddam Hussein was captured Saturday, December 13 at about 8:30 PM local in a cellar in the town of ad-Duar, which is some 15 kilometers south of Tikrit.

Before Dr. Pachachi, who is the acting president of the Governing Council, and Lt. General Sanchez speak, I want to say a few words to the people of Iraq.

This is a great day in your history.

For decades hundreds of thousands of you suffered at the hands of this cruel man. For decades, Saddam Hussein divided you citizens against each other. For decades he threatened and attacked your neighbors.

Those days are over forever.

Now it is time to look to the future, to your future of hope, to a future of reconciliation.

Iraq's future, your future, has never been more full of hope.

The tyrant is a prisoner.

The economy is moving forward.

You have before you the prospect of sovereign government in a few months.

With the arrest of Saddam Hussein, there is a new opportunity for members of the former regime, whether military or civilian, to end their bitter opposition.

Let them come forward now in a spirit of reconciliation and hope, lay down their arms and join you, their fellow citizens, in the task of building the new Iraq.

Now is the time for all Iraqis—Arabs and Kurds, Sunnis, Shias, Christians and Turkomen—to build a prosperous, democratic Iraq at peace with itself and with its neighbors.

Source: Bremer, L. Paul. Opening Remarks at News Conference on the
Capture of Saddam Hussein. Coalition Provisional Authority, Baghdad,
Iraq, December 14, 2003. www.cpa-iraq.org/transcripts/
20031214_Dec14_Saddam_Capture.htm (accessed March 14, 2004).

President Bush's Address to the Nation on the Capture of Saddam Hussein

Good afternoon. Yesterday, December the 13th, at around 8:30 p.m. Baghdad time, United States military forces captured Saddam Hussein alive. He was found near a farmhouse outside the city of Tikrit, in a swift raid conducted without casualties. And now the former dictator of Iraq will face the justice he denied to millions.

The capture of this man was crucial to the rise of a free Iraq. It marks the end of the road for him, and for all who bullied and killed in his name. For the Baathist holdouts largely responsible for the current violence, there will be no return to the corrupt power and privilege they once held. For the vast majority of Iraqi citizens who wish to live as free men and women, this event brings further assurance that the torture chambers and the secret police are gone forever.

And this afternoon, I have a message for the Iraqi people: You will not have to fear the rule of Saddam Hussein ever again. All Iraqis who take the side of freedom have taken the winning side. The goals of our coalition are the same as your goals—sovereignty for your country, dignity for your great culture, and for every Iraqi citizen, the opportunity for a better life.

In the history of Iraq, a dark and painful era is over. A hopeful day has arrived. All Iraqis can now come together and reject violence and build a new Iraq.

The success of yesterday's mission is a tribute to our men and women now serving in Iraq. The operation was based on the superb work of intelligence analysts who found the dictator's footprints in a vast country. The operation was carried out with skill and precision by a brave fighting force. Our servicemen and women and our coalition allies have faced many dangers in the hunt for members of the fallen regime, and in their effort to bring hope and freedom to the Iraqi people. Their work continues, and so do the risks. Today, on behalf of the nation, I thank the members of our Armed Forces and I congratulate them.

I also have a message for all Americans: The capture of Saddam Hussein does not mean the end of violence in Iraq. We still face terrorists who would rather go on killing the innocent than accept the rise of liberty in the heart of the Middle East. Such men are a direct threat to the American people, and they will be defeated.

We've come to this moment through patience and resolve and focused action. And that is our strategy moving forward. The war on terror is a different kind of war, waged capture by capture, cell by cell, and victory by victory. Our security is assured by our perseverance and by our sure belief in the success of liberty. And the United States of America will not relent until this war is won.

May God bless the people of Iraq, and may God bless America. Thank you.

Source: U.S. Bush, George W. Address to the Nation on the Capture of Saddam Hussein. *Weekly Compilation of Presidential Documents* 39, no. 51 (December 22, 2003): 1799–1800. Washington, D.C.: National Archives and Records Administration. www.gpoaccess.gov/ wcomp/v39no51.html (accessed January 7, 2004).

Israeli Prime Minister on "Disengagement" from the Palestinians

December 18, 2003

A flurry of plans to bring peace to the Israeli-Palestinian conflict emerged in the last half of 2003, but peace itself still seemed far away. An internationally sponsored "roadmap" to peace, which was unveiled by U.S. president George W. Bush at the end of April, stalled after just four months and appeared to offer little hope for a negotiated settlement of the conflicting territorial claims by Israel and Palestinians. Moderates on both sides crafted two alternative peace plans, each of which generated broad support—especially internationally—but neither of which had any chance of being adopted by the Israeli government of Prime Minister Ariel Sharon. Sharon himself sought to break the diplomatic impasse in December with his own plan for a unilateral separation of Israelis and Palestinians. He called it "disengagement," a concept that was growing increasingly popular within Israel. Sharon appeared likely to move ahead with at least part of his plan in 2004, starting with the evacuation of Jewish settlements in the Palestinian-dominated Gaza Strip.

For their part, Palestinians formed a new government—their second of the year. But the government, dominated by longtime Palestinian leader Yasir Arafat, was unable to resurrect a limited cease-fire that during the summer had brought a temporary lull in the violent uprising, called the Intifada, that had started in 2000. Suicide bombings and other terrorist attacks killed about two hundred Israelis during the year; in retaliation the Israeli government killed more than six hundred Palestinians. (*Roadmap and previous events of the year, p. 191*)

New Palestinian Prime Minister

Under pressure from U.S. and European diplomats, Arafat had agreed early in the year to appoint a prime minister to manage the Palestinian Authority on a daily basis and to represent the Palestinians in peace talks with

Israel. Arafat named a longtime aide, Mahmoud Abbas (better known as Abu Mazen), to the post in March but then undermined his authority by refusing to give up control of key Palestinian security services. Abbas's resignation on September 6 represented a short-term political victory for Arafat but pounded another nail in the coffin of the U.S.-sponsored peace process.

Arafat immediately chose another veteran Palestinian official, Ahmed Qureia, as the new prime minister. Qureia (also known as Abu Ala) was the speaker of the Palestinian parliament and had been a key negotiator of the 1993 Israeli-Palestinian peace agreement known as the Oslo accord. Qureia at first said he would accept the job only if Arafat gave him the powers that had been denied Abbas, but after a two-month power struggle Qureia backed down. On November 8 Qureia agreed to an arrangement under which Arafat retained control of Palestinian police and other security services; four days later the parliament approved Qureia's cabinet and Arafat swore the new government into office.

Israeli officials immediately suggested that Sharon would meet with Qureia soon, but that prospective session kept being postponed as each side focused on its domestic constituency. With the help of Egyptian officials, Qureia tried to persuade Palestinian extremist groups to accept a cease-fire in violent attacks against Israel. The truce would have replaced one that had curtailed the level of violence during much of the summer before it was shattered by a suicide bombing on August 19. Qureia's effort had failed by mid-December, however, and a new outburst of violence at the end of the year appeared to damage any prospects for a cease-fire ageement. For his part, Sharon turned his attention to unilateral actions intended to end the Israeli-Palestinian conflict by permanently separating the two sides.

The back-and-forth over the shape of the Palestinian government had been overshadowed, for a few days in mid-September, by the latest Israeli threat against Arafat. The Israeli cabinet on September 11 voted, in principle, to give Sharon power to "remove" Arafat as the Palestinian leader. The policy left unstated which of several options Sharon could use, including forcing Arafat into exile, putting him in prison, or simply killing him. Israel effectively had Arafat under house arrest; since early 2002 he had been unable to leave his compound in Ramallah, on the West Bank. Israeli officials made it clear the decision essentially was a warning to Arafat, not a threat of immediate action against him. Even so, the decision—coupled with an explicit statement by one of Sharon's senior aides that killing Arafat was indeed an option—brought harsh international criticism down on Sharon's government. On September 15 foreign minister Silvan Shalom said killing Arafat was "not an official policy of the Israeli government." The next day a majority of the United Nations Security Council voted for a resolution demanding that Israel not deport Arafat, another of Sharon's options; the United States vetoed the measure.

Israel Strikes in Syria

For at least a couple weeks in early October the risk of a wider conflict between Israel and its Arab neighbors suddenly loomed on the horizon. The risk appeared on October 5 when Israel bombed what it called a "terrorist training camp" deep inside Syria, near the capital, Damascus. Israel said the camp was run by Islamic Jihad (one of the Palestinian extremist groups) and was in retaliation for a suicide bombing the previous day that killed nineteen people at a restaurant in Haifa; Islamic Jihad had claimed responsibility for the bombing. The strike was Israel's first direct attack inside Syria since the October 1973 Arab-Israeli war.

Syria and other Arab nations denounced the attack, and Damascus hotly denied Israel's allegation that the bombed target had been used by Palestinian terrorists. The Syrian government long had allowed Palestinian extremist groups to operate openly in Damascus; earlier in 2002 it closed the offices of Hamas and Islamic Jihad in response to U.S. pressure. Israel received important support for its action from President Bush, who said on October 6 he had told Sharon that "Israel's got a right to defend herself, that Israel must not feel constrained in defending the homeland."

Israel's raid produced several days worth of hot rhetoric on both sides of the Arab-Israeli divide but not a further escalation. Syria, which was not strong enough to challenge Israel militarily, ultimately was forced to live with the humiliating reality that Israeli warplanes could strike inside its territory with impunity. Sharon's government had made the point that it could, when it chose, hold Arab governments responsible for the continuing Palestinian terrorism.

Attack on U.S. Guards

As soon as the Israel-Syria confrontation calmed down, another serious incident raised new concerns about a broadened conflict. On October 15 a remote-controlled bomb exploded as a U.S. diplomatic convoy was traveling in the Gaza Strip. Three American security guards assigned to the U.S. embassy in Tel Aviv were killed and a U.S. diplomat was wounded. Diplomats in the convoy were on their way to interview Palestinian candidates for the Fulbright scholarships, which provided funding for foreigners to study in the United States. It was the first fatal attack on U.S. officials in either Israel or the Palestinian territories since 1967.

Observers said the attack appeared to have been carefully planned. U.S. officials routinely drove along the route where the attack took place, and a previously undisclosed attack had taken place nearby in June; no one was hurt. The subsequent successful attack appeared to create new dangers in a conflict that previously had been confined to mutual violence between

Israelis and Palestinians. Palestinian police on October 16 arrested three members of a small extremist group that had ties to Arafat's security services. The group, the Popular Resistance Committees, issued a statement denying responsibility. No further action had been taken as of year's end.

Unofficial Peace Plans

The failure of the U.S.-led roadmap stood in contrast to what appeared to be substantial popular support, among both Israelis and Palestinians, for two other peace plans that emerged during the year. Both plans were drawn up by prominent public figures, but neither plan had any official standing. The plans demonstrated that fundamental disagreements between Israelis and Palestinians could be resolved, although not to the satisfaction of hardliners on both sides.

The first of the two to be made public was a statement called the "People's Voice," issued July 27 by Ami Ayalon, a retired admiral and former head of Israel's Shin Bet domestic intelligence service, and Sari Nusseibeh, the president of the Palestinian Al-Quds University and one of the most prominent Palestinian intellectuals. The statement was a general call for compromise by both sides on the hot-button issues; each side would get some of its basic demands but would have to give up others. It called for an independent Palestinian state within the West Bank and Gaza Strip but did not indicate where the borders would be; proposed that Jerusalem would be "an open city" serving as the capital of both states, with each side administering its own holy sites; stated that no Israeli settlers would remain within the borders of the new Palestinian state; and required Palestinians to acknowledge that refugees who fled or were pushed out of Israel during and after the 1948 war would not have the right to return to their former homes. The statement was far from a complete peace plan because it lacked crucial details for each of these controversial points. Even so, it sketched the general parameters for an agreement that might be broadly accepted on both sides.

Ayalon and Nusseibeh circulated their plan in the form of a petition and by year's end had gathered more than 200,000 signatures from both Israelis and Palestinians. The two men also won diplomatic support from UN Secretary General Kofi Annan, who met with them on October 29 and said their initiative "can play an essential role in generating the momentum needed for peace." Another endorsement came from an unexpected quarter: U.S. deputy secretary of defense Paul Wolfowitz, one of the Bush administration's most hawkish conservatives.

The year's other peace proposal was a detailed, formal version of a potential agreement between Israel and the Palestinians. It was negotiated, over a two-year period with the help of the Swiss government, by Yossi

Beilin, a former Israeli justice minister during the administration of prime minister Ehud Barak, and Abed Rabbo, a former Palestinian Authority information minister. A member of the Knesset, Beilin had no connection with the current Sharon government, but Rabbo was a close associate of Arafat's and reportedly had his tacit approval.

Beilin and Rabbo completed work on the agreement on October 13 and formally signed it on December 1 at a celebrity-filled ceremony in Geneva hosted by American movie actor Richard Dreyfuss and attended by former U.S. president Jimmy Carter (1977–1981) and former Polish president Lech Walesa, among others. The negotiators had received a letter of encouragement from Secretary of State Colin Powell and messages of outright support from dozens of current and former world leaders, including former president Bill Clinton (1993–2001), British prime minister Tony Blair, French president Jacques Chirac, and Egyptian president Hosni Mubarak. Carter, who had mediated the 1978–1979 peace agreements between Israel and Egypt, lavished praise on the agreement, saying: "It is unlikely that we will ever see a more promising foundation for peace." Notable by their absence were Arafat and Sharon, the two antagonists whose hard-line positions Beilin and Rabbo were trying to overcome. Arafat had made noncommittal remarks about the peace plan, but Sharon had rejected it outright and implied that Beilin was a traitor for participating in the negotiations.

The fifty-page agreement, called the Geneva Accord because of its Swiss sponsorship, covered all major issues between Israel and the Palestinians in great detail, even including maps showing potential borders. Its general thrust was similar to the Ayalon-Nusseibeh declaration, calling on both sides to give up key aspects of what had long been their bottom-line demands. Israel's main concessions would include withdrawing from all of the Gaza Strip and 98 percent of the West Bank, and dismantling all Jewish settlements in Gaza and all but about twenty settlements in the West Bank; those twenty would be annexed to Israel. The agreement provided a complex formula for determining the future status of Palestinian refugees that, in effect, ruled out any large-scale return of refugees to Israel; according to some estimates, 30,000 to 40,000 refugees might be allowed to return over a period of several years. The Geneva Accord called for Jerusalem to be split between Israel and the Palestinians, with several crossings allowing access through an international border. Each side would control its holy sites.

In most respects, the Geneva Accord was similar to a peace plan advanced by Clinton during failed negotiations at Camp David in July 2000 between Arafat and then-Israeli prime minister Barak. Barak accepted Clinton's plan but Arafat did not. The failure of those negotiations played a major role in the outbreak, two months later, of the Palestinian Intifada, which continued throughout 2003. *(Camp David negotiations, Historic Documents of 2000, p. 494)*

One important player—the Bush administration—appeared to take an ambivalent stance on the Geneva Accord. Administration officials repeatedly said the United States remained committed to the roadmap as the only agreement that had been endorsed by all major parties. Powell met with Beilin and Rabbo at the State Department on December 5 and explained why the administration was standing by the roadmap. Even so, that meeting amounted to something of a rebuff to Sharon, who had demanded that the United States have nothing to do with the Geneva Accord or its proponents.

The UN's special envoy for the Middle East, Terje Roed-Larsen, praised both initiatives in a December 12 report to the Security Council. "While civil initiatives do not substitute for the officials of the parties negotiating, there are significant indications that Israelis and Palestinians can work together to constructively bridge their differences," he said. These initiatives, coupled with recent polls indicating that most Israelis and Palestinians were eager for peace, "show what we can all feel on the ground, an intense weariness of the current tragic state of affairs and a desire for real change."

Sharon's Ultimatum

The roadmap had briefly raised hopes among both Israelis and Palestinians for a negotiated settlement to the decades-long conflict, and its failure led to some reassessments of positions on both sides, especially in Israel. The first signs of movement came in late October, when Sharon began to face pressure from some of his own military officers, who said the harsh tactics against the Palestinians were not working. A former army general who many Israelis considered a military hero, Sharon had been substantially invulnerable to domestic criticism about his security policies—until that criticism came from within the military.

Armed forces chief of staff Lt. Gen. Moshe Yaalon took the highly unusual step of telling columnists for three newspapers that Israel's repression had backfired and contributed to "hatred and terrorism" among Palestinians. "In our tactical decisions, we are operating contrary to our strategic interests," Yaalon was quoted as saying. Yaalon referred in particular to Israel's restrictions on travel by Palestinians within the West Bank, and between the West Bank and Israel. The general also criticized the government's plans for driving a security wall deep into the West Bank. Other military officials said Yaalon decided to make his views known publicly out of frustration because senior government officials, including Sharon, had overruled his appeals for policy changes. Sharon rebuked Yaalon and demanded that he keep his opinions within government circles, but the damage had been done.

The Israeli military long had been deeply divided about how to deal with the Palestinians. At any given time one-half or more of Israelis serving in the military were reservists fulfilling mandatory terms of duty. Dozens of reservists, and even some active-duty service personnel, had refused to serve in the Palestinian territories or had otherwise made public their disagreements with government policy. One such incident had occurred in September when twenty-seven reserve pilots had signed a public letter opposing air strikes against Palestinian militants in civilian neighborhoods. Even so, Yaalon's statements created an enormous controversy within Israel because they appeared to undercut the principal justification for Sharon's hard-line policies.

That controversy grew a month later when four former directors of Israel's domestic intelligence agency—the Shin Bet—said in a joint newspaper interview that Sharon's policies were leading only to further conflict and possibly the eventual destruction of Israel as a Jewish state. One of the four was Ayalon, the coauthor of the peace pledge with Nusseibeh.

Yet another sign of a political shift in Israel came December 5 when Sharon's deputy prime minister, Ehud Olmert, said Israel would have no choice but to withdraw from the Gaza Strip and much of the West Bank if it was to remain a Jewish-majority state. A former mayor of Jerusalem, Olmert was considered one of the most hard-line members of Sharon's Likud Party. His remark essentially paralleled an argument that many of Israel's leftist leaders had long been making—that if Israel insisted on maintaining control of the territories, within a few years Jews would become a minority in the lands controlled by Israel because of the more rapid population growth among Palestinians. As of 2003, about 5.2 million Jews lived within Israel and the territories. By contrast, 1.3 million Palestinian Arabs lived in Israel (most were citizens) and about 3.5 million Palestinians lived in the territories, most of them without any formal citizenship. Unless Israel was able to encourage a sudden influx of Jewish immigrants or somehow shed its control over large numbers of Palestinians in the territories, the combined total of about 4.8 million Palestinians would grow to exceed the Jewish population within ten years, according to most projections. Once that happened, Israel's Jews would find themselves a minority governing a majority population of Arabs, who could then demand a unified state rather than a separate state for themselves.

These population projections had been well-known in Israel for years, but Olmert's sudden acknowledgment of them set off a round of soul-searching within Sharon's Likud Party. Some party members agreed with Olmert and suggested abandoning or modifying Likud's long-held position in favor of holding on to every acre of territory that Israel had conquered in the 1967 war. Others went to the opposite extreme, saying Israel should embrace the "transfer" solution that the nation's earliest leaders reportedly had considered but rejected: forcing the Palestinians across the Jordan River into Jordan so Israel could claim all the West Bank for itself.

It was in that context that Sharon sought to seize the initiative with a bold proposal making formal what had become the government's de facto policy: the physical separation of Israelis and Palestinians. Sharon announced his policy on December 18 in a speech to an annual national security conference in Herzliya, a Tel Aviv suburb.

Sharon said he still supported the roadmap peace plan, which he called "a balanced program for phased progress toward peace." Israel would fulfill the commitments it had made when accepting the roadmap in June, he said, including dismantling the unauthorized Jewish settlements in the West Bank and banning the construction of new settlements; this latter point did not rule out expansion of existing settlements. He made no mention of fourteen major objections that his government had lodged against the roadmap in May.

Sharon had a warning, however: If, "in a few months," the Palestinians had not implemented their obligations under the roadmap (which he had defined as permanently stopping all terrorist attacks), Israel would launch "the unilateral security step of disengagement from the Palestinians." Sharon offered only a general description of what he called a "disengagement plan." He said the plan would include the redeployment of the Israeli military "along new security lines" and "a change in the deployment of settlements" to reduce the number of Israelis living in what he called "the heart of the Palestinian population" in the Gaza Strip and West Bank. Sharon refused to name the settlements to be "relocated" but said they would include those that would not fall within Israel as part of "any possible future permanent agreement." Israel also would "greatly accelerate" the construction of its security barrier around the West Bank, he said. Overall, Sharon said "the disengagement plan will reduce friction between us and the Palestinians."

Sharon's speech provoked wide-ranging reactions. Within Israel, political and religious leaders to the right of Sharon denounced any action that would diminish Israel's claim to, or hold on, the occupied territories, especially the West Bank. Residents in some of the Jewish settlements blasted Sharon's plan as a "betrayal" and a "surrender" to terrorism. To Sharon's left, Labor Party leader Shimon Peres and others said only a negotiated settlement with the Palestinians could resolve the underlying conflict between the two sides, while a unilateral withdrawal would leave age-old enmities in place and not guarantee Israel's security. Palestinian leaders rejected Sharon's new plan as a unilateral action intended to solve Israel's problem at the expense of Palestinians. "They may make peace between Israelis and Israelis," Palestinian negotiator Saeb Erekat told the CNN network. "They will not make peace with the Palestinians."

The Bush administration's immediate response was to emphasize its support of the roadmap and to reject what White House spokesman Scott McClellan called a unilateral attempt by Israel to "impose a settlement." One day later, however, the administration backed away from its criticism and emphasized, instead, the parts of Sharon's speech that talked about pursuing the roadmap. Weeks later, administration officials appeared to embrace elements of the Sharon plan, including the likely first step: an Israeli withdrawal of Jewish settlements and military forces from the Gaza Strip.

The Wall in Dispute

For much of the previous two decades, one of the principal issues between Israel and the Palestinians had been Israel's policy of building settlements for Jews in parts of the Gaza Strip and in substantial portions of the West Bank, including in what formerly were Palestinian neighborhoods of East Jerusalem. More than 400,000 Israelis lived in the settlements, all of which were in what the United Nations considered to be "occupied territories." Under U.S. pressure, Israel in June dismantled several small settlements that the government had not authorized, but it continued to expand settlements built with government money.

By 2003 the longstanding controversy over the settlements had been overtaken by a new dispute over Israel's plan to build what it called a "fence" or "security barrier" around much of the West Bank. Israel already had a barrier along its borders with the Gaza Strip. The government said the new barrier was intended to prevent terrorists from entering Israel from the West Bank. The barrier consisted of fencing (in some urban areas the fences were twenty-five-foot-high concrete walls), barbed wire, ditches, electronic monitors, and a road on the Israeli side for use by security forces. Palestinians and most international observers called the barrier a "wall" and said it would constitute a de facto border between Israel and the West Bank.

Sharon's cabinet approved the first segment of the barrier in April 2002, and by the middle of 2003 more than 100 miles had been completed along portions of what was known as the "green line" separating Israel proper from the West Bank. On October 1 the cabinet approved plans for a complete barrier stretching about 430 miles entirely around the West Bank, including along the Jordan River valley that separated Israel from Jordan.

Most Palestinian leaders said they accepted Israel's right to build a fence or wall along the internationally recognized green line, so long as it was on Israeli territory. But Palestinians, backed by most international governments, objected to the actual route of the wall, which in some cases thrust deep into the West Bank to separate Jewish settlements from surrounding Palestinian communities. The first phase of the wall, completed at the end of July, entirely encircled the Palestinian city of Qalqilya (with a population of about 41,000) and three nearby villages with a total population of about 7,000. Long stretches of the wall were about four miles inside the West Bank, and the route approved on October 1 showed the wall running as deep as thirteen miles inside the West Bank in places. If the wall was completed along that route, the United Nations estimated that about 160,000 Palestinians would be encircled by it, and another 237,000 (most of them in East Jerusalem) would find themselves trapped between the wall to the east and the Israeli border to the west.

In addition to challenging the route of the wall, Palestinians argued that the very process of building it had caused hardships among civilians. The Israeli military demolished dozens of homes and businesses and seized several thousand acres of agricultural lands, including fruit orchards and olive groves, that stood in the way of the wall. Ironically, Palestinians provided the manual labor for much of the work on the wall—as they had for the Jewish settlements built on formerly Palestinian land in the territories.

The wall posed an acute political problem for the Bush administration, which sympathized with Israel's security concerns but feared that the planned route undermined the prospects for an eventual peace settlement. The administration's ambivalence was clear in late June when Bush met at the White House with then-Palestinian prime minister Abbas and called the wall a "problem" but two days later did not raise the matter during a meeting with Sharon.

Seeking to draw more international attention to the wall, Arab nations on October 21 pushed a resolution through the United Nations General Assembly demanding that Israel halt further construction and tear down the sections that had been built inside the West Bank. Foreign ministers of the European Union (EU) followed suit on November 18, issuing a statement calling for a halt to the wall before it caused "further humanitarian and economic hardship" for the Palestinians. That statement contained a broader demand for Israel to ease travel restrictions on Palestinians and halt "punitive measures," such as the demolition of the homes of Palestinians suspected of engaging in or supporting terrorism. The EU statement also denounced Palestinian terrorism and called on Arafat to take more aggressive action against it.

The increased international attention to the wall put more pressure on the Bush administration, which was in the process of reviewing Israel's request for U.S. guarantees of Israeli bonds issued on world financial markets. After several weeks of negotiations, the White House announced on November 25 that the United States would cut $289.5 million from the $1.4 billion it had previously pledged to guarantee for the current fiscal year, 2004. The decision did not affect direct U.S. aid to Israel, which averaged $3 billion annually. National Security Council spokesman Sean McCormack said the action "acknowledges U.S. policy concerns," a reference to the route of the West Bank wall and Israel's continued expansion of Jewish settlements.

In an unusually harsh report to the General Assembly, Secretary General Annan on November 26 described Israel's construction of the wall within the West Bank as "a deeply counterproductive act." Israel had a "right and duty" to provide security for its citizens, Annan said. "However, that duty should not be carried out in a way that is in contradiction to international law, that could damage the longer-term prospects for peace by making the creation of an independent, viable, and contiguous Palestinian state more difficult, or that increases suffering among the Palestinian people."

Violence Continues

The violence between the Israelis and Palestinians had caused casualties on both sides, but throughout the first three years of the Intifada about three Palestinians died for each Israeli. According to the Israeli human rights group B'Tselem (a left-leaning organization), between September 2000 and the end of 2003 the violence had taken the lives of 2,337 Palestinians and 653 Israelis. B'Tselem's figures for 2003 were 589 Palestinians and 185 Israelis. Sharon's office gave a higher figure for the number of Israelis killed during the year, saying there had been 213 deaths, which it said included 163 civilians and 50 members of security forces. Whatever the precise numbers, only about half as many died on each side as a result of violence in 2003 as in 2002, when 1,018 Palestinians and 419 Israelis were killed, according to B'Tselem's figures. The Israeli government offered another measure of the relatively lower violence during the year. It listed 3,838 "terrorist attacks" against Israeli targets, compared to 5,301 the previous year; the government's definition of a terrorist attack was a broad one, including every reported case of violence or attempted violence by a Palestinian against Israeli citizens or property. *(Previous years' violence, Historic Documents of 2002, p. 927)*

As in previous years, the vast majority of Palestinian casualties occurred in the territories, and most of the Israeli deaths took place inside Israel. All but a handful of Palestinian deaths resulted from operations by the Israeli army and security forces; some operations were direct retaliation for specific terrorist attacks and others were part of a broader crackdown on what the government called the Palestinian "terrorist infrastructure." The majority of Israeli deaths during the year came in large-scale suicide bombings, all of which took place in or near Israel's major cities: Jerusalem, Haifa, and Tel Aviv.

The year's violence was significantly different from that of the previous two years in one major respect: Palestinian extremist groups in late June called a cease-fire that lasted for nearly seven weeks, reducing the overall number of attacks, and killings, for the year. The suicide bombing of a bus in Jerusalem on August 19 effectively ended that cease-fire. Two bombings on September 9—one near Tel Aviv killing eight soldiers and another at a restaurant in Jerusalem killing seven civilians—appeared to herald a new wave of violence, but that did not occur. Only one large-scale suicide bombing hit

Israel afterward, an October 4 attack at a restaurant in Haifa, which killed nineteen people. The seaside restaurant was co-owned by Israeli Arabs and Jews. Another suicide bomber struck a bus stop in a Tel Aviv suburb on December 25, killing four people.

Israeli reprisals for these and other incidents killed more than 160 Palestinians during the last four months of the year, according to B'Tselem. Most of the attacks by Israeli security forces took place in Gaza, where the Palestinian extremist groups Hamas and Islamic Jihad were strongest. One of the most extensive Israeli operations was on October 20, when planes and helicopters carried out five attacks on Palestinian targets in Gaza. Eleven Palestinians, including two members of Hamas, were killed and more than ninety people were wounded. Israel eased its restrictions on much of the West Bank early in November but then reimposed them after the December 25 bombing in Tel Aviv.

Economic and Social Distress

Israel and the Palestinian territories experienced strong economic growth during the last half of the 1990s and into 2000. Israel essentially had a European economy based on tourism, modern industry including high-technology, and exports of high-value agricultural products such as flowers and fruits. In 2000 Israel's per capita income hovered around $20,000, on par with the middle tier of European nations. Israel's economic boom, plus aid and investment from Europe and the United States, also had stimulated economic growth in the Palestinian territories. Even so, the best jobs for Palestinians were in Israel, as day laborers.

The outbreak of the Palestinian uprising in September 2000 sent the economies of both Israel and the Palestinian territories plummeting. Tourism came to a halt. More importantly, both sides were hurt economically by Israel's blanket policy of barring Palestinians from crossing into Israel to find work. Israeli businesses lost the workers they needed for menial tasks that Israelis did not want to perform, and tens of thousands of Palestinians lost their jobs. Israel's economy went into recession. In both 2001 and 2002, according to Bank of Israel figures, the gross domestic product fell by nearly 1 percent. Israeli employers rapidly replaced Palestinian laborers with imported workers from eastern Europe and southeast Asia, and by the last half of 2003 the Israeli economy had started growing again as exports resumed and there were signs that tourism might be picking up. Preliminary Bank of Israel figures showed slow but positive economic growth in Israel for 2003 and continuing into 2004.

Across the green line, the Palestinian economy remained in a deep depression. A report issued March 5 by the World Bank presented a litany of statistics documenting the near-collapse of economic activity in the Gaza

Strip and the West Bank. In just two years (2001 and 2002), the report said, the number of Palestinians in poverty (defined as living on less than $2 a day) had tripled from 637,000 to nearly 2 million; unemployment exceeded 50 percent; per capita food consumption had dropped by 30 percent; and Palestinians had lost an estimated $5.4 billion in total income, the equivalent of their entire income for a full year before the uprising began. The report said the Palestinian economy would have collapsed without the continued functioning of Arafat's government, the Palestinian Authority, which still received enough aid from Arab and European countries to pay monthly salaries to 125,000 people—one-third of all Palestinians still working.

The violence also made it difficult for international aid agencies to provide services in the territories. Ever since the 1948 war, a United Nations agency, the Relief and Works Agency for Palestinian Refugees (known as UNRWA) had provided food, housing, medical care, and other services for hundreds of thousands of Palestinians in the territories and neighboring countries (notably Jordan). That agency issued emergency appeals in 2002 and 2003 for money to provide additional services because of the economic difficulties. It announced major cutbacks on November 10 because donor nations had supplied less than half the requests. Among other things, UNRWA said it would cut in half the amount of food it provided to the 1 million Palestinians it had been feeding in the territories.

More cutbacks were announced November 18 by the International Committee of the Red Cross, which said it was ending two food assistance programs begun in mid-2002 to help about 50,000 Palestinians dislocated by Israeli military operations in the West Bank. The Red Cross openly acknowledged that its action was a political statement intended to put pressure on Israel to ease its restrictions on the Palestinians. "This program was not designed to substitute for the responsibility of the occupying power, which is Israel," Red Cross Jerusalem spokesman Vincent Bernard said.

The Israeli government placed the entire blame for the Palestinian economic crisis on Arafat, saying his failure to prevent terrorist attacks against Israel had left Israel no choice but to clamp down on border crossings and other aspects of Palestinian daily life. In mid-November Israel also gave the Bush administration details of plans to build factories in the West Bank that could employee more than 100,000 Palestinians. The factories would be built only after terrorist attacks against Israelis had been stopped, officials said.

Following are excerpts from a speech delivered December 18, 2003, by Israeli prime minister Ariel Sharon to a national security conference in Herzliya, outside Tel Aviv, in which he outlined plans for a possible "disengagement" between Israelis and the Palestinians.

"Prime Minister's Speech at the Herzliya Conference"

We are all entrusted with the duty of shaping the face of the Jewish and democratic State of Israel a state where there is an equal distribution of the burden, as well as the acceptance of rights and shouldering of duties by all sectors, through different forms of national service. A state where there is a good and efficient education system which educates a young generation imbued with values and national pride, which is capable of confronting the challenges of the modern world. A country whose economy is adapted to the advanced global market of the 21st century, where the product per capita crosses the $20,000 line and is equal to that of most developed European countries. An immigrant-absorbing state which constitutes a national and spiritual center for all Jews of the world and is a source of attraction for thousands of immigrants each year. Aliyah [the "return" or emigration to Israel of all Jews] is the central goal of the State of Israel.

This is the country we wish to shape. This is the country where our children will want to live.

I know that there is sometimes a tendency to narrow all of Israel's problems down to the political sphere, believing that once a solution is found to Israel's problems with its neighbors, particularly the Palestinians, the other issues on the agenda will miraculously resolve themselves. I do not believe so. We are facing additional challenges, which must be addressed the economy, educating the young generation, immigrant absorption, enhancement of social cohesion and the improvement of relations between Arabs and Jews in Israel.

Like all Israeli citizens, I yearn for peace. I attach supreme importance to taking all steps, which will enable progress toward resolution of the conflict with the Palestinians. However, in light of the other challenges we are faced with, if the Palestinians do not make a similar effort toward a solution of the conflict I do not intend to wait for them indefinitely.

Seven months ago, my Government approved the Roadmap to peace, based on President George Bush's June 2002 speech. This is a balanced program for phased progress toward peace, to which both Israel and the Palestinians committed themselves. A full and genuine implementation of the program is the best way to achieve true peace. The Roadmap is the only political plan accepted by Israel, the Palestinians, the Americans and a majority of the international community. We are willing to proceed toward its implementation: two states Israel and a Palestinian State living side by side in tranquility, security and peace.

The Roadmap is a clear and reasonable plan, and it is therefore possible and imperative to implement it. The concept behind this plan is that only security will lead to peace. And in that sequence. Without the achievement of full security within the framework of which terror organizations will be dismantled it will not be possible to achieve genuine peace, a peace for generations. This is the essence of the Roadmap. The opposite perception, according to which the very signing of a peace agreement will produce security out of thin air, has already been tried in the past and failed miserably. And such will be the fate of any other plan which promotes this concept. These plans deceive the public and create false hope. There will be no peace before the eradication of terror.

The government under my leadership will not compromise on the realization of all phases of the Roadmap. It is incumbent upon the Palestinians to uproot the terrorist groups and to create a law-abiding society, which fights against violence and incitement. Peace and terror cannot coexist. The world is currently united in its unequivocal demand from the Palestinians to act toward the cessation of terrorism and the implementation of reforms. Only a transformation of the Palestinian Authority into a different authority will enable progress in the political process. The Palestinians must fulfill their obligations. A full and complete implementation will at the end of the process lead to peace and tranquility.

We began the implementation of the Roadmap at Aqaba [a meeting in June 2003 between Sharon and then-Palestinian prime minister Mahmoud Abbas, mediated by President Bush], but the terrorist organizations joined with Yasser Arafat and sabotaged the process with a series of the most brutal terror attacks we have ever known.

Concurrent with the demand from the Palestinians to eliminate the terror organizations, Israel is taking and will continue to take steps to significantly improve the living conditions of the Palestinian population: Israel will remove closures and curfews and reduce the number of roadblocks; we will improve freedom of movement for the Palestinian population, including the passage of people and goods; we will increase the hours of operation at international border crossings; we will enable a large number of Palestinian merchants to conduct regular and normal economic and trade relations with their Israeli counterparts, etc. All these measures are aimed at enabling better and freer movement for the Palestinian population not involved in terror.

In addition, subject to security coordination, we will transfer Palestinian towns to Palestinian security responsibility.

Israel will make every effort to assist the Palestinians and to advance the process.

Israel will fulfil the commitments taken upon itself. I have committed to the President of the United States that Israel will dismantle unauthorized outposts. It is my intention to implement this commitment. The

State of Israel is governed by law, and the issue of the outposts is no exception. I understand the sensitivity; we will try to do this in the least painful way possible, but the unauthorized outposts will be dismantled. Period.

Israel will meet all its obligations with regard to construction in the settlements. There will be no construction beyond the existing construction line, no expropriation of land for construction, no special economic incentives and no construction of new settlements.

I take this opportunity to appeal to the Palestinians and repeat, as I said at Aqaba: it is not in our interest to govern you. We would like you to govern yourselves in your own country. A democratic Palestinian state with territorial contiguity in Judea and Samaria and economic viability, which would conduct normal relations of tranquility, security and peace with Israel. Abandon the path of terror and let us together stop the bloodshed. Let us move forward together towards peace.

We wish to speedily advance implementation of the Roadmap towards quiet and a genuine peace. We hope that the Palestinian Authority will carry out its part. However, if in a few months the Palestinians still continue to disregard their part in implementing the Roadmap then Israel will initiate the unilateral security step of disengagement from the Palestinians.

The purpose of the Disengagement Plan is to reduce terror as much as possible, and grant Israeli citizens the maximum level of security. The process of disengagement will lead to an improvement in the quality of life, and will help strengthen the Israeli economy. The unilateral steps which Israel will take in the framework of the Disengagement Plan will be fully coordinated with the United States. We must not harm our strategic coordination with the United States. These steps will increase security for the residents of Israel and relieve the pressure on the IDF [Israeli Defense Forces] and security forces in fulfilling the difficult tasks they are faced with. The Disengagement Plan is meant to grant maximum security and minimize friction between Israelis and Palestinians.

We are interested in conducting direct negotiations, but do not intend to hold Israeli society hostage in the hands of the Palestinians. I have already said we will not wait for them indefinitely.

The Disengagement Plan will include the redeployment of IDF forces along new security lines and a change in the deployment of settlements, which will reduce as much as possible the number of Israelis located in the heart of the Palestinian population. We will draw provisional security lines and the IDF will be deployed along them. Security will be provided by IDF deployment, the security fence and other physical obstacles. The Disengagement Plan will reduce friction between us and the Palestinians.

This reduction of friction will require the extremely difficult step of changing the deployment of some of the settlements. I would like to repeat what I have said in the past: In the framework of a future agreement, Israel will not remain in all the places where it is today. The relocation of settlements will be made, first and foremost, in order to draw the most efficient security line possible, thereby creating this disengagement between Israel and the Palestinians. This security line will not constitute the permanent border of the State of Israel, however, as long as implementation of the Roadmap is not resumed, the IDF will be deployed along that line. Settlements which will be relocated are those, which will not be included in the territory of the State of Israel in the framework of any possible future permanent agreement. At the same time, in the framework of the Disengagement Plan, Israel will strengthen its control over those same areas in the Land of Israel which will constitute an inseparable part of the State of Israel in any future agreement. I know you would like to hear names, but we should leave something for later.

Israel will greatly accelerate the construction of the security fence. Today we can already see it taking shape. The rapid completion of the security fence will enable the IDF to remove roadblocks and ease the daily lives of the Palestinian population not involved in terror.

In order to enable the Palestinians to develop their economic and trade sectors, and to ensure that they will not be exclusively dependent on Israel, we will consider, in the framework of the Disengagement Plan, enabling in coordination with Jordan and Egypt the freer passage of people and goods through international border crossings, while taking the necessary security precautions.

I would like to emphasize: the Disengagement Plan is a security measure and not a political one. The steps which will be taken will not change the political reality between Israel and the Palestinians, and will not prevent the possibility of returning to the implementation of the Roadmap and reaching an agreed settlement.

The Disengagement Plan does not prevent the implementation of the Roadmap. Rather, it is a step Israel will take in the absence of any other option, in order to improve its security.

The Disengagement Plan will be realized only in the event that the Palestinians continue to drag their feet and postpone implementation of the Roadmap.

Obviously, through the Disengagement Plan the Palestinians will receive much less than they would have received through direct negotiations as set out in the Roadmap.

According to circumstances, it is possible that parts of the Disengagement Plan that are supposed to provide maximum security to the citizens of Israel will be undertaken while also attempting to implement the Roadmap.

Ladies and Gentlemen,

My life experience has taught me that for peace, as well as for war, we must have broad consensus. We must preserve our unity, even in the midst of a difficult, internal debate.

In the past three years, the Palestinian terrorist organizations have put us to a difficult test. Their plan to break the spirit of Israeli society has not succeeded. The citizens of Israel have managed to step into the breach, support each other, lend a helping hand, volunteer and contribute.

I believe that this path of unity must be continued today. Whether we will be able to advance the Roadmap, or will have to implement the Disengagement Plan, experience has taught us that, together, through broad national consensus, we can do great things.

Let us not be led astray. Any path will be complicated, strewn with obstacles, and obligate us to act with discretion and responsibility. I am confident that, just as we have managed to overcome the challenges of the past, we will stand together and succeed today. . . .

Source: Prime Minister's Office, Israel. "Prime Minister's Speech at the Herzliya Conference" (English translation). December 18, 2003. www.pmo.gov.il/english/ts.exe?tsurl=0.41.7635.0.0.

Libyan, U.S., and British Statements on Libya's Nuclear Weapons Programs

December 19, 2003

INTRODUCTION

A man of many surprises, Libyan leader Muammar Qaddafi in December 2003 pulled off the biggest surprise of his long career, renouncing his country's attempts to build biological, chemical, and nuclear weapons. Qaddafi opened secret weapons facilities to international inspection and pledged to eliminate the programs he had built secretly in defiance of treaties he had signed.

The inspections were certain to expose details of how Libya had acquired equipment and technology for its weapons programs from Pakistan and other suppliers. Recently uncovered evidence appeared to show that Pakistan also had provided components for nuclear weapons programs in Iran and North Korea. *(North Korea, p. 592; Iran, p. 1025)*

In retrospect, most Western experts said it appeared that Qaddafi for many years had been rethinking his policies, which had squandered Libya's oil wealth and made him a pariah both within his region and on the world stage. Perhaps most important domestically, his decision to give up his ambitions for weapons of mass destruction improved the chances for Western-financed economic development in Libya and a revitalization of the country's sagging oil industry.

Qaddafi's decision on weapons came just four months after Libya settled another important aspect of its dispute with the West: British and U.S. claims stemming from Libya's role in the 1988 bombing of a U.S. airliner over Lockerbie, Scotland. After years of denying responsibility, Libya in August acknowledged that its agents had planted the bomb that blew up the plane, killing 270 people. Libya also agreed to pay the victim's families $2.7 billion in damages. *(Lockerbie case, Historic Documents of 1990, p. 301)*

The Lockerbie bombing—along with a similar bombing of a French airliner over Africa in 1989—had been the climax of Libya's status as one of the handful of countries that most concerned Western leaders because of their sponsorship of terrorism and their efforts to develop weapons of mass destruction. Libya had headed the list of those "rogue" countries in the mid-1980s. In 1986 President Ronald Reagan (1981–1989) sent U.S. Air Force and Navy warplanes to bomb Libyan targets, including Qadaffi himself, in retaliation for what Reagan said was Libyan sponsorship of the terrorist bombing earlier that year of a nightclub in Berlin, Germany, which killed three people, including two U.S. servicemen. Libya said the U.S. attack killed seventy people, including Qaddafi's infant daughter, but Qaddafi himself was unhurt. Many observers said the Lockerbie bombing was Qaddafi's revenge. During the 1990s and into the early years of the twenty-first century, however, Washington's focus switched to other countries with allegedly anti-Western agendas, notably Iran, Iraq, and North Korea—the three countries President George W. Bush described in 2002 as an "axis of evil."

Whether he intended it or not, Qaddafi's decision to give up his weapons drew renewed attention to the only country in the Middle East known to possess nuclear weapons: Israel. Some Arab leaders and Western commentators said the day was approaching—with Iraq under U.S. control, with Libya in the process of being disarmed, and with Iran's nuclear program under intense international scrutiny—when Israel could no longer justify its reportedly large nuclear arsenal. "Once foes like Iraq, Iran, and Libya have all been certified as free of WMD [weapons of mass destruction], Israel will have little excuse for retaining the nuclear option—and America will have just as little excuse for not pressing it to give up the bomb," the British *Economist* magazine editorialized on December 29. *(Iraq WMD inspections, p. 974)*

A Surprise Announcement

Although Libya for years had been moving to improve its relations with the United States and other Western nations, the coordinated announcements on December 19 by Qadaffi, President Bush, and British prime minister Tony Blair that Libya would open its weapons programs to international inspection came as a major surprise. In contrast to many such developments, there had been no advance leaks or public indications of any sort that negotiations were under way.

The first statement came from Libya's foreign ministry, which announced that Libya had "decided with its free will to dispose of these [weapons] materials, equipment and programs and to be completely free from internationally banned weapons." The statement also said Libya would give up any missiles capable of flying more than 180 miles—a limit imposed by an international agreement Libya had not previously signed. Qaddafi was quoted by Jana, the official Libyan news agency, as endorsing the foreign ministry statement as "a wise decision and a courageous step which deserves the support of the Libyan people." Qaddafi added that Libya "will encourage the world, especially the countries of the Middle East, Africa, and the Third World, to get rid of weapons of mass destruction programs."

In back-to-back announcements a few hours later, Blair in London and Bush in Washington praised Qaddafi's decision. "This courageous decision by Colonel Qaddafi is an historic one," Blair said. "It will make the region and the world more secure." Bush recited Qaddafi's pledges to renounce terrorism as well as to give up Libya's weapons programs. "As the Libyan government takes these essential steps, its good faith will be returned," Bush said. "Libya can regain a secure and respected place among the nations and, over time, achieve far better relations with the United States."

A Long Process of Diplomacy

The rapprochement between Libya and the United States and Britain had developed gradually over a number of years before suddenly lurching forward in 2003. Qaddafi's decision to give up his weapons was the culminating step, but it had been preceded by much diplomacy and the resolution of other troubling issues.

The process began in 1999 when the Clinton administration, with British encouragement, secretly urged Libya to end its isolation by resolving the Lockerbie case, ending support for Middle Eastern terrorists, and giving up its chemical and nuclear weapons programs. Qaddafi responded with a concession on the Lockerbie case and by deporting Abu Nidal, a Palestinian terrorist who had been living in Libya since 1987. Qaddafi took no concrete steps at that time to dismantle his weapons programs, however, U.S. officials said.

In September 2002—as Bush was pressing for international diplomatic support for his potential war against Iraq—Blair sent Qaddafi a confidential letter suggesting steps he could take to improve his relations with the West, especially the United States. Chief among them, according to news reports, was a final resolution of the Lockerbie case and a decision by Libya to halt its programs to build weapons of mass destruction. The letter may have helped speed up long-running negotiations on the Lockerbie case, and it likely contributed to Qaddafi's decision to open secret talks on weapons issues, experts said.

Also in late 2002 and early 2003, Qaddafi engaged in what appeared to be a campaign to burnish his image in the West, particularly the United States. He gave interviews to *Newsweek* magazine, the *New York Times,* and other new organizations, and said he, too, felt threatened by the brand of Islamist extremism that Osama bin Laden and the al Qaeda terrorist network represented. Qaddafi even suggested that he had come to accept Israel's existence.

Signs of a warming trend toward Libya occurred in the United States, as well. In May 2003 a panel sponsored by the Atlantic Council, a Washington think tank, called on the Bush administration to reach out to Libya by testing its willingness to abandon its weapons programs. "By all indications, Libya has changed its policy on terrorism," the panel said.

The diplomacy on Libya's weapons began in March 2003 when Libyan intelligence chief Musa Kusa approached the British foreign intelligence service, MI6, to discuss how the United States could be persuaded to lift its sanctions in return for Libya's ending its weapons programs. That approach came a few days before the United States and Britain launched their invasion of Iraq. *(Iraq war, p. 135)*

Negotiations continued for months thereafter and were given a sense of urgency in September when the British and U.S. intelligence agencies raised suspicions about a German-flag ship heading to Libya from the United Arab Emirates. The ship was seized, in secret, and found to be carrying parts for centrifuges (used to enrich uranium to weapons-grade) that had been made in Malaysia. U.S. and British officials used that discovery to pressure Libya, which then agreed to allow intelligence officials from the two countries to examine secret weapons sites.

In two visits in October and December, the officials were allowed to inspect ten facilities where the Libyan military had stored several dozen tons of mustard gas (a chemical weapon); a rudimentary program of experimentation with biological weapons; equipment, including centrifuges, used to process highly enriched uranium for nuclear weapons; and North Korean–supplied Scud-C missiles capable of flying 500 miles. Neither the chemical weapons nor the missiles came as a surprise to the British and U.S. experts. Libya had used mustard gas in 1987, when it intervened in a civil war in neighboring Chad. In 1999 and 2000 shipments of North Korean missile parts, believed destined for Libya, were discovered by authorities in India and Britain. Despite the earlier seizure of centrifuges bound for Libya, the extent of Libya's nuclear equipment did surprise the U.S. and British officials. They reported back to their capitals that Libya's program—while still far short of actually producing a bomb—was more advanced than had been assumed.

On December 16, in a meeting at the posh Travelers' Club in London, British and Libyan officials worked out the details of an agreement under which Libya would renounce its weapons programs in return for praise and vague commitments from Blair and Bush. Two days later Blair and Qaddafi talked by telephone for a half hour—their first-ever direct contact. After further negotiations over the final wording, Libya's stunning announcement was made public the next day. The announcement capped a week of very good news for Blair and Bush, who had earlier celebrated the capture in Iraq of the deposed leader, Saddam Hussein. *(Saddam capture, p. 1189)*

Most Western leaders praised Qaddafi's decision and expressed hope that it would encourage other countries—notably Iran and North Korea—to drop their nuclear weapons ambitions as well. French foreign minister Dominique de Villepin also used the occasion to praise the use of diplomacy, rather than military force, as a means of getting countries to accept international norms. "This confirms the efficiency of the political approach to bringing a peaceful response to the major challenge of the risk of proliferation in today's world," he said. France had been among the most vocal U.S. allies opposing the war in Iraq. Arab leaders, whose relations with Qaddafi were cool at best, used the event to focus attention on Israel's nuclear weapons.

Any lingering doubt that Libya intended to follow through on its pledge appeared to be erased in the last days of the year. On December 20 a Libyan delegation met in Vienna with Mohamed El Baradei, director general of the UN's International Atomic Energy Agency (IAEA) and invited the agency to inspect all of Libya's nuclear facilities. Libya had ratified the UN's 1970 Nonproliferation Treaty and had long allowed the IAEA to inspect a Soviet-supplied nuclear research reactor, but it had kept its weapons-related facilities hidden from the agency. The Libyan officials also said Tripoli would sign an agreement, called an Additional Protocol to the Nonproliferation Treaty, formally allowing the IAEA to conduct surprise inspections of all its nuclear facilities.

El Baradei and a team of IAEA weapons experts arrived in Libya on December 28 and visited some of the same facilities that British and U.S. experts had inspected months earlier. "What we have seen is a [nuclear weapons] program in the very initial stages of development," El Baradei told reporters the next day. Libya had been building a program to enrich uranium for use in weapons, he said, but it would have been "a question of years, not a question of months" before it actually generated enough weapons-grade uranium for a bomb.

El Baradei's visit resulted in yet another dust-up between his agency and U.S. officials. Early in the year, El Baradei had angered the Bush administration by saying that IAEA inspections had shown that Iraq had not been able to revive its nuclear weapons program—despite U.S. contentions that Baghdad was actively working to develop such weapons. Following El Baradei's visit to Libya, U.S. officials suggested to reporters that the IAEA was still allowing itself to be misled by the Libyans, who had not shown the agency's inspectors all of the country's weapons facilities. As a result, White House aides said the United States and Britain—not the IAEA—would oversee the dismantlement of Libya's weapons. Upon his return to Vienna on December 30, El Baradei rejected that idea. "I'm not familiar with anything they plan to do on a bilateral basis," he said of the United States. "But as far as I'm concerned, we have the mandate, and we intend to do it alone."

The Lockerbie Case

For both Britain and the United States, the single most important impediment to improved relations with Libya had long been that country's alleged sponsorship of the bombing of Pan American Airways flight 103 over Lockerbie, Scotland, in December 1988. All 259 passengers (most from the United States), along with 11 people on the ground, where killed in the crash of the plane. Libya denied claims that it was responsible, but in 1992 the United Nations imposed sanctions against Libya until it accounted for its role; the measures included diplomatic sanctions and an international ban on sales of spare parts for Libya's oil industry. The United States also imposed its own sanctions against Libya, which were more extensive than the UN measures.

After secret negotiations, Libya in April 1999 handed over two government officials who Britain had accused of planning the bombing. Those negotiations reportedly were aided by South African president Nelson Mandela and Prince Bandar bin Sultan bin Adul Aziz, the Saudi Arabian ambassador to the United States. In response the UN suspended, but did not repeal, its sanctions against Libya. The two men were tried in a special British court that was held in the Netherlands. In January 2001 the court found Libyan intelligence agent Abdel Basset Ali Megrahi guilty of murder but acquitted his colleague, Lamen Khalifa Fhimah, who was sent back to Libya, where he received a hero's welcome. Ali Megrahi was imprisoned in Scotland on a life sentence.

That verdict led to further negotiations that resulted in Libya's tentative agreement in late 2002 to pay $10 million in damages to relatives of each of the victims—$2.7 billion in total. Under that agreement, Libya was to pay $4 million to each family once the UN lifted its sanctions, another $4 million once the United States lifted its sanctions related to the Lockerbie case, and the final $2 million once the United States took Libya off its list of countries that supported terrorism (Libya was subject to further sanctions because of its role in terrorism). The provisions relating to U.S. actions included a twist, however. If the United States had not lifted all its sanctions within eight months (or by mid-March 2004), Libya would pay each family only $1 million of the remaining commitment (for a total of $5 million) and retrieve the balance of its pledge. The effect was to give the families a major financial incentive to press the United States to lift its sanctions.

That agreement was made final and announced formally on August 13, 2003, when Libya set up an escrow account in a Swiss bank for the $2.7 billion. Two days later Libya sent a letter to the United Nations officially acknowledging blame for the Lockerbie bombing. "Libya as a sovereign state accepts responsibilities for the actions of its officials," the letter from Libyan ambassador Ahmed Own said.

In response to Libya's announcement, the Bush administration said it would "not oppose" the lifting of UN sanctions against Libya, even though Secretary of State Colin Powell said the United States would retain its own sanctions for several reasons, most importantly Libya's "pursuit of weapons of mass destruction." On August 15 Britain introduced a resolution in the UN Security Council lifting the sanctions.

An obstacle to UN action, however, was the French government, which was angered that the Lockerbie settlement was far more generous than another one Libya had reached with the families of the 170 people who were killed in the September 1989 bombing of a French UTA airliner over Niger. After a French court found Libya responsible for that bombing, Libya agreed in July 1999 to pay $34 million to the families. When the Lockerbie settlement was announced, France threatened to block the lifting of UN sanctions, and Qaddafi on August 31 said Libya had agreed to offer a new payment to the UTA victims. "Our problem with the UTA case is over and the Lockerbie case is now behind us," he said in an address to the nation. "We are opening a new page in our relations with the West." French and Libyan official said on September 11 that they had concluded a final deal. They offered no details, however, and the exact amount of Libya's new payment to the UTA families had not been made public as of year's end.

The next day, September 12, the Security Council voted 13–0, with France and the United States abstaining, to lift the UN sanctions against Libya. That action did not affect the U.S. sanctions, which Bush administration officials said would remain in effect until Libya had met Washington's other conditions, including ending its weapons programs and all involvement with terrorism. In a statement, the Bush administration said the UN vote "should not be construed by Libya or by the world community as tacit U.S. acceptance that the government of Libya has rehabilitated itself." British foreign secretary Jack Straw was more effusive, saying the lifting of UN sanctions "marks and new and welcome chapter in Libya's relationship with the international community based on cooperation, not confrontation."

Libya and September 11

Qaddafi's actions on the Lockerbie case and Libya's weapons programs drew new attention during 2003 to his response to the September 11, 2001, terrorist attacks against the United States. Qaddafi had immediately denounced the attacks and pledged to help the United States fight the al Qaeda terrorist network, which Bush had accused of sponsoring the attacks. He also followed up his words with actions, sending Kusa, his intelligence chief, to give British and U.S. officials Libya's intelligence files concerning al Qaeda and its leader, bin Laden. The full extent of Libya's cooperation had not been made public as of the end of 2003.

Qaddafi's expression of solidarity with the United States was out of character, but his denunciation of Islamist extremism was not. Qaddafi for years had positioned himself as an opponent of such groups, having closed down the Muslim Brotherhood in Libya in the 1970s and acted against other extreme groups that tried to oppose his regime during the mid-1980s. In 1998, after the Clinton administration blamed al Qaeda for the bombing of the U.S. embassies in Kenya and Tanzania, Libya issued an arrest warrant for bin Laden. Qaddafi told a reporter from the *New York Times* in January, 2003: "It's strange, as far as Libya is concerned, that we find ourselves today in one trench fighting one common enemy with America." *(Embassy bombings, Historic Documents of 1998, p. 555)*

Qaddafi's Motives

President Bush and his aides portrayed Qaddafi's decision to give up his weapons as stemming directly from U.S. resolve toward Iraq. Most experts, however, said economic and internal Libyan political considerations—rather than a fear of a potential U.S. invasion—were Qaddafi's principal motivations in shifting course.

Economically, Libya had fallen on hard times by 2003 despite its oil wealth. Oil was discovered in Libya in the late 1950s, and a decade later U.S. oil companies with concessions in Libya were pumping an average of more than 3 million barrels of oil a day—a level generating enough revenue to build a strong, lasting economic foundation for a country of only about 5 million people. But after seizing power in 1969 at the head of a military coup, Qaddafi imposed his own version of socialism on the economy. Putting in place a doctrine he called the Third Universal Theory (an alternative to both capitalism and communism), he ousted the U.S. oil companies, nationalized the oil industry, barred nearly all other forms of private commerce, and imposed rules limiting private wealth, for example by prohibiting families from owning more than one house or saving large amounts of money. Libya's oil earnings went to support the government and the military and to subsidize consumer goods, such as staple food products and televisions. Qaddafi also spent billions of dollars on an enormous system of water pipelines (called the Great Man-Made River Project) tapping into underground aquifers in the southern part of the country. Qaddafi accompanied his economic policies with a unique political theory he called the *Jamahiriya*—or rule by the people, who supposedly made all important decisions. Qaddafi himself held no formal government position but was referred to as the "Leader of the Revolution."

If Qaddafi's theories succeeded in giving Libyans food and televisions, they failed to produce a working economy. Oil, the only steady industry other than small-scale agriculture, began to deteriorate after 1992, when UN sanctions barred the international sale to Libya of spare parts. By 2003 oil production had fallen by more than 50 percent, to an average of about 1.4 million barrels a day, and unemployment had reached 30 percent.

In an apparent two-step process to reverse his economic policies, Qaddafi in 2002 installed a U.S.-educated technocrat, Shokri Ghanem, as his economics and trade minister. In June 2003 Qaddafi made Ghanem prime minister and said much of the economy would be privatized so that Libya could attract foreign investment. After the December 19 announcement, Ghanem was quoted as saying he had urged Qaddafi to give up his nuclear weapons program as "useless" and focus instead on improving the economy.

Qaddafi's about-face fit into a long-time pattern in which he demonstrated a remarkable ability to maneuver in response to internal or external circumstances. In the 1970s and 1980s, for example, Qaddafi spent much of his personal energy, and Libya's oil wealth, attempting to put himself and his country at the forefront of the Arab world. Qaddafi routinely adopted some of the most extreme positions among Arabs on questions involving Israel—funding radical Palestinian groups, cutting relations with neighboring Egypt for a full decade after its 1979 peace treaty with Israel, and opposing the 1993 Oslo agreement between Israel and the Palestinians even though most other Arab countries supported it. Qaddafi's drive for regional power went far beyond public diplomacy. In addition to the Lockerbie bombing and other terrorism, Qaddafi's agents were accused of attempting to stir rebellions in Egypt and Tunisia, and Libya fought a border war with Egypt in 1977 and intervened in Chad's civil war in the 1980s.

By the 1990s Qaddafi's constant hectoring of his fellow Arab leaders had isolated him, and so he abruptly leaped onto another stage: Africa. Qaddafi began courting African leaders, promising to share some of Libya's oil wealth in return for a leading role in the Organization of African Unity (OAU). Starting in 1999 Qaddafi went further, mounting a campaign for what he called a "United States of Africa." That plan went nowhere, but African leaders did accept Qaddafi's money to finance studies for transforming the OAU along the lines of the European Union. The fifty-three African leaders agreed in 2001 to replace the OAU with a new African Union, which came into being the following year. Even so, Qaddafi's colleagues kept their distance from Qaddafi himself, refusing to give him an important leadership role. African leaders also overrode Qaddafi's objections to a proposed set of common standards intended to promote democracy, end ethnic conflicts, and create free-market economic systems on the continent. Qaddafi pointedly was excluded from a joint summit in June 2002 between African leaders and the leaders of the Group of Eight industrialized countries. *(African Union, Historic Documents of 2001, p. 506; G-8 summit on African development, Historic Documents of 2002, p. 446)*

Qaddafi also acted directly to prop up some of his fellow African leaders but with little success. In May 2001 Libya sent several hundred soldiers to protect Ange-Felix Patasse, the president of the Central African Republic, who had faced several coup attempts. The Libyan guards helped Patasse survive in office, but their presence provoked sharp criticism from other leaders in the region. At the end of 2002 Libya quietly withdrew its troops, and soldiers from several neighboring countries took over the task of guarding Patasse in his presidential palace. That effort failed, however, and Patasse was overthrown in a March 2003 coup.

Qaddafi in 2002 agreed to provide fuel to Zimbabwe, which was on the verge of economic collapse because of the failed policies of its autocratic president, Robert Mugabe. After a year, however, Mugabe failed to deliver the agricultural supplies that he had promised in return for the fuel, and Qaddafi stopped the fuel shipments. U.S. officials said Libya also repeatedly supplied weapons to Liberian leader Charles Taylor, some of which helped fuel the guerrilla war that Taylor supported in Sierra Leone. Libya reportedly was still shipping weapons to Taylor in mid-2003, just weeks before he was forced from power. *(Liberia, p. 767; Zimbabwe, p. 1110)*

Following are four documents, all issued December 19, 2003, dealing with Libya's decision to give up its programs to develop weapons of mass destruction: first, a statement from the Libyan foreign ministry; second, a report by the Libyan news agency, Jana, on a statement attributed to Libya's leader, Muammar Qaddafi; third, a statement delivered by British prime minister Tony Blair; and fourth, a statement delivered by U.S. president George W. Bush.

"Statement of the Foreign Liaison Secretary"

Due to the international climate during the Cold War and tensions in the Middle East, the Great Socialist Peoples Libyan Arab Jamahiriya [Libya's formal name] called on countries in the region to free the Middle East and Africa from weapons of mass destruction. As its call didn't receive a serious response the Great Socialist Peoples Libyan Arab Jamahiriya tried to develop its defense capabilities.

Libyan, American and British experts conducted discussions over the activities of the Great Socialist Peoples Libyan Arab Jamahiriya in this field as the Libyan experts told their counterparts about the materials, equipment and programs which led to the manufacture of internationally banned weapons with centrifuges and containers for the transfer of chemical materials.

Therefore according to talks conducted between the Jamahiriya, the USA and Britain, permanent members of the Security Council which are responsible for international peace and security, Libya decided with its free will to dispose of these materials, equipment and programmes and to be completely free from internationally banned weapons.

It also decided to keep missiles of agreed standards in accordance with the control systems "MTC [Missile Technology Control Regime, a voluntary agreement imposing limits on international trade in missile components and systems]. These steps will be taken clearly and can be improved through immediate international monitoring.

In addition, it affirmed that it will comply with the [1979] Nuclear Non-Proliferation Weapons Treaty and the securities agreement of the International Nuclear Energy Agency [a reference to the United Nations' International Atomic Energy Agency] and the [1972] Biological Weapons Agreement. It also accepts any other obligations including the additional protocol of the security agreement of the International Atomic Energy Agency and the chemical and biological weapons agreement.

As the Jamahiriya [the Libyan people as a collective] believes that the weapons arms race does not serve its security or the security of the region and is contrary to its efforts to create peace and security in the world, the Jamahiriya is eager that this initiative should also be undertaken by other countries in the Middle East without exemption or a policy of double standards.

The Great Socialist Peoples Libyan Arab Jamahiriya will inform the Security Council about that.

> **Source:** Libya. Jana [official Libyan news agency]. "Statement of the Foreign Liaison Secretary." *English News Bulletin.* Tripoli, Libya. December 20, 2003. www.jamahiriyanews.com/displayNews.php?lang=en&day =sat&tim=pm (accessed December 21, 2003).

"The Leader of the Revolution"

In a statement to Jana [Jamahiriya News Agency] the Leader of the Revolution [Qaddafi] said that the statement of the Secretary of the General Peoples Committee for Foreign Liaison and International Co-operation reflects a wise decision and a courageous step which deserves the support of the Libyan people.

The Great Socialist Peoples Libyan Arab Jamahiriya will encourage the world, especially the countries of the Middle East, Africa, and the Third World, to get rid of weapons of mass destruction programmes. It will enable the Jamahiriya to play its international role of building a new world free from weapons of mass destruction and all kinds of terrorism. This decision is aimed at preserving international peace and security and advancing the progress of humanity in the fields of development and peoples democracy and confronting the challenges of the environment until the green colour [a reference to Qaddafi's economic and political theories expressed in his "Green Book"] prevails throughout the world.

Source: Libya. Jana [official Libyan news agency]. "The Leader of the Revolution." Tripoli, Libya. December 20, 2003. www.jamahiriyanews.com/displayNews.php?lang=en&day=sat&tim=pm (accessed December 21, 2003).

"PM Welcomes Libyan WMD Announcement"

This evening Colonel Qadhafi has confirmed that Libya has in the past sought to develop WMD [weapons of mass destruction] capabilities, as well as longer range missiles. Libya came to us in March following successful negotiations on Lockerbie [the 1988 bombing of a U.S. airliner over Lockerbie, Scotland] to see if it could resolve its WMD issue in a similarly co-operative manner. Nine months of work followed with experts from the US and UK, during which the Libyans discussed their programs with us. As a result, Libya has now declared its intention to dismantle its weapons of mass destruction completely and to limit the range of Libyan missiles to no greater than 300 kms, in accordance with the parameters set by the Missile Technology Control Regime.

The Libyan government has undertaken that this process will be transparent and verifiable. Libya will immediately adhere to the [1992] Chemical Weapons convention and conclude with the International Atomic Energy Agency an Additional Protocol to its Safeguards Agreement [the Additional Protocol authorized the IAEA to conduct short-notice inspections of a country's nuclear facilities]. We have offered our support to Libya in presenting its programs to these international bodies and are prepared to offer assistance with dismantlement.

This courageous decision by Colonel Qadhafi is an historic one. I applaud it. It will make the region and the world more secure. It shows that problems of proliferation can, with good will, be tackled through discussion and engagement, to be followed up by the responsible international agencies. It demonstrates that countries can abandon programs voluntarily and peacefully. The Libyan government has stated that weapons of mass destruction are not the answer for Libya's defence. No more are they the answers for the region. Libya's actions entitle it to rejoin the international community. I have spoken to Colonel Qadhafi to say that, as the process of dismantlement goes forward, I now look forward to developing a productive relationship with him and with Libya.

Today's announcement is a further step in making the world a safer place. The UK, US and our partners are determined to stop the threat of WMD. We have played a leading role in the IAEA, with our closest allies, on the issue of Iran and nuclear weapons. We strongly support the Six Party talks on North Korea [negotiations held in 2003 among China, Japan, North Korea, South Korea, Russia, and the United States]. We have enforced Security Council resolutions relating to Iraq. We have played a leading role in the Proliferation Security Initiative designed to interdict the passage of cargoes which could be used in WMD programs. These actions show that we are serious about effective multilateral action against WMD.

And today's decisions show that recent events and political determination are opening up possibilities which just a few years ago would have been unthinkable. We must work now to create new partnerships, across geographical and cultural divides, backed by tough international rules and action.

We have identified the security threat of the early 21st century. It is the combination of terrorism and the development of nuclear or chemical or biological weapons of mass destruction.

September 11th [terrorist attacks against the United States on September 11, 2001] showed the world this new form of terrorism knows no limits to the innocent lives it will take. WMD are the means by which it could destroy our world's security, and with it our way of life.

Today's announcement shows that we can fight this menace through more than purely military means; that we can defeat it peacefully, if countries are prepared, in good faith, to work with the international community to dismantle such weapons. Those countries who pursue such a path will find ready partners in the US and in the UK, as Libya will see. We never have wanted, as our opponents falsely claim, to dominate the world, to wage war on Muslims or Arabs, to interfere with the legitimate rights of sovereign nations.

We have only ever wanted to make peace in our world lasting and stable, built on sure foundations, peace for people of all faiths, all cultures, all nations who desire the good of their citizens and the wider world.

Tonight is a further step on that journey.

Source: United Kingdom. Prime Minister's Office. "PM Welcomes Libyan WMD Announcement." December 19, 2003. www.number-10.gov.uk/output/Page5086.asp (accessed December 20, 2003).

Bush's Remarks on Libya's Decision to Dismantle Its WMD Programs

Good evening. I have called you here today to announce a development of great importance in our continuing effort to prevent the spread of weapons of mass destruction. Today in Tripoli, the leader of Libya, Colonel Muammar al-Qadhafi, publicly confirmed his commitment to disclose and dismantle all weapons of mass destruction programs in his country. He has agreed immediately and unconditionally to allow inspectors from international organizations to enter Libya. These inspectors will render an accounting of all nuclear, chemical, and biological weapons programs and will help oversee their elimination. Colonel Qadhafi's commitment, once it is fulfilled, will make our country more safe and the world more peaceful.

Talks leading to this announcement began about 9 months ago when Prime Minister Tony Blair and I were contacted, through personal envoys, by Colonel Qadhafi. He communicated to us his willingness to make a decisive change in the policy of his Government. At the direction of Colonel Qadhafi himself, Libyan officials have provided American and British intelligence officers with documentation on that country's chemical, biological, nuclear, and ballistic missile programs and activities. Our experts in these fields have met directly with Libyan officials to learn additional details.

Opposing proliferation is one of the highest priorities of the war against terror. The attacks of September the 11th, 2001, brought tragedy to the United States and revealed a future threat of even greater magnitude. Terrorists who kill thousands of innocent people would, if they ever gained weapons of mass destruction, kill hundreds of thousands without hesitation and without mercy. And this danger is dramatically increased when regimes build or acquire weapons of mass destruction and maintain ties to terrorist groups.

The United States and our allies are applying a broad and active strategy to address the challenges of proliferation, through diplomacy and through the decisive actions that are sometimes needed. We've enhanced our intelligence capabilities in order to trace dangerous weapons activities. We've organized a proliferation security initiative to interdict dangerous materials and technologies in transit. We've insisted on multilateral approaches, like that in North Korea, to confront threats. We are supporting the work of the International Atomic Energy Agency to hold the Iranian regime to its treaty obligations. We obtained an additional United Nations Security Council resolution requiring Saddam Hussein to prove that he had disarmed, and when that resolution was defied, we led a coalition to enforce it.

All of these actions by the United States and our allies have sent an unmistakable message to regimes that seek or possess weapons of mass destruction: Those weapons do not bring influence or prestige. They bring isolation and otherwise unwelcome consequences.

And another message should be equally clear: Leaders who abandon the pursuit of chemical, biological, and nuclear weapons and the means to deliver them will find an open path to better relations with the United States and other free nations.

With today's announcement by its leader, Libya has begun the process of rejoining the community of nations. And Colonel Qadhafi knows the way forward. Libya should carry out the commitments announced today. Libya should also fully engage in the war against terror. Its Government, in response to the United Nations Security Council's Lockerbie demands, has already renounced all acts of terrorism and pledged cooperation in the international fight against terrorism. We expect Libya to meet these commitments as well.

As the Libyan Government takes these essential steps and demonstrates its seriousness, its good faith will be returned. Libya can regain a secure and respected place among the nations and, over time, achieve far better relations with the United States. The Libyan people are heirs to an ancient and respected culture, and their country lies at the center of a vital region. As Libya becomes a more peaceful nation, it can be a source of stability in Africa and the Middle East. Should Libya pursue internal reform, America would be ready to help its people to build a more free and prosperous country.

Great Britain shares this commitment, and Prime Minister Blair and I welcome today's declaration by Colonel Qadhafi. Because Libya has a troubled history with America and Britain, we will be vigilant in ensuring its Government lives up to all its responsibilities. Yet, as we have found with other nations, old hostilities do not need to go on forever. And I hope that other leaders will find an example in Libya's announcement today.

Our understanding with Libya came about through quiet diplomacy. It is a result, however, of policies and principles declared to all. Over the last 2 years, a great coalition of nations has come together to oppose terror and to oppose the spread of weapons of mass destruction. We've been clear in our purposes. We have shown resolve. In word and in action, we have clarified the choices left to potential adversaries. And when leaders make the wise and responsible choice, when they renounce terror and weapons of mass destruction, as Colonel Qadhafi has now done, they serve the interest of their own people, and they add to the security of all nations.

Thank you.

Source: U.S. Bush, George W. "Remarks on the Decision by Colonel Muammar Abu Minyar al-Qadhafi of Libya to Disclose and Dismantle Weapons of Mass Destruction Programs." *Weekly Compilation of Presidential Documents* 39, no. 52 (December 29, 2003): 1835–1836. Washington, D.C.: National Archives and Records Administration. www.gpoaccess.gov/wcomp/v39no52.html (accessed February 9, 2004).

Secretary of Agriculture on Finding Mad Cow Disease

December 23 and 30, 2003

INTRODUCTION

In a hastily convened news conference held December 23, 2003, Secretary of Agriculture Anne M. Veneman announced that a milk cow in Washington state had tested positive for bovine spongiform encephalopathy (BSE), known more commonly as "mad cow disease." It was the first case of mad cow disease ever detected in the United States. Consumption of certain parts of infected cows could cause a rare but incurable wasting brain disease in humans known as variant Creutzfeldt-Jakob disease. Veneman tried to reassure the nation that the food supply was safe and the risk to human health extremely low. She said she planned to serve beef to her family for Christmas dinner. But the announcement frightened American consumers, caused more than thirty foreign countries to ban imports of American beef products, and prompted "I told you so" charges from consumer advocacy groups, animal rights activists, legislators, and others who said the U.S. Department of Agriculture had not taken adequate steps to keep BSE from entering the food supply.

A week later, on December 30, Veneman announced new rules that she said would offer additional protections against BSE. These included stopping all sick or "downer" cattle from entering the human food chain and prohibiting the use in food of certain body parts from older cattle implicated in transmitting the disease to humans. Veneman also announced that she was establishing an international panel of scientific experts to review the new procedures and to recommend any others they thought might be necessary. Many of the new rules were measures consumer groups had long been advocating over the strong resistance of the American beef industry.

Although consumer fears appeared to be easing by the end of the year, bans on U.S. beef exports remained in force, representing a potentially devastating blow to ranchers and meat packers. Officials were still trying to determine where the infected cow had lived before coming to Washington, in an effort to track and quarantine any other cattle in contact with her that might also have BSE. Officials were also still trying to trace meat from the sick cow, which had already been mixed with meat from several other cows, ground into hamburger, and shipped to eight states and Guam before the BSE was discovered. The Agriculture Department on December 24 issued a recall of 10,000 pounds of meat from cattle slaughtered along with the sick cow. The recall was simply a precaution, the department said, again assuring consumers that there was little risk of infection from eating meat.

Origin of BSE

First identified in 1986 in Britain, mad cow disease attacked the nervous system of infected cattle, ultimately destroying the brain and causing death. Televised images of infected cows, stumbling around their fields as if they were deranged, led to the "mad cow" nickname. Britain confirmed 181,376 cases of BSE between 1986 and 2002 and killed about 4 million cattle during that period in an effort to stop the spread of the disease. The United States banned importation of British cattle in 1989. *(BSE in Britain, Historic Documents of 2000, p. 880)*

Mad cow disease was thought to be caused by abnormal protein cells, called prions, which appeared to lodge in the brains, spinal columns, and bone marrow of infected cattle. The disease, which took four or five years to develop, was not contagious and did not spread from animal to animal. Rather, its spread was linked to the use of feed that contained ground meat and bone products from infected animals. Using such animal protein in livestock feed had been a common practice since World War II. Since 1997, however, Canada and the United States made it illegal to feed protein from cattle, sheep, and other ruminants (cud-chewing animals) to ruminants. Sheep were susceptible to a similar disease, known as scrapie, and deer and elk herds in North America suffered from a related wasting disease.

Humans could contract the human variant of mad cow disease by consuming meat products containing tissue from the brain, the spinal cord, and other parts of an infected cow's central nervous system. There were no known cases of humans contracting the disease by consuming beef muscle tissue, milk, or milk products. About 150 people had died from variant Creutzfeldt-Jakob disease since it was first identified in Britain in 1996. Most of those who died were British.

A "Downer" in Washington State

Before 2003 the only case of known BSE in North America was in Canada in 1993. Authorities reported a case in a cow imported from Britain; the rest of its herd was eventually slaughtered to keep the disease out of the food chain. Ten years later, in May 2003, Canadian authorities reported finding another cow with BSE, this one on a farm in Alberta. The cow was sent to a rendering plant and did not go into the food chain. The herd she was part of was destroyed for testing, and herds at two other farms where she had lived earlier were quarantined. Ultimately 1,700 cattle were destroyed. The Canadian beef industry lost an estimated $1 billion in sales after May, as countries around the world, including the United States, banned imports of Canadian beef and cattle. The United States began to relax its ban later in the year. The mad cow scare was the second major blow to Canada in the spring of 2003; it was still struggling to control a serious outbreak of Severe Acute Respiratory Syndrome (SARS) in the Toronto area. *(SARS, p. 121)*

About seven months later, on December 22, routine tests on a slaughtered Holstein cow from a farm in Washington state near Yakima proved positive for mad cow disease. The cow had been tested because she was a *downer,* the term used for animals unable to stand or walk on their own because of injury, age, or disease. BSE frequently prevented infected cows from standing. The farm was immediately placed under quarantine, and officials began to trace what happened to the animal's carcass after it had been slaughtered on December 9. They also tried to determine how and where the cow became infected. It was quickly learned that meat from the cow had been processed and put in the food chain. But the cow's brain and spinal column, the parts considered at highest risk for conveying BSE, had been sent to a rendering plant, where cattle parts deemed unfit for human consumption were turned into pet foods, fertilizers, and other products.

Tracing the cow back to its birth herd proved to be a more difficult task. The Agriculture Department said that the cow apparently was born on a farm in Alberta, Canada, where it may have been infected by contaminated feed before the 1997 ban was put in place prohibiting certain cattle parts in feed. DNA tests were being performed at the end of the year to confirm the cow's identity. Officials were also trying to locate eighty-one other cows that might have been shipped to the United States with the mad cow. The birth of the cow before the feed supplement ban went into effect was viewed as good news by many. Initially it had been thought that the infected cow had been born two or three years after the ban went into effect, which raised question about the effectiveness both of the ban and its enforcement.

Although they were both from Alberta, the two mad cows of 2003 did not appear to be linked. They did not come from the same farm in Canada, the two farms did not exchange animals, and feed records did not show a common source of possible contamination. The chief veterinarian of Canada said officials would investigate whether the feed mills involved bought raw materials from same source.

The announcement that mad cow disease had been found in the United States had immediate repercussion worldwide. Nearly three dozen countries banned or limited imports of U.S. beef or cattle, including Mexico, Japan, and South Korea, the three biggest importers of U.S. beef. Other countries that imposed bans included Canada, Chile, Jamaica, Malaysia, Russia South Africa, and Thailand. Australia and Brazil, beef-producing countries that stood to gain financially from the bans, also limited U.S. imports.

New Protections against Mad Cow Disease

The new rules announced by Veneman on December 30 banned all downer cows from the human food chain. Of the 36 million cattle slaughtered in the United States every year, about 200,000 were downers. Any cattle tested for BSE would be held until tests confirmed that the they were disease-free. The holding period was likely to range from thirty-six to forty-eight hours, using new, rapid tests developed in Europe but not yet widely used in the United States. Under existing regulations, tested animals—like the one that tested positive for mad cow—were stamped "inspected and passed" and put back into the food chain before the results of the tests were known.

The new rules prohibited small intestines of all cattle and the heads, spinal cords, and other central nervous system tissues from cattle older than thirty months from being used in products for human consumption. Tonsils had already been declared unfit. Because of the long incubation period for BSE, the heads, and nervous tissues of younger cattle, were considered safe. Slaughterhouses would be required to develop and implement procedures to ensure that banned materials could not enter the human food supply.

New limits were placed on products obtained by using high pressure to remove the last vestiges of meat from bones. Federal regulations already prohibited spinal cord in any advanced meat recovery (AMR) products labeled as meat, and the new rules extended that prohibition to dorsal root ganglia, which are clusters of nerve cells connected to the spinal cord. Vertebral columns and skulls of cattle older than thirty months were also banned from ARM use. All meat that was mechanically separated from bone with scrapers was prohibited from use as human food.

To prevent brain tissue from being dislodged and possibly contaminating muscle tissue, animals were no longer to be stunned with air-injection guns applied to the head. Finally, Veneman said the department would speed up its development and implementation of a national animal identification program. This was an area in which the United States lagged far behind most other industrial countries, which had already installed sophisticated electronic identifying programs to trace cattle as they moved from the farm to the feed lot to the slaughterhouse. The absence of such a system in the Washington case had made it more difficult to determine where the mad cow had been infected and what other cattle might be at risk.

The beef industry, cattle ranchers, and food companies by and large supported, if grudgingly, the new rules as the best way to restore confidence in American beef both at home and abroad. "We do believe that these are extraordinary measures that go well beyond what the international standards would dictate," a spokesperson for the American Meat Institute said. "In light of these, our trading partners should re-establish beef trade with us immediately." The institute stated that the new bans on using downers and certain cow parts went beyond what was necessary to protect the food supply. Many of the larger food companies said they had already been practicing much of what the new rules required.

Consumer groups, while applauding the government for acting quickly in a crisis, said the agriculture department should have acted much sooner and had still not gone far enough to protect the public. Consumer groups and animal rights activists had been trying to keep downers out of the human food supply since at least 1992, but the meat industry had strongly resisted the move. In November, for the second year in a row, the Republican-controlled Congress killed legislation that would have barred the use of downers. "I said on the floor of the House that you will rue the day," Rep. Gary Ackerman, D-N.Y., the chief House sponsor of the prohibition, said after learning of the BSE-infected cow.

Carolina Smith DeWaal, executive director of food safety at the Center for Science in the Public Interest, said the new rules should make the beef supply safer than it had been, but "it's still not safe enough." She said her group had been lobbying the federal government since 2001 to bar the use of spinal column and neck bone meat in the food supply. She noted that the new rules still allowed use of vertebral columns and skulls of young cattle.

Several consumer groups said the incident demonstrated the need to broaden the BSE testing program. The Agriculture Department had increased BSE testing from 219 cows in 1997 to more than 20,000 in 2002 and was planning, even before the discovery of the mad cow, to nearly double that number to 38,000 in 2004. But the Consumers Union and others noted that European countries tested 10 million cattle in 2002. Japan tested every cow it slaughtered—1.2 million in 2002. Veneman pointed out that the United States already was testing nearly fifty times as many cattle as called for under international standards. Ron DeHaven, chief veterinarian at the Agriculture Department, said universal testing was unnecessary, likening it to "a doctor testing every patient who comes through the door for prostate cancer." Others said that the money required for more BSE could be better on testing for food-borne pathogens such as salmonella and E-coli, which killed an estimated 5,000 people in the United States every year and sickened as many as 76 million.

Several consumer advocates and their supporters were concerned that the federal government was not adequately enforcing the ban on certain cow parts in animal feed. The Food and Drug Administration, which regulated animal feed, said that there was 99 percent compliance with the regulation. But investigations by the General Accounting Office in 2000 and 2002 found serious shortcomings in enforcement. The comprehensiveness of the ban was also at issue. While brain and central nervous system tissue from cattle, sheep, and goats could not be mixed into animal feed for those animals, it could be used in chicken feed. The government allowed chicken waste to be used in cattle feed, which opened another possible route for transmitting BSE. Sen. Richard J. Durbin, D-Ill., said he planned to introduce legislation addressing some of these issues early in 2004.

Following are excerpts from remarks by Secretary of Agriculture Anne M. Veneman at a December 23, 2003, news conference announcing that a case of mad cow disease had been detected in the United States for the first time and at a December 30, 2003, news conference announcing several steps the Agriculture Department was taking to increase protections against mad cow disease.

"News Conference on BSE"

. . . Today we received word from USDA's National Veterinary Services Laboratories in Iowa that a single Holstein cow from Washington State has tested as presumptive positive for BSE [Bovine Spongiform Encephalopathy] or what is widely known as mad cow disease.

Despite this finding we remain confident in the safety of our food supply. The risk to human health from BSE is extremely low. The animal tested was a downer cow or nonambulatory at the time of slaughter and was identified as part of USDA's [U.S. Department of Agriculture's] targeted surveillance program.

The sample was taken on December 9th. It was tested and retested at our Ames facility using two tests including immuno-histo-chemistry, which is recognized as the "gold standard" for the detection of BSE by the World Health Organization and OIE, the Organization of International Epizootics.

A sample from this animal is being flown on a military aircraft to the central veterinary laboratory in Weybridge, England in order to confirm this finding. Our traceback indicates that the animal comes from a farm in Mabton, Washington, about 40 miles southeast of Yakima, Washington.

As part of our response plan that farm has been quarantined. After the animal was slaughtered meat was sent for processing to Midway Meats in Washington State. USDA's Food Safety Inspection Service is working quickly to accurately determine the final disposition of the products from the animal.

Even though the risk to human health is minimal based on current evidence, we will take all appropriate actions out of an abundance of caution.

Since 1990 the U.S. Department of Agriculture has had an aggressive surveillance program in place to ensure detection and a swift response in the event of the introduction of BSE in this country. As part of that program we developed a response plan to be used if BSE is identified in the United States.

While this is a presumptive finding, we have activated that response plan today. We are making the appropriate notifications and confirmations under the plan and start-up activities are beginning.

I have been in contact with Secretary [of Homeland Security Tom] Ridge and I would emphasize that based on the information available this incident is not terrorist related nor is it related in any way to our nation's heightened alert status. I cannot stress this point strongly enough.

The safety of our food supply and public health are high priorities of this Administration and high priorities of USDA. In the last year we have tested 20,526 head of cattle for BSE, which is triple the level of the previous year of 2002. The presumptive positive today is a result of our aggressive surveillance program. This is a clear indication that our surveillance and detection program is working.

USDA has been training and planning for several years in case this situation presented itself. We continue to protect the U.S. food supply and the public health and safeguard American agriculture.

In October we announced findings from the Harvard Center for Risk Analysis that found that even if an infected animal were introduced into the U.S. animal agriculture system, the risk of spreading is low based on the safeguards and controls we have already put in place.

As part of our response to this situation we will provide daily briefings to update the public on the status. We will continue to provide you all of the information that we possibly can and do so as quickly as possible.

We have released this finding even before final confirmation in the U.K. because of our confidence in the testing that has already been carried out, and in the interest of protecting the food supply and public health. Information is available on our web site at www.usda.gov, and we will be updating that information frequently. . . .

While this incident would represent the first finding of BSE in the United States, we have worked hard to ensure that our response is swift and effective. We will continue to work with partners such as the Food and Drug Administration and the Department of Homeland Security to protect our food supply and the public health.

At this time of year many Americans are making plans for the holidays and for food. We see no need for people to alter those plans or their eating habits or to do anything but have a happy and healthy holiday season. I plan to serve beef for my Christmas dinner. And we remain confident in the safety of our food supply. . . .

> **Source:** U.S. Department of Agriculture. Office of Communications. "Transcript of News Conference with Agriculture Secretary Ann M. Veneman on BSE." Washington, D.C.: December 23, 2003. www.usda.gov/news/releases/2003/12/0433.htm (accessed January 6, 2004).

"Protection Measures to Guard Against BSE"

. . . It was just one week ago today that I stood here before you hours after learning of a single presumptive positive case of BSE [Bovine Spongiform Encephalopathy], or what we call "Mad Cow Disease," in Washington State, and I stood here to make that announcement. In that short period of time, exhaustive efforts have been made, countless hours have been spent, to investigate this finding.

My thanks to everyone who has assisted in these efforts including our partners at the federal, state and industry and international level especially all of the hosts—and many did this—they altered their holiday plans significantly to ensure our swift and effective response to this incident.

While this investigation is still in its early phases we've made a lot of progress in both the trace-back and the trace-forward from the indexed cow. Our investigative team on the ground, working with the state of Washington and Canadian authorities, has done an outstanding job. I especially want to thank Canadian officials for their excellent cooperation throughout this process.

As our technical experts have informed you, our main line of inquiry indicates that the cow slaughtered in Washington State and found to have BSE may have been born in Canada. We know that higher risk materials from the animal did not—did not—enter the food chain. Recalls of meat and product from this cow and others slaughtered at the same facility on the same day have been implemented, and we continue to be guided by an abundance of caution.

But I will stress again that our food supply and the public health remain safe.

Judging by recent market actions, consumer confidence and demand for beef are still relatively strong. We have initiated discussions with our trading partners which are ongoing to assure them of the actions that we are taking, and continue to take, to investigate this finding. Our USDA [U.S. Department of Agriculture] trade team has been in Tokyo and South Korea. Our goal is to see trade resume as quickly as possible.

We are also making information available to the public as soon as it becomes known to us. As you know, we have been updating on a daily basis and our updates are virtually up to the minute. They are webcast across the country and around the world and our materials are posted on our USDA website at www.usda.gov.

Sometimes we will tell you that this information is in a preliminary form, but we make it available quickly in the public interest.

For more than a decade the United States has had in place an aggressive surveillance detection and response program for BSE. That program has evolved over time as our understanding of BSE has changed. But sound science continues to be our guide.

We have tested about 20,000 head of cattle for BSE in each of the last two years—47 times the recommended international standard. Since 1989 USDA has banned imports of live ruminants and most ruminant product from the United Kingdom and other countries having BSE. In 1997 the FDA [Food and Drug Administration] prohibited the use of most mammalian protein in the manufacture of animal feed intended for cattle and other ruminants.

I would note . . . that the indexed cow appears to have been born before the feed ban was in place. And we are now awaiting the results of a DNA test to obtain positive identification on this animal.

Currently in the United States every animal going to slaughter is inspected by a USDA veterinarian for attributes such as ability to walk and central nervous system impairment. An independent analysis of our systems by Harvard University in the years 2001 and then again this year in 2003 shows that the risk of BSE spreading in the U.S. is extremely low, and possible spread would have been reversed by the controls that we have already put in place.

While we are confident that the United States has safeguards and firewalls needed to protect our food supply and public health as well as our animal health, today I am announcing steps we are taking to further protect our system.

In most instances these actions are the results of work that was underway long before the discovery last week in Washington State and prior to the announcement of BSE last May in Alberta, Canada.

First, effective immediately USDA will ban all downer cattle from the human food chain. We will also continue an aggressive surveillance program for BSE. However, these animals tested for BSE will no longer be marked "inspected and passed" until there is confirmation that they have tested negative for BSE. In other words, any animal tested under our surveillance program, that will continue, will be held until the test results are known.

Next, in order to further prevent human exposure to high-risk tissues and protect public health, USDA will implement new regulations. These actions are consistent with those taken by Canada following the BSE case discovered there in May of this year. These regulations deal with specified risk materials or SRMs.

Scientific studies have indicated that specific tissues from cattle of certain ages can harbor prions believed to cause BSE. Therefore, we are declaring those high-risk tissues primarily contained in the head and spinal column in cattle 30 months or older to be unfit for human consumption, and we are prohibiting their presence in human food.

In addition, for all cattle the small intestines will also be considered unfit for human consumption and prohibited from inclusion in human food.

Tonsils will remain prohibited from the human food chain.

Another area we are addressing in the regulations will provide additional process controls for facilities that use a process called advanced meat recovery, or AMR systems. AMR is a technical process that enables processors to remove smaller amounts of meat from carcasses without breaking bones. This rule will codify an existing USDA policy that prohibits the presence of spinal cord tissue in beef obtained through the AMR process.

USDA Food Safety and Inspection Service currently verifies the presence of spinal cord tissue through testing of the product. The new AMR rule will ensure that spinal cord tissue and another central nervous system tissue known as dorsal root ganglia are not present in the AMR product.

We will also specify that the skull cannot be used in AMR systems. These new regulations will become effective immediately on publication, which will take place as soon as possible.

In addition, FSIS is issuing a regulation to prohibit air injection stunning of cattle. This will further strengthen our systems by decreasing the risk of any brain material becoming dislodged during the slaughter of an animal.

USDA is also working to take the next steps toward implementation of a verifiable system of national animal identification. This is a process that has been underway for more than a year and a half. USDA has led an effort among partners at the federal and state levels, along with industry, which has resulted in the adoption of standards for a nationwide animal

ID system. Currently many animals can be identified through some system of animal ID. In fact, the cow in question was subject to an animal ID system which has facilitated our investigation in this case over the past week.

Such a system will help enhance the speed and accuracy of our response to disease outbreaks across many different animal species. With the standards now in place, I have asked USDA's chief information officer to make it his top priority to work with the committee that's working on this issue to develop the technology architecture necessary to implement an effective and verifiable system throughout the United States.

Our goals are to achieve uniformity, consistency, and efficiency across the national system.

And finally today, I am announcing the appointment of an international panel of scientific experts to provide an objective review of our response actions and areas for potential enhancement. This team will function almost identically to the panel that lent expertise to Canada after the May 20 discovery of BSE in Alberta.

In fact, we anticipate that the team members from the Canada incident will also serve on the panel that we are announcing today.

It is important that USDA seek credible, objective scientists from countries that have had experience with BSE in implementing the most effective response possible.

The actions that we're taking today are steps to enact additional safeguards to protect the public health and maintain the confidence of consumers, industry, and our trading partners in our already strong food safety and protection systems. Along with our scientific review panel we will continue to look at other potential actions that may be appropriate. USDA remains committed to taking every appropriate step along with our partners to protect our food supply and the well-being of American agriculture . . . .

Source: U.S. Department of Agriculture. Office of Communications. "Transcript of Agriculture Secretary Ann M. Veneman Announcing Additional Protection Measures to Guard Against BSE." Washington, D.C.: December 30, 2003. www.usda.gov/news/releases/2003/12/0450.htm (accessed January 6, 2004).

Cumulative Index, 1999–2003